Best Practices in School Neuropsychology

Guidelines for Effective Practice, Assessment, and Evidence-Based Intervention

Edited by

Daniel C. Miller

WILEY

John Wiley & Sons, Inc.

Library of Congress Cataloging-in-Publication Data:

Best practices in school neuropsychology: guidelines for effective practice, assessment, and evidence-
based intervention/edited by Daniel C. Miller.
  p. cm.
 Includes bibliographical references and index.
 ISBN 978-0-470-42203-8 (cloth)
1. Pediatric neuropsychology.   2. Clinical neuropsychology.   3. School psychology.   4. School
children—Mental health services.   5. Crisis intervention (Mental health services)   6. Evidence-based
psychiatry.   I. Miller, Daniel C.
 RJ486.5.B47 2010
 618.92′8—dc22

                                                                          2009010839

Printed in the United States of America
SKY10028692_081021

This book is dedicated to all school psychology practitioners who believe that "Minds Do Matter: All Children Can Learn"; to my loving wife Michie, my best friend and supporter; and to my parents who have provided me support and love throughout all my years.

Contents

Foreword

WE ARE SO lucky to be school psychologists in this day and age. The face of psychology, in general, has been changed by neuroscience in the last two decades and it promises more knowledge, better tools, and improved outcomes and quality of life for individuals who need our help. An avalanche of research on the brain is rushing into the clinical practice of all specialties in psychology. For example, geropsychology is rapidly becoming geroneuropsychology because research is enlightening practitioners about differential diagnosis of aging problems. Research on the dementias, vascular irregularities, stroke, and depression in the elderly population is abundant and well funded; therefore practitioners who work with senior patients meld much of this new research into their daily practice. They use the information because it is critical to successful outcomes. When a clinician improves differential diagnosis, then the interventions used are more specific to the etiology of the problem and confounding variables in the single-patient research design are kept to a minimum. This is simply good practice. It requires that the clinician keep up with the latest developments in research that might improve his or her diagnostic skills. Indeed, this also is mandated by professional ethical standards.

The reverse is true as well. For example, exponential growth in the numbers of children identified with neurodevelopmental disorders, that are very difficult to diagnose and treat, is pressing for expansion of neuroscientific research. Disorders such as autism and Asperger's disorder are clearly brain-related and the understanding of the brain processes involved is critical not only for treatment, but also for prevention. Psychologists working with children understand that the treatments for autism are very different than the treatments for mental retardation, metabolic disorders, learning disorders, and seizure disorders. Children with the later disorders may exhibit a few of the behavioral characteristics associated with autism and therefore the chance of misdiagnosis, inflated incidence/prevalence numbers, inappropriate treatment, and poor outcomes is high. The need for neuroscientific information to assist practice has never been more pressing and essential. The collective plea for more information has never been so loud.

This bilateral relationship between research and practice is not an accident. The National Institutes of Health (NIH) have been calling for and funding "translational research" efforts for some time. The NIH have long recognized that while excellent research on the brain was being conducted in laboratories around the country and the world, the findings of that research was not being translated down to prospective patients. Hence, the NIH continues to push for research information in the neurosciences to go from "bench to bedside." So far, significant translational research results have been obtained regarding polio, memory, blindness, Parkinson's disease, multiple sclerosis, stroke, stress, depression, bipolar disorder, schizophrenia, and drug addiction.

Leading universities are also naturally pushing the boundaries of neuroscientific inquiry. Advances in technology, and imaging in particular, have allowed researchers such as Sally Shaywitz, Jack Fletcher, Bob Schultz, Erin Bigler, Margaret Semrud-Clikeman (to name just a few) to look inside the brain and glean important information about neuroanatomical correlates of reading disabilities, Attention Deficit Hyperactivity Disorder, and autism. The findings about reading disabilities, for example, have translated into more effective differential diagnosis of dyslexia and remediative activities. These research studies have also shed light on how plastic the brain is and how we can influence that plasticity to achieve long-term positive reading outcomes. When neuroscience translates directly into the classroom for positive outcomes, we have the perfect marriage. Of course, the perfect marriage requires that both partners are aware of what the other is doing. Researchers who conduct brain imaging studies must be interested in the functional application of their findings and clinicians must be interested in the neuropsychological makeup of the problems that they see in the classroom. We have seen enough of research that does not see the outside of the laboratory, and we have seen enough of clinical and educational personnel not understanding why academic problems exist.

Up until this day and age, the field of school psychology was ruled by certain ideas about who and how we practice. Those ideas were results of preconceived values and the level of knowledge that we had about the brain. For example, it was thought that intelligence could be represented by a single number that adequately described the ability of a child, was immutable, and precisely predicted success. That genes unilaterally dictated how development would unfold. It was thought that a discrepancy between two numbers could describe and remediate differences in learning. That differences in behavior could only be described by behavioral observations. We thought that once a child was disabled, that they would always be disabled. Autism was caused by "refrigerator mothers." Reading problems existed because of minimal brain damage. These types of beliefs carved out the role of the school psychologist. They dictated our job descriptions and directed our professional boundaries.

Why don't we believe these things anymore? And if we do not believe them, what do we believe and how does it influence our roles as school psychologists? What forces proved these ideas to be incorrect or off the mark? The answer is: Neuroscience. The 1990s was called the "Decade of the Brain" and the only trouble with sectioning off the 1990s for the brain is that the decades after the 1990s have been far more exciting and continue to grow more exciting every year! It seems that the force of outstanding neuropsychological findings is pushing every decade to be the decade of the brain. Advances in technology and imaging are developing so fast it is very difficult to translate the avalanche of new research findings into clinical practice, but new ideas and beliefs are emerging. The concept of "neural Darwinism" has emerged where we are beginning to understand how the individual brain develops a dynamic and plastic dance between genes and experiences. Another new belief that guides treatment of early childhood normal and problematic development is "use it or lose it." This concept reflects new understanding of neural pruning of information that is learned but not used by the young brain. A new understanding of "automaticity," how the brain must get information to an automatic level, is also important because it will help us understand how fluid a skill must be before we pursue another new skill. Perhaps the most exciting new belief that guides practice is "neurons that fire together, wire together" suggesting that remediation of learning issues can be enhanced by helping new axonal growth tap into existing neural networks. Of course, to apply these new beliefs we must change our usual way of doing business, or more specifically, we must change our practice methods and standards.

Neuropsychological practice principles are being drawn into everyday school psychology practice because neuroscience has localized areas of brain function that are imperative to the understanding of academic difficulties. Executive functions, for example, are critical to reading comprehension and it is becoming just plain silly to evaluate a child for reading problems without examining how that child organizes, plans, and evaluates what he or she has just read! We could say that we are assessing a child's organizing skills or we could say that we are assessing a child's executive functions, and in general, the terms mean the same thing. The difference in this day and age, as opposed to what went before, is that when the school psychologist assesses executive functions, he or she is also seeing how those functions relate to working memory, short-term memory, and several forms of attention. Why would the school psychologist want to do that?—because differentiating memory, attention, and executive function skills will determine which evidence-based interventions will work with a certain child and which ones will not. This is school psychology at a higher level of competence and at a level that is commensurate with knowledge translated down from the neurosciences. Of course, the school psychologist could always just informally estimate the child's organizational skills, omit any evaluation of organizational skills, or not relate deficits in organizational skills to academic problems. Indeed, this is how it has been done for years. But the main question in this day and this age is: *Should we charge school psychologists with the task of keeping abreast of new neuroscientific research developments that translate into psychoeducational evaluation practice?*

This book, *Best Practices in School Neuropsychology: Guidelines for Practice, Assessment, and Evidence-Based Intervention* edited by Dr. Dan Miller answers the question with a resounding "yes!" It begins the long journey of establishing guidelines that reflect the advances in neuroscience critical to good practice. It sets down the minimal knowledge that school psychologists of the future will need to know to adequately carry out a comprehensive assessment of a child who experiences sustained academic difficulties despite having exposure to differentiated instruction with highly qualified teachers. This is not a "nice to have" book. It is an essential book for school psychologists in training and those who are in practice. For the school psychologist in training, it will imprint the highest standards of the day as a base of future practice. For the practicing school psychologist, it will help retool and redesign the current level of practice to knowledge that incorporates neuroscience. The later was omitted from training because technology and findings in genetics and imaging simply were not present in older training programs: At that time, a cohesive understanding of the research did not exist, and beliefs and outcomes were commensurate with the level of knowledge. Now it does exist, and incorporating neuropsychological principles into school psychology practice is a seamless and natural process that will advance good outcomes.

Readers will find that Dr. Miller and his co-authors have labored very hard to present a balanced and comprehensive set of practice standards for school psychologists. Dr. Miller provides a detailed explanation of the breadth and depth of knowledge that is needed for basic practice. He addresses the complex and sometimes difficult issues that present with the redefinition of the role of the school psychologist and the leaning toward subspecialization with detailed analyses and wisdom. The clinical applications, special populations, medical disorders, and resource sections grow into a comprehensive view of applying neuropsychological principles to the practice of school psychology and also show the outstanding wealth of expertise and experience of the respective authors.

This work indicates that the authors and editor have insatiable curiosity about the brain! It demonstrates that the authors and editor are pushing the boundaries of what school psychologists believe because it is the ethical thing to do. Beliefs, ideas, and ethics direct how we act. It is obvious that the individuals involved in the writing of this book take their ethical obligation to incorporate neuroscience into practice very seriously and are acting on that obligation. We are all very lucky to have these colleagues with us in school psychology in this day, and in this age.

Elaine Fletcher-Janzen, Ed.D., NCSP
Cleveland, Ohio
April, 2009

Preface

AFTER SPENDING MOST of 2006 writing my first book, *Essentials of School Neuropsychological Assessment*, I told family, friends, and colleagues that I would probably not jump into writing a new book too soon. Writing a book is akin to childbirth: nine months of labor following by the blessed event, or publication in this case. Women tell me they forget the pain of childbirth and soon look forward to having another child. I must have forgotten the arduous process of putting a book together because two years later I suggested to my publisher that this book needed to be published. This time around I am blessed with many gifted, talented, and insightful colleagues that have joined me in crafting this edited book.

For me, scholarly writing must be guided by a passion for the topic, and I have been passionate about school neuropsychological theory and practice since I entered the field of school psychology in 1980. After working as a school psychologist practitioner for six years, I decided to go back to school for a doctoral degree. I was very fortunate to be offered a full-time graduate research position in the Brain Behavior Laboratory at Ohio State University (OSU) working with my mentor Dr. Marlin Languis. Dr. Languis established the first U.S. laboratory using the relatively new technology of quantitative EEG or topographic brain mapping to study children with learning disorders. I spent three years at OSU obtaining a one-of-a-kind doctoral degree that blended school psychology, pediatric neuropsychology, and electrophysiology. As a result of my doctoral studies, I realized the importance of recognizing the biological bases of behavior and their influences on individual differences.

In 1990, after I completed my doctoral studies, I accepted a faculty position at Texas Woman's University to develop an area of specialization in school neuropsychology for school psychology and counseling psychology doctoral students. Eighteen year later, and counting, I have continued to train future psychologists to integrate neuropsychological principles into their professional practices. The integration of neuropsychological principles into the practice of school psychology specifically has emerged as a subspecialization within school psychology since the early 1990s.

From 2003 to 2004, I had the privilege of serving as the President of the National Association of School Psychologists. I set the theme for the 2004 annual conference as "Minds Matter: All Children Can Learn." That conference theme still resonates for me today. In this new era of implementation of response-to-intervention models across the country, our profession has become polarized between those who advocate for a strict behavioral, curriculum-based measurement approach to identifying children with disabilities and those who continue to see the value of assessing individual differences and tailoring interventions to assessment data.

Another major impetus for this book comes from my review of the most recent *Best Practices in School Psychology V*. I was discouraged that in this comprehensive five-volume set there was not a single chapter that addressed the biological bases of behavior. This book, *Best Practices in School Neuropsychology: Guidelines for Effective Practice, Assessment, and Evidence-Based Intervention* will attempt to fill that void. The best practice of school psychology is not complete without considering the biological bases of behavior. This book is organized into three broad sections: Professional Issues in School Neuropsychology, Practice Issues in School Neuropsychology, and Clinical Applications of School Neuropsychology.

PROFESSIONAL ISSUES IN SCHOOL NEUROPSYCHOLOGY

In this section, Chapter 1 provides a rationale for why school neuropsychology is an emerging subspecialty within school psychology. Chapter 2 discusses the issue of what constitutes competency in school neuropsychology, reviews training standards in related fields (e.g., clinical neuropsychology), compares certification requirements in clinical and school neuropsychology, and proposes a set of school neuropsychology training standards. Chapter 3 provides a succinct review of legal and ethical issues that arise in the practice of school neuropsychology. Chapter 4 covers the unique challenges in working with culturally diverse populations using school neuropsychological techniques.

PRACTICE ISSUES IN SCHOOL NEUROPSYCHOLOGY

There are six chapters in this section of the book. Chapter 5 describes current school neuropsychological assessment and intervention models. Chapter 6 describes best practices in assessing for cognitive processes. Chapter 7 provides an overview of what neuroscience offers to the practice of school neuropsychology currently and in the future. Chapter 8 presents a comprehensive model of how school neuropsychology fits within a response-to-intervention model. Chapter 9 presents a rationale for the importance of school neuropsychologists collaborating with parents, educators, and other professionals to maximize services to children. Chapter 10 describes the various roles and responsibilities a school neuropsychologist can assume when children return to school after serious neurological injuries.

CLINICAL APPLICATIONS OF SCHOOL NEUROPSYCHOLOGY

The third section of the book is divided into four sections: clinical applications of school neuropsychology with: 1) special populations, 2) academic disabilities, 3) processing deficits, and 4) medical disorders. The special populations section presents the best practices for assessing and intervening with: ADD/ADHD children (Chapter 11), children with autism (Chapter 12), children with Asperger's Syndrome (Chapter 13), children with developmental delays (Chapter 14), children with externalizing disorders (Chapter 15), children with internalizing disorders (Chapter 16), children who are deaf or hard of hearing (Chapter 17), and children who are visually impaired (Chapter 18).

The academic disabilities Section (Section IV) presents the best practices for assessing and intervening with: children with reading disorders (Chapter 19), children with writing disorders (Chapter 20), children with math disorders (Chapter 21), children with speech and language disorders (Chapter 22), and children with nonverbal learning disabilities (Chapter 23).

The processing deficits section presents the best practices for assessing and intervening with children who have executive function disorders (Chapter 24), memory and learning disorders (Chapter 25), and sensory-motor impairments (Chapter 26).

The medical disorders Section (Section V) presents the best practices for assessing and intervening with children with chronic illnesses (Chapter 27), brain tumors (Chapter 28), seizure disorders (Chapter 29), and traumatic brain injury (Chapter 30).

Writing this book has been a collaborative effort. The chapter authors represent a well-respected group of school psychologists, school neuropsychologists, neuropsychologists, clinicians, professors, and advanced doctoral students committed to sharing their knowledge and expertise. My sincere thanks goes to all of the authors who took time from their busy schedules to contribute to this project.

Special thanks to my colleague at work, Glenda Peters, who tirelessly proofed every chapter and covered the department while I hid away from the phones, e-mail, students, and faculty to write. Also special thanks to Isabel Pratt, my editor at Wiley, who kept me on track. Special thanks to the doctors and staff at the Denton Regional Hospital who gave me a second lease on life in December 2008, which afforded me the opportunity to finish this book project. Last but not least, I want to thank my wife Michie for her continued support as my best friend, live-in editor, and chief supporter.

Daniel C. Miller
April, 2009

About the Editor

DANIEL C. MILLER, Ph.D., is a Professor and Department Chair in the Department of Psychology and Philosophy at Texas Woman's University in Denton, Texas. He is also the Director of a national school neuropsychology post-graduate certification program available at multiple locations across the country. Dr. Miller has more than 25 years of experience working in the field of school psychology and the emerging specialty of school neuropsychology as a practitioner and trainer. Dr. Miller is credentialed as a Licensed Psychologist, Licensed Specialist in School Psychology, Diplomate in School Psychology from the American Board of Professional Psychology, Diplomate in School Neuropsychology from the American Board of School Neuropsychology, and a National Certified School Psychologist. Dr. Miller has been an active leader in both school psychology and school neuropsychology. He was the founding president of the Texas Association of School Psychologists (1993) and a past president of the National Association of School Psychologists (2003–2004). Dr. Miller is a frequent presenter at state and national conferences about school neuropsychology-related topics. He is an active researcher and the author of the *Essentials of School Neuropsychological Assessment* (2007) by John Wiley & Sons, Inc.

Contributors

Vincent C. Alfonso, Ph.D.
Professor and Associate Dean for
    Academic Affairs
Graduate School of Education
Fordham University
New York, New York

Erin Avirett, B.A.
Doctoral Student
Department of Psychology and
    Philosophy
Texas Woman's University
Denton, Texas

Elizabeth L. Begyn, Ph.D.
Postdoctoral Fellow
Department of Psychiatry
Neuropsychology Service
Children's Medical Center Dallas
Dallas, Texas

Virginia W. Berninger, Ph.D.
Professor
Department of Educational
    Psychology
University of Washington
Seattle, Washington

Jessica L. Blasik, MS.Ed.
Doctoral Student
Department of Counseling,
    Psychology, and Education
Duquesne University
Pittsburgh, Pennsylvania

Christine L. Castillo, Ph.D.
Neuropsychologist
Department of Psychiatry,
    Neuropsychology Service
Children's Medical Center Dallas
Dallas, Texas
and
University of Texas Southwestern
    Medical Center
Dallas, Texas

Ginger Depp Cline, Ph.D.
Postdoctoral Fellow
Texas Children's Hospital
Houston, Texas

Beth Colaluca, Ph.D.
Neuropsychologist
Department of Neuropsychology
Cooks Children's Medical Center
Fort Worth, Texas

Andrew Davis, Ph.D.
Associate Professor
Department of Educational
    Psychology
Ball State University
Muncie, Indiana

Scott L. Decker, Ph.D.
Assistant Professor
College of Education
Department of Counseling and
    Psychological Services
Georgia State University
Atlanta, Georgia

Philip A. DeFina, Ph.D., ABSNP
Chief Executive Officer and
    Chief Scientific Officer
International Brain Research
    Foundation, Inc.
Edison, New Jersey

**Douglas A. Della Toffalo, Ph.D.,
    ABSNP**
School Neuropsychologist
Licensed Psychologist
Cranberry Area School
    District
Seneca, Pennsylvania

Kathy DeOrnellas, Ph.D.
Assistant Professor
Department of Psychology and
    Philosophy
Texas Woman's University
Denton, Texas

Catherine L. Dial, B.S.
Vocational Services Coordinator
Clinical & Consulting
    Neuropsychology
Dallas, Texas

Jack G. Dial, Ph.D.
Licensed Psychologist and Licensed
    Specialist in School Psychology
Clinical & Consulting
    Neuropsychology
Dallas, Texas

Cristin Dooley, Ph.D.
Psychologist
Lewisville Independent School
    District
Lewisville, Texas

Agnieszka M. Dynda, Psy.D.
Adjunct Assistant Professor
St. John's University
Queens, New York

Jonelle Ensign, M.S.
Licensed Specialist in School
    Psychology
Fort Worth Independent School
    District
Fort Worth, Texas
and
Doctoral Student
Texas Woman's University
Denton, Texas

Eleazar Eusebio, M.A.
Doctoral Student
Department of Psychology
Philadelphia College of
    Osteopathic Medicine
Philadelphia, Pennsylvania

**Steven G. Feifer, D.Ed., ABSNP,
    NCSP**
School Psychologist
Frederick County Public
    Schools
Frederick, Maryland

Dawn P. Flanagan, Ph.D.
Professor
Department of Psychology
St. John's University
Queens, New York

Lisa Hain, Psy.D.
Doctoral Student
Department of Psychology
Philadelphia College of Osteopathic
    Medicine
Philadelphia, Pennsylvania

James Brad Hale, Ph.D., ABSNP
Associate Professor
Department of Psychology
Philadelphia College of Osteopathic
    Medicine
Philadelphia, Pennsylvania

Julie Henzel, M.A.
Doctoral Student
Department of Psychology
Philadelphia College of Osteopathic
    Medicine
Philadelphia, Pennsylvania

Jacqueline Hood, Ph.D.
Psychologist, Center for Pediatric
    Psychiatry
Children's Medical Center Dallas
and
Assistant Professor of Psychiatry
University of Texas Southwestern
    Medical School

Colleen Jiron, Ph.D., ABCN
Clinical Neuropsychologist
Professional School Psychologist
Boulder Valley School District
Boulder, Colorado

Wendi Johnson, Ph.D.
Licensed Specialist in School
    Psychology
Denton Independent School District
Denton, Texas

Mary Joann Lang, Ph.D., ABPN
Neuropsychologist
Irvine School of Medicine
Department of Pediatrics
University of California
Irvine, California
and
Beacon Day School
Orange, California

**Ann Marie T. Leonard-Zabel, Ph.D.,
    ABSNP, NCSP**
Associate Professor
Psychology Department
Curry College
Milton, Massachusetts
and
School Neuropsychologist
President of N.E.A.L.A.C.
    Clinic
Plymouth, Massachusetts

Denise E. Maricle, Ph.D.
Associate Professor
Department of Psychology and
    Philosophy
Texas Woman's University
Denton, Texas

Robb N. Matthews, M.A.
Doctoral Student
Department of Educational
    Psychology
Texas A & M University
College Station, Texas

Marie C. McGrath, Ph.D., NCSP
Assistant Professor
Department of Graduate
  Psychology
Immaculata University
Immaculata,
  Pennsylvania

Amy McLaughlin, M.A.
Doctoral Student
Department of Psychology
Philadelphia College of Osteopathic
  Medicine
Philadelphia, Pennsylvania

Kurt Metz, Ph.D., ABSNP
Researcher
The Madrillon Group, Inc.
Vienna, Virginia

**Daniel C. Miller, Ph.D., ABPP,
  ABSNP, NCSP**
Professor
Department of Psychology and
  Philosophy
Texas Woman's University
Denton, Texas

Jeffrey A. Miller, Ph.D., ABPP
Associate Professor
Department of Counseling,
  Psychology, and Special
  Education
Duquesne University
Pittsburgh,
  Pennsylvania

Margery Miller, Ph.D.
Professor
Psychology Department
Gallaudet University
Washington, D.C.

Jennifer Morrison, Ph.D.
Neuropsychologist
Kids Brains, LLC
Dallas, Texas

Raychel C. Muenke, B.S.
Doctoral Student
Department of Psychology
  and Philosophy
Texas Woman's University
Denton, Texas

Brooke Novales, Ph.D.
Licensed Specialist in School
  Psychology
Denton Independent School District
Denton, Texas

Samuel O. Ortiz, Ph.D.
Associate Professor
Department of Psychology
St. John's University
Jamaica, New York

H. Thompson Prout, Ph.D., ABSNP
Professor
Department of Educational and
  Counseling Psychology
University of Kentucky
Lexington, Kentucky

Susan M. Prout, Ed.S.
School Psychologist
Fayette County Schools
Lexington, Kentucky

Lynsey Psimas-Fraser, B.A.
Doctoral Student
Department of Psychology and
  Philosophy
Texas Woman's University
Denton, Texas

Mittie T. Quinn, Ph.D.
Licensed School Psychologist
Adjunct Faculty
George Mason University
Fairfax, Virginia

Linda A. Reddy, Ph.D.
Associate Professor
Rutgers Graduate School of Applied
    and Professional Psychology
Piscataway, New Jersey

Robert L. Rhodes, Ph.D.
Professor, Department
Special Education & Communication
    Disorders
New Mexico State University
Las Cruces, New Mexico

Cynthia Riccio, Ph.D.
Professor
Department of Educational
    Psychology
Texas A & M University
College Station, Texas

Amy Stern, M.S.
Doctoral Student
Department of Psychology
Philadelphia College of Osteopathic
    Medicine
Philadelphia, Pennsylvania

Tania N. Thomas-Presswood,
    Ph.D., ABSNP
Associate Professor
Psychology Department
Gallaudet University
Washington D.C.

Nichole Wicker, M.A.
Doctoral Student
Department of Educational
    Psychology
Texas A & M University
College Station, Texas

Gabrielle Wilcox, M.S.
Doctoral Student
Department of Psychology
Philadelphia College of Osteopathic
    Medicine
Philadelphia, Pennsylvania

Jed Yalof, Ph.D., ABSNP
Professor
Department of Graduate Psychology
Immaculata University
Immaculata, Pennsylvania

Audrea R. Youngman, B.A.
Doctoral Student
Department of Educational
    Psychology
Texas A & M University
College Station, Texas

PROFESSIONAL ISSUES IN SCHOOL NEUROPSYCHOLOGY

CHAPTER 1

School Neuropsychology, an Emerging Specialization

DANIEL C. MILLER

"WE BELIEVE IT is no longer possible for the school psychologist to master all of the areas of knowledge needed to function ethically and effectively in so many domains. The time for the development of specializations in school psychology has come" (Hynd & Reynolds, 2005, pp. 11–12).

The preceding quote is from George Hynd and Cecil Reynolds, the principal pioneers behind the development of the school neuropsychology specialty. The purpose of this chapter is to provide a rationale for why the time is right for our national school psychology organizations to recognize specialties/subspecialties. The focus of this chapter will be on the need to specifically recognize school neuropsychology as a subspecialty. The chapter will also review the various roles and functions of a school neuropsychologist, review the history of school neuropsychology, and review the common reasons for referral for a school neuropsychological evaluation.

THE NEED FOR PROFESSIONAL ORGANIZATIONS TO RECOGNIZE SPECIALIZATIONS

In this chapter, the term *emerging specialty* or *emerging specialization* will be used in reference to school neuropsychology, which implies that the author believes that the practice of school psychology has matured into a separate and distinct profession from the practice of psychology in general.

For the past forty years there has been a debate between the American Psychological Association (APA) and the National Association of School

Psychologists (NASP) about how school psychology relates to the broader field of psychology. The question remains whether the practice of school psychology has become a separate profession or remains a recognized specialty within the broader field of psychology. If school psychology were considered a separate and distinct profession from psychology in general, then school neuropsychology would be viewed as an "emerging specialization/specialty" within school psychology. In APA, school psychology is already a recognized specialty area within the broader field of psychology. If specializations were recognized within the specialty of school psychology, then school neuropsychology would be viewed as an emerging "subspecialization or subspecialty."

Another long-standing controversy in school psychology is the use of the title "school psychologist." Again, this contentious debate has been between APA and NASP. Within APA's Model Act for State Licensure of Psychologists (American Psychological Association, 1987) there has been a long-standing exemption that allows nondoctoral practitioners to use the title "school psychologist" if they are state certified for practice. In 2007, APA proposed that the language granting this exemption be removed and the title school psychologist only be reserved for doctoral licensed practitioners. At the time this chapter was written, this issue was still unresolved. In this chapter, the term *school psychologist* will be used to describe specialist-level and doctoral-level practitioners who offer the full array of school psychological services.

The evidence exists to suggest that the days of being a school psychologist generalist are numbered. The term *generalist* implies that a broad array of entry-level knowledge and skills within the field of school psychology are known and demonstrated respectively. Fagan (2002) noted "that the point has been exceeded where a school psychologist can be trained to perform all roles and functions with competence" (p. 7). The challenge for trainers and their students has been to remain abreast at the entry-level depth of knowledge and skills required within each domain of practice (Miller, DeOrnellas, & Maricle, 2008).

Miller et al. (2008) and Miller, DeOrnellas, and Maricle (2009) stated that the increase in specialized knowledge within our field has led many school psychology practitioners to choose (voluntarily or through necessity) to specialize within a particular area. It is important to realize that such specialization is a luxury afforded to school districts that have a sizable number of school psychologists. School psychologists working in large school districts, often in urban areas, have opportunities for specialization that are not afforded to those school psychologists working in rural, and often underserved, areas. In rural areas, school psychologists are "generalists" by necessity. Therefore, as the profession enters into discussing the merits of recognizing specializations within the field of school psychology, the urban versus rural service delivery differences need to be considered.

Another issue that must be weighed is the impact of recognizing specializations on the existing shortage of school psychologists. Curtis, Hunley, and Chesno-Grier (2004) reviewed the potential negative impact of the shortage of school psychologists on service delivery to children. Any time a profession makes credentialing of its practitioners more difficult, the risk increases that there will be fewer practitioners to offer services. Specialization within a profession may be a natural progression that takes place within a profession with specialization being viewed as a sign of organizational maturity (Fagan, 2002; Hynd & Reynolds, 2005; Miller et al., 2008, Miller, DeOrnellas, & Maricle, 2009); however, professional organizations should carefully consider the potential impact of recognizing specializations on the shortage of school psychologists and on rural service delivery.

Miller, Maricle, and DeOrnellas (2009) conducted a random survey of 1,000 regular members of the National Association of School Psychologists (NASP), and 80.9 percent of the respondents were in favor of NASP recognizing subspecialties with school neuropsychology being one of the top ten recommended areas of specialization. Specialization occurs when a school psychologist is either asked, or volunteers through interest, to assume the duties within a narrow range of focus. For example, a school psychologist may be assigned to work on the autism assessment team. While the school psychologist may have some basic training in differential diagnosis in the identification of autism spectrum disorders, he or she is often lacking in the specialized expertise required to expertly perform the required duties. In order to hone professional skills in autism, the ethical practitioner will seek out training, supervision, and professional resources (e.g., books, tests). The question then becomes what ultimately constitutes entry-level competency within a specialization. This question will be discussed in Chapter 2 of this book entitled School Neuropsychology Training and Credentialing.

SCHOOL NEUROPSYCHOLOGY AS A SPECIALTY

The body of specialized school psychology knowledge has grown exponentially in recent years. We truly live in an amazing age of vast information. The training requirements for entry-level school psychology practitioners have increased dramatically since the early 1990s. Trainers of school psychologists do their best to train entry-level and advanced practitioners in a variety of roles and functions, including data-based problem solving, assessment, consultation, counseling, crisis intervention, and research. Most school psychology curriculums at the specialist-level have a class that covers the biological bases of behavior, but there is no in-depth exposure to neuropsychology. School psychology trainers often feel that they only have enough time to introduce specialist-level students to the broad array of roles and functions available to them as practitioners. Increased specializations in areas such as school neuropsychology must occur either through organized, competency-based postgraduate certification programs or through doctoral school psychology programs that offer specialization in school neuropsychology.

There are several reasons for recognizing school neuropsychology as a specialty within school psychology, including the following:

- The growing acknowledgment within the medical and education communities of the neurobiological bases of childhood learning and behavioral disorders.
- The influences of federal education laws such as IDEA, which have included traumatic brain injury as a disability and continued to empha-size the identification of processing deficits in specific learning disabled children.
- The increased number of children with medical conditions that affect their school performance.
- The increased use of medications with school-aged children often including multiple medications with unknown combined risks or po-tential interactions.
- Limited access to neuropsychological services within the schools. There is a tremendous need for school psychologists to receive enhanced training in school neuropsychological practice. When neuropsychological ser-vices are provided to the school by outside professionals, the reports are often not useful to the schools in developing educationally relevant interventions (see Miller, 2007, for a review).

THE ROLES AND FUNCTIONS OF A SCHOOL NEUROPSYCHOLOGIST

ASSESSMENT

One of the specialized roles that a school neuropsychologist can perform is specialized assessment. School neuropsychological assessments are more in-depth than traditional psychoeducational or psychological evaluations. School neuropsychological assessments typically measure a wider variety of neurocognitive constructs such as sensory-motor functions, attentional processes, visual-spatial processes, language processes, memory and learn-ing, executive functions, speed and efficiency of cognitive processing, general intellectual ability, academic achievement, and social-emotional functioning (see Miller, 2007, for a review and Chapter 5 in this book, which reviews the best practices in school neuropsychological assessment and intervention).

CONSULTATION

A school neuropsychologist will have specialized knowledge of brain-behavior relationships and an awareness of how education is affected by impairment of function. School neuropsychologists can assist in the interpretation of neuropsychological findings or medical records from outside agencies. School neuropsychologists can help translate brain research into educational practice by consulting with educators and parents about specific child-related issues and about broader systemic educational issues. See Chapter 9 in this book for a more thorough discussion of the best practices in school neuropsychology collaboration with home, school, and outside professionals.

AGENCY/SCHOOL LIAISON

An important role of a school neuropsychologist is to monitor interventions and to facilitate re-entry planning for children and youth who are medically incapacitated due to a neurological insult or injury. As an example, a school neuropsychologist should act as a liaison between the hospital and the schools when a child is being treated for a traumatic brain injury. Finding out for the first time about "Johnny," who experienced a head injury six months ago and is now sitting in your office wanting to be educationally served, is not good practice. Miller (2007, pp. 79–80) detailed several activities that a school neuropsychologist can perform as a liaison between the schools and a medical facility. Also see Chapter 10 of this book for a more thorough discussion of the best practices in school reentry for children recovering from neurological conditions.

EDUCATOR

School neuropsychologists can conduct inservice trainings for parents and teachers about neuropsychological factors that relate to common childhood disorders. As an example, a school neuropsychologist could offer a workshop on the biological bases of ADHD and discuss how psychopharmacology assists in managing the disability in some cases.

EVIDENCE-BASED RESEARCHER

Another important role and function for a school neuropsychologist is to conduct both basic and applied educational research to continually investigate the assessment–intervention linkage and to evaluate the efficacy of neuropsychologically based interventions and consultations (Miller, 2007). In the last two decades, many new assessment instruments and interventions have been made available to school neuropsychologists. As a good consumer of new products or techniques, the school neuropsychologist must continually evaluate the quality and the applicability of these new tools. When evaluating a new assessment instrument or a new intervention, the practitioner should always be asking the questions: How does this new assessment offer new insight into the neuropsychological processing of the child compared to established assessment techniques? or What is the effectiveness of this new intervention compared to other established interventions?

The emerging specialty of school neuropsychology has been historically influenced by the disciplines of clinical neuropsychology, school psychology, and education. The state of the art and a review of the history of school neuropsychology are discussed in the next section.

STATE OF THE ART OF SCHOOL NEUROPSYCHOLOGY

In order to appreciate the current state of the art in school neuropsychological assessment, it is important to review some of the historical approaches to neuropsychological assessment. Rourke (1982) labeled three stages to describe the history of clinical neuropsychology: (1) the single-test stage, (2) the test battery/lesion specification stage, and the (3) functional profile stage. Miller (2007) labeled the current state-of-the-art practice in neuropsychology as the integrative and predictive stage.

The **single-test stage** dominated the early years (1900–1950s) of clinical neuropsychology in the United States. As the name of the stage implies, clinicians attempted to use a single test to differentially classify patients with and without brain damage. Clinicians looked for signs of organicity or brain dysfunction in patients using single tests such as the *Bender Visual-Motor Gestalt*, *Benton Visual Retention*, or the *Memory for Designs* tests (Miller, 2007). In current practice, school neuropsychologists may use a few stand-alone tests that have been created to assess specific neurocognitive skills. For example, the *Wisconsin Card Sorting Test* (Heaton, 1981) assesses executive functions, and the *Bender-Gestalt Second Edition* (Brannigan & Decker, 2003) assesses visual perceptual-motor ability. The single-test approach to differentiate brain damage did not work with sufficient validity (Rourke, 1982), so the field progressed to using fixed test batteries.

During the **test battery/lesion specification stage** (1940–1980s), there were several major test batteries that were designed to provide multiple measures of the same neuropsychological constructs, thereby improving the reliability and validity of the tests. In the 1940s, World War II shaped the required role and function of early clinical neuropsychologists, which was to use a battery of tests designed to determine the source of possible brain dysfunction. In 1955, Ralph Reitan published the *Halstead-Reitan Neuropsychological Test Battery* (HRNTB), which became the gold standard in clinical neuropsychological assessment. The HRNTB is still used in adult clinical neuropsychology practice today, largely due to updated norms that were developed in the early 1990s (Heaton, Grant, & Matthews, 1991).

Reitan and Davidson (1974) published a downward extension of the HRNTB for children ages 9 to 14 called the *Halstead-Reitan Neuropsychological Test Battery for Older Children* (also see Reitan & Wolfson, 1992). Reitan and Wolfson (1985) also published a version of the HRNTB for young children ages 5 to 8 called the *Reitan-Indiana Neuropsychological Test Battery.* These versions of the HRNTB for children had several limitations, including poor conceptualization of childhood developmental disorders, inadequate norms, covariance with measures of intelligence, an inability to distinguish psychiatric from neuropsychological conditions in children, and the inability to localize dysfunction or predict recovery of function after brain injury (see Teeter & Semrud-Clikeman [1997] for a review).

It is not state-of-the-art practice to use the Halstead-Reitan Batteries to assess neuropsychological functions in children. Unlike the adult versions of the test, which have updated norms, the children's versions of the HRNTB have not been renormed in over fifty years. In current practice, many of the HRNTB tests have been modified and updated and included in more recent neuropsychological test batteries. For example, the *Reitan-Klove Sensory-Perceptual Examination* from the HRNTB has been restandardized, updated, and serves as the foundation for the *Dean-Woodcock Sensory-Motor Battery* (DWSMB; Dean & Woodcock, 2003). One of the advantages of using the DWSMB is the fact that the test is co-normed with the *Woodcock-Johnson III Tests of Cognitive Abilities* (Woodcock, McGrew, & Mather, 2001). As another example, the Trail Making Test (TMT) from the HRNTB has been widely used in isolation by practitioners. An updated version of the TMT was included in the *Delis-Kaplan Executive Function System* (D-KEFS; Delis, Kaplan, & Kramer, 2001). The D-KEFS version of the TMT is co-normed with a battery of other executive function measures, and it includes detailed process assessment information to aid in clinical interpretation.

Another early "gold standard" in the practice of adult clinical neuropsychology was the *Luria-Nebraska Neuropsychological Battery* (LNNB) for adults (Golden, Hammeke, & Purish, 1978). The LNNB was an attempt by U.S. neuropsychologists to standardize the largely qualitative approach to clinical neuropsychology used by the Russian neuropsychologist, Alexander Luria. Luria's theory of brain functioning has provided the foundation for many of the more modern neuropsychological assessment instruments used today (e.g., *Cognitive Assessment System* [Naglieri & Das, 1997]; *Kaufman Assessment Battery for Children, 2nd Edition* [Kaufman & Kaufman, 2004]). Golden (1986) also published a children's version of the LNNB for ages 8 to 12 called the *Luria-Nebraska Neuropsychological Battery: Children's Revision*

(LNNB-CR). Teeter and Semrud-Clikeman (1997) provided an extensive review of the LNNB-CR. They found studies that supported the use of the LNNB-CR for differentiating LD from non-LD children, but there was little evidence that the LNNB-CR was effective in differentiating neurologically impaired from nonclinical groups.

The third major clinical approach that emerged during the test battery/lesion specification stage became known as the process assessment approach. In the 1960s and 1970s, a group of clinicians and researchers (e.g., Norman Geschwind, Harold Goodglass, Nelson Butters, Heinz Warner, Edith Kaplan) investigated variations in cognitive functions across clinical populations, but did not use the typical fixed batteries (e.g., HRNTB or the LNNB) (see Hebben & Milberg, 2002 for a review). The process assessment approach used a flexible, rather than fixed, battery approach and put emphasis on the qualitative aspects of behavior. As clinicians, those trained in the process assessment approach were just as interested in the strategies that an individual used to derive a test score, if not more than the test score itself. The principle of "testing the limits" to determine why a particular test was difficult for an individual was developed by these process assessment clinicians.

In current practice, the process assessment approach has been integrated into tests such as the *Cognitive Assessment System* (Naglieri & Das, 1997), the *Wechsler Intelligence Scale for Children, 4th Edition Integrated* (Wechsler, 2004), the *Kaufman Assessment Battery for Children, 2nd Edition* (Kaufman & Kaufman, 2004), the D-KEFS (Delis, Kaplan, & Kramer, 2001), and the NEPSY-II (Korkman, Kirk, & Kemp, 2007).

In summary, the HRNB, the LNNB, and the process assessment approach emerged during the test battery/lesion specification stage, and each has produced a lasting impact upon clinical neuropsychological assessment. However, the need to move beyond assessment only for the sake of diagnosis to a model that links assessment to prescriptive interventions laid the foundation for the next stage in clinical neuropsychology, called the functional profile stage (Miller, 2007).

The **functional profile stage** (1970s–1990s) described the period in clinical neuropsychology and the emerging specialization of school neuropsychology. In the 1970s, there were three major factors that helped to reshape neuropsychology: (1) Neuropsychologists who specialized in working with children started to question the logic of using downward extensions of adult assessment models and applying these to children, (2) neuropsychologists started to question the validity of neuropsychological test batteries to localize brain lesions and predict recovery of functions, and (3) the emergence of noninvasive brain imaging techniques that replaced the need for neuropsychological tests to make inferences regarding the site of brain lesions or dysfunction (Miller, 2007). The focus of neuropsychological testing during this period shifted away from localizing lesions to identifying functional strengths and weaknesses that would aid in the remediation of impaired abilities.

Rourke (1982) referred to this *functional profile stage* as the *cognitive stage* because clinicians integrated the principles of cognitive psychology into the practice of neuropsychology. However, despite the call for neuropsychologists to provide more functional assessments of cognitive strengths and weaknesses and for better linkages to prescriptive interventions, the assessment tools available to neuropsychologists did not change until the early 1990s.

The **integrative and predictive stage** was a term used by Miller (2007) to describe the period of neuropsychological assessment from the 1990s to present time. Within the past two decades, there has been a convergence of research on brain–behavior relationships that has influenced school neuropsychology and the assessment tools. School neuropsychology started to emerge as a specialization in earnest in the 1990s. The multidisciplinary influences on school neuropsychology include the development of tests specifically designed for children, advancements in neuroimaging techniques (see Chapter 7 in this book for a review of the best practices in the application of neuroscience to the practice of school neuropsychology), advancements in the theoretical foundations for neuropsychological tests, cross-battery assessment, the process assessment approach, focus on ecological validity, and the emphasis on linking assessment with evidence-based interventions (Miller, 2007).

Table 1.1 presents the major tests of cognitive abilities and school neuropsychological tests published since the 1990s. The tests of cognitive abilities were included in this table because the major tests of cognition have increasingly incorporated neuropsychological constructs (e.g., processing speed, working memory, executive functions). The wealth of theoretically based and psychometrically sound assessment instruments that we as practitioners have at our current disposal is unprecedented in the history of school psychology or the emerging specialization of school neuropsychology. However, many of these neuropsychological constructs now mainstream in assessment require the practitioner to have better training in the biological bases of behavior and understanding of neuropsychological theories. Training issues will be discussed in more depth in Chapter 2 of this book.

WHEN TO REFER FOR A SCHOOL NEUROPSYCHOLOGICAL ASSESSMENT OR CONSULTATION

It would not be prudent or practical to conduct a comprehensive school neuropsychological assessment on every child experiencing learning difficulties. Neuropsychological evaluations are more in-depth than psychoeducational and psychological evaluations because they assess a wider variety of

Table 1.1

Major School Neuropsychological Tests Published Since 1990

Tests of Cognitive Ability	Neuropsychological Tests
• Cognitive Assessment System (Naglieri & Das, 1997) • Woodcock-Johnson III Tests of Cognitive Abilities (Woodcock, McGrew, & Mather, 2001) • Wechsler Preschool and Primary Scales of Intelligence – Third Edition (Wechsler, 2002) • Stanford-Binet Intelligence Scales: Fifth Edition (Roid, 2003) • Wechsler Intelligence Scale for Children – Fourth Edition (Wechsler, 2003) • Kaufman Assessment Battery for Children – Second Edition (Kaufman & Kaufman, 2004) • Differential Ability Scales – Second Edition (Elliott, 2007).	• Wide Range Assessment of Memory and Learning (WRAML: Sheslow & Adams, 1990) • Test of Memory and Learning (Reynolds & Bigler, 1994) • California Verbal Learning Test: Children's Version (Delis, Kramer, Kaplan, & Ober, 1994) • Children's Memory Scale (Cohen, 1997) • Wechsler Memory Scale – Third Edition (Wechsler, 1997) • NEPSY (Korkman, Kirk, & Kemp, 1998) • WISC-III as a Process Instrument (Kaplan, Fein, Kramer, Delis, & Morris, 1999) • Test of Everyday Attention (Manly, Robertson, Anderson, & Nimmo-Smith, 1999) • Delis-Kaplan Executive Functions System (Delis, Kaplan, & Kramer, 2001) • Dean-Woodcock Neuropsychological Battery (Dean & Woodcock, 2003) • Wide Range Assessment of Memory and Learning – Second Edition (Sheslow & Adams, 2003) • Wechsler Intelligence Scale for Children – Fourth Edition Integrated (Wechsler, 2004) • Test of Memory and Learning – Second Edition (Reynolds & Voress, 2007) • NEPSY-II (Korkman, Kirk, & Kemp, 2007)

constructs (e.g., sensory-motor functions, memory and learning, executive functions, and others). One of the first roles a school neuropsychologist must assume with a school district is to set some policies and procedures for educators and parents about when to refer for a school neuropsychological evaluation.

Table 1.2 lists some of the common reasons for a school neuropsychological assessment.

Children with a Known or Suspected Neuropsychological Disorder

This is a broad category of potential referral candidates. It could be argued that all learning and behavior has a neuropsychological basis; however,

Table 1.2

Common Reasons for a School Neuropsychological Evaluation

- Children with a known or suspected neuropsychological disorder.
- Children with a past or recent history of a head injury who are currently having academic or behavioral problems.
- Children with acquired or congenital brain damage.
- Children with neuromuscular diseases.
- Children with brain tumors.
- Children with a central nervous system infection or compromise.
- Children with neurodevelopmental risk factors.
- Children returning to school after a head injury.
- Children who have rapid declines in academic achievement and behavioral deterioration that cannot be explained by social-emotional or environmental factors.
- Children who have not responded to multiple evidence-based interventions.

Adapted from Miller (2007).

the targeted referral source in this case is more specific. Many school districts are implementing a Response-to-Intervention approach to monitor educational interventions and perhaps lead to more comprehensive diagnosis of a disability. When a child consistently does not respond to a variety of evidence-based interventions, a comprehensive school neuropsychological assessment could help identify a profile of the child's neurocognitive strengths and weaknesses and perhaps an underlying neuropsychological condition. The goal of the school neuropsychological evaluation will be to develop appropriate educational interventions based on the neurocognitive assessment data.

It is important to keep in mind that not all children with known or suspected neuropsychological disorders will be experiencing current academic or behavioral difficulties. Ideally, school neuropsychologists should work with educators in a preventive manner to maximize the learning environment for all children in an effort to minimize future learning and behavioral difficulties. However, if a child with a known or suspected neuropsychological disorder starts to manifest educational problems, appropriate assessments and interventions should be taken to help that child.

CHILDREN WITH HEAD INJURIES WHO ARE HAVING ACADEMIC OR BEHAVIORAL PROBLEMS

During the early years of development many children have incidences of hitting their heads. Bumps and bruises seem to be a normal process of growing up for most children. However, when a hit to a child's head causes loss of consciousness, the potential adverse impact of that injury dramatically increases. It is not uncommon for a child to sustain a head injury and to appear afterward (perhaps for days, weeks, or years) as if there were no side effects, only to have academic or behavioral difficulties surface at a later date that are related to the head injury. At a minimum, school neuropsychologists should monitor those children who have suffered head traumas to make sure there are no lasting effects. A comprehensive school neuropsychological evaluation would provide baseline data about the child's neurocognitive strengths and weaknesses that could aid in intervention planning. See Chapter 30 in this book for a review of the best practices of assessing and intervening with children who have traumatic brain injuries.

Children with Acquired or Congenital Brain Damage

Not all head injuries are caused by traumatic events such as blows to the head. Some head injuries caused by disorders of the brain, such as anoxia or meningitis, can adversely affect some brain functions. A comprehensive school neuropsychological evaluation for children with acquired or congenital brain damage would provide baseline data about the child's neurocognitive strengths and weaknesses that could aid in intervention planning. See Miller (2007, pp. 65–66) and Chapter 27 in this book for a comprehensive review of the best practices of assessing and intervening with children who have chronic illnesses.

Children with Neuromuscular Diseases

Children with neuromuscular disorders may or may not have neurocognitive deficits associated with their primary disorder. The very nature of neuro-muscular disorders makes traditional assessment methods difficult to apply. An example would be children with cerebral palsy, which prohibits or impairs motor movements, interfering with motor output, including speech and gross and fine motor control. In such as cases, school neuropsychologists will need to collaborate with other specialized practitioners such as occupa-tional and physical therapists when assessing children with neuromuscular diseases. See Miller (2007, pp. 66–72) for a review of cerebral palsy and muscular dystrophy disorders and their potential related neuropsychological deficits.

Children with Brain Tumors

School neuropsychologists will ultimately work with children who have been identified as having a brain tumor or with children who are coming back to school after medical interventions to treat a brain tumor. Brain tumors occur in different sizes and locations. Some brain tumors are more readily treatable, while others shorten a child's life considerably. Children with brain tumors and their families and peers will need emotional support while coping with the medical treatment. A school neuropsychologist can play a direct role in providing counseling support services to the child, family, and peers or in acting as a referral agent to facilitate those services. Regardless of how one provides those counseling support services, these services cannot be ignored. A comprehensive school neuropsychological assessment will provide information about which neurocognitive functions are impaired and which ones are spared in a child with a brain tumor. Chapter 28 in this book reviews the best practices of assessing and intervening with children who have brain tumors.

CHILDREN WITH A CENTRAL NERVOUS SYSTEM INFECTION OR COMPROMISE

Many children in the schools have medical disorders that compromise the central nervous system (CNS) and may lead to transient or chronic neurocognitive deficits. These disorders include, but are not limited to, asthma, HIV/AIDS, hydrocephalus, juvenile diabetes, leukemia, and end-stage renal disease. These disorders and their associated neuropsychological deficits are reviewed by Miller (2007, pp. 68–75), and Chapter 27 of this book reviews the best practices of assessing and intervening with children who have chronic illnesses. School neuropsychological assessments may or may not be warranted with these children who have CNS infections or compromises. Educational need will be the determinant as to when to refer for a school neuropsychological evaluation for these types of children.

CHILDREN WITH NEURODEVELOPMENTAL RISK FACTORS

There are a wide variety of neurodevelopmental risk factors that can affect a child's neuropsychological functions. Unfortunately, some of these are preventable such as fetal exposure to drugs and alcohol. Other examples include exposure to environmental toxins (e.g., lead, PCBs, mercury) and low birth weight or prematurity. These disorders and their associated neuropsychological deficits are reviewed by Miller (2007, pp. 75–77), and Chapter 27 of this book reviews the best practices of assessing and intervening with children who have chronic illnesses. If one of these neurodevelopmental risk factors is found in the developmental history of a child, it may be prudent to conduct a school neuropsychological assessment specifically in the areas of known deficits. For example, fetal alcohol exposure has been linked to fine motor deficits, so an assessment that includes a test of visual-motor functioning or fine motor control would be warranted.

CHILDREN RETURNING TO SCHOOL AFTER EXPERIENCING A NEUROLOGICAL CONDITION

An important role of a school neuropsychologist is to assist in the planning and transition for children who are coming back to school after hospitalization for a neurological condition or a chronic illness. As previously mentioned, it is better to plan for a smooth transition for a child returning to school after a neurological insult rather than to have the child show up at a school without any prior warning or preparation. Sometimes a child comes back to school with a recently completed comprehensive neuropsychological assessment. However, if the child did not receive a neuropsychological assessment while in the hospital or as part of the outpatient care, the school neuropsychologist should conduct an evaluation to establish a functional profile of the child's neurocognitive strengths and weaknesses. Chapter 10 in this book reviews the best practices in school reentry for children recovering from neurological conditions.

CHILDREN WHO HAVE RAPID DECLINES IN ACADEMIC ACHIEVEMENT AND BEHAVIORAL DETERIORATION THAT CANNOT BE EXPLAINED BY SOCIAL-EMOTIONAL OR ENVIRONMENTAL FACTORS

It is important for a school neuropsychologist to recognize the limits of his or her expertise and competency. There will be occasions when a school neuropsychologist will need to refer a child to a neurologist due to a suspected neurological condition such as a brain tumor or severe seizure disorder. School neuropsychologists should be concerned about a child who has a rapid decline in his or her academic performance and or behavioral functioning that cannot be explained by social-emotional or environmental factors. If the condition of the child is not too severe, a comprehensive school neuropsychological evaluation might be helpful to the neurologist to determine the extent of any neuropsychological impairment (Miller, 2007).

SUMMARY

It is an exciting time to specialize in school neuropsychology. Many of the constructs of neuropsychology, such as working memory and executive functions, are becoming part of mainstream assessment. There has never been a time in the history of school neuropsychology that offers practitioners a myriad of choices of theoretically and psychometrically sound assessment instruments to use in evaluating children with special needs. The challenge for school neuropsychology is the same challenge for school psychology—to establish strong evidence-based linkages between assessment and interventions and to broaden our approaches to culturally diverse populations. The remainder of this book will cover many of these topics in greater detail.

REFERENCES

American Psychological Association. (1987). Model Act for state licensure of psychologists. *American Psychologist, 42*, 696–703.

Brannigan, G. G., & Decker, S. L. (2003). *Bender-Gestalt II examiner's manual*. Itasca, IL: Riverside Publishing.

Cohen, M. J. (1997). *Children's memory scale*. San Antonio, TX: Harcourt Assessment, Inc.

Curtis, M. J., Hunley, S. A., & Chesno-Grier, J. E. (2004). The status of school psychology: Implications of a major personnel shortage. *Psychology in the Schools, 41*, 431–442.

Dean, R. S., & Woodcock, R. W. (2003). *Dean-Woodcock neuropsychological battery*. Itasca, IL: Riverside Publishing.

Delis, D., Kaplan, E., & Kramer, J. H. (2001). *Delis-Kaplan executive function system examiner's manual*. San Antonio, TX: The Psychological Corporation.

Delis, D. C., Kramer, J. H., Kaplan, E., & Ober, B. A. (1994). *California verbal learning test: Children's version*. San Antonio, TX: Harcourt Assessment, Inc.

Elliott, C. D. (2007). *Differential ability scales – II*. San Antonio, TX: Harcourt Assessment, Inc.

Fagan, T. K. (2002). School psychology: Recent descriptions, continued expansion, and an ongoing paradox. *School Psychology Review, 31*, 5–10

Golden, C. J. (1986). *Manual for the Luria-Nebraska neuropsychological battery: Children's revision*. Los Angeles: Western Psychological Services.

Golden, C. J., Hammeke, T. A., & Purish, A. D. (1978). Diagnostic validity of a standardized neuropsychological battery derived from Luria's neuropsychological tests. *Journal of Consulting and Clinical Psychology, 46*, 1258–1265.

Heaton, R. K. (1981). *Wisconsin card sorting test manual*. Odessa, FL: Psychological Assessment Resources.

Heaton, R. K., Grant, I., & Matthews, C. G. (1991). *Comprehensive norms for expanded Halstead-Reitan battery: Demographic corrections, research findings, and clinical applications*. Odessa, FL: Psychological Assessment Resources.

Hebben, N., & Milberg, W. (2002). *Essentials of neuropsychological assessment*. New York: John Wiley & Sons.

Hynd, G. W., & Reynolds, C. R. (2005). School neuropsychology: The evolution of a specialty in school psychology. In R. C. D'Amato, E. Fletcher-Janzen, & C. R. Reynolds (Eds.), *Handbook of school neuropsychology* (pp. 3–14). Hoboken, NJ: John Wiley & Sons.

Kaplan, E., Fein, D., Kramer, J., Delis, D., & Morris, R. (1999). *WISC-III PI manual*. San Antonio. TX: The Psychological Corporation.

Kaufman, A. S., & Kaufman, N. L. (2004). *Kaufman assessment battery for children* (2nd ed.). Circle Pines, MN: American Guidance Service Publishing.

Korkman, M., Kirk, U., & Kemp, S. (1998). *NEPSY: A developmental neuropsychological assessment*. San Antonio, TX: The Psychological Corporation.

Korkman, M., Kirk, U., & Kemp, S. (2007). *NEPSY-II: A developmental neuropsychological assessment*. San Antonio, TX: The Psychological Corporation.

Manly, J., Robinson, I. H., Anderson, V., & Nimmo–Smith, I. (1999). *Test of everyday attention for children (TEA-Ch) manual*. San Antonio, TX: Harcourt Assessment.

Miller, D. C. (2007). *Essentials of school neuropsychological assessment*. Hoboken, NJ: John Wiley & Sons.

Miller, D. C., DeOrnellas, K., & Maricle, D. (2008). Is it time for our organization to recognize subspecialties within school psychology? *Communiqueé, 36*(5), 40–41.

Miller, D. C., DeOrnellas, K., & Maricle, D. (2009). What is so special about the specialist degree? In E. García-Vázquez, T. Crespi, and C. Riccio (Eds.), *Handbook of education, training and supervision of school psychologists in school and community— Volume I: Foundations of professional practice*. United Kingdom: Routledge.

Miller, D. C., Maricle, D., & DeOrnellas, K. (2009). Survey: Is it time for our organization to recognize subspecialties within school psychology? *Communiqué, 37*(5), 23–24.

Nagileri, J., & Das, J. P. (1997). *Das-Naglieri cognitive assessment system*. Itasca, IL: Riverside Publishing Company.

Reitan, R. M. (1955). Discussion: Symposium on the temporal lobe. *Archives of Neurology and Psychiatry, 74*, 569–570.

Reitan, R. M., & Davidson, L. A. (Eds.). (1974). *Clinical neuropsychology: Current status and applications*. Washington, DC: V. H. Winston & Sons.

Reitan, R. M., & Wolfson, D. (1985). *The Halstead-Reitan neuropsychological test battery: Theory and clinical interpretation*. Tucson, AZ: Neuropsychological Press.

Reitan, R. M., & Wolfson, D. (1992). *Neuropsychological evaluation of older children*. Tucson, AZ: Neuropsychology Press.

Reynolds, C. R., & Bigler, E. D. (1994). *Tests of memory and learning examiner's manual*. Austin, TX: PRO-ED, Inc.

Reynolds, C. R., & Voress, J. K. (2007). *Test of memory and learning* (2nd ed.). Lutz, FL: PAR, Inc.

Roid, G. H. (2003). *Stanford-Binet intelligence scales* (5th ed.). Itasca, IL: Riverside Publishing.

Rourke, B. P. (1982). Central processing deficits in children: Toward a developmental neuropsychological model. *Journal of Clinical Neuropsychology, 4*, 1–18.

Sheslow, D., & Adams, W. (1990). *Wide range assessment of memory and learning*. Wilmington, DE: Wide Range, Inc.

Sheslow, D., & Adams, W. (2003). *Wide range assessment of memory and learning* (2nd ed.). Wilmington, DE: Wide Range, Inc.

Teeter, P. A., & Semrud-Clikeman, M. (1997). *Child neuropsychology: Assessment and interventions for neurodevelopmental disorders*. New York: Allyn and Bacon.

Wechsler, D. (1997). *Wechsler memory scales* (3rd ed.). San Antonio, TX: Harcourt Assessment, Inc.

Wechsler, D. (2002). *Wechsler preschool and primary scales of intelligence* (3rd ed.). San Antonio, TX: Harcourt Assessment, Inc.

Wechsler, D. (2003). *Wechsler intelligence scale for children* (4th ed.). San Antonio, TX: Harcourt Assessment, Inc.

Wechsler, D. (2004). *WISC-IV integrated*. San Antonio, TX: Harcourt Assessment.

Woodcock, R. W., McGrew, K. S., & Mather, N. (2001). *Woodcock-Johnson III tests of cognitive abilities*. Itasca, IL: Riverside Publishing.

CHAPTER 2

School Neuropsychology Training and Credentialing

DANIEL C. MILLER

T HE PURPOSE OF this chapter is to discuss the question of what constitutes competency in school neuropsychology, review existing training standards in clinical neuropsychology, discuss the need for school psychologists to integrate neuropsychological principles into practice, review the controversies about professional titles used in the field, review and compare the board certified credentials that are available to neuropsychology specialists, present proposed guidelines for training in school neuropsychology, and finally, illustrate a model school neuropsychology training program.

THE ISSUE OF COMPETENCY

The American Psychological Association (APA) and the National Association of School Psychologists (NASP) have each adopted guidelines for ethical behavior by their membership. Both documents address the issue of competency.

"Psychologists provide services, teach, and conduct research with populations and in areas only within the boundaries of their competence, based on their education, training, supervised experience, consultation, study, or professional experience" (APA, 2002, p. 4).

"School psychologists recognize the strengths and limitations of their training and experience, engaging only in practices for which they are qualified" (NASP, 2000, p. 16).

The question that often arises in practice is, What constitutes competency within a specialty area, such as school neuropsychology? Competency is often poorly defined in many professions as the concept relates to continued professional development. Miller (2007) provides the example of typical continued professional development training in school psychology. When a new version of a widely used test of cognitive abilities comes on the market, practitioners flock to Countinuing Education Unit workshops around the country that are often sponsored by the test publisher. The question raised is, If a practitioner sits in a three-hour workshop on this newly revised test instrument and has the Continuing Education Unit (CEU) certificate to prove attendance, does that make the practitioner competent to administer and interpret the newly revised version of the test? The answer should be a resounding no, but many practitioners in the fields of psychology and education commonly use this method of professional development.

In this example, for true professional competency to occur, continued professional development must have a supervised practice component built into the training. For example, the practitioner could take a basic CEU workshop on the steps to administer the new version of a test, but it would then be a best practice to send the practitioner back to his or her daily job to practice using the new test. Ideally, the practitioner would then return for a follow-up advanced CEU workshop for small group supervision to review questions he or she has about administration and interpretation of the test. Miller noted:

> If the practitioner demonstrated evidence of mastery of the new test, then that new test could be confidently integrated into practice. If the practitioner could not demonstrate mastery of the new test, additional time for supervised practice should be mandated. This model of competency-based workshop and training should be used more often in the ever changing and often technically and theoretically complex field of school psychology [and the emerging specialization of school neuropsychology]. (2007, p. 43)

Competency in school neuropsychology is not based on learning how to administer and interpret a battery of neuropsychological tests. Neuropsychological tests are tools, but knowing how to use those tests does not make a practitioner a school neuropsychologist (Miller, 2007). The professional competency of school neuropsychology resides with the meaningful interpretation of test results from a brain–behavior perspective and their linkage with evidence-based interventions. Too many professionals claim competency in a specialization because they know how to use a few tools of the trade. In the field of clinical neuropsychology, it was common for psychologists to claim expertise in neuropsychology after attending a three-day workshop on the *Halstead-Reitan Neuropsychological Battery*. Test publishers share responsibility in this regard by offering trainings on their newer tests that are based on neuropsychological theory only to those practitioners who have prior graduate training in psychological foundations. Competency in school neuropsychology must include a broad range of skills, which are later defined in this chapter in a set of proposed training guidelines.

After school psychologists receive advanced training in school neuropsychology, they often report that their perceptions of children are unequivocally changed (Miller, 2007). Rather than being test dependent, school neuropsychology has basically a qualitative understanding of brain–behavior relationships and how they are manifested through behavior and learning. A competent school neuropsychology clinician can recognize neuropsychological conditions based on a variety of samples of behavior, starting with observing the child in the normal course of daily activities and including interpreting data from formal testing. In school neuropsychology, competency is initially achieved through supervised formal training and maintained by a commitment to lifelong learning.

TRAINING STANDARDS IN CLINICAL NEUROPSYCHOLOGY

In the broader field of psychology, there are too many practitioners who claim competency and even expertise in neuropsychology, yet they have minimal training (Shordone & Saul, 2000). In an effort to define entry-level competency in clinical neuropsychology, several of the major professional organizations representing the field have attempted to create national training guidelines. In the realm of United States clinical neuropsychology, there have been two major training guidelines suggested for the education and training of clinical neuropsychologists: (1) the Guidelines of the INS-Division 40 Task Force on Education, Accreditation, and Credentialing (1987), and (2) the Houston Conference on Specialty Education and Training in Clinical Neuropsychology (Hannay et al., 1998).

With major differences between the two sets of training guidelines, the clinical neuropsychology field is struggling with ways to fully implement them in training programs and in certification boards. The INS-Division 40 Guidelines represent a broader view of neuropsychology than the Houston Conference Policy Statement. The INS-Division 40 Guidelines state that a neuropsychologist may or may not be a psychologist, which suggests that neuropsychology is viewed in a broad interdisciplinary context, whereas the Houston Conference Policy Statement suggests that neuropsychology is a specialty area within psychology only. Many concerns have been expressed about the Houston Conference Policy Statement, ranging from the lack of a broad base of constituents when the document was developed (Reitan, Hom, Van De Voorde, Stanczak, & Wolfson, 2004; Reynolds, 2002), to lacking in content (e.g., not providing enough background training in basic neuropsychology knowledge [Ardila, 2002]), and for concerns about the restrictive definition of a clinical neuropsychologist (Reitan et al., 2004). Koffler (2002) suggested that the INS-Division 40 Guidelines serve to outline training programs in clinical neuropsychology, whereas the Houston Conference Policy Statement sets aspirational goals for individuals wanting to be trained in clinical neuropsychology.

Despite the differences between these sets of clinical neuropsychology guidelines, both training guidelines take the position that a clinical neuropsychologist is a doctoral-level service provider. In 2001, the National Academy of Neuropsychologists (NAN) adopted a definition of a clinical neuropsychologist (Barth et al., 2003), including the following minimal criteria:

1. A doctoral degree in psychology from an accredited university training program.
2. An internship, or its equivalent, in a clinically relevant area of professional psychology.
3. The equivalent of two (full-time) years of experience and specialized training, at least one of which is at the postdoctoral level, in the study and practice of clinical neuropsychology and related neurosciences. These two years include supervision by a clinical neuropsychologist.
4. A license in his or her state or province to practice psychology and/or clinical neuropsychology independently, or employment as a neuropsychologist by an exempt agency.

Most clinical neuropsychology training programs take place within Ph.D. or Psy.D. clinical psychology programs. On the APA Division 40s web page (www.div40.org) there is a list of twenty-nine doctoral programs that are self-identified as providing doctoral training in clinical neuropsychology and thirty-nine internship training sites with a clinical neuropsychology rotation or focus (retrieved August 10, 2008). Most clinical neuropsychology training programs and internships have an adult focus, with few programs offering a pediatric track (Miller, 2007).

TRAINING SCHOOL PSYCHOLOGISTS TO INTEGRATE NEUROPSYCHOLOGICAL PRINCIPLES INTO PRACTICE

Chapter 1 in this book and Miller (2004, 2007) provide a comprehensive review of reasons why neuropsychological services are needed within the schools. For example, children are increasingly coming to school with known or suspected neuropsychological conditions that include, but are not limited to: traumatic or acquired brain injuries, neuromuscular disorders, central nervous system infection or compromise, neurodevelopmental risk factors (e.g., prematurity, low-birth weight), or prenatal exposure to drugs or alcohol. These conditions may lead to a neuropsychological evaluation being requested by a parent, educator, school district, or impartial hearing officer. When a neuropsychological evaluation is requested by the schools, educators are faced with services that are often very difficult to find, require a long wait to be evaluated, and are expensive.

In 2003, Rohling, Lees-Haley, Langhinrichsen-Rohling, and Williamson estimated that there were approximately 3,500 to 4,000 professionals who practice as clinical neuropsychologists. The majority of those practitioners specialized in working with adults. When schools need a neuropsychological evaluation completed, they prefer contracting with a pediatric neuro-psychologist. However, today pediatric neuropsychologists are often found in hospital or rehabilitation settings and may or may not take outside referrals. Therefore, finding access to a professional who can conduct a neuropsychological evaluation for the schools is often difficult at best.

When a school district is fortunate enough to find a clinical neuro-psychologist to conduct an evaluation on a school-aged child, it is often the case that the neuropsychological evaluation is not very helpful to the schools. Clinical neuropsychological evaluations are generally geared toward identifying brain dysfunction, and clinical neuropsychologists typically do not understand how educational systems work in regard to identifying and working with children with disabilities. The downside to contracting with any specialists outside of the schools is that they may not be familiar with the IDEA rules and regulations and are therefore limited in having successful results (Miller, 2004). As a result of these limitations, school districts are often frustrated with the results, and the schools do not seem to appreciate the services of the specialists.

For neuropsychological principles to be successfully integrated into the schools, there needs to be greater cross-discipline or interdisciplinary training (Miller, 2004). School psychologists are uniquely poised to integrate neuro-psychological principles into educational practice because they have direct daily access to children in the schools. Currently, there are over 30,000 school psychologists in the United States.

A limitation for school psychologists providing neuropsychological assess-ments, consultations, and interventions in the schools is lack of training in neuropsychology. The majority of school psychology training programs are modeled after the 60+ hours of graduate training (the specialist-level) as recommended by the National Association of School Psychologists. In a comprehensive review of all U.S. and Canadian training programs, Miller (2008) found that out of the total 220 nondoctoral school psychology training programs, only three U.S. and three Canadian school psychology nondoctoral training programs require fewer than 60 hours of graduate training. The data revealed that the school psychology profession is largely a field dominated by professionals trained at the specialist level. Unfortunately, most specialist-level training programs provide minimal training in the biological bases of behavior and rarely cover neuropsychological assessment and intervention techniques (Miller, 2004). Recent studies by McGrath and Yalof (2007, 2008) found that minimal training in the biological bases of behavior occurs at both the specialist level and doctoral levels of school psychology training programs.

McGrath and Yalof (2007) surveyed all of the U.S. school psychology training programs regarding the extent to which they are covering school neuropsychological content. Their survey yielded a 26.6 percent return rate. The average number of training programs that required a course on the study of neuropsychological principles was less than one course (mean = .68). The training directors reported that neuropsychological principles were covered in other courses to a lesser degree, and most training directors indicated a desire to increase the level of training in school neuropsychology. In a follow-up study, McGrath and Yalof (2008) surveyed a random sample of 500 NASP members about their school neuropsychology training experiences, their perception of the adequacy of their school neuropsychology training, and their confidence level in incorporating neuropsychological principles into their professional practice. The survey yielded a 22.6 percent return rate. The respondents reported that the median number of courses that they had in which school neuropsychology was the principal content was one. Eight-five percent of the respondents reported that they would like to have more training in school neuropsychology. Likewise, 84 percent of the respondents agreed that neuropsychologically informed assessment methods are essential to a school psychologist's skill set.

Based on convergent evidence, such as the McGrath and Yalof (2007, 2008) survey results, the consistently filled workshops on school neuropsychology–related topics at national- and state-level association meetings, and the high volume of school neuropsychology–related book sales, there seems to be a strong interest among school psychologists to receive more training in the content area. Many of the newest tests already being administered by school psychologists measure constructs based on neuropsychological theory (e.g., K-ABC-II, NEPSY-II, D-KEFS). School psychologists and educators will need to improve their knowledge base about brain–behavior relationships if they are going to appropriately interpret these newer tests. In order to achieve a professionally accepted level of competency to conduct school-based neuro-psychological assessments, school psychologists must receive more formal training than what they are receiving in most school psychology specialist-level training programs.

Finding such formal training remains a challenge for most school psychol-ogy practitioners. There are few school psychology doctoral programs that offer a specialization in school neuropsychology in addition to the Doctorate in School Psychology (e.g., Ball State University, Georgia State University, Texas A&M University, Texas Woman's University). In order to document the highest recognized level of competency in school neuropsychology, practitioners interested in the content area are encouraged to obtain a Doctoral in School Psychology with a specialization in school/pediatric neuropsychology.

Another possible training alternative in school neuropsychology is for school psychologists to complete a postgraduate, competency-based school neuropsychology certification program. Several programs have operated in the past, but currently there is only one national program. In 2002, Miller started a postgraduate certification program in school neuropsychology (see www.schoolneuropsych.com for complete program details). Since 2002, this training program has been held twenty-seven times in seventeen different cities across the United States and graduated over 400 students. The structure has changed over the years from a full-year program to the current training in which students meet eighteen hours once a month on a weekend for eight months. The school neuropsychology postgraduate certification is open to state-certified or licensed school psychologists (graduates of both doctoral and nondoctoral school psychology programs) or to licensed psychologists who work with school-aged children. The course is rigorous and competency-based. Students must pass a 200-item multiple-choice comprehensive exam at the end of the course, and they must complete three comprehensive school neuropsychological evaluations during the course of the program. The course is designed to teach professionals how to use current school neuropsychological assessment instruments and link assessment data to evidence-based interventions.

Most psychologists and other mental health professionals would not argue about the growing need for providing neuropsychological services within the schools. However, there is a major difference of opinion about what level of graduate training should be required to offer neuropsychological services within the schools. Within the fields of psychology and school psychology, it is certainly a guild issue that is related to the long-standing doctoral versus nondoctoral debate of service delivery that has been going on for the past forty years. Crespi and Cooke (2003) raised the question, "What constitutes appropriate education and training for the school psychologist interested in practicing as a neuropsychologist?" This question has sparked a great deal of debate in the literature (see Lange, 2005; Parrish, 2005; Pelletier, Hiemenz, & Shapiro, 2004). In an ideal world, all school psychologists who are interested in becoming competent in neuropsychological assessment and intervention would obtain a doctoral degree in school psychology with a specialization in neuropsychology or a doctoral degree in clinical neuropsychology with a specialization in pediatric neuropsychology. However, the practice of school psychology as it is principally housed within the confines of the public schools is now, and will continue to be, dominated by specialist-level-trained school psychologists. Given that reality of who principally has access to school-aged children and the growing need for neuropsychological services within the schools, this author has taken the position that both specialist-level and doctoral-level school psychologists can be trained to become competent in the integration of neuropsychological principles into their professional practices.

WHAT'S IN A NAME?

The term *psychologist* is a protected term in most states by Psychology Licensing Acts. If a practitioner wants to be called a psychologist, a doctorate in psychology and licensure as a psychologist is generally required. Licensure as a psychologist in most states is generic, meaning that a doctoral psychologist trained in the specialties of clinical, school, counseling, or industrial/organization psychology is uniformly licensed as a psychologist. The title *neuropsychologist* is usually not regulated by state licensing acts, but rather is regulated by the level of attained professional experience and training and through board certification (Miller, 2007).

Hynd and Obrzut (1981) were the first to refer to neuropsychology as a specialty area within doctoral school psychology. The term *school neuropsychology* does not evoke the same degree of response as the title *school neuropsychologist*. For example, one claiming competency in school neuropsychology does not seem to be as inflammatory to some constituencies compared to using the title school neuropsychologist. Pelletier et al. (2004) stated that: "use of the title 'school neuropsychologist' can only serve to diminish the practice of school psychology and clinical neuropsychology alike" (p. 20). Pelletier and her colleagues went on to say that "We believe that the use of this title is not clear, nor fair, and can easily be misconstrued by the lay public" (p. 20). The title school neuropsychologist is not confusing to the public if the title is backed by proficiencies of practice. Peer-reviewed specialty certification (i.e., ABSNP) that attests to the competency of a practitioner who claims expertise in school neuropsychology is designed in part to protect the public and lead to ethical practice. It is hoped that the guidelines for training school neuropsychologists proposed in this chapter will generate a healthy debate in the profession and that additional training programs will adopt these guidelines. The next section of this chapter will focus on credentialing options for clinical neuropsychology and school neuropsychology.

WHO OFFERS CREDENTIALING IN THE NEUROPSYCHOLOGY AREAS?

SPECIALTY CERTIFICATION IN CLINICAL NEUROPSYCHOLOGY

In 1947, the American Psychological Association (APA) set up an independent certification board known today as the American Board of Professional Psychology (ABPP) (Bent, Packard, & Goldberg, 1999). Contrary to popular belief, "APA does not endorse or recognize any examining board in psychology" (Goldstein, 2001, p. 57). ABPP recognized school psychology as a specialty area in 1968; however, it was not until 1984 that the ABPP formally recognized a specialty in clinical neuropsychology (Goldstein, 2001).

In 1982, two certification boards issuing diplomates in clinical neuropsychology were formed: the American Board of Clinical Neuropsychology (ABCN) and the American Board of Professional Neuropsychology (ABPN) (Goldstein, 2001; Horton, Crown, & Reynolds, 2001). The ABCN board was formally recognized by ABPP in 1984, while the ABPN remains autonomous. In 1985, the ABCN and ABPN held discussions about merging the two organizations, but agreement was not reached (Horton et al., 2001). Since the mid-1980s, the two clinical neuropsychology certification boards have continued to independently certify clinical neuropsychologists. The NAN definition of a clinical neuropsychologist (previously presented) also included a statement indicating that board certification is currently not required for practice in clinical neuropsychology.

RECOGNIZING THE INCREASED SPECIALIZATION IN CLINICAL NEUROPSYCHOLOGY

Similar to school psychology, which has become increasingly specialized, subspecialization is also occurring in clinical neuropsychology. The ABCN has a generic focus on clinical neuropsychology; however, the emphasis is more on adult neuropsychology. In 1996, a group of pediatric neuropsychologists expressed concern that neither the ABCN nor ABPN provided board examinations that were sufficient to the task of assessing the unique skills set of pediatric neuropsychologists. As a result of these concerns, a third certification board was formed and called the American Board of Pediatric Neuropsychology (ABPdN). The ABPdN was reorganized in 2002, but it remains a small board compared to the ABCN and the ABPN. In 2007, the ABPdN submitted an application to become a recognized ABPP member, but the application was denied.

The ABPN has recently taken an important step by recognizing the increased specialization within clinical neuropsychology. Similar to the ABCN, the ABPN also has a generic focus on applied clinical neuropsychology; however, in 2007, it created an Added Qualifications Certificate, in addition to the Diplomate, that recognizes competency in one of four subspecialty areas: child and adolescent neuropsychology, forensic neuropsychology, geriatric neuropsychology, and rehabilitation neuropsychology. This is a positive move on the part of the ABPN because clinical neuropsychologists with subspecialties will be more inclined to apply for the Diplomate credential with the Added Qualifications Certificate that attests to their area of competency.

In summary, psychologists at the doctoral level who are licensed psychologists and have documented expertise in clinical neuropsychology have several options to choose from when it comes to board certification. The ABCN and the ABPN are the two principal Board Certified Diplomate credentials. The recent Added Qualifications Certificate that the ABPN has approved as an extension to its Diplomate credential in recognition of one of four subspecialties should be well received by the profession. If a clinical neuropsychologist has specialized expertise in working with populations, the ABPN Diplomate with the child and adolescent Added Qualifications Certification would be one option for a professional to pursue when applying for the ABPdN Diplomate.

SPECIALTY CERTIFICATION IN SCHOOL NEUROPSYCHOLOGY

In 1999, another certification board was created, called the American Board of School Neuropsychology (ABSNP). The ABSNP was established to provide a peer-reviewed credential for those school psychologists claiming expertise in applying neuropsychological principles with children in school-based settings. The ABSNP issues a Diplomate in School Neuropsychology credential. The ABSNP Diplomate is not a license to practice in any state; rather, it is a peer-reviewed credential that certifies entry-level competency in school neuropsychology. Applicants must be certified or licensed as a school psychologist (or equivalent), or be a licensed psychologist with specialization in school/pediatric neuropsychology, or be an ABPP Diplomate in School Psychology with additional specialization in school/pediatric neuropsychology.

The distinction between the ABSNP and the other certification boards previously mentioned is that the ABSNP awards the Diplomate in School Neuropsychology to professionals with graduate training in school psychology at both the doctoral and nondoctoral levels. This distinction is not without controversy; however, the founders of the ABSNP believed that there needed to be a peer-reviewed credential for all school psychologist practitioners who claim competency in applying neuropsychological principles in school-based settings. As of 2007, all but three school psychology training programs in the United States are based on the specialist level

(Miller, 2008), and this entry-level training in school psychology combined with additional competency-based training in school neuropsychology serves as an adequate baseline for applying to the ABSNP for the Diplomate in School Neuropsychology credential.

Whenever a new certification board is created, there is a tendency for some members of existing boards to accuse a new entity as being just a "vanity board." In the mid-1980s, when both the ABCN and ABPN were created, the ABPN was not affiliated with the ABPP; therefore, the ABPN was accused by some as being a vanity board (Goldstein, 2001). Goldstein made it clear that he did not think the ABPN was a vanity board, but he cautioned against the proliferation of vanity boards. Shordone and Saul (2000) also cautioned that a number of "vanity boards" had surfaced in recent years, "which would offer a Diplomate in clinical neuropsychology to virtually any psychologist who applies and is willing to pay a rather hefty fee" (p. 23). There are several credentialing boards that require no formal peer review of work samples, no passage of an objective written exam based on a knowledge base of the field, and no oral exam to gauge the professional skills and ethical practice of the candidate.

Contrary to some accounts (see Pelletier et al., 2004), the ABSNP is not a vanity board. The ABSNP does require minimal training and experience in school neuropsychology as part of the initial application. If the applicant to the ABSNP is admitted to candidacy, the candidate must pass a 200-item multiple-choice exam and an oral exam based upon a submitted case study and knowledge of the field. Table 2.1 presents the certification requirements for the four neuropsychology-related certification boards. The ABSNP Diplomate in School Neuropsychology requirements are as adequately rigorous as the other specialty certification boards in neuropsychology. Any school psychologist who meets the eligibility requirements may apply for the ABSNP Diplomate. The Diplomate credential is not limited to graduates of one or two programs. A recent review of the ABSNP Diplomates showed that 32 percent hold a doctorate (Ph.D., Psy.D., Ed.D.), and the remaining 68 percent hold either a Specialist Degree or a Master's Degree in school psychology. All of the ABSNP Diplomates are credentialed school psychologists within their state (personal communication, ABSNP office, February 1, 2009).

The interest in the school neuropsychology Diplomate credential has been strong the past two years (2006–2008), with a 79.7 percent increase in the number of ABSNP Board Certified Diplomates. During this same two-year period, there has been a 12.5 percent increase in the number of ABCN Board Certified Diplomates, a 43.7 percent increase in ABPN Board Certified Diplomates, and only a 2.5 percent increase in ABPdN Board Certified Diplomates.

Table 2.1

Comparison of Requirements for Specialty Board Certification in Neuropsychology

Requirement	ABCN[a]	ABPN[b]	ABPdN[c]	ABSNP[d]
Completed Doctorate in Psychology	Yes[e]	Yes	Yes	No[f]
Completed Specialist-Level Training (60+ hrs.) in School Psychology	n/a	n/a	n/a	Yes
Completion of an APA, CPA[g], or APPIC[h] listed internship	Yes	No	Yes	No
Completion of a 1,200 hour internship with at least 600 hours in the schools	No	No	No	Yes
Licensed as a psychologist	Yes	Yes	Yes	No
State Credentialed as a School Psychologist or an NCSP[i]	No	No	No	Yes
3 years of experience in the field	Yes	Yes	No	Yes
2 years postdoctoral residency	Yes	No	Yes	No
Minimum of 500 hours each of the past 5 years providing neuropsychological services	No	Yes	No	n/a
Documentation of approved ongoing CEU workshops	No	Yes	No	Yes
Objective Written Exam	Yes	Yes	Yes	Yes
Work samples peer reviewed	Yes	Yes	Yes	Yes
Oral Exam	Yes	Yes	Yes	Yes
Number of board certified individuals (as of 1999)	444[j]	217[j]	Not known	10[k]
Number of board certified individuals (as of 10/25/06)[l]	562	197	40	197
Number of board certified individuals (as of 10/25/08)[m]	632	283	41	354
Percentage increase in a two-year period	+12.5%	+43.7%	+2.5%	+79.7%

[a]For complete ABCN application guidelines visit www.theabcn.org.
[b]For complete ABPN application guidelines visit www.abpn.net.
[c]For complete ABPdN application guidelines visit www.abpdn.org.
[d]For complete ABSNP application guidelines visit www.absnp.com.
[e]For persons receiving their doctorate after 1/1/2005, the training program must have conformed with the Houston Conference (Hannay et al., 1998).
[f]A doctorate in psychology (school or clinical) with a specialization in neuropsychology is recognized but not required. An ABPP Diplomate in School Psychology is also recognized.
[g]CPA stands for the Canadian Psychological Association.
[h]APPIC stands for the Association of Psychology Postdoctoral and Internship Centers.
[i]NCSP stands for Nationally Certified School Psychologist.
[j]As cited in Rohling, Lees-Haley, Langhinrichsen-Rohling, & Williamson, 2003.
[k]Review of historical records from the ABSNP, Inc.
[l]Cited in Miller (2007, p. 46). Includes board certified professionals from the U.S. and Canada.
[m]Includes board certified professionals from the U.S. and Canada.

PROPOSED SCHOOL NEUROPSYCHOLOGY TRAINING STANDARDS

Currently, there are no professional standards or guidelines for the practice of school neuropsychology that have been endorsed by a national professional organization. NASP has a set of practice standards for the practice of school psychology (Standards for Training and Field Placement Standards in Psychology, 2002), but NASP currently does not endorse specialties within the field of school psychology, despite a challenge by some to do just that (Hynd & Reynolds, 2005; Miller, DeOrnellas, & Maricle, 2008, 2009).

Shapiro and Ziegler (1997), writing as trainers of pediatric neuropsychologists at the University of Minnesota, proposed that students should receive the following knowledge base in their program:

- Basic neuroanatomy, neurophysiology, and some neurochemistry and psychopharmacology.
- Clinical neurology: Functional relationships in both adult and child patients. Basic knowledge of imaging techniques, EEG, and other neurophysiological methods.
- Normal psychological development of the child (both cognitive and emotional/behavioral).
- Developmental neuroscience: Brain–behavior relationships across the lifespan.
- Clinical child psychology: Psychopathology, clinical methods, and personality assessment.
- Educational psychology: Psychoeducational assessment methods for both academic achievement and behavior; methods of intervention in the classroom for neurologically and neurodevelopmentally impaired children.
- Pediatric neuropsychology: Functional brain–behavior relationships in a developmental context; assessment of infants through adolescents.
- Research methods especially as applied to pediatric neuropsychology.
- Intervention methods: Educational, rehabilitational, psychological, and medical (pp. 227–228).

In the *Essentials of School Neuropsychological Assessment* book, Miller (2007) proposed a set of professional guidelines to train school neuropsychologists (see Table 2.2). The training guidelines for pediatric neuropsychology (Shapiro & Ziegler, (1997)) are similar to the training guidelines for school neuropsychology (Miller, 2007), but with some important differences. The proposed pediatric neuropsychology guidelines emphasize the more germane medical aspects of neuropsychology, such as neurophysiology, neurochemistry, basic knowledge of imaging techniques, and cognitive and medical rehabilitation in medical settings (Miller, 2007). The proposed school neuropsychology training guidelines emphasize the theoretical bases for

Table 2.2
Proposed Training Guidelines for School Neuropsychologists

A school neuropsychologist must first have a clear professional identity as a school psychologist. The school neuropsychologist:

- must be trained at the specialist or doctoral level [preferred] in school psychology from a regionally accredited university.
- must have completed a minimum 1,200-hour internship, of which 600 hours must be in the school setting.
- must be state credentialed (certified or licensed) as a school psychologist or equivalent title; or be certified as a Nationally Certified School Psychologist (NCSP), or hold a Diplomate in School Psychology from the American Board of Professional Psychology (ABPP).
- should have a minimum of three years of experience working as a school psychologist before seeking to add the school neuropsychology specialization.

In addition, to the entry-level credentials as outlined above, the school neuropsychologist must have a documented knowledge base and competencies in the following areas:

- Functional neuroanatomy
- History of clinical neuropsychology, pediatric neuropsychology, and school neuropsychology
- Major theoretical approaches to understanding cognitive processing and brain behavior relationships related to learning and behavior
- Professional issues in school neuropsychology
- Neuropsychological disorder nomenclature
- Conceptual model for school neuropsychology assessment
- Specific theories of, assessment of, and interventions with:
  - Sensory-motor functions
  - Attention functions
  - Visual-spatial functions
  - Language functions
  - Memory and learning functions
  - Executive functions
  - Cognitive efficient, cognitive fluency, and processing speed functions
  - General cognitive abilities
- Genetic and neurodevelopmental disorders
- Childhood and adolescent clinical syndromes and related neuropsychological deficits
- Neuropsychopharmacology
- Neuropsychological intervention techniques
- Professional ethics and professional competencies (i.e., report writing skills, history taking, and record review, etc.)
- Competency-based supervised experiences (minimum of 500 hours)
- Continuing education requirements (minimum of 6 CEU hours per year)

Reprinted with permission from D. C. Miller, *Essentials of School Neuropsychological Assessment*, 2007, pp. 48–49.

basic cognitive processes, functional neuroanatomy, and the assessment and evidence-based interventions with various neurodevelopmental processes (e.g., memory, attention, executive functions) within the context of a school-based setting (Miller, 2007).

Miller stated that:

> The entry-level skills and competencies of a school neuropsychologist should first meet the specialist-level training standards as set forth by NASP (Standards for Training and Field Placement Standards in Psychology, 2002). Therefore, it is assumed that a school psychologist trained to become a school neuropsychologist would already have a base knowledge of psychological and educational principles gained as part of their specialist or doctoral-level of training (e.g., child psychopathology, diagnosis/intervention, special education law, professional ethics, etc.). Specialization in school neuropsychology at the doctoral level is the preferred model of training; however, some specialist-level school psychologists will seek out formal training in this area as well. (2007, p. 49)

FUNCTIONAL NEUROANATOMY

In the school setting, it is more important for the school neuropsychologist to have a working knowledge of functional neuroanatomy more so than structural neuroanatomy.

HISTORY OF CLINICAL NEUROPSYCHOLOGY, PEDIATRIC NEUROPSYCHOLOGY, AND SCHOOL NEUROPSYCHOLOGY

"In order to appreciate the current state of professional practice in the field, it is important for school neuropsychologists to review and appreciate the contributions of other related fields to the emerging school neuropsychology specialty" (Miller, 2007, p. 50).

MAJOR THEORETICAL APPROACHES TO UNDERSTAND BRAIN–BEHAVIOR RELATIONSHIPS

The tests of cognitive abilities published since 2000 have integrated many neuropsychological constructs, such as working memory, processing speed, executive functions, and others, based on neuropsychological theories. School neuropsychologists need to understand the major theoretical approaches related to the specialization.

PROFESSIONAL ISSUES IN SCHOOL NEUROPSYCHOLOGY

School neuropsychologists need to be knowledgeable about the professional issues within the field (e.g., credentialing issues, current practice trends).

NEUROPSYCHOLOGICAL DISORDER NOMENCLATURE

School neuropsychologists are frequently called upon to "translate" medical records or previous outside neuropsychological reports to educators and parents (Miller, 2007, p. 50). It is imperative that school neuropsychologists understand and can apply the neuropsychological nomenclature (e.g., knowing the subtypes of dyslexia or dysgraphia).

CONCEPTUAL MODEL FOR SCHOOL NEUROPSYCHOLOGY ASSESSMENT

School neuropsychologists must learn a conceptual model that can serve as a framework for neuropsychological assessments and interventions. Two such models are those proposed by Hale and Fiorello (2004) or Miller (2007).

SPECIFIC THEORIES, ASSESSMENT, AND INTERVENTIONS USED IN DIFFERENT CONSTRUCTS

- Sensory-motor functions
- Attention functions
- Visual-spatial functions
- Language functions
- Memory and learning functions
- Executive functions
- Speed and efficiency of cognitive processing
- General cognitive abilities
- Academic achievement
- Social-emotional functions

School neuropsychologists need to know the specific theoretical models that apply to the processes and functions in the preceding list and their relationship to manifestations in learning problems and in making differential diagnoses with the data. They also need to be proficient in the best assessment instruments designed to measure these individual constructs. The school neuropsychologist needs to know which empirically validated interventions can be linked with the assessment data to maximize the educational opportunities for students and demonstrate the efficacy of the interventions used to address the learning problems (Miller, 2007, p. 51).

GENETIC AND NEURODEVELOPMENTAL DISORDERS

As the front-line psychological service providers in the schools, school psychologists are often one of the first professionals to observe the neurobehavioral consequences of low-incidence genetic and neurodevelopmental disorders. School neuropsychologists should be able to recognize the characteristics associated with the major genetic and neurodevelopmental disorders in children and the related neuropsychological correlates.

CHILDHOOD AND ADOLESCENT CLINICAL SYNDROMES AND RELATED NEUROPSYCHOLOGICAL DEFICITS

School neuropsychologists must be familiar with the research related to the known or suspected neuropsychological correlates of common childhood disorders (e.g., ADHD, Tourette's, pervasive developmental disorders, etc.) and empirically validated interventions in a school setting (Miller, 2007, p. 51).

NEUROPSYCHOPHARMACOLOGY

School-aged children and adolescents are increasingly being medicated to control their behavior and facilitate their learning. "School neuropsychologists need to understand the mechanism of drug actions on brain neurochemistry. They also need to know the medications used to treat common childhood disorders and the potential side effects in order to consult effectively with medical, health personnel, parents, and educators" (Miller, 2007, pp. 51–52).

NEUROPSYCHOLOGICAL INTERVENTION TECHNIQUES

The major challenge for school psychology and school neuropsychology is linking assessment data with evidence-based interventions and monitoring the effectiveness of those interventions. A curriculum for training in school neuropsychology must have a strong focus on evidence-based interventions.

PROFESSIONAL ETHICS AND PROFESSIONAL COMPETENCIES

"School neuropsychologists must understand, appreciate, and integrate professional ethics into their daily practice. School neuropsychologists must gain proficiencies in skills such as integrative report writing, history taking, record review, clinical interviewing, etc." (Miller, 2007, p. 52).

COMPETENCY-BASED SUPERVISED EXPERIENCES

Mastering the knowledge base of school neuropsychology is not sufficient to claim competency in school neuropsychology. Supervised experience where the knowledge base can be applied to real-world experiences is a basic requirement of formal training in school neuropsychology. Miller stated that "[i]ndividual supervision or a 'grand rounds' group type of supervision must be incorporated into a training program to ensure that the trainee is getting practice and quality feedback on emerging skills before putting those skills into actual practice" (2007, p. 52). Miller (2007) recommended that the school neuropsychologist document a minimum of 500 hours of supervised, field-based experiences.

CONTINUING EDUCATION REQUIREMENTS

Miller (2007) recommended that a school neuropsychologist be committed to lifelong learning. School neuropsychology is an emerging specialization, and new resources are becoming available on a regular basis. In order to keep up with the rapid advances in the specialization, school neuropsychologists must maintain their professional skills. The ABNSP requires current Diplomates in School Neuropsychology to obtain a minimum of 6 hours of continuing education credit annually in order to maintain their Diplomate status. Other organizations also require CEUs to renew certification or licensure. For example, NASP requires 75 continuing professional development (CPD) units every three years for renewal of the NCSP credential.

MODEL SCHOOL NEUROPSYCHOLOGY TRAINING PROGRAM

Table 2.3 presents a doctoral school neuropsychology curriculum that was modeled after the 27- to 29-hour school neuropsychology area of specialization within the School Psychology Doctoral Program at Texas Woman's University, Denton, Texas.

Table 2.3
Model Doctoral School Neuropsychology Curriculum

Area of Focus	Possible Class Title
• Functional neuroanatomy	Functional Neuroanatomy, Advanced Behavioral Neuroscience, Advanced Neurophysiology (3 semester hour class)

• History of clinical neuropsychology, pediatric neuropsychology, and school neuropsychology
 • Professional ethics
 • Major theoretical approaches and professional issues
 • Conceptual model for school neuropsychology
 • Neuropsychological disorder nomenclature
 • Theories of, assessment of, and interventions with:
   ○ Sensory-motor functions
   ○ Attention functions
   ○ Executive functions
   ○ Speed and efficiency of cognitive processing
	School Neuropsychology I (3 semester hour class)

Table 2.3
Continued

Area of Focus	Possible Class Title
• Report writing • Supervised practice (minimum 50 hours)	

• Theories of, assessment of, and interventions with:
  ○ Memory and learning functions
  ○ Language functions
  ○ Visual-spatial functions
  ○ Social-emotional functions
• Childhood/adolescent clinical syndromes and related neuropsychological deficits
• Report writing (reinforced)
• Professional ethics (reinforced)
• Supervised practice (minimum 50 hours)
	School Neuropsychology II
	(3 semester hour class)

• Genetic and neurodevelopmental disorders	Genetic and Neurodevelopmental Disorders (3 semester hour class)
• Neuropsychopharmacology	Neuropsychopharmacology (3 semester hour class)
• Neuropsychological intervention techniques	Neuropsychological Intervention Techniques -or- Neurocognitive Intervention Techniques (3 semester hour class)
• Competency-based supervised experiences (minimum of 225 hours, preferred 500 hours)	Supervised Practicum (3 semester hour class)
• Internship hours (minimum of 600 hours in school neuropsychology experiences)	Internship (6–8 semester hour classes)
• Totals	27–29 hours of concentrated study in school neuropsychology

Adapted from the School Psychology Doctoral Training Program at Texas Woman's University, Denton, Texas. Reprinted with permission from D. C. Miller, *Essentials of School Neuropsychological Assessment*, 2007, pp. 53–54.

SUMMARY

xThis chapter presented the issue of what constitutes competency within the school neuropsychology specialization. Entry-level competency in school neuropsychology must include a broad range of knowledge and a supervised skill set. Because the knowledge base for school neuropsychology is so rapidly expanding, continued competency in school neuropsychology can only be maintained through a professional commitment to lifelong learning.

This chapter reviewed the bifurcated past in the clinical neuropsychology specialty with the two sets of training guidelines and two principal certification boards. This dual set of standards at the doctoral level has created a great deal of tension in the clinical neuropsychology field. Miller pointed out that "as basic research in cognitive neuroscience and neuropsychology becomes more readily translated into educational practice, there will be a need to define what constitutes competency for practitioners who want to apply this knowledge base with school-aged children and youth" (2007, p. 54). Undoubtedly, controversy will continue unabated about the appropriate entry level of graduate training for practice in specialty areas such as school neuropsychology. The need for providing neuropsychological services to school-aged children to help them optimize their learning and behavioral potentials is undeniable, and credentialed school psychologists are uniquely poised to provide those services if they seek out additional competency-based training in school neuropsychology. The increased interest in school neuropsychology and the demand for more training will undoubtedly help shape credentialing issues in the future.

REFERENCES

American Psychological Association (APA) (2002). *Ethical principles of psychologists and code of conduct*. Washington, DC: Author.

Ardila, A. (2002). The Houston Conference: Need for more fundamental knowledge in neuropsychology. *Neuropsychology Review, 12*, 127–130.

Barth, J. T., Pliskin, N., Axelrod, B., Faust, D., Fisher, J., Harley, J. P., Heilbronner, R., Larrabee, G., Puente, A., Ricker, J., & Silver, C. (2003). Introduction to the NAN 2001 definition of a clinical neuropsychologist: NAN Policy and Planning Committee. *Archives of Clinical Neuropsychology, 18*, 551–555.

Bent, R. J., Packard, R. E., & Goldberg, R. W. (1999). The American Board of Professional Psychology, 1947 to 1997: A historical perspective. *Professional Psychology: Research and Practice, 30*, 65–73.

Crespi, T., & Cooke, D. T. (2003). Specialization in neuropsychology: Contemporary concerns and considerations for school psychology. *The School Psychologist, 57*, 97–100.

Goldstein, G. (2001). Board certification in clinical neuropsychology: Some history, facts and opinions. *Journal of Forensic Neuropsychology, 2*, 57–65.

Guidelines of the INS-Division 40 Task Force on Education, Accreditation, and Credentialing. (1987). *Clinical Neuropsychologist, 1*, 29–34.

Hale, J. B., & Fiorello, C. A. (2004). *School neuropsychology: A practitioner's handbook*. New York: Guilford Press.

Hannay, H. J., Bieliauskas, L. A., Crosson, B. A., Hammeke, T. A., Hamsher, K. S., & Koffler, S. P. (1998). Proceedings: The Houston conference on specialty education and training in clinical neuropsychology. *Archives in Clinical Neuropsychology Special Issue, 13*, 157–250.

Horton, A. M., Crown, B. M., & Reynolds, C. R. (2001). American Board of Professional Neuropsychology: An update—2001. *Journal of Forensic Neuropsychology, 2*, 67–78.

Hynd, G. W., & Obrzut, J. E. (1981). School neuropsychology. *Journal of School Psychology, 19*, 45–50.

Hynd, G. W., & Reynolds, C. R. (2005). School neuropsychology: The evolution of a specialty in school psychology. In R. C. D'Amato, E. Fletcher-Janzen, & C. R. Reynolds (Eds.), *Handbook of school neuropsychology* (pp. 3–14). Hoboken, NJ: John Wiley & Sons.

Koffler, S. (2002). Commentary on the Houston conference. *Neuropsychology Review, 12*, 141.

Lange, S. (2005). School neuropsychology redux: Empirical versus arbitrary conclusions? *The School Psychologist, 59*, 113–116.

McGrath, M. C., & Yalof, J. (2007, March). *School neuropsychology: Impact on school psychology programs.* Poster presented at the annual meeting of the National Association of School Psychologists. New York.

McGrath, M. C., & Yalof, J. (2008, February). *School neuropsychology: Practitioners' perceptions of training.* Poster presented at the annual meeting of the National Association of School Psychologists. New Orleans, LA.

Miller, D. C. (2004). Neuropsychological assessment in the schools. In *Encyclopedia of applied psychology* (pp. 657–664). San Diego, CA: Academic Press.

Miller, D. C. (2007). *Essentials of school neuropsychological assessment.* Hoboken, NJ: John Wiley & Sons.

Miller, D. C. (2008). Appendix VII—School psychology training programs. In A. Thomas and J. Grimes (Eds.), *Best practices in school psychology V* (pp. clv–cxcviii). Bethesda, MD: National Association of School Psychologists.

Miller, D. C., DeOrnellas, K., & Maricle, D. (2008). The time for recognizing subspecialties in school has come. *Communiqué*, Bethesda, MD: National Association of School Psychologists.

Miller, D. C., DeOrnellas, K., & Maricle, D. (2009). What is so special about the specialist degree? In E. García-Vázquez, T. Crespi, & C. Riccio (Eds.), *Handbook of education, training and supervision of school psychologists in school and community—Volume I: Foundations of professional practice.* London: Taylor Francis/Routledge.

National Association of School Psychologists. (2000). *Professional conduct manual: Principles for professional ethics.* Bethesda, MD: Author.

Parrish, S. D. (2005). The future of neuropsychology: Read your horoscope lately? *The School Psychologist, 59*, 146–150.

Pelletier, S. L. F., Hiemenz, J. R., & Shapiro, M. B. (2004). The application of neuropsychology in the schools should not be called school neuropsychology: A rejoinder to Crespi and Cooke. *The School Psychologist, 58*, 17–24.

Reitan, R. M., Hom, J., Van De Voorde, J., Stanczak, D. E., & Wolfson, D. (2004). The Houston Conference revisited. *Archives of Clinical Neuropsychology, 19*, 375–390.

Reynolds, C. R. (2002). An essay on the Houston Conference policy statement: Static yet incomplete or a work in progress? *Neuropsychology Review, 12,* 143–145.

Rohling, M. L., Lees-Haley, P. R., Langhinrichsen-Rohling, J., & Williamson, D. J. (2003). A statistical analysis of board certification in clinical neuropsychology. *Archives of Clinical Neuropsychology, 18,* 331–352.

Shapiro, E. G., & Ziegler, R. (1997). Training issues in pediatric neuropsychology. *Child Neuropsychology, 3,* 227–229.

Shordone, R. J., & Saul, R. E. (2000). *Neuropsychology for health care professionals and attorneys.* New York: CRC Press.

Standards for Training and Field Placement Standards in Psychology. (2002). Bethesda, MD: National Association of School Psychologists.

CHAPTER 3

Ethical and Legal Issues Related to School Neuropsychology

MARY JOANN LANG and ANN MARIE T. LEONARD-ZABEL

Always do right, this will gratify some people and astonish the rest.

—Mark Twain

THIS CHAPTER PRESENTS an initial exploration of the ethical and legal issues in the practice of school neuropsychology. Areas include ethical principles related to the practice of school neuropsychology, legal mandates that affect the practice of school neuropsychology, and the initial handling of due process or legal proceedings related to school neuropsychology. We will discuss the importance of developing awareness to recognize issues of ethical significance, and we will provide a model for processing information for best practices with decision making in this regard.

Professional standards and codes of ethics address issues of right and wrong and govern performance. Professional ethics includes rules specific to a profession or industry and broad principles as well as specific requirements enforceable through disciplinary proceedings or in lawsuits. The goal of this chapter is to assist practicing school neuropsychologists "to pursue high standards of practice, minimize the potential for ethical conflict, and appropriately resolve ethical challenges when they occur" (Bush, 2007).

In order to understand the ethics and laws that apply to school neuropsychologists, we will begin by defining school neuropsychology and the main roles and functions of school neuropsychologists in their school districts.

Miller summarized the roles and functions of the school neuropsychologist in *Essentials of Neuropsychological Assessment* (2007) as follows:

- Provide neuropsychological assessment and interpretation services to schools for children with known or suspected neurological conditions.
- Assist in the interpretation of neuropsychological findings from outside consultants or medical records.
- Seek to integrate current brain research into educational practice.
- Provide educational interventions that have a basis in the neuropsychological or educational literature.
- Act as a liaison between the school and the medical community for transitional planning for TBI and other health-impaired children and adolescents.
- Consult with curriculum specialists in designing approaches to instruction that more adequately reflect what is known about brain–behavior relationships.
- Conduct in-service training for educators and parents about the neuropsychological factors that relate to common childhood disorders.
- Engage in evidence-based research to test for the efficacy of neuropsychologically based interventions (p. 35).

School neuropsychologists must be competent to perform the tasks required by the profession, cognizant of laws and regulations that apply to their work, and motivated to abide by the ethical standards established by the profession.

ETHICAL PRINCIPLES RELATED TO THE PRACTICE OF SCHOOL NEUROPSYCHOLOGY

Ethics apply to individual decision-making processes, but guidelines are well established within professional circles. Currently, there is not a separate professional organization for school neuropsychology with a distinct set of ethical guidelines. School neuropsychologists are typically members of either the American Psychological Association (APA) or the National Association of School Psychologists (NASP), both of which have established ethical guidelines. The principles discussed in this chapter reflect guidelines derived from these organizations. The guidelines of professional organizations establish "a common set of principles and standards from which members of the organization or the profession can determine appropriate behaviors" (Bush, 2007, p. 6).

Membership in APA, NASP, and local professional organizations is recommended for practicing psychologists. The benefits of membership include financial services, career planning, as well as advocacy programs, information resources, and continuing education opportunities. Active involvement in professional organizations encourages practitioners to operate at the highest professional standards. These associations require members to uphold their ethical codes, which address "clinical activities, counseling, and school practice of psychology; research; teaching; supervision of trainees; public service; policy development; social intervention, development of assessment instruments; conducting assessments, educational counseling, organizational counseling, forensic activities; program design and evaluation; and administration" (APA, 2002, p. 2).

Professional ethics may require school neuropsychologists to work, individually and/or collectively, to change laws and regulations, which they believe require them to violate professional ethical standards. "School psychologists understand the intimate nature of consultation, assessment, and direct service. They engage only in professional practices that maintain the dignity and integrity of children and other clients" (NASP, 2000, p. 20).

The APA Ethics Code of Introduction and Applicability (APA, 2002) states the following:

> Psychologists must meet the higher ethical standard. If psychologists' ethical responsibilities conflict with law, regulations, or other governing legal authority, psychologists should make known their commitment to this Ethics Code and take steps to resolve the conflict in a responsible manner. If the conflict is irresolvable via such means, psychologists may adhere to the requirements of the law, regulations, or other governing authority in keeping with basic principles of human rights. (APA, 2002, p. 2)

The APA Ethics Code highlights five general principles: beneficence and nonmaleficence, fidelity and responsibility, integrity, justice, and respect for people's rights and dignity (APA, 2002). The APA code's standards and principles provide a basis for encouraging "voluntary efforts to live our moral ideals" within the profession (Knapp & VandeCreek, 2006, p. 3). The APA Ethics Code is typically the first resource to consider when determining ethical conduct (Bush, 2007, p. 8).

The NASP Ethics Code (2000) states:

> At times, Ethics may require a higher standard of behavior than the prevailing policies and pertinent laws. Under such conditions, members should adhere to the Ethics. Ethical behavior may occasionally be forbidden by policy or law, in which case members are expected to declare their dilemma and work to bring the discrepant regulations into compliance with the Ethics. To obtain additional assistance in applying these principles to a particular setting, a school psychologist should consult with experienced school psychologists and seek advice

from the National Association of School Psychologists or the state school psychology association. (p. 14)

"Ethical principles articulate the standards of NASP regarding the conduct expected of a professional school psychologist. Guidelines for the provision of services are intended to inform both the profession and the public of the hallmark of quality services that should be the goal of every school psychologist and every school psychological services delivery unit" (NASP, 2000, p. 6).

REVIEW OF LEGISLATION THAT IMPACTS THE ROLES AND FUNCTIONS OF SCHOOL NEUROPSYCHOLOGISTS

The roles and functions of school neuropsychologists dictate that they become knowledgeable about legislation that impacts their profession, as well as protecting rights of students and parents in the school setting (Jacobs & Hartshorne, 2007). A brief review of the following legislation will assist the school neuropsychologist in complying with relevant legislation and prevent legal action that can result from failure to comply with governing laws.

REHABILITATION ACT OF 1973, SECTION 504 AND THE AMERICANS WITH DISABILITIES ACT (ADA), 1973 AND 1990

The Rehabilitation Act of 1973 was written to address the need for persons with disabilities to have equal access to federally funded programs. Within its text, the act addresses the failure of public schools to educate disabled students (Richards, 2002).

Section 504 is a single paragraph that stipulates:

No otherwise qualified individual with a disability in the United States, as defined in section 796(8) of this title, shall, solely by reason of her or his handicap, be excluded from participation in, be denied the benefits of, or be subjected to discrimination under any program or activity receiving federal financial assistance or under any program or activity conducted by any Executive agency or by the United States Postal Service. (29 U.S.C. § 794(a) (1973))

The Americans with Disabilities Act of 1990 (U.S. Department of Health Human Services, 2000) is considered the most significant federal law regarding the rights of individuals with disabilities. The law guarantees equal opportunity in many areas including: employment, public services, and transportation, and Title II, Subtitle A pertains specifically to education.

The Office for Civil Rights (OCR) of the U.S. Department of Health and Human Services (DHHS) governs the nondiscrimination requirements of

Section 504 of the Rehabilitation Act of 1973 and Title II of the Americans with Disabilities Act (ADA) of 1990, involving health care and human service providers and institutions. Several of the clauses in the document apply to education, as well as other areas of concern.

Both Section 504 and the ADA prohibit covered entities from discriminating against persons with disabilities in the provision of benefits or services or the conduct of programs or activities on the basis of their disability (U.S. DHHS, 2000). Section 504 applies to programs or activities that receive federal financial assistance. Title II of the ADA covers all of the services, programs, and activities conducted by public entities (state and local governments, departments, agencies), including licensing (U.S. DHHS, 2000).

Covered entities *must not*:

- Establish eligibility criteria for receipt of services or participation in programs or activities that screen out or tend to screen out individuals with disabilities, unless such criteria are necessary to meet the objectives of the program.
- Provide separate or different benefits, services, or programs to individuals with disabilities, unless it is necessary to ensure that the benefits and services are equally effective (U.S. DHHS, 2000).

Covered entities *must*:

- Provide services and programs in the most integrated setting appropriate to the needs of qualified individuals with disabilities.
- Make reasonable modifications in their policies, practices, and procedures to avoid discrimination on the basis of disability, unless it would result in a fundamental alteration in their program or activity.
- Ensure that buildings are accessible.
- Provide auxiliary aids to individuals with disabilities, at no additional cost, where necessary to ensure effective communication with individuals with hearing, vision, or speech impairments. (Auxiliary aids include such services or devices as qualified interpreters, assistive listening headsets, television captioning and decoders, telecommunications devices for the deaf [TDDs], videotext displays, readers, taped texts, Braille materials, and large-print materials.) (U.S. DHHS, 2000.)

No Child Left Behind (NCLB), 2001

This legislative act lets states define proficiency, but requires them to reach it, "leaving no student behind," by 2014. NCLB was composed to correct the absence of research-based reading instruction in schools and to address underachievement witnessed on the part of specific groups, including students with disabilities. Among its provisions are the following:

- Sets forth requirements for districts to document progress.
- Requires "highly qualified teachers" in each classroom.
- Requires use of standardized tests to evaluate teaching and learning.
- Stipulates remedies, including school transfers and tutoring services, for students in consistently "failing" schools.

No Child Left Behind is based on the goal to improve accountability for results, to provide more freedom for states and communities, to require proven education methods, and to offer more choices for parents (U.S. Department of Education, *Overview: Four Pillars of NCLB*, n.d.).

INDIVIDUALS WITH DISABILITIES EDUCATION IMPROVEMENT ACT (IDEA)

IDEA (Individuals with Disabilities Education Improvement Act of 2004) addresses the educational needs of children with disabilities, including early intervention, special education, and related services and requires that research-based interventions be used to the extent practicable. The provisions of IDEA are far-reaching and include the following:

- Requirement that state and local funds supplement, not supplant, the proportionate share of federal funds (34 CFR §300.133(d)).
- Right to file due process complaints regarding child find and state complaints regarding equitable participation requirements (34 CFR §300.140).
- Requirements that funds not benefit a private school (34 CFR §300.141).
- Requirements regarding use of public and private school personnel to provide equitable services (34 CFR §300.142).
- Prohibition of separate classes based on school enrollment or religion under certain circumstances (34 CFR §300.143).
- Funds for equitable participation remaining in control of public agency (34 CFR §300.144(a)).
- Definition of child with a disability (34 CFR §300.8).
- Special procedures for identifying specific learning disabilities (34 CFR §§300.307–300.311).
- Requirements for highly qualified public school special education teachers (34 CFR §300.18).
- Parental consent for evaluation and provision of services (34 CFR §300.300).

- Sixty-day evaluation timeline or state-established timeline (34 CFR §300.301(c)).
- State advisory panel (34 CFR §§300.167–300.169).
- Arrangement for a bypass (if local education agencies (LEAs) are barred by state law from providing services to private school students or if a public agency has failed or is unwilling to provide for equitable participation) (34 CFR §300.190).
- Prohibition of mandatory medication (34 CFR §300.174).
- Changing services plans without a formal team meeting (34 CFR §300.324(a)(4)).
- Accommodation guidelines/alternate assessments (if private school children with disabilities participate in statewide assessments) (34 CFR §300.160).
- Reducing litigation to provide an opportunity for resolution within 30 days following a due-process complaint regarding the Child Find process (34 CFR §300.510).

The 2004 Amendments to IDEA expand upon the 1997 reauthorization and include new requirements to ensure that LEAs provide parentally placed private school children with disabilities an opportunity for equitable participation in programs assisted or carried out under IDEA, the foundation of which is the consultation process (see U.S. Department of Education: *Building the Legacy: IDEA 2004*, n.d.).

FAMILY EDUCATIONAL RIGHTS AND PRIVACY ACT (FERPA)

The Family Educational Rights and Privacy Act (FERPA) (20 U.S.C. § 1232g; 34 CFR Part 99) protects the privacy of student education records. The law applies to all schools that receive funds under an applicable program of the U.S. Department of Education. FERPA gives parents certain rights with respect to their children's educational records. These rights transfer to the student when he or she reaches the age of 18 or attends a school beyond the high school level and becomes an "eligible student." Rights include:

- Inspection and review of student education records.
- Requesting that a school correct records which the student believes to be inaccurate or misleading.
- If the school declines to amend the record, the parent or eligible student then has the right to a formal hearing.
- After the hearing, if the school still decides not to amend the record, the parent or eligible student has the right to place a statement with the record, setting forth his or her view about the contested information.

For further information, contact the United States Department of Education web site.

ETHICAL AND LEGAL ISSUES RELATED TO THE PRACTICE OF SCHOOL NEUROPSYCHOLOGY

What Can Persons Trained in School Neuropsychology Call Themselves?

State governments across the United States, in an effort to protect the public, enacted legislation/laws to regulate the practice of psychological services. According to Jacobs and Hartshorne (2007), there exist two forms of legislation acts regulating school psychological services: a title or certification act (typically granted from the state department of education) and a licensing act (usually issued by the state licensing board). School neuropsychologists may provide services in either a school-based and/or private practice setting. In addition, nonpractice credentials recognize islands of competence and the quality of one's professional preparation for training such as the National Association of School Psychology Certification system or the American Board of School Neuropsychology Certification system. If one desires to call him- or herself a school neuropsychologist, one would need to contact the state in which he or she desires to practice for the proper procedures about what is needed to provide practice.

The professional trained in school neuropsychology should consider becoming board certified by the American Board of School Neuropsychology (ABSNP). The purpose of holding this specialty credential is to

> promote the active involvement of school psychologists in training and application of neuropsychological principles to the individuals they serve. The ABSNP does require that applicants for the Diplomate in School Neuropsychology be certified or licensed school psychologists, or licensed psychologists with specialization in school neuropsychology, or ABPP Diplomate in School Psychology with additional specialized training in school neuropsychology. (Miller, 2007, p. 45)

According to Fagan and Wise (2000), a nonpracticing credential does not provide sole authorization for a psychologist to provide services. Rather, the school psychologist must first hold a valid certificate or license in the state he or she desires to practice. Thus, it would serve the school neuropsychologist to consult with legal council as to what he or she needs to specifically practice within his or her state using the title of school neuropsychologist.

Issue of Competency in School Neuropsychology

School neuropsychological professional competency should be considered the foundation of ethical practice. One should not practice in area(s) in which one is not professionally skilled or proficient. According to Jacobs and Hartshorne (2007) school psychologists (e.g., school neuropsychologists) should provide services with students/clients in the area(s) only within the boundaries of their training and competence. School practitioners hold the responsibility to be aware of the boundaries of their competence. In addition, Knapp and VandeCreek (2006) describe competence as a process involving three major areas: technical knowledge of skills within one's chosen field, social skills, and emotional well-being. Of note, Knapp and VandeCreek further stipulate that the ability to withstand emotionally challenging issues with clients and the ability of the psychologist to convey positive emotions related to good interpersonal relationships, such as compassion and empathy, are essential ingredients when it comes to exercising ethical competence. See Chapter 2 in this book for a further discussion of what constitutes competency in school neuropsychology.

INFORMED CONSENT: WHY THIS IS IMPORTANT—GENERAL RULES

The American Psychological Association's (APA, 2002) ethics code states, "When psychologists conduct research or provide assessment, therapy, counseling or consulting services . . . they obtain the informed consent of the individual or individuals using language that is reasonably understandable to that person or persons except when conducting such activities without consent is mandated by law or governmental regulations or as otherwise provided in this Ethics Code" (APA, 2002, Section 3.10).

Informed consent requires that the individual granting consent be knowing, competent, and voluntarily making decisions (Dekraal, Sales, & Hall, 1998). The person must have a clear understanding of the situation to which he or she is consenting. The practitioner must divulge enough information about the services offered, the expected time to complete assessments, treatment goals and possibilities, the costs to parent (if any), and the confidentiality measures that will be taken for the individual to make an informed decision. "This information must be provided in language (or by other mode of communication) understandable to the person giving consent" (Weithorn, 1983).

Who is legally authorized to grant consent for assessments, IEP agreements, and other educational issues? Typically, parents are authorized to grant consent, but other persons can have that right/responsibility. Legal guardians, conservators, foster parents, stepparents, caregivers, court appointees, and others may hold the legal right to grant consent and speak on behalf of a student. Be sure to address consent issues with persons legally authorized to grant or deny consent (California Medical Association, 2001).

Consent issues are also open to ethical and legal challenge. Consent must be voluntary, informed, obtained without coercion, duress, and misrepresentation of undue inducement. In the school setting, informed consent is typically sought from the parent or guardian of a minor child (Dekraal et al., 1998; Jacobs & Hartshorne, 2007). For children and adolescents, legal consent rights are typically assigned to parents; however, in the absence of practical "assent" by the student, assessment and remediation may be impossible. An adult's refusal to consent to assessments or services on his or her child's behalf may under certain circumstances justify nonprovision of the assessment or services. This is a complex legal area, because at times school districts should take action regardless of consent, and often there are disputes as to whether a parent's refusal to consent was based on sufficient and truthful information. For instance, a parent who was told that "special education" would be a stigmatizing, isolating way of dealing with a child's learning difficulties or emotional struggles would be able to credibly claim that his or her lack of consent was based on disinformation. Had the student's right to be educated to the maximum extent appropriately alongside nondisabled peers been explained, assessment and services would have been welcomed.

Provisions of IDEA and state law dictate who is authorized to give consent for a student. Consent is typically sought from a parent or guardian, unless the student is an adult. In addition to the natural or adoptive parent, other individuals can sometimes act as the parent in giving consent, including grandparents, stepparents, or other relatives living with the child. Legally responsible adults can include foster parents, but state laws vary. School neuropsychologists should consult their school administrators or attorney with questions regarding consent (Jacobs & Hartshorne, 2007).

ETHICAL AND LEGAL ISSUES RELATED TO CONFIDENTIALITY

What Is Confidentiality?   "Psychologists have a primary obligation and take reasonable precautions to protect confidential information obtained through or stored in any medium, recognizing that the extent and lists of confidentiality may be regulated by law. . . ." (APA, 2002, Section 4.01). Confidentiality obligations relating to the handling of student information are governed by the Family Educational Rights and Privacy Act (FERPA), by state law provisions for sharing of information with other agencies, and by professional ethics. Parents have a right to see anything that is in educational records and to decide with whom to share that information; however, "personal notes" maintained by a school neuropsychologist to refresh his or her memory, which are not shared with anyone else, are not subject to disclosure.

It is "an ethical decision not to reveal what is learned in the professional relationship" (Hummel, Talbutt, & Alexander, 1985, p. 54). Confidentiality is a matter of ethical behavior, and school psychologists must respect the importance of keeping information private (NASP, 2000, III, A, #9). The extent of confidentiality, which is accorded to oral communications with students and parents, is complex, and there are reasonable exceptions that justify the suspension of confidentiality norms. These include the following: "Where there is a reasonable suspicion of child maltreatment, when the examinee poses a physical threat to another person, or when the examinee is a minor and poses a threat to himself or herself" (Sattler, 2008, p. 71). Confidentiality helps build trust, which is essential to successful assessments and treatments. However, there are situations that obligate the school neuropsychologist to disclose information to others: at the student's request, when the student's behavior involves danger to the student or to others, or when the psychologist is legally obligated to testify in court (Hummel et al., 1985).

Collaboration and Confidentiality   School neuropsychologists typically work with teachers, parents, and others to assist students. Information is typically shared with those involved in the collaborative effort, and the school neuropsychologist should discuss the bonds of confidentiality with teachers and others before divulging information about a student. "In collaboration, the individuals involved carry joint responsibility for assisting the student . . . and information will most likely be shared by those individuals" (Hansen, Himes, & Meier, 1990).

Occasionally, school neuropsychologists are approached by teachers and other staff members for advice. Voluntary consultations by teachers with school neuropsychologists form consultant–consultee relationships, implying that communications between psychologists and teachers must be kept confidential by the psychologist, even at the request of administrators in the school district (Davis & Sandoval, 1982). Often "consultation" is not a purely voluntary process: It can be specified in a student's Individual Education Program (IEP).

If a school neuropsychologist learns that a teacher is failing to implement a student's IEP, lacks behavioral control over the class in general, or is having personal problems that make competent job performance impossible, and if the psychologist has enough information to realize that consultations are not going to fix significant problems, the psychologist may have an overriding duty to the student to reveal quality problems to whomever can compel improvements, such as an administrator or parent. The general rule of the National Association of School Psychologists is that the school psychologist's primary duty in cases of conflicting interests is to the student. Teacher/psychologist privileged communications apply to this special relationship, which prevents "disclosure in legal proceedings" (Davis & Sandoval, 1982).

ETHICAL AND LEGAL ISSUES IN SCHOOL NEUROPSYCHOLOGICAL ASSESSMENT

What is the difference between testing and assessment? Testing is used to gather information that can be used in the assessment process, but assessment is the complete process of collecting data with the goal of giving meaning to a particular student's characteristics (Mowder, 1982). School neuropsychologists must consistently apply ethical principles to the assessment process. Students are referred for a school neuropsychological evaluation for a variety of reasons, such as a decline in academic performance, medical conditions, psychiatric conditions. The important issue is that each child or adolescent be seen as an individual, and the assessment focuses on the referral question and ensures that the assessment process leads to evidence-based interventions that facilitate the child's growth and development, as well as to accessing educational opportunities.

Preassessment responsibilities have been outlined in IDEA, Section 300.304 (IDEA, 2004) and include selection of appropriate assessment tools, which are current, unbiased, fair, administered in the child's native language, and use tools and strategies that provide relevant information (U.S. Department of Education, *Building the Legacy: IDEA 2004*, n.d.). Assessment tools must be multifaceted, comprehensive, fair, valid, and useful. Decisions regarding a student's diagnosis should never be made on the basis of a single evaluation tool or test score. Children with suspected disabilities should be evaluated on the basis of health, emotional status, communication status, as well as in areas related to the disabilities (IDEA, 2004, 34 CFR §300.304).

Responsibilities to pupil and parent include exchange of key information. IDEA 2004 requires that school districts obtain written consent from the parent (or other appointed person) before testing, assessment, or reassessment procedure can begin. This communication may be the first communication with the family and can help set the stage for effective collaborations (Jacobs & Hartshorne, 2007). Parent consent is not needed for reevaluation of existing data or for determining effective instructional strategies, and any questions regarding consent requirements may be answered in IDEA 2004 or by your school administrator or attorney.

Assessment tools are developed to meet the needs of children of various ages, genders, disabilities, languages, ethnic backgrounds, and socio-economic backgrounds. Tools must be selected to fit the individual being tested (NASP, 2000, IV, C, #1). Individuals selected to administer the tests must be trained and proficient. The tools should be selected according to their likelihood to provide relevant information that can be useful in planning for the educational needs of the individual child (IDEA, 2004, 34 CFR §300.304).

Only technically adequate instruments should be used to assess students. Evidence-based practices lay the groundwork for selection of tools that have been proven to provide reliable results (NASP, 2000, IV, C). Test reliability and validity of assessment are critical to obtaining accurate diagnostic results, and therefore it is an important ethical responsibility of the school psychologist to select tools that are consistent with responsible evidence-based practice (NASP, 2000, IV, C). Test reliability (consistency) demonstrates similar results from using the same test on a student at different times. Reliability of a test can be measured by administering it to the same group of examinees at different times and comparing the results (Sattler, 2008). However, one can expect some variance in testing, with coefficients of .80 to .85 being acceptable, but .90 is desirable for tests that strongly influence decisions (Hammill, Brown, & Bryant, 1989; Sattler, 2008).

Validity is a measure of how closely a given test actually measures what it is designed to measure. How can you evaluate validity of a test? Available evidence in the literature should be considered, in respect to quality and quantity. "Although the test manual and supportive materials are starting points for test review, practitioners are obligated ethically to keep abreast of the research related to the validity of tests used in psychoeducational diagnosis" (Jacobs & Hartshorne, 2007, p. 100).

Practitioners should familiarize themselves with the technical manuals for the tests they administer, as they contain very valuable information regarding all aspects of the tests at hand. For example, the Woodcock-Johnson Technical Manual starts with an overview of the tests, clusters, and discrepancy calculations. Succeeding chapters provide information of development, standardization, reliability, and validity. The manuals for each battery include detailed discussion for administering, scoring, and interpreting results (Woodcock, McGrew, & Mather, 2001). These documents can help the practitioner to stay on track regarding selection and use of available tools.

Training needs occur when a clinician is new at using particular diagnostic tools or when the tools are revised by their publishers. In order to keep current with new research regarding brain–behavior relationships, publishing houses update assessment instruments. Frequently, the publishing companies, professional organizations, and universities provide in-service education for administration of tests and interpretation of test results. This is consistent with a variety of ethical standards, including competency of the practitioner and appropriate use, analysis, and interpretation of assessment tools.

ETHICAL AND LEGAL ISSUES IN EVIDENCE-BASED INTERVENTIONS

Evidence-based practice (EBP) is now recognized as the gold standard for decision making and delivering high-quality care (Levin & Feldman, 2005). EBP originated in the field of medicine as doctors began demanding scientific proof that diagnostic measures and treatment regimes were effective. David Hargreaves describes EBP as operating on two levels, "to utilize existing evidence from worldwide research and literature on education and related subjects" and "to establish sound evidence where existing evidence is lacking or questionable" (Hargreaves, 1999). Other fields, including nursing and education, adopted the desire for EBP measures in response to a "spirit of inquiry" that has developed in these fields (Mazurekk-Melnyk, 2005).

Evidence-based education is defined as "the integration of professional wisdom with the best available empirical evidence in making decisions about how to deliver instruction," according to Grover J. Whitehurst, Assistant Secretary for Educational Research and Improvement in the U.S. Department of Education (Whitehurst, 2003). The term *evidence-based education* was first used in 1996 by Hargreaves (Hargreaves, 1999) in a lecture to teachers. He later explained, "Doctors and teachers are similar in that they make decisions involving complex judgments" (Hargreaves, 1999, p. 407).

Evidence-based teaching relies on methods that have been tested and proven effective. In order to prove that a method is effective, one must develop a measure to evaluate the outcome of a teaching activity. The measured outcomes relate to evidence, and a procedure that includes a randomized control trial is the "golden standard" for research that produces "evidence" (Davies, 1999). Educators must support evidence-based education in order to comply with measures stated in the No Child Left Behind Act of 2002, and, according to Whitehurst, "Scientifically based research is really the mantra of the bill" (Kersting, 2003). Whitehurst stated that school districts should track their progress to determine which programs work for their students.

Evidence-based educational practice is the conscientious use of current best evidence in making decisions about the education of individuals or the delivery of developmental services. EDPs promote reliability based on clinical trials, literature reviews, and in-the-field scientific evaluation of goal-oriented theories and tools. The best available evidence, tailored to circumstances and preferences, is applied to improve the chances for meeting the goals for the individual, with respect to clinical judgment and cost-effective educational care (Jacobs & Hartshorne, 2007).

Ethical and Legal Issues in Continued Professional Development

There exists an ethical, moral, and legal obligation to continue to be committed to lifelong learning in one's chosen specialty in the field of psychology. According to the NASP Principles for Professional Ethics, Section II, Professional Competency (2000), "School psychologists engage in continuing professional development. They remain current regarding developments in research, training, and professional practices that benefits children, families, and schools" (NASP, 2000, p. 16). The APA (2002) Ethical Principles of Psychologists and Code of Conduct Standard 2.01, Boundaries of Competence, section (3) stipulates "Psychologists planning to provide services, teach, or conduct research involving populations, areas, techniques, or technologies new to them undertake relevant education, training, supervised experience, and consultation, or study" (APA, 2002). Therefore, many state departments of education and psychology licensing boards require continued education in order to renew one's credential(s) to practice.

Ethical and Legal Issues in the Use of Technology

The use of computers in the school neuropsychological assessment process is playing an increasing role in test administration and scoring, interviewing, recording and analyzing behavioral observation and analysis, report preparation, and data transmission (Sattler, 2008). However, one must be vigilant that a computer program is only as smart as the person who programmed it. Therefore, school neuropsychologists need to use caution and good common sense when using computer technology in their clinical practice. To avoid potential pitfalls and problems that may come with the use of computer technology in school neuropsychological assessment practice, computer data and/or generated reports should never be used in isolation but rather as a tool to assist the school neuropsychologist in conjunction with his or her clinical judgment when analyzing a case.

Ethical and Legal Issues in Due Process and Legal Proceedings

There is a possibility at some point in a school neuropsychologist's career of being called into a due process hearing and/or court proceeding to testify on behalf of a student/client. The school neuropsychologist may be deemed an "expert witness" by the judge at a court proceeding. If this should occur, one's role and function is to act as an expert, not an advocate. There are several ways of exhibiting effectiveness as an expert witness:

- How you consider all the relevant facts in the case.
- How confident you are regarding the accuracy of the facts supporting your professional opinion.
- How you demonstrate an adequate understanding of scientific and clinical principles involved in your case.
- How you use best practices within the field for methods and analysis of assessment data.
- How you draw your hypotheses and/or inferences and whether your approach is logical, reasonable, and objective.
- How clear and ethically convincing your testimony is.
- How honest and unbiased you appear instead of being viewed as a "hired gun" (Sattler, 2008).

If you are called into a hearing or court setting on a school neuro-psychological case, there are several things you may need to know about testifying: Most of the time you do not testify since most civil cases settle; most testimony usually involves questioning that is routine and the scope can be modest; you know more than you are consciously aware of, especially since many attorneys possess a superficial knowledge of your field. Stay focused on what you know and see past the hearing or courtroom equivalent of jesters and jousters; the best preparation does not take place right before the hearing or trial but during ongoing study and training, which will make an enormous differ-ence in your testimony. You do not have to have an answer for every question posed to you, and be honest with your responses without making up references, guessing, and/or denying authentic mistakes in the field or in your work. Remember: Testifying depends on organization, preparation, and confidence.

What to Do When School Records Are Subpoenaed   There comes a time when the school and/or private practice neuropsychological records may be subpoe-naed for a variety of reasons. Therefore, it is imperative that school neuro-psychologists understand what a subpoena entails and what to do if one encounters this situation in his or her practice.

A subpoena "is a command to produce certain documents or to appear at a certain time and place to give testimony, which is typically issued by the clerk of the court. Attorneys use subpoenas to gather information relevant to a case. Strategies for coping with subpoenas or compelled testimony regarding client records are outlined in APA Committee on Legal Issues (1996)" (Jacobs & Hartshorne, 2007, p. 71).

Recently requests from school personnel, parents, and attorneys regarding access to test protocols have become very common. Such practice is noted in the Individuals with Disabilities Education Law Report (IDELR; Sattler, 2008). However, the Family Educational Rights and Privacy Act (FERPA), initially enacted in 1974 by the United States Congress, protects the privacy of students' educational records, files, and documents and applies to all feder-ally funded school districts (Sattler, 2008). In addition, under FERPA, parents and eligible students have the absolute right to review and inspect all records, including psychological testing protocols. This legal right often conflicts with the school neuropsychologist's ethical obligation and commitment to pre-serve the integrity to maintain test security. Therefore, it is best practice to encourage that parents and/or eligible students review the protocols under supervision of the school neuropsychologist or with another appropriately trained professional psychologist, including a discussion of sample questions and answers. In addition, establishing a good rapport early in the assessment process, explaining the conflict between the school neuropsychologist's professional obligation to maintain test security versus parental/student rights to record review and communicating assessment results in a manner that assists parents/students to fully understand strengths and weaknesses may prove to be a proactive response to ward off contentious issues. Keep in mind that some states allow parents to obtain copies of their child's test protocols (Jacobs & Hartshorne, 2007).

Table 3.1
Further Information

Office of Non-Public Education
Office of Innovation and Improvement
U.S. Department of Education
400 Maryland Ave. S.W.
Washington, DC 20202–5940
Phone: 202–401–1365
Fax: 202–401–1368
E-mail: OIINon-PublicEducation@ed.gov
http://www.ed.gov/about/offices/list/oii/nonpublic/index.html

Office of Special Education Programs
U.S. Department of Education
550 12th St. S.W.
Washington, DC 20202
Phone: 202–245–7629
Fax: 202–245–7614
http://www.idea.ed.gov

For ADA Information:
Office for Civil Rights
U.S. Department of Health and Human Services
200 Independence Avenue, SW—Room 506-F
Washington, DC 20201
Hotlines: 1–800–368–1019 (Voice) 1–800–537–7697 (TDD)
E-mail: ocrmail@hhs.gov
http://www.hhs.gov/ocr (H-141/June 2000)

FERPA Information:
Family Policy Compliance Office
U.S. Department of Education
400 Maryland Avenue, SW
Washington, DC 20202–5920
Phone: (202) 260–3887
http://www.ed.gov/about/offices/list/ocr/index.html

SUMMARY

Remaining vigilant about the legal and ethical aspects of school neuro-psychology is a continual ongoing process. The desire to help students and the use of best practices give practitioners the foundation for providing and maintaining a high standard of care and professionalism, reducing potential for ethical challenges. While some practitioners will be fortunate enough to work in organizations featuring similarly high levels of integrity and professional responsibility, others will encounter conflicts between personal and institutional self-interest, on the one hand, and client needs on the other. In some cases, actual ethical dilemmas will occur, pitting one ethical principle against another or involving a conflict between a practitioner's duty to professional standards and his or her duty to obey the law. Through awareness and foresight, ethical dilemmas can be prevented and/or resolved. When ethical choices become difficult, the practitioner should remember that he or she is not alone. In order to make an informed decision—and to keep out of trouble—reliable resources should be consulted, and those consultations should be carefully documented.

> When facing situations that create an ethical dilemma, be sure to choose the best path for all concerned. Whenever you have questions about propriety or legalities, don't hesitate to use available consultation resources: colleagues, school administrators, the APA Ethics Code, or published literature. Let your conscience be your guide, and above all else—do no harm!

Make notes about your decision—and the process you used to make your choices, including any opinions given by those you consulted. While some ethical choices are obvious, others require some thought to understand the cause and possible effects of any actions taken.

Help can be found in the form of ethics codes or codes of conduct. These important documents establish guidelines for professional behavior and have been composed and endorsed by groups, such as APA and NASP. Many professional organizations provide guidelines, discussions, and experts for consultation. Professional journals, academic papers, books and chapters, and notes from presentations delivered at conferences provide guidance should you need clarification on an important issue. When confronted with an ethical dilemma, professionals should consult with experts: legal counsel, professional liability insurance carriers, and scholars. Don't overlook the guidelines of your own institution and even your job description as resources. Remember that you are never alone.

Make concerted efforts to base your decisions on facts, and be sure that your facts are well documented. Include notes from conversations with experts, testing and student records, as well as contributing factors that influence your judgment. Take logical steps to assess each aspect of a case, and avoid the tendency to jump to conclusions. Be confident in your final decision, and act with the knowledge that facts and opinions are available to support your conclusions

As a closing thought, we would like to leave you with the following statement by Francis Wellman (1936/1997), author of the classic text, *The Art of Cross-Examination*, and ask you to apply this to the practice of School Neuropsychology: "It requires the greatest ingenuity; a habit of logical thought; clearness of perception in general; infinite patience and self control . . . ability to act with force and precision; a masterful knowledge of the subject-matter itself; and extreme caution . . ." It involves all shades of complexions of human morals, human passions, and human intelligence.

REFERENCES

American Psychological Association (APA). (2002). Ethical principles of psychologists and code of conduct. *American Psychologist, 57*, 1060–1073.

Brusling, C. (2005, November). *Evidence-based practice in teaching and teacher education*. Paper presented at the Conference of Professional Development of Teachers in a Lifelong Perspective: Teacher Education, Knowledge Production and Institutional Reform. Center for Higher Education Greater Copenhagen in Collaboration with OECD. Retrieved July 8, 2008 from http://www.samford.edu/ctls/evidence-basedpracticeinteachingcb.pdf.

Bush, S. S. (2007). Ethical decision making in clinical neuropsychology. *American Academy of Clinical Neuropsychology*. New York: Oxford University Press.

California Medical Association. (2001, August). *How to consent to medical care for minors*. Retrieved September 15, 2008 from http://www.cmanet.org/publicdoc.cfm/15/4/GENER/165.

Davies, P. (1999). What is evidence-based education? *British Journal of Educational Studies, 47*, 108–121.

Davis, J. M., & Sandoval, J. (1982). Applied ethics for school-based consultants. *Professional Psychology, 13*, 543–551.

Dekraal, S. T., Sales, B., & Hall, S. (1998). Informed consent, confidentiality, and duty to report laws in the conduct of child therapy. In T. R. Kratochwill & R. J. Morris (Eds.), *The practice of child therapy* (3rd ed., pp. 540–559). Boston: Allyn and Bacon.

Fagan, T. K., & Wise, F. S. (2000). *School psychology: Past, present, and future* (2nd ed.). New York: Longman.

Hammill, D. D., Brown, L., & Bryant, B. R. (1989). *A consumer's guide to tests in print*. Austin, TX: Pro-Ed.

Hansen, J. C., Himes, B. S., & Meier, S. (1990). *Consultation: Concepts and practices*. Englewood Cliffs, NJ: Prentice-Hall.

Hargreaves, D. (1999). In defense of research for evidence-based teaching: A rejoinder to Martyn Hammersley. [Electronic version]. *British Educational Research Journal, 23*, 405–419.

Hummel, D. L., Talbutt, L. C., & Alexander, M. D. (1985). *Law and ethics in counseling.* New York: Van Nostrand-Reinhold.

Individuals with Disabilities Education Improvement Act of 2004. (PL No. 108-446, 20 USC 1400).

Jacobs, S., & Hartshorne, T. S. (2007). *Ethics and law for school psychologists* (5th ed.). Hoboken, NJ: John Wiley & Sons.

Kersting, K. (2003, October). Bolstering evidence-based education. [Electronic version]. *Monitor on Psychology,* 34.

Knapp, S., & VandeCreek, L. (2006). *Practical ethics for psychologists: A positive approach.* Washington, DC: American Psychological Association.

Levin, R., & Feldman, H. (2005). *Teaching evidence-based practice in nursing: A guide for academic and clinical settings.* New York: Springer.

Mazurekk-Melnyk, B. (2005) *Teaching evidence-based practice in nursing: A guide for academic and clinical settings.* New York: Springer.

Miller, D. C. (2007). *Essentials of school neuropsychological assessment.* Hoboken, NJ: John Wiley & Sons.

Mowder, B. A. (1982). Assessment and intervention in school psychological services. In G. W. Hynd (Ed.), *The school psychologist* (pp. 145–167). Syracuse, NY: Syracuse University Press.

National Association of School Psychologists (NASP). (2000). *Principles for professional ethics. Guidelines for the provision of school psychological services. Professional conduct manual.* Bethesda, MD: Author.

Richards, D. M. (2002). *An overview of §504.* Retrieved September 14, 2008, from http://www.504idea.org/504_Overview_Fall_2006.pdf.

Sattler, J. M. (2008). *Assessment of children: Cognitive applications* (5th ed.). La Mesa, CA: Jerome M. Sattler.

U.S. Department of Education. (n.d.). *Building the legacy: IDEA 2004.* Retrieved September 14, 2008 from http://www.idea.ed.gov.

U.S. Department of Education. (n.d.). *Overview: Four pillars of NCLB.* Retrieved September 14, 2008 from http://www.ed.gov/nclb/overview/intro/4pillars.html.

U.S. Department of Health and Human Services (DHHS). (2000, June). *Your rights under Section 504 and the Americans with Disabilities Act.* Retrieved September 14, 2008 from http://www.hhs.gov/ocr/504ada.html.

Weithorn, L. A. (1983) Involving children in decisions affecting their own welfare: Guidelines for professionals. In G. B. Melton, G. P. Koocher, & M. J. Saks (Eds.), *Children's competence to consent* (pp. 235–260). New York: Plenum Press.

Wellman, F. L. (1936/1997). *The art of cross-examination* (4th ed., rev. and enl.). New York: Touchstone. Adapted from: Dye, T. R. (1995). *Understanding public policy.* Englewood Cliffs, NJ: Prentice-Hall.

Whitehurst, J. J. (2003). *Evidence-based education.* Retrieved September 18, 2008 from http://www.ed.gov/admins/tchrqual/evidence/whitehurst.html?exp=0.

Woodcock, R. W., McGrew, K. S., & Mather, N. (2001). *Woodcock-Johnson III battery.* Itasca, IL: Riverside Publishing.

CHAPTER 4

Multicultural School Neuropsychology

ROBERT L. RHODES

T HE UNITED STATES public school system includes speakers of over 400 different languages (Kindler, 2002). The majority of students who speak a language other than English (77 percent) are Spanish speakers (National Clearinghouse for English Language Acquisition and Language Instruction Educational Programs [NCELA], 2002). Vietnamese (2.3 percent), Hmong (2.2 percent), Haitian Creole (1.1 percent), Korean (1.1 percent), Cantonese (1.0 percent), Arabic (0.9 percent), Russian (0.9 percent), Navajo (0.9 percent), and Tagalog (0.8 percent) round out the list of top ten languages spoken by students in the United States (NCELA, 2002).

The most recent nationwide census (U.S. Bureau of the Census, 2001) revealed that among the 48.7 million students in the United States, one in ten students (10 percent) were born outside the United States, and one in five (20 percent) had a parent born outside the United States. During the past decade, the overall K-12 student population within the nation increased by only 2.6 percent. The English language learner (ELL) student population increased by 60.8 percent during that same period, with the highest rate of growth in states that did not have historically high numbers of ELL students (NCELA, 2006).

The purpose of this chapter is to discuss best practices for the referral, assessment, and intervention of multicultural and linguistically diverse students within a school neuropsychology framework. Key considerations related to differentiation of language difference and disability, legislative requirements, language acquisition, acculturation, neuropsychological assessment instruments and procedures, and intervention selection will be discussed.

HISTORY OF DIFFERENCE VERSUS DISABILITY DIFFERENTIATION ATTEMPT

The differentiation between culture and language differences and actual disabilities is a multifaceted task that has been attempted for decades and one that has particular implication for school-based neuropsychological practice. One of the most documented indicators of difficulty in this area is the long-standing overrepresentation of diverse students across various special education categories. Forty years ago, Lloyd Dunn (1968) highlighted the problem of disproportional representation of students from minority groups in special education and offered several recommendations to address this concern (e.g., alternative diagnostic procedures, heterogeneous service delivery models, prescriptive/diagnostic teaching). Central to Dunn's recommendations was a move toward "a more precise science of clinical instruction based on diagnostic instruments which yield a profile of abilities and disabilities about a specific facet of behavior and which have incorporated within them measures of a child's ability to learn samples or units of materials at each of the points on a profile" (Dunn, 1968, pp. 13–14). Four decades later, few of Dunn's recommendations have been consistently implemented, and the discrepancy that he urgently alerted us to has, in large part, remained (Donovan & Cross, 2002; Gravois & Rosenfield, 2006; Trent & Artiles, 1998).

Twenty years ago, Garcia and Ortiz (1988) differentiated between three broad categories of student experiences leading to academic failure. Type I, as it was termed, occurs when students are in educational environments that do not accommodate their individual differences or learning styles. An example of this situation would be a student with LEP who needs native language or ESL instruction who is taught solely in English without any adaptation of the curricula. Type II is when students have achievement difficulties that cannot be attributed to a specific disability. A student who has not learned to read because of excessive absences, for example, can overcome these deficits through individualized instruction or remediation. In contrast, Type III represents students who have major disorders that interfere with the teaching-learning process. These students have an actual disability and require special education assistance to achieve their maximum potential.

Garcia and Ortiz (1988) added that failure to differentiate Types I and II from Type III learning problems results in the inappropriate referral of culturally and linguistically diverse (CLD) students to special education and contributes to the disproportionate representation of these students in special education. They recommended an examination of the quality of instruction provided in the regular classroom environment and the validity of the referral process in order to address this concern. Also recommended was an effective prereferral process that included a prereferral problem-solving committee comprised of regular classroom teachers to help distinguish achievement difficulties that are associated with failure to accommodate individual differences from problems that stem from actual disabilities (Garcia & Ortiz, 1988).

Now, twenty years removed from Garcia and Ortiz's accurate differentiation of difference versus disability and forty years from Dunn's revolutionary recommendations, we continue to struggle to meet the spirit of the law in our assessment of CLD students. The flexible approach and individualized nature of school neuropsychology offer many potential advantages for work in this area if approached in an informed and thoughtful manner and practiced within the guidelines of public laws regulating school-based practice.

LEGISLATIVE HISTORY RELATED
TO NONDISCRIMINATORY ASSESSMENT

The following sections provide a history of legislation related to the identification of learning disabilities and nondiscriminatory assessment. Each successive revision of public law has served to establish more specific and extensive minimal standards of practice when working with CLD students.

PUBLIC LAW 94–142

Rhodes (2006) noted that the need to differentiate difference from disability among CLD students was addressed in this first federal law requiring special education services. Section 4 of the exclusionary clause for Public Law 94–142 states that a child should not be identified as learning disabled if the "discrepancy between ability and achievement is primarily the result of environmental, cultural, or economic disadvantage" (U.S. Office of Education, 1977, p. 65083). Although students who have unique environmental, cultural, or economic circumstances may be identified as having a learning disability, the extent to which these external factors affect their academic performance must be established and may not be the primary cause of the performance deficit in question.

PUBLIC LAW 105–17 (IDEA 1997)

Each successive revision of public law related to special education has addressed the appropriate identification of CLD students suspected of having a disability and the continued mislabeling and disproportionate identification of these same students. PL 105–17 concluded that "[g]reater efforts are needed to prevent the intensification of problems connected with mislabeling minority children with disabilities" [601 (c) (8) (A)] and "[m]ore minority children continue to be served in special education than would be expected given the percentage of minority students in the general population" [601 (c) (8) (B)]. PL 105–17 added provisions related to lack of effective instruction and limited English proficiency as a safeguard against these concerns, stating that "[i]n making a determination of eligibility under paragraph 4(A), a child shall not be determined to be a child with a disability if the determinant factor for such determination is lack of instruction in reading or math or limited English proficiency" [Section 614 (b) (5)]. Within this law, Congress further required states to (1) collect ethnic data by type of disability, (2) determine if disproportionality exists, and (3) address the problem via corrective action measures.

Public Law 108–446 (IDEA 2004)

According to IDEA 2004, states must work to prevent the inappropriate overidentification or disproportionate representation by race and ethnicity of children as children with disabilities, including children with disabilities with a particular impairment (U.S. Department of Education, 2007). PL 108–446 further establishes policies and procedures to prevent disproportionality or overidentification by race and ethnicity and provides for the collection and examination of data regarding disproportionality. This current legislation also outlines requirements when reviewing policies and procedures and extends opportunities for technical assistance, demonstration projects, dissemination of information, and implementation of scientifically based research.

ISSUES AND CONSIDERATIONS PRIOR TO THE SELECTION OF INSTRUMENTS AND PROCEDURES

Prior to the selection of assessment instruments and procedures, one must consider several issues that may greatly influence the individual performance of students from multicultural and linguistically diverse backgrounds. These issues include, but are not limited to, an individual student's educational history, language history, bilingual and ESL program participation, current language proficiency, and level of acculturation. Listed below is a summary of these issues as detailed by Ochoa and Rhodes (2005).

Educational History

Inquiry should be made through record review and parent interview about the country (or countries) in which the student has been educated, the language (or languages) of instruction, previous bilingual education services, reason for termination or exit from bilingual education services, grades repeated, number of schools attended, areas of academic success, and areas of academic difficulty or concern. If academic difficulties exist, one should determine whether these difficulties are present across both languages or if they are manifest only when the student is required to perform academic tasks in English. Difficulties that are present only when the student is required to perform tasks in English may be an indication of second-language acquisition issues rather than a specific content knowledge deficit or disability.

LANGUAGE HISTORY

The language history of the child and family should be explored through record review (e.g., home language surveys) and parent interview. Questions that might be asked include the following: What language or languages are currently used at home? What language or languages have been used at home during the life of the student? What language appears to be preferred by the student? In what language does the student prefer to read? In what language does the student watch TV or listen to music?

The language of instruction, the student's language proficiency, and the language demands of the task and method of measurement should be clearly understood and carefully evaluated. School psychologists working with CLD students should have an awareness of language acquisition and the impact on a student's response to instruction and intervention. This pervasive concern is perhaps best illustrated by the tremendous difference in language exposure often experienced by ELL students in comparison to their monolingual peers. Ortiz (1997) reports that English language learners with an average of as much as two to three hours per day of exposure to the English language will still be 15,000 total hours behind their monolingual English speaking peers by kindergarten. By fifth grade, ELL students are nearly 24,000 total hours behind their monolingual English-speaking peers, on average, with respect to exposure and experience with the English language (Ortiz, 1997).

BILINGUAL AND ESL PROGRAM PARTICIPATION

Ochoa and Rhodes (2005) noted that there are several different educational programs used to educate ELL students in the United States, including English-only programs, pull-out English as a second language (ESL) programs, transitional bilingual programs, maintenance bilingual programs, and two-way or dual language bilingual education programs. The amount of English and native language instruction that is used varies markedly across the programs as does program effectiveness. The type of program(s) a student attended and the reason for exiting is key information for accurate problem analysis.

CURRENT LANGUAGE PROFICIENCY

The current language proficiency of the student should be examined through record review, teacher interview, and formal and informal assessment. A student's use of one particular language more frequently than another should not serve as an indicator of his or her language proficiency. Recently administered language proficiency measures (no more than six months old) should be used to determine the student's level of proficiency across both languages.

Cummins (1984) proposed basic interpersonal communication skills (BICS) and cognitive academic language proficiency (CALP) as two distinct types of language proficiency. BICS is the development of conversational language skills and is thought to take two to three years to acquire. CALP is the academic language skills that are necessary to fully understand instructions and produce verbal and written work unencumbered by issues of language acquisition and proficiency. CALP is a more advanced level of language acquisition and is estimated to take five to seven years to develop (Cummins, 1984).

In order to address issues of language proficiency in the context of the evaluation of academic performance, Ochoa (2005) recommended that evaluators compare the educational trajectory of the student in question with his or her same grade-level ELL peers. If the educational trajectories are similar and are within the time frame of BIC and CALP development, length of native language instructional programming and issues of language acquisition might be considered critical factors in the student's performance. However, there may be cause for concern if the educational trajectory of an ELL student across time is notably different from his or her ELL classmates who have been educated in a similar instructional setting for approximately the same number of years.

Familiarity with the process of second-language acquisition may be obtained through a review of several seminal studies in this area, including Cummins (1983, 1984), Ortiz and Polyzoi (1986), Collier (1987), and Thomas and Collier (1996, 1997, 2002). These and other studies provide critical information regarding the expected rate of second-language acquisition, the multiple factors that may influence language acquisition, the difference between basic communication and academic language skills, and the potential impact of second-language acquisition on academic achievement (Ochoa & Rhodes, 2005).

LEVEL OF ACCULTURATION

The student's current level of acculturation in relation to the appropriateness of instruction and procedures should be assessed. Although less readily and intuitively understood by many school psychologists, the degree to which the student is acculturated to the mainstream of U.S. society has a significant impact on student progress and participation in the classroom and the decisions and procedures used in evaluation. Bidimensional measurement of acculturation is recommended across cognitive styles, personality, identity, attitudes, and acculturative stress.

MULTICULTURAL SCHOOL NEUROPSYCHOLOGICAL ASSESSMENT INSTRUMENTS AND PROCEDURES

Once the issues of educational history, language history, bilingual and ESL program participation, current language proficiency, and level of acculturation have been considered, school-based practitioners can consider appropriate instruments and procedures to address key areas of communication and language skills; intelligence and cognitive skills; academic achievement; executive functions and problem solving; attention, memory, and learning; sensory, perception, and motor skills; and behavior and personality. An updated discussion of issues initially presented by Hess and Rhodes (2005) is provided next.

COMMUNICATION/LANGUAGE SKILLS

The *Woodcock-Muñoz Language Survey Revised* (WMLS-R; Woodcock & Muñoz-Sandoval, 2005) is one of the most frequently used measures of language proficiency for Spanish-speaking students and is one of the few measures that provides information about the student's academic language development in both the student's first language and in English. Another beneficial instrument is the *Bilingual Verbal Ability Test* (BVAT-NU; Muñoz-Sandoval, Cummins, Alvarado, & Ruef, 2005), which is available in eighteen languages in addition to English. Frequently spoken languages assessed by the BVAT include Vietnamese, Hmong, Haitian-Creole, Chinese, Arabic, Russian, and Navajo.

Rhodes, Kayser, and Hess (2000) recommended procedures to aid in the differential diagnosis of a language impairment and normal language development among LEP children during the neuropsychological assessment process. Information gathered from the comprehensive interview (e.g., parental concerns, language use) can be combined with teacher interviews and observations from the speech-language pathologist to develop a complete picture of the child's language use and skills. Children with language impairments typically have restricted abilities related to forms (syntax and phonology), use, and content (semantics) in both languages regardless of the context. Additionally, the practitioner will want to consider data related to sequencing, memory, and attention span. Language-impaired children often have difficulty in these areas in both languages. These data should all support the diagnosis of language impairment. The characteristics of acquired aphasia, dysarthria, apraxia, and traumatic brain injury will be present in both languages.

Hess and Rhodes (2005) noted that it is easy to recognize the impact of language when a child clearly speaks a language other than English as his or her first language. However, it is critical to consider the more subtle effects of language when a child speaks nontraditional English (e.g., Black English) or has specific culturally determined patterns of usage. For example, Manly et al. (1998) found that Black English use among African American adults was correlated with performance deficits on the Trail Making Test, part B, and the Information subtest on the *WAIS-R*. Furthermore, Native American children have been found to score lower on tests of verbal ability on the *WISC-III* (Tanner-Halverson, Burden, & Sabers, 1993) and language (Dauphinais & King, 1992), leading some to propose that for this population there is a cultural mismatch between the decontextualized format of test-taking and the culturally determined patterns of language use (Gopaul-McNicol & Armour-Thomas, 2002). Once school neuropsychologists have determined the level of language skill, they can make better decisions about which instruments to use and how to interpret the results in order to obtain the best information about the child's strengths and weaknesses.

Intelligence/Cognitive Skills

Hess and Rhodes (2005) observed that several researchers have reviewed the difficulties in using IQ and other cognitive ability tests to assess culturally and linguistically diverse children (e.g., Dent, 1996; Gopaul-McNicol & Armour-Thomas, 2002; Marlowe, 2000). The inclusion of children from diverse backgrounds into normative samples for a test does not justify using the test with those populations, because the minority group norms will not cluster within the distribution in large enough numbers to have any influence on the norms (Dent, 1996). On the Wechsler scales, African American, Hispanics, and Native American populations all have mean scores that are approximately 10 points to one standard deviation below the mean (Tanner-Halverson et al., 1993; Wasserman & Becker, 1999). Although mean score differences do not necessarily constitute test bias (Reynolds & Kaiser, 1992), the overrepresentation of minority children in special education classrooms has led some to discourage the use of verbally weighted measures of intelligence such as the

Wechsler scales and instead use alternative approaches (e.g., Naglieri, 1997; Sternberg, 1999).

Previously, there were two translated versions of the *WISC-III*, the *Escala de Inteligencia Wechsler par Ninos—Revisada* (EIWN-R; The Psychological Corporation, 1983) and the *Escala de Inteligencia Wechsler para Ninos – Revisada de Puerto Rico* (The Psychological Corporation, 1993). The former is considered a research edition and was published without normative data; the latter has a narrow norming base (Puerto Rican children) and may not be appropriate for most Hispanic groups in the United States (Echemendia & Julian, 2002). With the development of the WISC-IV, the *Escala de Inteligencia de Wechsler para Niños* (The Psychological Corporation, 2004) is the most current school-age translation available.

Two alternatives to translated versions of traditional ability tests are comprehensive nonverbal assessments (e.g., *Universal Nonverbal Intelligence Test*, UNIT; Bracken & McCallum, 1998) and measures based on neuropsychological theory (e.g., *Cognitive Assessment System*, CAS; Naglieri & Das, 1997a). Hess and Rhodes (2005) state that the UNIT was designed to be totally nonverbal and to measure memory and reasoning through symbolic (language-mediated) and nonsymbolic modalities. While not nonverbal, the *CAS* offers an alternative framework for examining and interpreting ability based on the Planning, Attention, Simultaneous, Successive (PASS) model of cognitive processing theory (Naglieri & Das, 1997b). Early studies suggested that there is less discrepancy between the scores of White and African American children on this measure and that fewer African American children were identified as mentally retarded using the CAS rather than the WISC-III (Naglieri & Rojahn, 2001). This instrument is also beneficial because its emphasis on processing strengths and weaknesses facilitates academic intervention planning, although the interpretation of the Planning and Attention factors remains questionable (Sattler, 2001).

ACADEMIC ACHIEVEMENT

Common areas of academic achievement measurement include reading, mathematics, spelling, and writing. Because academic performance is based on experientially dependent skills and abilities, the assessment of achievement can be an exceedingly complex process with children from culturally and linguistically diverse backgrounds who may have educational and life experiences that are unique in comparison to the normative population of many commonly used measures. As noted by Duran (1989), until a student is proficient in English, measures of academic achievement may really only be a crude test of English competence rather than an accurate assessment of academic growth and development.

Standardized measures of academic achievement, curriculum-based measurement, or a combination of these two approaches are common methods of assessing the academic achievement of students who are culturally and linguistically diverse. Frequently used standardized measures of academic achievement include the *Woodcock-Johnson III NU Tests of Achievement* (Woodcock, McGrew, & Mather, 2006), the *Batería III Woodcock-Muñoz: Pruebas de Aprovechamiento* (Woodcock, Muñoz-Sandoval, McGrew, & Mather, 2006) a parallel Spanish version of the *Woodcock-Johnson Psychoeducational Battery III*, and the *Aprenda: La Prueba de Logros en Español, Tercera Edición* (The Psychological Corporation, 2006) a measure of academic achievement for Spanish-speaking students in the areas of reading, language arts, and mathematics. Unfortunately, there are not many options available if the child's first language is not Spanish. Curriculum-based measurement is one of the most widely used methods of curriculum-based assessment and has been suggested as a potential strategy for making educational decisions with CLD students (Baker & Good, 1995; Shinn, 1989).

Executive Functions/Problem Solving

In nearly all measures of neuropsychological functioning, the amount of schooling that an individual has experienced will play a role in his or her functioning (Rosselli, 1993). Some tests have been observed to be more sensitive to educational variables (e.g., language tests) than others (e.g., *Wisconsin Card Sorting Test*, WCST; Heaton, 1981) as exemplified in the work of Rosselli and Ardila (1993). Furthermore, research has demonstrated that the educational effect on neuropsychological test performance is not linear. That is, differences between zero and three years of education are usually highly significant, whereas there are virtually no differences found between individuals with twelve and fifteen years of education (Puente & Ardila, 2000). With this caution in mind, there are a few promising instruments available that provide comprehensive assessments of individual functioning.

The NEPSY II (Korkman, Kirk, & Kemp, 2007) is a developmental neuropsychological test that was developed to identify neuropsychological problems in children. The NEPSY II measures five Core Domains: (a) Attention and Executive Functioning, (b) Sensorimotor, (c) Visuospatial, (d) Language, and (e) Memory. Hess and Rhodes (2005) reported that two studies suggest the utility of the original version of the NEPSY with diverse populations. Mulenga, Ahonen, and Aro (2001) tested forty-five literate school children in Zambia with the NEPSY and concluded that although there were differences between the norm group and the Zambian group of children (e.g., lower Language and Attention and Executive Functioning scores and higher Visuospatial scores for the Zambian population), the

NEPSY did not appear to be overly sensitive to language and cultural differences. McCloskey (2001) found support for use of the NEPSY with a group of fifty-five low-income Hispanic children based on the similarities between the correlations for this group and for the standardization sample. Hess and Rhodes (2005) cautioned that the practitioner would want to use care in selecting the subtests that would be least impacted by the child's language and/or schooling history as well as using care in the interpretation of the results pending additional research support.

ATTENTION/MEMORY/LEARNING

Hess and Rhodes (2005) recommended that memory should be measured using both verbal and nonverbal stimuli because of the impact of SES, schooling, and language differences. It is important to recognize that even if the child speaks the dominant language, he or she may be limited English proficient. Harris, Cullum, and Puente (1995) found that nonbalanced (proficient in conversational English, but not equally adept in both languages) Spanish-English bilinguals learned fewer words and had poorer retention scores when tested in English as compared to Spanish on the *California Verbal Learning Test* (CVLT). The results of this study suggested that the relative degree of bilingualism was significant and that it systematically altered the learning and retention of verbal information. When assessed in their dominant language, no significant differences were found in groups. Therefore, when possible, the practitioner would want to assess the child in both the first and second language.

SENSORY, PERCEPTUAL, AND MOTOR SKILLS

In general, measures used to assess gross and fine motor skills will be similar across cultures (Hess & Rhodes, 2005). However, it is important to keep in mind the degree of familiarity an individual might have with the tools used to measure fine motor skills (e.g., pencil use, scissors). This type of information can be gathered during the interview to determine the most appropriate test as well as how to interpret individual items. Cultural differences might also impact test behaviors. For example, Puente and Ardila (2000) cautioned that Hispanic children often respond differently on timed tests in that they tend to work at their own pace rather than compete with a clock.

BEHAVIOR AND PERSONALITY

An important component of a thorough neuropsychological assessment includes an evaluation of individual social-emotional functioning. The

Behavior Assessment System for Children, 2nd Edition (BASC II; Reynolds & Kamphaus, 2004), used extensively to identify behavioral and emotional disorders in children and adolescents, also has a Spanish version, *el Sistema Multidimensional de Evaluación de la Conducta de los Niños* (*el Sistema*). McCloskey, Hess, and D'Amato (2003) generally supported the use of the *Escalas Evaluativas de los Padres*, the Spanish version of the BASC Parent Rating Scale, with low-income Hispanic children, particularly with the Internalizing, Externalizing, and Adaptive Composites. However, there were some noted differences between this sample and the normative sample in that significant differences were noted between the Adaptive Composite and scales from other composites. Similar studies are needed for African American, Asian, and Native American populations to assist practitioners in interpreting their findings.

The *Tell-Me-A-Story* evaluation procedure (TEMAS; Constantino, 1987) provides another clinical measure for use with diverse populations. Constantino, Flanagan, and Malgady (2001) noted that the Tell-Me-A-Story procedure is one of the only comprehensive personality measures that offers nonminority and minority norms for four groups (African American, Puerto Rican, other Hispanic, and White).

SELECTION OF CULTURALLY AND LINGUISTICALLY APPROPRIATE INTERVENTIONS

Culturally and linguistically appropriate interventions designed to meet the particular need of the student should take into account whether the data indicates that the student fits a Type I (when students are in educational environments that do not accommodate their individual differences or learning styles), Type II (when students have achievement difficulties not attributed to a specific disability that can be addressed through individualized instruction or remediation), or Type III profile (when students have an actual disability and require special education assistance to reach their desired performance) as defined by Garcia and Ortiz (1988).

The selection of an intervention with empirical validity or one that is evidenced-based is a particular challenge. Ingraham and Oka (2006) stated that very few evidence-based interventions are currently available for use with CLD students, and the generalizability and portability of models validated on other populations is unknown. They make the following observations regarding the use of interventions currently available:

1. Interventions that have not included diverse populations (among the intervention recipients, interventionists, and researchers) are yet unknown in terms of their effectiveness with other groups.

2. More intervention research with other, more diverse groups must be conducted with designs that provide data regarding the transferability, generalization, and cultural validity of the intervention.
3. It is expected that adjustments may be needed for the intervention to be meaningful and successful for different cultural groups and/or in different contexts. Whether this will affect the outcome of the intervention is an empirical question that requires the collection and evaluation of data.

SUMMARY

This chapter discussed best practices for the referral, assessment, and intervention of multicultural and linguistically diverse students within a school neuropsychology framework. The differentiation of language difference and disability, legislative requirements, language acquisition, acculturation, neuropsychological assessment instruments and procedures, and intervention selection were reviewed in light of the needs of this important and heterogeneous population. The individualized and innovative nature of school-based neuropsychology offers opportunities to incorporate these unique concepts and considerations into a comprehensive assessment and intervention strategy. Practitioners should become well versed in each of the areas discussed in order to provide the breadth and depth of services required for best practices.

REFERENCES

Baker, S. K., & Good, R. (1995). Curriculum based measurement of English reading with bilingual Hispanic students: A validation study with second-grade students. *School Psychology Review, 24,* 561–578.

Bracken, B., & McCallum, S. (1998). *Universal Nonverbal Intelligence Test.* Itasca, IL: Riverside.

Collier, V. (1987). Age and rate of acquisition of second language for academic purposes. *TESOL Quarterly, 21,* 617–641.

Constantino, G. (1987). *Picture cards: The TEMAS (Tell-Me-A-Story) Test.* Los Angeles: Western Psychological Services.

Constantino, G., Flanagan, R., & Malgady, R. G. (2001). Narrative assessments TAT, CAT, and TEMAS. In L. A. Suzuki, J. G. Ponterotto, & P. J. Meller (Eds.), *Handbook of multicultural assessment* (2nd ed., pp. 217–236). San Francisco: Jossey-Bass.

Cummins, J. (1983). Bilingualism and special education: Program and pedagogical issues. *Learning Disability Quarterly, 6,* 373–386.

Cummins, J. (1984). *Bilingualism and special education: Issues in assessment and pedagogy.* San Diego: College-Hill.

Dauphinais, P. L., & King, J. (1992). Psychological assessment with American Indian children. *Applied & Preventive Psychology, 1,* 97–110.

Dent, H. E. (1996). Non-biased assessment or realistic assessment? In R. Lewis (Ed.), *Handbook of tests and measures for Black populations* (pp. 103–122). Hampton, VA: Cobb & Henry.

Donovan, S., & Cross, C. (Eds.). (2002). *Minority students in special and gifted education.* Washington, DC: National Academy Press.

Dunn, L. (1968). Special education for the mildly mentally retarded: Is much of it justifiable? *Exceptional Children, 23,* 5–21.

Duran, R. P. (1989). Assessment and instruction of at-risk Hispanic students. *Exceptional Children, 56,* 154–158.

Echemendía, R. J., & Julian, L. (2002). Neuropsychological assessment of Latino children. In F. R. Ferraro (Ed.), *Minority and cross-cultural aspects of neuropsychological assessment* (pp. 181–203). Lisse, The Netherlands: Swets & Zeitlinger Publishers.

Garcia, S. B., & Ortiz, A. A. (1988). Preventing inappropriate referrals of language minority students to special education. *National Clearinghouse for Bilingual Education Focus, 5,* 1–21.

Gopaul-McNichol, S., & Armour-Thomas, E. (2002). *Assessment and culture: Psychological tests with minority populations.* San Diego: Academic Press.

Gravois, T. A., & Rosenfield, S. (2006). Impact of instructional consultation teams on the disproportionate referral and placement of minority students in special education. *Remedial and Special Education, 27,* 42–52.

Harris, J. G., Cullum, C. M., & Puente, A. E. (1995). Effects of bilingualism on verbal learning and memory in Hispanic adults. *Journal of the International Neuropsychological Society, 1,* 10–16.

Heaton, R. K. (1981). *A manual for the Wisconsin Card Sort Test.* Odessa, FL: Psychological Assessment Resources.

Hess, R., & Rhodes, R. L. (2005). Providing neuropsychological services to culturally and linguistically diverse learners. In R. C. D'Amato, E. Fletcher-Janzen, & C. R. Reynolds (Eds.), *Handbook of school neuropsychology* (pp. 637–660). Hoboken, NJ: John Wiley & Sons.

Ingraham, C. L., & Oka, E. R. (2006). Multicultural issues in evidence-based interventions. *Journal of Applied School Psychology, 22,* 127–149.

Kindler, A. L. (2002). Survey of the states' limited English proficient students and available educational programs and services 1999–2000 summary report. Washington, DC: National Clearinghouse for English Acquisition and Language Instruction Educational Programs.

Korkman, M., Kirk, U., & Kemp, S. (2007). *NEPSY II: A developmental neuropsychological assessment manual.* San Antonio, TX: Harcourt Brace.

Manly, J. J., Miller, S. W., Heaton, R. K., Byrd, D., Reilly, J., Velasquez, R. J., Saccuzzo, D. P., & Grant, I. (1998). The effect of African-American acculturation on neuropsychological test performance in normal and HIV-positive individuals. *Journal of the International Neuropsychological Society, 4,* 291–302.

Marlowe, W. B. (2000). Multicultural perspectives on the neuropsychological assessment of children and adolescents. In E. Fletcher-Janzen, T. L. Strickland, & C. R.

Reynolds (Eds.), *Handbook of cross-cultural neuropsychology* (pp. 145–168). New York: Kluwer Academic/Plenum.

McCloskey, D. (2001). Evaluating the neuropsychological and behavioral abilities of migrant children and non-migrant children of Hispanic background. *Dissertation Abstracts International, 61,* 12-B. (UMI No. 6755).

McCloskey, D., Hess, R. S., & D'Amato, R. C. (2003). Evaluating the utility of the Spanish version of the Behavior Assessment System for Children - Parent Report System. *Journal of Psychoeducational Assessment, 21,* 325–337.

Mulenga, K., Ahonen, T., & Aro, M. (2001). Performance of Zambian children on the NEPSY: A pilot study. *Developmental Neuropsychology, 20,* 375–383.

Muñoz-Sandoval, A. F., Cummins, J., Alvarado, C. G., & Ruef, M. L. (2005). *Bilingual verbal ability tests normative update.* Itasca, IL: Riverside Publishing.

Naglieri, J. A. (1997). Planning, attention, simultaneous, and successive theory and the Cognitive Assessment System: A new theory-based measure of intelligence. In D. P. Flanagan, J. L. Genschaft, & P. L. Harrison (Eds.), *Contemporary intellectual assessment: Theories, tests, and issues* (pp. 247–267). New York: Guilford Press.

Naglieri, J. A., & Das, J. P. (1997a). *Cognitive assessment system.* Itasca, IL: Riverside.

Naglieri, J. A., & Das, J. P. (1997b). *Cognitive assessment system interpretive handbook.* Itasca, IL: Riverside.

Naglieri, J. A., & Rojahn, J. (2001). Intellectual classification of Black and White children in special education programs using the WISC-III and the Cognitive Assessment System. *American Journal on Mental Retardation, 106,* 359–367.

National Clearinghouse for English Language Acquisition and Language Instruction Educational Programs (NCELA). (2002). *United States most commonly spoken languages.* Retrieved September 10, 2007, from http://www.ncbe.gwu.edu/askn-cela/05toplangs.html.

National Clearinghouse for English Language Acquisition and Language Instruction Educational Programs (NCELA). (2006). *United States rate of LEP growth.* Retrieved September 10, 2007, from http://www.ncbe.gwu.edu/states/stateposter.pdf.

Ochoa, S. H. (2005). Bilingual education and second-language acquisition: Implica tions for assessment and school-based practice. In R. L. Rhodes, S. H. Ochoa, & S. O. Ortiz (Eds.), *Assessing culturally and linguistically diverse students: A practical guide.* New York: Guilford.

Ochoa, S. H., & Rhodes, R. L. (2005). Assisting parents of bilingual students to achieve equity in public schools. *Journal of Educational and Psychological Consultation, 16,* 75–94.

Ortiz, A. A., & Polyzoi, E. (1986). *Characteristics of limited English proficient Hispanic students in programs for the learning disabled: Implications for policy, practice and research. Part I. Report summary.* (ERIC Document Reproduction Service No. ED 267 578) Austin, TX.

Ortiz, S. O. (1997). *Implications of English only instruction: When do English learners catch up?* Unpublished manuscript. St. John's University.

The Psychological Corporation. (1983). *Escala de inteligencia Wechsler para Niños - Revisada.* San Antonio: Author.

The Psychological Corporation. (1993). *Escala de inteligencia Wechsler para Niños - Revisada de Puerto Rico.* San Antonio: Author.

The Psychological Corporation. (2004). *Escala de inteligencia Wechsler para Niños - IV.* San Antonio: Author.

The Psychological Corporation. (2006). *Aprenda: La Prueba de Logros en Español, Tercera Edición.* San Antonio: Author.

Puente, A. E., & Ardila, A. (2000). Neuropsychological assessment of Hispanics. In E. Fletcher-Janzen, T. Strickland, & C. R. Reynolds (Eds.), *The handbook of cross-cultural neuropsychology* (pp. 87–104). New York: Plenum Press.

Reynolds, C. R., & Kaiser, S. (1992). Test bias in psychological assessment. In T. B. Gutkin & C. R. Reynolds (Eds.), *The handbook of school psychology* (2nd ed., pp. 487–525). New York: John Wiley & Sons.

Reynolds, C. R., & Kamphaus, R. W. (2004). *Behavioral assessment system for children* (2nd ed.). Circle Pines, MN: American Guidance Service.

Rhodes, R. L. (2006). Implementing the problem-solving model with culturally and linguistically diverse students. In R. Ervin, G. Gimpel, E. Daly, & K. Merrell (Eds.), *Handbook of school psychology: Effective practices for the 21st century.* New York: Guilford.

Rhodes, R., Kayser, H., & Hess, R. S. (2000). Neuropsychological differential diagnosis of Spanish-speaking preschool children. In E. Fletcher-Janzen, T. L. Strickland, & C. R. Reynolds (Eds.), *Handbook of cross-cultural neuropsychology* (pp. 317–333). New York: Kluwer Academic/Plenum.

Rosselli, M. (1993). Neuropsychology of illiteracy. *Behavioral Neuropsychology, 6,* 107–112.

Rosselli, M., & Ardila, A. (1993). Developmental norms for the Wisconsin Card Sorting Test in 5- to 12-year-old children. *Clinical Neuropsychologist, 7,* 145–154.

Sattler, J. M. (2001). *Assessment of children: Cognitive applications* (4th ed.). San Diego: Sattler.

Shinn, M. R. (1989). *Curriculum-based measurement: Assessing special children.* New York: Guilford.

Sternberg, R. J. (1999). A triarchic approach to the understanding and assessment of intelligence in multicultural populations. *Journal of School Psychology, 37,* 145–160.

Tanner-Halverson, P., Burden, T., & Sabers, D. (1993). WISC-III normative data for Tohono O'odham Native American children. *Journal of Psychoeducational Assessment. Monograph Series: Wechsler Intelligence Scale for Children-III,* 125–133.

Thomas, W., & Collier, V. (1996). *Language minority student achievement and program effectiveness.* Fairfax, VA: George Mason University, Center for Bilingual/Multicultural/ESL Education.

Thomas, W. P., & Collier, V. (1997). *School effectiveness for language minority students.* Washington, DC: National Clearinghouse for Bilingual Education.

Thomas, W. P., & Collier, V. P. (2002). *A national study of school effectiveness for language minority students' long-term academic achievement.* Retrieved September 4, 2002, from http://www.crede.uscu.edu/research/llaa1.html.

Trent, S. C., & Artiles, A. J. (1998). Multicultural teacher education in special and bilingual education. *Remedial and Special Education, 19,* 2–7.

U.S. Bureau of the Census. (2001). *Percent of persons who are foreign born: 2000.* Washington, DC: Author.

U.S. Department of Education (2007). *Disproportionality and overidentification.* Washington, DC: U.S. Government Printing Office.

U.S. Office of Education. (1977). Definition and criteria for defining students as learning disabled. *Federal Register, 42:250, p.* 65083. Washington, DC: U.S. Government Printing Office.

Wasserman, J. D., & Becker, K. A. (1999). *Recent advances in intellectual assessment of children and adolescents: New research on the Cognitive Assessment System (CAS).* Itasca, IL: Riverside Publishing Research Report.

Woodcock, R. W., McGrew, K. S., & Mather, N. (2006). *The Woodcock-Johnson III NU.* Itasca, IL: Riverside.

Woodcock, R. W., & Muñoz-Sandoval, A. F. (2005). *Woodcock-Muñoz Language Survey Revised.* Itasca, IL: The Riverside Publishing Company.

Woodcock, R. W., Muñoz-Sandoval, A. F., McGrew, K. S., & Mather, N. (2006). *Batería III Woodcock-Muñoz.* Itasca, IL: The Riverside Publishing Company.

SECTION II

PRACTICE ISSUES IN SCHOOL NEUROPSYCHOLOGY

CHAPTER 5

School Neuropsychological Assessment and Intervention

DANIEL C. MILLER

THIS PURPOSE OF this chapter is to discuss the importance of using a conceptual model to guide the assessment and intervention practices of school neuropsychologists. Three major theoretical models will be briefly reviewed, including Lurian theory, Carroll-Horn-Cattell (CHC) approach, and the process assessment approach. These are the principal theories that shape contemporary assessment. The chapter will then focus on how school neuropsychological assessment fits within several response-to-intervention (RTI) models. Finally, a comprehensive school neuropsychological model for assessment and intervention will be presented.

IMPORTANCE OF A CONCEPTUAL MODEL TO GUIDE ASSESSMENT AND INTERVENTION

THEORIES THAT GUIDE ASSESSMENT

There are three models that guide contemporary practice in school neuropsychology: (1) Lurian theory, (2) Carroll-Horn-Cattell (CHC) model, and the process assessment approach. Lurian theory provides the foundation for tests such as the *Cognitive Assessment System* (CAS: Naglieri & Das, 1997), the *Kaufman Assessment Battery for Children, 2nd Edition* (K-ABC-II: Kaufman & Kaufman, 2004), and the NEPSY-II (Korkman, Kirk, & Kemp, 2007).

The CHC model was developed using a factor analytic approach (see Flanagan & Harrison, 2005 for a review). Measures from multiple cognitive abilities were factor analyzed, and the resulting factors were labeled as neurocognitive constructs (e.g., processing speed, short-term memory, auditory processing, etc.). The CHC model provides the foundation for tests such as the *Woodcock-Johnson-III Tests of Cognitive Abilities* (Woodcock, McGrew, &

Mather, 2001), the *Stanford-Binet Intelligence Scales: 5th Edition* (Roid, 2003), the *K-ABC-II* (Note: May be interpreted using either Lurian theory or CHC model) (Kaufman & Kaufman, 2004), and the *Differential Ability Scale, 2nd Edition* (Elliott, 2007).

The third model of assessment that guides contemporary practice is the process assessment approach. This approach was named the Boston Process Approach in 1986 (Milberg, Hebben, & Kaplan, 1996) and has been called the Boston Hypothesis Testing Approach (Teeter & Semrud-Clikeman, 1997). The approach is now generically called the process assessment approach and has been incorporated into tests such as the *CAS* (Naglieri & Das, 1997), the *WISC-III as a Process Instrument* (Kaplan, Fein, Kramer, Delis, & Morris, 1999), the *Delis-Kaplan Executive Functions System* (Delis, Kaplan, & Kramer, 2001), and the NEPSY-II (Korkman, Kirk, & Kemp, 2007). All of these tests have one thing in common: The scores for qualitative behaviors are noted during the administration of the test, in addition to the traditional quantitative scores. The process assessment approach assists school neuropsychologists in determining which strategies a child is using during the performance of a particular task. The test publishers and authors of the preceding tests have established base rates for common qualitative behaviors. For example, a child asking for repetitions is a common qualitative behavior that provides insight into the child's receptive language skills or selective attention. Base rates reflect the frequency of children the same age that exhibit a particular qualitative behavior.

An important distinction needs to be made between these three approaches. The Lurian approach is the only one of the three based on a neuropsychological theory, whereas the CHC approach is based on a statistical classification of human performance factors, and the process assessment approach is more of an interpretative model based on qualitative behavioral analysis and limit testing. With all three of these assessment approaches, basis research is needed that correlates brain function with what the tests are reportedly measuring. For example, does a test that is designed to measure the transfer of information in immediate memory to long-term memory stores actually activate the hippocampus area of the brain, which is the neuro-anatomical location for such neurocognitive activities? In the near future, brain-imaging techniques such as functional magnetic resonance imaging (fMRI) will help researchers and clinicians validate behavioral assessments and may become a direct measurement of intervention efficacy (Fletcher, 2008). Simos et al. (2002) already demonstrated how dyslexic-specific brain activation normalized after remediation using fMRI. These approaches hold the promise of more precise assessment and targeted intervention in the future, but where does that leave those in current practice? In the next section of this chapter, the response-to-intervention model that is being widely touted in educational circles will be reviewed as well as Cognitive Hypothesis Testing (CHT) model, and a proposed model that blends these two together.

RESPONSE-TO-INTERVENTION (RTI) MODEL

In 2004, the Individuals with Disabilities Education Improvement Act was enacted. Over the past several decades, school psychologists came to rely on psychoeducational testing as a means of identifying specific learning disabilities (SLD). The most commonly used method was ability–achievement discrepancy. Researchers and public policy makers realized that the discrepancy model for SLD identification was flawed and created a "wait-to-fail" process (Lyon & Fletcher, 2001), which resulted in overidentification of minority children (Donovan & Cross, 2002).

As a result of these problems with using a discrepancy model in SLD identification, the IDEA 2004 law and subsequent federal rules allow the state to use alternative models. The conceptual approach to special education that is currently sweeping the nation is Response to Intervention (RTI). The implementation of RTI has been controversial and has sparked a great deal of debate in school psychology and education.

Most RTI models are conceptualized in three tiers. In Tier I, the goal is to provide all students within the general education environment positive behavioral supports and high-quality instruction. The progress of each student is regularly monitored. If a child makes adequate educational progress, the child continues to receive services within the general educational environment. If a child does not make adequate educational progress in one or more areas, the child is referred to Tier II for targeted intervention(s).

In the second tier of an RTI model, children with learning and behavioral problems are referred to a Student Assistance Team (referred to by multiple names across states), which is typically composed of general and special educators. The Student Assistance Team is responsible for (see Figure 5.1): (1) clarifying the presenting problem, (2) reviewing the effectiveness of previous interventions tried to remediate the problem, and (3) consulting with the child's parent(s), teacher(s), and educational specialists to choose a new evidence-based intervention for implementation. The educators, hopefully in collaboration with the parent(s), will implement the new intervention and then (4) collect objective data for progress monitoring. The Student Assistance Team, or the educators implementing the intervention, will then (5) determine the intervention efficacy. This is a (6) decision point in the intervention process. If the intervention is working, it may be continued to reach performance goals or may be discontinued if performance goals are met. If the intervention does not appear to be effective, the child may be referred back to the Student Assistant Team to develop another intervention. As illustrated in

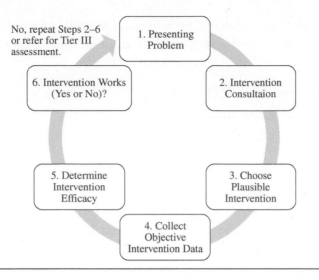

Figure 5.1 An illustration of the processes within a Tier II RTI model.

Figure 5.1, steps 2–6 may be repeated multiple times with iterations, each involving another intervention plan.

Questions remain in the implementation of RTI, such as:

- How long should one intervention be tried before moving on to the next intervention?
- How many Tier II interventions should be tried before a formal comprehensive individualized assessment is requested?
- How can the RTI process ensure that interventions are being implemented in a timely manner with integrity?
- What do we do with the child who has not responded to multiple interventions?

The question of "what to do with the child who has not responded to multiple interventions" has sparked a great deal of debate. Most RTI models suggest that when the child "fails to respond" to multiple interventions, the child would be referred to Tier III for a comprehensive assessment and possible referral for special education. Tier III is viewed as the place where comprehensive individualized assessment is used for continued intervention planning and perhaps qualification for special education. It should be noted here that failure of prior interventions does not mean those implementing the programs have failed, but rather the complexity of problems requires specialized assessment to determine an individualized approach.

Some proponents of the RTI assert that children who have not responded to multiple evidence-based interventions should be considered, by default, to have a specific learning disability and placed in special education (Reschly, 2005a; 2005b; Shinn, 2005). Those who share this view of the identification of SLD within the RTI model also assert that there is no need for further assessment for diagnostic purposes or for modifying instructional interventions within a third tier of RTI. Furthermore, advocates for this narrower view of RTI argue that there is no need to administer measures of cognitive abilities as part of SLD identification because the results do not contribute to the understanding of specific learning problems (Gresham et al., 2005; Reschly, 2005a; 2005b).

The proponents of this narrower and strict behavioral approach to the identification of SLD have conveniently ignored two important realities: (1) the federal definition of SLD and (2) thirty years of empirical research that shows a biological basis for SLD. Hale et al. (2008) pointed out that SLD is not simply a learning delay or unresponsiveness to instruction, but rather a reflection of a specific learning deficit caused by a disorder in "one or more of the basic psychological processes" (Individuals with Disabilities Education Act of 2004: 34 C.F.R. 300.8). By equating SLD as a default diagnosis due to unresponsiveness to instruction, practitioners ignore the SLD federal definition.

The past thirty years have yielded substantial evidence for the biological bases of specific learning disorders caused by specific neuropsychological deficits, not delays (Hale et al., 2008; Miller, 2007). There is strong neuropsychological evidence for:

- *Reading disorders* (Feifer & Della Toffalo, 2007; Francis, Shaywitz, Stuebing, Shaywitz, & Fletcher, 1996; Shaywitz, Lyon, & Shaywitz, 2006);
- *Writing disorders* (Berninger & Holdnack, 2008; Feifer & De Fina, 2002);
- *Math disorders* (Feifer & De Fina, 2005; Geary, Hamson, & Hoard, 2000; Geary, 2004); and
- *All types of SLD* (Berninger & Richards, 2002; Collins & Rourke, 2003; Fischer, Daniel, Immordino, Stern, Battro, & Koizumi, 2007); Semrud-Clikeman, Fine, & Harder, 2005).

The salient feature of a traditional RTI model, which needs to be reiterated, is that intervention comes early in the process. Early intervention is ideal if it produces educational gains. One concern with a traditional RTI model is that repeated interventions will be tried within Tier II, most often, using the "one-size-fits-all" approach. For example, if a first grader is not making adequate progress in reading, the most common intervention is to provide additional instructional time in phonological awareness. If the child does not respond to the added instruction, instructional time is increased or another phonological awareness curriculum is added. The most fundamental concern about this approach is that there is a lack of comprehensive assessment data that can target prescriptive interventions and thereby maximize the intervention's success. If educators only refer a child for a comprehensive individual evaluation after repeated lack of responsiveness to interventions, we run the risk of having the same "wait-to-fail" problems, even with RTI, that we had with the use of discrepancy models. Assessment must be used to help target intervention, which leads to the next section where the Cognitive Hypothesis Testing (CHT) Model will be reviewed.

The Cognitive Hypothesis Testing (CHT) Model

Hale and Fiorello (2004) introduced the cognitive-hypothesis-testing model as a comprehensive framework for assessing and intervening with children who have special educational needs. The authors combine two approaches into their model: (1) individual psychoeducational assessment and (2) intervention development and monitoring, using both behavioral interventions and problem-solving consultation. Inherent in their model is a respect for assessing the child's behavior within the confines of their environment and for assessing the influences of the neuropsychological constraints on the child's behavior. The authors advocate using behavioral analyses to track intervention progress and they stress the importance of single-subject designs. However, unlike the strict behaviorists who advocate for behavioral assessment and monitoring exclusively, Hale and Fiorello (2004) also recognized the importance of using information about the child's cognitive functioning in forming appropriate and effective interventions.

The CHT model has four major components (theory, hypothesis, data collection, and interpretation) that traverse thirteen steps (see Figure 5.2). Steps 1 through 5 represent the procedures used in a traditional psychoeducational assessment. There is a decision point that is reached after a psychoeducational evaluation is completed. One decision could be that the child qualifies for special education services. Another decision could be that the child does not qualify for special education services but requires continued regular education intervention with or without 504 accommodations. Finally, another decision could be that additional assessment information is needed for diagnosis and/or treatment planning, and the child is referred for additional assessment.

Steps 6 through 8 in the CHT Model relate to specialized assessment, such as school neuropsychological testing. For example, a child is referred for learning difficulties that seem to relate to poor memory. The child is administered a psychoeducational battery of tests that includes the WISC-IV, and the child performed well below expected levels on the working memory subtests. In this example, a test would be chosen that is designed to assess memory functions in more detail, such as the WRAML-2. The additional

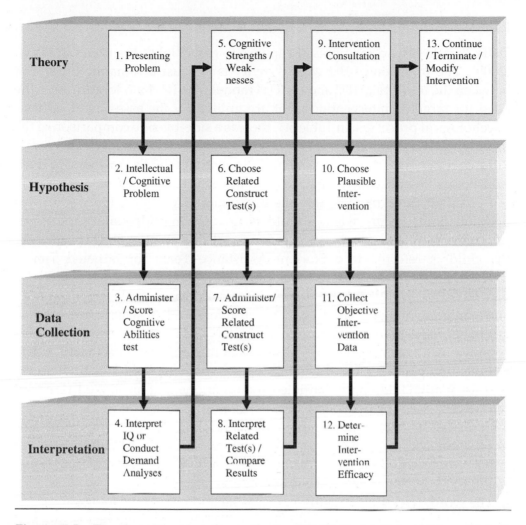

Figure 5.2　The Cognitive Hypothesis Testing (CHT) Model (Adapted from Hale & Fiorello, 2004)

assessment data would be used to help clarify diagnosis decisions and facilitate further intervention planning.

Steps 9 through 13 in the CHT Model are similar to the Tier II level in the RTI Model. The difference is that in the CHT Model, the interventions are guided by assessment data. Hale et al. stated that "the goal of CHT is to develop individualized single subject interventions that are subsequently monitored to determine their effectiveness" (2008, p. 127). The CHT Model can be easily integrated within a traditional RTI model. The CHT Model principally addresses Tier III assessment and subsequent interventions, whereas the RTI Model emphasizes interventions early in Tier II. A proposed blending of these two models is presented in the next section called the Response-to-the-Right-Intervention Model.

RESPONSE-TO-THE-RIGHT-INTERVENTION (RTrI) MODEL

Della Toffalo coined the phrase Response to the "Right" Intervention (RTrI) (2008). The insertion of the word "right" is not just a semantic difference between the traditional RTI and an RTrI model. The RTrI model addresses the need for targeted interventions that are guided by the assessment of basic psychological processes. In Table 5.1, there is a side-by-side comparison of the traditional RTI model, the CHT model, and an RTrI model. The major difference between these assessment/intervention models is where the decision points lie and which data are used at each decision point.

Across all three models, there is a common Tier I decision point. This decision point occurs when a child is not making adequate educational progress using general education services. At this point in all three models, the child is referred to a Student Assistance Team for targeted Tier II interventions. Differences between the three models become evident in Tier II. In the traditional RTI model, informal measures, classroom grades, and some curriculum-based or criterion-referenced measures are used to guide the selection of interventions. In the CHT model, comprehensive cognitive and neuropsychological assessment data are collected to aid in intervention planning, but these data are not collected until Tier III. It seems that for many children, the targeted interventions that are linked to norm-referenced assessment data will come after multiple failures in Tier II. In the RTrI model, *selective cognitive processing and neuropsychological assessment data*, in addition to informal measures, classroom grades, and curriculum-based or criterion-referenced measures are collected early in the RTI process to better guide the selection of evidence-based interventions.

The words "selective cognitive processing and neuropsychological assessment data" are used in contrast to "comprehensive cognitive processing and neuropsychological assessment data" in recognition of the fact that it is not necessary to conduct a comprehensive cognitive processes evaluation of every child who is initially identified as having learning problems. Comprehensive evaluations would still be conducted in the third tier of these models. However, selective assessment of the neurocognitive constructs related to the current presenting problems may be warranted at the earlier second tier. Norm-referenced assessment data should be used to provide additional insight into the child's cognitive processing strengths and weaknesses and link that information to evidence-based prescriptive interventions.

Let us consider again the example of the first grader who is not reading. In a traditional RTI model, data are collected, revealing that classroom grades are poor in reading, the instructional level for basal reading is below grade level expectations, criterion-referenced measures indicate that the child cannot identify basic phonemes or sound out simple words, and the child achieves low scores on the DIEBELS. Based on these data, the child is placed in

Table 5.1

The RTI, CHT, and RTrI Models Compared

	Traditional Response-to-Intervention Model	CHT Model (Hale & Fiorello, 2004)	Response-to-the-Right-Intervention Model
Tier I	General Education Positive Behavioral Support and High Quality Instruction for All Students		
	DECISION POINT: If child is not making adequate educational progress for general education services, refer for Student Assistant Team for Tier II intervention(s).		
Tier II	1. Presenting Problem See Figure 5.1	The CHT Model assumes that Tier I & II interventions have been tried and the educational progress has not been adequate. The CHT Model starts with Tier III assessment, but loops back to targeted Tier II interventions.	1. Presenting Problem(s) Evaluated by Student Assistance Team.
	2. Curriculum-Based Measurement (CBM) data collected to aid in selecting a targeted intervention (e.g., informal and formal measures as needed).		2. CBM and select norm-referenced psychological process data collected to aid in selecting a targeted intervention (e.g., informal and formal measures as needed).
	3. Choose Plausible Intervention		3. Choose Plausible Intervention
	4. Collect Objective Intervention Data		4. Collect Objective Intervention Data
	5. Determine Intervention Efficacy		5. Determine Intervention Efficacy
	DECISION POINT		**DECISION POINT**
	6a. Continue Intervention (if it is working), or		6a. Continue Intervention (if it is working), or
	b. Modify or Change Intervention (if it is not fully working). Go back to steps 2–6, or		b. Modify or Change Intervention (if it is not fully working). Go back to steps 2–6, or
	c. Terminate Intervention (if progress goals met), or		c. Terminate Intervention (if progress goals met), or

(continued)

Table 5.1
Continued

Traditional Response-to-Intervention Model	CHT Model (Hale & Fiorello, 2004)	Response-to-the-Right-Intervention Model
d. If adequate interventions have been tried unsuccessfully, refer for Tier III assessment.		d. If adequate interventions have been tried unsuccessfully, refer for Tier III assessment.
7. Presenting problem re-examined	1. Presenting problem(s) examined	7. Presenting problem reexamined
8. Hypothesize intellectual/cognitive problem(s)	2. Hypothesize intellectual/cognitive problem(s)	8. Hypothesize intellectual/cognitive problem(s)
9. Administer/score cognitive abilities test	3. Administer/score cognitive abilities test	9. Administer/score cognitive abilities test
10. Interpret cognitive abilities scores and conduct demands analyses	4. Interpret cognitive abilities scores and conduct demands analyses	10. Interpret cognitive abilities scores and conduct demands analyses
11. Identify cognitive strengths and weaknesses	5. Cognitive strengths and weaknesses	11. Cognitive strengths and weaknesses
DECISION POINT	**DECISION POINT**	**DECISION POINT**
12a. Child qualifies for special education services and corresponding interventions.	a. Child qualifies for special education services and corresponding interventions—go to step 9.	12a. Child qualifies for special education services and corresponding interventions.
b. Child does not qualify for special education but requires continued regular education intervention(s)—go back to Tier II.	b. Child does not qualify for special education but requires continued regular education intervention(s)—go to step 9.	b. Child does not qualify for special education but requires continued regular education intervention(s)—go back to Tier II.
c. Additional assessment information is needed for diagnosis and treatment planning. Refer child for additional testing—go to step 13.	c. Additional assessment information is needed for diagnosis and treatment planning. Refer child for additional testing—go to step 6.	c. Additional assessment information is needed for diagnosis and treatment planning. Refer child for additional testing—go to step 13.

Tier III: Traditional Psychoeducational and/or Psychological Assessment

6. Choose related construct test(s)

7. Administer/score related construct test(s)

8. Interpret related test(s) and compare results

DECISION POINT

a. Child qualifies for special education services and corresponding interventions. Use assessment data obtained in steps 1–8 and pre-referral intervention efficacy data to plan for targeted, evidence-based interventions. Go to step 9 (same as steps in Tier II).

b. Child does not qualify for special education but requires continued Tier II intervention(s)—go to step 9 (same as steps in Tier II).

13. Choose related construct test(s)

14. Administer/score related construct test(s)

15. Interpret related test(s) and compare results

DECISION POINT

16a. Child qualifies for special education services and corresponding interventions. Use assessment data obtained in steps 1–8 and pre-referral intervention efficacy data to plan for targeted, evidence-based interventions. Go to step 17 (same as steps in Tier II).

b. Child does not qualify for special education but requires continued Tier II intervention(s)—go to step 17 (same as steps in Tier II).

(continued)

Tier III: Specialized Assessment
(e.g., School Neuropsychological Assessment)

Table 5.1
Continued

Traditional Response-to-Intervention Model	CHT Model (Hale & Fiorello, 2004)	Response-to-the-Right-Intervention Model
	9. Intervention consultation	17. Intervention consultation
	10. Choose plausible intervention	18. Choose plausible intervention
	11. Collect objective intervention data	19. Collect objective intervention data
	12. Determine intervention efficacy	20. Determine intervention efficacy
	DECISION POINT	**DECISION POINT**
	13a. Continue intervention (if it is working), or	21a. Continue intervention (if it is working), or
	b. Modify or change intervention (if it is not fully working). Go back to steps 9–12, or	b. Modify or change intervention (if it is not fully working). Go back to steps 9–12, or
	c. Terminate intervention (if progress goals met), or	c. Terminate intervention (if progress goals met), or
	d. If multiple interventions have been tried unsuccessfully, consider additional Tier III assessment.	d. If multiple interventions have been tried unsuccessfully, consider additional Tier III assessment.

Targeted Interventions

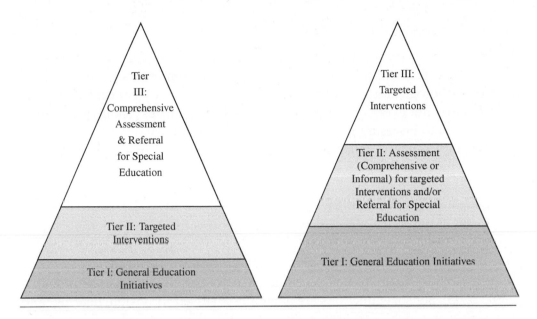

Figure 5.3 The figure on the left illustrates the traditional RTI model. The figure on the right illustrates the CHT Model and a Modified RTrI Model.

remedial reading instruction that emphasizes phonological processing. In this example, there is ample objective evidence detailing the symptoms of the child's reading difficulties; however, the question left unanswered is, "Why is this child experiencing these reading problems?" The proponents of a traditional, behaviorally oriented RTI approach are not interested in addressing the why question, only in modifying the targeted behavior(s). However, answering the why question will generally help educators more effectively select interventions that will produce positive results.

In the CHT model, the question of why a child is not reading is addressed much later in the RTI process. In the RTrI model, a selective, norm-referenced assessment battery could be used to determine that the child has a subtype of dyslexia such as dysphonetic dyslexia that would suggest alternative reading interventions other than phonological (see Figure 5.3). Similar selective batteries could be used to identify subtypes of math disorders, writing disorders, or language disorders.

Within tier III of each of the assessment/intervention models presented in this chapter, there is a section for specialized assessment. School neuropsychological assessment is a specialized assessment and is warranted for some children (see Miller, 2007, for a discussion on when to refer for a school neuropsychological assessment, pp. 62–87). It is important to approach school neuropsychological assessment and interventions with a conceptual model in mind. Miller introduced such a model in 2007, which is the focus of the next section of this chapter.

School Neuropsychological Conceptual Model

Miller (2007) introduced a comprehensive school neuropsychological conceptual model. The model provides a conceptual framework for both school neuropsychological assessment and intervention. A key concept to understand is that not every child referred for a school neuropsychological assessment needs to be tested in each of the areas. The battery of tests, across and within the domains, must be individualized to (1) ultimately answer the referral questions, (2) identify a profile of neurocognitive strengths and weaknesses, and (3) provide information for targeted, prescriptive, and evidence-based interventions.

The essential school neuropsychological assessment components are presented in Table 5.2. Within the school neuropsychological conceptual model, sensory-motor functions and attentional processes "serve as the essential building blocks for all of the other higher-order cognitive processes" (Miller, 2007, p. 95). Sensory functions are generally assessed for vision, hearing, and the sense of touch. The assessment of motor functions typically includes measures of both fine and gross motor skills. The *Dean-Woodcock Sensory-Motor Battery* (Dean & Woodcock, 2003), which is part of the *Dean-Woodcock Neuropsychology Battery*, is a good choice for assessing both sensory and motor functions in school-aged children.

Table 5.2
Essential School Neuropsychological Assessment Components

Sensorimotor Functions

- Sensory Functions
  - Visual
  - Auditory
  - Kinesthetic
- Motor Functions
  - Fine motor coordination
  - Gross motor coordination

Attentional Processes

- Selective/focused attention
- Shifting attention
- Sustained attention
- Divided attention
- Attentional capacity
- Behavioral rating of attention

Visual-Spatial Processes

- Visual perception (motor response)
- Visual perception (motor-free response)
- Visual-perceptual organization
- Visual scanning/tracking

Language Processes

- Auditory/phonological processing
- Oral expression
- Receptive language (listening comprehension)

Memory and Learning Processes

- Verbal immediate memory (with and without context)
- Visual immediate memory (with and without context)

Executive Functions

- Concept generation
- Problem solving, reasoning, and planning
- Shifting and sustained attention

Table 5.2
Continued

- Verbal-visual associative memory
  - Verbal-visual associative learning
  - Verbal-visual delayed associative memory
- Verbal (delayed) long-term memory
  - Verbal learning
  - Verbal delayed recall
  - Verbal delayed recognition
  - Semantic memory (comprehension-knowledge)
- Visual (delayed) long-term memory
  - Visual learning
  - Visual delayed recall
  - Visual delayed recognition
- Working memory
  - Verbal working memory
  - Visual working memory

- Retrieval fluency
- Working memory
- Behavioral/emotional regulation
  - Inhibition
  - Motivation

Speed and Efficiency of Processing

- Cognitive efficiency
- Processing speed
- Cognitive fluency

General Intellectual Functioning

- Overall indices of general intellectual functioning

Academic Achievement

- Basic reading skills
- Reading comprehension
- Reading fluency
- Mathematics computations
- Mathematical reasoning
- Written expression
- Oral expression
- Listening comprehension

Social-Emotional Functioning

- Behavioral ratings of social emotional functioning
- Behavioral observations

Attention is not a unitary construct (see Miller, 2007, for a review). It is important for a school neuropsychologist to understand how *attentional processes* can be subdivided into selective/focused attention, sustained attention, shifting attention, and attentional capacity components. A word of caution must be noted here. While attention is most probably multi-dimensional, many of the tests that are designed to measure attention (e.g., Auditory Attention and Response Set subtest from the NEPSY-II:

Korkman et al., 2007) do not isolate the subcomponents of attention very well. Many of the common tests of attention measure, as one unit, multiple subcomponents of attention such as selective and sustained attention. The *Test of Everyday Attention* (TEA-Ch: Manly, Robertson, Anderson, & Nimmo-Smith, 1999) is a good choice for assessing the unique subcomponents of attention in school-aged children.

Visual-spatial processes are subdivided into four major areas: (1) visual perception (with motor response), (2) visual perception (motor-free), (3) visual-perceptual organization, and (4) visual scanning/tracking. Other visual-spatial processes such as visual reasoning, visual-motor functioning, visual planning, are covered in other portions of the school neuropsychological conceptual model. The visuomotor domain subtests of the NEPSY-II (Korkman et al., 2007) provide a good baseline assessment of visual-spatial processes for school-aged children.

Within the school neuropsychological conceptual model, language functions are subdivided into three areas: (1) auditory/phonological processing, (2) oral expression, and (3) receptive language. The language domain subtests of the NEPSY-II (Korkman et al., 2007) provide a good baseline assessment of language functions for school-aged children.

Memory and learning are higher-order cognitive skills that are dependent upon sensory-motor, attention, visual-spatial, and language processes. It is imperative to determine if memory and learning difficulties are caused by neurocognitive memory deficits or by lower-level neurocognitive deficits, such as attention. As an example, memory encoding will be compromised if attention is impaired. Memory and learning within the school neuropsychological conceptual model are subdivided into multiple components including verbal, visual, and verbal-visual associative immediate memory; verbal, visual, and verbal-visual associative (delayed) long-term memory, auditory and visual working memory; and semantic memory. No one test can measure all of these subcomponents of memory in school-aged children. Recommended tests for memory function are the short-term memory, long-term memory, and semantic memory clinical cluster subtests from the *Woodcock-Johnson III Tests of Cognitive Abilities* (WJIII-COG; Woodcock et al., 2001), the memory domain subtests of the NEPSY-II (Korkman et al., 2007), or a stand-alone memory test such as the *Wide Range Assessment of Memory and Learning, 2nd Edition* (WRAML-2; Sheslow & Adams, 2003).

Executive functions are the command and controls for the other cognitive processes (Miller, 2007). Executive functions are difficult to categorize because they overlap with other cognitive processes such as attention and memory. Within the school neuropsychological conceptual model, the principal subdivisions of executive functions include concept generation, problem solving, reasoning, planning, shifting and sustained attention, retrieval fluency, working memory, and behavioral/emotional regulation (e.g., inhibition and motivation). Many tests measure components of executive functions, so generally a cross-battery approach is warranted. The *Delis-Kaplan Executive Function System* (Delis et al., 2001) provides a good baseline assessment of executive functions for school-aged children.

Speed and efficiency of cognitive processing encompasses all of the processes. The principal subdivisions within this category include: processing speed, cognitive efficiency, and cognitive fluency. All of the processes are directly measured on the WJIII-COG (Woodcock et al., 2001) and indirectly measured by any test that measures completion time and accuracy.

Unlike traditional psychoeducational evaluations that often report the intelligence test results first in a school neuropsychological assessment, the scores from the cognitive abilities measures are separated by the principal construct being measured (e.g., visual-spatial processing) and reported in that section of the report. Miller noted that "Intelligence tests measure a combined sum of the various processes presented in the conceptual model. From a school neuropsychological perspective, the overall 'g' of intelligence will be the least useful measure; rather, the quantitative and qualitative performance on the individual tests will be utilized the most" (2007, p. 96). The child's academic achievement must be considered in light of the child's neurocognitive strengths and weaknesses. Finally, the child's cognitive profile and current levels of academic achievement must be considered within the context of the child's social-emotional, cultural, environmental, and situational influences. Miller (2007) provides a comprehensive list of the assessment instruments that were designed to measure the various domains with the school neuropsychological assessment model.

SUMMARY

In the practice of contemporary school neuropsychology, practitioners should use assessment instruments that include the following: a solid theoretical foundation; a broad-based, representative standardization sample; good psychometrics; the capability of using a subset of tests from a common core battery; both qualitative and quantitative scores; and a direct linkage with prescriptive interventions. The three major approaches to contemporary school neuropsychological assessment were reviewed: Lurian theory, CHC model, and the process assessment approach. As districts begin to use the RTI approach to assessment and intervention, they are encouraged to selectively use norm-referenced cognitive and neurocognitive assessments early in tier II to help target interventions that will most likely be effective.

REFERENCES

Berninger, V., & Holdnack, J. (2008). Neuroscientific and clinical perspectives on the RTI initiative in learning disabilities diagnosis and intervention: Response to questions begging answers that see the forest and the trees. In C. Reynolds & E. Fletcher-Janzen (Eds.), *Neuroscientific and clinical perspectives on the RTI initiative in learning disabilities diagnosis and intervention* (pp. 66–81). New York: John Wiley & Sons.

Berninger, V., & Richards, T. L. (2002). *Brain literacy for educators and psychologists.* Boston: Academic Press.

Collins, D. W., & Rourke, B. P. (2003). Learning-disabled brains: A review of the literature. *Journal of Clinical and Experimental Neuropsychology, 25,* 1011–1034.

Dean, R. S., & Woodcock, R. W. (2003). *Dean-Woodcock Neuropsychological Battery.* Itasca, IL: Riverside Publishing.

Delis, D., Kaplan, E., & Kramer, J. H. (2001). *Delis-Kaplan Executive Function System examiner's manual.* San Antonio, TX: The Psychological Corporation.

Della Toffalo, D. A. (2008, February). *School neuropsychology and RTrI (Response to the Right Intervention).* Mini Skills presentation at the National Association of School Psychologist Annual Convention. New Orleans: LA.

Donovan, M. S., & Cross, C. T. (Eds.). (2002). *Minority students in special and gifted education.* Washington, DC: National Academy Press.

Elliott, C. D. (2007). *Differential Ability Scales—II.* San Antonio, TX: Harcourt Assessment, Inc.

Feifer, S. G., & De Fina, P. A. (2002). *The neuropsychology of written language disorders: Diagnosis and intervention.* Middletown, MD: School Neuropsych Press.

Feifer, S. G., & De Fina, P. A. (2005). *The neuropsychology of mathematics disorders: Diagnosis and intervention.* Middletown, MD: School Neuropsych Press.

Feifer, S. G., & Della Toffalo, D. A. (2007). *Integrating RTI with cognitive neuroscience: A scientific approach to reading.* Middletown, MD: School Neuropsych Press.

Fischer, K. W., Daniel, D. B., Immordino, M. H., Stern, E., Battro, A., & Koizumi, H. (2007). Why mind, brain, and education? Why now? *Mind, Brain, and Education, 1,* 1–2.

Flanagan, D. P., & Harrison, P. L. (2005). *Contemporary intellectual assessment: Theories, tests, and issues* (2nd ed.). New York: Guilford.

Fletcher, E. (2008). Knowing is not enough—we must apply. Willing is not enough—we must do, Goethe. In E. Fletcher-Janzen, & C. R. Reynolds, (Eds.), *Neuropsychological perspectives on learning disabilities in the era of RTI: Recommendations for diagnosis and intervention.* Hoboken, NJ: John Wiley & Sons, Inc.

Francis, D. J., Shaywitz, S. E., Stuebing, K. K., Shaywitz, B. A., & Fletcher, J. M. (1996). Developmental delay versus deficit models of reading disability: A longitudinal, individual growth curve analysis. *Journal of Educational Psychology, 88,* 3–17.

Geary, D. C. (2004). Mathematics and learning disabilities. *Journal of Learning Disabilities, 37,* 4–15.

Geary, D. C., Hamson, C. O., & Hoard, M. K. (2000). Numerical and arithmetical cognition: A longitudinal study of process deficits in children with learning disabilities. *Journal of Experimental Child Psychology, 77,* 236–263.

Gresham, F. M., Reschly, D. J., Tilly, D. W., Fletcher, J., Burns, M., Crist, T., et al. (2005). Comprehensive evaluation of learning disabilities: A response to intervention perspective. *The School Psychologist, 59*, 26–29.

Hale, J. B., & Fiorello, C. A. (2004). *School neuropsychology: A practitioner's handbook.* New York: Guilford.

Hale, J. B., Fiorello, C. A., Miller, J. A., Wenrich, K., Teodori, A., & Henzel, J. N. (2008). WISC-IV interpretation for specific learning disabilities identification and intervention: A cognitive hypothesis testing approach. In A. Prifitera, D. H. Saklofske, & L. G. Weiss (2008). *WISC-IV clinical assessment and intervention,* (2nd ed., pp. 109–171). San Diego, CA: Academic Press.

Individuals with Disabilities Education Improvement Act of 2004. (PL No. 108–446, 20 USC 1400).

Kaplan, E., Fein, D., Kramer, J., Delis, D., & Morris, R. (1999). *WISC-III PI Manual.* San Antonio. TX: The Psychological Corporation.

Kaufman, A. S., & Kaufman, N. L. (2004). *Kaufman Assessment Battery for Children* (2nd ed.). Circle Pines, MN: American Guidance Service Publishing.

Korkman, M., Kirk, U., & Kemp, S. (2007). *NEPSY-II: A developmental neuropsychological assessment.* San Antonio, TX: The Psychological Corporation.

Lyon, R., & Fletcher, J. M. (2001). Early warning system: How to prevent reading disabilities. *Education Matters, 1*, 22–29.

Manly, T., Robertson, I. H., Anderson, V., & Nimmo-Smith, I. (1999). *Test of everyday attention for children (TEA-Ch) manual.* San Antonio, TX: Harcourt Assessment.

Milberg, W. P., Hebben, N., & Kaplan, E. (1996). *The Boston process approach to neuropsychological assessment.* In I. Grant & K. M. Adams (Eds.), New York: Oxford University Press.

Miller, D. C. (2007). *Essentials of school neuropsychological assessment.* Hoboken, NJ: John Wiley & Sons.

Nagileri, J., & Das, J. P. (1997). *Das-Naglieri cognitive assessment system.* Itasca, IL: Riverside Publishing Company.

Reschly, D. (2005a). Learning disabilities identification: Primary intervention, secondary intervention, and then what? *Journal of Learning Disabilities, 38*, 510–515.

Reschly, D. (2005b, August). *RTI paradigm shift and the future of SLD diagnosis and treatment.* Paper presented to the Annual Institute for Psychology in the Schools of the American Psychological Association, Washington, DC.

Roid, G. H. (2003). *Stanford-Binet intelligence scales.* (5th ed.). Itasca, IL: Riverside Publishing.

Semrud-Clikeman, M., Fine, J., & Harder, L. (2005). The school neuropsychology of learning disabilities. In R. K. D'Amato, E. Fletcher-Janzen, & C. R. Reynolds (Eds.), *Handbook of school neuropsychology.* New York: John Wiley & Sons.

Shaywitz, B. A., Lyon, G. R., & Shaywitz, S. E. (2006). The role of functional magnetic imaging in understanding reading and dyslexia. *Developmental Neuropsychology, 30*, 613–632.

Sheslow, D., & Adams, W. (2003). *Wide range assessment of memory and learning* (2nd ed.). Wilmington, DE: Wide Range, Inc.

Shinn, M. (2005, August). *Who is LD? Theory, research, and practice.* Paper presented to the Annual Institute for Psychology in the Schools of the American Psychological Association, Washington, D.C.

Simos, P. G., Fletcher, J. M., Bergman, E., Brier, J. I., Foorman, B. R., Castillo, E. M., Davis, R. M., Fitzgerald, M., & Papanicolaou, A. C. (2002). Dyslexia-specific brain activation profile becomes normal following successful remedial training. *Neurology, 58,* 1203–1213.

Teeter, P. A., & Semrud-Clikeman, M. (1997). *Child neuropsychology: Assessment and interventions for neurodevelopmental disorders.* New York: Allyn and Bacon.

Woodcock, R. W., McGrew, K. S., & Mather, N. (2001). *Woodcock-Johnson III Tests of Cognitive Abilities.* Itasca, IL: Riverside Publishing.

CHAPTER 6

Integrating Cognitive Assessment in School Neuropsychological Evaluations

DAWN P. FLANAGAN, VINCENT C. ALFONSO, SAMUEL O. ORTIZ,
and AGNIESZKA M. DYNDA

SINCE THE INCEPTION of the profession itself, assessment has been one of the more common activities for school psychologists and use of standardized, norm-referenced tests has been the most frequently conducted service in the schools (Alfonso, Oakland, LaRocca, & Spanakos, 2000; Alfonso & Pratt, 1997). Over the past decade however, methods for school-based evaluations have been influenced by the emergence of three significant developments, primarily in approaches designed to evaluate students with suspected learning difficulties.

The first notable development is the integration of Fluid Crystallized (*Gf Gc*) theories of intelligence (i.e., the Cattell-Horn-Carroll [CHC] theory of cognitive abilities) and the Cross-Battery Assessment (XBA) approach to measurement and interpretation of cognitive abilities and processes that is based on CHC theory. Prior to the emergence of both CHC theory and XBA procedures, evaluation of learning problems in educational settings was seldom sufficiently individualized or based on empirically supported theory. As such, conclusions and interpretations based on data from cognitive tests often reflected faulty logic and, therefore, were not defensible. With greater attention paid to CHC theory, coupled with the emergence of the XBA method, practitioners appear to be making more theoretically and psychometrically defensible interpretations of cognitive test performance.

The second significant development is Response-to-Intervention (RTI), which uses primarily academic achievement instruments, curriculum-based measures, and progress monitoring to measure the effectiveness of scientifically based interventions for students who are at risk for academic failure. Such approaches have helped to shift the initial focus on school-based learning problems from the child to the curriculum and have shed significant light on the importance and merit of ensuring that students receive effective and appropriate classroom instruction (see for example, Mather & Kaufman, 2006).

The third development is the use of neuropsychological theories and evaluation approaches in the schools to better understand cognitive processing strengths and weaknesses in students suspected of having significant learning difficulties (Miller, 2007). School neuropsychological assessment has been lauded for providing information considered to be both useful and relevant for tailoring interventions to meet the unique learning needs of students having difficulty mastering school-based skills, such as reading, writing, and arithmetic (Hale & Fiorello, 2004; Kaufman, 2009).

The growing popularity of all three developments suggests that each provides information that is seen as helpful and relevant in understanding why some students appear to have difficulties in the acquisition and development of various academic skills. Clearly, each assessment method focuses on different aspects of the presumptive causes of significant learning difficulties. In addition, each method generates different types of information and data from which to understand a student's learning needs within the educational context. In some cases, similar data may be generated by two different approaches, but the manner in which these data are interpreted may differ as a function of the conceptual framework underlying each approach. Although these approaches can be and often are viewed as distinct, they are far from mutually exclusive. In fact, it is our belief that these recent assessment approaches are complementary and can be viewed together as an enhancement to the manner in which we have typically addressed referrals for suspected learning disability. A conceptual framework based on recent assessment developments is illustrated in Figure 6.1, and the stepped design is intended to depict a continuum of assessment- and intervention-related activities that range from those that are least intensive and narrow in scope or purpose to those that are most intensive and comprehensive. It should also be noted that the progression from one tier to another is not strictly linear and that after engaging in activities in one tier, it is natural and expected that activities will return to other tiers over time, as may be necessary and appropriate. The continuum is intended to emphasize the wide range of assessment and intervention activities that may be employed in attempts to understand and improve the learning process for a given student and to reinforce the idea that assessment-related activities, whether based on response-to-intervention, cognitive assessment, neuropsychological assessment, or

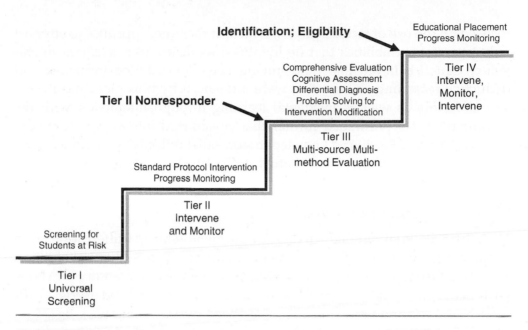

Figure 6.1 A Continuum of Assessment and Intervention Activities. The steps repersent an increase in the breadth, depth, and intensity of evaluation and intervention. The sequence, however, need not be linear and movement among and between the levels is expected.

some combination thereof, are not mutually exclusive. Moreover, the link between assessment and intervention can be accomplished via a wide range of activities that are carried out at different points in time based on a student's response to instruction and intervention.

In this chapter we provide a discussion regarding how the three recent assessment developments hold promise for enhancing the manner in which professionals are able to understand and interpret findings in alternative ways and for promoting more effective communication among professionals regarding the link between assessment data and interventions. Attention is paid to describing the manner in which the approaches are related, in particular CHC theory and neuropsychology, and how, when integrated, they have the potential to better inform diagnosis and treatment. To that end, we begin with a brief description of each recent assessment development in the field of school psychology and its contribution to the various levels of assessment in the schools.

INTEGRATED FLUID-CRYSTALLIZED THEORIES OF COGNITIVE FUNCTIONING AND CROSS-BATTERY ASSESSMENT

The original *Gf-Gc* theory was a dichotomous conceptualization of human cognitive ability put forth by Raymond Cattell in the early 1940s. Cattell focused on the use of factor analysis, which, at the time, appeared to support only two distinct abilities that he identified as *fluid* and *crystallized* intelligence. Cattell believed that fluid intelligence (*Gf*) included inductive and deductive reasoning abilities that were influenced by biological and neurological factors as well as incidental learning through interaction with the environment. He postulated further that crystallized intelligence (*Gc*) consisted primarily of acquired knowledge stores that reflected, to a large extent, the influences of acculturation (Cattell, 1957, 1971).

The Cattell-Horn *Gf-Gc* Theory

In his 1965 dissertation conducted under the mentorship of Cattell, John Horn expanded the dichotomous *Gf-Gc* model to include four additional abilities, including visual perception or processing (*Gv*), short-term memory (or short-term acquisition and retrieval [*Gsm*]), long-term storage and retrieval (or tertiary storage and retrieval [*Glr*]), and speed of processing (*Gs*). Based on subsequent research over the next two decades, Horn added auditory processing ability (*Ga*) to the theoretical model and refined the definitions of *Gv*, *Gs*, and *Glr* (Horn, 1968; Horn & Stankov, 1982).

   In the early 1990s, Horn added a factor representing an individual's quickness in reacting (or reaction time) and making decisions (i.e., decision speed), which he labeled *Gt* (Horn, 1991). Finally, a quantitative knowledge (*Gq*) factor and a broad reading and writing (*Grw*) factor were added to the model based mainly on the continued program of collaborative research conducted by Horn (1991) and Woodcock (1994), respectively. As a result of Horn and colleagues' research, *Gf-Gc* theory eventually expanded into a ten-factor model that became known as the Cattell-Horn theory or modern *Gf-Gc* theory (see Horn & Blankson, 2005, for a summary).

Carroll's Three-Stratum Theory

In his seminal survey of the large body of literature on human cognitive abilities, Carroll (1993) proposed that the structure of cognitive abilities could be understood best via three strata that differed in breadth and generality. The broadest and most general level of ability is represented by stratum III. According to Carroll, stratum III represents a general factor, consistent with Spearman's (1927) concept of *g*, and subsumes both broad (stratum II) and narrow (stratum I) abilities. Consistent with the designations used by Cattell and Horn, the various broad, stratum II abilities are denoted with an upper-case G followed by a lowercase letter or letters (e.g., *Gf* and *Glr*). Unlike Cattell-Horn *Gf-Gc* theory, however, Carroll only delineated eight broad abilities, but his theory did subsume a large number of narrow, stratum

I abilities. To date, approximately 100 narrow abilities have been discussed in the literature (Carroll, 1993, 1997; McGrew, 1997, 2005).

SIMILARITIES AND DIFFERENCES IN THE CATTELL-HORN AND CARROLL THEORIES

In general, there are significant similarities between the Cattell-Horn and Carroll conceptualizations. For example, each theory posits that there are multiple broad (stratum II) abilities, and, for the most part, the names and codes associated with these abilities (e.g., *Gv*) are similar or identical. That is, there is substantial overlap in the major constructs specified by both frameworks and both provide specification of abilities at both a broad (stratum II) and narrow (stratum I) level. Nevertheless, there are four major structural differences between the Cattell-Horn and Carroll theories. First, Carroll's theory includes a general ability factor (stratum III), whereas the Cattell-Horn theory does not. This difference reflects a continuing and, as of yet, unresolved debate regarding the presumed existence of an overarching or global intelligence construct. Second, the Cattell-Horn theory includes quantitative knowledge and quantitative reasoning as a separate broad ability (i.e., *Gq*). In contrast, Carroll's theory includes quantitative reasoning as a narrow ability subsumed by *Gf*. Third, the Cattell-Horn theory includes a broad reading/writing (*Grw*) factor, but Carroll's theory includes reading and writing as narrow abilities subsumed by *Gc*. And fourth, Carroll's theory includes short-term memory with other memory abilities such as associative memory, meaningful memory, and free recall memory under *Gy* (or General Memory and Learning). On the other hand, the Cattell-Horn theory separates short-term memory (*Gsm*) from associative memory, meaningful memory, and free recall memory because the latter abilities were purported to measure long-term retrieval (*Glr*). These differences notwithstanding, Carroll concluded upon completion of his meta-analytic survey that the Cattell-Horn *Gf-Gc* theory represented the most empirically supported and reasonable approach to the structure of cognitive abilities currently available (Carroll, 1993).

THE CATTELL-HORN-CARROLL (CHC) THEORY OF COGNITIVE ABILITIES

In the late 1990s, McGrew (1997) attempted to resolve some of the differences between the Cattell-Horn and Carroll models. Based on his own research, McGrew proposed an "integrated" *Gf-Gc* theory in Flanagan, McGrew, and Ortiz (2000). This integrated theory eventually became known as the CHC (in order of author contribution) theory of cognitive abilities shortly thereafter (see McGrew, 2005). An illustration of the integrated CHC theoretical model is depicted in Figure 6.2. This figure shows the most commonly referenced broad and narrow abilities within the CHC framework.

Figure 6.2 Integrated CHC Theoretical Framework

Fluid Intelligence (Gf)	Quantitative Knowledge (Gq)	Crystallized Intelligence (Gc)	Reading and Writing (Grw)	Short-Term Memory (Gsm)	Visual Processing (Gv)	Auditory Processing	Long-Term Storage & Retrieval	Processing Speed	Decision Reaction Time / Speed
- General Sequential Reasoning - Induction - Quantitative Reasoning - Piagetian Reasoning - Speed of Reasoning	- Math Knowledge - Math Achievement	- Language Development - Lexical Knowledge - Listening Ability - General Information - Information about Culture - General Science Information - Geography Achievement - Communication Ability - Oral Production & Fluency - Grammar Sensitivity - Foreign Language Proficiency - Foreign Language Aptitude	- Reading Decoding - Reading Comprehension - Verbal Language Comprehension - Cloze Ability - Spelling Ability - Writing Ability - English Usage Knowledge - Reading Speed	- Memory Span - Learning Abilities	- Visualization - Spatial Relations - Visual Memory - Closure Speed - Flexibility of Closure - Spatial Scanning - Serial Perceptual Integration - Length Estimation - Perceptual Illusions - Perceptual Alterations - Imagery	- Phon. Cdg: Analysis - Phon. Cdg: Synthesis - Speech Snd. Discrim. - Resp. to Aud. Stim. Distortion - Mem. for Sound Patterns - General Snd. Discrim. - Temporal Tracking - Musical Discrim. & Judgment - Maintaining & Judging Rhythm - Sound Intensity Duration Discrim. - Sound Freq. Discrim. - Hearing & Speech Threshold - Absolute Pitch - Sound Localization	- Associative Memory - Meaningful Memory - Free Recall Memory - Ideational Fluency - Associative Fluency - Expressional Fluency - Naming Facility - Word Fluency - Figural Fluency - Figural Flexibility - Sensitivity to Problems - Orginality/ Creativity - Learning Abilities	- Perceptual Speed - Rate-of-Test Taking - Number Facility	- Simple Reaction Time - Choice Reaction Time - Semantic Processing Speed - Mental Comparison Speed

What may be noted initially upon an examination of Figure 6.2 is that CHC theory omits a *g*, or general ability factor, primarily because the utility of the theory (in assessment-related disciplines) is in understanding functioning in distinct ability and processing domains, which are understood best through the operationalization of broad and narrow cognitive abilities and processes (Flanagan & Ortiz, 2001; Flanagan, Ortiz, & Alfonso, 2007). Despite the ongoing debate regarding the existence of the construct itself, others continue to accept the reality of *g* and many believe it to be the most important ability to assess because it predicts various outcomes, such as academic and occupational functioning, better than other indices (e.g., Glutting, Watkins, & Youngstrom, 2003). Such a view may have been more tenable when both the theoretical foundations and psychometric organizations of intelligence tests were quite poor. Recent advances in both areas have made it clear that regardless of the predictive ability of *g*, there is now considerable evidence that both broad and narrow CHC cognitive abilities and processes explain substantial variance in specific academic abilities over and above the variance accounted for by *g* (e.g., Floyd, Keith, Taub, & McGrew, 2007; McGrew, Flanagan, Keith, & Vanderwood, 1997; Vanderwood, McGrew, Flanagan, & Keith, 2002).

Despite the various revisions of and refinements to CHC theory over the past several decades, and its expansive network of validity evidence, it has only recently begun to have considerable influence on cognitive test development and interpretation. Authors and publishers of mental tests acknowledge readily the importance of CHC theory in defining and interpreting mental ability and processing constructs, and most have used this theory to guide directly the development of their own cognitive and intelligence batteries (e.g., Elliott, 2007; Kaufman & Kaufman, 2004; Roid, 2003; Woodcock, McGrew, & Mather, 2001). Consider for example, that within just the last eight years, most of the major cognitive ability and intelligence batteries have been revised in a manner that incorporates CHC theory directly. The XBA approach and its corresponding CHC classifications of the major intelligence, achievement, and special purpose tests helped pave the way for this new CHC-based generation of intelligence tests (Alfonso, Flanagan, & Radwan, 2005; McGrew, 2005).

CROSS-BATTERY ASSESSMENT

Cross-Battery Assessment (XBA) was introduced to the field in the late 1990s as a practical method of assessment and interpretation that was fully grounded in CHC theory and research (Flanagan & McGrew, 1997; McGrew & Flanagan, 1998). In general terms, XBA provides a set of principles and procedures that allows practitioners to measure and interpret a wider range of abilities than that represented by most single cognitive or achievement batteries in a manner that is both psychometrically and theoretically defensible. More specifically, the approach guides practitioners in the selection of cognitive batteries, both core and supplemental, that allows for measurement of abilities and processes that is sufficient in both breadth and depth for the purpose of addressing referral concerns that seek to understand cognitive function and dysfunction. Furthermore, the XBA approach includes detailed interpretive guidelines that are based on current research and best practices in assessment (Flanagan, Ortiz, Alfonso, & Dynda, 2008; Kaufman, 2000). The approach is best understood as encompassing three foundational sources of information or pillars.

THE THREE PILLARS OF THE XBA APPROACH

The first pillar of the XBA approach is CHC theory. This theory was selected to guide assessment and interpretation because, as noted previously, it is based on a more thorough network of validity evidence than any other contemporary psychometric theory (Daniel, 1997; Flanagan, Ortiz, & Alfonso, 2007; Horn & Blankson, 2005; Horn & Noll, 1997; McGrew, 2005; Messick, 1992; Sternberg & Kaufman, 1998). According to Daniel (1997), the strength of the multiple (CHC) cognitive abilities model is that it was arrived at "by synthesizing hundreds of factor analyses conducted over decades by independent researchers using many different collections of tests. Never before has a psychometric ability model been so firmly grounded in data" (pp. 1042–1043).

The second pillar of the XBA approach is the CHC broad (stratum II) ability classifications of tests and subtests (including intelligence, academic, neuropsychological, speech-language, and other special purpose tests (we will refer to this group of tests hereafter as *ability tests*). Specifically, based on the results of a series of confirmatory factor analysis studies of the major cognitive batteries as well as the task analyses of over sixty test experts, Flanagan and colleagues classified ability tests according to the particular CHC broad abilities and processes they measured (Flanagan et al., 2000; Flanagan & Ortiz, 2001; Flanagan, Ortiz, Alfonso, & Mascolo, 2006; Flanagan et al., 2007; McGrew & Flanagan, 1998). To date, several hundred CHC broad ability and processing test classifications have been made based on the results of these studies. Ability test classifications assist practitioners in identifying measures that assess the various broad CHC abilities (such as *Gf*, *Gc*, *Gq*, and *Grw*) represented in CHC theory. Classification of ability tests at the broad ability level is necessary to improve upon the validity of cognitive assessment and interpretation. Specifically, broad ability test classifications ensure that the CHC constructs that underlie assessments are minimally affected by construct irrelevant variance (Messick, 1989, 1995). In other words, knowing what subtests measure what abilities allows clinicians to organize subtests into construct relevant clusters. It is clear that current cognitive batteries (viz., intelligence tests) have paid close attention to this source of invalidity in assessment, as most "IQ" tests include only *construct relevant* composites, clusters, scales, factors, indexes, and the like (Flanagan et al., 2007).

The third pillar of the XBA approach is the CHC narrow (stratum I) ability and processing classifications of ability tests. These classifications were originally reported in McGrew (1997). Subsequently, Flanagan and colleagues (Rosengarten, Alfonso, & Flanagan, 2009; Flanagan & Ortiz, 2001; Flanagan, Ortiz, Alfonso, & Mascolo, 2002, 2006; Flanagan et al., 2007) provided content validity evidence for the narrow ability classifications of ability tests. Use of narrow ability and processing test classifications is necessary to ensure that the CHC constructs that underlie assessments are adequately represented. That is, the narrow ability and processing classifications of subtests assist practitioners in combining qualitatively different indicators (or *subtests*) of a given broad ability into *composites* (so that appropriate inferences can be made about performance in a broad ability domain). Alternatively, (sub)tests with the same narrow ability classification may be combined to form narrow ability composites, thereby improving upon the reliability and validity of the construct measured by these tests (see Flanagan et al., 2007, for details). The better the construct representation in assessment, the more effective practitioners will be in interpreting the precise nature of a student's learning strengths and weaknesses.

Taken together, the three pillars underlying the XBA approach provide the necessary foundation from which to organize assessments of a variety of ability tests that are theoretically driven, comprehensive, and valid. Since the 1990s, both CHC theory and the XBA classifications of hundreds of tests have not only influenced cognitive test development and interpretation, but have paved the road for more advanced and sophisticated methods of psychological and educational practice, particularly within the school setting (Kaufman, 2000). This impact has occurred primarily at Tier III of the assessment continuum in Figure 6.1. The XBA assessment and interpretation guidelines provide practitioners with a more defensible method for evaluating learning disabilities in a comprehensive manner than that provided by previous methods. At Tier III of the assessment continuum in Figure 6.1, CHC theory and XBA have also begun to inform school neuropsychological evaluations, where extensive information is derived regarding the cognitive capabilities of individuals and their relation to the learning process (e.g., Fiorello et al., 2008).

CHC theory and XBA have and continue to make significant inroads in the schools, particularly for the purpose of conducting comprehensive and thorough cognitive evaluations of children suspected of having SLD (e.g., Hanson, Sharman, & Esparza-Brown, 2008). In addition, an alternative assessment method, known as Response to Intervention (RTI), has quickly permeated the schools following the reauthorization of IDEA in 2004. This assessment method is discussed next.

RESPONSE TO INTERVENTION

At the most general level, Response to Intervention (RTI) is a multitiered approach to the early identification of students with academic or behavioral difficulties. For the purpose of this chapter, we will focus on RTI for academic difficulties only. The RTI process begins with the provision of quality instruction for all children in the regular education classroom along with universal screening to identify children who are at risk for academic failure, primarily in the area of reading (Tier I). Children who are at risk for reading failure, that is, those who have not benefitted from the instruction provided to all children in the classroom, are then identified and given scientifically based interventions, usually following a standard treatment protocol (Tier II). If for any reason, a student does not respond to the intervention provided at Tier II, he or she may be identified as a nonresponder and selected to receive additional and more intensive interventions in an attempt to increase his or her rate of learning. When one type of intervention does not appear to result in gains for the student, a new intervention is provided until the desired response is achieved.

To implement an RTI approach effectively, each child's response to intervention must be monitored closely at each tier, typically by regular education and special education teachers. Ultimately, in an RTI model, children who repeatedly fail to demonstrate an adequate response to increasingly intensive interventions may be deemed to have a specific learning disabled (SLD) simply by default. Others, however, suggest that such failure to respond may be attributable to many factors, only one of which is SLD, and therefore, nonresponders should be given a comprehensive evaluation (at Tier III, for example; see Figure 6.1), at which time decisions are often made about special education eligibility and placement (e.g., Flanagan, Kaufman, Kaufman, & Lichtenberger, 2008; Flanagan, Ortiz, Alfonso, & Dynda, 2006; Hale & Fiorello, 2004; Kavale, Kauffman, Bachmeier, & LeFever, 2008; Reynolds & Shaywitz, 2009). Whether referred for a comprehensive evaluation or not, in an RTI service delivery model (including the one illustrated in Figure 6.1), the focus never strays far from understanding the ongoing instructional needs of the child, regardless of where instruction is delivered (i.e., in the regular or special education setting).

RTI has been an influential force in the schools in recent years, particularly with respect to shaping Tier I and Tier II assessment. The emphasis on ensuring that students are benefitting from empirically supported instruction and verifying their response to instruction, via a systematic collection of various types of data, has elevated screening procedures and classroom progress monitoring to new heights. Notwithstanding improvements in screening and progress monitoring procedures, RTI approaches to date are not proven to be appropriate as a standalone method for SLD identification (e.g., Reynolds & Fletcher-Janzen, 2008). Based on the lack of data to support the diagnostic utility of RTI, it is our view that this approach should be seen mainly as a model for the *prevention* of early academic failure.

It would be difficult to accept as valid any practice that diagnoses non-responders as having a learning disability simply because they did not respond to scientifically-based instruction. Not all students respond to the same types of instruction and intervention, and not all interventions work for every student. When a student repeatedly fails to demonstrate an adequate response to an intervention that has been empirically supported, we find it is necessary to gather additional data using diagnostic tools. Specifically, non-responders should be given a comprehensive evaluation to determine more definitively the nature and extent of their presumed learning difficulties. That evaluation may include educational, psychological, cognitive, and neuro-psychological assessments as may be appropriate following review and analysis of data already available from Tiers I and II.

Comprehensive evaluations are seen as informative because they offer the type of data practitioners need to generate hypotheses about why certain interventions were not effective (despite the fact that they were supposed to be) and to assist in selecting or developing different interventions and approaches to instruction. To date, a systematic study of the benefits of comprehensive evaluations for Tier II nonresponders is lacking. And, an important reality that RTI-only advocates often overlook is that there is no evidence demonstrating that comprehensive evaluations *do not benefit* Tier II nonresponders. In fact, some agree that in order to understand the role that cognitive assessment plays in learning and achievement, we need to look outside the school psychology and special education literature and pay closer attention to the fields of neuropsychology and neuroscience (McGrew, 2008). Indeed, the budding field of school neuropsychology offers many insights into the value of assessing cognitive function and dysfunction for the purpose of instructional planning and intervention (D'Amato, Fletcher-Janzen, & Reynolds, 2005; Hale & Fiorello, 2004).

SCHOOL NEUROPSYCHOLOGICAL ASSESSMENT

Based largely on Luria's (1973) theory of brain functioning, neuropsychology has sought from the very beginning to connect cognitive activity (or processing patterns) with performance on cognitive and academic tasks (Languis & Miller, 1992). The purpose and intent of school neuropsychology is quite consistent with Luria's belief that "to understand the brain's foundations for psychological activity, one must be prepared to study both the brain and the system of activity" (Luria, 1979, p. 173). Thus, a Luria-based approach in school neuropsychology is ideal because it is not merely one that seeks to label dysfunction, but rather it is a system where the brain's mechanisms responsible for the dysfunction are delineated and connected directly to the actual performance of real-world tasks, in this case academic skills. Moreover, Luria's model appears to describe well some of the aspects of observable functioning in academic settings because it emphasizes an understanding of the integration of the three functional units ("blocks") of the brain. That is, learning in the classroom is based upon successful integration and application of the brain's basic functional systems, conceptualized as three blocks: Block 1 consists of reticular structures, which regulate cortical tone and arousal; Block 2 encompasses the posterior occipital (visual), parietal (somatosensory), and temporal (auditory) lobes and is responsible for analyzing, coding, and storing information; Block 3 encompasses the anterior frontal cortex and is responsible for acting upon information, including formulating plans and monitoring higher level thinking and reasoning (Hale & Fiorello, 2004; Luria, 1973, 1979). Development of the specific structures of the brain has been observed to occur in utero and continue throughout the lifespan (Kolb & Fantie, 1997, as cited in Hale and Fiorello, 2004).

A variation of Luria's theory that was adapted for evaluation and intervention in academic settings is the Planning, Attention, Simultaneous, and Successive (PASS) processing theory (Naglieri & Das, 1988), which was later operationalized by the *Cognitive Assessment System* (CAS; Das & Naglieri, 1997). In PASS theory, there are four processing components, attention (Block 1), simultaneous (part of Block 2), successive (another part of Block 2), and planning (Block 3). In Luria-based models, mental activity is the result of all three functional units working in concert. School learning, particularly reading, writing, and math, can be analyzed as the product of these functional units working together in identifiable and predictable ways. However, "because the brain operates as an integrated functional system . . . even a small disturbance in an area can cause disorganization in the entire functional system" (Naglieri & Das, 2005, p. 122). Identification of the area or areas of disturbance, via the use of cognitive and neuropsychological assessment tools, therefore, is critical to understanding learning difficulties and for explaining why learning is not taking place as expected. This type of information is considered necessary for making instructional adjustments and curricular modifications as well as for developing interventions. It is important to note that because the functional system governing brain activity is "always undergoing modification due to the interaction of internal and environmental demands" (Fiorello, Hale, Snyder, Forrest, & Teodori, 2008, p. 234), the development of learning and memory is ongoing, suggesting that "the relationship between an individual's brain structure and function is readily malleable and adaptable to environmental demands. As a result, providing differentiated instruction in the classroom will not only improve achievement, but it could improve brain functioning as well" (p. 234).

The need and value of both cognitive and neuropsychological assessment for children who fail to respond to intervention is clear to many (e.g., Flanagan, Ortiz, & Alfonso, 2008; Hale, Flanagan, & Naglieri, 2008; Reynolds & Fletcher-Janzen, 2008; Reynolds & Shaywitz, 2009; Semrud-Clikeman, 2005). In our view, nowhere is theory-based testing and interpretation more critical than in the schools where high stakes decisions regarding the future of many children are made daily. In an attempt to better understand and serve children with significant learning needs, practitioners who use diagnostic tools in the schools may derive more clinically rich information from them if interpretation is informed by more than one theoretical perspective.

AN INTEGRATIVE FRAMEWORK BASED ON PSYCHOMETRIC, NEUROPSYCHOLOGICAL, AND LURIAN PERSPECTIVES

Scientific understanding of the manner in which the brain functions and how mental activity is expressed on psychometric tasks has increased dramatically in recent years, but there is still much to be learned. All efforts to create a framework that guides test interpretation benefit from diverse points of view. For example, according to Fiorello et al. (2008), "the compatibility of the neuropsychological and psychometric approaches to cognitive functioning suggests converging lines of evidence from separate lines of inquiry, a validity dimension essential to the study of individual differences in how children think and learn" (p. 232). Their analysis of the links between the neuropsychological and psychometric approaches not only provides validity for both, but also suggests that each approach may benefit from knowledge of the other. As such, a framework that incorporates the neuropsychological and psychometric approaches to cognitive functioning holds the promise of increasing knowledge about the etiology and nature of academic skill deficits and the manner in which such deficits are treated. This type of framework must not only connect the elements and components of both assessment approaches, but it must also allow for interpretation of data within the context of either model. In other words, the framework should serve as a "translation" of the concepts, nomenclature, and principles of one approach into their equivalent counterparts in the

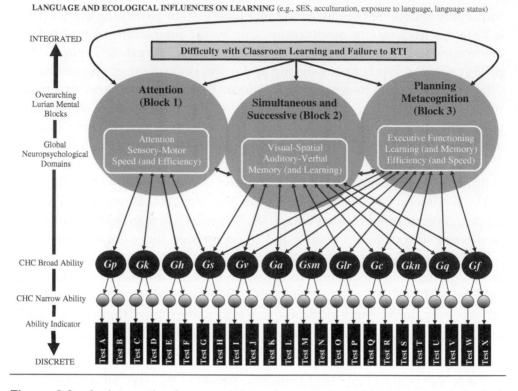

Figure 6.3   An integrative framework based on psychometric, neuropsychological, and Lurian perspectives.

other. The remainder of this chapter provides a brief discussion of just such a framework, which we have illustrated in Figure 6.3.

Figure 6.3 represents a first attempt to describe a broad interpretive framework that links Luria's blocks, neuropsychological domains, and CHC abilities. This interpretive framework draws on prior research and sources, most notably Dehn (2007), Fiorello et al. (2008), Reynolds and Fletcher-Janzen (2008), Miller (2007), and Strauss, Sherman, and Spreen (2006). In understanding the manner in which Luria's blocks, the neuropsychological domains, and CHC broad abilities may be linked to inform test interpretation and mutual understanding among assessment professionals, four important observations deserve mention. First, there is a hierarchical structure among the three theoretical conceptualizations. Second, the hierarchical structure parallels a continuum of interpretive complexity, spanning the broadest levels of cognitive functioning, where mental activities are fully "integrated," to the narrowest level of cognitive functioning where mental activity is reduced to more "discrete" processes and abilities (see far left side of Figure 6.3). Third, all mental activity takes place within a given ecological and societal context and is heavily influenced by language as well as other factors external to the individual. As such, the dotted line surrounding Figure 6.3 represents "language and ecological influences on learning," which includes factors such as exposure to language, language status (English learner vs. English speaker), opportunity to learn, and socioeconomic status (SES). Fourth, because the administration of cognitive and neuropsychological tools should not typically be conducted in the schools unless a student fails to respond to scientifically based instruction and intervention (at Tier II, for example; see Figure 6.1), a rectangle is included at the top of Figure 6.3 that is labeled, "Difficulty with Classroom Learning and Failure to RTI." Thus, the framework in Figure 6.3 is a representation of the cognitive constructs that may be measured, at the "comprehensive evaluation" tier of an RTI model, and the manner in which they relate to one another.

The arrows leading from the "Difficulty with Classroom Learning and Failure to RTI" rectangle to Luria's three functional units of the brain (represented as large circles in Figure 6.3) demonstrate the beginning of a school-based hypothesis-generation, testing, and interpretation process. Luria's functional units are depicted in Figure 6.3 as overarching cognitive concepts. The interaction between, and the interconnectedness among, the functional units are represented by double-headed arrows. Because Luria's functional units are primarily descriptive concepts designed to guide applied clinical evaluation practices, neuropsychologists have had considerable independence in the manner in which they align their assessments with these concepts. School psychologists, however, have made more direct links between the Lurian functional units and psychometric tests (e.g., Das & Naglieri, 1997; Kaufman & Kaufman, 1983, 2004).

Although a few psychoeducational batteries have been developed to operationalize one or more of Luria's functional units, for the most part, neuropsychologists have typically couched Luria's blocks within clinical and neuropsychological domains. In doing so, the Lurian blocks have been transformed somewhat from overarching concepts to domains with more specificity. These domains are listed in rectangles within each of the three functional units (large circles) in Figure 6.3. For example, the neuropsychological domains include: *attention, sensory-motor, and speed (and efficiency)*, corresponding to Block 1; *visual-spatial, auditory-verbal, memory (and learning)*, corresponding to Block 2; and *executive functioning, learning (and memory)*, and efficiency (and speed) corresponding to Block 3. Noteworthy is the fact that the memory and learning domain spans Blocks 2 and 3, and its placement and use of parentheses is intended to convey that memory may be primarily associated with Block 2 (simultaneous/successive) whereas the learning component of this domain is probably more closely associated with Block 3 (planning/metacognition). Likewise, speed and efficiency spans

Blocks 1 and 3, and its placement and use of parentheses denote that speed may be more associated with Block 1 (i.e., attention) whereas efficiency seems to be more associated with Block 3.

Perhaps the most critical juncture of the proposed integrative framework is the distinction between functioning at the neuropsychological domain level and functioning at the broad CHC level. As compared to the neuro-psychological domains, CHC theory allows for greater specificity of cognitive constructs. Because of structural differences in the conceptualization of neuro-psychological domains and CHC broad abilities vis-à-vis factorial complexity, it is not possible to provide a precise, one-to-one correspondence between these conceptual levels. This is neither a problem nor an obstacle, but simply the reality of differences in perspective among these two lines of inquiry.

As compared to the neuropsychological domains, CHC constructs within the psychometric tradition tend to be unidimensional because the intent is to measure a single broad ability as purely and independently as possible. This is not to say, however, that the psychometric tradition has completely ignored shared task characteristics in favor of a focus on precision in measuring a single ability. For example, Kaufman provided a "shared characteristic" approach to individual test performance for several intelligence tests includ-ing the KABC-II (Kaufman & Kaufman, 2004) and the various Wechsler Scales (Kaufman, 1979; see also McCloskey, 2009, McGrew & Flanagan, 1998, and Sattler, 1998). This practice has often provided insight into the underlying cause(s) of learning difficulties, and astute practitioners continue to make use of it. Despite the fact that standardized, norm-referenced tests of CHC abilities were designed primarily to provide information about relatively discrete constructs, performance on these tests can still be viewed within the context of the broader neuropsychological domains. That is, when evaluated within the context of an entire battery, characteristics that are shared among groups of tests on which a student performed either high or low, for example, often provide the type of information necessary to assist in further under-standing the nature of an individual's underlying cognitive function or dysfunction, conceptualized as neuropsychological domains.

The double-headed arrows between neuropsychological domains and CHC abilities in Figure 6.3 demonstrate that the relationship between these constructs is bidirectional. That is, one can conceive of the neuropsychological domains as global entities that are comprised of various CHC abilities, just as one can conceive of a particular CHC ability as involving aspects of more than one neuropsychological domain. Our conceptualization of the relations between the neuropsychological domains and the CHC broad abilities fol-lows. For the purpose of parsimony we grouped the neuropsychological domains according to their relationship with the Lurian blocks and thus, we discuss these domains as clusters, rather than separately.

CORRESPONDENCE BETWEEN THE NEUROPSYCHOLOGICAL DOMAINS AND CHC BROAD ABILITIES

At least six CHC broad abilities comprise the *Attention/Sensory-Motor/Speed (and Efficiency)* neuropsychological domain, including Psychomotor Abilities (*Gp*), Tactile Abilities (*Gh*), Kinesthetic Abilities (*Gk*), Decision/Reaction Time or Speed (*Gt*),[1] Processing Speed (*Gs*), and Olfactory Abilities *(Go)*.[2] *Gp* involves the ability to perform body movements with precision, coordination, or strength. *Gh* involves the sensory receptors of the tactile (touch) system, such as the ability to detect and make fine discriminations of pressure on the surface of the skin. *Gk* includes abilities that depend on sensory receptors that detect bodily position, weight, or movement of the muscles, tendons, and joints. Because *Gk* includes sensitivity in the detection, awareness, or movement of the body or body parts and the ability to recognize a path the body previously explored without the aid of visual input (e.g., blindfolded). It may involve some visual-spatial process, but the input remains sensory-based and thus better aligned with the sensory-motor domain. *Gt* involves the ability to react and/or make decisions quickly in response to simple stimuli, typically measured by chronometric measures of reaction time or inspection time. *Gs* is the ability to automatically and fluently perform relatively easy or over-learned cognitive tasks, especially when high mental efficiency is required. As measured by current intelligence tests (e.g., WISC-IV Coding, Symbol Search, and Cancellation), *Gs* seems to capture the essence of both speed and efficiency, which is why there are double headed arrows from *Gs* to Block 1 (where *Speed* is emphasized) and Block 3 (where *Efficiency* is emphasized) in Figure 6.3. *Go* involves abilities that depend on sensory receptors of the main olfactory system (nasal chambers). Many of the CHC abilities comprising the Attention/Sensory-Motor/Speed (and efficiency) domain are measured by neuropsychological tests (e.g., Dean-Woodcock; see Table 6.1 for examples).

Prior research suggests that virtually all broad CHC abilities may be subsumed by the *Visual-Spatial/Auditory-Verbal/Memory (and Learning)* neuropsychological domain. That is, the vast majority of tasks on neuropsychological, intelligence, and cognitive ability tests require either visual-spatial or auditory-verbal input. Apart from tests that relate more to discrete sensory-motor functioning and that utilize sensory input along the kinesthetic, tactile, or olfactory systems, all other tests will necessarily rely either on visual-spatial or auditory-verbal stimuli. Certainly, visual (*Gv*) and

---

1. *Gt* is omitted from Figure 6.3 because we did not include any tests in Table 6.1 that primarily measure this ability.
2. *Go* is omitted from Figure 6.3 because we did not include any tests in Table 6.1 that primarily measure this ability and the cognitive and perceptual aspects of this ability have not been studied extensively (McGrew, (2005).

Table 6.1

Neurocognitive Demand Task Analyses of the Major Neuropsychological Test Batteries According to Lurian Blocks, Neuropsychological Domains, and CHC Abilities

Battery	Subtest	Lurian Block: Attention	Simultaneous and Successive	Planning and Metacognition	Sensory-Motor	Speed and Efficiency	Attention	Visual-Spatial	Auditory-Verbal	Memory and/or Learning	Executive	Language	Gf	Gc	Gkn	Gq	Gsm	Glr	Gv	Ga	Gs	Gh	Gk	Gp
NEPSY-II	Affect Recognition	✓	✓					✓		✓					✓				✓					
	Animal Sorting	✓		✓			✓				✓		✓	✓										
	Arrows		✓					✓											✓					
	Auditory Attention & Response Set	✓	✓	✓	✓		✓	✓	✓	✓	✓		✓				✓							
	Block Construction		✓	✓				✓			✓								✓					
	Body Part Naming and Identification			✓	✓			✓		✓		√E/R		✓			✓							
	Clocks	✓	✓	✓	✓		✓			✓	✓	√R		✓					✓					
	Comprehension of Instructions	✓	✓	✓			✓			✓	✓	√R		✓			✓							
	Design Copying	✓	✓		✓		✓	✓											✓					

118

Design Fluency	✓	✓	✓	✓	✓	✓				✓						✓	✓			✓
Fingertip Tapping	✓	✓	✓	✓		✓		✓									✓			
Geometric Puzzles		✓			✓										✓		✓			
Imitating Hand Positions	✓	✓	✓	✓	✓										✓		✓			
Inhibition	✓	✓	✓	✓	✓	✓	✓^R			✓	✓	✓				✓	✓		✓	
List Memory and List Memory Delayed	✓	✓			✓	✓	✓					✓				✓				
Manual Motor Sequences	✓	✓	✓	✓	✓	✓				✓	✓	✓				✓				
Memory for Designs	✓	✓			✓	✓				✓	✓						✓			
Memory for Designs Delayed	✓	✓			✓	✓				✓							✓			
Memory for Faces and Memory for Faces Delayed	✓	✓			✓	✓														
Memory for Names and Memory for Names Delayed	✓	✓			✓					✓	✓				✓					
Narrative Memory	✓	✓			✓	✓	✓^E/R			✓	✓	✓				✓				
Oromotor Sequences	✓	✓			✓	✓	✓^E/R			✓		✓								
Phonological Processing		✓			✓		✓^E/R				✓				✓					
Picture Puzzles	✓	✓	✓		✓					✓						✓				
Repetition of Nonsense Words	✓	✓	✓		✓	✓	✓^E/R			✓	✓					✓		✓		
Route Finding	✓	✓	✓		✓	✓	✓				✓						✓			
Sentence Repetition	✓	✓			✓	✓	✓^E/R			✓	✓		✓			✓				
Speeded Naming	✓	✓			✓	✓					✓								✓	
Statue	✓	✓	✓			✓	✓													

(continued)

Table 6.1
Continued

Battery	Subtest	Lurian Block			Neuropsychological Domains								CHC Broad Abilities											
		Attention	Simultaneous and Successive	Planning and Metacognition	Sensory-Motor	Speed and Efficiency	Attention	Visual-Spatial	Auditory-Verbal	Memory and/or Learning	Executive	Language	Gf	Gc	Gkn	Gq	Gsm	Glr	Gv	Ga	Gs	Gh	Gk	Gp
NEPSY-II - cont.	Theory of Mind	✓	✓				✓		✓	✓		✓E/R		✓										
	Visuomotor Precision	✓	✓		✓	✓	✓				✓								✓		✓			✓
	Word Generation		✓	✓		✓		✓	✓	✓	✓	✓E						✓						
	Word List Interference	✓	✓	✓					✓	✓	✓	✓E/R					✓							
	Color-Word Interference: Color-Naming	✓	✓	✓		✓	✓	✓	✓									✓			✓			
	Color-Word Interference: Inhibition	✓	✓	✓		✓	✓	✓	✓	✓	✓							✓			✓			
	Color-Word Interference: Inhibition/Switching	✓	✓	✓	✓	✓	✓	✓	✓	✓	✓							✓			✓			
	Color-Word Interference: Word Reading	✓	✓		✓	✓	✓	✓	✓									✓			✓			
	Design Fluency Test: Filled Dots	✓	✓	✓	✓	✓	✓	✓			✓								✓		✓			
	Design Fluency Test: Unfilled Dots Only	✓	✓	✓	✓	✓	✓	✓			✓								✓		✓			

Delis-Kaplan Executive Function System (D-KEFS)														
Design Fluency Test: Switching	✓	✓	✓	✓		✓							✓	✓
Proverb Test: Free Inquiry		✓	✓		✓	✓	✓^E/R	✓						
Proverb Test: Recognition		✓	✓		✓	✓	✓^R	✓						✓
Sorting Test: Free Sorting	✓	✓	✓	✓	✓	✓	✓^R	✓						
Sorting Test: Sort Recognition	✓	✓	✓	✓	✓	✓	✓^E	✓						
Tower	✓	✓	✓	✓	✓	✓		✓	✓			✓		
Trail Making Test: Letter Sequencing	✓	✓	✓	✓	✓									✓
Trail Making Test: Motor Speed		✓	✓	✓	✓									✓
Trail Making Test: Number Sequencing	✓	✓	✓	✓	✓									✓
Trail Making Test: Number-Letter Switching	✓	✓	✓	✓	✓	✓								✓
Trail Making Test: Visual Scanning	✓	✓	✓	✓	✓	✓								✓
Twenty Questions Test		✓			✓	✓	✓^E	✓						
Verbal Fluency Test: Category Fluency	✓	✓	✓		✓	✓	✓^E			✓				
Verbal Fluency Test: Category Switching	✓	✓	✓	✓	✓	✓	✓^E	✓	✓					
Verbal Fluency Test: Letter Fluency	✓	✓	✓		✓	✓	✓^E			✓				
Word Context Test	✓	✓	✓		✓	✓	✓^E/R	✓	✓					
Auditory Acuity	✓	✓	✓											
Construction	✓	✓	✓								✓			
Coordination	✓	✓	✓	✓										

(continued)

121

Table 6.1
Continued

Battery	Subtest	Lurian Block: Attention	Lurian Block: Simultaneous and Successive	Lurian Block: Planning and Metacognition	Neuro: Sensory-Motor	Neuro: Speed and Efficiency	Neuro: Attention	Neuro: Visual-Spatial	Neuro: Auditory-Verbal	Neuro: Memory and/or Learning	Neuro: Executive	Neuro: Language	CHC: Gf	CHC: Gc	CHC: Gkn	CHC: Gq	CHC: Gsm	CHC: Glr	CHC: Gv	CHC: Ga	CHC: Gs	CHC: Gh	CHC: Gk	CHC: Gp
Dean-Woodcock Neuropsychological Battery (DWNB)	Expressive Speech		✓		✓				✓			✓E/R					✓							
	Finger Tapping	✓			✓		✓																	✓
	Gait and Station	✓			✓		✓																	✓
	Grip Strength																							
	Lateral Preference Scale	✓					✓																	
	Left-Right Movements			✓						✓		✓R												
	Mime Movements			✓						✓		✓R		✓										
	Naming Pictures of Objects			✓						✓		✓E		✓										

Near-Point Visual Acuity	✓	✓	✓										
Romberg	✓	✓	✓	✓								✓	
Tactile Examination: Finger Identification	✓	✓	✓								✓		
Tactile Examination: Object Identification	✓	✓	✓								✓		
Tactile Examination: Palm Writing	✓	✓	✓								✓		
Tactile Examination: Simultaneous Localization	✓	✓	✓								✓		
Visual Confrontation	✓	✓	✓										
Arithmetic	✓		✓	✓	✓	✓	✓^R ✓			✓			
Arithmetic – Process Approach			✓	✓	✓	✓	✓^R ✓						
Block Design (BD) and BD No Time Bonus	✓	✓	✓	✓	✓			✓					
Block Design – Process Approach	✓	✓	✓	✓	✓			✓					
Block Design Multiple Choice (BDMC) and BDMC No Time Bonus	✓		✓					✓					
Cancellation	✓	✓	✓	✓	✓						✓		
Coding Copying	✓	✓	✓	✓	✓	✓					✓		
Coding Recall	✓	✓	✓	✓	✓	✓			✓		✓		
Comprehension	✓		✓	✓	✓ ✓	✓^{E/R}	✓						

Wechsler Intelligence Scale for Children–Fourth Edition (WISC-IV) and WISC-IV Integrated

(continued)

123

Table 6.1
Continued

Battery	Subtest	Lurian Block			Neuropsychological Domains								CHC Broad Abilities											
		Attention	Simultaneous and Successive	Planning and Metacognition	Sensory-Motor	Speed and Efficiency	Attention	Visual-Spatial	Auditory-Verbal	Memory and/or Learning	Executive	Language	Gf	Gc	Gkn	Gq	Gsm	Glr	Gv	Ga	Gs	Gh	Gk	Gp
Wechsler Intelligence Scale for Children–Fourth Edition (WISC-IV) and WISC-IV Integrated	Comprehension Multiple Choice		✓					✓	✓	✓		✓R		✓										
	Digit Span	✓	✓	✓			✓		✓	✓	✓						✓							
	Elithorn Mazes (EM) and EM No Time Bonus	✓	✓	✓	✓		✓	✓			✓								✓					
	Information		✓						✓	✓		✓E		✓										
	Information Multiple Choice		✓	✓				✓	✓	✓		✓R		✓										
	Letter Span	✓	✓	✓			✓		✓	✓	✓						✓							
	Letter-Number Sequencing	✓	✓	✓			✓		✓	✓	✓						✓							
	Letter-Number Sequencing – Process Approach	✓	✓	✓			✓	✓	✓		✓			✓										
	Matrix Reasoning		✓	✓				✓					✓											
	Picture Completion		✓					✓		✓				✓					✓					

124

Test															
WISC-IV & WISC-IV Integrated															
Picture Concepts		✓				✓		✓		✓					
Picture Vocabulary Multiple Choice		✓			✓	✓	✓	✓	✓^F	✓				✓	
Similarities		✓			✓	✓	✓	✓	✓^E	✓					
Similarities – Multiple Choice		✓		✓	✓	✓	✓	✓	✓^R	✓					
Spatial Span Forward and Backward	✓	✓	✓	✓	✓	✓					✓	✓			
Symbol Search	✓	✓	✓			✓					✓				✓
Visual Digit Span	✓	✓		✓	✓	✓					✓				
Vocabulary		✓			✓	✓	✓								
Vocabulary – Multiple Choice		✓			✓	✓	✓	✓^E	✓						
Word Reasoning		✓		✓	✓	✓	✓	✓^R	✓						
Written Arithmetic		✓		✓	✓	✓	✓	✓^{E/R}	✓						
Woodcock-Johnson Third Edition Tests of Cognitive Abilities															
Analysis-Synthesis		✓		✓	✓	✓	✓	✓^R	✓						
Auditory Attention	✓	✓	✓		✓	✓	✓	✓^R						✓	
Auditory Working Memory	✓	✓		✓	✓	✓	✓				✓				
Concept Formation		✓			✓	✓	✓	✓^R	✓						
Decision Speed	✓	✓	✓	✓	✓	✓	✓		✓						
DR: Visual Auditory Learning		✓			✓	✓	✓					✓			
General Information		✓			✓	✓		✓^{E/F}	✓						
Incomplete Words		✓			✓	✓		✓^{E/F}	✓						✓
Memory for Words	✓	✓		✓	✓	✓	✓			✓					

(continued)

Table 6.1
Continued

Battery	Subtest	Lurian Block: Attention	Lurian Block: Simultaneous and Successive	Lurian Block: Planning and Metacognition	Neuro: Sensory-Motor	Neuro: Speed and Efficiency	Neuro: Attention	Neuro: Visual-Spatial	Neuro: Auditory-Verbal	Neuro: Memory and/or Learning	Neuro: Executive	Neuro: Language	Gf	Gc	Gkn	Gq	Gsm	Glr	Gv	Ga	Gs	Gh	Gk	Gp
Woodcock-Johnson Third Edition Tests of Cognitive Abilities	Numbers Reversed	✓	✓	✓			✓		✓	✓	✓						✓							
	Pair Cancellation	✓	✓	✓		✓	✓	✓			✓										✓			
	Picture Recognition	✓	✓				✓	✓		✓									✓					
	Planning	✓	✓	✓	✓		✓	✓			✓		✓						✓					
	Rapid Picture Naming	✓	✓			✓			✓	✓	✓	✓E						✓						
	Retrieval Fluency		✓			✓			✓	✓	✓	✓E						✓						
	Sound Blending		✓		✓				✓	✓		✓E/R								✓				
	Spatial Relations		✓					✓											✓					
	Verbal Comprehension	✓	✓	✓	✓		✓		✓	✓		✓E/R		✓										
	Visual Matching	✓	✓	✓		✓				✓	✓										✓			
	Visual-Auditory Learning		✓	✓					✓	✓	✓							✓						

Kaufman Assessment Battery for Children–Second Edition (KABC-II)																		
Atlantis		✓	✓					✓	✓	✓					✓	
Atlantis Delayed		✓	✓			✓	✓	✓	✓				✓	✓	
Block Counting		✓			✓	✓	✓					✓	✓
Conceptual Thinking		✓	✓		✓	✓	✓	✓	✓			✓	✓
Expressive Vocabulary		✓			✓	✓	✓	✓^E		✓	✓^E
Face Recognition	✓	✓		✓					✓
Gestalt Closure		✓		✓	✓	✓			✓
Hand Movements	✓	✓	✓	✓	✓	✓		✓	✓
Number Recall	✓	✓	✓	✓	✓		✓
Pattern Reasoning		✓	✓	✓	✓	✓	✓		✓
Rebus		✓	✓	✓	✓	✓	✓		✓
Rebus Delayed		✓	✓	✓	✓	✓		✓
Riddles		✓	✓	✓	✓	✓	✓^E/R	✓
Rover		✓	✓	✓	✓	✓	✓
Story Completion		✓	✓	✓	✓	✓	✓	✓
Triangles		✓	✓	✓	✓		✓
Verbal Knowledge		✓	✓	✓	✓^R
Word Order	✓	✓	✓	✓	✓	✓		✓

(continued)

Table 6.1
Continued

Battery	Subtest	Lurian Block — Attention	Simultaneous and Successive	Planning and Metacognition	Neuropsychological Domains — Sensory-Motor	Speed and Efficiency	Attention	Visual-Spatial	Auditory-Verbal	Memory and/or Learning	Executive	Language	CHC Broad Abilities — Gf	Gc	Gkn	Gq	Gsm	Glr	Gv	Ga	Gs	Gh	Gk	Gp
Wechsler Adult Intelligence Scale-Fourth Edition (WAIS-IV)	Arithmetic	✓	✓	✓			✓		✓	✓	✓	✓R	✓			✓	✓							
	Block Design		✓	✓	✓	✓		✓			✓								✓					
	Cancellation	✓	✓	✓	✓		✓	✓			✓										✓			
	Comprehension		✓	✓					✓	✓		✓E/R		✓										
	Digit Span	✓	✓	✓			✓		✓	✓	✓						✓							
	Coding	✓	✓	✓	✓	✓	✓	✓			✓										✓			
	Figure Weights		✓	✓				✓			✓		✓											
	Information		✓	✓					✓	✓		✓E		✓										
	Letter-Number Sequencing	✓	✓	✓			✓		✓	✓	✓						✓							

	Col1	Col2	Col3	Col4	Col5	Col6	Col7	Col8	Col9	Col10	Col11	Col12	Col13	Col14	Col15	Col16
Matrix Reasoning	✓	✓							✓		✓					
Picture Completion	✓	✓				✓		✓			✓	✓				
Similarities	✓	✓			✓	✓	✓^{E}	✓								
Symbol Search	✓	✓	✓	✓	✓	✓	✓^{E}	✓	✓							✓
Visual Puzzles	✓				✓	✓					✓					
Vocabulary	✓	✓			✓	✓	✓^{E}	✓	✓							
Nonverbal Fluid Reasoning	✓	✓			✓	✓	✓	✓			✓					
Nonverbal Knowledge	✓	✓			✓	✓	✓$^{E/R}$	✓	✓	✓	✓					
Nonverbal Quantitative Reasoning	✓	✓			✓	✓	✓^{R}	✓	✓	✓	✓					
Nonverbal Visual-Spatial	✓	✓	✓	✓	✓		✓	✓								
Nonverbal Working Memory	✓	✓		✓	✓		✓	✓			✓	✓				
Verbal Fluid Reasoning	✓	✓			✓	✓	✓$^{E/R}$	✓	✓			✓				
Verbal Knowledge	✓	✓			✓	✓	✓^{E}	✓	✓							
Verbal Quantitative Reasoning	✓	✓			✓	✓	✓$^{E/R}$	✓	✓	✓						
Verbal Visual-Spatial	✓	✓			✓	✓	✓^{R}	✓	✓		✓					
Verbal Working Memory	✓	✓		✓	✓	✓	✓$^{E/R}$	✓	✓	✓	✓					

SB5

(continued)

129

Table 6.1
Continued

Battery	Subtest	Attention (Lurian)	Simultaneous and Successive	Planning and Metacognition	Sensory-Motor	Speed and Efficiency	Attention	Visual-Spatial	Auditory-Verbal	Memory and/or Learning	Executive	Language	Gf	Gc	Gkn	Gq	Gsm	Glr	Gv	Ga	Gs	Gh	Gk	Gp
		Lurian Block			**Neuropsychological Domains**								**CHC Broad Abilities**											
Differential Ability Scales-Second Edition (DAS-II)	Copying		✓		✓			✓											✓					
	Early Number Concepts		✓					✓	✓	✓		✓[R]		✓		✓								
	Matching Letter-Like Forms		✓					✓											✓					
	Matrices		✓	✓				✓					✓											
	Naming Vocabulary								✓	✓		✓[E]		✓										
	Pattern Construction		✓	✓	✓			✓			✓								✓					
	Phonological Processing		✓				✓		✓	✓		✓[E/R]								✓				
	Picture Similarities			✓			✓	✓		✓	✓	✓[E]	✓											
	Rapid Naming	✓				✓				✓								✓			✓			
	Recall of Designs	✓	✓		✓			✓		✓									✓					

130

DAS	Recall of Digits – Forward/Backward	✓	✓	✓					✓		✓								✓		
	Recall of Objects Immediate and Delayed	✓	✓	✓				✓		✓										✓	
	Recall of Sequential Order	✓	✓	✓				✓	✓	✓	✓^{R}				✓		
	Recognition of Pictures	✓	✓	✓				✓	✓	✓						✓	
	Sequential and Quantitative Reasoning	✓	✓	✓			✓	✓			✓					
	Speed of Information Processing	✓	✓	✓			✓	✓	✓					✓		
	Verbal Comprehension		✓			✓	✓	✓	✓^{R}	✓			
	Verbal Similarities	✓	✓			✓	✓	✓	✓^{E}	✓		
	Word Definitions	✓			✓	✓	✓	✓^{E}	✓	
Cognitive Assessment System (CAS)	Expressive Attention	✓	✓	✓		✓	✓	✓				✓	
	Figure Memory	✓			✓	✓					✓
	Matching Numbers	✓	✓	✓		✓	✓	✓			
	Nonverbal Matrices		✓	✓		✓	✓	✓	✓		
	Number Detection	✓	✓	✓		✓	✓	✓				✓
	Planned Codes	✓	✓	✓		✓	✓	✓				✓
	Planned Connections	✓	✓	✓		✓	✓	✓				✓
	Receptive Attention	✓	✓	✓		✓	✓	✓				✓
	Sentence Questions	✓	✓			✓	✓	✓	✓$^{E/R}$		✓	
	Sentence Repetition	✓	✓			✓	✓	✓	✓$^{E/R}$		✓	

(continued)

131

Table 6.1

Continued

Battery	Subtest	Lurian Block: Attention	Simultaneous and Successive	Planning and Metacognition	Sensory-Motor	Speed and Efficiency	Attention	Visual-Spatial	Auditory-Verbal	Memory and/or Learning	Executive	Language	Gf	Gc	Gkn	Gq	Gsm	Glr	Gv	Ga	Gs	Gh	Gk	Gp
CAS	Verbal Spatial Relations	✓	✓				✓	✓		✓		✓R		✓			✓							
	Word Series	✓	✓				✓		✓	✓							✓							

Note: *Gf* = Fluid intelligence/reasoning; *Gc* = Crystallized intelligence/knowledge; *Gkn* = General (domain-specific) knowledge; *Gq* = Quantitative knowledge; *Gsm* = Short-term memory; *Glr* = Long-term storage and retrieval; *Gv* = Visual-spatial abilities; *Ga* = Auditory processing; *Gs* = Cognitive processing speed; *Gh* = Tactile abilities; *Gk* = Kinesthetic abilities; *Gp* = Psychomotor abilities. The following CHC broad abilities are omitted from this table because none is a primary ability measured by the tests included herein: *Gt* (Decision/Reaction Time or Speed); *Grw* (Reading and Writing Ability); *Go* (Olfactory Abilities); and *Gps* (Psychomotor Speed). Most Cattell-Horn-Carroll (CHC) test classifications are from *Essentials of Cross-Battery Assessment, second edition* (Flanagan, Ortiz, & Alfonso, 2007). Classifications according to neuropsychological domains were based on the authors' readings of neuropsychological texts (e.g., Hale & Fiorello, 2004; Lezak, 1995; Miller, 2007; Reynolds & Fletcher-Janzen, 1997). Classifications according to Lurian blocks were based on the relations between the blocks and the neuropsychological domains, as conceptualized in Figure 6.1.

auditory (*Ga*) processing are measured well on neuropsychological and cognitive instruments. Furthermore, tests of Short-Term Memory (*Gsm*) and Long-Term Storage and Retrieval (*Glr*) typically rely on visual (e.g., pictures) or verbal (digits or words) information for input. Tasks that involve reasoning (*Gf*), stores of acquired knowledge (viz., *Gc*), and even speed (*Gs*) also use either visual-spatial and/or auditory-verbal channels for input. Furthermore, it is likely that such input will be processed in one of two possible ways—simultaneously or successively.

And last, we believe that prior research suggests that the *Executive Functioning/Learning (and Memory)/Efficiency (and Speed)* neuropsychological domain is thought to correspond well with perhaps eight broad CHC abilities, including Fluid Intelligence (*Gf*), Crystallized Intelligence (*Gc*), General (Domain-Specific) Knowledge Ability (*Gkn*), Quantitative Knowledge (*Gq*), Broad Reading and Writing Ability (*Grw*), Processing Speed (*Gs*), Short-Term Memory (*Gsm*), and Long-Term Storage and Retrieval (*Glr*). *Gf* generally involves the ability to solve novel problems using inductive, deductive, and/or quantitative reasoning and, therefore, is most closely associated with executive functioning. *Gc* represents one's stores of acquired knowledge or "learned" information and is entirely dependent on language, the ability that Luria believed was necessary to mediate all aspects of learning. Therefore, in a neuropsychological framework, stores of acquired knowledge related to general cultural information, science, geography, and so forth are not likely to be as important for the purposes of assessment as are the lexical aspects of *Gc*, which include vocabulary, lexical knowledge, and language development. As such, *Gc*, as well as more domain-specific knowledge (*Gkn*), together with knowledge of reading/writing (*Grw*) and math (*Gq*) reflect the *learning* component of "memory and learning." Therefore, *Gc*, *Gkn*, *Grw*, and *Gq* are included as part of this domain. *Gsm*, especially working memory, and *Glr* appear to require executive functioning as well as planning and metacognition.

As may be seen in Figure 6.3, we have placed the CHC *narrow* abilities at the *discrete* end of the integrated-discrete continuum. Due to space limitations, it is not possible to list the narrow abilities that make up each broad ability (this information may be found in Flanagan et al., 2007 and McGrew, 2005). Figure 6.3 shows that each CHC broad ability should be represented by at least two qualitatively different narrow ability indicators (or subtests). This is a fundamental principle in psychometrics (Messick, 1995) and an important part of XBA.

Noteworthy is the fact that narrow ability deficits tend to be more amenable to remediation, accommodation, or compensatory interventions as compared to broad and more overarching abilities. For example, poor memory span, a narrow ability subsumed by the broad ability, *Gsm*, can often be compensated for effectively via the use of strategies such as writing things down or recording them in some manner for later reference. In contrast, when test performance suggests more pervasive dysfunction, as may be indicated by deficits in one or more global neuropsychological domains, for example, the greater the likelihood that intervention will need to be broader, perhaps focusing on the type of instruction being provided to the student and how the curriculum ought to be modified and delivered to improve the student's learning (Fiorello et al., 2008).

Because CHC theory is the basis for XBA, neuropsychologists who follow XBA principles and procedures can identify the cognitive constructs that are presumed to be part of any given global neuropsychological domain, thereby strengthening interpretation. This holds true irrespective of the collection of tests or batteries used in evaluation, as long as those tests have been classified according to CHC theory. The following section assists in understanding popular and recently normed tests from the three theoretical perspectives discussed in this chapter with the intent of improving test interpretation.

INTEGRATED INTERPRETATION OF COGNITIVE TESTS

Figure 6.3 provided a conceptual framework from which clinicians can understand and interpret their data. The applicability of this framework may be seen in Table 6.1, which includes several popular cognitive and neuropsychological tests used by school and clinical psychologists as well as neuropsychologists. These tests include the NEPSY-II, D-KEFS, DWNB, WISC-IV, WISC-IV Integrated, WJ III COG, KABC-II, WAIS-IV, SB5, DAS-II, and CAS. Each subtest from the batteries included in this table has been classified according to the Lurian blocks, neuropsychological domains, and broad CHC abilities it measures.

We find that analyzing data according to the blocks, domains, and abilities listed in Table 6.1 leads to more theoretically defensible interpretations and allows clinicians to understand and communicate findings more consistently within and across assessment-related fields. The classifications of tests may also be used to generate and test hypotheses regarding the nature of a student's learning difficulties (e.g., *Gsm* is deficient, but is it deficient using auditory-verbal stimuli, visual-spatial stimuli, or both?). This information can then be used to understand why a particular intervention was not effective and to assist in selecting or developing one that may prove more effective for a student who struggles academically.

SUMMARY

Assessment in the schools continues to evolve in many significant ways. It is clear that the trend is toward application of both empirically supported assessment practices and theoretically guided conceptualizations and interpretations of cognitive performance. School neuropsychology and cognitive assessment have been enhanced by developments in theory (i.e., Luria, CHC) as well as in test selection and interpretation (e.g., XBA). In this chapter, we provided an overview of the various levels of an assessment continuum that are defined by the depth and breadth of assessment and intervention activities. Approaches that are based on screening, probes, progress monitoring, and curriculum-based measures represent Tiers I and II of the assessment continuum depicted in Figure 6.1. These approaches, referred to collectively as RTI, provide a systematic means of measuring a students response to scientifically based instruction and intervention. When a student fails to respond to intervention, it is necessary to gather more data via a comprehensive evaluation (Tier III in Figure 6.1) to determine the specific reason for the lack of response and to inform the next steps of a treatment plan for the student (Tiers III and IV in Figure 6.1).

Assessment at Tier III, in particular, seeks to understand learning problems and cognitive function and dysfunction within the context of the students' curriculum, as well as the types of instruction and intervention that the student received. Comprehensive assessments, as described in the fields of school psychology (e.g., Flanagan et al., 2007) and neuropsychology (e.g., Hale & Fiorello, 2004; Miller, 2007; Reynolds & Fletcher-Janzen, 2008) have introduced levels of sophistication related to theory and measurement that are more advanced and that have created stronger links to intervention and remediation than previous atheoretical methods. In keeping with these developments, we offered here a broad, integrative framework for organizing cognitive and neuropsychological test data across three different but related theoretical conceptualizations— the Lurian blocks, common neuropsychological domains, and broad CHC abilities. It is our contention that when data are evaluated within and across different conceptualizations (Table 6.1), a better understanding of an individual's learning strengths and weaknesses, and most important, his or her learning needs is obtained. For us, the ultimate goal of assessment is to identify the cognitive abilities and processes that are inhibiting response to intervention so that they can be remediated, accommodated, or otherwise bypassed in the learning process. Noteworthy is the fact that an understanding of an individual's cognitive strengths and how they interact with the learning environment is also considered necessary for determining how to proceed with interventions for students who have been nonresponsive to intervention. The classifications provided in Table 6.1 are meant to assist in these efforts. Unless and until the cognitive ability profiles of *nonresponders* are understood within the context of *contemporary* theory and research and attempts to match intervention to these profiles are studied empirically, the conclusion that cognitive tests are irrelevant to intervention planning is without merit.

REFERENCES

Alfonso, V. C., Flanagan, D. P., & Radwan, S. (2005). The impact of Cattell-Horn-Carroll theory on test development and interpretation of cognitive and academic abilities. In D. P. Flanagan & P. L. Harrison (Eds.), *Contemporary intellectual assessment: Theories, tests and issues* (2nd ed., pp. 185–202). New York: Guilford.

Alfonso, V. C., Oakland, T., LaRocca, R., & Spanakos, A. (2000). The course on individual cognitive assessment. *School Psychology Review, 29,* 52–64.

Alfonso, V. C., & Pratt, S. (1997). Issues and suggestions for training professionals in assessing intelligence. In D. P. Flanagan, J. L. Genshaft, & P. L. Harrison (Eds.), *Contemporary intellectual assessment: Theories, tests, and issues* (pp. 326–344). New York: Guilford.

Carroll, J. B. (1993). *Human cognitive abilities: A survey of factor-analytic studies.* Cambridge, UK: Cambridge University Press.

Carroll, J. B. (1997). The three-stratum theory of cognitive abilities. In D. P. Flanagan, J. L. Genshaft, & P. L. Harrison (Eds.), *Contemporary intellectual assessment: Theories, tests, and issues* (pp. 122–130). New York: Guilford.

Cattell, R. B. (1957). *Personality and motivation structure and measurement.* New York: World Book.

Cattell, R. B. (1971). *Abilities: Their structure, growth, and action.* Boston: Houghton Mifflin.

D'Amato, R. C., Fletcher-Janzen, E., & Reynolds, C. R. (Eds.). (2005). *Handbook of school neuropsychology.* New York: John Wiley & Sons.

Daniel, M. H. (1997). Intelligence testing: Status and trends. *American Psychologist, 52,* 1038–1045.

Das, J. P., & Naglieri, J. A. (1997). *Das-Naglieri Cognitive Assessment System.* Chicago: Riverside Publishing.

Dehn, M. J. (2007) *Working memory in academic learning: Assessment and intervention.* Hoboken, NJ: John Wiley & Sons.

Elliott, C. D. (2007). *Differential ability scales* (2nd ed.). *San Antonio, TX: PsychCorp.*

Fiorello, C. A., Hale, J. B., Snyder, L. E., Forrest, E., & Teodori, A. (2008). Validating individual differences through examination of converging psychometric and neuropsychological models of cognitive functioning. In S. K. Thurman & C. A. Fiorello (Eds.), *Applied cognitive research in K-3 classrooms* (pp. 232–254). New York: Routledge.

Flanagan, D. P., Kaufman, A. S., Kaufman, N. L., & Lichtenberger, E. O. (2008). *Agora: The marketplace of ideas—Best practices: Applying response to intervention (RTI) and comprehensive assessment for the identification of specific learning disabilities.* Minneapolis, MN: Pearson.

Flanagan, D. P., & McGrew, K. S. (1997). A cross-battery approach to assessing and interpreting cognitive abilities: Narrowing the gap between practice and cognitive science. In D. P. Flanagan, J. L. Genshaft, & P. L. Harrison (Eds.), *Contemporary intellectual assessment: Theories, tests, and issues* (pp. 314–325). New York: Guilford.

Flanagan, D. P., McGrew, K. S., & Ortiz, S. O. (2000). *The Wechsler intelligence scales and Gf-Gc theory: A contemporary interpretive approach.* Boston: Allyn and Bacon.

Flanagan, D. P., & Ortiz, S. O. (2001). *Essentials of cross-battery assessment.* New York: John Wiley & Sons.

Flanagan, D. P., Ortiz, S. O., & Alfonso, V. C. (2007). *Essentials of cross-battery assessment* (2nd ed.). New York: John Wiley & Sons.

Flanagan, D. P., Ortiz, S. O., & Alfonso, V. C. (2008). Response to intervention (RTI) and cognitive testing approaches provide different but complimentary data sources that inform SLD identification. *NASP Communiqué, 36,* 16–17.

Flanagan, D. P., Ortiz, S. O., Alfonso, V. C., & Dynda, A. M. (2006). Integration of response-to-intervention and norm-referenced tests in learning disability identification: Learning from the tower of Babel. *Psychology in the Schools, 43,* 807–825.

Flanagan, D. P., Ortiz, S. O., Alfonso, V., & Mascolo, J. (2002). *The achievement test desk reference (ATDR): Comprehensive assessment and learning disability.* New York: Allyn and Bacon.

Flanagan, D. P., Ortiz, S., Alfonso, V. C., & Mascolo, J. (2006). *The achievement test desk reference (ATDR): A guide to learning disability identification* (2nd ed.). New York: John Wiley & Sons.

Fletcher-Janzen, E., & Reynolds, C. R. (Eds.) (2008). *Neuropsychological perspective on learning disabilities in the era of RTI: Recommendations for diagnosis and intervention.* Hoboken, NJ: John Wiley & Sons.

Floyd, R., Keith, T., Taub, G., & McGrew, K. (2007). Cattell-Horn-Carroll cognitive abilities and their effects on reading decoding skills: *g* has indirect effects, more specific abilities have direct effects. *School Psychology Quarterly, 22,* 200–223.

Glutting, J. J., Watkins, M. W., & Youngstrom, E. A. (2003). Multifactored and cross-battery ability assessments: Are they worth the effort? In C. R. Reynolds & R. W. Kamphaus (Eds.), *Handbook of psychological and educational assessment of children: Intelligence, aptitude, and achievement* (2nd ed., pp. 343–374). New York: Guilford.

Hale, J. B. & Fiorello, C. A. (2004). *School neuropsychology: A practitioner's handbook.* New York: Guilford.

Hale, J. B., Flanagan, C. P., & Naglieri, J. A. (2008). Alternative research-based methods for IDEA 2004 identification of children with specific learning disabilities. *Communique, 36,* 8, pp. 1, 14–17.

Hanson, J., Sharman, L. A., & Esparza-Brown, J. (2008). Pattern of strengths and weaknesses in specific learning disabilities: What's it all about? *Technical assistance paper presented to the Oregon Department of Education.*

Horn, J. L. (1968). Organization of abilities and the development of intelligence. *Psychological Review, 75,* 242–259.

Horn, J. L. (1991). Measurement of intellectual capabilities: A review of theory. In K. S. McGrew, J. K. Werder, & R. W. Woodcock (Eds.), *Woodcock-Johnson technical manual: A reference on theory and current research* (pp. 197–246). Allen, TX: DLM Teaching Resources.

Horn, J. L., & Blankson, N. (2005). Foundation for better understanding cognitive abilities. In D. P. Flanagan & P. Harrison (Eds.), *Contemporary intellectual assessment* (2nd ed., pp. 41–68). New York: Guilford.

Horn, J. L., & Noll, J. (1997). Human cognitive capabilities: *Gf-Gc* theory. In D. P. Flanagan, J. L. Genshaft, & P. L. Harrison (Eds.), *Contemporary intellectual assessment: Theories, tests, and issues* (pp. 53–91). New York: Guilford.

Horn, J. L., & Stankov, L. (1982). Comments about a chameleon theory: Level I/Level II. *Journal of Educational Psychology, 74*, 874–878.

Kaufman, A. S. (1979). *Intelligent testing with the WISC-R*. New York: John Wiley & Sons.

Kaufman, A. S. (2000). Foreword. In D. P. Flanagan, K. S. McGrew, & S. O. Ortiz (Eds.), *The Wechsler intelligence scales and Gf-Gc theory: A contemporary approach to interpretation*. Boston: Allyn and Bacon.

Kaufman, A. S. (2009, February). Invited Debate: Cognitive/Neuropsychological Assessment is Critical for Learning Disabilities—or is it? Presented at the International Neuropsychological Conference, Atlanta, GA.

Kaufman, A. S., & Kaufman, N. L. (1983). *K-ABC interpretative manual*. Circle Pines, MN: American Guidance Service.

Kaufman, A. S., & Kaufman, N. L. (2004). *Kaufman assessment battery for children* (2nd ed.). Circle Pines, MN: AGS Publishing.

Kavale, K. A., Kauffman, J. M., Bachmeier, R. J., & LeFever, G. B. (2008). Response-to-intervention: Separating the rhetoric of self-congratulation from the reality of specific learning disability identification. *Learning Disability Quarterly, 31*, 135–150.

Kolb, B., & Fantie, B. D. (1997). Development of the child's brain and behavior. In C. E. Reynolds & E. Fletcher-Janzen (Eds.), *Handbook of clinical child neuropsychology* (2nd ed., pp. 17–41). New York: Plenum.

Languis, M. L., & Miller, D. C. (1992). Luria's theory of brain functioning: A model for research in cognitive psychophysiology. *Educational Psychologist, 27*, 493–512.

Lezak, M. (1995). *Neuropsychological assessment, 3rd edition*. New York: Oxford University Press.

Luria, A. R. (1973). *The working brain*. New York: Basic Books.

Luria, A. R. (1979). *The making of mind: A personal account of Soviet psychology*. Cambridge, MA: Harvard University Press.

Mather, N., & Kaufman, N. (Eds.). (2006). Introduction to the special issue, Part Two: It's about the what, the how well, and the why. *Psychology in the Schools, 43*, 7–8.

McGrew, K. S. (1997). Analysis of the major intelligence batteries according to a proposed comprehensive *Gf-Gc* framework. In D. P. Flanagan, J. L. Genshaft, & P. L. Harrison (Eds.), *Contemporary intellectual assessment: Theories, tests, and issues* (pp. 151–179). New York: Guilford.

McGrew, K. S. (2005). The Cattell-Horn-Carroll theory of cognitive abilities: Past, present, and future. In D. P. Flanagan, J. L. Genshaft, & P. L. Harrison (Eds.), *Contemporary intellectual assessment: Theories, tests, and issues* (pp. 136–182). New York: Guilford.

McGrew, K. S. (2008). Interview. In D. P. Flanagan, A. S. Kaufman, N. L. Kaufman, & E. O. Lichtenberger (Eds.), *AGORA: Best practices in applying response to intervention (rti) and comprehensive assessment for the identification of specific learning disabilities*. Bloomington, IN: Pearson Education.

McGrew, K. S., & Flanagan, D. P. (1998). *The intelligent test desk reference (ITDR): Gf-Gc cross-battery assessment.* Boston: Allyn and Bacon.

McGrew, K. S., Flanagan, D. P., Keith, T. Z., & Vanderwood, M. (1997). Beyond *g:* The impact of *Gf-Gc* specific cognitive abilities research on the future use and interpretation of intelligence tests in the schools. *School Psychology Review, 26,* 177–189.

Messick, S. (1989). Validity. In R. L. Linn (Ed.), *Educational measurement* (3rd ed., pp. 13–103). New York: Macmillan.

Messick, S. (1992). Multiple intelligences or multilevel intelligence? Selective emphasis on distinctive properties of hierarchy: On Gardner's Frames of Mind and Sternberg's Beyond IQ in the context of theory and research on the structure of human abilities. *Psychological Inquiry, 3,* 365–384.

Messick, S. (1995). Validity of psychological assessment: Validation of inferences from persons' responses and performances as scientific inquiry into score meaning. *American Psychologist, 50,* 741–749.

Miller, D. C. (2007). *Essentials of school neuropsychological assessment.* New York: John Wiley & Sons.

Naglieri, J. A., & Das, J. P. (1988). Planning-arousal-simultaneous-successive (PASS): A model for assessment. *Journal of School Psychology, 26,* 35–48.

Naglieri, J. A., & Das, J. P. (2005). Planning, attention, simultaneous, and successive (PASS) theory: A revision of the concept of intelligence. In D. P. Flanagan and P. Harrison (Eds.), *Contemporary intellectual assessment* (pp. 120–135). New York: Guilford.

Reynolds, C. R., & Fletcher-Janzen, E. (Eds.). (1997). *Handbook of clinical child neuropsychology* (2nd ed.). New York: Plenum Press.

Reynolds, C. R., & Fletcher-Janzen, E. (Eds.). (2008). *Handbook of clinical child neuropsychology* (3rd ed.). New York: Plenum.

Reynolds, C. R., & Shaywitz, S. E. (2009). Response to intervention: Prevention and remediation, perhaps. Diagnosis, No. *Child Development Perspectives.*

Roid, G. H. (2003). *Stanford-Binet intelligence scale* (5th ed.). Itasca, IL: Riverside Publishing. *[Test battery, Examiners Manual, Technical Manual, Scoring Pro software, and Interpretive Manual].*

Rosengarten, M. E., Alfonso, V. C., & Flanagan, D. P. (2009). *CHC abilities in young children measured by the WJ III COG.* Poster presented at the annual conference of the National Association of School Psychologists, Boston, MA.

Sattler, J. M. (1998). *Clinical and forensic interviewing of children and families.* San Diego, CA: Jerome M. Sattler.

Semrud-Clikeman, M. (2005). Neuropsychological aspects for evaluating learning disabilities. *Journal of Learning Disabilities, 38,* 563–566.

Spearman, C. (1927). *The abilities of man.* New York: Macmillan.

Sternberg, R. J., & Kaufman, J. C. (1998). *Annual Review of Psychology, 49,* 479–502.

Strauss, E., Sherman, E. M. S., & Spreen, O. (2006). *A compendium of neuropsychological tests: Administration, norms, and commentary* (3rd ed.). New York: Oxford University Press.

Vanderwood, M. L., McGrew, K. S., Flanagan, D. P., & Keith, T. Z. (2002). The contribution of general and specific cognitive abilities to reading achievement. *Learning and Individual Differences, 13,* 159–188.

Woodcock, R. W. (1994). Measures of fluid and crystallized theory of intelligence. In R. J. Sternberg (Ed.), *Encyclopedia of human intelligence* (pp. 452–456). New York: Macmillan.

Woodcock, R. W., McGrew, K. S., & Mather, N. (2001). *Woodcock-Johnson III.* Itasca, IL: Riverside Publishing.

CHAPTER 7

The Application of Neuroscience to the Practice of School Neuropsychology

DANIEL C. MILLER and PHILIP A. DEFINA

T HERE HAVE BEEN many rapid advances in the cognitive neurosciences in the past twenty years. The 1990s were declared by the U.S. Congress to be the "decade of the brain," and starting in the year 2000, they dubbed it the "millennium of the brain," which resulted in grants of many federal funds to basic and translational clinical research in neuroscience. In 2003, after thirteen years of intense effort, the Human Genome Project identified all of the 20,000–25,000 genes in the human DNA. The future unlocking of the genetic code in relation to neuropathology has major implications for identifying risk factors of childhood disorders that have a known genetic basis. A parallel development in the past two decades has been the advancement of brain neuroimaging techniques. Researchers and clinicians now have a window into the brain that can be used to facilitate early diagnosis of childhood disorders, provide validation for behavioral measures of brain functions, and monitor the effectiveness of educational interventions.

The purpose of this chapter is to review how recent advances in neuroscience can contribute to school neuropsychology and developmental aspects of clinical neuroscience. The chapter is divided into five sections. The first section of this chapter will review the emerging movement to translate brain research into educational practice. The second section will review the role genetics will play in future educational practice. The third section of the chapter will review the role of brain imaging on current and future educational practice. The fourth section will review the role of neurofeedback in the treatment of childhood disorders. The fifth section of the chapter will speculate about what lies ahead for the brain research–education linkage.

TRANSLATING BRAIN RESEARCH INTO EDUCATIONAL PRACTICE

The goal of brain-based education is to translate brain research into the optimization of the school learning environment. While there are some general principles from brain research that can be readily translated into educational practice, the global notion of brain-based education has led to some questionable practices. Advocates for brain-based education often claim that there are basic summary principles of neuroscience that, can be used as the foundation for brain-based educational practices. Well-known educational consultants such as Drs. David A. Sousa and Eric Jensen have popularized brain-based education with the publication of books such as *How the Brain Learns* (Sousa, 2000), *How the Brain Learns How to Read* (Sousa, 2004), *How the Brain Influences Behavior: Management Strategies for Every Classroom* (Sousa, 2008), *Teaching with the Brain in Mind* (Jensen, 2005), and *Brain-Based Learning: The New Paradigm of Teaching* (Jensen, 2008). Two school neuropsychologists wrote a series of popular books that emphasized a neuropsychological model for diagnosis and intervention of academic disorders: *The Neuropsychology of Reading Disorders* (Feifer & DeFina, 2000), *The Neuropsychology of Written Language* (Feifer & DeFina, 2002), and *The Neuropsychology of Mathematics* (Feifer & DeFina, 2005). See Appendix A in this book for a list of the most recent major school neuropsychology publications. In addition to these publications, the International Mind, Brain, and Education Society was formed in 2003 and has provided additional support for the interest in brain-based education.

Bruer (2008) referred to brain-based education as an emerging discipline and labeled it as *"neuroeducation."* Neuroeducation emphasizes the focus of education on transdisciplinary connections (Battro, Fischer, & Léna, 2008a; 2008b). With the emergence of this new discipline, some researchers warn educators to exercise caution in overgeneralizing brain research into educational practice. It is very easy to state the claim that "research shows" and misleads the public (Bruer, 1997). Swanson (2008) states that: "Although correlational research between brain and behavior has a long history in the field of specific learning disabilities (SLD), there is a gap in the application of this research to instruction. Recent work with the advent of fMRI procedures and treatment outcomes is beginning to bridge this gap. However, the bridge between brain studies and education is not well developed (e.g., Bruer, 1997). Knowing precisely which brain centers are activated over time and how they are associated with instruction is rudimentary" (p. 30).

THE ROLE OF GENETICS ON EDUCATIONAL PRACTICE

Psychologists have long recognized the interaction between the influences of genetics (nature) versus the influences of the environment (nurture). A school neuropsychologist should treat a child with a reading disorder and a known genetic predisposition to dyslexia differently from a child with a reading disorder and no genetic predisposition to dyslexia. The child with a known genetic predisposition to dyslexia should be screened for the various subtypes of dyslexia (see Chapter 19 in this book for a discussion of dyslexia subtypes or Feifer & DeFina, 2000; Feifer & Della Toffalo, 2007), and appropriate interventions should be based on the assessment data. The child with no genetic predisposition to dyslexia may not be reading due to environmental factors (e.g., poor instruction, lack of instructional opportunity, attention difficulties, dysexecutive functioning), which should be appropriately evaluated and addressed.

As noted, reading disorders seem to have a genetic determinant. Pennington and Olson (2005) reported that a child of a parent with a reading disability is eight times more likely to have problems with reading compared to the offspring of the general population. Specific learning disabilities all have a genetic basis to them. See Fletcher, Lyon, Fuchs, and Barnes (2007) for a review of the genetic basis for specific learning disabilities such as: word recognition deficits (pp. 123–128), word fluency deficits (p. 176), reading comprehension deficits (pp. 195–196), mathematics disabilities (pp. 224–226), and written expression disabilities (pp. 247–248).

Berninger and Holdnack stated: "Neuroscience and genetics research findings are increasing rapidly. Parents are likely, in the not-so-distant future, to show up to an Individual Education Plan (IEP) meeting with brain images and genotyping results attached to independent evaluations" (2008, p. 75). Genetic and neuroimaging will become powerful diagnostic tools in the near future, but our diagnoses of disabilities will be much stronger and accurate when these emerging diagnostic tools are combined with the results of neuropsychological, academic, and psychological testing (Berninger & Holdnack, 2008).

THE ROLE OF BRAIN IMAGING IN EDUCATIONAL PRACTICE

The advancement in recent years of neuroimaging techniques has allowed cognitive neuroscientists to develop a window into the brain never before available. Through the use of functional neuroimaging, one can look not only at brain structure to determine differences between SLD and non-SLD children, but also can examine perceptual-motor and cognitive functions during task performance. Research using these techniques has demonstrated that SLD children show specific differences as compared to developmentally aged-matched normal children. Based on numerous empirically based studies demonstrating specific differences in brain functions with neuroimaging procedures, it is possible to develop individualized interventions that are more efficacious in children with atypical neurodevelopment in relation to their functional needs and deficits. The functional neuroimaging data is most helpful when coupled with psychometrically valid neuropsychological tests, which can elucidate qualitative aspects related to the student's educational needs.

While caution is certainly warranted about translating brain research into educational practice, there are exciting contributions from neuroscience that offer insight into the neurological basis of a variety of learning disorders. As an example, Shaywitz (2005) provided an overview of the important role that neuroimaging is playing in pinpointing brain systems related to specific functions, thereby using neuroimaging to monitor the effectiveness of educational interventions:

> Modern brain imaging technology now allows scientists to noninvasively peer into, and literally watch, the brain at work—in children and adults. Using this new technology, we and other laboratories around the world have now identified the specific neural systems used in reading, demonstrated how these system differ in good and struggling readers, pinpointed the systems used in compensation, and identified the systems used in skilled or fluent reading. In addition, we have identified the different types of reading disabilities and also demonstrated the malleability or plasticity of the neural circuitry for reading in response to an evidence-based reading intervention. These and other studies have provided a new and unprecedented level of insight and understanding about common neuropsychological disorders affecting children and adults, their mechanisms, their identification, and their effective treatment. (p. vii)

TYPES OF NEUROIMAGING TECHNIQUES

Structural neuroimaging describes techniques that determine the integrity of brain structures and include computerized tomography (CT) and magnetic resonance imaging (MRI). *Functional neuroimaging* techniques measure aspects of brain function with the goal of understanding the relationship between activity in brain regions and specific mental functions. Measures include cortical electrical activity (electroencephalography [EEG]), glucose metabolism (Positron Emission Tomography [PET] scans), blood flow (PET, functional magnetic resonance imaging [fMRI] scans, and near infrared spectroscopy [NIRS]), magnetic activity (magnetic source imaging [MSI] scans or Diffusion Tensor Imaging [DTI]), or brain chemistry (magnetic resonance spectroscopy [MRS]). The changes in brain activity are usually recorded during cognitive tasks to determine differences in brain functions in different brain regions between normal and neurologically atypical populations. Functional neuroimaging measures are most often superimposed on structural MRI images to relate behavioral function with brain structure (Fletcher et al., 2007).

Neuroimaging techniques such as EEG, fMRI, MSI, MRS, and DTI do not involve radiation and are noninvasive, so they can be readily used with children. PET scans, on the other hand, must rely on recording the metabolic uptake of a radioactive isotope injected into the blood stream. Typically, PET scans are not used on children, unless medically necessary, because of the exposure to radiation and its invasive nature.

Diffusion Tensor Imaging (DTI) examines the structural organization of white matter tracts. What makes DTI unique compared to other imaging techniques is that it evaluates processing efficiency as opposed to localization of function (Fletcher-Janzen, 2008). Noble and McCandliss (2005) used DTI and found microstructural abnormalities of the perisylvian white matter tracts in children and adults with reading deficits. Beaulieu et al. (2005) also used DTI with healthy children who were good readers and found that regional connectivity in the left temporo-parietal white matter is an indicator of enhanced reading performance. DeFina and colleagues at the International Brain Research Foundation are currently examining white matter differences and electromagnetic and chemical signatures in various types of TBI that will predict clinical outcomes and guide treatments.

Electroencephalography is unique in its ability to detect real-time changes (milliseconds) in cortical neuronal firing and communication between regions of the brain. Based on the size and speed of the electrical activity in brain regions, one can determine the amount of activation occurring at specific brain regions at specific time periods. When used in conjunction with cognitive tasks, the EEG provides a window into "how" the brain is working in real time to process information while under task.

EEG quantifies brainwave activity (a quantitative EEG [qEEG]) and can compare an individual's brainwave patterns to an age-matched normative database. Databases allow for the comparison of brain function at rest and under task conditions such as reading and arithmetic, thus allowing for a diagnosis specifying which brain regions are defective under task. Since certain brain waves are better able to be evaluated through EEG/qEEG and others through analysis from Magnetoencephalography or MEG, it is much more powerful to use both measures simultaneously to assess electrical mapping more comprehensively.

One of the main advantages of using EEG and qEEG as assessment measures is that, based on the electroencephalographic diagnostic criteria and their comparison to known norms, remediation programs can be developed that target abnormal brain regions or connections using EEG training as a remediation tool. EEG-feedback, or neurofeedback as it is commonly called, is an operant conditioning technique by which persons learn to control and modify their brainwave (EEG) activity to meet preset criteria. Neurofeedback is widely used in practice but has not been fully accepted by the entire medical community. The majority of insurance companies do not pay for neurofeedback. In 2008, the National Institute of Mental Health (NIMH) funded researchers at Ohio State University to conduct a double-blind study of the effectiveness of neurofeedback (retrieved from http://www.nimh.nih.gov/about/advisory-boards-and-groups/namhc/reports/directors-report-to-the-national-advisory-mental-health-council-september-19–2008.shtml).

In neurofeedback, a training protocol is developed based on a qEEG assessment to teach a person to regulate his or her brainwaves to enhance or reduce specific electrical frequencies in specific brain regions and alter them toward normal functioning. As the neural regions and pathways are exercised using EEG feedback, subjects develop a sense of what these changed patterns feel like and how they can be accessed. After practicing these exercises over a period of time, the pathways involved in attention and learning work more efficiently, and this enhanced brain activity becomes a natural part of the subject's functioning. As the brain learns during the EEG-feedback process, the brain changes structurally by forming and reinforcing small connections between neurons. The brain naturally develops and expands pathways that are used, and "prunes" connections that are not. EEG-feedback training takes advantage of this "growth-through-utilization." Through visual and/or auditory rewards, the process allows the client to see when he or she is meeting preset criteria, thus reinforcing the positive connections and strengthening these pathways.

EEG feedback also has the advantage of being able to be combined with more conventional interventions used to treat learning disorders. Once a subject is consistently meeting the EEG criteria, then it is known that the brain is functioning optimally to perform the task that is being treated, such as a reading disorder. At this time, while the feedback reward continues, the subject can engage in traditional reading training techniques. By pairing the reading remediation techniques with the optimal brainwave production, the subject learns through classical conditioning to produce the specified brainwaves and neural connections while performing a reading task. The use of EEG feedback thus improves the efficiency and effectiveness of traditional remediation methods by ensuring that the subject engages the correct pathways and mental states during traditional interventions. EEG-directed neurofeedback can optimize the electrical potentials in a child's brain that can make the brain more responsive to traditional speech and language, cognitive remediation, and occupational therapies. Additional noninvasive neuromo-dulation techniques such as transcranial Direct Current Stimulation (tDCS) and repeated Transcranial Magnetic Stimulation (rTMS) are being studied to enhance cognition and emotion in neurodevelopmental disorders, depression, anxiety, PTSD, and TBI.

EXAMPLES OF NEUROIMAGING STUDIES WITH CHILDHOOD DISORDERS

General Studies   Diagnostic uses for neuroimaging are helping neuropsychologists understand the neural basis of SLD. Lubar et al. (1985) used qEEG to assess SLD children compared to a group of normal children. Their research determined that SLD children exhibited slower brainwave patterns than the normal control group and that it was possible to predict SLD versus normal group membership with greater than 95 percent accuracy. More recently, Chabot, di Michele, Prichep, and John (2001) demonstrated that over 80 percent of children with attentional difficulties had abnormal EEG patterns compared to a matched normal group.

Reading Disorders   One of the most researched areas of learning disabilities is dyslexia and associated reading disorders. This area has been studied using multiple neuroimaging techniques that when taken together allow for a comprehensive view of neural abnormalities associated with reading disorders.

Shaywitz (2003) reviewed several major studies that used functional brain imaging techniques (e.g., fMRI) to study efficient and inefficient readers. Studies revealed differing brain activation patterns between skilled and nonskilled readers. Skilled readers engage only one pathway that is very quick and efficient, whereas dyslexic readers engage two pathways, making their reading slow and inefficient. Efficient readers were found to activate an occipital-temporal pathway, which uses a whole-word approach to reading. This neural circuitry allows words to be recognized automatically by sight, rather than by deconstructing words phonetically. When the occipital-temporal pathway is activated, an exact neural form of the word is retrieved along with the word's spelling, pronunciation, and meaning (Shaywitz, 2003). The parietal-temporal system is required for phonetic decoding. This system initially analyzes a word, separates it by phonemes, and links letters to sounds. Children learning to read initially use the parietal-temporal system exclusively until the child memorizes the whole word and increases fluency using the occipital-temporal pathway. The third area of the brain activated in reading is the area surrounding Broca's area in the left frontal region. This part of the brain also relies on phonological processing but is not as efficient as the occipital-temporal pathway. Nonimpaired readers activate primarily posterior portions of left hemisphere, while impaired readers underactivate posterior regions and activate primarily frontal areas (Shaywitz, 2003).

Generally speaking, "brain-based research in dyslexia has focused on the planum temporale, gyral morphology of the perisylvian region, corpus callosum, as well as cortical abnormalities of the temporal-parietal region (e.g., Fine, Semrud-Clikeman, Keith, Stapleton, & Hynd, 2007; see Miller, Sanchez, & Hynd, 2003, for review)" (Swanson, 2008, p. 39). Children with dyslexia have consistently been found to have smaller regions in language areas (left planum, bilateral insular regions, and right anterior region) than children who are efficient readers (Foster, Hynd, Morgan, & Hugdahl, 2002; Paul, Bott, Helm, Eulitz, & Elbert, 2006; Pugh et al., 2000; Shaywitz et al., 2003). Maisog, Einbinder, Flowers, Turkeltaub, and Eden (2008) reported a meta-analysis of functional neuroimaging studies of dyslexia. The review revealed that there are two main differences between typical readers and dyslexics. First, normal readers show more activity in left-sided brain areas, including two left extrastriate areas within Brodmann area 37, precuneus, inferior parietal cortex, superior temporal gyrus, thalamus, and left inferior frontal gyrus. The second finding revealed areas that demonstrate hyper-activity in dyslexics compared to normals. These areas were located in the right hemisphere and included the right thalamus and anterior insula.

Structural neuroimaging studies have also shown difference between normal subjects and children with developmental dyslexia (DD). Menghini et al. (2008) used structural neuroimaging to measure grey matter (GM) volume in dyslexics. They found that compared to normal subjects, DD subjects demonstrated significantly smaller GM volume in the right posterior superior parietal lobule and precuneus and in the right supplementary motor area. Mody, Wehner, and Ahlfors (2008) performed a study to determine the mechanism behind reading disabilities in a group of children. By using magnetoencephalography while administering a speech perception task, they revealed that poor readers process phonologically similar incongruent stimuli as congruent, thus leading to their reading difficulties.

MATHEMATICAL CALCULATIONS

Neuroimaging work in the area of dyscalculia has shed light upon regions associated with the representation and processing of numerical magnitude. Price, Holloway, Räsänen, Vesterinen, and Ansari (2007) used neuroimaging techniques to demonstrate that both adults and children with dyscalculia demonstrate deficits in the same region, the intraparietal sulcus, during math tasks. Through the application of neuroimaging, this research was able to localize the deficit structure in both adults and children with dyscalculia thus demonstrating a common dysfunctional area in dyscalculia.

Subtypes of dyscalculia are also able to be revealed using neuroimaging. For instance, fMRI was used by Kucian et al. (2006) to look at differences in neural activation between approximate calculation and exact calculation. Results of this work showed a positive correlation between accuracy of approximate calculation and neural activation in the left intraparietal sulcus, the inferior frontal gyrus, and the right middle frontal gyrus. Normal individuals showed high activity in these regions, whereas subjects with dyscalculia were less accurate and showed less activation in these regions. However, this population demonstrated no significant differences in exact calculation accuracy, and there were no significant differences between groups in neural activation during exact calculation. This study demonstrates the ability of neuroimaging to accurately assess subtle neurologic activity differences between subgroups of people with dyscalculia. (See Feifer & DeFina, 2005; or Chapter 21 in this book for reviews of the various subtypes of mathematics disorders from a brain-behavioral perspective.)

Molko et al. (2003) demonstrated further evidence of the important role the intraparietal sulcus plays in developmental dyscalculia. This work used a combination of functional and structural imaging during arithmetic tasks. Functional magnetic resonance imaging showed an abnormal modulation of intraparietal activations during arithmetic, while structural imaging revealed an abnormal length, depth, and sulcal geometry in the right intraparietal sulcus. It was therefore concluded that "a genetic form of developmental dyscalculia can be related to both functional and structural abnormalities of the right intraparietal sulcus" (Molko et al., 2003).

In another study that sought to reveal the neurologic origins of different subtypes of dyscalculia, Stanescu-Cosson et al. (2000) used fMRI and event-related potentials (ERPs) to study differences in the regions activated and the temporal dynamics during calculation processes of normal subjects compared to subjects with dyscalculia. The results of their study revealed two difference cerebral networks that were used for number processing. Left regions were used more in the operations involving small numbers, while both left and right parietal cortices were highly active during calculations with large numbers. One of the most interesting findings in this work involved the temporal dynamics of the calculation process. Differences between task and number size were apparent in the ERP data as early as 200–300 ms after problem presentation.

BRAIN IMAGING FOR MONITORING THE EFFECTIVENESS OF INTERVENTION

One of the most exciting applications of functional neuroimaging is the use of these technologies to monitor the effectiveness of treatment interventions. Based on neuroimaging measures that compare pretreatment to posttreatment scans, one can determine if neurologic changes have taken place that can account for the effectiveness, or in some cases ineffectiveness, of interventions. By determining the effectiveness of treatment interventions via neuroimaging, remediation techniques become an evidence-based practice where effectiveness is quantifiable and measurable. Additionally, treatment programs can be altered in a stepwise progression to address deficits in neural functioning in a logical manner based on deviations from normative databases.

Thompson and Thompson (1998) demonstrated the effectiveness of pairing neuroimaging diagnostic techniques with specific treatment interventions. In this study 111 subjects with an official diagnoses of Attention Deficit Disorder (ADD) were assessed using traditional techniques including the *Wechsler Intelligence Scale* (WISC-R, WISC-III, WAIS-R), the *Wide Range Achievement Test* (WRAT 3) and the *Test of Variables of Attention* (TOVA), as well as a qEEG. Based on the results of the assessment, subjects underwent EEG-feedback training paired with metacognitive strategies. After forty sessions of this intervention, changes were measured in full-scale IQ, TOVA, and EEG brainwave patterns. The results of the study showed that ADD symptoms (impulsivity, inattention, and variability in response times), brainwave patterns, and full IQ score changes were significant, with an average gain in full scale IQ of 12 points. Work like this demonstrates the effectiveness of neuroimaging in assessing and guiding treatment interventions.

As previously discussed, imaging as an assessment tool can serve to demonstrate the underlying mechanism by which external changes have occurred. Richards et al. (2000) used magnetic resonance spectroscopy (MRS) imaging to study changes pre- and postintervention for remediating deficits in phonological processing, word decoding, reading comprehension, and listening comprehension. In this study and a follow-up study by Richards et al. (2002), the students showed significant changes in lactate activation in the areas of the brain responsible for reading efficiency.

Aylward et al. (2003) used fMRI to evaluate the effectiveness of a word recognition intervention in a reading disabled group of students. Prior to the comprehensive reading instruction, the children with dyslexia demonstrated significantly less activation in brain regions associated with efficient reading. Following the comprehensive reading instruction, the scans were repeated on both groups, and the reading disabled group showed an increase in left hemispheric activation, which was more similar to matched controls. Simos et al. (2002a) used magnetic source imaging (MSI) to evaluate changes in dyslexic children after an intensive phonologically based intervention. They found similar findings to the Aylward et al. study with the dyslexia brain activation being overly focused in the right hemisphere before intervention and an increased left hemispheric activation after intervention. These early neuroimaging studies showed changes in the activation of neural networks as a result of intervention; however, they did not provide evidence of compensatory changes (Fletcher et al., 2007). Subsequent neuroimaging studies (Simos et al., 2002b; Simos et al., 2005; Temple et al., 2003) have all shown increased activation in the left temporo-parietal and inferior frontal regions with evidence of compensatory changes.

Shaywitz et al. (2004) used fMRI to baseline image students who were poor readers and students with average reading achievement from a study conducted by Blachman et al. (2004). Blachman and colleagues separated the poor readers into two groups: One received the typical educational instruction offered in the classroom, and the other group of poor readers participated in a one-year experimental phonologically based reading intervention. Shaywitz and colleagues obtained postintervention fMRI data and found that the experimental group of poor readers who had the targeted reading intervention showed a normalization of the left occipito-temporal pathway that is related to the automaticity of reading, and less reliance of the frontal phonological pathway for reading. "The activation patterns were comparable to those obtained from normal children who had always been good readers" (Shaywitz, 2003, p. 85–86).

In a study similar to the work of Shaywitz and colleagues, Simos and colleagues (Simos et al., 2006; Simos et al., 2007a; Simos et al., 2007b) found that intensive training in phonics and word recognition normalized the activation of brain functioning in children (recorded using magnetic source imaging [MSI]) with reading problems, but only if the children were positive responders to the intervention behaviorally. Richards and Berninger (2008) used fMRI imaging to study connectivity patterns in children with dyslexia and demonstrated that these children showed abnormal fMRI connectivity on a phoneme task before treatment but not after treatment.

Meyler, Keller, Cherkassky, Gabrieli, and Just (2008) used fMRI in a longitudinal study to measure the impact of intensive remedial instruction on cortical activation among fifth-grade poor readers during a sentence comprehension task. FMRI measures were taken at three different time periods. Prior to instruction, the poor readers had significantly less activation than good readers in bilateral parietal regions. Immediately after instruction, poor readers made substantial gains in reading ability, and demonstrated significantly increased activation in the left angular gyrus and the left superior parietal lobule. Activation in these regions continued to increase among poor readers one year post-remediation and eventually resulted in a normalization of the activation of these regions. This study is important in that it demonstrates changes in cortical activation following an intervention in brain regions known to be involved in reading, and it demonstrates that this intervention had lasting positive effects.

WHAT LIES AHEAD FOR THE BRAIN RESEARCH–EDUCATION LINKAGE?

A genetic predisposition for a disorder does not guarantee that the individual will at some point manifest the symptoms of that disorder. The environment is a major determinant to whether a genetic predisposition manifests itself. From a prevention model, it would be a significant advance for educators to know if a child had a genetic predisposition for a neurodevelopmental disorder so that the educational environment could be modified. Berninger and Holdnack (2008) pointed out that once genetic typing of children who are at risk for various neurodevelopmental disorders becomes commonplace, it would be expected that school districts would implement large-scale screening and early intervention programs. Undoubtedly, school psychologists and school neuropsychologists could play a major role in developing and monitoring interventions for these children who would be genetically at risk for neurodevelopmental disorders.

The use of neuroimaging has not become mainstream due to its invasive nature for some techniques and for its cost. However, a recent neuroimaging technology called near infrared spectropy (fNIRS) could change these limitation factors. fNIRS is a noninvasive, portable, and low-cost method of monitoring brain functions (Zabel & Chute, 2002). "This technology, although still in its infancy, requires more refinement and validation efforts with other neurotechnologies but holds the future potential for describing in greater detail brain–behavior relationships in brain disorders and can be integrated with neuropsychological testing as well" (Breiger & Majovski, 2008, pp. 146–147). Intervention approaches such as neurofeedback are gaining in popularity as well. Parents and educators like the idea of directly training the brain to respond in a proper and efficient manner. Clinicians and researchers will need to continue to demonstrate the treatment efficacy of neurofeedback before it is more widely accepted.

As neuroimaging becomes more accessible, it will be used as a tool to validate what neuropsychological tests were designed to measure (Miller, 2008). Test developers in the past have relied on correlational data to validate a test's construct validity. Neuroimaging could help school neuropsychologists by creating functional profiles for children that would predict the presence or absence of a learning disorder and guide us toward specific interventions (Reynolds, 2008). As reported earlier in this chapter, the use of neuroimaging to monitor the effectiveness of interventions will become more commonplace in the foreseeable future. It will not be unusual for a parent to bring to an IEP meeting neuroimages that show her child's brain functions during a particular task, like reading, as still showing an inefficient pathway activation, thus requiring modified interventions.

SUMMARY

In summary, ongoing research in neurogenetics, advances in brain-imaging technology, establishment of brain-imaging databases, imaging validation of psychometric instruments that measure brain functions, and measurement of processing changes through remediation are powerful scientific advances already influencing our understanding, assessment, and treatment of learning disabilities (Fletcher-Janzen, 2008, pp. 319–320).

In the future, the use of computerized cognitive enhancement training programs will be more commonplace, designed to augment special education services and language therapies and improve attention, memory, and executive skills to assist with reading, written language, and math disorders. In addition, the development of valid and reliable functional imaging "neuro-markers" that can predict outcomes and guide treatments of neurobehavioral disorders will be the way of the future (DeFina, 2008). Interdigitating these imaging algorithms with psychometric algorithms will be much more valuable in understanding the nuances of how to maximize the potential of compromised brains. Emerging research protocols for moderate-to-severe TBI, PDD, and other more debilitating neurodevelopmental disorders are being treated with combinations of specifically targeted nutraceuticals, hyperbaric oxygen, stem cells, and brain-computer interface systems. We are embarking on a new frontier in brain science that can impact disorders once thought to be refractory to interventions. The future is also shaping up for normal individuals to reach much higher levels of potential, by piquing perceptual, cognitive, motor and emotional boundaries. The limits of our brain's capabilities are only constrained by our lack of knowledge of brain–behavioral functions and neural plasticity.

REFERENCES

Aylward, E. H., Richards, T. L., Berninger, V. W., Nagy, W. E., Field, K. M., Grimme, A. C., et al. (2003). Instructional treatment associated with changes in brain activation in children with dyslexia. *Neurology, 22,* 212–219.

Battro, A. M., Fischer, K. W., & Léna, P. J. (2008a). *The educated brain: Essays in neuroeducation.* New York: Cambridge University Press.

Battro, A. M., Fischer, K. W., & Léna, P. J. (2008b). Introduction: Mind, brain, and education in theory and practice. In A. M. Battro, K. W. Fischer, & P. J. Léna (Eds.), *The educated brain: Essays in neuroeducation.* (pp. 3–19). New York: Cambridge University Press.

Beaulieu, C., Plewes, C., Paulson, L. A., Roy, D., Snook, L., Concha, L., & Phillips, L. (2005). Imaging brain connectivity in children with diverse reading ability. *Neuroimage, 25,* 1266–1271.

Berninger, V. W., & Holdnack, J. A. (2008). Nature-nurture perspectives in diagnosing and treating learning disabilities: Response to questions begging answers that see the forest and the trees. In E. Fletcher-Janzen & C. R. Reynolds (Eds.), *Neuropsychological perspectives on learning disabilities in the era of RTI* (pp. 66–81). Hoboken, NJ: John Wiley & Sons.

Blachman, B. A., Schatschneider, C., Fletcher, J. M., Clonan, S., Shaywitz, B., et al. (2004). Effects of intensive reading remediation for second and third graders. *Journal of Educational Psychology, 96,* 444–461.

Breiger, D., & Majovski., L. V. (2008). Neuropsychological assessment and RTI in the assessment of learning disabilities: Are they mutually exclusive? In E. Fletcher-Janzen & C. R. Reynolds (Eds.), *Neuropsychological perspectives on learning disabilities in the era of RTI* (pp. 141–158). Hoboken, NJ: John Wiley & Sons.

Bruer, J. T. (1997). Education and the brain. *Educational Researcher, 26,* 4–16.

Bruer, J. T. (2008). Building bridges in neuroeducation. In A. M. Battro, K. W. Fischer, & P. J. Léna (Eds.), *The educated brain: Essays in neuroeducation* (pp. 43–58). New York: Cambridge University Press.

Chabot, R. J., di Michele, F., Prichep, L., & John, E. R. (2001). The clinical role of computerized EEG in the evaluation and treatment of learning and attention disorders in children and adolescents. *Journal of Neuropsychiatry and Clinical Neuroscience, 13,* 171–186.

DeFina, P. A. (2008, November). *New trends in brain research.* Paper presented at the international workshop on BCI. Rome, Italy.

Feifer, S. G., & DeFina, P. A. (2000). *The neuropsychology of reading disorders: Diagnosis and intervention.* Middletown, MD: School Neuropsych Press.

Feifer, S. G., & DeFina, P. A. (2002). *The neuropsychology of written language disorders: Diagnosis and intervention.* Middletown, MD: School Neuropsych Press.

Feifer, S. G., & DeFina, P. A. (2005). *The neuropsychology of mathematics disorders: Diagnosis and intervention.* Middletown, MD: School Neuropsych Press.

Feifer, S. G., & Della Toffalo, D. (2007). *Integrating RTI with cognitive neuropsychology: A scientific approach to reading:* Middletown, MD: School Neuropsych Press.

Fine, J. G., Semrud-Clikeman, M., Keith, T. Z., Stapleton, L. M., & Hynd, G. W. (2007). Reading and the corpus callosum: An MRI family study of volume and area. *Neuropsychology, 21,* 235–241.

Fletcher, J. M., Lyon, G. R., Fuchs, L. S., & Barnes, M. A. (2007). *Learning disabilities: From identification to intervention.* New York: Guilford.

Fletcher-Janzen, E. (2008). Knowing is not enough—we must apply. Willing is not enough—we must do. In E. Fletcher-Janzen & C. R. Reynolds (Eds.), *Neuropsychological perspectives on learning disabilities in the era of RTI* (pp. 315–325). Hoboken, NJ: John Wiley & Sons.

Foster, L. M., Hynd, G. W., Morgan, A. E., & Hugdahl, K. (2002). Planum temporale asymmetry and ear advantage in dichotic listening in developmental dyslexia and attention-deficit/hyperactivity disorder (ADHD). *Journal of International Neuropsychological Society, 8,* 22–36.

Jensen, E. (2005). *Teaching with the brain in mind* (rev. 2nd ed.). Thousand Oaks, CA: Corwin Press.

Jensen, E. (2008). *Brain-based learning: The new paradigm of teaching* (2nd ed.). Thousand Oaks, CA: Corwin Press.

Kucian, K., Loennecker, T., Dietrich, T., Dosch, M., Martin, E., & von Aster, M. (2006). Impaired neural networks for approximate calculation in dyscalculic children: A functional MRI study. *Behavioral and Brain Functions* [Electronic Resource]: BBF, 2, 31.

Lubar, J. F., Bianchini, K. J., Calhoun, W. H., Lambert, E. W., Brody, Z. H., & Shabsin, H. S. (1985). Spectral analysis of EEG differences between children with and without learning disabilities. *Journal of Learning Disabilities, 18,* 403–408.

Maisog, J. M., Einbinder, E. R., Flowers, D. L., Turkeltaub, P. E., & Eden, G. F. (2008). A meta-analysis of functional neuroimaging studies of dyslexia. *Annals of the New York Academy of Sciences, 1145,* 237–259.

Menghini, D., Hagberg, G. E., Petrosini, L., Bozzali, M., Macaluso, E., Caltagirone, C., & Vicari, S. (2008). Structural correlates of implicit learning deficits in subjects with developmental dyslexia. *Annals of the New York Academy of Sciences, 1145,* 212–221.

Meyler, A., Keller, T. A., Cherkassky, V. L., Gabrieli, J. D. E., & Just, M. A. (2008). Modifying the brain activation of poor readers during sentence comprehension with extended remedial instruction: A longitudinal study of neuroplasticity. *Neuropsychologia, 46,* 2580–2592.

Miller, C. J., Sanchez, J., & Hynd, G. W. (2003). Neurological correlates of reading disabilities. In H. L. Swanson, K. R., Harris, & S. Graham (Eds.), *Handbook of Learning Disabilities* (pp. 242–255). New York: Guilford.

Miller, D. C. (2008). The need to integrate cognitive neuroscience and neuropsychology in a RTI model. In E. Fletcher-Janzen & C. R. Reynolds (Eds.), *Neuropsychological perspectives on learning disabilities in the era of RTI* (pp. 131–140). Hoboken, NJ: John Wiley & Sons.

Mody, M., Wehner, D. T., & Ahlfors, S. P. (2008). Auditory word perception in sentence context in reading-disabled children. *Neuroreport, 19,* 1567–1571.

Molko, N., Cachia, A., Rivière, D., Mangin, J. F., Bruandet, M., Le Bihan, D., Cohen, L., & Dehaene, S. (2003). Functional and structural alterations of the intraparietal sulcus in a developmental dyscalculia of genetic origin. *Neuron, 40,* 847–858.

National Institute of Mental Health web site. *Director Report to the National Advisory Mental Health Council.* Retrieved on February 3, 2009. from http://www.nimh. nih.gov/about/advisory-boards-and-groups/namhc/reports/directors-report-to-the-national-advisory-mental-health-council-september-19-2008.shtml.

Noble, K. G., & McCandliss, B. D. (2005). Reading development and impairment: Behavioral, social, and neurobiological factors. *Developmental and Behavioral Pediatrics, 26,* 370–376.

Paul, I., Bott, C., Helm, S., Eulitz, C., & Elbert, T. (2006). Reduced hemispheric asymmetry of the auditory N260m in dyslexia. *Neuropsychologia, 44,* 785–794.

Pennington, B. F., & Olson, R. K. (2005). Genetics of dyslexia. *The science of reading: A handbook* (pp. 453–472). Oxford, UK: Blackwell.

Price, G. R., Holloway, I., Räsänen, P., Vesterinen, M., & Ansari, D. (2007). Impaired parietal magnitude processing in developmental dyscalculia. *Current Biology, 17,* R1042–43.

Pugh, K. R., Mencl, W. E., Jenner, A. R., Katz, L., Frost, S. J., Lee, J. R., et al. (2000). Functional neuroimaging studies of reading and reading disabilities (developmental dyslexia). *Mental Retardation and Developmental Disabilities Research Reviews, 6,* 207–213.

Reynolds, C. R. (2008). RTI, neuroscience, and sense: Chaos in the diagnosis and treatment of learning disabilities. In E. Fletcher-Janzen & C. R. Reynolds (Eds.), *Neuropsychological perspectives on learning disabilities in the era of RTI* (pp. 14–27). Hoboken, NJ: John Wiley & Sons.

Richards, T. L., & Berninger, V. W. (2008). Abnormal fMRI connectivity in children with dyslexia during a phoneme task: Before but not after treatment. *Journal of Neurolinguistics, 21,* 294–304.

Richards, T. L., Berninger, V., Sylward, E., Richards, A., Thomson, J., Nagy, W., et al. (2002). Reproducibility of proton MR spectroscopic imaging (PEPSI): Comparison of dyslexic and normal reading children and effects of treatment on brain lactate levels during language tasks. *American Journal of Neuroradiology, 23,* 1678–1685.

Richards, T. L., Corina, D., Serafini, S., Steury, K., Echelard, D. R., Dagar, S. R., et al. (2000). The effects of a phonologically driven treatment for dyslexia on lactate levels as measured by proton MRSI. *American Journal of Neuroradiology, 21,* 916–922.

Shaywitz, B. A., Shaywitz, S. E., Blachman, B. A., Pugh, K. R., Fulbright, R. K., Skudlarski, P., Mencl, W. E., Constable, R. T., Holahan, J. M., Marchione, K. E., et al. (2004). Development of left occipitotemporal systems for skilled reading in children after a phonologically-based intervention. *Biological Psychiatry, 55,* 926–933.

Shaywitz, S. (2003). *Overcoming dyslexia: A new and complete science-based program for reading problems at any level.* New York: Knopf.

Shaywitz, S. E. (2005). Foreword. In R. D'Amato, E. Fletcher-Janzen, & C. R. Reynolds (Eds.), *Handbook of school neuropsychology* (pp. vii–viii). New York: John Wiley & Sons.

Shaywitz, S. E., Shaywitz, B. A., Fulbright, R. K., Skudlarski, P., Mencl, W. E., Constable, R. T., et al. (2003). Young adult outcome of childhood reading disability. *Biological Psychiatry, 54,* 25–33.

Simos, P. G., Fletcher, J. M., Bergman, E., Breier, J. L., Foorman, B. R., Castillo, E. M., et al. (2002a). Dyslexia-specific brain activation profile becomes normal following successful remedial training. *Neurology, 58,* 1–10.

Simos, P. G., Fletcher, J. M., Denton, C., Sarkari, S., Billingsley-Marshall, R., & Papanicolaou, A. C. (2006). Magnetic source imaging studies of dyslexia interventions. *Developmental Neuropsychology, 30,* 591–661.

Simos, P. G., Fletcher, J. M., Foorman, B. R., Francis, D. J., Castillo, E. M., Davis, R. N., et al. (2002b). Brain activation profiles during the early stages of reading acquisition. *Journal of Child Neurology, 17,* 159–163.

Simos, P. G., Fletcher, J. M., Sarkari, S., Billingsley, R. L., Denton, C., & Papanicolaou, A. C. (2007a). Altering the brain circuits for reading through intervention: A magnetic source imaging study. *Neuropsychology, 21,* 485–496.

Simos, P. G., Fletcher, J. M., Sarkari, S., Billingsley-Marshall, R., Denton, C. A., & Papanicolaou, A. C. (2007b). Intensive instruction affects brain magnetic activity associated with oral word reading in children with persistent reading disabilities. *Journal of Learning Disabilities, 40,* 37–48.

Simos, P. G., Fletcher, J. M., Sarkari, S., Billingsley, R. L., Francis, D. J., Castillo, E. M., et al. (2005). Early development of neurophysiological processes involved in normal reading and reading disability. *Neuropsychology, 19,* 787–798.

Sousa, D. A. (2000). *How the brain learns* (2nd ed.). Thousand Oaks, CA: Corwin Press.

Sousa, D. A. (2004). *How the brain learns how to read.* Thousand Oaks, CA: Corwin Press.

Sousa, D. A. (2008). *How the brain influences behavior: Management strategies for every classroom.* Thousand Oaks, CA: Corwin Press.

Stanescu-Cosson, R., Pinel, P., van De Moortele, P. F., Le Bihan, D., Cohen, L., & Dehaene, S. (2000). Understanding dissociations in dyscalculia: A brain imaging study of the impact of number size on the cerebral networks for exact and approximate calculation. *Brain, 123,* 2240–2255.

Swanson, H. L. (2008). Neuroscience and RTI: A complementary role. In E. Fletcher-Janzen & C. R. Reynolds (Eds.), *Neuropsychological perspectives on learning disabilities in the era of RTI* (pp. 28–53). Hoboken, NJ: John Wiley & Sons.

Temple, E., Deutsch, G. K., Oldrack, R. A., Miller, S. L., Tallal, P., Merzenich, M. M., et al. (2003). Neural deficits in children with dyslexia ameliorated by behavioral remediation: Evidence from functional MRI. *Proceedings of the National Academy of Sciences, 12,* 46–65.

Thompson, L., & Thompson, M. (1998). Neurofeedback combined with training in metacognitive strategies: Effectiveness in students with ADD. *Applied Psychophysiology and Biofeedback, 23,* 243–263.

Zabel, T. A., & Chute, D. L. (2002). Educational neuroimaging: A proposed neuropsychological application of near-infrared spectroscopy (nIRS). *Journal of Head Trauma Rehabilitation, 17,* 477–488.

CHAPTER 8

Linking School Neuropsychology with Response-to-Intervention Models

DOUGLAS A. DELLA TOFFALO

THE PURPOSE OF this chapter is to provide a brief review of historical practices of identifying learning disabilities (LD), discuss the benefits and pitfalls of Response-to-Intervention (RTI) models of LD identification, review the need for an improved model, and present an integrated model for LD identification that combines the merits of RTI with modern methods of neurocognitive assessment driven by an evidence-based understanding of LD that is informed by advances in modern neuroscience.

HISTORICAL IDENTIFICATION OF LD

Debate over the methods used to accurately identify and effectively educate students with learning disabilities has reached a new level of fervor since the 2004 reauthorization of the Individuals with Disabilities Education Act (IDEA). At the heart of this debate is a long-criticized method for identifying LD, referred to as the "discrepancy model," that has operationally defined learning disabilities as a significant discrepancy between a student's measured intellectual abilities and his or her actual level of acquired skills in one or more primary curricular areas such as reading, math, written expression, and so forth. This discrepancy model has been the lone method for identifying learning disabilities within the schools since the inception of special education services with the signing of Public Law 94–142 in 1975. PL 94–142 provided a definition of LD that has not changed in thirty-three years.

Even in the most recent revision of this law, the term *specific learning disability* continues to be defined as:

> a disorder in one or more of the basic psychological processes involved in understanding or in using language, spoken or written, which may manifest itself in the imperfect ability to listen, think, speak, read, write, spell, or do mathematical calculations. Such term includes such conditions as perceptual disabilities, brain injury, minimal brain dysfunction, dyslexia, and developmental aphasia. Such term does not include a learning problem that is primarily the result of visual, hearing, or motor disabilities, of mental retardation, of emotional disturbance, or of environmental, cultural, or economic disadvantage. (20 U.S.C. 1401 [30])

For many years before this law was passed, LDs were described as learning problems of a presumed neurological origin. In fact, the symptoms of LDs were often referred to collectively as *minimal brain dysfunction*. This language clearly denotes the enduring (and increasingly validated) perspective that the heterogeneous symptoms, which constitute LDs, are largely attributable to neurological atypicalities. Clearly, the attribution of LD symptoms to a neurological origin represented a greater leap of faith when 94–142 was passed than it does today. While much remains to be explored, neuroscience has already shown us unequivocally that some types of learning disabilities have very specific neural signatures that can be observed with modern neuroimaging techniques such as fMRI (Shaywitz, 2003). It is only reasonable to assume that neuroscientific replication of these pivotal and illuminating research studies will eventually document the neural signatures of additional types of learning disabilities.

The language in PL 94–142 outlined a rather loose definition of LDs and, in doing so, failed to establish the manner in which LDs were to be operationally defined and diagnosed. The lack of specific inclusionary criteria in the definition of LD in PL 94–142 prompted the U.S. Department of Education in 1977 to make recommendations for a more specific manner of operationalizing the definition of LD. Its statement included explicit phrasing that described LD as "a severe discrepancy between achievement and intellectual ability in one or more areas . . . " According to Fletcher, Lyon, Fuchs, and Barnes (2007), this was supported by some then-current research by Rutter and Yule (1975) that appeared to validate the IQ-achievement discrepancy as a way of identifying LDs. The prevailing (and enduring) operational definition of LD thereafter emerged as one in which individuals acquired skills in one or more major academic skill domains (as measured by norm-referenced achievement tests) were "significantly lower than expected," or "discrepant," from their measured cognitive ability level (as estimated by individual measures of intelligence). While the research by Rutter and Yule that initially appeared to support the discrepancy model "has not stood up over time" (Fletcher, et al., 2002, p. 186) the discrepancy model remains, to this day, the most widely utilized method of defining LD.

PROBLEMS WITH THE DISCREPANCY MODEL

A variety of criticisms and concerns have been raised about the use of the discrepancy model over the years. These criticisms and concerns are many, and an exhaustive review of them is beyond the scope of this chapter. Instead, a brief review of the more frequently cited issues is offered. Perhaps most frequently mentioned is that the discrepancy model results in a wait-to-fail method of identifying LDs because many kids do not display a large enough discrepancy between IQ and achievement until the third grade or later (Mather & Goldstein, 2001). This is particularly problematic because this means that their eligibility for specially designed interventions typically occurs near the chronological end of a closing developmental window of opportunity (especially in reading skill development) for intensive efforts to sufficiently remediate learning problems (Shaywitz, 2003).

Another criticism of the discrepancy model is that it can actually discourage intervention in some ways. Specifically, intervention can backfire if it results in a temporary increase in an individual's score(s) on academic skill measures that causes the all-too-important discrepancy between IQ and achievement scores from being significant enough to qualify him or her for special education services. Such simple comparison of IQ and achievement scores from assessment may not reveal a significant discrepancy, and a simple numerical analysis of test scores ignores a consideration of the level of intensity of intervention that was required to yield the achievement test scores that was produced. By ignoring the intensity of the interventions involved in producing the achievement scores yielded by assessment and by measuring achievement with the notoriously limited samples of academic skills that are available on norm-referenced measures, it becomes increasingly likely that diagnosticians will make both false-positive and false-negative errors in identifying LD based upon the discrepancy model.

The discrepancy model has resulted in an overreliance upon an unempirically supported and arbitrarily selected set of discrepancy calculations that have been selected and applied with widely varying degrees of consistency and precision from school to school and even among educational diagnosticians within the same school (Mather & Goldstein, 2001). At various times and in various settings, both organizational policies and individual practitioner ideologies have dictated which discrepancy formulas have been used. Because of this variability, students could be considered eligible for special education in one school district and not in the next (Berninger & Holdnack, 2008).

Some practitioners have opted to use a simple difference method of establishing a threshold for the significance of discrepancy. In addition to insensitivity to the statistical imprecision of this technique, wide variations even within this practice have been noted in the number of points that practitioners considered to be significant. Most practitioners using this method selected a 15-point difference while others applied thresholds ranging from 10 or 12 points through as many as 25 points (Mather & Goldstein, 2001). Some practitioners have chosen to use a 1.5 standard deviation threshold that, on most IQ and achievement measures, equates to a more rare 22.5 standard score point difference. Others have attempted to utilize greater statistical precision and employ a predicted achievement method that takes into account the degree of measured correlation between the ability and achievement measures used and also corrects for statistical concerns such as regression to the mean (Sattler, 2008). Other practitioners, in complying with mandates for reevaluation, readministered IQ and achievement tests and terminated a student's previously established special education program when they failed to observe a significant discrepancy among the test scores acquired during reevaluation (thereby ignoring in such an approach a host of key considerations such as statistical regression to the mean, the potentially beneficial and intended influence of intervention on test performance, etc.).

Ultimately, operationalizing LDs as a significant discrepancy between IQ and achievement has led to an incredible amount of variability in the practice of identifying students with LDs. This variability appears massive enough even without considering additional sources of variance and error in scores due to how those scores were obtained. Examples include examiner deviation from standardized test administration procedures, variance introduced by selection of instruments of varying correlations with each other, and the difficult-to-quantify impact of nonneurostructural factors affecting examinee performance (such as variations in motivation, compliance with examination procedures, etc). According to Simpson and Buckhalt, "Though the formula method may have some appeal because it requires less clinical competence and judgment, the fact remains that reducing an important diagnostic decision to a mathematical equation gives a false sense of objectivity to a contrived procedure that is still essentially subjective" (1990, p. 197). It seems as though the price paid for the false sense of diagnostic precision and resultant false sense of security offered by the use of a discrepancy model is a history of LD identification that is, perhaps ironically so, marked by extreme variability. This widespread variability appears so substantial that a large portion of the body of research on LD and educational or treatment outcomes that has been conducted thus far might be considered to be of uncertain validity and therefore of limited utility. Specifically, this concern most clearly pertains to any research whose methodology involved aggregating the highly heterogeneous data that results from the assessment of LD individuals into group-level data consisting of multiple individuals diagnosed as LD. Any such approach "washes out" or homogenizes the clinically relevant heterogeneity in skill levels displayed by such individuals and therefore limits the ability of such research to draw accurate conclusions about such important issues as treatment or intervention outcomes.

THE RESPONSE-TO-INTERVENTION (RTI) APPROACH TO THE IDENTIFICATION OF LD

With the 2004 reauthorization of IDEA, states are no longer allowed to require school districts to consider a discrepancy between IQ and achievement as being a necessary condition to identify students as having a learning disability. IDEA 2004 established that individual states were allowed to opt-out of using a discrepancy model to identify learning disabilities, and to utilize a Response-to-Intervention (RTI) model. Now, instead of being confined to measuring a student's level of academic achievement and intelligence and then applying any number of formulas to determine if a significant discrepancy exists between ability and achievement in one or more areas, states are empowered with the ability to permit schools to employ an alternate method of diagnosing LD. This alternate approach consists of systematic progress-monitoring in an evidence-based core curriculum provided to all learners with increasingly intensive intervention processes and more frequent progress monitoring provided for students who do not show appropriate progress in skill development. This RTI model allows for students who do not respond adequately to evidence-based instructional practices and curricula to be considered eligible for special education services. Perhaps most importantly, this approach allows for earlier and more systematic intervention for struggling learners, and it promotes a data-driven process of instruction that is poised to potentially reduce the numbers of children who encountered learning difficulties as a result of poor instruction.

RTI is not new. Rather, it is the name of one specific model that can be used in an attempt to meet the legal requirement for prereferral intervention that has been a mandated component of the special education identification process since 1975, when PL 94–142 was passed. As such, prereferral intervention models with widely varying degrees of resemblance to RTI have been in use as schoolwide prevention programs within districts for several decades. What is new, however, is the explicit support in federal special education law specifically naming RTI as a viable alternative to less effective traditional models of determining student eligibility for special education services (Canter, 2006). Also new is a degree of apparent confusion about whether RTI may, in and of itself, be sufficient to warrant the educational diagnosis of LD. This would be in direct contradiction to the long-standing (and still-present) wording in IDEA that requires the LD diagnosis to be based on evidence of processing deficits; such deficits can only be documented through individual neurocognitive assessment, and without such assessment they can only be inferred (Reynolds, 2008).

RTI has enjoyed considerable support, especially from organizations such as the National Association of School Psychologists (NASP), because it circumvents many of the shortcomings of the traditional discrepancy model. Additionally, RTI emphasizes the use of evidence-based approaches to instruction that serve to reduce academic problems that result from deficient curricula and/or poor instructional methodologies rather than from neurologically based learning problems. In other words, RTI provides a framework for instruction and progress monitoring that encourages sound instructional practices for all students, not just those with disabilities. RTI also incorporates the well-established benefits of prereferral intervention strategies meant to ensure that, when poor student progress is observed, it is addressed as early as possible and through the least intrusive means possible.

Curriculum-based progress monitoring data is an extremely critical component of all RTI models because it forms the basis for educational programming decisions, not only for individual at-risk learners but also for the entire student population. Some low achieving students, (particularly those for whom a lack of early skill exposure, rather than an inherent learning disability, was the primary reason for observed skill delays) may eventually make appropriate progress without individualized or small-group interventions. Such students may simply require more time or a mild or temporary increase in instructional intensity, as opposed to special educational services and supports, in order to narrow the initial gap in skill development between their progress and that of students who are not considered to be at risk.

THE TIERED ASPECT OF RTI MODELS

RTI models specifically identify different levels or tiers of increasing intensity in instruction and related instructional supports. Various RTI models differ in the number of tiers that they include (usually three or four), but the first three tiers in nearly all RTI models are essentially the same. Tier 1 consists of evidence-based core curricula that are used for all students and typically consist of specific commercially available curricula in reading and math, which may or may not be from the same publisher.

Often, a writing curriculum is incorporated into the reading series as a language arts component.

Tier 1

In addition to providing evidence-based core curricula, Tier 1 is intended to incorporate evidence-based instructional methodologies that are not tied to specific curricula. Examples include instructional practices that have been concluded through a formidable body of research to constitute best practices in learning. Examples include high academic engaged time, high success rates, direct and supervised teaching, scaffolded instruction, differentiated instruction, opportunities for reteaching material, and strategic and explicit instruction (Ysseldyke & Christenson, 2002). Performance data is gathered via curriculum-based assessment and other evidence-based assessment (such as the DIBELS, etc.) at least three times per year in Tier 1 (usually in September, January, and April). This data not only allows for conclusions to be drawn regarding the efficacy of the core curriculum but also serves as a screener to identify students who are not making appropriate progress and may need more intensive intervention.

Some schools incorporate results from other forms of assessment, such as criterion-referenced statewide assessment tests, to provide additional analysis of the efficacy of their core curriculum and to help identify and guide any necessary changes to the core curricula. Changes to the core curriculum are generally advised when a larger than normal number (i.e., in excess of 20 percent) of students do not make appropriate academic progress from it alone. Individual student data is analyzed in each curricular area to determine which students should be considered at risk, and such students are provided with more intensive levels of intervention (Tier 2). Definitions of at risk vary among RTI models, but a commonly suggested criterion is a student who scores at or below the 10th percentile during a progress-monitoring assessment (McCook, 2006). District and class norms are generally preferable for these determinations, although such norms are often not available for many schools (particularly when they are just beginning to implement a systematic progress monitoring system). Tier 1 data is compiled, recorded, and analyzed by school system personnel in regular education, although it is clearly ideal to include special educators and school psychologists in the analysis of such data. The primary role or function of the school psychologist or special education team in this stage is essentially one of professional consultation. All progress-monitoring data should be interfaced with, and verified by, other sources of information that can additionally be indicative of at-risk status such as parent and teacher input and/or behavior ratings, grades, and disciplinary and attendance records (McCook, 2006).

TIER 2

Following the data collection application of Tier 1, students who are classified as at risk begin to receive increased instructional supports classified as Tier 2 supports, and they are monitored more frequently (every one to four weeks) with curriculum-based measures. These students are not labeled as having an educational disability that would warrant special education services; rather, they are deemed in need of additional instructional supports and assistance within the regular educational setting. Certainly, definitions of adequate and inadequate progress vary from school to school, although criteria have been suggested that involve students who are making less weekly progress (a lower skill growth rate) than 10 to 25 percent of their local grade peers.

Students who are identified as at risk due to low academic skills acquisition or poor progress after an initial six- to eight-week period in Tier 1 (general core curriculum instruction) are recommended for Tier 2 interventions. Tier 2 instruction is intended to accommodate approximately 20 to 30 percent of students who do not display sufficient skill development in an evidence-based core (Tier 1) curriculum. Note that any progress monitoring data that identifies more than approximately 30 percent of students as at risk should trigger an analysis of the core curriculum for appropriateness in areas such as content and pacing. Students who have not made sufficient progress in Tier 1 are judged to require supplementary supports and services in addition to the regular core curriculum. Screening measure data for such individuals should be analyzed in depth and choices made regarding the intensity, setting, and/or nature of the Tier 2 interventions that will be delivered. Tier 2 interventions are generally provided for a specified period of time in order to provide the opportunity for measuring student response to the increases in targeted skill instruction, support, and interventions that are delivered in this tier.

Tier 2 interventions typically involve an increase in direct instructional time in the specific area(s) of weakness identified by progress monitoring data. Most RTI models recommend that Tier 2 interventions entail an additional 30 minutes of direct small-group instruction and support in the academic domain and/or specific skills areas that are most critical to development of the identified skill deficits displayed by the student. Current literature in this area suggests that appropriate intervention durations of nine to twelve weeks are commonly recommended for Tier 2 interventions (Kovaleski & Prasse, 2004; McCook, 2006). Tier 2 interventions tend to be delivered by individuals other than the regular classroom teacher (such as a reading specialist) and are generally provided in small groups of three to five students having similar skill deficits (e.g. reading fluency). Students who respond well to Tier 2 interventions are those who close the achievement gap and progress to a point where they are substantially on grade level. Students who do not display sufficient progress through Tier 2 interventions are provided with an array of even more intensive intervention procedures referred to as Tier 3.

Tier 3

Students at Tier 3 in an RTI model receive even more direct and explicit instruction than is provided to students at Tiers 1 or 2. In some cases, scheduling changes are needed to allow for an even greater amount of direct instruction beyond that provided in Tier 1, and this ideally involves at least one-half hour more of daily direct instruction than in Tier 2. Furthermore, these scheduling changes may require the sacrifice of nonacademic classes (such as art, music, gym, etc.) in order to allow ample time for instruction within one or more research-supported programs of remedial instruction. Tiers 2 and 3 generally make use of similar evidence-based intervention programs; however, the intensity and duration of instruction within these programs is greater in Tier 3 (McCook, 2006). Progress monitoring requirements become even more intensive at Tier 3 with recommended measurement of progress occurring a minimum of one to two times per week.

Educators must be aware that a lack of sufficient response to Tier 3 interventions does not automatically indicate eligibility for special education services as a student with LD, but it does suggest that a disability may exist. Thus, nonresponders to Tier 3 interventions could be interpreted legally as "thought to be exceptional," which would therefore entitle them to the rights and protections under IDEA. This can potentially be problematic from the perspective that, under IDEA, once a student is considered thought to be exceptional, schools have only a limited amount of time within which to gather any additional data necessary and arrive at a decision regarding the student's eligibility for special education services. Especially in the integrated model of RTI proposed in the last section of this chapter, this should not pose a problem as all data necessary for this eligibility determination is gathered by the time a student is demonstrating failure to respond to Tier 3 interventions.

In an RTI-only model of LD identification that does not provide for assessment other than with standard progress monitoring measures, it is conceivable that a student may progress to the status of Tier 3 failure (to respond to intervention) because important neurocognitive or other vital barriers to learning were not identified early enough in the process (if at all) to allow for consideration of such barriers when selecting or implementing interventions. In an RTI-only model with no comprehensive assessment even after Tier 3, such learning constraints may never be identified. Conversely, in an RTI model that provides for comprehensive assessment after failure to RTI at the level of Tier 3, at least there remains a chance (albeit late) for the process to unveil critical barriers to learning and responding to interventions so that they may be addressed.

While many RTI models specify only three tiers, the outcome of Tier 3 interventions is treated similarly regardless of whether a fourth tier is referenced. Students who either fail to respond sufficiently to Tier 3, or those who do demonstrate adequate response but remain dependent upon the high levels of support in Tier 3 for adequate skill growth to continue may be considered potentially eligible for special education services due to a learning disability (provided there is also other data to suggest that the students meet the required inclusionary component of the LD definition (that they display evidence of a processing disorder) and that they did not fail to benefit from RTI due to any of the exclusionary criteria specified in the LD definition (sensory impairments, health factors, cultural factors, etc.).

TIER 4

When specifically named as one of the tiers in an RTI model, Tier 4 is generally regarded as the stage at which a comprehensive multidisciplinary evaluation (MDE) is conducted to determine a student's potential eligibility for special education services. As stated earlier, this evaluation must include a comprehensive review of all possible barriers to learning and intervention response. In RTI models that specify only three tiers, MDE is indicated in lieu of a fourth tier as "what occurs after insufficient response to Tier 3." It is important to emphasize here that a student's lack of response to specific intervention(s) in and of itself is not a legally sufficient procedure or criterion for determination of a student's eligibility or need for special education services (Hale, Kaufman, Naglieri, & Kavale, 2006; Reynolds, 2008). School teams must still conduct relevant and thorough evaluations of students in all areas of suspected disability before determining eligibility for special education services. However, this does not mean that school psychologists should simply revert back to administering individual IQ and achievement tests and then utilize the discrepancy model to confirm the presence of a learning disability. As proposed later in this chapter, a better use of the skills and time of school psychologists would be to conduct a targeted assessment to identify as many sources of possible barriers to a student's ability to learn and respond to interventions before attempting to select, implement, and monitor responses to interventions. Indeed, targeted assessment could help to boost the efficacy of the RTI model by increasing the chance that interventions attempted at Tiers 2 and 3 might, in fact, be the *right* interventions for each student based upon his or her unique neurocognitive profile.

PITFALLS OF THE RTI MODEL

Citing an inability to link results meaningfully to intervention, some proponents of an RTI-only model of LD identification have proposed the elimi-
nation of intelligence testing altogether for LD identification (Reschly, 2005).
This would substantially decrease the ability to detect features of students'
neurocognitive profiles that could impact their ability to respond to a set of
interventions. As well, this omission would also curtail the ability to identify
additional disabilities and/or other educationally relevant weaknesses that
might serve as primary or additive barriers to students' abilities to respond to
otherwise appropriate intervention(s). For example, we know that a substantial number of learning-disabled individuals also display features of ADHD
and executive function deficits and that estimates of the comorbidity of
ADHD and LDs vary widely (from 10 to 92 percent) "most likely (as) a
result of inconsistencies in the criteria used to define LD in different studies"
(Fletcher et al., 2007, p. 266). Research in this area suggests that the actual comorbidity of ADHD and LDs in reading or math likely varies between 17 and
43 percent (Semrud-Clikeman et al., 1992). This should come as no surprise
given what we have learned through neuroscience about the underlying
neurobiology of reading disorders, which, among other areas, involves
atypical neural functioning in the brain areas responsible for controlling
attention and executive functions.

The elegant and groundbreaking fMRI research of Shaywitz (2003) and her
colleagues has documented aberrant frontal lobe activation patterns in
dyslexic individuals. With ADHD known to be closely tied to abnormal
functioning of the frontal lobes and prefrontal cortex, it should also be of little
surprise, then, that Hynd and colleagues (1991) found evidence of a commonality between many individuals with ADHD and individuals with
reading and math LDs. They found that children with ADHD without
hyperactivity displayed significantly lower performance on rapid naming
measures than children diagnosed as ADHD with hyperactivity. Deficits on
rapid naming measures have been shown to be one of the strongest early
predictors of reading disorders (Shaywitz, 2003; Wolf & Bowers, 1999). Hynd
and his colleagues found that 60 percent of the children with ADHD (without
hyperactivity) had a codiagnosis of a developmental reading or arithmetic
disorder, whereas none of the children with ADHD (with hyperactivity)
carried such a diagnosis (Hynd et al.).

As already discussed, deficits in rapid naming have long been known to be
a cardinal feature of reading disorders. But, because this deficit can also be a
distinct indicator of other deficits (such as language, memory, etc) that may
constitute an entirely different set of barriers to learning (Fletcher et al., 2007),
this empirically proven predictor of reading disorders provides just one of

a wide variety of processing disorder symptoms that requires further specialized assessment before intervention(s) can be accurately prescribed (Feifer & Della Toffalo, 2007). Clearly, any intervention(s) prescribed solely to address just one aspect of deficit runs the risk of lower efficacy. By ignoring the very real likelihood that a reading problem, for example, coexists with other neurologically based processing deficits, educators will substantially limit their ability to select and/or design interventions that account for the actual deficits and therefore have the greatest possible chance of meaningful educational impact.

The systematic instruction and progress monitoring components of the RTI model are clearly necessary, but not sufficient, as an approach to identifying LDs because they do not take into account the highly heterogeneous nature of LDs. Employing standard protocol interventions with fidelity in a lock-step fashion may work for the majority of learners who are not truly learning disabled (but who might have otherwise appeared LD in the absence of systematic evidence-based instruction and accountability through progress monitoring). However, standard protocol interventions provided in a lock-step fashion will not address at least a portion of the learning barriers that exist for individuals with neurologically based LDs. This suggests that educators who promote RTI alone as a cure for the wait-to-fail risks of the discrepancy model method of LD identification have traded one problematic model for another that uses systematic progress monitoring to "watch them fail" (Reynolds, 2008, p. 18).

An important conclusion to be emphasized from the previous paragraphs is that many disorders of learning, behavior, and emotion share a common underlying neurobiology that must be understood to the greatest degree possible when attempting to design or evaluate a program of individualized interventions for students (Fletcher et al., 2007). ADHD, as discussed earlier, is merely one example among many disorders that are correlated with underlying cognitive profiles that can impact the likelihood that an individual will respond to standard protocol interventions. Some other disorders, such as Asperger's syndrome, consist of highly unique and clearly educationally relevant cognitive profiles that might actually prevent students with this disability from being recognized as at-risk through standard progress monitoring methods. Specifically, some individuals with Asperger's are hyperlexic (which is an almost uncanny ability to read words with correct pronunciation at a very high rate of speed despite having other significant neurocognitive limitations). Therefore, such individuals would not likely be identified as at-risk by analysis of progress monitoring data on skills such as word identification. Table 8.1 lists a variety of disorders or conditions that are often associated with highly unique sets of learning assets and deficits that are likely to be extremely challenging for RTI models to address without the

Table 8.1

Disorders Often Involving LD for Whom RTI Alone May Not Be Successful

- Autism Spectrum Disorders (especially Asperger's Syndrome)
- Tourette's Syndrome
- OCD and other anxiety-related conditions
- Seizure Disorders
- Medical Disorders (diabetes, cancer, etc.)
- Fetal Alcohol Syndrome
- Lead Poisoning
- Traumatic Brain Injuries
- Low Incidence Disorders (metabolic, genetic, and neurodevelopmental syndromes such as hydrocephalus, callosal agenesis, tuberous sclerosis, etc.)
- Emotional disturbance

benefit of data from cognitive neuropsychological assessment to guide intervention design and implementation.

The more that we learn from neuroscience about functional cortical organization and the complex interplay of neural networks in both normal and learning-disabled individuals, the less appropriate the word *comorbid* appears. This term implies that two or more separate conditions or distinct disorders coexist when, in reality, many seemingly distinct disorders or sets of symptoms can be attributed to the same common underlying neurological dysfunction. Without a full appreciation (through targeted assessment) of the many potentially coexisting and interrelated cognitive barriers to learning, standard protocol interventions are less likely to be effective, and the responses to such interventions are more likely to yield an inappropriate or incomplete conclusion if employed as a method of LD diagnosis. Without carefully selected assessment techniques to determine the presence or absence of comorbid conditions described as one of the "major sources of heterogeneity in learning disabilities" (Fletcher et al., 2007, p. 266), interventions will be weaker, outcomes will look less promising, and otherwise beneficial interventions may appear deceivingly useless.

THE OPPORTUNITY FOR A BETTER MODEL OF LD IDENTIFICATION

One interpretation of IDEA 2004 is that school psychologists and educational diagnosticians have finally been liberated from a tireless obligation to obtain a full-scale IQ and administer most or all subtests of an achievement test for every special education eligibility evaluation involving suspected LD. Practitioners are now legally permitted to employ a process of disability prevention, identification, and intervention that is structured in a way to have a more selective, efficient, and targeted assessment, thereby allowing the referral question(s) and hypotheses formed during assessment to flexibly guide the selection of assessment instruments. The goals of such assessment are to find out (1) why the student is struggling to acquire skills and (2) which intervention methods are most likely to reduce or eliminate those struggles and remediate learning problems.

The search for answers to these questions demands that we acquire data about the integrity of the core cognitive constructs that may contribute to, or be responsible for, the student's area of learning difficulties (Hale et al., 2006). To accomplish this, the underlying neurocognitive processes responsible for processing information in the academic area(s) of struggle need to be isolated, measured, and analyzed to determine why a student is not, or has not been, responding to evidence-based core instruction and interventions. This also should be accomplished in part by the systematic progress monitoring that is a clear strength of RTI models. This also can, and should, be augmented by data from cognitive neuropsychological assessment for a portion of at-risk individuals who display evidence of learning constraints beyond that of merely slower academic skill acquisition. In order to fuse the benefits of RTI and an assessment model of LD identification, it is vital to realize that *cognitive neuropsychological assessment can occur at any point in a prereferral intervention process* and does not always need to be (nor should it be) deferred until the final tier (Della Toffalo, 2006; Hale et al., 2006). If such assessment was restricted to the final tier, then RTI would run the risk of imposing yet another wait-to-fail process not unlike the one that has plagued the discrepancy model paradigm (Della Toffalo, 2006). Or, perhaps more accurately stated, the emphasis of RTI on increasingly intensive progress monitoring would likely allow such delayed assessment to turn the RTI model into a "watch-them-fail" process (Reynolds, 2008, p. 18).

Most important, the assessment process should yield information that can be used to help determine the type(s) of intervention(s) to which the student may be more responsive. This is critical regardless of whether the student eventually goes on to receive special education services. If special education services are needed, then data from the assessment process will be useful in designing interventions as well as identifying necessary disability-related supports, services, and accommodations. However, the hope is that targeted assessment during the prereferral intervention process may yield clues to selecting interventions that the at-risk student can respond to, thereby ultimately preventing the need for special education services. This is the defining characteristic of the model referred to in the remainder of this chapter as an integrated model or RTRI.

Such an integrated model is not without challenges. Proponents of an RTI-only model of identifying LD have suggested that the attempt to use assessment to individualize interventions endeavor is akin to an approach that has been referred to in the literature as Aptitude-Treatment Interaction (ATI)

(Hale & Fiorello, 2004; Reschly, 2005). The rather young field of school neuropsychology has been plagued by this aging ghost of a small but clearly influential corpus of literature pertaining to ATI. Various groups of individuals have, over time, quoted several rather old but seminal articles by Cronbach (1957, 1975), who denounced the practice of using assessment to identify aptitudes (cognitive or academic strengths) for the purpose of designing treatments or interventions to address educational weaknesses or deficits. From his review of research on the efficacy of such practices that began over fifty years ago, Cronbach concluded that the assessment of aptitudes did not consistently lead to the ability to design better treatments or instructional methods.

The applicability of Cronbach's conclusions to modern cognitive neuropsychological research is limited at best (Hale et al., 2006). The research that he reviewed to arrive at his conclusions employed a wide variety of methods for defining aptitudes based upon assessment data. Those methods that did involve norm-referenced standardized measures were based upon assessment instruments that had little to no resemblance to the much better-normed, more precise (factorially pure), and neuroscientifically based and validated neuropsychological measures that are widely available today, especially within the past decade (Hale et al., 2006).

Proponents of an RTI-only model of identifying LDs represent yet another group of individuals who have found it convenient to cite Cronbach. Some such individuals take it a bit further by arguing that Cronbach's (aged) conclusions, along with the myriad shortcomings of the discrepancy model of LD identification, mean that cognitive assessment is irrelevant for the purpose of identifying individuals with LD. This extremist perspective is legally problematic in that it ignores the continued presence in the LD definition of a statement indicating that evidence of an information-processing deficit, from more than one source of data, must be established in order to conclude that a LD exists (Reynolds, 2008). This perspective is also conceptually flawed in that it ignores decades of burgeoning evidence from the field of neuroscience that has clearly demonstrated some directly observable profiles of neurocognitive functioning that often correspond to LDs and can be predicted rather consistently by the judicious use of data from intelligence, achievement, and information-processing measures (Elliott, 2008). Being judicious about the use of such assessment data means simply not being content to restrict the use of such data to interpreting global metrics of g, such as full-scale IQs (Hale et al., 2006).

An RTI-only approach to LD identification represents a step in the wrong direction by ignoring the countless contributions from neuroscience that have told us so much more about the complexity of learning disabilities. Initial attempts to define LDs were, due to still unresolved disagreement regarding the exact nature of LDs, based upon a default position of inference. In the absence of more definitive knowledge about the nature of LDs, the eligibility criteria for LDs were written in an intentionally vague manner to allow LDs to be concluded inferentially on the basis of exclusionary criteria—on "what a learning disability is not rather than what it is" (Berninger & Holdnack, 2008, p. 66). Advances in neuroscience have, at last, begun to firmly place practitioners at the point where we can now begin to focus more on inclusionary criteria that relies more heavily upon neuroscientific data about what LDs *are* more so than what they *are not* (Reynolds, 2008). An RTI-only model of LD identification would return our field to a position of diagnosing LD by default based solely upon exclusionary data.

Consider the hypothetical example of a third-grade student reading at just 18 words per minute who displays an insufficient increase in reading fluency through Tier 2 interventions. Suppose that observations and teacher input revealed that the student was also manifesting attention problems in the classroom, struggling with written language skills, displaying difficulty with the rapid and automatic retrieval of math facts, and demonstrating both expressive and receptive language difficulties. Due to the potential for any one of these symptoms to represent evidence of one or more neurocognitive deficits that might reduce or prevent responsiveness to interventions, targeted assessment would clearly be warranted prior to advancing the student to the next tier or attempting any further interventions in Tier 2. The goal of this targeted assessment would be to use a variety of data and tools, including cognitive neuropsychological measures, to ascertain the full extent and nature of this student's additional difficulties in order to determine the full range and scope of interventions needed in order to address the variety of difficulties (above and beyond reading fluency) that the student is displaying. Without such data from targeted assessment conducted as an integrated RTI model, there would be very little data for the purpose of identifying and reducing as many barriers as possible for this student. In an RTI-only model, this student would simply be moved into a Tier 3 level intervention to receive a greater intensity of intervention(s) likely including variants of some that had not worked thus far. Given that such interventions would likely have been restricted to those of a standard protocol nature, they would almost certainly have proven insufficient by not accounting for the additional aspects of learning constraints beyond that of the student's reading problems.

In recognizing the critical shortcomings of using either an RTI-only model or an assessment-only approach, multiple individuals of prominence in the RTI movement have advocated for a more balanced approach to RTI that includes the respective benefits from each approach. Examples include Hale and Fiorello's (2004) Concordance-Discordance Model, the Dual-Discrepancy Model advocated by Kovaleski and Prasse (2004), and the 4 Factor Model of

LD Identification (Feifer & Della Toffalo, 2007). While the names and assorted elements of these models vary, each of these models advocates for the same basic principles, specifically, these principles being that in order to identify a learning disability, academic deficits should be evidence based on progress monitoring data that corresponds to (concordant with) deficits in cognitive processing and that academic deficits do not correspond to (discordant with) processing strengths.

INTRODUCTION TO A RESPONSE TO THE RIGHT INTERVENTION (RTRI) MODEL

It is important to recognize that many disorders stem from underlying neurological abnormalities that often include learning difficulties, and many of these will be rather challenging for any RTI model to address without the benefit of data from concurrent neurocognitive assessment. Attempting to address the unique constellation of deficits presented by such disabilities with a pure RTI framework would likely yield another wait-to-fail scenario unless incorporated within a framework that includes cognitive neuropsychological assessment as part of the problem-solving process. Many disabilities encountered in the school setting result in highly unique sets of cognitive and learning characteristics, and many of the standard protocol interventions that are successful for most struggling learners may be insufficient to address the needs of these more unique learners. When an RTI process is implemented for identifying and intervening with struggling learners, it is imperative that schools use all available tools to ensure that they are using data to identify and employ interventions that have a reasonable chance of being successful for at-risk learners. Ultimately, it will be anathema to the fundamental goals of the RTI process to risk imposing a wait-to-fail scenario by engaging a student in a lock-step process of standard protocol interventions when there is reason to believe that such interventions are not likely to meet the full scope of his or her needs. Knowledge of an existing diagnosis of a psychiatric disorder or observations of notably unique learner characteristics by the teacher and/ or intervention team members are examples of the type of information that could form the basis of a reason to believe (data or information to suggest) that standard protocol interventions may not be sufficient. Instead, an RTI model integrated with a cognitive neuropsychological assessment can offer targeted assessment early in the RTI process in order to help determine the types of interventions that are most likely to assist unique learners. Perhaps, then, the true emphasis of this integrated model is RT<u>RI</u> (Response <u>T</u>o the <u>R</u>IGHT <u>I</u>ntervention).

Simply stated, the RTRI model proposed by this author involves the combination of RTI as a method of prevention and systematic progress monitoring integrated with the process of cognitive neuropsychological assessment employed at any of the tiers necessary and in a fashion consistent with that of the problem-solving model of assessment. The distinguishing characteristic of an RTRI model is the assertion that educationally relevant cognitive neuropsychological assessment (hereafter referred to as school neuropsychological assessment) can and should occur at any time (any tier) in the RTI process when an intervention team has good reason to believe that standard protocol interventions may not be adequate to address the needs of an at-risk student.

THE PROCESS OF SCHOOL NEUROPSYCHOLOGICAL ASSESSMENT

A pragmatic approach to educationally relevant cognitive neuropsychological or school neuropsychological assessment has been proposed by Hale and Fiorello (2004) in their Cognitive Hypothesis Testing (CHT) model. In this model, all available sources of information regarding a child's functioning are brought together to form specific hypotheses about the potential source(s) of constraint(s) upon academic performance. In an integrated (RTRI) model, this information is gathered as part of the data analysis teaming process during which both group and individual data are analyzed to make inter- or intratier movement recommendations. Each hypothesis is then tested through a combination of assessment techniques and instruments selected to specifically explore cognitive factors that may potentially be hindering the learning process of an at-risk student. For example, if a student who has been identified as at risk by the RTI process additionally displayed difficulty in following verbal directions in the classroom, then a task analysis is conducted to develop an inventory of the neurocognitive skills that are required by the tasks on which the student performed poorly. With joint consideration of the tasks on which, or situations in which, the student performed adequately or better, a list of hypotheses is then generated that includes all conceivable skill deficits that could be responsible for observed difficulties. In the aforementioned example dealing with following directions, the skills identified for exploration through CHT assessment would include neurocognitive constructs such as auditory perception and discrimination, receptive language, sustained auditory attention, and executive functioning skills, including working memory.

Each hypothesis is then explored through a combination of four primary data collection techniques. The first includes a formal assessment of the particular construct(s) in question. For instance, subtests such as Auditory Attention and Response Set from the NEPSY-II (Korkman, Kirk, & Kemp, 2007) and Understanding Directions from the WJ-III NU—Tests of Cognitive Abilities (Woodcock, McGrew, & Mather, 2001) may be administered to assess sustained attention to auditory stimuli and various relevant aspects of executive functions including working memory. Second, qualitative information is gathered through observations that include not only the classroom or other relevant school settings but also by observing *how* a student performed on a given set of assessment tasks. For instance, perhaps this hypothetical student made many errors of commission, especially during part B of the NEPSY Auditory Response Set, thus implying that the student has difficulty inhibiting cognitive impulses. This might then result in further hypothesis generation and/or revision thereby creating the need for further hypothesis testing, such as by administering the D-KEFS Color-Word Interference subtest (Delis, Kaplan, & Kramer, 2001) or the *Conners' Continuous Performance Test, 2nd Edition* (CPT-2; Conners, 2000) to see if the observed difficulty in inhibiting cognitive impulses is limited to tasks involving auditory stimuli or if it is a broader deficit (because neither the CPT-2 or Color-Word Interference involve auditorily presented stimuli). Third, data is collected through teacher- and parent-completed checklists, rating scales, and observations. This can be helpful in determining the frequency and types of classroom situations where learning problems and/or behaviors of concern occur most often (and sometimes more importantly where they DO NOT occur). Last, nonnormative data including teacher observations, work samples, grades, and task analysis of actual classroom performance is gathered and examined. Each of these four data collection techniques must occur simultaneously as each provides data that are interdependent upon one another to form, explore, and refine cognitive hypotheses.

Thorough evaluation of a child's specific neurocognitive skill set typically requires the use of specialized assessment techniques and tools selected to permit exploration of hypotheses and to generate further hypotheses, which then require further assessment. Such endeavors require more than simple lock-step administration of common intelligence tests or achievement measures because such measures involve assessment tasks that are too "factorially complex." That is, the typical subtests on common IQ and achievement tests often require a wide variety of neurocognitive skills in order to successfully complete the task. Consequently, when trying to determine the factors that influenced a student's performance on a particular task, there may be too many factors (neurocognitive skills) to consider. For example, if a student performs poorly on the Digit Span subtest from the WISC-IV (Wechsler, 2003), there would be a vast set of possible deficits to explore in order to isolate the cognitive factor(s) responsible for this observed poor performance. Examples would include auditory acuity deficits, auditory-processing problems, poor attention, poor working memory, limited understanding of the test directions due to language deficits, or even non-neurocognitive factors such as low motivation or test anxiety.

The goal of school-based cognitive neuropsychological assessment is to determine what underlying factors are responsible for hindering learning, test performance, and classroom performance. Therefore, if a student displays difficulty with following verbal directions in class or on an assessment, then the prudent practitioner must explore an array of underlying factors in an attempt to understand the cause of this weakness. Further testing of multiple cognitive constructs needs to be conducted, in a fashion that is well represented by the Cognitive Hypothesis Testing (CHT) model, in order to begin ruling in and ruling out potential source(s) of neurocognitive difficulty responsible for the observed poor test performance. In this example, if the student performs well on individually administered tests of following verbal directions, then hypotheses about the reason for the student's difficulty in displaying this skill in the classroom setting would begin to focus less on factors such as auditory perception and receptive language deficits and shift focus toward assessing factors such as attention. If the student also performs well on multiple measures of various aspects of attention, then analysis and hypothesis testing would begin to focus more on extrinsic factors such as motivation and emotional functioning. It is important to recall that, as stated earlier, this process of CHT is not restricted solely to the use of standardized test components or batteries. Rather, the task analysis required for CHT can be performed on nearly any formal or informal assessment administered to a student (Hale & Fiorello, 2004). This includes homework, classroom-based tests, standardized group achievement tests, curriculum-based measures, and so forth.

Table 8.1 includes a variety of disabilities whose manifestations often include learning difficulties that will likely require targeted assessment very early in the RTI process in order to design more individualized interventions to which a student's response would need to be monitored. Students with these types of disabilities typically display cognitive profiles notable for significant variability and generally include unique profiles of strengths and weaknesses in processing different types of information. To expound upon a previous example, many students with Asperger's syndrome tend to display hyperlexia. For these students, curriculum-based measures of reading skills commonly yield little to no information regarding their learning difficulties, since these students typically struggle with comprehension rather than decoding or fluency. In fact, many of the progress monitoring measures used for reading skills in an RTI framework would be likely to miss their specific type of reading problems (which, in the area of reading skills, are most commonly in the area of comprehension deficits due to difficulties with the semantic and pragmatic qualities of language that are often an integral part of such disorders on the autism spectrum). These difficulties certainly have educational implications that are far more pervasive than simply one aspect of reading problems.

Many students with Asperger's syndrome also display a rather unique profile of cognitive strengths and weaknesses associated with right hemispheric dysfunction, and this type of learning profile has been thoroughly described in the literature as Nonverbal Learning Disability Syndrome (Rourke, van der Vlugt, & Rourke, 2002). This syndrome generally consists of cognitive features such as markedly stronger verbal skills than nonverbal reasoning skills, poor gross and fine motor coordination, difficulties learning new information and recognizing its applicability to previously learned information, social skill deficits related to difficulties in understanding the perspective of others and understanding nonverbal social cues such as facial expressions and body postures, and impaired ability to engage in novel reasoning (Rourke et al., 2002). Of further interest, the syndrome of Nonverbal Learning Disability (NLD) has been described by Rourke (1995) as a "final common pathway" for many other disorders—meaning that the unique cognitive profile characterized by this label often results from a wide variety of genetic, metabolic, acquired, and neurodevelopmental disorders. Examples include but are not limited to: Sotos syndrome, Williams syndrome, Callosal Agenesis, Early Hydrocephalus, Noonan's syndrome, Fetal Alcohol Syndrome, Multiple Sclerosis, Turner syndrome, Congenital Hypothyroidism, and Traumatic Brain Injury (Rourke, 1995).

Conditions involving seizures, exposure to ingested or environmental toxins, and traumatic brain injuries also result in highly individualized profiles of cognitive deficits that are inherently unpredictable in nature and often dynamic in their course. While individuals with these types of conditions often display symptoms that overlap with those of LDs, they often require highly individualized approaches to instruction in order to learn new information or skills, frequently need assistance relating new skills or information to previously acquired skills and often require support to retrieve and/or demonstrate previously acquired knowledge (Della Toffalo, 2006). Fortunately, students who manifest these types of disorders constitute a relatively small percentage of children; however, they are at great risk for having their educational needs neglected if not provided with an appropriate assessment detailing their unique needs as a first step toward meeting them. Clearly, an inflexible implementation of RTI in which students progressed through each of the tiers in lock-step fashion *before* being comprehensively assessed would almost certainly result in a wait-to-fail scenario for such students. Even worse, such students are at risk for having their unique educational needs go undetected by the measures used for Tier 1 school-wide screenings, which, at present, are heavily biased toward reading skills.

Make no mistake, this hybrid or integrated model of identifying (and serving) students with LDs does not arrive prepackaged along with dozens of studies touting its "scientific validation." However, it is *evidence-based* because it emanates from the marriage of a collective body of knowledge that has been acquired through research in the fields of neuroscience, pedagogy, assessment, and intervention. The process advocated by this hybrid model is one that requires a type of validation that has yet to be well documented because it cannot be appropriately represented by the types of research methods traditionally used to measure LD outcomes (assigning multiple individuals to treatment groups, delivering a treatment or intervention, and then examining group means to determine outcome). The heterogeneity of learning disabilities renders this research methodology weak at best for the purpose of measuring the efficacy of the integrated RTRI model proposed in this chapter. At minimum, any attempts to conduct intervention outcomes research with this specific model will require more rigor than has historically been employed. Examples include more careful control over the heterogeneity of the individuals grouped together as a treatment group (beginning with increased consistency in the criteria used to diagnose individuals as learning disabled), improved control over other factors both within and external to the student (such as psychiatric disorders, SES, etc.), and improved attention paid to measuring the fidelity with which the interventions are delivered. It is worth noting here that such improved controls in outcomes research, especially for the within-student variables that need controlled for, will require the prudent use of specialized diagnostic assessment instruments, such as modern neuropsychological and information-processing measures. Some researchers even contend that outcomes research, especially of the aforementioned integrated model of LD identification, will require research of single-subject design (Feifer & Della Toffalo, 2007; Hale et al., 2006). A corpus of such research will likely be built slowly, but nevertheless, it shall be built. This integrated model then arrives to you with a call to duty—the duty of the scientist practitioner to engage simultaneously in both practice and research calculated to evaluate current practice in order to guide future practice.

SUMMARY

The field of school psychology has changed substantially since the term learning disability was first described by Samuel Kirk (1963). Our scientifically based understanding of brain–behavior relationships is stronger than ever before, and our assessment technology has advanced rapidly to reflect this progress. However, school psychologists are faced with a reactionary movement in educational practice that threatens to ignore such advances and attempts to discredit psychometric assessment as a foundation for disability identification and intervention. It is vital for school psychologists to seek out and acquire advanced training in cognitive neuropsychological assessment methodology in order to integrate assessment-for-intervention into their practice of identifying and intervening with students. It has become abundantly clear that to choose either a pure RTI model or a pure psychometric model for identifying and intervening with learning problems will only serve to perpetuate historically problematic practices and/or create new shortcomings. A marriage of these two approaches, greater than the sum of their collective parts, will be essential in order to ensure that no child is left behind. Suffice it to say, anything less may very well constitute educational malpractice.

REFERENCES

Berninger, V. W., & Holdnack, J. A. (2008). Nature-nurture perspectives in diagnosing and treating learning disabilities: Response to questions begging answers that see the forest and the tress. In E. Fletcher-Janzen & C.R. Reynolds (Eds.), *Neuropsychological perspectives on learning disabilities in the era of RTI* (pp. 66–81). Hoboken, NJ: John Wiley & Sons.

Canter, A. (2006, February). Problem solving and RTI: New roles for school psychologists. *Communiqué, 34*(5), insert. Available: http://www.nasponline.org/advocacy/rtifactsheets.aspx

Conners, C. K. (2000). *Continuous Performance Test II*. Toronto: Multi-Health Systems.

Cronbach, L. J. (1957). The two disciplines of scientific psychology. *American Psychologist, 12,* 671–684.

Cronbach, L. J. (1975). Beyond the two disciplines of scientific psychology. *American Psychologist, 30,* 671–684.

Delis, D., Kaplan, E., & Kramer, J. H. (2001). *Delis-Kaplan Executive Function System examiner's manual*. San Antonio, TX: The Psychological Corporation.

Della Toffalo, D. A. (2006, October 18). *Neuropsychology and RTI: The odd couple?* Workshop presented at the Annual Fall Conference of the Association of School Psychologists of Pennsylvania, State College, PA.

Elliott, C. D. (2008). Identifying a learning disability: Not just product, but process. In E. Fletcher-Janzen & C. R. Reynolds (Eds.), *Neuropsychological perspectives on learning disabilities in the era of RTI* (pp. 210–218). Hoboken, NJ: John Wiley & Sons.

Feifer, S. G., & Della Toffalo, D. A. (2007). *Integrating RTI with cognitive neuropsychology: A scientific approach to reading*. Middletown, MD: School Neuropsych Press.

Fletcher, J. M., Lyon, G. R., Barnes, M., Stuebing, K. K., Francis, D. J., Olson, R. et al. (2002). Classification of learning disabilities: An evidence-based evaluation. In R. Bradley, L. Danielson, & D. P. Hallahan (Eds.), *Identification of learning disabilities: Research to practice* (pp. 185–250). Mahwah, NJ: Erlbaum.

Fletcher, J. M., Lyon, G. R., Fuchs, L. S., & Barnes, M. A. (2007). *Learning disabilities: From identification to intervention.* New York: Guilford.

Hale, J. B., & Fiorello, C. A. (2004). *School neuropsychology: A practitioner's handbook.* New York: Guilford.

Hale, J. B., Kaufman, A., Naglieri, J. A., & Kavale, K. A. (2006). Implementation of IDEA: Integrating response to intervention and cognitive assessment methods. *Psychology in the Schools, 43,* 753–770.

Hynd, G. W., Lorys, A. R., Semrud-Clikeman, M., Nieves, N., Huettner, M. I. S., & Lahey, B. B. (1991). Attention deficit disorder without hyperactivity: A distinct behavioral and neurocognitive syndrome. *Journal of Child Neurology, 6*(Suppl.), S35–S41.

Individuals with Disabilities Education Improvement Act of 2004. (PL No. 108–446, 20 USC 1400).

Kirk, S. A. (1963). Behavioral diagnosis and remediation of learning disabilities. *Conference on exploring problems of the perceptually handicapped child, 1,* 1–23.

Korkman, M., Kirk, U., & Kemp, S. (2007). *NEPSY-II: A developmental neuropsychological assessment.* San Antonio, TX: The Psychological Corporation.

Kovaleski, J. F., & Prasse, D. P. (2004). Response to instruction in the identification of learning disabilities: A guide for school teams. *Communiqué, 32*(5) insert.

Mather, N., & Goldstein, S. (2001). *Learning disabilities and challenging behaviors: A guide to intervention and classroom management.* Baltimore, MD: Paul H. Brookes.

McCook, J. E. (2006). *The RTI guide: Developing and implementing a model in your schools.* Horsham, PA: LRP Publications.

Reschly, D. (2005, August). *RTI paradigm shift and the future of SLD diagnosis and treatment.* Paper presented to the Annual Institute for Psychology in the Schools of the American Psychological Association, Washington, DC.

Reynolds, C. R. (2008). RTI, neuroscience, and sense: Chaos in the diagnosis and treatment of learning disabilities. In E. Fletcher-Janzen & C. R. Reynolds (Eds.), *Neuropsychological perspectives on learning disabilities in the era of RTI* (pp. 14–27). Hoboken, NJ: John Wiley & Sons.

Rourke, B. P. (1995). *Syndrome of nonverbal learning disabilities: Neurodevelopmental manifestations.* New York: Guilford.

Rourke, B. P., van der Vlugt, H., & Rourke, S. B. (2002). *Practice of child clinical neuropsychology; An introduction.* The Netherlands: Swets & Zeitlinger.

Rutter, M., & Yule, W. (1975). The concept of specific reading retardation. *Journal of Child Psychology and Psychiatry, 16,* 181–197.

Sattler, J. M. (2008). *Assessment of children: Cognitive foundations.* La Mesa, CA: Jerome M. Sattler.

Semrud-Clikeman, M., Biederman, J., Sprich-Buckminster, S., Lehman, B. K., Faraone, S. V., & Norman, D. (1992). Comorbidity between ADDH and learning disability: A review and report in a clinically referred sample. *Journal of the American Academy of Child and Adolescent Psychiatry, 31,* 439–448.

Shaywitz, S. (2003). *Overcoming dyslexia: A new and complete science-based program for reading problems at any level.* New York: Alfred A. Knopf.

Simpson, R. G., & Buckhalt, J. A. (1990). A non-formula discrepancy model to identify learning disabilities. *School Psychology International, 11,* 273–279.

Wechsler, D. (2003). *Wechsler Intelligence Scale for Children* (4th ed.). San Antonio, TX: Harcourt Assessment.

Wolf, M., & Bowers, P. G. (1999). The double deficit hypothesis for the developmental dyslexias. *Journal of Educational Psychology, 91,* 415–438.

Woodcock, R. W., McGrew, K. S., & Mather, N. (2001). *Woodcock-Johnson III Tests of Cognitive Abilities.* Itasca, IL: Riverside Publishing.

Ysseldyke, J. E., & Christenson, S. (2002). *Functional assessment of academic behavior: Creating successful learning environments.* Arden Hills, MN: Sopris West.

CHAPTER 9

School Neuropsychology Collaboration with Home, School, and Outside Professionals

ROBB N. MATTHEWS

RRENDONDO, SHEALY, NEALE, and Winfrey (2004) regard collaboration as a historically practiced concept in the field of psychology. Working across specialty areas and consultation models with other stakeholders (e.g., social workers, educators) and teaming for the best interest of a client (e.g., individual, family, system) is evident in numerous arenas. The continuing paradigm shift away from guild issues toward collaboration, acknowledges complementary perspectives and methods offered across professional boundaries and "represents a 'best practice' strategy for responding to real-world complexit[ies] in education, training, research, and practice" (p. 790). This chapter will review the role of the school neuropsychologist as a consultant/collaborator with children, families, educators, caretaker(s), and outside agency personnel with regard to known or suspected neurological conditions.

THE ROLE OF THE SCHOOL NEUROPSYCHOLOGIST CONSULTANT

Given the popularity of current classroom interventions such as Response-to-Intervention (RTI) and curriculum-based measurement, the importance of the school neuropsychologist as a consultant to the educational planning team cannot be underestimated. It is the role of the consulting school neuropsychologist to review school, hospital, and community-based neuropsychological assessments, to recommend and oversee the implementation of evidence-based interventions, and to monitor the educational progress of children with known or suspected neuropsychological deficits. The school neuropsychologist can also serve as a collaborative consultant with student assistance teams when a child is struggling with educational progress to recommend process-oriented neurocognitive approaches to assessment and intervention as needed. Table 9.1 presents an overview of the collaborative consultation roles of a school neuropsychologist.

The collaborative role of the school neuropsychologist is diverse, traversing traditional models of consultation and collaboration with components of

Table 9.1

Possible Collaborative Consultation Roles and Functions of a School Neuropsychologist

Consultee	Possible Roles and Functions
• Child with a known or suspected neurological impairment.	• Provide diagnostic assessment services to the child to determine the child's neurocognitive strengths and weaknesses and link those results to providing an optimal learning environment. • Provide the child with emotional support related to educational or behavioral issues. • Provide the child with information about his/her disability and strategies to accommodate that disability.
• Caregiver (e.g., parent, guardian, relative)	• Serve as a consultant to families of children with known or suspected neuropsychological disabilities. They will have many questions about the nature of the disability, intervention outcomes, and prognosis for the future. • Provide or arrange for emotional support (e.g., counseling) for families of children with neuropsychological disabilities. • Conduct inservice trainings for caregivers about topics that pertain to disability services.
• Teachers	• Provide consultation services to teachers about evidence-based interventions that are designed to maximize the learning and behavior of children. • Provide consultation to teacher about when to refer a child for a comprehensive school neuropsychological evaluation. • Serve as a consultant on student assistance teams.

Table 9.1
Continued

Consultee	Possible Roles and Functions
• Related Special Education Personnel (e.g., speech and language pathologist, occupational therapist)	• Serve as a collaborative partner in the diagnostic assessment of children with known or suspected neuropsychological disabilities. Working as a transdisciplinary team with other related special education personnel will strengthen the quality of the services provided to the child and family. • Serve as a collaborative partner in the coordinated implementation of evidence-based interventions.
• School administrators (e.g., principals, special education directors)	• Communicate the need to build a caseload of children with suspected or known neuropsychological impairments. • Communicate the need to develop early identification procedures for children that have sustained a traumatic or acquired head injury and are not in school but are receiving medical services from a hospital or rehabilitation agency. • Advocate for environmental modifications needed in the school environment to accommodate the needs of children with disabilities (e.g., removing physical barriers to mobility)
• Outside agency personnel caregivers	• Coordinate the individualized education goals and objectives that are being implemented in the schools with the goals and objectives that are being implemented by outside agency personnel (e.g., private speech and language pathologists). It is important that all service delivery personnel, in and out of the schools, are providing coordinated services to children with neuropsychological impairments. The school neuropsychologist can help facilitate this coordinated service delivery.
• Medical personnel	• Act as a liaison between the medical community and the schools when dealing with children who are hospitalized for neurologically related illnesses. • Work with the hospital staff to ensure the child's smooth transition from the acute care facility back into an educational environment.

sociocultural and psychoeducational issues relevant to children, families, and systems. Many times the school neuropsychologist is tasked with educating stakeholders from a variety of backgrounds on the neuropsychological, neurobehavioral, and/or neuropsychoeducational issues surrounding a client or situation. These challenges require the integration of traditional assessment roles with effective communication and advocacy skills, as well as a broad-based knowledge of appropriate intervention strategies, the inner workings of available educational, community and home-based services, and the expertise of diverse stakeholders.

Essential elements of effective collaboration vary considerably within and across disciplines. The first step the school neuropsychologist must take for successful collaboration is to identify stakeholders as well as their roles and concerns (Timmins, Bahm, McFadyen, & Ward, 2006). School neuropsychologists will consult/collaborate with direct stakeholders (i.e., children, caretakers), indirect stakeholders (e.g., teachers, therapists, administrators), and community stakeholders (e.g., peers, medical personnel), each of which represents a diverse collection of influences, knowledge, and ideas (Eckert & Hintze, 2000). The school neuropsychologist should clarify the issues surrounding the request for consultation including program or systemic operation and traditions, as well as individual perceptions and cultural issues that could impact the method and focus of information gathered in addressing the referral question(s).

A primary consideration for the school neuropsychologist is the purpose of a referral or the goal(s) for the requested information. Considering underlying factors will help define useful techniques, reporting strategies, and support (emotional, material, instructional, etc.) needed in a given situation, because collaboration can take both a proactive and reactive focus (Kratochwill, Elliot, & Callan-Stoiber, 2002). Of utmost importance in defining and building effective collaborative relationships is working toward others viewing themselves as active *partners* rather than obligatory participants (Gilman & Medway, 2007). Ultimately, the ability of the school neuropsychologist to change the previously unsuccessful behavior of the consultee (i.e., exert social influence), with regard to the issue at hand, largely impacts collaborative success (Erchul, Raven, & Ray, 2001).

Given the extensive knowledge base necessary for successful school neuropsychological practice, the lack of a comprehensive model underlying consultation practices, and the rapidly growing body of available information, practitioners may be best served by first collaborating with one another (Fuqua, Newman, & Dickman, 1999). Peer collaboration allows the school neuropsychologist to incorporate advances in established and promising practices, as well as to maintain awareness of unreliable information being circulated in the popular media, among groups, or on the Internet. Additionally, peer collaboration can improve professionalism, case conceptualization, and problem solving, while lessening feelings of stress and burnout. Thus, peer collaboration may take on an even greater role for those with less experience in the practice of school neuropsychology (Zins & Murphy, 1996).

Research has demonstrated the effectiveness of the peer collaboration process, regardless of the training or experience level of those involved (Prinze & Sanders, 2007). Practical training in effective consultation methods and issues varies widely across educational programs. It is possible for a school neuropsychologist to have graduated with only a conceptual understanding of consultation and little practical experience (Kratochwill & Van Someren, 1995). Thus, less-experienced school neuropsychologists may need to seek out specific support in developing a functional skill set for efficacious practice through peer collaboration. While supportive peer collaboration structured around recognized goals, comparable interests and commitments, and knowledge of local issues is a necessary component for experienced and inexperienced practitioners alike, the practice of school neuropsychology is still emerging as a specialty and often there may be only one school neuropsychologist working within a given geographical region. This poses a challenge to the practitioner who would like to engage in peer collaboration, yet is lacking appropriately trained peers. Consequently, the school neuropsychologist may need to be proactive in seeking out support through national, regional, and local trainings/associations, and/or some type of distance-based (e.g., Internet) peer support groups.

IMPORTANCE OF CONJOINT COLLABORATION AND WORKING WITH OUTSIDE AGENCIES

Working in a collaborative fashion with others from diverse backgrounds benefits the school neuropsychologist as well as the community served. Collaboration among stakeholders fosters sharing of experience and knowledge from various personal and professional backgrounds, occupations, and specialty areas. Effective relationships, based on trust and cooperation, are built from collaborative efforts, and many times challenge participants to improve their existing skill set (Arredondo et al., 2004). In the end, collaboration among stakeholders both enhances and is enhanced by serving consultees/clients in need.

Many times external agencies have programs, personnel, and funding streams not available in primary educational settings. Thus, interagency collaboration allows for consistency across environments, highlights potential future problems, and lends a higher degree of support to families (Prinze & Sanders, 2007). Ultimately, each stakeholder gives only a small percentage of his or her time to address the needs of a specific child, while the family is tasked with rearing a child into adulthood, and at times, throughout adulthood. Effective collaboration gives the best opportunity for children and families to be informed and prepared for current and future issues as they arise. The overarching goal of consultation should not only be addressing current concerns, but building capacity in consultees and clients as well (Lewis & Newcomer, 2002).

As is true in the majority of situations, when people (teachers, parents, etc.) have more confidence in their ability (e.g., skills, resources) to meet a challenge, they are more flexible in their approach. Respect for the limitations (e.g., time) and the perceptions of the consultee are central considerations in successful collaboration (Kratochwill et al., 2002). Recommendations may require re-sources the consultee lacks and/or resources existing in competition with other opportunities and demands in a given environment (Noell et al., 2005). Recommendations and strategies must, therefore, demonstrate deference to collaborators and consultees while being "user-friendly," meaningful, and relevant to the situation at hand. Ultimately, changing the behavior of a client results from changes in the consultee's behavior (Hiralall & Martens, 1998; Sterling-Turner, Watson, Wildmon, Watkins, & Little, 2001). Thus, school neuropsychologists need to support others with formal and informal instruc-tion in necessary strategies and application of those strategies before tasking those people with providing services (Sterling-Turner et al., 2001).

Adequate consultee training and support have been found to result in enduring perceptions of personal or professional efficacy (Tschannen-Moran, Hoy, & Hoy, 1998). With regard to training, direct methods (e.g., role play, rehearsal) have been found to yield higher confidence and intervention integrity than indirect methods (e.g., reading materials, outline of suggestions) when developing a skill set through consultation (Sterling-Turner et al., 2001; Tschannen-Moran et al., 1998). As new skills are developing, direct and indirect stakeholders may benefit from the support provided by a generalized script that could be adapted to various situations and/or could be used as a self-monitoring device for the skills being practiced (Hiralall & Martens, 1998).

How to accomplish training and coordination without adding significant stress to the consultee is a primary concern for the consultee, administrators, and school neuropsychologists alike. Anderson, Klassen, and Georgiou (2007) found the most requested teacher support to be training in the specific need(s) of the children being taught. However, as the number of stakeholders involved in a collaborative consultation increases, the need for coordination with a variety of additional personnel similarly increases and may serve to intensify the consultee's stress level and negatively impact the effectiveness of the consultation (Lewis & Newcomer, 2002). An example of a frequently used support for more severely impaired clients is the assignment of auxiliary personnel to assist in the classroom, home, and work place. This strategy however raises a number of potentially stressful issues surrounding supervision, training and changes in the environment. At issue in the use of auxiliary personnel could be a consultee's lack of knowledge, which would certainly negatively impact one's ability to train and direct someone else. Moreover, adding people to any environment can serve to increase stress and decrease efficiency unless sufficient structure exists.

Effective consultation/collaboration results in changes in the consultee (e.g., skill development) and in the environment (e.g., positive behavioral supports), as both components are necessary to positively impact long-term outcomes (Martens & Ardoin, 2002). Successful collaboration by a school neuropsychologist requires both organizational and individual consultee endorsement of the process (Prinze & Sanders, 2007). Resistance, generally systemic in nature, is "anything that impedes problem solving or plan implementation and ultimately problem resolution" (Wickstrom & Witt, 1993, p. 160) Many times it is not the idea(s), but the practicalities of implementation that meet resistance in systems and individuals. Incorporating existing skill sets and preferences for intervention into recommendations may work to lessen resistance and increase efficacy (Kratochwill et al., 2002; Prinze & Sanders, 2007). Finally, research suggests ongoing support is necessary for the successful continuation of consultatively developed interventions (Martens & Ardoin, 2002).

COLLABORATING WITH OTHERS TO ADDRESS THE NEEDS OF THE CHILD

Consultation focuses on the development of competencies addressing the presenting problem and preventing future problems (Aldrich & Martens, 1993; Kratochwill, Sheridan, Rotto, & Salmon, 1991). In recent years, the focus of intervention has shifted from the traditional reactive (medical) model of service delivery to a prevention/early intervention focused, multitiered public heath model (Blom-Hoffman & Rose, 2007; Hojnoski, 2007). Services are no longer delayed by lack of a clearly defined diagnosis, but instead focus on early detection and intervention services as risk factors are noted. Continuing services are then targeted and defined based on data sets, which may be beneficial as the initial structure of a collaborative relationship is often defined around a request for assistance rather than by data-driven needs (Hojnoski, 2007).

Matching one's approach to the circumstances surrounding a consultation request is supported in the literature (Graham, 1998). Research indicates both consultants and consultees find a positive and supportive collaborative relationship is associated with greater implementation of the recommendations (Erchul et al., 2001). Generalization is hypothesized to increase, based on the acceptability of the professional (i.e., social influence) in combination with consultation processes, recommendations, and outcomes (Blom-Hoffman &

Rose, 2007). The consultant developing causal hypotheses and initial recommendations following the first consultation session may also be vital to the consultee joining in the collaborative process (Graham, 1998; Hughes & DeForest, 1993). Eckert and Hintze (2000) suggest discussing the overall effectiveness of a strategy with consultees may also improve acceptability of neuropsychologically based interventions.

The attributional tendencies of the individual or group should be a primary consideration of the school neuropsychologist. Research has demonstrated that the perspective of the information presented can significantly shift reaction and/or authenticity of implementation (Soodak & Podell, 1994). Ysseldyke, Christenson, Algozzine, and Thurlow (1983) found 85 percent of the teachers in their study attributed children's difficulties to intrinsic issues, and 20 percent of those difficulties were attributed to the home dynamic. Thus, respondents were less likely to have a "stake" in the student's success as the issues perceived as negatively impacting the child's performance were outside the teacher's realm of influence or expertise. Blom-Hoffman and Rose (2007) contend the outward appearance of resistance (or negative perspective taking) does not preclude a collaborative approach. Rather, the school neuropsychologist has to consider both the consultee's willingness to address the concern(s) as well as his or her ability to address the underlying neuropsychological issue(s).

Considering the larger value (i.e., social validity) of recommendations, the requested service, or acceptability to stakeholders, gives insight into the likelihood of intervention adoption and implementation (Eckert & Hintze, 2000). If a service is not deemed essential to the task at hand or is too cumbersome or disruptive to be effectively implemented, it is unlikely to be viewed as acceptable (Truscott, Cosgrove, Meyers, & Eidle-Barkman, 2000). Similarly, the lack of some degree of positive change following implementation of recommendations or services will lessen the likelihood of continuation, even with stakeholder acknowledgment of the usefulness of the service/recommendation. Given these considerations, stakeholder acceptance as the only measure of potential implementation or success is of little value to practitioners or researchers (McDougal, Nastasi, & Chafouleas, 2005; Noell et al., 2005).

Collaborating with Parents/Guardians/Foster Parents   Caregivers can present with a wide variety of skills and needs related to the child and/or their condition(s) of concern. Improving skills and insight into issues surrounding a child may be addressed by the school neuropsychologist in a parent-focused or conjoint (parent-teacher) relationship, by using technology training, or some combination of the three approaches. Conjoint consultation works to balance home and school expectations and supports (Kratochwill et al., 2002). McDougal and colleagues (2005) consider conjoint collaboration to be a crucial factor in generalization and maintenance of skills acquisition. Frequent communication across environments at regular intervals allows for the development of consistent expectations as well as a wider range of contingency plans and supports.

Parents in general have contact with a number of care providers (e.g., hospital, rehabilitation center, home care) on a regular basis; however, many of the providers have little or no consultation expertise (Prinze & Sanders, 2007). Thus, collaborative conjoint consultation allows parents to gain critical understanding and skills, as well as communicate their child's needs and request assistance of others who may need to care for their child. Collaborative consultation then works to build a network of support for the child across environments and care providers, allowing the child to meet the demands of his or her environment(s) and continue with the most appropriate neurocognitive interventions.

Collaborating with Indirect Stakeholders   Collaboration can be difficult to implement because intervention success is many times mediated by the thoughts, actions, and abilities of consultee(s) (Elliott, Witt, Galvin, & Peterson, 1984; Erchul et al., 2001). Teachers may or may not request outside assistance with classroom difficulties. However, when outside assistance is requested, externalizing behaviors are the most common referral issue (Alderman & Gimpel, 1996). This finding reinforces the idea of more discreet problems potentially continuing without appropriate intervention and is one of the reasons why the school neuropsychologist should consult with the school's student assistance team at the earliest signs of a child's neurodevelopmental dysfunction (including failure to improve after repeated intervention). It is not in the best interest of a child or those working with the child to wait until struggles become well established, and subsequently, more difficult to change.

Collaborative consultation will occasionally be sought by those wanting an outcome other than success (e.g., placement in a different environment). The disparity between collaborator goals must be addressed at the outset of the relationship to find successful intervention and generalization of acquired skills (Blom-Hoffman & Rose, 2007). To this end, ongoing consultative support is a more effective way of structuring the implementation of evidenced-based strategies than brief presentations or written materials alone (DuPaul, 2003). Additionally, linking strategies to consultation outcomes has also been found helpful in improving implementation (Noell, Duhon, Gatti, & Connell, 2002).

Collaborating with Speech and Language Pathologists   The American Speech-Language-Hearing Association (ASHA) has adopted a diverse policy of essential knowledge, roles, activities, and settings in defining the practice of speech language pathology (2007). ASHA describes the function of Speech Language Pathologists (SLPs) as undertaking activities targeted at reducing or preventing communication problems. In concert with efforts to remediate or alleviate communication difficulties, SLPs many times focus on educating families and other professionals about the nature and management of communication problems (ASHA, 1996, 2005). Collaborative consultation and contextually based services have been recognized by ASHA as representing the most productive approach when multiple settings or service providers are working toward a common goal (2005). Collaboration may include varying degrees of "role release" between professionals, where one professional assumes the role of primary service provider, while collaborating professionals (i.e., professionals from other disciplines) provide consultation to the primary provider (ASHA, 2008).

Traditionally, the SLPs role has focused primarily on individual service delivery, but the service delivery model has shifted focus toward education and generalization through strategies, such as whole-language methodologies, delivered in less restrictive environments (ASHA, 1991). Thus, SLPs have expanded their collective vision as a profession to include a collaborative model of service delivery allowing for acquisition of or improvement in functional communication and learning strategies among all students, rather than only in those with an identified impairment. Collaboration with the SLP can be a major facet of successful evaluation, planning, and intervention. The focus of school neuropsychology and that of speech language pathology may intersect at points such as the effect of individual (e.g., executive skills, attention, semantics, pragmatics) and environmental factors as well as in the participation and success of students. Like school neuropsychologists, SLPs provide services to individuals, families, and groups in a variety of situations. In many cases, an SLP may be the first contact with children demonstrating a range of neurodevelopmental difficulties or acquired impairments and may be faced with particularly difficult behavioral issues in need of support by a school neuropsychologist.

Collaborating with Educators   In the information age, methodologies are no longer idiosyncratic but are likely to be examined across professional boundaries. As policies shift, educators are given increasingly varied duties from differentiating instruction in a Response-to-Intervention (RTI) model to meaningfully including children with disabilities in general education classrooms. Increasing homogeneity of expectations require teachers to divide their time into smaller units, ultimately targeting only the greatest needs when planning, teaching, and conferencing (Anderson et al., 2007).

Strategic support has been identified as the most necessary consultation component for classroom success, with little credence given to "feel-good" recommendations. While teachers may see the benefit(s) of expanding traditional educational roles/models/methodologies, they clearly require additional support to be effective educators (Noell, Witt, Gilberton, Ranier, & Freeland, 1997). Like school neuropsychologists, teachers seek knowledge to enhance their professional skills. Thus, clearly defined collaborative goals and strategies as well as a broad knowledge base to support the operationalization of those goals and strategies are fundamental requirements for effective school neuropsychology consultation with educators.

Soodak and Podell (1994) reported that teacher-focused strategies designed to assist students were more amenable to teachers with increased concern related to symptom severity or greater teaching efficacy (beliefs about professional effectiveness), suggesting attributions impact service preferences. More easily implemented interventions have been found acceptable in instances of lower perceived difficulty, but increased teacher involvement is acceptable in the face of more severe issues (Elliott et al., 1984). Teacher efficacy is highly related to a teacher's previous success with students and the overall quality of student-teacher relationships (Bogler, 2001). Teachers with higher professional efficacy were found to be more accepting of consultation and the resulting intervention plans. Their perception of additional control over problems also seems to result in greater use of consultation/problem solving than in referral for outside appraisal (DeForest & Hughes, 1992).

In the Soodak and Podell (1994) study asking teachers to list possible interventions to help a hypothetical student, about 88 percent of the teachers made teacher-focused suggestions, while about 95 percent made suggestions involving outside assistance, with outside assistance being indicated as the most likely effective strategy. Interestingly, the most frequently rated nonteaching strategy thought to bring about positive change was parent participation (about 78 percent), a finding suggesting conjoint consultation could be viewed positively in numerous situations. Finally, more than 52 percent of participating teachers suggested an assessment by an interdisciplinary team was indicated. In a similar observation, Aldrich and Martens (1993) found focusing consultation on environmental information resulted in greater attribution given to the setting and issues under the teacher's control than simple behavior analysis information that teachers tended to attribute to the child's intrinsic and home dynamic, issues outside their realm of expertise.

It appears issues without an easily defined cause or solution are more likely to result in referral to someone or some group perceived as having greater knowledge or influence, when a problem has moved beyond the teacher's professional means (Hughes, Baker, Kemenoff, & Hart, 1993). Moreover, lower feelings of efficacy tend to be associated with authoritarian classroom management practices, and thus manipulation to force compliance (Erdem & Demirel, 2007). Bandura (1997) points out that teachers may have differing levels of efficacy for individual tasks, thus consideration of necessary skills should be multifaceted.

Being attentive to a collaborator's or consultee's milieu (time, funding, administration, climate, etc.) is a key component in effective service delivery. Alderman and Gimpel (1996) found educators perceived formal evaluation as the least effective method of assistance, because results often lack practical assistance and realistic school-based interventions. Additionally, the study established that educators were more likely to seek consultation from each other than from an outside consultant for a variety of concerns, including attention-related issues. This tendency may be related to the proximity, familiarity, or access to consultants (Gonzalez, Nelson, Gutkin, & Shwery, 2004). In many instances, the school neuropsychologist has far less contact with general education teachers than with special education teachers (Gilman & Medway, 2007). A "whole school" approach may support client change in a manner similar to teachers seeking peer support, such that a culture of structured, systematic methodologies addressing academic and behavioral concerns is implemented by all stakeholders (Hojnoski, 2007). Added support for this method may also be given in the form of other indirect stakeholders (including peers) assisting with attainment, maintenance, and generalization (e.g., peer-mediated consultation).

Further consideration should be given to other external educator influences such as social circles, family life, and so on. One cannot consider indirect influences needing to be addressed in children without considering the indirect influences impacting collaborators or consultees. A vital aspect of effectively impacting the performance of consultees and clients alike may be the school neuropsychologist's skill in the development and support of explicit and practical recommendations from evaluation results. As educators tend to seek assistance from one another, precise and well-supported consultative interventions may well impact the educational community beyond the present issue, collaborator or consultee.

Hiralall and Martens (1998) developed a six-step scripted protocol for use by teachers in an instructional sequence. They found teachers were more likely to adopt and effectively implement the scripted sequence of strategies than imprecise suggestions surrounding strategies. High levels of intervention specification have been found reasonable and effective (McDougal et al., 2005) and can be used as an efficient method for giving performance feedback regarding intervention integrity. Additionally, scripted sequences may become part of the implementers' managerial and instructional approaches, thus generalizing the strategies across circumstances (Hiralall & Martens, 1998).

Studies of implementation suggest teachers' efforts at implementing treatment plans following sufficient training for consultees and clients is initially high, but decreases over time. Giving performance feedback supported with graphic representations of treatment integrity and client performance has resulted in substantial increases in long-term implementation (Noell et al., 1997, 2002, 2005). Implementation also remained high as consultative support for the interventions was reduced following performance feedback. Finally, performance feedback has been shown effective despite the absence of a hierarchical relationship between collaborators (Noell et al., 1997, 2002). Besides considerations of reliability and validity, monitoring techniques should be feasible, efficient and sensitive to incremental change (McDougal, et al., 2005; Prinze & Sanders, 2007). Additionally, more frequent feedback and changes in intervention strategies as necessary within the first year following neurological insult appear to have better results, while overtraining makes little difference in implementation quantity or quality.

Motivational Interviewing (MI) is one evidence-based consultation style developed in behavioral medicine that has been found effective through meta-analysis and successfully employed in a number of helping professions (Blom-Hoffman & Rose, 2007). While a comprehensive discussion of this technique is beyond the focus of this chapter, general principles and considerations are worthy of review. MI focuses on enhancing motivation for and addressing barriers to behavior change by supporting the self-realization of needed change(s) in the consultee's previous approaches to a situation (similar to consultee-focused consultation).

Blom-Hoffman and Rose (2007) present the structure of MI as based on clear collaborative relationship principles. The consultant's behavior can reinforce or reduce a consultee's fluctuating attitude toward change. An empathic style results in greater willingness to make necessary change(s), while a confrontational or impassioned approach may increase resistance (Erchul, Raven, & Whichard, 2001). Cognitive dissonance is an expected result of behavior change, and consultants must recognize the arguments opposing change. Consultants then provide support through ideas and alternatives with the goal of consultees taking ownership of the change initiative, process, and result.

Consulting with Administrators A collaborative model of service delivery requires administrative support to lessen systemic resistance to change, particularly as the redirection of resources may be necessary to shift from a direct to an indirect intervention focus (ASHA, 1991; Prinze & Sanders, 2007). Leadership supporting collaboration between staff members in decision making and problem solving assistance tends to develop a climate supportive of higher professional efficacy (Tschannen-Moran et al., 1998). Ross and Gray (2006) found collective efficacy was predictive of both student achievement and the school's relationship with parents. Thus, the relationship between student success and parental involvement is directly impacted by administrative leadership style.

Transactional leadership focuses on maintaining the status quo through meeting only the vital needs of the organization. This management style can be best described as top-down imposition of change. There is little consultation with, input from, or ownership of needs or program changes by the staff designated to implement it. This lack of collaboration may serve to increase staff resistance to any change (Webster-Stratton & Taylor, 1998) and result in essential changes not being implemented (Prinze & Sanders, 2007). The transactional environment is stable but monotonous and lacks a strong sense of community (Bogler, 2001). Transactional leaders may reward underlings for fulfilling expectations or may respond to a perceived problem but lack the necessary vision to create a collaborative environment. Educators wishing to create proactive change in their system rather than have change imposed on them need a broad collaborative mindset, an ethical commitment to effectively meet children's needs, and insightful administrative support (Hazel, 2007). In a school neuropsychological service delivery model, it is particularly necessary to integrate flexibility into teaching, the student's schedule, and consultation style.

Transformational leaders build goals through foresight, offer intellectual inspiration, provide personal support, model best practices, maintain expectations, and build a participatory structure (Leithwood & Jantzi, 2000). Transformational leaders enter into a collaborative change relationship with others, many times inspiring them to attain new heights or adopt a new approach (Ross & Gray, 2006). The resulting environment is accessible and novel. Leithwood, Jantzi, and Steinbach's (1999) review of transformational leadership studies found that teachers' willingness to exert extra effort in changing classroom practices and/or attitudes were consistently predicted by a transformational leadership style.

Transformational leadership improves the collective professional efficacy beliefs of staff members. Collective professional efficacy is simply the staff members' belief in their collective capacity to positively impact students and reach their goals. Ross and Gray (2006) observed that individuals who believe in their potential success are more likely to achieve success as they adopt more challenging goals, work toward achievement, persist when hindered, and develop more effective coping mechanisms. Further, they believe the relationship between efficacy and outcomes to be reciprocal, as positive efficacy contributes to higher attainment while poor efficacy contributes to lower overall attainment.

A consistent empirical link to teacher outcomes (particularly commitment to the organization) is clearly delineated by transformational leadership research (Ross & Gray, 2006). Bogler (2001) found that job satisfaction is related to the degree of autonomy given to teachers and staff, the opportunities to participate in the decision-making process, and the style of administration. Greater job satisfaction was noted in teachers who perceive their administrator as an open communicator and a delegator in management style. Thus, increasing teacher control over their professional lives increases efficacy, liveliness, diligence, and flexibility (Tschannen-Moran et al., 1998).

Given these findings, school neuropsychologists must do more than convince administrators to allow collaborative consultation. District leaders, like teachers, need to be aware of the potential positive impact not only on the students but on staff and parents as well. Many transactionally based leaders and staff with low efficacy may tend to view collaborative consultation as just another program with unrealistic expectations. This is where sharing a broader vision of commitment to the learning community and the research-based outcome literature can begin to move them toward a transformational mindset. Strategic support of the process will likely be the most necessary component in building a collaborative consultation community from one where the status quo has been the acceptable standard.

Consultation with Daily Care Providers   Consultation needs to be provided to early childhood providers when a child has sustained a neuropsychological insult or when neuropsychological deficits are interfering with the child's learning and behavior. Successful intervention appears to be related to the quality of relationships in the child's life, which can be mediated by the frequency of contact and supportive (collaborative) relationships available to caretakers (Green, Everhart, Gordon, & Gettman, 2006). The interplay of developmental, mental health, socioeconomic, and environmental factors has a significant impact on a child's ability to progress and meet the expectations of others. Early life experiences (e.g., cognitive stimulation, social opportunities, unexpected illness or injury) can have significant immediate and long-term impact on the overall functioning of children as they progress through the educational system toward the end goal of functional independence.

Many times daycare and birth to 3 (e.g., Head Start) personnel lack the background in neurodevelopmental sequence, classroom management, and effective instruction commonly found in public school teachers (Barnett, Ihlo, Nichols, & Wolsing, 2006). Thus, the role of the school neuropsychologist may not only encompass evaluation and intervention development and support, but may also include significant training in neurodevelopmental pathways, appropriate expectations, and classwide strategies as well. Ensuring parents and other caretakers understand these basic principles will be a necessary first step in the child's academic and social readiness. As is the case with other collaborative relationships, Barnett and colleagues (2006) found relationships and teambuilding to be necessary components of effective preschool program consultation. Simply building better skill sets is insufficient to impact long-term outcomes. Likewise, school neuropsychologists can facilitate intervention strategy sharing among educators, families, and outside agency personnel.

Consultation with Medical Personnel Medical practitioners must learn to cope with a variety of stressors in addition to patient care issues as part of clinical practice. This may heighten their stress level and decrease their tendency toward empathic communication. Van Dulmena, Tromp, Grosfeld, ten Catec, and Bensing (2007) examined physiological stress indicators among medical students role-playing communicating bad news to their patients. The study supported previous results suggesting medical practitioners tend to communicate the purely medical information most effectively, with much less emphasis placed on the psychosocial impact of the information being presented. The authors believe stress reactions decrease with experience, but the model of communication may remain. Thus, patients and families may require additional emotional support not previously available to them.

Neuropsychological intervention is generally valued by the medical community, especially in relation to the potential positive impact on medical concerns. However, healthcare administration is many times overshadowed by fiscal needs rather than psychological functioning. Given this focus, patients and families may indeed see signs of physical improvement when they leave a medically supported environment, while at the same time their emotional well-being may flounder (Robinson & Baker, 2006). Collaboration with medical professionals allows the school neuropsychologist to facilitate communication and clarify transition issues with the patient and family. This can be accomplished by communicating with service providers (e.g., nurses, motor therapists), reading and interpreting progress notes, and interviewing and educating the patient and family. Communication to non-mental health professionals should be succinct, reasoned, and valuable in a medical context.

For recently hospitalized clients, the attending nurse may be the most knowledgeable source for behavior and/or current condition information, but progress notes and consultant reports can also be a wealth of information. Level of care may be an issue as clients have received significantly more care in a facility than available in the community. By involving many different service providers who work with families on the "front line" in collaborative consultation, a program has a much greater chance of success without getting mired in guild or turf issues (Robinson & Baker, 2006).

COMMUNICATING SCHOOL NEUROPSYCHOLOGICAL RESULTS

Athanasiou, Geil, Hazel, and Copeland (2002) found attributional styles are expressed in the most pronounced fashion in etiology and treatment plans. Further, in summarizing and making recommendations, school neuropsychologists tend to adopt an external attributional style while teachers appear to adopt an internal one with regard to the child's difficulties. Conoley, Conoley, Ivey, and Scheel (1991) found teachers were more receptive to interventions presented from a perspective similar to their own. Thus, when communicating results, the school neuropsychologist may be able to positively impact the receptiveness of the information as well as intervention integrity, at least initially, by framing results and recommendations from a perspective similar to the audience receiving the information (Wickstrom & Witt, 1993).

In communicating needs, Kratochwill et al. (2002) believe consultees are best served when recommendations are proactive, built on existing competencies, and include existing resources. Athanasiou and colleagues (2002) support incorporating teachers' causal attributions into consultative work. In reporting results or developing strategies or goals, school neuropsychologists may need to adopt a more eclectic approach in their focus (e.g., include academic issues) as well as in the selection of treatment modalities. Additionally, specific support (e.g., emotional, material) for those using the information presented in a report may be necessary prior to focusing on implementation.

SUMMARY

This chapter reviewed the literature related to effective approaches to collaborative consultation by school neuropsychologists. The benefits of having the school neuropsychologist assist the educational planning team in reviewing and interpreting medical records, neurocognitive and neuro-developmental assessments, and in intervention planning and progress monitoring have been examined. The school neuropsychologist can play a major role in coordinating the service delivery for children with suspected or known neuropsychological impairments, while collaboratively consulting with various consultees (e.g., child, caregiver, educators, outside agency personnel).

REFERENCES

Alderman, G. L., & Gimpel, G. A. (1996). The interaction between type of behavior problem and type of consultant: Teachers' preferences for professional assistance. *Journal of Educational and Psychological Consultation, 7*, 305–313.

Aldrich, S. F., & Martens, B. K. (1993). The effects of behavioral problem analysis versus instructional environment information on teachers' perceptions. *School Psychology Quarterly, 8,* 110–124.

American Speech-Language-Hearing Association (ASHA). (1991). *A model for collaborative service delivery for students with language-learning disorders in the public schools.* [Relevant paper]. Retrieved November 29, 2008, from http://www.asha.org/policy.

American Speech-Language-Hearing Association (ASHA). (1996). Scope of practice in speech-language pathology. *ASHA, 38,* 16–20.

American Speech-Language-Hearing Association (ASHA). (2005). *Roles and responsibilities of speech-language pathologists serving persons with mental retardation/developmental disabilities* [Guidelines]. Retrieved November 29, 2008, from http://www.asha.org/policy.

American Speech-Language-Hearing Association (ASHA). (2007). *Scope of practice in speech-language pathology* [Scope of Practice]. Retrieved November 29, 2008, from http://www.asha.org/policy.

American Speech-Language-Hearing Association (ASHA). (2008). *Roles and responsibilities of speech-language pathologists in early intervention* [Guidelines]. Retrieved November 29, 2008, from http://www.asha.org/policy.

Anderson, C. J. K., Klassen, R. M., & Georgiou, G. K. (2007). Inclusion in Australia: What teachers say they need and what school psychologists can offer. *School Psychology International, 28,* 131–147.

Arredondo, P., Shealy, C., Neale, M., & Winfrey, L. L. (2004). Consultation and interprofessional collaboration: Modeling for the future. *Journal of Clinical Psychology, 60,* 787–800.

Athanasiou, M. S., Geil, M., Hazel, C. E., & Copeland, E. P. (2002). A look inside school-based consultation: A qualitative study of the beliefs and practices of school psychologists and teachers. *School Psychology Quarterly, 17,* 258–298.

Bandura, A. (1997). *Self-efficacy: The exercise of control.* New York: W. H. Freeman.

Barnett, D. W., Ihlo, T., Nichols, A., & Wolsing, L. (2006). Preschool teacher support through class-wide intervention: A description of field-initiated training and evaluation. *Journal of Applied School Psychology, 23,* 77–96.

Blom-Hoffman, J., & Rose, G. S. (2007). Applying motivational interviewing to school-based consultation: A commentary on "Has consultation achieved its primary prevention potential?" an article by Joseph E. Zins. *Journal of Educational and Psychological Consultation, 17,* 151–156.

Bogler, R. (2001). The influence of leadership style on teacher job satisfaction. *Educational Administration Quarterly, 37,* 662–683.

Conoley, C. W., Conoley, J. C., Ivey, D. C., & Scheel, M. J. (1991). Enhancing consultation by matching the consultee's perspectives. *Journal of Counseling & Development, 69,* 546–549.

DeForest, P. A., & Hughes, J. N. (1992). Effect of teacher involvement and teacher self-efficacy on rating of consultant effectiveness and intervention acceptability. *Journal of Education and Psychological Consultation, 3,* 301–316.

DuPaul, G. J. (2003). Commentary: Bridging the gap between research and practice. *School Psychology Review, 32,* 178–180.

Eckert, T. L., & Hintze, J. M. (2000). Behavioral conceptions and applications of acceptability: Issues related to service delivery and research methodology. *School Psychology Quarterly, 15*, 123–148.

Elliott, S. N., Witt, J. C., Galvin, G. A., & Peterson, R. (1984). Acceptability of positive and reductive behavioral interventions: Factors that influence teachers' decisions. *Journal of School Psychology, 22*, 353–360.

Erchul, W. P., Raven, B. H., & Ray, A. G. (2001). School psychologists' perceptions of social power bases in teacher consultation. *Journal of Educational and Psychological Consultation, 12*, 1–23.

Erchul, W. P., Raven, B. G., & Whichard, S. M. (2001). School psychologist and teacher perceptions of social power in consultation. *Journal of School Psychology, 39*, 483–497.

Erdem, E., & Demirel, O. (2007). Teacher self-efficacy belief. *Social Behavior and Personality, 35*, 573–586.

Fuqua, D. R., Newman, J. L., & Dickman, M. M. (1999). Barriers to effective assessment in organizational consultation. *Consulting Psychology Journal: Practice and Research, 51*, 14–23.

Gilman, R., & Medway, F. J. (2007). Teachers' perceptions of school psychology: A comparison of regular and special education teacher ratings. *School Psychology Quarterly, 22*, 145–161.

Gonzalez, J. E., Nelson, J. R., Gutkin, T. B., & Shwery, C. S. (2004). Teacher resistance to school-based consultation with school psychologists: A survey of teacher perceptions. *Journal of Emotional and Behavioral Disorders, 12*, 30–37.

Graham, D. (1998). Consultant effectiveness and treatment acceptability: An examination of consultee requests and consultant responses. *School Psychology Quarterly, 13*, 155–168.

Green, B. L., Everhart, M., Gordon, L., & Gettman, M. G. (2006). Characteristics of effective mental health consultation in early childhood settings: Multilevel analysis of a national survey. *Topics in Early Childhood Special Education 26*, 142–152.

Hazel, C. E. (2007). Timeless and timely advice: A commentary on "Consultation to facilitate planned organizational change in schools," an article by Joseph E. Zins and Robert J. Illback. *Journal of Educational and Psychological Consultation, 17*, 125–132.

Hiralall, A. S., & Martens, B. K. (1998). Teaching classroom management skills to preschool staff: The effects of scripted instructional sequences on teacher and student behavior. *School Psychology Quarterly, 13*, 94–115.

Hojnoski, R. L. (2007). Promising directions in school-based systems level consultation: A commentary on "Has consultation achieved its primary prevention potential?" an article by Joseph E. Zins. *Journal of Educational and Psychological Consultation, 17*, 157–163.

Hughes, J. N., Baker, D., Kemenoff, S., & Hart, M. (1993). Problem ownership, causal attributions, and self-efficacy as predictors of teachers' referral decisions. *Journal of Educational and Psychological Consultation, 4*, 369–384.

Hughes, J. N., & DeForest, P. A. (1993). Consultant directiveness and support as predictors of consultation outcomes. *The Journal of School Psychology, 31*, 355–373.

Kratochwill, T. R., Elliot, S. N., & Callan-Stoiber, K. (2002). Best practices in school-based problem-solving consultation. In A. Thomas & J. Grimes (Eds.), *Best practices in school psychology IV* (pp. 583–608). Bethesda, MD: National Association of School Psychologists.

Kratochwill, T. R., Sheridan, S. M., Rotto, P. C., & Salmon, D. (1991). Preparation of school psychologists to serve as consultants for teachers of emotionally disturbed children. *School Psychology Review, 20,* 530–550.

Kratochwill, T. R., & Van Someren, K. R. (1995). Barriers to treatment success in behavioral consultation: Current limitations and future directions. *Journal of Educational and Psychological Consultation, 6,* 125–143.

Leithwood, K., & Jantzi, D. (2000). Transformational leadership: How principals can help reform school cultures. *School Effectiveness and School Improvement, 1,* 249–280.

Leithwood, K. A., Jantzi, D., & Steinbach, R. (1999). *Changing leadership for changing times.* Buckingham, UK: Open University Press.

Lewis, T. J., & Newcomer, L. L. (2002). Examining the efficacy of school-based consultation: Recommendations for improving outcomes. *Child & Family Behavior Therapy, 24,* 165–181.

Martens, B. K., & Ardoin, S. P. (2002). Training school psychologists in behavior support consultation. *Child & Family Behavior Therapy, 24,* 147–163.

McDougal, J. L., Nastasi, B. K., & Chafouleas, S. M. (2005). Bringing research into practice to intervene with young behaviorally challenging students in public school settings: Evaluation of the behavior consultation team (BCT) project. *Psychology in the Schools, 42,* 537–551.

Noell, G. H., Duhon, G. J., Gatti, S. L., & Connell, J. E. (2002). Consultation, follow-up, and implementation of behavior management interventions in general education. *School Psychology Review, 31,* 217–234.

Noell, G. H., Witt, J. C., Gilberton, D. N., Ranier, D. D., & Freeland, J. T. (1997). Increasing teacher intervention implementation in general education settings through consultation and performance feedback. *School Psychology Quarterly, 12,* 77–88.

Noell, G. H., Witt, J. C., Slider, N. J., Connell, J. E., Gatti, S. L., Williams, K. L., Koenig, J. L., Resetar, J. L., & Duhon, G. J. (2005). Treatment implementation following behavioral consultation in schools: A comparison of three follow-up strategies. *School Psychology Review, 34,* 87–106.

Prinze, R. J., & Sanders, M. R. (2007). Adopting a population-level approach to parenting and family support interventions. *Clinical Psychology Review, 27,* 739–749.

Robinson, J. D., & Baker, J. (2006). Psychological consultation and services in a general medical hospital. *Professional Psychology: Research and Practice, 37,* 264–267.

Ross, J. A., & Gray, P. (2006). Transformational leadership and teacher commitment to organizational values: The mediating effects of collective teacher efficacy. *School Effectiveness and School Improvement, 17,* 179–199.

Soodak, L. C., & Podell, D. M. (1994). Teachers' thinking about difficult-to-teach students. *Journal of Educational Research, 88,* 44–51.

Sterling-Turner, H. E., Watson, T. S., Wildmon, M, Watkins, C., & Little, E. (2001). Investigating the relationship between training type and treatment integrity. *School Psychology Quarterly, 16*, 56–67.

Timmins, P., Bahm, M., McFadyen, J., & Ward, J. (2006). Teachers and consultation: Applying research and development in organizations (RADIO). *Educational Psychology in Practice, 22*, 305–319.

Truscott, S. D., Cosgrove, G., Meyers, J., & Eidle-Barkman, K. A. (2000). The acceptability of organizational consultation with prereferral intervention teams. *School Psychology Quarterly, 15*, 172–206.

Tschannen-Moran, M., Hoy, A. W., & Hoy, W. K. (1998). Teacher efficacy: Its meaning and measure. *Review of Educational Research, 68*, 202–248.

van Dulmena, S., Tromp, F., Grosfeld, F., ten Catec, O., & Bensing, J. (2007). The impact of assessing simulated bad news consultations on medical students' stress response and communication performance. *Psychoneuroendocrinology, 32*, 943–950.

Webster-Stratton, C., & Taylor, T. K. (1998). Adopting and implementing empirically supported interventions: A recipe for success. In A. Buchanan & B. L. Hudson (Eds.), *Parenting, schooling and children's behaviour: Interdisciplinary approaches* (pp. 127–160). Hampshire, UK: Ashgate.

Wickstrom, K. F., & Witt, J. C. (1993). Resistance within school-based consultation. In J. E. Zins, T. R. Kratochwill, & S. N. Elliott (Eds.), *Handbook of consultation services for children: Applications in educational and clinical settings* (pp. 159–178). San Francisco: Jossey-Bass.

Ysseldyke, J. E., Christenson, S., Algozzine, B., & Thurlow, M. L. (1983). *Classroom teachers' attributions for students exhibiting different behaviors* (Report No. BBB17903). Minneapolis, MN: Minneapolis Institute for Research on Learning Disabilities (ERIC Document Reproduction Service No. ED236848)

Zins, J. E., & Murphy, J. J. (1996). Consultation with professional peers: A national survey of the practices of school psychologists. *Journal of Educational and Psychological Consultation, 17*, 175–184.

CHAPTER 10

School Reentry for Children Recovering from Neurological Conditions

H. THOMPSON PROUT, GINGER DEPP CLINE, and SUSAN M. PROUT

S TUDENTS WITH VARIOUS neurological conditions may be absent from school for some time due to their illness or injury. This chapter will highlight several medical conditions such as meningitis, sickle cell disease and stroke, childhood cancer, and traumatic brain injury that are known to cause secondary neuropsychological deficits. Depending on the chronicity or longer term effects of these conditions, students may qualify for educational services under Section 504 of the Rehabilitation Act of 1973 or through Individuals with Disabilities Education Act as a student with an Other Health Impairment (OHI) or Traumatic Brain Injury (TBI) if a negative educational impact can be demonstrated subsequent to the health condition or head injury. The purpose of this chapter is to discuss the neuropsychological aspects of four impairments (meningitis, sickle cell disease and stroke, cancer, and traumatic brain injury) that typically involve school absence and often have neuropsychological residuals. Additionally, issues with school reentry and roles for a school neuropsychologist in the reentry process will also be discussed.

MENINGITIS

Meningitis, an infection of the membranes in the brain, has several causative agents, including viruses, fungi, traumatic brain injury, and surgery. However, bacterial meningitis is the most common form, affecting 10 to 30 individuals per 100,000 (Palumbo, Davidson, Peloquin, & Gigliotti, 1995). The three most common variants include *Haemaphilus influenzae B*, Neisseria meningitis, and

Streptoccus pneumonia (Berg, Trollfors, Hugosson, Fernell, & Svensson, 2002). A vaccination was introduced in 1993, which helped to reduce the incidence (Koomen et al, 2005); however, certain populations remain at risk (e.g., the very young, very old, and any person who is immunosuppressed) with mortality rates ranging from 5 to 20 percent (Palumbo et al., 1995).

Initial symptoms of meningitis typically include an upper respiratory infection with progression to neck rigidity, irritability, fever, loss of appetite, headache, and light/sound sensitivity. Standards of care in assessment and treatment include a lumbar puncture and high-dose antibiotics. With the advent of more efficacious treatment, more children/adolescents are requiring long-term services following neurocognitive effects from meningitis (Koomen et al., 2005).

EFFECTS OF MENINGITIS

Patients have been found to have more abnormal neurological exams than controls and significantly lower IQ scores (Casella et al., 2004). Functionally, children with a history of meningitis have repeated more grades and been referred more frequently for special education services (Koomen, Grobbee, Jennekens-Schinkel, Roord, & van Furth, 2003). Long-term effects may occur in 25 to 35 percent of patients, including seizures (15 to 25 percent), hydrocephalus (30 percent), sensorineural hearing loss, blindness, cranial nerve damage, cerebral palsy, symptoms of inattention and hyperactivity/ impulsivity, learning disabilities, mental retardation, motoric disabilities, and deficits in visuomotor coordination, general cognition, processing speed, motor steadiness memory, executive functioning, and behavioral competence (Casella et al., 2004; Koomen, van Furth, et al., 2004; Palumbo et al., 1995). Anderson, Anderson, Grimwood, and Nolan (2004) followed up children who had meningitis at a young age, twelve years after their illness. They found that these children continued to show neurobehavioral sequelae into adolescence. The deficits were not considered severe compared to typically developing peers, but the adolescents with a history of meningitis were twice as likely to need special services. The most notable residuals were deficits in the executive functioning domain. Identified risk factors for negative effects included male gender, young age at diagnosis, acute neurological symptoms, and having Streptoccus pneumonia (Koomen, Grobbee, et al., 2004). Children whose meningitis involved additional medical complications (e.g., seizures, hemiparesis, coma) were found to have deficits on several nonverbal tasks, were rated as performing less well in school, and showed lower levels of adaptive behavior (Taylor, Barry, & Schatschneider, 1993). Taylor, Minich, and Schatschneider (2000) found indications that children with a history of meningitis appeared to be at risk for "late-emerging" sequalae. Last, there also appeared to be some adjustment issues for children who have had meningitis. Shears, Nadel, Gledhill, Gordon, and Garralda (2007) followed up on a cohort of children and adolescents one year after having meningitis. In over half of the younger children (under age 6), there were indications of psychiatric disorders, most notably depressive, oppositional defiant, and anxiety disorders sometime during the year, with disorders persisting for about one-third of the children at the one-year point. About one-quarter of the older children were experiencing some type of disorder after one year.

School Reintegration Following Meningitis

With known challenges, an individualized plan put in place by medical and educational professionals for reintegration into the schools and everyday life is important for survivors of meningitis. Close communication begins with notification and preventive medication for students who were in close proximity to the affected student. Treatment for the affected student may require an extended absence, thus homebound/hospital school services may be appropriate once he or she is neurologically stable. Supplementary support services may also be initiated while the student is recovering and upon school reentry (e.g., physical therapy [PT], occupational therapy [OT], speech/language therapist [SLT]). Furthermore, an audiological exam is recommended for all children/adolescents with meningitis due to the high frequency of hearing loss (5 to 20 percent) (Berg et al., 2002).

Koomen, van Furth, et al., (2004) viewed a comprehensive neuropsychological evaluation as essential to allow for the planning of an individualized education plan (IEP) or Section 504 support services (U.S. Department of Education, n.d.). While this may be useful in some cases, the need for a complete neuropsychological battery should be based on the individual case and the point in recovery. Based on common neurocognitive effects, the following recommendations may be appropriate: giving directions in quiet settings without distractions, shortened/direct instruction to assist with auditory attention/processing weaknesses, and shortened assignments to accommodate decreased motor and/or visuomotor skills (Grimwood et al., 1995). Education for staff is certainly essential for understanding the child's condition and subsequent impact on learning. With parental permission, preparation for classmates may be beneficial in establishing a supportive social environment for the student's return (Koomen et al., 2005; Palumbo et al., 1995). Finally, frequent monitoring of progress is essential to allow for an evolving plan of support with appropriate expectations and an understanding of current needs. Until specific cognitive skills are challenged, some symptoms/difficulties may not be apparent.

SICKLE CELL DISEASE AND STROKE

Sickle cell disease (SCD) or anemia is a genetic blood disorder yielding an abnormal form of hemoglobin, which interferes with oxygen transportation throughout the body. The variants of SCD affect diverse ethnic groups including a predominance in African American (1:396) and Latino (1:36,000) populations (Lindsey et al., 2005). Pain crises are common due to sickling of hemoglobin S and obstruction to blood flow (Morse & Shine, 1998). Most children/adolescents with SCD are at risk for stroke, which occurs when there is a diminished supply of blood to the brain (Phelps, 1998). By 14 years of age, 11 percent of individuals with SCD will have an overt stroke, while 22 percent will experience a silent stroke by the age of 18 years (Berkelhammer et al., 2007; Lindsey et al., 2005). DeBaun, Derdeyn, and McKinstry (2006) noted that 30 percent of persons with SCD will experience a stroke at some point in their lifetime, which typically occurs relatively early in their development. Silent strokes are diagnosed when MRI results are suggestive of stroke within the context of a normal neurological exam and no known history of stroke (Schatz, Brown, Pascual, Hsu, & DeBaun, 2001).

EFFECTS OF SICKLE CELL DISEASE AND STROKE

Resultant deficits following a stroke depend on the particular area of insult. General intellectual functioning has been found to be reduced (i.e., 10 to 15 point loss), along with accompanying difficulties in academic skills (e.g., recommendations for special education and retention), attention and executive functioning, visual-motor integration, language skills, behavioral regulation, and memory (King, Tang, Ferguson, & DeBaun, 2005; Schatz & McClellan, 2006). Frontal lobe damage is associated with skill loss in memory and attention, while more diffuse damage of the frontal and parietal lobes leads to increased difficulties with memory, attention, and visual-spatial processing (King et al., 2006). Effects from silent strokes seem to be less severe, but have similar outcomes to those of overt strokes (Schatz & McClellan, 2006).

SCHOOL REINTEGRATION FOLLOWING SICKLE CELL DISEASE AND STROKE

Based on these risks, students with SCD who experience a stroke are more likely to require specialized services upon their return to school, possibly qualifying for special education under the Other Health Impairment (OHI) category or through Section 504. Intensive educational planning including professional education regarding SCD and stroke is essential for school staff (King et al., 2006). Teacher awareness of early warning signs of stroke may lead to early recognition of a stroke. Signs of a stroke may include sudden weakness/numbness of a part or side of the body, sudden loss of vision or speech, difficulty talking or understanding others, a severe headache, and unexplained dizziness/falls. Symptoms of a silent stroke include a general decrease in performance, increased forgetfulness, and difficulty following directions (Lindsey et al., 2005). Frequent absences due to pain crises may also warrant occasional homebound educational services, and teachers should be aware of health precautions for students with SCD (e.g., avoiding temperature extremes, drinking plenty of water) (King et al., 2005). Accurate knowledge about SCD and its effects will lead to more positive/situational educational outcomes for students. King et al. (2006) highlighted a program that was developed to increase teacher knowledge about this condition with significant, positive effects.

Following a stroke, a comprehensive neuropsychological exam is often viewed as essential to allow for individualized planning for areas of support along with frequent monitoring, assessing for continuing improvement and need for services (King et al., 2005, 2006). Again, the need for full neuropsychological evaluation is contingent on the specific aspects of an individual child's condition. Specific accommodations/modifications may include resource room instruction, extended time, preferential seating, attentional strategies, note-taking assistance, computer assistance, homebound instruction, and related service support (e.g., OT, PT, SLT) (King et al., 2005, 2006). Psychosocial support for students with SCD and stroke may also be necessary in order to strengthen/support coping strategies, adjustment skills (e.g., related to pain, delayed growth/puberty, changes following a stroke), and peer relationships. Support in both school and clinical settings is optimal.

CANCER

Children/adolescents are diagnosed with numerous forms of cancer, or abnormal cell growth, each year. Malignancies of the blood are the most common childhood cancer diagnoses, followed by solid tumors (Li & Wendt, 1998). The National Cancer Institute (n.d.) reports that the incidence of childhood cancer has risen slightly in recent years (11.5 per 100,000 children in 1975 to 14.8 per 100,000 in 2004). Death rates have declined dramatically in approximately the same time frame with five-year survival rates increasing from 58.1 to 79.6 percent. While survivability has improved significantly, radical/intense treatments may have residual effects (Reinfjell, Lofstad, Veenstra, Vikan, & Diseth, 2007). It is often the nature of and the associated residuals of the treatments that impact neurocognitive functioning. However, brain tumors obviously have the most direct impact on neurocognitive outcome in addition to treatment side effects. The size, location, and extent of the tumor have significant and direct impact on the residual functional capacity of the child. Additionally, the invasiveness of the intervention (e.g., surgery) may impact the specific area of the tumor as well as surrounding areas in the brain. Brain tumors are often associated with global cognitive decline, deficits in function associated with frontal cortex, nonverbal abilities, visual-motor skills, attention and concentration, processing speed, and memory (Armstrong, Blumberg, & Toledano, 1999). Armstrong et al. also note that deficits may emerge in the years following treatment, rather than immediately.

Effects of Cancer Treatment

Chemotherapy and radiation involve several noxious physical effects including nausea/vomiting, fatigue, mouth sores, hair loss, growth retardation, and endocrine difficulties, along with the longer-term effects of a decrease in cognition, academics, visual-motor skills, attention, short-term memory, and a higher incidence of learning disabilities (Li & Wendt, 1998; Reinfjell et al., 2007). Espy et al. (2001) followed children with acute lymphoblastic leukemia (ALL) who had been treated with prophylactic chemotherapy and found modest declines in math skills, verbal fluency, and visual-motor integration abilities, as well as deficits in visual-motor skills that appeared to persist at four years post treatment.

School Reintegration After Cancer Treatment

Prolonged treatment necessitates the early involvement of the school. Students may be provided with home/hospital instruction since consistent communication among the family, school, and medical team ensure appropriate recommendations and services. Teachers and peers, with parental consent, may be provided education about the child's condition, treatment, and prognosis/expected effects. Once back in the classroom, specific instruction in skills to strengthen attention/memory and organizational strategies, as well as social skills support, are recommended. Specific academic modifications may be beneficial in reducing limitations imposed by physical side effects (e.g., decreased writing expectations, oral exams, increased time for assignments, calculator use). A comprehensive neuropsychological evaluation may delineate student strengths and areas of weakness that will require educational accommodations and modifications. Long-term follow-up information for educators will increase their knowledge and awareness of residual effects that may only emerge once the student encounters more cognitively demanding work (Li & Wendt, 1998). Armstrong et al. (1999) suggested repeated evaluations at twelve- to eighteen-month intervals, specifically including measures of attention, concentration, memory, visual-spatial and visual-motor, fine motor, and processing speed skills. They also suggested that curriculum-based or performance based measures may also identify children whose academic growth potential is not progressing as it was prior to medical treatment. These measures can also interface with more traditional neuropsychological measures.

TRAUMATIC BRAIN INJURY (TBI)

A reported one million children/adolescents experience a TBI each year (Tremont, Mittenberg, & Miller, 1999), with 15- to 24-year-olds falling at greatest risk (Hooper et al., 2004). TBI may result from multiple etiologies including falls, assaults, sporting events, and motor vehicular accidents (MVAs) (Hooper et al., 2004; Tremont et al., 1999). Two types of damage may result from TBI: closed and open head injuries. In a closed head injury, the brain bounces off the bony structures within the skull. This movement may lead to shearing of nerve fibers and blood vessels, which can lead to hemorrhages and swelling in the brain (Rotto, 1998). Open head injuries occur when there is penetration of the skull by an object that reaches brain tissue. Specific effects vary based on the severity of the injury, the location of the injury(ies) (e.g., most commonly the frontal and temporal lobes), and pre-morbid functioning (Harvey, 2002; Rotto, 1998). However, the majority of TBIs are considered mild (Yeates & Taylor, 2005). Younger children are more likely to exhibit worse outcomes due to having fewer previously established cognitive skills at the time of injury (Gil, 2003).

EFFECTS OF TRAUMATIC BRAIN INJURY

Determining neurocognitive effects from a TBI is difficult based on medical technology (e.g., CT scan, MRI). Neuropsychological assessments have been found to be the most sensitive to subtle changes with the most common difficulties found in novel learning, processing speed, and word finding or recall (dysnomia) (Miller & Donders, 2003). Diffuse effects tend to include difficulty concentrating, confusion, irritability, fatigue, and the need for increased effort to complete tasks. Memory skills are frequently initially depressed, although improvement during the first year following the injury may occur for individuals with mild-to-moderate TBI. Academic performance may remain more stable, although math tends to be more at risk for negative change with some findings of mild decrements in reading comprehension (Ewing-Cobbs & Bloom, 2004). Research suggests that negative effects are more noticeable as the student ages and becomes responsible for his or her own executive functioning (Gil, 2003; Savage, Pearson, McDonald, Potoczny-Gray, & Marchese, 2001).

Psychiatric symptoms that may occur following a TBI include depression, irritability, posttraumatic stress disorder (PTSD), aggression and difficulty regulating behavior, and obsessive-compulsive symptoms (Massagli et al., 2004). Due to increased efforts required for mastery of cognitive tasks, mental fatigue may lead to further reduced efficiency and increased frustration (Tremont et al., 1999). Also, aspects of these symptoms may result in children/adolescents with TBI having fewer friends than their classmates (Prigatano & Gupta, 2006). Physical symptoms may include insomnia, appetite changes, headache, nausea, vestibular changes (e.g., altered sense of balance), and fatigue (Rotto, 1998; Yeates & Taylor, 2005).

Project ACCESS documented a reduction in neurological symptoms ten months following a TBI, while neurocognitive symptoms increased during that time. Many were able to return to school by one month postinjury, while some required several months' recovery prior to reentry (Hooper et al., 2004). It is important to note, however, that 9 percent of students in this study experienced new learning/behavioral problems one month following their injury. Even at four months, 15.2 percent experienced difficulties, while 10 percent still exhibited deficits ten months later, including continued headaches, difficulties with attention and learning, and impaired frustration tolerance (Hooper et al., 2004). Overall, symptoms have lasted for up to five years following a mild TBI with the most rapid recovery occurring six to twelve months from the injury date (Harvey, 2002).

SCHOOL REINTEGRATION FOLLOWING TRAUMATIC BRAIN INJURY

Schools are increasingly providing primary intervention services as access to rehabilitation facilities/services wanes (Ewing-Cobbs & Bloom, 2004). Further, TBI was added as a category within the special education service delivery system in 1990 (Gil, 2003). In 2006, 1,027 children between the ages of 3 to 5 were being served under TBI, and 23,867 children between the ages of 6 to 21 were being served (Data Accountability Center, 2006). In order to develop appropriate services, specific assessment of cognitive skills (e.g., short-term memory, attention) is required, as opposed to broad cognitive assessment (intelligence) (Gil, 2003). The consideration of pain as a confound during assessment is also vital, as decreased performance may be caused by the injury, pain, or both (Nicholson, Martelli, & Zasler, 2001). It is recommended that neuropsychological assessment not occur during the acute recovery phase due to rapid changes in cognitive status, and an IEP or 504 plan should be reevaluated every six to eight weeks as most appropriate to accommodate the student's gradual recovery (Thomas & Grimes, 2002). Annual reevaluation of deficit areas for the first three years postinjury will help to capture areas of skill recovery and those areas with continuing difficulties (Ewing-Cobbs & Bloom, 2004). Other classroom-based indices of progress monitoring may also be useful.

A designated school case manager may engage in early communication with the family/medical team in order to begin planning to support the child's needs (Ewing-Cobbs & Bloom, 2004). The school neuropsychologist is in a good position to fill this role due to knowledge regarding school systems/services, consultation skills, and knowledge of empirically supported assessment/intervention techniques.

A flexible schedule for the student to reenter school, such as part-time attendance, is recommended. General skills necessary for reentry include ability to sustain attention for 10 to 15 minutes, ability to complete 20 to 30 minutes of class work, ability to function within a group, ability to communicate needs, and ability to follow directions. Specific instructional approaches including direct instruction, which involves preteaching, modeling, shaping, reinforcement, and continuous assessment, and error-less learning have been found to lead to the successful learning in students with TBI (Bigler, Clark, & Farmer, 1997; D'Amato & Rothlisberg, 1997; Semrud-Clikeman, 2001; Wilson, Baddeley, & Evans, 1994).

Possible classroom accommodations/modifications include adding a rest period to the school day, implementing recognition versus recall tasks, increasing classroom structure, implementing organizational tools such as a daily planner, multimodal instruction, transitional programming for older students (e.g., career education and training), increasing communication among settings, providing education for teachers/staff/students, offering counseling support (Harvey, 2002; Savage et al., 2001), and increasing communication between educators during the student's educational transition to assist with appropriate educational expectations. The student with TBI may be less likely to be perceived as "lazy" or "unmotivated" if teachers are appropriately informed about the effects of TBI and the specific child's learning profile (Ewing-Cobbs & Bloom, 2004). Related services may be necessary compliments in order to address sensory and/or psychosocial needs (Savage et al., 2001).

Antecedent control techniques (e.g., prevention of problems) are most beneficial in managing behavior due to the inability of some individuals with TBI to effectively learn from consequences of their behavior (Savage et al., 2001; Ylvisaker et al., 1995). Possible suggestions include actively planning to avoid sensory overload (e.g., quiet classroom/work area), planning for transitions (Savage et al., 2001), allowing choices when possible, and establishing a routine (Harvey, 2002). Finally, intense protection from further injury is necessary, as subsequent TBI tends to have cumulative effects.

BEST PRACTICES IN SCHOOL REENTRY

Obviously, a great deal of variance and differences in neuropsychological sequelae across the conditions are covered in this chapter, with additional variance within each condition. Additionally, these conditions may yield more generalized impairment, or more specific impairment in cases where neurological impact is more localized. However, due to the complexity of many cognitive processes, even localized damage may impact many neurocognitive tasks, which involve multiple areas of the brain. Nonetheless, some general guidelines appear to be applicable in most cases when a child reenters school after experiencing an illness or injury that impacts neurocognitive functioning:

- If feasible, a school neuropsychologist should meet with medical personnel who have been providing the most recent care for the student. Medical records should be obtained and reviewed to evaluate the severity of illness/injury and to determine whether there are indications of specific neurological dysfunction or if the impact was fairly generalized. Any delineated cognitive or behavioral residuals should be noted. If any objective assessments of function have been completed, those records should be specifically reviewed. Prior school records may be provided to medical and psychological personnel providing acute care and/or initial rehabilitation for the child or adolescent for information about pretreatment or injury performance.

- The school neuropsychologist should gather as much information as possible about the student's functioning prior to the illness or injury. If the child has previously received special or remedial services, those associated educational and psychological records will be useful. If the child has been typically developing, any general evaluations of academic or cognitive skills will be useful. It may be helpful for the teachers and/or parents to complete rating scales or checklists to describe the child's functioning prior to the illness or injury. The *Behavior Rating Inventory of Executive Functioning (BRIEF)* (Gioia, Isquith, Guy, & Kenworthy, 2000) or the *Neuropsychological Processing Concerns Checklist for School-age Children and Youth* (Miller, 2007) would be useful for this type of evaluation.

- The school neuropsychologist should meet with the parents to gain their perspective on residual problems and to establish a home-school collaborative relationship for planning reentry.

- If the child is still considered to be in an "acute" phase of the injury or illness, a full neuropsychological battery is probably not indicated at this point. The school neuropsychologist may complete some brief assessments to establish current baselines of neurocognitive status.

- The school neuropsychologist should consult with receiving teachers to provide an overview of any deficits at initial reentry and to describe the potential educational impacts and needed accommodations for initial reentry. These accommodations might include shortened school days, alternative modes of testing, note-takers, and development of a consistent routine. Specific training and/or information may need to be provided to teachers and other school personnel.
- After the child has been in school for a few days (five to ten days), it may be useful for the teacher to complete one of the checklists used to evaluate pre-illness/injury status, and also for baseline comparisons.
- Many children may experience social-emotional residuals and/or specific behavioral residuals related to their condition. It may be useful for the school neuropsychologist to meet with the child's peers, within the limits of confidentiality, to discuss some of the associated changes in the student. Additionally, it may be beneficial to plan specific activities for the social reintegration of the student.
- Depending on the apparent needs of the child, the school neuropsychologist along with other educational personnel may initiate the process for either a 504 plan or for possible disability for special education services under either Traumatic Brain Injury (TBI) or Other Health Impaired (OHI). Individual 504 plans typically are for more mild disabilities and conditions with minimal educational impact and can be implemented on a shorter-term basis. The 504 plan also requires less formal assessment and involves accommodations within the educational program and setting rather than in the direct provision of services. If there appears to be longer term or more significant residual educational impact of the injury or illness, the student may be referred for evaluation and services under Other Health Impaired (OHI) or Traumatic Brain Injury (TBI) special education categories. While the residuals of different conditions may be similar and both are "acquired" to some extent, the specific classification appears related to the basis of the residuals; (i.e., illness vs. injury).
- Related to the initiation of consideration for accommodations or educational services, a full comprehensive neuropsychological battery may be useful at this point. As discussed previously, a full battery may not be indicated in cases where the child's neurological status is not fully stabilized or is still considered to be in an acute or recovery phase. Partial batteries may be indicated in these cases. A full battery may also not be indicated in two other situations. First, if there appears to be minimal neurocognitive or educationally relevant residuals, a full battery may not be warranted. This does not mean that some accommodations and/or psychosocial supports are not provided, but it may be

that a comprehensive battery is not likely to yield substantive educationally relevant recommendations. However, caution in these cases should be taken to ensure that subtle deficits are not ignored. Second, in cases where there are very severe residuals, formal neuropsychological assessment may not be helpful. For example, if a child has experienced very severe general cognitive loss and now functions in the lower ranges of intellectual disability, standard neuropsychological assessment may not yield meaningful information. Similarly, if there are severe physical or sensory residuals, testing may not be feasible.

- Where comprehensive assessment is indicated, the recommendation is that Miller's (2007) conceptual model be followed. This model is also described in other sections of this volume. This model dictates an orderly progression of assessment through sensory-motor, attentional, visual-spatial, language, memory and learning, executive, cognitive speed and efficiency, intellectual, and academic functions and processes. Based on medical information and information from parents, teachers, and others, the neuropsychological assessment should be individually planned to focus on apparent residuals from the illness or injury and the possible educational impact. The *Neuropsychological Processing Concerns Checklist for School-Aged Children and Youth* (Miller, 2007) would be useful in planning the formal assessment. Also, since many of these children and adolescents may have social-emotional residuals related to their injury or illness, assessment of both internalizing and externalizing behavioral and emotional concerns should be considered to supplement the model.

- The assessment and related educational plans should delineate the various accommodations and related services. In many cases, the child with neurocognitive residuals will need an interdisciplinary approach involving occupational therapy, physical therapy, and speech and language services. Professionals from these disciplines often assess and intervene in areas related to Miller's (2007) conceptual model.

- In many cases, children with neurological disorders may warrant more frequent evaluations of status. While special education laws and regulations typically indicate a three-year evaluation cycle, this may be too infrequent for these children. The first twelve to eighteen months after return to school may be an appropriate time for additional reevaluation.

- Last, children who have experienced neurologically related illness or injury may present atypical patterns after their return to school. Some data suggests there may be "late-emerging" problems even several years after the illness or injury. Some children may appear to have had minimal, educationally related residuals when they were younger, but problems may emerge with additional development and/or changing demands of the school curriculum. Children with significant history of neurological illness or injury may need evaluation and/or services later in their educational career.

SUMMARY

Children and adolescents returning to school after experiencing a serious neurological condition or injury present special challenges for the school neuropsychologist and other educational professionals. The disorders covered in this chapter share some commonalities in terms of the residuals, but also yield unique impairments related to their condition. It is important to know the specific residuals of the condition and collaboration with medical personnel is important in planning a successful reintegration program. Dealing with reintegration issues often requires the school to be able to quickly develop a plan for the child's return. The school neuropsychologist is often the ideal individual to coordinate a reintegration team. A variety of activities may include assessment, consultation with and education for other school personnel, developing accommodations, monitoring progress of school readjustment, and dealing with associated social-emotional or behavioral issues.

REFERENCES

Anderson, V., Anderson, P., Grimwood, K., & Nolan, T. (2004). Cognitive and executive function 12 years after childhood bacterial meningitis: Effect of acute neurologic complications and age of onset. *Journal of Pediatric Psychology, 29*, 67–81.

Armstrong, F. D., Blumberg, M. J., & Toledano, S. R. (1999). Neurobehavioral issues in childhood cancer. *School Psychology Review, 28*, 194–203.

Berg, S., Trollfors, B., Hugosson, S., Fernell, E., & Svensson, E. (2002). Long-term follow-up of children with bacterial meningitis with emphasis on behavioural characteristics. *European Journal of Pediatrics, 161*, 330–336.

Berkelhammer, L. D., Williamson, A. L., Sanford, S. D., Dirksen, C. L., Sharp, W. G., Margules, A. S., & Prengler, R. A. (2007). Neurocognitive sequelae of pediatric sickle cell disease: A review of the literature. *Child Neuropsychology, 13*, 120–131.

Bigler, E. D., Clark, E., & Farmer, J. E. (Eds.). (1997). *Childhood traumatic brain injury: Diagnosis, assessment, and intervention.* Austin, TX: Pro-Ed.

Casella, E. B., Cypel, S., Osmo, A. A., Okay, Y., Lefvre, B. H., Lichtig, I., & Marques-Dias, M. J. (2004). Sequelae from meningococcal meningitis in children. *Arq Neuropsiquiatr, 62*, 421–428.

D'Amato, R. C., & Rothlisberg, B. A. (1997). How education should respond to students with traumatic brain injury. In E. D. Bigler, E. Clark, & J. E. Farmer (Eds.), *Childhood traumatic brain injury: Diagnosis, assessment, and intervention* (pp. 213–237). Austin, TX: Pro-Ed.

Data Accountability Center. (2006, Fall). *Children and students ages 3 through 5 served under IDEA, Part B, by disability category and state.* Retrieved September 26, 2008 from https://www.ideadata.org/arc_toc8.asp#partbCC.

DeBaun, M. R., Derdeyn, C. P., & McKinstry, R. C. (2006). Etiology of strokes in children with sickle cell anemia. *Mental Retardation and Developmental Disability Research Reviews, 12,* 192–199.

Espy, K. A., Moore, I. M., Kaufman, P. M., Kramer, J. H., Matthay, K., & Hutter, J. J. (2001). Chemotherapeutic CNS prophylaxis and neuropsychologic change in children with acute lymphoblastic leukemia: A prospective study. *Journal of Pediatric Psychology, 26,* 1–9.

Ewing-Cobbs, L., & Bloom, D. R. (2004). Traumatic brain injury: Neuropsychological, psychiatric, and educational issues. In R. T. Brown (Ed.), *Handbook of pediatric psychology in school settings* (pp. 313–331). Hillsdale, NJ: Lawrence Erlbaum Associates.

Gil, A. M., (2003). Neurocognitive outcomes following pediatric brain injury: A developmental approach. *Journal of School Psychology, 41,* 337–353.

Gioia, G. A., Isquith, P. K., Guy, S. C., & Kenworthy, L. (2000). *Behavior rating inventory of executive functioning.* Odessa, FL: Psychological Assessment Resources.

Grimwood, K., Anderson, V. A., Bond, L., Catroppa, C., Hore, R. L., Keir, E. H., Nolan, T., & Roberton, D. M. (1995). Adverse outcomes of bacterial meningitis in school-age survivors. *Pediatrics, 95,* 646–656.

Harvey, J. M. (2002). Best practices in working with students with traumatic brain injury. In A. Thomas & J. Grimes (Eds.), *Best practices in school psychology—IV* (pp. 1433–1445). Bethesda, MD: National Association of School Psychologists.

Hooper, S. R., Alexander, J., Moore, D., Sasser, H. C., Laurent, S., King, J., Bartel, S., & Callahan, B. (2004). Caregiver reports of common symptoms in children following a traumatic brain injury. *NeuroRehabilitation, 19,* 175–189.

King, A., Herron, S., McKinistry, R., Bacak, S., Armstrong, M., White, D., & DeBaun, M. (2006). A multidisciplinary health care team's efforts to improve educational attainment in children with sickle-cell anemia and cerebral infarcts. *Journal of School Health, 76,* 33–37.

King, A. A., Tang, S., Ferguson, K. L., & DeBaun, M. R. (2005). An education program to increase teacher knowledge about sickle cell disease. *Journal of School Health, 75,* 11–14.

Koomen, I., Grobbee, D. E., Jennekens-Schinkel, A., Roord, J. J., & van Furth, A. M. (2003). Parental perception of educational, behavioural and general health problems in school-age survivors of bacterial meningitis. *Acta Paediatrica, 92,* 177–185.

Koomen, I., Grobbee, D. E., Roord, J. J., Jennekins-Schinkel, A. J., van der Lei, H. D. W., Kraak, M. A. C., & van Furth, A. M. (2004). Prediction of academic and behavioural limitations in school-age survivors of bacterial meningitis. *Acta Paediatrica, 93,* 1378–1385.

Koomen, I., Raat, H., Jennekens-Schinkel, A., Grobbee, D. E., Roord, J. J., & van Furth, M. (2005). Academic and behavioral limitations and health-related quality of life in school-age survivors of bacterial meningitis. *Quality of Life Research, 14,* 1563–1572.

Koomen, I., van Furth, A. M., Kraak, M. A. C., Grobbee, D. E., Roord, J. J., & Jennekins-Schinkel, A. J. (2004). Neuropsychology of academic and behavioral limitations in school age survivors of bacterial meningitis. *Developmental Medicine & Child Neurology, 46,* 724–732.

Li, C., & Wendt, R. N. (1998). Cancer (childhood). In L. Phelps (Ed.), *Health-related disorders in children and adolescents* (pp. 114–120). Washington DC: American Psychological Association.

Lindsey, T., Watts-Tate, N., Southwood, E., Routhieaux, J., Beatty, J., Diane, C., Phillips, M., Lea, G., Brown, E., & DeBaun, M. R. (2005). Chronic blood transfusion therapy practices to treat strokes in children with sickle cell disease. *Journal of the American Academy of Nurse Practitioners, 17,* 277–282.

Massagli, T. L., Fann, J. R., Burington, B. E., Jaffe, K. M., Katon, W. J., & Thompson, R. S. (2004). Psychiatric illness after mild traumatic brain injury in children. *Archives of Physical Medicine and Rehabilitation, 85,* 1428–1434.

Miller, D. C. (2007). *Essentials of school neuropsychological assessment.* Hoboken, NJ: John Wiley & Sons.

Miller, L. J., & Donders, J. (2003). Prediction of educational outcome after pediatric traumatic brain injury. *Rehabilitation Psychology, 48,* 237–241.

Morse, L. W., & Shine, A. E. (1998). Sickle cell anemia. In L. Phelps (Ed.), *Health-related disorders in children and adolescents* (pp. 596–602). Washington, DC: American Psychological Association.

National Cancer Institute (n.d.). Childhood cancers: Questions and answers. Retrieved October 10, 2008, from http://www.cancer.gov/cancertopics/factsheet/Sites-type/childhood.

Nicholson, K., Martelli, M. F., & Zasler, N. D. (2001). Does pain confound interpretation of neuropsychological test results? *NeuroRehabilitation, 16,* 225–230.

Palumbo, D. R., Davidson, P. W., Peloquin, L. J., & Gigliotti, F. (1995). Neuropsychological aspects of pediatric infectious diseases. In M. C. Roberts (Ed.), *Handbook of pediatric psychology* (pp. 342–361). New York: Guilford.

Phelps, L. (Ed.). (1998). *Health-related disorders in children and adolescents.* Washington DC: American Psychological Association.

Prigatano, G. P., & Gupta, S. (2006). Friends after traumatic brain injury in children. *Journal of Head Trauma and Rehabilitation, 21,* 505–513.

Reinfjell, T., Lofstad, G. E., Veenstra, M., Vikan, A., & Diseth, T. H. (2007). Health-related quality of life and intellectual functioning in children in remission from acute lymphoblastic leukaemia. *Acta Paediatrica, 96,* 1280–1285.

Rotto, P. C. (1998). Traumatic brain injury. In L. Phelps (Ed.), *Health-related disorders in children and adolescents* (pp. 652–671). Washington, DC: American Psychological Association.

Savage, R. C., Pearson, S., McDonald, H., Potoczny-Gray, A., & Marchese, N. (2001). After hospital: Working with schools and families to support the long term needs of children with brain injuries. *NeuroRehabilitation, 16,* 49–58.

Schatz, J., Brown, R. T., Pascual, J. M., Hsu, L., & DeBaun, M. R. (2001). Poor school and cognitive functioning with silent cerebral infarcts and sickle cell disease. *Neurology, 56,* 1109–1111.

Schatz, J., & McClellan, C. B. (2006). Sickle cell disease as a neurodevelopmental disorder. *Mental Retardation and Developmental Disabilities Research Reviews, 12,* 200–207.

Semrud-Clikeman, M. (2001). *Traumatic brain injury in children and adolescents: Assessment and intervention.* New York: Guilford.

Shears, D., Nadel, S., Gledhill, J., Gordon, F., & Garralda, M. E. (2007). Psychiatric adjustment in the year after meningococcal disease in childhood. *Journal of the American Academy of Child and Adolescent Psychiatry, 46,* 76–82.

Taylor, H. G., Barry, C. T., & Schatschneider, C. (1993). School-age consequences of Haemophilus influenza type b meningitis. *Journal of Child Clinical Psychology, 22,* 196–206.

Taylor, H. G., Minich, N. M., & Schatschneider, C. (2000). Longitudinal outcomes of Haemophilus influenzae in school-age children. *Neuropsychology, 14,* 509–518.

Thomas, A., & Grimes, J. (Eds.). (2002). *Best practices in school psychology—IV.* Bethesda, MD: The National Association of School Psychologists.

Tremont, G., Mittenberg, W., & Miller, L. J. (1999). Acute intellectual effects of pediatric head trauma. *Child Neuropsychology, 5,* 104–114.

U.S. Department of Education. (n.d.). Protecting students with disabilities: Frequently asked questions about Section 504 and the education of children with disabilities. Retrieved August 8, 2008 from http://www.ed.gov/about/offices/list/ocr/504faq.html.

Wilson, B., Baddeley, A., & Evans, J. (1994). Errorless learning in the rehabilitation of memory impaired people. *Neuropsychological Rehabilitation, 4,* 307–326.

Yeates, K. O., & Taylor, H. G. (2005). Neurobehavioral outcomes of mild head injury in children and adolescents. *Pediatric Rehabilitation, 8,* 5–16.

Ylvisaker, M., Feeney, T. J., Maher-Maxwell, N., Mesere, N., Greary, P., & DeLorenzo, J. (1995). School reentry following severe traumatic brain injury: Guidelines for educational planning. *Journal of Head Trauma Rehabilitation, 10,* 25–41.

SECTION III

CLINICAL APPLICATIONS OF SCHOOL NEUROPSYCHOLOGY: SPECIAL POPULATIONS

CHAPTER 11

Assessment and Intervention Practices for Children with ADHD and Other Frontal-Striatal Circuit Disorders

JAMES B. HALE, LINDA A. REDDY, GABRIELLE WILCOX, AMY MCLAUGHLIN, LISA HAIN, AMY STERN, JULIE HENZEL, and ELEAZAR EUSEBIO

MOST CHILDREN REFERRED for a school neuropsychological evaluation present with an attention problem, and when behavioral criteria are gathered by informant report, many will meet criteria for Attention Deficit Hyperactivity Disorder (ADHD). No longer considered *just* a "disruptive behavior disorder," ADHD is now widely understood to be a frontal-subcortical circuit disorder (Castellanos et al., 2002), with affected brain regions potentially contributing to both cognitive and behavioral symptom expression (Voeller, 2001). Although this clarifies the nature and manifestation of ADHD, most frontal-subcortical circuit disorders lead to impaired attention (see Lichter & Cummings, 2001), suggesting differential diagnosis of ADHD can be difficult using only behavioral criteria (Hale, Fiorello, & Brown, 2005). In fact, the conflicting evidence regarding frontal-subcortical-executive causes of ADHD may be due to considerable population heterogeneity found when behavioral diagnostic criteria are used (Sonuga-Barke, Sergeant, Nigg, & Willcutt, 2008).

With so many causes of inattention, both cortical and subcortical, school neuropsychological evaluations are needed for greater diagnostic sensitivity and specificity of ADHD and other frontal-subcortical circuit disorders (Hale & Fiorello, 2004). Although the empirical investigation of ADHD in relation to other causes of attention problems, including other frontal-subcortical circuit disorders, is in its relative infancy, this chapter seeks to clarify these relationships for both school neuropsychological assessment and intervention purposes, with the premise being that such practice leads to more accurate identification of disorders and greater ecological and treatment validity as a result.

THE BIOLOGICAL BASIS OF ADHD

Most often an inherited disorder that results in catecholamine (e.g., dopamine and/or norepinephrine) neurotransmitter dysregulation (Arnsten, 2001; Faraone, 2008; Kieling, Goncalves, Tannock, & Castellanos, 2008; Pliszka, 2005), the main cortical areas implicated in ADHD include the prefrontal cortex (e.g., Castellanos et al., 2002; Filipek, 1999), specifically the dorsolateral prefrontal and inferior prefrontal cortices (Dickstein, Bannon, Castellanos, & Milham, 2006) and their associated frontal-subcortical circuit structures, including the striatum and the thalamus (Denckla & Reiss, 1997; Halperin & Schultz, 2006; Semrud-Clikeman et al., 2000; Wolosin et al., 2007). Described by Luria (1973) as the brain's "superstructure," these governing executive areas are responsible for planning, organizing, strategizing, problem solving, monitoring, evaluating, and changing behavior (Hale & Fiorello, 2004). Other structures affected include the anterior cingulate (e.g., Rubia et al., 2005; Schulz et al., 2004) and corpus callosum (e.g., Giedd et al., 1994; Semrud-Clikeman et al., 1994), both of which affect information transfer and control according to anterior-posterior and left-right axes respectively in ADHD populations (Hale & Fiorello, 2004; Liotti et al., 2007; Moll et al., 2000).

Specifically, the right prefrontal, globus pallidus, caudate nucleus, and cerebellar regions have been found to be reduced in volume and/or hypo-active using neuroimaging techniques (Castellanos et al., 2002; Durston, 2003; Rubia et al., 1999; Valera et al., 2007; Vaidya et al., 1998), suggesting ADHD does not only affect the frontal lobes, but a number of interrelated midline circuits and tracts extending from the subcortical cerebellar to the cortical prefrontal regions. Thus, in addition to a left-right hemisphere and anterior-posterior axes of interpretation in understanding ADHD and other disorders (Hale & Fiorello, 2004), a third superior-cortical to inferior-subcortical mid-line axis can be inferred during school neuropsychological assessment and intervention, and this axis is likely the seat of most known psychopathologies, including ADHD (see Lichter & Cummings, 2001). This midline axis impairment found in ADHD suggests that the inattention, impulsivity, and hyper-activity typically addressed during ADHD evaluations is only but one facet of the disorder, with multiple executive, memory, and perceptual systems likely affected. Although behavioral symptoms remain relevant in ADHD diagnosis, and the simplicity of such an approach is alluring, the ubiquity of attention problems and their numerous causes suggests behavioral criteria are insufficient for ADHD diagnosis (Hale, Fiorello, & Brown, 2005; Hale et al., 2009; Hale, Blaine-Halperin, & Beakley, 2007; Reddy & Hale, 2007).

Table 11.1

Cognitive/Neuropsychological and Achievement Characteristics of Children with ADHD

Construct	Likely Impairment Level	Reliability
Inhibitory Control	Moderate to Severe	Consistent
Attention Deficit	None to Mild	Consistent
Executive Attention/Vigilance	Moderate to Severe	Consistent
Motor Activity (Hyperactivity)	Moderate (Old) to Severe (Young)	Consistent
Frontal Fine Motor/Praxis	Mild to Moderate	Inconsistent
Motor Timing/Cerebellar Motor	Mild to Moderate	Inconsistent
Somatosensory/Tactile, Auditory, Visual	None to Mild	Inconsistent
Executive Functioning/Fluid Reasoning	Mild to Severe[1]	Inconsistent
Working Memory	Mild to Severe[2]	Inconsistent
Long-Term Memory	None to Mild	Consistent
Long-Term Memory Encoding	None to Mild	Consistent
Long-Term Memory Retrieval	Moderate to Severe	Inconsistent
Processing Speed	Mild to Severe	Inconsistent
Visual-Spatial-Holistic Ability	None to Moderate	Inconsistent
Auditory-Verbal-Crystallized	None to Mild	Inconsistent

Note: [1]Depends on cortical-subcortical circuit examined.
[2]Verbal impairment < visual impairment.

The frontal-striatal abnormalities inherent in ADHD may manifest in several areas of functional impairments in inhibitory control, attention regulation, sensory-motor, executive functions including working memory and processing speed and efficiency, and to a lesser extent language/crystallized abilities and visual/spatial skills, all of which affect academic achievement and behavior. These findings are summarized briefly below and highlighted in Table 11.1. We largely focus on frontal-subcortical functions such as inhibitory control, sustained attention (vigilance), motor functioning, working memory/processing speed, and emotion regulation, as these variables discriminate a vast majority of ADHD children and controls (Berlin, Bohlin, Nyberg, & Janols, 2004; Willcutt et al., 2005).

COGNITIVE/NEUROPSYCHOLOGICAL FUNCTIONING IN ADHD

INHIBITORY CONTROL

Often related to emotion regulation, inhibitory control is widely understood as the ability to suppress responses to irrelevant stimuli. Impulsivity is a common problem with inhibitory control and results in a wide array of maladaptive externalizing behaviors such as sensation-seeking, risk-taking, carelessness, indulgence, and fearlessness (Hollander & Evers, 2001). In typically developing children, the frontal lobes tend to regulate this process (Posner & Raichle 1994), with dorsolateral and orbital prefrontal regions responsible for stimulus judgment, goal setting and maintenance, and determining adaptive response patterns (D'Amato, Fletcher-Janzen, & Reynolds, 2005). In particular, the right inferior or ventrolateral prefrontal cortex is the cortical region most often associated with impulsivity and is heavily involved in motor control and emotion regulation (Congdon & Canli, 2005). This could explain why internalization of language is a critical feature of behavioral control (Barkley, 1997) and could also explain why impulsivity and hyperactivity problems are commonly seen in children with ADHD.

Children with ADHD can respond without consideration of consequences, act upon stimuli irrelevant to the task at hand, or begin responding before instructions are completed (Solanto, Arnsten, et al., 2001). Neuropsychological performance on both executive attention and behavioral regulation measures correlates with inhibitory more than attention behavioral symptoms (Hale et al., 2006), so children presenting with poor inhibitory control could show deficits related to multiple cortical and subcortical regions, as has been suggested by Barkley's (1997) theory of ADHD. As Nigg (2000) suggests, there are many types of inhibitory control problems including cognitive and behavioral inhibition and interference control, thought to be a "top-down" executive-mediated cortical inhibitory problem, while "bottom-up" sub-cortical problems are related to response to reinforcement and punishment.

Determining the interrelationship among inhibitory mechanisms and structures remains a challenge. Using quantitative meta-analytic activation likelihood estimation (ALE) techniques, the dorsolateral and inferior prefrontal cortex, precentral gyrus, anterior cingulate, and basal ganglia were all important for inhibition (Dickstein et al., 2006). Apparently, the right prefrontal cortex is more involved in representation and maintenance of adaptive responding, and suppression to salient, but irrelevant events, while the basal ganglia is more involved in suppression or execution of response (Casey et al., 1997; 2002). Prefrontal, anterior cingulate, and posterior cingulate involvement may depend on the triggering, monitoring, and evaluation stages of inhibitory control (Liotti et al., 2007). Castellanos (2001) found cortical-striatal-thalamic circuit hypofunctioning to correlate with inhibitory functions in individuals with ADHD. Children with ADHD not only have difficulty with response inhibition, but they may rely on multiple frontal and even posterior parietal regions in an attempt to compensate for poor ventrolateral inhibitory function (e.g., Durston, 2003), suggesting multiple frontal-subcortical circuits and posterior cortical areas can be implicated in inhibitory control and dysfunction.

Thus, differentiation of inhibitory mechanisms could follow a bottom-up (e.g., striatal→prefrontal) or top-down (e.g., prefrontal-striatal) approach to understanding the pathophysiology of response inhibition deficits in ADHD. More likely it is the bottom-up striatal cause of poor behavioral regulation, given that dopamine and inhibitory control are highly related, and stimulants are dopamine agonists that largely have their effect in the striatum. However, it is well known that depletion of dopamine and norepinephrine affects many prefrontal functions (Arnsten, 1997), so attention arousal, maintenance, and selection may play an important interactive role with inhibitory mechanisms, suggesting their interaction requires diagnostic consideration and further empirical elucidation.

ATTENTION DEFICIT OR SUSTAINED ATTENTION (VIGILANCE) DEFICIT?

The most commonly reported referral symptom for children with ADHD is attention problems (Reddy & Hale, 2007), yet there are multiple attention systems that can result in disordered attention (Mirsky, 1996; Posner & Petersen, 1990). As a result, a distinction is necessary between attention activation or allocation (Sergeant, 2005) versus executive control of attentional resources (Huang-Pollock, Nigg, & Halperin, 2006) in the pathophysiology of ADHD. Because inattention affects so many areas of cognitive functioning, these children are at considerable risk for school failure and social problems (Biederman et al., 2004; Clark, Prior, & Kinsella, 2002; Lawrence et al., 2004). Understanding the neural mechanisms that contribute to this domain is therefore important for assessment and future treatment implications, extending well beyond the use of stimulant medication.

As with inhibition control, recent studies have linked specific frontal-striatal abnormalities to attention dysfunction in individuals with ADHD (Brieber et al., 2007; Castellanos et al., 2006; Williams, Stott, Goodyer, & Sahakian, 2000). Again, the ventrolateral and dorsolateral prefrontal cortical areas, basal ganglia, and parietal lobe (Brieber et al., 2007; Casey, Nigg, & Durston, 2007; Castellanos et al., 2006) have been associated with attention deficits as they are with inhibitory control. Additionally, Brieber et al. (2007) found attention correlated with frontal gray matter, and gray and white matter volume reductions have been reported in several frontal areas (Mostofsky, Cooper, Kates, Denckla, & Kaufmann, 2002). The posterior parietal attention network, although likely the cause of some children's attention problems (e.g., Hale, Kaufman, Naglieri, & Kavale, 2006), is not likely the cause of ADHD (Huang-Pollock & Nigg, 2003).

Modulation of attention could be due to dysfunctional interconnectivity between frontal and posterior attention systems (Gazzaley et al., 2005), but a recent direct comparison of the posterior attention system (e.g., parietal, pulvinar, superior colliculus), anterior attention system (e.g., anterior cingulate, supplementary motor cortex), and vigilance system (e.g., right prefrontal circuits, locus coeruleus), found support for vigilance impairment in ADHD (Huang-Pollock et al., 2006), consistent with previous meta-analytic findings (Huang-Pollock & Nigg, 2003). Therefore, these prefrontal-striatal circuits likely impact executive control of attention (Willis & Weiler, 2005), thereby *secondarily* affecting the posterior and anterior attention systems. Directly comparing selective attention and response inhibition causes of ADHD using fMRI, Booth et al. (2005) showed the primary region of interest differences between ADHD and controls were found on the inhibitory task, not the attention one.

As a result, ADHD, at least the subtype (i.e., endophenotype) that benefits from stimulant medication, is probably best understood as a disorder of *intention* or *attention control* rather than a primary attention problem (Denckla, 1996; Hale et al., 2006). Interestingly, then, children with ADHD *do not* have a primary attention deficit, but difficulty with executive *control* of attention. While evidence of specific neural regions affecting attention exists, it remains unclear as to what extent these regions are responsible for attention dysfunction in children with ADHD and how these deficits are manifested in ADHD endophenotypes (Doyle et al., 2005; Nigg, 2005). Hale et al. (2006) found attention symptoms did not correlate with executive and self-regulation factors, but hyperactive/impulsive symptoms did, and children with impaired executive function were more likely to have combined type ADHD and respond to stimulants. However, other studies suggest little neuropsychological difference between ADHD subtypes, and support has been limited for a pure executive model of ADHD (Geurts, Verte, Oosterlaan, Roeyers, & Sergeant, 2004). As a result, the inattentive type of ADHD is probably quite heterogeneous, with some children having mild ADHD and others having other causes for their attention problems (Hale, et al., 2006; 2007, February; Reddy & Hale, 2007). Since multiple disorders with their associated brain dysfunction can lead to attention problems, heterogeneity among children referred for attention problems must be considered and explored carefully, with differential diagnosis and alternative treatment strategies considered for ADHD, endophenotypes, and other disorders affecting attention.

ACTIVITY LEVEL AND SENSORY-MOTOR FUNCTIONING

Sensory-motor functioning should dissociate for children with ADHD, with motor impairments more likely than sensory deficits given the frontal-subcortical motor circuit involvement and motor overactivity associated with the disorder. Hyperactivity has been linked to dysfunctional frontal-subcortical circuits due to dopaminergic insufficiency, and stimulants (e.g., methylphenidate) reduce motor activity primarily by binding to the dopamine transporter, thereby increasing extracellular dopamine (see Swanson et al., 2007). This is consistent with findings that children with ADHD have been found to have midbrain dopamine transporter deficits, and dopamine receptor binding in the right caudate has been related to hyperactivity (Jucaite et al., 2005), with variations in dopamine transporter candidate genes identified for children with hyperactive/impulsive symptoms (Mazei-Robison et al., 2005). However, children with predominantly inattentive ADHD are often characterized as being slow moving, sluggish, and *hypoactive*, which could suggest a different etiology and treatment course (Angold, Costello, & Erkanli, 1999; Milich, Balentine, & Lynam, 2001).

As would be expected given their frontal-cerebellar midline axis deficits, children with ADHD have difficulty with motor precision and consistency (Rommelse et al., 2008), which frequently results in comorbid developmental coordination disorder diagnosis (Sergeant, Piek, & Oosterlaan, 2006; Watemberg, Waiserberg, Zuk, & Lerman-Sagie, 2007). In addition to premotor and/or supplementary motor deficits associated with the cortical-subcortical circuits (Mostofsky et al., 2002; Suskauer et al., 2008), especially the basal ganglia for maintaining motor control execution (Wang et al. 2007; Castellanos et al., 2006; Halperin & Schulz, 2006), reduced gray matter found in the cerebellum, perirolandic area, and rolandic operculum could also account for motor deficits (Carmona et al., 2005). As a result, it would be important to evaluate whether motor deficits are the result of a cortical motor or subcortical cerebellar problem, or likely both (e.g., Castellanos et al., 2006). In addition, children with ADHD have difficulties with sequential processing of motor patterns and motor timing, but basic motor skills appear to be largely intact (Mostofsky et al., 2003; Rommelse et al., 2008). Certainly, apraxia is commonly associated with frontal dysfunction (Zanini, 2008), but it is likely the coordination of motor actions over time that is impaired (Piek, Dyck, Francis, & Conwell, 2007), and this could be due to cortical motor areas, basal ganglia, and/or cerebellar deficits as well (Berquin et al., 1998; Hale & Fiorello, 2004).

Children with ADHD have more sensory processing deficits than controls (e.g., Mangeot et al., 2001; Yochman, Parush, & Ornoy, 2004). This leads us to the question of how a frontally based disorder can affect sensory functioning. One possibility is that sensory impairments could be due to impaired thalamic functioning in ADHD (Rowe et al., 2005), as this is the only structure associated with afferent processing in the frontal-subcortical circuits. Certainly, the corpus callosum problems noted earlier could lead to difficulty with sensory-motor integration and bimanual coordination during motor performance (e.g., Klimkeit, Sheppard, Lee, & Bradshaw, 2004; Moll et al.,

2000). Finally, sensory problems could be the result of poor connectivity or efficiency of white matter connections between the anterior and posterior regions, either through the anterior and posterior cingulate (e.g., Liotti et al., 2007) and/or the superior and inferior longitudinal fasciculi (see Hale & Fiorello, 2004; Kraus et al., 2007).

Executive Functioning, Fluid Reasoning, Working Memory, and Processing Speed

Probably the most consistent, albeit still controversial, neuropsychological finding is that children with ADHD have considerable deficits in executive function due to their cortical-subcortical circuit impairments (Castellanos et al., 2006). As noted earlier, meta-analyses have found dorsolateral and inferior prefrontal cortices, anterior cingulate, basal ganglia, thalamus, prefrontal motor, and associated parietal areas to be impaired (Dickstein et al., 2006), so it is likely that executive deficits can be found in tasks that require planning, organizing, strategizing, monitoring, evaluating, and shifting/changing behaviors (Hale & Fiorello, 2004). Despite the growing body of evidence supporting frontal-striatal-thalamic circuit dysfunction in ADHD, the neuropsychological findings have been inconsistent, likely because of the behavioral diagnostic criteria used to define groups (Reddy & Hale, 2007), with heterogeneity diminishing the utility of these measures (e.g., Sonuga-Barke et al., 2008).

To examine the primacy of executive deficits in ADHD, several neuropsychological test meta-analyses have been conducted to document the extent of these executive deficits (e.g., Willcutt et al., 2005; Homack & Riccio, 2004; Romine et al., 2004; Sergeant, Guerts, & Oosterlaan, 2002). The most comprehensive to date has been the Wilcutt et al. (2005) study, which found that ADHD was best characterized by executive deficits in response inhibition, vigilance, working memory, and planning, with average effect sizes for measures in the medium range. Importantly, these deficits could not be explained by intelligence, achievement, or comorbidities, and were evident in both community and clinic samples. Independent meta-analyses for executive decision making, online performance monitoring, and interference control (i.e., Stroop Color-Word Test), and problem solving, mental flexibility, cognitive set shifting, and response to feedback (i.e., Wisconsin Card Sorting Test) found the measures were sensitive to ADHD, but not specific for the disorder (Homack & Riccio, 2004; Romine et al., 2004).

Similar analyses of sustained attention and inhibitory control on continuous performance tests (CPT) have yielded similar results (see Riccio, Reynolds, Lowe, & Moore, 2002). Interestingly, CPT deficits may be more sensitive to children with combined type ADHD (Collins, 2003), consistent with earlier arguments regarding response inhibition as the primary cause of "true" ADHD (e.g., Barkley, 1997; Castellanos et al., 2006; Hale et al., 2005). However, the discriminant validity problem of executive measures remains a significant one, as executive deficits are common in many types of childhood psychopathology (Sergeant et al., 2002; Sonuga-Barke et al. 2008).

Although fluid reasoning is often considered a "cognitive" test, there are similarities among measures of fluid reasoning and executive function (Decker, Hill, & Dean, 2007; Miller & Hale, 2008; Saggino et al., 2006) as both require novel problem solving, the ability to benefit from feedback, and adaptive as opposed to vertical responding (Goldberg, 2001). As the complexity of problem solving increases, so does dorsolateral prefrontal functioning (Kroger et al., 2002). Children with ADHD and social problems have deficits on fluid reasoning and visual organization/praxis measures with high executive demands (Schafer & Semrud-Clikeman, 2008), suggesting fluid reasoning is in part a measure of right dorsolateral prefrontal functioning (Kane & Engle, 2002), with deficits in this area consistently associated with ADHD (Castellanos et al., 2006; Swanson et al., 2007). A strong predictor of fluid abilities is working memory (Conway et al., 2002), which is a common deficit found in children with ADHD (Willcutt et al., 2005).

Likely most related to dorsolateral prefrontal functioning (Levy & Goldman-Rakic, 2000), working memory deficits are common in children with ADHD (Barkley, 1997) and frequently observed on cognitive tests (Marusiak & Janzen, 2005; Mayes & Calhoun, 2006). Although both verbal and nonverbal working memory impairments in ADHD have been reported, with meta-analyses revealing moderate and large effect sizes respectively, spatial working memory appears to be more impaired than verbal working memory (Martinussen et al., 2005; Willcutt et al., 2005). Executive factors that include working memory have been found to be related to DSM-IV reported hyperactive-impulsive symptoms (Hale et al., 2005), which would be consistent with visual-spatial working memory and inhibition deficits both being related to right frontal dysfunction (Clarke et al., 2007), but executive functions have been found to be most related to inattentive symptoms in other studies (Chhabildas et al., 2001; Martinussen & Tannock, 2006). Perhaps differences in part might reflect the divided (left) and sustained (right) prefrontal attention influences on verbal and nonverbal working memory respectively (e.g., Pasini, Paloscia, Allesandrelli, Porfirio, & Curatolo, 2007; Smith & Jonides, 1997), which could be differentially impaired based on ADHD sample composition. However, one must also consider how the dorsolateral prefrontal circuit might exert a top-down attentional control over behavioral (dis)inhibition resulting from ventrolateral impairment when working memory is engaged (e.g., Sandrini, Rossini, & Miniussi, 2008).

Children with ADHD also exhibit deficits in processing speed and efficiency (Mayes & Calhoun, 2006). In typically developing children, the prefrontal cortices interact with posterior brain regions to determine the efficiency of information processing (D'Amato et al., 2005). Known to be impaired in ADHD and other disorders, the cingulate seems to be the critical structure for maintaining this online regulation of anterior-posterior communication (Hale & Fiorello, 2004). Russell et al. (2006) posited that slow and variable performance on information processing and rapid continuous responses tasks could result from a lack of energy supply to rapidly firing neurons, consistent with the tenets of Sergeant's (2000) cognitive-energetic model, which appears to apply specifically to the inattentive ADHD subtype (Weiler, Holmes Bernstein, Bellinger, & Waber, 2000). Kalff et al. (2005) found processing speeds were slower and more variable on focused and divided attention tasks in both the ADHD at-risk and "borderline" ADHD groups. As noted earlier, visuomotor deficits in ADHD are more related to motor timing, organization, and control, as opposed to actual motor performance (Mostofsky et al., 2003; Piek et al., 2007; Rommelse et al., 2008), so processing speed impairments may not be comparable across ADHD subtypes. Several studies have found processing speed deficits in both subtypes (Chhabildis et al., 2001; Nigg, Blaskey, Huang-Pollock, & Rappley, 2002). Rucklidge and Tannock (2002) noted that while variability in reaction time was inherent in both ADHD subtypes, the inattentive subtype was notable for processing speed variability, while interference control was predictive of hyperactive/impulsive ADHD. The difference may be one of arousal for processing speed deficits in the inattentive type, versus sustained attention or persistence interfering with processing efficiency for the combined type (Lockwood, Marcotte, & Stern, 2001).

Learning and Memory

Although at first glance children with ADHD (more anterior problem) would appear to be different than children with specific learning disabilities (SLD; more posterior problem), inhibitory control, attention, sensory-motor, executive function, processing speed, and working memory deficits can severely impact a child's ability to encode, store, and retrieve information, making learning a difficult process for many children with ADHD. Academic deficits have long been considered the final common pathway for children with ADHD (Shaywitz & Shaywitz, 1988), so the impact on learning and memory is clearly evident. Not surprisingly, the comorbidity of SLD and ADHD ranges from 25 to 70 percent (Kellner, Houghton, & Douglas, 2003), with SLD diagnosed more often in inattentive and combined subtypes than the hyperactive/impulsive subtypes (Tannock & Brown, 2000).

New learning requires executive functions for governing a gradiential shift from right frontal to left posterior regions (Goldberg, 2001; Hale & Fiorello, 2004), which would be consistent with the executive-fluid connection discussed previously (Decker et al., 2007; Kane & Engle, 2002). As a result, new learning can be difficult for children with ADHD, especially if they have difficulty attending to the novel information presented, but long-term memory storage does not seem to be impaired in children with ADHD (Kaplan, Dewey, Crawford, & Fisher, 1998). The difficulty may be the overload in working memory rather than memory or procedural knowledge, however, as children with ADHD have difficulty filtering out irrelevant information, which overloads working memory (Passolunghi, Marzocchi, & Fiorillo, 2005). Even if a child could control attention and have adequate long-term memory, a well-known fact is that a working memory is important for both long-term memory encoding and retrieval, which is consistently deficient in children with ADHD, as noted earlier (Martinussen et al., 2005; Willcutt et al., 2005). Specifically, encoding does not appear to be as impaired as retrieval, which would be consistent with the importance of the right frontal lobe deficits implicated in ADHD (Clarke et al., 2007) affecting retrieval from long-term memory (Tulving & Markowitsch, 1997). Gitten et al. (2006) found that children with ADHD were impaired on spatial learning, but not on object learning tasks, due to inconsistency in response due to poor executive control of strategic responding, suggesting that meaning facilitates learning. Consistent with this finding, Krauel et al. (2007) used fMRI to show that emotional salience increased episodic memory in those with ADHD and that parietal lobe activation could be used to compensate for low anterior cingulate activation during encoding tasks.

Subcortical structures are also implicated in ADHD learning and memory deficits. The basal ganglia is particularly important in associative, procedural, and habit learning (Myers et al., 2003; Packard & Knowlton, 2002). Sagvolden et al. (2005) argue that dopaminergic hypoactivity affects several different cortical/subcortical functions with limited reinforcement strength, impulsivity, poor sustained attention, and hyperactivity (mesolimbic branch); poor attention orienting and executive deficits (mesocortical branch); and non-declarative habit learning and memory, and motor impairments (nigrostriatal branch) differentially affected. In particular, nucleus accumbens deficiencies may lead to deficient motivation or reinforcement during new learning situations (Sonuga-Barke, 2005). Finally, implicated in these findings are learning problems associated with cerebellar deficits in ADHD (Castellanos et al., 2006), as this subcortical structure is not only important in motor function, but also critical in executive coordination of cognitive functions, including learning, memory, timing, and automaticity (Doya, 2000; Ivry, 1993; Rapoport, van Reekum, & Mayberg, 2000).

VISUAL-SPATIAL-HOLISTIC AND AUDITORY-VERBAL-CRYSTALLIZED FUNCTIONING

Associated with more posterior brain functions (Hale & Fiorello, 2004), visual-spatial-holistic and auditory-verbal-crystallized psychological processes are not as impaired as executive processes (e.g., working memory, processing speed) in children with ADHD (Mayes & Calhoun, 2006). However, since the frontally mediated executive functions govern all other aspects of cognition (Luria, 1973), the fact that children with ADHD also experience visual-spatial-holistic right hemisphere and auditory-verbal-crystallized left hemisphere dysfunction should not be surprising. In addition, as noted earlier, frontal-striatal-thalamic circuit impairment likely affects sensory processing because of thalamus involvement. In addition, because of the superior and inferior longitudinal fasciculi (frontal-posterior white matter tracts that foster information processing), corpus callosum (left-right hemisphere communication) cingulate (regulation of decision making and anterior-posterior communication), and cerebellar (learning, memory, automaticity) involvement (e.g., Castellanos et al., 2002; Durston, 2003; Hale & Fiorello, 2004; Rubia et al., 1999; Valera et al., 2007; Vaidya et al., 1998), the executive regulation/output impairments common in ADHD affect processing of information as well. Even though some children with attention problems could have visual or auditory processing problems that cause problems with attention, these children do not have "primary" or "true" ADHD (Hale et al., 2005).

There is some debate in the literature regarding the extent to which visual-spatial-holistic deficits in children with ADHD are directly related to executive dysfunction or whether these deficits are in fact due to comorbid processing problems. Visual-spatial-holistic processes are often associated with right hemisphere function (Hale & Fiorello, 2004). Not surprisingly, there appears to be a right hemisphere dominance for attention in general, with posterior regions necessary for attention orienting and the anterior regions responsible for sustained attention and inhibition (Aman, Roberts, & Pennington, 1998; Berger & Posner, 2000; Casey et al., 1997; Mirsky, 1996; Pliszka et al., 2000). Studies have suggested that right hemisphere dysfunction, specifically right frontal lobe dysfunction (Aron, Robbins, & Poldrack, 2004; Castellanos, 2001; Congdon & Canli, 2005; Durston, 2003; Rubia, 2002; Sandson, Bachna, & Morin, 2000; Vaidya et al., 2005), is clearly evident in ADHD. While right frontal impairment seems likely in ADHD, meta-analyses suggest that these children have few problems with visual orienting, which could suggest more right posterior attention problems (e.g., Huang-Pollock & Nigg, 2003).

Visual-spatial-holisitic processes, especially visual working memory ones, appear to be more impaired than auditory-verbal-crystallized ones

(Martinussen et al., 2005), and these visual deficits improve with medication treatment (Bedard et al., 2004). Visual sustained attention may be particularly helpful in discriminating children with ADHD from children with psychosis who have difficulty with selective attention (Karatekin & Asarnow, 1999). Visual-spatial-holistic memory impairments in ADHD are also evident, but they are more related to executive processes involved in initial encoding and/or retrieval deficits reflecting more frontal-executive rather than in posterior dysfunction (e.g., Barnett, Maruff, & Vance, 2005). So while visual-spatial-holistic processing deficits are evident in ADHD, this may be due to the strong relationship between executive functions and visual-perceptual tasks (e.g., Denckla, 1996). However, given that attention orienting and attentional neglect can occur with right posterior dysfunction (Gross-Tsur, Shalev, Manor, & Amir, 1995; Reddy & Hale, 2007; Posner & Petersen, 1990), it is important for differential diagnosis to determine if visual-spatial-holistic processes are primary, such would be the case in "nonverbal" learning disabilities (Hain, Hale, & Glass-Kendorski, 2008) or secondary to executive dysfunction and true "ADHD" because only the latter problem is likely to be ameliorated by stimulant medication (e.g., Hale, et al., 2005; 2006; 2007, February; in press; Reddy & Hale, 2007).

Despite evidence that visual-spatial-holistic impairments are more likely than auditory-verbal-crystallized ones in ADHD (Martinussen et al., 2005; Sandson et al., 2000), attention deficits also overlap with auditory processing and language disorders (Moss & Sheiffele, 1994), which can interfere with the learning, behavioral, and social outcomes of affected children (Irwin, Carter, & Briggs-Gowan, 2002). In early research, 48 percent of children who had speech/language disorders met criteria for ADHD (Love & Thompson, 1988), and verbal working memory has been found to be more indicative of language impairment than ADHD (Cohen et al., 2000). In addition, children with central auditory processing disorder often meet criteria for ADHD (Riccio et al., 1994), with the CAPD deficits suggested as possible causes for, or intensifying of, the behavioral issues experienced by children with ADHD (Sundheim & Voeller, 2004). In fact, Barkley (1997) argues that poor internalization of language in ADHD is in part responsible for poor behavior regulation and impulse control, consistent with findings that ventrolateral frontal regions are responsible for response inhibition tasks (Liddle, Kiehl, & Smith, 2001).

Early reports of auditory and language deficits in ADHD have not been substantiated, leading some to question the language-ADHD relationship (Ors et al., 2005; Williams, Stott, Goodyer, & Sahakian, 2000). Clearly, children who do not process language efficiently will appear inattentive in the classroom (Buttross, 2000), and could meet "comorbid" ADHD when asked the DSM-IV-TR criteria, but is this really ADHD? Early research in this area often did not screen for comorbid SLD and, when directly tested, auditory processing and language deficits were more often associated with SLD than ADHD (Gomez & Condon, 1999; Pisecco, Baker, Silva, & Brooke, 2001; Purvis & Tannock, 2000). ADHD executive deficits appear to be independent of SLD (Klorman et al., 1999; McInnes, Humphries, Hogg-Johnson, & Tannock, 2003), suggesting these are related but distinct disorders (Chermak, Hall, & Musiek, 1999). Perhaps the language deficits in ADHD are more related to the executive/expressive aspects of language (Goodyer, 2000), such as working memory required during verbal retrieval, language organization/formulation, and pragmatic language, which are known to be impaired in ADHD and affected by frontal-executive dysfunction (e.g., Hale et al., 2005; Hurks et al., 2004; Kim & Kaiser, 2000; Kourakis et al., 2004; Purvis & Tannock, 1997; Tannock & Schachar, 1996; Thorell, 2007; Westby & Cutler, 1994). These findings suggest that right hemisphere implicit or indirect language processes (e.g., metaphors, humor, idioms, pragmatics) may be more impaired (e.g., Bryan & Hale, 2001) and consistent with earlier arguments regarding right hemisphere impairment in ADHD. In fact, while the inferior frontal cortex may be responsible for response inhibition as suggested by Barkley's (1997) arguments, it appears to be a *right*—not left—sided predominance for this function.

ACADEMIC ACHIEVEMENT AND DISABILITY IN ADHD

Given the etiology and manifestation of ADHD symptoms, it should not be surprising that these children are frequently found to have significant comorbid academic and behavior disorders. The question of academic achievement and disability in ADHD is one that requires some elucidation. The question of whether ADHD and SLD comorbidity reflects different or similar disorder processes is an important one. SLD is defined by IDEA (2004) as a "deficit in the basic psychological processes" that adversely affects academic achievement (see Hale, Kaufman, Naglieri, & Kavale, 2006). As suggested in previous sections, ADHD is clearly not only a behavior disorder, but it also affects basic psychological processes such as attention control and other executive functions. If these executive deficits significantly interfere with academic achievement, then clearly the child has ADHD and SLD, and both disorders are due to the same cause. However, if a child also has auditory-verbal-crystallized or visual-spatial-holistic processing deficits, a diagnostic dilemma becomes apparent.

Are these "comorbid" deficits due to executive dysfunction, a possibility discussed in the previous section, or are they a separate problem? If a separate problem, could the child have different genetic causes for each disorder, inherited separately from each parent (see Isles & Humby, 2008), perhaps the ADHD symptoms from one parent and the SLD ones from the other? Could the attention and behavioral deficits, if left unaddressed in school settings, resulted in a delay in learning (e.g., DuPaul & Stoner, 2003; Silver, 1990), even though there really isn't a cognitive explanation for the comorbid SLD? Could the child have an undiagnosed coup–contre coup incident where damage has occurred in the front and back of the brain (e.g., Konrad et al., 2000; McDonald, Flashman & Saykin, 2002), thereby mimicking ADHD with comorbid SLD? Could the child have a primary SLD, speech/language disorder, or even other psychiatric condition that could lead to attention problems, so ADHD is misdiagnosed? All these possibilities must be considered when evaluating a child with suspected ADHD, suggesting that careful diagnostic procedures must not only consider ADHD, executive dysfunction, and behavior problems, but also academic functioning as well.

In general, research has shown children with ADHD perform on average one standard deviation lower than typical children on pre-academic and cognitive measures (DuPaul, McGoey, Eckert, & VanBrakle, 2001), so these deficits are identifiable early in development. Decreased persistence coupled with increased fidgeting and distractibility in first-graders has been linked to poor academic achievement in fifth grade (Martin, Olejnik, & Gaddis, 1994). Similar results have been found between reading and math achievement scores and child temperament among adolescents (Guerin, Gottfried, Oliver, & Thomas, 1994). Temperament factors such as persistence, distractibility, and activity level can also influence peer and teacher responses to children with ADHD, negatively influencing academic self-concept and performance as a result (Martin, 1988). Clearly, given that their executive deficits are likely to interfere with planning, organizing, monitoring, evaluating, and revising academic work (Hale & Fiorello, 2004), it is not surprising that attention, impulsivity, and hyperactivity are often associated with academic deficits in children with ADHD (Reddy & Hale, 2007). These deficits lead to difficulty with work completion, poorer academic achievement including grades, more disciplinary problems such as suspension and expulsion, lower standardized test scores in all academic areas, and increased risk of grade retention as compared to same age peers (DuPaul & Stoner, 2003).

Not surprisingly, ADHD and SLD comorbidity rates tend to be quite high. In one study, 71 percent of the ADHD Combined Type and 66 percent of the ADHD Inattentive Type children were diagnosed with comorbid SLD, with written language SLD commonly found in ADHD and other psychiatric disorders (Mayes & Calhoun, 2006; Mayes, Calhoun, & Crowell, 2000), consistent with the importance of executive functions and writing (Hale & Fiorello, 2004). The Inattentive Type may show more academic impairment in math calculation and written expression than the Combined Type

(Riccio, Homack, Jarratt, & Wolfe, 2006), suggesting an interrelationship between attention, executive, and academic dysfunction (Biederman et al., 2004; Thorell, 2007). However, other studies have suggested that reading SLD is more common in children with ADHD than math or written language disorders (Del'Homme, Kim, Loo, Yang, & Smalley, 2007), with as many as 50 percent showing reading difficulties (Semrud-Clikeman et al., 1992). In another large-scale study ($N = 476$), children diagnosed with ADHD had prevalence rates of comorbid reading (16%), math (8%), and both reading and math (10%) SLD, with rates similar across subtypes (Capano et al., 2008), suggesting there is no uniform type of SLD in ADHD. Regardless, high rates of reading, math, and writing, SLD are often reported in children with ADHD (Mayes & Calhoun, 2006; Semrud-Clikeman, 2005). While consensus is lacking regarding the prevalence of SLD in children with ADHD, academic deficits may be the final common pathway among children with ADHD (Shaywitz & Shaywitz, 1988). Finally, children diagnosed with ADHD and learning disabilities tend to be at greater risk for social deficits than children with ADHD alone (Kellner et al., 2003), which is the focus on the next section.

DIFFERENTIATING ADHD AND OTHER FRONTAL-SUBCORTICAL CIRCUIT DISORDERS: THE COMORBIDITY PERSPECTIVE

Comorbid Conduct Disorder/Oppositional Defiant Disorder

Children with ADHD often present with noncompliant, impulsive, and aggressive behavior, which result in considerable peer and familial conflicts (e.g., Harada, Yamazaki, & Saitoh, 2002; Johnston & Mash, 2001). This could be due to elevated levels of interpersonal intensity, problems with social information processing and friendship development, and more aggressive and noisier play (Whalen & Henker, 1998). Children with combined type ADHD are often more aggressive in their social interactions and exhibit impaired emotional and behavioral inhibition (Barkley, 1997). Although it was once suggested that these externalizing behaviors resulted in the executive deficits seen in ADHD, executive function deficits appear to be specific to those with comorbid ADHD (Clark et al., 2000; Klorman et al., 1999).

Not surprisingly, comorbid conduct disorder (CD) and/or oppositional defiant disorder (ODD) are found in approximately 40 to 90 percent of community samples (Pfiffner et al., 1999). The most common comorbid condition is ODD, which occurs in 40 to 60 percent of children with ADHD (Biederman et al., 2007), and these children are at increased risk for developing CD (Biederman et al., 2008). Males are more likely to be diagnosed with ODD and CD than females (Levy, Hay, Bennett, & McStephen, 2005), with CD occurring in 9 percent of males and 7 percent of females (Nock, Kazdin,

Hiripi, & Kessler, 2006). Comorbid symptoms include hyperactivity, impulsive behavior, social skills deficits, and cognitive and learning problems (Turgay, 2005). Children with comorbid ADHD and ODD/CD have more hyperactive, impulsive learning and social skills problems (Turgay, 2005), and higher rates of teacher conflict and school refusal than children with ADHD or ODD alone (Harada et al., 2002). As suggested previously, poor executive functioning appears to be primarily related to ADHD, which results in poor strategy generation and self-monitoring of behavior (Clark, Prior, & Kinsella, 2002) and leads to the comorbid ODD symptoms (Thorell & Wahlstedt, 2006). However, executive deficits are also a common finding among children with CD (Moffit, 1993); this may not be specific to CD, but instead a manifestation of the ADHD (Klorman et al., 1999).

Comorbid Mood Disorders

Rates of comorbidity with depressive disorders range from 10 to 50 percent (Souza, Pinheiro, Denardin, Mattos, & Rohde, 2004; Pfiffner et al., 1999), with estimates overall suggesting about a 14 percent comorbidity rate (Kessler et al., 2005). Deficits in both executive and attention are common in Major Depressive Disorder (MDD) (Mayberg, 2001), so affected children experience significant impairment in addition to symptoms such as low self-esteem, poor concentration, and irritability (American Psychiatric Association, 2000; Wasserstein, 2005). Children with inattentive type ADHD are more likely to have internalizing disorders and later onset of ADHD diagnosis (Drabick, Gadow, & Sprafkin, 2006) than those diagnosed with combined type ADHD (Clarke et al., 2007), a finding confirmed in meta-analyses (Angold et al., 1999). However, combined type males are more likely than similarly diagnosed females to have MDD, perhaps due to increased rates of grade failure, suspensions, and expulsions (Bauermeister et al., 2007). Females are also severely affected, with those diagnosed with ADHD having a fivefold risk of developing major depression than controls, and this comorbidity results in a more severe prognosis (Biederman, Ball, et al., 2008; Blackman, Ostrander, & Herman, 2005).

Among children with Bipolar Disorder (BPD), the comorbidity of ADHD is very high (approximately 60 to 80 percent; Shear, DelBello, Lee-Rosenberg, & Strakowski, 2002; Wozniak et al., 2004), while 22 percent of ADHD children also have BPD (Butler, Arredondo, & McCloskey, 1995). Symptoms common to both BPD and ADHD may include distractibility, emotional lability/irritability, pressured speech, and increased energy or activity level (Wozniak, 2005). As is the case with comorbid depression, attention and executive deficits are common in both ADHD and BPD (Shear et al., 2002). This comorbidity increases the risk of neurocognitive deficits

(Rucklidge, 2006) and poor treatment response (Adler et al., 2005) because mania, often mistaken for ADHD in children, requires treatment with a mood stabilizer, not stimulants (Biederman, Hammerness, et al., 2008; Henin et al., 2007).

COMORBID ANXIETY, OBSESSIVE-COMPULSIVE, AND TOURETTE DISORDERS

Approximately one-third of youth with ADHD are diagnosed with anxiety disorders (e.g., Perrin & Last, 1996; Safren, Lanka, Otto, & Pollack, 2001; Souza et al., 2004), yet only 25 percent meet DSM-IV criteria for an anxiety disorder (Biederman, Newcorn, & Sprich, 1991). As with other comorbidities, ADHD-anxiety prevalence rates vary considerably, ranging from 13 to 34 percent, with this comorbidity resulting in a less robust response to stimulant medication (Jarrett & Ollendick, 2008; Kratochvil et al., 2005; Levy, 2004). Researchers have found anxiety to be primarily associated with the ADHD Inattentive symptoms, but not hyperactive/impulsive symptoms (Angold et al., 1999; Lahey, Schaughency, Hynd, Carlson, & Nieves, 1987; Newcorn et al., 2001; Pliszka, 1992). A more severe form of anxiety, obsessive-compulsive disorder (OCD), also co-occurs with ADHD in approximately 30 percent of affected children (Geller, Biederman, Griffin, & Jones, 1996), which is not surprising given that both are related to cortical-subcortical circuit and executive dysfunction (e.g., Lichter & Cummings, 2001).

Several studies have found that many children with Tourette Syndrome (TS) also have ADHD (Towbin & Riddle, 1993, Freeman, 2007; Olson, 2004), with the prevalence of this comorbidity ranging from 35 to 90 percent across studies (Erenberg, 2005). It is well known that the involuntary tics wax and wane, with attentional problems found to precede or follow the onset of tics (APA, 2000). ADHD symptoms likely impact the anger control, self-regulation, sleep disturbance, school performance, and impaired executive functions seen in children with TS (Freeman, 2007; Singer et al., 1995). Although OCD and ADHD seem to be different disorders, TS occurs comorbidly with ADHD and OCD (Spencer et al., 1998). In a recent large-scale study ($N = 5060$), TS with ADHD resulted in significant internalizing and externalizing comorbidity in childhood, but only externalizing and mood problems in adolescence, whereas TS without ADHD was largely associated with less comorbidity, and only comorbid internalizing/OCD symptoms in adolescence (Roessner et al., 2007). Associated autistic-like features (Ivarsson & Melin, 2008), OCD in combination with TS results in self-monitoring, error detection, and response inhibition deficits (Muller et al., 2003), but as noted earlier, these are hallmark characteristics of children with ADHD. As Denckla (2006) suggests, differences in motor, dorsolateral, and orbital circuits may elucidate the relationship among these apparently disparate disorders.

DIFFERENTIATING ADHD AND OTHER FRONTAL-SUBCORTICAL CIRCUIT DISORDERS: THE SCHOOL NEUROPSYCHOLOGY PERSPECTIVE

Establishing Symptom Coherence for ADHD Differential Diagnosis

We have come a long way since seeing ADHD merely as a disruptive behavior disorder. Genetic, neurochemical, and psychopharmacological evidence supports the role of dopaminergic-striatal dysfunction in ADHD (Castellanos et al., 2002; Durston., 2003; Rubia et al., 1999; Swanson et al., 2007; Valera et al., 2007; Vaidya et al., 1998), and this fits well with our knowledge of how stimulants inhibit reuptake via blockade of the dopamine transporter, resulting in increased dopamine availability and reduction in symptoms as a result (Madras, Miller, & Fischman, 2005). Despite this apparent clarity in understanding ADHD, much controversy exists over whether this dopamine deficiency provides a sufficient explanation for the disorder, or whether this, combined with other abnormal catecholamine (e.g., norepinephrine) and other neurotransmitters (e.g., serotonin, GABA), best explains the heterogeneity seen in the disorder (Comings et al., 2000; Frank et al., 2007; Sergeant et al., 2003; Solanto, Arnsten, & Castellanos, 2001).

For conducting school neuropsychological evaluations, some executive function measures are more effective than others in the diagnosis of ADHD, especially those that measure response inhibition, interference control, vigilance, working memory, and planning (Homack & Riccio, 2004; Willcutt et al., 2005; see Table 11.2). They generally have better sensitivity than specificity for ADHD, because several other disorders also show impaired performance on these and other executive measures (Sergeant et al., 2002) In Table 11.2 we also report the findings of our recent large-scale standardization study (Typical $N = 306$; ADHD $N = 64$) results for Trails B Errors and the Hale-Denckla Cancellation Test (HDCT; Hale et al., 2009). Other assessment tools that have limited ADHD research on their use, but considerable promise in the diagnosis of ADHD, include the *Delis-Kaplan Executive Function Scale* (D-KEFS; Delis, Kaplan, & Kramer, 2001), NEPSY-II (Korkman, Kirk, & Kemp, 2007; selected executive measures), *California Verbal Learning Test-Children's Version* (Delis, Kramer, Kaplan, & Ober, 1994), *Controlled Oral Word Association Test* (COWAT; Benton, Hamsher, & Sivan, 1983), Luria's *Response Inhibition Task* (Go-No-Go Test, see Trommer, Hoeppner, & Zecker, 1991), and *WISC-IV Integrated Elithorn Mazes* (Kaplan et al., 2004). Another measure that holds promise for differential diagnosis of ADHD is the *Test of Everyday Attention* (TEA-Ch; Manly, Anderson, Robertson, & Nimmo-Smith, 1999). The TEA-Ch was normed on an Australian population, but validation is now being undertaken in the United States (Miller & Belloni, 2009).

Table 11.2

Executive Function Measures for ADHD Differential Diagnosis

Measure	Mean Effect Size/ Supportive Studies	Test Author(s)
Tower of Hanoi	.69 4/7 (57%)[1]	Borys et al., 1982
Continuous Performance Test Omissions	.64 23/30 (77%)[1]	Newcorn et al., 1989[2]
Spatial Working Memory (Self-Order Pointing)	.63 6/8 (75%)[1] (Spatial WM)	Petrides & Milner, 1982 Owen et al., 1996
Stop Signal Reaction Time	.61 22/27 (82%)[1]	Logan et al., 1997
Porteus Mazes	.58 4/5 (80%)[1]	Porteus, 1965
Trail Making Test Part B Time	.55 8/14 (57%)[1]	Reitan & Wolfson, 1985
Verbal Working Memory (Digits Backward)	.55 6/11 (55%)[1]	Wechsler, 1991
WM Sentence Span		Siegel & Ryan, 1989
CPT Commission Errors	.51 17/28 (61%)[1]	Newcorn et al., 1989
Tower of London	.51 3/6 (50%)[1]	Shallice, 1982
Wisconsin Card Sort Test Perseverative Errors	.46 11/24 (46%)[1]	Heaton et al., 1993
Rey Complex Figure Copy Organization	.43 5/9 (56%)[1]	Waber & Holmes, 1985
Stroop Color-Word Test – Color Word	.52[3]	Golden, 1978
Stroop Color-Word Test – Interference	.75[3]	Golden, 1978
Trail Making Test – Part B Errors	.68[4]	Reitan & Wolfson, 1985
Hale-Denckla Cancellation Test Correct	.64[4]	Hale et al., 2009

Notes: [1]Wilcutt et al., 2005 meta-analysis, ratio is number of studies that show significant ADHD-control group differences; [2]There are a number of Continuous Performance Tests on the market (e.g., CPT-II, TOVA, GDT), and this does not suggest preference of one over another; [3]Homack and Riccio (2004) Stroop meta-analysis; [4]Hale et al. (2009) study.

As no single assessment tool is sufficiently diagnostic of ADHD, the school neuropsychologist should use a variety of direct assessment tools for ADHD diagnosis and intervention purposes (Doyle et al., 2000; Reddy & Hale, 2007; Teeter & Semrud-Clikeman, 1995), as well as indirect measures of ADHD symptoms, such as objective behavior rating scales typically used in identification of the disorder. These indirect measures are important assessment tools in a comprehensive ADHD evaluation, but they are not sufficient for differential diagnosis of ADHD (Hale et al., 2009). Most commonly used behavior rating measures that have been shown to be sensitive (but not specific) for ADHD differential diagnosis include the *Behavior Rating Inventory of Executive Functions* (Gioia, Isquith, Guy, & Kenworthy, 2000), *Behavior Assessment System for Children-2* (Reynolds &

Kamphaus, 2004), *Achenbach Child Behavior Checklist* (Achenbach, 1991), and *Conners Comprehensive Behavior Rating Scales* (Conners, 2008). Although some may prefer to use rating scales specific to ADHD (e.g., Brown *ADD Rating Scales*, Brown, 2001; *ADHD Rating Scale*, DuPaul, Power, Anastopoulos, & Reid, 1998), these scales may be useful for hypothesis testing or progress monitoring of response to intervention. Their use in differential diagnosis may be limited because of the items do not cover a broad range of child psychopathology.

ADHD Comorbidity: "Primary" versus "Secondary" ADHD

Children with ADHD clearly present with a wide variety of symptoms and comorbid conditions, which may lead to a parsimonious albeit reductionistic conclusion that ADHD is a risk factor for developing other disorders. ADHD has long been the diagnosis *du jour* for children who present with significant attention problems, but the question remains whether ADHD diagnoses are correct for all these children. It is tempting to adopt a pragmatic reliance on overt behavioral symptoms of inattention, impulsivity, and hyperactivity using rating scales and DSM-IV-TR diagnostic nomenclature to identify ADHD, and then determine the presence of comorbidity. As we have seen, comorbidity is the norm—not the exception—among psychiatric disorders, including ADHD (Angold et al., 1999), and only through examination of underlying deficits can these interrelationships be clarified (Rhee et al., 2005). What if the comorbid disorder for a child who meets behavioral criteria for ADHD is actually the *primary* disorder, which subsequently results in *secondary* attention problems? Given that this suggests inadequate diagnostic specificity, which is never a good thing, what are the implications of such findings? For these questions to be relevant, two fundamental empirical questions must be addressed:

1. To what extent do psychiatric disorders have similar or different etiologies, and can knowledge of these differences lead to more accurate diagnostic techniques?
2. If etiological and diagnostic differences among disorders can be established, do these differences lead to more effective treatment practices and outcomes?

At the present time, the answer to these fundamental and enigmatic questions remains a tentative "maybe." When we examine the structural and functional neuroimaging findings, we find considerable overlap between

Table 11.3

Functional Neuroimaging Evidence of Frontal-Subcortical Impairment
in Select Psychiatric Disorders

Disorder	Study	Sample Characteristics	Clinical Group Circuit Findings
Anxiety Disorders	Krain et al., 2008	Generalized anxiety disorder/social phobia and control groups	Increased frontal-limbic region activation that reported higher intolerance of uncertainty.
	McClure et al., 2007	Generalized anxiety disorder & control groups	Increased activation in ventral prefrontal, anterior cingulate, and amygdala.
Attention Deficit Hyperactivity Disorder (ADHD)	Booth et al., 2005	Children with ADHD & control group	Decreased activation in inferior, middle, superior & medial fronto-striatal regions, caudate nucleus & globus pallidus.
	Cao et al., 2008	Adolescent males & control group	Decreased activation in frontal (middle & superior frontal gyrus), putamen, & inferior parietal lobe.
	Durston 2003	Children with ADHD and controls	ADHD underactivated ventrolateral prefrontal, anterior cingulate, and caudate during response inhibition.
	Pliszka et al., 2006	ADHD treatment naïve & previously medicated groups, & control group	ADHD treatment naïve less cingulate and left ventrolateral activation during impulsive responding than controls.
	Rubia et al., 2005	ADHD adolescents & matched controls	ADHD less right inferior frontal activation during inhibition.
	Scheres et al., 2007	ADHD adolescents and matched controls	Reduced ventral striatum activity during reward anticipation.
	Schulz et al., 2004	Male adolescents with ADHD & control group	Increased left & right ventrolateral inferior frontal gyrus, left & right frontopolar regions of the middle frontal gyrus, right dorsolateral middle frontal gyrus, left anterior cingulate gyrus, & left medial frontal gyrus.
	Tamm et al., 2002	Children with ADHD and controls	Hypoactivation of anterior cingulated and hyperactivation temporal compensatory regions.
	Vaidya et al., 1998	Children with ADHD and controls	Frontal activity possible compensation for striatal

Table 11.3
Continued

Disorder	Study	Sample Characteristics	Clinical Group Circuit Findings
			hypoactivity normalized with stimulant treatment.
Bipolar Disorder	Adler et al. 2005	Children with Bipolar Disorder with and without ADHD	Children with comorbid ADHD showed decreased ventrolateral and cingulated activity.
	Blumberg et al., 2003	Adolescents with Bipolar Disorder & control group	Increased left putamen & thalamus; depressive symptoms and ventral striatum positively correlated.
	Adler et al., 2005	Youth with BD + ADHD & BD groups	Decreased activation of ventrolateral prefrontal cortex & anterior cingulated (BD + ADHD group).
	Chang et al., 2004	Youth with Bipolar Disorder and controls	Increased activation in anterior cingulated, left dorsolateral prefrontal, right inferior, and right insula.
	Gruber et al. 2003	Bipolar Disorder and Controls	Increased dorsolateral and decreased cingulated.
	Nelson et al., 2007	Adolescents with Bipolar Disorder and controls	Increased left dorsolateral prefrontal and premotor activity interfere with flexibility.
	Rich et al., 2006	Adolescents with Bipolar Disorder and controls	Greater putamen, accumbens, amygdala, and ventral prefrontal with emotional face processing.
Obsessive Compulsive Disorder	Nakao et al., 2005	Patients with OCD pre and posttreatment	Hyperactivity in orbital frontal and cingulate reduced with SSRI medication treatment.
	Rosenberg & Keshaven, 1998	Children with OCD and controls	Increased ventral prefrontal.
	Szeszesko et al., 2004	Children with OCD and controls	Increased cingulate gray matter volume.
	Szeszesko et al., 2004	Children with OCD and controls	Increased cingulate gray matter volume.
	Viard et al., 2005	Adolescents with OCD & control group	Abnormal activation in parietal, temporal & precuneus regions; hyperactivity in anterior

(continued)

Table 11.3
Continued

Disorder	Study	Sample Characteristics	Clinical Group Circuit Findings
			cingulate & left parietal subregions.
	Woolley et al, 2008	Adolescent males with OCD & control group	Reduced activation in right orbitofrontal cortex, thalamus, cingulate & basal ganglia during response inhibition.
	Yucel et al., 2007	Adolescents with OCD and controls	Hyperactivation of medial frontal cortex compensatory for reduced dorsal anterior cingulated.
Unipolar Depression/ Major Depression (MDD)	Forbes et al., 2006	Youth with MDD, generalized anxiety disorder, & control group	Decreased amygdala and orbital frontal cortex in response to reward, inconsistent with anxiety group.
	Grimm et al., 2008	Adults with MDD (unmedicated) & control group	Hypoactivity in left dorsolateral, hyperactivity in right dorsolateral prefrontal correlated with depression severity.
	Steingard et al., 2002	Adolescents with MDD & control group	Decreased white matter/ increased gray matter in frontal lobe.
	Wagner et al., 2006	Adult females with MDD (unmedicated) & control group	Hyperactivity in rostral anterior cingulate gyrus & left dorsolateral prefrontal cortex in during Interference phase.

ADHD and other disorders, inconsistency within disorder subtypes, and different results for different samples. For instance, as can be seen in Table 11.3, several disorders with different clinical presentations have similar cortical-subcortical structures affected, but to different degrees and sometimes in different directions (for comprehensive review of ADHD neuroimaging, see Bush, Valera, & Seidman, 2005). Neurochemical, structural, and functional imaging differences among disorders add further confusion to the diagnostic picture. Studies of ADHD circuit function may also result in different findings due to prior treatment history (Pliszka, Lancaster, Liotti, & Semrud-Clikeman, 2006) or methodologies and analyses used (Cabeza & Kingstone, 2006). Finally, to further complicate matters, circuits are influenced by both indirect and direct pathways (Chow & Cummings, 2007) and differences in white and gray matter volumes/functions, such as white matter hyperintensities in psychiatric disorders (e.g., Lyoo, Lee, Jung, Noam, & Renshaw, 2002).

While these complex and sometimes conflicting findings limit diagnostic clarity, the conclusion from these studies is that most— if not all— psychopathologies have a basis in the frontal-subcortical circuits (Lichter & Cummings, 2001; Nigg, 2000), and their dysfunction leads to observable learning and behavior problems (Compton, 2003; Middleton & Strick, 2000). Not unlike a global intelligence or "g" perspective, this global frontal-subcortical circuit/executive problem approach allows us to speak to the *level* of dysfunction, but not the *pattern* of dysfunction. The level of dysfunction orientation results in conflicting clinical presentations, poor diagnostic specificity, and limited treatment efficacy because the focus is on the *need* for services, not the *type* of services needed. While the former may suffice for a traditional school psychologist role, the latter, in essence, defines the role of the school neuropsychologist.

What we do know is that there are at least five frontal-subcortical circuits (see Figure 11.1) according to most nomenclatures (Miller & Cummings, 2007) and dozens of so-called executive functions related to these interdependent circuits (Garavan, Ross, Murphy, Roche, & Stein, 2002; Stuss & Alexander, 2000), all of which are necessary for acting successfully in the natural environment. Although these interdependent circuits exert executive control over thought and behavior, a critical question arises from our knowledge of these circuits: How can there be so many different executive functions, with their dysfunction leading to so many different psychiatric disorders, yet so few frontal-subcortical circuits?

There are several possible reasons for this perplexing enigma. It is possible that different gene-environment interactions lead to different diagnoses with and without comorbidities. Certainly the interaction of midline structures, including frontal-striatal-limbic-cerebellar circuits, is exceedingly complex and is modulated by both direct and indirect pathways, gray and white matter volumes, and coinciding neurotransmitter actions in each of these (see Miller & Cummings, 2007). Perhaps the problem lies in part on our measures, which currently lack sufficient specificity for circuit function, and neuroimaging results are confounded by experimental and control tasks that elicit brain structures and functions. These measures have adequate sensitivity (e.g., level of dysfunction), but limited specificity (e.g., pattern of dysfunction), for ADHD and other disorders. Another issue has to do with how we *define* disorders. Clearly, delineating frontal-subcortical circuit function is difficult when we use behavioral diagnostic

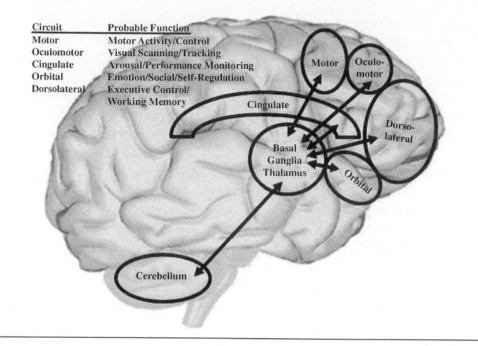

Figure 11.1 Frontal-subcortical circuits and probable functions.

criteria and nomenclature to define disorders. Behavioral diagnostic methods lead to heterogeneous samples of children diagnosed with ADHD and other disorders, making behavioral measures more meaningful for diagnosis than neuropsychological measures (Hale et al., 2009).

Although no child with ADHD has all the comorbid learning and psychopathologies described earlier, they all exist in some children diagnosed with ADHD. This leads us to a very simple question: Why do these differences among children with ADHD exist, and why are they not consistent across children? This simple question leads us to several diagnostically relevant questions, which are much more difficult to answer and require careful clinical evaluation (Reddy & Hale, 2007). The school neuropsychologist must determine if ADHD is the proper diagnosis if:

- Comorbid SLD and/or Language Disorder lead to inattention because comprehension is impaired when the teacher gives oral instructions or lecture?
- Comorbid MDD is the cause of significant inattention, difficulty with decision making, and slow psychomotor speed?
- Comorbid anxiety and/or OCD leads to motor restlessness/fidgeting, internal distraction (i.e. obsessions), and inflexible, compulsive behavior?

- Comorbid BPD and/or CD explains the distractibility, racing thoughts, impulsivity, and antisocial tendencies?
- Comorbid Pervasive Developmental Disorder and/or Prodromal Schizophrenia leads to poor focused attention, limited working memory language formulation difficulties, slow psychomotor speed, and social problems?
- Comorbid "nonverbal" SLD with poor visual-spatial-holistic processing, novel problem-solving deficits, and math disability results in poor attention of self and the environment?

For an individual child, a school neuropsychologist conducting a thorough comprehensive evaluation might successfully have the answers to these questions after careful scrutiny of all diagnostic information. However, this may be more challenging if evaluations are limited or behavioral criteria are considered sufficient for "comprehensive" evaluations. Comprehensive evaluations should use multiple cognitive, neuropsychological, academic, and behavioral/personality measures, and include multiple informants. This way both the level and pattern of child functioning can be explored, differential diagnosis can be achieved, and individualized interventions established.

Focusing solely on overt behavioral symptoms not only diminishes our ability to identify and treat individual children, it also obfuscates empirical study results. When behaviorally defined individuals with ADHD are collapsed for large sample empirical studies of ADHD, the clarity of results diminishes, effect sizes for diagnostic tests are attenuated, and findings are inconsistent across studies. Although a behavior rating item such as "has difficulty paying attention" may be sensitive for a global *level* of functioning decision, such as determining the need for services, it is hardly specific for children with ADHD. Behavioral symptoms of ADHD vary across environments (Wolraich et al., 2004), seldom show adequate parent and teacher inter-rater agreement (Angtrop, Roeyers, Oosterlaan, & Van Oost, 2002; Mitsis et al., 2000; Wolraich et al., 2004), have limited discriminant validity for ADHD subtypes and other disorders (Hale, How, DeWitt, & Coury, 2001; Mahone et al., 2002; Sullivan & Riccio, 2007), and may be due to multiple underlying causes (Reddy & Hale, 2007). Given these significant limitations, it is astonishing that some still argue that behavioral approaches are sufficient for ADHD diagnoses (e.g., Brown & LaRosa, 2002).

IMPLICATIONS FOR INTERVENTION: ACHIEVING CIRCUIT BALANCE

Moving beyond behavioral definitions to conceptualize ADHD (and other frontal-subcortical circuit disorders) as a central nervous system disorder

(Clarke, Barry, McCarthy, Selikowitz, & Brown, 2002) that impacts neuro-psychological and behavioral functioning (Voeller, 2001) may lead to more accurate diagnoses and targeted interventions (Hale & Fiorello, 2004; Hale et al., 2009). Like ADHD diagnoses, ADHD interventions have been plagued by a lack of specificity. Diagnoses have always been made on the basis of overt behavioral criteria, the symptoms a child displays, and as a result, interventions have typically focused on improving self-awareness and regulation (see Table 11.4). Although these strategies can be accomplished by the school neuropsychologist or a special education teacher, meta-analy-ses show these methods are best incorporated within the context of the child's educational environment (Hattie, Biggs, & Purdie, 1996). Although behavioral methods are highly successful in meeting the needs of children with ADHD (Barkley, 2005), they are beyond the scope of this chapter. The reader is referred to DuPaul and Stoner's (2003) excellent book *ADHD in the Schools: Assessment and Intervention Strategies* for more traditional behavioral interventions.

We can modify the environment, expectations, instructional techniques, or provide specific interventions for children with ADHD and other exec-utive disorders (Dawson & Guare, 2004), but it is important to realize that we are still at the stage of offering "global" interventions instead of specific ones. Individualization requires a better understanding than this global intervention perspective. What if we turned the tables diagnostically and, instead, diagnosed children on the basis of frontal-subcortical circuit dys-function and on the types of executive strengths and deficits they displayed during our evaluations? We believe this will be the future of school neuropsychology. As science progresses and our measurement tools be-come more sensitive and specific, we will one day be examining behavioral criteria and ratings scales for their diagnostic utility. Instead of offering global interventions designed to generally improve executive function, we can start to use targeted interventions for specific types of executive deficits.

Obviously, a paradigm shift is needed. What seems apparent is that there must be *differences* in circuit function and *differences* in executive function that result in *different* disorders. As long as behavioral criteria are used to define disorders, we will continue to consider differential diagnosis chal-lenging, and comorbidity rates will be high. However, what if we started to diagnose children on the basis of their cortical-subcortical circuit function and differentiated their neuropsychological patterns of performance? For instance, Hale and colleagues (2005; 2006; Reddy & Hale, 2007) found that some children carefully diagnosed with ADHD had executive dysfunction and showed significant medication response, while those who did not appear to show circuit impairment were less likely to respond. All children were diagnosed by physicians and psychologists as having "ADHD," but

Table 11.4
Interventions for Children with ADHD

Intervention	Source
Metacognitive Strategies	
Think Alouds	Davey, 1983
Self-Regulated Strategy Development	Graham & Harris, 1999
Self-Monitoring	Harris, 1986
Goal Setting and Attainment	Zimmerman & Schunk, 2001
Mnemonics	Allsopp, 1999
Cognitive Behavior Intervention	Bloomquist et al., 1991
Child Generated Strategy Instruction	Naglieri & Gottling, 1995
Semantic Feature Analysis	Anders & Bos, 1986
Anticipation Guide	Tierney & Readance, 2004
Semantic Maps/Advance Organizers	Bos & Vaughn, 2002
Graphic Organizers	Kim et al. 2004
Self-Advocacy Skills	Ozonoff & Schetter, 2007
Learning Strategy Curriculum	Deshler & Schumaker, 1988
Drive to Thrive Strategy Instruction	Meltzer et al., 2004
Benchmark Method	Gaskins, Sallou, & Pressley, 2007
Improving Classroom Performance	
Cornell Method	Pauk, 1993
Three-Column Method	Saski et al., 1983
AWARE Method	Suritsky & Hughes, 1996
PIRATES Test-Taking Strategy	Hughes & Schumaker, 1991
PORPE Test Preparation and Comprehension	Simpson, Stahl, & Hayes, 1988
STAR Writing Strategy	Meltzer et al., 2006

circuit-impaired responders were more likely to be classified with Combined Type ADHD, whereas Inattentive Type diagnoses were more common in the non-responders with little executive impairment. These findings are consistent with Barkley's arguments regarding difference in ADHD subtypes (1997) and Angold's et al. (1999) meta-analysis showing little concordance between children with ADHD with comorbid internalizing and externalizing disorders.

Differences among frontal-subcortical circuits and executive functions are beginning to emerge in the literature. Once they become clearer, studies of differential treatment efficacy can take place. Although individual studies vary, it is possible that these interconnected circuits guide behavior in relation to the environment in a reciprocal manner, with optimal executive function being *average* executive function, with attention regulation problems likely being the outcome for all disorders regardless of the type of circuit dysfunction displayed. By using the term *average*, we mean that there is an optimal amount of executive function that allows for an individual to balance internal experiences and external responsiveness to environmental stimuli to maximize adaptive responding. If there is too little or too much circuit function, a disorder may occur and limit an individual's capability to adjust to environmental demands. For instance, too little (e.g., ADHD) or too much (e.g., OCD) executive function due to circuit hypoactivity or circuit hyperactivity, respectively, can lead to poor attention because the former child is often *externally* distracted, while the latter child is often *internally* distracted. The externally-distracted child has difficulty focusing on a particular stimulus or event in the environment because he is paying attention to all external stimuli, while the internally-distracted child is too focused on internal stimuli to pay attention to the stimulus or event in the environment.

Both the externally distracted and internally distracted child would be given a problematic caregiver and/or teacher rating on "Has difficulty paying attention," and if enough similar items were endorsed, both children could be diagnosed with "ADHD." Perhaps the child with OCD would receive an Inattentive Type ADHD diagnoses, while the "true" ADHD child would receive a Combined Type diagnosis, but would each child respond equally well to stimulant medication? Research is emerging that only those with "true" ADHD are likely to respond to stimulant medication (Hale et al., 2005; 2006; 2007). Not only do these findings impact our interventions, but collapsing these and other children with attention problems into heterogeneous large groups obscures and attenuates study findings. While beyond the scope of this chapter, similar findings regarding hemispheric balances and psychopathology have also been noted. For instance, several studies suggest left hemisphere activity leads to positive affect and left deficits lead to depressive symptoms, while right hemisphere activity can lead to avoidance patterns, and right deficits can lead to indifference and disinhibition (see Davidson, 2000; Hale & Fiorello, 2004).

With this balance premise in mind, achieving circuit *equilibrium* may hold the key to successful interventions for children with ADHD and other psychopathologies. This is not just relevant for psychosocial interventions, but for medication interventions as well. Optimal stimulant medication dosage appears to be different for the orbital-ventral and dorsolateral-dorsal circuits (Hale et al., 2005; 2006). As a result, using a combination of medication and behavioral therapies will likely produce the most positive outcomes, as has been demonstrated in large-scale treatment studies of ADHD (e.g., Multimodal Treatment Study of ADHD; Jensen et al., 2001). Optimizing medication dosages based on executive function results and then using adjunct behavioral or metacognitive therapies could lead to this balance (Hale et al., 2005, 2006, 2007). A lower dosage for dorsolateral executive functions could be supplemented with behavior management strategies to foster optimal executive and behavioral regulation (Reddy & Hale, 2007). This would even apply for other circuit disorders that lead to secondary ADHD symptoms. For instance, if one has an overactive orbital circuit and an underactive dorsolateral one (e.g., comorbid anxiety and depression), the key may be increasing dorsolateral function by fostering working memory, mental flexibility, and environmental interaction, and using systematic desensitization, relaxation techniques, and thought stopping to reduce orbital dysfunction.

Obviously, given the complexity of frontal-subcortical circuit function and its relationship to symptom expression, behavioral criteria alone are insufficient to determine specific, targeted interventions for children with ADHD and other circuit disorders. Until we are well versed in these complex interrelationships, it is best to use multimethod, multisource assessments to develop hypotheses about the interventions that might work best within the context of the natural environment. Part of any successful intervention is educating those who will carry out the interventions (e.g., teachers, aides, parents) regarding the nature and course of ADHD (DuPaul & Stoner, 2003; Barkley, 2005) because of conflicting and sometimes inaccurate understanding of the disorder (Bekle, 2004; Snider, Busch, & Arrowood, 2003). Sometimes using the analogy of a "brain boss" or "brain manager" can be useful in helping parents and teachers understand the nature of ADHD (Hale & Fiorello, 2004). By asking them what a manager or boss does and then suggesting that their child's boss is half asleep (consistent with circuit hypoactivity) can be illuminating for them. It also helps them understand that stimulants work because they "wake the brain boss" to help manage the rest of the brain.

Using an approach such as the cognitive hypothesis testing model (Fiorello et al., 2007; Hale & Fiorello, 2004; Reddy & Hale, 2007) can be useful in maximizing both diagnostic decision making and developing targeted interventions. However, regardless of the intervention(s) attempted, it is critical to use CHT to develop, monitor, evaluate, and recycle interventions until efficacy is achieved. Although all interventions should be carefully monitored, this is an especially important requirement when children are treated with psychotropic medications. Using a combination of neuropsychological assessment, behavior ratings, and observation data can help practitioners, teachers, parents, and the child determine whether medication is effective, and if so, what is the best dose for their learning and behavior. This careful monitoring of response to medication treatment can help determine the need for other interventions, and ultimately lead to academic and behavioral success for children with ADHD (Hale & Fiorello, 2004; Hale et al., 2005; 2006; 2007; 2009; Reddy & Hale, 2007).

SUMMARY

This chapter marks an important transitional period for our understanding of ADHD and best practices in school neuropsychological assessment and intervention strategies for the disorder. The outdated belief that ADHD is merely a "disruptive behavior disorder" has been replaced with a more sophisticated understanding of the neurobiology of ADHD. Although behavioral diagnostic approaches lead to heterogeneous ADHD samples with disparate characteristics and comorbidities, it is best to think of several endophenotypes as representing different disorders. Those with "true" ADHD are likely to have dopaminergic insufficiency in the striatum, which leads to poor executive control of attention, inhibition, and motor activity. As a result, children with ADHD do not have a primary attention deficit; rather, it is executive control of attention that is impaired in the disorder. As Martha Denckla (1996) has suggested, ADHD is a disorder of *intention* not attention. Although other causes of attention impairment are clearly evident in the neuropsychological literature, and a majority of psychiatric disorders present with attention problems, we suggest that these be considered separately, because it appears that only those with "true" ADHD due to frontal-subcortical circuit hypoactivity respond to stimulant treatment.

As we develop a clearer understanding of frontal-subcortical circuit functions and how they interact in affected individuals, the path to differential diagnosis of ADHD and other psychiatric disorders will become clearer. It would appear that these circuits, given their interdependence, work to balance circuit function, with imbalance leading to various types of psychopathology. This perspective not only helps school neuropsychologists in differential diagnosis of ADHD and other disorders, but it could also lead to more targeted interventions designed to create circuit balance or equilibrium. Although these advances will certainly foster clarity in ADHD diagnoses and increase the sensitivity and specificity of neuropsychological measures, the real value in these new discoveries will be found in our ability to design more targeted interventions that have both ecological and treatment validity for children with ADHD and other circuit disorders.

Multimethod, multisource evaluations using cognitive, neuropsychological, behavioral, and academic data are necessary for accurate identification and treatment of ADHD, as the traditional physician interview and rating scale *level of dysfunction* approach is woefully inadequate in defining the *pattern of dysfunction* indicative of ADHD or other frontal-subcortical circuit disorders. Similarly, monitoring response-to-intervention following diagnosis is critical, both to ensure optimal treatment strategies are attempted and to establish treatment efficacy. Although stimulants are the most common treatment for ADHD, it is clear that multiple interventions, including cognitive, academic, and behavioral ones, are often needed. In addition, when medication is attempted, it is important to note that the best dose for cognitive and neuropsychological functions may actually be lower than the best dose for behavior. Titrating medication based on cognitive and neuropsychological functioning and then providing adjunct behavior therapy may result in more efficacious outcomes, including improvement in academic performance (Hale et al., 2009).

The school neuropsychologist is especially well suited to provide both diagnostic and treatment services for children with ADHD. Through comprehensive CHT evaluations, school neuropsychologists can not only ensure accurate diagnosis of ADHD, but also determine the cognitive, neuropsychological, behavioral, and academic strengths and needs of affected individuals. With specific CHT diagnostic information in hand, the school neuropsychologist is then prepared to meet with parents, teachers, physicians, and other affiliated professionals to develop, implement, monitor, evaluate, and recycle interventions as necessary to ensure both ecological and treatment validity for children with ADHD.

REFERENCES

Achenbach, T. M. (1991). *Manual for the child behavior checklist/4–18 and 1991 profile.* Burlington: University of Vermont.

Adler, C. M., DelBello, M. P., Mills, N. P., Schmithorst, V., Holland, S., & Strakowski, S. (2005). Comorbid ADHD is associated with altered patterns of neuronal activation in adolescents with bipolar disorder performing a simple attention task. *Bipolar Disorders, 7*, 577–588.

Allsopp, D. H. (1999). Using modeling, manipulatives, and mnemonics with eighth-grade math students. *Teaching Exceptional Children, 32*, 74–81.

Aman, C. J., Roberts, R. J., Jr., & Pennington, B. F. (1998). A neuropsychological examination of the underlying deficit in attention deficit hyperactivity disorder: Frontal lobe versus right parietal lobe theories. *Developmental Psychology, 34*, 956–969.

American Psychiatric Association. (2000). *Diagnostic and statistical manual of mental disorders* (4th ed., text rev.). Washington, DC: Author.

Anders, P. L., & Bos, C. S. (1986). Semantic feature analysis: An interactive strategy for vocabulary development and text comprehension. *Journal of Reading, 29*, 10–16.

Angold, A., Costello, E. J., & Erkanli, A. (1999). Comorbidity. *Journal of Child Psychology and Psychiatry, and Allied Disciplines, 40*, 57–87.

Angtrop, I., Roeyers, H., Oosterlaan, J., & Van Oost, P. (2002). Agreement between parent and teacher ratings of disruptive behavior disorders in children with clinically diagnosed ADHD. *Journal of Psychopathology and Behavioral Assessment, 24*, 67–73.

Arnsten, A. F. T. (1997). Catecholamine regulation of the prefrontal cortex. *Journal of Psychopharmacology, 11*, 151–162.

Arnsten, A. (2001). Neurobiology of executive functions: Catecholamine influences on prefrontal cortical functions. *Biological Psychiatry, 57*, 1377–1384.

Aron, A. R., Robbins, T. W., & Poldrack, R. A. (2004). Inhibition and the right inferior prefrontal cortex. *Trends in Cognitive Sciences, 8*, 170–177.

Barkley, R. A. (1997). *ADHD and the nature of self-control.* New York: Guilford.

Barkley, R. A. (2005). *Attention-deficit hyperactivity disorder* (3rd ed.). New York: Guilford.

Barnett, R., Maruff, P., & Vance, A. (2005). An investigation of visuospatial memory impairment in children with attention deficit hyperactivity disorder (ADHD), combined type. *Psychological Medicine, 35*, 1433–1443.

Bauermeister, J. J., Shrout, P. E., Ramirez, R., Milagros, B., Alegria, M., Martinez-Taboas, A., et al. (2007). ADHD correlates, comorbidity, and impairment in community and treated samples of children and adolescents. *Journal of Abnormal Child Psychology, 35*, 883–898.

Bedard, A. C., Martinussen, R., Ickowicz, A., & Tannock, R. (2004). Methylphenidate improves visual-spatial memory in children with attention-deficit/hyperactivity disorder. *Journal of the American Academy of Child and Adolescent Psychiatry, 43*, 260–268.

Bekle, B. (2004). Knowledge and attitudes about attention-deficit hyperactivity disorder (ADHD): A comparison between practicing teachers and undergraduate education students. *Journal of Attention Disorders, 7*, 151–161.

Benton, A. L., Hamsher, K., & Sivan, A. B. (1983). *Multilingual aphasia examination* (3rd ed.). Iowa City, IA: AJA Associates.

Berger, A., & Posner, M. I. (2000). Pathologies of brain attentional networks. *Neuroscience and Biobehavioral Reviews, 24*, 3–5.

Berlin, L., Bohlin, G., Nyberg, L., & Janols, L. O. (2004). How well do measures of inhibition and other executive functions discriminate between children with ADHD and controls? *Child Neuropsychology, 10*, 1–13.

Berquin, P. C., Giedd, J. N., Jacobsen, L. K., Hamburger, S. D., Krain, A. L., Rapoport, J. L., & Castellanos, F. X. (1998). Cerebellum in attention-deficit hyperactivity disorder: A morphometric MRI study. *Neurology, 50*, 1087–1093.

Biederman, J., Ball, S. W., Monuteaux, M. C., Kaiser, R., & Faraone, S. V. (2008). CBCL clinical scales discriminate ADHD youth with structured-interview derived diagnosis of oppositional defiant disorder (ODD). *Journal of Attention Disorders, 12*, 76–82.

Biederman, J., Hammerness, P., Doyle, R., Joshi, G., Aleardi, M., & Mick, E. (2008). Risperidone treatment for ADHD in children and adolescents with bipolar disorder. *Neuropsychiatric Disease and Treatment, 4*, 203–207.

Biederman, J., Monuteaux, M. C., Doyle, A. E., Seidman, L. J., Wilens, T. E., Ferrero, F., et al. (2004). Impact of executive function deficits and attention-deficit/hyperactivity disorder (ADHD) on academic outcomes in children. *Journal of Consulting and Clinical Psychology, 72*, 757–766.

Biederman, J., Newcorn, J., & Sprich, S. (1991). Comorbidity of attention deficit hyperactivity disorder with conduct, depressive, anxiety, and other disorders. *American Journal of Psychiatry, 148*, 564–577.

Biederman, J., Spencer, T. J., Newcorn, J. H., Gao, H., Milton, D. R., Feldman, P. D., & Witte, M. M. (2007). Effect of comorbid symptoms of oppositional defiant disorder on responses to atomoxetine in children with ADHD: A meta-analysis of controlled clinical trial data. *Psychopharmacology, 190*, 31–41.

Blackman, G. L., Ostrander, R., & Herman, K. C. (2005). Children with ADHD and depression: A multisource, multimethod assessment of clinical, social, and academic functioning. *Journal of Attention Disorders, 8*, 195–207.

Bloomquist, M. L., August, G. J., & Ostrander, R. (1991). Effects of a school-based cognitive-behavior intervention for ADHD children. *Journal of Abnormal Child Psychology, 19*, 591–605.

Blumberg, H. P., Leung, H. C., Skudlarski, P., Lacadie, C. M., Fredericks, C. A., Harris, B. C., et al. (2003). A functional magnetic resonance imaging study of bipolar disorder: State- and trait-related dysfunction in ventral prefrontal cortices. *Archives of General Psychiatry, 60*, 601–609.

Booth, J. R., Burman, D. D., Meyer, J. R., Lei, Z., Trommer, B. L., Davenport, N. D., et al (2005). Larger deficits in brain networks for response inhibition than for visual selective attention in attention deficit hyperactivity disorder (ADHD). *Journal of Child Psychology and Psychiatry, 46*, 94–111.

Borys, S. V., Spitz, H. H., & Dorans, B. A. (1982). Tower of Hanoi performance of retarded young adults and nonretarded children as a function of solution length and goal state. *Journal of Experimental Child Psychology, 33*, 87–110.

Bos, C. S., & Vaughn, S. (2002). *Strategies for teaching students with learning and behavior problems* (5th ed.). Needham Heights, MA: Allyn & Bacon.

Brieber, S., Neufang, S., Bruning, N., Kamp-Becker, I., Remschmidt, H., Herpertz-Dahlmann, B., et al. (2007). Structural brain abnormalities in adolescents with autism spectrum disorder and patients with attention deficit/hyperactivity disorder. *Journal of Child Psychology and Psychiatry, 48*(12), 1251–1258.

Brown, R. T. (2001). *Brown Attention Deficit Disorder Scales*. San Antonio, TX: The Psychological Corporation.

Brown, R. T., & LaRosa, A. L. (2002). Recent developments in the pharmacotherapy of attention-deficit/hyperactivity disorder (ADHD). *Professional Psychology, Research and Practice, 33*, 591–595.

Bryan, K. L., & Hale, J. B. (2001). Differential effects of left and right cerebral vascular accidents on language competency. *Journal of the International Neuropsychological Society, 7*, 655–664.

Bush, G., Valera, E. M., & Seidman, L. J. (2005). Functional neuroimaging of attention-deficit/hyperactivity disorder: A review and suggested future directions. *Biological Psychiatry, 57,* 1273–1284.

Butler, S. F., Arredondo, D. E., & McCloskey, V. (1995). Affective comorbidity in children and adolescents with attention deficit hyperactivity disorder. *Annals of Clinical Psychiatry, 7,* 51–55.

Buttross, S. (2000). Attention deficit-hyperactivity disorder and its deceivers. *Current Problems in Pediatrics, 30,* 41–50.

Cabeza, R., & Kingstone, A. (2006). *Handbook of functional neuroimaging of cognition.* Cambridge, MA: MIT Press.

Cao, Q., Zang, Y., Zhu, C., Cao, X., Sun, L., Zhou, X., & Wang, Y. (2008). Alerting deficits in children with attention deficit/hyperactivity disorder: Event-related fMRI evidence. *Brain Research, 1219,* 159–168.

Capano, L., Minden, D., Chen, S. X., Schachar, R. J., & Ickowicz, A. (2008). Mathematical learning disorder in school-age children with attention-deficit hyperactivity disorder. *The Canadian Journal of Psychiatry, 53,* 392–399.

Carmona, S., Vilarroya, O., Bielsa, A., Tremols, V., Soliva, J. C., Rovira, M., et al. (2005). Global and regional gray matter reductions in ADHD: A vowel-based morphometric study. *Neuroscience Letters, 389,* 88–93.

Casey, B. J., Castellanos, F. X., Giedd, J. N., Marsh, W. L., Hamburger, S. D., Schubert, A. B., et al. (1997). Implications of right frontostriatal circuitry in response inhibition and attention-deficit/hyperactivity disorder. *Journal of the American Academy of Child and Adolescent Psychiatry, 36*(3), 374–383.

Casey, B. J., Nigg, J. T., & Durston, S. (2007). New potential leads in the biology and treatment of attention deficit-hyperactivity disorder. *Current Opinion in Neurology, 20,* 119–124.

Casey, B. J., Tottenham, N., & Fossela, J. (2002). Clinical, imaging, lesion, and genetic approaches toward a model of cognitive control. *Developmental Psychobiology, 40,* 237–254.

Castellanos, F. X. (2001). Neuroimaging studies of attention-deficit/hyperactivity disorder. In M. Solanto, A. Arnsten, & F. X. Castellanos (Eds.), *Attention-deficit/ hyperactivity disorder and stimulants: Basic and clinical neuroscience* (pp. 243–258). New York: Oxford University Press.

Castellanos, F. X., Lee, P. P., Sharp, W., Jeffries, N. O., Greenstein, D. K., Clasen, L. S., et al. (2002). Developmental trajectories of brain volume abnormalities in children with attention-deficit/hyperactivity disorder. *Journal of the American Medical Association, 288,* 1740–1748.

Castellanos, F. X., Sonuga-Barke, E. J., Milham, M. P., Tannock, R. (2006). Characterizing cognition in ADHD: beyond executive dysfunction. *Trends in Cognitive Science, 10,* 117–123.

Chang, K., Adleman, N. E., Dienes, K., Simeonova, D., Menon, V., & Reiss, A. (2004). Anomalous prefrontal-subcortical activation in familial pediatric bipolar disorder: A functional magnetic resonance imaging investigation. *Archives of General Psychiatry, 61,* 781–792.

Chermak, G. D., Hall, J. W., & Musiek, F. E. (1999). Differential diagnosis and management of central auditory processing disorder and attention deficit hyperactivity disorder. *Journal of the American Academy of Audiology, 10,* 289–303.

Chhabildas, N., Pennington, B. F., & Willcutt, E. G. (2001). A comparison of the neuropsychological profiles of the DSM-IV subtypes of ADHD. *Journal of Abnormal Child Psychology, 29,* 529–540.

Chow, T. W., & Cummings, J. L. (2007). Frontal-subcortical circuits. In B. L. Miller & J. L. Cummings (Eds.), *The human frontal lobes: Functions and disorders* (2nd ed.). New York: Guilford.

Clark, C., Prior, M., & Kinsella, G. J. (2000). Do executive function deficits differentiate between adolescents with ADHD and oppositional defiant-conduct disorder? A neuropsychological study using the Six Elements Test and Hayling Sentence Completion Test. *Journal of Abnormal Psychology, 28,* 403–414.

Clark, C., Prior, M., & Kinsella, G. (2002). The relationship between executive function abilities, adaptive behaviour, and academic achievement in children with externalizing behaviour problems. *Journal of Child Psychology and Psychiatry, 43,* 785–796.

Clarke, A. R., Barry, R. J, McCarthy, R., Selikowitz, M., & Brown, C. R. (2002). EEG evidence for a new conceptualization of attention deficit hyperactivity disorder. *Clinical Neurophysiology, 113,* 1036–1044.

Clarke, S. D., Kohn, M. R., Hermens, D. F., Rabbinge, M., Clark, C. R., Gordon, E., et al. (2007). Distinguishing symptom profiles in adolescent ADHD using an objective cognitive test battery. *International Journal of Adolescent Medicine & Health. 19,* 355–367.

Cohen, N. J., Vallance, D. D., Barwick, M., Im, N., Menna, R., Horodezky, N. B., & Isaacson, L. (2000). The interface between ADHD and language impairment: An examination of language, achievement, and cognitive processing. *Journal of Child Psychology and Psychiatry, 41,* 353–362.

Collins, R. D. (2003). Differences between ADHD inattentive and combined types on the CPT. *Journal of Psychopathology and Behavioral Assessment, 25,* 177–189.

Comings, D. E., Gade-Andavolu, R., Gonzalez, N., Wu, S., Muhleman, D., Blake, H., et al. (2000). Comparison of the role of dopamine, serotonin, and noradrenaline genes in ADHD, ODD and conduct disorder: Multivariate regression analysis of 20 genes. *Clinical Genetics, 57,* 178–196.

Compton, R. J. (2003). The interface between emotion and attention: A review of evidence from psychology and neuroscience. *Behavioral and Cognitive Neuroscience Reviews, 2,* 115–129.

Congdon, E., & Canli, T. (2005). The endophenotype of impulsivity: Reaching consilience through behavioral, genetic, and neuroimaging approaches. *Behavioral and Cognitive Neuroscience Reviews, 4,* 262–281.

Conners, C. K. (2008). *Conners comprehensive behavior rating scales.* North Tonawanda, NY: Multi-Health Systems.

Conway, A. R. A., Cowan, N., Bunting, M. F., Therriault, D. J., & Minkoff, S. R. B. (2002). A latent variable analysis of working memory capacity, short-term memory capacity, processing speed, and general fluid intelligence. *Intelligence, 30*, 163–184.

D'Amato, R. C., Fletcher-Janzen, E., & Reynolds, C. R. (2005). *Handbook of school neuropsychology*. Hoboken, NJ: John Wiley & Sons.

Davidson, R. J. (2000). Affective style, psychopathology, and resilience: Brain mechanisms and plasticity. *American Psychologist, 55*, 196–214.

Davey, B. (1983). Think Aloud-Modeling the Cognitive Processes of Reading Comprehension. *Journal of Reading, 27*, 44–47.

Dawson, P., & Guare, R. (2004). *Executive skills in children and adolescents*. New York: Guilford.

Decker, S. L., Hill, S. K., & Dean, R. S. (2007). Evidence of construct similarity in executive functions and fluid reasoning abilities. *International Journal of Neuroscience, 117*, 735–748.

Del's Homme, M., Kim, T. S., Loo, S. K., Yang, M. H., & Smalley, S. L. (2007). Family association and frequency of learning disabilities in ADHD sibling pair families. *Journal of Abnormal Child Psychology, 35*, 55–62.

Delis, D. C., Kaplan, E., & Kramer, J. H. (2001). *Delis-Kaplan Executive Function System*. San Antonio, TX: The Psychological Corporation.

Delis, D. C., Kramer, J. H., Kaplan, E., & Ober, B. A. (1994). *CVLT-C: California Verbal Learning Test-Children's Version*. San Antonio, TX: The Psychological Corporation.

Denckla, M. B. (1996). Biological correlates of learning and attention: What is relevant to learning disability and attention-deficit hyperactivity disorder? *Journal of Developmental and Behavioral Pediatrics, 17*, 114–119.

Denckla, M. B. (2006). *Attention deficit hyperactivity disorder: The childhood comorbidity that most influences the disability burden in Tourette syndrome*. Philadelphia: Lippincott Williams & Wilkins Publishers.

Denckla, M. B., & Reiss, A. L. (1997). Prefrontal-subcortical circuits in developmental disorders. In N. Krasnegor, G.R. Lyon and P. S. Goldman-Rakic (Eds.), *Prefrontal cortex: Evolution, development, and behavioral neuroscience* (pp. 283–293). Baltimore, MD: Brooke Publishing.

Deshler, D., & Schumaker, J. B. (1988). An instructional model for teaching students how to learn. In J. L. Graden, J. E. Zins, & M. J. Curtis (Eds.), *Alternative educational delivery systems: Enhancing instructional options for all students* (pp. 391–411). Washington, DC: National Association of School Psychologists.

Dickstein, S. G., Bannon, K., Castellanos, F. X., & Milham, M. P. (2006). The neural correlates of attention deficit hyperactivity disorder: An ALE meta-analysis. *Journal of Child Psychology and Psychiatry, 47*(10), 1051–1062.

Doya, K. (2000). Complementary roles of basal ganglia and cerebellum in learning and motor control. *Current Opinion in Neurobiology, 10*, 732–739.

Doyle, A. E., Biederman, J., Seidman, L. J., Weber, W., & Faraone, S. V. (2000). Diagnostic efficiency of neuropsychological test scores for discriminating boys with and without attention deficit-hyperactivity disorder. *Journal of Consulting and Clinical Psychology, 68*, 477–488.

Doyle, A. E., Willcutt, E. G., Seidman, L. J., Biederman, J., Chouinard, V. A., Silva, J., et al. (2005). Attention-deficit/hyperactivity disorder endophenotypes. *Biological Psychiatry, 57,* 1324–1335.

Drabick, D. G., Gadow, K. D., & Sprafkin, J. (2006). Co-occurrence of conduct disorder and depression in a clinic-based sample of boys with ADHD. *Journal of Child Psychology and Psychiatry, 47,* 766–774.

DuPaul, G. J., McGoey, K. E., Eckert, T. L., & VanBrakle, J. (2001). Preschool children with attention-deficit/hyperactivity disorder: Impairments in behavioral, social, and school functioning. *Journal of the American Academy of Child & Adolescent Psychiatry, 40,* 508–515.

DuPaul, G. J., Power, T. J., Anastopoulos, A. D., & Reid, R. (1998). *ADHD rating scale— IV: Checklists, norms, and clinical interpretation.* New York: Guilford.

DuPaul, G. J., & Stoner, G. (2003). *ADHD in the schools: Assessment and intervention strategies* (2nd ed.). New York: Guilford.

Durston, S. A. (2003). A review of the biological bases of ADHD: What have we learned from imaging studies? *Mental Retardation and Developmental Disabilities Research Reviews, 9,* 184–195.

Erenberg, G. (2005). The relationship between Tourette syndrome, attention deficit hyperactivity disorder, and stimulant medication: A critical review. *Seminars in Pediatric Neurology, 12,* 217–221.

Faraone, S. V. (2008). Statistical and molecular genetic approaches to developmental psychopathology: The pathway forward. In J. J. Hudziak (Ed.), *Developmental psychopathology and wellness: Genetic and environmental influences* (pp. 245–265). Arlington, VA: American Psychiatric Publishing.

Filipek, P. A. (1999). Neuroimaging in the developmental disorders: The state of the science. *Journal of Child Psychology and Psychiatry, 40,* 113–128.

Fiorello, C. A., Hale, J. B., Holdnack, J. A., Kavanagh, J. A., Terrell, J., & Long, L. (2007). Interpreting intelligence test results for children with disabilities: Is global intelligence relevant? *Applied Neuropsychology, 14,* 2–12.

Forbes, E. E., May, J. C., Siegle, G. J., Ladouceur, C. D., Ryan, N. D., Carter, C. S., et al. (2006). Reward-related decision-making in pediatric major depressive disorder: An fMRI study. *Journal of Child Psychology and Psychiatry, 47,* 1031–1040.

Frank, M. J., Santamaria, A., O'Reilly, R. C., & Willcutt, E. (2007). Testing computational models of dopamine and noradrenaline dysfunction in attention deficit/ hyperactivity disorder. *Neuropsychopharmacology, 32,* 1583–1599.

Freeman, R. D., and Tourette Syndrome International Database Consortium. (2007). Tic disorders and ADHD: Answers from the world-wide clinical dataset on Tourette syndrome. *European Child and Adolescent Psychiatry, 16,* 15–23.

Garavan, H., Ross, T. J., Murphy, K., Roche, R. A. P., & Stein, E. A. (2002). Dissociable executive functions in the dynamic control of behavior: Inhibition, error detection, and correction. *Neuroimage, 17,* 1820–1829.

Gaskins, I. W., Satlou, E., & Pressley, M. (2007). Executive control of reading comprehension in the elementary school. In L. Meltzer (Ed.), *Executive function in education. From theory to practice* (pp. 165–193). New York, NY: Guilford.

Gazzaley, A., Cooney, J. W., McEvoy, K., Knight, R. T., & D'Esposito, M. (2005). Top-down enhancement and suppression of the magnitude and speed of neural activity. *Journal of Cognitive Neuroscience, 17,* 507–517.

Geller, D. A., Biederman, J., Griffin, S., & Jones, J. (1996). Comorbidity of juvenile obsessive-compulsive disorder with disruptive behavior disorders. *Journal of the American Academy of Child & Adolescent Psychiatry, 35,* 1637–1646.

Geurts, H. M., Verte, S., Oosterlaan, J., Roeyers, H., & Sergeant, J. A. (2004). ADHD subtypes: Do they differ in their executive functioning profile? *Archives of Clinical Neuropsychology, 20,* 457–477.

Giedd, J. N., Castellanos, F. X., Casey, B. J., Kozuch, P., et al. (1994). Quantitative morphology of the corpus callosum in attention deficit hyperactivity disorder. *American Journal of Psychiatry, 151,* 665–669.

Gioia, G. A., Isquith, P. K., Guy, S. C., & Kenworthy, L. (2000). *Behavior rating inventory of executive function.* Odessa, FL: Psychological Assessment Resources.

Gitten, J. C., Winer, J. L., Festa, E. K., & Heindel, W. C. (2006). Conditional associative learning of spatial and object information in children with attention deficit/hyperactivity disorder. *Child Neuropsychology, 12,* 39–56.

Goldberg, E. (2001). *The executive brain: Frontal lobes and the civilized mind.* New York: Oxford University Press.

Golden, C. J. (1978). *The Stroop color-word test.* Chicago, IL: Stoelting.

Gomez, R., & Condon, M. (1999). Central auditory processing ability in children with ADHD with and without learning disabilities. *Journal of Learning Disabilities, 32,* 150–158.

Goodyer, I. M. (2000). Language difficulties and psychopathology. In D. V. M. Bishop & L. B. Leonard (Eds.), *Speech and language impairments in children: Causes, characteristics, intervention and outcome* (pp. 227–244). New York: Psychology Press.

Graham, S., & Harris, K. R. (1999). Assessment and intervention in overcoming writing difficulties. An illustration from the self-regulated strategy development model. *Language, Speech, and Hearing Services in Schools, 30,* 255–264.

Grimm, S., Beck, J., Schuepbach, D., Hell, D., Boesiger, P., Bermpohl, F., et al. (2008). Imbalance between left and right dorsolateral prefrontal cortex in major depression is linked to negative emotional judgment: An fMRI study in severe major depressive disorder. *Biological Psychiatry, 63,* 369–376.

Gross-Tsur, V., Shalev, R. S., Manor, O., & Amir, N. (1995). Developmental right-hemisphere syndrome: Clinical spectrum of the nonverbal learning disability. *Journal of Learning Disabilities, 28,* 80–86.

Gruber, S., Rogowska, J., & Yurgelun-Todd, D. (2003). Decreased activation of the anterior cingulate in bipolar patients: An fMRI study. *Journal of Affective Disorders, 82,* 191–201.

Guerin, D. W., Gottfried, A. W., Oliver, P. H., & Thomas, C. W. (1994). Temperament and school functioning during early adolescence. *The Journal of Early Adolescence, 14,* 200–225.

Hain, L. A., Hale, J. B., & Glass-Kendorski, J. G. (2008). The enigmatic population of specific learning disabilities: Comorbidity of psychopathology in cognitive and academic subtypes. In S. G. Feifer, & G. Rattan (Eds.), *Emotional disorders: A neuropsychological, psychopharmacological, and educational perspective.* Middletown, MD: School Neuropsych Press.

Hale, J. B., Blaine-Halperin, D., & Beakley, K. (2007, February). *Executive impairment determines ADHD response to methylphenidate treatment.* Paper presentation at the 35th Annual Meeting of the International Neuropsychological Society, Portland, OR.

Hale, J. B., & Fiorello, C. A. (2004). *School neuropsychology: A practitioner's handbook.* New York: Guilford.

Hale, J. B., Fiorello, C. A., & Brown, L. (2005). Determining medication treatment effects using teacher ratings and classroom observations of children with ADHD: Does neuropsychological impairment matter? *Educational and Child Psychology, 22,* 39–61.

Hale, J. B., Fiorello, C. A., Kavanagh, J. A., Holdnack, J. A., & Aloe, A. M. (2007). Is the demise of IQ interpretation justified? A response to special issue authors. *Applied Neuropsychology, 14,* 37–51.

Hale, J. B., How, S. K., DeWitt, M. B., & Coury, D. L. (2001). Discriminant validity of the Conners' scales for ADHD subtypes. *Current Psychology, 20,* 231–249.

Hale, J. B., Kaufman, A., Naglieri, J. A., & Kavale, K. A. (2006). Implementation of IDEA: Integrating response to intervention and cognitive assessment methods. *Psychology in the Schools, 43,* 753–770.

Hale, J. B., Reddy, L. A., Decker, S. L., Thompson, R., Henzel, J., Teodori, A., Forrest, E., Eusebio, F., & Denckla, M. B. (2009). Development and validation of an ADHD executive function and behavior rating screening battery. *Journal of Clinical and Experimental Neuropsychology. 1,* 1–16.

Halperin, J. M., & Schulz, K. P. (2006). Revisiting the role of the prefrontal cortex in the pathophysiology of attention-deficit/hyperactivity disorder. *Psychological Bulletin, 132:4,* 560 581.

Harada, Y., Yamazaki, T., & Saitoh, K. (2002). Psychosocial problems in attention deficit hyperactivity disorder with oppositional defiant disorder. *Psychiatry and Clinical Neuroscience, 56*(4), 365–369.

Harris, K. R. (1986). Self-monitoring of attentional behavior versus self-monitoring of productivity: Effects on on-task behavior and academic response rate among learning disabled children. *Journal of Applied Behavior Analysis, 19,* 417–423.

Hattie, J., Biggs, J., & Purdie, N. (1996). Effects on learning skills interventions on student learning: A meta-analysis. *Review of Educational Research, 66,* 99–136.

Heaton, R. K., Chelune, G. J., Talley, J. L., Kay, G. G., & Curtiss, G. (1993). *Wisconsin card sorting test manual: Revised and expanded.* Odessa, FL: Psychological Assessment Resources.

Henin, A., Mick, E., Biederman, J., Fried, R., Wozniak, J., Faraone, S. V., et al. (2007). Can bipolar disorder-specific neuropsychological impairments in children be identified? *Journal of Consulting and Clinical Psychology, 75,* 210–220.

Hollander, E., & Evers, M. (2001). New developments in impulsivity. *The Lancet, 358,* 949–950.

Homack, S., & Riccio, C. A. (2004). A meta-analysis of the sensitivity and specificity of the Stroop color and word test with children. *Archives of Clinical Neuropsychology, 19,* 725–743.

Huang-Pollock, C. L., & Nigg, J. T. (2003). Searching for the attention deficit in attention deficit hyperactivity disorder: The case of visuospatial orienting. *Clinical Psychology Review, 23,* 801–830.

Huang-Pollock, C. L., Nigg, J. T., & Halperin, J. M. (2006). Single dissociation findings of ADHD deficits in vigilance but not anterior or posterior attention systems. *Neuropsychology, 20,* 420–429.

Hughes, C. A., & Schumaker, J. B. (1991). Test-taking strategy instruction for adolescents with learning disabilities. *Exceptionality, 2,* 205–221.

Hurks, P. P., Hendriksen, J. G., Vles, J. S., Kalff, A. C, Feron, F. J., Kroes, M., et al. (2004). Verbal fluency over time as a measure of automatic and controlled processing in children with ADHD. *Brain and Cognition, 55,* 535–544.

Irwin, J. R., Carter, A. S., & Briggs-Gowan, M. J. (2002). The social-emotional development of "late-talking" toddlers. *Journal of the American Academy of Child & Adolescent Psychiatry, 41,* 1324–1332.

Isles, A. R., & Humby, T. (2008). Modes of imprinted gene action in learning disability. *Journal of Intellectual Disability Research, 50,* 318–325.

Ivarsson, T., & Melin, K. (2008). Autism spectrum traits in children and adolescents with obsessive-compulsive disorder (OCD). *Journal of Anxiety Disorders, 22,* 969–978.

Ivry, R. B. (1993). Cerebellar involvement in the explicit representation of temporal information. *Annals of the New York Academy of Sciences, 682,* 214–230.

Jarrett, M. A., & Ollendick, T. H. (2008). A conceptual review of the comorbidity of attention-deficit/hyperactivity disorder and anxiety: Implications for future research and practice. *Clinical Psychology Review, 28,* 1266–1280.

Jensen, P. S., Hinshaw, S. P., Kraemer, H. C., Lenora, N., Newcorn, J. H., Abikoff, H. B., et al. (2001). ADHD comorbidity findings from the MTA study: Comparing comorbid subgroups. *Journal of the American Academy of Child & Adolescent Psychiatry, 40,* 147–158.

Johnston, C., & Mash, E. J. (2001). Families of children with attention-deficit/hyperactivity disorder: Review and recommendations for future research. *Clinical Child and Family Psychology Review, 4,* 183–207.

Jucaite, A., Fernell, E., Halldin, C., Forssberg, H., & Farde, L. (2005). Reduced midbrain dopamine transporter binding in male adolescents with attention-deficit/hyperactivity disorder: Association between striatal dopamine markers and motor hyperactivity. *Biological Psychiatry, 57,* 229–238.

Kalff, A. C., De Sonneville, L. M., Hurks, P. P., Hendriksen, J. G., Kroes, M., Feron, F. J., et al. (2005). Speed, speed variability, and accuracy of information processing in 5- to 6-year-old children at risk of ADHD. *Journal of the International Neuropsychological Society, 11,* 173–183.

Kane, M. J., & Engle, R. W. (2002). The role of the prefrontal cortex in working memory capacity, executive attention, and fluid intelligence: An individual differences perspective. *Psychonomic Bulletin and Review, 9,* 637–671.

Kaplan, B. J., Dewey, D. M., Crawford, S. G., & Fisher, G. C. (1998). Deficits in long-term memory are not characteristic of ADHD. *Journal of Clinical and Experimental Neuropsychology, 20,* 518–528.

Kaplan, E., Fein, D., Kramer, J., Morris, R., Delis, D., & Maerlender, A. (2004). *Wechsler Intelligence Scale for Children, 4th Edition Integrated*. San Antonio, TX: The Psychological Corporation.

Karatekin, C., & Asarnow, R. F. (1999). Exploratory eye movements to pictures in childhood-onset schizophrenia and attention-deficit/hyperactivity disorder (ADHD). *Journal of Abnormal Child Psychology, 27*, 35–49.

Kellner, R., Houghton, S., & Douglas, G. (2003). Peer-related personal experiences of children with attention-deficit/hyperactivity disorder with and without comorbid learning disabilities. *International Journal of Disability, Development and Education, 50*, 119–136.

Kessler, R. C., Adler, L. A., Barkley, R., Biederman, J., Conners, C. K., Faraone, S. V., Greenhill, L. L., Jaeger, S., Secnik, K., Spencer, T., Ustun, T. B., & Zaslavsky, A. M. (2005). Patterns and predictors of attention-deficit/hyperactivity disorder persistence into adulthood: Results from the national comorbidity survey replication. *Biological Psychiatry, 57*, 1442–1451.

Kieling, C., Goncalves, R. R., Tannock, R., & Castellanos, F. X. (2008). Neurobiology of attention-deficit/hyperactivity disorder. *Child and Adolescent Clinics of North America, 17*, 285–307.

Kim, A.-H., Vaughn, S., Wanzek, J., & Wei, S. (2004). Graphic organizers and their effects on the reading comprehension of students with LD: A synthesis of the research. *Journal of Learning Disabilities, 37*, 105–118.

Kim, O. H., & Kaiser, A. P. (2000). Language characteristics of children with ADHD. *Communication Disorders Quarterly, 21*, 154–165.

Klimkeit, E. I., Sheppard, D. M., Lee, P., & Bradshaw, J. L. (2004). Bimanual coordination deficits in attention deficit/hyperactivity disorder (ADHD). *Journal of Clinical and Experimental Neuropsychology, 26*, 999–1010.

Klorman, R., Hazel-Fernandez, L. A., Shaywitz, S. E., Fletcher, J. M., Marchione, K. E., Holohan, J., et al. (1999). Executive functioning deficits in attention-deficit/hyperactivity disorder are independent of oppositional defiant or reading disorder. *Journal of the American Academy of Child and Adolescent Psychiatry, 38*, 1148–1155.

Konrad, K., Gauggel, S., Manz, A., & Scholl, M. (2000). Inhibitory control in children with traumatic brain injury (TB1) and children with attention deficit/hyperactivity disorder (ADHD). *Brain Injury, 14*, 859–875.

Korkman, M., Kirk, U., & Kemp, S. (2007). *NEPSY-II*. San Antonio, TX: The Psychological Corporation.

Kourakis, L. E., Katachanakis, C. N., Vlahonikolis, L. G., & Paritsis, N. K. (2004). Examination of verbal memory and recall time in children with attention deficit hyperactivity disorder. *Developmental Neuropsychology, 26*, 565–570.

Krain, A., Gotimer, K., Hefton, S., Ernst, M., Castellanos, F., Pine, D., & Milham, M. (2008). A functional magnetic resonance imaging investigation of uncertainty in adolescents with anxiety disorders. *Biological Psychiatry, 63*, 563–568.

Kratochvil, C. J., Newcorn, J. H., Arnold, L. E., Duesenberg, D., Emslie, G. J., Quintana, H., et al. (2005). Atomoxetine alone or combined with fluoxetine for treating ADHD with comorbid depressive or anxiety symptoms. *Journal of the American Academy of Child & Adolescent Psychiatry, 44,* 915–924.

Krauel, K., Duzel, E., Hinrichs, H., Santel, S., Rellum, T., & Baving, L. (2007). Impact of emotional salience on episodic memory in attention-deficit/hyperactivity disorder: A functional magnetic resonance imaging study. *Biological Psychiatry, 61,* 1370–1379.

Kraus, M. F., Susmaras, T., Caughlin, B. P., Walker, C. J., Sweeney, J. A., & Little, D. M. (2007). White matter integrity and cognition in chronic brain injury: A diffusion tensor imaging study. *Brain, 130,* 2508–2519.

Kroger, J. K., Sabb, F. W., Fales, C. L., & Bookheimer, M. S. (2002). Recruitment of anterior dorsolateral prefrontal cortex in human reasoning: A parametric study of relational complexity. *Cerebral Cortex, 12,* 477–485.

Lahey, B. B., Schaughency, E. A., Hynd, G. W., Carlson, C. L., & Nieves, N. (1987). Attention deficit disorder with and without hyperactivity: Comparison of behavioral characteristics in clinic-referred children. *Journal of the American Academy of Child and Adolescent Psychiatry, 28,* 718–723.

Lawrence, V., Houghton, S., Douglas, G., Durkin, K., Whiting, K., & Tannock, R. (2004). Executive function and ADHD: A comparison of children's performance during neuropsychological testing and real-world activities. *Journal of Attention Disorders, 7,* 137–149.

Levy, F. (2004). Synaptic gating and ADHD: A biological theory of comorbidity of ADHD and anxiety. *Neuropsychopharmacology, 29,* 1589–1596.

Levy, F., Hay, D. A., Bennett, K. S., & McStephen, M. (2005). Gender differences in ADHD subtype comorbidity. *Journal of the American Academy of Child and Adolescent Psychiatry, 44,* 368–376.

Levy, R., & Goldman-Rakic, P. S. (2000). Segregation of working memory functions within the prefrontal cortex. *Experimental Brain Research, 133,* 21–32.

Lichter, D. G., & Cummings, J. L. (Eds.). (2001). *Frontal-subcortical circuits in psychiatric and neurological disorders.* New York: Guilford.

Liddle, P. F., Kiehl, K. A., & Smith, A. M. (2001). Event-related fMRI study of response inhibition. *Human Brain Mapping, 12,* 100–109.

Liotti, M., Pliszka, S. R., Perez, R., Luus, B., Glahn, D., & Semrud-Clikeman, M. (2007). Electrophysiological correlates of response inhibition in children and adolescents with ADHD: Influence of gender, age, and previous treatment history. *Psychophysiology, 44,* 936–948.

Lockwood, K. A., Marcotte, A. C., & Stern, C. (2001). Differentiation of attention-deficit/hyperactivity disorder subtypes: Application of a neuropsychological model of attention. *Journal of Clinical and Experimental Neuropsychology, 23,* 317–330.

Logan, G. D., Schachar, R., J., & Tannock, R. (1997). Impulsivity and inhibitory control. *Psychological Science, 8,* 60–64.

Love, A. J., & Thompson, M. G. (1988). Language disorders and attention deficit disorders in young children referred for psychiatric services: Analysis of prevalence and a conceptual synthesis. *American Journal of Orthopsychiatry, 58,* 52–64.

Luria, A. R. (1973). *The working brain.* New York: Basic Books.

Lyoo, I. K., Lee, H. K., Jung, J. H., Noam, G. G., & Renshaw, P. F. (2002). White matter hyperintensities on magnetic resonance imaging of the brain in children with psychiatric disorders. *Comprehensive Psychiatry, 43,* 361–368.

Madras, B. K., Miller, G. M., & Fischman, A. J. (2005). The dopamine transporter and attention-deficit/hyperactivity disorder. *Biological Psychiatry, 57,* 1397–1409.

Mahone, E. M., Cirino, P. T., Cutting, L. E., Cerrone, P. M., Hagelthorn, K. M., Hiemenz, J. R., et al. (2002). Validity of the behavior rating inventory of executive function in children with ADHD and/or Tourette syndrome. *Archives of Clinical Neuropsychology, 17,* 643–662.

Mangeot, S. D., Miller, L. J., McIntosh, D. N., McGrath-Clarke, J., Simon, J., Hagerman, R. J., et al. (2001). Sensory modulation dysfunction in children with attention-deficit-hyperactivity disorder. *Developmental Medicine & Child Neurology, 43,* 399–406.

Manly, T., Anderson, V., Robertson, I., & Nimmo-Smith, I. (1999). *Test of everyday attention for children.* London, UK: Thames Valley Test Company.

Martin, R. P. (1988). *Assessment of personality and behavior problems.* New York: Guilford.

Martin, R. P., Olejnik, S., & Gaddis, L. (1994). Is temperament an important contributor to schooling outcomes in elementary school? Modeling effects of temperament and scholastic ability on academic achievement. In W. B. Carey & S. C. McDevitt (Eds.), *Prevention and early intervention: Individual differences us risk factors for the mental health of children: A festschrift for Stella Chess and Alexander Thomas* (pp. 59–68). Philadelphia, PA: Brunner/Mazel.

Martinussen, R., Hayden, J., Hogg-Johnson, S., & Tannock, R. (2005). A meta-analysis of working memory impairments in children with attention-deficit/hyperactivity disorder. *Journal of the American Academy of Child & Adolescent Psychiatry, 44,* 377–384.

Martinussen, R., & Tannock, R. (2006). Working memory impairments in children with attention-deficit hyperactivity disorder with and without comorbid language learning disorders. *Journal of Clinical and Experimental Neuropsychology, 28,* 1073–1094.

Marusiak, C. W., & Janzen, H. L., (2005). Assessing the working memory abilities of ADHD children using the Stanford-Binet intelligence scales (5th ed.). *Canadian Journal of School Psychology, 20,* 84–97.

Mayberg, H. (2001). Depression and frontal-subcortical circuits: Focus on prefrontal-limbic interactions. In D. G. Lichter & J. L. Cummings (Eds.), *Frontal-subcortical circuits in psychiatric and neurological disorders* (pp. 177–206). New York: Guilford.

Mayes, S. D., & Calhoun, S. L. (2006). WISC-IV and WISC-III profiles in children with ADHD. *Journal of Attention Disorders, 9,* 486–493.

Mayes, S. D. Calhoun, S. L., & Crowell, E. W. (2000). Learning disabilities and ADHD: Overlapping spectrum disorders. *Journal of Learning Disabilities, 33,* 417–424.

Mazei-Robison, M. S., Couch, R. S., Shelton, R. C., Stein, M. A., & Blakely, R. D. (2005). Sequence variation in the human dopamine transporter gene in children with attention deficit hyperactivity disorder. *Neuropharmacology, 49,* 724–736.

McClure, E. B., Adler, A., Monk, C. S., Cameron, J., Smith, S., Nelson, E. E., et al. (2007). fMRI predictors of treatment outcome in pediatric anxiety disorders. *Psychopharmacology, 191,* 97–105.

McDonald, B. C., Flashman, L. A., & Saykin, A. J. (2002). Executive dysfunction following traumatic brain injury: Neural substrates and treatment strategies. *NeuroRehabilitation, 17,* 333–344.

McInnes, A., Humphries, T., Hogg-Johnson, S., & Tannock, R. (2003). Listening comprehension and working memory are impaired in attention-deficit hyperactivity disorder irrespective of language impairment. *Journal of Abnormal Child Psychology, 31,* 427–443.

Meltzer, L., Reddy, R., Pollica, L., & Roditi, B. (2004). Academic success in students with learning disabilities: The roles of self-understanding, strategy use, and effort. *Thalamus, 22,* 16–32.

Meltzer, L., Roditi, B., Steinberg, J., Biddle, K. R., Taber, S., Caron, K. B., et al. (2006). *Strategies for success: Classroom teaching techniques for students with learning differences* (2nd ed.). Austin, TX: Pro-Ed.

Middleton, F. A., & Strick, P. L. (2000). Basal ganglia output and cognition: Evidence from anatomical, behavioral, and clinical studies. *Brain and Cognition, 42,* 183–200.

Milich, R., Balentine, A. C., & Lynam, D. R. (2001). ADHD combined type and ADHD predominantly inattentive type are distinct and unrelated disorders. *Clinical Psychology: Science and Practice, 8,* 463–488.

Miller, B. L., & Cummings, J. L. (Eds.). (2007). *The human frontal lobes: Functions and disorders* (2nd ed.). New York: Guilford.

Miller, D. C., & Belloni, K. (2009). *U.S. validation sample for the test of everyday attention (TEACH).* Denton, TX: Texas Woman's University and The Psychological Corporation.

Miller, D. C., & Hale, J. B. (2008). Neuropsychological applications of the WISC-IV and WISC-IV Integrated. In A. Prifitera, D. H. Saklofske, & L. G. Weiss (Eds.), *WISC-IV clinical assessment and intervention* (2nd ed.) (pp. 445–495). New York: Elsevier.

Mirsky, A. F. (1996). Disorders of attention: A neuropsychological perspective. In G. R. Lyon, & N. A. Krasnegor (Eds.), *Attention, memory, and executive function* (pp. 71–95). Baltimore, MD: Paul H. Brookes.

Mitsis, E. M., McKay, K. E., Schulz, K. P., Newcorn, J. H., & Halperin, J. M. (2000). Parent-teacher concordance for DSM-IV attention-deficit/hyperactivity disorder in a clinic-referred sample. *Journal of the American Academy of Child & Adolescent Psychiatry, 39,* 308–313.

Moffit, T. E. (1993). The neurobiology of conduct disorder. *Development and Psychopathology, 5,* 135–151.

Moll, G. H., Heinrich, H., Trott, G., Wirth, S., & Rothenberger, A. (2000). Deficient intracortical inhibition in drug-naive children with attention-deficit hyperactivity disorder is enhanced by methylphenidate. *Neuroscience Letters, 284,* 121–125.

Moss, W. L., & Sheiffele, W. A. (1994). Can we differentially diagnose an attention deficit disorder without hyperactivity from a central auditory processing problem? *Child Psychiatry and Human Development, 25,* 85–96.

Mostofsky, S. H., Cooper, K. L., Kates, W. R., Denckla, M. B., & Kaufmann, W. E. (2002). Smaller prefrontal and premotor volumes in boys with attention-deficit/hyperactivity disorder. *Biological Psychiatry, 52,* 785–794.

Mostofsky, S. H., Newschaffer, C. J., & Denckla, M. B. (2003). Overflow movements predict impaired response inhibition in children With ADHD. *Perceptual and Motor Skills, 97,* 1315–1331.

Muller, S. V., Johannes, S., Wieringa, B., Weber, A., Muller-Vahl, K., Matzke, M., et al. (2003). Disturbed monitoring and response inhibition in patients with Gilles de la Tourette syndrome and comorbid obsessive compulsive disorder. *Behavioural Neurology, 14.*

Myers, C. E., Shohamy, D., Gluck, M. A., Grossman, S., Kluger, A., Ferris, S., et al. (2003). Dissociating hippocampal versus basal ganglia contributions to learning and transfer. *Journal of Cognitive Neuroscience, 15,* 185–193.

Naglieri, J. A., & Gottling, S. H. (1995). A study of planning and mathematics instruction for students with learning disabilities. *Psychological Reports, 76,* 1343–1354.

Nakao, T., Nakagawa, A., Yoshiura, T., Nakatani, E., Nabeyama, M., Yoshizato, C., et al. (2005). Brain activation of patients with obsessive-compulsive disorder during neuropsychological and symptom provocation tasks before and after symptom improvement: A functional magnetic resonance imaging study. *Biological Psychiatry, 57,* 901–910.

Nelson, E. E., Vinton, D. T., Berghorst, L., Hommer, R. E., Dickstein, D. P., & Rich, B. A. (2007). Brain systems underlying response flexibility in healthy and bipolar adolescents: An event-related fMRI study. *Bipolar Disorders, 9,* 810.

Newcorn, J. H., Halperin, J. M., Healey, J. M., O'Brien, J. D., Pascualvaca, D. M., Wolf, L. E., et al. (1989): Are ADDH and ADHD the same or different? *Journal of the American Academy of Child & Adolescent Psychiatry, 285,* 734–738.

Newcorn, J. H., Halperin, J. M., Jensen, P. S., Abikoff, H. B., Arnold, E., Cantwell, D. P., et al. (2001). Symptom profiles in children with ADHD: Effects of comorbidity and gender. *Journal of the American Academy of Child & Adolescent Psychiatry, 40,* 137–146.

Nigg, J. T. (2000). On inhibition/disinhibition in developmental psychopathology: Views from cognitive and personality psychology and a working inhibition taxonomy. *Psychological Bulletin, 126,* 220–246.

Nigg, J. T. (2005). Neuropsychologic theory and findings in attention-deficit/hyperactivity disorder: The state of the field and salient challenges for the coming decade. *Biological Psychiatry, 57,* 1424–1435.

Nigg, J. T., Blaskey, L. G., Huang-Pollock, C. L., & Rappley, M. D. (2002). Neuropsychological executive functions and DSM-IV ADHD subtypes. *Journal of the American Academy of Child and Adolescent Psychiatry, 41,* 59–66.

Nock, M. K., Kazdin, A. E., Hiripi, E., & Kessler, R. C. (2006). Prevalence, subtypes, and correlates of DSM-IV conduct disorder in the National Comorbidity Survey Replication. *Psychological Medicine, 36,* 699–710.

Olson, S. (2004). Making sense of Tourette's. *Science, 305,* 1390–1392.

Ors, M., Ryding, E., Lindgren, M., Gustafsson, P., Blennow, G., & Rosen, I. (2005). SPECT findings in children with specific language impairment. *Cortex, 41,* 316–326.

Owen, A. M., Doyon, J., Petrides, M., & Evans, A. C. (1996). Planning and spatial working memory: A positron emission tomography study in humans. *European Journal of Neuroscience, 8*, 353–364.

Ozonoff, S., & Schetter, P. L. (2007). Executive dysfunction in autism spectrum disorders: From research to practice. In L. Meltzer (Ed.), *Executive function in education. From theory to practice* (pp. 133–160). New York, NY: Guilford.

Packard, M. G., & Knowlton, B. J. (2002). Learning and memory functions of the basal ganglia. *Annual Review of Neuroscience, 25*, 563–593.

Pasini, A., Paloscia, C., Alessandrelli, R., Porfirio, M. C., Curatolo, P. (2007). Attention and executive functions profile in drug naïve ADHD subtypes. *Brain & Development, 29*, 400–408.

Passolunghi, M. C., Marzocchi, G. M., & Fiorillo, F. (2005). Selective effect of inhibition of literal or numerical irrelevant information in children with attention deficit hyperactivity disorder (ADHD) or arithmetic learning disorder (ALD). *Developmental Neuropsychology, 28*, 731–753.

Pauk, W. (1993). *How to study in college* (5th ed.). Boston, MA: Houghton Mifflin.

Perrin, S., & Last, C. G. (1996). Relationship between ADHD and anxiety in boys: Results from a family study. *Journal of the American Academy of Child & Adolescent Psychiatry, 35*, 988–996.

Petrides, M., & Milner, B. (1982). Deficits on subject ordered tasks after frontal and temporal lobe lesions in man. *Neuropsychologia, 20*, 249–262.

Pfiffner, L. J., McBurnett, K., Lahey, B. B., Loeber, R., Green, S., Frick, P. J., et al. (1999). Association of parental psychopathology to the comorbid disorders of boys with attention deficit-hyperactivity disorder. *Journal of Consulting and Clinical Psychology, 67*, 881–893.

Piek, J. P., Dyck, M. J., Francis, M., & Conwell, A. (2007). Working memory, processing speed, and set-shifting in children with developmental coordination disorder and attention-deficit-hyperactivity disorder. *Developmental Medicine & Child Neurology, 49*, 678–683.

Pisecco, S., Baker, D. B., Silva, P. A., & Brooke, M. (2001). Boys with reading disabilities and/or ADHD: Distinctions in early childhood. *Journal of Learning Disabilities, 34*, 98–106.

Pliszka, S. (2005). The neuropsychopharmacology of attention-deficit/hyperactivity disorder. *Biological Psychiatry, 57*, 1385–1390.

Pliszka, S. R. (1992). Comorbidity of attention deficit hyperactivity disorder and overanxious disorder. *Journal of the American Academy of Child & Adolescent Psychiatry, 31*, 197–209.

Pliszka, S. R., Lancaster, J., Liotti, M., & Semrud-Clikeman, M. (2006). Volumetric MRI differences in treatment-naive vs. chronically treated children with ADHD. *Neurology, 67*, 1023–1027.

Pliszka, S. R., Liotti, M., & Woldorff, M. G. (2000). Inhibitory control in children with attention-deficit/hyperactivity disorder: Event related potentials identify the processing component and timing of an impaired right-frontal response-inhibition mechanism. *Biological Psychiatry, 48*, 238–246.

Porteus, S. D. (1965): *Porteus Maze Test: Fifty years application.* New York: Psychological Corporation

Posner, M. I., & Petersen, S. E. (1990). The attention system of the human brain. *Annual Review of Neuroscience, 13*, 25–42.

Posner, M. I., & Raichle, M. E. (1994). *Images of mind.* New York: Scientific American Library/Scientific American Books.

Purvis, K., & Tannock, R. T. (2000). Phonological processing, not inhibitory control, differentiates ADHD and reading disorder. *Journal of the American Academy of Child & Adolescent Psychiatry, 39*, 485–494.

Rapoport, M., van Reekum, R., & Mayberg, H. (2000). The role of the cerebellum in cognition and behavior: A selective review. *Journal of Neuropsychiatry & Clinical Neurosciences, 12*, 193–198.

Reddy, L. A., & Hale, J. B. (2007). Inattentiveness. In A. R. Eisen (Ed.), *Clinical handbook of childhood behavior problems: Case formulation and step-by-step treatment programs* (pp. 156–211). New York: The Guilford Press.

Reitan, R. M., & Wolfson, D. (1985) *Neuroanatomy and neuropathology: A guide for neuropsychologists.* Tucson, AZ: Neuropsychology Press.

Reynolds, C. R., & Kamphaus, R. W. (2004). *Behavior assessment system for children,* (2nd ed.). Circle Pines, MN: American Guidance Service.

Rhee, S. H., Hewitt, J. K., Corley, R. P., Willcutt, E. G., & Pennington, B. F. (2005). Testing hypotheses regarding the causes of comorbidity: Examining the underlying deficits of comorbid disorders. *Journal of Abnormal Psychology, 114*, 346–362.

Riccio, C., Homack, S., Jarratt, K. P., & Wolfe, M. E. (2006). Differences in academic and executive function domains among children with ADHD predominantly inattentive and combined types. *Archives of Clinical Neuropsychology, 21*, 657–667.

Riccio, C. A., Hynd, G. W., Cohen, M. J., Hall, J., et al. (1994). Comorbidity of central auditory processing disorder and attention-deficit hyperactivity disorder. *Journal of the American Academy of Child & Adolescent Psychiatry, 33*, 849–857.

Riccio, C. A., Reynolds, C. R., Lowe, P., & Moore, J. J. (2002). The continuous performance test: A window on the neural substrates for attention? *Archives of Clinical Neuropsychology, 17*, 235–272.

Rich, B. A., Vinton, D. T., Roberson-Nay, R., Hommer, R. E., Berghorst, L. H., McClure, E. B., et al. (2006). Limbic hyperactivation during processing of neutral facial expressions in children with bipolar disorder. *PNAS Proceedings of the National Academy of Sciences of the United States of America, 103*, 8900–8905.

Roessner, V., Becker, A., Banaschewski, T., Freeman, R. D., & Rothenberger, A. (2007). Developmental psychopathology of children and adolescents with Tourette syndrome: Impact of ADHD. *European Child & Adolescent Psychiatry, 16*(Suppl. 1), 24–35.

Romine, C. B., Lee, D., Wolfe, M. E., Homack, S., George, C., & Riccio, C. A. (2004). Wisconsin card sorting test with children: A meta-analytic study of sensitivity and specificity. *Archives of Clinical Neuropsychology, 19*, 1027–1041.

Rommelse, N. N. J., Altink, M. E., Oosterlaan, J., Beem, L., Buschgens, C. J. M., Buitelaar, J., et al. (2008). Speed, variability, and timing of motor output in ADHD: Which measures are useful for endophenotypic research? *Behavior Genetics, 38*, 121–132.

Rosenberg, D. R., & Keshavan, M. S. (1998). Toward a neurodevelopmental model of obsessive-compulsive disorder. *Biological Psychiatry, 43*, 623–640.

Rowe, D. L., Robinson, P. A., Lazzaro, I. L., Powles, R. C., Gordon, E., & Williams, L. M. (2005). Biophysical modeling of tonic cortical electrical activity in attention deficit hyperactivity disorder. *International Journal of Neuroscience, 115,* 1273–1305.

Rubia, K. (2002). The dynamic approach to neurodevelopmental psychiatric disorders: Use of fMRI combined with neuropsychology to elucidate the dynamics of psychiatric disorders, exemplified in ADHD and schizophrenia. *Behavioural Brain Research, 130,* 47–56.

Rubia, K., Overmeyer, S. O., Taylor, E., Brammer, M., Williams, S. C. R., Simmons, A., et al. (1999). Hypofrontality in attention deficit hyperactivity disorder during higher order motor control: A study with functional MRI. *American Journal of Psychiatry, 156,* 891–896.

Rubia, K., Smith, A. B., Brammer, M. J., Toone, B., & Taylor, E. (2005). Abnormal brain activation during inhibition and error detection in medication-naive adolescents with ADHD. *American Journal of Psychiatry, 162,* 1067–1075.

Rucklidge, J. J. (2006). Impact of ADHD on the neurocognitive functioning of adolescents with bipolar disorder. *Biological Psychiatry, 60,* 921–928.

Rucklidge, J. J., & Tannock, R. (2002). Neuropsychological profiles of adolescents with ADHD: Effects of reading difficulties and gender. *Journal of Child Psychology and Psychiatry, 43,* 988–1003.

Russell, V. A., Oades, R. D., Tannock, R., Killeen, P. R., Auerback, J. G., Johansen, E. B., et al. (2006). Response variability in attention-deficit/hyperactivity disorder: A neuronal and glial energetic hypothesis. *Behavioral and Brain Functions, 2:30,* 1–25.

Safren, S. A., Lanka, G. D., Otto, M. W., & Pollack, M. H. (2001). Prevalence of childhood ADHD among patients with generalized anxiety disorder and a comparison condition, social phobia. *Depression and Anxiety, 13,* 190–191.

Saggino, A., Perfetti, B., Spitoni, G., & Galati, G. (2006). Fluid intelligence and executive functions: New perspectives. In L. V. Wesley (Ed.), *Intelligence: New research* (pp. 1–22). Hauppauge, NY: Nova Science Publishers.

Sagvolden, T., Aase, H., Johansen, E. B., & Russell, V. A. (2005). A dynamic developmental theory of attention-deficit/hyperactivity disorder (ADHD) predominantly hyperactive/impulsive and combined subtypes. *Behavioral and Brain Sciences, 28,* 397–468.

Sandrini, M., Rossini, P. M., & Miniussi, C. (2008). Lateralized contribution of prefrontal cortex in controlling task-irrelevant information during verbal and spatial working memory tasks: RTMS evidence. *Neuropsychologia, 46,* 2056–2063.

Sandson, T. A., Bachna, K. J., & Morin, M. D. (2000). Right hemisphere dysfunction in ADHD: Visual hemispatial inattention and clinical subtype. *Journal of Learning Disabilities, 33,* 83–90.

Saski, J., Swicegood, P., & Carter, J. (1983). Notetaking formats for learning disabled adolescents. *Learning Disability Quarterly, 6,* 265–272.

Schafer, V., & Semrud-Clikeman, M. (2008). Neuropsychological functioning in subgroups of children with and without social perception deficits. *Journal of Attention Disorders, 12,* 177–190.

Scheres, A., Milham, M. P., Knutson, B., & Castellanos, F. X. (2007). Ventral striatal hyporesponsiveness during reward anticipation in attention-deficit/hyperactivity disorder. *Biological Psychiatry, 61,* 720–724.

Schulz, K. P., Fan, J., Tang, C. Y., Newcorn, J. H., Buchsbaum, M. S., Cheung, A. M., et al. (2004). Response inhibition in adolescents diagnosed with attention deficit hyperactivity disorder during childhood: An event-related fMRI study. *American Journal of Psychiatry, 161,* 1650–1657.

Semrud-Clikeman, M. (2005). Neuropsychological aspects for evaluating learning disabilities. *Journal of Learning Disabilities, 38,* 563–569.

Semrud-Clikeman, M., Filipek, P. A., Biederman, J., Steingard, R., et al. (1994). Attention-deficit hyperactivity disorder: Magnetic resonance imaging morphometric analysis of the corpus callosum. *Journal of the American Academy of Child & Adolescent Psychiatry, 33,* 875–881.

Semrud-Clikeman, M., Steingard, R. J., Filipek, P., Biederman, J., Bekken, K., & Renshaw, P. F. (2000). Using MRI to examine brain-behavior relationships in males with attention deficit disorder with hyperactivity. *Journal of the American Academy of Child & Adolescent Psychiatry, 39,* 477–484.

Semrud-Clikeman, M., Biederman, J., Sprich-Buckminster, S., Lehman, B. K., et al. (1992). Comorbidity between ADDH and learning disability: A review and report in a clinically referred sample. *Journal of the American Academy of Child & Adolescent Psychiatry, 31,* 439–448.

Sergeant, J. (2000). The cognitive-energetic model: An empirical approach to attention-deficit hyperactivity disorder. *Neuroscience & Biobehavioral Reviews, 24,* 7–12.

Sergeant, J. (2005). Modeling attention-deficit/hyperacticity disorder: A critical appraisal of the cognitive-energetic model. *Biological Psychiatry, 57,* 1248–1255.

Sergeant, J. A., Geurts, H., Huijbregts, S., Scheres, A., & Oosterlaan, J. (2003). The top and the bottom of ADHD: A neuropsychological perspective. *Neuroscience & Biobehavioral Reviews, 27,* 583–592.

Sergeant, J. A., Geurts, H., & Oosterlaan, J. (2002). How specific is a deficit in executive functioning for attention-deficit/hyperactivity disorder? *Behavioural Brain Research, 130,* 3–28.

Sergeant, J. A., Piek, J. P., & Oosterlaan, J. (2006). ADHD and DCD: A relationship in need of research. *Human Movement Science, 25,* 76–89.

Shallice, T. (1982): Specific impairments of planning. *Philosophical Transactions of the Royal Society of London, 298,* 199–209.

Shaywitz, S. E., & Shaywitz, B. A. (1988). Increased medication use in attention-deficit hyperactivity disorder: Regressive or appropriate? *Journal of the American Medical Association, 260,* 2270–2272.

Shear, P. K., DelBello, M. P., Lee-Rosenberg, H., & Strakowski, S. M. (2002). Parental reports of executive dysfunction in adolescents with bipolar disorder. *Child Neuropsychology, 8,* 285–295.

Siegel, L. S., & Ryan, E. B. (1989). The development of working memory in normally achieving and subtypes of learning disabled children. *Child Development, 60,* 973–980.

Silver, L. B. (1990). Attention deficit-hyperactivity disorder: Is it a learning disability or a related disorder? *Journal of Learning Disabilities, 23,* 394–397.

Simpson, M. L., Stahl, N. A., & Hayes, C. G. (1988). PORPE: A comprehensive study strategy utilizing self-assigned writing. *Journal of College Reading and Learning, 22,* 51–55.

Singer, H. S., Schuerholz, L. J., & Denckla, M. B. (1995). Learning difficulties in children with Tourette syndrome. *Journal of Child Neurology, 10*(Suppl. 1), S58–S61.

Smith, E. E., & Jonides, J. (1997). Working memory: A view from neuroimaging. *Cognitive Psychology, 33,* 5–42.

Snider, V. E., Busch, T., & Arrowood, L. (2003). Teacher knowledge of stimulant medication and ADHD. *Remedial and Special Education, 24,* 46–56.

Solanto, M. V., Abikoff, H., Sonuga-Barke, E., Schachar, R., Logan, G. D., Wigal, T., et al. (2001). The ecological validity of delay aversion and response inhibition as measures of impulsivity in AD/HD: A supplement to the NIMH multi-modal treatment study of AD/HD. *Journal of Abnormal Child Psychology, 29,* 215–228.

Solanto, M. V., Arnsten, A. T., Castellanos, F. X. (2001). *Stimulant drugs and ADHD: Basic and clinical neuroscience.* New York: Oxford University Press.

Sonuga-Barke, E. J. S. (2005). Causal models of attention-deficit/hyperactivity disorder: From common simple deficits to multiple developmental pathways. *Biological Psychiatry, 57,* 1231–1238.

Sonuga-Barke, E. J. S., Sergeant, J. A., Nigg, J., & Willcutt, E. (2008). Executive dysfunction and delay aversion in attention deficit hyperactivity disorder: Nosologic and diagnostic implications. *Child and Adolescent Psychiatric Clinics of North America, 17,* 367–384.

Souza, I., Pinheiro, M. A., Denardin, D., Mattos, P., & Rohde, L. A. (2004). Attention-deficit/hyperactivity disorder and comorbidity in Brazil: Comparisons between two referred samples. *European Child & Adolescent Psychiatry, 13,* 243–248.

Spencer, T., Biederman, J., Harding, M., O'Donnell, D., Wilens, T. Faraone, S., et al. (1998). Disentangling the overlap between Tourette's disorder and ADHD. *Journal of Child Psychology and Psychiatry, 39,* 1037–1044.

Steingard, R. J., Renshaw, P. F., Hennen, J., Lenox, M., Cintron, C. B., Young, A. D., et al. (2002). Smaller frontal lobe white matter volumes in depressed adolescents. *Biological Psychiatry, 52,* 413–417.

Stuss, D. T., & Alexander, M. P. (2000). Executive functions and the frontal lobes: A conceptual view. *Psychological Research, 63,* 289–298.

Sullivan, J. R., & Riccio, C. A. (2007). Diagnostic group differences in parent and teacher ratings on the BRIEF and Conners' scales. *Journal of Attention Disorders, 11,* 398–406.

Sundheim, S. T. P., & Voeller, K. K. S. (2004). Psychiatric implications of language disorders and learning disabilities: Risks and management. *Journal of Child Neurology, 19,* 814–826.

Suritsky, S. K., & Hughes, C. A. (1996). Notetaking strategy instruction. In D. D. Deshler, E. S. Ellis, & B. K. Lenz (Eds.), *Teaching adolescents with learning disabilities* (2nd ed., pp. 267–312). Denver, CO: Love Publishing.

Suskauer, S. J., Simmonds, D. J., Caffo, B. S., Denckla, M. B., Pekar, J. J., & Mostofsky, S. H. (2008). fMRI of intrasubject variability in ADHD: Anomalous premotor activity with prefrontal compensation. *Journal of the American Academy of Child & Adolescent Psychiatry, 47,* 1141–1150.

Swanson, J. M., Kinsbourne, M., Nigg, J., Lanphear, B., Stefanatos, G. A., Volkow, N., et al. (2007). Etiologic subtypes of attention-deficit/hyperactivity disorder: Brain imaging, molecular genetic and environmental factors and the dopamine hypothesis. *Neuropsychology Review, 17*, 39–59.

Szeszko, P. R., MacMillan, S., McMeniman, M., Chen, S., Baribault, K., Lim, K. O., et al. (2004). Brain structural abnormalities in psychotropic drug-naive pediatric patients with obsessive-compulsive disorder. *American Journal of Psychiatry, 161*, 1049–1056.

Tamm, L., Menon, V., & Reiss, A. L. (2002). Maturation of brain function associated with response inhibition. *Journal of the American Academy of Child & Adolescent Psychiatry, 41*, 1231–1238.

Tamm, L., Menon, V., Ringel, J., & Reiss, A. L. (2004). Event-related fMRI evidence of frontotemporal involvement in aberrant response inhibition and task switching in attention-deficit/hyperactivity disorder. *Journal of the American Academy of Child & Adolescent Psychiatry, 43*, 1430–1440.

Tannock, R., & Brown, T. E. (2000). Attention-deficit disorders with learning disorders in children and adolescents. In T. E. Brown (Ed.), *Attention-deficit disorders and comorbidities in children, adolescents, and adults* (pp. 231–295). Arlington, VA: American Psychiatric Publishing, Inc.

Tannock, R., & Schachar, R. (1996). Executive dysfunction as an underlying mechanism of behavior and language problems in attention deficit hyperactivity disorder. In J. H. Beitchman, N. J. Cohen, M. M. Konstantareas, & R. Tannock (Eds.), *Language, learning, and behavior disorders: Developmental, biological, and clinical perspectives* (pp. 128–155). New York: Cambridge University Press

Teeter, P. A. & Semrud-Clikeman, M. (1995). Integrating neurobiological, psychosocial, and behavioral paradigms: A transactional model for the study of ADHD. *Archives of Clinical Neuropsychology, 10*, 433–461.

Thorell, L. B. (2007). Do delay aversion and executive function deficits make distinct contributions to the functional impact of ADHD symptoms? A study of early academic skill deficits. *Journal of Child Psychology and Psychiatry, 48*, 1061–1070.

Thorell, L. B., & Wahlstedt, C. (2006). Executive functioning deficits in relation to symptoms of ADHD and/or ODD in preschool children. *Infant and Child Development, 15*, 503–518.

Tierney, R. J., & Readance, J. E. (2004). *Reading strategies and practices: A compendium.* New York, NY: Allyn & Bacon.

Towbin, K. E., & Riddle, M. A. (1993) attention deficit hyperactivity disorder. In R. Kurlan (Ed.), *Handbook of Tourette's syndrome and related tic and behavioural disorders* (pp. 89–109). New York: Marcel Dekker.

Trommer, B. L., Hoeppner, J. B., & Zecker, S. G. (1991). The go-no-go test in attention deficit disorder is sensitive to methylphenidate. *Journal of Child Neurology, Vol. 6*, S128–S131.

Tulving, E., & Markowitsch, H. J. (1997). Memory beyond the hippocampus. *Current Opinion in Neurobiology, 7*, 209–216.

Turgay, A. (2005). Treatment of comorbidity in conduct disorder with attention-deficit hyperactivity disorder (ADHD). *Essential Psychopharmacology, 6*, 277–290.

Vaidya, C. J., Austin, G., Kirkorian, G., Ridlehuber, H. W., Desmond, J. E., Glover, G. H., et al. (1998). Selective effects of methylphenidate in attention deficit hyperactivity disorder: A functional magnetic resonance study. *Proceedings of the National Academy of Sciences, 95*, 14494–14499.

Vaidya, C. J., Bunge, S. A., Dudukovic, N. M., Zalecki, C. A., Elliott, G. R., & Gabrieli, J. D. E. (2005). Altered neural substrates of cognitive control in childhood ADHD: Evidence from functional magnetic resonance imaging. *American Journal of Psychiatry, 162*, 1605–1613.

Valera, E. M., Faraone, S. V., Murray, K. E., & Seidman, L. J. (2007). Meta-analysis of structural imaging findings in attention-deficit/hyperactivity disorder. *Biological Psychiatry, 61*, 1361–1369.

Viard, A., Flament, M. F., Artiges, E., Dehaene, S., Naccache, L., Cohen, D., et al. (2005). Cognitive control in childhood-onset obsessive-compulsive disorder: A functional MRI study. *Psychological Medicine, 35*, 1007–1017.

Voeller, K. K. S. (2001). attention-deficit/hyperactivity disorder as a frontal-subcortical disorder. In D. G. Lichter, & J. L. Cummings (Eds.), *Frontal-sub-cortical circuits in psychiatric and neurological disorders* (pp. 334–371). New York: Guilford.

Waber, D., & Holmes, J. H. (1985). Assessing children's copy production of the Rey Osterrieth complex figure. *Journal of Clinical and Experimental Neuropsychology, 7*, 264–280.

Wagner, G., Sinsel, E., Sobanski, T., et al. (2006). Cortical inefficiency in patients with unipolar depression: An event-related FMRI study with the Stroop task. *Biological Psychiatry, 59*, 958–965.

Wang, J., Jiang, T., Cao, Q., & Wang, Y. (2007). Characterizing anatomic differences in boys with attention-deficit/hyperactivity disorder with the use of deformation-based morphometry. *American Journal of Neuropsychology, 28*, 543–547.

Wasserstein, J. (2005). Diagnostic issues for adolescents and adults with ADHD. *Journal of Clinical Psychology, 61*, 535–547.

Watemberg, N., Waiserberg, N., Zuk, L., & Lerman-Sagie, T. (2007). Developmental coordination disorder in children with attention-deficit-hyperactivity disorder and physical therapy intervention. *Developmental Medicine & Child Neurology, 49*, 920–925.

Wechsler, D. (1991). *Wechsler intelligence scales for children*, (4th ed.). San Antonio, TX: The Psychological Corporation.

Weiler, M. D., Holmes Bernstein, J., Bellinger, D. C., & Waber, D. P. (2000). Processing speed in children with attention deficit/hyperactivity disorder, inattentive type. *Child Neuropsychology, 6*, 218–234.

Westby, C. E., & Cutler, S. K. (1994). Language and ADHD: Understanding the bases and treatment of self-regulatory deficits. *Topics in Language Disorders, 14*, 58–76.

Whalen, C. K., & Henker, B. (1998). attention-deficit/hyperactivity disorders. In T. H. Ollendick, & M. Hersen (Eds.), *Handbook of child psychopathology* (3rd ed., pp. 181–211). New York: Plenum Press.

Willcutt, E. G., Doyle, A. E., Nigg, J. T., Faraone, S. V., & Pennington, B. F. (2005). Validity of the executive function theory of attention-deficit/hyperactivity disorder: A meta-analytic review. *Biological Psychiatry, 57*, 1336–1346.

Williams, D., Stott, C. M., Goodyer, I. M., & Sahakian, B. J. (2000). Specific language impairment with or without hyperactivity: Neuropsychological evidence for frontostriatal dysfunction. *Developmental Medicine & Child Neurology, 42*, 368–375.

Willis, W. G., & Weiler, M. D. (2005). Neural substrates of childhood attention-deficit/hyperactivity disorder: Electroencephalographic and magnetic resonance imaging evidence. *Developmental Neuropsychology, 27*, 135–182.

Wolosin, S. M., Richardson, M. E., Hennessey, J. G., Denckla, M. B., & Mostofsky, S. H. (2007). Abnormal cerebral cortex structure in children with ADHD. *Human Brain Mapping, 30*, 175–184.

Wolraich, M. L., Lambert, E. W., & Bickman, L. (2004). Assessing the impact of parent and teacher agreement on diagnosing attention-deficit hyperactivity disorder. *Journal of Developmental & Behavioral Pediatrics, 25*, 41–47.

Woolley, J., Heyman, I., Brammer, M., Frampton, I., McGuire, P. K., & Rubia, K. (2008). Brain activation in pediatric obsessive-compulsive disorder during tasks of inhibitory control. *British Journal of Psychiatry, 192*, 25–31.

Wozniak, J. (2005). Recognizing and managing bipolar disorder in children. *Journal of Clinical Psychiatry, 66*(Suppl. 1), 18–23.

Wozniak, J., Spencer, T., Biederman, J., Kwon, A., Monuteaux, M., Rettew, J., et al. (2004). The clinical characteristics of unipolar vs. bipolar major depression in ADHD youth. *Journal of Affective Disorders, 82*(Suppl. 1), S59–S69.

Yochman, A., Parush, S., & Ornoy, A. (2004). Responses of preschool children with and without ADHD to sensory events in daily life. *American Journal of Occupational Therapy, 58*, 294–302.

Yucel, M., Harrison, B. J., Wood, S. J., Fornito, A., Wellard, R. M., Pujol, J., et al. (2007). Functional and biochemical alterations in the medial frontal cortex in obsessive-compulsive disorder. *Archives of General Psychiatry, 64*, 946–955.

Zanini, S. (2008). Generalised script sequencing deficits following frontal lobe lesions. *Cortex, 44*, 140–149.

Zimmerman, B. J., & Schunk, D. H. (2001). *Self-regulated learning and academic achievement*. New York, NY: Lawrence Erlbaum.

CHAPTER 12

Assessing and Intervening with Children with Autism Spectrum Disorders

MARY JOANN LANG

UTISM IS A complex neurodevelopmental disorder that can be challenging to diagnose and manage due to wide variation in expression. The National Institute of Neurological Disorders and Strokes estimates 6 out of 1,000 (approximately 1 in 150) children born today will have autism, and males are four times more likely to have autism than females (National Institute of Neurological Disorders and Stroke/ [NINDS]/NIH, 2008). Autism Spectrum Disorders (ASD) must be considered a major public health problem due to early onset, life-long persistence, and high levels of associated impairment as documented by Simonoff et al. (2008).

It is important to emphasize that autism is a spectrum disorder. Individual differences in presentation occur, making each case unique. Although we can observe strong and consistent commonalities among children with autism (especially in social deficits), no single behavior is diagnostic or always present. Furthermore, the absence of any of the ASD behaviors would not automatically exclude an individual from a diagnosis of ASD. Differences are seen among individuals in the severity of symptoms, the age of onset, and the expression of specific features. Since features can change considerably over time, ASD definitely affects children's overall potential development and ability to be successful in the academic setting. Due to the nature and complexity of this disorder, it is critical to follow best practices based on documented research when planning for the developmental and educational needs of a child with ASD.

This chapter is organized to assist the reader in understanding the nature and extent of the expression of ASD and its core deficits. In addition, comorbid psychological disorders and neurocognitive challenges will be explored. Interventions and recommendations will be presented to assist in formulating individual therapeutic plans.

CORE DEFICITS IN AUTISM

Autism is defined in the *Diagnostic and Statistical Manual of Mental Disorders* (American Psychiatric Association [APA], 2000) as a spectrum disorder that includes three core deficits: (1) social interaction, (2) language and communication, and (3) restricted interests and repetitive behaviors. Manifestations of the disorder vary greatly, depending on each individual's age and developmental level. The main core deficits appear consistently in some form in all children with the diagnosis. These core deficits dramatically impact the child's academic performance and activities of daily living.

1. **Social interactions** challenge individuals with autism, and these difficulties can be expressed throughout a lifetime. Children with autism experience difficulty initiating and sustaining social exchanges and relationships. They tend to avoid situations where they might be expected to engage in shared activities with others. Limited ability to include the perspective of others is commonly seen in individuals with autism. Nonverbal messages often are misunderstood and can lead to failure to develop social relationships appropriate to the child's level of development.

2. **Communication** (verbal or nonverbal) presents great challenges for these children. Symptoms can include delay in language development and failure to develop expressive language. If a child with autism is unable to use expressive language, there may be a limited ability to initiate and sustain a conversation with others. At times, spoken language in children with autism can be echolalic, and these children can exhibit pronoun reversal. Individuals with autism often have difficulties with syntax and oral expression (Williams, Goldstein, & Minshew, 2006.

3. **Restricted and stereotypic patterns of behavior** in daily living may also characterize children with this disorder. Typical behaviors include fascination with a particular object, motor mannerisms, or ongoing preoccupation with parts of objects or toys. Sometimes a child's body movement may include unusual hand movements, such as finger flicking, or can involve the entire body, as seen in rocking. Abnormal postures may be present and can include toe walking or a general lack of coordination associated with motor activities (APA, 2000, p. 75).

SCREENING FOR AUTISM SPECTRUM DISORDERS

The Pervasive Development Disorders (PDD) include: Autistic Disorder, Asperger's Disorder, and Pervasive Developmental Disorder—Not Otherwise Specified (PDD-NOS), according to *DSM-IV-TR* (APA, 2004, p. 75). AD is characterized by difficulties in the areas of communication, lack of reciprocal social interaction, and restricted/repetitive behaviors and interests, with onset often occurring before age 3. Children and adults with Asperger's Disorder do not usually have cognitive delays and do not typically appear to have significant delay in acquisition of language. Their communication problems are less severe than those seen in children who are more severely impacted with the spectrum disorder. These children will display frustration when trying to communicate. In addition, they have tendencies to exhibit restrictions and repetitions of a single topic. PDD-NOS children can exhibit similar symptoms, but do not meet the full diagnostic criteria for AD. School psychologists perform assessments to evaluate children with respect to these disorders, and best practice procedures include use of standardized tests.

Tools have been developed to determine diagnoses, the severity of symptoms, and to help identify appropriate interventions. The following has been identified as best practice in the diagnosis of ASD based on the *DSM IV-TR* (APA, 2000).

The *Autism Diagnostic Observation Schedule* (ADOS) (Lord, Rutter, DiLavore, & Risi, 1989) is a semi-structured assessment of communication, social interaction, and play, or the imaginative use of materials for individuals suspected of having autism or other pervasive developmental disorders (PDD). The ADOS consists of four modules, each of which is appropriate for children and adults of differing developmental and language levels. The ADOS is an appropriate standardized diagnostic observation tool (California Department of Developmental Services, 2002; National Research Council, 2001) for evaluating social interactions, communication, and repetitive behaviors.

In a study by Akshoomoff, Corsello, & Schmidt (2006), ASD diagnostic practices among school psychologists and clinical psychologists were examined, with attention given to those who used the ADOS. Findings showed that school psychologists often relied on home observations and reports from the child's teacher for diagnosis, rather than the ADOS. Among those who used the ADOS, perceived strengths include the ability to capture ASD-specific behaviors. The cost of the kit and the time to administer the test were seen as drawbacks. The ADOS accounted for the developmental age of the child and allowed for direct observation of behavior, which many considered to provide great advantages.

The *Autism Diagnostic Interview—Revised* (ADI-R) (Le Couteur, Lord, & Rutter, 2003) is a standardized, semi-structured clinical interview format for caregivers of children and adults suspected to have ASD. The interview includes 93 items and focuses on behavior in three areas: (1) quality of social interaction; (2) sharing, offering, and seeking comfort; and (3) social smiling and responding to other children. Aside from providing an assessment, this structured interview incorporates features relevant for planning therapy. The interview takes about two hours to administer and can be used with children as young as 2 years of age. The interviewer is required to have extensive training to develop competence.

Other practical evaluation tools are supported by research and experience, including those presented in Table 12.1.

These tools help to clarify the diagnosis of autism but may not be sufficient for planning educational goals and treatment planning. The following sections will further identify aspects of the individual profile, leading to construction and implementation of appropriate educational planning.

COMORBIDITY AND ASSOCIATED DISORDERS

For the purpose of this chapter, comorbidity is defined as the coexistence of two or more forms of psychopathology in one individual (Matson & Nebel-Schwalm, 2007). Discussion regarding comorbidity in ASD has only sporadically appeared in previous literature. Currently, more attention is being given to issues of comorbidity. Obtaining a comprehensive profile of a child's condition is critical to formulating effective interventions and treatments. The clinician should first identify the primary disorder and then consider comorbid possibilities. Identifying the "primary" disorders is important for several reasons: The clinician can then determine the degree to which daily living is disrupted, assess the availability of resources dictated by the primary diagnosis, and determine the total impact of the treatment planning by considering the features of ASD and comorbid disorders together. The nature and severity of the combined effects can be significant.

Psychiatric disorders are common in individuals with autism, and these may provide targets for intervention and should be routinely evaluated in the clinical assessment. This section will focus primarily on the most common comorbid psychological conditions associated with autism.

In a study that focused on ASD prevalence, comorbidity, and associated factors, Simonoff et al. (2008) recognized that little is known about the associated psychiatric disorders that contribute to impairment in ASD. They found in their clinical ASD sample, that 70 percent of children with ASD exhibited at least one comorbid disorder, and 41 percent displayed two or more. The most common coexisting psychological disorders were social

Table 12.1
Common Additional Assessment Instruments Used in the Diagnosis of ASD

Name of Instrument	Age	Time Required	Overview
Autism Behavior Checklist (ABC: Krug, Arick, & Almond, 1980)	Children as young as 3 years	30–40 Minutes	Fifty-seven questions divided into sections, relating body and object use, language, social interaction and self-help. Completed by parent or teacher.
Autism Diagnostic Interview – Revised (ADI-R: Le Couteur, Lord, & Rutter, 2003)	Children and adults with a mental age above 2.0 years	$1\frac{1}{2}$ to $2\frac{1}{2}$ hours	Ninety-three interview items that evaluate three functional domains: language/ communication; reciprocal social interactions; and restricted, repetitive and stereotyped behaviors and interests.
Autism Diagnostic Observation Schedule (ADOS: Lord et al., 1989)	Toddlers to adults	30–45 minutes	A semistructured assessment of communication, social interaction, and play or imaginative use of materials for individuals suspected of having autism or other pervasive developmental disorders (PDD).
Checklist for Autism in Toddlers (CHAT: Baren-Cohen 1992)	Toddlers	5–10 Minutes	Nine yes/no questions answered by the parent. Topics include social play, interest in other children, pretend play, and developmental progress of the child.
Childhood Autism Rating Scale (CARS: Schopler, Reichler, & Rochen Renner, 1988)	Children as young as 2 years	20–30 minutes	The most widely used standardized instrument specifically geared to the assessment of children suspected to have ASD. Fifteen items are included to address relationships, imitation, body use, anxiety, verbal communication, and nonverbal communication. Completed by a clinician.
Gilliam Autism Rating Scale – Second Edition (GARS-II: Gilliam, 1995)	3–22 years	5–10 minutes	Assists teachers, parents, and clinicians in identifying and diagnosing. It also helps estimate the severity of the child's disorder.
Parent Interview for Autism (PIA: Stone & Hogan, 1993)	Preschool and younger	30–45 minutes	Respondent based interview. Parents report occurrence of specific behaviors.

(*continued*)

Table 12.1

Continued

Name of Instrument	Age	Time Required	Overview
Pre-Linguistic Autism Diagnostic Observation Schedule (PL-ADOS: Dilavore, Lord, & Rutter, 1995)	Children under age 6, who are not using phrase speech	30 minutes	This is a version of ADOS, modified to use with young children, and inclusive of semi-structured assessment of play, interaction and social communication.
Social Communication Questionnaire (SCQ: Rutter, Bailey, & Lord, 2003)	4 years and over—with a mental age of 2 years or over	10 minutes	Forty questions for parental responses. Total score can be interpreted with respect to various cutoff points.
Social Responsiveness Scale (SRS: Constantino & Gruber, 2005)	4–18 years	20 minutes	Standardized rating scale for parents and/or teachers responding to questions regarding social deficits and treatment scale scores for five areas of socialization.

anxiety disorder, ADHD, oppositional defiant disorder, and mental retardation. The list of other psychological conditions that can be comorbid with ASD is quite extensive. The discussion is limited here to those conditions most often comorbid with ASD.

Mental Retardation

Associated mental retardation is a common concern for families and professionals who care for children with autism. However, challenges are presented in obtaining accurate data because of the nature of the autism (for example, limited language ability) and the compounding variable of language in published standardized tests (Dawson, Soulieres, Gernsbacher, & Mottron, 2007). If a child with autism has a comorbid condition of mental retardation, the range of involvement can be mild to profound. However, in the recent literature, facts concerning the nature and extent of mental retardation as a comorbid condition with autism are inconsistent. For example, Edelson (2006) questioned the fundamental assumptions that most children with autism are mentally retarded. Dawson, Mottron, and Gernsbacher (2008) indicated that a fraction of children with autism who met the criteria for mental retardation varied from 25 to 70 percent. This poses a challenge for families and the professionals who provide educational care and psychological support.

ATTENTION-DEFICIT HYPERACTIVITY DISORDER (ADHD)

Although researchers have recently reported high levels of comorbidity, the DSM IV-TR (APA, 2004) prohibits the co-diagnosis of ADHD and ASD. However, co-occurrence of clinically significant ADHD and autistic symptoms are common, and several studies support this finding (Mulligan et al., 2008; Reierson & Todd, 2008; Ronald, Simonoff, Kuntsi, Asherson, & Plomin, 2008). Reierson and Todd concluded that: "Studies indicate that co-occurrence of clinically significant ADHD and autistic symptoms is common, and that some genes may influence both disorders" (p. 657). The Mulligan et al. and Ronald et al. findings indicated evidence for overlapping genetic influences of autism and ADHD in a twins sample. The results indicate that common genetic influences operate in both of these conditions.

MOOD DISORDERS

Mood Disorders are defined in the DSM IV-TR as "disorders that have a disturbance in mood as the predominant feature" (APA, 2004, p. 345), and these disorders are subdivided into:

- Depressive Disorders
- Bipolar Disorders
- Additional Specific Phobias

Generalized Anxiety Disorders frequently coexist with Mood Disorders or with other anxiety disorders, including Panic Disorder, Social Phobia, and Specific Phobias, or they can appear with substance abuse. Phobias, depression, and other childhood disorders have been described for almost thirty years, and research has consistently demonstrated comorbidity with ASD. Several investigators have studied comorbidity of ASD with mood disorders and anxieties, and their results are consistent:

- Matson, González, Terlonge, Thorson, and Laud (2007) suggested that comorbid features of ASD and Mood Disorders do exist. These authors suggested that depression frequently coexists with autism, and several researchers have supported their findings.
- For example, Ghaziuddin, Ghaziuddin, and Greden (2002) published numerous articles on depression and comorbidity with ASD. They found that depression was probably the most frequent form of psychopathology in ASD.
- Gold (1993) also stressed that the co-occurrence of depression and ASD is critical in planning treatment. Gold presented the following rationale:

1. Depression can negatively impact the long-term outcome of personal and academic success.
2. Depression may put a child or adolescent with ASD at risk to be a danger to him- or herself, others, and property.
3. And finally, the coexistence of depression in autism can cause an increase in behavioral difficulties, such as withdrawal, aggression, and noncompliance, which can limit access to education as well as interactions with family, community, and society.

- Children with autism can develop depression and anxiety comorbid with ASD. Major depression and bipolar disorder are often debilitating, and Matson and Nebel-Schwalm (2007) stressed that identifying comorbid depression in ASD is important. Depression can negatively affect the outcome of any interventions for autism, and in turn, these problems can impact the family, resulting in increased stress and conflict.
- Brereton, Tonge, and Einfeld (2006) found that depressive symptoms increased with age, and the identification and management of these symptoms can improve the ability to target interventions for treatment of ASD.
- Matson and Love (1990) conducted the first research study on phobias in children with ASD and matched controls. The results of the study indicated that children with autism were fearful of such things as dark places, large crowds, closets, and going to bed in the dark. Evans, Canavera, Klinepeter, Taga, and Maccubbin (2005) replicated and extended Matson and Love's study, with similar findings.
- Obsessive/Compulsive Disorder (OCD), anxiety, and phobias were studied by Ivarsson and Melin (2008) in children and adolescents with autism. They indicated that autistic traits are prevalent in OCD patients and seem to be intricately associated with the comorbidities, as well as with OCD itself. Behaviors related to OCD are characterized by anxiety.
- According to Matson et al. (2007) a child or individual with OCD demonstrates repetitive behaviors with the purpose of decreasing anxiety. Symptoms of ASD could also be described in this manner, which suggest that the two conditions may be intricately related.

Although researchers may agree that mood disorders are comorbid with ASD, there may be some differences relating to commonly occurring situations. Munesue et al. (2008) concluded that the major comorbid mood disorder in patients with high-functioning ASD is bipolar disorder, not major depressive disorder. The investigators suggested that genetic predispositions may exist that put ASD children at risk for bipolar disorder.

In summary, school neuropsychologists need to be aware of the possible existence of comorbid conditions in children with ASD. This leads to a better understanding of the individual and to more effective interventions.

NEUROPSYCHOLOGICAL APPROACH: BRAIN/BEHAVIOR FUNCTIONING IN AUTISM

In the past twenty years, we have seen growing interest in the neurocognitive domains that go beyond the ASD three core deficits mentioned in the DSM-IV-TR (APA, 2004). In 1997 Minshew, Goldstein and Siegel discussed the neuropsychological functions in autism. They looked beyond the basic signs and symptoms of autism to the relationship of autism as an information processing disorder. This research—and similar studies—help us to understand the global effects of ASD on academic functioning as well as in activities of daily living.

Studies show that beyond the core deficits, motor praxis, lack of motor planning and imitation appear to be major components of autism (Dawson & Watling, 2000). Recently, various researchers and experts have developed a growing appreciation for the involvement of other areas of cognitive and neurological function among persons with ASD. Models of autism have been expanded to consider broader cognitive neurologic and brain involvement in ASD. These hypotheses evolved when a neuropsychological test battery was administered by Williams, Goldstein and Minshew (2006) to 33 individuals diagnosed with autism (IQ > 80) and 33 matched controls. The neuropsychological profile of the individuals with autism was defined by impairments in motor skills, complex memory, complex language, and reasoning domains and by intact or superior performance in the attention, simple memory, simple language, and visual-spatial domains. This neuropsychological profile is consistent with a complex information-processing deficit.

A model proposed by Minshew and Williams stated: "Autism is a selective impairment in the neural processing of complex information across domains and sensory modalities, with intact or enhanced simple abilities in the same domains as impairments. In this model complexity is a proxy for the level of demand placed on the brain's processing capacity by tasks or situations" (2007, p. 280).

The school neuropsychologist must look at symptoms in connection with the overall functional capacity of the child, and then he or she must break down these behaviors to neurocognitive issues that affect behavior. A school neuropsychological model (see Miller, 2007, 2009) focuses on assessments of brain/behavior relationships, which allow us to understand the child's needs and abilities. The foundation upon which all other neurocognitive abilities comprises sensory-motor functioning and attentional processing. The school neuropsychologist can use Miller's school neuropsychology model in order to understand brain/behavior relationships and the information processing concepts reported by Minshew and Williams (2007) in order to conceptualize the neurocognitive and emotional functioning of children.

It's also important to remember that a child who demonstrates adequate language skills (expressive/receptive), or who appears "within normal limits" in many categories, can still be on the autism spectrum. The cognitive profile of a child must consider social-emotional, cultural, environmental, and situational components. In a study of students with autism, developmental improvements were observed as children progress to adolescence, but "speed of processing and response preparation or executive control of behavior is abnormal in autism. . . . Results from the study show that while brain processes such as myelination may be sufficiently intact to support basic information processing, they may be impaired in heteromodal cortex including prefrontal regions that support executive function" (Luna, Doll, Hegedus, Minshew, & Sweeney, 2007, p. 479).

ASSESSMENT OF NEUROCOGNITION

In addition to considering parent and teacher observations, formalized assessment processes help clinicians make an accurate and thorough diagnosis of autism. Professional judgment needs to be considered, and the major diagnostic tools at this time are the *Autism Diagnostic Observation Schedule* (ADOS: Lord et al., 1989) and the *Autism Diagnostic Interview—Revised* (ADI-R: Le Couteur et al., 2003). However, these measures do not sufficiently explore neurocognitive functioning to lead to specific recommendations.

It is critical to remember that children impacted by autism can have average or high IQs but remain moderately to severely impacted by the disorder. A flexible approach is essential to provide a comprehensive understanding of the child's neurocognitive abilities. The assessment should be based on the referral concerns and observational data, as well as quantitative and qualitative information. The analysis and interpretation of the data for children with autism and related disabilities include aspects such as asking the child how he or she approaches the task, using a vector analysis to confirm hypotheses, and appreciating multiple causes of behavior.

A wide variety of assessment instruments is available to clinicians, and these tools can provide an accurate perception of a child's condition. Selection of test materials must be evaluated in respect to each child's needs, and school psychologists can choose assessment tools with a specific purpose in mind. Students may be best served by taking a variety of tests or by taking targeted components of instruments, which can provide the clinician with information necessary to form conclusions. Selected tests or batteries of tests should be administered to answer specific referral questions and to confirm or rule out suspicions of the clinician. Table 12.2 provides an overview of commonly used diagnostic instruments.

Table 12.2
Educational and Treatment Planning Tools

Name of Instrument	Age	Time Required	Overview
Assessment of Basic Language and Learning Skills (Revised) (ABLLS-R: Parrington, 2006).	3–9 years	Up to 14 hours	Covers twenty-five areas assessing current skills. Requires direct behavior observations and provides option to include caretaker interview.
Autism Screening Instrument for Educational Planning: Third Edition (ASIEP-3: Krug, Arick, & Almond, 2008).	2 years to 13.11 years	One and a half to two hours	Designed to identify functional needs and classroom behaviors. Scores for five subtests.
Psychoeducational Profile (Third Edition) (PEP-3: Schopler, Lansing, & Reichler, 2005).	6 months to 7 years	45 minutes to an hour and a half	Ten subtests of performance and a caregiver report are rated on quantified pass/emerge/fail basis. Areas include Motor and Maladaptive Behaviors with ten subtest scores.
PDD Behavior Inventory (PDDBI: Cohen & Sudhalter, 2005).	1.6 years to 12.5 years	20–30 minutes	Rating scales are completed by parents and teachers, regarding two broad categories: Approach/Withdrawal Problems, and Receptive/Expressive Social Communication.
Process Assessment of the Learner II (PAL-II: Berninger & Abbott, 2007).	Elementary school students of any age	Varies by child	Research-Based Reading and Writing Lessons, which is a more general education tool that can be especially valuable when working with children with autism. PAL-II was developed to assess reading and writing disabilities, and to offer intervention and treatment strategies.

In selecting any instrument, it is important to identify the neurocognitive demands and consequently understand what the assessment measure or subtest actually measures. Miller (2007) recommended that school neuropsychologists ask: What are the primary abilities, secondary abilities, unique abilities, and error variances of the task? Once deficits are identified, tools can be used to address specific needs.

In Table 12.3, the neurocognitive functions, behaviors, and symptoms in ASD and relevant interventions are presented. Interventions are presented with regard to environmental and instructional, as well as bypass strategies.

Table 12.3

Intervention Strategies for ASD Children Based on Neurocognitive Deficit Areas

Function/Description	Examples	Intervention Strategies
Sensory Processing: Ability to perceive and respond to information that is seen, heard, smelled, tasted, and felt.	• Bothered by loud noises or bright light. • Fussy about clothing and how it feels. • Constant movement. • Avoids grooming. • Picky about foods. • Distracted by any noise or movements.	• Minimize distractions. • Keep structure in daily activities. • Encourage physical activities. • Explore resources including Occupational Therapy, Physical Therapy and Speech Therapy. • Use sensory integration techniques. • Apply deep pressure for a calming effect. • Create a routine to help the child adjust to the stimulation that occurs throughout the day. • Break up long periods of sitting with structured activity.
Gross Motor Control: Ability to coordinate use of the large muscles.	• Tight muscles. • Unsteady movements. • Toe walking. • Walks with feet wide apart. • Appears clumsy. • Avoids sports and playground activities. • Jerky movements.	• Encourage physical activity. • Teacher or Aid joins in games and sports. • Involve Occupational Therapy (OT) and/or Physical Therapy (PT) in educational plan. • Involve child in physical activities, such as pushing a wheelbarrow or a piece of furniture, to help at home or school.
Fine Motor Control: Ability to control small muscles, such as those of the hand.	• Awkward pencil grip. • Difficulty using utensils, such as forks, spoons, etc.	• Occupational Therapy involvement is very helpful in developing muscles and skills. • Practice managing tools. • Encourage coloring, painting and writing—even in short sessions. • Make sure the work area is physically supportive (desk or table is correct height, chair fits).

		• Steady paper with a clipboard, or tape paper to the table. • Use wide-spaced paper or colored line paper for assignments. • Allow for accommodations in some work.
Attentional Processes: Ability to sustain focus for learning or for completing a task.	• Easily distracted. • Fails to complete assignments. • Talks excessively. • Moves around in seat. • Loses possessions, assignments, etc. • Interrupts conversations.	• Seat the child near the teacher or speaker. • Eliminate distractions as much as possible. • Make sure that the assignment meets the child's ability level. • Keep lessons short enough to sustain attention. • Develop visual aids. • Include response requirements. • Provide breaks as needed. • Divide material into manageable segments.
Visual Perception: Ability to interpret information from visible light reaching the eyes.	• Difficulty learning new words. • Fails to recognize written words and numbers. • Misses operation signs in math (e.g., +/–). • Inaccurate copying of written work. • Struggles to interpret graph, charts, etc. • Transposes numbers and letters. • Poor handwriting, even with great effort. • Difficulty with space and time. • Poor spelling. • Fails to recognize faces.	• Seat the student in prime position at the front of the room. • Provide copies of handouts, visual aids, etc. • Assign a "copy buddy" to take class notes and reproduce them. • Discuss theories in math to help understand process and create strong interest in numbers. • Provide large-typed materials, texts, and tests when possible. • Keep sessions short, and provide breaks. • Give extra time to complete assignments. • Teach concept and words by explaining and repeating. • Review spelling using multi-sensory tools. • Take pictures of key people, and discuss who they are on a daily or regular basis.
Perceptual Organization: Ability to perceive visual components as organized	• Puzzles. • Reading a map. • Difficulty aligning columns of numbers.	• Employ bypass strategies where appropriate. • Use one-on-one instruction to clarify details. *(continued)*

293

Table 12.3
Continued

Function/Description	Examples	Intervention Strategies
patterns or wholes, instead of many different parts.	• Difficulty understanding size and location relationships. • Struggles with sequential ordering.	• Work at rate that allows student to grasp information. • Point and review relationships. • Ask probing questions to see if student understands concepts before moving to next concept. • Practice arranging items in sequences, and discuss why they are arranged in a particular order.
Visual Scanning and Tracking: Ability to coordinate eye movement to identify salient details rapidly and accurately.	• Difficulty with reading, writing, performing paper and pencil tasks. • Difficulty telling time.	• Use assisted technologies, such as computers and adding machines • Demonstrate telling time and allow the child to move the arms on the clock. • Underline key words and phrases. • Develop outlining techniques. • Allow sufficient time for student to be successful. • Divide tasks into small blocks of information. • Have accessible notebook within reach at all times. • Use highlighters to underline, circle comments in margins to point out key information.
Oral Expression: Ability to use words and sentences to communicate.	• Frequently misunderstood. • Poor grammar and usage skills. • Difficulty relaying information. • Speaks slowly. • Unclear or slurred speech.	• Review common word meanings. • Provide practice using phrases. • Explain sentence structure and parts of speech. • Reinforce key information with repetition. • Provide time extensions for assignments. • Adjust teaching style to allow for reinforcements. • Integrate sentence formation practice into all subject lessons.

Receptive Language: Ability to understand words and sentences.

- Reading comprehension problems.
- Trouble understanding homework assignments.
- Fails to follow conversations.
- Doesn't "get" jokes.

- Speak to the child in specific and clear language.
- Talk about daily events.
- Provide books on tape.
- Give extra time for verbal responses in conversations.
- Check the child's attention before you begin to speak.
- Eliminate distractions.
- Ask the child to identify the most important point in discussions.

Nonverbal Communication: Ability to acquire and absorb social and academic information that is not expressed in language.

- Lacks meaningful friendships.
- Struggles with charts, maps, and graphs.
- Poor problem-solving skills.
- Lacks a sense of humor.
- Poor reading comprehension.
- Doesn't see the "big picture."

- Help your student understand how activities in his or her life relate to a bigger picture.
- Role-play situations using expressions and body language to convey messages.
- Discuss daily life situations that can be confusing.
- Pre-teach difficult concepts that may appear in science or social studies.
- Involve student in structured and supervised activities with peers.

Learning: Ability to acquire knowledge.

- Slow to learn new skills.
- Requires several repetitions to master a thought or act.
- Is literal, or concrete in thinking.
- Receives facts, but can't apply them.
- Fails to identify the "main idea."

- Provide a variety of strategies for learning.
- Explain details and relationships—don't assume that information is obvious.
- Keep the environment relaxed and pressure-free.
- Determine the best time of day for a specific student to work on challenging tasks.
- Provide one-on-one assistance, and discuss how relationships occur in all situations.

Memory: Ability to store and retrieve information.

- Can't remember facts or details.
- Fails to remember recent events.
- Forgets names or details about a person.

- Repeat important information.
- Explain information and relate to key messages.
- Use multisensory teaching strategies.

(continued)

Table 12.3
Continued

Function/Description	Examples	Intervention Strategies
	• Forgets important events. • Gets lost in an assignment.	• Make lists, charts and other aids to support memory. • Break down information into small parts.
Executive Functions: Ability to plan and organize behavior toward a goal.	• Disorganized. • Has trouble beginning an activity. • Messy desk, backpack, and room. • Becomes upset with changes. • Fails to complete tasks.	• Provide structure and priorities for daily activities. • Make student responsible for personal items (at a level that is appropriate for the individual). • Provide organizational tools. • Assist/support as needed. • Set up folders, calendars, etc. • Review assignments, calendars and personal goals regularly.
Emotional/Self-Regulation: Ability to think and act appropriately—even when emotionally upset and the ability to manage emotions and to control behaviors.	• Gets upset by little things. • Runs out of classroom. • Temper tantrums. • Throws objects. • Kicks/hits. • Can't tolerate changes. • Often angry with siblings. • Impulsive. • Mood changes. • Plays too rough. • Can't calm oneself.	• Discuss/explain situations that trigger outbursts. • Role-play situations that involve interactions. • Reduce stress by letting the child know that it's OK to make mistakes. • Teach the child how to respond to various situations; include phrases and language used in these situations. • Describe model behaviors to the child. • Reward good behaviors and not tantrums. • Develop a list of things the child can do to calm himself. • Provide assistants for controlling behaviors, such as toys to occupy thoughts through rough periods.
Speed and Efficiency of Cognitive Processing:	• Needs repetition of directions. • Becomes tired easily.	• Reduce distractions as much as possible. • Wait for the student to "digest" information before moving on.

Ability to receive, efficiently process and respond to information.

- Acts like he doesn't understand.
- Difficulty multitasking (listening to teacher and taking notes at the same time).
- Becomes easily frustrated.
- Has blank look.
- Fails to complete work.

- Repeat information, and remain patient.
- Allow extended time for completing assignments.
- Reduce the number of assignments.
- Provide positive feedback when success are seen—even small successes!

Social Functioning:
Ability to promote successful interaction with people and in groups of people.

- Acts younger than age.
- Can't keep friends.
- Is a "follower."
- Prefers younger children for friends.
- Doesn't participate in conversations.
- Says inappropriate things.

- Discuss how other people may feel in specific situations.
- Practice and expect manners.
- Reward good behaviors.
- Model appropriate language and action.
- Use recreational activities to facilitate communication.
- Use non-threatening environments to boost communication skills.
- Teach skills—such as reading expressions—that would typically seem natural.

EFFECTIVE INTERVENTION RECOMMENDATIONS

Once deficits are revealed, plans can be written to address each need. Early intervention is the key to maximizing success. Other characteristics of effective intervention include:

- Active engagement in intensive instruction.
- Organized and structured classroom presentations.
- A minimum of five days/week with full year intervention.
- Brief sessions to avoid overload.
- Repetition and opportunities for overlearning of basic concepts.
- One-to-one teacher/student ratio or small group sessions.
- Integrative education and encouragement of community-based instruction.
- Home/school consistency, such as regular communication with parents/guardians.

Goals begin with a general compliance behavior—sit at your desk, look at the teacher, and respond to simple directions such as "point to your head." Later, goals can include more advanced skills such as language or academic material. Growth is demonstrated in the length of attention paid to a topic, vocabulary development, the complexity of sentences, and abstract thinking. Similar progress can be seen in interpretation of written language, math skill usage, and community-based activities. Intervention approaches include a menu of evidence-based strategies, including the following:

- Applied Behavioral Analysis (ABA) is an intensive system of reward-based training that focuses on teaching specific skills. (This is the most fully researched treatment specifically developed for autism.)
- *Speech Therapy.* Speech and language problems are extremely common among individuals with autism, although these issues vary from person to person. Including a speech and language therapist in the educational planning team and scheduling regular sessions for speech therapy should be recommended for every child with ASD.
- *Occupational Therapy and Physical Therapy.* Delays in motor skills (gross or fine) can be addressed by an occupational therapist (OT) and/or a physical therapist (PT). An OT can work on general living skills, or he or she can address specific needs such as sensory integration therapy to overcome hypersensitivities. For children with gross motor delays, and/or low muscle tone, PT will address muscle tone, coordination, and even basic sport skills such as swimming, kickball, or dance.

- *Social Skills Therapy*. Every child with ASD needs help learning how to connect with others, how to interpret words and nonverbal expressions, and how to participate in a conversation. Building these skills is especially challenging for children with autism, and remedies to this "core deficit" are needed for the child to function in everyday settings. Strategies can include play therapy, including activities that are pleasurable to the individual.
- *Educational Strategies*. The best-case learning conditions that apply to all children are especially helpful to children with autism. Structure is the key to success, and it applies to environment, activities, and schedules. Be as *consistent* as possible with routines, with word choices, and with rewards and adverse stimuli. Providing a *predictable environment* and *daily routine helps children relax and focus. In situations that require changes, be sure to prepare the child in advance and allow for questions*. Curriculum-based strategies offer a wide variety of options for presenting materials; therefore the teacher and the psychologist must look for ways to reach each individual. When one intervention strategy is not working, change to another.

Keep distractions to a minimum, especially when communicating. Be aware of background noise, eliminating sounds and motions that can become distractions to the child. Keep communication (especially instructions) simple and direct. Allow ample time for each child to process information, and this may differ for each child. Reinforce messages with repetition and a variety of cues, such as pictures or other visual aids that are of great help in encoding messages and in supporting memory functions.

The National Academy of Sciences Committee on Educational Interventions for Children with Autism stresses the role of families as key to successful education strategies, stating that "Families should be involved in the education of young children with ASD as both advocates and participating partners in . . . their child's education. Educators should implement a family oriented orientation that considers the needs and strengths of the family as a unit." (National Research Council, 2001, p. 215).

SUMMARY

Autism, a prevalent disorder, affects individuals, families, communities, and society. Core deficits in three areas characterize autism: language and communication, social interaction, and restricted and stereotypic patterns of behavior (APA, 2004). These behaviors can range in impact from mild to severe and drastically affect an individual's ability to function. In order to provide appropriate care for children with autism, we must understand the condition as it appears in the individual child. In this spectrum disorder, characteristics of autism present differently among those affected; therefore, careful assessment of each child is needed to identify strengths and weaknesses.

Several conditions can be comorbid to autism, including mental retardation, Attention-Deficit Disorder, and Mood Disorders. Interventions and therapies should address ASD and any other existing mental or physical conditions. Once we have a clear picture of the child's condition, we can formulate plans for providing effective interventions and therapies, which can include Applied Behavioral Analysis, speech therapy, occupational therapy, physical therapy, and social skills training. A combination of evidence-based therapies may be appropriate for an individual child. Additionally, appropriate educational strategies and parental support greatly enhance the chances for success for children with autism. A diagnosis of autism is the first step to help the child and family, and early intervention provides the best opportunity for success. Communication between the school and the home is critical in order to facilitate the child's educational career.

Autism is now recognized as a critical issue in public health. Researchers continue to search for the etiology of autism and are seeking intervention strategies to minimize the potentially devastating impact of this developmental disorder. Educational and social research also must be enhanced for this population in order to ensure quality of life for the individual children, adolescents, adults, their families, community and society.

REFERENCES

Akshoomoff, N., Corsello, C., & Schmidt, H., (2006). The role of the autism diagnostic observation schedule in the assessment of autism spectrum disorders in school and community settings. *California School Psychologist, 11*, 7–19.

American Psychiatric Association. (2000). *Diagnostic and statistical manual of mental disorders* (4th ed.), *TR*. Washington, DC: Author.

Baren-Cohen, S. (1992). *Checklist for autism in toddlers*. Retrieved August 26, 2008, http://www.depts.washington.edu/dataproj/chat.html.

Berninger, V. W., & Abbott, S. P. (2003). *Process assessment of the learner (PAL)*. San Antonio, TX: Pearson Assessment.

Brereton, A. V., Tonge, B. J., & Einfeld, S. L. (2006). Psychopathology in children and adolescents with autism compared to young people with intellectual disability. *Journal of Autism and Developmental Disorders, 36*, 863–870.

California Department of Developmental Services. (2002). *Autistic spectrum disorders: Best practice guidelines for screening, diagnosis and assessment*. Sacramento, CA: Author.

Cohen, I. L., & Sudhalter, V. (2005). *PDD behavior inventory (PDDBI)*. Lutz, FL: Psychological Assessment Resources.

Constantino, J., & Gruber, C. F. (2005). *Social responsiveness scale (SRS)*. Los Angeles: Western Psychological Services.

Dawson, M., Mottron, L., & Gernsbacher, M. A. (2008). Learning in autism. In J. H. Byrne (Series Ed.) & H. Roediger (Vol. Ed.), *Learning and memory: A comprehensive reference: Cognitive psychology* (pp. 759–772). New York: Elsevier.

Dawson, M., Soulieres, I., Gernsbacher, M. A., & Mottron, L. (2007). The level and nature of autistic intelligence. *Psychological Science, 8*, 657–662.

Dawson, G., & Watling, R. (2000). Interventions to facilitate auditory, visual, and motor integration in autism: A review of the evidence. *Journal of Autism and Developmental Disorders, 30*, 423–425.

DiLavore, P. C., Lord, C., & Rutter, M. (1995). The pre-linguistic autism diagnostic observation schedule. *Journal of Autism and Developmental Disorders, 25*, 355–379.

Edelson, M. G. (2006). Are the majority of children with autism mentally retarded? A systematic evaluation of the data. *Focus on Autism and Other Developmental Disabilities, 21*, 66–83.

Evans, D. W., Canavera, K., Klinepeter, F. L., Taga, K., & Maccubbin, E. (2005). The fears, phobias and anxieties of children with autism spectrum disorders and Down syndrome: Comparisons with developmentally and chronologically age matched children. *Child Psychiatry and Human Development, 36*, 3–36.

Ghaziuddin, M., Ghaziuddin, N., & Greden, J. (2002). Depression in persons with autism: Implications for research and clinical care. *Journal of Autism and Developmental Disorders, 32*, 299–306.

Gilliam, J. E. (1995). *Gilliam autism rating scale (GARS)*. Austin, TX: Pro-Ed.

Gold, N. (1993) Depression and social adjustment in siblings of boys with autism. *Journal of Autism and Developmental Disorders, 23*, 147–163.

Ivarsson, T., & Melin, K. (2008) Autism spectrum traits in children and adolescents with obsessive-compulsive disorder (OCD). *Journal of Anxiety Disorders, 22*, 969–978.

Krug, D. A., Arick, J. R., & Almond, P. J. (1980). *Autism behavior checklist (ABC)*. Los Angeles: Western Psychological Services.

Krug, D. A., Arick, J. R., & Almond, P. J. (2008). *Autism Screening Instrument for Educational Planning: Third Edition (ASIEP-3)*. Los Angeles: Western Psychological Services.

Le Couteur, A., Lord, C., & Rutter, M. (2003). *Autism diagnostic interview, revised*. Los Angeles: Western Psychological Services.

Lord, C., Rutter, M., DiLavore, P. C., & Risi, S. (1989). *Autism diagnostic observation schedule (ADOS)*. Los Angeles: Western Psychological Services.

Luna, B., Doll, S. K., Hegedus, S. J., Minshew, J. J., & Sweeney, J. A. (2007). Maturation of executive function in autism. *Biological Psychiatry, 61*, 474–481.

Matson, J. L., González, M. L., Terlonge, C., Thorson, R. T., & Laud, R. B. (2007). What symptoms predict the diagnosis of mania in persons with severe/profound intellectual disability: Focusing on observable behaviours. *Journal of Intellectual Disability Research, 51*, 25–31.

Matson, J. L., & Love, S. (1990). Diagnostic instruments to aid depressed mentally retarded individuals. In A. Dosen, & F. J. Menolascino (Eds.), *Depression in mentally retarded children and adults*. The Netherlands: Logon Publications.

Matson, J. L., & Nebel-Schwalm, M. S. (2007). Comorbid psychopathology with autism spectrum disorder in children: An overview, *Research in Developmental Disabilities, 28*, 341–352.

Miller, D. C. (2007). *Essentials of school neuropsychological assessment*. Hoboken, NJ: John Wiley & Sons.

Minshew, N. J., Goldstein, G., & Siegel, D. J. (1997). Neuropsychologic functioning in autism: Profile of a complex information processing disorder. *Journal of the International Neuropsychological Society, 3*, 303–316.

Minshew, N. J., & Williams, D. L. (2007). The new neurobiology of autism: Cortex, connectivity, and neuronal organization. *Archives of Neurology, 64*, 945–950.

Mulligan, A., Anney, R. J., O'Regan, M., et al. (2008). Autism symptoms in attention-deficit/hyperactivity disorder: A familial trait which correlates with conduct, oppositional defiant, language and motor disorders, *Journal of Autism and Developmental Disorders*, July 19. Advance online publication. Retrieved September 15, 2008. PMID: 18642069.

Munesue, T., Ono, Y., Mutoh, K., Shimoda, K., Nakatani, H., & Kikuchi, M. (2008). High prevalence of bipolar disorder comorbidity in adolescents and young adults with high-functioning autism spectrum disorder: A preliminary study of 44 outpatients. *Journal Affective Disorders*, March 28. Advance online publication. Retrieved September 15, 2008. PMID: 18378000.

National Institute of Neurological Disorders and Stroke (NIND) and National Institute of Health (NIH). (2008). Accessed September 10, 2008, from http://www.ninds.nih.gov/disorders/autism/detail_autism.htm, Autism Fact Sheet, "What is Autism?"

National Research Council. (2001). *Educating children with autism*. Washington, DC: National Academy Press.

Parrington, J. W. (2006). *Assessment of basic language and learning skills (revised) (ABLLS-R)*. Los Angeles: Western Psychological Services.

Reierson, A. M., & Todd, R. D. (2008). Co-occurrence of ADHD and autism spectrum disorders: Phenomenology and treatment. *Expert Review of Neurotherapeutics, 8*, 645–669.

Ronald, A., Simonoff, E., Kuntsi, J., Asherson, P., & Plomin, R. (2008). Evidence for overlapping genetic influences on autistic and ADHD behaviours in a community twin sample. *Journal of Child Psychology and Psychiatry, 499*, 535–542.

Rutter, M., Bailey, A., & Lord, C. (2003). *Social communication questionnaire (SCQ)*. Los Angeles: Western Psychological Services.

Schopler, E., Lansing, M. D., and Reichler, R. J. (1988). *Psychoeducational profile (PEP-3)*. Austin, TX: PRO-ED.

Schopler, E., Reichler, R. L., & Rochen Renner, B. (1998). *Childhood autism rating scale*. Los Angeles: Western Psychological Services.

Simonoff, E., Pickles, A., Charman, T., Chandler, S., Loucas, T., & Baird, G. (2008). Psychiatric disorders in children with autism spectrum disorders: Prevalence, comorbidity, and associated factors in a population-derived sample. *Journal of American Academy Child Adolescent Psychiatry, 47,* 921–929.

Stone, W. L., & Hogan, K. L. (1993). *Parent interview for autism (PIA).* Los Angeles: Western Psychological Services.

Williams, D. L., Goldstein, G., Carpenter, P. A., & Minshew, N. J. (2005) Verbal and spatial working memory in autism. *Journal of Autism and Developmental Disorders, 35,* 747–56.

Williams, D. L., Goldstein, G., & Minshew, N. J. (2006). Neuropsychologic functioning in children with autism: Further evidence for disordered complex information-processing. *Child Neuropsychology, 12,* 279–298.

CHAPTER 13

Assessing and Intervening with Children with Asperger's Disorder

KATHY DEORNELLAS, JACQUELINE HOOD, and BROOKE NOVALES

THE NEUROPSYCHOLOGICAL FUNCTIONING of individuals with Asperger's Disorder (AD), also known as Asperger's Syndrome, has been a topic of research interest for quite some time. Many of the original assumptions regarding neuropsychological profiles in children with AD may not be supportable (Ambery, Russell, Perry, Morris, & Murphy, 2006; Macintosh & Dissanayake, 2004), which calls into question the very reason for performing such measures in routine evaluations. However, it is important to assess for strengths and weaknesses within the neuropsychological profile of children with AD, not for the purpose of making diagnostic distinctions, but because some of these factors have been found to correlate to later outcome levels (Hill, Pierce, Rogers, & Wehner, 2001). Moreover, while it may be parsimonious to make assumptions about treatment planning based on a diagnosis such as AD (i.e., the need for occupational therapy or instruction in language pragmatics), children with AD present a broad neuropsychological phenotype, and interventions must be tailored to actual functioning levels based on measured need. In order to help guide such assessments, current findings regarding the functioning of children with AD across a number of neuropsychological domains have been provided.

NEUROPSYCHOLOGICAL FUNCTIONING IN ASPERGER'S DISORDER

SENSORY FUNCTIONING

Sensory sensitivities are not listed among the current diagnostic criteria for AD, and there continues to be a debate as to whether sensory issues should be considered as important features of the disorder. While there is anecdotal evidence of sensory dysfunction in Asperger's, there have been few studies to date that have empirically evaluated this using direct assessment methods.

However, the existing literature does support the hypothesis of poor sensory modulation in AD. In a study by Dunn, Myles, and Orr (2002), the *Sensory Profile* parent questionnaire was used to compare the functioning of 23 children with AD with 23 typically developing (TD) children on a number of sensory domains. In this study, the authors found significant group differences on 22 of 23 measured items, with a trend toward greater difficulty in the AD group. Notably, the authors found both hypo- and hypersensory responsiveness, suggesting the possibility of a problem with sensory modulation rather than a particular trend of responsiveness in either direction. A few other studies have directly investigated sensory issues in AD. Specifically, Blakemore et al. (2006) provided evidence of lower tactile perceptual thresholds in AD than in TD controls (for a particular frequency); they additionally found that self-reported measures of intensity of stimuli were higher for subjects with AD. Furthermore, McAlononan et al. (2002) found reduced prepulse inhibition when they measured the eye blink component of the startle response to acoustic stimulus (a prepulse is a lower level stimulus that inhibits subsequent startle response to a higher-level stimulus). Suzuki, Critchley, Rowe, Howlin, and Murphy (2003) detected evidence of impaired olfactory identification in AD versus TD controls. Finally, Pfeiffer, Kinnealy, Reed, and Herzberg (2005) found a particularly compelling motivation for attempting to measure directly sensory responsivity in children with AD. Specifically, they found a significant positive correlation between sensory overreponsiveness and anxiety symptoms in AD, as well as a significant positive correlation between sensory underresponsiveness and depression.

MOTOR FUNCTIONING

Motor functioning has been a significant subject of investigation in AD, particularly as it has been listed as an associated feature of the disorder in the *DSM-IV-TR* (APA, 2000); furthermore, Hans Asperger identified clumsiness as one of the core features of AD in his first clinical account (Wing, 1981). In general, studies have shown that motor functioning is indeed likely to be impaired in individuals with AD, as it is in other Autism Spectrum Disorders (ASD). Research subjects with AD have been noted to demonstrate deficits relative to typically functioning children in multiple aspects of motor functioning, including gross motor, fine motor, upper limb coordination, manual dexterity, ball skill, and balance tasks (see Ghaziuddin & Butler, 1998; Ghaziuddin, Butler, Tsai, & Ghaziuddin, 1994; Manjiovina & Prior, 1995). Notably, these studies generally have not shown statistically significant differences between children with AD and high functioning autism (HFA) on these measures, although a study by Ghaziuddin and Butler did find that individuals with AD appeared to be less clumsy. Similarly, in the Manjiovina and Prior study, it was found that 50 percent of participants with AD as compared to 66.7 percent of children with HFA demonstrated motor functioning scores that were significantly lower than that of same-aged peers.

ATTENTION/EXECUTIVE FUNCTION

Children with AD have well-documented deficits in the areas of attention and executive function (see Pennington & Ozonoff, 1996, for a review). Difficulties with executive functioning may appear as problems with self-control or self-direction (emotional lability, affective flattening, irritability, excitability, carelessness, rigidity, and difficulties in shifting attention), impaired ability to initiate or inhibit activity, decreased or absent motivation, and defects in planning and carrying out goal-directed behaviors (Lezak, Howieson, & Loring, 2004). Multiple studies have been conducted on the subject of attention and executive functioning in ASD, although few have been tailored specifically to AD. Over time, studies have begun to reveal specific patterns of executive function deficits rather than global impairment. In particular, specific deficits have been found on tasks measuring cognitive flexibility (e.g., cognitive set switching, particularly for language-based information), planning, and generativity/creativity (Hill, 2004). Notably, a number of studies with both children and adults with ASD have demonstrated evidence of preserved response inhibition capability (see Hill, 2004, for a review; Ozonoff & Strayer, 1997). Moreover, there is evidence that the executive function deficits in children with ASD may be less severe and persistent than those found in children with ADHD (Ambery et al., 2006; Happe, Booth, Charlton, & Hughes, 2006; Hill, 2004). Also noteworthy is the evidence from recent research that children with AD may actually have an attentional advantage when it comes to divided attention; that is, children with AD performed better on tasks of divided attention when measured against their TD peers (Rutherford, Richards, Moldes, & Sekuler, 2007). Not only does this perhaps change preconceived ideas of deficit functioning in these children, it may provide some direction in terms of learning preference and ultimate career choice for children with AD.

VISUAL SPATIAL ABILITY

One of the areas of neuropsychological functioning that is often considered spared in ASD is visual spatial ability. In fact, in certain aspects of visual spatial functioning, children with ASD have been shown to outperform TD controls. Specifically, children with ASD (including both HFA and AD) have been shown to demonstrate superior performance, relative to TD children, on embedded figures identification tasks and finding targets in a visual array

(Jolliffe & Baron-Cohen, 1997; see Mitchell & Ropar, 2004 for a review.). In particular, children with ASD are more quickly able to identify figure from ground. Some authors have contended that this strength reflects a cognitive style better equipped to discern local versus global information. However, a study by Edgin and Pennington (2005) suggests that although children with ASD demonstrated decreased reaction times on an embedded figures task, there was no evidence of superior (or inferior) functioning on any other of multiple visual spatial measures. Notably, in this study, participants with AD as well as HFA were included, and when compared, no significant difference between spatial skills arose between the AD and HFA group, contrary to the notion of a nonverbal learning disability profile in individuals with AD.

LANGUAGE

One of the features that distinguishes AD from autism is the absence of a language delay. Thus, in individuals with AD, language is thought to be a spared skill. However, due to the nature of AD as a social disorder, it is generally accepted that children with AD will have pragmatic language deficits, meaning that in the face of spared verbal abilities, they will demonstrate deficits in the practical and social aspects of language. Specifically, children with AD demonstrate subtle linguistic differences from children with autism, even when matched by verbal ability on IQ tests. Prior to the *DSM-IV-TR* (APA, 2000) definition of AD, a number of authors included particular speech peculiarities in their definition of AD. For example, Gillberg and Ehlers (1998, p. 82) noted "superficially perfect expressive language," "formal pedantic language," "odd prosody, peculiar voice characteristics," and "impairments of comprehension including misinterpretations of literal/ implied meanings." Szatmari, Bremner, and Nagy (1989) noted odd speech and suggested abnormalities in inflection, quantity of speech (too much or too little), lack of cohesion to conversation, idiosyncratic use of words, and repetitive patterns of speech. In general, studies have shown that although children with AD may have spared verbal abilities, individuals with AD do demonstrate language atypicalities. Specifically, studies have borne out differences in use of pedantic speech (Ghaziuddin & Gerstein, 1996) and language pragmatics (conversational structure, nonverbal communication, and prosody) (Ramberg, Ehlers, Nyden, Johansson, & Gillberg, 1996). It should be noted that subtle differences have been noted in the pragmatic language skills between individuals with HFA and those with AD (Seung, 2007); that is, children with HFA tend to have slightly more difficulty with pragmatic language, possibly reflecting lasting subtle deficits from language delay (as there is no language delay in AD).

MEMORY AND LEARNING

AD, along with other ASDs, has been linked to deficits in memory functioning (Bowler, Matthews, & Gardiner, 1997). In general, ASDs are hypothesized to be related to intact rote memory along with impaired ability to utilize complex organizational strategies in encoding and retrieving items from memory; however, the picture may be more complex than this (see Kamio & Toichi, 2007, McCrory, Henry, & Happe, 2007). Specifically, individuals with ASD are thought to utilize techniques such as semantic coding, categorizing, and use of context less frequently when learning. A number of studies have looked into this phenomenon, although few studies have specifically targeted AD. In a recent study in which individuals with AD and autism were compared to TD children, the results indicated the possibility that the aforementioned pattern of learning differences may not hold true for children with AD, as no significant differences were found between TD children and children with AD on measures of semantic cueing and contextual coding, with only subtle, nonsignificant differences separating the groups on memory measures (Kamio & Toichi, 2007).

GENERAL COGNITIVE PROFILE

The evidence to date suggests that as a group, there is not enough evidence to support the existence of a specific pattern of performance by children with AD on measures of intelligence, such as verbal versus nonverbal ability (see Macintosh & Dissanayake, 2004, for a review). Specifically, although once prevalent, the hypothesis that children with AD possess deficits in nonverbal intelligence similar to children with Nonverbal Learning Disability (NLD) has not been empirically validated. Thus, the use of cognitive profile analysis in making a determination of AD diagnosis is not currently supportable. However, performance on certain tasks, such as those taxing fine motor ability or focused attention, might be expected to be lower in children with AD; certain others (e.g., detecting figure from ground) might be expected to be spared, while still others might be noted as strengths (e.g., fluid intelligence; Koyama, Tachimori, Osada, Takeda, & Kurita, 2007). Therefore, as part of a comprehensive evaluation for a child suspected of AD, it will be critical to perform a direct assessment of a child's specific strengths and weaknesses, particularly because these factors are not consistent across the population of children with AD and because these factors may relate to treatment planning and outcome.

ACADEMIC ACHIEVEMENT

Little research focuses specifically on academic achievement in individuals with AD. Available evidence suggests that children and adolescents with AD tend to score in the average range on measures of academic achievement, though there is significant variability among scores. For instance, a study by Griswold, Barnhill, Myles, Hagiwara, and Simpson (2002) found children with AD attained scores on the *Wechsler Individual Achievement Test* (WIAT) ranging from significantly above average (e.g., 151 in Oral Expression) to well below average (e.g., 63 in Listening Comprehension). Mean scores on all measures from the WIAT were in the average range; however, the lowest scores were obtained in the areas of Written Expression, Listening Comprehension, and Numerical Operations. Similarly, Reitzel and Szatmari (2003) found mean academic achievement scores of children with AD were in the average range, although individuals did have some difficulties with math. Reading comprehension is also reported to be an area of concern for children and adolescents with AD (Church, Alisanski, & Amanullah, 2000; Nation, Clarke, Wright, & Williams, 2006).

COMORBIDITY WITH OTHER DISORDERS

Comorbidity has been somewhat difficult to assess given the disagreement among authors as to what constitutes AD (Macintosh & Dissanayake, 2004). Indeed, much of the research assessing comorbidity relies on case reports. Given these limitations, however, AD has been found to co-occur with Attention-Deficit/Hyperactivity Disorder (ADHD) (Ghaziuddin, Weidmer-Mikhail, & Ghaziuddin, 1998; Lee & Ousley, 2006)—although this picture is also complicated by the fact that the *DSM-IV-TR* specifies a diagnosis of ADHD should be subsumed under the autism spectrum diagnosis (APA, 2000). It has been noted, however, that symptoms of inattention and hyperactivity frequently occur in children with AD, and many individuals receive a diagnosis of ADHD prior to receiving a diagnosis of AD (APA, 2000). Kim, Szatmari, Bryson, Streiner, and Wilson (2000) investigated the prevalence of anxiety and depression in individuals with AD and HFA and determined children with these disorders were significantly more likely to experience anxiety and depression problems than TD peers. Other case reports and studies document the comorbidity of AD/autism spectrum disorders with mood disorders, tic disorders, and obsessive-compulsive disorder (Gillberg & Billstedt, 2000).

Evidence also suggests children and adolescents with AD have comorbid learning differences. For instance, Sturm, Fernell, and Gillberg (2004) reported that of 95 children with ASD (and an IQ of 70 or above), 66 evidenced learning problems at school, although specific academic areas were not listed. Impairments have been documented in the areas of reading, particularly in terms of reading comprehension (Nation et al., 2006) and, more specifically, inferential comprehension, as compared to comprehension of rote facts

(Myles et al., 2002). Written language has also been reported as an area of weakness, and research has documented that children and adolescents with AD produce shorter, less complex writing samples when compared to TD peers (Myles et al., 2003). A recent review of literature indicated a majority of individuals with AD and HFA have average abilities in math (Chiang & Lin, 2007).

COMPONENTS OF A SCHOOL NEUROPSYCHOLOGICAL EVALUATION TO ADDRESS ASPERGER DISORDER

INITIAL DIAGNOSIS

If a student has not been identified as having AD at the time the school neuropsychological evaluation is requested, then a comprehensive evaluation specifically for autism spectrum disorders (completed by a multidisciplinary team) will be recommended in additional to the neuropsychological assessment. Such an evaluation might include the use of instruments such as the *Autism Diagnostic Observation Schedule–Generic* (Lord, Rutter, DiLavore, & Risi, 2000) and the *Autism Diagnostic Interview–Revised* (Rutter, Le Couteur, & Lord, 2003). However, it should be noted these instruments are not specific to AD but rather evaluate for the presence of ASD as well as for behavioral observations across multiple settings, including a thorough developmental history. Rating scales, such as the *Gilliam Asperger's Disorder Scale* (Gilliam, 2001), the *Asperger Syndrome Diagnostic Scale* (Myles, Bock, & Simpson, 2001), or the *Krug Asperger's Disorder Index* (Krug & Arick, 2003), are also useful in determining whether characteristics of AD are present, although it should be noted that there are weaknesses associated with these rating scales, which work best when used in conjunction with other data (Campbell, 2005). Finally, the NEPSY-II (Korkman, Kirk, & Kemp, 2007), which includes subtests measuring social perception in the areas of Affect Recognition and Theory of Mind, might also yield information that would help corroborate a diagnosis of AD.

SCHOOL NEUROPSYCHOLOGICAL EVALUATION

After the initial diagnosis of AD is made, or during the course of testing for an autism spectrum disorder, a school neuropsychological evaluation may be requested to identify patterns of learning strengths and weaknesses so that appropriate interventions can be put into place in the educational setting. As with any thorough evaluation, typical components include a developmental history, educational history, clinical interview, information from parents and teachers, and behavioral observations across multiple settings (Miller, 2007). A particular strength of working in the context of a school setting is the availability of specialized evaluation personnel such as speech-language pathologists (SLPs) and occupational therapists (OTs); hence, additional information could also be gathered from these professionals and incorporated into the neuropsychological evaluation. For instance, when evaluating a student with AD or suspected AD, speech/language evaluations to assess pragmatic language can be completed by an SLP if necessary, and specific intervention strategies implemented by the SLP in the school setting if the IEP team determines such interventions are warranted. Similarly, an OT might complete parts of the assessment in the areas of sensory and motor perform-ance. Regardless of who completes each specific piece of the evaluation, the following measures may prove useful during the course of the school neuropsychological assessment.

Sensory Functioning   Sensory hyper- and hyposensitivities with difficulties in sensory modulation have been reported in individuals with AD (Blakemore et al., 2006; Dunn et al., 2002; McAlononan et al., 2002; Pfeiffer et al., 2005; Suzuki et al., 2003). In order to determine whether sensory sensitivities affect a child's educational performance, one might first administer a general screening instrument such as the *Sensory Profile* (Dunn, 1999). This measure is completed by caregivers and yields information regarding aspects of sensory processing that may affect academic and behavioral performance. In a school setting, this measure is often administered and the results interpreted by an OT. Additionally, if specific sensory deficits are suspected (e.g., difficulty with auditory or tactile perception), then selected tests from the *Dean-Woodcock Sensory-Motor Battery* (Dean & Woodcock, 2003) might be used to investigate these areas.

Motor Functioning   Sensory-motor deficits, such as poor gesture imitation, poor motor planning, and motor clumsiness, as well as concerns with visual-motor integration and fine motor performance, are often reported for indi-viduals with AD (Ghaziuddin & Butler, 1998; Ghaziuddin et al., 1994; Manjiovina & Prior, 1995; Mesibov, Shea, & Adams, 2001; Wing, 1981). The administration of measures of visual-motor ability is helpful in order to investigate potential skill deficits in this area. The NEPSY-II (Korkman et al., 2007) includes several measures of sensory-motor ability, including Fingertip Tapping, Imitating Hand Positions, and Visuomotor Precision. Although Fingertip Tapping can be administered to youth aged 5 to 16, Imitating Hand Positions and Visuomotor Precision are normed on youth aged 3 to 12. For older students, then, other measures will be necessary. These might include the *Beery-Buktenica Developmental Test of Visual-Motor Integra-tion, 5th Edition* (Beery, Buktenica, & Beery, 2003), which includes tests of Visual Motor Integration, Visual Perception, and Motor Coordination and can be administered to individuals aged 2 to 18. The *Dean-Woodcock Sensory-Motor Battery*, part of the *Dean-Woodcock Neuropsychological Battery* (Dean & Woodcock, 2003), includes multiple sensory and motor tasks and may be administered to individuals aged 4 to 80 years. Tests can be selected based on the referral question (e.g., difficulties with finger dexterity, tactile difficulties), and one advantage to this battery is that it allows for assessment of both gross motor and fine motor difficulties.

Attention/Executive Function   Attentional processing deficits in the areas of sustained attention and shifting attention have been documented in individuals with AD, while strengths in the area of divided attention have been noted (Rutherford et al., 2007). There are multiple measures available to address attention concerns, and only a few will be mentioned here. First, it is important to gather information from parents and school personnel to determine when and in what settings attention is an issue. General rating scales and behavioral checklists such as the *Behavior Assessment System for Children, 2nd Edition* (BASC-2; Reynolds & Kamphaus, 2004) and the *Conners Rating Scales, 3rd Edition* (Conners, 2008b) are useful in this regard, as are rating scales more specific to characteristics of attention, such as the *Brown Attention Deficit Disorder Scales for Children and Adolescents* (Brown, 2001), although these measures are not specific to a particular type of attention (e.g., shifting attention).

In order to evaluate a child's ability to sustain attention, the NEPSY-II (Korkman et al., 2007) includes the Auditory Attention and Response Set task (parts A and B) that can be administered to individuals aged 5 to 16 years. It should be noted this measure assesses both sustained attention and shifting attention. Other measures of sustained attention include the Cancellation task on the *Wechsler Intelligence Scale for Children, 4th Edition* (WISC-IV; Wechsler, 2003) and the Pair Cancellation task on the *Woodcock-Johnson III Tests of Cognitive Abilities* (WJIII-COG; Woodcock, McGrew, & Mather, 2001a). The *Test of Everyday Attention for Children* (TEA-Ch; Manly, Robertson, Anderson, & Nimmo-Smith, 1999) also includes several subtests that measure sustained attention (specifically, Score!, Score DT, Walk Don't Walk, and Code Transmission) and includes norms for children aged 6 to 16 years. Unlike the NEPSY-II, TEA-Ch, and WISC-IV, the WJ III-COG can be used with individuals older than 16. Finally, there are multiple continuous performance tests that measure sustained attention. *The Integrated Visual and Auditory Continuous Performance Test* (IVA+ Plus; Sandford & Turner, 1993-2006) tests both the auditory and visual modalities and can be administered to individuals aged 6 to 96. The *Test of Variables of Attention* (Greenberg, 1996) also has both an auditory and a visual version, although the upper age limit for this measure is 16 years.

Instruments that measure shifting attention include the NEPSY-II (Auditory Attention and Response Set, Part B) and the TEA-Ch (Creature Counting, Opposite Worlds). The *Wisconsin Card Sorting Test* (Heaton, Chelune, Talley, Kay, & Curtiss, 1993) is a measure of shifting attention as well as perseveration and abstract thinking, making it especially useful when testing students with AD, and it can be used with individuals aged 6.5 to 89 years. Children are required to sort cards according to different principles or rules that are changed during the course of the administration. Additionally, the *Delis-Kaplan Executive Function System* (D-KEFS; Delis, Kaplan, & Kramer, 2001) includes four measures of shifting attention. These include the Trail-Making Test (Condition 4), the Verbal Fluency Test (Condition 3), the Design Fluency Test (Condition 3), and the Color-Word Interference Test (Condition 4). The D-KEFS can be administered to individuals aged 8 to 89 years. Additionally, because divided attention is often an area of strength, tests such as Sky Search DT (from the TEA-Ch) and Auditory Working Memory (WJIII-COG) might also be administered in order to yield information relevant to educational programming.

Executive function deficits have been associated with AD. Areas of impairment often include motor planning, response inhibition, cognitive flexibility (rigidity), perseveration, and difficulty in self-monitoring (Hill, 2004; Lezak et al., 2004; Ozonoff & Strayer, 1997). The *Behavior Rating Inventory of Executive Function* (BRIEF; Gioia, Isquith, Guy, & Kenworthy, 2000) is useful to obtain parent and teacher input on everyday executive function abilities in the home and school settings. It is intended for use with children and adolescents aged 5 to 18 years; a preschool version is also available. Additionally, a self-report form is available for use with adolescents aged 11 to 18 years.

For a more in-depth evaluation of executive function performance, several measures are available. The D-KEFS (Delis et al., 2001) is a comprehensive battery of tests designed to measure multiple aspects of executive functions, including those areas thought to be impaired in individuals with AD. For instance, parts of the Color-Word Interference Test, Design Fluency, Trail-Making, and Verbal Fluency measures are useful in assessing cognitive flexibility. The NEPSY-II (Korkman et al., 2007) includes measures of inhibition (Auditory Attention and Response Set, Knock and Tap, Statue, Inhibition) and set shifting (Auditory Attention and Response Set, Part B). The *Wisconsin Card Sorting Test* (Heaton et al., 1993) is a measure of cognitive flexibility, and the WJIII-COG (Woodcock et al., 2001a) includes measures of inhibition (Pair Cancellations) and motor planning (Planning).

Visual-Spatial Ability   Visual-spatial abilities tend to be relatively spared in individuals with AD (Edgin & Pennington, 2005; Jolliffe & Baron-Cohen,

1997). If there are specific referral concerns, an omnibus test such as the NEPSY-II may prove useful, as it includes measures of visual perception (including a motor-free measure, Arrows) as well as visual scanning. The WJIII-COG (Woodcock et al., 2001a) also includes both a motor-free measure of visual perception (Spatial Relations) and a test for visual scanning (Pair Cancellation).

Language Language ability is also relatively spared in individuals with AD, although deficits are reported in the area of prosody and pragmatic language (Ghaziuddin & Gerstein, 1996; Gillberg & Ehlers, 1998; Ramberg et al., 1996; Szatmari et al., 1989). In the school setting, a full speech/language evaluation would likely be conducted by an SLP. Tests administered might include the *Test of Pragmatic Language, 2nd Edition* (Phelps-Terasaki & Phelps-Gunn, 2007), which can be administered to children aged 6 to 18 years, and the *Comprehensive Assessment of Spoken Language* (CASL; Carrow-Woolfolk, 1999). The CASL can be administered to individuals aged 3 to 21 years and includes measures of nonliteral language, inference abilities, and social language.

Memory and Learning Impairments in episodic memory have been reported in children and adolescents with AD, although recent evidence suggests these abilities may be spared more than was previously thought (Kamio & Toichi, 2007; McCrory et al., 2007). If specific concerns were noted as part of the referral, it may be helpful to administer a stand-alone measure of memory and language in order to investigate a broad range of abilities. Measures used to assess memory and learning performance include the *Children's Memory Scale* (Cohen, 1997), the *Test of Memory and Learning, 2nd Edition* (TOMAL-2; Reynolds & Voress, 2007), and the *Wide Range Assessment of Memory and Learning, 2nd Edition* (WRAML2; Sheslow & Adams, 2003). These measures test both verbal and visual memory performance—both immediately and after a short delay. The TOMAL-2 and WRAML2 include measures of verbal-visual associative learning, though the subtest on the WRAML2 (Sound-Symbol) is intended only for children aged 5 to 8 years.

Speed and Efficiency of Processing Individuals with AD often exhibit slowed processing speed, although it is difficult to determine whether this is related to AD itself or to the fact that many of these children take psychotropic medication that affects processing speed. The WJIII-COG (Woodcock et al., 2001a) includes a specific processing speed cluster, while other measures include tests or subtests where completion time is recorded—an indirect measure of processing speed. Both the NEPSY-II (Korkman et al., 2007) and the D-KEFS (Delis et al., 2001) include timed tests, and slow completion times might indicate slow processing speed; however, caution should be exercised as other explanations for slow completion times might be equally valid (e.g., medication side effects, perfectionistic response style, poor fine motor abilities).

General Cognitive Abilities   In the school setting, particularly if a student has already been identified as a child with AD, cognitive testing has likely already been performed. If testing has not been done, or if additional information is sought beyond that already provided by previous cognitive testing, there are multiple cognitive measures available. However, it is important to report the results of the cognitive testing within the framework of the school neuro-psychological evaluation, with emphasis given to the basic cognitive processes tested (e.g., processing speed, visual-spatial processing, long-term retrieval) rather than on a single IQ score (Miller, 2007). The WJIII-COG (Woodcock et al., 2001a) yields the broadest results in terms of the number of cognitive processes tested. Other measures include the WISC-IV (Wechsler, 2003), the *Kaufman Assessment Battery for Children, 2nd Edition* (Kaufman & Kaufman, 2004) and the *Stanford-Binet Intelligence Scales, 5th Edition* (Roid, 2003).

Academic Achievement   As with cognitive testing, academic testing may have been completed by the time a school neuropsychological evaluation is requested. Areas of academic difficulty associated with AD include reading comprehension, math calculations, and written language (Church et al., 2000; Griswold et al., 2002; Nation et al., 2006; Reitzel & Szatmari, 2003). Multiple measures exist to evaluate academic achievement, including the *Woodcock-Johnson III Tests of Achievement* (WJIII-ACH; Woodcock, McGrew, & Mather, 2001b), the *Wechsler Individual Achievement Test, 2nd Edition* (Wechsler, 2001), and the *Kaufman Test of Educational Achievement, 2nd Edition* (Kaufman & Kaufman, 2005). The WJIII-ACH includes measures of reading and writing fluency that are useful in teasing apart potential sources for academic difficulty (e.g., is a student experiencing reading difficulty because of issues with reading comprehension or reading fluency, or both); however, it should be noted the Writing Samples test on the WJIII-ACH is limited to writing a single sentence at a time, which is generally not the type of writing required in the school setting (e.g., paragraphs, essays, reports).

Social/Emotional Functioning   Children and adolescents with AD exhibit multiple social deficits; they have difficulty with both verbal and nonverbal social communication (such as interpreting the facial expression or nonverbal cues of others). Additionally, adolescents with AS may experience depression or anxiety because of their social difficulties. As part of the school neuro-psychological evaluation, it is important to gather information regarding the child's or adolescent's own perception of his or her social/emotional functioning, as well as the perceptions of parents and teachers. Specific measures administered will depend upon the age of the child but might include a general behavioral screening instrument such as the BASC-2 (Reynolds & Kamphaus, 2004), *Conners Rating Scales, 3rd Edition* (Conners, 2008b), or the *Conners Comprehensive Behavior Rating Scales* (Conners, 2008a). Each of these instruments has separate forms for teachers and parents, as well as self-report forms for children (ages 8 to 21 for the BASC-2 and ages 12 to 17 for the Conners; the BASC-2 also includes an interview-format self-report form for children ages 6–7). In order to solicit information regarding the child's perception of his or her levels of anxiety or depression, scales such as the *Multidimensional Anxiety Scale for Children* (March, 1999), the *Revised Children's Manifest Anxiety Scale, 2nd Edition* (Reynolds & Richmond, 1998), the *Multi-score Depression Inventory for Children* (Berndt & Kaiser, 1996), and the *Children's Depression Inventory* (Kovacs, 2003) are commonly used. Additionally, the *Piers-Harris Children's Self-Concept Scale, 2nd Edition* (Piers, Harris, & Herzberg, 2002) can be used as an overall measure of the child's self-concept.

INTERVENTION APPROACHES FOR WORKING WITH STUDENTS WITH ASPERGER'S DISORDER

SENSORY FUNCTIONS

Sensory overload can be a significant problem for students with AD, and the average school setting provides a number of stressing situations on a daily basis (Bolick, 2001). The first step in intervening is to recognize the signs of overload. In some individuals, the first sign may be a slight rocking back and forth followed by hand wringing or flapping, pacing, or talking to him- or herself. If the student's distress is overlooked, behavioral acting out may occur in the form of verbal or physical aggression. As an intervention, it is important to teach the student how to monitor his or her own reactions to the environment and the resulting behaviors. Next, evaluate the strategies used by the individual with AD for handling sensory overload. Are they efficient and appropriate for the setting? If not, additional strategies will be required. Teaching relaxation techniques such as counting to ten, deep breathing, imagery, and progressive muscle relaxation can be useful (Bolick, 2001).

It is equally important to identify the situations that are most likely to result in sensory overload. Environmental characteristics (e.g., crowds, noise, and lighting), social demands, academic demands, and the behavior of others place great demands on the resources of the individual with AD (Bolick, 2001). The effects can be cumulative, making the end of the day or week a time of greater stress. Modifying the environment whenever possible can be very helpful. Bolick gives the examples of allowing the student with AD to have the locker at the end of the row so that the student endures less jostling by others or giving students with AD copies of class notes so they do not have to take notes while trying to listen to the lecture.

MOTOR FUNCTIONS

Clumsiness and motor function deficits are frequently associated with AD, but participation in exercise programs is beneficial in reducing acting-out behavior and increasing skills (Jordan, 2003). In schools that specialize in students with AD, swimming, jumping on a trampoline, rock climbing, cycling, and jogging are used to introduce physical activity in a pleasurable fashion. Other advantages of physical activity include increased motor coordination, learning to take turns, learning to participate in group activities, and increased self-esteem. Students with AD who have difficulty with balance, who have difficulty walking on uneven ground, or who are uncomfortable with their feet off the ground may benefit from a consultation with an OT (Jordan, 2003).

In the classroom, using a computer for writing is helpful to those students with AD who have difficulty with motor coordination and producing legible handwriting (Jordan, 2003). Although learning to write with a pencil or pen is an important life skill, using a computer for writing makes creativity attainable because the student is not focused on the difficulty of manipulating a pencil. When writing by hand is required, pencil grips and posture supports such as those used by individuals with cerebral palsy can be helpful (Jordan, 2003).

ATTENTION/EXECUTIVE FUNCTION

Students with AD frequently have difficulty maintaining adequate attention and concentration. They are easily distracted and subject to irrelevant thoughts and behaviors (Bolick, 2001). They have difficulty staying on track during a conversation and can wander onto another topic very easily. When this happens, it is important to redirect the conversation by reminding the student about the topic of the discussion. With time and repetition, students with AD can internalize this direct feedback and begin to redirect their own conversations. Bolick suggests the "OHIO: Only Handle it Once" method (p. 36) in which the student with AD is advised to finish one activity before moving on to another. Breaking tasks into chunks is also helpful. If there are 100 math problems, the student is encouraged to finish ten before taking a bite of his or her snack, then ten more, and so on (Bolick, 2001).

With regard to executive function-related tasks, students with AD have difficulty organizing materials and tasks (Bolick, 2001). They also do not know the same information that other students know. For example, TD students know what it means when they are told to get ready to go home at the end of the school day; students with AD may need a checklist that describes which materials go in the backpack, as well as other basic items. Checklists, diagrams, and concept maps can all be used in the classroom to help students with AD make connections (Bolick, 2001). If a project is due several weeks from now, make sure it is listed on the student's assignment sheet every day. Teach the student how to keep a calendar or record information into an electronic device such as a BlackBerry®. Students with AD also have little flexibility in problem solving. Their insistence on sameness results in using the same techniques for problem solving in every situation, regardless of whether the method is effective (Bolick, 2001).

LANGUAGE

Students with AD do not have the language delays typical of other individuals with ASD. They tend to speak quite well, and many use language beyond their years. Some use grammatical structures and vocabulary that could be considered precocious. While this may seem like an advantage, teachers may mistake language ability for language comprehension and expect more from them in terms of understanding than they are capable of (Jordan, 2003). When students with AD do not respond appropriately, teachers may interpret this as willful disobedience rather than lack of comprehension. Upon entering school, students with AD are just beginning to understand the rules of conversation. In the classroom, students are exposed to a different set of rules (i.e., raise your hand before you speak), and the teacher models a communication style they find easy to emulate or may have already mastered (i.e., talk about a subject for a long time regardless of whether anyone seems to be listening, ask many questions.). When students with AD use these communication styles in the rest of the world (or even within the classroom), they find themselves in trouble (Jordan, 2003).

To intervene with language problems, it is important to make conversational intentions clear in the classroom. Students with AD need to be taught two different sets of conversational rules—one for formal situations, such as the classroom, and one for more informal situations, such as on the playground or in the neighborhood (Jordan, 2003). Raising one's hand to ask a question may be appropriate in the classroom but will be a source of ridicule during games at recess. Teachers should also attempt to be specific when asking questions rather than leaving it to the student with AD to guess what information the teacher is wanting. For example, ''Tell me how Great Britain's economic policy influenced the outcome of the

U.S. Civil War" instead of "Tell me about Great Britain and the Civil War" (Jordan, 2003).

Students with AD frequently ask repetitive questions, and attempting to discern the reason for the questions may be helpful (Jordan, 2003). In some cases, the students may be trying to introduce a preferred topic while in other cases they may be feeling anxious and need reassurance by hearing the answer over and over. Giving the students the opportunity to talk about their favorite topics or finding another way of reassuring them may prove helpful. In some cases, however, the students with AD enjoy hearing the sound of their own questions and answers, or they enjoy watching the teacher's mouth as he or she is responding. In that instance, limits will have to be set as to how many times the teacher will respond (Jordan, 2003).

Bolick offers several other suggestions for intervening with language difficulties (2001):

- Be sure that your words match your nonverbal signals and your meaning. Do not expect students with AD to understand sarcasm or figures of speech. They are unlikely to be able to "read between the lines."
- Allow time for processing when giving verbal instructions and talk slowly. Students with AD may be able to remember directions and to follow directions, but they are unlikely to be able to remember and follow directions at the same time. Provide written lists of directions.
- Model the language you expect from students with AD. When adults are sarcastic with each other, students with AD are likely to be sarcastic with those same adults.
- Teach students with AD definitions of the slang their peers are using to help them avoid embarrassing situations.

Emotional/Behavioral

Emotional and behavioral problems in students with AD are frequently the result of sensory overload, misunderstanding or misreading of social situations, lack of knowledge of the unwritten rules, or compulsive behaviors (Mesibov et al., 2001). Students with AD do not respond well to changes in the routine or to not being allowed to finish a task. Punishing this behavior is not typically effective; determining the reason for the behavior and changing the environment are more effective. For example, if a student with AD had a tantrum during lunch, it may be that he or she did not finish eating before it was time to go because the line was longer than usual. Preparing the student for changes in the routine or creating an alternate plan when things do not go as scheduled is more helpful than sending the student to the principal's office (Mesibov et al., 2001).

Myles and Simpson (2003) outline a series of steps important in developing appropriate interventions for students with AD. They reported:

> It is unlikely that intervention will succeed without a clearly defined and measured target behavior such as; a thorough analysis of salient antecedent variables (e.g., curriculum or activity most associated with a target behavior, personnel connected to a problem, environments most likely to be associated with a target response, time of day when a targeted behavior is most and least apt to occur); and an understanding of functions that motivate a particular response (e.g., attention, failure to understand, communication, avoidance of an undesired activity). (p. 101)

Unfortunately, gathering this information, while helpful, is not sufficient when designing interventions. Students with AD are individuals, and there is no one type of intervention that can be used successfully for all. Tailoring the intervention to the preferences of the student while taking into consideration the student's tolerance level will be most successful. Myles and Simpson describe two types of interventions that have proven successful. The first is to provide structure within the environment by establishing clear expectations for behavior, setting up routines, and providing support. The second involves behavioral interventions. Behavioral interventions include cognitive behavior modification, use of reinforcers, and behavior contracts (see Myles & Simpson, 2003, for detailed instructions).

MEMORY AND LEARNING

Students with AD frequently have excellent rote memory ability, particularly for their topic of interest. However, they must be taught the meaning of what they have learned, how it relates to what they have already learned, and how the information can be used in the future (Jordan, 2003). Other memory interventions include teaching strategies, such as mnemonics, using chunking, writing down information that is likely to be forgotten, and breaking down tasks into smaller, more manageable parts (Bolick, 2001).

LEARNING/ACADEMIC PROBLEMS

Students with AD have exceptional potential in the classroom if teachers take the time to develop strategies for helping them learn. Zager and Shamow (2005) recommend the following for creating a supportive learning environment for students with AD:

- Provide visual aids such as schedules, maps, signs, charts, and lists.
- Develop task organizers that can be reviewed prior to lectures.

- Use precise, clear language to minimize confusion.
- Have clear expectations for the student and rehearse desired behaviors if necessary.
- Be certain you have the student's attention before beginning the lecture.
- Be consistent when giving directions.

Introducing information prior to its use in a lecture (priming) is very helpful to students with AD. It makes the material more familiar and less anxiety provoking and increases the likelihood that the student will be successful (Myles & Simpson, 2003). Priming can be done by the student's parent at home the evening before the material is to be presented in class. Alternatively, the teacher, an aide, or a trusted peer can go over the material with the student the day or morning before the lecture. Using the actual textbook or worksheet is recommended, but a description of the activity can also be helpful (Myles & Simpson, 2003).

Modifying assignments is also required for many students with AD. Because they have trouble with handwriting, have slower processing, and can usually demonstrate competency with fewer repetitions, it is best practice to match the length of the assignment to the amount of time the student would spend on it (Myles & Simpson, 2003). Lengthy writing assignments are especially well suited to alternative assignments such as conducting and recording interviews; creating art work, journaling, or writing songs; developing presentations using computer skills; or creating timelines. While some students with AD enjoy reading, particularly non-fiction books about their topic of interest, others are laborious readers. Long reading assignments can be difficult, and students with AD may lack motivation. Providing study guides, identifying the most important aspects of the reading, and providing models of assignments are helpful interventions (Myles & Simpson, 2003).

Motivating students to work can be difficult, but this is especially true for students with AD. They frequently refuse to complete a task if it does not make sense to them. Providing a rationale for completing the assignment, assuring the student that everyone else is working on the assignment, or relating the assignment to the student's area of interest should prove helpful (Myles & Simpson, 2003). Another method of motivation is based on the Premack principle in which the student must complete one assignment before engaging in another more enjoyable task. Working on assignments with a peer or in a small group can also be motivating for the student with AD. If these techniques are not successful, the teacher should attempt to determine the reason the student is balking at the assignment. In some cases, the format of the assignment (e.g., long writing or reading assignments) may need to be modified (Myles & Simpson, 2003).

SOCIAL

Much has been written about the need for social skills training for children with AD. Developing social skills, including awareness of social cues, is especially important given the complexity of the school setting (Jordan, 2003). Students with AD will need to be taught the skills required for successfully navigating the confusing world into which they walk every day. Problems with social interactions are compounded by the difficulties students with AD have using and interpreting nonverbal language. They have difficulty reading facial expressions and understanding the significance of tone of voice (Mesibov et al., 2001). Teachers, parents, and other students often make faulty assumptions regarding the facial expressions worn by students with AD. Teachers and others should not assume that they know how students with AD feel simply by observing their body language.

In addition to informing students about the rules and regulations of the school setting, students need to be told of the hidden curriculum of the school. Examples of the hidden curriculum include learning which students to avoid, how to respond to sarcasm from teachers or peers, how to behave in a fire drill, when to ask questions or make comments, or what to do if a peer asks you to do something that could get you in trouble (Myles & Simpson, 2003). Some schools have found it helpful to set up buddy systems for students with AD in which they are paired with another student who is patient and behaves appropriately. Circle of Friends groups are also used to help students with AD get to know peers who are helpful, supportive, and serve as good role models (Jordan, 2003). Two books, in particular, offer curricula for small-group instruction that can be adapted to the individual: *Navigating the Social World* (McAfee, 2002) and *Social Skills Training* (Baker, 2003). Comic strip conversations and social stories (Gray, 1995) can be useful tools for developing scripts for social interactions.

SUMMARY

In this chapter, we have described the neurological deficits most frequently found in individuals diagnosed with AD, the mildest form of autism spectrum disorders. Although these deficits are quite mild when compared to those of children with autism, children with AD stand out from TD children in the classroom. Their difficulties with social interaction, pragmatic language, and adherence to routines can be challenging to teachers and other students. We have suggested a number of assessment instruments that can be used to evaluate these students' strengths and weaknesses and offered a number of recommendations for intervening with them in the classroom. By building on their strengths and remediating or accommodating their weaknesses, students with AD can be among the best and brightest in the classroom.

REFERENCES

Ambery, F. Z., Russell, A. J., Perry, K., Morris, R., & Murphy, D. G. M. (2006). Neuropsychological functioning of adults with Asperger syndrome. *Autism, 10,* 551–564.

American Psychiatric Association. (2000). *Diagnostic and statistical manual of mental disorders* (4th ed., text revision). Washington, DC: Author.

Baker, J. E. (2003). *Social skills training for children and adolescents with Asperger syndrome and social-communication problems.* Shawnee Mission, KS: Autism Asperger Publishing Company.

Beery, K. E., Buktenica, N. A., & Beery, N. A. (2003). *Beery-Buktenica Developmental Test of Visual-Motor Integration* (5th ed.). Minneapolis, MN: Pearson Assessments.

Berndt, D. J., & Kaiser, C. F. (1996). *Multiscore depression inventory for children.* Los Angeles: Western Psychological Services.

Blakemore, S. J., Tavassoli, T., Calo, S., Thomas, R. M., Catmur, C., Frith, U., et al. (2006). Tactile sensitivity in Asperger syndrome. *Brain and Cognition, 61,* 5–13.

Bolick, T. (2001). *Asperger syndrome and adolescents. Helping preteens and teens get ready for the real world.* Gloucester, MA: Fair Winds Press.

Bowler, D. M., Matthews, N. J., & Gardiner, J. M. (1997). Asperger's syndrome and memory: Similarity to autism but not amnesia. *Neuropsychologia, 35,* 65–70.

Brown, T. E. (2001). *Brown attention-deficit disorder scales for children and adolescents.* San Antonio, TX: Harcourt Assessment.

Campbell, J. M. (2005). Diagnostic assessment of Asperger's disorder: A review of five third-party rating scales. *Journal of Autism and Developmental Disorders, 35,* 25–35.

Carrow-Woolfolk, E. (1999). *Comprehensive assessment of spoken language.* Circle Pines, MN: American Guidance Service Publishing.

Chiang, H. M., & Lin, Y. H. (2007). Mathematical ability of students with Asperger syndrome and high-functioning autism. *Autism, 11,* 547–556.

Church, C., Alisanski, S., & Amanullah, S. (2000). The social, behavioral, and academic experiences of children with Asperger syndrome. *Focus on Autism and Other Developmental Disabilities, 15,* 12–20.

Cohen, M. J. (1997). *Children's memory scale.* San Antonio, TX: Harcourt Assessment.

Conners, C. K. (2008a). *Conners comprehensive behavior rating scales* (3rd ed.). North Tonawanda, NY: Multi-Health Systems.

Conners, C. K. (2008b). *Conners rating scales* (3rd ed.). North Tonawanda, NY: Multi-Health Systems.

Dean, R. S., & Woodcock, R. W. (2003). *Dean-Woodcock neuropsychological battery.* Itasca, IL: Riverside Publishing.

Delis, D., Kaplan, E., & Kramer, J. H. (2001). *Delis-Kaplan executive function system examiner's manual.* San Antonio, TX: Harcourt Assessment.

Dunn, W. (1999). *Sensory profile.* San Antonio, TX: Harcourt Assessment.

Dunn, W., Myles, B. S., & Orr, S. (2002). Sensory processing issues associated with Asperger syndrome: A preliminary investigation. *American Journal of Occupational Therapy, 56,* 97–102.

Edgin, J. O., & Pennington, B. F. (2005). Spatial cognition in autism spectrum disorders: Superior, impaired, or just intact? *Journal of Autism and Developmental Disorders, 35*, 729–745.

Ghaziuddin, M., & Butler, E. (1998). Clumsiness in autism and Asperger syndrome: A further report. *Journal of Intellectual Disability Research, 42*, 43–48.

Ghaziuddin, M., Butler, E., Tsai, L., & Ghaziuddin, N. (1994). Is clumsiness a marker for Asperger syndrome? *Journal of Intellectual Disability Research, 38*, 519–527.

Ghaziuddin, M., & Gerstein, L. (1996). Pedantic speaking style differentiates Asperger syndrome from high-functioning autism. *Journal of Autism and Developmental Disorders, 26*, 585–595.

Ghaziuddin, M., Weidmer-Mikhail, E., & Ghaziuddin, N. (1998). Comorbidity of Asperger syndrome: A preliminary report. *Journal of Intellectual Disability Research, 42*, 279–283.

Gillberg, C., & Billstedt, E. (2000). Autism and Asperger syndrome: Coexistence with other clinical disorders. *Acta Psychiatrica Scandinavica, 102*, 321–330.

Gillberg, C., & Ehlers, G. (1998). High-functioning people with autism and Asperger syndrome: A literature review. In E. Schopler & G. B. Mesibov (Eds.), *Asperger syndrome or high-functioning autism?* (pp. 79–106). New York: Plenum.

Gilliam, J. E. (2001). *Gilliam Asperger's disorder scale.* Austin, TX: Pro-Ed.

Gioia, G. A., Isquith, P. K., Guy, S. C., & Kenworthy, L. (2000). *Behavior rating inventory of executive function professional manual.* Odessa, FL: Psychological Assessment Resources.

Gray, C. (1995). *Social stories unlimited: Social stories, comic strip conversations, and related instructional techniques.* Jenison, MI: Jenison Public Schools.

Greenberg, L. M. (1996). *Test of variables of attention.* Los Alamitos, CA: Universal Attention Disorders

Griswold, D. E., Barnhill, G. P., Myles, B. S., Hagiwara, T., & Simpson, R. L. (2002). Asperger syndrome and academic achievement. *Focus on Autism and Other Developmental Disabilities, 17*, 94–102.

Happe, F., Booth, R., Charlton, R., & Hughes, C. (2006). Executive function deficits in autism spectrum disorders and attention-deficit/hyperactivity disorder: Examining profiles across domains and ages. *Brain and Cognition, 6*, 25–39.

Heaton, R. K., Chelune, G. J., Talley, J. L., Kay, G., & Curtiss, G. (1993). *Wisconsin card sorting test manual.* Odessa, FL: Psychological Assessment Resources.

Hill, E. L. (2004). Evaluating the theory of executive dysfunction in autism. *Developmental Review, 24*, 189–233.

Hill, R. L., Pierce, R. A., Rogers, S. J., & Wehner, B. (2001). Predictors of treatment outcomes in young children with autism. *Autism, 15*, 407–429.

Jolliffe, T, & Baron-Cohen, S. (1997). Are people with autism and Asperger syndrome faster than normal on the Embedded Figures Test? *Journal of Child Psychology and Psychiatry, 38*, 527–534.

Jordan, R. (2003). School-based interventions for children with specific learning disabilities. In M. Prior (Ed.), *Learning and behavior problems in Asperger syndrome* (pp. 212–243). New York: Guilford.

Kamio, Y., & Toichi, M. (2007). Memory illusion in high-functioning autism and Asperger's disorder. *Journal of Autism and Developmental Disabilities, 37*, 867–876.

Kaufman, A. S., & Kaufman, N. L. (2004). *Kaufman assessment battery for children* (2nd ed.). Circle Pines, MN: American Guidance Service Publishing.

Kaufman, A. S., & Kaufman, N. L. (2005). *Kaufman test of educational achievement* (2nd ed.). Circle Pines, MN: American Guidance Service Publishing.

Kim, J. A., Szatmari, P., Bryson, S. E., Streiner, D. L., & Wilson, F. J. (2000). The prevalence of anxiety and mood problems among children with autism and Asperger syndrome. *Autism, 4*, 117–132.

Korkman, M., Kirk, U., & Kemp, S. (2007). *NEPSY-II: A developmental neuropsychological assessment*. San Antonio, TX: The Psychological Corporation.

Kovacs, M. (2003). *Children's depression inventory*. North Tonawanda, NY: Multi-Health Systems.

Koyama, T., Tachimori, H., Osada, H., Takeda, T., & Kurita, H. (2007). Cognitive and symptom profiles in Asperger's syndrome and high-functioning autism. *Psychiatry & Clinical Neurosciences, 61*, 99–104.

Krug, D. A., & Arick, J. R. (2003). *Krug Asperger's disorder index*. Austin, TX: Pro-Ed.

Lee, D. O., & Ousley, O. Y. (2006). Attention-deficit hyperactivity disorder symptoms in a clinic sample of children and adolescents with pervasive developmental disorders. *Journal of Child and Adolescent Psychopharmacology, 16*, 737–746.

Lezak, M. D., Howieson, D. B., & Loring, D. W. (2004). *Neuropsychological assessment* (4th ed.). New York: Oxford.

Lord, C., Rutter, M., DiLavore, P., & Risi, S. (2000). *Autism diagnostic observation schedule*. Los Angeles: Western Psychological Services.

Macintosh, K. E., & Dissanayake, C. (2004). Annotation: The similarities and differences between autistic disorder and Asperger's disorder: A review of the empirical evidence. *Journal of Child Psychology and Psychiatry, 45*, 421–434.

Manjiovina, J., & Prior, M. (1995). Comparison of Asperger syndrome and high-functioning autistic children on a test of motor impairment. *Journal of Autism and Developmental Disorders, 25*, 23–39.

Manly, T., Robertson, I. H., Anderson, V., & Nimmo-Smith, I. (1999). *Test of everyday attention for children*. San Antonio, TX: Harcourt Assessment.

March, J. S. (1999). *Multidimensional anxiety scale for children*. North Tonawanda, NY: Multi-Health Systems.

McAfee, J. (2002). *Navigating the social world*. Arlington, TX: Future Horizons.

McAlononan, G. M., Daly, E., Kumari, V., Critchley, H. D., van Amelsvoort, T., Suckling, J., et al. (2002). Brain anatomy and sensorimotor gating in Asperger syndrome. *Brain, 127*, 1594–1606.

McCrory, E., Henry, L. A., & Happe, F. (2007). Eyewitness memory and suggestibility in children with Asperger syndrome. *Journal of Child and Adolescent Psychiatry, 48*, 482–489.

Mesibov, G. B., Shea, V., & Adams, L. W. (2001). *Understanding Asperger syndrome and high functioning autism*. New York: Kluwer Academic.

Miller, D. C. (2007). *Essentials of school neuropsychological assessment*. Hoboken, NJ: John Wiley & Sons.

Mitchell, P., & Ropar, F. (2004). Visual-spatial abilities in autism: A review. *Infant and Child Development, 13*, 185–198.

Myles, B. S., Bock, S. J., & Simpson, R. L. (2001). *Asperger syndrome diagnostic scale.* Austin, TX: Pro-Ed.

Myles, B. S., Hilgenfeld, T. D., Barnhill, G. P., Griswold, D. E., Hagiwara, T., & Simpson, R. L. (2002). Analysis of reading skills in individuals with Asperger syndrome. *Focus on Autism and Other Developmental Disabilities, 17*, 44–47.

Myles, B. S., Huggins, A., Rome-Lake, M., Hagiwara, T., Barnhill, G. P., & Griswold, D. E. (2003). Written language profiles of children and youth with Asperger syndrome: From research to practice. *Education and Training in Developmental Disabilities, 38*, 362–369.

Myles, B. S., & Simpson, R. L. (2003). *Asperger syndrome. A. guide for educators and parents* (2nd ed.). Austin, TX: Pro-Ed.

Nation, K., Clarke, P., Wright, B., & Williams, C. (2006). Patterns of reading ability in children with autism spectrum disorder. *Journal of Autism and Developmental Disorders, 36*, 911–919.

Ozonoff, S., & Strayer, D. L. (1997). Inhibitory function in nonretarded children with autism. *Journal of Autism and Developmental Disabilities, 27*, 59–77.

Pennington, B. F., & Ozonoff, S. (1996). Executive functions and developmental psychopathology. *Journal of Child Psychology and Psychiatry, 37*, 51–87.

Pfeiffer, B., Kinnealy, M., Reed, C., & Herzberg, G. (2005). Sensory modulation and affective disorders in children and adolescents with Asperger's disorder. *American Journal of Occupational Therapy, 59*, 335–345.

Phelps-Terasaki, D., & Phelps-Gunn, T. (2007). *Test of pragmatic language* (2nd ed.). Austin, TX: Pro-Ed.

Piers, E. V., Harris, D. B., & Herzberg, D. S. (2002). *Piers-Harris Children's self-concept scale* (2nd ed.). Los Angeles: Western Psychological Services.

Ramberg, C., Ehlers, S., Nyden, A., Johansson, M., & Gillberg, C. (1996). Language in addition, pragmatic functions in school-age children on the autism spectrum. *European Journal of Disorders of Communication, 31*, 387–413.

Reitzel, J., & Szatmari, P. (2003). Cognitive and academic problems. In M. Prior (Ed.), *Learning and behavior problems in Asperger syndrome* (pp. 35–54). New York: Guilford.

Reynolds, C. R., & Kamphaus, R. W. (2004). *Behavior assessment system for children* (2nd ed.). Circle Pines, MN: American Guidance Service Publishing.

Reynolds, C. R., & Richmond, B. O. (1998). *Revised children's manifest anxiety scale* (2nd ed.). Los Angeles: Western Psychological Services.

Reynolds, C. R., & Voress, J. K. (2007). *Test of memory and learning* (2nd ed.). Lutz, FL: PAR.

Roid, G. H. (2003). *Stanford-Binet intelligence scales* (5th ed.). Itasca, IL: Riverside Publishing.

Rutherford, M. D., Richards, E. D., Moldes, V., & Sekuler, A. B. (2007). Evidence of a divided attention advantage in autism. *Cognitive Neuropsychology, 24*, 505–515.

Rutter, M., Le Couteur, A., & Lord, C. (2003). *ADI-R: Autism diagnostic interview, revised.* Los Angeles: Western Psychological Services.

Sandford, J. A., & Turner, A. (1993–2006). *Integrated visual and auditory continuous performance test.* Richmond, VA: BrainTrain.

Seung, H. K. (2007). Linguistic characteristics of individuals with high functioning autism and Asperger's syndrome. *Clinical linguistics and phonetics, 21,* 247–259.

Sheslow, D., & Adams, W. (2003). *Wide range assessment of memory and learning* (2nd ed.). Wilmington, DE: Wide Range.

Sturm, H., Fernell, E., & Gillberg, C. (2004). Autism spectrum disorders in children with normal intellectual levels: Associated impairments and subgroups. *Developmental Medicine and Child Neurology, 46,* 444–447.

Suzuki, Y., Critchley, H. D., Rowe, A., Howlin, P., & Murphy, D. G. M. (2003). Impaired olfactory identification in Asperger's syndrome. *Journal of Neuropsychiatry and Clinical Neurosciences, 15,* 105–107.

Szatmari, P., Bremner, R., & Nagy, J. (1989). Asperger's syndrome: A review of clinical features. *Canadian Journal of Psychiatry, 34,* 554–560.

Wechsler, D. (2001). *Wechsler individual achievement test* (2nd ed.). San Antonio, TX: Harcourt Assessment.

Wechsler, D. (2003). *Wechsler intelligence scale for children* (4th ed.). San Antonio, TX: Harcourt Assessment.

Wing, L. (1981). Asperger's syndrome: A clinical account. *Psychological Medicine, 11,* 115–129.

Woodcock, R. W., McGrew, K. S., & Mather, N. (2001a). *Woodcock-Johnson III tests of cognitive abilities.* Itasca, IL: Riverside Publishing.

Woodcock, R. W., McGrew, K. S., & Mather, N. (2001b). *Woodcock-Johnson III tests of achievement.* Itasca, IL: Riverside Publishing.

Zager, D., & Shamow, N. (2005). Teaching students with autism spectrum disorders. In D. Zager (Ed.), *Autism spectrum disorders. Identification, education, and treatment* (3rd ed., pp. 296–326). Mahway, NJ: Lawrence Erlbaum Associates.

CHAPTER 14

Assessing and Intervening with Children with Developmental Delays

CRISTIN DOOLEY

W ITH THE 1975 congressional passing of P.L. 94–142, states were required to provide a free and appropriate public education to all children identified as having a disability. If public schools were to receive federal funding for educational programs, they were then expected to offer services to children with handicapping conditions. This was later expanded through the 1986 passing of P.L. 99–457, in which services were also federally granted to preschool children who were identified as having a disability (components of which additionally included the Handicapped Infants and Toddler Program). The establishment of these laws, along with the reauthorized Individuals with Disabilities Education Improvement Act (IDEA) in 2004 and the No Child Left Behind Act (NCLB) in 2001 made it increasingly clear that screening for and identification of early developmental delay was crucial.

DEFINITIONS OF DEVELOPMENTAL DELAYS

The concept of developmental delay is rather multifaceted. The more traditional categorical descriptions for a child with a disability were defined by IDEA as the following:

- Autism
- Deaf-Blindness
- Deafness
- Emotional disturbance
- Hearing impairment

- Mental retardation
- Multiple disabilities
- Other health impairment
- Orthopedic impairment
- Specific learning disability
- Speech or language impairment
- Traumatic brain injury
- Visual impairment (including blindness)

These categorical descriptions, however, were not always well received by early childhood educators and service providers (Snyder, Bailey, & Auer, 1994). It was thought premature to "label" a child with such a disability before he or she ever attended a kindergarten classroom. For example, the idea of describing a 3-year-old preschool student as having a learning disability or an emotional disturbance might be considered untimely or "premature." This 3-year-old student might never have previously attended any type of school or daycare setting where structured activities or routines were expected. Additionally, research would suggest that this 3-year-old student did not yet have a "stable" intelligence quotient (Alfonso & Flanagan, 1992) to compare with academic performance for patterns of a recognized learning difference. Last, many clinicians would be hesitant to definitively diagnose this 3-year-old student with depression and/or anxiety, but would preferably use such descriptors as regulatory disorders or multisystem developmental disorders (Zero to Three, 2005) until later clarification could be made.

EARLY IDENTIFICATION ISSUES

In addition to the difficulty in describing early delay, Lifter (1999) indicated that controversy existed over the concept of educational need—in the sense that along with a categorical description, there needed to be proof that a child's educational performance was "adversely affected." This has traditionally been the practice of identifying students for special education services within the public schools in that not only must there be a qualifying eligibility, but also a demonstrated need for support services. Formulating evidence of educational need for the preschool-aged child without a history of school performance would therefore be significantly difficult, if not impossible.

Instead, federal regulations guided states to use the term "developmental delay" or incorporate a "non-categorical eligibility" to account for the inherent difficulty in "labeling" young children. Support services would be offered to children with suspected developmental delay in one or more of the following areas: physical, cognitive, communicative, social/emotional and/or adaptive development (Brassard & Boehm, 2007). Federal law allowed for both types of descriptors, categorical and non-categorical, to be used in identifying young children with disabilities through the age of 9 years (Lifter, 1999). It was ultimately, however, left to the discretion of the state and local education agency (Brassard & Boehm, 2007) as to how they wished to identify children with special needs within this age group.

Derrington and Lippitt (2008) explained that due to this flexibility in early identification for states, as allowed through IDEA, children receive services based upon "clinical opinion, biological risk factors, and/or environmental risk factors." Determining the percentages of children identified with developmental delay was rather difficult due to the varying definitions (Derrington & Lippitt, 2008). However, much of the current research in early assessment procedures has stressed the importance of linking the identified eligibility with instructional needs (Brassard & Boehm, 2007). For example, a child can be identified with a developmental delay in speech and language, but must also have an individual education plan to address those noted difficulties within the classroom setting.

Assessing or screening for developmental delay is somewhat complicated by the inherent nature of a developmental continuum. Although there are milestones to accomplish and concepts to master, which formally originated in Arnold Gessell's initial "developmental schedule" of 150 items (Nuttall, Nuttall-Vasquez, & Hampel, 1999), these steps of mastery can have broad expected age ranges and do not always appear linear. For example, it may be assumed that a child will vocalize his or her first words anywhere between the ages of 10 to 15 months (Edwards, 1999), but there may be qualitative differences in the acquisition of that developmental skill, and/or there may also be qualitative differences in how "delay" is determined outside the expected or "typically developing" age range. For instance, a child may have demonstrated initial speech and language delay and then began to speak in two-word sentences, skipping over the traditional milestone of one-word phrasing.

The majority of early childhood intervention programs have generally qualified children for programming services based upon a three- to six-month "delay" range (dependent upon state definitions). This means that a child who is not vocalizing words by the age of 18 months would typically qualify for support in the area of speech and language. Children in these early intervention programs (including Head Start and state pre-kindergarten classes) have shown improvement in both intellectual and social performance, but then have a tendency to lose those early gains during later primary grades (Brassard & Boehm, 2007). However, other research has shown later benefits in decreased grade retention and decreased enrollment in special education programs, lower rates of dropout from school, and lower overall "delinquency" (Berrueta-Clement, Schweinhart, Barnett, Epstein, & Weikart, 1984; Lazar & Darlington, 1982; Schweinhart & Weikart, 1998).

Global developmental delay has been identified as the most common subtype of childhood developmental disability (Shevell, Majnemer, Platt, Webster, & Birnbaum, 2005), perhaps due to the flexibility in diagnosis and the tendency to "defer diagnosis" for those young children with an unclear etiology (Brassard & Boehm, 2007). Global developmental delay typically entails the identification of significant delay in two or more areas, and children receiving support services with this eligibility seem to have "persistent significant difficulties at school age, in both developmental and functional outcomes" (Shevell et al., 2005).

Most modern clinicians accept that the previous epistemological philosophies of Locke and Hume, where an individual begins life as "tabula rasa," does not fully explain the transactional processes that take place between a person and his/her environment (Sameroff, 1993). When considering early identification and screening for delay, especially as it pertains to a neuropsychological perspective, it is important to consider a more transactional or interactionist approach, where an individual's actions affect an active environment and vice versa (Sameroff, 1993). For instance:

> There is no logical possibility of considering development of an individual independently of the environment. Continuity cannot be explained as a characteristic of the child, because each new achievement is an amalgam of characteristics of the child and his or her experience. Neither alone is predictive of later levels of functioning. If continuities are found, it is because there is continuity in the relationship between the child and the environment, not because of continuities in either taken alone. (Sameroff, 1993, p. 5)

COMPETENCY-BASED PERFORMANCE MONITORING

In addition to the current laws advocating for increased or expanded services to young children and the type of descriptor used for handicapping conditions, there are also national trends shaping school curriculum that rely on "standards-based curricula, prescribed instructional approaches, and standardized testing for younger and younger children" (Litty & Hatch, 2006). The NCLB legislation of 2001 has mandated annual assessments for children in grades 3 through 8, using scientifically based or research-based instruction. These accountability measures (supported through national, state, and local governing boards) have posed some distress for teachers and school administrators who have to sometimes accommodate severely delayed children who do not necessarily meet the minimal academic expectations. Litty and Hatch explained that these current expectations, especially for young children, have become much more stringent in recent years. For example, "Five-year-olds are now assumed to have already acquired social understandings and capacities that used to comprise a central place in the kindergarten curriculum" (Litty & Hatch, 2006). Brassard and Boehm (2007) similarly explain that there is a perceived trend of "pushing academic activities typical of first grade down to younger and younger children" (p. 173).

Accountability testing designated by state laws (e.g., the Texas Assessment of Knowledge and Skills, or TAKS, the Academic Performance Index in California) have expanded to include otherwise "untouched" grade levels. For example, the Texas Education Agency has recently determined that school districts within the state will begin to more strategically measure demonstrated improvement for preschool children who have individual education plans (IEPs). Improvement is measured by determining the child's functioning levels at "entry" into the special education program and at his or her "exit" from early childhood services. Improvement is ideally attained in social-emotional development, knowledge/skill set, and behavior. This data is being used to determine the efficacy of early childhood programs.

Trends in educational policy and current research (the benefits for early intervention) seem to therefore support the need for early identification of developmental delay (regardless of how it is defined). Perspectives from neuropsychology or school neuropsychology seem to correlate nicely with the early identification of developmental concerns—the focus on processes related to skill acquisition and an understanding of subtle deficits related to relative weaknesses. The identification of developmental dysfunction should support interventions and programming that have ecological validity within the school, daycare, or home setting.

THE RELEVANCE OF NEUROPSYCHOLOGICAL PROCESSES

A young child's behavior is unquestionably variable daily, so most clinicians stress the importance of assessing "patterns" over time as well as interpreting developmental outcomes in relationship to all other skill areas (Brassard & Boehm, 2007). For example, a noticed deficit in communication would be interpreted within the context of social, emotional/behavioral, and cognitive domains. There should be an examination of the "vertical" or "nomothetic" and horizontal or "idiographic" developmental variations of each skill (Hale & Fiorello, 2004). These examinations should also place greater emphasis on *understanding* the deficit rather than describing the "localized brain damage" that is thought to cause the particular deficit (Hale & Fiorello, 2004). Current practice within school neuropsychology, including the early assessment of developmental delay, would stress the importance of everyday functioning and "prescriptive recommendations," rather than "diagnostic conclusions" (Miller, 2007). Both school neuropsychological and developmental evaluations have evolved to stressing this concept of "ecological validity."

Neuropsychological assessment of the young child, especially as it pertains to the identification of developmental delay, must consider this "interplay between development, recovery of function, and environmental influences" (Aylward, 1997). Aylward stressed that even though the idea of developmental delay has traditionally implied that a child will "catch up" over time, this concept may be somewhat inaccurate. Instead, the identification of dysfunction "could be related to (1) a maturational delay, (2) neural dysfunction, (3) motor deficits, or (4) the influence of variables external to the infant or young child." Aylward additionally explained that conducting an assessment for a young child is similar to "shooting at a moving target" in the sense that accuracy is determined by the "size of the target" and "when the shot is fired." For example, Aylward provided an example of ataxia (significant difficulty with coordination of movement), explaining that the identification of this disorder is usually not apparent until after the young child begins to walk. This is considered an "age-related manifestation," where deficits in skill become more noticeable as the child grows and develops (Aylward, 1997). Therefore, the timing of a developmental evaluation is of importance and should always be considered by the clinician.

Some of the basic concepts and theories related to school neuropsychology involve an understanding of subtle processing deficits. Miller (2007) explained that school neuropsychology is defined by the (1) integration of neuropsychological and educational principles, (2) the incorporated assessment and intervention processes, (3) the facilitated learning and behavior within the school and family system, and (4) the importance in determining optimal learning environments. The school neuropsychological assessment, as it has been explained in previous chapters within this book, relies upon the identification of processes related to (1) sensory-motor functions, (2) attention functions, (3) visual-spatial functions, (4) language functions, (5) memory and learning functions, (6) executive functions, (7) speed and efficiency of cognitive processing, (8) general cognitive abilities, (9) academic achievement, and (10) social-emotional functions. These same processes are involved in the identification of developmental delay for young children, although the clinician will want to take into account the variable developmental continuum, the controversial nature of identifying disability within the first five years of life, and the demonstrated need in relating eligibility for support services to individual classroom instruction. The only difference may be that the processes that are typically involved within a school neuropsychological evaluation may commingle in respect to early development, in that one process is often interchangeable from the other.

Within the remainder of this chapter, which describes the intricacies of developmental assessment or neurocognitive deficits associated with developmental delay, the neuropsychological processes may be combined for better effect. For example, although attention and executive function skills are often thought to be related, but usually discussed separately in evaluations for school-aged children or adolescents, the foundation of these skills within an early developmental assessment are, many times, indistinguishable. However, the relationship or "risk factors" between these processes can still be identified at an early age. The "art" in developmental assessment is using the available science to more fully explain established neuropsychological processes to functional applications. There is a growing need for this in terms of both early evaluation and early intervention. Singer (2001) explained that "societal concern for and public health focus on the growing numbers of high-risk infants have contributed to an interest in developing assessments of brain-behavior relationships that can be used as early in life as possible" (p. 11).

THE ASSESSMENT OF DEVELOPMENTAL DELAY USING A NEUROPSYCHOLOGICAL PERSPECTIVE: COMPONENTS OF A SCHOOL NEUROPSYCHOLOGICAL EVALUATION

IMPORTANCE OF A DEVELOPMENTAL HISTORY (INCLUDING HEALTH AND EDUCATIONAL BACKGROUND)

Although all thorough psychological or school neuropsychological evaluations contain a developmental and/or medical history, the importance of this within an evaluation for a preschool-aged child cannot be overly stressed. There must be consideration of prenatal, perinatal, and postnatal experience, along with acknowledgment of the number of days the child remained in the hospital after birth. Aylward (1997) explained that this factor of "days in the hospital" post-delivery is perhaps the "best gross measure of medical risk" and somewhat "analogous to using maternal education as a measure of the environment."

The developmental history should also contain a description of early developmental skill acquisition (from the first month to the age at the time of the evaluation). Medical history should be accounted for, which includes any use of medications (both past and present). In addition, all pertinent sociological information (e.g., "makeup" of the family, living arrangements, second language issues, multicultural factors) should be addressed. Kalesnik (1999) explained that the developmental history helps to establish contact with the child's primary caregivers early in the evaluation process, provides background clues on current functioning and developmental status, guides evaluators in choosing appropriate test measurements, provides a "broader and more meaningful context," and "guides the formulation of recommendations and action plans." It is essentially the foundation of the assessment process and often provides clarification with later data interpretation. It should also be noted that in many instances, parental concerns about their child's development have been highly correlated to results from developmental screening (Glascoe, 1997). It would therefore seem reasonable that parent concerns should be addressed within the developmental history section of a report assessing for delay.

As there is much ambiguity in the definition of what constitutes developmental delay (described earlier within this chapter), there are a variety of risk factors that should play into the overall evaluation process of early childhood. Brassard and Boehm (2007) indicated a list of possible considerations when interpreting "early risk" that ultimately pertain to the child, the family, the school or childcare setting, and the community. Some of these factors are provided below.

- Risk factors related specifically to the child:
  - Low birth weight or prematurity
  - Biological risk factors (e.g., exposure to harmful events during the prenatal, perinatal, and/or postnatal periods)
  - Poor prenatal care
  - Previous medical diagnoses
  - Malnutrition
  - Temperament (difficulty with regulatory processes)
  - Poor peer relationships
  - Difficulty with cognitive tasks
  - History of family mental illness
  - Need for remedial education (e.g., previous referral to early childhood intervention program)
- Risk factors related specifically to the family:
  - Exposure to child maltreatment
  - Lower maternal educational level
  - Poverty
  - Disorganized routines
  - High degree of family mobility
  - Birth spacing less than two years
  - Unlimited television watching
- Risk factors related specifically to the school or childcare setting:
  - Rigid or skill-focused curriculum
  - Less opportunity to interact with other children
  - Retention during early years
- Risk factors related specifically to the community:
  - Social isolation
  - Violence frequently observed
  - Few community supports for families

IMPORTANCE OF ADMINISTRATOR FLEXIBILITY

When describing "best practices" in assessing early developmental delay, it is necessary to discuss the importance of being flexible with test administration—not to a point where standardization is compromised (even though at times, "testing of limits," may be justified), but to allow for the inherent complications that arise with the early childhood population. For example, Hale and Fiorello (2004) discuss the need to "maintain rapport while moving quickly through measures, keeping the child engaged and interested in the test materials." They also explain the importance of remembering developmental trajectories when interpreting data (being flexible as to how typical development relates to interpretation), providing an example that young children will often demonstrate articulation errors or pronoun reversals that are not necessarily related to signs of pathology (Hale & Fiorello, 2004).

An early childhood assessor needs to be aware of possible distracters within the testing environment and be open to alternative methods of sustaining the child's attention (e.g., providing "play time" between a designated number of tasks, removing extraneous materials within the room that are not a part of test administration). These variations or accommodations to the evaluation process should, of course, be noted within the subsequent assessment report.

Other aspects to consider within the evaluation of developmental delay are listed below (Brassard & Boehm, 2007).

- The child may demonstrate possible difficulty when separating from the parent or caregiver.
- The child may have a lower tolerance for frustration (which could be compounded by language difficulties and an inability to express emotions).
- There may be variances within the preschool or structured daycare setting (which could affect the reaction or familiarity to test administration).
- The child's physical well-being may be compromised (e.g., hunger and fatigue), which may affect the younger child more than an older child, in the sense that coping skills are not yet as refined.

IMPORTANCE OF QUALITATIVE DATA TO AID INTERPRETATION

Qualitative data is interrelated to quantitative data in the process of assessing for developmental delay—and both are essential to establishing a clinical conclusion and ultimate ecological validity (Lezak, 1995). Miller (2007) refers to the inclusion of qualitative data as part of a "broader process assessment approach." This would include test authors' providing opportunities for assessors to note how a child uses particular strategies and techniques to solve a specific problem. For example, on the NEPSY-II subtest of Affect Recognition (administered to children between the ages of 3 and 16 years), the evaluator is given the opportunity to note how many times a child spontaneously makes comments during the administration. The NEPSY-II even allows for behavioral observations made during the evaluation process to be "quantified and compared to the frequency with which those behaviors were present in the normative and clinical samples" (Korkman, Kirk, & Kemp, 2007).

These types of observations further help to clarify a child's difficulty, or what Lezak, Howieson, and Loring (2004) refer to as diagnostic discrimination, requiring differential diagnosis from a broad range of disorders that may involve variables not always noticeable to a "naïve observer" or revealed through standard questionnaires. These qualitative observations typically include behaviors that seem atypical from the majority of responses and then those behaviors that are not necessarily atypical, but that have a "quality of uniqueness" (Lezak, Howieson, & Loring, 2004).

In addition, when assessing aspects of gross and fine motor functioning within an early childhood evaluation (which is extremely common as part of a full battery), the school neuropsychologist evaluating developmental delay could note qualitative aspects of motor functioning (e.g., muscle tone). Although the clinician should always be sensitive to not overstepping diagnostic boundaries (e.g., physical or neurological diagnoses), the qualitative notation of gait or movement can be helpful in the final analysis and relevance to ecological validity (Aylward, 1997). It is not uncommon for health clinics that serve populations of young children at risk (e.g., Low Birth Weight Clinic) to involve a multidisciplinary team in helping to distinguish the qualitative aspects of motor movement. For example, it may be difficult for the attending physician to note whether abnormal movements in a 3-year-old child are more related to spastic diplegia (bilateral lower extremity hypertonicity) or to spastic hemiplegia (hypertonicity on one side of the body). Differential diagnosis can sometimes be assisted through qualitative observations made during the developmental/neuropsychological examination (e.g., noted right-hand difficulty with drawing tasks or inability to complete certain gross motor activities).

POSSIBLE ASSESSMENT INSTRUMENTS TO INCORPORATE INTO A DEVELOPMENTAL EVALUATION WITH A SCHOOL NEUROPSYCHOLOGICAL PERSPECTIVE

NEONATAL ASSESSMENT INSTRUMENTS

There has been an increase over the last several decades in being able to assess not only an infant's neurological status, but also his or her neuropsychological status. For example, Aylward (1997) explained that although initially clinicians were more focused on the presence of neonatal reflexes, more interest is now shown toward quality of movement or tone and behavioral components associated with infancy (e.g., postural control, orientation, habituation, temperament, and behavioral states). Some of the more known assessments in this area include the following:

- *Assessment of Preterm Infants' Behavior* (Als, Lester, Tronick, & Brazelton, 1982)
- *Brazelton Neonatal Behavioral Assessment Scale* (Brazelton & Nugent, 1995)
- *Neonatal Neurodevelopmental Examination* (Allen & Capute, 1989)
- *Neurobehavioral Assessment of the Preterm Infant* (Richardson et al., 1993)

There is a general consensus that the more "optimal" responses an infant displays (which will depend upon the infant's age), the better prognosis is then predicted (Aylward, 1997). However, neurodevelopmental examinations within the infancy period are usually best when there are repeated tests over time, rather than only a single assessment of comparison to a normative group.

Bayley Scales of Infant and Toddler Development, Third Edition (BSID-III)   The BSID-III was revised in 2006 with the third edition. It is an individually administered instrument that measures the developmental functioning of infants and young children between 1 month and 42 months of age. Its primary purpose is to identify children with developmental delay and provide information for educational programming (Bayley, 2006). The BSID-III contains three scales, which are administered directly to the child. This includes a Cognitive Scale, a Language Scale (which assesses for both receptive and expressive communication) and a Motor Scale (which assesses for both gross motor and fine motor ability). In addition, there is a Social-Emotional Questionnaire and an Adaptive Behavior Questionnaire—both of which are completed by the primary caregiver. Last, the BSID-III offers a cognitive growth chart, a gross motor growth chart, and a social-emotional growth chart, which offer visual representations of a child's relative progress over periodic testing (e.g., for continued follow-up in a health clinic or school setting).

The BSID-III provides an option for assessors who are evaluating the development of children born prematurely (under 37 weeks gestation) to use "an adjusted age" for the child when calculating standard scores for interpretation. The use of adjusted or corrected age for children born prematurely is common and is predominantly supported within the research literature. Siegel (1983) found that when the corrected age for prematurity was used during the first year of life, the infants' performance was significantly correlated with performance on cognitive assessments at three and 5 years of age. Similarly, Lems, Hopkins, and Samson (1993) reported that the majority of psychologists who use the BSID-II (earlier version) corrected for prematurity up to the age of two years. Hunt and Rhodes (1977) had previously recommended full correction of prematurity up to the age of two years within an influential report that appeared to set the standard for later practice. Currently, "best practices" would recommend reporting both the adjusted score and then also the uncorrected score (Brassard & Boehm, 2007).

Bayley Infant Neurodevelopmental Screener (BINS)   This screening instrument, which was designed in 1995 by Glen P. Aylward, uses items selected from the *Bayley Scales of Infant Development, 2nd Edition*. It can be administered to children between the ages of 3 months to 24 months. Results from the screening test classify the child's performance within a low-risk category, a medium-risk category, or a high-risk category. It is not considered to be a "smaller version" of the BSID-II, but instead emphasizes "a process approach by considering how an ability is expressed, rather than simply whether the ability is exhibited" (Aylward, 1997, p. 79). Administration time takes approximately 10 minutes and the overall cost of test materials seems both practical and effective for routine screening. Hess, Papas, and Black (2004) noted that the BINS may be a better measure of developmental delay for infants and children with biological risk (e.g., prematurity, low birth weight) as opposed to environmental risk (e.g., poverty, adolescent parent, etc.).

NEPSY-II   The NEPSY-II, recently revised, is a comprehensive individually administered instrument for children between the ages of 3 and 16 years that assesses overall neuropsychological development across six specific domains (Attention and Executive Functioning, Language, Memory and Learning, Sensorimotor, Social Perception, and Visuospatial Processing). Not only is this assessment instrument able to aid in understanding neuropsychological processes, it also stresses the importance of linking diagnostic information to programming and intervention decisions (Korkman et al., 2007). It is also one of the few instruments that very obviously addresses neuropsychological components for young children.

Temperament and Atypical Behavior Scale (TABS)   The TABS is completed by a child's parent/caregiver or a professional who has worked closely with the child and is able to comment on "daily behaviors" (Neisworth, Bagnato, Salvia, & Hunt, 1999). It is intended to measure dysfunctional behavior for children between the ages of 11 months and 71 months. It assists in identifying those children who are either already demonstrating atypical behavior or are at risk for demonstrating such behavior. Within the test manual,

Neisworth et al. explained that although many infants and preschool children do not qualify for early intervention or preschool services through public school, they may still exhibit certain difficulties in temperament and self-regulation that can later result in behavioral difficulties or delayed development without early intervention. This aspect of the assessment instrument seems to correlate nicely with neuropsychological processes of behavior in early childhood.

Other Assessment Instruments   There are certainly many other assessment instruments that can assist in formulating diagnosis and programming interventions for the early childhood age group (e.g., *Gesell Developmental Schedules* [Knobloch et al., 1980]; *Infant Mullen Scales of Early Learning* [Mullen, 1984]; *Stanford-Binet Intelligence Scale, 5th Edition* [Roid, 2003]; *Wechsler Preschool and Primary Scale of Intelligence, 3rd Edition,* [Wechsler, 2002]; *Woodcock Johnson Tests of Cognitive Ability, 3rd Edition* [Woodcock, McGrew, & Mather, 2001]; *Differential Ability Scales, 2nd Edition* [Elliott, 2007]; *Cognitive Assessment System* [Naglieri & Das, 1997], *Preschool Language Scale, 4th Edition,* [Zimmerman, Steiner, & Pond, 2002]), not all of which are necessarily considered assessment instruments for developmental delay, but again, do definitively measure aspects of development. The list can be quite exhaustive, all with relatively good to very good reliability and validity. There are also other screening measures commonly referenced within the literature and used within health clinics, pediatric offices, and hospitals that should be familiar to school psychologists. These might include the *Denver Developmental Screening Test, 2nd Edition* (Frankenburg, Dodds, Archer, Shapiro, & Bresnick, 1992) or the *Ages and Stages Questionnaire, 3rd Edition* (Squires, Twombly, Bricker, & Potter, 2009). The importance, however, when holistically formulating a depiction of a young child's functioning, should rely not upon one single test, but on an assortment of data. For the school neuropsychologist, that data should then be considered based upon the relationships between brain and behavior.

NEUROCOGNITIVE DEFICITS ASSOCIATED WITH DEVELOPMENTAL DELAY

SENSORY-MOTOR FUNCTIONS

Within the standard developmental evaluation, specific notice should be given to gross motor skill, fine motor skill, and sensory development. These are truly the basic processes by which the infant or preschool child interacts with the environment. Although there are many excellent instruments available to assess each of these domains, such as The *Beery-Buktenica Developmental Test of Visual Motor Integration, 5th Edition* (Beery, Buktenica, & Beery, 2006), the

Pediatric Evaluation of Disability Inventory (Haley, Coster, Ludlow, Haltiwanger, & Andrellos, 1992), and the *Peabody Developmental Motor Skills, 2nd Edition* (Folio & Fewell, 2000), an examiner must also utilize good observational techniques. Many of the standard assessment instruments measuring global development have subtests or composite scores dedicated to investigating motor abilities, so qualitative information through observation can assist in the overall interpretation of developmental level. Furthermore, it is often advantageous to consult with other available professionals who may have expertise in this area (e.g., physical therapists and occupational therapists). They can often provide unique viewpoints or suggestions for interventions in later programming.

The assessment of sensory-motor functions includes processing issues related to environmental stimuli (e.g., hyporesponsiveness versus hyper-responsiveness). Sensory symptoms are often associated with pervasive developmental disorders, but can also be present with other diagnoses (e.g., global developmental delay, mental retardation, attentional disorders, secondary symptoms due to hearing or visual impairments). As stated earlier, clinicians often have difficulty differentiating overlapping symptoms within the early childhood population, simply due to the nature of the developmental continuum. For example, Baranek, David, Poe, Stone, and Watson (2006) found that there appears to be a "developmental nature of sensory features in young children"—meaning that "as children mature and gain life experiences, their repertoire of coping strategies expands in number and sophistication." So while there may be initial difficulty, those challenges with sensory processing may later evolve into more typically developing behavior with additional positive changes in executive functions and discriminating "novel stimuli" (Baranek et al., 2006).

Along with assessing for responsiveness to environment, there also must be notice to overall motor movement (which includes hand dominance, grasp on writing utensil, coordination with cutting/drawing/writing, etc.) There should also be a focus on qualitative movements noticed during the assessment process. This may include some of the following questions:

- Does the child have an abnormal gait?
- Does the child consistently touch the walls of the school while walking down the hallway?
- Does the child react aversively when someone "pats" him or her on the back?

Although one or two such atypicalities do not necessarily determine developmental dysfunction, the accumulation of such observations can impact the holistic interpretation. Aylward (1997) noted that if a child "passes all motor milestones but has some abnormal physical findings, the likelihood of later neurodevelopmental problems is decreased." For example, if a child has demonstrated a "tip-toe walking pattern," but has no difficulty with any other motor milestone, the probability of later problems from a neurodevelopmental perspective is decreased. Again, it seems as though the optimal approach is relevant, in the sense that with more appropriate behaviors, it is less likely that dysfunction in development is present.

The differential diagnosis involved with young children who demonstrate sensory-motor atypicalities usually involves some of the following possibilities (when hearing and vision are within normal limits and there are no other medical risk factors): autism or a pervasive developmental disorder; attentional disorders; developmental coordination disorder; chronic motor disorder; various tic disorders, which include vocal tics, transient tics, and tics not otherwise specified; and stereotypic movement disorder. Developmental delay within the motor domain, however, or global developmental delay, is often the initial classification until further clarification can be made.

ATTENTION AND EXECUTIVE FUNCTIONS

For the young child especially, attention is often considered to be the foundation for important processes in perceptual, cognitive, and social functioning. There is some research that would suggest that early focused attention (different from casual attention) may actually be predictive of later cognitive performance (Lawson & Ruff, 2001). Lawson and Ruff helped to delineate two of the biobehavioral systems that develop for the young child within the first year of life with respect to focused attention: (1) orienting to and investigating of objects and events and (2) controlling complex sequences of action. The first system involves the parietal cortex and subcortical areas, such as the superior colliculus and the frontal eye fields (Lawson & Ruff, 2001). This system involves habituation and becoming motivated to new objects or experiences within the environment—a skill that is found in early infancy. The second system involves the frontal cortex and relates to inhibitory control and the "increasing complexity of action." Lawson and Ruff explain that by 12 months of age, attention may still be governed by the first system, but note that the second system begins to influence behavior as an emerging skill. Both the quantity and quality of attention are often characterized as having "increased variability and inconsistency" (Lawson & Ruff, 2001) due to the very nature of brain development in early childhood. This often makes it difficult to assess for possible developmental delay in either domain of attention and executive function, which could help explain why difficulty in either area is often not specified until a later time (after the age of 5 years) and, instead, is often explained as "behavioral difficulties."

Both systems theorized by Lawson and Ruff (2001) incorporate known aspects of attentional theory and executive function theory. However, when discussing these neurocognitive concepts, one must also consider the idea of "self-regulation" and how it pertains to early assessment. Although current research has clearly shown delineation between attentional factors and executive functions (Barkley, 1998), the precursors in their development are often difficult to distinguish within the early childhood population, especially during initial times of screening for developmental delay. Self-regulation, or emotional regulation, has been recently identified as a possible precursor to later cognitive and behavioral outcome (Davis & Burns, 2001). It involves the ability to choose, make appropriate decisions, plan for the future, judge the value of rewards, control impulsive behavior, and use effective strategies to accomplish a task (Bronson, 2000). Barkley (1998) explained that for self-control or self-regulation of control to occur, an individual must have the neuropsychological faculty to sense time and to conjecture the future, which ultimately allows that individual to organize and execute behavior. Self-regulation in some capacity is also related to the neuropsychological concept of executive functioning, allowing an individual to possess self-directed actions (Barkley, 2004).

Symptoms of Attention-Deficit/Hyperactivity Disorder (ADHD) tend to appear at an early age, with an average onset between 3 and 4 years of age (Barkley, 1998). Although many clinicians often remark that diagnosis within the early childhood age range is difficult due to the variant activity level within typically developing children, there are perhaps some common features that seem to connect behavior with later diagnosis. Barkley (1998) noted that this might include the following *persistent* problems:

- Problems with social interaction with parents and peers (This does not necessarily pertain to the ability to engage with others, but rather with the quality of interactions. For example, social engagement is often chaotic and disorganized.)
- Excessive activity
- Inattention
- Emotional difficulties such as aggression or fearfulness
- Negative temperament (e.g., being demanding of others, irritability, quickness to anger, decreased adaptability to change)
- Irregularity of sleep-wake cycle

It should be recognized, however, that these features of maladaptive difficulty could also be associated with a variety of other disorders, not just ADHD or concerns with executive dysfunction. Therefore, in addition to a direct examination of the child (which would include naturalistic observations and individual testing), it would also be necessary to utilize parent information. Barkley (1998) explained that ADHD symptoms are often linked to parent psychiatric distress (e.g., family history of ADHD) and dynamics within the family environment (e.g., marital discord, poor maternal health during pregnancy).

VISUAL-SPATIAL FUNCTIONS

Visual-spatial functioning within the early childhood age (where developmental delay is typically assessed) includes aspects of visual memory (e.g., visual recognition). Usually, task items assessing such abilities are related to cognitive indexes, where it might be more difficult to "tease" out such processes from an overall development score.

However, the clinician should not only note quantitative performance on standard visual-spatial items, but also qualitative performance as well. For example, when visual items are administered on any assessment instrument of early childhood, the clinician should notice deviations in eye gaze, "aberrant eye positioning," or uncoordinated eye movement (Aylward, 1997). Abnormalities can include nystagmus (involuntary, rhythmic eye movements), strabismus (one or both eyes deviating either outward or inward), or "downward eye deviations with paresis of upward gaze," often referred to as the "setting sun sign," which could indicate abnormalities in intracranial pressure (Aylward, 1997).

LANGUAGE FUNCTIONS

Language abilities are crucial to early developmental assessment and are intricately linked to cognition (Brassard & Boehm, 2007). Wetherby and Prizant (1993) indicated that 70 percent of all children between the ages of 3 and 5 years were identified as having speech and language eligibility within the schools.

A simple definition of language is complicated by a variety of constructs (e.g., phonology, semantics, morphology, syntax, and pragmatics), but is perhaps most concretely defined by expressive communication (what is produced) and receptive communication (what is understood). Other communicative skills involve the use and understanding of gestures, sounds, facial expressions, and other nonverbal behaviors.

Language abilities are not only closely linked to cognition, but also to aspects of social and behavioral functioning. Early childhood is often the age at which concern is initially expressed for possible signs of autism. The difficulty in differentiating language from social difficulties is perhaps best illustrated by a diagnosis of Mixed Receptive-Expressive Language Disorder in which the delay in language is so severe that social deficits are seen. Upon further analysis, however, it becomes clear that the child demonstrates an ability to engage with others, but just does not have the speech-language skills to do so.

Along with issues of differential diagnosis come extraneous factors that affect the overall interpretation of results in a developmental evaluation. This would include culture and linguistic diversity (Brassard & Boehm, 2007). It is not always clear in differentiating a true developmental delay in language abilities from the influences of a second or third language. It is also not always clear when a child's "delay" is a part of the typical developmental continuum. Consultation may be needed with a speech-language pathologist. Regardless, it is important for clinicians to learn to distinguish which children are perhaps "late to talk," but who will "catch up" as opposed to those children with true language difficulties that continue into school entry (Brassard & Boehm, 2007).

MEMORY AND LEARNING FUNCTIONS

As with language, memory and learning tasks are linked very closely to the concept of cognition, especially for very young children, when distinctions are not made for such abilities on tests of global development. Nevertheless, the development of these constructs begins at birth (some would argue even before birth). Learning and memory initially take form as habituation within the infancy period (Fagan & Ohr, 2001). When problems arise with young children not reacting to novel items, the clinician should note such difficulty, especially if this is persistent over time and situation.

GENERAL COGNITIVE ABILITIES

The research literature on early childhood cognition often cites the controversy surrounding the predictability factor in developmental evaluations. The question has always been: Is the performance of infants and preschool-aged children on developmental assessments predictive of later performance on standardized intelligence tests? Sattler (1992) explained that it may be somewhat "exaggerated" to state that "developmental tests in infancy bear no relationship to intelligence test scores obtained in childhood." It would appear that while there are varying correlations between the two performances (dependent upon the instrument used), there does seem to be evidence linking significantly delayed performance with risk factors in later intelligence testing (Aylward, 1997; Brassard & Boehm, 2007; Sattler, 1992). This would mean that a young child who was evaluated at 2 years of age (perhaps with the BSID-III) and performed within a significantly delayed range (Mental Developmental Index < 50) would have a statistically good chance of performing at lower levels on an intelligence test administered at the age of 5 years (perhaps the *Wechsler Preschool and Primary Scale of Intelligence, 3rd Edition*).

Studies that looked at specific predictive validity with high-risk subgroups appeared to demonstrate positive results. For example, within a group of infants at biological risk, performance on the BSID (previous version) at 12 months of age significantly correlated with cognitive and motor performance at 4½ years of age (Crowe, Deitz, & Bennett, 1987). Similarly, within a group of infants who were at risk due to a "deprived environment," the BSID MDI at 6 months of age correctly predicted later performance on the *Stanford-Binet* at 24 and 48 months of age (Farran & Harber, 1989).

Unless a child is found to meet criteria for mental retardation, cognitive delays are usually not described as learning disabilities or learning differences until exposure to a kindergarten or primary grade curriculum is offered. Cognitive delays found for children under the age of 3 years that qualify for early intervention services can often be associated with later deficits that integrate other areas of skill (e.g., speech and language deficits or fine motor deficits). These deficits become known later with "age-known manifestations" (Aylward, 1997).

Speed and Efficiency of Cognitive Processing

The speed and efficiency of cognitive processing is more definitively assessed with standard intelligence tests (e.g., *Wechsler Preschool and Primary Scale of Intelligence, 3rd Edition* or the *Stanford Binet Intelligence Scales, 5th Edition*), but the quality of such behavior can still be noted within the context of a developmental evaluation. For example, notice should be given to how long it takes for the young child to complete certain tasks and whether he or she utilizes efficient strategies for completion. Many developmental assessments (e.g., BSID-III) will require the assessor to time specific items that relate to such abilities (e.g., calculating the amount of time it takes for a child to complete a puzzle board). Although deficits in this area are not as identifiable as they may be within the older school-aged child, qualitative differences can be commented upon, and consideration is given to standard developmental scores. For example, if a child were to take a significantly longer time in completing a specific task, such as correctly placing puzzle pieces in slots, then this difficulty would be accounted for in the subsequent standard score.

Academic Achievement

Although there are recognized curriculum guidelines for preschool aged children (e.g., through the National Association for the Education of Young

Children; Copple, & Bredekamp, 2009) and certainly measurements are available that assess for early academic skills in young children (e.g., *Young Children's Achievement Test*; Hresko, Peak, Herron, & Bridges, 2000), the ability to identify low performance is often difficult. Children present with different levels of experience in a structured school environment, and there are varying levels of parental involvement with promoting academic concepts within the home setting. It is not atypical for the first level of identification in lower academic performance to be related to cognitive deficits found through developmental evaluations or preschool testing. Kindergarten readiness tests also seem to identify possible difficulties early on. However, Brassard and Boehm (2007) note that there is a significant difference between the two types of evaluation (developmental assessment versus kindergarten readiness test). Poor performance on a readiness test is many times attributed to limited prior experience, whereas poor performance on a developmental evaluation is more often attributed to an "impairment that affects the child's ability to acquire knowledge." Regardless, assessing academic achievement in young children should be gauged with caution, since there are many variables to consider.

Social-Emotional Functions

Within the context of developmental evaluation, social and emotional development are usually assessed—if not formally, then informally by observation within the assessment process. Throughout early childhood, key milestones must be achieved in order to attain "emotional competence" (Brassard & Boehm, 2007). According to Brassard and Boehm, these milestones include "emotional knowledge or understanding" (being able to identify emotions in oneself and others), "emotional expressiveness" (related to initiating and maintaining relationships), and "emotional regulation" (described earlier within this chapter, but related to monitoring, evaluating, and modifying emotional responses). It could be noted, however, that each of these milestones is somewhat subsumed under the construct of emotional or self-regulation (McCabe, Cunnington, & Brooks-Gunn, 2004).

Cole, Martin, and Dennis (2004) surveyed the recent literature regarding emotional regulation and discussed some of the theoretical difficulties involving such a broad construct (e.g., difficulty in defining emotion, physiological activity affecting emotion, difficulty with distinguishing "good" and "bad" emotions, and understanding emotions in terms of context). However, these researchers recognized that emotional regulation appears to signify changes associated with activated emotions. This includes changes within the emotion, changes that appear to result from activated emotion, and changes that occur in others as a result of the emotion (Cole, Martin, & Dennis, 2004).

Temperament is often discussed with the concept of emotional regulation. Some research has suggested early regulatory behavior, or temperament, was predictive of later functioning. For example, Eisenberg, Fabes, et al. (1997) found that teacher reports of regulatory behavior at the early elementary school grades were able to predict later functioning between 8 to 10 years of age. Similarly, difficult temperaments at age 2 were found to predict significant behavioral problems at age 4 (Pettit & Bates, 1989).

When describing early difficulty with social and/or emotional functioning, many clinicians who have experience with the early childhood population choose to use the revised 2005 Zero to Three classification system (DC:0-3) established through the National Center for Clinical Infant Programs. These guidelines were established to complement other types of classification systems (e.g., DSM-IV-TR). Many of the classifications within this system take the construct of emotional regulation into account and provide a descriptive approach in recording patterns of symptoms and behaviors. For example, three types of regulatory disorders are explored—(1) Hypersensitive (Type A: Fearful/Cautious or Type B: Negative/Defiant; (2) Hyposensitive/Underresponsive; and (3) Sensory Stimulation-Seeking/Impulsive all of which include a specific behavior pattern coupled with a sensory, sensory-motor, or organizational processing difficulty ultimately affecting daily function (including relationships and across settings).

EVIDENCE-BASED INTERVENTIONS FOR CHILDREN WITH DEVELOPMENTAL DELAYS

After conducting a thorough evaluation and identifying patterns of strengths and weaknesses for a particular child, the next question of the caregiver or professional inevitably seems to be, "So now what do I do?" It's not enough to find a possible answer as to why a situation or concern may be occurring, the evaluator assessing developmental delay must also be able to identify possible solutions for intervention. Interestingly, neuropsychological evaluations have always been designed to consider functionality, so the formulation of useful interventions should be a somewhat natural process.

Barnett, Bell, and Carey (1999) explained that the preschool period is often considered to be the "most significant period of development." While there has been some previous controversy over the long-term effectiveness of early intervention, research does seem to suggest that there are overall benefits detected (Barrera, Kitching, Cunningham, Doucet, & Rosenbaum, 1990; Boyce, Saylor, & Price, 2004; Hack, Klein, & Taylor, 1995). These benefits should not only consider the current educational setting, but should also recognize potential future environments. For example, a young student may currently be placed within a preschool classroom designed specifically for children with disabilities, but that same student will eventually reach the age to enter kindergarten. Interventions should be considered to help prepare that student for the least restricted placement, or, in this case, the general kindergarten classroom.

Brassard and Boehm (2007) explain that when developing interventions for educational programming, clinicians should not only focus on supporting detected weaknesses, but should also focus on relative strengths found within developmental testing. They provide an example of a child found to have strengths in the area of visual processing. This child may ultimately benefit from using picture supports or visual cues within the classroom setting, which will ideally provide support for detected weaknesses. The noted cognitive or academic strength of the child is a foundation from which to formulate effective interventions at school (Brassard & Boehm, 2007).

Along with considering the "next educational placement" and relative strengths and weaknesses of the child, it is also critical to recognize the transactional influences of the family. This is especially important for the area of early childhood, since factors involved within the family system are so influential in early development (e.g., parenting style, attachment processes, socioeconomic status, cultural influences, supports within the community). Successful early intervention programs seem to use this component within their framework—mitigating identified stressors to the family patterns of interaction (Guralnick, 2005).

While considering the key components of school neuropsychological testing and the unique characteristics of early childhood/developmental delay, it is important to think in terms of two types of strategies: (1) intervening at the level of the environment and (2) intervening at the level of the person (Dawson & Guare, 2004). Both have shown levels of effectiveness dependent on the individual situation. Table 14.1 presents a possible set of evidence-based interventions for children with developmental delays by neuropsychological area.

Figure 14.1 provides a reference list specifically for early childhood interventions.

FOR CONSIDERATION: THE USE OF DEVELOPMENTAL ASSESSMENTS FOR OLDER CHILDREN

There are instances when an older child (above the age of 5 years) is severely delayed to a point where traditional measures of intellectual assessment are not either practical in determining current functioning or helpful in establishing appropriate interventions. In such instances, certain assessment instruments are able to provide developmental age equivalents, which can be helpful in formulating educational programming. Developmental age equivalents "represent the average age in months at which a given total raw score is typical" (Bayley, 2006). Although these equivalents are helpful in providing

Table 14.1
Evidence-Based Interventions for Children with Developmental Delays

Neuropsychological Area	Evidence-Based Interventions
Sensory-Motor Functioning	• Sensory diet strategies (e.g., weighted vests, vestibular cushions, etc.). Although there is some inherent controversy with strategies for sensory integration, there is some research which supports its use (Baranek, 2002). • Environmental modifications (e.g., decreasing stimulation, providing added structure, providing support during transitional situations, etc.).
Attention and Executive Functions	• Increase external controls. • Cue the child to control impulses (can be both visual or verbal). • Break tasks into smaller steps. • Arrange for a visual cue to prompt the child to begin a specific task. • Use of organizational systems.
Visual-Spatial Functioning	• Reteach uniform spacing using pencil tip by prompting, tracing and then finally, fading. • Review size concept. • Provide models. • Ambient prism lenses. Although there is some controversy with such a technique, some case studies support its effectiveness (Baranek, 2002).
Language Functioning	• Use of visual cues or supports. • Picture exchange system. • Sign language. • Picture communication boards. • Aided language stimulation. • Vocal output devices. • Integrate communication and play.
Memory and Learning Functioning	• Arranging for verbal reminders. • Visual cues. • Teaching mental rehearsal. • Providing meaning and context.
General Cognitive Abilities	• Embedding instruction into daily activities. • Targeting cognitive goals to individual strengths and weaknesses.
Speed and Efficiency of Cognitive Processing	• Noting start and stop times when tasks are completed. • Setting a timer and challenging child to complete task within time allotted. • Teaching organizational strategies.
Academic Achievement	• Embedding instruction into daily activities. • Curriculum-based instruction.
Social-Emotional Functioning	• Family resources for supportive home environment. • Positive behavior supports. • Differential reinforcement. • Response cost.

(continued)

Table 14.1
Continued

Neuropsychological Area	Evidence-Based Interventions
	• Peer mediation or role-modeling. • Social stories or social scripts. • Use of incentive systems. • Teaching coping strategies (especially for dealing with intense feelings, such as anger or frustration). • Embedding friendship opportunities into daily schedule. • Using children's literature to support social emotional development. • Response-contingent learning opportunities.

an easy way to comprehend current functioning, they do not provide information on the child's relative standing to his or her same-aged peer group (Bayley, 2006). For example, an evaluator may be faced with having to assess the skills of an 8-year-old female who presents with global

Barnett, D. W., Bell, S. H., & Carey, K. T. (1999). *Designing preschool interventions: A practitioner's guide*. New York: Guilford.

Copple, C., & Bredekamp, S. (2009). *Developmentally appropriate practice in early childhood programs: Serving children from birth through age 6*. Washington, DC: NAEYC.

Dawson, P., & Guare, R. (2004). *Executive skills in children and adolescents: A practical guide to assessment and intervention*. New York: Guilford.

Greenspan, S. I., & Wieder, S. (2006). *Infant and early childhood mental health: A comprehensive developmental approach to assessment and intervention*. Arlington, VA: American Psychiatric Publishing.

Hirschland, D. (2008). *Collaborative intervention in early childhood: Consulting with parents and teachers of 3 to 7 year olds*. New York: Oxford University Press.

Karoly, L. A. (2005). *Early childhood interventions: Proven results, future promises*. Santa Monica, CA: RAND Corporation.

Jongsma, A. E., & Winkelsten, J. A. (2006). *The early childhood education intervention treatment planner*. Hoboken, NJ: John Wiley & Sons.

Randall, S., Mclean, M. E., & Smith, B. J. (2000). *DEC recommended practices in early intervention/early childhood special education*. Arlington, VA: Council for Exceptional Children.

Zeanah, C. H. (Ed.). (2005). *Handbook of infant mental health, second edition*. New York: Guilford.

Zigler, E. F., Shonkoff, J. P., & Meisels, S. J. (Eds.). (2000). *Handbook of early childhood intervention, second edition*. Cambridge, UK: Cambridge University Press.

Figure 14.1   Reference list specifically for early childhood interventions.

developmental delay and estimated cognitive skills less than 1 year of age. Administering a more traditional cognitive assessment, such as the *Wechsler Intelligence Scale for Children, 4th Edition,* would not be practical, considering the child's verbal and motor abilities. In cases such as this, it may be appropriate to administer a developmental assessment that targets skills and functions more applicable to the child's developmental level. Although a standardized score is not attainable with such a measure, a developmental level is attainable. Some might argue this approach would be the more practical in terms of formulating individualized educational goals.

SUMMARY

With federal and state legislation continually emphasizing the importance of early detection for possible disabilities (e.g., Child Find Initiatives), developmental assessment and identifying developmental delay becomes crucial for the practice of school neuropsychology. Not only is it important to know some of the more common assessment instruments that incorporate a neuropsychological perspective, it is necessary to understand the link between neuropsychological processes and early childhood concepts. This understanding helps to facilitate the formulation of prescriptive interventions, which can be used both in the home and school setting. The goal would then be to assist the young child to function within a least restricted setting upon entrance into kindergarten.

REFERENCES

Alfonso, V. C., & Flanagan, D. P. (1992). Assessment of cognitive functioning in preschoolers. In E. V. Nuttall, I. Romero, & J. Kalesnik (Eds.), *Assessing and screening preschoolers: Psychological and educational dimensions* (pp. 186–217). Needham Heights, MA: Allyn and Bacon.

Allen, M. C., & Capute, A. J. (1989). Neonatal neurodevelopmental examination as a predictor of neuromotor outcome in premature infants. *Pediatrics, 83,* 498–506.

Als, H., Lester, B. M., Tronick, E., & Brazelton, T. B. (1982). Towards a systematic assessment of preterm infants' behavioral development. In H. E. Fitzgerald, B. M. Lester, & M. W. Yogman (Eds.), *Theory and research in behavioral pediatrics* (pp. 35–63). New York: Plenum Press.

Aylward, G. P. (1995). *Bayley infant neurodevelopmental screener.* San Antonio, TX: Harcourt Assessment.

Aylward, G. P. (1997). *Infant and early childhood neuropsychology.* New York: Plenum Press.

Baranek, G. T. (2002). Efficacy of sensory and motor interventions for children with autism. *Journal of Autism and Developmental Disorders, 32,* 397–422.

Baranek, G. T., David, F. J., Poe, M. D., Stone, W. L., & Watson, L. R. (2006). Sensory experiences questionnaire: Discriminating sensory features in young children with autism, developmental delays and typical development. *Journal of Child Psychology and Psychiatry, 47,* 591–601.

Barkley, R. A. (1998). *Attention-deficit/hyperactivity disorder: A handbook for diagnosis and treatment* (2nd ed.), New York: Guilford.

Barkley, R. A. (2004). Attention-deficit/hyperactivity disorder and self-regulation. In R. F. Baumeister, & K. D. Vohs (Eds.), *Handbook of self-regulation: Research, theory and applications* (pp. 301–323). New York: Guilford.

Barnett, D. W., Bell, S. H., & Carey, K. T. (1999). *Designing preschool interventions: A practitioner's guide.* New York: Guilford.

Barrera, M. E., Kitching, K. J., Cunningham, C. C., Doucet, D., & Rosenbaum, P. L. (1990). A 3-year early home intervention follow-up study with low birth weight infants and their parents. *Topics in Early Childhood Special Education, 10,* 14–28.

Bayley, N. (2006). *Bayley scales of infant and toddler development* (3rd ed.). San Antonio, TX: Harcourt Assessment.

Beery, K. E., Buktenica, N. A., & Beery, N. A. (2006). *The Beery-Buktenica developmental test of visual-motor integration* (5th ed.). Minneapolis, MN: Pearson Assessments.

Berrueta-Clement, J., Schweinhart, L., Barnett, W., Epstein, A., & Weikart, D. (1984). *Changed lives: The effects of the Perry preschool program on youths through age 19.* Ypsilanti, MI: High/Scope Press.

Boyce, G. C., Saylor, C. F., & Price, C. L. (2004). School-age outcomes for early intervention participants who experienced intraventricular hemorrhage and low birth weight. *Children's Health Care, 33,* 257–274.

Brassard, M. R., & Boehm, A. E. (2007). *Preschool assessment: principles and practices.* New York: Guilford Press.

Brazelton, T. B., & Nugent, J. K. (1995). *Neonatal behavioral assessment scale.* London: MacKeith Press.

Bronson, M. B. (2000). *Self-regulation in early childhood.* New York: Guilford.

Cole, P. M., Martin, S. E., & Dennis, T. A. (2004). Emotion regulation as a scientific construct: Methodological challenges and directions for child development research. *Child Development, 75,* 317–333.

Copple, C., & Bredekamp, S. (2009). *Developmentally appropriate practice in early childhood programs: Serving children from birth through age 6.* Washington DC: NAEYC.

Crowe, T. K., Deitz, J. C., & Bennett, F. C. (1987). The relationship between the Bayley scales of infant development and preschool gross motor and cognitive performance. *The American Journal of Occupation Therapy, 41,* 374–378.

Davis, D. W., & Burns, B. (2001). Problems of self-regulation: A new way to view deficits in children born prematurely. *Issues in Mental Health Nursing, 22,* 305–323.

Dawson, P., & Guare, R. (2004). *Executive skills in children and adolescents: A practical guide to assessment and intervention.* New York: Guilford.

Derrington, T. M., & Lippitt, J. A. (2008). State-level impact of mandated referrals from child welfare to Part C early intervention. *Topics in Early Childhood Special Education, 28,* 90–98.

Edwards, C. P. (1999). Development in the preschool years: The typical path. In E. V. Nuttall, I. Romero, and J. Kalesnik (Eds.), *Assessing and screening preschoolers: Psychological and educational dimension* (pp. 9–24). Boston: Allyn & Bacon.

Eisenberg, N., Fabes, R. A., Shephard, S. A., Murphy, B. C., Guthrie, I., Jones, S. et al. (1997). Contemporaneous and longitudinal prediction of children's social functioning from regulation and emotionality. *Child Development, 68,* 642–664.

Elliott, C. D. (2007). *Differential ability scales – II.* San Antonio, TX: Harcourt Assessment.

Fagan, J. W., & Ohr, P. S. (2001). Learning and memory in infancy: Habituation, instrumental conditioning and expectancy formation. In L. T. Singer & P. S. Zeskind (Eds.), *Biobehavioral assessment of the infant* (pp. 233–273). New York: Guilford.

Farran, D. C., & Harber, L. A. (1989). Responses to a learning task at 6 months and I.Q. test performance during the preschool years. *International Journal of Behavioral Development, 12,* 101–114.

Folio, M. R., & Fewell, R. R. (2000). *Peabody developmental motor skills* (2nd ed.). San Antonio, TX: Pearson Assessment.

Frankenburg, W. K., Dodds, J., Archer, P., Shapiro, H., & Bresnick, B (1992). The DENVER II: A major revision and restandardization of the Denver developmental screening test. *Pediatrics, 89,* 91–97.

Glascoe, F. P. (1997). Parents' concerns about children's development: Prescreening technique or screening test? *Pediatrics, 99,* 522–528.

Guralnick, M. J. (2005). Early intervention for children with intellectual disabilities: Current knowledge and future prospects. *Journal of Applied Research in Intellectual Disabilities, 18,* 313–324.

Hack, M., Klein, N. K., & Taylor, H. G. (1995). Long-term developmental outcomes of low birth weight children. In R. Behrman (Ed.), *The future of children* (pp. 176–196). Los Altos, CA: Center for the Future of Children.

Hale, J. B., & Fiorello, C. A. (2004). *School neuropsychology: A practitioner's handbook.* New York: Guilford.

Haley, S. M., Coster, W. J., Ludlow, L. H., Haltiwanger, J. T., & Andrellos, P. J. (1992). *Pediatric evaluation of disability inventory.* San Antonio, TX: Pearson Assessment.

Hess, C. R., Papas, M. A., & Black, M. M. (2004). Use of the Bayley infant neurodevelopmental screener with an environmental risk group. *Journal of Pediatric Psychology, 29,* 321–330.

Hresko, W. P., Peak, P. K., Herron, S. R., & Bridges, D. L. (2000). *Young children's achievement test.* Austin, TX: Pro-Ed.

Hunt, J. V., & Rhodes, L. (1977). Mental development of preterm infants during the first year. *Child Development, 48,* 204–210.

Individuals with Disabilities Education Improvement Act of 2004 (PL No. 108–446, 20 USC 1400).

Kalesnik, J. (1999). Developmental history. In E. V. Nuttall, I. Romero, & J. Kalesnik (Eds.), *Assessing and screening preschoolers: Psychological and educational dimension* (pp. 94–111). Boston: Allyn & Bacon.

Knobloch, H., Stevens, S. & Malone, A. E. (1980). *Manual of developmental diagnosis.* New York: Harper & Row.

Korkman, M., Kirk, U., & Kemp, S. (2007). *NEPSY-II second edition administration manual.* San Antonio, TX: Harcourt Assessment.

Lawson, K. R., & Ruff, H. A. (2001). Focused attention: Assessing a fundamental cognitive process in infancy. In L. T. Singer & P. S. Zeskind (Eds.), *Biobehavioral assessment of the infant.* New York: Guilford.

Lazar, I., & Darlington, R. (1982). Lasting effects of early education: A report from the consortium for longitudinal studies. *Monographs of the Society for Research in Child Development, 47(2–3, Serial No. 195),* 1–151.

Lems, W., Hopkins, R., & Samson, J. F. (1993). Mental and motor development in preterm infants: The issue of corrected age. *Early Human Development, 34,* 113–123.

Lezak, M. D. (1995). *Neuropsychological assessment* (3rd ed.). New York: Oxford University Press.

Lezak, M. D., Howieson, D. B., & Loring, D. W. (2004). *Neuropsychological assessment* (4th ed.). New York: Oxford University Press.

Lifter, K. (1999). Descriptions of preschool children with disabilities or at-risk for developmental delay. In E. V. Nuttall, I. Romero, & J. Kalesnik (Eds.), *Assessing and screening for preschoolers: Psychological and educational dimensions* (pp. 25–49). Boston: Allyn & Bacon.

Litty, C. G., & Hatch, J. A. (2006). Hurry up and wait: Rethinking special education identification in kindergarten. *Early Childhood Education Journal, 33,* 203–208.

McCabe, L. A., Cunnington, M., & Brooks-Gunn, J. (2004). The development of self-regulation in young children: Individual characteristics and environmental contexts. In R. F. Baumeister & K. D. Vohs (Eds.), *Handbook of self-regulation: Research, theory and applications* (pp. 340–356). New York: Guilford.

Miller, D. C. (2007). *Essentials of school neuropsychological assessment.* Hoboken, NJ: John Wiley & Sons.

Mullen, E. M. (1984). *Mullen Scales of Early Learning.* Circle Pines, MN: American Guidance Service.

Nagileri, J., & Das, J. P. (1997). *Das-Naglieri cognitive assessment system.* Itasca, IL: Riverside.

Neisworth, J. T., Bagnato, S. J., Salvia, J., & Hunt, F. M. (1999). *TABS manual for the temperament and atypical behavior scale: Early childhood indicators of developmental dysfunction.* Baltimore, MD: Paul H. Brooks Publishing Company.

No Child Left Behind Act of 2001 (Pub. L. No. 107–110). Most recent set of amendments to the Elementary and Secondary Education Act of 1965. Available at http://www.nochildleftbehind.gov/.

Nuttall, E. V., Nuttall-Vasquez, K., & Hampel, A. (1999). Introduction. In E. V. Nuttall, I. Romero, & J. Kalesnik (Eds.), *Assessing and screening preschoolers* (pp. 1–8). Boston: Allyn & Bacon.

Pettit, G. S., & Bates, J. E. (1989). Family interaction patterns and children's behavior problems from infancy to 4 years. *Developmental Psychology, 25,* 413–420.

Richardson, D. K., Gray, J. E., McCormick, M. C., et al. (1993). Score for neonatal acute physiology: A physiologic severity index for neonatal intensive care. *Pediatrics, 91,* 617–623.

Roid, G. H. (2003). *Stanford-Binet intelligence scales* (5th ed.). Itasca, IL: Riverside.

Sameroff, A. J. (1993). Models of development and developmental risk. In C. H. Zeanah, Jr. (Ed.), *Handbook of infant mental health* (pp. 3–13). New York: Guilford.

Sattler, J. M. (1992). *Assessment of children* (Rev. and updated 3rd ed.). San Diego, CA: Author.

Schweinhart, L. J., & Weikart, D. P. (1998). High/Scope Perry Preschool Program effects at age twenty-seven. In J. Crane (Ed.), *Social programs that work* (pp. 148–162). New York: Russell Sage Foundation.

Shevell, M., Majnemer, A., Platt, R. W., Webster, R., & Birnbaum, R. (2005). Developmental and functional outcomes at school age of preschool children with global developmental delay. *Journal of Child Neurology, 20,* 648–654.

Siegel, L. S. (1983). Correction for prematurity and its consequences for the assessment of the very low birth weight infant. *Child Development, 54,* 1176–1188.

Singer, L. T. (2001). General issues in infant assessment and development. In L. T. Singer & P. S. Zeskind (Eds.), *Biobehavioral assessment of the infant* (pp. 3–17). New York: Guilford.

Snyder, P., Bailey, D. B., & Auer, C. (1994). Preschool eligibility determination for children with known or suspected learning disabilities under IDEA. *Journal of Early Intervention, 18,* 380–390.

Squires, J., Twombly, E., Bricker, D., & Potter, L. (2009). *Ages and stages questionnaires, ASQ: A parent-completed child-monitoring system* (3rd ed.). Baltimore, MD: Paul D. Brookes Publishing.

Wechsler, D. (2002). *Wechsler preschool and primary scales of intelligence* (3rd ed.). San Antonio, TX: Harcourt Assessment.

Wetherby, A. M., & Prizant, B. M. (1993). Profiling communication and symbolic activities in young children. *Journal of Childhood Communication Disorders, 15,* 23–32.

Woodcock, R. W., McGrew, K. S., & Mather, N. (2001). *Woodcock-Johnson III tests of cognitive abilities.* Itasca, IL: Riverside Publishing.

Zero to Three. (2005). *Diagnostic classification of mental health and developmental disorder of infancy and early childhood* (Rev. ed.). Washington, DC: Author.

Zimmerman, I. L., Steiner, V. G., & Pond, R. E. (2002). *Preschool language scale* (4th ed.). San Antonio, TX: Harcourt Assessment.

CHAPTER 15

Assessing and Intervening with Children with Externalizing Disorders

COLLEEN JIRON

The growing neuropsychological literature on violent and antisocial behavior is confirming beyond a reasonable doubt what some have argued for a long time—that antisocial and violent offenders have neuropsychological impairments. (Raine et al., 2005, p. 38)

THE TERM "*EXTERNALIZING behavior*" describes chronically impulsive, op positional, aggressive, destructive, or delinquent behavior. Externalizing Disorders in children often are grouped into two subtypes, consisting of impulsive disorders such as Attention Deficit Hyperactivity Disorder (ADHD) versus disruptive conditions such as Oppositional-Defiant Disorder (ODD) and Conduct Disorder (CD).

ADHD the most commonly diagnosed childhood mental health condition, often co-occurs with one of the disruptive disorders, which poses a high risk for adult antisocial behavior and other psychiatric and psychosocial problems (Simonoff et al., 2004). Childhood hyperactivity is believed to be a predictor of adult antisocial behavior (Lilienfeld & Waldman, 1990), and childhood aggression is a predictor of adult crime and violence (Farrington, 2001). These longitudinal outcomes make sense in light of findings from Nestor (2002), who reviewed the literature concerning mental disorders and violence and concluded (in part) that low impulse control and poor affect regulation increase the risk of violence across the different types of disorders. These two characteristics have consistently emerged as salient features of externalizing disorders.

In addition to the long-term personal and familial costs of childhood externalizing and subsequent adult antisocial behaviors, there are sobering and increasing societal impacts, as well. The number of child delinquents seen in U.S. juvenile courts increased 33 percent from 1991 to 2001 (Snyder, 2001), with offense patterns reflecting more serious crimes, and child offenders being two to three times more likely to become serious, violent, and chronic offenders than "late starters." The age of onset factor permeates much of the research on child externalizing behaviors. Moffitt (2007) conducted and reviewed ten years of research and proposed two subtypes of youths engaging in externalizing behaviors, defined as "life-course persistent" (LCP) offenders, versus "adolescence-limited" (AL) offenders. She suggested that that life-course persistent (LCP) offenders' antisocial behavior has its origins in neurodevelopmental processes, begins in childhood, and continues persistently thereafter. In contrast, adolescence-limited (AL) offenders' antisocial behavior has its origins in social processes, begins in adolescence, and desists in young adulthood.

A review of the juvenile delinquency literature (see Giancola, Mezzich, & Tarter, 1998; Henry, Caspi, Moffitt, & Silva, 1996; Taylor, Iacono, & McGue, 2000) yields a slightly different conceptualization of two subtypes in terms of etiology and presentation (although both of these groups may, in fact, be comprised of LCP offenders):

- Earlier Starters, primarily developmentally disabled:
  - Medical/neurological factors resulting in neurocognitive deficits.
  - Poor familial attachments, dysfunctional verbal interactions, and maltreatment.
  - Family distress.
  - School failures.
  - Negative peers.
  - Difficulty with planning and with subterfuge (more likely to be caught).
- Later Starters, primarily personality disordered:
  - Medical/neurological factors resulting in low autonomic nervous system arousal.
  - Poor attachments, inconsistent discipline, and maltreatment.
  - Dysfunctional beliefs about self and others.
  - Deficits in empathy, more likely to use others for their own purposes.
  - Able to plan and to engage in subterfuge.

In any event, the school neuropsychological model of cognition provides a conceptualization for the underpinnings of prosocial skills and the ability to exert what is termed "effortful control" over attentional and response mechanisms in various situations. Effortful control was first defined by Rothbart and Bates as "the ability to inhibit a dominant response to perform a subdominant response" (1998, p. 137).

Several aspects of externalizing behavior have shown a link to neurocognitive factors (Riggs, Greenberg, Kusche, & Pentz, 2006), such as frontal lobe function (ability to exert executive control over one's behavior), speech/language centers (ability to use language effectively for both inner speech and interpersonal communication), and areas of the brain involved in visuospatial processing (ability to perceive and express nonverbal information). Moreover, some research suggests that social experience and environment can alter neurobiological function (Fishbein, 2000), as well as neurocognition (Dowsett & Livesey, 2000).

NEUROPSYCHOLOGY AND NEUROBIOLOGY CONTRIBUTING FACTORS

With respect to the neurocognitive aspects of the externalizing disorders, certain key elements have repeatedly surfaced in the literature, including the following:

- Difficulty with effortful control
- Difficulty with self management
- Specific cognitive deficits (see Table 15.1)
- Difficulty with socio-emotional functioning and affective regulation

While there are multiple factors involved in the etiology of these conditions, there is compelling evidence from research in the area of juvenile delinquency to suggest that some of the characteristics of these disorders represent outward manifestations of anomalies in neurobiology, some of which appear to have a genetic component.

NEUROTRANSMITTER SYSTEMS

One line of research involves the neurotransmitter genetics of externalizing behavior. Young et al. (2002) identified a particular allele (variant) of the dopamine transporter 1 gene (DAT1), the 9-repeat allele, as a risk factor for externalizing behavior at ages 4 and 7 years. A related variant of the DAT1 allele, the 10-repeat variant, is tentatively linked to ADHD. DeYoung et al. (2006) reported that the 7-repeat allele of the dopamine D4 receptor gene appears to play a moderating role in the relationship between low cognition and externalizing behavior. Individuals lacking the allele showed a negative

Table 15.1

Neurocognitive Correlates Associated with Externalizing Disorders

Function	Deficits Reported
Sensory-Motor	• Children ages 4–6 years diagnosed with ADHD and ODD exhibited autonomic underarousal similar to that found in older adolescents with CD and antisocial adults. Heart rate changes in the clinical group were mediated exclusively by the parasympathetic system, whereas in the controls, heart rate changes were mediated by both autonomic branches (Crowell et al., 2006). • Meta-analysis of forty studies between 1971–2002 found that low resting heart rate was the best-replicated biological correlate of antisocial behavior in children and adolescents (Ortiz & Raine, 2004).
Attention	• In a five-year prospective study with repeated testing, omission errors on the Conners' CPT were significantly higher for unmedicated girls diagnosed with either subtype of ADHD, compared to controls (Hinshaw et al., 2007). Hinshaw et al. also found that on a timed visual cancellation task, unmedicated girls with either subtype of ADHD scored significantly worse than controls. • Meta-analysis found consistently significant deficits in this arena for both subtypes of ADHD groups, compared to normal controls (Frazier, Demaree & Youngstrom, 2004). • Children with ADHD made more omission and commission errors during the Conners' CPT than controls, which has been a generally consistent finding in the literature (Sartory et al., 2002).
Visual-Spatial	• Girls with both subtypes of ADHD scored significantly lower than controls on copying the Taylor Complex Figure on repeated testings (although the delayed recall condition did not differentiate the groups) (Hinshaw et al., 2007). • Life course persistent (LCP) juvenile offenders scored significantly lower on Block Design compared to controls (Raine et al., 2005). • Persistently antisocial 8-year-old children showed spatial (but not verbal) deficits when 3 years old (Raine et al., 2002). • Children with callous-unemotional traits showed intact speech/language skills, but had visuospatial deficits (Loney, Frick, Ellis, & McCoy, 1998).
Language	• In the Minnesota Twin Family Study (Taylor et al., 2000), boys ages 10–12 years old showed verbal skills deficits, indicated by VIQ, which predicted "early" vs. "late" behavior problems. • Speltz et al. (1999) found that in 80 preschool boys with ODD, 19% had undiagnosed language impairment. All had lower VIQ. • Cohen et al. (1998) reported that formal language impairment and deficits in social cognition had been found in one-third to half of children referred for psychiatric services.

Table 15.1
Continued

Function	Deficits Reported
Working Memory	• Reddy, Braunstein, and Dumont (2008) reported that the DAS Recall of Digits and Recall of Objects-Immediate were significantly lower in children with ADHD vs. controls, noting that Recall of Digits alone (at a cutoff score of 40), yielded high specificity, low sensitivity, and moderate positive predictive power.
	• Prospective study with repeated testing of unmedicated girls with both subtypes of ADHD found significantly worse Wechsler Digit Span (forward and backward) performance, compared to controls (Hinshaw et al., 2007).
	• Mayes and Calhoun (2007) reported that the WISC-IV WMI Index (together with PSI and Comprehension score) was a powerful predictor of learning disabilities in children with ADHD.
	• Meta-analysis found significant deficits in working memory for both subtypes of ADHD groups, compared to normal controls (Frazier, Demaree & Younstrom, 2004).
Visual Memory	• Spatial memory deficits were the strongest neurocognitive deficit differentiating three juvenile offender groups (Life Course persistent, Childhood Limited, Adolescent Limited) from the comparison control subjects (Raine et al., 2005).
Executive Function	• Barkley (2008)—deficits in self-control lead to secondary impairments in four executive functions: 1. *nonverbal working memory*—sensing to the self 2. *verbal working memory*—internalized speech 3. *emotional/motivation self regulation*—private emotion/motivation to the self. 4. *reconstruction or generativity*—behavioral simulation to the self.
	• Meta-analysis found significant deficits in behavioral inhibition for both subtypes of ADHD groups, compared to normal controls. Results for other types of executive function were mixed (Frazier, Demaree, & Youngstrom, 2004).
	• Children with ADHD demonstrate deficits in planning and organizing academic material, and in self-monitoring academic tasks (as do children with learning disabilities) (Cutting & Denckla, 2003).
	• In 1998, Oosterlaan, Logan, and Sergeant published a meta-analysis of eight studies of children with ADHD, CD, or both, (as well as anxiety-disordered and control groups) in which response inhibition was assessed with a "stop task." Four hundred and fifty-six children ages 6–12 years were included. Results demonstrated consistently significant deficits in response inhibition for the ADHD, CD, and combined groups as compared to anxiety-disordered or control groups.

(*continued*)

Table 15.1
Continued

Function	Deficits Reported
	• Seguin et al. (1995) followed 893 white, 6-year-old, French-speaking boys from 53 low SES Montreal schools with annual assessments. Physically aggressive behavior was assessed at ages 6, 10, 11, and 12 years. Nineteen percent of the sample were found to be "Stable Aggressives," and physical aggression was most strongly associated with tests of executive function (even when controlling for social factors).
	• Among 118 male children ages 9–22 years with ADHD (and other comorbid conditions), significant impairments were noted on the Wisconsin Card Sorting Test, Stroop test, and Rey-Osterreith Complex Figure, compared to controls. Comorbidity did not produce significantly different findings (Seidman et al., 1997).
Processing Speed/ Efficiency	• Mayes and Calhoun (2007) reported that a relatively lower WISC-IV PSI Index (especially in combination with a lower WMI Index and Comprehension subtest score) was a significant predictor of learning disabilities in children with ADHD (this finding was not replicated for children with ODD, according to earlier findings from these same authors).
General Cognition	• In a meta-analysis reviewing cognitive performance in ADHD vs. control groups, Frazier et al. (2004) reported that ADHD groups displayed significantly lower FSIQ scores relative to controls, with VIQ and PIQ also showing significant sensitivity. The weighted mean effect size was roughly equivalent to a 9-point difference in FSIQ for most commercial IQ tests. FSIQ was not significantly different between ADHD subtypes.
	• Level of IQ was associated with childhood conduct disorder and also with juvenile delinquency, for both any and all violent crime under age 17 years (Simonoff et al., 2004).
	• Speltz et al. (1999) studied 80 preschool boys with diagnosis of ODD, and all had lower IQs.
	• In a longitudinal study of mother-infant dyads, 83% of the behavior disordered 7-year-olds had shown a disorganized attachment pattern *and* low mental development at 18 months (Lyons-Ruth, Easterbrooks, & Cibelli, 1997).
Academic Functioning	
Reading	• Reading disability predicted persistent problem behavior from children ages 5–11 years (Henry et al., 1996).
Written Language	• Seventy percent of children with ADHD were found to have a comorbid learning disability in written expression (twice as common as disabilities in reading or math in this cohort) (Mayes & Calhoun, 2000).

Table 15.1
Continued

Academic Functioning *Continued*

Socio-Emotional	• Speltz et al. (1999) studied 80 preschool boys with the diagnosis of ODD. They found that all ODD boys had poorer ability to link an emotion word with a cartoon picture.
	• Difficult temperament in 3- to 5-year-old boys predicted convictions for violent offenses at age 18 years (Henry et al., 1996).
	○ At-risk temperament was characterized by:
	▪ Emotional lability, with intense reactions
	▪ Irritability, pervasive negative mood
	▪ Withdrawal from novel stimuli, low adaptability
	▪ Distractibility, poor frustration tolerance
	▪ Irregular biological functioning

---

correlation between cognition and externalizing behaviors, which did not manifest in individuals having at least one copy of the allele. While not fully accounting for externalizing behaviors, these findings make sense, in view of the role of the dopamine system in both child and adult externalizing disorders and the medication interventions that have proven effective for some of them.

NEUROANATOMY

Neuroanatomical dysfunction has also been implicated in the role of both externalizing disorders and deficit in memory and learning. For example, the limbic system is involved in regulating intensity of rage and aggression, but more important, the hippocampus in particular is also involved in encoding new information, especially spatial-temporal information that is known to include nonverbal communication critical for building and maintaining healthy social relationships. Hippocampal dysfunction has been found in brain imaging studies with convicted murderers (Raine, Buchsbaum, & LaCasse, 1997), violent offenders (Soderstrom et al., 2000), violent inpatients (Critchley et al., 2000), and both alcoholic and unsuccessful psychopaths (Laakso et al., 2001; Raine et al., 2004).

The prefrontal cortex is involved in regulating emotions, or self-management of responses, and the right orbital frontal cortex is involved in associating bad behavior with punishment (ostensibly facilitating development of a conscience). Yang et al. (2005) found that "unsuccessful" psychopaths showed lower prefrontal gray matter volume compared to controls on MRI ("successful" psychopaths did not). Raine et al. (2001) conducted PET scans of

38 male/female murderers and found that among the 26 subjects who came from non-abusive home environments, there was 5.7 percent less activity in the medial prefrontal cortex, as compared to 14.2 percent less activity in the right orbitofrontal cortex. Among violent offenders with a history of abuse, there was reduced right temporal cortex blood flow during a working memory task.

Hill et al. (2003) found that male and female children diagnosed with ADHD without comorbid learning disabilities showed several differences on MRI compared to the normal sample. Differences included smaller total brain, superior prefrontal, and right superior prefrontal volumes, as well as significantly smaller areas for cerebellar lobules I-V and VIII-X, total corpus callosum area, and splenium. Furthermore, greater right superior prefrontal volume was inversely correlated with Conners' CPT performance in the ADHD (but not control) group. The authors suggested that the latter finding may have been explained by the additional outcome with a subset of children receiving a magnetic resonance spectroscopy (MRS) study, which suggested possible right superior neurometabolite dysfunction in those with ADHD (i.e., greater dysfunctional right frontal tissue and/or activity would negatively impact CPT performance). While other studies have reported differences in caudate volume, these authors reported this finding only for children who were comorbid for ADHD and ODD. This group showed a significantly larger caudate measurement than those diagnosed only with ADHD.

BRAIN ACTIVITY

Anomalous EEG findings around event-related potentials (ERP) have also been reported consistently in both children and adults with externalizing disorders. One of the most robust features of the ERP is the P300, a positive deflection in voltage that occurs approximately 300 milliseconds after an unpredictable stimulus is presented. Hicks et al. (2007) reported that the P300 amplitude was strongly linked to symptoms of externalizing behavior in a sample of over 1,000 adolescent male twins and suggested that reduced P300 amplitude is a broad marker of neurobiological vulnerability underlying externalizing disorders with a strong genetic correlation.

Children with ADHD have also shown abnormalities in EEG studies measuring both event- and movement-related potentials while completing sustained attention tasks, such as a visual search (Trails Test) or a computerized Continuous Performance Test (CPT), which some authors have interpreted as deficits in both stimulus processing and response execution (Sartory et al., 2002).

Santesso, Reker, Schmidt, and Segalowitz (2006) reported significantly greater relative right frontal EEG activity at rest in children with externalizing behaviors, compared to controls. We know that the right hemisphere is relatively more attuned to novel stimuli from both visual fields, relative to the left hemisphere, so this EEG finding would also make sense in terms of deficits with sustained, selective, and divided attention, which have been hallmarks of ADHD. It would also make sense in terms of children who come from disruptive psychosocial environments where they have needed to be vigilant to potential threat. In fact, exposure to long- term threat has been shown to alter hippocampus anatomy (and presumably, functioning), which in turn impacts memory and learning (see Bremner, Randall, Vermetten, & Staib, 1997; Phelps et al., 2001).

ACQUIRED DYSFUNCTION

Traumatic Brain Injury (TBI) is more common among incarcerated prisoners than among the general population. Lewis et al. (1988) reported that all of the fifteen adults and fourteen juveniles on death row in the mid-1980s had a history of TBI. Among the juveniles, nine had major neurological impairment, seven had psychotic disorders antedating incarceration, seven showed organic dysfunction on neuropsychological testing, twelve scored lower than a standard score of 90 on their FSIQ, and twelve had been the target of brutal physical and/or sexual abuse.

OTHER CONTRIBUTING FACTORS

MEDICAL

Other risk factors can be as basic as sleep (see Gregory, Van der Ende, Willis, & Verhulst, 2008), nutrition (Liu, Raine, Venables, & Mednick, 2004), or headache (Virtanen et al., 2004), as well as many medical disorders, possibly due to the related stress on the child and the family.

FAMILY ENVIRONMENT

Family variables are an obvious component of externalizing disorders, including psychosocial stressors, parenting and disciplines practices, and family medical and psychiatric status. This is especially important given the correspondence between maternal depression and exposure to violence on the one hand, and CD with academic failure and poor self-control on the other (Levin, 2006).

Van den Oord, Boomsma, & Verhulst (2000) examined 446 MZ and 912 DZ pairs of 3-year-old twins from the Netherlands Twin Register, using multivariate genetic models fitted to a broad spectrum of behaviors. They reported that genetic factors accounted for 37 percent of shared variance, whereas shared environment accounted for 51 percent (see more on this topic under the following Comorbidity section).

Gender

There also appears to be a gender-based difference in the etiology of externalizing disorders, with history of physical and/or sexual abuse comprising a more salient risk factor for girls. Acoca (1998) reported on findings from a study conducted by the National Council on Crime and Delinquency, with a sample of nearly 1,000 California female offenders age 17 years or less. A large majority (81 percent) of their subjects, as young as 5 years of age, reported physical and/or sexual abuse that was often repeated. Intensity and longevity of abuse also yielded a significant effect: Violent female offenders who had experienced physical abuse at home outnumbered their male counterparts by a ratio of 2:1, and outnumbered their nonviolent female peers by a ratio of 3:1. More than 90 percent of the total sample had been suspended, expelled, retained, or were in Special Education.

A Commonwealth Fund survey (Harris, 1997) of 7,000 high school students found that 20 percent of the girls reported a history of physical/sexual abuse (approximately twice that of boys), and Harris (1997) hypothesized that boys may follow many developmental paths to delinquency, whereas girls seem to follow primarily a "delayed onset" path. They noted that the data indicated greater homogeneity in onset and adult outcomes of female juvenile delinquents, compared to boys.

COMORBIDITY WITH OTHER CHILDHOOD DISORDERS AND LEARNING DISABILITIES

Not surprisingly, comorbidity carries a more negative prognosis for continued dysfunction over the lifespan of children with externalizing disorders. In Simonoff et al.'s (2004) longitudinal study with a clinical sample of 225 twins over a ten- to twenty-five-year period, only 13 percent of those participants below the threshold for both hyperactivity and conduct disorder had early adult antisocial personality disorder, compared with 65 percent of those in whom both disorders were present. Mayes and Calhoun (2006) reported that their clinic-referred sample of children with ADHD had comorbid learning disabilities at the rates of 71 and 66 percent for combined and inattentive types, respectively. In contrast, 18 to19 percent of children referred for ODD also had a learning disability. Problems with written expression were twice as common as disabilities in reading or math. These authors suggested that learning and attention problems both range on a continuum, are interrelated, and usually coexist (Mayes & Calhoun, 2002).

Pliszka (1989) reported that ADHD was frequently comorbid with other disorders, including ODD or CD (approximately 47 percent) and anxiety disorder (approximately 26 percent). Several authors have argued that internalizing and externalizing disorders are both rooted in negative emotion, with impulsivity and effortful control being the characteristics that mediate how the child presents (Eisenberg et al., 2005). Mayes and Calhoun (2007) reported on findings from 678 children with ADHD, noting that approximately 76 percent were identified with a learning disability, most frequently in written expression.

Ezpeleta, Domenech, and Angold (2006) reported a high degree of comorbidity between ODD/CD and depressive disorders, with comorbid children demonstrating more irritability, substance abuse, and negative outcomes, as well as antisocial or destructive behaviors. Comorbidity was reported to accentuate emotional symptoms and functional impairment with no dramatic difference between children without comorbidity. According to Sartory et al. (2002), children with ADHD often present with comorbid oppositional and conduct disorder, as well as depression, anxiety, and functional enuresis. Undoubtedly, these conditions are mutually exacerbating and have a cumulatively negative effect on both academic and socio-emotional status.

Last, some authors have argued that while the individual externalizing disorders have a high degree of heritability, environmental factors play a large part in comorbidity. In an adoption study, Ge, Conger, Cadoret, and Neiderhiser (1996) reported that parental discipline and child antisocial behavior are mutually interactive, each impacting the other. Patterson, DeGarmo, and Knutson (2000) suggested that psychosocial factors, including disruptive parental discipline, accounted for the correlation between hyperactivity and antisocial behaviors. In a large multivariate study of 11-year-old twins from the Minnesota Twin Family Study, Burt, Krueger, McGue, and Iacono (2001) reported that (related to ADHD, ODD and CD), "although each disorder is significantly influenced by genetic factors at the individual level, the presence of a *comorbid* disorder is largely a function of a single shared environmental factor that is common to all disorders" (italics added, p. 523). The authors also noted that ". . . psychosocial adversity within the family system appears to be a prime candidate for the shared environmental vulnerability revealed in this study" (p. 524).

SCHOOL NEUROPSYCHOLOGICAL EVALUATION

1. Background Interview. Figure 15.1 depicts all of the variables that have been linked (to a greater or lesser degree) with externalizing behaviors. This chart is included in order to emphasize the importance of obtaining a thorough and careful background interview when conducting an assessment of a student with symptoms of an externalizing disorder.

them. This type of positively framed attention and feedback from an adult can be unique to the student's experience and can provide a valuable opportunity to identify dysfunctional self-talk and challenge some of the maladaptive beliefs which are molding self-concepts and behaviors.

6. Rule-Outs. There also needs to be careful consideration of other conditions that can present with comorbid or similar symptomatology, such as anxiety-related disorders, some medical conditions, or Bipolar Disorder as well as a Learning Disability confounded with ODD.

7. Give Feedback to the Student and the Parent at Separate Times, Apart from the IEP Meeting. Novice school psychologists can sometimes forget that assessment is conducted with an eye toward helping students and families improve in their overall functioning. The demands of the school setting, the IEP team, and the written report sometimes override the primary goal of discerning the problem and providing a proactive solution.

Setting aside time to give a student and parent individual feedback not only lets them know that they are important members of the school community, it also establishes rapport for future interactions and interventions and increases the likelihood that recommendations will be carried out with integrity.

The feedback session, even if brief or conducted over the phone, can be a critical juncture for effective intervention with both the parent(s) and the student and is the setting in which the school neuropsychologist can "pull it all together" in lay terms, with recommendations couched in language that the student can understand and apply. Younger students often enjoy seeing visuals depicting their strengths and visual cue cards to help with their weaknesses. Older students respond well to a bullet-point list of salient features from their assessment, with suggestions included, which they can take home.

In essence, in this author's opinion, if this type of feedback is not provided, the school neuropsychologist has not applied the basic principles of good psychology. For a sample case study of a student with conduct disorder, see Jiron (2004), particularly chapters six, seven, and eight (assessment report and intervention recommendations, respectively).

EVIDENCE-BASED INTERVENTIONS FOR THE TREATMENT OF EXTERNALIZING DISORDERS

One way of conceptualizing the development of more serious externalizing behavior might be as follows:

- We have emotional brain patterns and potentials.
- Environmental factors can reinforce or reduce them.
- Patterns are also influenced by attachment and cognitive skills.
- The person's view on the world is formed by emotion-brain-cognition interaction.
- Dysfunctional views hinder self-talk and self-regulation.
- Self-regulation impacts upon teachability.
- Teachability impacts upon success and self-perception.
- All of this impacts on functional social ability.

We can see that there are several paths to intervention for children with externalizing disorders, including the cognitive, psychosocial, and medical arenas. Intervention plans that include all three will undoubtedly yield the best results.

MEDICAL INTERVENTIONS

Although school practitioners generally have little direct means of ensuring that children receive the pharmacological interventions indicated for their symptom profile, they can assert a considerable amount of influence when collecting and presenting data, educating staff and parents about medications that have proven effective for ADHD or mood disorders contributing to disruptive behavior, and acting as liaisons with the practice sector to facilitate medical followup. Most parents are appreciative of this type of help, although some will be resistant. Medical intervention should never be included in a student's educational plan, but communication with the private practitioner can be mentioned as an augmentative facet of the comprehensive intervention. This can range from a simple phone contact between the classroom teacher and physician, to a more formal rating scale completed by school staff on a regular basis, to help with monitoring the effects of a medication protocol.

If school staff members are observing symptoms of a bona fide medical disorder, they are obligated to advise the parents and, if necessary, to enlist the services of the school nurse in order to ensure that the child receives appropriate medical care.

THE BASICS: CLASSROOM ENVIRONMENT

Some of the time-honored environmental interventions for ADHD continue to have merit. For example, the basic strategy of minimizing distractions was proven effectively in a clever study by Pugzles Lorch, et al. (2004). The authors presented children with ADHD and comparison controls with two televised stories, both with and without toys in the room, and then measured the children's visual attention and responses to factually and causally related questions about the stories. Not surprisingly, the toys-present condition yielded the most significant contrast between groups, with the ADHD group showing fewer "long looks" and less ability to respond to causal relation questions than the controls.

Current trends in education toward students seated in work groups or tables raise serious questions regarding the effect of this type of arrangement on children with externalizing disorders, or even on neurotypical children. Most adults would have difficulty working elbow-to-elbow with peers, and the distraction of having other children inches away is obvious to any observer of a student with ADHD. This author recently visited a classroom where a well-intended teacher had hung rows of artwork from the ceiling, so that they dangled over students' heads, covered nearly every inch of wall space with words and pictures clipped from magazines, and brought her pet poodle into the classroom on a regular basis. Although students were seated at individual desks, they were grouped into closely spaced clusters, and when it came time to do text work, the teacher asked them to sit in groups on the floor. Needless to say, many students were unable to balance their textbooks, read, think, and write on their assignment sheet while sitting on the floor. The classroom was very friendly and inviting, but the student being observed commented aloud, "I really hate working on the floor," and had significant difficulty resisting all of the distractions in the room.

At a different school, a new resource teacher who was highly receptive to ideas to help her with classroom management immediately implemented suggestions that each student have her or his own desk with necessary supplies and books at hand (to reduce out-of-seat behavior) and a "work plan" that involved a sequence of steps to be followed prior to asking the for teacher's help. One week later, she contacted the author and expressed her astonishment at how greatly negative behaviors had diminished after structuring the classroom with these few and simple techniques. She also reported having more time for both actual teaching and positive interactions with students.

In short, it can be helpful to a teacher for a trusted observer to make concrete suggestions about classroom environment. For example, artwork can be displayed on one section of one wall, or in the hallway, and changed out regularly. The clutter of open shelves can be minimized by hanging solid color sheets or curtains from Velcro attachments, and desks can replace student tables so that student belongings are not piled on the floor. Word lists can be arranged neatly on a removable display, rather than taped randomly all over the wall. These are all suggestions that will help not only the children with attention problems, but will also help all students understand how to organize and structure their own work environments.

COGNITIVE-BEHAVIORAL INTERVENTIONS

Following is a list of characteristics of students who are more "teachable" and who experience more academic success, according to teachers (Blair, 2002):

- Less distractible
- More positively balanced
- Moderate emotional intensity
- Intact friendship skills
- Perceived control over learning

We can see that many of these characteristics have to do with self-regulation and, at a more fundamental level, with effective self-talk.

Robinson, Smith, Miller, and Brownell (1999) conducted a meta-analysis combining twenty-three studies in nonclinical school-based populations that involved cognitive behavior modification interventions with children and adolescents who were impulsive or aggressive. Authors reported that in 89 percent of the studies, intervention with a cognitive component yielded greater improvement on both posttest and maintenance measures than comparison treatments. Moreover, there were no significant differences between posttest and follow-up measures, suggesting that the interventions had resulted in lasting positive change.

The cognitive-behavioral approach was also supported in several other meta-analytic literature reviews as one of the most effective behavior therapy techniques in adults (Miller & Berman, 1983; Smith & Glass, 1977). In children, this approach is largely patterned after Meichenbaum and Goodman (1971) and Meichenbaum (1977).

Cognitive-behavioral therapy is based on the model that disruptive behavior results from maladaptive inner speech (possibly, but not always, due to speech/language deficits in general) and that metacognitive skills are reliant on effective inner speech. An abundance of literature from the 1970s and 1980s supports this model as an appropriate intervention resource for the academic setting. For example, self-monitoring and selective strategy use differentiate skilled versus unskilled learners and are relevant to learning disabilities (Borkowski, Weyhing, & Carr, 1988).

Effective self-talk:

- Creates the "connection" between a behavior and an outcome.
- Creates the ability to pause before reacting.
- Creates the ability to stop a feeling from becoming a reaction.
- Creates the ability to form new strategies.

Some examples of maladaptive self-statements include the following:

- No one will meet my needs; I have to take care of myself.
- People can't be trusted.
- Relationships are a way to get what you want, but they don't last.
- The best way to avoid being hurt is to attack first.
- I have to get revenge when people hurt me.
- I can't let my guard down.
- Most people just think about themselves.
- If I keep pestering, I'll get my way.
- I shouldn't have to follow everybody else's rules.
- I never get to have enough _____.
- Life is boring, then you die.

These statements reflect just some of the beliefs expressed by externalizing students and often lead them to respond to the world in negative ways.

See Jiron (2004) for a comprehensive review of cognitive-behavioral research, as well as concrete examples and applications. Briefly, to implement cognitive-behavioral interventions for different types of students:

- Speech/Language deficits:
  - State child's feelings, beliefs, needs, watch for affirmation/refusal.
  - Provide visual means of communicating.
  - Provide speech/language therapy.
- Visuospatial deficits:
  - State what has happened, use sequences, empathy.
  - Coach child to notice others' nonverbal communication.
  - Practice social situations and teach strategies to "buy time" or understand.

PARENT TRAINING

Early studies indicated that 75 percent of children who did *not* have a good relationship with one parent (marked by warmth and the absence of criticism) developed a Conduct Disorder, compared to only 25 percent of children who did have a good relationship but later developed Conduct Disorder (Rutter et al., 1979). Lyons-Ruth et al. (1997) reported that in mother-infant dyads with a Disorganized Attachment pattern, mothers had poor fluency/conversation skills, made inappropriate responses to infant cues, and also conveyed "mixed messages." In addition, 83 percent of the behavior-disordered 7-year-olds had shown a Disorganized Attachment pattern *and* low mental development at 18 months.

Farmer, Compton, Burns, and Robertson (2002) conducted a literature review of controlled research studies on treatments for childhood externalizing behavior disorders, organized around the two subsets (disruptive versus hyperactive), for children ages 6 to 12 years. Results suggested positive outcomes for parent training and community-based interventions for disruptive disorders and also for medication for hyperactivity.

DeGarmo, Patterson, and Forgatch (2004) reported significant reductions in both externalizing and internalizing behaviors following an intervention of Parent Management Training for externalizing problems alone. An earlier study (Mendlowitz et al., 1999) concluded that children's use of active coping strategies and overall emotional functioning improved with parent involvement. Based on a literature review and their own study with children with ODD, Chase and Eyberg (2008) stated that "Parent involvement and early intervention are key aspects of many successful treatment programs for externalizing behavior problems" (p. 274). They also described effective parent management training as not problem-specific, but rather focused on increasing desirable behaviors and decreasing undesirable behaviors through coaching and application of proactive skills.

OVERALL SCHOOL ENVIRONMENT

Evidence suggests that many school characteristics, including the following, may be linked to antisocial behavior in children (Herrenkohl et al., 2001):

- Low levels of teacher satisfaction
- Little cooperation among teachers
- Poor student-teacher relations
- The prevalence of norms and values that support antisocial behavior
- Poorly defined rules and expectations for conduct
- Inadequate rule enforcement

In contrast, successful schools share certain characteristics:

- Emphasis on academics
- Clear expectations and regulations
- High levels of student participation
- Alternative resources such as library facilities, vocational work opportunities, art, music, and extracurricular activities

Rutter et al. noted that "One of the most significant findings is that the longer students attend these successful schools, the more their problem behaviors decrease" (1979, p. 83).

Although many school-wide programs have emerged over the past few decades, school neuropsychologists will be happy to know that some of the more recent programs incorporate understanding of the impact of cognition on behavior. Riggs et al. (2006) asserted that programs designed to promote social and emotional development should consider comprehensive models that attend to neurocognitive functioning and development in order to ensure the optimal outcomes. Those authors examined the Promoting Alternative Thinking Strategies (PATH) Curriculum (Kusche & Greenberg, 1994), a school-wide prevention program that incorporates neurocognitive models of development in elementary age children (such as the link between limbic-level emotion processing and prefrontal cortex systems involved in self-regulation). Children are systematically coached and given practice in verbal mediation (self-talk) and inhibitory control, as well as in identifying and labeling their own and others' emotions.

The Conduct Problems Prevention Research Group (1992) reported significant improvement in child aggression and disruptive behavior from a randomized trial with forty-eight schools in four U.S. communities using PATHS as a model for the Fast Track program, with both regular education and Special Education students. In addition, positive effects were maintained at one- and two-year followups. Most recently, Kam, Greenberg, and Kusche (2004) reported significant improvements in both internalizing and externalizing behaviors, as well as self-report of child depression in special needs children. (For a complete description of PATHS, and review of five clinical trials over two decades, see Greenberg & Kusche, 2006.)

In addition, Shriver and Weissberg reported in the *New York Times* (2005) on the positive academic effects of school-wide affective curriculums and positive behavior supports, noting that emotions and academic performance are "intimately connected." Their article was based on the results of Durlak and Weissberg (2005), who conducted a meta-analysis of more than 300 studies. The meta-analysis consistently showed that social and emotional learning programs significantly improved students' *academic performance* (italics added by this author). In fact, they reported that the average student enrolled in a social and emotional learning program ranked at least 10 percentile points higher on achievement tests than students who did not participate in such programs. Students enrolled in a socio-emotional learning program also:

- Had significantly better attendance records.
- Had more constructive (less disruptive) classroom behavior.
- Liked school more.
- Had better grade point averages.
- Were less likely to be suspended or disciplined.

INTEGRATED SCHOOL AND COMMUNITY

Loeber, Farrington, and Petechuk (2003) reporting on the Department of Justice website, recommended integrating the following types of school and community prevention programs:

- Classroom and behavior management programs
- Multicomponent classroom-based programs
- Social competence promotion curriculums
- Conflict resolution and violence prevention curriculums
- Bullying prevention
- Afterschool recreation programs
- Mentoring programs
- School organization programs
- Comprehensive community interventions

INTERVENTIONS: BOTTOM LINE

- Start early, in preschool if possible.
- Relationships matter and provide positive adult-child interactions.
- Effective self-talk is a key component of self-management.
- Use positive, specific language.
- Establish and maintain consistent limits and expectations.
- Provide social coaching and role modeling.
- Gently challenge dysfunctional beliefs.
- Provide family support and parent training.

When kids feel safe, valued, confident, challenged, and have clear behavioral and social expectations and skills, they do better in school, and in life.

SUMMARY

In this chapter, the factors shown to contribute to externalizing behaviors, as well as the longitudinal outcomes for children diagnosed with externalizing types of disorders, such as ADHD, ODD, and CD were reviewed. ADHD was noted to be not only the most commonly diagnosed childhood mental health condition, but often a comorbid condition with one of the other disruptive disorders, thereby posing a high risk for subsequent antisocial behavior, as well as other psychiatric and psychosocial problems. It was also noted that low impulse control and poor affect regulation consistently emerge as salient features of the externalizing disorders and also appear to increase the risk of violence across the different diagnoses.

The juvenile delinquency literature suggests that two subtypes consistently emerge, comprised of "adolescence-limited" versus "life-course persistent" offenders. Age of onset appears to also play a role, with early starters considered to have poorer neurocognitive function, compared to later starters who may be cognitively intact, but who demonstrate low autonomic nervous system arousal. In addition, there appears to be gender-based differences in the development of externalizing behavior.

Neurocognitive deficits associated with externalizing disorders span virtually every cognitive domain, including sensory-motor, attention, visual-spatial, language, memory and learning, executive function, and professing speed/efficiency. Not surprisingly, academic deficits have also been reported, most specifically in reading and writing. Underlying neurological etiologies have been implicated in the presence of externalizing disorders, including atypical development of neuroanatomical and neurotransmitter systems, as well as acquired dysfunction. Other risk factors include medical disorders, maladaptive family and home environment, and gender. It was also noted that the externalizing behaviors often present as comorbid diagnoses, with comorbidity associated with higher incidence of learning disabilities and school failure.

Last, a comprehensive school neuropsychological assessment approach for children with externalizing symptomatology was described and interventions ranging from the individual to community-wide levels were reviewed.

REFERENCES

Acoca, L. (1998). Outside/inside: The violation of American girls at home, on the streets and in the juvenile justice system. *Crime & Delinquency, 44*, 562–589.

Barkley, R. (1997). Attention-deficit/hyperactivity disorder, self-regulation, and time: Toward a more comprehensive theory. *Journal of Developmental & Behavioral Pediatrics, 18*, 271–279.

Barkley, R. (2008). About ADHD—A fact sheet by Dr. Barkley. Retrieved on June 27, 2008, from http://www.russellbarkley.org/adhd-facts.htm.

Blair, C. (2002). School readiness: Integrating cognition and emotion in a neuro-biological conceptualization of children's functioning at school entry. *American Psychologist, 57*, 111–127.

Borkowski, J. G., Weyhing, R. S., & Carr, M. (1988). Effects of attributional retraining on strategy-based reading comprehension in learning disabled students. *Journal of Educational Psychology, 80*, 46–53.

Bremner, J. D., Randall, P., Vermetten, E., & Staib, L. (1997). Magnetic resonance imaging-based measurement of hippocampal volume in posttraumatic stress disorder related to childhood physical and sexual abuse: A preliminary report. *Biological Psychiatry, 41*, 23–32.

Burt, S. A., Krueger, R. F., McGue, M., & Iacono, W. G. (2001). Sources of covariation among attention-deficit/hyperactivity disorder, oppositional defiant disorder, and conduct disorder: The importance of shared environment. *Journal of Abnormal Psychology, 110,* 516–525.

Chase, R. M., & Eyberg, S. M. (2008). Clinical presentation and treatment outcome for children with comorbid externalizing and internalizing symptoms. *Journal of Anxiety Disorders, 22,* 273–282.

Cohen, N. J., Menna, R., Vallance, D. D., Barwick, M. A., Im, N., & Horodezky, N. B. (1998). Language, social cognitive processing, and behavioral characteristics of psychiatrically disturbed children with previously identified and unsuspected language impairments. *Journal of Child Psychology & Psychiatry & Allied Disciplines, 39,* 853–864.

Conduct Problems Prevention Research Group. (1992). A developmental and clinical model for the prevention of conduct disorder: The fast track program. *Development and Psychopathology, 4,* 509–527.

Critchley, H. D., Simmons, A., Daly, E. M., Russell, A., van Amelsvoort, T., & Robertson, D. M. (2000). Prefrontal and medial temporal correlates of repetitive violence to self and others. *Biological Psychiatry, 47,* 928–934.

Crowell, S. E., Beauchaine, T. P., Gatske-Kopp, L., Sylvers, P., Mead, H., & Chipman-Chacon, J. (2006). Autonomic correlates of attention-deficit/hyperactivity disorder and oppositional defiant disorder in preschool children. *Journal of Abnormal Psychology, 115,* 174–178.

Cutting, L. E. & Denckla, M. B. (2003). Attention: Relationships between attention-deficit hyperactivity disorder and learning disabilities. In H. Lee Swanson, Karen R. Harris, & Steve Graham (Eds.) *Handbook of learning disabilities.* (pp. 125–213). New York: Guilford Press.

DeGarmo, D. S., Patterson, G. R., & Forgatch, M. S. (2004). How do outcomes in a specified parent training intervention maintain or wane over time? *Prevention Science, 5,* 73–89.

DeYoung, C. G., Peterson, J. B., Seguin, J. R., Mejia, J. M., Pihl, R. O., Beitchman, J. H., Jain, U., Tremblay, R. E., Kennedy, J. L., & Palmour, R. M. (2006). The dopamine D4 receptor gene and moderation of the association between externalizing behavior and IQ. *Archives of General Psychiatry, 63,* 1410–1416.

Dowsett, S. M., & Livesey, D. J. (2000). The development of inhibitory control in preschool children: Effects of "executive skills" training. *Developmental Psychobiology, 36,* 161–174.

Durlak, J., & Weissberg, R. (2005, August). *A major meta-analysis of positive youth development programs.* Presentation at the Annual Meeting of the American Psychological Association, Washington, DC.

Eisenberg, N., Sadovsky, A., Spinrad, T. L., Fabes, R. S., Losoya, S. H., Valiente, C., Reiser, M., Cumberland, A., & Shepard, S. A. (2005). The relations of problem behavior status to children's negative emotionality, effortful control, and impulsivity: Concurrent relations and prediction of change. *Developmental Psychology, 41,* 193–211.

Ezpeleta, L., Domenech, J. M., & Angold, A. (2006). A comparison of pure and comorbid CD/ODD and depression. *Journal of Child Psychology and Psychiatry, 47*(7), 704–712.

Farmer, E. M. Z., Compton, S. N., Burns, J. B., & Robertson, E. (2002). Review of the evidence base for treatment of childhood psychopathology: Externalizing disorders. *Journal of Consulting and Clinical Psychology, 70*, 1267–1302.

Farrington, D. P. (2001). Predicting adult official and self-reported violence. In G. F. Pinard & L. Pagani (Eds.), *Clinical assessment of dangerousness: Empirical contributions* (pp. 66–88). New York: Cambridge University Press.

Fishbein, D. (2000). The importance of neurobiological research to the prevention of psychopathology. *Prevention Science, 1*, 89–106.

Frazier, T. W., Demaree, H. A., & Youngstrom, E. A. (2004). Meta-analysis of intellectual and neuropsychological test performance in attention-deficit/hyperactivity disorder. *Neuropsychology, 18*, 543–555.

Ge, X., Conger, R. D., Cadoret, R. J., & Neiderhiser, J. M. (1996). The developmental interface between nature and nurture: A mutual influence model of child antisocial behavior and parent behaviors. *Developmental Psychology, 32*, 574–589.

Giancola, P. R., Mezzich, A. C., & Tarter, R. E. (1998). Executive cognitive functioning, temperament, and antisocial behavior in conduct-disordered adolescent females. *Journal of Abnormal Psychology, 107*, 629–641.

Greenberg, M. T., & Kusche, C. A. (2006). Building social and emotional competence: The PATHS curriculum. In S. R. Jimerson & M. Furlong (Eds.), *Handbook of school violence and school safety: From research to practice* (pp. 395–412). Mahwah, NJ: Lawrence Erlbaum Associates.

Gregory, A. M., Van der Ende, J., Willis, T. A., & Verhulst, F. C. (2008). Parent-reported sleep problems during development and self-reported anxiety/depression, attention problems, and aggressive behavior later in life. *Archives of Pediatric & Adolescent Medicine, 162*, 330–335.

Hale, J. B., Fiorello, C. F., Kavanagh, J. A., Hoeppner, J. B., & Gaither, R. A. (2001). WISC-III predictors of academic achievement for children with learning disabilities: Are global and factor scores comparable? *School Psychology Quarterly, 16*, 31–55.

Harris, L. & Associates. (1997). *The Commonwealth Fund survey of the health of adolescent girls*. New York: Commonwealth Fund.

Henry, B., Caspi, A., Moffitt, T. E., & Silva, P. A. (1996). Temperamental and familial predictors of violent and nonviolent criminal convictions: Age 3 to age 18. *Developmental Psychology 32*, 614–623.

Herrenkohl, T. I., Hawkins, J. D., Chung, I. J., Hill, K. G., & Battin-Pearson, S. (2001). School and community risk factors and interventions. In R. Loeber & D. P. Farrington (Eds.), *Child delinquents: Development, intervention, and service needs*, (pp. 211–246). Thousand Oaks, CA: Sage Publications.

Hicks, B. M., Bernat, E., Malone, S. M., Iacono, W. G., Patrick, C. J., Krueger, R. F., & McGue, M. (2007). Genes mediate the association between P3 amplitude and externalizing disorders. *Psychophysiology, 44*, 98–105.

Hill, D. E., Yeo, R. A., Campbell, R. A., Hart, B., Vigil, J., & Brooks, W. (2003). Magnetic resonance imaging correlates of attention-deficit/hyperactivity disorder in children. *Neuropsychology, 17*, 496–506.

Hinshaw, S. P., Carte, E. T., Fan, C., Jassy, J. S., & Owens, E. B. (2007). Neuropsychological functioning of girls with Attention-Deficit/Hyperactivity Disorder followed prospectively into adolescence: Evidence for continuing deficits? *Neuropsychology, 21*(2), 263–273.

Jiron, C. (2004). *Brainstorming: Using neuropsychology in the schools.* Los Angeles: Western Psychological Services.

Kam, C. M., Greenberg, M. T., & Kusche, C. A. (2004). Sustained effects of the PATHS curriculum on the social and psychological adjustment of children in special education. *Journal of Emotional and Behavioral Disorders, 12*, 66–78.

Kusche, C. A., & Greenberg, M. T. (1994). *The PATHS (promoting alternative thinking strategies) curriculum.* South Deerfield, MA: Channing-Bete Co.

Laakso, M. P., Vaurio, O., Koivisto, E., Savolainen, L., Eronen, M., & Aronen, H. J. (2001). Psychopathy and the posterior hippocampus. *Behavioral Brain Research, 118*, 187–193.

Levin, A. (2006). Depression, violence formula for poor school performance. *Psychiatric News, 41*, 20.

Lewis, D. O., Pincus, J. H., Bard, B., Richardson, E., et al. (1988). Neuropsychiatric, psychoeducational, and family characteristics of 14 juveniles condemned to death in the United States. *American Journal of Psychiatry, 145*, 584–589.

Lilienfeld, S. O., & Waldman, I. D. (1990). The relation between childhood attention-deficit hyperactivity disorder and adult antisocial behavior reexamined: The problem of heterogeneity. *Clinical Psychology Review, 10*, 699–725.

Liu, J., Raine, A., Venables, P. H., & Mednick, S. A. (2004). Malnutrition at age 3 years and externalizing behavior problems at ages 8, 11 and 17 years. *American Journal of Psychiatry, 161*, 2005–2013.

Loeber, R., Farrington, D. P., & Petechuk, D. (2003). Child delinquency: Early intervention and prevention. *Child Delinquency Bulletin Series*, U.S. Dept. of Justice, http://www.ojjdp.ncjrs.org

Loney, B., Frick, P., Ellis, M., & McCoy, M. (1998). Intelligence, callous-unemotional traits, and antisocial behavior. *Journal of Psychopathology & Behavioral Assessment, 20*, 231–247.

Lyons-Ruth, K., Easterbrooks, M., & Cibelli, C. (1997). Disorganized attachment strategies and mental lag in infancy: Prediction of externalizing problems at age seven. *Developmental Psychology, 33*, 681–692.

Mayes, S. D., & Calhoun, S. (2000). Prevalence and degree of attention and learning problems in ADHD and LD. *ADHD Reports, 8*(2), 1.

Mayes, S. D., & Calhoun, S. L. (2002). Learning disabilities and ADHD: Overlapping spectrum disorders. *Journal of Learning Disabilities, 33*, 417–424.

Mayes, S. D., & Calhoun, S. L. (2004). Similarities and differences in WISC-III profiles: Support for subtest analysis in clinical referrals. *The Clinical Neuropsychologist, 18*, 559–572.

Mayes, S. D., & Calhoun, S. L. (2006). Frequency of reading, math and writing disabilities in children with clinical disorders. *Learning and Individual Differences, 16*, 145–157.

Mayes, S. D., & Calhoun, S. L. (2007). Wechsler intelligence scale for children—third and fourth edition predictors of academic achievement in children with attention-deficit/hyperactivity disorder. *School Psychology Quarterly, 22,* 234–249.

Mendlowitz, S. L., Manassis, K., Bradley, S., Scapillato, D., Miezitis, S., & Shaw, B. F. (1999). Cognitive-behavioral group treatments in childhood anxiety disorders: The role of parental involvement. *Journal of the American Academy of Child and Adolescent Psychiatry, 38,* 1223–1229.

Meichenbaum, D. H. (1977). *Cognitive-behavior modification: An integrative approach.* New York: Plenum Press.

Meichenbaum, D. H., & Goodman, J. (1971). Training impulsive children to talk to themselves: A means of developing self-control. *Journal of Abnormal Psychology, 77,* 115–126.

Miller, D. C. (2007). *Essentials of school neuropsychological assessment.* Hoboken, NJ: John Wiley & Sons.

Miller, R. C., & Berman, J. S. (1983). The efficacy of cognitive behavior therapies: A quantitative review of research evidence. *Psychological Bulletin, 94,* 39–53.

Moffitt, T. E. (2007). A review of research on the taxonomy of life-course persistent versus adolescence-limited antisocial behavior. In D. J. Flannery, A. T. Vazsonyi, & I. D. Waldman (Eds.), *The Cambridge handbook of violent behavior and aggression* (pp. 49–74). New York: Cambridge University Press.

Nestor, P. (2002). Mental disorder and violence: Personality dimensions and clinical features. *American Journal of Psychiatry, 159,* 1973–1978.

Oosterlaan J., Logan G. D., & Sergeant J. A. (1998). Response inhibition in AD/HD, CD, comorbid AD/HD + CD, anxious, and control children: A meta-analysis of studies with the stop task. *Journal of Child Psychology & Psychiatry, 39,* 411–25.

Ortiz, J., & Raine, A. (2004). Heart rate level and antisocial behavior in children and adolescents: A meta-analysis. *Journal of the American Academy of Child & Adolescent Psychiatry, 43,* 154–162.

Patterson, G. R., DeGarmo, D. S., & Knutson, N. (2000). Hyperactive and antisocial behaviors: Comorbid or two points in the same process? *Development & Psychopathology, 12,* 91–106.

Phelps, E. A., O'Connor, K. J., Gatenby, J. C., Gore, J. C., Grillon, C., & Davis, M. (2001). Activation of the left amygdala to a cognitive representation of fear. *Nature Neuroscience, 4,* 437–441.

Pliszka, S. R. (1989). Effect of anxiety on cognition, behavior, and stimulant response in ADHD. *Journal of the American Academy of Child & Adolescent Psychiatry, 28,* 882–887.

Pugzles Lorch, E., Eastham, D., Milich, R., Lemberger, C. C., Polley Sanchez, R., Welsh, R., van den Broek, P. (2004). Difficulties in comprehending causal relations among children with ADHD: The role of cognitive engagement. *Journal of Abnormal Psychology, 113,* 56–63.

Raine, A., Buchsbaum, M., & LaCasse, L. (1997). Brain abnormalities in murderers indicated by positron emission tomography. *Biological Psychiatry, 24,* 495–508.

Raine, A., Ishikawa, S. S., Arce, E., Lencz, T., Knuth, K. H., Birhle, S., Lacasse, L., & Colletti, P. (2004). Hippocampal structural asymmetry in unsuccessful psychopaths. *Biological Psychiatry, 55,* 185–191.

Raine, A., Moffitt, T. E., Caspi, A., Loeber, R., Stouthamer-Loeber, M., & Lynam, D. (2005). Neurocognitive impairments in boys on the life-course persistent antisocial path. *Journal of Abnormal Psychology, 114*, 38–49.

Raine, A., Venables, P. H., Dalais, C., Mellingen, K., Reynolds, C., & Mednick, S. A. (2001). Early educational and health enrichment at age 3–5 years is associated with increased autonomic and central nervous system arousal and orienting at age 11 years: Evidence from the Mauritius Child Health Project. *Psychophysiology, 38*, 254–266.

Raine, A., Yaralian, P. S., Reynolds, C., Venables, P. H., & Mednick, S. A. (2002). Spatial but not verbal cognitive deficits at age 3 years in persistently antisocial individuals. *Development & Psychopathology, 14*, 25–44.

Reddy, L., Braunstein, D., & Dumont, R. (2008). Use of the differential ability scales for children with attention-deficit/hyperactivity disorder. *School PsychologyQuarterly, 23*, 139–148.

Riggs, N. R., Greenberg, M. T., Kusche, C. A., & Pentz, M. A. (2006). The mediational role of neurocognition in the behavioral outcomes of a social-emotional prevention program in elementary school students: Effects of the PATHS curriculum. *Prevention Science, 7*, 91–102.

Robinson, R. T., Smith, S. W., Miller, M. D., & Brownell, M. T. (1999). Cognitive behavior modification of hyperactivity-impulsivity and aggression: A meta-analysis of school-based studies. *Journal of Educational Psychology, 91*, 195–203.

Rothbart, M. K., & Bates, J. E. (1998). Temperament. In W. Damon & N. Eisenberg (Eds.), *Handbook of child psychology, Vol. 3, Social, emotional and personality development* (pp. 105–176). New York: John Wiley & Sons.

Rutter, M., Maughan, B., Mortimore, P., Ouston, J., & Smith, A. (1979). *Fifteen thousand hours*. Cambridge, MA: Harvard University.

Santesso, D., Reker, D., Schmidt, T. A., & Segalowitz, S. J. (2006). Frontal electroencephalogram activation asymmetry, emotional intelligence, and externalizing behaviors in 10-year-old children. *Child Psychiatry & Human Development, 36*, 311–328.

Sartory, G., Heine, A., Muller, B. W., & Elvermann-Hallner, A. (2002). Event-and motor-related potentials during the continuous performance task in attention-deficit/hyperactivity disorder. *Journal of Psychophysiology, 16*, 97–106.

Seguin, J. R., Pihl, R. O., Harden, P. W., Tremblay, R. E., & Boulerice, B. (1995). Cognitive and neuropsychological characteristics of physically aggressive boys. *Journal of Abnormal Psychology, 104*, 614–624.

Seidman, L. J., Biederman, J., Faraone, S. V., Weber, W., & Ouellette, C. (1997). Toward defining a neuropsychology of attention deficit-hyperactivity disorder: Performance of children and adolescents from a large clinically referred sample. *Journal of Consulting and Clinical Psychology, 65*, 150–160.

Shriver, T. P., & Weissberg, R. P. (2005, August 16). No emotion left behind [Op Ed article]. *New York Times*.

Simonoff, E., Elander, J., Holmshaw, J., Pickles, A., Murray, R., & Rutter, M. (2004). Predictors of antisocial personality: Continuities from childhood to adult life. *British Journal of Psychiatry, 184*, 118–127.

Smith, M., & Glass, G. (1977). Meta-analysis of psychotherapy outcome studies. *American Psychologist, 32*, 752–760.

Snyder, H. N. (2001). Epidemiology of official offending. In R. Loeber & D. P. Farrington (Eds.), *Child delinquents: Development, intervention, and service needs* (pp. 25–46). Thousand Oaks, CA: Sage Publications.

Soderstrom, H., Tullberg, N., Wikkelsoe, C., Ekholm, S., & Forsman, A. (2000). Reduced regional cerebral blood flow in non-psychotic violent offenders. *Psychiatry research: Neuroimaging, 98*, 29–41.

Speltz, M. L., DeKlyen, M., Calderon, R., Greenberg, M. T., & Fisher, P. A. (1999). Neuropsychological characteristics and test behaviors of boys with early onset conduct problems. *Journal of Abnormal Psychology, 108*, 315–325.

Taylor, J., Iacono, W. G., & McGue, M. (2000). Evidence for a genetic etiology of early-onset delinquency. *Journal of Abnormal Psychology, 109*, 634–643.

Van den Oord, E. J. C. G., Boomsma, D. I., & Verhulst, F. C. (2000). A study of genetic and environmental effects on the co-occurrence of problem behaviors in three-year-old twins. *Journal of Abnormal Psychology, 109*, 360–372.

Virtanen, R., Aromaa, M., Koskenvuo, M., Sillanpaa, M., Pulkkinen, L., Metsahonkala, L., Pulkkinen, L., Metsahonkala, L., Suominen, S., Rose, R. J., Helenius, H., & Kaprio, J. (2004). Externalizing problem behaviors and headache: A follow-up study of adolescent Finnish twins. *Pediatrics, 114*, 981–987.

Yang, Y., Raine, A., Lencz, T., Bihrle, S., LaCasse, L., & Colletti, P. (2005). Volume reduction in prefrontal gray matter in unsuccessful criminal psychopaths. *Biological Psychiatry, 57*, 1103–1108.

Young, S. E., Smolen, A., Corley, R. P., Krauter, K. S., DeFries, J. C., Crowley, T. J., & Hewitt, J. K. (2002). Dopamine transporter polymorphism associated with externalizing behavior problems in children, *American Journal of Medical Genetics, 114*, 144–149.

CHAPTER 16

Assessing and Intervening with Children with Internalizing Disorders

JEFFREY A. MILLER

A LTHOUGH THE FOCUS for neuropsychologists may be on acquired brain damage or developmental brain dysfunction, it is critical that they are also aware of neuropsychiatric disorders for diagnostic accuracy, understanding of the course of disorders, and for proper treatment selection (Smith, 2007). One such class of neuropsychiatric disorders commonly associated with neuropsychological dysfunction is internalizing disorders. Internalizing disorders include depression and anxiety and are associated with significant impairment in psychosocial and academic functioning as well as suicide. Internalizing disorders are called *internalizing* because the primary symptoms are typically experienced internally by the child (Teeter & Semrud-Clikeman, 1997). These internal experiences include worry, feelings of worthlessness, rumination, and inaccurate social perception. Internalized experience manifests in apparent behavioral symptoms including withdrawal, isolation, flat affect, and panic. However, it is the rich internal, cognitive-emotional world of the child with an internalizing disorder in which the disorder resides.

RELATIONSHIP BETWEEN NEUROPSYCHOLOGY AND INTERNALIZING DISORDERS

With regard to neuropsychiatric disorders, there has been a general emphasis on the psychological aspects because many theories of their emergence focus on cognitions and family systems. Further, there is an emphasis on the psychiatric aspects of internalizing disorders with explanatory theories at the neurotransmitter level indicating pharmacotherapy treatment regimens. On the other hand, neurodevelopmental disorders such as learning disabilities appear to encourage an emphasis on the neuropsychological causes (Teeter & Semrud-Clikeman, 1997; Tramontana & Hooper, 1997). However, evidence suggests neuropsychiatric disorders may result from manifest brain dysfunction, either developmental or acquired (Tramontana & Hooper, 1997). Therefore, the neuropsychologist must both attend to the acquired or developmental brain dysfunction and be aware of the likely neuropsychiatric sequelae.

There are at least three pathways that may account for neuropsychological (e.g., inattention) or neuropsychiatric symptoms (e.g., worry). First, there is the neuropsychiatric disorder in the absence of clear evidence of a neuropsychological deficit, such as early onset major depression. Second, there is clear evidence of brain-related causes of the psychopathology, such as in social phobia for a child with nonverbal learning disability. Finally, psychopathology resulting in temporary cognitive deficits that result in impairment on neuropsychological tests (Semrud-Clikeman, Kamphaus, Teeter, & Vaughn, 1997; Smith, 2007), such as sustained attention associated with depression-related rumination. It is very possible that poor sustained attention is a secondary symptom of depression and only evident during depressive episodes. Without a comprehensive evaluation of the child's psychosocial functioning, including measures of internalizing disorders, it is very possible that the evaluator will miss, in this example, the differential diagnosis of depression. Misdiagnosis of internalizing disorders can have deleterious outcomes such as substance abuse and suicide.

DIRECT AND INDIRECT EFFECTS

The second pathway described above, brain dysfunction leading to psychopathology, can be accounted for by both direct and indirect effects. Direct effects include disruption of the neurotransmitter balance as a result of the natural course of acquired head injury (Arffa, 2006) or decreased frustration tolerance related to direct insults to the frontal lobe via coup or contra coup injury (Oddy, 1993). Indirect effects are typically associated with the transactional experiences of the child with peers or family due to his or her acquired or developmental brain dysfunction and the child's inability to cope with those stressful experiences. For example, family members' overprotecting or scapegoating or feelings of failure associated with repeated academic failure (Tramontana & Hooper, 1997).

CLASSIFICATION OF INTERNALIZING DISORDERS

Most children experience temporary, mild feelings of depression and anxiety. More chronic and severe bouts of depression and anxiety are classified by in the *Diagnostic and Statistical Manual of Mental Disorders, 4th Edition, Text Revision* (DSM-IV-TR; American Psychiatric Association, 2000). In addition, schools utilize a classification system described in the federal special education law *Individuals with Disabilities Education Improvement Act* (IDEA; P.L. 108–446, 2004). In the following, DSM diagnoses for mood and anxiety disorders will be discussed followed by IDEA regulations. Internalizing disorders include numerous disorders. For this reason, the focus of the literature review for this chapter will primarily be on the most common and general internalizing disorders found in children—major depression and generalized anxiety disorder (GAD).

MOOD DISORDERS

Depression as described in the DSM-IV-TR is a class of mood disorders including Depressive Disorder (Major Depression and Dysthymic Disorder) and Bipolar Disorder (Bipolar I, Bipolar II, and Cyclothymic Disorder). The diagnosis of Major Depression in children includes depressed mood, irritable mood, or anhedonia (loss of interest or pleasure), as well as other symptoms such as weight loss or gain, changes in sleep patterns, psychomotor agitation or retardation, fatigue, feelings of worthlessness, or recurrent thoughts of death (American Psychiatric Association, 2000). As many as 2.5 percent of children and 8.5 percent of adolescents are diagnosed with Major Depression (Miller, 1998).

The course of major depression for children includes depressive episodes that last from seven to nine months (Miller, 1998). It is notable that for children, a major depressive episode can span the length of a typical school year. Recurrence of a depressive episode occurs between 54 and 72 percent of the time (Kowatch, DelBello, Mayes, Kennard, & Emslie, 2006). When there is a relapse, the chances of a recurrence continue to increase. Further, with each depressive episode, it takes less stress to activate the next depressive episode, and the time between episodes diminishes. About 70 percent of the time, children with more than one episode of depression will experience depression in adulthood with poorer outcomes the younger the index episode occurred (Miller, 1998).

ANXIETY DISORDERS

The DSM-IV-TR lists numerous types of clinical anxiety disorders including Panic Disorder, Obsessive-Compulsive Disorder, Generalized Anxiety Disorder, Social Phobia, and Posttraumatic Stress Disorder. Specific to children, Separation Anxiety is identified as a disorder usually diagnosed in infancy, childhood, or adolescence. The overwhelming feature of anxiety disorders is a subjective feeling of apprehension about impending danger or misfortune.

Children diagnosed with GAD experience excessive worry and anxiety as the essential symptom accompanied by any of the following: restlessness, easily fatigued, difficulty concentrating, irritability, muscle tension, or sleep disturbance (American Psychiatric Association, 2000). It is notable that both irritability and sleep disturbance are symptoms for both Major Depression and GAD. Over half of individuals with GAD report onset during childhood (American Psychiatric Association, 2000; Kessler, Keller, & Wittchen, 2001). Prevalence rates vary substantially across studies. Teeter and Semrud-Clikeman (1997) summarized prevalence studies of anxiety and found estimates as low as 2.9 percent and as high as 8 percent. More recently, twelve-month prevalence rates for school-aged children and adolescents were found to range between 8.6 and 20.9 percent for children and adolescents (Costello, Egger, & Angold, 2005), suggesting anxiety is more widespread than once thought.

The course of GAD is notable for frequent childhood onset and association with the onset of depression. High comorbidity with other neuropsychiatric disorders makes tracking the course of anxiety difficult due to a high percentage of individuals receiving a different diagnosis on followup (Pathak & Perry, 2006). However, there is evidence that anxiety persists into adulthood (Feng, Shaw, & Silk, 2008; Sweeny & Pine, 2004). In a study of boys, Feng and colleagues (2008) observed multiple trajectories for anxiety over the developmental period. From ages 2 though 10, about 50 percent of the boys in the study maintained a low level of anxiety. The other 50 percent maintained a high level of anxiety over that period with 17 percent of them showing elevating anxiety over time. The latter 50 percent were at a much great risk of developing an internalizing disorder later in life (Feng et al., 2008).

SCHOOL-BASED CLASSIFICATION OF INTERNALIZING DISORDERS

Public Law 108–446, *Individuals with Disabilities Education Improvement Act* (IDEA; 2004) is the third reauthorization of the Education for all Handicapped Children Act of 1975 (PL 94–142, 1975). IDEA includes definitions for the different disabilities that can be identified to entitle individuals for services, including the development of an individualized education program (IEP) and the opportunity to receive an education in the least restrictive environment (LRE). *Emotional Disturbance* (ED) is the category used to identify individuals with internalizing disorders such as depression and anxiety. The definition for ED is quite different from the DSM diagnostic categories. There are three main parts to the criteria for the classification of ED. First, the behavior must occur for a long time, to a severe degree, and adversely impact the child's school functioning. Second, the behavior must fall into one of the following five categories: (1) inability to learn that can't be accounted by factors such as intellectual, sensory, or health factors; (2) inability to build interpersonal relationships with peers and teachers; (3) inappropriate behaviors or feelings under normal circumstances; (4) a general, pervasive mood of depression or unhappiness; or (5) a tendency to develop physical symptoms or fears associated with personal or school problems. Finally, the term ED does not apply to children who are socially maladjusted unless it is determined they also have an emotional disturbance. Although vague, it is relatively clear that mood disorders and anxiety disorders qualify for services under numbers 4 and 5 in the ED definition. There is no mention of etiological considerations, so internalizing disorders secondary to brain dysfunction would qualify a child for services under IDEA.

MIXED ANXIETY-DEPRESSION

It has been argued that Major Depression and Generalized Anxiety Disorder are closely associated in children, sometimes referred to as mixed anxiety-depression, and may be variations of the same disorder (Cannon & Weems, 2006; Clark & Watson, 1991; Moffitt et al., 2007). Andrade and colleagues (2003) found major depression to be comorbid with GAD in ten countries from North America, Latin America, Europe, and Asia. Further, during the developmental period, anxiety and depression in children follows a heterotypic course, that is, sometimes changing symptomatic patterns between anxiety and depression (Caspi, Elder, & Bem, 1988; Ferdinand, Dieleman, Ormel & Verhulst, 2007). The issue of comorbidity has particular relevance because there is consideration being given to including Major Depression and GAD in the same diagnostic category in upcoming revisions of the DSM. It should be noted that Kessler et al. (2008) argue, based on a longitudinal, prospective study of comorbidity, that their finding of different risk factors for GAD and Major Depression suggests these two disorders are not manifestations of the same underlying factor. Despite this finding, the majority of published studies provide convincing evidence for the association between major depression and anxiety.

TRIPARTITE MODEL OF INTERNALIZING DISORDERS

The tripartite model of anxiety and depression has been provided as a framework for interpreting the high comorbidity and heterotypic nature of these two internalizing disorders (Chorpita, Plummer, & Moffitt, 2000; Clark & Watson, 1991). The model posits that the primary feature shared by anxiety and depression is *negative affect*. It is further hypothesized that *physiological hyperarousal* is associated with anxiety and *low positive affect* is related to depression. Subsequent studies have shown physiological hyperarousal to be positively related to panic disorder and negatively related to generalized anxiety disorder (Brown, Chorpita, & Barlow, 1998; Chorpita et al., 2000). However, Greaves-Lord and colleagues (2007) have argued, based on physiological measurement data, that it is an oversimplification to say that physiological hyperarousal is specific to anxiety and not to depression. What appears to be clear from the literature is that negative affectivity undergirds both anxiety and depression. The research on the neural basis of negative affectivity (discussed below) is therefore particularly relevant to neuropsychological understanding of internalizing disorders.

DEVELOPMENTAL PSYCHOPATHOLOGY

Applying neuropsychological methodologies to school-aged children and adolescents requires attention to developmental features of internalizing disorders. In very general terms the emergence of an internalizing disorder can be traced to the interaction of a physiological and biological vulnerability (diathesis) and the introduction of environmental stress, known as the *diathesis-stress model* (Charney & Manji, 2004; Earnheart et al., 2007; Miller, 1998). Studies indicate that the organization of the developing child may be affected by pervasive anxiety that is out of context or extreme reactions to neutral threats (Pathak & Perry, 2006). For example, parent modeling of affective responses inconsistent to the situation can produce a diathesis during critical early developmental periods. In regard to depression, the model was extended to identify *cognitive diatheses*, that is, a pattern of negative cognitions, and was called the *cognitive diathesis-stress model* (Hilsman & Garber, 1995). This notion of the development of internalizing disorders, that there is a predisposition toward psychopathology that is activated by stressful events, is a useful framework on which to link the burgeoning literature base on the developmental psychopathology of internalizing disorders.

BRAIN SYSTEMS AND INTERNALIZING DISORDERS

As indicated above, children with brain dysfunction are more susceptible to internalizing disorders (Tramontana & Hooper, 1997). This is likely due to the complex circuits that account for emotion in the human brain. That is, there is a good probability that some of the circuits involved in emotion could be involved in the general brain dysfunction. Further, as discussed above, the indirect effects of brain dysfunction in the absence of well-developed coping skills could result in internalizing symptoms such as withdrawal and feelings of helplessness.

BEHAVIOR INHIBITION SYSTEM

Gray (1995) theorized that internalizing disorders are associated with the behavioral inhibition system (BIS). The BIS is localized in the hippocampus and amygdala of the limbic system and the dorsal and ventral striatal systems of the basal ganglia. If the BIS does not develop normally and functions in an overactive state, the individual tends to experience negative affect as well as physiological arousal (Carver & Bell, 2006). This is consistent with the tripartite model of internalizing disorders previously discussed. Hale and Fiorello (2004) go on to conclude that children with depression and anxiety tend to have an overactive BIS accompanied by cortical overarousal that extends to the autonomic nervous system in the form of high parasympathetic reactivity.

NEUROBIOLOGY OF ANXIETY

Anxiety is a natural response associated with fundamental, primal survival instincts and is associated with the fight-or-flight response. Specifically, the activation of the threat response system by a real threat results in feelings of anxiety and fear (Pathak & Perry, 2006). The complex brain structures and circuits that have evolved over time to protect humans are also activated in anxiety disorder in which threats are generated internally. Because the threat response is so primal, some of the phylogenetically oldest parts of the brain are engaged in the response. After sensory information enters the brain, the afferent signals synapse in the ascending reticular activating system, causing arousal and alarm. Sensory information is integrated in the thalamus and transmitted to the limbic system including the amygdala and hippocampus. The subjective interpretation of the threat signals is conducted in the orbitofrontal cortex in concert with limbic-mediated activity (Pathak & Perry, 2006).

NEUROBIOLOGY OF DEPRESSION

As opposed to anxiety, which focuses on complex circuits throughout the brain, the neurobiology of depression is characterized by dysfunction and abnormalities of neurotransmitter and neuroendocrine (hormonal) systems. The primary neurotransmitters studied for depression are norepinephrine, serotonin, and acetylcholine (Kowatch et al., 2006). Studies of medications such as selective-serotonin reuptake inhibitors (SSRI) indicate insufficient norepinephrine and serotonin are associated with depression. Abnormal functioning of the hypothalamic-pituitary-adrenal (HPA) axis has been associated with depression. Specifically, the HPA axis is activated in times of stress and results in instructions to the hypothalamus to produce corticotrophin-releasing factor (CRF) that results in elevations of the hormone cortisol (Miller, 1998). Chronically elevated cortisol levels result in increased sensitivity to future stress, leading to an open feedback loop of increasing cortisol levels. Recent studies have revealed that prolonged, intense maternal stress during pregnancy increases cortisol levels and can alter functioning of the HPA axis in both the mother and fetus. Such alterations are associated with structural changes in the hippocampus, amygdala, and frontal cortex (Weinstock, 2008). Such changes can have systemic influence because the frontal lobe is the largest of the brain's lobes and performs diverse functions. Along with planning appropriate behavioral responses and working memory, it functions with other parts of the brain in regard to learning, memory, motivation, and attention. The frontal cortex integrates perceptual information from the parietal and temporal lobes, as well as the sensory and motor areas during learning (Buchsbaum, 2004).

These findings correlate with the course of depression described above in which the time between depressive episodes and the stress needed to activate a depressive episode decrease over time. Soares and Mann (1997) conducted a review of existing morphological neuroimaging studies and found consistent evidence for decreased volume of the frontal lobe, cerebellum, caudate, and putamen in adults with depression. These findings have not been replicated in children due to difficulties with conducting MRI studies with children (Kowatch et al., 2006). However, the limited functional neuroimaging studies of cerebral blood flow have pointed to abnormalities in the limbic-thalamic-cortical network (Drevets et al., 1992; Soares & Mann, 1997).

NEUROCOGNITIVE DEFICITS ASSOCIATED WITH INTERNALIZING DISORDERS

SENSORY-MOTOR DEFICITS

Baron (2004) pointed out that sensory-motor assessments have been minimized or marginalized in the typical child neuropsychological evaluation. This is evidenced by the very minimal information about sensory-motor functioning in the empirical literature base. Nevertheless, Baron concluded that sensory-motor assessment should be routine in child neuropsychological evaluations. For example, Hale and Fiorello (2004) report that right hemisphere dysfunction has been associated with internalizing disorders. Therefore, it would be important to assess hemispheric laterality through lateral dominance testing to assist in the interpretation of other assessment data. Depression has been associated with psychomotor retardation, which would likely impact sensory-motor tasks. In a study with adults, Zarrinpar, Deldin, and Kosslyn (2006) found that individuals with major depression evidence slower response times for visual-spatial tasks. They concluded that psychomotor retardation associated with depression may be a stimulus-encoding or motor-output deficit rather than a cognitive deficit.

Replication studies are necessary to extend this finding to children, but the findings do suggest children may exhibit longer response times for visual-spatial tasks while in a depressive episode.

ATTENTIONAL PROCESSING DEFICITS

Inattention is often observed during the early childhood period of children who later become depressed. In fact, the DSM-IV-TR indicates that Major Depression in young children is often comorbid with attention-deficit disorders (American Psychiatric Association, 2000). Throughout the developmental period there is substantial evidence for the co-occurrence of Attention-Deficit/Hyperactivity Disorder (ADHD) and Major Depression (Ostrander, Crystal, & August, 2006). Despite the early appearance of inattention as a prodromal symptom in very young children, inattention may not be the primary attentional problem in school-aged children. Blackman, Ostrander, and Herman (2005) compared depressed and non-depressed school-age children to determine if the depressed children exhibited higher rates of ADHD inattentive type than combined type. They found no difference in rates of inattentive type and combined type compared to the control subjects suggesting that children with depression and ADHD may present either as inattentive or as overactive/impulsive. On the other hand, Hurtig and colleagues (2007) studied 457 adolescents with ADHD and found that those with primarily inattentive symptoms had increased probability of comorbid Major Depression. Blackman et al. (2005) further found that children with ADHD and depression exhibit great social impairment than normal controls.

VISUAL-SPATIAL PROCESSING DEFICITS

As with sensory-motor deficits, visual-spatial deficits in children with internalizing disorders are not frequently reported in the literature. In a non-clinical sample of 66 children ages 6 to 13 years, Aronen, Vuontela, Steenari, Salmi, and Carlson (2005) found that children with internalizing symptoms performed poorly on visual working memory tasks. Additionally, there was a positive correlation between anxious/depressed symptoms and the number of incorrect, multiple, and missed responses on the visual working memory tasks. McClure, Rogeness, and Thompson (1997) found subtle differences between subclinically depressed adolescent females and nondepressed peers in terms of visuospatial perception and organization.

LANGUAGE DEFICITS

When examining the relationship between language deficits and internalizing disorders, it is difficult to determine if neuropsychological dysfunction accounts for the development of both language deficits and internalizing disorders or if the stigma from having difficulty speaking results in increased levels of anxiety or depression. It does appear, however that increased rates of both anxiety and depression as well as other internalizing disorders are strongly correlated with language disorders such as combined speech/language disorder, stuttering, selective mutism, and Tourette syndrome.

General Speech/Language Disorders   Vallance, Cummings, and Humphries (1998) studied school-aged students diagnosed with language learning disorders (LLD) who were found to have lower social discourse than the control students. The *Test of Language Development* (TOLD-2: Hammill & Newcomer, 1988) was used to measure expressive and receptive language, while the *Test of Language Competence—Expanded Edition* (TLC-E: Wiig & Secord, 1989) was used to measure social discourse. The students with LLD were also found to be less social overall as well as demonstrating more problem behaviors. The researchers hypothesized that the language problems may interfere with a student's language, cognitive, and social processes, thus increasing in the display of behavior problems including internalizing disorders.

Language disorders also appear to manifest in higher levels of anxiety as well. In a fourteen-year longitudinal study conducted by Beitchman and colleagues (2001), students who had both speech and language impairments (S/L) were found to have a higher prevalence of anxiety disorders (most of which were social phobic disorder) later in life than the control group or those with only a speech impairment or language impairment group. Early onset of S/L impairments was found to be associated with a higher likelihood of developing an anxiety disorder later in adolescence. These findings point to the accumulation of risk factors leading to poorer adaptive outcomes.

Specific Speech Disorders   Specific speech disorders are also associated with internalizing behaviors. Selective mutism (SM), for example, is highly correlated with symptoms of anxiety. Ford, Sladeczek, Carlson, and Kratochwill (1998) found that individuals with SM showed similar symptoms on the parent and self-report behavior rating scales as individuals with only anxiety disorders. Manassis and colleagues (2007) found that children with SM performed poorer on tasks involving verbal comprehension or visual memory than normal controls. The children with SM also had a higher prevalence of social anxiety

Craig, Hancock, Tran, and Craig (2003) examined the link between stuttering and anxiety in a sample of adolescents and adults. Individuals who stuttered had higher scores for anxiety than those who did not stutter. The researchers also found that of the people in the group who stuttered, the ones who sought treatment for their stuttering were more anxious. It was inferred that these individuals sought treatment because they demonstrated more severe stuttering and that their severe stuttering could also lead to stigmatization in school and social settings, resulting in higher levels of anxiety. Meanwhile, the individuals who did not seek treatment may not have viewed their symptoms as serious and were less likely to get treatment or feel as anxious.

Depression, like anxiety, is also found in people with language impairments. Tourette syndrome (TS) is usually accompanied by vocal tics that start between ages 11 and 15. Robertson, Banerjee, Eapen, and Fox-Hiley (2002) found that students diagnosed with TS had significantly higher levels of depression than a control group. The students diagnosed with TS were also more likely to show compulsions as well.

MEMORY AND LEARNING DEFICITS

Memory and learning deficits have been linked to internalizing disorders primarily through the association of internalizing disorders and frontal lobe dysfunction (Buchsbaum, 2004). Günther, Holtkamp, Jolles, Herpertz-Dahlmann, and Konrad (2004) examined performance differences on attention and memory tasks in children and adolescents diagnosed with anxiety or depression compared to controls. Both anxiety and depression were found to be associated with verbal memory deficits but not with attention. The authors pointed out that the small sample size should be taken into consideration in the interpretation of findings. Aronen et al. (2005) found visual memory deficits for children rated with mixed anxiety and depression. Lauer, Giordani, Boivin, and Halle (1994) examined performance on automatic memory tasks, effortful memory tasks and a meta-memory battery. Results indicated that depressed children performed more poorly on the meta-memory battery and that severity of depression differentiated overall performance. Hartlage, Alloy, Vázquez, and Dykman (1993) found that depression interferes with effortful processing, and the degree of interference is determined by severity of the depression.

There is an emerging literature on autobiographical memory and depression. Depressed adolescents tended to remember personal experiences from an observer perspective, thought their memories were personally important, and tended to rehearse negative memories more often than non-depressed youth (Kuyken & Howell, 2006).

With regard to anxiety, Vasa et al. (2007) examined visual and verbal memory deficits in common childhood anxiety disorders and whether specific deficits are associated with particular anxiety disorders, as well as children with risk factors such as parental history of internalizing disorders, including panic disorder or major depressive disorder. Results indicated that children with social phobia history demonstrated lower visual memory performance. No other anxiety disorder predicted memory performance. Neither parental panic disorder nor major depressive disorder was associated with their children's memory performance.

EXECUTIVE FUNCTION DEFICITS

As with memory deficits, internalizing disorders are associated with compromised executive function abilities in relation to frontal lobe functioning (Emerson, Mollet, & Harrison, 2005). Emerson et al. (2005) looked at executive function deficits in anxious and depressed boys (ages 9–11). They found that anxious/depressed boys showed deficits in problem-solving, sequencing, and alternation tasks. Frontal lobe involvement was evidenced by increased response times and frequency of errors compared to controls. Cataldo, Nobile, Lorusso, Battagila, and Moteni (2005) examined impulsivity on clinic-based measures of executive function and parent rating of impulsivity/restlessness. Children with depression were found to exhibit a conservative response style, slow reaction times, and inattention. These findings were considered consistent with executive functioning deficits in adults with depression. It is notable that children with depression were not more impulsive/restless on behaviorally based parent reports. Kyte, Goodyer, and Sahakian (2005) investigated the cognitive ability of adolescents with first-episode Major Depression. They concluded that these children were more impulsive when making decisions, paid more attention to sad stimuli, but were more able to switch attentional set to neutral stimuli than their normal peers. Bucci and colleagues (2007) found deficits in visuospatial abilities in adults with Obsessive-Compulsive Disorder. The authors also examined executive functions and concluded that their findings supported previous findings that internalizing disorders involve dysfunction of frontostriatal circuits in the right hemisphere.

With regard to anxiety, Toren and colleagues (2000) examined executive function indicators from neuropsychological tests with nineteen children and adolescents. They concluded that youth with overanxious and separation anxiety disorders slowed less cognitive flexibility than controls as evidenced by more perseverations, errors, and incorrect responses to negative feedback. Similar findings were noted by Andres and colleagues (2008) with children with obsessive-compulsive disorder. Specifically, they showed more perseverations, errors, and slower response times than normal controls.

SPEED AND EFFICIENCY OF PROCESSING DEFICITS

Results of studies of executive function suggest that processing speed will be slower for individuals with internalizing disorders. This is consistent with

Kaufman's (1994) hypothesis that neurocognitive dysfunction could adversely impact processing speed. Calhoun and Mayes (2005) examined 980 children with various clinical disorders and found a relative weakness on the Processing Speed Index (PSI) of the WISC-III (Wechsler, 1991) for children diagnosed with depression ($n = 11$). However, children with anxiety ($n = 17$) did not evidence low PSI scores. Using a similar methodology, Mayes and Calhoun (2007) did not find a significant difference in terms of processing speed when comparing children diagnosed with mixed depression and anxiety ($n = 25$) to a community sample. It appears the introduction of anxiety moderates the slow processing speed for youth with depression.

GENERAL COGNITIVE DEFICITS

Overall, the literature shows that there are two approaches to looking at cognitive ability and internalizing disorders: (1) how neuropsychological ability impacts internalizing symptoms and (2) how internalizing symptoms can impact neuropsychological functioning. There is most likely a reciprocal relationship between these factors. Children who have trouble with academic performance because of cognitive deficits can become anxious and depressed as a result.

Rapport, Denney, Chung, and Hustace (2001) linked IQ to withdrawal and mixed anxiety and depression. They generated a reciprocal model with the three factors, the dual pathway model. All three factors impacted each other and together could predict cognitive functioning, achievement, and classroom performance.

Lundy (2007) measured whether having anxious/depressed or withdrawn symptoms was associated with cognitive and academic measures. There were significant decrements found for children who were anxious/depressed and withdrawn than those without internalizing symptoms on the following cognitive and academic measures: general intelligence including verbal and nonverbal abilities, language, specific executive function skills, attention and processing speed, psychomotor speed and coordination with the dominant hand, the interference and/or delayed recall trial of a memory task, and basic reading, math problem solving, and early spelling/writing skills. The conclusion was that having symptoms of anxiety and depression do have an impact on cognitive and academic measures in children.

ACADEMIC DEFICITS

In recent years, the area of internalizing disorders has become increasingly studied as it relates to school-age children and adolescents due to the potential negative impact it may have on students' education (Herman,

Lambert, Reinke, & Ialongo, 2008; Herman & Ostrander, 2007; Lundy, 2007; Maughan, Rowe, Loeber, & Stouthamer-Loeber, 2003; Rapport et al., 2001). Rapport et al. (2001), among others, suggest that anxiety/depression and social withdrawal contribute to academic underachievement above and beyond intelligence levels.

Studies have shown that academic underachievement leads to depression later in one's academic career (Herman et al., 2008; Maughan et al., 2003; Rapport et al., 2001). In a study conducted by Herman and colleagues (2008), it was found that academic underachievement and depression can be linked to the underlying cognitive problem of perceptions of a lack of control. This lack of control stems from a long history of failure and not being able to succeed in an academic setting, something often found in children diagnosed with a learning disability, which can be generalized to other areas of life (Sideridis, 2007). Children use external cues to assess themselves and make conclusions about their self-control and competence; in school, the classroom and peers serve as two of these moderators (Herman et al., 2008). Thus, school neuropsychologists ought to be aware of how the external world may be affecting the internal processes of children in school.

Because memory and learning are highly dependent on optimal performance of the frontal cortex, they are often comorbid with neuropsychiatric internalizing disorders (Semrud-Clikeman, 2005). Martínez and Semrud-Clikeman (2004) found that adolescents with multiple learning disabilities reported poorer functioning at school and clinical maladjustment, emotional symptoms, atypicality, and depression than typical achieving peers. Students with single and multiple learning disabilities perceived a greater sense of inadequacy than the typical peer group. Regarding gender, girls reported more emotional symptoms, social stress, and depression, while boys reported school maladjustment and sensation-seeking concerns.

A recent study examined children who were at risk for the development of anxiety or depression and their performance on reading and spelling tasks. Results indicated that children at risk for depression made more spelling errors during dictation. There were no differences on reading tasks in the group of children at risk for anxiety (Bonifacci, Candria, & Contento 2008).

Maughan et al. (2003) found that reading problems occurred prior to any depressive symptoms in children. They ascertained that even after controlling for other variables often associated with depression, such as family problems, conduct problems, and inattention, 7- to 10-year-old boys with severe reading problems were three times more likely be depressed in a followup assessment after a period of struggling with the reading problems (Maughan et al., 2003). However, the study did not support the reverse path of depression leading to academic underachievement. One possible conclusion is that low self-control and negative feelings of school competence lead to more generalized negative feelings about the self as a child grows into adolescence, and that the underlying cognitive problem can be seen early on in school achievement (Herman et al., 2008; Maughan et al., 2003).

Herman and Ostrander (2007) use the term *"school maladjustment"* to describe problems at school, such as learning problems, school dissatisfaction, and impaired peer relationships, which can be observed and are also associated with depression and inattention. These researchers suggested additional developmental considerations for children's school maladjustment. For example, it was found young children under age 10 often experience depression in relation to the environment around them, often visible in their school maladjustment, and as children get older, their depression becomes more cognitively related and internalized. Consequently, control-related beliefs tend to develop over time as the child matures. This supports the notion of helping children as early as possible. If children with school maladjustment are identified at a young age, before experiencing negative control related beliefs, their ultimate depression and internalizing disorder may be diminished.

In addition to various reasons for underachievement, there are different achievement strategies students use, which often are affected by their feelings of control and self-esteem (Aunola, Stattin, & Nurmi, 2000). The different strategies that students use tend to be either adaptive (e.g., mastery and task oriented, belief in one's own success, and optimism) or maladaptive (e.g., failure expectations, learned helplessness, belief of lack of control, and task avoidance (Aunola et al., 2000; Dweck, 1986). It is suggested that self-esteem, which is developed through internal understandings of individual experiences, plays a key role in a student's achievement strategy usage. It was found that as maladaptive strategy usage increased, so did the number of reported depressive symptoms; low self-esteem was related to both problem behaviors and low achievement (Aunola et al., 2000). It was concluded that students' self-esteem is related substantially to a student's achievement strategy, school adjustment, and, if these previous areas are negative, internalizing disorder symptomatology.

Social-Emotional Functioning   In a study on anxiety by Hughes, Lourea-Waddell, and Kendall (2008) it was found that children who endorsed symptoms of anxiety and internalizing disorders also had increased somatic complaints. Additionally, the increased somatic complaints significantly contributed to poor academic performance. Findings supported previous research whereby high rates of anxiety are also associated with high dropout rates and poor school attendance, and that there is a relationship between somatic complaints and internalizing disorders such as anxiety and depression. Hughes and colleagues further suggested that somatic complaints may be one way children express their underlying desire to avoid anxiety-provoking situations.

In summary, a variety of neuropsychological deficits are associated with depression and anxiety. The related neuropsychological deficits should be assessed in a comprehensive evaluation of a child suspected of having an internalizing disorder.

LIKELIHOOD OF COMORBIDITY WITH OTHER CHILDHOOD DISORDERS AND LEARNING DISABILITIES

Internalizing disorders are obviously highly comorbid with other neuropsychiatric disorders in children and adolescents (American Psychiatric Association, 2000). As discussed above, depression and anxiety are often comorbid with each other. Further, internalizing disorders are comorbid with ADHD (Ostrander et al., 2006), speech/language disorders (Beitchman et al., 2001), memory disorders (Semrud-Clikeman, 2005), and learning disabilities (Herman et al., 2008; Rapport et al., 2001).

An area of potential comorbidity not discussed is between depression, Oppositional Defiant Disorder (ODD), and/or Conduct Disorder (CD), which have been shown to be comorbid at a rate of over 25 percent (Angold, Costello, & Erkanli, 1999). Herman and Ostrander (2007) theorized that depression would be a secondary disorder to Conduct Disorder due in part to academic failure as a cumulative stressor. Conduct Disorder in the presence of inattention would lead to increased depression. However, the path models did not support this theory with regard to Conduct Disorder. As discussed above, the role of inattention and school maladjustment was predictive of later depression. In a longitudinal study, researchers examined relationships between academic achievement and externalizing/internalizing symptoms over a twenty-year period. The study found that externalizing behavior problems in childhood appeared to lead to academic underachievement in adolescence, which then led to internalizing problems in young adulthood (Masten et al., 2005). One explanation for mixed findings may have to do with the developmental ordering of Conduct Disorder in relation to learning problems. Wisniewski, Hughes, Loeber, and Miller (under review) examined eleven-year longitudinal data from 503 youth concerning the development of attention problems, learning problems, and delinquency. It was found that on average learning problems develop before delinquency. Of course, ADHD was evidenced before either problem. With regard to the emergence of depression in association with conduct problems, it is likely that both conduct problems and depression emerge after attention and learning problems, but that remains to be verified empirically.

Studies are emerging suggesting Autism Spectrum Disorder may be comorbid with internalizing disorders. Simonoff et al. (2008) studied 112 children 10 to 14 years old diagnosed with either Pervasive Developmental Disorder or childhood autism to identify comorbid neuropsychiatric conditions. With regard to anxiety, any anxiety disorder was found in 41.9 percent of the children, with social anxiety disorder as the most frequent (29.2 percent). Only 1.4 percent had any comorbid depressive disorder. Using a different methodology, Pine, Guyer, Goldwin, Towbin, and Leibenluft (2008) found significant associations between depression and ratings of autism symptoms, but not between anxiety and autism symptoms after controlling for potential confounding variables. Two studies of cognitive behavioral treatments for children with comorbid autism and anxiety disorders found that after treatment there were significant reductions in anxiety symptoms (Chalfant, Rapee, & Carroll 2007; Sze & Wood, 2007). The treatment findings suggest that the internalizing disorder in comorbid disorders may respond to treatment even if the other disorder is more intractable. Taken together, there is evidence of comorbidity between autism and internalizing disorders, but this research is still in an early stage of development.

COMPONENTS OF A SCHOOL NEUROPSYCHOLOGICAL EVALUATION TO ADDRESS INTERNALIZING DISORDERS

Internalizing disorders are best assessed with assessment procedures designed to measure personality functioning. Smith (2007) thoroughly examines the integration of personality assessment with neuropsychology. The gist of his argument is that neuropsychological or personality assessment in isolation does not provide a complete picture of the individual's functioning. Personality assessment in isolation may result in false conclusions because individual responses may be impacted by neuropsychological deficits. As a basic example, a child's ratings to a self-report measure of behavior could be impacted by a reading learning disability resulting invalid responses due to poor reading ability. On the other hand, as has been discussed, neuropsychiatric conditions can appear as neuropsychological deficits. Without personality assessment to identify the underlying internalizing problem, invalid conclusions could be drawn. Finally, due to the significant comorbidity of internalizing problems with cognitive functioning in children, personality assessment should be a standard protocol for the school neuropsychologist.

The primary assessment procedures that should augment the neuropsychological battery for internalizing problems are clinical interview, behavioral observation, behavior ratings, and personality tests. Each of these classes of assessment procedures will be briefly described in the following sections.

CLINICAL INTERVIEW

Child clinical interviewing requires a diverse set of skills because the contexts of a child's life are complex and are set along a developmental trajectory (McConaughy, 2005). Younger children are heavily influenced by parents, and as the child develops, influence increasingly comes from peers. Given these interrelated forces and the frequency of comorbidity of internalizing disorders, one of the first goals of the interview is to clarify the referral questions. After the referral questions are clear and some initial hypotheses have been generated, the school neuropsychologist could employ a structured, semistructured, or unstructured interview approach (Semrud-Clikeman, Fine, & Butcher, 2007). Structured interviews typically require proprietary training to administer, and include the *Diagnostic Interview for Children and Adolescents* (DISC-IV; Reich, Welner, & Herjanic, (1997) and the *Kiddie Schedule for Affective Disorders and Schizophrenia for School-age Children* (K-SADS; Ambrosini, 2000; Puig-Antich & Chambers, 1978). Semistructured interviews tend to generate a list of questions that provide a sequence to the interview, but give the interviewer the flexibility to explore responses as needed. Sattler (1998) provides a compendium of semistructured interviews as well as instruction on clinical interviewing. Unstructured interviews with children may include an informal discussion, the use of games to encourage the child to talk about his or her thoughts and feelings, or art-related activities such as drawing or playing with clay in which the child is encouraged to talk about what the artwork creation represents to him or her.

When working with children, interviewers should include the child's guardians or teachers. It is important to get a family history of internalizing disorders as well as treatment histories (Semrud-Clikeman et al. 2007). It may be helpful to draw a genogram with the guardian to establish a familial pattern of internalizing disorders (McGoldrick, Gerson, & Petry, 2008).

BEHAVIORAL OBSERVATION

Behavioral observation is an integral assessment process for use with children and adolescents (Merrell, 2003; Sattler, 1998). Behavioral observation occurs in the child's environment and is based on the notion of *situational specificity*, that is, the assumption that the target behaviors are caused by variables in the immediate setting (Shapiro, 1988). By observing the interaction between the child's behavior and the antecedents and consequences in the setting, one can make inferences about the causes of the behavior. School neuropsychologists have an advantage over clinic-based neuropsychologists in that they can conduct observations of referred children in situ, i.e., the school building. This is of course a challenge for both types of practitioners when it comes to home-schooled children. Miller and Leffard (2007) provide comprehensive coverage of informal behavioral observation as well as published direct observation systems. Two popular published observation systems include the *Behavior Assessment System for Children, 2nd Edition, Student Observation System* (BASC-2 SOS; Reynolds & Kamphaus, 2004) and the *Achenbach System of Empirically Based Assessment Direct Observation Form* (ASEBA DOF; Achenbach & Rescorla, 2001). Finally, there has been an emergence of computer-based observation systems that may simplify the collection of behavioral data (Miller & Leffard, 2007).

BEHAVIORAL RATING SCALES

Broad-Band Rating Scales   Behavior rating scales are very popular assessment procedures in school settings because they allow for indirect behavioral data to be collected from multiple informants in a rapid, cost-efficient manner. Most popular behavior rating systems employ the multi-informant approach because each rater provides incremental validity to the assessment results (Merrell, 2003). Multi-informant scales typically include child self report, parent report, and teacher report forms. Broad-band rating scales, meaning that they assess multiple behavioral constructs at the same time, are useful for providing hypotheses about comorbid problems and patterns of behavioral strengths and weaknesses. Popular broad-band rating scale systems are the *Behavior Assessment System for Children, 2nd Edition* (BASC-2; Reynolds & Kamphaus, 2004) and the *Achenbach System of Empirically Based Assessment* (ASEBA; Achenbach & Rescorla, 2001)

Narrow-Band Rating Scales   Numerous narrow-band rating scales, meaning they only assess one or a few related constructs, are available for the assessment of depression and anxiety. Popular narrow-band measures of depression include the *Children's Depression Inventory* (CDI; Kovacs, 1992) and the *Reynolds Adolescent Depression Scale – II* (RADS-II; Reynolds, 2005). Measures of anxiety demonstrating very good psychometric properties include the *Multidimensional Anxiety Scale for Children* (MASC; March, 1997) and the *Screen for Child Anxiety Related Emotional Disorders* (SCARED; Muris, Merckelback, Schmidt, & Mayer, 1999).

PERSONALITY TESTS

Self-Report Measures   Self-report measures of personality tend to measure a wide variety of personality constructs that are interpreted in a profile manner on a strong theoretical base. Frequently used personality tests include the *Millon Pre-Adolescent Clinical Inventory* (M-PACI; Millon, Tringone, Millon, & Grossman, 2005), the *Millon Adolescent Clinical Inventory*

(MACI; Millon, 1993), and the *Personality Inventory for Youth* (PIY; Lachar & Gruber, 1995). However, the most frequently used youth personality test is the *Minnesota Multiphasic Personality Inventory-Adolescent* (MMPI-A; Archer, Krishnamurthy, & Stredny, 2007). The MMPI-A includes validity scales as well as the classic Basic Scales such as Depression and Psychasthenia. Also included are the content and supplementary scales. The content scales are particularly useful to the school neuropsychologist because they provide assessments of many common problems faced by adolescents including depression, health concerns, alienation, bizarre mentation, anger, cynicism, conduct problems, low self-esteem, low aspirations, social discomfort, family problems, school problems, anxiety, obsessiveness, and negative treatment indicators. Finally, the Harris-Lingoes scales, scored routinely with the MMPI-A Basic Scales, provide more fine-grained interpretation of the several of the Basic Scales.

Projective Techniques   Projective assessment techniques continue to be popular child assessment procedures and have been advocated as complementary to self-report measures of personality (Butcher & Rouse, 1996). Projective techniques have been shown to be particularly useful with children (Erdberg, 2007; Hughes, Gacono, & Owen, 2007). Among the projective techniques appropriate for the assessment internalizing disorders are the *Rorschach Inkblot Measure, Roberts Apperception Technique, Kinetic Family Drawing*, and *Sentence Completion* (Semrud-Clikeman et al., 2007). Kearney and Bensaheb (2007) note that projective techniques are particularly useful when the child being assessed cannot identify a clear external cause to the reported symptomatology.

EVIDENCE-BASED INTERVENTIONS FOR THE TREATMENT OF INTERNALIZING DISORDERS

PHARMACOTHERAPY

Recent studies have shown that psychotherapy may not add variance to the treatment gains of pharmacotherapy (Apter, Kronenberg, & Brent, 2005; Segool & Carlson, 2008) for internalizing disorders. However, it should be noted that there is significant concern with the safety of pharmacotherapy for children. As such, it is recommended that psychotherapy be included as a conjoint therapy to pharmacotherapy (Apter et al., 2005). Boylan, Romero, & Birmaher (2007) provide a current overview of pharmacotherapy for Major Depression in children as well as an analysis of the safety issues with regard to suicide, interactions, and side effects. The American Academy of Child and Adolescent Psychiatry (2007) supports a multi-method approach to conjoint pharmacotherapy, cognitive-behavioral therapy, and family therapy for children with anxiety. The professional organization details the current literature on pharmacotherapy for anxiety disorders. For useful reviews of the current status of pharmacotherapy for anxiety disorders, see Birmaher, Yelovich, and Renaud (1998) and Compton, Kratochvil, and March (2007).

COGNITIVE-BEHAVIORAL INTERVENTIONS

There has been an abundance of research on treatment of adults with internalizing disorders. Fortunately, there has been a burgeoning of research on cognitive-behavioral intervention as applied to children (Ammerman & Coe, 2006). It should be noted that treating neuropsychiatric disorders in children poses unique challenges, as not all techniques and treatments can be easily adapted for use with children (Asarnow & Carlson, 1988). However, among the treatments available, cognitive-behavior therapy (CBT) arguably has the largest corpus of evidence-based outcome studies to date, with many studies supporting the positive outcomes of CBT for children (Kendall, Hudson, Gosch, Flannery-Schroeder, & Suveg, 2008; Muñoz-Solomando, Kendall, & Whittington, 2008; Stice, Rohde, Seeley, & Gau, 2008). The National Institute for Health and Clinical Excellence recommends that the first line of action for child and adolescent depression/anxiety not be pharmacological treatment, but rather psychosocial approaches such as CBT (Muñoz-Solomando et al., 2008).

CBT is designed to reduce negative thought patterns and can include an increase in pleasant activities and homework assignments to practice newly learned skills (Stice et al., 2008). With the reduction of negative thoughts and a supportive environment, children can experience decreased levels of depressive thoughts and the associated negative outcomes (Stice et al., 2008). The National Institute of Health *Treatment of Adolescent Depression Study* (The TADS Team, 2007) was a six-year study involving thirteen different sites with a nationally representative sample (Apter et al., 2005). It was concluded that CBT plus fluoxetine (Prozac) treatment resulted in the quickest treatment response and greatest treatment gains at the end of twelve weeks of treatment (Apter et al., 2005; The TADS Team, 2007).

Muñoz-Solomando and colleagues (2008) summarized recent findings in meta-analyses of treatments for internalizing disorders in children and adolescents. It was suggested that CBT is highly effective and has evidence-based support from numerous studies. Specifically, it was also recommended that the ideal CBT time frame is 8 to 16 sessions for 40 to 60 minutes each over a period of five to eight weeks. The authors concluded CBT is most successful with Generalized Anxiety Disorder and moderately successful for children with depression.

Kendall et al. (2008) suggests that involving parents as clients while treating children with anxiety can be helpful, but not entirely necessary. It was hypothesized that children with anxiety often have parents who have similar personality traits, and so treating just the child might not prove to be efficient. Interestingly, Kendall and colleagues found that involving parents in treatment, as co-clients did not significantly increase the positive results the children experienced. It should not be assumed that including parents is not beneficial, however. Parental involvement as a collaborator is critical in the treatment process (Kendall et al., 2008).

It is important to note that often times in the studies mentioned, CBT was used in conjunction to different psychopharmacologic inventions (i.e., The TADS Team, 2007). These studies found that conjoint therapy was more effective and produced larger results faster; however, one advantage CBT had was its lasting effects in social adjustment. The TADS researchers point out that using conjoint medication and CBT may help prevent suicide attempts because of the added understanding provided about what the child is going through with CBT.

Psychoeducational Interventions

Miller, Bagnato, Dunst, and Mangis (2006) summarized seven principles of psychoeducational interventions. They should include functional intervention goals, developmental perspective on change, linkages between functional assessment and interventions, functional instructional strategies, attention to functional contexts and settings, integrated support services, and collaborative teamwork. In addition, Miller and colleagues pointed out that family-centered care is critical. Connell and Dishion (2008) supported this position in a three-year longitudinal study of family-centered therapy of middle school youth where they found that inclusion of family therapy prevented an increase in depressive symptoms in a high-risk group compared to a control group.

More specific to the classroom setting and educational environment, educational modifications and accommodations can be put into place to help children with internalizing disorders succeed in the classroom. Recommendations include providing extra time on homework assignments and tests that can give the child time to calm down and concentrate. The school can provide weekly counseling and *as needed* trips to the counselor when the child feels overwhelmed. A designated person can be assigned to check to make sure the child is bringing all homework home and documenting assignments in a day planner. The child can have the ability to retake tests or turn in homework a little late for days when symptoms are bad. The teachers can also send emails to the parents notifying them of the child's progress.

If the child is taking medication, someone in the school can be designated to make sure the child gets his or her medication. Other things such as increasing the light, putting up bright-colored posters, or having the teachers speak more positively about assignments can help the child feel more comfortable in the classroom. With these modifications, students with internalizing disorders can be helped to achieve higher levels of academic success.

SUMMARY

Internalizing disorders are characterized as having symptoms that are typically internal, cognitive-emotional experiences. Internalizing disorders include depression and anxiety and are associated with significant impairment of psychosocial and academic functioning. The school neuropsychologist should be concerned with internalizing disorders for at least two reasons. First, internalizing disorders may emerge as a result of either the direct or indirect effects of acquired or developmental brain dysfunction. Second, in the absence of evidence of brain dysfunction, internalizing disorders are associated with a number of neuropsychological deficits that are amenable to intervention or accommodation.

Depression can have a global impact on neuropsychological functioning. Involvement of the frontal lobes in youth with depression is related to executive function deficits, general cognitive deficits, psychomotor retardation, inattention, and memory deficits. Anxiety involves complex brain systems because of the adaptive and phylogentically old nature of the fear response. Youth with anxiety may have comorbid language deficits, memory and learning problems, executive function deficits, slower speed of information processing, and general cognitive deficits.

Also, internalizing disorders have been shown to be highly comorbid with each other and with other classes of disorders. Thus, it is important to conduct a comprehensive neuropsychological evaluation of children presenting with internalizing disorders as well as to assess for internalizing disorders in those who have experienced brain injury. Cognitive-behavioral interventions have been shown as one of the most effective treatments for children with internalizing disorders. In addition, pharmacotherapy and adjustments to the educational milieu are indicated forms of treatment.

REFERENCES

Achenbach, T. M., & Rescorla, L. A. (2001). *Manual for ASEBA school age forms and profiles*. Burlington, VT: University of Burlington Center for Children, Youth and Families.

Ambrosini, P. J. (2000). Historical development and present status of the schedule for affective disorders and schizophrenia for school-aged children (K-SADS). *Journal of the American Academy of Child and Adolescent Psychiatry, 39*, 49–58.

American Academy of Child and Adolescent Psychiatry. (2007). Practice parameter for the assessment and treatment of children and adolescents with anxiety disorders. *Journal of the American Academy of Child and Adolescent Psychiatry, 46*, 267–283.

American Psychiatric Association. (2000). *Diagnostic and statistical manual of mental disorders* (4th ed., Text Revision ed.). Washington, DC: American Psychological Association.

Ammerman, R. T., & Coe, M. E. (2006). Psychological and behavioral interventions. In C. E. Coffey, R. A. Brumback, D. R. Rosenberg, & K. Voeller (Eds.), *Textbook of essential pediatric neuropsychiatry* (pp. 685–699). Philadelphia: Lippincott Williams & Wilkins.

Andrade, L., Caraveo-Anduaga, J. J., Berglund, P., Bijl, R. V., De Graaf, R., Vollebergh, W., et al. (2003). The epidemiology of major depressive episodes: Results from the international consortium of psychiatric epidemiology (ICPE) surveys. *International Journal of Methods in Psychiatric Research, 12*, 3–21.

Andres, S., Lazaro, L., Salamero, M., Boget, T., Penades, R., & Castro-Fornieles, J. (2008). Changes in cognitive dysfunction in children and adolescents with obsessive-compulsive disorder after treatment. *Journal of Psychiatric Research, 42*, 507–514.

Angold, A. E., Costello, J., & Erkanli, A. (1999). Comorbidity. *Journal of Child Psychology and Psychiatry, 40*, 57–87.

Apter, A., Kronenberg, S., & Brent, D. (2005). Turning darkness into light: A new landmark study on the treatment of adolescent depression. Comments on the TADS study. *European Child & Adolescent Psychiatry, 14*(3), 113–116.

Archer, R. P., Krishnamurthy, R., & Stredny, R. V. (2007). The Minnesota multiphasic personality inventory-adolescent. In S. R. Smith & L. Handler (Eds.), *The clinical assessment of children and adolescents: A practitioner's handbook* (pp. 237–266). Mahwah, NJ: Lawrence Erlbaum.

Arffa, S. (2006). Traumatic brain injury. In C. E. Coffey, R. A. Brumback, D. R. Rosenberg, & K. Voeller (Eds.), *Textbook of essential pediatric neuropsychiatry* (pp. 507–548). Philadelphia: Lippincott Williams & Wilkins.

Aronen, E. T., Vuontela, V., Steenari, M.-R., Salmi, J., & Carlson, S. (2005). Working memory, psychiatric symptoms, and academic performance at school. *Neurobiology of Learning and Memory, 83*, 33–42.

Asarnow, J. R., & Carlson, G. A. (1988). Childhood depression: Five-year outcome following combined cognitive-behavior therapy and pharmacotherapy. *American Journal of Psychotherapy, 42*, 456–464.

Aunola, K., Stattin, H., & Nurmi, J. (2000). Adolescents' achievement strategies, school adjustment, and externalizing and internalizing problem behaviors. *Journal of Youth and Adolescence, 29*, 289–306.

Baron, I. S. (2004). *Neuropsychological evaluation of the child.* New York: Oxford University Press.

Beitchman, J. H., Wilson, B., Johnson, C. J., Atkinson, L., Young, A., Adlaf, E., et al. (2001). Fourteen-year follow-up of speech/language-impaired and control children: Psychiatric outcome. *Journal of the American Academy of Child & Adolescent Psychiatry, 40*, 75–82.

Birmaher, B., Yelovich, K., & Renaud, J. (1998), Pharmacologic treatment for children and adolescents with anxiety disorders. *Pediatric Clinics of North America, 45*, 1187–1204.

Blackman, G. L., Ostrander, R., & Herman, K. C. (2005). Children with ADHD and depression: A multisource, multimethod assessment of clinical, social, and academic functioning, *Journal of Attention Disorders, 8*, 195–207.

Bonifacci, P., Candria, L., & Contento, S. (2008). Reading and writing: What is the relationship with anxiety and depression? *Reading and Writing, 21*, 609–625.

Boylan, K., Romero, S., & Birmaher, B. (2007). Psychopharmacologic treatment of pediatric major depressive disorder. *Psychopharmacology, 191*, 27–38.

Brown, T. A., Chorpita, B. F., & Barlow, D. H. (1998). Structural relationships among dimensions of the DSM-IV anxiety and mood disorders and dimensions of negative affect, positive affect, and autonomic arousal. *Journal of Abnormal Psychology, 107*, 179–192.

Bucci, P., Galderisi, S., Catapano, F., Di Benedetto, R., Piegari, G., Mucci, A., et al. (2007). Neurocognitive indices of executive hypercontrol in obsessive-compulsive disorder. *Acta Psychiatrica Scandinavica, 115*, 380–387.

Buchsbaum, M. S. (2004). Frontal cortex function. *The American Journal of Psychiatry, 161*, 2178.

Butcher, J. N., & Rouse, S. V. (1996). Personality: Individual differences and clinical assessment. *Annual Review of Psychology, 47*, 87–111.

Calhoun, S. L., & Mayes, S. D. (2005). Processing speed in children with clinical disorders. *Psychology in the Schools, 42*, 333–343.

Cannon, M. F., & Weems, C. F. (2006). Do anxiety and depression cluster into distinct groups?: A test of Tripartite model predictions in a community sample of youth. *Depression and Anxiety, 23*, 453–460.

Carver, L. J., & Bell, M. A. (2006). Clinical electrophysiology of the developing human brain. In C. E. Coffey, R. A. Brumback, D. R. Rosenberg, & K. Voeller (Eds.), *Textbook of essential pediatric neuropsychiatry* (pp. 135–148). Philadelphia: Lippincott Williams & Wilkins.

Caspi, A., Elder, G. H., & Bem, D. J. (1988). Moving away from the world: Life-course patterns of shy children. *Developmental Psychology, 24*, 824–831.

Cataldo, M. G., Nobile, M., Lorusso, M. L., Battaglia, M., & Molteni, M. (2005). Impulsivity in depressed children and adolescents: A comparison between behavioral and neuropsychological data. *Psychiatry Research, 136*, 123–133.

Chalfant, A. M., Rapee, R., & Carroll, L. (2007). Treating anxiety disorders in children with high functioning autism spectrum disorders: A controlled trial. *Journal of Autism and Developmental Disorders, 37*, 1842–1857.

Charney, D. S., & Manji, H. K. (2004). Life stress, genes, and depression: Multiple pathways lead to increased risk and new opportunities for intervention. *Science Signaling, 2004*(225), re5.

Chorpita, B. F., Plummer, C. M., & Moffitt, C. E. (2000). Relations of tripartite dimensions of emotion to childhood anxiety and mood disorders. *Journal of Abnormal Child Psychology, 28,* 299–310.

Clark, L. A., & Watson, D. (1991). Tripartite model of anxiety and depression: Psychometric evidence and taxonomic implications. *Journal of Abnormal Psychology, 100,* 316–336.

Compton, S. N., Kratochvil, C. J., & March, J. S. (2007). Pharmacotherapy for anxiety disorders in children and adolescents: An evidence-based medicine review. *Psychiatric Annals, 37,* 504–517.

Connell, A. M., & Dishion, T. J. (2008). Reducing depression among at-risk early adolescents: Three-year effects of a family-centered intervention embedded within schools. *Journal of Family Psychology, 22,* 574–585.

Costello, E. J., Egger, H. L., & Angold, A. (2005). The developmental epidemiology of anxiety disorders: Phenomenology, prevalence, and comorbidity. *Child and Adolescent Psychiatric Clinics of North America, 14,* 631–648.

Craig, A., Hancock, K., Tran, Y., & Craig, M. (2003). Anxiety levels in people who stutter: A randomized population study. *Journal of Speech, Language, and Hearing Research, 46,* 1197–1206.

Drevets, W. C., Videen, T. O., Price, J. L., Preskorn, S. H., Carmichael, S. T., & Raichle, M. E. (1992). A functional anatomical study of unipolar depression. *Journal of Neuroscience, 12,* 3628–3641.

Dweck, C. S. (1986). Motivational processes affecting learning. *American Psychologist, 41,* 1040–1048.

Earnheart, J. C., Schweizer, C., Crestani, F., Iwasato, T., Itohara, S., Mohler, H., et al. (2007). GABAergic control of adult hippocampal neurogenesis in relation to behavior indicative of trait anxiety and depression states. *The Journal of Neuroscience, 27,* 3845–3854.

Education for All Handicapped Children Act of 1975 (Pub. L. No. 94–142).

Emerson, C. S., Mollet, G. A., & Harrison, D. W. (2005). Anxious-depression in boys: An evaluation of executive functioning. *Archives of Clinical Neuropsychology, 20,* 539–546.

Erdberg, P. (2007). Using the Rorschach with children. In S. R. Smith & L. Handler (Eds.), *The clinical assessment of children and adolescents: A practitioner's handbook* (pp. 139–147). Mahwah, NJ: Lawrence Erlbaum.

Feng, X., Shaw, D. S., & Silk, J. S. (2008). Developmental trajectories of anxiety symptoms among boys across early and middle childhood. *Journal of Abnormal Psychology, 117,* 32–47.

Ferdinand, R. F., Dieleman, G., Ormel, J., & Verhulst, F. C. (2007). Homotypic versus heterotypic continuity of anxiety symptoms in young adolescents: Evidence for distinctions between DSM-IV subtypes. *Journal of Abnormal Child Psychology, 35,* 325–333.

Ford, M. A., Sladeczek, I. E., Carlson, J., & Kratochwill, T. R. (1998). Selective mutism: Phenomenological characteristics. *School Psychology Quarterly, 13,* 192–227.

Gray, J. A. (1995). A model of the limbic system and basal ganglia: Applications to anxiety and schizophrenia. In M. S. Gazzaniga (Ed.), *The cognitive neurosciences* (pp. 1165–1176). Cambridge, MA: MIT Press.

Greaves-Lord, K., Ferdinand, R. F., Sondeijker, F. E. P. L., Dietrich, A., Oldehinkel, A. J., Rosmalen, J. G. M., et al. (2007). Testing the tripartite model in young adolescents: Is hyperarousal specific for anxiety and not depression? *Journal of Affective Disorders, 102,* 55–63.

Günther, T., Holtkamp, K., Jolles, J., Herpertz-Dahlmann, B., & Konrad, K. (2004). Verbal memory and aspects of attentional control in children and adolescents with anxiety disorders or depressive disorders. *Journal of Affective Disorders, 82,* 265–269.

Hale, J. B., & Fiorello, C. A. (2004). *School neuropsychology: A practitioner's handbook.* New York: Guilford.

Hammill, D. D., & Newcomer, P. L. (1988). *Test of Language Development-2: Intermediate.* Austin, TX: Pro-Ed.

Hartlage, S., Alloy, L. B., Vázquez, C., & Dykman, B. (1993). Automatic and effortful processing in depression. *Psychological Bulletin, 113,* 247–278.

Herman, K. C., Lambert, S. F., Reinke, W. M., & Ialongo, N. S. (2008). Low academic competence in first grade as a risk factor for depressive cognitions and symptoms in middle school. *Journal of Counseling Psychology, 55,* 400–410.

Herman, K. C., & Ostrander, R. (2007). The effects of attention problems on depression: Developmental, academic, and cognitive pathways. *School Psychology Quarterly, 22,* 483–510.

Hilsman, R., & Garber, J. (1995). A test of the cognitive diathesis-stress model of depression in children: Academic stressors, attributional style, perceived competence, and control. *Journal of Personality and Social Psychology, 69,* 370–380.

Hughes, A. A., Lourea-Waddell, B., & Kendall, P. C. (2008). Somatic complaints in children with anxiety disorders and their unique prediction of poorer academic performance. *Child Psychiatry & Human Development, 39,* 211–220.

Hughes, T. L., Gacono, C. B., & Owen, P. F. (2007). Current status of Rorschach assessment: Implications for the school psychologist. *Psychology in the Schools, 44,* 281–291.

Hurtig, T., Ebeling, H., Taanila, A., Miettunen, J., Smalley, S. L., McGough, J. J., et al. (2007). ADHD symptoms and subtypes: Relationship between childhood and adolescent symptoms. *Journal of the American Academy of Child & Adolescent Psychiatry, 46,* 1605–1613.

Individuals with Disabilities Education Improvement Act (IDEA), P.L. 108–446, 20 U.S.C. 1400–87 December, 2004.

Kaufman, A. S. (1994). *Intelligence testing with the WISC-III.* New York: Wiley.

Kearney, C. A., & Bensaheb, A. (2007). Assessing anxiety disorders in children and adolescents. In S. R. Smith & L. Handler (Eds.), *The clinical assessment of children and adolescents: A practitioner's handbook* (pp. 467–483). Mahwah, NJ: Lawrence Erlbaum.

Kendall, P. C., Hudson, J. L., Gosch, E., Flannery-Schroeder, E., & Suveg, C. (2008). Cognitive-behavioral therapy for anxiety disordered youth: A randomized clinical trial evaluating child and family modalities. *Journal of Consulting and Clinical Psychology, 76,* 282–297.

Kessler, R. C., Gruber, M., Hettema, J. M., Hwang, I., Sampson, N., & Yonkers, K. A. (2008). Comorbid major depression and generalized anxiety disorders in the national comorbidity survey follow-up. *Psychological Medicine, 38,* 365–374.

Kessler, R. C., Keller, M. B., & Wittchen, H.-U. (2001). The epidemiology of generalized anxiety disorder. *Psychiatric Clinics of North America, 24*, 19–39.

Kovacs, M. (1992). *Children's Depression Inventory manual.* North Tonawanda, NY: Multi-Health Systems.

Kowatch, R., DelBello, M., Mayers, T., Kennard, B., & Emslie, G. (2006). Pediatric mood disorders. In C. E. Coffey, R. A. Brumback, D. R. Rosenberg, & K. Voeller (Eds.), *Textbook of essential pediatric neuropsychiatry* (pp. 263–283). Philadelphia: Lippincott Williams & Wilkins.

Kuyken, W., & Howell, R. (2006). Facets of autobiographical memory in adolescents with major depressive disorder and never-depressed controls. *Cognition & Emotion, 20*, 466–487.

Kyte, Z. A., Goodyer, I. M., & Sahakian, B. J. (2005). Selected executive skills in adolescents with recent first episode major depression. *Journal of Child Psychology and Psychiatry, 46*, 995–1005.

Lachar, D., & Gruber, C. P. (1995). *Personality Inventory for Youth (PIY) manual: Administration and interpretation guide.* Los Angeles: Western Psychological Services.

Lauer, R. E., Giordani, B., Boivin, M. J., & Halle, N. (1994). Effects of depression on memory performance and metamemory in children. *Journal of the American Academy of Child & Adolescent Psychiatry, 33*, 679–685.

Lundy, S. M. (2007). The relationship between anxious/depressed and withdrawn symptoms on cognitive and academic measures in elementary school children. *Dissertation Abstracts International, 68*, 2658.

Manassis, K., Tannock, R., Garland, E. J., Minde, K., McInnes, A., & Clark, S. (2007). The sounds of silence: Language, cognition and anxiety in selective mutism. *Journal of the American Academy of Child & Adolescent Psychiatry, 46*, 1187–1195.

March, J. (1997). *Multidimensional Anxiety Scale for Children.* North Tonawanda, NY: Multi-Health Systems.

Martínez, R. S., & Semrud-Clikeman, M. (2004). Emotional adjustment and school functioning of young adolescents with multiple versus single learning disabilities. *Journal of Learning Disabilities, 37*, 411–420.

Masten, A. S., Roisman, G. I., Long, J. D., Burt, K. B., Obradovic, J., Riley, J. R., et al. (2005). Developmental cascades: Linking academic achievement and externalizing and internalizing symptoms over 20 years. *Developmental Psychology, 41*, 733–746.

Maughan, B., Rowe, R., Loeber, R., & Stouthamer-Loeber, M. (2003). Reading problems and depressed mood. *Journal of Abnormal Child Psychology, 31*, 219–229.

Mayes, S. D., & Calhoun, S. L. (2007). Learning, attention, writing, and processing speed in typical children and children with ADHD, autism, anxiety, depression, and oppositional-defiant disorder. *Child Neuropsychology, 13*, 469–493.

McClure, E., Rogeness, G. A., & Thompson, N. M. (1997). Characteristics of adolescent girls with depressive symptoms in a so-called 'normal' sample. *Journal of Affective Disorders, 42*, 187–197.

McConaughy, S. H. (2005). *Clinical interviews for children and adolescents: Assessment to intervention.* New York: Guilford.

McGoldrick, M., Gerson, R., & Petry, S. (2008). *Genograms: Assessment and intervention* (3rd ed.). New York: W. W. Norton & Co.

Merrell, K. W. (2003). *Behavioral, social, and emotional assessment of children and adolescents*. Mahwah, NJ: Lawrence Erlbaum.

Miller, J. A. (1998). *The childhood depression sourcebook*. Chicago: McGraw-Hill/Contemporary Books.

Miller, J. A., Bagnato, S. J., Dunst, C. J., & Mangis, H. (2006). Psychoeducational interventions in pediatric neuropsychiatry. In C. E. Coffey, R. A. Brumback, D. R. Rosenberg, & K. Voeller (Eds.), *Textbook of essential pediatric neuropsychiatry* (pp. 701–714). Philadelphia: Lippincott Williams & Wilkins.

Miller, J. A., & Leffard, S. A. (2007). Behavioral assessment. In S. R. Smith & L. Handler (Eds.), *The clinical assessment of children and adolescents: A practitioner's handbook* (pp. 115–137). Mahwah, NJ: Lawrence Erlbaum.

Millon, T. (1993). *Millon adolescent clinical inventory (MACI) manual*. Minneapolis, MN: National Computer Systems.

Millon, T., Tringone, R., Millon, C., & Grossman, S. (2005). *Millon Pre-Adolescent Clinical Inventory manual*. Minneapolis, MN: Pearson.

Moffitt, T. E., Harrington, H., Caspi, A., Kim-Cohen, J., Goldberg, D., Gregory, A. M., et al. (2007). Depression and generalized anxiety disorder: Cumulative and sequential comorbidity in a birth cohort followed prospectively to age 32 years. *Archives of General Psychiatry, 64*, 651–660.

Muñoz-Solomando, A., Kendall, T., & Whittington, C. J. (2008). Cognitive behavioural therapy for children and adolescents. *Current Opinion in Psychiatry, 21*, 332–337.

Muris, P., Merckelbach, H., Schmidt, H., & Mayer, B. (1999). The revised version of the screen for child anxiety related emotional disorders (SCARED-R): Factor structure in normal children. *Personality and Individual Differences, 26*, 99–112.

Oddy, J. (1993). Head injury during childhood. *Neuropsychological Rehabilitation, 3*, 301–320.

Ostrander, R., Crystal, D. S., & August, G. (2006). Attention deficit-hyperactivity disorder, depression, and self- and other-assessments of social competence: A developmental study. *Journal of Abnormal Child Psychology, 34*, 773–787.

Pathak, S., & Perry, B. (2006). Anxiety disorders. In C. E. Coffey, R. A. Brumback, D. R. Rosenberg, & K. Voeller (Eds.), *Textbook of essential pediatric neuropsychiatry* (pp. 285–305). Philadelphia: Lippincott Williams & Wilkins.

Pine, D. S., Guyer, A. E., Goldwin, M., Towbin, K. A., & Leibenluft, E. (2008). Autism spectrum disorder scale scores in pediatric mood and anxiety disorders. *Journal of the American Academy of Child & Adolescent Psychiatry, 47*, 652–661.

Puig-Antich, J., & Chambers, W. (1978). *The schedule for affective disorders and schizophrenia for school-aged children*. New York: New York State Psychiatric Association.

Rapport, M. D., Denney, C. B., Chung, K., & Hustace, K. (2001). Internalizing behavior problems and scholastic achievement in children: Cognitive and behavioral pathways as mediators of outcome. *Journal of Clinical Child Psychology, 30*, 536–551.

Reich, W., Welner, Z., & Herjanic, B. (1997). *Diagnostic interview for children and adolescents-IV computer program*. North Tonawanda, NY: Multi-Health Systems.

Reynolds, C. R., & Kamphaus, R. W. (2004). *BASC-2 behavior assessment system for children* (2nd *ed.*) Circle Pines, MN: AGS Publishing.

Reynolds, W. M. (2005). *Reynolds adolescent depression scale.* Lutz, FL: Psychological Assessment Resources.

Robertson, M. M., Banerjee, S., Eapen, V., & Fox-Hiley, P. (2002). Obsessive compulsive behaviour and depressive symptoms in young people with Tourette syndrome: A controlled study. *European Child & Adolescent Psychiatry, 11,* 261–265.

Sattler, J. M. (1998). *Clinical and forensic interviewing of children and families: Guidelines for the mental health, education, pediatric, and child maltreatment fields.* San Diego: Author.

Segool, N. K., & Carlson, J. S. (2008). Efficacy of cognitive-behavioral and pharmacological treatments for children with social anxiety. *Depression and Anxiety, 25,* 620–631.

Semrud-Clikeman, M. (2005). Neuropsychological aspects for evaluating learning disabilities. *Journal of Learning Disabilities, 38,* 563–568.

Semrud-Clikeman, M., Fine, J. G., & Butcher, B. (2007). The assessment of depression in children and adolescents. In S. R. Smith & L. Handler (Eds.), *The clinical assessment of children and adolescents: A practitioner's handbook* (pp. 487–503). Mahwah, NJ: Lawrence Erlbaum.

Semrud-Clikeman, M., Kamphaus, R. W., Teeter, P., & Vaughn, M. (1997). Assessment of behavioral and personality in the neuropsychological diagnosis of children. In C. R. Reynolds & E. Fletcher-Janzen (Eds.), *Handbook of clinical child neuropsychology* (2nd ed., pp. 320–341). New York: Plenum Press.

Shapiro, E. S. (1988). Behavioral assessment. In J. C. Witt, S. N. Elliott, & F. M. Gresham (Eds.), *Handbook of behavior therapy in education* (pp. 67–98). New York: Plenum Press.

Sideridis, G. D. (2007). Why are students with LD depressed? A goal orientation model of depression vulnerability. *Journal of Learning Disabilities, 40,* 526–539.

Simonoff, E., Pickles, A., Charman, T., Chandler, S., Loucas, T., & Baird, G. (2008). Psychiatric disorders in children with autism spectrum disorders: Prevalence, comorbidity, and associated factors in a population-derived sample. *Journal of the American Academy of Child & Adolescent Psychiatry, 47,* 921–929.

Smith, S. R. (2007). Integrating neuropsychology and personality assessment with children and adolescents. In S. R. Smith & L. Handler (Eds.), *The clinical assessment of children and adolescents: A practitioner's handbook* (pp. 37–51). Mahwah, NJ: Lawrence Erlbaum.

Soares, J. C., & Mann, J. J. (1997). The anatomy of mood disorders: Review of structural neuroimaging studies. *Biological psychiatry, 41,* 86–106.

Stice, E., Rohde, P., Seeley, J. R., & Gau, J. M. (2008). Brief cognitive-behavioral depression prevention program for high-risk adolescents outperforms two alternative interventions: A randomized efficacy trial. *Journal of Consulting and Clinical Psychology, 76,* 595–606.

Sweeny, M., & Pine, D. (2004). Etiology of fear and anxiety. In T. Ollendick & J. March (Eds.), *Phobic and anxiety disorders in children and adolescents: A clinician's guide to effective psychosocial and pharmacological interventions* (pp. 34–60). New York: Oxford University Press.

Sze, K. M., & Wood, J. J. (2007). Cognitive behavioral treatment of comorbid anxiety disorders and social difficulties in children with high-functioning autism: A case report. *Journal of Contemporary Psychotherapy, 37*, 133–143.

The TADS Team. (2007). The treatment for adolescents with depression study (TADS): Long-term effectiveness and safety outcomes. *Archives of General Psychiatry, 64*, 1132–1144.

Teeter, P., & Semrud-Clikeman, M. (1997). *Child neuropsychology: Assessment and interventions for neurodevelopmental disorders.* Boston: Allyn and Bacon.

Toren, P., Sadeh, M., Wolmer, L., Eldar, S., Koren, S., Weizman, R., et al. (2000). Neurocognitive correlates of anxiety disorders in children: A preliminary report. *Journal of Anxiety Disorders, 14*, 239–247.

Tramontana, M. G., & Hooper, S. R. (1997). Neuropsychology of child psychopathology. In C. R. Reynolds & E. Fletcher-Janzen (Eds.), *Handbook of clinical child neuropsychology* (2nd ed., pp. 120–139). New York: Plenum Press.

Vallance, D. D., Cummings, R. L., & Humphries, T. (1998). Mediators of the risk for problem behavior in children with language learning disabilities. *Journal of Learning Disabilities, 31*, 160–171.

Vasa, R. A., Roberson-Nay, R., Klein, R. G., Mannuzza, S., Moulton, J. L., III, Guardino, M., et al. (2007). Memory deficits in children with and at risk for anxiety disorders. *Depression and Anxiety, 24*, 85–94.

Wechsler, D. (1991). *Wechsler intelligence scale for children* (3rd ed.). New York: Psychological Corporation.

Weinstock, M. (2008). The long-term behavioural consequences of prenatal stress. *Neuroscience & Biobehavioral Reviews, 32*, 1073–1086.

Wiig, E. H., & Secord, W. (1989). *Test of language competence—Expanded edition: Administration manual.* San Antonio, TX: Psychological Corporation.

Wisniewski, K. G., Hughes, T. L., Loeber, R., & Miller, J. A. (under review). A longitudinal examination of delinquency, academic underachievement, and ADHD in children and adolescents.

Zarrinpar, A., Deldin, P., & Kosslyn, S. M. (2006). Effects of depression on sensory/motor vs. central processing in visual mental imagery. *Cognition & Emotion, 20*, 737–758.

CHAPTER 17

Assessing Children Who Are Deaf or Hard of Hearing

KURT METZ, MARGERY MILLER, and TANIA N. THOMAS-PRESSWOOD

THE INTENT OF this chapter is to provide the background and knowledge required to make prudent and responsible decisions regarding assessment practices and to make appropriate intervention recommendations when serving the highly heterogeneous, yet low-incidence population of school-age learners who are Deaf and Hard of Hearing (DHH).[1] Indeed, the seemingly limitless implications of any hearing loss, whether audiologically classified as slight, mild, moderate, severe, or profound, are daunting even for the veteran evaluators who are fluent and conversant in one or more communication modalities such as American Sign Language (ASL), Signed English (SE), Manual Codes on English (MCE), or the Oral approach. Moreover, deafness can also indicate a DHH child's identity within a particular culture or social milieu (i.e., Deaf culture; see Woll & Ladd, 2003) as opposed to purely conceptualizing a child's hearing loss within the scope of a medical condition.

But even when such critical considerations are addressed, a well-reasoned grasp of these aspects alone will not necessarily heighten either the sensitivity to or the discernment of a DHH child's unique cognitive and learning styles relative to both the DHH and "hearing"[2] populations; that is, adequate communication skills between the DHH child and examiner (although important) does not always guarantee a more appropriate or fair assessment of neurocognitive skills and abilities. By the same token, appreciation of Deaf culture will not necessarily lead to a well-rounded formulation of a particular

---

1. The classification "Deaf and Hard of Hearing" (DHH) will be used to address the broad range of children with educationally significant bilateral hearing loss ranging from mild to profound.

2. The term "hearing" refers to the majority group of individuals whose hearing levels are within normal limits.

case where, for instance, a DHH learner is desperately struggling to keep up with his or her DHH peers. Additional assessment and interpretive factors must be employed in such cases in order to more fully capture the nuances of a struggling DHH child's overall school neuropsychological assessment profile. This chapter will go beyond the controversies of the cultural versus medical models of deafness by addressing the following from a school neuropsychological (SNP) perspective: frequency, classification, and types of hearing loss in children; neurocognitive deficits, etiologies, and syndromes associated with hearing loss; DHH demographics and SNP assessment; diversity, deafness, and SNP assessment; putting together the SNP model and the DHH contextual template; interventions; and summary and conclusions.

FREQUENCY, CLASSIFICATION, AND TYPES OF HEARING LOSS IN CHILDREN: AN OVERVIEW

Clearly, detection and discrimination of basic audition is at issue for the DHH school-age population. Audiologists and ear-nose-throat (ENT) medical professionals trained to evaluate hearing loss conduct hearing evaluations and convey the test results by means of an audiogram with an accompanying written report. Epidemiological data will be presented here as well as the classification schemes frequently used for describing the nature of a child's hearing loss (Petit & Weil, 2001): age of onset, location, and degree of severity.

EPIDEMIOLOGICAL DATA

Most sources (e.g., Petit & Weil, 2001; Smith, Bale, & White, 2005) suggest that in the United States roughly one child out of 1000 births is born with congenital hearing loss. Smith, Bale, and White (2005) further estimate that this results in about "4000 infants born each year with severe to profound bilateral hearing loss, and another 8000 are born with unilateral or mild to moderate bilateral [sensorineural hearing loss]" (p. 881).

For the academic year 2006–2007, the Gallaudet University Research Institute conducted its annual survey of over 35,000 DHH children in the schools for which responses were based on school administrator/teacher report. The data suggested that over half (51.4 percent) of these students were reportedly identified as having additional disabilities (Gallaudet Research Institute, 2006; see Table 17.1). In addition, approximately 70 percent (see Table 17.2) were regarded as having so-called functional limitations[3] (Gallaudet Research Institute, January 2005). These limitations were in the areas of thinking/reasoning; maintaining attention to classroom tasks; social

---

3. The 2003–2004 survey contains the most recent functional limitations data available.

Table 17.1

Additional Disabilities Data from the 2006–2007 Annual Survey

Additionally Relevant Conditions	%
None	48.6
Speech or language impairment	24.9
Mental retardation	8.0
Specific learning disability	8.0
Attention Deficit Disorder (ADD/ADHD)	5.1
Orthopedic impairment (includes cp)	4.0
Developmental delay	3.8
Other health Impairments	3.6
Visual impairment	3.6
Emotional disturbance	1.8
Deaf-blindness	1.4
Autism	1.3
Traumatic Brain Injury	0.3

Source: Gallaudet Research Institute, December 2006.
N = 35,706

Table 17.2

Functional Limitations Data from the 2003–2004 Annual Survey

Functional Limitations*	%
No functional limitations	30.5
1 or more functional limitation	69.5
• Receptive communication	53.2
• Expressive communication	52.7
• Maintaining attention to classroom tasks	38.9
• Thinking/reasoning	34.6
• Social interaction/classroom behavior	30.8
• Vision	12.5
• Use of hands, arms, and legs	12.4
• Overall physical health	11.2
• Balance	10.4

Source: Gallaudet Research Institute, January 2005.
N = 36,953
*Percent totals more than 100.0 because multiple responses were allowed.

interaction/classroom behavior; use of hands, arms, and legs; balance; and compromised physical health. Miller (2006) cautioned, however, that these data may in fact underestimate the prevalence of disabilities among DHH students since many assessment protocols used with deaf children, especially when the practitioner is not able to communicate effectively with the child (see Contextual Template section), rely solely on nonverbal measures of general cognitive ability and potentially fail to notice accompanying disabilities (e.g., language learning disorders) or co-existing conditions. In any case, latent explanations for the increased risk for concomitant conditions are as varied as the DHH population's heterogeneity.

Some of the key demographic issues that will help examiners to better understand the child and to frame the test results in meaningful ways without overdiagnosing developmental disabilities or underdiagnosing disabilities in the DHH population are as follows (Gallaudet Research Institute, 2006):

- More than 90 percent of all DHH children have hearing parents.
- Race and Ethnicity:
  ○ White, 47 percent
  ○ Hispanic, 28 percent
  ○ Black, 15 percent
- Hearing Loss:
  ○ Profound, 28 percent
  ○ Severe, 14 percent
  ○ Less than severe, 58 percent
- Use of Cochlear Implants:
  ○ 12 percent (This statistic is much higher for young DHH students and is expected to grow, so the majority of this population will have cochlear implants in the near future.)
- Hearing Aid Use: 58 percent
- Educational Placement Settings:
  ○ Special/Center school: 26 percent (This includes both day and residential schools.)
  ○ Regular school: 42 percent
  ○ Self-contained class in regular school: 20 percent
  ○ Resource room in regular school: 12 percent
  ○ Integrated more than 26 hours weekly: 33 percent
- Classroom Communication:
  ○ Speech only, 51 percent
  ○ Sign plus speech, 35 percent
  ○ Sign only, 11 percent
- No Condition Other Than Deafness: 48 percent

In addition, it is reported that approximately 75 percent of these students are educated in their local public schools (Karchmer & Mitchell, 2003).

DEGREE OF SEVERITY

An audiological examination begins at a frequency of 125 hertz (Hz) (low; i.e., akin to "bass-like" pitches) and progresses to 8000 Hz. Conversational speech frequencies typically occur in the middle frequencies, 500 Hz, 1000 Hz, and 2000 Hz, and better ear averages (BEA) for unilateral or bilateral losses may be calculated to obtain an index of hearing levels. For example, if a student's left ear presents with 60, 65, and 70 decibels (dB) (level at which each tone is heard) across the respective frequencies of 500–2000 Hz, then a BEA of 65 dB for that ear is obtained, which falls within moderately severe range of hearing loss. (However, much like composite IQ scores, merging of data that results in "a number" may obfuscate other important audiological pieces of the puzzle, and the school neuropsychologist is always advised to consult with speech and hearing specialists for fuller explanations of audiological data.) The classification of hearing loss as measured using pure tone average at 500 Hz, 1000 Hz, and 2000 Hz frequencies is presented in Table 17.3.

LOCATION AND AGE OF ONSET

Hearing loss determined to be due to damage of the auditory nerve (i.e., "nerve deafness") is considered sensorineural (damage to the inner ear). Conductive hearing losses, on the other hand, refer to damage to the outer

Table 17.3

Hearing Loss Classifications (as measured using pure tone averages at 500, 1000, and 2000 frequencies[1])

Classification	Decibel (dB) range
Normal	−20 to 25
Mild	26 to 40
Moderate	41 to 55
Moderately Severe	56 to 70
Severe	71 to 90
Profound	91 to 120

[1]The frequencies 500, 1000, and 2000 represent the conversational range for the majority of speech.
Sources: Martin & Clark, 2009; Musiek & Baran, 2007.

Table 17.4

Audiological Terms Associated with Hearing Loss

- *Audiogram*—a graph that shows the results of a hearing test conducted by an audiometer at various frequencies and levels of sound.
- *Bilateral hearing loss*—present in both ears.
- *Conductive hearing loss*—involves hearing loss in the outer or middle ear (i.e., the *conductive* apparatus for hearing).
- *Congenital hearing loss*—present at birth.
- *Mixed hearing loss*—a combination of conductive and sensorineural hearing loss.
- *Postlingual hearing loss*—occurs after the acquisition of spoken language.
- *Prelingual hearing* loss—occurs before the acquisition of spoken language (includes congenital hearing loss).
- *Sensorineural hearing loss*—involves hearing loss in the inner ear.
- *Unilateral hearing loss*—present in one ear.

Sources: Martin & Clark, 2009; Musiek & Baran, 2007.

or middle ear (e.g., due to chronic middle ear infections). Mixed hearing loss is both sensorineural and conductive. If a child is born with a hearing loss, it is classified as congenital. Hearing loss occurring either at birth or before the acquisition of incidental language (e.g., prior to 6 months) is described as prelingual in nature. Hearing loss that occurs following early acquisition of spoken language (e.g., 24 months) is considered to be postlingual. This distinction holds important educational ramifications for language and learning in the schools since prelingually DHH children are precluded from hearing a spoken form of language. The common audiological terms associated with hearing loss are presented in Table 17.4.

NEUROCOGNITIVE DEFICITS, ETIOLOGIES, AND SYNDROMES ASSOCIATED WITH HEARING LOSS

IS HEARING LOSS A NEUROCOGNITIVE DEFICIT?

Aside from the obvious inability to hear, children with hearing loss often discriminate speech sounds, produce speech as intelligibly as hearing students do, and struggle with mastery of the graphemic-phonemic code that supports literacy learning for hearing children; intrinsic neurocognitive deficits are not necessarily manifest in DHH children who present without co-existing conditions. Although reduced academic learning trajectories do frequently occur for many DHH students and may lead to associated delays or developmental differences, particularly in the print literacy areas, searching for neurocognitive deficits with the goal of attributing them to a student's deafness or hearing loss is a pointless pursuit. It is important to understand that deafness *per se* does not create neurocognitive deficits for all DHH students.

Having no identifiable neurocognitive deficits is entirely plausible for many DHH children, just as there is none expected for the hearing population unless a neurological injury, disorder, or disease (documented or assumed) is present. Historically, clichéd views of deafness tend to center on the medical model, which give emphasis to an abnormal version of a hearing child's development (i.e., a "pathological view" of deafness) versus an "audiological, educational, social, and linguistic" view of deafness (Kannapell, 1989; see also Woll & Ladd, 2003).

SYNDROMAL/NONSYNDROMAL HEARING LOSS

Syndromal deafness is typically genetic in nature; however, rubella, toxoplasmosis, and cytomegalovirus (CMV) infections are the three embryopathies that are exceptions to the rule (Petit & Weil, 2001). Of the children born with prelingual deafness, 30 percent of the etiologies are syndromic (Petit & Weil, 2001; Smith & Van Camp, 2007). The most common autosomal dominant syndromic hearing loss is Waardenburg syndrome (four types), while Usher syndrome (three types) is the most common autosomal recessive syndromic hearing loss (Smith & Van Camp, 2007). The majority of the syndromes indicated in Table 17.5 are subsequently discussed below.

Table 17.5
Examples of Genetic Syndromes Related to Hearing Loss

Syndrome	Hearing Loss Characteristics	Concomitant Conditions or Deficits
Alport	Progressive sensorineural hearing loss of varying severity; usually not present before age 10	Progressive glomerulonephritis (may lead to end-stage renal disease), variable ophthalmologic deficiencies
Alstrom	Mild to moderate bilateral hearing loss	Retinitis Pigmentosa (RP), childhood obesity, dilated cardiomyopathy
Biotinidase deficiency	Sensorineural hearing loss (severity varies)	Seizures; hypertonia, developmental delay, ataxia, visual problems, cutaneous features may be observed
Branchio-oto-renal (BOR)	Conductive, sensorineural, or mixed	Branchial cleft cysts, external ear malformations, renal anomalies
CHARGE	May involve malformation of ossicles and/or cochlea; small or absent semicircular canals;	Coloboma, choanal atresis or stenosis, cranial nerve abnormalities

(continued)

Table 17.5
Continued

Syndrome	Hearing Loss Characteristics	Concomitant Conditions or Deficits
	chronic history of otitis media may be present	
Down	May present with conductive hearing loss due to narrow ear canals and chronic history of otitis media	Mental retardation, heart defects
Goldenhar (also known as keratitis-ichthyosis-deafness [KID] syndrome)	Severe sensorineural hearing loss	RP, hemifacial microsomia, erythrokeratoderma
Hypoparathyroidism-deafness-renal dysplasia (HDR)	Bilateral sensorineural hearing loss of varying severity	Renal dysfunction, mental retardation, seizures, syncope
Jervell and Lange-Niesen (JLN)	Congenital profound hearing loss	Syncope, cardiac arrhythmia that may be life threatening
Pendred	Congenital severe to profound sensorineural hearing loss	Euthyroid goiter that develops in early puberty or adulthood, vestibular dysfunction often seen
Refsum	Severe progressive sensorineural hearing loss	RP, peripheral neuropathy, ataxia, ichthyosis
Stickler	Progressive sensorineural hearing loss	Cleft palate, spondyloepiphyseal dysplasia, resulting in osteoarthritis, three types identified of which two are characterized as severe myopia
Treacher-Collins	Conductive or mixed hearing loss	Craniofacial abnormalities, external and middle ear malformations
Usher	Most common autosomal recessive type of hearing loss; congenital and sensorineural in nature	RP often manifest after age 10, three types identified, vestibular dysfunction often seen in Types I and III
Waardenburg	Most common autosomal dominant type of hearing loss; variable degrees of sensorineural deafness	Pigmentary abnormalities of skin, hair (white forelock), and eyes, four types of WS based on presence of additional abnormalities

Sources: Alstrom Syndrome website: http://www.alstrom.org/professionals/clinical_features.html; CHARGE web site—http://www.chargesyndrome.org; GeneTests web site: http://www.geneclinics.org/profiles/deafness-overview/details.html; Genetics Home Reference web site—http://www.ghr.nlm.nih.gov/; NORD web site—http://www.rarediseases.org/search/rdbsearch.html; Schein & Miller, 2008; Watanabe, Zako, Tamada, & Matsumoto, 2007.

Nonsyndromal hearing loss, on the other hand, is characterized as an inherited isolated physical finding (Smith et al., 2005) and comprises 70 percent of children with prelingual deafness (Petit & Weil, 2001; Smith & Van Camp, 2007). Of the nonsyndromic genetic cases of hearing loss, 80 percent are autosomal recessive in nature; in addition, King, Hauser, and Isquith (2006) report that "[a]utosomal recessive forms of deafness tend to be more severe, and sensorineural in etiology in comparison to the conductive loss that typifies most syndromic forms of deafness. Nonsyndromic causes of deafness are, almost by definition, less likely to be associated with other neurological, cognitive, behavioral, or psychiatric concerns" (p. 410).

ADDITIONAL ETIOLOGICAL CAUSES OF HEARING LOSS

Children can acquire hearing loss secondary to prenatal infections. The "TORCH" organisms—toxoplasmosis, other infections (e.g., syphilis), rubella, cytomegalovirus, and herpes (see Table 17.6)—in addition to postnatal infections, such as bacterial meningitis (see the following table), are frequent

Table 17.6
Examples of "TORCH" Etiologies of Hearing Loss

Teratogen	Hearing Loss Characteristics	Concomitant Conditions or Deficits
Toxoplasmosis	Sensorineural losses range from mild unilateral to bilateral profound.	Vision impairment, mental retardation, psychomotor anomalies, seizures, hematological abnormalities, hepatosplenomegaly, hydrocephalus.
Other infections (e.g., syphilis)	Sensorineural loss with either sudden, progressive, or fluctuating course.	Blindness, facial deformities, skin lesions, neurological involvement, vestibular dysfunction.
Rubella	If occurs, bilateral severe to profound sensorineural loss is seen in 50% of cases, may be progressive.	Vision impairment, heart disorder, low birth weight, mental retardation.
Cytomegalovirus (CMV)	Sensorineural loss varying in severity and often progressive, may be delayed onset and unilateral.	Mental retardation, approximately 90% exhibit no symptoms at birth (i.e., "silent" infection).
Herpes Simplex Virus (HSV)	Severe to profound sensorineural hearing loss may result.	Mental retardation, visual impairment, seizures, liver and adrenal gland damage.

Sources: Joint Commission on Infant Hearing, 2000; King et al., 2006; Montoya & Remington, 2008; Northern & Downs, 2001; Stach & Ramachandran, 2008.

etiologies of acquired hearing loss (King et al., 2006; Smith & Van Camp, 2007; Smith et al., 2005). Such damage to the central nervous system occurs when a bacterial or viral agent enters the blood stream of the fetus by way of the placenta (King et al., 2006).

DHH DEMOGRAPHICS AND SCHOOL NEUROPSYCHOLOGICAL ASSESSMENT: A CONTEXTUAL TEMPLATE

ANALYZING AND INTERPRETING TEST RESULTS WITH DHH STUDENTS

Regardless of hearing loss levels, a valid assessment is only possible when an understanding occurs of the key contexts in which to frame the evaluation results, observations, and ratings from teachers, staff, and parents. This is particularly true when testing and evaluating DHH students with the same degree of hearing loss (e.g., a cohort of children with moderately severe hearing loss) who may have considerably different educational, communication, home environments, and additional related experiences. This in turn impacts developmental progress, academic achievement levels, and the ability to demonstrate various kinds of cognitive competencies (Miller, 2006).

In addition, the occurrence of diagnostic overshadowing (Mason & Scior, 2004; Reiss, Levitan, & Szyszko, 1982) may preclude sound clinical acumen during the evaluation process. Specifically, diagnostic overshadowing occurs when an evaluator ascribes a given feature of a particular condition (e.g., ritualistic behaviors endemic to the autism spectrum disorders) and in its place ascribes such features to the fact that the child is DHH; or, along slightly different lines, an evaluator may overlook a particular feature (e.g., cluster of symptoms suggesting dysthymia) and assume that educational needs should take precedence (i.e., focusing on the physical elements of possible learning delays; e.g., child needs an FM system in the classroom), rather than incorporating the social-emotional components into the school neuropsychological profile. When a school neuropsychologist accepts a referral in which the presenting conditions are outside the scope of his or her practice, the risk for diagnostic overshadowing is heightened.

AN ASSESSMENT TEMPLATE

Miller (2006) suggested an assessment framework to assist practitioners in interpreting score results, observations, and related findings. To begin, a thorough knowledge of age-expected behaviors for DHH children and adolescents, which will serve as an internal template of expected normal development and behavior for the DHH population, is essential. The gold standard for the ideal linguistic environment would be a Deaf child born and reared by Deaf parents[4] whose native language is American Sign Language (ASL). As would be the case also for the vast majority of hearing infants born to hearing parents, immediate and consistent linguistic exposure is provided throughout the formative years because of a shared language between the Deaf child and Deaf parents.

Keeping this in mind, assessment plans are then formulated around this ideal linguistic environment. Evaluation findings that suggest potential areas of concern (e.g., a language or learning disability) for a DHH child born to hearing parents may be attributable to external rather than internal factors; additionally, these may or may not reflect the lack of an early, rich, linguistic environment. For example, the younger the DHH child, then the fewer years of educational intervention or parental instruction on parent-child communication would have occurred; for that reason, many indications of possible deficits may be less meaningful. On the contrary, the longer a DHH child has had the benefit of more intense intervention and educational experiences alongside excellent parent-child communication skills and fluency, the more likely the school neuropsychologist must search for other more plausible explanations that can account for performance below expectation relative to other DHH children *with similar audiological, educational, familial, and linguistic profiles*. As such, this model views both external and internal factors that can influence the DHH child's development.

COMMUNICATION AND LANGUAGE DURING THE EVALUATION PROCESS

The communication issues related to DHH children and youth are of obvious overriding importance for school neuropsychologists (see also "Using Educational Interpreters as Part of the Assessment Process" below). Prior to the start of testing, the child's major language and communication modality must be determined; in addition, the related language competencies of the evaluator need to be gauged to establish the appropriateness between the two parties. Given the array of language and communication modalities, determining which language to use and for which particular components of the evaluation process is an extremely critical part of validly assessing the skills and competencies of any DHH child. While there are numerous variations, the following communication approaches and languages tend to be used by most DHH children:

- American Sign Language (ASL) may be used as the primary language (particularly for DHH children with Deaf parents).

---

4. One or both parents may also be hearing and use ASL as the native language; oftentimes they are referred to as CODAs (children of Deaf adults).

- The oral approach or method of communicating the language used in the home and/or at school (sometimes referred to as the oral/aural or auditory/verbal [i.e., spoken language] approach).
- The Cued Speech method of communicating the language used in the home and/or at school.
- The Manual Codes on English (MCE) approach, such as Signed English, Signing Exact English (SEE I, SEE II), etc., where English word order is used and signs are imposed on the existing English language structure and lexicon.
- The multiple sign language approach incorporating a combination of sign languages such as ASL and some form of MCE. (Informally these students are called "Code Switchers," and they often vary the language and language system used based on situational needs, the skills of the information receiver, or other factors.).

In the general sense, the language and modality used most frequently by the child in educational contexts should be used during the evaluation process; however, there are several caveats that need to be considered.

Alterations in Mode of Test Presentation   Adapting test items to the preferred language of the child (e.g., ASL) may not be viable for all tests or all items within a test because of some inherent characteristics of the source language (i.e., spoken English), which make signed adaptations, though possible, entirely inappropriate for testing purposes. For instance, a child may be asked to define the word "interrupt" with a scorable correct response of "bother." When using an ASL interpretation, however, the sign for the stimulus word "interrupt" is also the identical sign for the acceptable response "bother," in which case the desired response was divulged by the examiner. This example can be analogously applied to numerous other instances, and even when ASL signs are available for a term, phrase, or sentence, these may consequently reduce the item difficulty (discussed below), resulting in the alteration of the item discrimination ability of the stimulus word.

Also, for some literacy test items, examiners try to combat the test presentation and language format issue by fingerspelling target words. However, whether trying to test a student's knowledge of vocabulary, an academic area (i.e., science or math), or another area of development without the confounding variable of reading, the fingerspelling of words changes the test to that of literacy knowledge as opposed to the academic construct to be assessed. Much controversy exists in the field with deafness experts about the validity of fingerspelling target items, but Miller (2006) cautioned against using correlation data to resolve this issue. If fingerspelled test results (or using written words) are correlated to academic achievement, then it would be safe to conclude that reading and English vocabulary skills using fingerspelling as the testing format are related to the same skills required in school (i.e., print literacy). Otherwise, differentiation between mastery of knowledge without the reading requirements involved in the task versus literacy skills used to demonstrate knowledge and conceptual development (when hearing peers are not asked to do this) has not been accomplished. As a result of absent research to this issue, defining what constitutes a language and/or a learning disability in the DHH population continues to be a conundrum.

Alterations to Test Item Difficulty   From a test development perspective, items placed at particular points of difficulty level are done to either screen out younger children or those demonstrating developmental delays or disabilities; conversely, an item may also be designed and placed in a certain hierarchical order of item difficulty to prevent older children who are developmentally comparable to their peers in the standardization sample from progressing through ever-increasingly difficult test items before ceiling criteria are met, thus terminating the test. In the case of DHH children, however, the ordering of particular items on any "hearing" test cannot be assumed to follow the same developmental rank or position on an equivalently designed test for the DHH school-age population. King et al. (2006), Maller (1996), and Maller and Braden (1993), among others, have described the various impacts of signed test adaptations in addition to the care that must be taken with them (Miller, 2006) and/or how the family and school experiences of DHH children may impact development and learning, which, again, may make item difficulty order selection different than it is for hearing students comprising the norm samples.

Mode of Presentation When Evaluating Literacy, Reading, and Writing Skills   When evaluating literacy, reading, and writing skills, English in print form should always be used (Miller, 2006). Altering the format of the test from printed English to sign language interpretation does not yield information regarding how efficaciously the student can independently access and express knowledge through written formats, such as through print English. Despite the fact that this point seems patently obvious, this practice is oftentimes placed aside. For example, parents (unaware of the pitfalls of their actions) will successfully advocate for sign-interpreted access to standardized tests of achievement involving reading and writing in English. While this is not good testing practice for obvious reasons, it may be a good "testing the limits" approach subsequent to completion of the initial literacy-related tests. If appropriately used in this particular manner, then the examiner can partition out the student's literacy skills in English or language and obtain qualitative information regarding his fund of knowledge.

USING EDUCATIONAL INTERPRETERS AS PART OF THE ASSESSMENT PROCESS

Clearly, if a DHH student uses sign language, American Sign Language (ASL), Signed English (SE), Cued Speech (CS), or any of the numerous variations referred to as Manual Codes on English (MCE), then the school neuropsychologist must be fluent in sign language with excellent receptive as well as expressive sign skills (Lukomski, 2002; Miller, 2006). An overwhelming majority of school neuropsychologists, however, possess either negligible or rudimentary sign language and communication skills; a six-week community class in sign language hardly qualifies as having sign language skills.

The next seemingly reasonable course of action would be to secure the services of a nationally certified sign language interpreter (i.e., one who holds the credential from the Registry of Interpreters for the Deaf [RID] that sanctions the individual to provide this service); however, locating a RID-certified interpreter can be a challenge, particularly in rural school districts (Yarger, 2001). Individual skill levels, state certification requirements, and interpreter training programs may vary considerably; furthermore, most educational interpreters have not received formal training in child and adolescent development and education (Schick, 2008) nor in psychological principles and assessment.

In spite of this, although a sign language interpreter may be used, the sign translation issues often become a confounding variable such that results are often not a valid representation of the student's true skills, particularly for language-based tests. Also, bringing a "third party" into the evaluation process creates a dynamic that may be to the detriment of rapport building and elicits possible concerns about confidentiality.

For example, although there may be a sign for a target word on a vocabulary test, it may be the same sign used for a more difficult term. If the sign language interpreter uses the correct sign, the item difficulty of the target word can be drastically lowered, thus showing competence for even those children who do not know the higher-level word targeted on the test. If the interpreter decides to fingerspell the item in order to maintain the item difficulty, the test becomes one of a reading test, since hearing children taking this test listen to the words and do not have to read them or know their spelling. We only want students to read for tests that are assessing reading skills or academic skills through print literacy. As a result, merely obtaining a highly skilled professional sign language interpreter is not necessarily the answer for which school neuropsychologists should be looking.

On the other hand, with DHH children using Cued Speech (CS), interpreters may be appropriate and useful. CS is a manual system that supports speechreading (lipreading) and spoken English. Thus, since the DHH child using CS has English (or whichever native language) as his or her first language, using an interpreter would not necessarily be inappropriate from a translation perspective. However, the school neuropsychologist would still have to understand how to interpret the findings relative to the child's hearing status and the other key variables, as is true with this population regardless of the communication system or language being used. The same holds true for DHH children who are orally educated. However, being able to give the tests is only the initial portion of the assessment process. Being able to frame the tests in the appropriate context based on numerous key variables and characteristics requires expertise that goes well beyond being able to communicate orally or being able to utilize a Cued Speech interpreter for the assessment process.

FRAMING THE REFERRAL QUESTION

Questions that must be answered when assessing DHH children and adolescents and that help frame the interpretation of the test results include the following (Miller & Thomas-Presswood, 2008):

- Does the child demonstrate any developmental delays or weaknesses in the areas of language, cognition, sensory-motor, attention, social-emotional development, executive functioning, and pre-academic or academic learning?
- Does the child have any underlying memory, attention, language processing, sensory-motor, executive functioning, or other weaknesses that could account for any difficulties she or he is having achieving age-appropriate levels of development and pre-academic or academic achievement?
- Are any observed delays or differences in the child's development and academic achievement levels attributable to him or her being Deaf rather than to other neurodevelopmental issues?

The above could be considered general referral questions. More specific ones might include (Miller & Thomas-Presswood, 2008):

- At this time, what is the best type of educational program and school-related communication approach for this child that would maximize language, cognitive, motor, and social-emotional growth, and improve skills related to English language usage necessary for advancing levels of print literacy?
- How does this relate to DHH children using ASL, MCE, Cued Speech, or Spoken English?

In addition, appropriate reasons for referral might include examples such as:

- Language development (American Sign Language and spoken English; or American Sign Language and Signed English; or ASL only; or PSE/Contact Signs and ASL, etc.).
- Sensory-motor skills.
- Overall levels of activity, attention, impulse control, and social-emotional maturity.
- Delineation of her or his strengths and weaknesses and provision of specific intervention strategies for home and school, if needed.
- Advice about school and class placement options for the child who is DHH.

TEST VALIDITY AND MODIFICATIONS: REPORT EXAMPLES

Following an assessment, the practitioner must make a determination as to the validity of the test results. Some examples of assessment validity notations (Miller & Thomas-Presswood, 2008) for use with DHH evaluations might read as follows:

- The results of this assessment should not be considered as a valid estimate of the child's overall current level of functioning in the assessed areas and are (or are not) indicative of his or her current strengths and needs in cognitive, memory, attention, academic, behavioral, and related neurodevelopmental and neurocognitive areas. Thus, results are viewed as accurately reflecting (or not reflecting) the child's abilities at this time, except where noted.
- Procedures used were selected with consideration for age, culture, language (bilingual-English and American Sign Language, or others), and experiential background. Both validated tests and alternatives that were used and considered to be the most appropriate available include observations, interviews, achievement samples, and scales.

Finally, notations in the report regarding use of modifications will need to be made. An example might read as:

- Test modifications were incorporated as appropriate for testing a deaf child and are noted throughout the report. This child uses spoken English, American Sign Language, and an alternating form of communication going back and forth between ASL and spoken English. All directions were signed and/or spoken, and comprehension of instructions was checked before testing was initiated (Miller & Thomas-Presswood, 2008).

Previous Testing Results

Previous testing results are usually included for all new assessments, but are particularly important when evaluating DHH children. It is important to note the qualifications of the examiners who administered tests, if they were fluent in the language and communication system used by the student, if test selection was in keeping with best practices, and if interpretation of test results reflected knowledge of and experience with large numbers of DHH students. Statements about how a test was or was not adapted for the child should be included along with how this adaptation may or may not interfere with test reliability and validity, as well as how ceiling rules were used and how item difficulty variations for DHH children may have interfered with the true representation of skill levels based on the scores achieved. The current examiner must then decide if any tests should be repeated to determine the previous score's utility in educational planning. Explanations should be given if different results and subsequent recommendations are given by the current examiner. If different tests are included that had not been included previously, a notation by the current examiner should be made with explanations for test selection and the relevance to understanding the child's development and overall developmental and educational needs (Miller & Thomas-Presswood, 2008).

DIVERSITY, DEAFNESS, AND SCHOOL NEUROPSYCHOLOGICAL ASSESSMENT

Diversity within the DHH Population

The diversity within the DHH population in the United States schools demands focus on areas of assessment and intervention. In 1993, Christensen and Delgado recognized that classrooms for DHH children reflected ethnic and racial diversity along with Deaf culture and use of signed communication. In its Annual Survey of DHH Children and Youth, Gallaudet provided statistics on the ethnic profile of this population in the United States (Gallaudet Research Institute, December, 2005). The results are as follows: White, 50.7 percent; African American, 15.3 percent; Hispanic/Latino, 25.0 percent; American Indian, 0.8 percent; Asian/Pacific Islander, 4.1 percent; and Multiethnic and Other, 4.1 percent. Deaf individuals from diverse ethnic backgrounds are also unique in their experiences, which are shaped by their socioeconomic and linguistic backgrounds.

The experience of a DHH African American individual is not only shaped by being deaf but also by social and political realities of being Black in America and by being deaf in the African American community. Due to the low-incidence of deafness in the African American community, Corbett (1999) noted that African Americans are unaware of DHH people in their own communities, and this often leads to marginalization and misunderstandings. Native Americans who are DHH also struggle to receive recognition as members of a distinct cultural community (Hammond & Meiners, 1993). The diversity even within Native American cultures is great: No two tribes share exact cultural characteristics; many native languages are widely spoken; the size of tribal group varies; differences in socioeconomic conditions exist; differing levels of acculturation and traditionalism can be observed; and geographical place of residence (urban vs. reservations) impact resources and living conditions (Hammond & Meiners, 1993). The Native American deaf population is heterogeneous in levels of acculturation, first language, tribal affiliation, tradition, and history (Hammond & Meiners, 1993).

DHH children of other ethnic groups who immigrated to the United States face similar challenges to African American and Native American DHH children. They too are members of various cultural groups and have the additional burden of learning to communicate in another language and negotiate the ways of the mainstream American culture. Many challenges emerge. Spoken language interpreters may not be familiar with particular sign languages (e.g., Mexican Sign Language or British Sign Language). Immigrant families with DHH children must become familiar with special educational laws or disability laws as they impact employment (e.g., Section 504, American Disability Act [ADA], and Individual Disability and Education Improvement Act [IDEA]). The immigrant DHH child or youth and his or her family must learn about new resources and technologies available to Deaf people in the United States (e.g., sidekicks, TTYs, pagers, teleconferencing). Most of all, however, the immigrant DHH child must learn what it means to be Deaf in the United States. In order to interact with the Deaf community in the United States and to benefit from the resources available via networking within the Deaf community, the immigrant DHH child needs to learn ASL in addition to learning English in order to navigate the American hearing culture (Humphries, 1993). There are similarities in the immigrant experience that transcends ethnic groups; these similarities surround the broader dynamics of immigrants and immigration. Gopaul-McNichol and Thomas-Presswood (1998) discussed these factors: acculturation, social support and network, language proficiency, education and socioeconomic status. DHH immigrant individuals must reconcile the new culture with that of their own; that is, expectations, roles definitions, educational programs, social structures and values may be different (Humphries, 1993).

Another source of diversity is socioeconomic status (SES). Thomas-Presswood and Presswood (2007) indicated that poverty affects children's cognitive and social development in addition to factors such as nutritional deficiencies during pregnancy (in addition to children's diets as they develop), substandard living conditions, health issues, and even neighborhood violence can have a detrimental effect on children's neurocognitive development. Other factors such as sociopolitical and educational practices (e.g., school funding) also influence the school performance of children living in homes and communities characterized by poverty. Children living in poverty have a higher chance of being identified with educational needs that require special education services than children from more affluent backgrounds (Thomas-Presswood & Presswood, 2007), thus increasing the likelihood that school neuropsychological services may be needed to discern the nature of the learning and behavioral deficits. The impact of poverty is also present in the classroom for children who are DHH (Rose, McNally, & Quigley, 2004). In addition to the impacts noted above, families living in poverty who have DHH children may experience difficulty purchasing and maintaining hearing aids and supporting and participating in literacy efforts due to limited resources, time, and knowledge of strategies.

Assessment Considerations with Diverse DHH Children

Considering these multiple factors that impact the educational development of ethnically and linguistically diverse DHH children, it is critical that we embrace assessment models that focus on empirically supported interventions that are sensitive to these ecological contexts (Hess & Rhodes, 2005). One goal of a school neuropsychological assessment is to identify children who may need specialized services, instruction, and intervention. Three strategies have been documented in the literature as best practice in assessing culturally and linguistically diverse children (Gopaul-McNichol & Thomas-Presswood, 1998; Rhodes, Ochoa, & Ortiz, 2005): evaluating language proficiency, using formal and informal measures, and determining the child's language development. As argued by Rhodes et al. (2005), evaluating the language proficiency of the child's native language and English is not only best practice but also a legal directive in special education regulation (Individuals with Disabilities Education Improvement Act [IDEA], 2004). If a comprehensive interview reveals another language (in addition to the ones used in school) is present in the child's life, it is best to begin a neuropsychological assessment with an examination of the child's receptive language ability in each language (Hess & Rhodes, 2005). Assessing all languages used allows a practitioner to establish which language is most appropriate to conduct the majority of evaluation; ascertain if the child's current language of instruction is appropriate; determine the impact of second language acquisition on learning, achievement, and on the current evaluation; and to consider if concerns that precipitated a referral are due to a possible disability or to second language acquisition factors (Gopaul-McNichol & Thomas-Presswood, 1998; Rhodes et al., 2005; Thomas-Presswood & Presswood, 2007). Specific to the case of DHH children from multicultural and multilingual background, these findings emphasize that not only should these children be evaluated in their native language but also in the second language. This can become complicated for the following reasons: (1) There is typically another spoken language being used by the child's family at home, (2) the second language is typically the language of instruction, and (3) the child might also have a native signed language (that could be different from the language of the home and the language of instruction in school; e.g., the child uses Mexican Sign Language, but his parents speak and only use Spanish).

Evaluating language proficiency presents its own challenge because standardized language proficiency tests exist mostly for spoken languages. Formal and informal methods need to be employed for evaluating proficiency in signed and spoken languages when assessing a DHH child. Presently, there are fewer than ten measures that assess ASL language proficiency in children. French (1999b) recognized the need to assess language proficiency in deaf children and suggested using *The Kendall Conversational Proficiency Levels* (Pre-College National Mission Programs, 1999b) and the *Stages of Language Development* (Pre-College National Mission Programs, 1999a), which include features of ASL to informally assess language proficiency. The *Kendall Conversational Proficiency Levels* (Pre-College National Mission Programs, 1999b) is a rating scale that evaluates deaf children's communicative competency (French, 1999a), while the *Stages of Language Development* (Pre-College National Mission Programs, 1999a) was designed to provide criteria describing language skills at various stages of development in English and ASL and is essentially an observational tool.

BASIC INTERPERSONAL COMMUNICATION SKILLS, COGNITIVE ACADEMIC LANGUAGE PROFICIENCY, AND MULTIDIMENSIONAL ASSESSMENT MODEL FOR BILINGUAL INDIVIDUALS

Most DHH children in the United States are enrolled in programs where the primary method of teaching is speech only (47 percent) followed by sign and speech (39 percent); only 11 percent are in sign-only program (Gallaudet Research Institute, December 2005). There have been a number of tests commercially available that formally assess spoken language proficiency.

For example, the *Woodcock-Muñoz Language Survey* (WMLS; Woodcock & Muñoz-Sandoval, 2001) was designed to evaluate language proficiency in English and Spanish, and it also provides information about Basic Interpersonal Communication Skills (BICS) and Cognitive Academic Language Proficiency (CALP). Nevertheless, Rhodes et al. (2005) noted that with low-incidence languages, informal methods might be the only appropriate choice. The informal assessment should draw information from multiple sources using a variety of strategies such as observing the child (classroom, home, and playground), analyzing authentic data generated in the classroom (e.g., portfolio language assessment, language sampling, collecting language data from instructional staff like ESL teachers, and curriculum based language assessments), and conducting comprehensive assessments by evaluating all major aspects of language development (expressive and receptive language skills) and second language acquisition (BICS and CALP).

The effect of language cannot be underestimated, because it has the power to profoundly impact all aspects of assessment (Hess & Rhodes, 2005). Ortiz and Ochoa (2005) asserted that a fair and non-biased assessment of individuals from diverse backgrounds cannot be accomplished by using a single method; it demands an integration of appropriate procedures and strategies into an assessment paradigm that is nondiscriminatory. This involves using formal and informal methods (Gopaul-McNichol & Thomas-Presswood, 1998; Lidz, 2003; Losardo & Notari-Syverson, 2001; Rhodes et al., 2005; Thomas-Presswood & Presswood, 2007).

The belief that by administering a test in the child's native language and adding nonverbal psychological instruments to achieve equitable and fair assessment of children from diverse background is a myth (Ortiz & Ochoa, 2005). Nondiscriminatory assessment is supported by the application and use of a systematic, comprehensive framework where methods purposely developed to minimize bias are used within the context of a thorough sociocultural and background history (Ortiz & Ochoa, 2005). Based on this knowledge, Ortiz and Ochoa proposed the Multidimensional Assessment Model for Bilingual Individuals (MAMBI) to help practitioners determine the best approach to use in assessing children from diverse background and to gather valid data on which to base educational decisions (Ortiz & Ochoa, 2005).

The MAMBI combines into a comprehensive framework four significant variables: the current grade level of the child, the approach to assessment (reduced culture, native language, English, or both languages), the current and previous types of educational program, and the child's current degree of language proficiency in both English and the native language (for details, please see Ortiz & Ochoa, 2005) must be balanced. Ortiz and Ochoa's assessment model is applicable to deaf children from multilingual and multicultural backgrounds. Assessment can be achieved by including information relevant to this group:

1. Linguistic history
2. Educational programming: type of education (ASL, Oral, Total Communication, Bi-Bi, ESL services, mainstream, residential school, etc.)
3. Grade level and literacy data
4. Level of acculturation

It is important to note that if one is to obtain the most accurate and truthful picture of the cognitive abilities of a DHH child from a culturally and linguistically diverse background, one cannot strictly adhere to a standardized and traditional assessment procedure because such procedure will not accurately reflect the neurodevelopmental strength and weaknesses of the DHH child. Formal as well as informal procedures for collecting data must be utilized. In determining the approach of the assessment, Ortiz and Ochoa (2005) recommended first identifying language proficiency level (i.e., BICS & CALP), instructional programming, and current grade level (for DHH children, knowing the type of educational program: Bi-Bi, ESL, Oral, Total Communication, Manually Coded English, etc.) since these impact the development of CALP in both languages. When working with the DHH population from a diverse background, test instructions often need to be given in a visual mode (e.g., gesturing, signing, cueing, or lipreading) or a combination of verbal and visual modalities, depending on which communication mode is most appropriate for the child. Based on the information gathered regarding language proficiency, instructional programming and grade level, the examiner chooses an assessment procedure:

1. A nonverbal assessment strategy (reduced language and reduced culture);
2. An assessment strategy in the native language (test directions are provided in the native or first language); or
3. A bilingual administration where the language of instruction and the native language are both used as part of the assessment strategy.

The first choice (total nonverbal administration) is more appropriate for culturally and linguistically diverse children who show limited proficiency in their first and second languages, regardless of whether they use a signed or spoken language. It is possible that in this case CALP has not been acquired in any of the languages the deaf child has had access to. The second strategy works best for culturally and linguistically diverse deaf or hard of hearing children from an oral background and those who had appropriate access to their first language. The third strategy would be appropriate for a culturally and linguistically diverse child who has developed CALP in both the first and second languages. For a deaf or hard of hearing child, these two languages could be spoken for oral children (e.g., English and Spanish), and for a deaf child who signs, two signed languages or a signed and a spoken language (e.g., Spanish and ASL via simultaneous communication) could be used. However, the likelihood of having a practitioner who signs another language other than ASL, one who speaks another language other than English, and one who has expert knowledge of assessment of deaf individuals is small. When such an individual is not available, a more nonverbal procedure is the better option.

PUTTING IT INTO PRACTICE: THE SNP MODEL OF ASSESSMENT AND THE DHH CONTEXTUAL TEMPLATE

When evaluating DHH children, it is critical to always remember that standardized procedures for test administration are rarely followed for a range of reasons, from giving the instructions in sign language (instead of spoken English), or the child's responses are signed instead of spoken, or recorded stimuli (i.e., on CD/cassette) are signed, and so forth. As discussed in previous sections, the school neuropsychologist must consider all educational, medical, demographic, communication, and etiological information when developing an appropriate evaluation plan.

SENSORY-MOTOR

Vision Given the heightened risk among the DHH school-age population for visual difficulties (Prickett & Prickett, 1992), visual screenings and tests are essential to establish that bilateral vision is within normal limits. Administration of the Near Point Visual Acuity and Visual Confrontation tests on the *Dean-Woodcock Sensory-Motor Battery* (DWSMB; Dean & Woodcock, 2003) may be appropriate depending on the communication needs and profile of the child and the examiner's ability to effectively communicate test instructions. Results indicating possible visual acuity deficiencies or visual neglect outside of normal limits coupled with a family history of visual abnormalities and other physical defects will likely warrant a referral to ophthalmological experts knowledgeable about deafness and vision to rule out any associated conditions, syndromal etiologies, or other anomalies. In any case, a DHH child who presents with blindness/visual impairments will likely experience an atypical, if not delayed, developmental trajectory in this area.

Hearing Auditory perception tests (i.e., on the DWSMB) are neither necessary nor appropriate for administration. The school neuropsychologist will instead depend on the audiologist's findings contained in the audiological evaluation report. Ideally, a consultation meeting with the audiologist can occur to allow the school neuropsychologist to ask questions and gain comprehensive background information in order to better understand the nature of the DHH child's hearing loss profile.

Gross and Fine Motor Skills   King et al. (2006) noted that "[t]here is widespread agreement that deaf children's early gross and fine motor development is quantitatively and qualitatively similar to that of hearing children (Paul & Jackson, 1993)" (p. 412). Furthermore, King et al. referred to literature highlighting the fact that DHH children of Deaf parents exhibited better manual speed performance than DHH children of hearing parents.

On the other hand, the 2003–2004 Annual Survey (Gallaudet Research Institute, January 2005) reported that 12.4 percent of DHH school-age children possessed functional limitations in the use of hands, arms, and legs, while 10.4 percent were considered as having problems with balance. Pisoni, Conway, Kronenberger, Horn, Karpicke, and Henning (2008) also pointed out that a number of studies yielded results for which DHH children exhibited below-expected performance on tasks such as balance, running, throwing, and figure drawing. However, caution is needed since samples (particularly from earlier studies) may have included DHH children who presented with other neurological and cognitive sequelae.

Thus, given the higher incidence of concomitant conditions for the DHH population, diagnosing any gross or fine motor delays needs to be made in light of the DHH assessment template and attributed to some other etiology, not to the child's hearing loss.

ATTENTION AND EXECUTIVE FUNCTIONING

Like sensory-motor functions, attention is an essential building block for higher-order processes (Miller, 2007), and it is critical for classroom learning. Attention refers to the brain's ability to focus on and select information (Baars, 2007), and oftentimes in an academic environment, perceiving and interpreting classroom information entail cross-modal integration of cognitive resources via audition and vision. For DHH learners, however, one sensory modality is compromised (i.e., audition), thus necessitating the need for students with hearing loss to rely more heavily on their vision to perceive and interpret visually relevant information while at the same time capitalizing upon whatever amount of residual audition they have.

Many practitioners in the field of deafness have long assumed that DHH children, in general, exhibited difficulties with attentional control and inhibition (e.g., see Altshuler, Deming, Vollenweider, Ranier, & Tendler, 1976);

however, Dye, Hauser, and Bavelier (2008) provided evidence of behavioral and neuroimaging studies that revealed reallocation of processing resources to the use of vision as an adaptive response when DHH individuals monitored their environments. For instance, many hearing students may be distracted by peripheral auditory noise that is loud and sudden occurring outside classroom door; DHH students, on the other hand, are easily distracted by "visual noise" as registered in their peripheral vision, such as someone entering the room when attempting to remain focused on the teacher or sign language interpreter (i.e., the "noise" is outside of their overt gaze). Dye et al. (2008) also stated that for DHH individuals the "redistribution of visual attention to the periphery can compensate for the lack of peripheral auditory cues provided by the environment, such as the sound of an approaching vehicle or the creak of an opening door" (p. 256).

Because DHH students are likely to have enhanced visual peripheral attention and may therefore appear to be "excessively looking around and noticing" minor visual changes in the environment that hearing students can access auditorily (in the peripheral sense), practitioners must resist the temptation to ascribe a DHH student's propensity for "looking around the room" as either substantiating or supporting evidence of any sort of attentional processing problem. Rather, this observation needs to be framed within the context of reallocation of attentional resources to the visual system as a consequence of deafness,[5] and these behaviors are to be expected for any DHH child without concomitant disabilities. Thus, the focus should not be on the DHH child's behavior but instead on restructuring the classroom to maximize a visually predictable environment that enhances optimal learning.

All this being said, a portion of DHH students may well exhibit attentional processing difficulties, not to mention any additional neuropsychological factors unrelated to attention that could also account for inattentiveness or impulsivity (e.g., delayed sign and/or oral language skills relative to native signers who are DHH). Referring again to the 2003–2004 Annual Survey (Gallaudet Research Institute, January 2005), 6.6 percent of DHH students were considered as having "attention deficit disorder" while 38.9 percent were reported as having a functional limitation in "maintaining attention to classroom tasks." Given the nature of this survey, it is impossible to know the accuracy of the reported conditions and limitations for these students; however, these statistics appear to suggest that a number of DHH students may not have been successfully evaluated for attentional processing deficits,

---

5. This reallocation is not observed in hearing individuals who are native signers; therefore, "deafness appears to be the leading factor in this reorganization of the attentional system" (Dye et al., 2008, p. 256).

especially after taking the visual reallocation of attentional resources into consideration.

Executive function has been described as the control and self-regulatory system involving planning, organizing, initiating, self-monitoring, memorizing, shifting, and prioritizing (Meltzer, 2007). Executive functions are integral to higher-order cognitive processes that are responsible for metacognition and behavior regulation (Hauser, Lukomski, & Hillman, 2008). The development of executive function skills is greatly influenced by experiences in one's environment (home and school), especially linguistic experiences. In the case of DHH children, Hauser et al. (2008) indicated that DHH children seem to develop executive function in accordance with expected milestones if they receive effective linguistic input or access during the first few years of life and are trained how to use their eyes to learn from their environment. For example, the development of visual attention control is essential to DHH individuals in order to maximize their access to language and incidental learning (Please refer to Hauser et al. for discussion). The *Behavior Rating Inventory of Executive Functions* (BRIEF; Gioia, Isquith, Guy, & Kentworthy, 2000) has been used successfully with DHH individuals. Rhine (2002) found that while some elevation was shown on the Inhibit, Shift, and Working Memory scales of the BRIEF rating of DHH children, none of the measured scales or indexes fell within the clinical range. These findings suggest that BRIEF is appropriate to use with this population.

VISUAL SPATIAL FUNCTIONING

In terms of face validity, visual-spatial tasks appear to be "nonverbal" in nature; however, careful inspection of certain tasks (e.g., WISC-IV Picture Completion subtest) shows these measures to include pictorial items that can be named (such as chair, house, etc.), thus requiring an element of linguistic processing (i.e., "internal speech"). A simple response via pointing or declaring whether the correct answer is "a" or "b" still necessitates a "verbal" component in order for a DHH student to elicit a correct response based on the pictorial stimuli as portrayed. If a DHH child's vocabulary base and/or linguistic experience are limited, then it stands to reason that these factors may confound the child's true visual-spatial abilities. In addition, Pisoni et al. (2008) found that higher posttest VMI scores were a result of improved language abilities for children with cochlear implants (CIs). The message, then, is that visual-spatial and language abilities do interact in some way, and relatively few visual-spatial tasks are truly "nonverbal." School neuropsychologists unfamiliar with deafness and deaf children thus need to refrain from the temptation of giving a multitude of visual-spatial measures in order to collect substantiating evidence of any

DHH child's "true abilities" (e.g., the WISC-IV POI standard score used as a proxy full-scale IQ score). It is entirely possible that a DHH child happens to possess a weakness in this particular area. As Clark (2003) incisively pointed out, if "a deaf child evidences deficits on measures of visual-perceptual or visual-motor abilities, then results obtained on nonverbal cognitive measures must be interpreted with extreme caution" (p. 127). Clearly, the practice of utilizing visual-spatial scores to draw broad-based inferences of a DHH child's cognitive profile is flawed.

Visuoconstructive and Visual-motor Skills   Hauser, Cohen, Dye, and Bavelier (2007) found that their tests selected for study with deaf native young adult signers, the *Beery-Buktenica Developmental Test of Visual-Motor Integration* (Beery, Buktenica, & Beery, 2003), the *Rey Complex Figure Test and Recognition Trial* (Myers & Myers, 1995), the *Wechsler Memory Scale* (Wechsler, 1997) *Visual Reproduction* subtest, and the *Stanford-Binet Intelligence Scale* (Roid, 2003) *Paper Folding and Cutting* subtests, yielded performance comparable to matched hearing controls, thus establishing "the robustness of these tests in the face of altered experience such as deafness or signing" (p. 153). Insofar as the mode of communication used during a school neuropsychological evaluation allows maximal visual accessibility when conveying test instructions, then it is reasonable for school neuropsychologists to use these instruments, notably the VMI and *Rey Complex Figure Test and Recognition Trial* (Meyers & Meyers, 1995), as part of the assessment repertoire for use with DHH students. A caveat required for further study is needed to document the appropriateness of similar tests for the school-age DHH population to preclude the potentially inaccurate assumption that a downward extension of DHH young adult findings also apply to younger cohorts. To our knowledge, we know of no studies that address this issue.

LANGUAGE FUNCTIONING

The assessment of language for deaf and hard of hearing students is a complex process and can take into account expressive and receptive components, through the air communication (sign or speech or cues) and print, and various elements of communication such as phonemic, morphemic, syntactic, semantic, and pragmatic elements and corresponding elements of signed languages (cheremes, etc.). In addition, there are age considerations as well as situational factors. Formative (ongoing) assessments of the development of a child in a social setting, such as with a family or with peers, can take place and be reported. More formal evaluations, especially the administration of tests or the scoring of language samples, can occur as part of the required assessment process. Standardized tests may also be administered for purposes of academic placement and always as support for educational planning, intervention, and general educational goal and objective setting for students.

A major issue, which must be addressed, is the purpose of the assessment for each child at a particular stage of development. For a very young child, there are significant milestones in typical language development that can be utilized, as well as tests specifically developed for deaf children (Akamatsu, 1994; Bradley-Johnson & Evans, 1991; Leigh, 2008; Schow & Nerbonne, 2002). For school-age children, language assessment can help in identifying areas of strength and weakness as the foundation for the development and implementation of an individualized educational plan (IEP), to monitor progress on a regular basis, and to document long-term development. Curriculum-based assessment procedures and criterion-referenced tests can be meaningful for deaf students in addition to analyses of language samples for form, meaning, and use (Schirmer, 1994). Easterbrooks and Baker (2002) recommended "checklists, tallies, assessment rubrics, artifacts from a portfolio of products, interviews, and analysis of language samples" (p. 202). Schirmer (1994) set a figure of 100 language samples as a goal for the teacher, so part of the school neuropsychology assessment can include a review of these samples, if available.

Formal assessment can include standardized tests based on hearing norms such as the Stanford Achievement Test (SAT) (although these are more academically oriented and will be discussed in the section about achievement testing and assessment), criterion-referenced tests such as the state assessments mandated by the No Child Left Behind legislation, and tests specifically developed for use with deaf students. Reviews of the most commonly used assessment instruments in this category are provided by Akamatsu (1994); Bradley-Johnson and Evans (1991); Schirmer (1994); Schow and Nerbonne (2002); Thompson, Biro, Vethivelu, Pious, and Hatfield (1987). Although some tests used with deaf and hard of hearing children are outdated and some have weakly designed test construction and normative data, this is all that is available with specific norms for this population. Many psychologists with expertise in assessing deaf children rely on these tests, but include numerous tests designed and normed with hearing students with adaptations based on the test purpose, test administration design, and the key and salient characteristics of the child being tested. Some of the most commonly used tests developed for deaf students include the following:

Test of Syntactic Abilities (TSA; Quigley, Steinkamp, Power, & Jones, 1976) The TSA is a paper-and-pencil test of the nine major syntactic structures of English, with norms for deaf students. In a study of reading and writing achievement of deaf adolescents using more than twenty measures, Moores and Sweet (1991) reported that the TSA had the highest correlation with reading and writing of all tests used.

Rhode Island Test of Language Structure (Engen & Engen, 1983)   This test consists of fifty simple sentences and fifty complex sentences. The student selects correct response from three choices.

Grammatical Analysis of Elicited Language (GAEL; Moog, Kozak, & Geers, 1983)   The GAEL tests expressive and receptive language in either spoken or signed English at three age levels: 3 to 6, 5 to 9, and 8 to 12. Games and activities are used to elicit responses. The grammar they are analyzing is clearly English and therefore does not provide an overview of linguistic fluency (receptively and expressively) for those children whose primary language is ASL.

Carolina Picture Vocabulary Test (Layton & Holmes, (1985)   This is a receptive test of signs for students from 5 to 18 years of age. The tester produces a sign and the student points to one of four pictures. This test of single sign receptive vocabulary is often used in spite of the outdated norms and some test items, that are not appropriate for some deaf children and their experiences. The score conversion process is not sophisticated, and scores tend to be very inflated for students. That said, it is a good starting point for receptive signed vocabulary assessment and the only test available that is normed for deaf and hard of hearing students. At the very least, it helps provide indications of typical development in this area from atypical development.

SKI-HI Language Development Scale (Tonelson & Watkins, 1979).   This is a parent observation report of the linguistic development of the deaf child.

Although a wealth of assessment protocols exist for deaf children of all ages, unfortunately, they are seldom used by teachers or other professionals. In a study of assessment practices used by teachers of deaf students, Luckner and Bowen (2006) reported that the individual statewide annual assessments were the most frequently used measurers of reading and writing. Teachers reported that they typically leave language and communication assessment to speech and language pathologists, because they are often seen as the sole experts in this area.

Spontaneous and elicited language samples (spoken, signed, or cued) are important components of the overall language assessment. The school psychologist has often relied on the speech and language pathologist to assess this area, and this is still a good source of language-based information from those professionals with expertise in the linguistic development and its variations among deaf and hard of hearing children. More frequently, school psychologists are including the language area in their overall assessment process, and information can be shared among all involved professionals. School neuropsychological tests that focus on receptive and expressive language and on verbal memory (testing both memory and language knowledge, as memory is often influenced by the automaticity of the language, just as language abilities may be facilitated or hampered by memory abilities) are often included in the test battery with deaf and hard of hearing students.

Although it would be nice and neat to state which tests and "subtests" and which exact items within these tests should and should not be used with the deaf and hard of hearing population, it is not possible. Inclusion of tests and test items is dependent on the individual child's skills, communication preferences, primary and preferred language or languages, and a number of other factors. However, it should be noted that without expertise in this area, these decisions are almost impossible to make; therefore, examiners not familiar with these issues and ways to make appropriate testing decisions followed by correct interpretations of the results should limit their testing to non-language based or minimally language loaded tests and request assistance for the language assessment components from other professionals with expertise in deafness (Miller, 2006).

MEMORY AND LEARNING

As previously stated above, intrinsic neurocognitive deficits are not necessarily manifest in DHH children who present without co-existing conditions. For DHH children born to Deaf parents (i.e., the "norm" group), this appears to be particularly true for memory skills; in fact, Wilson, Bettger, Niculae, and Klima's (1997) study found evidence to indicate that while the hearing control group in their sample displayed the as-expected longer recall of forward word sequences, the DHH children of Deaf parents sample, who use American Sign Language (ASL) as the native language and thus had language exposure since birth, performed similarly on *both* forward and backward trials of the memory span tasks. Wilson et al. suggested "that serial order information for ASL is stored in a form that does not have a preferred directionality" (p. 150). By extension then, DHH children who are native users of ASL may indeed exhibit relatively similar spans when assessing such skills on school neuropsychological tests (e.g., equal number spans forward and backward).

Moreover, Wilson et al. (1997) also found that the DHH children of Deaf parents outperformed the hearing controls on visuospatial tasks involving block-tapping sequences (i.e., Corsi blocks). Consequently, similar tasks, such as the WNV Spatial Span subtest, may yield useful information regarding visuospatial memory skills. Marschark (2003) also cited research that indicated DHH children as surpassing "hearing peers in short-term memory for complex visual figures, except when the task involved serial presentation of parts of a stimulus and serial (ordered) recall" (p. 470).

With respect to DHH readers and working memory, Paul (2003) pointed out that the "bulk of the evidence reveals that deaf students who use predominantly a phonological code in working tend to be better readers than deaf students who use predominantly a nonphonological code (e.g., Hanson, 1989; Leybaert, 1993; Musselman, 2000; Paul 1998)" (p. 104); he also adds that "[d]eaf adolescent readers who do not use a phonological code have difficulty simultaneously using syntactic and semantic information at the sentence level" (p. 104). In addition, Marschark (2003) cited a study that deaf 11- to 15-year-olds who use simultaneous communication showed multiple coding strategies for memory, including the effects of phonological coding. Consequently, DHH children of hearing parents exhibiting below-grade print literacy skills may present with compromised working memory skills (i.e., phonological loop) relative to DHH children of Deaf parents.

In addition, children with cochlear implants (who have participated in a period of rehabilitation) appear to perform below expectation relative to hearing cohorts such that results for digit spans, verbal rehearsal speeds, and processing and retrieving verbal information (though accurately recalled) were delayed (Pisoni et al., 2008). In addition, Pisoni et al. found that visual sequential memory and learning were deficient when using Simon learning conditions.

Therefore, a school neuropsychologist must exercise caution when assessing the different memory capacities of a DHH student. Important factors to consider include parental hearing and language status (i.e., households where ASL is the native language used), modality of the memory tasks (e.g., Baddeley's working memory model regarding the phonological loop or visuospatial sketch pad), mode of test presentation and response (e.g., visual or auditory-verbal), the amount of exposure to language (e.g., at what age was sign language or the oral method introduced?), the presence of any co-existing conditions, and the audiological profile (e.g., the severity and age of onset of the hearing loss, and so forth).

GENERAL COGNITION

Over the years, it has been the general practice of most evaluators trained and experienced to provide psychological evaluation services to obtain a non-verbal IQ score for use as the surrogate full-scale score in order to establish a student's eligibility for specially designed instruction under the special education classification of Hearing Impairment (HI).[6] Too often, however, this IQ score becomes (mis)construed as a valid "barometer reading" of overall cognitive ability and may in fact be a particularly inadequate, if not downright inaccurate, representation of the DHH student's cognitive strengths and weaknesses. Worse, an evaluator—with no knowledge or expertise in deafness—may even attempt to administer the entire battery in order to derive a full-scale IQ score (e.g., WISC-IV). While this may be appropriate for some DHH students with mild to moderate hearing loss who communicate fluently in spoken English, in large part, this practice is inappropriate for most DHH students for a variety of reasons (see Maller, 2003 for a discussion of the psychometric difficulties associated with this). The confounds of language exposure and communication modality—on both sides of the testing table—make it virtually impossible to validly interpret the results since these were obtained without a context in which to frame them.

This is not to say, however, that deafness categorically results in compromised cognition scores for the population. As mentioned throughout this chapter, the "norm" or reference group is DHH children with Deaf parents as they tend to use ASL as the native language in the home environment and this incidental exposure to language is begun at birth. Braden (1994) found through his investigation of meta-analytic data that DHH children with Deaf parents, as well as those who have Deaf siblings and hearing parents "who are assumed to be genetically deaf, have mean PIQs *above* the normal-hearing average" (p. 103). He further explains that these findings are consistent across studies involving samples from North America, England, and Israel, thus providing robustness to the overall results.

If cognitive assessment batteries must be given (i.e., as mandated by state departments of education), several measures are available that provide recommendations for administration, accommodations, and adaptations of its subtests. However, it is crucial to remember that "verbal" subtests contained within a test tend to reflect the English language learning for a DHH student as opposed to intelligence (Sattler, Hardy-Braz, & Willis, 2006). Sattler et al. further stipulated that the psychometric properties of tests used to measure overall cognitive ability are still largely unknown with the DHH population. In Miller's (2008) article on CHC assessment with DHH children, he pointed out that the manuals of the *Differential Ability Scales, 2nd Edition* (DAS-II; Elliott, 2007), *Kaufman Assessment Battery for Children, 2nd Edition* (KABC-II; Kaufman & Kaufman, 2004), and *Stanford-Binet Intelligence Scales,*

---

6. Many states maintain use of the term "hearing impairment"; however, it is considered derogatory by many in the Deaf community. The preferred term is Deaf and Hard of Hearing.

5th Edition (SB5; Roid, 2003) do provide information on clinical studies conducted with DHH students along with their respective administration considerations. Additional batteries for consideration include *Leiter International Performance Scale—Revised* (Leiter-R; Roid & Miller, 1998), *Universal Nonverbal Intelligence Test* (UNIT; Bracken & McCallum, 1998), *Wechsler Intelligence Scale for Children, 4th Edition* (WISC-IV; Wechsler, 2003), and the *Wechsler Nonverbal Scale of Ability* (WNV; Wechsler & Naglieri, 2006).

SOCIAL-EMOTIONAL FUNCTIONING

The presentation of psychiatric, behavioral, or emotional disorders and their assessment pose a challenge for most psychologists (Hindley & Kroll, 1998). Because DHH children develop in an environment significantly different than that of their hearing peers, it is essential that psychologists seek an understanding of how biological, familial, and social influences affect their development. This knowledge helps in the identification of psychopathology in DHH children. In general, assessment of children should be conducted within the context of a broad knowledge of developmental psychopathology (Kamphaus & Frick, 2001). This is true for deaf children as well; therefore, gathering and understanding family and school context and then interpreting this information in light of developmental psychopathology is key to the assessment of social and emotional functioning in deaf and hard of hearing children.

Research has consistently documented a high incidence of emotional and behavioral disorders among deaf and hard of hearing children (see Jensema & Trybus, 1975; Sinnott & Jones, 2005; Willis & Vernon, 2002). The prevalence of other disabilities, besides deaf and hard of hearing, in this population is estimated to be three times larger (30.2 percent) than in the general school population (Pollack, 1997). The reason for this high incidence is the etiologies of childhood deafness that are known to be associated with neurological impairments. These etiologies include maternal rubella, prematurity, cytomegalovirus, and meningitis (see also King et al., 2006; Moores, 1987). Deaf children with co-occurring emotional or behavioral disorders exhibit characteristics such as inappropriate, disruptive, and aggressive behaviors that interfere with learning (Pollack, 1997). Their behaviors are atypical in comparison to other deaf and hard of hearing children. Sinnott and Jones summarized a database on deaf and hard of hearing children in Illinois diagnosed with emotional disabilities. These children were different from the general population of deaf and hard of hearing children in that they had higher incidences of prematurity, prenatal and perinatal trauma; experienced later onset of hearing loss; lived in single-parent homes; belonged to an ethnic minority group; lived in an urban or suburban area; had a history of abuse;

and qualified for low-income health care. However, some of these character-istics are similar to those reported for children receiving services for emo-tional disabilities in the general population in that they too tend to be male members of ethnic minority groups, live in urban areas, live in single-parent homes, and experience poverty (Thomas-Presswood & Presswood, 2007).

INTERVENTIONS

LANGUAGE

There are several different types of language intervention approaches with deaf and hard of hearing children, with some relying on spoken language com-pletely, others on American Sign Language (ASL), and others on a combination of spoken language, ASL, and a form of English-based signing. There are two approaches to intervention relying on spoken language completely. The first, labeled oral-aural instruction, concentrates on the development of speech, speechreading, and auditory training without any reliance on ASL or English-based signs. Instruction primarily is on an elemental, step-by-step building block process beginning with drill and practice starting with phonemes and expanding to syllables, whole words, and sentences. Auditory-verbal training is another oral, non-manual approach. It concentrates on maximal development of residual hearing with less emphasis on speechreading. The impact of cochlear implants with very young deaf children has resulted in an increase in the popularity of the auditory-verbal approach. Similar to oral-aural training, there is a concentration on elemental building block drill and practice (Moores, 2006).

Bilingual-Bicultural (Bi-Bi) programs, in contrast, rely exclusively on ASL as the primary form of person-to-person, through-the-air communication. Speech and auditory training may be conducted separately, but not in con-junction with ASL use. English-based sign systems also are not used. Spoken language is bypassed in the development of reading, and thus the phonolog-ical decoding of print is not taught or used to assist reading advancement. Interventions tend to be by the whole language approach (Moores, 2006) and are not typically referred to as interventions but rather as a communication/language, cultural, and educational approach. Using the term *intervention* implies a pathology or disability and proponents of this model tend to view deaf people through a cultural and linguistic lens and not through the traditional medical model approach.

Total Communication (TC) usually employs sign-based English, auditory training, ASL, speech, and speechreading, depending on individual needs. As the name implies, TC is somewhat more eclectic than other intervention systems. Recently, there has been a move to emphasize the impor-tance of phonology and phonologically related skills in the acquisition of

English (Wang, Trezek, Luckner, & Paul, 2008), and many programs are moving toward a phonologically based elemental program of instruction, but, unlike oral programs, continue to emphasize the importance of sign communication.

READING

Research-based instruction in the area of reading is severely lacking in the field of deaf education. Musselman (2000) summarized her review for the article, "How Do Children Who Can't Hear Learn to Read an Alphabetic Script? A Review of the Literature on Reading and Deafness," she concluded:

> To answer the question posed by the title of this article: No one knows yet how deaf children learn to read. And the jury is still out on whether they use processes that are qualitatively similar or dissimilar to those used by hearing children, for whom printed language is primarily an alternative representation of spoken language. This is essentially the crux of the matter: Since few deaf children succeed in acquiring functional levels of spoken language, it is perhaps surprising that they learn to read at all. (p. 25)

In fact, for nearly a century, reading achievement levels for DHH students completing high school have remained at or around fourth grade (Holt, 1993; Pintner & Patterson, 1916; Traxler, 2000). Today, debates regarding appropriate reading instruction methods and approaches for DHH students continue in spite of this persistent finding.

A number of educators teaching reading to DHH students espoused a whole language approach (i.e, "top-down") under the premise that a lack of audition precludes phonological awareness and processing, and therefore, any methods utilizing this "bottom-up" approach to acquiring reading literacy skills were regarded as inappropriate for the population. Others, however, purport that phonologically based reading strategies are indeed appropriate (e.g., Trezek & Malmgren, 2005; Wang et al., 2008) by drawing predominantly from the premise that cracking the phonological code is a *cognitive* skill, not an auditory skill (see Conrad, 1979). In addition, Wang et al. stressed that "[e]vidence of phonological coding among skilled deaf readers has been available for more than 30 years" (p. 399).

- Schirmer and McGough (2005) reviewed the reading research literature on DHH students and juxtaposed the data with the findings of the National Reading Panel (NRP, 2000) to determine how DHH readers compare versus normally achieving and disabled hearing readers. Four topical areas were reviewed: alphabetic, fluency, comprehension, and computer technology. A condensed summary of Schirmer and

McGough's (2005, pp. 116–117) findings related to DHH readers is presented next):

- ○ Alphabetics: For the phonemic awareness subarea, skilled DHH readers in particular are able to "crack the phonological code," although the strength of such phonological knowledge is not known. For word recognition skills, fingerspelling and sign language appear to be used as visual codes by DHH readers, but the effectiveness of such coding use remains unproven. In addition, the instructional strategies for teaching DHH readers to use visual codes are not yet successfully proven. In the subarea of phonics instruction, no research exists; however, research on word recognition strategies appears to center on sight word recognition. As for automatic word recognition, DHH readers do seem to learn this, and matching written words with sign and/or sign print may assist younger readers.
- ○ Fluency: No studies were conducted in the subarea of guided repeated oral reading. For independent silent reading, two studies suggest a positive association between reading ability and reading engagement.
- ○ Comprehension: The subarea of vocabulary instruction, either direct or indirect, appears to be a vital component of enhancing DHH readers' skills and shows good promise as an intervention. As for the subarea of text comprehension, the majority of these centered on syntax—an area *not* addressed directly by NRP; regardless, improved comprehension is apparently not observed when syntactic structures are simplified. Instruction in building and activating background knowledge, mental imagery, and inference making appear to enhance understanding of text. However, the question of whether DHH readers develop knowledge of text structure at a slower rate relative to hearing readers is inconclusive. Finally, weak comprehension-monitoring skills require interventions for many DHH readers, but no existing studies were available for this area.
- ○ Computer technology: For the NRP area of computer technology, hypertext and word processing technologies reveal potential. Hypertexting would allow signed versions of printed text to be accessed while integration of reading and writing instruction could be accomplished via word processing software.

A coherent research agenda based on the NRP framework needs to be developed, refined, and endorsed by school neuropsychologists, educators, reading specialists, and researchers alike. Accordingly, Schirmer and McGough (2005) provided their conclusions:

Do the conclusions of the National Reading Panel apply to the reading development and instruction of children who are deaf? Our review indicates that in areas for which there is sufficient research on deaf readers to compare with the NRP review, the answer is yes. Are deaf readers different enough from hearing readers to suggest that there are paths worth following in the research on deaf readers that are unique to this population of students? This answer is also yes; for example, research on the use of fingerspelling and sign codes for word recognition certainly would be worth pursuing. (p. 111)

Until a body of research-based interventions is presented as substantiating evidence of successful instructional methods for teaching DHH students to develop reading mastery skills on a level comparable to hearing peers, a "balanced literacy" approach to reading instruction is proposed by Marschark, Lang, and Albertini (2002). Rather than adhering strictly to a particular instructional paradigm (i.e., top-down vs. bottom-up approaches to reading), integration of authentic (original) texts combined with opportunities for learning component skills such as word decoding strategies, among others, is good practice. In fact, Kelly (2003) highlights a number of options for instruction with respect to helping DHH readers acquire a viable coding system: phonological, orthographic, morphological, logographic processing, sign coding, and coding through fingerspelling. Regardless of the reading interventions incorporated into an integrated curriculum, active participation on the part of the DHH learners is strongly indicated so that reading is viewed as fun and exciting, rather than a chore (Kelly, 2003; Marschark et al., 2002). In this manner, there is still a chance that the almost-century-old ceiling of the pejorative "fourth grade reading level" for DHH readers exiting high school can be surpassed as a result of efficacious teaching of reading instructions, practices, and interventions before the 100-year anniversary mark of this statistic is reached.

WRITING

Paul (1999) and Schirmer (2000) provided in-depth treatments of the literature on writing instruction for deaf students, with disappointing results. Relatively little time is spent on writing in classrooms with deaf students. We find such descriptors as *limited vocabulary, concrete, lack of function words, poor mastery of verb inflections and plurals, repetitive, simple structure,* and *bland.* There is interest now in adapting the traditional approach to writing used in regular education for use with deaf students. Kluwin and Kelly (1992) expanded the process to include prewriting, organizing, writing, feedback, and revision in order to provide the opportunity for more feedback throughout the process of writing instruction. There has been an increased interest in writing due to the emphasis on state mandated standardized testing. Several "Writing Across the Curriculum" programs are now in place for deaf students.

MATHEMATICS

As with other content areas, mathematics achievement of deaf students has lagged behind that of hearing students. A concerned committee of mathematics' educators and deaf education professionals produced a document, *A National Action Plan for Mathematics Education for the Deaf* (Dietz, 1995). The plan called for a reform-based constructivist curriculum for deaf students based on the standards of the National Council of Teachers of Mathematics. Pagliaro (2006) noted that teachers of the deaf continue to encourage rote memorization of facts, formulas, and algorithms through drill and practice with few opportunities to engage in higher-order cognitive functioning and thinking skills, such as analyzing, synthesizing, and evaluating information in response to authentic problems. She advocated for a reform in teacher preparation programs to change mathematics instruction for deaf learners. This information can be used to guide teachers working with deaf and hard of hearing students and for family and school related consultations.

SUMMARY

The population of school-age learners with educationally significant hearing loss is a highly heterogeneous, low-incidence group. Whether the level of hearing loss is slight or profound, children who are deaf or hard of hearing (DHH) frequently present with coexisting conditions and educational challenges, particularly in the print literacy areas. By factoring in the DHH child's etiology, audiological profile, communication needs, educational history, family mode of communication, use of assistive listening devices, demographics and more, contrasting and integrating this information alongside of the school neuropsychological evaluation data will allow the school neuropsychologist to better identify the unmet needs of the DHH child so that academic progress can proceed.

REFERENCES

Akamatsu, T. (1994). Language and communication development. In R. Nowell & L. Marshak (Eds.), *Understanding deafness and the rehabilitation process* (pp. 13–34). Boston: Allyn & Bacon.

Alstrom Syndrome web site. Retrieved January 14, 2009, from http://www.alstrom .org/professionals/clinical_features.html.

Altshuler, K. Z., Deming, W. E., Vollenweider, J., Ranier, J. D., & Tendler, R. (1976). Impulsivity and early profound deafness: A cross-cultural inquiry. *American Annals of the Deaf, 121,* 331–345.

Baars, B. J. (2007). Attention and consciousness. In B. J. Baars & N. M. Gage (Eds.), *Cognition, brain, and consciousness: Introduction to cognitive neuroscience* (pp. 225–253). London: Academic Press.

Beery, K. E., Buktenica, N. A., & Beery, N. A. (2003). *Beery-Buktenica developmental test of visual-motor integration* (5th ed.). Minneapolis, MN: Pearson Assessments.

Bracken, B. A., & McCallum, R. S. (1998). *Universal nonverbal intelligence test*. Itasca, IL: Riverside Publishing Co.

Braden, J. P. (1994). *Deafness, deprivation, and IQ*. New York: Plenum Press.

Bradley-Johnson, S., & Evans, L. (1991). *Psychoeducational assessment of hearing impaired students*. Austin, TX: Pro-Ed.

Branigan, G. G., & Decker, SL. (2003). *Bender visual-motor Gestalt test* (2nd ed.). Itasca, IL: Riverside Publishing.

CHARGE web site. Retrieved January 14, 2009, from http://www.chargesyndrome.org.

Clark, T. A. (2003). Psychological evaluation of deaf children. In N. S. Glickman & S. Gulati (Eds.), *Mental health care of deaf people: A culturally affirmative approach* (pp. 109–144). Mahwah, NJ: Lawrence Erlbaum Associates.

Conrad, R. (1979). *The deaf schoolchild: Language and cognitive function*. London: Harper & Row.

Corbett, C. (1999). Mental health issues for African American deaf people. In I. W. Leigh (Ed.), *Psychotherapy with deaf clients from diverse groups* (pp. 151–176). Washington, DC: Gallaudet University Press.

Dean, R. S., & Woodcock, R. W. (2003). *Dean-Woodcock neuropsychological battery*. Itasca, IL: Riverside Publishing.

Dietz, C. H. (Ed.). (1995). *Moving towards the standards: A national action plan for mathematics education reform for the deaf*. Washington, DC: Gallaudet University, Pre-College Programs.

Dye, M. W. G., Hauser, P. C., & Bavelier, D. (2008). Visual attention in deaf children and adults. In M. Marschark & P. C. Hauser (Eds.), *Deaf cognition: Foundation and outcomes* (pp. 250–263). New York: Oxford University Press.

Easterbrooks, S., & Baker, S. (2002). *Language learning in children who are deaf and hard of hearing*. Boston: Allyn & Bacon.

Elliott, C. (2007). *Differential ability scales* (2nd ed.) (DAS-II). San Antonio, TX: PsychCorp.

Engen, E., & Engen, T. (1983). *The Rhode Island test of language structure*. Austin, TX: Pro-Ed.

French, M. (1999a). Stages of language development including features of ASL. In M. French (Ed.), *The toolkit: Appendices for starting with assessment* (pp. 45–50). Washington, DC: Pre-College National Mission Programs.

French, M. (1999b). The Kendall conversational proficiency levels. In M. French (Ed.), *The toolkit: Appendices for starting with assessment* (pp. 25–42). Washington, DC: Pre-College National Mission Programs.

Gallaudet Research Institute. (2005, January). *Regional and national summary report of data from the 2003–2004 Annual Survey of Deaf and Hard of Hearing Children and Youth*. Washington, DC: GRI, Gallaudet University.

Gallaudet Research Institute. (2005, December). *Regional and national summary of data from the 2002–2003 Annual Survey of Deaf and Hard of Hearing Children and Youth*. Washington, DC: GRI, Gallaudet University.

Gallaudet Research Institute. (2006, December). *Regional and national summary of data from the 2006–2007 Annual Survey of Deaf and Hard of Hearing Children and Youth.* Washington, DC: GRI, Gallaudet University.

GeneTests web site information page. Retrieved January 14, 2009 from http://www.geneclinics.org/profiles/deafness-overview/details.html.

Genetics Home Reference web site. Retrieved January 14, 2009 from http://www.ghr.nlm.nih.gov.

Gioia, G. A., Isquith, P. K., Guy, S. C., & Kentworthy, L. (2000). *Behavior rating inventory of executive function (BRIEF) professional manual.* Odessa, FL: Psychological Assessment Resources.

Gopaul-McNichol, S., & Thomas-Presswood, T. (1998). *Working with linguistically and culturally different children: Innovative clinical and educational approaches.* Boston: Allyn & Bacon.

Hammond, S. A., & Meiners, L. H. (1993). American Indian deaf children and youth. In K. M. Christensen & G. L. Delgado (Eds.), *Multicultural issues in deafness* (pp. 143–166). New York: Longman Publishing Group.

Hanson, V. (1989). Phonology and reading: Evidence from profoundly deaf readers. In D. Shankweiler & I. Lieberman (Eds.), *Phonology and reading disability: Solving the reading puzzle* (pp. 69–89). Ann Arbor, MI: University of Michigan Press.

Hauser, P. C., Cohen, J., Dye, M. W. G., & Bavelier, D. (2007). Visual constructive and visual-motor skills in deaf native signers. *Journal of Deaf Studies and Deaf Education, 12,* 148–157.

Hauser, P. C., Lukomski, J., & Hillman, T. (2008). Development of deaf and hard-of-hearing students' executive functions. In M. Marschark and P. Hauser (Eds.), *Deaf cognition: Foundations and outcomes* (pp. 286–308). New York: Oxford University Press.

Hess, R. S., & Rhodes, R. L. (2005). Providing neuropsychological services to culturally and linguistically diverse learners. In R. C. D'Amato, E. Fletcher-Janzen, & C. R. Reynolds (Eds.), *Handbook of school neuropsychology* (pp. 637–660). Hoboken, NJ: John Wiley & Sons.

Hindley, P., & Kroll, L. (1998). Theoretical and epidemiological aspects of attention deficit and overactivity in deaf children. *Journal of Deaf Studies and Deaf Education, 3,* 64–72.

Holt, J. (1993). Stanford Achievement Test, 8th edition: Reading comprehension subgroup results. *American Annals of the Deaf, 138,* 172–175.

Humphries, T. (1993). Deaf cultures and cultures. In K. M. Christensen & G. L. Delgado (Eds.), *Multicultural issues in deafness* (pp. 3–27). New York: Longman Publishing Group.

Individuals with Disabilities Education Improvement Act of 2004. (PL No. 108–445, 20 USC 1400).

Jensema, C. J., & Trybus, R. J. (1975). *Reported emotional/behavioral problems among hearing impaired children in special education programs: United States 1972–1973* (Series R, No. 1). Washington, DC: Gallaudet College, Office of Demographic Studies.

Joint Committee on Infant Hearing. (2000). Year 2000 position statement: Principles and guidelines for early hearing detection and intervention programs. *Pediatrics.*

106, 798–817. Retrieved January 14, 2009, Health Module database. (Document ID: 62956190).

Kamphaus, R. W., & Frick, P. J. (2001). *Clinical assessment of child and adolescent personality and behavior* (2nd ed.). Boston: Allyn & Bacon.

Kannapell, B. (1989) Inside the deaf community In S. Wilcox (Ed.), *American deaf culture: An anthology* (pp. 21–28). Burtonsville, MD: Linstok Press.

Karchmer, M., & Mitchell, R. E. (2003). Demographic and achievement characteristics of deaf and hard-of-hearing students. In M. Marschark & P. E. Spencer (Eds.), *Oxford handbook of deaf studies, language, and education* (pp. 21–37). New York: Oxford University Press.

Kaufman, A. S., & Kaufman, N. L. (2004). *Kaufman assessment battery for children* (2nd ed.). Circle Pines, MN: American Guidance Service Publishing.

Kelly, L. P. (2003). Considerations for designing practice for deaf readers. *Journal of Deaf Studies and Deaf Education, 8*, 171–186.

King, B. H., Hauser, P. C., & Isquith, P. K. (2006). Neuropsychiatric aspects of blindness and severe visual impairment, and deafness and severe hearing loss in children. In C. E. Coffey & R. A. Brumback (Eds.), *Pediatric neuropsychiatry* (pp. 397–434). Philadelphia: Lippincott, Williams, & Wilkins.

Kluwin, T., & Kelly, A. (1992). Implementing a successful writing program in public schools for children who are deaf. *Exceptional Children, 59*, 41–53.

Layton, T., & Holmes, D. (1985). *The Carolina picture vocabulary test*. Austin, TX: Pro-Ed.

Leigh, G. (2008). Changing parameters in deafness and deaf education. In M. Marschark & P. Hauser (Eds.), *Deaf cognition: Foundations and outcomes* (pp. 24–51). New York: Oxford University Press.

Leybaert, J. (1993). Reading in the deaf: The roles of phonological codes. In M. Marschark & M. D. Clark (Eds.), *Psychological perspectives on deafness* (pp. 269–309). Hillsdale, NJ: Lawrence Erlbaum Associates.

Lidz, C. (2003). *Early childhood assessment*. Hoboken, NJ: John Wiley & Sons.

Losardo, A., & Notari-Syverson, A. (2001). *Alternative approaches to assessing young children*. Baltimore: Paul H. Brookes Publishing.

Luckner, J., & Bowen, S. (2006). Assessment practices of professionals serving students who are deaf or hard of hearing. *American Annals of the Deaf, 151*, 410–417.

Lukomski, J. (2002). Program planning for deaf and hard of hearing learners. In A. Thomas & J. Grimes (Eds.), *Best practices in school psychology IV* (pp. 1393–1403). Bethesda, MD: NASP Publications.

Maller, S. J. (1996). WISC-III verbal item invariance across samples of deaf and hearing children of similar measured ability. *Journal of Psychoeducational Assessment, 14*, 152–165.

Maller, S. J. (2003). Intellectual assessment of deaf people. In M. Marschark & P. E. Spencer (Eds.), *Oxford handbook of deaf studies, language, and deaf education* (pp. 451–463). New York: Oxford University Press.

Maller, S. J., & Braden, J. P. (1993). The construct and criterion-related validity of the WISC-III with deaf adolescents. *Journal of Psychoeducational Assessment, WISC-III Monograph Series: WISC-III*, 105–113.

Marschark, M. (2003). Cognitive functioning in deaf adults and children. In M. Marschark & P. E. Spencer (Eds.), *Oxford handbook of deaf studies, language, and deaf education* (pp. 464–477). New York: Oxford University Press.

Marschark, M., Lang, H. G., & Albertini, J. A. (2002). *Educating deaf students: From research to practice*. New York: Oxford University Press.

Martin, F. B., & Clark, J. G. (2009). *Introduction to audiology* (10th ed.). Boston: Pearson.

Mason, J., & Scior, K. (2004). Diagnostic overshadowing amongst clinicians working with people with intellectual disabilities in the UK. *Journal of Applied Research in Intellectual Disabilities, 17,* 85–90.

Meltzer, L. (2007). Preface. In L. Meltzer (Ed.), *Executive functions in education: From theory to practice* (pp. xi-xiii). New York: Guilford.

Meyers, J. E., & Meyers, K. R. (1995). *Rey Complex Figure Test and Recognition Trial.* Odessa, FL: Psychological Assessment Resources.

Miller, B. D. (2008). Cattell-Horn-Carroll (CHC) theory-based assessment with deaf and hard of hearing children in the school setting. *American Annals of the Deaf, 152,* 459–466.

Miller, D. C. (2007). *Essentials of school neuropsychological assessment.* New York: John Wiley & Sons.

Miller, M. (2006). Individual assessment and educational planning: Deaf and hard of hearing students viewed through meaningful contexts. In D. F. Moores & D. S. Martin (Eds.), *Deaf learners: Developments in curriculum and instruction* (pp. 161–177). Washington, DC: Gallaudet University Press.

Miller, M., & Thomas-Presswood, T. (2008, November). *Impact of being deaf on the assessment process.* Paper presented at the conference of Making Connections: Neuropsychological Assessment and Applications with Individuals Who Are Deaf and Hard of Hearing, Washington, DC.

Montoya, J. G., & Remington, J. S. (2008). Management of *Toxoplasma gondii* infection during pregnancy [Abstract]. *Clinical Infectious Diseases, 47,* 554.

Moog, J. S., Kozak, V. J., & Geers, A. E. (1983). *Grammatical analysis of elicited language.* St. Louis, MO: Central Institute for the Deaf.

Moores, D. (2006). Print literacy. In D. Moores & D. Martin (Eds.), *Deaf learners: Developments in curriculum and instruction* (pp. 41–55). Washington, DC: Gallaudet University Press.

Moores, D. F. (1987). *Educating the deaf: Psychology, principles, and practices* (3rd ed.). Boston: Houghton Mifflin.

Moores, D., & Sweet, C. (1991). Factors predictive of academic achievement. In D. Moores & K. Meadow-Orlans (Eds.), *Educational and developmental aspects of deafness* (pp. 154–201). Washington, DC: Gallaudet University Press.

Musiek, F. E., & Baran, J. A. (2007). *The auditory system: Anatomy, physiology, and clinical correlates.* Boston: Pearson.

Musselman, C. (2000). How do children who can't hear learn to read an alphabetic script? A review of the literature of reading and deafness. *Journal of Deaf Studies and Deaf Education, 5,* 9–31.

National Reading Panel (NRP). (2000). *Report of the National Reading Panel. Teaching children to read: An evidence-based assessment of the scientific research literature on reading and its implications for reading instruction.* Washington, DC: U.S. Department of Health and Human Services.

NORD web site. Retrieved January 14, 2009 from http://www.rarediseases.org/search/rdbsearch.html.

Northern, J. L., & Downs, M. P. (2001). *Hearing in children.* Philadelphia: Lippincott, Williams, & Wilkins.

Ortiz, S. O., & Ochoa, S. H. (2005). Advances in cognitive assessment of culturally and linguistically diverse individuals: A nondiscriminatory interpretive approach. In D. P. Flanagan & P. L. Harrison (Eds.), *Contemporary intellectual assessment: Theories, tests and issues* (2nd ed., pp. 234–268). New York: Guilford.

Pagliaro, C. (2006). Mathematics education and the deaf learner. In D. Moores & D. Martin (Eds.), *Deaf learners: Developments in curriculum and instruction* (pp. 29–40). Washington, DC: Gallaudet University Press.

Paul, P. (1998). *Literacy and deafness: The development of reading, writing, and literate thought.* Boston: Allyn & Bacon.

Paul, P. (1999). *Literacy and deafness.* Boston: Allyn & Bacon.

Paul, P. V. (2003). Processes and components of reading. In M. Marschark & P. E. Spencer (Eds.), *Oxford handbook of deaf studies, language, and deaf education* (pp. 97–109). New York: Oxford University Press.

Paul, P. V., & Jackson, D. W. (1993). *Toward a psychology of deafness: Theoretical and empirical perspectives.* Boston: Allyn and Bacon.

Petit, C., & Weil, D. (2001). Deafness. *Encyclopedia of life sciences.* Nature Publishing Group. Available at http://www.els.net. Retrieved January 14, 2009.

Pintner, R., & Patterson, D. (1916). A measure of the language ability of deaf children. *Psychological Review, 23,* 413–436.

Pisoni, D. B., Conway, C. M., Kronenberger, W. G., Horn, D. L., Karpicke, J., & Henning, S. C. (2008). Efficacy and effectiveness of cochlear implants in deaf children. In M. Marschark & P. C. Hauser (Eds.), *Deaf cognition: Foundation and outcomes* (pp. 52–101). New York: Oxford University Press.

Pollack, B. J. (1997). *Educating children who are deaf/hard of hearing: Additional learning problems.* ERIC Digest #E548. ERIC Clearinghouse on Disabilities and Gifted Education, Reston, VA. (ERIC Document Reproduction Service No. ED 414 666).

Pre-College National Mission Programs. (1999a). Stages of language development including features of ASL. In M. French, *The toolkit: Appendices for starting with assessment: A developmental approach to deaf children's literacy* (pp. 45–50). Washington, DC: Author.

Pre-College National Mission Programs. (1999b). The Kendall conversational proficiency levels. In M. French, *The toolkit: Appendices for starting with assessment: A developmental approach to deaf children's literacy* (pp. 25–42). Washington, DC: Author.

Prickett, H. T., & Prickett, J. G. (1992). Vision problems among students in schools and programs for deaf children. *American Annals of the Deaf, 137,* 56–60.

Quigley, S., Steinkamp, M., Power, D., & Jones, B. (1976). *The test of syntactic abilities.* Eugene, OR: Dormac.

Reiss, S., Levitan, G. W., & Szyszko, J. (1982). Emotional disturbance and mental retardation: Diagnostic overshadowing. *American Journal of Mental Deficiency, 86,* 567–574.

Rhine, S. (2002). *Assessment of executive function.* Unpublished master's thesis, Gallaudet University, Washington, DC.

Rhodes, R. L., Ochoa, S. H., & Ortiz, S. O. (2005). *Assessing culturally and linguistically diverse students: A practical guide.* New York: Guilford.

Roid, G. H. (2003). *Stanford-Binet intelligence scales* (5th ed.). Itasca, IL: Riverside Publishing.

Roid, G. H., & Miller, L. J. (1998). *Leiter international performance scale—Revised.* Wood Dale, IL: Stoelting Co.

Rose, S., McNally, P. L., & Quigley, S. P. (2004). *Language learning practices with deaf children* (3rd ed.). Austin, TX: Pro-Ed.

Sattler, J. M., Hardy-Braz, S. T., & Willis, J. O. (2006). Hearing impairments. In J. M. Sattler (Ed.) *Assessment of children: Behavioral, social, and clinical foundations* (5th ed., pp. 478–492). San Diego: Jerome M. Sattler.

Schein, J. D., & Miller, M. H. (2008). Genetics and deafness: Implications for education and life care of deaf students. *American Annals of the Deaf, 153,* 408–10. Retrieved January 14, 2009, from Health Module database. (Document ID: 1626474091).

Schick, B. (2008). A model of learning within an interpreted K-12 educational setting. In M. Marschark & P. Hauser (Eds.), *Deaf cognition: Foundations and outcomes* (pp. 351–386). New York: Oxford University Press.

Schirmer, B. (1994). *Language and literacy development in children who are deaf.* New York: Macmillan.

Schirmer, B. (2000). *Language and literacy development in children who are deaf.* Boston: Allyn & Bacon.

Schirmer, B. R., & McGough, S. M. (2005). Teaching reading to children who are deaf: Do the conclusions of the National Reading Panel apply? *Review of Educational Research, 75,* 83–117.

Schow, R., & Nerbonne, M. (2002) *Introduction to audiologic rehabilitation.* Boston: Allyn & Bacon.

Sinnott, C. L., & Jones, T. W. (2005). Characteristics of the population of deaf and hard of hearing students with emotional disturbance in Illinois. *American Annals of the Deaf, 150,* 268–273.

Smith, R. J. H., Bale, J., Jr., & White, K. (2005). Sensorineural hearing loss in children. *Lancet, 365,* 879–890.

Smith, R. J. H., & Van Camp, G. (2007). Deafness and hereditary hearing loss overview. *GeneReviews at GeneTests: Medical Genetics Information Resource* [database online]. Retrieved January 14, 2009, from http://www.geneclinics.org.

Stach, B. A., & Ramachandran, V. S. (2008). Hearing disorders in children. In J. R. Madell & C. A. Flexer (Eds.), *Pediatric audiology* (pp. 3–12). New York: Thieme Medical Publishers.

Thomas-Presswood, T. N., & Presswood, D. (2007) *Meeting the needs of students and families of poverty: A handbook for school and mental health professionals.* Baltimore: Paul H. Brookes Publishing.

Thompson, M., Biro, P., Vethivelu, S., Pious, C., & Hatfield, N. (1987). *Language assessment of hearing-impaired school age children.* Seattle, WA: University of Washington Press.

Tonelson, S., & Watkins, S. (1979). *SKI*HI language development scale*. Logan UT: Hope.

Traxler, C. B. (2000). The Stanford Achievement Test, 9th edition: National norming and performance standards for deaf and hard-of-hearing students. *Journal of Deaf Studies and Deaf Education, 5*, 337–348.

Trezek, B. J., & Malmgren, K. W. (2005). The efficacy of utilizing a phonics treatment package with middle school deaf and hard-of-hearing students. *Journal of Deaf Studies and Deaf Education, 10*, 256–271.

Wang, Y., Trezek, B., Luckner, J., & Paul, P. (2008). The role of phonology and phonologically related skills in reading instruction for students who are deaf or hard of hearing. *American Annals of the Deaf, 153*, 396–407.

Watanabe, D., Zako, M., Tamada, Y., & Matsumoto, Y. (2007). A case of keratitis-ichthyosis-deafness (KID) syndrome. *International Journal of Dermatology, 46*, 400–402.

Wechsler, D. (1997). *Wechsler memory scale* (3rd ed.). San Antonio, TX: Harcourt Assessment.

Wechsler, D. (2003). *Wechsler intelligence scale for children* (4th ed.). San Antonio, TX: Harcourt Assessment.

Wechsler, D., & Naglieri, J. A. (2006). *Wechsler nonverbal scale of ability (WNV)*. San Antonio, TX: PsychCorp.

Willis, W. G., & Vernon, M. (2002). Residential psychiatric treatment of emotionally disturbed deaf youth. *American Annals of the Deaf, 47*, 31–38.

Wilson, M., Bettger, J. G., Niculae, I., & Klima, E. S. (1997). Modality of language shapes working memory: Evidence from digit span and spatial span in ASL signers. *Journal of Deaf Studies and Deaf Education, 2*, 152–162.

Woll, B., & Ladd, P. (2003). Deaf communities. In M. Marschark & P. E. Spencer (Eds.), *Oxford handbook of deaf studies, language, and education* (pp. 151–163). New York: Oxford University Press.

Woodcock, R. W., & Muñoz-Sandoval, A. F. (2001). *Woodcock-Muñoz language survey normative update*. Chicago: Riverside.

Yarger, C. C. (2001). Educational interpreting: Understanding the rural experience. *American Annals of the Deaf, 146*, 16–30.

CHAPTER 18

Assessing and Intervening with Visually Impaired Children and Adolescents

JACK G. DIAL and CATHERINE L. DIAL

T HERE IS A significant need for neuropsychological assessment of children and adolescents who are visually impaired or blind (VI/B). Although the numbers vary considerably from one source to another, some authors report that there are over 400,000 individuals under the age of 18 who have "significant impairment of vision which cannot be further improved by corrective lenses" (Hupp, 2003; Leonard, 2002). Of this number, only 93,600 as of 1998 were technically receiving special education services in the public schools (Kirchner & Diament, 1999) and, according to the National Center for Educational Statistics, only 28,772 were being served under the "Individuals with Disabilities Education Act" in 2004 (NCES, 2007). However, the disparity in numbers may be explained by considering that many students with vision loss do not meet the technical definition of VI/B, or they have other significant disabilities under which they may be classified for special education purposes and, thus, are not formally reported as VI/B to federal census agencies. Still others are under school age and are not accounted for in special education records.

In a retrospective study of adults with vision loss, 73 percent had onset of vision loss prior to the age of 18 and 75 percent had significant secondary disabilities, of which 44 percent were neuropsychological in nature. Although these percentages are likely inflated somewhat by referral bias (all individuals were referred for vocational and/or psychological evaluations), they are nevertheless alarming and indicative of the fact that persons with visual impairment or blindness are at much greater risk of having

465

neuropsychological and other disabilities than are sighted persons (Bouchard & Tetreault, 2000; Mukaddes, Kilincaslan, Kucukyazici, Sevketoglu, & Tuncer, 2007; Stores & Ramchandani, 1999; Stuart, 1995). Furthermore, of those persons with the onset of significant vision loss occurring before age 18, there were over twenty-three different etiologies, many of which give rise to other disabilities or medical conditions that, in addition to vision loss, may interfere with learning and consequently require accommodations and interventions in the school setting apart from those normally utilized with students who are only blind or visually impaired (Dial et al., 1990; Hill-Briggs, Dial, Morere, & Joyce, 2007; Joyce, Isom, Dial, & Sandel, 2004; MacCluskie, Tunick, Dial, & Paul, 1998; Miller & Skillman, 2003). Given the heterogeneity and complexity of this population, the school neuropsychologist is confronted with numerous issues when evaluating a student with significant vision loss. Among these, the most critical issues appear to be limitations in test adaptation and development, impact of heterogeneity of the population on test norming, impact of visual functioning level, age at onset, etiology, and level of educational attainment on interpretation of neuropsychological test results (Hill-Briggs et al., 2007).

ISSUES RELATED TO TEST DEVELOPMENT

Relatively few successful efforts have been made to adapt or design instrumentation for application to a VI/B population, especially in the area of cognitive assessment. For example, the historical development and adaptation of performance cognitive measures such as the *Perkins-Binet Tests of Intelligence for the Blind* (Davis, 1980) and *Hayes-Binet Intelligence Scale for the Blind* (Hayes, 1942; 1943) were adversely affected by small normative samples of blind children, many of whom had secondary disabilities (Gutterman, Ward, & Genshaft, 1985; Hills-Briggs et al., 2007). Commercial investment in test development for this population has been almost nonexistent for a number of reasons, among which is the limited vertical market of potential users and the difficulty in defining a representative normative sample (Bylsma & Doninger, 2004; Miller & Skillman, 2003; Miller et al., 2007). For example, instruments such as the *Vocational Intelligence Scale for Adult Blind* (Jones & Tears, 1964, as referenced in Reid, 2002), *Haptic Version of the Raven Standard Progressive Matrices* (Rich & Anderson, 1965), the *Stanford Ohwki-Kohs Tactile Block Design Intelligence Test* (cited in Bylsma et al., 2004), *Adapted Kohs Block Design Test* (Reid, 2002), and many others are no longer marketed.

These issues have also plagued independent researchers in the study of blindness. For example, during the development of a neuropsychological and vocational test battery (the *Comprehensive Vocational Evaluation System* for visually impaired/blind—CVES), Dial et al. (1990) found that only 25 percent of the original normative sample of adolescents and adults were "normal" with reference to having only a visual impairment or blindness; 75 percent of the sample had multiple and varying other disabilities or medical disorders. To counter this problem, only those individuals who had no other disorder or disability were included in the sampling process, thereby increasing the sensitivity of the CVES battery in detecting the effects of other disorders or disabilities, if present, in a person being tested. This operational definition of "normal VI/B" was found to be particularly helpful in detecting and diagnosing neuropsychological disabilities (Dial et al., 1990; Nelson, Dial, & Joyce, 2002). However, since only a quarter of those involved in the data collection process met the operational definition of "normal VI/B," massive numbers of individuals had to be tested in order to obtain an adequate sample size. This process required many years of effort (1982 to present), a commitment not possible for many researchers or commercial test developers.

In addition to normative problems, test developers have been hampered by the wide variation in level of visual functioning and the specific nature of the person's visual loss. Since approximately 80 percent (National Center for Health Statistics, 1994 & 1995) of the VI/B population have some useful vision that may vary from being able to read regular print to almost no functional vision, how does a test developer control for the effects of residual vision on test performance? Dial et al. (1990) reasoned that tests for those with vision loss should allow for vision-free administration when possible, regardless of the individual's level of visual functioning, and this strategy worked particularly well when developing the CVES battery.

A variety of traditional tests have been adapted for use with the VI/B population; for example, the Tactual Performance Test (TPT), Grip Strength (GS), Finger Oscillation (FO), and Seashore Rhythm (SR) subtests from the *Halstead-Reitan Battery* (HRB) have been used to assess individuals with visual impairment or blindness (Bigler & Tucker, 1981; Reitan & Davison, 1974; Reitan & Wolfson, 1993). However, these measures are limited to assessing selected perceptual and motor functions and lack appropriate norms for the VI/B population, particularly for children and adolescents comprising the typical school-age range. There have also been significant efforts from other clinicians and researchers to adapt or develop instruments that could be administered to a person with visual impairment or blindness (Mangiameli & Peters, 1998; Mangiameli, Roderick, Moses, & Dohen, 1999). The lack of sufficient numbers of blind subjects (particularly children) for norming purposes, as well as appropriate controls for residual vision and age at onset, have adversely affected the researcher's progress and, consequently, the utility of these measures with a student population. One promising cognitive test for younger VI/B school age students is the *Intelligence Test for Visually Impaired Children* (ITVIC) developed by Dekker and associates (Dekker, 1989;

1993). This test was originally normed on 156 blind Braille-reading children ages 6 to 15 from Belgium and Holland. It is now available in English, as well as Dutch and German. However, the norms do not account for the issues of age at onset or level of visual functioning, etc., and cultural differences between Western Europe and the United States may be a factor. Even traditional verbal-cognitive tests, included in instruments such as the *Wechsler Adult Intelligence Test—III/IV* (WAIS-III; Wechsler, 1977a) or WAIS-IV (Wechsler, 2008), the *Wechsler Intelligence Scales for Children, 4th Edition* (WISC-IV; Wechsler, 2003), and the verbal sections of the *Wechsler Memory Scales, 3rd Edition* (WMS-III; Wechsler, 1997b) that would appear intuitively appropriate for use with the VI/B population cannot necessarily be directly interpreted in many cases without considering age at onset, level of visual functioning, and level of educational attainment (Bylsma & Doninger, 2004; Hill-Briggs et al., 2007; Miller & Skillman, 2003; Miller et al., 2007).

Level of visual functioning, age at onset, and level of educational attainment may interact such that interpretation of results from traditional verbal intelligence tests utilizing sighted norms may be compromised. For example, in a study by Hupp (2003), "sighted and totally blind adults performed significantly better on the *WAIS-III* VIQ than did a group of legally blind persons." Furthermore, persons with congenital onset of their vision loss (onset within the first two years of age) performed significantly better than all other VI/B groups (early: 2 to 5 years, 11 months; school age: 6 to 17 years, 11 months; and adults: 18 years and older) on tests of immediate and working verbal memory (Hill-Briggs, 2007). Differences were also observed between groups of congenital versus adult onset in verbal conceptualization (MacCluskie et al., 1998). Dekker et al. (1989) also observed that "congenital blindness had a positive influence on verbal memory and a negative influence on spatial ability" as measured by the ITVIC. Congenitals out-performed all other groups on specific subtests and factors included in the *Cognitive Test for the Blind* (CTB), a component of the CVES battery (Dial et al., 1990); namely, on measures of haptic nonverbal abstract learning and rote verbal learning (Hupp, 2003). Not surprisingly, when Hupp conducted analyses to remove the effects of age at onset and level of visual functioning, post-hoc tests revealed that level of education significantly impacted cognitive performance on CTB subtests of Letter-Number Learning and Category Memory, both, in part, measures of executive functioning. In both instances, the sighted group outperformed the VI/B groups. When taken in concert, Hupp (2003) concluded, "Vision is, indeed, an essential factor in cognitive development independent of one's educational opportunities. However, education does become a significant factor in terms of priming and accommodating for complex information processing."

Interactions among age at onset, level of visual functioning, and other variables have also been observed to affect perceptual-motor functions. For example, Joyce et al. (2004) observed that persons who became blind earlier in life were able to discriminate shapes and textures better than persons who became blind as adults, and persons who were totally blind outperformed those who retained vision. With respect to motor functions, adult onset groups were observed to perform better on tasks requiring slow, careful persistent motor movement (continuous performance) than the early onset groups, while the school-age groups were observed to perform better on bimanual tasks than the early onset groups. All VI/B groups demonstrated poorer fine and gross motor functioning when compared to sighted individuals (Bouchard & Tetreault, 2000; Joyce et al., 2004).

The school neuropsychologist should also be aware that etiology of VI/B can be an underlying factor that may predispose a student to have a greater risk for higher cortical dysfunction that will adversely affect the learning process. To cite just one example, Nelson, O'Brien, Dial, and Joyce (2001) observed a significantly greater chance of neuropsychological deficits in individuals with retinopathy of prematurity (ROP) as the etiology of their vision loss compared to other groups with different etiologies; namely, congenital cataracts and retinitis pigmentosa. This is an important finding since ROP constitutes the etiology of vision loss for a significant number of VI/B children entering school systems (Centers for Disease Control and Prevention, National Center on Birth Defects and Developmental Disabilities, 2008). Specifically, the ROP group demonstrated greater deficits in spatial functioning and performance cognitive functioning on the CTB, haptic-memory matching abilities on the left side of the body, as measured by the Haptic Sensory Discrimination Test (HSDT), and left side motor functions on the McCarron Assessment of Neuromuscular Development—VI/B version (MAND-VI); the latter tests are components of the CVES Battery. The patterns and relationships among the aforementioned results are consistent with right parietal lobe dysfunction, likely correlated to gestational age at birth, birth weight, and the specific cause of premature birth (although typically not known). Nevertheless, the underlying systems that contribute to the mediation of such functions as spatial orientation, organizational abilities, mathematics and other nonverbal functions are compromised, thus leading to potential practical problems in orientation and mobility, specific mathematics disorders, and a disheveled arrangement of one's environment and/or work materials. Therefore, the school neuropsychologist who observes this pattern may be able to make valuable recommendations for intervention strategies, possibly averting some of the problems the student may encounter in the school environment and later in the world of work.

Although considerably more research is needed to understand the interaction among age at onset, level of visual functioning, etiology, level of education, etc. on neuropsychological functioning of the VI/B population, the recognition of the heterogeneity of this group greatly enhances the effectiveness of appropriately adapting or developing tests that can take into account these variables. More important, understanding the impact of such interactions may increase the accuracy of interpretation of neuro-psychological test results and lead to more useful and beneficial recommendations for educational intervention.

CONSIDERATIONS IN TEST SELECTION AND EVALUATION OF THE VI/B STUDENT

As previously mentioned, there is a dearth of instrumentation available for use in neuropsychological evaluation of VI/B children and adolescents as well as limitations in those tests that are available. However, there are tests and rating scales that, within limits, are applicable to this population and enable the school neuropsychologist to assess strengths and functional limitations or deficits associated with significant vision loss, concomitant disabilities, and possible neuropsychological impairment. Using a factor configuration and data gathering model proposed by McCarron and Dial (1986), the instrumentation used to assess problem or ability areas may be conceptualized under the following categories: Verbal-Spatial Cognitive (VSC), Perceptual-Motor (PM), and Emotional-Coping (EC) functioning. The VSC factor or domain includes verbal and nonverbal information processing, memory, learning, executive functions, and attention and concentration. A person's performance across this domain may have a significant bearing on his or her general academic and vocational success. The PM factor focuses on sensory integration and motor functions, which may impact the efficiency of performance, while the EC factor includes measures of emotional personality and adaptive behavioral functioning. Table 18.1 provides a brief listing of instruments that the school neuropsychologist may wish to consider when conducting a comprehensive evaluation of a person with significant vision loss (note that this is not a complete list and instruments that are not readily available have been excluded).

Limitations regarding the interpretation of the Wechsler Scales, the *Intelligence Test for Visually* Impaired Children, Wechsler Memory Scales, and Halstead/Reitan subtests have already been discussed. However, there are also limitations with reference to age norms for those instruments included in the CVES battery, e.g., CTB, HSDT, MAND-VI, EBC, OEI-R, and SFAB. With regard to the interpretation of levels of performance and patterns and relationships among scores, the CVES VI/B norms only extend down through age 14. Sighted norms for the MAND are available for ages $3\frac{1}{2}$ through older adults. Nevertheless, other methods of inference may be applied selectively to the CVES, Halstead-Reitan, and other instruments in the absence of VI/B norms. For example, pathognomic signs may emerge during the performance

Table 18.1

Instrumentation Utilized in Neuropsychological Assessment to Identify Strengths and Limitations in VI/B Children, Adolescents, and Young Adults

Factor	Tests	Accommodations
Verbal – Spatial Cognitive Factor	Wechsler Verbal Scales (WAIS-III, WISC-IV)	• Regular and VI/B norms. • No procedural or structural adaptations necessary.
	Cognitive Test for the Blind (CTB)	• VI/B norms. • No procedural or structural adaptations necessary.
	• Verbal Scales (Auditory Analysis, Immediate Digit Recall, Language Comprehension and Memory, Letter-Number Learning and Vocabulary). • Performance Scales (Category Learning, Category Memory, Memory Recognition, Spatial Pattern Recall and Spatial Analysis).	• VI/B norms. • Textured and raised rubber stimulus materials; response board, and screen to control residual functional vision.
	Intelligence Test for Visually Impaired Children (ITVIC)	• English version. • VI/B norms. • No procedural or structural adaptations necessary.
	Wechsler Memory Scales (WMS III, WMS IV)	• Regular norms available. • No procedural or structural adaptations necessary.
	Wide Range Achievement Test (WRAT- 3)	• VI/B norms. • Regular, large print or Braille reading (according to functional vision); regular or oral spelling; large print or oral arithmetic.
Perceptual (Sensory) Motor Factor	Haptic Sensory Discrimination Test (HSDT) • Discrimination and Immediate recall of shapes, sizes, textures and spatial configurations	• VI/B norms. • Textured and raised rubber stimulus materials; response board; screen to control residual functional vision. • Alternate (hands-on) methods of demonstration and instruction.
Perceptual (Sensory) Motor Factor – continued	McCarron Assessment of Neuromuscular Development (VI/B Version) (MAND VI) • Fine Motor Scales (Beads-in-Box, Beads on Rod, Finger-Tapping, Nut & Bolt and Rod Slide).	• VI/B norms. • Some subtests performed with eyes closed to control for residual functional vision. • Alternate (hands-on) methods of demonstration and instruction.

(continued)

Table 18.1
Continued

Factor	Tests	Accommodations
	• Gross Motor Scales (Hand Strength, Finger-Nose-Finger, Jumping, Heel-Toe-Walk and Standing on One Foot.	• VI/B norms. • Some subtests performed with eyes closed to control for residual functional vision; raised rubber or cloth line for gross coordination subtest. • Alternate (hands-on) methods of demonstration and instruction.
	Halstead-Reitan Neuropsychological Battery Tests: • Tactile Performance Test (TPT) • Grip Strength (GS) • Finger Oscillation (FO) • Seashore Rhythm Test (SRT) • Discrimination of non-language sound patterns	• No procedural or structural adaptations necessary. • Regular norms available; no procedural or structural adaptations necessary.
Emotional – Coping Factor	Observational Emotional Inventory—Revised (OEI-R)	• VI/B norms.
	Emotional—Behavioral Checklist (EBC) Seven areas of emotional-behavioral functioning are rated.	• VI/B norms.
	Minnesota Multiphasic Personality Inventory (MMPI-2 or A)	• Tape, oral, large print, or CCTV issues regarding presentation. • Interpretation in persons with chronic disabilities.
	Rotter Incomplete Sentence Blank (RISB)	• Oral, large print, or CCTV presentation.
	Beck Depression and Beck Anxiety Inventories (BDI and BAI)	• Oral, large print, or CCTV presentation.
	Survey of Functional Adaptive Behavior (SFAB)	• VI/B norms. • Interview and behavioral observations.

on any of the tests, and selected perceptual-motor subtests allow for the use of the individual as his or her own control by comparing measured functioning between the right and left sides of the body, e.g., grip strength, finger tapping (oscillation) and haptic-memory matching (HSDT). Furthermore, when appropriate sighted age norms are available, criteria referenced interpretations may provide valuable insight into how a person with vision loss compares to sighted peers with reference to a particular demand situation (academic or physical education standards, etc.).

ACCOMMODATION AND REMEDIATION OF IDENTIFIED DEFICITS

With regard to general accommodations for vision loss, traditional use of many different visual aids for magnification such as closed circuit televisions, magnifiers, and telescopes can enable the administration of instruments, such as the *Minnesota Multiphasic Personality Inventory—2/Adolescent* (Butcher, Dahlstrom, Graham, Tellegen, & Kaemmer, 1989; Butcher et al., 1992); *Rotter Incomplete Sentence Blank* (Rotter & Rafferty, 1950), to individuals with sufficient residual vision. Large print and high contrast materials may also suffice (Siddiqui, Rydberg, & Lennerstrand, 2005). Computer screen reading software (and hardware) and other adaptive technology can also facilitate the administration of some tests or provide the means by which a person with impaired vision can formulate written responses. Most of the necessary assistive technology is already in place in large school districts. Furthermore, traditional programs of orientation-mobility and rehabilitation or vision teacher interventions are routinely used in academic environments to support VI/B student needs. However, given the issues of comorbidity (50 to 75 percent), etiology, level of visual functioning, age at onset, and others, the student may require a comprehensive neuropsychological evaluation to identify specific needs that extend beyond accommodations and services that address vision loss. The school neuropsychologist may provide a unique contribution through specific individual recommendations for accommodations or strategies of remediation that address non-vision-related deficits identified from such an evaluation.

Through the evaluation process, the school neuropsychologist must first determine whether one or more comorbid conditions exist. There is a much greater probability within the VI/B, as contrasted to sighted population, that an undiagnosed neuropsychological disorder may be detected. In many instances the so-called "secondary disability" will have as much or even greater impact on educational programming than the vision loss. Examples of commonly diagnosed neuropsychological disorders include specific learning disabilities, developmental disorders, autistic spectrum disorders, and mild traumatic brain injuries. Traditional methods of inference are used to interpret the neuropsychological data: levels of performance, patterns and relationships among scores, pathognomic signs, and the comparison of perceptual or sensory-motor functions between the two sides of the body. In addition, criteria-referenced and predictive techniques can be used to weigh the impact of identified deficits on academic and physical challenges imposed by the school curriculum. From this process, the individual's learning style can also be determined and general placement recommendations can be made. For example, there is a greater risk that a VI/B student will need recommended adaptations in physical education such as trained peer role models and tutors, motor behavior assessment feedback to the student, and guided-discovery teaching techniques (Shapiro, Lieberman & Moffett, 2003; Wiskochil, Lieberman, Houston-Wilson, & Petersen, 2007).

The school neuropsychologist needs to also identify specific functional deficits (and strengths) within the major assessment domains: Verbal-Spatial-Cognitive, Perceptual (Sensory) Motor, and Emotional-Coping. This process overlaps with diagnostics but involves a different focus. The specific methods of intervention that are recommended depend on the enumeration of these deficits in concert with a consideration of the person's level of visual functioning, age, comorbid conditions, and other such factors. A software program entitled "PACS" to expedite this process is presently being field tested in Texas and North Dakota (Dial, Savaresy, Mezger, & Mihulka, 2005).

PACS (Profile Analysis and Consultation System) translates identified neuropsychological deficits into clustered "traits" for which specific recommendations, or guides to educational management, are generated. Data from the WAIS-III (Wechsler, 1997a), WAIS-IV (Wechsler, 2008), or the WISC-IV (Wechsler, 2003), as well as the WRAT-3 (Wilkinson, 1993) and the CVES (Dial et. al., 1990) measures are analyzed by levels of performance, patterns, and relationships among scores and are converted to common trait clusters.

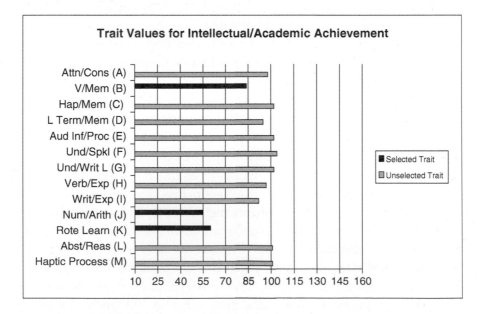

Figure 18.1 Intelligence-achievement trait selection. Note that three deficits were identified and selected: (B) short term verbal-auditory memory; (J) numerical concepts and arithmetic reasoning; and (K) rote learning.

Trait scores are corrected for age and gender differences, and those traits that meet deficit cut-off criteria or are determined to be "relatively lower" than factor composite scores are selected. A database of recommendations generated by professionals (including psychologists, neuropsychologists, vocational evaluators, and educators with expertise in VI/B) is searched. Recommendations are selected and sorted by the person's level of visual functioning. The result is a report that can be further individualized and transmitted to appropriate educational programming staff and teachers. The report contains no "test data" and is written in common sense language. Figure 18.1 presents the trait selection results within the "Intelligence-

NUMBER CONCEPTS & ARITHMETIC REASONING: Understanding numbers and solving simple arithmetic problems

Functional Implications:

This student may experience significant problems in learning number and/or measurement concepts and in solving problems that require basic arithmetic and/or measurement skills. Difficulties in this area may include inability to recognize money equivalents, careless errors in simple arithmetic problems, inability to recognize and correct errors in arithmetic, errors in linear measurement, and occasional counting errors.

Recommendations:

- Review basic arithmetic operations and reinforce successful attempts.
- Ensure this student's attention before giving instructions and encourage questions.
- Use a peer tutor and break assignments into smaller units.
- Use visual and tactile materials if possible for multi-sensory learning of new concepts and skills.
- Teach new materials in terms of already learned material when possible.
- Limit the number of problems and verbally walk through the process of solving each.
- Continually emphasize old learning and links; help this student see the "big picture."
- Continuously reinforce concepts; play different games to learn the same concepts.
- Apply simple counting and arithmetic exercises to practical, real-life situations as much as possible, such as using a vending machine.
- Consider using an applied approach to the fundamentals of mathematics with hands-on manipulatives including talking calculator, marked ruler, gauges, money, etc.
- Use simplified materials that provide instructional organization.
- Use counting games, and work with textured patterns.
- Play games requiring the exchange of money (e.g., Monopoly).
- Have this student show more than one way to work out problems (grouping, drawing pictures).
- Use a calendar/agenda for homework assignments and parent/teacher feedback.
- Consider taking community outings to demonstrate real-life applications of math.

Figure 18.2   Example recommendations for remediation of deficits in number concepts and arithmetic reasoning.

Achievement Factor" (Verbal-Spatial-Cognitive domain) for a 15-year-old male student with moderate functional vision loss (levels of functional vision are operationally defined within the system).

A recommendation report is then generated. Examples of specific recommendations selected by PACS to address the identified deficit trait, "numerical concepts and arithmetic reasoning," are included in Figure 18.2.

Whether developed manually or derived from a program such as PACS, it is incumbent on the school neuropsychologist to contribute, when possible, more than just a differential diagnosis and general recommendations. Data collected through a comprehensive neuropsychological evaluation provide an excellent base from which specific educational recommendations can be generated.

SUMMARY

Given the number of students with vision loss and the comorbidity of other disabilities and disorders (50 to 75 percent), a comprehensive neuropsychological evaluation is a valuable service that can help distinguish problems that, in addition to visual impairment, may adversely affect the learning process. However, the school neuropsychologist is faced with many obstacles and issues that affect the delivery of this service. The most important issues encountered by the neuropsychologist include the lack of appropriate instrumentation specifically adapted or developed for VI/B population, the lack of suitable norms (especially for younger children), the effect of age at onset, the level of visual functioning, the etiology of VI/B on norming and interpretation, and the lack of research in the subspecialty field of neuropsychological evaluation of persons with vision loss.

Despite these limitations, some progress has been made toward resolving these issues. Instruments such as the *Comprehensive Vocational Evaluation System* (CVES) for visually impaired/blind, the *Intelligence Test for Visually Impaired Children*, subtests of the Halstead-Reitan Battery, and others have proven useful in neuropsychological evaluation of the VI/B student population. Furthermore, research has begun to delineate possible directions for more appropriate norming procedures and issues regarding the effects of age at onset, level of visual functioning, and etiology on interpretation; the impact of such is gradually being understood. Nevertheless, continued efforts to advance the field are obviously needed.

Regarding the evaluation process, the school neuropsychologist is encouraged to go beyond diagnostics and reporting of generic programming recommendations. The rich database extracted from a comprehensive neuropsychological evaluation provides the information necessary to develop specific recommendations, which contribute to interventions that may be helpful to teachers and other programming staff in the school setting. This process may be intuitively based on the experience of the professional neuropsychologist and/or augmented by systems, such as "PACS," that identify student profile deficits and translate these into specific recommendations for "Guides for Educational Management." Continued educational development and research in the field of neuropsychological evaluation of the VI/B population is essential.

REFERENCES

Bigler, E. D., & Tucker, D. M. (1981). Comparison of verbal I.Q., tactual performance, seashore rhythm, and finger oscillation tests in the blind and brain-damaged. *Journal of Clinical Psychology, 37,* 849–851.

Bouchard, S., & Tetreault, S. (2000). The motor development of sighted children and children with moderate low vision aged 8–13. *Journal of Visual Impairment and Blindness, 4,* 564.

Butcher, J. N., Dahlstrom, W. G., Graham, J. R., Tellegen, A., & Kaemmer, B. (1989). *Minnesota multiphasic personality inventory—2 (MMPI-2): Manual for administration and scoring.* Minneapolis: University of Minnesota Press.

Butcher, J. N., Williams, C. L., Graham, J. R., Archer, R., Tellegen, A., Ben-Porath, Y. S., & Kaemmer, B. (1992). *MMPI-A manual for administration, scoring and interpretation.* Minneapolis: University of Minnesota Press.

Bylsma, F. W., & Doninger, N. (2004). Neuropsychological assessment in individuals with severe visual impairment. *Topics in Geriatric Rehabilitation, 20,* 196–203.

Centers for Disease Control and Prevention, National Center on Birth Defects and Developmental Disabilities (CDC, NCBDDD, DD). (2008). Vision impairment: how common is vision impairment? Retrieved September 19, 2008, from http://www.cdc.gov/ncbddd/dd/vision3.htm.

Davis, C. J. (1980). *The Perkins-Binet tests of intelligence for the blind.* Watertown, MA: Perkins School for the Blind.

Dekker, R. (1989). Cognitive development of visually handicapped children. In R. Dekker, P. J. D., Drenth, & J. N. Zaal (Eds.), *Intelligence test for visually impaired children aged 6 to 15* (pp. 1–21). The Nederlands: Bartimeus Zeist.

Dekker, R. (1993). Visually impaired children and haptic intelligence test scores: Intelligence Test for Visually Impaired Children (ITVIC). *Developmental Medicine & Child Neurology, 35,* 478–489.

Dial, J. G., Mezger, C., Gray, S., Massey, T., Chan, F., & Hull, J. (1990). *Manual: Comprehensive Vocational Evaluation System.* Dallas, TX: McCarron-Dial Systems.

Dial, J. G., Savaresy, M., Mezger, C., & Mihulka, D. (2005). PACS: Profile Analysis and Counsulting System. Dallas, TX: McCarron-Dial Systems.

Gutterman, J., Ward, M., & Genshaft, J. (1985). Correlations of scores of low vision children on the Perkins-Binet tests of intelligence for the blind, the WISC-R and the WRAT. *Journal of Visual Impairment & Blindness, 79,* 55–58.

Hayes, S. P. (1942). Alternative scales for the mental measurement of the visually handicapped. *Outlook for the Blind, 36,* 225–230.

Hayes, S. P. (1943). A second test scale for the mental measurement of the visually handicapped. *Outlook for the Blind, 37,* 37–41.

Hill-Briggs, F., Dial, J. G., Morere, D. A., & Joyce, A. (2007). Neuropsychological assessment of persons with physical disability, visual impairment or blindness, and hearing impairment or deafness. *Archives of Clinical Neuropsychology, 22,* 389–404.

Hupp, G. S. (2003). *Cognitive differences between congenitally and adventitiously blind individuals.* Unpublished doctoral dissertation, University of North Texas, Denton, TX.

Joyce, A., Isom, R., Dial, J. G., & Sandel, M. G. (2004). Implications of perceptual-motor differences within blind populations. *Journal of Applied Rehabilitation Counseling, 35,* 3–7.

Kirchner, C., & Diament, S. (1999). Usable data report: Estimates of the number of visually impaired students, their teachers, and orientation and mobility specialists: Part I. *Journal of Visual Impairment & Blindness, 93,* 600–660.

Leonard, R. (2002). *Statistics on vision impairment: A resource manual* (5th ed.). New York: Arlene R. Gordon Research Institute of Lighthouse International.

MacCluskie, K. C., Tunick, R. H., Dial, J. G., & Paul, D. S. (1998). The role of vision in the development of abstraction ability. *Journal of Visual Impairment and Blindness, 92,* 189–199.

Mangiameli, L. J., & Peters, L. J. (1998). A non-visual battery for assessment of spatial abilities [Abstract]. *Archives of Clinical Neuropsychology, 14,* 86.

Mangiameli, L. J., Roderick, R., Moses, J. A., & Dohen, D. A. (1999). The Limited Vision Block Sorting Tests: A vision independent test of executive functioning [Abstract]. *Archives of Clinical Neuropsychology, 14,* 701–702.

McCarron, L., & Dial, J. (1986). *McCarron-Dial evaluation system: A systematic approach to vocational, educational, and neuropsychological assessment* (2nd ed.). Dallas, TX: McCarron-Dial Systems.

Miller, J. C., & Skillman, G. D. (2003). Assessors' satisfaction with measures of cognitive ability applied to persons with visual impairments. *Journal of Visual Impairment and Blindness, 97,* 769–774.

Miller, J. C., Skillman, G. D., Benedetto, J. M, Holtz, A., Nassif, C. L., & Weber, A. D. (2007). A three-dimensional haptic matrix test of nonverbal reasoning. *Journal of Visual Impairment & Blindness, 101,* 514–557.

Mukaddes, N. M., Kilincaslan, A., Kucukyazici, G., Sevketoglu, T., & Tuncer, S. (2007). Autism in visually impaired individuals. *Psychiatry and Clinical Neurosciences, 61,* 39–44.

National Center for Education Statistics (NCES). (2007). Number and percentage of children ages 3 to 5 and 6 to 21 served under the Individuals with Disabilities Education Act (IDEA), by race/ethnicity and type of disability: 2004. Retrieved September 19, 2008, from http://www.nces.ed.gov/pubs2007/minoritytrends/tables/table_8_1b.asp?referrer=report.

National Center for Health Statistics. (1994 & 1995). *Estimate of overall legal blindness. National Health Interview Survey—Disability Supplement*. Retrieved September 19, 2008, from http://www.cdc.gov/nchs/nhis.htm.

Nelson, P. A., Dial, J. G., & Joyce, A. (2002). Validation of the cognitive test for the blind as an assessment of intellectual functioning. *Rehabilitation Psychology, 47*, 184–193.

Nelson, P. A., O'Brien, E. P., Dial, J. G., & Joyce, A. (2001). Neuropsychological correlates of retinopathy of prematurity (ROP) compared to other causes of blindness [Abstract]. *Archives of Clinical Neuropsychology, 16*, 766–767.

Reid, J. M. V. (2002). Testing non-verbal intelligence of working age visually impaired adults: Evaluation of the adapted Kohs block design test. *Journal of Visual Impairment & Blindness, 96*, 585–595.

Reitan, R. M., & Davison, L. A. (1974). *Clinical neuropsychology: Current status and applications*. Washington, DC: Winston & Sons.

Reitan, R. M., & Wolfson, D. (1993). *The Halstead-Reitan neuropsychological test battery: Theory and clinical interpretation*. Tucson, Arizona: Neuropsychology Press.

Rich, C. C., & Anderson, R. P. (1965). A tactual form of the progressive matrices for use with blind children. *Personnel & Guidance Journal, 43*, 912–919.

Rotter, J. B., & Rafferty, J. E. (1950). *The Rotter incomplete sentences blank manual*. Cleveland, OH: Psychological Corporation.

Shapiro, D. R., Lieberman, J., & Moffett, A. (2003). Statistics to improve perceived competence in children with visual impairments. *RE:view, 35*(2), 69–80.

Siddiqui, A. P., Rydberg, A., & Lennerstrand, G. (2005). Visual contrast functions in children with severe visual impairment and the relation to functional ability. *Visual Impairment Research, 7*, 43–52.

Stores, G., & Ramchandani, P. (1999). Sleep disorders in visually impaired children. *Developmental Medicine & Child Neurology, 41*, 348–352.

Stuart, I. (1995). Spatial orientation and congenital blindness: A neuropsychological approach. *Journal of Visual Impairment & Blindness, 89*, 129–142.

Wechsler, D. (1997a). *Wechsler adult intelligence scale* (3rd ed.). San Antonio, TX: The Psychological Corporation.

Wechsler, D. (1997b). *Wechsler memory scale* (3rd ed.). San Antonio, TX: The Psychological Corporation.

Wechsler, D. (2003). *Wechsler intelligence scale for children* (4th ed.). San Antonio, TX: The Psychological Corporation.

Wechsler, D. (2008). *Wechsler adult intelligence scale* (4th ed.). San Antonio, TX: The Psychological Corporation.

Wilkinson, G. S. (1993). *Wide range achievement test* (3rd ed.). Wilmington, DE: Wide Range.

Wiskochil, B., Lieberman, L., Houston-Wilson, C., & Petersen, S. (2007). The effects of trained peer tutors on the physical education of children who are visually impaired. *Journal of Visual Impairment & Blindness, 101*, 339–350.

CLINICAL APPLICATIONS OF SCHOOL NEUROPSYCHOLOGY: ACADEMIC DISABILITIES

CHAPTER 19

Assessing and Intervening with Children with Reading Disorders

STEVEN G. FEIFER

A CCORDING TO THE National Center for Educational Statistics (2008), the number of students receiving special education services since the inception of the Individuals with Disabilities Education Act (IDEA) in 1975 has increased every year until reaching its pinnacle during the 2004–2005 year. Today, some 6.7 million children receive special education services under IDEA, which corresponds to approximately 9 percent of all children aged 3 to 21 in public education. Furthermore, approximately 40 percent of those children receiving services are classified as being *"learning disabled,"* due primarily to reading and/or written language deficiencies. Clearly, literacy is the single most important educational attribute paving the road for not only school success, but perhaps for successful life endeavors as well. For instance, consider the following statistics as highlighted by the Literacy Company (2008) (see Table 19.1).

CONTROVERSIES IN ASSESSMENT PRACTICES

Current research in neuroscience has revealed a number of important insights with respect to the neural underpinnings of literacy. For instance, there are certain universal truths in how the human brain acquires linguistic codes pertaining to reading. First, in all word languages studied to date, children with developmental reading disorders (dyslexia) primarily have difficulties in both recognizing and manipulating phonological units at all linguistic levels (Goswami, 2007). Second, children in all languages initially become aware of larger acoustical units within the words themselves such as syllable, onset, and rime. However, in a complex language such as English, when one letter may map to as many as five distinct phonemes or sounds, English-speaking children tend to develop phonemic awareness more slowly than children in more phonologically consistent languages such as Spanish or

Table 19.1

Literacy Facts

- The educational careers of 25 to 40 percent of American children are imperiled because they don't read well enough, quickly enough, or easily enough (Snow, Burns, & Griffin, 1998).
- It is estimated that more than $2 billion is spent each year on students who repeat a grade because they have reading problems.
- Research has shown that even 15 minutes a day of independent reading can expose students to more than a million words of text in a year (Anderson, Wilson, & Fielding, 1988).
- Children who have not developed some basic literacy skills by the time they enter school are three to four times more likely to drop out in later years.
- Over one million children drop out of school each year, costing the nation over $240 billion in lost earnings, forgone tax revenues, and expenditures for social services.
- Approximately 50 percent of the nation's unemployed youth age 16–21 are functionally illiterate, with virtually no prospects of obtaining good jobs.
- More than 20 percent of adults read at or below a fifth-grade level—far below the level needed to earn a living wage.
- More than three out of four of those on welfare, 85 percent of unwed mothers and 68 percent of those arrested are illiterate. About three in five of America's prison inmates are illiterate.

Italian (Goswami, 2007). Third, specific neuroimaging techniques have demonstrated that phonological processing is a by-product of the functional integrity of the *temporal-parietal* junctures in the left hemisphere (Paulesu et al., 1996; Rumsey, 1996). In particular, neuroimaging studies have noted a decreased activation in the left temporal-parietal regions and the superior temporal gyrus (plana temporale) during phonological processing tasks such as rhyming or segmenting various sounds in words (Pugh et al., 2000; Sandak et al., 2004). As Temple (2002) observed, most dyslexics have difficulty with phonological processing, which may indeed stem from disorganization of white matter tracts connecting the temporal-parietal regions with other cortical areas involved in the reading process.

Nevertheless, traditional school psychologists have continued to debate over the best practices to assess reading disorders in children without acknowledging the role of neurocognitive processes in reading. The discrepancy model had been the long-standing method that school systems have used to qualify students for special education services. This method involves assessing academic achievement in one or more major curricular areas, such as reading, math, or written language, and determining whether the student's achievement is significantly discrepant from his or her overall intelligence. The discrepancy model does not focus upon specific neurocognitive processes inherent in reading, but rather focuses upon more global attributes of cognition and achievement. There have been numerous shortcomings inherent within the discrepancy model including the overreliance upon a Full Scale

IQ score to capture the dynamic properties of one's reasoning skills (Hale & Fiorello, 2004) and the lack of agreement on the magnitude of the discrepancy at various ages and grades (Feifer & De Fina, 2000). According to Kavale and Forness (2000), nearly 50 percent of students classified as having a learning disability do not demonstrate a significant discrepancy between aptitude and achievement due in part to the statistical impreciseness of this method. Perhaps the most notable shortcoming of the discrepancy model was that it resulted in a *wait-to-fail* scenario in which a student must display a certain level of reading failure in order to qualify for special educational services. This was especially at odds with the National Reading Panel's (2000) conclusion highlighting the importance of early intervention services for children with reading difficulties. For many school neuropsychologists, the discrepancy model propagates an age-old educational myth that views reading disabilities along a one-dimensional continuum between those students with the disorder, and those without.

Subsequent to the 2004 reauthorization of IDEA, states were no longer allowed to require school districts to consider a discrepancy between IQ and achievement as being a necessary condition to identify students as having a reading disability. Among the many provisions in this bill, states were finally allowed to opt out of using a discrepancy model to identify reading disorders and replace it by using a Response-to-Intervention (RTI) model. In other words, rather than comparing a student's level of academic achievement with an intelligence measure to determine the presence of a reading disability, school districts were given the flexibility to craft a policy whereby students who do not respond to evidence-based early reading programs may be considered eligible for special education services. In addition, the law also required districts with significant overidentification of minority students to consider eliminating IQ testing and establish procedures to reduce disproportional representation of minorities in special education. Certainly, there are many different variations, critical components, and subtle nuances embedded within most versions of RTI. Nevertheless, McCook (2006) described six critical components (see Table 19.2) that must be addressed in the application of any RTI model.

RTI has enjoyed considerable support, especially from organizations such as the National Association of School Psychologists (NASP), because it circumvents many of the shortcomings of the traditional discrepancy model. Additionally, RTI emphasizes the use of evidence-based approaches to instruction in hopes of eliminating academic problems that are frequently due to deficient curricula or poor instructional methodologies. Therefore, RTI provides a framework for instruction and progress monitoring that prioritizes sound instructional practices for all students, not just those with disabilities. RTI also incorporates the well-established benefits of prereferral intervention

Table 19.2

Six Components of an Effective RTI Model

1. *Universal Screening*—must be conducted with all students at least three times per year, ideally in the fall, winter, and spring, beginning in kindergarten.
2. *Baseline Data*—must be gathered for all students using curriculum-based data in order to monitor individual and group response-to-instruction.
3. *Measurable Terms*—must be used to define problem areas for both individual students and groups of students.
4. *Accountability Plan*—must be developed once problems have been identified and interventions have been selected. The plan should specify critical features used to monitor intervention fidelity including the type, duration, intensity, setting, and parties responsible for each intervention component.
5. *Progress Monitoring Plan*—must address how, when, and where intervention results will be measured, recorded, and reviewed.
6. *Data-Based Decision Making*—involves the ongoing analysis of progress monitoring data to drive future instructional or intervention decisions for entire school populations, smaller instructional groups, and individual students who are at risk.

strategies meant to ensure that, when poor student progress is observed, it is addressed as early as possible and through the least intrusive means possible.

Nevertheless, there remains an inordinate amount of confusion regarding just how far the tentacles of RTI can stretch with respect to the identification of a specific reading disability. According to Reynolds (2007), a disability is recognized as constituting a particular condition residing intrinsically within the child, whereas RTI models focus more upon extrinsic factors highlighting child-school interactions. In essence, RTI is more of a delivery service model, not necessarily a diagnostic methodology to determine a specific reading disability. Although curriculum-based measurement (CBM) techniques are highlighted in most RTI models and can be extremely useful in assisting educators to effectively monitor progress, CBM as a standalone measure is not sufficient to determine the presence of a disability. In summary, the National Joint Commission on Learning Disabilities (2005) concluded that RTI is an insufficient means to diagnose a reading disability. Table 19.3 depicts the major pitfalls of RTI when inappropriately used as a diagnostic model for the identification of a reading disability (Reynolds, 2007):

According to the U.S. Department of Education's Learning Disabilities Roundtable Discussion report (2002), the process of determining student eligibility for special education services can be enhanced by the use of neuropsychological measures. The assessment process should attempt to document areas of cognitive strengths and weaknesses in order to make informed decisions about eligibility for services. Furthermore, it was recommended that IQ testing should continue to be an important component of the assessment process, especially when questions of cognitive level arise. Still,

Table 19.3

Major Pitfalls of RTI When Used as a Diagnostic Model of Reading Disabilities

- RTI assumes that all students have an IQ of 100 and that all students should more or less progress at equal rates.
- RTI lacks a universal and consistent means of establishing "responsiveness" thus creating the possibility of a student being disabled in one school district, but not another.
- RTI runs the potential of creating ability tracking as lower IQ students who naturally learn at slower rates will be disproportionately identified as having a reading disability.
- RTI ignores the needs of the top 10 percent of students with academic aptitude at the top of their class.
- RTI is nothing more than a model of "diagnosis by treatment failure," which has long been proven to be a poor model in medicine.
- RTI is incapable of differential diagnosis and offers little in the evaluation of other emotional conditions or attention factors hindering learning.
- RTI models that promote standard protocol interventions assume a "one-size-fits-all" approach to remediation.
- RTI promotes itself unabashedly as being based on a scientific process, though it blatantly ignores scores of neuroscientific research clearly demonstrating that reading disorders have a neurological origin.

there continue to be proponents of RTI who tend to denigrate neuropsychological assessment procedures as being nothing more than an extension of, or a thinly disguised version of, the discrepancy model. The incorrect notion that cognitive neuropsychological assessment and the discrepancy model are one in the same has led some to conclude that most nationally normed tests are irrelevant in the identification and remediation of learning disorders (Fuchs, Mock, Morgan, & Young, 2003; Reschly, 2003). Nevertheless, the true culprits are not the tests themselves, but rather, the psychologists, administrators, special educators, and other educational personnel interpreting these measures in a pseudoscientific context.

THE NEUROBIOLOGY OF READING

There are multiple linguistic avenues comprising the literacy highways of the human brain. Why? Simply put, the brain has evolved for the development of language, and not necessarily reading, thereby creating the need for multiple neural systems to modulate the process. Most reading disabilities derive from multiple genetic contributions to the overall process. According to Grigorenko (2007), there are nine candidate chromosomal regions involved in developmental dyslexia abbreviated as chromosomes 15q, 6p, 2p, 6q, 3cen, 18p, 11p, 1p, and Xq. These genetic transcriptions lay down the bylaws for the development and overall functional integrity of the reading brain. Based upon this genotype, Feifer and Della Toffalo (2007) have highlighted four major phenotypes of

Table 19.4

Four Subtypes of Reading Disorders

1. *Dysphonetic Dyslexia*—difficulty sounding out words in a phonological manner thus causing students to overrely on the orthographic and semantic properties of words. Neuroanatomical deficits mainly lie in the left temporal-parietal regions.
2. *Surface Dyslexia*—difficulty with the rapid and automatic recognition of words in print. Neuroanatomical deficits mainly lie with the fusiform gyrus of the left hemisphere.
3. *Mixed Dyslexia*—multiple reading deficits characterized by impaired phonological and orthographic processing skills. This is the most severe form of dyslexia. Neuroanatomical deficits lie in multiple brain regions including the left temporal-parietal regions, angular gyrus, and fusiform gyrus.
4. *Comprehension Deficits*—the reading process itself remains intact, but difficulty persists deriving meaning from print. Neuroanatomical deficits primarily lie in the left dorsolateral prefrontal cortex modulating working memory and executive functioning skills.

reading disabilities, each of which stems from a distinct neurophysiological dysfunction and can be readily measured by most psychologists.

SUBTYPES OF READING DISORDERS

DYSPHONETIC DYSLEXIA

The four subtypes of reading disorders are shown in Table 19.4. The first reading disorder subtype is called *dysphonetic dyslexia* and is characterized by an inability to utilize a phonological route to successfully bridge letters and sounds. Instead, there tends to be an overreliance on visual and orthographic cues to identify words in print.

Since there is little reliance on letter to sound conversions, these readers tend to frequently guess on words based upon the initial letter observed. For instance, the word "cat" may be read as "couch" or perhaps "corn." Hence, these students have tremendous difficulty incorporating strategies to allow them to crash through words in a sound-based manner, are often inaccurate oral readers, and tend to approach reading by simply memorizing whole words. According to Noble and McCandliss (2005), poor phonological processing in the early years leads to inefficient neural mappings between letters and sounds. Therefore, early intervention emphasizing the development of phonemic awareness and phonological processing is vital to remediating this type of reading deficiency. Specific testing in phonological awareness and phonological processing should assist in teasing out this subtype.

It is important to note there are separate brain regions to tackle the rigors of phonemic awareness and other brain regions to handle the more complex chore of phonological processing. In particular, the top portion of the left temporal lobes, particularly in the areas around Heschl's gyrus, are responsible for basic sound discrimination skills, rhyming skills, and processing pitch changes in the auditory cortex (Ritter, Gunter, Specht, & Rupp, 2005). Conversely, phonological processing refers to actually mapping out sounds to letters and thus requires more cross-modal associations between visual and verbal precepts. The *supramarginal gyrus*, located at the juncture of the temporal and parietal lobes, appears to be the key brain region responsible for phonological processing (McCandliss & Noble, 2003; Sandak et al., 2004; Shaywitz, 2004). The *supramarginal gyrus* functions to integrate the categorical representations of sounds (temporal lobe) with the spatial appreciation underlying sounds and symbols (inferior parietal lobe), thereby contributing to the temporal ordering of acoustical information.

Surface Dyslexia

The second reading disorder subtype is often referred to as *surface dyslexia* and is the opposite of the dysphonetic subtype. These students are readily able to sound out words, although they lack the ability to automatically and effortlessly recognize words in print. Consequently, these students tend to be letter-by letter and sound-by sound readers, as there is an *overreliance* upon the phonological properties of the word and an underappreciation of the spatial properties of the visual word form. Most words are painstakingly broken down to individual phonemes and read very slowly and laboriously. Fluency tends to suffer the most, although phonological processing skills are relatively intact. Specific interventions should focus on automaticity and fluency goals, and not necessarily on an explicit phonological approach. The prudent examiner should utilize rapid naming measures and reading fluency measures to parcel out this subtype.

There is compelling evidence that reading fluency is established by activating the quicker, more automatic pathways to decipher words in print (McCandliss & Noble, 2003; Owen, Borowski, & Sarty, 2004; Pugh et al., 2000; Shaywitz, 2004). This pathway is primarily situated in the posterior portions of the brain, along the interface of the occipital and temporal lobes, in a brain region called the *fusiform gyrus*. It is interesting to note that students with developmental dyslexia do not activate these pathways but instead rely on slower and less efficient pathways to assist with word recognition skills (Shaywitz & Shaywitz, 2005).

Mixed Dyslexia

The third reading disorder subtype is called *mixed dyslexia* and constitutes the most severe type of reading disability for students. Generally, these readers have difficulty across the language spectrum and are characterized by a combination of poor phonological processing skills, slower rapid and automatic word recognition skills, inconsistent language comprehension skills, and bizarre error patterns in their reading. The term *double-deficit hypothesis* often applies here, as there are numerous deficits, that disrupt the natural flow of rapidly and automatically recognizing words in print. When assessing these students, specific deficits will often be found utilizing a combination of phonological processing measures, rapid naming measures, verbal memory measures, and reading fluency measures. Most interventions should focus on a *balanced literacy* approach, which targets multiple aspects of the reading process in order to yield the best opportunity for success.

COMPREHENSION DEFICITS

The final reading disorder subtype involves deficits in *reading comprehension* skills. It has been estimated that some 10 percent of all school-aged children have good decoding skills, although they possess specific difficulties with reading comprehension skills (Nation & Snowling, 1997). In essence, these readers struggle to derive meaning from print despite good reading mechanics. A school neuropsychological assessment model can be extremely beneficial in dissecting the critical components necessary for effective reading comprehension. Often, this includes measuring constructs such as *executive functioning*, which involves the strategies students use to organize incoming information with previously read material; *working memory*, which is the amount of memory needed to perform a given cognitive task; and *language foundation skills*, which represents the fund of words with which a student is familiar.

Children with reading comprehension difficulties often display marked deficits on selected aspects of *executive functioning* skills (Reiter, Tucha, & Lange, 2004), especially working memory skills (Reiter et al., 2004; Vargo, Grosser, & Spafford, 1995; Wilcutt et al., 2001). Working memory involves the ability to hold representational knowledge of the world around us in mind and works in tandem with executive functioning. In essence, the longer the information is available, the greater the mental flexibility to manipulate, store, and slot this information in a manner that facilitates retrieval. Therefore, school psychologists should focus their assessments on cognitive constructs such as verbal IQ, executive functioning, working memory, attention, and reading fluency measures when testing for deficits in reading comprehension. In summary, specifying the underlying linguistic and cognitive factors associated with poor reading comprehension skills may be helpful toward developing more effective intervention strategies to assist children throughout their learning journey.

SCHOOL NEUROPSYCHOLOGICAL ASSESSMENT OF READING

The fundamental purpose of using a school-based neuropsychological assessment method with respect to reading is to determine the underlying neurocognitive causes hindering a child's reading performance. For instance, there may be significant deficits with phonemic awareness or phonological processing, so vital in the early acquisition of literacy skills. On the other hand, there may be significant deficits surrounding the automatic recognition of the visual word form (orthography), leading to poor fluency skills. Perhaps there are multiple cognitive constructs impairing the reading process, resulting in severe reading impairments. Last, there may be significant language-related deficits, working memory issues, or executive dysfunction hindering the comprehension process. It is crucial for school neuropsychologists to decipher the underlying cognitive constructs responsible for modulating the reading process. These constructs need to be isolated, measured, and analyzed in order to determine the specific subtype of reading impairment, as well as to help determine what intervention may work. The relative contribution of the following neurocognitive processes with respect to reading will be explored, with an assessment summary highlighted at the end of this section in Table 19.6.

ATTENTIONAL PROCESSES

Attention is a complex, multifaceted construct comprised of multiple domains, which influence academic performance (Miller, 2007). The process of reading primarily involves attending to visual stimuli for a protracted period of time to attain optimum performance. Attention can be viewed as the foundation for many other higher-level processing tasks and, if compromised, can adversely affect the process of reading, especially reading comprehension skills. There are five subtypes of attention measured.

Focused/Selective Attention   This concept refers to the ability to discriminate among competing auditory or visual stimuli to select only relevant information for the task at hand. With respect to reading, this may involve the child's ability to track words appropriately across each line of text without losing his or her 'place.

Sustained Attention   This refers to vigilance, or the ability to maintain attention over a prolonged period of time. With respect to reading, this often refers to the child's ability to engage in the continuous reading of a passage to completion.

Shifting or Switching Attention   This refers to the amount of cognitive flexibility a student possesses by disengaging his or her attention from one task and directing attention toward another task. With respect to reading, this may involve reading a passage from one text, then rapidly switching to another reading assignment.

Divided Attention   This concept refers to the ability to attend to multiple stimuli at the same time. An example might be reading a passage from the text while simultaneously listening to instructions from the teacher.

Attention Capacity   This refers to the sheer volume of information a student can attend before becoming overwhelmed. With respect to reading, this may involve reading a complex piece of literature while keeping track of numerous characters.

Visual-Spatial Processes

Reading is, first and foremost, a highly complex linguistic endeavor, although the initial stages of the reading process involve recognizing visual symbols. The visual system can be divided into two main types of cells. Approximately 90 percent are smaller types of cells called *parvo cells*, which basically respond to color and fine detail (Stein, 2000). However, the remaining 10 percent are *magno* (large) *cells*, and these cells in particular have noted implications to the reading process. Magno cells are not only larger but also are more heavily myelinated, meaning that these nerve signals have great conduction velocities and can respond much faster than parvo cells. Hence, the magno cells tend to respond very quickly to visual motion, especially the saccadic movements of the eyes when scanning across a page of text while reading. Both types of cells ultimately carry visual information from the retina, then to the lateral geniculate nucleus of the thalamus, and finally the information is relayed to various visual cortices housed in the occipital lobes.

Livingston, Rosen, Drislane, and Galaburda (1991) noted that dyslexics have up to 27 percent fewer neurons in the magno-cellular pathways, thereby resulting in much slower visual processing. Therefore, the magno-cellular deficit hypothesis may provide, in part, an anatomical explanation for slower reading speed and fluency. According to Stein (2000), about 75 percent of children and adults with dyslexia have poor motion sensitivity. Nevertheless, it is important to emphasize that while reading may begin as a visual process, it ends as a linguistic one. Consequently, interventions need to be tailored toward enhancing linguistic skills and not necessarily visual perceptual processes. The educational community has probably seen enough of specialized visual training to cure reading problems. This includes treatments such as using rose-colored paper or *dyslexic glasses*, both of which were intended to stimulate reading by altering contrast sensitivity between the print and paper. The days of visual perceptual training have long passed as an appropriate intervention for dyslexia.

PHONOLOGY AND LANGUAGE SKILLS

According to the National Reading Panel (2000), two of the five core linguistic skills that children need to acquire in order to become functionally independent readers are *phonemic awareness* (the manipulation of spoken syllables in words) and *phonics* (letter-sound correspondences. Of critical importance is a working knowledge of the serial position of the sounds that comprise the acoustical properties of the word. In the English language, there are forty-four phonemes that represent the sound properties of words. As Temple (2002) observed, most students with reading deficits have difficulty with phonological processing, which may stem from a neural disorganization of the temporal-parietal regions in the left hemisphere. Therefore, both phonemic awareness and phonological processing need to be explicitly measured, especially when assessing the reading skills of younger children.

As previously mentioned, language skills are a critical component in the development of a highly linguistic endeavor such as reading. There is overwhelming support in the literature that children with poor reading comprehension skills also have deficits in receptive vocabulary development as well as semantic processing (Catts, Adlof, & Weismer, 2006; Nation, Clarke, Marshall, & Durand, 2004; Nation & Snowling, 1998). Furthermore, students with poor reading comprehension skills especially struggled to draw inferences from passages (Cain, Oakhill, & Elbro, 2003). According to Catts et al. (2006), most of the language problems of students with poor reading comprehension skills, such as poor vocabulary development and limited grammatical development, are subclinical in nature and do not meet the standard diagnostic criteria for language impairment in kindergarten. Since the vast majority of these children do not receive speech and language therapy services at the early elementary level, there is an increased burden among school neuropsychologists to directly measure language skills. As Nation et al. (2004) noted, there is no support for the view that children with poor reading comprehension at the secondary level have residual phonological processing deficits. Instead, students with poor reading comprehension skills are less successful due to language-based deficits including semantic processing, morph-syntax, and higher-level aspects of linguistic reasoning skills.

MEMORY AND LEARNING PROCESSES

Working memory subserves the reading process by temporarily suspending previously read information and simultaneously allowing the reader to acquire new information. Deficits in working memory can certainly disrupt a student's ability to make appropriate linkages among information in the text and, therefore, hinder reading comprehension skills. The ability to utilize background knowledge and draw inferences from the text can facilitate the comprehension process by allowing for a deeper and more enriched engagement with the passage. Brosnan et al. (2002) suggested that deficits in working memory can also hinder a child's ability to recall the sequential order of events in a story and prevent the child from organizing contextual information in a cohesive manner. It is not surprising, then, that most classroom teachers often lament the organizational difficulties of children with reading disabilities.

According to Reiter et al. (2004), children with dyslexia often demonstrate impairments in tasks that measure both visual and verbal working memory systems. Therefore, working memory deficits can not only impair reading comprehension, but also hinder the ability to automatically recognize words in printed form. For instance, the inability to recall the orthography of words can lead to inconsistencies in recalling spelling rules and boundaries and thus restrict reading fluency skills. In addition, deficits in auditory working memory can also hinder the ability to connect sounds from multisyllabic words as a child may forget the actual sequential arrangement of sounds.

EXECUTIVE FUNCTIONING

The cognitive culprits responsible for a host of reading comprehension difficulties are a constellation of higher-level problem solving skills known collectively as executive functioning skills. Barkley (2001) defined executive functioning skills as a set of mind tools that facilitate adaptive behavior functioning during real-world encounters. Hence, executive functions can be thought of as a set of multiple cognitive processes that act in a coordinated way to direct cognition, emotion, and motor functions. A litany of research has demonstrated that most executive functioning skills have a generalized neuroanatomical base housed within the prefrontal cortex (Malloy & Richardson, 1994; Mega & Cummings, 1994; Moffitt & Henry, 1989). Children with dyslexia often display marked deficits on selected aspects of executive functioning skills (Reiter et al., 2004). According to Feifer and Della Toffalo (2007), the following reading attributes are compromised due to faulty executive skills (see Table 19.5).

SPEED AND EFFICIENCY OF COGNITIVE PROCESSING

Wolf and Bowers (1999) have highlighted the importance of early rapid naming skills with the subsequent development of reading fluency. Rapid

Table 19.5
Executive Functioning and Reading

Executive Functioning Skills	Reading Attribute
• Planning Skills	• Read with a specific question or purpose in mind when seeking specific information.
• Organizational Skills	• Connect together text in a coherent manner. Also when distracted, the ability to return back to the text and resume the story flow.
• Working Memory	• Temporarily suspending previously read information while simultaneously linking to new information being read.
• Cognitive Flexibility	• Shifting patterns of thought processes to the organizational parameters of the text being read, and not perseverating on material.
• Verbal Fluency	• Speed of processing linguistic information at the word level to facilitate passage comprehension at the text level.
• Concept Formation	• Depth of understanding of the text.
• Response Inhibition	• Refraining from jumping ahead when reading text and missing aspects of the passage.
• Sustained Attention	• The ability to stay focused on the text for prolonged periods of time and to resist distractions.

Source: Adapted from Feifer & Della Toffalo (2007).

naming involves the ability to look at a visual stimulus and assign a verbal tag to that stimulus. It is important to note that effective rapid naming requires numerous cognitive operations including attention skills, executive functioning skills, accurate retrieval skills, and processing speed. Most learning-disabled students have difficulty with automatic and rapid naming tasks because their ability to rapidly recall archived information, albeit letters, numbers, or words, tends to be compromised (Wolf & Bowers, 1999). It is interesting to note that naming speed, and not phonological awareness skills, tends to be a better predictor of reading difficulty in languages that are more phonologically consistent such as German, Dutch, Finnish, and Spanish (Wolf, 1999).

Recent studies conducted by Mirsa, Katzir, Wolf, and Poldrack (2004) have suggested that not all rapid naming tasks were created equal. For instance, rapid and automatic *letter naming* tasks were more predictive of word level reading skills than tasks involving the rapid and automatic naming of *familiar objects*. Therefore, school neuropsychologists who generally use tests of rapid naming such as the *Comprehensive Test of Phonological Processing* (CTOPP;

Wagner, Torgesen, & Rashotte, 1999) or the *Process Assessment of the Learner-II* (PAL-II; Berninger, 2007) should differentiate between the ability to rapidly name letters and phonemes versus rapidly naming objects. School neuropsychologists may want to explore the *Dynamic Indicators of Basic Early Literacy Skills* (DIBELS; Good & Kaminski, 2002) as a more viable measure of rapid naming skills as they pertain specifically to reading. See Table 19.6 for a comprehensive list of school neuropsychological assessments for developmental dyslexia.

INTELLIGENCE TEST MEASURES

The fundamental goal of intelligence testing should be to tease out specific patterns of cognitive strengths and weaknesses that contribute to the learning process. Clearly, intelligence is a concept underscored by multiple cognitive and social constructs that contribute to the expression of intelligent behavior. However, the prudent examiner must avoid asking the question of *"How smart are you?"* and begin asking a new question namely, *"How are you smart?"* School neuropsychologists recognize that intelligence is not a unitary construct but, rather, is comprised of multiple aspects of cognition, as reflected by the complexities inherent in newer tests such as the *Wechsler Intelligence Scale 4th Edition* (WISC-IV; Wechsler, 2003), *Woodcock Johnson Scales of Cognitive Abilities 3rd Edition* (WJIII-COG; Woodcock, McGrew, & Mather, 2001), and *Stanford-Binet 5th Edition* (SB-V; Roid, 2003). Kaufman (1994) has stressed that intelligence testing should be interpreted within a conceptual model around given cognitive constructs, no matter the test of choice. Therefore, the emphasis should not revolve around the measurement of *intelligence* per se, but rather on the measurement of *cognition*, which refers to the underlying constructs necessary to perform a given task. With respect to reading, it is important to particularly examine Verbal IQ scores, since they pertain to language development skills and ultimately reading comprehension skills.

It is important to reiterate the multivariate nature of reading, as there are numerous brain regions modulating phonological awareness, reading fluency, as well as passage comprehension skills. However, despite the popular notion that a child must have average ability to be classified as having a reading disability, there is no indication that a minimum intelligence score is needed. In fact, most research suggests that measures of intelligence account for little more than a meager 10 to 35 percent of the variance on measures of reading achievement (Vellutino, Scanlon, & Lyon, 2000). Furthermore, Shaywitz (2004) argues that measures of intelligence have virtually

Table 19.6

School Neuropsychological Assessment Battery for Developmental Dyslexia

School Neuropsychological Construct	Suggested Assessment Instruments
Attentional Processes	• Behavior Rating Scales (Metritech Staff, 1998), Attention Deficit Evaluation Scale (McCarney, 2004a, 2004b), Brown Attention-Deficit Disorder Scales for Children and Adolescents (Brown, 2001), Behavioral Assessment System for Children – Second Edition (Reynolds & Kamphaus, 2004), Conners 3rd Edition (Conners, 2008). • Cognitive Assessment System (CAS): Number Detection, and Receptive Attention (Naglieri & Das, 1997). • Kaufman Assessment Battery for Children – Second Edition (KABC-II): Number Recall (Kaufman & Kaufman, 2004). • NEPSY-II: Auditory Attention and Response Set (Korkman, Kirk, & Kemp, 2007). • Test of Everyday Attention (TEA-Ch: Manly, Robertson, Anderson, & Nimmo-Smith, 1999). • Woodcock Johnson III Tests of Cognitive Abilities (WJIII-COG): Numbers Reversed, and Auditory Attention (Woodcock, McGrow, & Mather, 2001).
Visual-Spatial Processes	• Beery-Buktenica Developmental Test of Visual-Motor Integration, 5th Ed. (Beery, Buktenica, & Beery, 2003). • Bender Visual-Motor Gestalt Test, Second Edition (Brannigan, & Decker, 2003). • Jordan Left-Right Reversal Test (Jordan, 1990). • KABC-II: Gestalt Closure (Kaufman & Kaufman, 2004). • NEPSY-II: Arrows and Design Copying (Korkman, Kirk, & Kemp, 2007). • PAL-II: Receptive Coding (Berninger, 2007). • Rey Complex Figure Test and Recognition Trial (Meyers & Meyers, 1995). • WJIII-COG: Spatial Relations (Woodcock, McGrew, & Mather, 2001).
Phonemic/Phonological Awareness	• Comprehensive Test of Phonological Processing (C-TOPP: Wagner, Torgesen, & Rashotte, 1999). • DIBELS (Good & Kaminski, 2002). • Gray Diagnostic Reading Tests – Second Edition (Bryant, Wiederholt, & Bryant, 2004). • Kaufman Test of Educational Achievement – Second Edition (Kaufman & Kaufman, 2005) • Lindamood Auditory Conceptualization Test (Lindamood & Lindamood, 2004). • NEPSY-II: Phonological Processing (Korkman, Kirk, & Kemp, 2007).
Phonemic/Phonological Awareness—continued	• PAL-II (Berninger, 2007). • Test of Phonological Awareness Skills (Newcomer & Barenbaum, 2003).

(continued)

Table 19.6

Continued

School Neuropsychological Construct	Suggested Assessment Instruments
Verbal Memory	• California Verbal Learning Test-Children's Version (CLVT-C: Delis, Kramer, Kaplan, & Ober, 1994). • Children's Memory Scales (CMS: Cohen, 1997). • Test of Memory and Learning-2 (TOMAL-II: Reynolds & Voress, 2007). • NEPSY-II Memory Scales (Korkman, Kirk, & Kemp, 2007). • Wide Range Assessment of Memory and Learning – Second Edition (WRAML-II: Sheslow & Adams, 2003).
Executive Functions	• Booklet Category Test (DeFilippis & McCampbell, 1979). • Behavior Rating Inventory of Executive Function (BRIEF: Gioia, Isquith, Guy, & Kenworthy, 2000). • Cognitive Assessment System (Naglieri & Das, 1997). • Delis-Kaplan Executive Functions Scale (D-KEFS: Delis, Kaplan, & Kramer, 2001). • NEPSY-II Subtests (Korkman, Kirk, & Kemp, 2007). • Stroop Test (Golden & Freshwater, 2002). • Wisconsin Card Sort Test (Heaton, 1981).
Speed and Efficiency of Cognitive Processing	• CTOPP (Wagner, Torgesen, & Rashotte, 1999) • DIBELS: Letter Naming (Good & Kaminski, 2002). • KTEA-II: Association Fluency and Naming Facility (Kaufman & Kaufman, 2005). • NEPSY-II: Word Generation and Speeded Naming) (Korkman, Kirk, & Kemp, 2007). • PAL-II: RAS/RAN (Berninger, 2007).
Cognitive Functioning	• Cognitive Assessment System (Naglieri & Das, 1997). • KABC-II (Kaufman & Kaufman, 2004). • Reynolds Intellectual Assessment Scales (RIAS: Reynolds & Kamphaus, 2003). • Stanford-Binet Intelligence Scale V (Roid, 2003). • WISC-IV (Wechsler, 2003). • WJIII-COG (Woodcock, McGrew, & Mather, 2001).
Reading Fluency	• Curriculum Based Measurement • DIBELS: Oral Reading Fluency (Good & Kaminski, 2002). • Informal Reading Inventories • Gray-Oral Reading Test – Fourth Edition (Weiderhold & Bryant, 2001). • KTEA-II (Word Recognition Fluency, Decoding Fluency) (Kaufman & Kaufman, 2005). • PAL-II (Silent Reading Fluency) (Berninger, 2007). • WIAT-II (Wechsler, 2001). • WJIII-COG: Rapid Picture Naming (Woodcock, McGrew, & Mather, 2001).

no relationship with certain aspects of the reading process, such as the acquisition of phonological awareness skills.

READING FLUENCY SKILLS

There is overwhelming evidence that skilled readers activate the quicker, more rapid, and automatic pathways to decipher words in print (McCandliss & Noble, 2003; Owen et al., 2004; Pugh et al., 2000; Shaywitz, 2004). These pathways are primarily situated in the posterior portions of the brain, along the interface of the occipital and temporal lobes, in a brain region called the *fusiform gyrus*. Shaywitz (2004) has referred to this brain region as the automatic word recognition center of the brain, since this neural system can respond in just 200 ms to the visual features of a word for proper identification.

The goal of any good reading program is to ultimately have the quicker paced pathways in the occipital-temporal regions of the brain assume responsibility for the reading process, thereby freeing up other cortical regions to assist in comprehension. Should the slower paced neural circuitry in the brain (*temporal-parietal regions*) assume full responsibility for the reading process, then fluency may become compromised and reading becomes an effortful and mundane process. It is important for educators to begin recording reading fluency and speed using a combination of both curriculum-based measurement techniques, as well as nationally normed-referenced tests. Instruments such as the *Kaufman Test of Educational Achievement-II* (KTEA-II; Kaufman & Kaufman, 2005), the *Process Assessment of the Learner - II* (PAL-II; Berninger, 2007), and *Gray-Oral Reading Test, 4th Edition* (GORT-4; Bryant, Wiederholt, & Bryant, 2004) can be excellent measures of reading fluency skills. This will help enable teachers to closely monitor reading proficiency and, from a neuropsychological standpoint, measure the extent with which these quicker pathways become acclimated to taking over the process of reading from the slower pathways.

SUMMARY

School neuropsychology finds itself at the forefront of a hotly contested debate regarding the proper methodology educators should adhere to when assessing reading disorders in children. Despite its flaws, the *discrepancy model* remains the more traditional approach to assessment, even as states begin to implement RTI standards into their identification process. There is clearly a third option. As proponents of RTI continue to mandate the need for "*scientifically*" based interventions, proponents of school neuropsychology must continue to stress the need for "*scientifically*" based assessments. In spite of all the legal posturing and maneuvering to redefine the true nature of a learning disorder, the scientific process must drive the debate, not the legislative one. School neuropsychology can be an invaluable diagnostic tool to assist educators in moving beyond nonspecific terms such as a "*learning disability*" and allow for a better understanding of the reading process by identifying specific reading subtypes that can derail successful learning. These subtypes are based upon individual neural circuitry housed within the brain that modulates the reading process. There is a crucial need for educators to fathom a basic understanding of brain-behavioral relationships, especially with respect to coinciding interventions with brain development. This chapter examined the core cognitive constructs contributing to each subtype of reading proposing that all educators begin to examine reading through the multidimensional lenses of brain-based learning.

REFERENCES

Anderson, R. C., Wilson, P. T., & Fielding, L. G. (1988). Growth in reading and how children spend their time outside of school. *Reading Research Quarterly, 23,* 285–303.

Barkley, R. (2001). The executive functions and self-regulation: an evolutionary neuropsychological perspective. *Neuropsychology Review, 11,* 1–29.

Beery, K. E., Buktenica, N. A., & Beery, N. A. (2003). *Beery-Buktenica developmental test of visual-motor integration* (5th ed.). Minneapolis, MN: Pearson Assessments.

Berninger, V. W. (2007). *Process assessment of the learner (PAL-II): Diagnostic assessment for reading and writing.* San Antonio, TX: Harcourt Assessment.

Brannigan, G. G., & Decker, S. L. (2003). *Bender visual-motor Gestalt test* (2nd ed.). Itasca, IL: Riverside Publishing Company.

Brosnan, M., Demetre, J., Hamill, S., Robson, K., Shepherd, H., & Cody, G. (2002). Executive functioning in adults and children with developmental dyslexia. *Neuropsychologia, 40,* 2144–2155.

Brown, T. E. (2001). *Brown attention-deficit disorder scales for children and adolescents.* San Antonio, TX: Harcourt Assessment.

Bryant, R. R., Wiederholt, J. L., & Bryant, D. P. (2004). *Gray diagnostic reading tests* (2nd ed.). Austin, TX: Pro-Ed.

Cain, K., Oakhill, J. V., & Elbro, C. (2003). The ability to learn new word meanings from context by school-age children with and without language comprehension difficulties. *Journal of Child Language, 30,* 681–694.

Catts, H. W., Adlof, S. M., & Weismer, S. E. (2006). Language deficits in poor comprehenders: A case for the simple view of reading. *Journal of Speech, Language, and Hearing Research, 49,* 278–293.

Cohen, M. J. (1997). *Children's Memory Scale.* San Antonio, TX: Harcourt Assessment.

Conners, C. K. (2008). *Conners* (3rd ed.). North Tonawanda, NY: Multi-Health Systems, Inc.

DeFilippis, N. A., & McCampbell, E. (1979). *Manual for the booklet category test: Research and clinical form.* Odessa, FL: Psychological Assessment Resources.

Delis, D., Kaplan, E., & Kramer, J. H. (2001). *Delis-Kaplan executive function system— Examiner's manual.* San Antonio, TX: The Psychological Corporation.

Delis, D. C., Kramer, J. H., Kaplan, E., & Ober, B. A. (1994). *California verbal learning Test: Children's version.* San Antonio, TX: Harcourt Assessment.

Feifer, S. G., & De Fina, P. D. (2000). *The neuropsychology of reading disorders: Diagnosis and intervention.* Middletown, MD: School Neuropsych Press.

Feifer, S. G., & Della Toffalo, D. (2007). *Integrating RTI with cognitive neuro- psychology: A scientific approach to reading.* Middletown, MD: School Neuropsych Press.

Fuchs, D., Mock, D., Morgan, P. L., & Young, C. L. (2003). Responsiveness-to- intervention: Definitions, evidence, and implications for the learning disabilities construct. *Learning Disabilities Research & Practice, 18,* 157–171.

Gioia, G. A., Isquith, P. K., Guy, S. C., & Kenworthy, L. (2000). *Behavior rating inventory of executive function professional manual.* Odessa, FL: Psychological Assessment Resources.

Golden, C. J., & Freshwater, S. M. (2002). *Stroop and color word test.* Odessa, FL: Psychological Assessment Resources.

Good, R. H., & Kaminski, R. A. (Eds.). (2002). *Dynamic indicators of basic early literacy skills* (DIBELS) (6th ed.). Eugene, OR: Institute for the Development of Educational Achievement. Available at: https://www.dibels.uoregon.edu/.

Goswami, U. (2007). Typical reading development and developmental dyslexia across languages. In D. Coch, G. Dawson, & K. W. Fischer (Eds.), *Human behavior, learning, and the developing brain* (pp. 145–167). New York: Guilford.

Grigorenko, E. L. (2007). Triangulating developmental dyslexia. In D. Coch, G. Dawson, & K. W. Fischer (Eds.), *Human behavior, learning, and the developing brain* (pp. 117–144). New York: Guilford.

Hale, J. B., & Fiorello, C. A. (2004). *School neuropsychology: A practitioner's handbook.* New York: Guilford.

Heaton, R. K. (1981). *Wisconsin card sorting test manual.* Odessa, FL: Psychological Assessment Resources.

Jordan, B. T. (1990). *Jordan left-right reversal test, revised.* Novato, CA: Academic Therapy Publications.

Kaufman, A. S. (1994). *Intelligent testing with the WISC III.* New York: John Wiley & Sons.

Kaufman, A. S., & Kaufman, N. L. (2004). *Kaufman assessment battery for children* (2nd ed.). Circle Pines, MN: American Guidance Service Publishing.

Kaufman, A. S., & Kaufman, N. L. (2005). *Kaufman test of educational achievement* (2nd ed.). Circle Pines, MN: American Guidance Service Publishing.

Kavale, K. A., & Forness, S. R. (2000). What definitions of learning disability say and don't say. *Journal of Learning Disabilities, 33,* 239–256.

Korkman, M., Kirk, U., & Kemp, S. (2007). *NEPSY-II: A developmental neuropsychological assessment.* San Antonio, TX: The Psychological Corporation.

Lindamood, P. C., & Lindamood, P. (2004). *Lindamood auditory conceptualization test.* Austin, TX: Pro-Ed.

The Literacy Company. (2008). *Reading, literacy, and educational statistics.* [Electronic Version]. Retrieved August 30, 2008, from http://www.readfaster.com/educa tion_stats.asp.

Livingstone, M. S., Rosen, G. D., Drislane, F. W., & Galaburda, A. M. (1991). Physiological and anatomical evidence for a magnocellular defect in developmental dyslexia. *Proceedings of the National Academy of Science, USA, 88,* 7943–7947.

Malloy, P. F., & Richardson, E. D. (1994). Assessment of frontal lobe functions. *Journal of Neuropsychiatry Clinical Neuroscience, 6,* 399–410.

Manly, T., Robertson, I. H., Anderson, V., & Nimmo-Smith, I. (1999). *Test of everyday attention for children (TEA-Ch)* Manual. San Antonio, TX: Harcourt Assessment.

McCandliss, B. D., & Noble, K. G. (2003). The development of reading impairment: A cognitive neuroscience model. *Mental Retardation and Developmental Disabilities, 9,* 196–205.

McCarney, S. B. (2004a). *Attention deficit disorders evaluation scale* (3rd ed.). Columbia, MO: Hawthorne Educational Services.

McCarney, S. B. (2004b). *Attention deficit disorders evaluation scale: Secondary-age student.* Columbia, MO: Hawthorne Educational Services.

McCook, J. E. (2006). *The RTI guide: Developing and implementing a model in your schools.* Horsham, PA: LRP Publications.

Mega, M. S., & Cummings, J. L. (1994). Frontal-subcortical circuits and neuropsychiatric disorders. *Journal of Neuropsychiatry Clinical Neuroscience, 6,* 358–370.

Metritech Staff. (1998). *ACTeRS Self Report.* Champaign, IL: Metritech.

Meyers, J. E., & Meyers, K. R. (1995). *Rey complex figure test and recognition trial.* Odessa, FL: Psychological Assessment Resources.

Miller, D. C. (2007). *Essentials of school neuropsychological assessment.* Hoboken, NJ: John Wiley & Sons.

Mirsa, M., Katzir, T., Wolf, M., & Poldrack, R. A. (2004). Neural systems for rapid automatized naming (RAN) in skilled readers: Unraveling the RAN-reading relationship. *Science Study of Reading, 8,* 241–256.

Moffitt, T. E., & Henry, B. (1989). Neuropsychological assessment of executive functions in self-reported delinquents. *Developmental Psycholopathology, 1,* 105–118.

Naglieri, J., & Das, J. P. (1997). *Das-Naglieri cognitive assessment system.* Itasca, IL: Riverside Publishing Company.

Nation, K., Clarke, P., Marshall, C. M., & Durand, M. (2004). Hidden language impairments in children: Parallels between poor reading comprehension and specific language impairments? *Journal of Speech, Language, and Hearing Research, 47,* 199–211.

Nation, K., & Snowling, M. (1997). Assessing reading difficulties: The validity and utility of current measures of reading skill. *British Journal of Educational Psychology, 67,* 359–370.

Nation, K., & Snowling, M. J. (1998). Individual differences in contextual facilitation: Evidence from dyslexia and poor reading comprehension. *Child Development, 69,* 994–1009.

National Center for Educational Statistics. (2008). *Children and youth with disabilities in public schools.* Washington DC: U.S. Department of Education.

National Joint Committee on Learning Disabilities. (2005). *Responsiveness to intervention and learning disabilities.* Retrieved August 30, 2008 from http://www.ldonline. org/njcld.

National Reading Panel. (2000). *Teaching children to read: An evidenced based assessment of the scientific research literature on reading and its implications for reading instruction.* Washington, DC: National Institutes of Child Health and Human Development.

Newcomer, P., & Barenbaum, E. (2003). *Test of phonological awareness skills.* Austin, TX: Pro-Ed.

Noble, K. G., & McCandliss, B. D. (2005). Reading development and impairment: Behavioral, social, and neurobiological factors. *Developmental and Behavioral Pediatrics, 26,* 370–376.

Owen, W. J., Borowsky, R., & Sarty, G. E. (2004). FMRI of two measures of phonological processing in visual word recognition: Ecological validity matters. *Brain and Language, 90,* 40–46.

Paulesu, E., Frith, U., Snowling, M., Gallagher, A., Morton, J., Frackowiak, R. S. J., & Frith, C. (1996). Is developmental dyslexia a disconnection syndrome? *Brain, 119,* 143–157.

Pugh, K. R., Mencl, W. E., Jenner, A. R., Katz, L., Frost, S. J., Lee, J. R., Shaywitz, S. E., Shaywitz, B. A. (2000). Functional neuroimaging studies of reading and reading disability (developmental dyslexia). *Mental Retardation and Developmental Disabilities Research Reviews, 6,* 207–213.

Reiter, A., Tucha, O., & Lange, K. W. (2004). Executive functions in children with dyslexia. *Dyslexia, 11,* 116–131.

Reschly, R. J. (2003). *What if LD identification changed to reflect research findings?* Paper presented at the National Research Center on Learning Disabilities Responsiveness-to-Intervention Symposium, Kansas City, MO.

Reynolds, C. R. (2007). RTI, neuroscience, and sense: Chaos in the diagnosis and treatment of learning disabilities. In E. Fletcher-Janzen, & C. R. Reynolds (Eds.), *Neuropsychological perspectives on learning disabilities in the era of RTI* (pp. 14–27). Hoboken, NJ: John Wiley & Sons.

Reynolds, C. R., & Kamphaus, R. W. (2003). *Reynolds intellectual assessment scales.* Lutz, FL: PAR, Inc.

Reynolds, C. R., & Kamphaus, R. W. (2004). *Behavioral assessment system for children* (2nd ed.). Circle Pines, MN: American Guidance Service Publishing.

Reynolds, C. R., & Voress, J. K. (2007). *Test of memory and learning* (2nd ed.). Austin, TX: Pro-Ed.

Ritter, S., Gunter, H. D., Specht, H. J., & Rupp, A. (2005). Neuromagnetic responses reflect the temporal pitch change of regular interval of sounds. *Neuroimage, 27,* 533–543.

Roid, G. H. (2003). *Stanford-Binet intelligence scales* (5th ed.). Itasca, IL: Riverside Publishing.

Rumsey, J. M. (1996). Neuroimaging in developmental dyslexia. In G. R. Lyon & J. M. Rumsey (Eds.), *Neuroimaging: A window to the neurological foundations of learning and behavior in children.* (pp. 57–77). Baltimore, MD: Paul H. Brookes.

Sandak, R., Mencl, W. E., Frost, S., Rueckl, J. G., Katz, L., Moore, D. L., Mason, S. A., Fulbright, R. K., Constable, R. T., & Pugh, K. R. (2004). The neurobiology of adaptive learning in reading: A contrast of different training conditions. *Cognitive, Affective, & Behavioral Neuroscience, 4,* 67–88.

Shaywitz, S. (2004). *Overcoming dyslexia.* New York: Random House.

Shaywitz, S., & Shaywitz, B. (2005). Dyslexia: Specific reading disability. *Biological Psychiatry, 57,* 1301–1309.

Sheslow, D., & Adams, W. (2003). *Wide range assessment of memory and learning* (2nd ed.). Wilmington, DE: Wide Range.

Snow, C. E., Burns, M., & Griffin, P. (Eds.). (1998). *Committee on the prevention of reading difficulties in young children.* Washington, DC: National Academy Press.

Stein, J. (2000). The neurobiology of reading. *Prostaglandins, Leukotrienes and Essential Fatty Acids, 63*(1/2), 109–116.

Temple, E. (2002). Brain mechanisms in normal and dyslexic readers. *Current Opinion in Neurobiology, 12,* 178–193.

U.S. Department of Education, Learning Disabilities Roundtable. (2002). *Specific learning disabilities: Finding common ground.* Washington, DC: U.S. Department of Education, Office of Special Education Programs, Office of Innovation and Development.

Vargo, F. E., Grosser, G. S., & Spafford, C. S. (1995). Digit span and other WISC-R scores in the diagnosis of dyslexia in children. *Perceptual and Motor Skills, 80,* 1219–1229.

Vellutino, F. R., Scanlon, D. M., & Lyon, G. R. (2000). Differentiating between difficult-to-remediate and readily remediate poor readers: More evidence against the IQ achievement discrepancy definition of reading disability. *Journal of Learning Disabilities, 33,* 223–238.

Wagner, R., Torgesen, J., & Rashotte, C. (1999). *Comprehensive test of phonological processing.* Minneapolis, MN: Pearson Assessments.

Wechsler, D. (2001). *Wechsler individual achievement test* (2nd ed.). San Antonio, TX: Harcourt Assessment.

Wechsler, D. (2003). *Wechsler intelligence scale for children* (4th ed.). San Antonio, TX: Harcourt Assessment.

Weiderhold, J. L., & Bryant, B. R. (2001). *Gray oral reading tests* (4th ed.). Austin, TX: Pro-Ed.

Willcutt, E. G., Olson, R. K., Pennington, B. F., Boada, R., Ogline, J. S., Tunick, R. A., & Chabildas, N. A. (2001). Comparison of the cognitive deficits in reading disability and attention deficit hyperactivity disorder. *Journal of Abnormal Psychology, 110,* 157–172.

Wolf, M. (1999). What time may tell: Towards a new conceptualization of developmental dyslexia. *Annals of Dyslexia, 49,* 3–23.

Wolf, M., & Bowers, P. G. (1999). The double deficit hypothesis for the developmental dyslexias. *Journal of Educational Psychology, 91,* 415–438.

Woodcock, R. W., McGrew, K. S., & Mather, N. (2001). *Woodcock-Johnson III tests of cognitive abilities.* Itasca, IL: Riverside Publishing.

CHAPTER 20

Assessing and Intervening with Children with Written Language Disorders

VIRGINIA W. BERNINGER

PREVALENCE ESTIMATES FOR written language disability range from 6.9 percent to 14.7 percent of the school-age population (Katusic, Barbaresi, Colligan, Weaver, & Jacobsen, 2009). However, the extent to which written language disability (writing impaired only) may co-exist with both writing and reading disability is unknown. Although significant gender differences are not associated with reading disability, boys are more impaired than girls for writing disability (Berninger, Nielsen, Abbott, Wijsman, & Raskind, 2008b).

Progress is being made toward evidence-based diagnoses of the written language disorders based on inclusionary criteria (what they are) in contrast to the exclusionary criteria (what they are not) used in the federal definition in special education law for qualifying students for services. Special education categories such as learning disabilities are based on criteria for qualifying students for services, rather than on evidence-based differential diagnoses that have specific treatment implications (Berninger & Holdnack, 2008). This distinction between diagnosis and qualification for services is important and a source of confusion to many parents and professionals. Many parents who participated in the NICHD-funded writing research at the University of Washington for over a decade, which generated evidence on which this chapter on written language disorders is based, expressed to the author that they were just as concerned with diagnosis as with qualification for services (Berninger, 2008c). In this chapter the research-supported definitions of written language disorders are based on family genetics research, brain-imaging research, and instructional treatment research (see Berninger, Raskind, Richards, Abbott, & Stock, 2008). Defining a developmental disorder is a necessary first step toward diagnosis linked to treatment.

DEFINITIONS

Dysgraphia is a Greek word whose prefix *dys* means "impaired" and whose base *graph* means "letter-form produced by hand." Its suffix *–ia* marks it as a noun, whereas the suffix *–ic* marks it as an adjective describing the condition of having impaired ability to process or produce letters and written words. Affected individuals with dysgraphia almost always have handwriting problems with or without associated spelling problems and sometimes have only orthographic spelling problems related to fluent access to precise spellings in long-term memory (Fayol, Zorman, Lété, 2009). As a result of these transcription problems related to handwriting and/or spelling, individuals with dysgraphia also have difficulties with written expression of ideas through composing (Berninger, Nielsen et al., 2008b). Also see Berninger (2004, 2006, 2008b) and Berninger, O'Donnell, and Holdnack (2008).

Dyslexia is a Greek word whose prefix *dys* means "impaired" and whose base *lex*, which is derived from lexicon, refers to "word"; thus, dyslexia (suffix *–ia* marks it as a noun) is a condition in which word processing is impaired—both for word reading and word spelling. Thus, for dyslexia, which is both a writing and a reading disorder, a hallmark feature is persisting spelling problems, which may interfere with written expression of ideas during composing (Berninger, Nielsen, Abbott, Wijsman, & Raskind, 2008a). However, in contrast to the spelling problems associated with dysgraphia, which tend to be orthographic, the spelling problems of dyslexics tend to be phonologically (e.g., Wijsman et al., 2000) and orthographically (Berninger, Abbott, Thomson et al., 2006) based. Also see Berninger (2008b), Berninger, Abbott, Thomson, & Raskind (2001), and Berninger, O'Donnell, et al. (2008).

The *Oral and Written Language Specific Learning Disability* (OWL LD) is an oral as well as written language disorder. Hallmark deficits of OWL LD are in morphological and syntactic awareness as well as in word retrieval. As a result, affected individuals have problems that include but are not restricted to word reading and spelling. They also have significant difficulty in reading comprehension and written expression of ideas (particularly in the syntax of the sentence construction) (Scott, 2002). See Berninger (2008b) and Berninger, O'Donnell, et al. (2008).

Many individuals have one of these specific written language disorders, all of which involve impaired writing but vary as to what other skills are also impaired. However, some may have a combination of two of these (e.g., dyslexia + dysgraphia) or all three, and as a result, their writing is extremely impaired (Berninger, Raskind, et al., 2008). Also, individuals with writing disabilities may have difficulty with paper-and-pencil math because of the written output required and present with dyscalculia even though they grasp underlying math concepts (Berninger, 2007a, 2007c).

DIAGNOSTIC ISSUES

In addition to identifying specific writing disabilities on the basis of their inclusionary criteria, one must differentiate the identified disabilities from other developmental or neuropsychological disorders in order to avoid communicating misleading and potentially harmful conclusions to parents, teachers, and other professionals about the etiology, diagnosis, and prognosis for the individual. Not all disorders of writing are specific learning disabilities interfering with written language acquisition. Individuals with a variety of developmental and neuropsychological disorders may also experience difficulties with written language, including reading and/or writing, but for very different reasons and with very different expected outcomes. For example, children with mental retardation, primary language disorder (developmental aphasia), primary motor disorder, pervasive developmental disorder (2 or more developmental domains affected), Down syndrome, fragile X syndrome, autism, head injury, spinal cord injury, seizure disorder, and severe social emotional disturbance may struggle with reading and/or writing at school, but for different reasons than those who have specific learning disabilities related to written language. In fact, the presence of these other conditions is grounds for ruling out a diagnosis of specific writing disability (Berninger, 2007a, 2007b).

Specific learning disabilities such as writing disability are developmental in origin rather than acquired disorders. Overall, children with specific learning disabilities fall within the normal range in the five domains of development: cognition and memory, receptive and expressive language, fine and gross motor skills, social and emotional maturity, and attention and executive function. However, within their profile of these developmental domains, academic achievement in specific reading, writing, and math skills, and related neuropsychological processes, they typically show intra-individual variation with selected abilities, skills, or processes falling outside the normal range (see Berninger, Abbott, Thomson et al., 2006) and discrepant from their overall level of functioning in their developmental and learning profile. See Berninger (2007a, 2007b) for specific guidelines for assessment of the five developmental domains and the profiles of intra-individual differences that characterize dysgraphia, dyslexia, and OWL LD. These specific learning disabilities occur in the absence of any other developmental or neuropsychological disorder (hence they are specific) even though they have a biological (genetic and brain) basis. Individuals may have both specific learning disabilities and attention-deficit/hyperactivity (inattentive, hyperactivity, or combined subtypes of ADHD) or one of these conditions without the other. The prognosis for these specific writing disabilities with or without comorbid ADHD depends on nature-nurture interactions. The appropriateness and quality of the instruction and learning environment influence their learning outcomes (see Berninger & Richards, 2002).

The three specific written language disorders are best understood and diagnosed within a verbal working memory architecture that consists of three kinds of word-form storage and processing (phonological, orthographic, and morphological), two loops (phonological and orthographic), and a panel of executive functions (inhibition, switching attention, self-monitoring, and revising, Berninger, Abbott, Thomson, et al., 2006). This working memory architecture may also support syntactic level processing for storing and processing multiple words within syntactic units within higher-level discourse schema (Berninger, 2008b). Impaired components in this architecture predict nature of disability:

- Children who are impaired only in the orthographic word-form storage and processing and/or the orthographic loop (from orthographic storage and processing to the hand's serial finger movement system) have, or are at risk for, *dysgraphia* (impaired handwriting and/or orthographic spelling) (Berninger, 2004, 2006, 2008b; Berninger, O'Donnell, et al., 2008; Berninger, Rutberg et al., 2006).
- Children who are impaired in phonological word-form storage and processing, the phonological loop (from phonological word-form storage and processing to mouth), orthographic word-form storage and processing, and/or the orthographic loop have or are at risk, for *dyslexia* (Berninger et al., 2001, Berninger, Abbott, Thomson et al., 2006; Berninger, 2006, 2008b; Berninger, O'Donnell, et al., 2008).
- Children who are impaired in orthographic, phonological, and morphological word-form storage and processing, syntactic storage and processing, the orthographic and/or the phonological loop, have, or are at risk for, OWL LD (Berninger, 2006, 2008b; Berninger, O'Donnell, et al., 2008; Berninger, Raskind et al. 2008).

Each of these written language disabilities has associated problems in executive functions. Each diagnosis has treatment implications. See Berninger (2007a, 2007b) for specific assessment procedures for making each of these differential diagnoses and linking them to treatment.

NEUROCOGNITIVE FUNCTIONS RELATED TO
DEVELOPMENTAL WRITING DISORDERS

Cross-sectional assessment studies have yielded considerable knowledge of which measures (a) most uniquely predict writing and reading achievement, (b) indicate that a child is probably a good candidate for early intervention in addition to the regular instructional program, (c) identify how the regular program might be modified to benefit an individual struggling child, and (d) can be used to diagnose a specific learning disability involving written language. These measures can also be used for assessing response to instructional interventions. See Berninger (2007a, 2007b) for specific guidelines on how to design and implement screening for Tier 1 early intervention and prevention of writing disabilities, Tier 2 problem-solving consultation for writing problems, and Tier 3 differential diagnosis of specific learning disabilities involving writing, The latter are based on family genetics research in which nuclear and extended family members across multiple generations completed the same test battery, yielding considerable knowledge about the behavioral expression of biologically based specific learning disabilities that have distinctive phenotypes (behavioral markers). Individual children vary as to whether they are impaired in all, a small subset, or just one or two of these behavioral markers. School neuropsychological assessment should be based on measures identified in research as best for Tier 1, Tier 2, or Tier 3 purposes (Berninger & Holdnack, 2008). See Berninger (2007a, 2007b) and Table 20.1 for guidance in selecting evidence-based assessment measures that can be used at Tier 1 for screening for early intervention for prevention, Tier 2 problem solving consultation to modify the regular program, and/or Tier 3 differential diagnosis and treatment planning.

EVIDENCE-BASED INTERVENTIONS FOR TREATMENT
OF WRITTEN LANGUAGE DISORDERS

Writing instruction that is explicit and teaches strategies children can apply to self-regulate their writing has been found to be effective (e.g., Graham & Perin, 2007a, 2007b). See Hooper, Knuth, Yerby, Anderson, and Moore (2009), Troia (2009), and Berninger (2008a) for reviews of evidence-based practices for prevention and treatment of specific writing disorders. Early intervention research has shown that explicit instruction in transcription skills (handwriting and spelling) in the early grades can prevent composition problems in the upper grades (see Berninger & Amtmann, 2003, for review). Also, integrating writing and reading instruction in the early grades has benefits for literacy learning in general (e.g., Berninger, Dunn, Lin, & Shimada, 2004; Berninger, Rutberg, et al., 2006). Each transcription mode—manuscript or

Table 20.1

Comprehensive Assessment of Evidence-Based Functions Associated
with Developmental Writing Disabilities

Function	General Principles Based on Research and Clinical Experience

Sensory
  Visual-Spatial
  Auditory
  Kinesthesia
  Motor
  Gross and Fine
  Finger Function—
  1) Planning serial finger
    movements
  2) Touch sensation
  3) Kinesthetic-
    Symbol
    Integration
	Vellutino (1979) showed that dyslexia is not a visual spatial disorder. Berninger et al. (2001) and Berninger, Abbott, Thomson et al. (2006) showed that dyslexia is associated with impaired orthographic coding in working memory (underlying orthographic awareness of spelling units in words). Visual-motor integration did not contributely uniquely to developing writing but orthographic coding did (Berninger, Yates, Cartwright, Rutberg, Remy, & Abbott, 1992). See Berninger and Richards (2002) for the distinction between visual and orthographic.
	
	Auditory discrimination does not explain writing disorders but impaired phonological coding in working memory (underlying awareness of phonemes, rimes, and syllables in spoken words) does (see Berninger & Richards, 2002).
	See first and third finger function under motor.
	Children with motor disorders have trouble writing (See Dewey and Tupper, 2004) for overview of developmental motor disorders.
	
	Finger functions are related to writing development in children whose motor development otherwise falls within the normal range. See Berninger (2007a, 2007b) for assessment measures for each of the finger function tasks below.
	
	Finger succession explained unique variance in handwriting and composing during the primary grades (Berninger et al., 1992) and composing during the intermediate grades (Berninger, Cartwright, Yates, Swanson, & Abbott, 1994) and showed robust brain differences between good and poor writers (Richards, Berninger, Stock, Altemeier, Trivedi, & Maravilla, 2009).
	
	Touch sensation during finger use is related to reading (Fletcher & Satz, 1982).
	
	Integration of sensation of movement sequences on fingers with symbols in memory is related to paper and pencil math computation (Shurtleff, Faye, Abbott, & Berninger, 1988).

Attention
  Focusing
  Switching
  Maintaining
	Focus on what is relevant and inhibit what is irrelevant
	Switching attention (changing set or what is relevant)
	Maintaining attention (staying on task over time)
	Difficulty in sustaining attention across rows on a RAN or RAS task (Amtmann, Abbott, & Berninger, 2007) predicted those who did not spell as well as during composing in response to writing instruction (Amtmann, Abbott, & Berninger, 2008). Pretreatment training in attention resulted in better response to writing instruction than pretreatment in reading fluency for students with persisting writing disabilities (Chenault, Thomson, Abbott, &

Table 20.1
Continued

Function	General Principles Based on Research and Clinical Experience
	Berninger, 2006). Forms for Rating Each Attention Component during Response to Instruction in Berninger (2007a).
Coding Words and Linguistic Awareness Phonological Orthographic Morphological	Family genetics research (e.g., Berninger, Raskind et al., 2008), brain imaging research (e.g., Richards et al., 2006; Richards, Berninger, Nagy, Parsons, Field, Richards, 2005), assessment (Berninger, Raskind et al. 2008; Garcia, 2007), and treatment research (e.g., Berninger & Fayol, 2008; Berninger, O'Donnelly, et al., 2008) show that phonological, orthographic, and morphological word forms (coding them into memory and reflecting on their parts to develop linguistic awareness) contribute to learning to spell and read words.
Levels of Language	Many studies have shown that all levels of language (word, sentence syntax discourse schema/text organization) contribute to writing in children with and without writing disorders (Berninger & Richards, 2002). Children may show intraindividual differences in these skills (Whitaker, Berninger, Johnston, & Swanson, 1994).
Memory	All memory systems (short-term, working, and long-term) contribute to writing but especially working memory (e.g, Swanson & Berninger, 1996). See Berninger (2007b) and Berninger, Abbott, Swanson, et al. (in press) for measures of working memory for different levels of written language.
Executive Functions— Self-Regulation	Executive functions contribute uniquely to writing acquisition (Altemeier, Abbott, & Berninger, 2008) and writing-reading integration (Altemeier, Jones, Abbott, & Berninger, 2006) and are likely to fall outside the normal range in students with written language disorders (e.g., Berninger, Abbott, Thomson et al., 2006). Low-level executive functions such as inhibition and switching attention explain substantial variance in word-level skills (Altemeier et al., 2008) but high-level executive functions like planning (Altemeier et al., 2006), goal-setting, self-monitoring and updating, and reviewing and revising explain text-level composition (see chapter 9 in Berninger & Richards, 2002).
Speed and Efficiency of Processing	Time can be used to assess automatic performance (e.g., automatic legible letter writing in alphabetic order during first 15 seconds on the alphabet writing task), speed (total time), rate (seconds per word), and sustained processing of written language over time in working memory. Not only automaticity but also flexibility (see Cartwright, 2008) or the ability to switch set, for example, as assessed by rapid automatic switching (RAS), is important in written language learning. (See Berninger, 2007a, 2007b.)

(continued)

Table 20.1

Continued

Function	General Principles Based on Research and Clinical Experience
Cognitive Abilities Verbal Comprehension Nonverbal Reasoning	For dyslexia, a cognitive measure of verbal reasoning can be used to evaluate whether an individual in underachieving in spelling and composing (e.g., Berninger et al., 2001, 2006). For dysgraphia-impaired handwriting, cognitive measures are not as relevant as they are for spelling. For OWL LD, a measure of nonverbal reasoning may be more appropriate for gauging underachievement in writing, given their language processing problems which may compromise performance on a measure of verbal reasoning with expressive language requirements. Nevertheless some children with OWL LD have strengths in verbal reasoning apart from their problems in expressive language and metalinguistic awareness. See Berninger, Raskind et al. (2008).
Academic Handwriting Spelling Composition Word Decoding and Reading Reading Comprehension Paper and Pencil Calculation	When assessing written language achievement, three writing skills should always be assessed; handwriting (legibility, automaticity, speed, and sustained writing over time, see Berninger, 2007b), spelling (pseudowords and real words with and without writing requirements), and composing—narrative and expository genre. See Berninger (2007a, 2007b). Also because children with writing disability often have reading disabilities as well (Berninger, 2008b) and classroom assignments typically require integrated writing-reading (Altemeier et al., 2006), ability to read pseudowords (decoding), real words, and reading comprehension should also be assessed. If concerns about written paper and pencil math have been expressed, math skills should also be assessed from the perspective of writing (Berninger, 2007c).
Social Emotional	Because children with writing disabilities become discouraged by their writing problems, they sometimes become writing-avoidant.

cursive writing by pen and keyboarding by computer—has unique processing requirements (Berninger, Abbott, Jones, et al., 2006). Keyboarding may not necessarily have advantages over writing by pen for students (2nd, 4th, and 6th grade): Both students with and without writing disabilities wrote longer essays, wrote words faster, and included more complete sentences by pen than keyboard (Berninger, Abbott, Augsburger, & Garcia, in press) and expressed more ideas (e.g., Hayes & Berninger, 2009). Children with writing disabilities need explicit instruction in writing whether or not they are given accommodations with computers (Berninger, 2006; Berninger, Abbott, Augsberger, et al., in press).

Excellent sources of instructional interventions for written language disorders include Birsh (2005), Morris and Mather (2008), and Troia (2009). The

Table 20.2
Evidence-Based School Neuropsychological Intervention for Writing Disabilities
within a Three-Tier Model

Tier	Handwriting	Spelling	Composing
Tier 1 Prevention	Lesson Set 3 (Berninger & Abbott, 2003)	Lesson Sets 4 and 5 (Berninger & Abbott, 2003)	Lesson Sets 7 and 10
For handwriting, spelling, and composing, see Berninger and Wolf (in press-a)	Also see Berninger, Rutberg et al. (2006)		(Berninger & Abbott, 2003)
Tier 2 Problem Solving Consultation	Handwriting Lessons, Berninger (1998)	Looking and Sound Games	See Instructional
		Talking Letters Berninger (1998)	Resources in Berninger (2007a) and Berninger and Abbott (2003)
Tier 3 Differential Treatment Based on Differential Diagnosis	Lesson Set 3	Lesson Set 12 (Berninger & Abbott, 2003)	Lesson Sets 8, 10, 13, 14 (Berninger & Abbott, 2003)
For handwriting, spelling, and composing, see Berninger and Wolf (in press-b)	(Berninger & Abbott, 2003)		

Source: From PAL Reading and Writing Lessons (Berninger and Abbott, 2003 for Tiers 1, 2, and 3), *PAL Guides for Reading and Writing Intervention* (Berninger, 1998), *PAL II User Guides* (Berninger, 2007a), *Teaching students with dyslexia and dysgraphia: Lessons from teaching and science* (Berninger & Wolf, in press-a) and *Helping students with dyslexia and dysgraphia make connections: Differentiated instruction lesson plans in reading and writing* (Berninger & Wolf, in press-b).
The User Guides, which are in PAL II Test Kits, contain the complete *PAL Guides for Reading and Writing Intervention* and *PAL Reading and Writing Lessons*, all of which can be downloaded to use as needed based on assessment.

following contain instructional recommendations that are teacher-friendly (Berninger & Dunn, 2008a, 2008b; Rosenfield & Berninger, 2009; Wong & Berninger, 2004). See Table 20.2 for instructional interventions based on the University of Washington writing research program. Participants in the Mark Twain Writers' Workshop showed significant improvement in both writing and motivation to write (Berninger & Hidi, 2006).

Without diagnosis, school professionals think that a single effective treatment for a specific writing disability may exist. We continue to get many referrals from schools, which have provided intensive phonological treatment and phonics for years, and students are not responding to the instruction. After diagnosis that pinpoints dysgraphia and associated handwriting and/or spelling problems, or that pinpoints OWL LD and associated morphological and syntactic awareness problems, a different kind of treatment is implemented—handwriting and spelling in the context of explicit composition instruction for the students with dysgraphia (e.g., Berninger, Winn, et al., 2008), or morphological and syntactic awareness training in the context of writing and reading activities (e.g., Berninger & Wolf, in press-a, in press-b). As a result, students become fast responders to instruction—once treatment is linked to diagnosis.

SUMMARY

School neuropsychology can improve understanding of the neuropsychological bases of specific written language disorders (Berninger, Nielsen et al., 2008a, 2008b; Berninger & Richards, 2002), measures to use in differential diagnoses (Berninger, 2004, 2006, 2007a, 2007b, 2008b, 2008c; Berninger, O'Donnell et al., 2008), and treatment planning based on differential diagnoses of specific writing disabilities (Berninger, 2008a; Berninger & Abbott, 2003; Berninger & Wolf, in press-a, in press-b).

REFERENCES

Altemeier, L., Abbott, R., & Berninger, V. (2008). Executive functions for reading and writing in typical literacy development and dyslexia. *Journal of Clinical and Experimental Neuropsychology, 30*, 588–606.

Altemeier, L., Jones, J., Abbott, R., & Berninger, V. (2006). Executive factors in becoming writing-readers and reading-writers: Note-taking and report writing in third and fifth graders. *Developmental Neuropsychology, 29*, 161–173.

Amtmann, D., Abbott, R., & Berninger, V. (2007). Mixture growth models for RAN and RAS row by row: Insight into the reading system at work over time. *Reading and Writing. An Interdisciplinary Journal, 20*, 785–813. Published Springer online: November 28, 2006.

Amtmann, D., Abbott, R., & Berninger, V. (2008). Identifying and predicting classes of response to explicit, phonological spelling instruction during independent composing. *Journal of Learning Disabilities, 41*, 218–234.

Berninger, V. (1998). *Process assessment of the learner (PAL). Guides for intervention. Reading and writing.* San Antonio, TX: The Psychological Corporation.

Berninger, V. (2004). Understanding the graphia in dysgraphia. In D. Dewey & D. Tupper (Eds.), *Developmental motor disorders: A neuropsychological perspective* (pp. 328–350). New York: Guilford.

Berninger, V. (2006). A developmental approach to learning disabilities. In I. Siegel & A. Renninger (Eds.), *Handbook of child psychology, Vol. IV, child psychology and practice* (pp. 420–452). New York: John Wiley & Sons.

Berninger, V. (2007a). *Process assessment of the learner II user's guide.* San Antonio, TX: Harcourt/PsyCorp. (CD format) ISBN 0158661818 Second Revision issued August 2008.

Berninger, V. (2007b). *Process assessment of the learner (2nd ed.). Diagnostic for reading and writing (PAL-II RW).* San Antonio, TX: The Psychological Corporation.

Berninger, V. (2007c). *Process assessment of the learner diagnostic for math (PAL II-M).* The San Antonio, TX: Psychological Corporation.

Berninger, V. (2008a). Evidence-based written language instruction during early and middle childhood. In R. Morris & N. Mather (Eds.), *Evidence-based interventions for students with learning and behavioral challenges* (pp. 215–235). New York: Lawrence Erlbaum Associates.

Berninger, V. (2008b). Defining and differentiating dyslexia, dysgraphia, and language learning disability within a working memory model. In E. Silliman & M. Mody (Eds.), *Language impairment and reading disability—interactions among brain, behavior, and experience* (pp. 103–134). New York: Guilford.

Berninger, V. (2008c). *Listening to parents of children with learning disabilities: Lessons from the University of Washington Multidisciplinary Learning Disabilities Center. Perspectives on language and literacy* (pp. 22–30). Wilmington, DE: International Dyslexia Association.

Berninger, V., & Abbott, S. (2003). *PAL research-supported reading and writing lessons.* San Antonio, TX: Harcourt/PsyCorp.

Berninger, V., Abbott, R., Augsburger, A., & Garcia, N. (in press). Comparison of pen and keyboard transcription modes in children with and without learning disabilities affecting transcription. *Learning Disability Quarterly.*

Berninger, V., Abbott, R., Jones, J., Wolf, B., Gould, L., Anderson-Youngstrom, M., et al. (2006). Early development of language by hand: Composing-, reading-, listening-, and speaking-connections, three letter writing modes, and fast mapping in spelling. *Developmental Neuropsychology, 29*, 61–92.

Berninger, V., Abbott, R., Swanson, H. L., Lovitt, D., Trivedi, P., Lin, S., et al. (in press). Relationship of word- and sentence-level working memory to reading and writing in second, fourth, and sixth grade. *Language, Speech, and Hearing Services in Schools.*

Berninger, V., Abbott, R., Thomson, J., & Raskind, W. (2001). Language phenotype for reading and writing disability: A family approach. *Scientific Studies in Reading, 5,* 59–105.

Berninger, V., Abbott, R., Thomson, J., Wagner, R., Swanson, H. L., Wijsman, E., et al. (2006). Modeling developmental phonological core deficits within a working-memory architecture in children and adults with developmental dyslexia. *Scientific Studies in Reading, 10,* 165–198.

Berninger, V., & Amtmann, D. (2003). Preventing written expression disabilities through early and continuing assessment and intervention for handwriting and/ or spelling problems: Research into practice. In H. L. Swanson, K. Harris, &

S. Graham (Eds.), *Handbook of research on learning disabilities* (pp. 345–363). New York: Guilford.

Berninger, V., Cartwright, A., Yates, C., Swanson, H. L., & Abbott, R. (1994). Developmental skills related to writing and reading acquisition in the intermediate grades: Shared and unique variance. *Reading and Writing: An Interdisciplinary Journal, 6*, 161–196.

Berninger, V., & Dunn, A. (2008a). Written language interventions for preschool and primary grades. In A. Carter, S. Carroll, L. Page, & I. Romero (Eds.). *Helping children at home and school: Handouts for families and educators*. Bethesda, MD: National Association of School Psychologists.

Berninger, V., & Dunn, A. (2008b). Written language interventions for intermediate and secondary school students. In A. Carter, S. Carroll, L. Page, & I. Romero (Eds.), *Helping children at home and school: Handouts for families and educators*. Bethesda, MD: National Association of School Psychologists.

Berninger, V., Dunn, A., Lin, S., & Shimada, S. (2004). School evolution: Scientist-practitioner educators creating optimal learning environments for all students. *Journal of Learning Disabilities, 37*, 500–508.

Berninger, V., & Fayol, M. (Published online: 2008-01-22 14:57:52 at Canadian Encyclopedia Entry\Encyclopedia of Language and Literacy Development.htm.). *Why spelling is important and how to teach it effectively.*

Berninger, V., & Hidi, S. (2006). Mark Twain' writers' workshop: A nature-nurture perspective in motivating students with learning disabilities to compose. In S. Hidi, & P. Boscolo (Eds.), *Motivation in writing* (pp. 159–179). Amsterdam, Elsevier.

Berninger, V., & Holdnack, J. (2008). Neuroscientific and clinical perspectives on the RTI initiative in learning disabilities diagnosis and intervention: Response to questions begging answers that see the forest and the trees. In C. Reynolds & E. Fletcher-Janzen (Eds.), *Neuroscientific and clinical perspectives on the RTI initiative in learning disabilities diagnosis and intervention* (pp. 66–81). New York: John Wiley & Sons.

Berninger, V., Nielsen, K., Abbott, R., Wijsman, E., & Raskind, W. (2008a). Writing problems in developmental dyslexia: Under-recognized and under-treated. *Journal of School Psychology, 46*, 1–21.

Berninger, V., Nielsen, K., Abbott, R., Wijsman, E., & Raskind, W. (2008b). Gender differences in severity of writing and reading disabilities. *Journal of School Psychology, 46*, 151–172.

Berninger, V., O'Donnell, L., & Holdnack, J. (2008). Research-supported differential diagnosis of specific learning disabilities and implications for instruction and response to instruction (RTI). In A. Prifitera, D. Saklofske, L. Weiss (Eds.), *WISC-IV clinical assessment and intervention* (2nd. ed., pp. 69–108). San Diego, CA: Academic Press (Elsevier).

Berninger, V., Raskind, W., Richards, T., Abbott, R., & Stock, P. (2008). A multidisciplinary approach to understanding developmental dyslexia within working-memory architecture: Genotypes, phenotypes, brain, and instruction.

Berninger, V., & Richards, T. (2002). *Brain literacy for educators and psychologists*. New York: Academic Press.

Berninger, V., Rutberg, J., Abbott, R., Garcia, N., Anderson-Youngstrom, M., & Brooks, A. (2006). Tier 1 and Tier 2 early intervention for handwriting and composing. *Journal of School Psychology, 44,* 3–30.

Berninger, V., Winn, W., Stock, P., Abbott, R., Eschen, K., Lin, C., et al. (2008). Tier 3 specialized writing instruction for students with dyslexia. *Reading and Writing. An Interdisciplinary Journal, 21,* 95–129.

Berninger, V., & Wolf, B. (in press-a). *Teaching students with dyslexia and dysgraphia: Lessons from teaching and science.* Baltimore: Paul H. Brookes.

Berninger, V., & Wolf, B. (in press-b). *Helping students with dyslexia and dysgraphia make connections: Differentiated instruction lesson plans in reading and writing.* Baltimore: Paul H. Brookes. Spiral book with teaching plans from University of Washington Research Program.

Berninger, V., Yates, C., Cartwright, A., Rutberg, J., Remy, E., & Abbott, R. (1992). Lower-level developmental skills in beginning writing. *Reading and Writing. An Interdisciplinary Journal, 4,* 257–280.

Birsh, J. (2005). *Multisensory teaching of basic language skills* (2nd ed.). Baltimore: Paul H. Brookes.

Cartwright, K. (Ed.), (2008). *Flexibility in literacy processes and instructional practice: Implications of developing representational ability for literacy teaching and learning* (pp. 114–139). New York: Guilford.

Chenault, B., Thomson, J., Abbott, R., & Berninger, V. (2006). Effects of prior attention training on child dyslexics' response to composition instruction. *Developmental Neuropsychology, 29,* 243–260.

Dewey, D., & Tupper, D. (2004). *Developmental motor disorders. A. neuropsychological perspective.* New York: Guilford.

Fayol, M., Zorman, M., & Lété, B. (2009). Associations and dissociations in reading and spelling French. Unexpecteadly poor and good spellers. *British Journal of Educational Psychology Monograph Series II (6).* British Psychological Society, Leicester, UK. 1476 9808.

Fletcher, J., & Satz, P. (1982). Kindergarten prediction of reading achievement: A seven-year longitudinal follow-up. *Educational and Psychological Measurement, 42,* 681–685.

Garcia, N. (2007, December). *Phonological, orthographic, and morphological contributions to the spelling development of good, average, and poor spellers.* Ph.D. dissertation. University of Washington.

Graham, S., & Perin, D. (2007a). *Writing next: Effective strategies to improve writing of adolescents in middle and high schools – A report to Carnegie Corporation of New York.* Washington, DC: Alliance for Excellent Education.

Graham, S., & Perin, D. (2007b). A meta-analysis of writing instruction for adolescent students. *Journal of Educational Psychology, 99,* 445–476.

Hayes, J. R., & Berninger, V. (2009). Relationships between idea generation and transcription: How act of writing shapes what children write. In C. Braverman, R. Krut, K. Lunsford, S. McLeod, S. Null, P. Rogers, & A. Stansell (Eds.), *Traditions of writing research.* New York: Routledge.

Hooper, S., Knuth, S., Yerby, D., Anderson, K., & Moore, C. (2009). A review of science supported writing instruction with implementation in mind. In

S. Rosenfield & V. Berninger (Eds.), *Implementing evidence-based interventions in school settings* (pp. 49–83). New York: Oxford University Press.

Katusic, S., Barbaresi, W., Colligan, R., Weaver, A., & Jacobsen, S. (2009). *The forgotten learning disability: Epidemiology of written language disorder in a population-based birth cohort (1976–1982).* Rochester, Minnesota. Pediatrics, 123, 1306-1313.

Morris, R., & Mather, N. (2007). *Evidence-based interventions for students with learning and behavioral challenges.* New York: Lawrence Erlbaum Associates.

Richards, T., Aylward, E., Raskind, W., Abbott, R., Field, K., Parsons, A., et al. (2006). Converging evidence for triple word form theory in children with dyslexia. *Developmental Neuropsychology, 30,* 547–589.

Richards, T., Berninger, V., Nagy, W., Parsons, A., Field, K., & Richards, A. (2005). Brain activation during language task contrasts in children with and without dyslexia: Inferring mapping processes and assessing response to spelling instruction. *Educational and Child Psychology, 22,* 62–80.

Richards, T., Berninger, V., Stock, P., Altemeier, L., Trivedi, P., & Maravilla, K. (2009). fMRI sequential-finger movement activation differentiating good and poor writers. *Journal of Clinical and Experimental Neuropsychology.* To link to this Article: DOI: 10.1080/13803390902780201 URL: http://www.dx.doi.org/10.1080/138033 90902780201

Rosenfield, S., & Berninger, V. (Eds.). (2009). *Implementing evidence-based interventions in school settings.* New York: Oxford University Press.

Scott, C. (2002). A fork in the road less traveled: Writing intervention based on language profile. In K. Butler & E. Silliman (Eds.), *Speaking, reading, and writing in children with language learning disabilities* (pp. 219–237). Mahwah, NJ: Lawrence Erlbaum Associates.

Shurtleff, H., Faye, G., Abbott, R., & Berninger, V. (1988). Neuropsychological and cognitive correlates of academic skills: A levels of analysis assessment model. *Journal of Psychoeducational Assessment, 6,* 298–308.

Swanson, H. L., & Berninger, V. (1996). Individual differences in children's working memory and writing skills. *Journal of Experimental Child Psychology, 63,* 358–385.

Troia, G. (Ed.). (2009). *Writing instruction and assessment for struggling writers from theory to evidence based practices.* New York: Guilford.

Vellutino, F. (1979). *Dyslexia, theory, and research.* Cambridge, MA: MIT Press.

Whitaker, D., Berninger, V., Johnston, J., & Swanson, L. (1994). Intraindividual differences in levels of language in intermediate grade writers: Implications for the translating process. *Learning and Individual Differences, 6,* 107–130.

Wijsman, E., Peterson, D., Leutennegger, A., Thomson, J., Goddard, K., Hsu, L., et al. (2000). Segregation analysis of phenotypic components of learning disabilities I. Nonword memory and digit span. *American Journal of Human Genetics, 67,* 631–646.

Wong, B., & Berninger, V. (2004). Cognitive processes of teachers in implementing composition research in elementary, middle, and high school classrooms. In B. Shulman, K. Apel, B. Ehren, E. Silliman, & A. Stone (Eds.), *Handbook of language and literacy development and disorders* (pp. 600–624). New York: Guilford.

CHAPTER 21

Assessing and Intervening with Children with Math Disorders

DENISE E. MARICLE, LYNSEY PSIMAS-FRASER,
RAYCHEL C. MUENKE, and DANIEL C. MILLER

S UCCESS IN MATHEMATICS is essential for academic success as well as future career success in a workforce that is growing in mathematics-intensive jobs (National Mathematics Advisory Panel, 2008). Since performing well in mathematics can be vital to healthy career prospects, it is important to understand how to assess and intervene with children identified as having math disorders. The focus of this chapter is to discuss the various types of math disorders, how they are subtyped neurologically, the brain structures and mechanisms that are thought to be responsible for math disorders, how math disorders are commonly assessed by school neuropsychologists, and some evidence-based interventions for the treatment of children with math disorders.

The *Diagnostic and Statistical Manual of Mental Disorders, 4th Edition, Text Revision (DSM-IV-TR;* APA, 2000) lists the prevalence of mathematic disorders at approximately 1 percent of school-age children. More recently, Pennington (2009) has suggested that the prevalence rates range from 3.0 to 6.5 percent. The statistics cited in the DSM-IV-TR were obtained from studies conducted with general clinical populations (Badian, 1983; Lewis, Hitch, & Walker, 1994; Shalev et al., 2001), although several of the studies do give estimates closer to Pennington's (e.g., 3.6 percent, Lewis et al., 1994; 5 to 6 percent, Shalev et al., 2001). Shalev and colleagues (2001) also discuss the strong concordance rates between family members such that 52 percent of individuals with dyscalculia have a parent or sibling with dyscalculia. According to Shalev and colleagues, the prevalence rate between family members is ten times higher than what occurs in the general population.

In the study by Lewis and colleagues, math disorders were divided into arithmetic-only disabilities (1.3 percent) and both arithmetic and reading disabilities (2.3 percent). It should be noted that some research (Fletcher, Lyon, Fuchs, & Barnes, 2007) suggests that children with learning disabilities in mathematics are referred at lower rates than children with learning disabilities in reading. Additionally, no consistent standards have been established to determine the presence or absence of a learning disability in math, which may account for the lower prevalence rates. There also appears to be a question as to whether a math disability is a unique learning disorder (Rourke, 1993) or a more generalized learning disorder, since it commonly co-occurs with other learning disorders (Fleishner, 1994). Math learning disorders often co-occur with learning disorders in reading, with approximately 56 percent of children with a reading disorder underperforming in mathematics, and 43 percent of children diagnosed with a math learning disorder underperforming in reading (Geary, 1993). This has led some researchers to conclude that there may be underlying cognitive mechanisms shared between students with a reading learning disorder and a mathematical learning disorder.

Mathematics appears to be especially vulnerable to learning difficulties. This may be due to the nature of mathematics instruction. Since mathematics is presented in a cumulative nature, failing to understand a simpler, foundational concept means that the learner will fail to understand the more complex concepts that build upon that foundation (Butterworth, 2008). This vulnerability emphasizes the importance of both well-designed and well-delivered mathematics instruction, as well as clearly targeted assessment and early intervention.

When students show high achievement in reading, they can be expected to continue to perform well over time in school. However, due to the evolving and multiple domain nature of mathematics, students who have a good start may not continue to be successful. Students may be proficient in understanding number sense but may have difficulty with a new skill introduced at the next grade level. This is due to the complex nature of mathematics domains and the various neuropsychological components necessary to be successful in all levels of mathematics. For example, the introduction of multiplication and division requires significant conceptual reorganization from concepts taught earlier (Clark, Baker, & Chard, 2002) The ability to identify the subtypes and components that make up math proficiency, much like reading being broken into component skills involving word recognition, fluency, and comprehension, is necessary to provide proper assessment and intervention (Fletcher et al., 2007).

The National Mathematics Advisory Panel (2008) convened to recommend targeting specific areas of math instruction. Of particular importance is the area of algebra because success in algebra is critical to success in higher-order mathematics. Critical foundations in mathematical skills necessary for success in algebra include proficiency in whole numbers, fractions, and certain aspects of geometry and measurement. The panel recommends that once a child has completed the fifth or sixth grade, he or she should have a deep understanding of numbers, including whole numbers; the understanding of place value; a firm grasp on addition, subtraction, multiplication, and division; knowledge of operational processes and general math facts; as well as the ability to estimate. Middle school students need to have fluency with fractions including the location of positive and negative fractions on a number line; the ability to compare fractions, decimals, and percentages; a firm grasp on how a fraction relates to a percentage; and a symbolic understanding of numbers. It is also important for middle school students to be familiar with geometry and measurement, such as understanding the properties of triangles, the ability to analyze the properties of shapes, and using formulas to determine concepts like perimeter, area, volume, and surface. According to the advisory panel, these recommended areas of mathematics instruction will give a child a secure base for instruction in algebra and higher-order mathematics.

DEFINITIONS

Several terms are commonly used to describe difficulties in mathematics. *Acalculia* is used to refer to acquired mathematical difficulties, often the result of a traumatic brain injury or other neurological insult. Acalculia is a form of aphasia characterized by the inability, or loss of ability, to perform mathematical tasks. Acalculia is often divided into three types (Gitelman, 2003). *Aphasic acalculia* (sometimes referred to in the literature as *agraphia* or *alexia*) is primarily the inability to recognize, read, or write numbers. Errors are related to reading numbers, writing numbers, or manipulating numbers. This type is almost always associated with left hemisphere damage. *Visual-spatial acalculia* is characterized by difficulties in the spatial representation of numerical information, such as difficulties with place value, misreading numerical signs, or misalignment of numbers. Visual-spatial acalculia is associated with damage to posterior regions of the right hemisphere. The third subtype of acalculia, *anarithmetia*, primarily involves the loss of calculation ability, including the inability to retrieve basic mathematical facts from long-term memory storage. It is associated with damage to the posterior regions of the left hemisphere. The term *dyscalculia* is also used to describe impairment in the ability to learn and perform mathematics. It is usually regarded as being developmental with no known or observable etiology. The term dyscalculia is often used to refer to a learning disability that affects an individual's ability to learn and/or comprehend mathematics (Geary, 1994). In the special education and child development literature dyscalculia is sometimes divided into *developmental dyscalculia*, which refers to difficulty in acquiring arithmetic competence at age-appropriate levels, and *math learning disability*, used to denote selective impairments of mathematical thinking or computational skills. Dyscalculia is often viewed as less severe than acalculia. The literature frequently refers to acalculia as the total inability to do math, whereas dyscalculia is posited to involve less severe difficulties in performing mathematics problems. Several other broad terms used to describe learning difficulties in mathematics include *developmental arithmetic disorder* (AD), *mathematics disability*, and *specific learning disability in mathematics* (SLD).

Under the definition of Specific Learning Disability (SLD) included within the *Individuals with Disabilities Education Improvement Act* (IDEIA [or sometimes referred to as IDEA] 2004), a child may be determined to have a disability in either mathematics calculation or mathematics problem solving. The 2004 revision of the IDEIA did not change how a specific learning disability was defined, but it did make changes in how a learning disability might be identified. According to IDEIA, a child may be determined to have a specific learning disability if the child does not make adequate progress for the child's age or does not meet state approved standards (§ 300.309 a) when provided with learning experiences and instruction appropriate for the child's age or grade; or the child does not make sufficient progress to meet age- or state-approved standards when using a process based on the child's response to scientific or research based interventions; or the child exhibits a pattern of strengths and weaknesses in academic performance below expected levels relative to age, intellectual development or state approved standards. In addition to a severe learning problem, the IDEIA's definition states that the child must demonstrate significant classroom delay relative to same-age peers and deficits in basic cognitive processes (such as working memory, executive functions, or long term retrieval). Additionally, the learning disability in mathematics cannot be the result of inadequate instruction, insufficient learning experiences, "a visual, hearing or motor disability, mental retardation, emotional disturbance, cultural factors, environmental or economic disadvantage, or limited English proficiency" (§ 300.309 a). The 2004 revision of IDEA gave states flexibility in how they identify specific learning disabilities. According to the IDEIA, states may continue to use a discrepancy procedure to identify specific learning disabilities; they may institute scientific researched based interventions that monitor student progress and use lack of progress to identify a specific learning disability, or they may use some other criteria established by the educational regulatory agency of the state.

According to the *DSM-IV-TR* (APA, 2000), a mathematics disorder is characterized by mathematical ability that is substantially below what is expected for the individual's age, intelligence, and access to adequate instruction. The mathematics disorder must significantly interfere with academic achievement or activities of daily living, and if the individual has a sensory deficit, then the mathematics difficulties are in excess of what would be expected or usually associated with it.

NEUROPSYCHOLOGICAL SUBTYPES

Math disorders, historically, have not received the same attention as reading disorders. As a result, neuropsychological explanations and imaging evidence for typically developing math abilities and math disabilities are still relatively limited and lacking in consensus.

Geary (1993, 1994, 1999, 2003) and Mazzocco (2001) found evidence for three types of learning disabilities in mathematics (Semantic, Procedural, and Visuo-Spatial). The *semantic subtype* appears to be the most common and is characterized by difficulties with fact retrieval and problems memorizing facts even with extensive drilling. In this subtype the normal processes that underlie memorization of math facts are interrupted. Individuals present with difficulties counting, difficulty with the rapid identification of numbers, and deficits retrieving or recalling math facts or overlearned math information. This subtype represents a disorder of the verbal representation of numbers and the inability to use language-based procedures to retrieve math facts. The semantic subtype is frequently associated with concomitant disorders in reading and spelling. Geary and colleagues (Geary, Hamson, & Hoard, 2000; Geary, Hoard, & Hamson, 1999) found that children with this math subtype had problems with phonological or semantic memory tasks, but not working memory tasks. Additionally, they concluded that when children with this subtype exhibited comorbid reading difficulties, their problems with encoding and retrieval of information from long-term memory impacted quantitative knowledge, number concepts and counting, calculation skills, and cognitive functioning beyond what would be within the expected range given their overall global intelligence.

The *procedural subtype* is characterized by a poor conceptual grasp of math procedures and difficulty in the use of math processes, although quantitative knowledge and quantity-symbol relationships are intact and adequate. This deficit is characterized by the use of procedures that are common to younger, yet academically normal children, slow processing speed, and frequent procedural errors. The procedural subtype has difficulty coding numeric systems into a meaningful language system, resulting in difficulty reading numbers aloud and writing dictated numbers. The deficiency is in processing and encoding numeric information. It tends to be localized in the left and right inferior occipital and temporal regions. This subtype is associated with processing disorders in working memory, long-term retrieval, fluid reasoning, and executive functions (Osmon, Patrick, & Andresen, 2008). The procedural subtype has been associated with attention-deficit/hyperactivity disorder (Marshall, Schafer, O'Donnell, Elliot, & Handwerk, 1999).

The *visuo-spatial subtype* demonstrates difficulties with spatial representation of numbers. Individuals exhibiting this subtype may have difficulties with column alignment, place value, and spatial orientation of numbers. Frequently there are spatial deficits in other areas as well. This subtype is often associated with nonverbal learning disorders (Hale & Fiorello, 2004; Rourke, 1994). Numerous studies by Rourke (1994) indicate that children with this subtype have poor visual-spatial-organizational skills, slow processing speed (psychomotor deficits), and deficient concept formation skills.

Geary's subtypes correspond well with the Cattell-Horn-Carroll (CHC) theory of cognitive functioning (Osmon et al., 2008) that currently pervades the assessment literature. This was exemplified in a study conducted by Floyd, Evans, and McGrew (2003), which determined that crystallized knowledge (Gc), fluid reasoning (Gf), processing speed (Gs), and long-term retrieval (Glr) were associated with mathematics performance and were often deficient in children with math disabilities. Floyd and colleagues did not find an association with the visual thinking factor (Gv); however, this is likely due to the nature of the tasks used to measure visual-spatial thinking on the *Woodcock Johnson III Tests of Cognitive Abilities* (WJ III COG; Woodcock, McGrew, & Mather, 2001a), which are not sensitive to the spatial deficits associated with math disabilities (Osmon et al., 2008).

More recently, Wilson and Dehaene (2007) reported that there are three subtypes of dyscalculia in adults that have been verified by lesion evidence and neuroimaging studies (see Table 19.1). Dehaene (1997, 2001), along with Wilson and Dehaene (2007), has suggested that the core aspect of numerical cognition is number sense, which is a description of the ability to understand, approximate, and manipulate numerical quantities. *Number sense dyscalculia* is one of the three adult dyscalculia subtypes. Based on adult neuroimaging studies (Dehaene, Piazza, Pinel, & Cohen, 2003), the neural substrate for number sense lies within the parietal cortex, specifically in the horizontal intraparietal sulcus (HIPS). The second adult dyscalculia subtype is referred to as *verbal dyscalculia*, which is characterized by difficulties with verbal numerical tasks such as multiplication and exact addition (Wilson & Dehaene, 2007). The neural substrate for verbal dyscalculia is the left angular gyrus. Damage to the left angular gyrus causes Gertsmann syndrome, which is characterized by acalculia, left-right confusion, agraphia, and finger agnosia (Gerstmann, 1940). The third adult dyscalculia subtype is referred to as *spatial attention dyscalculia*, which is characterized by difficulties with "numerical tasks that may require shifting of spatial attention, such as approximating, subtraction, and number comparison" (Wilson & Dehaene, 2007, p. 216).

Wilson and Dehaene (2007) pointed out that these three dyscalculia subtypes found in adults may be difficult to define in children. It may be common in children as math skills develop that deficits would occur across all of these areas and not specifically with just one subtype. Taking into account the neurodevelopmental influences in children, and extrapolating what is known about dyscalculia in adults, Wilson and Dehaene proposed that if there is a single core deficit that causes developmental dyscalculia, it would be related to one of the three possible subtypes (see Table 21.1).

Based on their research with adults, Wilson and Dehaene (2007) identified possible deficits that cause developmental dyscalculia:

- A deficit in number sense or nonsymbolic representation of number (i.e., 3).
- Impaired connections between symbolic and nonsymbolic representations.
- A deficit in verbal symbolic representation.
- A deficit in executive functions.
- A deficit in spatial attention.

In contrast to Wilson and Dehaene, Hale, Fiorello, Dumont, Willis, Rackley, and Elliott (2008) described five developmental subtypes of dyscalculia:

- Numeric Quantitative Knowledge
- Dyscalculia/Gertsmann Syndrome
- Mild Executive/Working Memory

Table 21.1
Dyscalculia Subtypes in Adults

Math Skill Deficit	Wilson & Dehaene (2007) Dyscalculia Adult Subtype Labels	Neural Substrate
• Comparing the size of numbers, estimating, subtracting, and approximating.	Number Sense Dyscalculia	Horizontal intraparietal sulcus within the parietal cortex
• Verbal numerical tasks such as multiplication and exact addition.	Verbal Dyscalculia	Left angular gyrus
• Approximating, subtraction, and number comparisons.	Spatial Attention Dyscalculia	Posterior superior parietal lobe

- Fluid/Quantitative Reasoning
- Nonverbal Learning Disability/Right Hemisphere

It is critical to recognize that not all children with developmental dyscalculia show difficulties in the same areas. There is little empirically based evidence regarding specific mathematic subtypes and how to measure each of these domains. Many authors have conducted research validating different subtypes of dyscalculia (e.g., Rourke, 1993, Jordan & Hanich, 2000, Geary, 2003, Kilpatrick, Swafford, & Findell, 2001). These inconsistencies in determining which specific cognitive dysfunctions are causing difficulty in mathematics makes it difficult to define specific math subtypes.

According to Hale, Fiorello, Dumont, et al. (2008) and Wilson and Dehaene (2007), there are multiple cognitive and neuropsychological functions necessary for understanding mathematics. The brain structures that Hale and colleagues propose to be involved in math computation and reasoning are the frontal, left, and right brain hemisphere systems. Research shows that disruption of one or more of these brain regions, whether *developmentally* or due to brain injury, can lead to various mathematics disabilities. Multiple neural networks appear to be involved in the processing of math tasks, with the specific cognitive strategy being deployed dictating which brain regions become the most active. However, three brain regions have been implicated through fMRI studies: The inferior frontal gyrus has been implicated in the breaking down of larger numbers into smaller numbers, so as to create more accessible units; the angular gyrus, which is at the intersection of the occipital and parietal lobes, appears to be the seat of symbolic representation in the human brain and is responsible for the visual spatial recognition of symbols and math facts; and the occipital-temporal regions of the left hemisphere appear to be involved in the automatic recognition of numbers and digits.

Most of the neuroimaging studies (Cohen, Dehaene, Chochon, Lehericy, & Naccache, 2000; Coswell, Eagan, Code, Harasty, & Watson, 2000; Gruber, Indefrey, Steinmetz, & Kleinschmidt, 2001; Rickhard et al., 2000) of math tasks have implicated bilateral hemispheric function, although the left hemisphere appears to be preferential for arithmetic/calculation tasks and the right hemisphere for determining numerical magnitude and visual-spatial orientation (Rickhard et al., 2000). Butterworth (1999), Cohen and colleagues (2000), Coswell and colleagues (2000), and Gruber et al. (2001) found that damage to the left frontal region, inferior parietal lobe, perisylvian region, and basal ganglia were all associated with deficits in mathematics. The majority of these studies indicate that the prefrontal and inferior parietal areas, including the angular gyrus and the supramarginal gyrus, are involved in computational/calculation skills.

Hale, Fiorello, Miller, et al. (2008) performed commonality analysis on *Wechsler Intelligence Scale for Children, 4th Edition* (WISC-IV; Wechsler, 2003) predictors for the Numerical Operations and Math Reasoning subtests from the *Wechsler Individual Achievement Test, 2nd Edition* (WIAT-II; Wechsler, 2001) using a group of typical children ($n = 846$) and a group of children with specific learning disabilities in math ($n = 63$). Hale and colleagues, using a forced entry discriminant analysis, identified five math subtypes in children (see Table 21.2) that closely approximate the developmental dyscalculia deficit areas proposed by Wilson and Dehaene (2007). The developmental dyscalculia subtypes revealed in research conducted by Hale, Fiorello, Miller, et al. (2008) and Wilson and Dehaene (2007) are demonstrated in the subsequent section.

In the research conducted by Hale, Fiorello, Miller, et al. (2008), the *Numeric-Quantitative Knowledge subtype* of developmental dyscalculia shows below average performance on numerical operations and slightly below average math reasoning, as well as low average functioning in other cognitive areas. More specifically, this group performed below average on Digits Forward, Arithmetic, and the Processing Speed subtests on the WISC-IV. Collectively, these scores imply that not all children with math problems have "nonverbal" specific learning disabilities (SLD) and support a comorbid language, reading, and math specific learning disability subtype (Helland, 2007). The Numeric-Quantitative Knowledge subtype can be compared to Wilson and Dehaene's (2007) first hypothesized developmental dyscalculia core deficit area, a deficit in number sense or nonsymbolic representation of numbers. Each of these deficits occurs in the horizontal intraparietal sulcus (HIPS) within the parietal cortex.

The *Dyscalculia-Gerstmann Syndrome subtype* shows severe deficits on numerical operation and math reasoning tasks, as well as low average verbal comprehension abilities. Wilson and Dehaene (2007) found an analogous deficit in verbal symbolic representation. Dyscalculia/Gerstmann Syndrome is a cognitive impairment in the left parietal lobe in the region of the angular gyrus, left inferior frontal, and/or temporal language areas, or the left basal ganglia. The research by Hale and his colleagues (Hale, Fiorello, Miller, et al., 2008) shows that children with this subtype display the lowest WISC-IV performance on verbal and nonverbal subtests including Information, Arithmetic, Block Design, Picture Completion, and the Processing Speed subtests. This could suggest general verbal-crystallized or left hemisphere dysfunction, which co-occurs with reading specific learning disabilities (Helland, 2007).

Hale's *Mild Executive/Working Memory subtype* and Wilson and Dehaene's (2007) deficit in executive functions show average performance in numerical operations and math reasoning, as well as average functioning in other

Table 21.2

Hypothesized Developmental Dyscalculia Subtypes as Validated by Math Subtypes
on the WIAT-II

Hypothesized Developmental Dyscalculia Core Deficit Areas (Wilson & Dehaene, 2007)	Developmental Math Subtypes Hale et al. (2008)	WIAT-II Math Deficits and WISC-IV Indices Deficits	Neural Substrate
• A deficit in number sense or nonsymbolic representation of numbers.	Numeric Quantitative Knowledge	• Below average numerical operations and slightly below average math reasoning. Low average in other cognitive areas.	Horizontal intraparietal sulcus (HIPS) within the parietal cortex.
• Impaired connections between symbolic and nonsymbolic representations.	Not reported	• Not reported	Disconnection between the HIPS and PSPL.
• A deficit in verbal symbolic representation.	Dyscalculia/ Gerstmann Syndrome	• Severe numerical operations and math reasoning deficits. Low average verbal comprehension abilities.	Left angular gyrus, the left inferior frontal, and/or temporal language areas, or the left basil ganglia.
• A deficit in executive functions.	Mild Executive/ Working Memory	• Average numerical operations and math reasoning. Generally average cognitive skills.	Frontal dysfunction
• A deficit in executive functions.	Fluid/ Quantitative Reasoning	• Average numerical operations but low average math reasoning. Generally average in other cognitive areas.	Left dorsolateral prefrontal
• A deficit in spatial attention.	Nonverbal Learning Disability/Right Hemisphere	• Borderline numerical operation and math reasoning deficits. Below average perceptual reasoning skills.	Posterior superior parietal lobe (PSPL).

Modified from Lerew, 2005, Feifer & DeFina, 2005.

cognitive areas on the WISC-IV and WIAT-II. When given the WISC-IV, children with the Mild Executive/Working Memory subtype show specific difficulty with Information, Digits Backward, Arithmetic, and Matrix Reasoning. Neuropsychological research suggests frontal-striatal dysfunction in this subtype. Overall, this subtype had the least difficulty of any other subtype, with only mild deficits on math subtests.

On the WISC-IV and WIAT-II, Hale, Fiorello, Miller, et al. (2008) found that average functioning in numerical operations, low average math reasoning, and generally average performance in other cognitive areas exemplified the Fluid/Quantitative Reasoning subtype. This proposed subtype shows the most difficulty with the following WISC-IV subtests: Matrix Reasoning, Picture Concepts, and Arithmetic. Math difficulties in fluid and quantitative reasoning appear to be the result of deficits in the left dorsolateral prefrontal cortex.

Children with Right Hemisphere SLD (e.g., NVLD), or right hemisphere dysfunction, show borderline numerical operation and math reasoning deficits on the WISC-IV and WIAT-II indices. They also performed in the below average range on skills of perceptual reasoning. These results are similar to Wilson and Dehaene's (2007) proposed deficit in spatial attention. In particular, these children performed poorly on the WISC-IV tests of Perceptual Reasoning and Processing Speed, as well as Information, Digits Backward, and Arithmetic. Interestingly, this group had well above average scores on Digits Forward, but deficits in Digits Backward. The neural substrate of children with right-hemisphere SLD is posited to be the posterior superior parietal lobe (PSPL).

There is still much to be learned about the particular brain mechanisms involved in dyscalculia, but significant research has been conducted on how mathematics is processed in a typically functioning individual. A key area that appears to be involved in mathematics processing is the left inferior parietal region posterior to the angular gyrus (Pennington, 2009). This area appears to be involved when normal-functioning adults perform arithmetic calculations or analyze the magnitude of a number; this appears to be true regardless of the modality of the input or output or even the individual's awareness of the numerical stimulus (Barth et al., 2006; Dehaene, 2003). Also of importance is the fact that individuals with lesions to the left inferior parietal region have deficits in even simple calculations and numerical comparisons that are severe enough to be called "pure semantic acalculia" (Pennington, 2009, p. 238).

According to Dehaene et al. (2003), posit a distributed bilateral cortical network involving areas of the parietal and frontal lobes such that lesions localized to different areas will differentially affect performance on various mathematical tasks. The notion of different brain-areas affecting math ability in different ways is supported by fMRI studies and corresponds to the five hypothesized subtypes of dyscalculia described by Hale, Fiorello, Miller, et al. (2008).

Dehaene and colleagues (2003) developed a tentative model based on brain imaging studies to enhance the understanding of the neuropsychological underpinnings of number processing. In their review, several brain areas appear to play key roles in number processing. The horizontal segment of the intraparietal sulcus (HIPS) appears to be strongly activated during (1) mental arithmetic, specifically semantic manipulation of numbers and estimation; (2) number comparison; (3) specificity for the number domain; (4) parametric modulation in which activation is stronger for large numbers; and (5) unconscious quantity processing. Another area that appears to play a key role is the angular gyrus, which is involved in the way numbers are encoded verbally (Dehaene et al., 2003). Therefore, this area may be essential for processing math problems that have strong linguistic demands.

Pennington (2009) calls for future research to develop a computational model to demonstrate how the brain regions accomplish the mathematical functions with clear delineations of the inputs and outputs to the various brain areas. In addition, researchers suggest that there may be other brain areas involved such that mathematical ability may not be as localized as other researchers have suggested (Dehaene et al., 2003; Pennington, 2009)

SCHOOL NEUROPSYCHOLOGICAL ASSESSMENT OF MATH DISORDERS

Unfortunately, there are no specific assessment measures used to diagnose a learning disorder in mathematics. Some assessment measures are more targeted than others, but the diagnosis is left up to the skills and discretion of the professional. Therefore, most school neuropsychologists rely on standardized measures of cognitive ability and achievement to determine if there is a discrepancy between the child's ability and his or her achievement in the area of mathematics; or if they are using the cross- battery approach to specific learning disability evaluation posited by Flanagan, Ortiz, and Alfonso (2007), identifying below expected normative performance on tasks of math achievement and concomitant tasks of the requisite CHC broad and narrow abilities hypothesized to be related to math ability. According to Geary (1999), the standardized achievement tests that are currently being utilized are too general and encompass too many different types of items to give the examiner useful information as to the cause of the poor mathematics performance.

Developing a neuropsychological understanding of the type of mathematical errors that a child is making is vital to conducting the correct assessment and implementing an effective intervention. To do this, a careful item analysis is recommended. An item analysis can be conducted on either a broad-based assessment, a focused-assessment, or a curriculum based measure (CBM) of performance, The examiner may develop a hypothesis about a particular area of mathematics that the child is having difficulty with, then administer extra math problems in that area to confirm the hypothesis. By linking a thorough assessment to evidence-based interventions, effective results may be seen in children with mathematical disabilities.

Hale and Fiorello (2004) describe five different types of error patterns: (1) math fact errors where the problem is with the automaticity of retrieving a basic math fact from long-term memory; (2) operand errors, where the examinee substitutes an incorrect operation (such as subtraction for addition); (3) algorithm errors in which the problem is performing the steps out of sequence (such as performing subtraction before multiplication); (4) place value errors, where the child performs the steps in proper order but makes a mistake in the place value of a number (possibly adding an extra 0), this could be a visual-spatial error or an algorithm error; and (5) regrouping errors, where the child unnecessarily regroups the numbers, adds regrouped numbers prior to multiplication, or forgets to subtract from the regrouped column. To effectively link measures of assessment with intervention, it is important to develop an understanding of the types of mathematical errors that the child is making and to link the error-types to targeted interventions.

CARROLL, HORN, AND CATTELL THEORY OF COGNITIVE ABILITIES: SPECIFIC AREAS INVOLVED IN MATHEMATICS

According to the Carroll-Horn-Cattell (CHC) theory of cognitive abilities, there are specific cognitive domains that influence one's ability to perform mathematically (Hale, Fiorello, Kavanaugh, Hoeppner, & Gaither, 2001; Keith, 1999; McGrew, Flanagan, Keith, & Vanderwood, 1997; McGrew & Hessler, 1995). The *Woodcock Johnson III: Tests of Cognitive Abilities* (WJIII-COG: Woodcock, McGrew, & Mather, 2001a) and the *Woodcock Johnson III: Tests of Achievement* (WJIII-ACH: Woodcock, McGrew, & Mather, 2001b) utilize the CHC theory as an interpretive framework for analyzing both cognitive and academic skill sets. The following section will discuss the CHC theory areas believed to impact mathematics ability as well as the tests utilized within the Woodcock Johnson system to analyze these abilities.

On the WJIII-ACH, quantitative knowledge and reasoning (Gq) is measured by four tests: calculation, math fluency, quantitative concepts, and applied problems. The Calculation subtest measures the ability to perform mathematical computations involving addition, subtraction, multiplication, division, fractions, algebra, and precalculus problems. The Math Fluency subtest involves the ability to solve simple addition, subtraction, and multiplication problems quickly. The Math Fluency subtest correlates strongly with processing speed and long-term retrieval at older ages, but at younger ages a certain amount of mathematics knowledge is required to complete the task. For younger children or children with disabilities, it may be more a measure of comprehension knowledge (Gc) than fluency with math facts. The Applied Problems subtest measures skills in analyzing and solving practical problems in math. It is thought to measure quantitative reasoning and math knowledge in an applied verbal format. The Quantitative Concepts subtest is found on the extended battery and serves as a measure of math concepts, symbols, and mathematical vocabulary. It is primarily a measure of mathematics knowledge and quantitative reasoning. CHC theory posits that the Gq factor measures an individual's acquired or stored mathematics knowledge, but that the use of mathematical reasoning while performing quantitative tasks falls under the purview of Fluid Reasoning (Gf) (Mather, Wendling, & Woodcock, 2001; McGrew, n.d.). A study by Floyd, Evans, and McGrew (2003) found a moderate to strong predictive relationship between the CHC areas of Comprehension Knowledge (Gc), Fluid Reasoning (Gf), Short-Term Memory-Working Memory (Gsm/Gsm-Wm), and Processing Speed (Gs) with mathematics performance and Quantitative Reasoning (Gq). At younger ages, Long-Term Retrieval (Glr) and Auditory Processing (Ga) also display a moderate relationship with math performance and Gq (Floyd et al., 2003).

Comprehension Knowledge (Gc) can be thought of as the child's encyclopedic knowledge of the world. Achievement in mathematics is strongly related to acquired comprehension knowledge of mathematics. Since mathematics skills are based on one another in a cumulative fashion, not learning a lower-level skill affects the learning of higher-order skills. If a child has a mathematics disorder, his or her encyclopedic knowledge of mathematics will shrink as he or she progresses through grades.

Memory, in particular working memory, which in CHC theory falls under the Gsm factor, plays an important role in mathematics performance. All math tasks from simple calculation to complex quantitative reasoning and problem solving involve memory skills such as short-term memory span, working memory, and long-term retrieval (Dehn, 2008). Empirical research has consistently implicated working memory as a central deficit in children with math disabilities. Hutton and Towse (2001) cited a correlation of .45 between digit span tasks and performance on mathematical tests, and Swanson and Beebe-Frankenberger (2004) noted a correlation of .54 between working memory tasks and mathematical problem solving. Furthermore, a study conduct by Hitch and McAuley (1991) concluded that children with math disorders have difficulty holding information in working memory while attending to more than one mathematics task. In a study conducted by Geary, Hoard, and Hamson (1999) the researchers found a significant difference between how individuals with a math disorder performed on digits backward tasks, but not on how they performed on digits forward when they were compared to normally functioning children. These results support the idea that children with a math disorder are able to store and retrieve information but that they have difficulty holding information in mind while manipulating that information. Children identified with a specific learning disability in math appear to suffer deficits in short-term retention and manipulation of verbal information (Swanson & Beebe-Frankenberger, 2004), although it appears that phonological short-term memory is most related to arithmetic during the learning of basic math concepts and facts (Dehn, 2008).

Processing Speed (Gs) can also affect mathematics performance. If automaticity of retrieval is an issue for the child, one would expect the child to perform better on tasks that are nontimed and perform more poorly on tasks where there are pressures of time and speed. Issues of processing speed are likely to broadly affect the child's performance, not just specifically in mathematics.

The area of Visual Spatial Thinking (Gv) measures a person's ability to think in visual spatial patterns, including the ability to perceive, analyze, rotate, store, and recall visual information. Visual spatial thinking is particularly important for mathematics tasks that require higher-level skills, but does not appear to be related to performance of basic math skills (McGrew & Flanagan, 1998).

WISC-IV/WIAT-II

Similar to the WJ III-COG and WJ III-ACH, careful analysis must be used when analyzing a mathematics disorder using the Wechsler series of assessments. The *Wechsler Intelligence Scale for Children- IV* (WISC IV; Wechsler, 2003) was designed using a CHC interpretive framework and purports to measure four domains of cognitive functioning: verbal comprehension, working memory, perceptual reasoning, and processing speed. However, Flanagan and Kaufman (2004) suggest that the WISC-IV is best viewed using a five-factor solution based on the CHC factors of Gv (visual spatial thinking), Gc (comprehension-knowledge), Gsm (short-term memory), Gf (fluid reasoning), and Gs (processing speed). The WISC IV retained the Arithmetic subtest as a supplemental subtest, which Flanagan and Kaufman classify as a measure of Gc and Gq (quantitative reasoning) with younger children and as measure of Gc and Gf at older ages. The Arithmetic subtest requires the child to answer simple to complex problems orally that involve math computation and numerical reasoning.

The *Wechsler Individual Achievement Test-II* (WIAT II; Wechsler, 2001; Lichtenberger & Smith, 2005) uses two subtests to assess mathematical ability. The Math Reasoning subtests consists of a series of problems that include concepts such as counting, quantity, geometric shapes, single and multistep word problems, telling time, money concepts, and the use of fractions, decimals, and percentages. This subtest measures quantitative concepts, multistep problem solving, and the application of quantitative concepts to practical problems (Strauss, Sherman, & Spreen, 2006). The Numerical Operations subtest consists of sets of problems for assessing the ability to identify and write numerals and solve calculation problems involving basic mathematical operations (addition, subtraction, multiplication, and division). It provides a measure of counting, one-to-one correspondence, numerical identification and writing, and calculation using basic math functions (Strauss et al., 2006).

The WISC-IV is commonly paired with the WIAT-II to measure discrepancies between predicted cognitive abilities and performance. It is essential when comparing scores across measures that the examiner analyzes the child's performance on the actual subtests because much of the variance is lost when the global scores are used (Berninger, O'Donnell, & Holdnack, 2008). The WIAT II manual states that the test allows detection of severe achievement difficulties; however, users should be aware that floor effects are evident at the lower end of the age spectrum. The score ranges at the youngest ages are insufficient for detecting pre-academic delays in young children with low average or lower intelligence. Additionally, insufficient ceilings are a problem if assessing high functioning older adolescents (Strauss et al., 2006).

KABC II/KTEA II

Similar to the Wechsler series and the Woodcock Johnson III series of assessments, careful analysis must be used when analyzing a mathematics disorder using the Kaufman series of assessments. The *Kaufman Assessment Battery for Children-II* (KABC II; Kaufman & Kaufman, 2004a) and the *Kaufman Test of Educational Achievement II* (KTEA II; Kaufman & Kaufman, 2004b) were co-normed and designed to be used together. The KABC II was designed to allow for two interpretive frameworks. Examiners may either use a Lurian perspective or the CHC theoretical approach when making interpretations with the KABC II (Kaufman, Lichtenberger, Fletcher-Janzen, & Kaufman, 2005). The CHC factors measured include Gsm (short-term memory), Gv (visual-spatial thinking), Glr (long-term retrieval), Gf (fluid reasoning) and Gc (comprehension-knowledge). The KTEA II contains two subtests that measure mathematical skills (Lichtenberger & Smith, 2005). Math Concepts and Applications measures arithmetic concepts and the application of mathematical principles and reasoning to real-life situations. Skills include numbers concepts, operations, time and money, measurement concepts, geometry and higher math concepts. All items are presented orally in combination with a visual stimulus. Mathematics Computation is a paper-and-pencil task where the child solves written computational problems. Skills include addition, subtraction, multiplication, division, fractions, decimals, square roots, exponents, and algebra.

KEYMATH 3 DIAGNOSTIC ASSESSMENT

The *KeyMath 3 Diagnostic Assessment* (KeyMath 3 DA; Connolly, 2008) is a comprehensive, norm-referenced measure of essential mathematical concepts and skills. This version of the KeyMath represents a substantial revision in concept and design, including the following:

- Updated content that extends through factoring and solving algebraic expressions.
- New subtests.
- Alignment with national math curriculum standards.
- Updated norms and new interpretive reports.
- Linkage to the *KeyMath 3 Essential Resources* companion instructional program.

Like previous versions, the KeyMath 3 DA is untimed and individually administered. The content of the KeyMath 3 DA covers the full spectrum of math concepts and skills that are typically taught in kindergarten through ninth grade and can be used with individuals aged 4½ through 21 years who are functioning at these instructional levels (Connolly, 2008). The items are grouped into ten subtests that represent three general math content areas:

- Basic Concepts (conceptual knowledge)
  - Numeration
  - Algebra
  - Geometry
  - Measurement
  - Data Analysis and Probability
- Operations (computational skills)
  - Mental Computation and Estimation
  - Written Computation: Addition and Subtraction
  - Written Computation: Multiplication and Division
- Applications (problem solving)
  - Foundations of Problem Solving
  - Applied Problem Solving

Each area is further divided into subtests with the content of each subtest spanning kindergarten through eighth- or ninth-grade math curricula. The five basic concept subtests parallel the five content standards of the National Council of Teachers of Mathematics (NCTM). Unlike the NCTM standards, which embed math operations in the numeration strand, the KeyMath 3 assessment includes two separately written computation subtests (Addition and Subtraction, Multiplication and Division), since operations skills are fundamental for success in mathematics and are often the source of math learning difficulties. The two applications subtests assess a student's ability to apply conceptual knowledge and operational skills to solve math problems. The Foundations of Problem Solving subtest includes items that require students to identify missing elements in a problem, operations needed to solve a problem, and optimal strategies for solving the problem. The Applied Problem Solving subtest presents math problems in real-world contexts and includes items that require standard and nonstandard problem-solving strategies.

The publisher notes that the KeyMath 3 DA has a substantial advantage over its predecessors in that it provides a means of monitoring an individual's progress over time. It includes two parallel forms (Form A and Form B), which can be administered in alternating sequence every three months, as well as growth scale values (GSVs), which are a type of developmental scale score. According to Connolly, GSVs enable users to accurately measure progress across the full range of math concepts and skills. Progress monitoring can be conducted with the KeyMath–3 DA ASSIST software, which (a) shows the amount of change across test administrations, (b) indicates whether an individual has made measurable progress, and (c) compares an individual's growth rate with the average growth rate of the representative population.

CURRICULUM BASED MEASURES (CBM)

CBMs usually consist of an examiner giving a child a timed series of problems based on grade-appropriate curriculum. CBMs are commonly used to analyze difficulties in mathematics, but according to Shapiro (2004), little systematic research has been conducted in this area. Since the areas of Fluid Reasoning (Gf) and Processing Speed (Gs) were found to be important predictors in mathematics abilities, Floyd, Evans, and McGrew (2003) hypothesize that a timed CBM may just be measuring how fast the child completes the problems, not what he or she knows.

OTHER CONSIDERATIONS

In addition to conducting measures of direct assessment, it is important to review samples of the child's work and speak with his or her teacher.

Reviewing the work can give the examiner an opportunity to view additional materials. Developing an understanding of how the child has performed on tasks of mathematics in the classroom, as homework, or on timed tests can strengthen the examiner's hypothesis as to what the underlying causes are for the mathematics difficulty.

Interviewing the teacher can help determine what the teacher considers to be the child's specific problems with math, the amount of time dedicated to mathematics, how the math instruction is delivered, and if the teacher has already implemented accommodations for the child (Shapiro, 2004). The teacher can give specific information on whether the child is having difficulties in the area of numerical representation, counting, recalling math facts, computation of basic math functions (addition, subtraction, multiplication, division), time, money, measurement, fractions, geometry, graphic representations of numbers, interpretations of numbers, and/or word problems (Shapiro, 2004). Speaking with the teacher can help to strengthen a hypothesis and inform areas of intervention.

As previously noted, the prevalence rates among family members is ten times what it is in the general population (Shalev et al., 2001); therefore, it is also essential to monitor any siblings of a child who have a mathematics learning disability as well as obtain information from parental interview about the history of learning disabilities within the family.

EVIDENCE-BASED INTERVENTIONS FOR THE TREATMENT OF CHILDREN WITH MATH DISORDERS

Understanding the foundation and specific effects of a math disability in conjunction with implementing evidence-based interventions can have a dramatic effect on the outcome of a child at risk or identified with a math disability. Providing effective interventions should be at the cornerstone of any evaluation. Unlike reading and writing, the research and literature available for neuropsychologically based interventions for math is narrow. Although limited, there are math interventions emerging for various subtypes of math skill deficits in areas such as numeric concepts, computational knowledge, working memory, long-term memory storage and/or retrieval, problem solving, and visual-spatial processes. Interventions for math disabilities often consist of not only skills training, but also explicit instruction in strategies such as self-regulation and mnemonic devices (Fletcher et al., 2007). Evidence-based interventions that are implemented must be appropriate for the child's neuropsychological profile. Deciding which intervention to use is a highly individualized process that depends on assessment results, response to previous intervention (e.g., Tier 1), the student's developmental level, current math skills, and requirements of the school district's math curriculum.

Lerew (2005) proposes a model that matches commonly used mathematics interventions to the student's neuropsychological and mathematics deficits. The modified table below (see Table 21.3) links these deficits to the affected brain region, further explaining the student's neuropsychological needs. The table provides a list of simple strategies that can be implemented for students who display a wide range of neuropsychological difficulties.

Quantitative Reasoning/Problem Solving

Executive functioning entails different domains of higher-order cognitive functioning. For example, planning, the ability to achieve a goal by working through a series of steps, is an essential component of higher-order cognitive processing such as problem solving. The following interventions appear to have the greatest amount of research support for problem solving deficits.

FAST DRAW   Students who are able to perform simple math skills, such as calculation, but have more difficulty with problem-solving tasks may benefit from the following intervention. FAST DRAW is an evidence-based problem-solving intervention that uses an eight-step strategy for solving word problems, in addition to incorporating self-regulation procedures (Rathvon, 2008). The mnemonic FAST DRAW helps students recall the eight steps that will assist them through a systematic series of problem solving stages. In order to solve word problems successfully, students must not only be able to perform the necessary calculations, but must also understand the question that is being asked, identify relevant information within the problem, and finally determine the specific operations needed to solve the problem. In the original study, as reported by Rathvon, two students with learning disabilities and two students with mild mental retardation showed significant improvement in math word problem-solving performance and maintained gains at six and eight-week followups. Furthermore, student attitudes toward word problems were reported to be much more positive. This intervention can be delivered successfully in a one-on-one format, small group, or class wide application.

A Neurocognitive Approach to Intervention: The Number Race (Wilson & Dehaene, 2007)   Wilson and Dehaene (2007) conducted research identifying the importance of uniting education and cognitive neuroscience in order to improve identification and understanding of mathematics disorders. These recommendations include developing a neurocognitive description of dyscalculia, developing and using core tests based on numerical cognition research, and developing and testing new educational remediation methods.

By developing a neurocognitive description of dyscalculia, Wilson and Dehaene (2007) suggest that the brain systems affected in math disorders

Table 21.3
Mathematics Interventions Based on Neuropsychological Deficits

Neuropsychological Deficit	Brain Region	Mathematics Deficit	Mathematics Interventions
Motor:			
		Numbers poorly formed and inaccurate.	Use a tape recorder for taking notes.
Graphomotor	Perisylvan Cortical Regions	Difficulty copying geometric shapes and letters.	Teach keyboarding skills instead of handwriting.
			Supplement oral-input software.
Cognitive Processes:			
		Retention and retrieval of math facts and tables.	Use mnemonic devices to teach math algorithms and sequential steps.
Working Memory	Left Temporal Lobes Prefrontal Lobes	Forgets math steps.	Use graph paper and pencils to line up and calculate equations.
		Poor regrouping skills.	Use a calculator.
			Use a tape recorder to review lectures.
Visuospatial Functions	Bilateral Inferior Parietal Regions	Misaligns numbers in columns.	Use visual reminders.
	Angular Gyrus	Confusion in carrying/borrowing.	Use verbal repetition.
		Misreads math signs.	Use a highlighter to help focus.
		Poor magnitude comparisons.	Attach a number line to the desk.
	Bilateral Occipital Parietal Lobes	Difficulty with mental rotation.	Turn visual problems into a verbal problems.
		Difficulty with mental math.	Present problems vertically rather than horizontally.
		Problems with direction (up, down, near, far, across).	

(*continued*)

Table 21.3
Continued

Neuropsychological Deficit	Brain Region	Mathematics Deficit	Mathematics Interventions
Auditory Processing	Bilateral Occipital-Temporal Lobes	Difficulty processing oral math drills quickly and efficiently.	Slow down the pace of instruction.
			Use pictures and other visual material.
			Focus on nonverbal cues
Linguistic-Verbal Processing	Left Hemisphere	Difficulty with concepts such as "less" or "more than."	Ask students to verbalize what they are doing.
			Slow down the pace of instruction.
Reasoning	Prefrontal Cortex	Unreasonable solutions.	Use graphic organizers to show relationships.
		Difficulty with estimation.	Teach generalization and application across contexts.
Attention	Anterior Cingulate	Difficulty sustaining attention.	Create routines with frequent breaks.
			Create cue sheets and mnemonics.
			Teach self monitoring/ self-talk techniques.
Executive Functions:			
Planning and Organization	Dorsolateral Prefrontal Cortex	Difficulty setting up math equations.	Create flow charts, graphs, and cognitive webs.
	Orbitofrontal Cortex	Applies only the practiced procedure.	Highlight and/or color code important information.
Problem Solving and Judgment	Dorsolateral Prefrontal Cortex	Difficulty with word problems.	Teach specific strategies to self-monitor and double-check work.

could be examined at the neural level. The results of understanding neural and behavioral systems would subsequently allow for better identification, treatment, and possibly prevention. For example, brain scans would allow for more specific identification of the deficit, which would sanction custom-built treatment plans. The possibility of prevention, as suggested by Wilson and Dehaene (2007), requires examining the plasticity of the brain circuits involved in dyscalculia, similar to current research suggesting this approach for dyslexia (Lyytinen et al., 2005).

Wilson and Dehaene (2007) also suggest the use of core ability tests to provide information on the core numerical cognition processes. Evidence-based core ability tests are currently very limited. Future research aims should include developing and implementing a standardized battery of core tests appropriate for all students.

Finally, by identifying specific neurocognitive deficits and subtypes, new evidence-based intervention techniques and strategies will emerge. Wilson and Dehaene (2007) have developed a software intervention program called "The Number Race," an adaptive program for the remediation of dyscalculia. This program, which is based on the number sense core deficit, provides intensive training on number sense tasks such as numerical comparison and serves to reinforce links between non-symbolic and symbolic representations of numbers. The program adapts to the individual child's performance continuously by increasing the difficulty of the numerical comparison, utilizing a speed limit, and increasing the ratio of symbolic to non-symbolic stimuli according to the child's performance. Thus far, pilot studies have shown significant improvements in numerical operations included in this program.

Working Memory

Learning-disabled children often have some degree of difficulty with working memory, an executive functioning deficit (Feifer & De Fina, 2005). This may result in many problems for the student, including forgetting the steps to solve a math word problem, the inability to remember a problem solving algorithm, or making place value errors. Feifer and De Fina (2005) offer five ways to facilitate working memory for students: (1) teach multiple ways to solve problems (visual-spatial and/or verbal strategies; (2) avoid anxiety-provoking skill drills; (3) link problem solving with passion to create personal meaning for the students; (4) set algorithmic procedures to a song (verbal strategies can be a key memory enhancer; and (5) encourage visual cues (jot down equations on scratch paper).

Nonverbal Leaning Disabilities (NVLD)

Rourke (1989, 1993, 1994) found that children with nonverbal learning disabilities also display poor academic achievement in mathematical reasoning and computation. Difficulties encountered often include limited concept formation, a poor understanding of cause-and-effect relationships, and limited problem-solving abilities (Rourke, 1989). Rourke encourages the use of rote memory strategies, such as the Concrete-Representational Model (Lerew, 2005). This model progressively moves from the concrete to the representational, and finally to abstract activities. The concrete level incorporates three-dimensional objects to solve problems. The representational level utilizes activities such as drawings to solve problems, and the abstract level removes objects and drawings from the problem-solving process. In a review by Lerew, the CRA model was effective for students with math difficulties in learning place value, basic math facts (Mercer & Miller, 1992), and multiplication facts.

BACK TO THE BASICS

As previously mentioned, it is critical to identify the cause of math difficulty prior to implementing an intervention. In a study of 9-year-olds (Butterworth, 2008), results show that oftentimes children with developmental dyscalculia do not understand the most simple math concepts. It is key to make sure that students grasp the concept introduced at the onset of the lesson. The children in this study rarely understood the concepts introduced, with the consequence being that the remainder of the lesson was wasted. This research further highlights the critical need for research for identifying an exact method for measuring a child's specific understanding of basic math concepts.

FUTURE RESEARCH

Given the potential impact of poor math on a child's educational and career opportunities, additional research on math disorders is necessary. Future research must consist of developing universal diagnostic criteria and gaining a better understanding of the brain structures and function involved in dyscalculia. Additional research is also critical to the continuation of effective neuropsychologically based mathematics interventions. While some research has been conducted on simple arithmetic, relatively little research has been conducted on understanding the cognitive and neuropsychological mechanisms that contribute to higher-order mathematics, such as problem solving. Research must serve to identify the causative factors contributing to math disorders, as well as effective interventions. Specific areas that are in need of attention include developing standardized, diagnostic instruments, and conducting cognitive and genetic research on the comorbidity of dyscalculia and other forms of learning disabilities (Geary, 2003). Researchers are continually attempting to link assessment to intervention, but certainly, more research is needed. While a new emphasis is being placed on mathematics, there is clearly a need for future research to better understand the underlying mechanisms and subtypes of math disability.

SUMMARY

Mathematics is a complex and dynamic field. The breadth and depth of the field make the identification and study of math-based learning disabilities a difficult endeavor (Geary, 2004). Research is just beginning to illuminate how typically developing children learn and process the concepts of mathematics, and although the research literature in math-based learning disabilities is very limited, it is growing. In the world today, mathematical knowledge, reasoning and skills are as critical as reading ability and the consequences of mathematic illiteracy carry significant ramifications. A first step in eradicating math illiteracy is to fully understand the cognitive and brain systems that support mathematical competency in typically developing children; this then should lead to a greater understanding of mathematical deficits, how such deficits should be evaluated and identified, and what interventions are successful at remediating math-based learning disabilities. Math-based learning disabilities are common, significant, and worthy of our attention.

REFERENCES

American Psychiatric Association. (2000). *Diagnostic and statistical manual of mental disorders* (DSM IV-TR, 4th ed., Text Revision). Washington, DC: Author.

Badian, N. A. (1983). Dyscalculia and nonverbal disorders of learning. In H. R. Myklebust (Ed.), *Progress in learning disabilities* (pp. 235–264). New York: Grune & Stratton.

Barth, H., La Mont, K., Lipton, J., Dehaene, S., Kanwisher, N., & Spelke, E. (2006). Nonsymbolic arithmetic in adults and young children. *Cognition, 8,* 199–222.

Berninger, V. W., O'Donnell, L., & Holdnack, J. (2008). Research-supported differential diagnosis of specific learning disabilities and implications for instruction and response to instruction. In A. Prifitera, D. H. Saklofske, & L. Weiss (Eds.), *WISC-IV clinical assessment and intervention* (2nd ed., pp. 69–108). New York: Elsevier.

Butterworth, B. (1999). *The mathematical brain*. London: Macmillan.

Butterworth, B. (2008). Developmental dyscalculia. In J. Reed & J. Warner-Rogers (Eds.), *Child neuropsychology: Concepts, theory, and practice* (pp. 357–374). Malden, MA: Wiley-Blackwell.

Clark, B., Baker, S., & Chard, D. (2002). Best practices in mathematics assessment and intervention with elementary students. In J. Grimes, & A. Thomas (Eds.), *Best practices in school psychology V* (pp. 453–463). Bethesda, MD: National Association of School Psychologists.

Cohen, L., Dehaene, S., Chochon, F., Lehericy, S., & Naccoche, L. (2000). Language and calculation with the parietal lobe: A combined cognitive, anatomical, and fMRI study. *Neuropsychologia, 38,* 1426–1440.

Connolly, A. J. (2008). *KeyMath 3 diagnostic assessment*. Bloomington, MN: Pearson.

Coswell, S. F., Eagan, G. F., Code, C., Harasty, J., & Watson, J. D. (2000). The functional neuroanatomy of simple calculation and number repetition: A parametric PET activation study. *Neuroimage, 12,* 565–573.

Dehaene, S. (1997). *The number sense: How the mind creates mathematics.* Oxford, UK: Oxford University Press.

Dehaene, S. (2001). Precis of the number sense. *Mind and Language, 16,* 16–36.

Dehaene, S. (2003). The neural basis of the Weber-Fechner law: A logarithmic mental number line. *Trends in Cognitive Neuroscience, 7,* 145–147.

Dehaene, S., Piazza, M., Pinel, P., & Cohen, L. (2003). Three parietal circuits for number processing. *Cognitive Neuropsychology, 20,* 487–506.

Dehn, M. J. (2008). *Working memory and academic learning: Assessment and intervention.* New York: John Wiley & Sons.

Feifer, S. G., & DeFina, P. A. (2005). *The neuropsychology of mathematics disorders: Diagnosis and intervention.* Middletown, MD: School Neuropsych Press.

Flanagan, D. P., & Kaufman, A. S. (2004). *Essentials of WISC IV assessment.* New York: John Wiley & Sons.

Flanagan, D. P., Ortiz, S. O., & Alfonso, V. C. (2007). *Essentials of cross battery assessment* (2nd ed.). New York: John Wiley & Sons.

Fleishner, J. E. (1994). Diagnosis and assessment of mathematics learning disabilities. In G. R. Lyon (Ed.), *Frames of references for the assessment of learning disabilities* (pp. 441–458). Baltimore, MD: Paul H. Brookes.

Fletcher, J. M., Lyon, G. R., Fuchs, L. S., & Barnes, M. A. (2007). *Learning disabilities: From identification to intervention.* New York: Guilford.

Floyd, R. G., Evans, J. J., & McGrew, K. S. (2003). Relations between measures of Cattell-Horn-Carroll (CHC) cognitive abilities and mathematics achievement across the school-age years. *Psychology in the Schools, 40,* 155–171.

Geary, D. (1993). Mathematical difficulties: Cognitive, neuropsychological, and genetic components. *Psychological Bulletin, 114,* 345–362.

Geary, D. (1994). *Children's mathematical development: Research and practical applications.* Washington, DC: American Psychological Association.

Geary, D. (1999). *Mathematical disabilities: What we know and don't know.* LD Online. Retrieved December 10, 2009, from http://www.ldonline.org/article/5881?theme=print.

Geary, D. (2003). Learning disabilities in arithmetic: Problem solving differences and cognitive deficits. In H. L. Swanson, K. Harris, & S. Graham (Eds.), *Handbook of learning disabilities* (pp. 199–212) New York: Guilford.

Geary, D. (2004). Mathematics and learning disabilities. *Journal of Learning Disabilities, 37,* 4–15.

Geary, D. C., Hamson, C. O., & Hoard, M. K. (2000). Numerical and arithmetical cognition: A longitudinal study of process and concept deficits in children with learning disability. *Journal of Experimental Child Psychology, 77,* 236–263.

Geary, D. C., Hoard, M. K., & Hamson, C. O. (1999). Numerical and arithmetical cognition: Patterns of functions and deficits in children as risk for mathematical disability. *Journal of Experimental Child Psychology, 74,* 213–239.

Gerstmann, J. (1940). Syndrome of finger agnosia disorientation for right and left agraphia and acalculia. *Archives of Neurology and Psychiatry, 44*, 398–408.

Gitelman, D. R., (2003). Acalculia: A disorder of numerical cognition. In M. D'Esposito (Ed.), *Neurological foundations of cognitive neuroscience*. Cambridge, MA: MIT Press.

Gruber, O., Indefrey, P., Steinmetz, H., & Kleinschmidt, A. (2001). Dissociating neural correlates of cognitive components in mental calculation. *Cerebral Cortex, 11*, 350–359.

Hale, J. B., & Fiorello, C. A. (2004). *School neuropsychology: A practitioner's handbook.* New York: Guilford.

Hale, J. B., Fiorello, C. A., Dumont, R., Willis, J. O., Rackley, C., & Elliott, C. (2008). Differential ability scales, 2nd edition: (Neuro)Psychological predictors of math performance for typical children and children with math disabilities. *Psychology in the Schools, 45*, 838–858.

Hale, J., Fiorello, C., Kavanagh, J., Hoeppner, J., & Gaither, R. (2001). WISC-III predictors of academic achievement for children with learning disabilities: Are global and factor scores comparable? *School Psychology Quarterly, 16*, 31–55.

Hale, J. B., Fiorello, C. A., Miller, J. A., Wenrich, K., Teodori, A., & Henzel, J. N. (2008). WISC-IV interpretation for specific learning disabilities identification and intervention: A cognitive hypothesis testing approach. In A. Prifitera, D. H. Saklofske, & L. Weiss (Eds.), *WISC-IV clinical assessment and intervention* (2nd ed., pp. 109–171). New York: Elsevier.

Helland, T. (2007). Dyslexia at a behavioural and cognitive level. *Dyslexia, 13*, 25–41.

Hitch, G., & McAuley, E. (1991). Working memory in children with specific arithmetical learning difficulties. *British Journal of Psychology, 82*, 375–386.

Hutton, U. M. Z., & Towse, J. N. (2001). Short-term memory and working memory as indices of children's cognitive skills. *Memory, 9*, 383–394.

Individuals with Disabilities Education Improvement Act of 2004, Pub. L. No. 108–446.

Jordan, N., & Hanich, L. (2000). Mathematical thinking in second grade children with different forms of LD. *Journal of Learning Disabilities. 33*, 567–578.

Kaufman, A. S., & Kaufman, N. (2004a). *Kaufman assessment battery for children-II.* Circle Pines, MN: American Guidance Service.

Kaufman, A. S., & Kaufman, N. (2004b). *Kaufman test of educational achievement-II.* Circle Pines, MN: American Guidance Service.

Kaufman, A. S., Lichtenberger, E., Fletcher-Janzen, E., & Kaufman, N. (2005). *Essentials of KABC II assessment.* New York: John Wiley & Sons.

Keith, T. (1999). Effects of general and specific abilities on student achievement: Similarities and differences across ethnic groups. *School Psychology Quarterly, 14*, 239–262.

Kilpatrick, J., Swafford, J., & Findell, B. (2001). *Adding it up: Helping children learn mathematics.* National Research Council. (pp. 407–432). Washington, DC: The National Academies Press.

Lerew, C. D. (2005). Understanding and implementing neuropsychologically based arithmetic interventions. In R. C. D'Amato, E. Fletcher-Janzen, & C. R. Reynolds

(Eds.), *Handbook of school neuropsychology* (pp. 758–776). New York: John Wiley & Sons.

Lewis, C., Hitch, G. J., & Walker, P. (1994). The prevalence of specific arithmetic difficulties and specific reading difficulties in 9- to 10-year-old boys and girls. *Journal of Child Psychology and Psychiatry, 25*, 283–292.

Lichtenburger, E. O., & Smith, D. R. (2005). *Essentials of WIAT II and KTEA II assessment.* New York: John Wiley & Sons.

Lyytinen, H., Guttorm, T., Huttunen, T., Hämäläinen, J., Leppänen, P., & Vesterinen, M. (2005). Psychophysiology of developmental dyslexia: A review of findings including studies of children at risk for dyslexia. *Journal of Neurolinguistics, 18*, 167–195.

Marshall, R. M., Schafer, V. A., O'Donnell, L., Elliot, J., & Handwerk, M. L. (1999). Arithmetic disabilities and ADD subtypes: Implications for DSM IV. *Journal of Learning Disabilities, 22*, 239–247.

Mather, N., Wendling, B. J., & Woodcock, R. W. (2001). *Essentials of WJ III tests of achievement assessment.* New York: John Wiley & Sons.

Mazzocco, M. M. M. (2001). Math learning disability and math LD subtypes: Evidence from studies of Turner syndrome, fragile X syndrome, and neurofribromatosis type 1. *Journal of Learning Disabilities, 34*, 417–424.

McGrew, K. (n.d.). Institute for Applied Psychometrics [Electronic source]. Retrieved January 2009 from http://www.iapsych.com.

McGrew, K., & Flanagan, D. (1998). *The intelligence test desk reference (ITDR): Gf-Gc cross-battery assessment.* Boston: Allyn & Bacon

McGrew, K., Flanagan, D., Keith, T., & Vanderwood, M. (1997). Beyond g: The impact of Gf-Gc specific cognitive abilities research on the future use and interpretation of intelligence tests in the schools. *School Psychology Review, 26*, 189–210. Retrieved January 23, 2009, from PsycINFO database.

McGrew, K., & Hessler, G. (1995). The relationship between the WJ—R Gf-Gc cognitive clusters and mathematics achievement across the life-span. *Journal of Psychoeducational Assessment, 13*, 21–38.

Mercer, C., & Miller, S. (1992). Teaching students with learning problems in math to acquire understanding, and apply basic math facts. *Remedial and Special Education, 13*, 19–35, 61.

National Mathematics Advisory Panel. (2008). *Foundations for success: The final report of the National Mathematics Advisory Panel.* Washington, DC: U.S. Department of Education.

Osmon, D. C., Patrick, C., & Andresen, E. (2008). Learning disorders. In A. MacNeill Horton & D. Wedding (Eds.), *The neuropsychology handbook* (3rd ed.). New York: Springer Publishing.

Pennington, B. F. (2009). *Diagnosing learning disorders: A neuropsychological framework* (2nd ed.). New York: Guilford.

Rathvon, N. (2008). *Effective school interventions: Evidence-based strategies for improving student outcomes* (2nd ed.). New York: Guilford.

Rickhard, T. C., Romero, S. G., Basso, G., Wharton, C., Flitman, S., & Grafman, J. (2000). The calculating brain: An fMRI study. *Neuropsychologia, 38*, 325–335.

Rourke, B. (1989). *Nonverbal learning disabilities: The syndrome and the model*. New York: Guilford.

Rourke, B. (1993). Arithmetic disabilities, specific and otherwise: A neuropsychological perspective. *Journal of Learning Disabilities, 26,* 214–226.

Rourke, B. (1994). Neuropsychological assessment of children with learning disabilities. In G. R. Lyon (Ed.), *Frames of reference for the assessment of learning disabilities*. Baltimore, MD: Paul H. Brookes.

Shalev, R. S., Manor, O., Kerem, B., Ayali, M., Badichi, N., Friedlander, Y., & Gross-Tsur, V. (2001). Developmental dyscalculia is a familial learning disability. *Journal of Learning Disabilities, 34,* 59–65.

Shapiro, E. S. (2004). *Academic skills problems*. New York: Guilford.

Strauss, E., Sherman, E. M. S., & Spreen, O. (2006). *A compendium of neuropsychological tests: Administration, norms and commentary* (3rd ed.). New York: Oxford University Press.

Swanson, H. L., & Beebe-Frankenberger, M. (2004). The relationship between working memory and mathematical problem solving in children at risk and not at risk for serious math difficulties. *Journal of Educational Psychology, 96,* 471–491.

Wechsler, D. (2001). *Wechsler individual achievement test* (2nd ed.). San Antonio, TX: Harcourt Assessment.

Wechsler, D. (2003). *Wechsler intelligence scale for children* (4th ed.). San Antonio, TX: Harcourt Assessment.

Wilson, A. J., & Dehaene, S. (2007). Number sense and developmental dyscalculia. In D. Coch, G. Dawson, & K. Fischer (Eds.), *Human behavior, learning, and the developing brain: Atypical development* (pp. 212–238). New York: Guilford.

Woodcock, R. W., McGrew, K. S., & Mather, N. (2001a). *Woodcock-Johnson III tests of cognitive abilities*. Itasca, IL: Riverside Publishing.

Woodcock, R. W., McGrew, K. S., & Mather, N. (2001b). *Woodcock-Johnson III tests of achievement*. Itasca, IL: Riverside Publishing.

CHAPTER 22

Assessing and Intervening with Children with Speech and Language Disorders

MITTIE T. QUINN

The level of language development reached in pre-school age has, since the 1970s, been considered the most reliable predictor of reading acquisition. (Termine et al., 2007)

THREE AREAS OF speech and language impairments (SLIs) can cause a disruption in a child's education: (1) phonological awareness, (2) receptive language, and (3) expressive language. From a neurological point of view, this division is not very exact. Where does the breakdown occur? Is the child actually hearing the sounds? Can the child interpret the sounds? Are the neural networks integrating those sounds into relevant and meaningful units, i.e., words? All of these acts involve the reception of language. But perhaps the breakdown is in the output or production. Does the child make the necessary sounds to create words? Are those sounds sequenced accurately to make words? And are the words produced in an order that makes sense to the listener? In other words, is the child's expressive language intact? Through careful investigation of a child's neuropsychological profile, strengths and weaknesses can be matched with appropriate evidence-based interventions designed to improve particular speech or language skills.

The Individuals with Disabilities Act (IDEA, 2004) suggests that a specific learning disability (SLD) can be a disorder in one or more of the basic psychological processes involved in understanding or in using language. A child with a SLD may also be a child with speech or language impairments. The statute goes on to say that SLDs cannot be the result of visual, hearing, or motor disabilities; mental retardation; emotional disturbance; or environmental, cultural, or economic disadvantage. Yet many children whose situations include these exclusionary factors have problems with language processing. The quality and content of their language is often the focus of Individualized Education Plan (IEP) goals. The law is further complicated by the allowance that children ages 3 to 9 years may be determined to have developmental delays in communication development, among other areas.

The vague guidelines of IDEA as well as disagreement among professionals have resulted in "speech and language disorders" being a broad umbrella term that is called by many different names. D'Amato, Fletcher-Janzen, and Reynolds (2005) include a chapter on "Otitis Media and Central Auditory Processing Disorders (CAPD)" in their *Handbook of School Neuropsychology*. CAPD is often associated with language disorders. In this chapter, McCloskey acknowledges that there is disagreement about CAPD and "whether it even actually exists" (McCloskey, 2005, p. 493). The American Speech-Language-Hearing Association (ASHA) describes a speech disorder as "having difficulty with the production of sounds and words," and a language disorder as "having difficulty with understanding language (a receptive disorder) or sharing ideas (an expressive language disorder)" (ASHA, 2008). "Verbal Learning Disabilities" and "Specific Language Impairment" are other terms often used to characterize these disorders. The World Health Organization (WHO) offers the *International Classification of Diseases* (World Health Organization, 2008), which suggests six different subtypes of speech and language disorders. For ease of communication, the acronym SLI (Specific Language Impairment) will be used to refer to speech and language disorders for the remainder of this chapter.

The Diagnostic and Statistical Manual of Mental Disorders, 4th Edition (American Psychiatric Association, 1994) suggests that approximately 3 to 5 percent of the population has expressive language disorders and another 3 percent has "mixed" expressive-receptive language disorders. Tomblin et al. (1997) estimated that 7.4 percent of the kindergarten students in the United States met the criteria for SLI. This epidemiological study also suggested that previous findings of a greater prevalence of these disorders among minority ethnic and racial groups were explained by factors such as level of parent education and income.

The exact causes of SLI are unknown. They often coexist with other disorders. Sometimes clinicians categorize SLI by the similarity of features to those of individuals with aphasia and apraxia. Aphasias are language impairments that occur subsequent to brain injury (Carlson, 2007). Apraxia is a speech disorder related to oral motor movement and the production of speech sounds. From the study of these speech and language disorders and their related brain lesions, researchers have determined areas of the brain that relate to language production.

Broca's and Wernicke's are the best known among the aphasias. Individuals with Broca's aphasia may understand language, that is, have intact receptive language, but because of Broca's proximity to the motor cortex, production of language (expressive language) can be impaired. Problems with word articulation, sequencing of sentences that are grammatically correct (agrammatism), or word-finding (anomia) may all be present (Carlson, 2007). Wernicke's area, on the other hand, is located at some distance from the motor cortex such that the individual maintains his or her capacity to create sounds, but the comprehension of language information, or receptive language, is impaired. "Word salad" is a frequent characteristic of Wernicke's aphasia. This is a pattern of speaking where the words may be recognizable, but the content is unintelligible. Other aphasias affect slightly different neurocortical areas and result in the impairment of different aspects of speech and language. An excellent summary of these may be found in Miller's *Essentials of School Neuropsychological Assessment* (2007, p. 179). Terminology developed for describing symptoms of these disorders can be useful in communicating the characteristics of a child with speech or language disorder and in developing relevant interventions.

Brain imaging technology (e.g., fMRIs) allows us to "watch the brain work," and as a result we are making progress in unlocking the mysteries behind speech and language production. While the left hemisphere continues to be a primary focus of language activity for 90 percent of the population, multiple sites are involved in more complex speech and language acts. For example, prosody, or the intonation and cadence of language, appears to require the cognitive processes housed in the right hemisphere (Carlson, 2007). We also know that some students with SLI have temporal lobe processing deficits (Tallal, Merzenich, Miller, & Jenkins, 1998). Dronkers, Ogar, Willock, and Wilkins (2004) affirmed the role of the superior precentral gyrus of the insula (SPGI) in apraxias, finding that this area is always damaged in patients with apraxia.

Brain imaging in infants is also informing our knowledge about language development. We now know that infants as young as 2 months old show differential brain responses to familiar words and nonsense words (Radicevic, Vujovic, Jelicic, & Sovilj, 2008). In cases of normal development, children's vocabulary increases rapidly from this point forward. Mean length of utterance (MLU) is frequently used as an indicator of language development in research. Rice, Redmond, and Hoffman (2006) found that the MLU increases incrementally over time and is a reasonable predictor of successful language development. Low MLU reliably predicted language disorders at later ages. Age of onset is also a predictor of receptive and expressive language delays. Rescorla (2005) found that "late talkers" were at greater risk for developing language disorders and reading difficulties. Deficits continued to be identified in students at age 13.

Families with a history of language delays or reading disorders are more likely to have children who start talking late and who ultimately develop language disorders. Children with a combination of late talking and measurable receptive or expressive language deficits also have the greatest chance for developing significant deficiencies in reading comprehension (Boscolo, Ratner, & Rescorla, 2002).

NEUROCOGNITIVE CORRELATES OF SPEECH AND LANGUAGE DISORDERS

Speech and language perception, encoding, and production require complex interactions of multiple brain regions. Table 22.1 highlights relevant research of neurocognitive deficits found among individuals with SLI.

Table 22.1

Neuropsychological Deficits Associated with Speech and Language Disorders

Function	Deficits Reported	Brain Region Impacted
Sensory-Motor	Disturbances in the development of lateral preference (atypical or unstable establishment) are more likely to be associated with disordered language than stable left or right lateral preference (Escalante-Mead, Minshew, & Sweeney, 2003).	Immature lateralization; lack of hemispheric dominance.
	Correlation found between difficulties with midline crossing and language impairment (Bishop, 2005).	Immature lateralization; corpus callosum.
	Child with unintelligible speech at 2 years, developed normal language comprehension, but little improvement in intelligibility at age 5 (Le Normand, Vaivre-Douret, Payan, & Cohen, 2000).	Enlarged ventricles, incomplete myelinazation of corpus callosum, intact basal ganglia.
Attentional Processing	Correlation found between performance on Stroop-type task and severity of language comprehension in Wernicke's aphasia (Wiener, Connor, & Obler, 2004).	Wernicke's area—left temporal (planum temporale).
	Processing conflicting simultaneous verbal information, e.g. two people speak at once, leads to increase activity of anterior cingulate cortex (Rota et al., 2008).	Anterior cingulate cortex.

Table 22.1
Continued

Function	Deficits Reported	Brain Region Impacted
	Interaction between complex language comprehension and attention (Leech, Aydelott, Symons, Carnevale, & Dick, 2007).	Prefrontal cortex (PFC) and planum temporale.
Visual-Spatial Processing	Less-skilled language comprehenders made more non-specific eye movements when scanning pictures related to spoken sentences (Nation, Marshall, & Altman, 2003).	PFC/planum temporale/ occipital/insular cortex.
Phonological Processing	Phonological processing task led to right hemisphere activity in poor readers versus left hemisphere in good readers (Breier et al., 2003).	Temporoparietal.
Receptive Language	Latency age girls may demonstrate faster activation of auditory processing networks than boys of the same age (Nanova, Lyamova, Hadjigeorgieva, Kolev, & Yordanova, 2008).	Parietal regions.
	Activation of LSTG during receptive language activity in nonclinical population versus zero activity among persons w/autism. Variations were also found in the growth of this area between the two groups (Bigler et al., 2007).	Left superior temporal gyrus (LSTG) gray matter.
Expressive Language	Speech prosody mediated primarily in the right hemisphere (Gandour et al., 2004).	Right hemisphere.
Memory and Learning	SLI group poorer than controls for encoding, recognition, slower reaction times on high complexity verbal tasks. Also SLIs < Controls executive functioning (Weismer, Plante, Jones, & Tamblin, 2005).	Nonlinguistic networks activated (Prefrontal Cortex).
Executive Function	Executive functioning in dyslexics with receptive language deficits worse than non-language impaired dyslexics (Helland & Asbjoernsen, 2000).	PFC.
	Students with SLI slower reaction time for correct answers on sentence memory recall and recognition tasks. fMRI results revealed significant hypoactivation (Weismer et al., 2005).	Parietal regions and precentral sulcus during encoding; and in planum temporale during recognition tasks.

(continued)

Table 22.1

Continued

Function	Deficits Reported	Brain Region Impacted
Speed and Efficiency of Processing	Generalized slow processing of auditory and visual information among SLI students (Miller, Kail, Leonard, & Tomblin, 2001).	PFC & Prefrontal Motor Cortex.
Social-Emotional Functioning	Connection between receptive and expressive language skills and emotion understanding, emotional regulation and social skills (Fujiki, Brinton, & Clarke, 2002).	PFC & Left and Right hemisphere.
	Two-year-olds with expressive and receptive language delays were also rated as having symptoms of depression, withdrawal, and low social relatedness (Irwin, Carter, & Briggs-Gowan, 2002).	Basal ganglia, left hemisphere speech centers.
	Children with complex (receptive/expressive) language impairments were rated as having more marked social difficulties with peers (Botting & Conti-Ramsden, 2000).	Left and right hemisphere speech centers.

COMORBIDITY WITH OTHER CHILDHOOD DISORDERS AND LEARNING DISABILITIES

CHILDHOOD DISORDERS

Numerous other disorders have revealed comorbid language disorders. Many of these disorders are evident in very young children, a fact that underscores the importance of early diagnosis and intervention.

Congenital Disorders Numerous congenital disorders have concomitant speech and/or language deficits that are part of the constellation of symptoms associated with the disorder. Individuals with congenital hypothyroidism have been found to exhibit receptive and expressive language deficits, sometimes identified as late as adolescence (Laws & Bishop, 2004b; Rovet, 1999). One study of children born with congenital heart defects found no lingering cognitive deficits of significance, but language disorders persisted (Miatton, De Wolf, Francois, Thiery, & Vingerhoets, 2006). Language acquisition delays among individuals with Down syndrome are well known (Laws &

Bishop, 2004b). Numerous studies of children with Williams syndrome have compared the similarities and differences of their language skills to those of children with spectrum disorders (Nonverbal Learning Disabilities, Asperger's, Autism). While children with Williams syndrome may have pragmatic language deficits that are similar to those found among children with spectrum disorders, children with Williams syndrome are much more socially engaging (Klein-Tasman, Mervis, Lord, & Phillips, 2007; Laws & Bishop, 2004a).

Low Birth Weight (LBW) Diverse language impairments are often evident in children with LBW (Miller et al., 1995). Korkman et al. (2008) followed a cohort of very low birth weight (VLBW) infants for five years. They identified that those with neuromotor involvement exhibited a broad spectrum of neurocognitive deficits at 5 years. While many deficits were related to attention and executive functioning, some atypicality in language functioning was also identified.

Cleft Palate Scherer, Williams, and Proctor-Williams (2008) found that vocabulary and vocalization deficits continue years after cleft is closed among children born with this condition.

Otitis Media with Effusion (OME) Inflammation of the inner ear that accompanies OME can result in intermittent hearing problems. There is inconsistent evidence about any connection between intermittent hearing loss in young children and later speech and language deficits (Pettinger & Force, 2003; Winskel, 2006). However, current recommendations for clinical practice from the American Academy of Pediatrics (2004) reiterate the importance of identifying children who are at risk for the development of more serious language disorders based on medical, genetic, familial, and environmental risk factors.

ADHD Not all students with ADHD have language disorders; however, some do have comorbid SLI and should be screened for that potentiality (Jonsdottir, Bouma, Sergeant, & Scherder, 2006).

Spectrum Disorders (Asperger's Syndrome, Autism) Students with Spectrum Disorders exhibit significant difficulties on language tasks that require more abstract skills, such as language comprehension, pragmatics, and social cognition. Varying degrees of language impairment appear to be related to the severity of the disorder. Deficits are evident early in development (prior to age 2 years) (Bishop & Norbury, 2002; Luyster, Kadlec, Carter, & Tager-Flusberg, 2008).

Traumatic Brain Injury (TBI)   TBI can impact persons of all ages. Brain plasticity of young children (< 4 years) allows for other regions of the brain to assume functions that may be injured (e.g. Bates et al., 1997; Kempler, Van Lancker, Marchman, & Bates, 1999). However, subtle deficits may continue. In one study, children who sustained perinatal brain injuries scored significantly below the control group on measures of receptive and expressive language (Ballantyne, Spilkin, & Trauner, 2007). Students who had experienced seizures subsequent to the injuries were significantly more likely to be affected. Anderson, Catroppa, Morse, Haritou, and Rosenfeld (2001) monitored children who sustained mild head injuries between ages 3 and 7 years. Neurocognitive assessments were completed immediately following injury, six and thirty months later. No deficits in most cognitive processes were identified when compared to matched controls, but verbal fluency and memory for narrative were significantly impaired even after thirty months of healing.

The location of the injury can also make a major difference in the aspect of language that is impacted (Bates, et al., 1997). Children ages 1 to 4 years who experienced focal head injuries showed no delays in many areas of cognitive functioning; however, ten to seventeen months after injury, those with right-hemisphere injuries showed significantly more delays in word comprehension and the use of gestures that are usually observed with beginning language. Children with left-hemisphere lesions showed greater deficits in expressive vocabulary and grammar development and frontal lobe injuries led to less expansion of expressive vocabulary and grammar regardless of which hemisphere was damaged.

TBI that involves anoxia (loss of oxygen) may result in language deficits (Zabel, Slomine, Brady, & Christensen, 2005). Individuals involved in any accident that causes anoxia should have a comprehensive neuropsychological evaluation.

Seizure Disorders   Seizure disorders have also been related to SLI. Participants with Benign Rolandic Epilepsy, while successfully treated for seizure activity, were identified to have continuing memory and phonological awareness deficits (Northcott et al., 2007).

OTHER ILLNESSES/DISORDERS ASSOCIATED WITH POTENTIAL LANGUAGE IMPAIRMENTS
Some of these disorders are rare but can be accompanied by SLI.

- Bacterial Meningitis (Pentland, Anderson, & Wrennall, 2000)
- Selective Mutism (Gray, Jordan, Ziegler, & Livingston, 2002)
- Hydrocephalus (Vachha & Adams, 2003)

- Encephalitis (Benjamin et al., 2007)
- Uncontrolled Diabetes with hypoglycemia (Hannonen, Tupola, Ahonen, & Riikonen, 2003)
- Lupus (Skeel, Johnstone, Yangco, Walker, & Komatireddy, 2000)

LEARNING DISABILITIES

Verbal Learning Disabilities   Longitudinal studies have shown that students with speech and language deficits identified prior to age 7 years continue to demonstrate language deficits into later elementary school (Tomblin, Xuyang Zhang, Buckwalter, & O'Brien, 2003) and into teen and adult years. Often these deficits continue despite involvement in speech and language therapy (Conti-Ramsden, Simkin, Botting, & Knox, 2001).

Reading/Dyslexia   The relationship between early language development and reading has been well documented. Catts, Fey, Tomblin, and Zhang (2002) determined that approximately 50 percent of students identified in kindergarten with SLI met criterion for a reading disability in second and fourth grades as opposed to roughly 8 percent of the non-impaired control group. Students with non-specific language impairment (NSLI = language skills measured < 1 standard deviation (SD) below the mean AND nonverbal IQ < 1 SD below the mean) were at even greater risk at second and fourth grades (63 and 67 percent likelihood respectively). Termine et al. (2007) emphasize the warning that other cognitive impairments put students with language deficits at higher risk. They also found that many students may have in tact phonological skills, but delayed receptive and/or expressive language development puts them at greater risk for later difficulties. These authors encourage early screening to identify these students for targeted intervention.

Dyscalculia   Current understanding of math conceptual development suggests that children first learn about numbers as words. It is logical to suspect that children with SLIs often have difficulty mastering a sense of number. fMRI studies of children with developmental dyscalculia (DD) suggest that two-thirds have other conditions, such as language disorders. Parietal areas, also active in language activities, were found to be underactive in children with DD (von Aster & Shalev, 2007).

SCHOOL NEUROPSYCHOLOGICAL EVALUATION FOR SLI

Some school-based professionals work with teams that include a social worker who completes the developmental history of a student. In these cases, it will be critical to brief him or her about essential factors relevant to language development that should be investigated. Key characteristics relevant to Specific Language Impairment are highlighted here. The *BASC-2 Structured Developmental History* (Reynolds & Kamphaus, 2004a) or the *Neuropsychological Processing Concerns Checklist for School-Aged Children and Youth* (Miller & Lang, 2005, see Miller, 2007) assure comprehensive coverage of relevant information.

Developmental History

Primary Language   The history should include a careful consideration of the primary language of the student as well as his or her family. While SLI is found among all world languages, there are some language disorders, such as selective mutism, that may actually be a stage of second language acquisition and should not be considered as a disorder. Information about how long the student has been exposed to English, how long English has been spoken, the degree to which English is spoken at home, and the quality of speech in his or her primary language (e.g., do parents observe errors in the spoken primary language?) should all be collected. The highest level of education attained by parents has also been found to be more predictive of SLI than other parental characteristics (Gasquoine, 1999; Lyytinen et al., 2004).

Family History   A comprehensive history of mother's and father's health and developmental history is an important element given what we know about genetic loading for SLI. Parents may not know about their early speech development, but may be aware of academic difficulties. Students with a family history of dyslexia are three times more likely to exhibit phonological processing deficits than their same age counterparts with no history (Lyytinen, Eklund, & Lyytinen, 2005). Other parent health-related issues that should be explored include drug use during pregnancy. Drugs used to treat various medical conditions are known to pose neurological dangers to the unborn fetus (e.g., epilepsy drugs, Rovet et al., 1995). The serious impact of illegal drugs on fetal development—stimulant drugs (Dixon, Thal, Potrykus, Dickson, & Jacoby, 1997), cocaine (Bandstra, Vogel, Morrow, Xue, & Anthony, 2004), and alcohol (Korkman, Kettunen, & Autii-Ramo, 2003)—are well documented. Attention deficits, neurological disorders, developmental delays, learning disabilities, or psychiatric disorders in addition to SLIs have also been reported among extended family members of students with SLIs.

Birth and Early Development   Many childhood disorders may be traced to prenatal or perinatal insult. See previous section for comorbid perinatal issues to consider.

Medical History   Cardiovascular and respiratory system development, seizures or high fevers, head injuries and/or loss of consciousness, allergies, and certain medications have all been shown in some cases to have links to intermittent hearing or language problems.

School History   Most children with SLIs come to the attention of school professionals prior to kindergarten age. Preschool experience, kindergarten performance, teachers comments, and educational supports previously attempted should all be considered.

ANCILLARY ASSESSMENTS

Audiological Exam   An audiological evaluation is essential for students with suspected speech and language deficits. A simple "hearing screening" may not be sufficient. Bellis and Ferre (1999) report that four different aspects of audiological processing can be identified through a comprehensive audiological examination: (1) dichotic listening, (2) monaural low-redundancy speech task, (3) temporal patterning, and (4) binaural interaction tasks. Each is related to a different aspect of auditory processing.

Previous Testing Results   If speech and language concerns were noted in preschool, the child may have had previous testing completed by speech - language specialists, audiologists or ENTs, other psychologists, or medical professionals.

Classroom Observation   When observing the SLI child in the classroom, look for nonverbal responses to instructions (an indication of receptive language processing) as well as verbal interactions with teachers and classmates, and "self-talk" (expressive language). Listen carefully to the target child's articulation. It is unusual for students beyond kindergarten age to evidence misarticulations and this could be a symptom of phonological processing deficits. Observations and notes related to the child's speech acts should continue in the standardized testing setting because it provides additional evidence of the child's language functions.

STANDARDIZED TESTING

As presented in Table 22.1, speech and language impairments often coexist with many other neurocognitive deficits. While a particular referral question may relate to speech and language issues, there are numerous other systems that could exhibit concomitant deficits. Working through a school neuropsychological assessment model provides information needed to determine what systems are compromised. This section will highlight some of the newer assessments and ones that may be particularly useful. Miller (2007) includes a comprehensive listing of available assessments for school neuropsychologists and speech-language clinicians.

Bilingual students with SLI present unique challenges for assessment. Chapter 4 in this book offers suggestions for working with culturally and linguistically diverse populations. Professionals who are routinely involved in bilingual psychological or school neuropsychological assessments may wish to consult one of the many comprehensive texts available (e.g., Ardila & Ramos, 2007).

Sensory-Motor Functions   Sensory-motor functions and attention are the first areas assessed by school neuropsychologists. Students with SLI may have comorbiddeficits in these areas. Screening for auditory perception with the *Dean-Woodcock Sensory Motor Battery* (Dean & Woodcock, 2003) may reveal problems with auditory acuity or auditory attention. If a comprehensive audiological exam has not already been completed, a referral to an audiologist would be in order.

Attention   When assessing attention functions, the typical school neuropsychological assessment will consider five primary areas of attention: selective/focus, shifting, divided, sustained, and attentional capacity (Miller, 2007). When there is a question of language processing involvement, one must augment this section by assessing visual and auditory attention in order to differentiate attention deficits from SLI.

Visual Processing   Research has not found any particular correlations between speech and language processing and visual processing per se. However, speech and language deficits are often a piece of a larger constellation of neurodevelopmental disorders that may include visual processing deficits.

Language Processing   Given the primary areas of neurocognitive compromise related to Speech and Language Impairments (phonological awareness, receptive and expressive language), the language portion of the school neuropsychological evaluation will be of significant importance (Wing et al., 2007).

Phonological Processing.   Wood, Hill, Meyer, and Flowers (2005) suggest that phonological processing is one of four critical skills (the others being rapid naming, picture vocabulary, and word identification) that together give 85 to 90 percent accuracy in identifying those children at the bottom 15 percent of their classmates in reading skills. It is one of the earliest skill deficiencies that classroom teachers recognize in students with SLI. See Miller (2007, pp. 182–183) for a comprehensive listing of relevant assessments.

Receptive Language.   Picture vocabulary or listening comprehension tests are both typical assessments for evaluating receptive language. An advantage of the *Peabody Picture Vocabulary Test* (Dunn & Dunn, 2006) and the *Receptive One-Word* (Brownell, 2000a) is that both have Spanish language versions (Brownell, 2000b; Dunn, Lugo, Padilla, & Dunn, 1986).

Expressive Language.   The *Test of Auditory Processing Skills, 3rd edition* (TAPS3; Martin & Brownell, 2005) has an "Auditory Cohesion" cluster that assesses comprehension of factual information and inferential and idiomatic language in addition to sections for phonological processing and short-term memory. The NEPSY-II (Korkman, Kirk, & Kemp, 2007) includes several new subtests that aid in the differential diagnosis of language impairments, verbal learning disabilities, and autism spectrum disorders. Garratt and Kelly (2008) found that the original U.S. version of the NEPSY (Korkman, Kirk, & Kemp, 1998) was not sensitive to language impairments in bilingual students, and although attempts have been made with this new edition to improve cultural and linguistic sensitivity, the new edition should be used with caution for that population.

Memory and Learning   A variety of assessments are available that allow examiners to assess various aspects of memory functioning. A comparison of verbal and visual memory modalities will provide important information related to intervention options for students with SLI.

General Intellectual Ability   Speech and language disorders will have a direct impact on full-scale IQ scores. As a result, this score may not be a suitable estimate of the child's cognitive potential and as such should be interpreted with caution. Most researchers who study speech-language disorders utilize an estimate of nonverbal skills as a better indicator of intellectual ability for this population. The *Wechsler Non-Verbal Scale of Ability* (Wechsler & Naglieri, 2006) is a recent addition to the library of available assessments.

Executive Functioning and Cognitive Efficiency   The examiner should be alert for potential problems with fluency, processing speed, and emotional regulation. Emotional regulation is related to one's ability to verbalize the nature of a problem, conflict, or one's emotional state. Denham et al. (2003) have found correlations between language development and emotional "intelligence," defined by the child's ability to assign words to faces showing emotions, as early as 2 to 3 years old. This in turn has been identified as a critical foundational skill for emotional regulation (Blair, Denham, Kochan-off, & Whipple, 2004).

Social Emotional   No causal relationship between SLI and social-emotional diagnoses has been identified, but assessments should include a screening for more serious emotional difficulties. Some clinicians suggest that difficulties with language may lead to low self-esteem, which is a gateway to numerous emotional reactions or adjustments, and over prolonged periods of time could become a more entrenched personality disorder (Glozman, 2004). The *Draw A Person: Screening Procedure for Emotional Disturbance* (*DAP: SPED*) (Naglieri, McNeish, & Bardos, 1991) and a comprehensive behavior survey such as the *BASC2* (Reynolds & Kamphaus, 2004b) provide a good basis. Given the possible impact on self-concept, the *Piers-Harris Children's Self Concept Scale-2* (Piers, Harris, & Herzberg, 2002) might also be included.

Academic Achievement   A comprehensive assessment of achievement will identify how the language disorder impacts reading, writing and math and guide the development of recommendations and interventions that extend beyond those specifically related to speech and language.

EVIDENCE-BASED INTERVENTIONS FOR THE TREATMENT OF CHILDREN WITH SLI

As we learn more about the nature of language, undoubtedly our interventions will change to address that new knowledge. If, for example, we were to accept Chomsky (2000) and colleagues' theory of an innate "grammar," are there interventions that can change something that is innate? At the present time, our interventions flow from our current understanding of SLI: phonemic awareness, receptive and expressive language.

Cirrin and Gillam (2008) completed a review of intervention research looking for evidence-based practice (EBP) for SLI. They identified over 500 published studies (1985–2005) related to interventions for school-aged children with language disorders. Among these, only twenty-one met criteria for classification as EBP: those following an experimental research design, those with a control group for comparison, and those with a systematic plan for pre- and post treatment evaluations. Feifer and De Fina (2000) found similar challenges in identifying EBP for reading. In a survey of speech and language clinicians, Law, Campbell, Roulstone, Adams, and Boyle (2008) found that they used research-based assessments, but offered no consistency or logic in their choice of interventions. Reported interventions varied depending on the age of the child. Skills were emphasized for young children, and metacognitive strategies were used with older students.

EARLY ASSESSMENT AND INTERVENTION

The importance of early intervention has been reiterated throughout this chapter. Research is now finding that as early as age 18 to 33 months predictors of receptive and expressive language deficits associated with Asperger's syndrome (AS) are present, including the quality of infant gestures and joint attention (Luyster et al., 2008).

Lyytinen et al. (2001) found that a combination of family history of language deficits and receptive language delays place children at higher risk for later language deficiencies than their same-aged counterparts without those risk factors. Speech and language screenings, even in early intervention clinics that routinely assess articulation deficits, may identify children at risk for phonological processing, but often fail to identify those children with language processing deficits (Lyytinen et al., 2005). They recommend engaging at-risk preschoolers in games that will strengthen vocabulary development, verbal memory, and sound awareness and discrimination.

Smith, Landry, and Swank (2006) found that mothers who talked to their children and "scaffolded" appropriate language models, particularly between age 2 and 3 years, had children who were faster to develop age-appropriate expressive language. They also found that children whose mothers asked more questions and guided exploration with verbal prompts scored higher on assessments of executive functioning.

Nutrition, medical care, and parent education in addition to learning activities that emphasized language development, were incorporated into a program specifically for children with low birth weight (LBW) and from low-income families. Upon entering kindergarten, they met or exceeded age-level expectations for many areas of development, but notably for language skills (Ramey, Campbell, & Ramey, 1999).

Early intervention is critical in the treatment of SLI. Roulstone, Peters, Glogowska, and Enderby (2003) assessed the "wait-and-see" approach and found that two-thirds of the children who were identified with language deficits at 3.5 years were still eligible for speech and language services after one year of "monitoring."

PHONOLOGICAL AWARENESS

Children older than 4 years of age who evidence sound errors in their speech are likely to have phonological processing deficits. Jenkins and Bowen (1994) provide a hierarchical progression of phonological skills that develop before age 6 years that can be used to develop relevant interventions. Three areas of skill development associated with phonological processing include: rhyming, blending, and segmenting.

Rhyming   By age 4 to 5 most children recognize rhyming sounds/phonemes and enjoy rhyming words and games. This is the age where children begin to appreciate Mother Goose rhymes, poetry, simple songs that rhyme, and Dr. Seuss books. Fazio (1996) found that children with SLI typically have difficulty memorizing Mother Goose rhymes.

Activities that reinforce rhyming:

- Teach children skipping rhymes, thereby adding gross motor reinforcement to the auditory stimuli (Fazio, 1996)
- Hand motions may also reinforce the rhymes and improve retention (Fazio, 1996)
- Expose small children to word "families"—those words with matching phonemes, e.g., the "at" family of cat, rat, bat, mat, sat, etc. (Smiley & Goldstein 1998)

Blending   Most preschoolers can assemble phonemes into a word. For example, if the teacher/evaluator says "c-a-t," children over 4 to 5 years of age are able to identify the word "cat." Rehearsal of this skill would, as with the rhyming, introduce families of words that are similar phonemically, for example, words that start with "s" or end with "p."

Other possibilities for improving blending skills:

- Have students practice listening to words broken into their phonemic parts and identifying the word.
- Create a "game" that requires blending sound parts into whole words.

Segmenting   Preschool children are able to break words into syllables or into sounds. One might observe a preschool class clapping while words are spoken. Recognizing the "rhythm" in a word is a common activity in preschool classes. Other activities to develop this skill:

- Substitute jumping for clapping to each syllable of a word.
- Do an activity that reverses the blending game described above. Have students break words into their component parts.
- Ask students to repeat a word with one syllable or sound omitted (e.g., say "birthday" without day). Older students enjoy creating "pig Latin" words, which provides practice in segmenting and reordering sounds.

Computer Programs   Research of Tallal et al. (1998) found that various acoustically modified speech sounds stimulated neural pathways in temporal lobe speech centers. They reported significant improvements in phonological processing skills of students identified with SLI who were exposed to these sounds over a period of time. Fast ForWord (FFW; Scientific Learning Corporation, 2001) is a computer intervention program based on this research. Hayes, Warrier, Nicol, Zecker, and Kraus, (2003) found improved speech perception, language comprehension, and increased brainstem activity in areas associated with processing of auditory information after an eight-week training program using FFW. However, Cohen et al. (2005) reported no difference in the gains made among students with severe receptive and expressive language impairments who participated in the FFW training and those who received typical speech and language therapy group for the same amount of time.

Pihko et al. (2007) implemented a program that incorporated lessons like FFW, using natural speech rather than computer-generated sounds and implementing methods similar to those used by the Lindamood Bell reading program to teach students the oral motor correlates of basic phonemes (Lindamood Bell Phoneme Sequencing [LiPS], 1975). The results identified increased brain activity in the speech centers in both left and right hemispheres after the eight-week training.

Earobics (Wasowicz, 1997) is another commercially available computer program that includes lessons on phonological awareness and language development as well as beginning reading and writing skills. Pokorni, Worthington, and Jamison (2004) compared Fast ForWord, Earobics, and LiPS with three matched groups of students identified with language and reading deficits. Results revealed improvements in phonological awareness for the Earobics and LiPS groups, but not in Fast ForWord. None of the trainings led to significant improvement on language or reading measures.

RECEPTIVE LANGUAGE

Cirrin and Gillam (2008) found several language EBPs that were effective in terms of vocabulary development. Their common feature was collaboration with the classroom teacher to develop target vocabulary that was integrated into class lessons. Integrating vocabulary into small group discussion opportunities also led to improved language performance.

Research related to the importance of reading to children is extensive. In addition to modeling accurate phonological patterns, reading and rereading stories (Neuman, 1995):

- Offers opportunities to hear language models.
- Exposes children to semantics and vocabulary, syntax, morphology, and pragmatic language.
- Provides content that invites questions, speculations, and character development.
- Provides topics of conversation for parents and their children at a level of understanding consistent with the child's age.

Owens and Robinson (1997) provide a list of young children's books in tandem with related language development goals.

Some students with receptive/expressive language deficits may find it difficult to categorize ideas. Son, Smith, and Goldstone (2008) identified that teaching students simple exemplars led to an expanding understanding of abstract concepts. However, attempting to teach them by introducing abstract information directly led to increased confusion and poorer performance.

Other suggestions that have led to improvements in language skills include talking to your toddler using vocabulary you might use with an older child (Weizman & Snow, 2001), not criticizing speech or language patterns (Bohannon III & Stanowicz, 1988), and responding to your child with expansions or slight restructuring of what they say (Chouinard & Clark, 2003).

Suggestions from school neuropsychological case studies:

- Work with speech/language therapist on listening comprehension strategies to enhance understanding of classroom lectures and social pragmatic conversation skills (McVay, 2007).
- Provide guided notes where the main content is provided and student fills in key words to enhance listening comprehension (McVay, 2007).
- Present all types of verbal information accompanied by visual stimuli that clearly illustrate the concepts being taught. Examples are pictures, charts, graphs, and semantic maps. (Vogel, 2007).
- Provide as much time as necessary for the student to respond to questions—"wait" time (Hiestand, 2007).
- Ensure that verbal directions are understood. Make eye contact, tell the student what to do, pause, and ask him or her to repeat back the instructions that have been given. Repeat as often as possible (Seeley-MacLeod, 2007).

EXPRESSIVE LANGUAGE

Early intervention is related to improved expressive language as well as overall language improvement. Numerous studies have considered the impact of positive verbal and emotional interactions and good models of language experience, such as reading, small group discussions, and one-on-one conversations in preschool settings, home, and childcare environments. These language experiences increased performance in expressive language, particularly among at-risk children (McGowan et al., 2008).

Gillum, Camarata, Nelson, and Camarata (2003) compared "analog" treatment, a mode of instruction where the clinician presents words or sentences and has the student repeat and imitate the words, with more naturalistic methods that emphasize conversation ("conversational recast treatment"). They found that students with poor performance on speech imitation (e.g., sentence repetition tasks) were poor candidates for analog treatment that relies on extensive repetition. Conversation recast was significantly more efficient in improving students' performances on expressive language measures. Gillum et al. suggest that it may be particularly important to review a student's learning profile to determine which method would be most efficient.

Alternative therapies that stimulate more nonverbal aspects of communication, such as art (Elkis-Abuhoff, 2008) and music (Schlaug, Marchina, & Norton, 2008), have also been used effectively to encourage increase self-expression and verbal expressiveness.

Suggestions from school neuropsychological case studies:

- Use specific mnemonic techniques to assist with development of vocabulary (Vogel, 2007).
- Provide experiential learning activities, such as trips, science activities, or role-playing events, to facilitate active involvement and focus on tasks (Vogel, 2007).
- Provide frequent repetition and review to develop automaticity with learned skills in order to reduce frustration (Vogel, 2007).

Pragmatic Language

Problems with language comprehension, social language, and pragmatics have been identified in some ADHD students although expressive language may be in tact. In one study (Bruce, Thernlund, and Nettelbladt, 2006), the majority of the students with ADHD (average age 11 years) demonstrated problems with aspects of pragmatic language that are often found in children with Asperger's syndrome (AS). Many interventions used with that population would be appropriate for students with pragmatic language deficits who do not exhibit other spectrum features.

Suggestions from school neuropsychological case studies:

- Provide small group oral expressive language therapy that focuses on social pragmatics skills, including initiating greeting and conversation, demonstrating nonverbal interest, learning verbal and non-verbal strategies to maintain conversations, and ending conversations (McVay, 2007).
- When doing small group work/projects in the classroom, pair the student with SLI with a student with good social pragmatic skills to model and facilitate conversational interaction (McVay, 2007).

INTERVENTION IMPLEMENTATION: CROSS-CULTURAL CONSIDERATIONS

When developing speech and language interventions for children from non-majority cultures or nonmajority language groups, alternative methods of service delivery may be advisable. Some cultural traditions discourage individualistic or competitive approaches to instruction. In these situations, involving a triadic or multiparty group, siblings, or friends may lead to more language gains. Some may respond more positively to highly structured tasks for language training as opposed to the conversational style encouraged in some research. Collaboration with a cultural consultant may also be beneficial to help identify other factors for consideration. Wing et al., (2007) apply these ideas to a preschool intervention but suggest that they are applicable for any age.

SUMMARY

Speech and language skills form the basis from which all other academic skills arise. The critical role that they play in origins of reading, writing, and even math cannot be overlooked. With interventions introduced early in the lives of children destined to have a speech or language disorder, many problems that arise from their difficulty communicating might be averted. Waiting until a child fails or monitoring his or her progress for a year has been shown to be ineffective. Identifying phonological processing deficits, and receptive, and expressive language delays before they interfere with reading is an important goal for school neuropsychologists working collaboratively with speech and language pathologists.

REFERENCES

American Academy of Pediatrics. (2004). Clinical practice guide: Otitis media with effusion. *Pediatrics, 113,* 1412–1429.

American Psychiatric Association. (1994). *Diagnostic and statistical manual of mental disorders* (4th ed.). Washington, DC: Author.

American Speech, Language, and Hearing Association. (2008). *Speech and language disorders and diseases.* Retrieved October 11, 2008, from http://www.asha.org/public/speech/disorders

Anderson, V., Catroppa, C., Morse, S., Haritou, F., & Rosenfeld, J. (2001). Outcome from mild head injury in young children: A prospective study. *Journal of Clinical and Experimental Neuropsychology* [Electronic Version], *23,* 705–718.

Ardila, A., & Ramos, E. (Eds.). (2007). *Speech and language disorders in bilinguals.* New York: Nova Science Publishers.

Ballantyne, A. O., Spilkin, A. M., & Trauner, D. A. (2007). Language outcome after perinatal stroke: Does side matter? *Child Neuropsychology, 13,* 494–509.

Bandstra, E. S., Vogel, A. L., Morrow, C. E., Xue, L., & Anthony, J. C. (2004). Severity of prenatal cocaine exposure and child language functioning through age seven years: A longitudinal latent growth curve analysis. *Substance Use and Misuse, 39,* 25–59.

Bates, E., Thal, D., Trauner, D., Fenson, J., Aram, D., Eisele, J., et al. (1997). From first words to grammar in children with focal brain injury. *Developmental Neuropsychology* [Electronic Version], *13,* 275–343.

Bellis, T. J., & Ferre, J. M. (1999). Multidimensional approach to the differential diagnosis of central auditory processing disorders in children. *Journal of the American Academy of Audiology, 10,* 319.

Benjamin, C., Anderson, V., Pinczower, R., Leventer, R., Richardson, M., & Nash, M. (2007). Pre- and post-encephalitic neuropsychological profile of a 7-year-old girl. *Neuropsychological Rehabilitation, 17,* 528–550.

Bigler, E. D., Mortensen, S., Neeley, E. S., Ozonoff, S., Krasny, L., Johnson, M., et al. (2007). Superior temporal gyrus, language function, and autism. *Developmental Neuropsychology, 31,* 217–238.

Bishop, D. V. M. (2005). Handedness and specific language impairment: A study of 6-year-old twins. *Developmental Psychobiology, 46,* 362–369.

Bishop, D. V. M., & Norbury, C. F. (2002). Exploring the borderlands of autistic disorder and specific language impairment: A study using standardized diagnostic instruments. *Journal of Child Psychology and Psychiatry* [Electronic Version], *43,* 917–929.

Blair, K. A., Denham, S. A., Kochanoff, A., & Whipple, B. (2004). Playing it cool: Temperament, emotion regulation, and social behavior in preschoolers. *Journal of School Psychology, 42,* 419–443.

Bohannon, III, J. N., & Stanowicz, L. (1988). The issue of negative evidence: Adult responses to children's language errors. *Developmental Psychology, 24,* 683–689.

Boscolo, B., Ratner, N. B., & Rescorla, L. (2002). Fluency of school-aged children with a history of specific expressive language impairment: An exploratory study. *American Journal of Speech-Language Pathology* [Electronic Version], *11,* 41.

Botting, N., & Conti-Ramsden, G. (2000). Social and behavioural difficulties in children with language impairment. *Child Language Teaching and Therapy, 16,* 105–120.

Breier, J. I., Simos, P. G., Fletcher, J. M., Castillo, E. M., Zhang, W., & Papanicolaou, A. C. (2003). Abnormal activation of temporoparietal language areas during phonetic analysis in children with dyslexia. *Neuropsychology, 17,* 610–621.

Brownell, R. (2000a). *Receptive one-word picture vocabulary test.* Novato, CA: Academic Therapy Publications.

Brownell, R. (2000b). *Receptive one-word picture vocabulary test: Spanish bilingual edition.* Novato, CA: Academic Therapy Publications.

Bruce, B., Thernlund, G., & Nettelbladt, U. (2006). ADHD and language impairment. *European Child and Adolescent Psychiatry, 15,* 52–60.

Carlson, N. R. (2007). *Physiology of behavior* (9th ed.). New York: Pearson Education.

Catts, H. W., Fey, M. E., Tomblin, J. B., & Zhang, X. (2002). A longitudinal investigation of reading outcomes in children with language impairments. *Journal of Speech, Language and Hearing Research, 45,* 1142.

Chomsky, N. (2000). *New horizons in the study of language and mind*. Cambridge, UK: Cambridge University Press.

Chouinard, M. M., & Clark, E. V. (2003). Adult reformulations of child errors as negative evidence. *Journal of Child Language, 30*, 637–669.

Cirrin, F. M., & Gillam, R. B. (2008). Language intervention practices for school-age children with spoken language disorders: A systematic review. *Language, Speech, and Hearing Services in Schools, 39*, S110–S137.

Cohen, W., Hodson, A., O'Hare, A., Boyle, J., Durrani, T., McCartney, E., et al. (2005). Effects of computer-based intervention through acoustically modified speech (Fast ForWord) in severe mixed receptive-expressive language impairment: Outcomes from a randomized controlled trial. *Journal of Speech, Language and Hearing Research, 48*, 715–729.

Conti-Ramsden, G., Simkin, Z., Botting, N., & Knox, E. (2001). Follow-up of children attending infant language units: Outcomes at 11 years of age. *International Journal of Language and Communication Disorders, 36*, 207–219.

D'Amato, R. C., Fletcher-Janzen, E., & Reynolds, C. R. (Eds.). (2005). *Handbook of school neuropsychology*. Hoboken, NJ: John Wiley & Sons.

Dean, R. S., & Woodcock, R. W. (2003). *Dean-Woodcock neuropsychological battery*. Itasca, IL: Riverside Publishing.

Denham, S., Blair, K., DeMulder, E., Levitas, J., Sawyer, K., Auerbach, M., et al. (2003). Preschool emotional competence: Pathway to social competence? *Child Development, 74*, 238–256.

Dixon, S., Thal, D., Potrykus, J., Dickson, T. B., & Jacoby, J. (1997). Early language development in children with prenatal exposure to stimulant drugs. *Developmental Neuropsychology, 13*, 371–396.

Dronkers, N. F., Ogar, J., Willock, S., & Wilkins, D. P. (2004). Confirming the role of the insula in coordinating complex but not simple articulatory movements. *Brain and Language, 91*, 23–24.

Dunn, L. M., & Dunn, L. M. (2006). *Peabody picture vocabulary test* (4th ed.) (PPVT-4). Minneapolis, MN: Pearson Assessments.

Dunn, L. M., Lugo, D. E., Padilla, E. R., & Dunn, L. M. (1986). *Test de Vocabulario en Imagenes Peabody*. Minneapolis, MN: Pearson Assessments.

Elkis-Abuhoff, D. L. (2008). Art therapy applied to an adolescent with Asperger's syndrome. *Arts in Psychotherapy, 35*, 262–270.

Escalante-Mead, R., Minshew, N., & Sweeney, J. (2003). Abnormal brain lateralization in high-functioning autism. *Journal of Autism and Developmental Disorders, 33*, 539–544.

Fazio, B. (1996). Serial memory in children with specific language impairment. Examining specific content areas for assessment and intervention. *Topics in Language Disorders, 17*, 58–71.

Feifer, S. G., & De Fina, P. A. (2000). *The neuropsychology of reading disorders: Diagnosis and intervention*. Middletown, MD: School Neuropsych Press.

Fujiki, M., Brinton, B., & Clarke, D. (2002). Emotion regulation in children with specific language impairment. *Language, Speech, and Hearing Services in Schools, 33*, 102–111.

Gandour, J., Tong, Y., Wong, D., Talavage, T., Dzemidzic, M., Xu, Y., et al. (2004). Hemispheric roles in the perception of speech prosody. *NeuroImage, 23,* 344–357.

Garratt, L. C., & Kelly, T. P. (2008). To what extent does bilingualism affect children's performance on the NEPSY? *Child Neuropsychology, 14,* 71–81.

Gasquoine, P. G. (1999). Variables moderating cultural and ethnic differences in neuropsychological assessment: The case of Hispanic Americans. *Clinical Neuropsychologist, 13,* 376–384.

Gillum, H., Camarata, S., Nelson, K. E., & Camarata, M. N. (2003). A comparison of naturalistic and analog treatment effects in children with expressive language disorder and poor preintervention imitation skills. *Journal of Positive Behavior Interventions, 5,* 171.

Glozman, J. M. (2004). *Communication disorders and personality.* New York: Kluwer Academic/Plenum Publishers.

Gray, R. M., Jordan, C. M., Ziegler, R. S., & Livingston, R. B. (2002). Two sets of twins with selective mutism: Neuropsychological findings. *Child Neuropsychology, 8,* 41.

Hannonen, R., Tupola, S., Ahonen, T., & Riikonen, R. (2003). Neurocognitive functioning in children with type-1 diabetes with and without episodes of severe hypoglycaemia *Developmental Medicine and Child Neurology, 45,* 262–270.

Hayes, E. A., Warrier, C. M., Nicol, T. G., Zecker, S. G., & Kraus, N. (2003). Neural plasticity following auditory training in children with learning problems. *Clinical Neurophysiology, 114,* 673–684.

Helland, T., & Asbjoernsen, A. (2000). Executive functions in dyslexia. *Child Neuropsychology, 6,* 37–48.

Hiestand, J. (2007). *A school neuropsychological case study.* Unpublished paper presented at school neuropsychology post-graduate certification program (Philadelphia, PA site). Hickory Creek, TX: KIDS.

Individuals with Disabilities Education Improvement Act of 2004. (PL No. 108–446, 20 USC 1400).

Irwin, J. R., Carter, A. S., & Briggs-Gowan, M. J. (2002). The social-emotional development of "late-talking" toddlers. *Journal of the American Academy of Child and Adolescent Psychiatry, 41,* 1324.

Jenkins, R., & Bowen, L. (1994). Facilitating development of preliterate children's phonological abilities. *Topics in Language Disorders, 14,* 26–39.

Jonsdottir, S., Bouma, A., Sergeant, J. A., & Scherder, E. J. A. (2006). Relationships between neuropsychological measures of executive function and behavioral measures of ADHD symptoms and comorbid behavior. *Archives of Clinical Neuropsychology, 21,* 383–394.

Kempler, D., Van Lancker, D., Marchman, V., & Bates, E. (1999). Idiom comprehension in children and adults with unilateral brain damage. *Developmental Neuropsychology, 15,* 327–349.

Klein-Tasman, B. P., Mervis, C. B., Lord, C., & Phillips, K. D. (2007). Sociocommunicative deficits in young children with Williams syndrome: Performance on the autism diagnostic observation schedule. *Child Neuropsychology, 13,* 444–467.

Korkman, M., Kettunen, S., & Autii-Ramo, I. (2003). Neurocognitive impairment in early adolescence following prenatal alcohol exposure of varying duration. *Child Neuropsychology, 9,* 117.

Korkman, M., Kirk, U., & Kemp, S. (1998). *NEPSY: A developmental neuropsychological assessment.* San Antonio, TX: The Psychological Corporation.

Korkman, M., Kirk, U., & Kemp, S. (2007). *NEPSY-II: A developmental neuropsychological assessment.* San Antonio, TX: The Psychological Corporation.

Korkman, M., Mikkola, K., Ritari, N., Tommiska, V., Salokorpi, T., Haataja, L., et al. (2008). Neurocognitive test profiles of extremely low birth weight five-year-old children differ according to neuromotor status. *Developmental Neuropsychology, 33,* 637–655.

Law, J., Campbell, C., Roulstone, S., Adams, C., & Boyle, J. (2008). Mapping practice onto theory: The speech and language practitioner's construction of receptive language impairment. *International Journal of Language and Communication Disorders, 43,* 245–263.

Laws, G., & Bishop, D. V. M. (2004a). Pragmatic language impairment and social deficits in Williams syndrome: A comparison with Down's syndrome and specific language impairment. *International Journal of Language and Communication Disorders, 39,* 45–64.

Laws, G., & Bishop, D. V. M. (2004b). Verbal deficits in Down's syndrome and specific language impairment: A comparison. *International Journal of Language and Communication Disorders, 39,* 423–451.

Le Normand, M. T., Vaivre-Douret, L., Payan, C., & Cohen, H. (2000). Neuromotor development and language processing in developmental dyspraxia: A follow-up case study. *Journal of Clinical and Experimental Neuropsychology* [Electronic Version], *22,* 408–418.

Lindamood Bell Phoneme Sequencing (LiPS). (1975). San Luis Obispo, CA: Gander Publishing.

Luyster, R., Kadlec, M., Carter, A., & Tager-Flusberg, H. (2008). Language assessment and development in toddlers with autism spectrum disorders. *Journal of Autism and Developmental Disorders, 38,* 1426–1438.

Lyytinen, H., Ahonen, T., Eklund, K., Guttorm, T., Kulju, P., Laakso, M. L., et al. (2004). Early development of children at familial risk for dyslexia: A follow-up from birth to school age. *Dyslexia, 10,* 146–178.

Lyytinen, H., Ahonen, T., Eklund, K., Guttorm, T. K., Laakso, M.-L., Leinonen, S., et al. (2001). Developmental pathways of children with and without familial risk for dyslexia during the first years of life. *Developmental Neuropsychology, 20,* 535–554.

Lyytinen, P., Eklund, K., & Lyytinen, H. (2005). Language development and literacy skills in late-talking toddlers with and without familial risk for dyslexia. *Annals of Dyslexia, 55,* 166–192.

Martin, N. A., & Brownell, R. (2005). *Test of auditory processing skills* (3rd ed.) (TAPS-3). Novato, CA: Academic Therapy Publications.

McCloskey, D. M. (2005). Providing neuropsychological services to learners with Otitis Media and Central Auditory Processing Disorders. In R. C. D'Amato,

E. Fletcher-Janzen, & C. R. Reynolds (Eds.), *Handbook of school neuropsychology* (pp. 487–510). Hoboken, NJ: John Wiley & Sons, Inc.

McGowan, M., Smith, L., Noria, C., Culpepper, C., Langhinrichsen-Rohling, J., Borkowski, J., et al. (2008). Intervening with at-risk mothers: Supporting infant language development. *Child and Adolescent Social Work Journal, 25,* 245–254.

McVay, B. (2007). *A school neuropsychological case study.* Unpublished paper presented at school neuropsychology post-graduate certification program (Philadelphia, PA site). Hickory Creek, TX: KIDS.

Miatton, M., De Wolf, D., Francois, K., Thiery, E., & Vingerhoets, G. (2006). Neuro-cognitive consequences of surgically corrected congenital heart defects: A review. *Neuropsychology Review, 16,* 65–85.

Miller, C. A., Kail, R., Leonard, L. B., & Tomblin, J. B. (2001). Speed of processing in children with specific language impairment. *Journal of Speech, Language and Hearing Research, 44,* 416.

Miller, C. L., Landry, S. H., Smith, K. E., Wildin, S. R., Anderson, A. E., & Swank, P. R. (1995). Developmental change in the neuropsychological functioning of very low birth weight infants. *Child Neuropsychology, 1,* 224–236.

Miller, D. C. (2007). *Essentials of school neuropsychological assessment.* Hoboken, NJ: John Wiley & Sons.

Miller, D. C., & Lang, M. J. (2005). *Neuropsychological processing concerns checklist for children and adolescents.* Hickory Creek, TX: Kids.

Naglieri, J. A., McNeish, T. J., & Bardos, A. N. (1991). *Draw A Person: Screening procedure for Emotional Disturbance* (DAP:SPED). Austin, TX: Pro-Ed.

Nanova, P., Lyamova, L., Hadjigeorgieva, M., Kolev, V., & Yordanova, J. (2008). Gender-specific development of auditory information processing in children: An ERP study. *Clinical Neurophysiology, 119,* 1992–2003.

Nation, K., Marshall, C. M., & Altmann, G. T. M. (2003). Investigating individual differences in children's real-time sentence comprehension using language-mediated eye movements. *Journal of Experimental Child Psychology, 86,* 314–330.

Neuman, S. B. (1995). Reading together: A community-supported parent tutoring. *Reading Teacher, 49,* 120.

Northcott, E., Connolly, A., Berroya, A., McIntyre, J., Christie, J., Taylor, A., et al. (2007). Memory and phonological awareness in children with Benign Rolandic Epilepsy compared to a matched control group. *Epilepsy Research, 75,* 57–62.

Owens, R. E., & Robinson, L. A. (1997). Once upon a time: Use of children's literature in the preschool classroom. *Topics in Language Disorders, 17,* 19–48.

Pentland, L. M., Anderson, V. A., & Wrennall, J. A. (2000). The implications of childhood bacterial meningitis for language development. *Child Neuropsychology, 6,* 87.

Pettinger, T., & Force, R. W. (2003). Tubes for otitis media do not improve developmental outcomes. *Journal of Family Practice, 52,* 939–940.

Piers, E. V., Harris, D. B., & Herzberg, D. S. (2002). *Piers-Harris children's self-concept scale* (2nd ed.). Los Angeles: Western Psychological Services.

Pihko, E., Mickos, A., Kujala, T., Pihlgren, A., Westman, M., Alku, P., et al. (2007). Group intervention changes brain activity in bilingual language-impaired children. *Cerebral Cortex, 17,* 849–858.

Pokorni, J. L., Worthington, C. K., & Jamison, P. J. (2004). Phonological awareness intervention: Comparison of Fast ForWord, Earobics, and LiPS. *Journal of Educational Research, 97*, 147–157.

Radicevic, Z., Vujovic, M., Jelicic, L., & Sovilj, M. (2008). Comparative findings of voice and speech: Language processing at an early ontogenetic age in quantitative EEG mapping. *Experimental Brain Research, 184*, 529–532.

Ramey, C. T., Campbell, F. A., & Ramey, S. L. (1999). Early intervention: Successful pathways to improving intellectual development. *Developmental Neuropsychology, 16*, 385–392.

Rescorla, L. (2005). Age 13 language and reading outcomes in late-talking toddlers. *Journal of Speech, Language and Hearing Research, 48*, 459–472.

Reynolds, C. R., & Kamphaus, R. W. (2004a). *BASC-2 structured developmental history*. Minneapolis, MN: Pearson Assessments.

Reynolds, C. R., & Kamphaus, R. W. (2004b). *Behavior assessment system for children* (2nd ed.). Minneapolis, MN: Pearson Assessments.

Rice, M. L., Redmond, S. M., & Hoffman, L. (2006). Mean length of utterance in children with specific language impairment and in younger control children shows concurrent validity and stable and parallel growth trajectories. *Journal of Speech, Language and Hearing Research, 49*, 793–808.

Rota, G., Veit, R., Nardo, D., Weiskopf, N., Birbaumer, N., & Dogil, G. (2008). Processing of inconsistent emotional information: An fMRI study. *Experimental Brain Research, 186*, 401–407.

Roulstone, S., Peters, T. J., Glogowska, M., & Enderby, P. (2003). A 12-month follow-up of preschool children investigating the natural history of speech and language delay. *Child: Care, Health and Development, 29*, 245.

Rovet, J., Cole, S., Nulman, I., Scolnik, D., Altmann, D., & Koren, G. (1995). Effects of maternal epilepsy on children's neurodevelopment. *Child Neuropsychology, 1*, 150–157.

Rovet, J. F. (1999). Long-term neuropsychological sequelae of early-treated congenital hypothyroidism: Effects in adolescence. *Acta Paediatrica, 88*, 88–95.

Scherer, N. J., Williams, A. L., & Proctor-Williams, K. (2008). Early and later vocalization skills in children with and without cleft palate. *International Journal of Pediatric Otorhinolaryngology, 72*, 827–840.

Schlaug, G., Marchina, S., & Norton, A. (2008). From singing to speaking: Why singing may lead to recovery of expressive language function in patients with Broca's aphasia. *Music Perception, 25*, 315–323.

Scientific Learning Corporation. (2001). *Fast ForWord—Language* (Version 2.01). Oakland, CA: Scientific Learning Corporation.

Seeley-MacLeod, A. (2007). *A school neuropsychological case study*. Unpublished paper presented at school neuropsychology post-graduate certification program (Philadelphia, PA site). Hickory Creek, TX: KIDS.

Skeel, R. L., Johnstone, B., Yangco, D. T., Walker, S. E., & Komatireddy, G. (2000). Neuropsychological deficit profiles in systemic lupus erythematosus. *Applied Neuropsychology, 7*, 96–101.

Smiley, L. R., & Goldstein, P. A. (1998). *Language delays and disorders: From research to practice*. San Diego: Singular.

Smith, K. E., Landry, S. H., & Swank, P. R. (2006). The role of early maternal responsiveness in supporting school-aged cognitive development for children who vary in birth status. *Pediatrics, 117*, 1608–1617.

Son, J. Y., Smith, L. B., & Goldstone, R. L. (2008). Simplicity and generalization: Short-cutting abstraction in children's object categorizations. *Cognition, 108*, 626–638.

Tallal, P., Merzenich, M., Miller, S., & Jenkins, W. (1998). Language learning impairment: Integrating research and remediation. *Scandinavian Journal of Psychology, 39*, 197–199.

Termine, C., Stella, G., Capsoni, C., Rosso, E., Binda, A., Pirola, A., et al. (2007). Neuropsychological profile of pre-schoolers with metaphonological difficulties: Results from a non-clinical sample. *Child: Care, Health and Development, 33*, 703–712.

Tomblin, J. B., Records, N. L., Buckwalter, P., Zhang, X., Smith, E., & O'Brien, M. (1997). Prevalence of specific language impairment in kindergarten children. *Journal of Speech, Language and Hearing Research, 40*, 1245–1260.

Tomblin, J. B., Xuyang Zhang, P., Buckwalter, M., & O'Brien, J. M. (2003). The stability of primary language disorders: Four years after kindergarten diagnosis. *Journal of Speech, Language and Hearing Research, 46*, 1283–1296.

Vachha, B., & Adams, R. (2003). Language differences in young children with mye-lomeningocele and shunted hydrocephalus. *Pediatric Neurosurgery, 39*, 184–189.

Vogel, M. (2007). *A school neuropsychological case study*. Unpublished paper presented at school neuropsychology post-graduate certification program (Philadelphia, PA site). Hickory Creek, TX: KIDS.

Von Aster, M., & Shalev, R. (2007). Number development and developmental dyscalculia. *Developmental Medicine and Child Neurology, 49*, 868–873.

Wasowicz, J. (1997). *Earobics Pro*. Evanston, IL: Cognitive Concepts.

Wechsler, D., & Naglieri, J. A. (2006). *Wechsler nonverbal scale of ability*. Minneapolis, MN: Pearson Assessments.

Weismer, S. E., Plante, E., Jones, M., & Tamblin, J. B. (2005). A functional magnetic resonance imaging investigation of verbal working memory in adolescents with specific language impairment. *Journal of Speech, Language and Hearing Research* [Electronic Version], *48*, 405–425.

Weizman, Z. O., & Snow, C. E. (2001). Lexical input as related to children's vocabulary acquisition: Effects of sophisticated exposure. *Developmental Psychology, 37*, 265.

Wiener, D., Connor, L. T., & Obler, L. (2004). Inhibition and auditory comprehension in Wernicke's aphasia. *Aphasiology, 18*, 599–609.

Wing, C., Kohnert, K., Pham, G., Cordero, K. N., Ebert, K. D., Kan, P. F., et al. (2007). Culturally consistent treatment for late talkers. *Communication Disorders Quarterly, 29*, 20–27.

Winskel, H. (2006). The effects of an early history of otitis media on children's language and literacy skill development. *British Journal of Educational Psychology, 76*, 727–744.

Wood, F. B., Hill, D. F., Meyer, M. S., & Flowers, D. L. (2005). Predictive assessment of reading. *Annals of Dyslexia* [Electronic Version], *55*, 193–216.

World Health Organization. (2008, September 24). *International classification of diseases* (ICD). Retrieved October 10, 2008, from http://www.who.int/classifications/apps/icd/icd10online/index.htm?gf80.htm+.

Zabel, T. A., Slomine, B., Brady, K., & Christensen, J. (2005). Neuropsychological profile following suicide attempt by hanging: Two adolescent case reports. *Child Neuropsychology*, *11*, 373–388.

CHAPTER 23

Assessing and Intervening with Children with Nonverbal Learning Disabilities

JED YALOF and MARIE C. MCGRATH

BEGINNING WITH JOHNSON and Myklebust's (1967) writings about children with learning problems in the areas of nonverbal processing and social perception, the term "nonverbal learning disability" (NLD) has become embedded within the fabric of educational, speech-language, occupational therapy, mental health, and medical lexicon and literature. A recent (August 13, 2008) search of *PsycARTICLES*, *PsycINFO*, and *PsycBOOKS* databases alone yielded a robust 565 entries for the key terms "nonverbal" and "learning disabilities," the majority of which reflect the growth of NLD in the past twelve years. Thus, NLD is clearly a hot topic. This chapter focuses on best practice guidelines for assessment and evidence-based intervention for NLD.

The NLD literature has been influenced heavily by the work of Rourke (1985, 1989, 1995), whose early research on distinctions between phonological processing and nonverbal learning disabilities gave rise to the syndrome deficit pattern that characterizes NLD. Rourke (1989) proposed a three-tiered model of NLD in which disturbances to the white matter tracts of the right hemisphere result in a particular syndrome that captures various diagnostic groups with varying degrees of concordance with Rourke's conception of prototypical NLD deficits (and assets). The right hemisphere is essential for appreciating NLD deficits because of its role in processing novel and heteromodal information (Goldberg & Costa, 1981), tactile-kinesthetic, visual-perceptual and motor functions, and nonverbal interpersonal cues, each of which help define the NLD profile. In Rourke's model, foundational deficits in tactile and visual perception, complex motor abilities, and novel problem-solving tasks lead to secondary deficits in attention and exploration and to tertiary deficits in memory and concept formation. Rourke also notes verbal deficits accompanying NLD that include speech prosody and language pragmatics. Tsatsanis and Rourke (1995) define the NLD syndrome on three levels ranging from disorders meeting almost all (e.g., Asperger syndrome) or many (e.g., multiple sclerosis in its early to middle stages) of the neuropsychological assets and deficits reflective of NLD.

Others have made substantive contributions to NLD classification. Palombo (2001, 2006), whose main focus has been on the integration of NLD cognition and social-emotional needs with disorders of self (e.g., self-cohesion, self-narrative) within a clinical-psychotherapeutic framework, has also noted NLD phenotypic variability and offered a different type of classification system (2006) highlighting four NLD subtypes organized around deficits in nonverbal perception and inferencing. Subtype I comprises individuals with core deficits in processing ". . . complex and nonlinguistic perceptual tasks . . ." who also develop social problems (p. 128). Subtype II comprises individuals who meet subtype I criteria and also have ". . . neuropsychological deficits in the areas of *attention and executive function* (italics in original, p. 131). Subtype III comprises individuals who meet subtype I criteria ". . . and have *social cognition impairments* (italics in original) that manifest in reciprocal social interactions, social communication, and emotional functioning . . ." (p. 134). Subtype IV comprises individuals who meet criteria for subtype II and have the ". . . same *social cognition impairments* (italics in original) as those described in subtype III" (p. 139). Hale and Fiorello (2004) suggested the possibility of two types of NLD associated with either the frontal (i.e., executive-novel problem solving) or posterior (visual-spatial holistic problem solving) right hemisphere. Pennington (1991) differentiated learning disability as a subset of learning disorders and cautioned against the direct correlation between right hemisphere and social-cognition deficits.

Despite the general consensus around descriptive features and hemispheric differences, NLD is not recognized as a distinct classification entity by such major nomenclatures as the *International Classification of Diseases* (ICD-10; World Health Organization, 1993), *Diagnostic and Statistical Manual of Mental Disorders* (4th ed., text revision; [DSM-IV-TR]; American Psychiatric Association, 2000), and Individuals with Disabilities Education Improvement Act (IDEIA: P.L. 108–446, 2004). Only the recent *Psychodynamic Diagnostic Manual* (PDM; PDM Task Force, 2006), however, identifies NLD as a specific diagnostic entity within the learning disability classifications. The PDM states:

> Children with nonverbal learning disabilities have a complex set of neuro-cognitive strengths and weaknesses: Strengths in rote verbal memory, in reading decoding, and in spelling; weaknesses in tactile and visual perception

and attention, concept formation, reading comprehension of complex materials, problem solving, and in dealing with novel materials. They tend to have problems in math and science, and they may show a pattern of socio-emotional difficulties involving the reception and expression of modulated affects and of nonverbal modes of communication. They typically have poor handwriting and may be deficient in arithmetic skills. Their reading comprehension is not on a par with their verbal skills; although they are good readers, they have great difficulty with art assignments. They also have problems with attention, novel materials, and new situations. (p. 279)

NLD ASSETS AND LIABILITIES

Miller (2007) provided a school neuropsychological model for categorizing expected assets and liabilities that guide the school neuropsychological evaluation. Miller's model focused on domain-specific expectations that guide the synthesis of data, and can be applied to NLD in the following way.

SENSORY-MOTOR DEFICITS

Miller (2007) noted that primary sensory-motor deficits underlie higher-level neuropsychological disturbances. The primary sensory areas and their associated cortical regions that are typically evaluated in a school neuropsychological assessment are the auditory/temporal lobe, the visual/occipital lobe, and the tactile-kinesthetic/parietal lobe. Olfaction and gustatory senses are the other two primary sensory areas. In the area of motor functioning, the premotor cortex is important for acquiring and implementing complex motor movements, whereas the primary motor cortex regulates motor movement, and the cerebellum is involved with motor coordination (Miller, 2007). Rourke (1995) identified tactile perception, visual perception, complex motor movements, and new learning as primary NLD deficit areas. Wodrich and Schmitt (2006) also noted that tactile and motor impairments, including delay in acquisition of motor skills, are "... hallmark deficits of NLD" (p. 97). Expected NLD findings might include contralateral (left side) sensory deficits and motor deficits; for example, relative impairment when asked to identify numbers drawn on the fingertips of the left hand (i.e., finger agnosia); relative left side motor weakness on a measure of motor strength (i.e., hypotonia); and motor clumsiness. Rote learning, simple motor skills, and auditory perception are preserved, although Keller, Tillery, and McFadden (2006) observed that NLD behaviors (e.g., deficits in reading comprehension and inference making, poor handwriting, internalizing problems) may co-occur with the tolerance-fading memory subtype of auditory processing disorder, suggesting that auditory-perceptual deficits are not the exclusive domain of individuals with language-based learning disorders.

ATTENTIONAL PROCESSING DEFICITS

Attention is processed through auditory, visual, and tactile modalities. Mirsky, Anthony, Duncan, Ahearn, and Kellam (1991) factor-analyzed attention tasks and identified four primary attention subcomponents with associated cortical and subcortical substrates: (a) encoding, which involved the temporal lobe; (b) sustaining, which involved the rostral-midbrain areas; (c) focus-executing, which involved superior temporal, parietal, and corpus striatum areas reticular activating system; and (d) shifting set, which involved the dorsolateral prefrontal cortex. Miller (2007) provided a brief but informative summary of studies on attention and augments Mirsky et al.'s (1991) findings with the constructs of divided attention and attention capacity. Rourke (1995) placed tactile and visual attention as areas of secondary NLD neuropsychological deficit and noted that auditory-verbal attention remained intact.

VISUAL-SPATIAL PROCESSING DEFICITS

Miller (2007) summarized literature and isolates several subskills in the area of visual-spatial processing. Some of these skills can be understood as parts of other neuropsychological systems, such as visual attention as part of the attention system, visual-motor integration as part of sensory-motor processing system, visual-motor planning as part of the executive system, and visual-spatial memory as part of memory and learning. Other visual-spatial processing skills include visual perception, visual-perceptual organization, visual perceptual reasoning, and visual scanning/tracking. The neuroanatomy of visual-spatial processing involves the visual cortex lobe and two major pathways: (a) the superior longitudinal fasciculus, which runs from the visual cortex to the parietal lobe, a pathway known as the "dorsal stream," and is specialized for object identification (i.e., location); and (b) the inferior longitudinal fasciculus, known as the "ventral stream," which runs from the visual cortex to inferior temporal lobe and is specialized for object perception (i.e., recognition). Visual-spatial processing deficits include deductive and inferential spatial reasoning, orthographic perception of shapes, visual search, constructional tasks that involve copying or building, and spatial orientation. Rourke (1995) described compromised visual-spatial-organizational abilities as one of the primary NLD deficits that affect exploratory behavior and supports NLD overreliance on verbal-linguistic skills for communication and learning. Forrest (2004) speculated that visual-perceptual deficits for locating objects in three-dimensional space might be related to the difficulty in gauging appropriate physical distance noted while observing individuals with NLD characteristics relate to other people.

LANGUAGE DEFICITS

Cortical regions that are important for language include Broca's area, in the frontal lobe, for expressive speech; Wernicke's area, in the posterior temporal lobe, for receptive language and speech comprehension; and the arcuate fasciculus, a fibrous band that connects Broca's and Wernicke's regions. Verbal-auditory skills represent an asset for individuals identified with NLD (Rourke, 1995) who tend to have strong language skills without expressive or receptive deficits but whose language prosody, semantics, and pragmatics, each of which are affected by the right hemisphere, are identified as neuropsychological deficits. The language of individuals with NLD tends to be rote, pedantic, and lacking the emotional nuancing and receptivity to the feeling states of others that characterize speech as a facilitator of interpersonal exchange. Rourke's (1995, p. 13) hierarchical model describes how underlying deficits in reasoning influence the way in which NLD individuals use language. Rourke stated: "The deficiencies in content and pragmatics are viewed as direct results of the difficulties in concept formation and other higher-order cognitive skills."

MEMORY AND LEARNING DEFICITS

Miller (2007, p. 198) cited research that provides an overview of basic neuropsychological processes involved in memory and learning. He described learning as the process of acquiring new information, and memory as " . . . the persistence of learning that can be assessed at a later time." The hippocampus, thalamus, and amygdala are involved in new learning. Memory involves encoding, storing, and retrieving information at a later time. The construct of memory includes several components. Immediate memory refers to information in conscious awareness. Working memory involves performing mental operations on this information and operates under an executive control. Verbal-auditory information is held in working memory by a phonological loop, whereas visual spatial information is under the direction of a visual-spatial sketchpad. Damage to the right occipital-parietal region results in greater compromise to the visual-spatial system compared to the phonological loop. Long-term memory includes factual and biographical information (i.e., declarative memory) and unconscious retrieval systems (i.e., procedural memory) for memories that have become automatized, cognitive (e.g., write left to right), and motoric (e.g., throwing a ball) skills. Retrieval from long-term storage is under the direction of the prefrontal cortex. NLD assets include auditory-verbal learning and memory, whereas deficits are likely to emerge on tasks that involve visual and visual-verbal learning, visual-spatial working memory, and long-term recall of visual information that includes associative learning, learning over repeated trials, and visual recognition. Learning and memory involving tactile-kinesthetic information is also a presumed weakness compared to auditory verbal learning and memory. Rourke (1995) identified tactile and visual memory as tertiary neuropsychological deficits. Liddell and Rasmussen (2005) identified visual memory to be poorer than verbal memory in conjunction with NLD, and also to be a specific NLD deficit on an immediate memory for faces test, which was linked to right hemisphere processing.

EXECUTIVE FUNCTION DEFICITS

Miller (2007) summarized terms and behaviors associated with executive functions. Executive functioning is associated with developing alternative solutions and strategic decision making, response inhibition, self-monitoring, motor programming, response fluency and sequencing, selective and focused attention, retrieval, and the ability to modify behavioral set in response to feedback. Miller provided a review of the five cortical-subcortical circuits that are involved in the executive system: (a) skeletal, (b) oculomotor, (c) dorso-lateral, (d) orbitofrontal, and (e) anterior cingulate. With respect to NLD, the first two circuits, respectively, involve regulation of motor movement and visual scanning and visual search strategies (Hale & Fiorello, 2004). Miller (2007) noted, however, that school neuropsychologists have a primary interest in the latter three circuits because of their role in behavior regulation and metacognition. The dorsolateral circuit is involved in such tasks as design fluency, visual-spatial search, and application of constructional strategies. The orbitofrontal cortex synthesizes emotion with response. The anterior cingulate is engaged when task requirements include selective attention, focused attention, and response inhibition. Rourke (1995) identified concept formation and problem solving as tertiary NLD deficits. Deficiencies in concept formation and problem solving are presumed to reflect underlying compromise in environmental manipulation and exploration using tactile, motor, and visual modalities, and limited ability to deal with novel situations. These are areas that are weaker in individuals identified as NLD. When these areas are weak, the ability to generate new ideas and solutions is at greater risk for impairment.

SPEED AND EFFICIENCY OF PROCESSING DEFICITS

Miller (2007) described speed and efficiency of cognitive processing in relation to processing speed and short-term memory, and notes the importance of efficient processing for success on complex academic tasks. Myelin, the white matter that covers axons, is important for information processing. Rourke (1995) identified disturbances to the white matter tracts of the right hemisphere as foundational to the deficit pattern of NLD. NLD assets are in the auditory-verbal realm, including sustained auditory attention, reading speed for simple words, and rapid oral word association. Performance deficits are expected on measures of visual attention, tracking and matching, decision-making speed, verbal-visual naming, color naming, and writing speed.

General Cognitive Deficits

Miller (2007) reviewed the general cognitive reasoning skills associated with standardized tests of intelligence. In keeping with the profile for NLD, deficits in the nonverbal areas of perceptual and quantitative reasoning are expected, relative to verbal reasoning. Perspective-taking, or "theory of mind" (Griffin et al., 2006) deficits, in which there is difficulty ascribing intentional states, especially second-order intention, or ". . . attributing knowledge about knowledge and the ability to detect deception" (p. 214), have been identified in relation to damage to the right hemisphere.

Academic Deficits

Miller (2007) discussed various academic skills that reflect the aforementioned processing and reasoning weaknesses, and Rourke (1995) highlighted academic deficits that are associated clinically with NLD. Feifer and De Fina (2000, 2002, 2005) and Hale and Fiorello (2004) provided thorough reviews of academic skills in relation to underlying neuropsychological processes.

Individuals with NLD characteristics share particular deficit patterns in the following areas. In the area of reading comprehension, individuals with NLD characteristics might have difficulty with reading assignments that require understanding people and motives; this difficulty would be secondary to the limited ability to generate the intuitive "gist" insights fostered by the right hemisphere that allow the reader to identify with the thoughts and feelings of protagonists. In the area of written expression, those with NLD might have early problems with orthographic identification of letters, spelling, graphomotor, tactile, and constructional deficits that affect legibility and accuracy of copy. In math and related subjects (e.g., physics), deficit areas of concern include spatial representation of abstract nonverbal concepts, visual learning, comprehension of graphs and diagrams, quantitative analysis, magnitude comparison, and misalignment of numbers during calculations. Forrest (2004) noted that NLD may be associated with mechanical math deficits that involving visual-perceptual errors more so than verbal reasoning errors. Rourke noted that problems with hypothesis testing and concept formation compromise performance in the more complex subject areas.

SOCIAL-EMOTIONAL DEFICITS

Rourke (1995) categorized five deficit areas that capture the social-emotional aspects of NLD. These areas are (a) social judgment secondary to problems with reasoning and concept formation, (b) face recognition and emotional expression secondary to problems with visual-organizational skill, (c) poor prosody and high verbal production that do not promote positive social feedback, (d) problems with emotional expression secondary to tactile and psychomotor deficits, and (e) problems with hypothesis testing secondary to poor adaptation to novelty.

Table 23.1 presents a sampling of NLD assets and liabilities.

Table 23.1
NLD Assets and Liabilities

Domain	Sampling of NLD Assets	Sampling of NLD Liabilities
Sensory-Motor	Auditory-Verbal	Tactile-Kinesthetic; Tactile Defensiveness; Motor Sequencing, Coordination, and Strength
Attention	Sustained Auditory; Rote Recall; Verbal	Sustained Visual; Divided Attention
Visual-Spatial	None	Visual Perception; Scanning-Tracking; Constructional
Language	Verbal Comprehension; Phonological; Expressive, Receptive, and Repetitive	Prosody; Semantics; Content; Tolerance-Fading Auditory Perceptual
Memory and Learning	Auditory-Verbal; Learning and Memory for Rote Information	Visual Immediate, Working; Delayed, and Recognition; Visual-Verbal Learning; Tactile-Kinesthetic Learning and Memory; Location Memory
Executive	Verbal Problem Solving	Hypothesis Generation and Flexible Problem Solving; Self-Monitoring; Behavior Regulation; Integration of Emotion with Context
Speed and Efficiency of Cognitive Processing	Verbal-Auditory; Word Retrieval; Rapid Verbal Word Association	Visual Tracking and Matching; Verbal-Visual Naming; Color Naming; Writing Speed
General Cognitive	Verbal Reasoning	Perceptual and Quantitative Reasoning; Theory of Mind
Academic Achievement	Literal Comprehension; Decoding; Verbal Arithmetic; Spelling	Mechanical Arithmetic; Science; Writing; Gist Reading Comprehension
Social-Emotional	General Knowledge; Verbal Skills	Language Pragmatics; Nonverbal Cues and Behavior; Social Judgment

COMORBIDITY OF NLD WITH OTHER CONDITIONS AND DISORDERS

As previously noted, the diagnostic and/or eligibility determination taxonomies (most notably, the DSM-IV-TR and IDEIA 2004) most frequently used by school psychologists and practitioners in related areas do not contain explicit diagnostic criteria for NLD. Therefore, individuals meeting criteria for identification with NLD using diagnostic criteria (i.e., the PDM), or existing theoretical frameworks, such as those described by Rourke or Palombo, may either receive alternative diagnoses characterized by NLD's core deficits (e.g., autism spectrum disorders, specific learning disabilities) or simply go undiagnosed. This lack of diagnostic consistency makes it difficult to examine the extent to which NLD co-occurs with other disorders or disabilities. Despite these difficulties, a number of recent studies have examined the comorbidity of a variety of high- and low-incidence conditions with NLD.

In a review of the NLD comorbidity literature, Sundheim and Voeller (2004) noted that individuals meeting diagnostic criteria for NLD frequently meet diagnostic criteria for conditions such as ADHD, anxiety disorders, and major depression. High rates of comorbidity between NLD and ADHD have been found in several studies (e.g., Gross-Tsur, Shalev, Manor, & Amir, 1995; Voeller, 1986). Cleaver and Whitman (1998) found that in a hospitalized sample of adolescents and young adults (n = 484), two-thirds of participants with NLD met diagnostic criteria for a depressive disorder, while only one-third of participants with reading disabilities demonstrated symptoms of depression. Similarly, Tsatsanis, Fuerst, and Rourke (1997) argued that the specific cognitive processing patterns seen in individuals with NLD, including organizational and novel reasoning difficulties, make individuals with NLD more susceptible to internalizing disorders. However, in a more recent study, Yu, Buka, McCormick, Fitzmaurice, and Indurkhya (2006) found that children with NLD were significantly less likely than individuals with verbal learning disabilities (i.e., disabilities in reading and writing) to exhibit externalizing behavior problems and somewhat (although not significantly) less likely to exhibit internalizing behavior problems, as rated by parents. Thus, it appears that further research is necessary to more clearly elucidate the relationship between internalizing disorders and NLD.

A number of studies have examined whether patterns of cognitive, motor, and socio-emotional deficits associated with various genetic disorders can be accounted for by NLD models. Don, Schellenberg, and Rourke (1999) found that children with Williams syndrome (WS) also tend to exhibit a pattern of cognitive strengths and deficits similar to that found in NLD, although overall level of cognitive performance tends to be lower in individuals diagnosed with WS. Further, the authors stated that the relative strengths in musical skill often seen in individuals with WS could represent a manifestation of the relative strengths in auditory processing often seen with NLD. Other studies have found linkages between subtypes of neurofibromatosis (also known as von Recklinghausen's disease) and NLD (e.g., Cutting, Clements, Lightman, Yerby-Hammack, & Denckla, 2004). Ryan, Crews, Cowen, Goering, and Barth (1998) reported the case of a girl with triple X syndrome (i.e., the presence of an extra X chromosome) who demonstrated a pattern of cognitive skills consistent with right-hemisphere impairment, although prior studies had suggested that triple X syndrome is characterized by impairment in verbal reasoning and language use; this case suggests that, while NLD-related traits may not be characteristic of triple X syndrome, they may co-occur with this genetic condition.

Swillen et al. (1999) found that children diagnosed with velo-cardio-facial syndrome (VCFS; also known as Shprintzen syndrome), a disorder involving a genetic deletion in chromosome 22q11, tend to demonstrate many traits characteristic of the NLD profile, including relatively strong verbal language, text decoding, and spelling skills; difficulties with arithmetic; visual-motor, and psychomotor weaknesses; poor visual attention and memory; and difficulty processing novel material. In a study comparing VCFS-linked NLD and idiopathic NLD, Antshel and Khan (1998) found that children with idiopathic NLD were significantly more likely to have relatives with ADHD, substance abuse disorders, and bipolar disorders than children with VCFS. In an attempt to further investigate the relationship between bipolar disorder and NLD, McDonough-Ryan et al. (2002) examined whether the children of individuals diagnosed with bipolar disorder exhibit patterns of cognitive of difficulties characteristic of NLD. They found that these children tended to demonstrate some difficulty with standardized visual-spatial and reasoning tasks; however, they did not demonstrate more significant difficulties with arithmetic than with text decoding and spelling tasks. These studies suggest a link between the two disorders; however, the precise nature of that link remains unclear.

Other researchers have investigated whether NLD symptoms can be caused by nongenetic medical conditions and/or treatments for those conditions. In a case study examining the cognitive skills of identical twins, one of whom had been diagnosed with periventricular leukomalacia (a condition involving white matter necrosis, increased ventricular size, and abnormal myelin development), Woods, Weinborn, Ball, Tiller-Nevin, and Pickett (2000) found that both twins demonstrated strong verbal reasoning and verbal memory skills. However, the twin who had been diagnosed with periventricular leukomalacia demonstrated NLD-linked impairments not exhibited by his twin, including motor impairments, difficulty with novel visual reasoning tasks, organizational difficulties, mild social isolation, and some emotional lability. Buono et al. (1998) examined the utility of NLD as a framework for understanding the cognitive sequelae of brain tumor treatment; specifically, they investigated whether white matter damage caused by radiation treatment leads to patterns of functioning consistent with an NLD diagnosis. Their sample consisted of 123 children who had previously been treated for brain tumors; approximately one-third ($n = 42$) of the sample demonstrated identifiable deficits in mathematical ability, while sixteen participants demonstrated reading deficits. The children with identified mathematical deficits also tended to demonstrate more significant visual-spatial and visual memory deficits than those with identified reading disorders, as well as lower (although not significantly so) adaptive ratings. As a result, Buono et al. noted that some brain tumor survivors seem to "show a phenotypic resemblance to children with NLD" (p. 154). A subsequent study by Carey, Barakat, Foley, Gyato, and Phillips (2001) also found that children who had been treated for brain tumors demonstrated relative weaknesses on cognitive tasks involving visual-spatial and visual reasoning skills. Carey et al. noted that the parents of participants in their study described their children as demonstrating social skills deficits, although the children themselves did not report significant social or emotional concerns. While no baseline psychoeducational data were reported for the participants in either of these studies, the consistencies in cognitive impairment seen across the studies seem to suggest that the NLD syndrome can be acquired, as well as genetically determined.

SCHOOL NEUROPSYCHOLOGICAL ASSESSMENT OF NLD

School neuropsychological assessment of NLD involves comprehensive evaluation of the core areas outlined by Miller (2007) as well as personality and social-emotional functioning that also impacts NLD psychosocial adjustment. The assessment is directed toward qualification of the aforementioned NLD assets and liabilities and toward a classification based upon a synthesis of multiple data points. Information is gathered, for example, from records, developmental-familial history, observation, and interviews. Interviewing involves the student, parent(s) or guardian(s), teachers, and other professionals who work with the student, including mental health practitioners, speech-language, and/or occupational therapists. Other contributors include pediatricians, psychiatrists, and/or neurologists whose input might have been sought for medication evaluation and for co-varying rule-outs that include pervasive developmental, anxiety, obsessive-compulsive, and specific learning disorders. Identifying any previous trials in response to interventions (Hale, 2008) and mapping changes in functioning over time is important because serial assessments can track the development and balance of the NLD asset-deficit profile. For older clients requesting evaluation for work or educational accommodations in which NLD is a potential rule-out, ecologically sensitive feedback can be sought from employers and others who observe and monitor the client's daily performance. However, because NLD is a developmentally based disability in which most initial and follow-up assessments are conducted during formative school years, the assessment approach recommended below conforms to a school neuropsychology model.

Early detection of NLD is challenging because of its covariance with other diagnoses and because symptoms may not be easy to isolate or may be in full ascension until such time that sensory-motor, cognitive, and social-emotional demands intensify. Cornoldi, Venneri, Marconato, Molin, and Montinari (2003) presented a visuospatial screening measure that has sensitivity and specificity for early identification of NLD characteristics. Miller (2007) offered a comprehensive review of tests and measures from which the school neuropsychologist can particularize the NLD assessment in the areas of sensory-motor functioning, attention, visual-spatial processing, language, memory and learning, executive functions, processing speed and efficiency, general cognitive factors, and academic achievement. Yalof and Abraham (2006) presented a sampling of tests and measures that provide both rating and thematic understanding of emotional disturbances that affect school-age children. Selection of particular instrumentation depends on the setting (e.g., public school, private school, private practice, outpatient clinic) and resources (e.g., tests/measures, time, access to resources available to the school psychologist). In the school setting, other members of school-based multidisciplinary teams are likely to directly participate in the assessment process; for example, occupational and/or physical therapists may evaluate visual-motor and psychomotor functioning, while speech and language therapists may be involved in assessing NLD-related language issues such as prosody, semantics, and pragmatic language use. The assessment should target a clear referral question with measures that are selected carefully in order to maximize comprehensiveness and to reduce excessive testing time. However, assessment of NLD is time-consuming because of the complex nature of problems, the need to qualify sensory-motor, cognitive, and social-emotional assets and deficits, the need for differential diagnostic/classification considerations, and the necessity for refinement of recommendations and interventions (Yalof, 2006).

NLD INTERVENTION

ELIGIBILITY DETERMINATION

As with all school-based special education eligibility determinations, the decision whether to identify a student with NLD as eligible for special education services must be made using the "two-pronged test": Does the student meet eligibility criteria for one or more of IDEIA 2004's disability categories, and does he or she require specially designed instruction? There is some ambiguity regarding the most appropriate eligibility category to choose when identifying students with NLD, since it is not included in the IDEIA regulations, either as its own eligibility category or among the eight specific learning disability (SLD) subtypes (i.e., oral expression; listening comprehension; written expression; basic reading skill; reading fluency skills; reading comprehension; mathematics calculation; and mathematics reasoning). The Analysis of Comments and Changes section of IDEIA 2004 specifically addressed the issue of inclusion of individuals with NLD under the SLD category as follows:

> Children with many types of disabilities or disorders may also have a specific learning disability. It is not practical or feasible to include all the different disabilities that are often associated with a specific learning disability. Therefore, we decline to add these specific disorders or disabilities to the definition of specific learning disability. (p. 46551)

It is clear from this excerpt that a student diagnosed with NLD must also meet criteria for identification with one of the eight SLD subtypes listed in the IDEIA 2004 regulations to be identified as a student with SLD. Given the nature of NLD, it is most likely that students with NLD would meet criteria for identification with one or both of the mathematical SLD subtypes, although it is possible that issues with pragmatic language, motor skills, or other NLD liability areas may affect reading comprehension or written expression significantly enough to permit identification in these areas. Basic reading skill, reading fluency, listening comprehension, and oral expression are less likely to be significantly affected, although skill in the latter two areas may be impacted by issues with prosody and/or pragmatic language. Other requirements for potential IDEIA eligibility include autism; if the student's NLD-related cognitive, sensory-motor, and socio-emotional difficulties also meet diagnostic criteria for an autism spectrum disorder or other health impairment; if students experience "limited strength, vitality, or alertness, including heightened alertness to environmental stimuli that results in limited alertness with respect to the educational environment," and concomitant educational difficulties as a result of NLD-related symptoms (p. 46757). Students with NLD who do not require specially designed instruction may still be eligible for accommodations and/or modifications under Section 504 of the Rehabilitation Act, which requires that individuals with physical or mental disabilities be provided with access to the same education as children without such conditions.

INTERVENTION SELECTION

Recent federal laws pertaining to both general and special education (e.g., IDEIA, No Child Left Behind) emphasize the use of empirically supported interventions in school settings. However, as Semrud-Clikeman, Fine, and Harder (2005) noted, there are no school-based interventions that have been specifically validated for use with students with NLD. Additionally, due to the heterogeneous nature of NLD, individuals with this diagnosis may require a variety of academic interventions. Therefore, school-based clinicians and/or multidisciplinary teams should consider the particular needs demonstrated by a student with NLD in designing intervention plans.

Specific academic interventions targeting mathematical, reading comprehension, or writing skills may be necessary. Organizations such as the What Works Clearinghouse (http://www.ies.ed.gov/ncee/wwc) and the Florida Center for Reading Research (http://www.fcrr.org), which review, synthesize, and disseminate intervention efficacy research, may be helpful in identifying educational interventions for students with NLD that are appropriate to those students' needs and that meet federal requirements regarding research support for interventions. School-based teams may also need to design and implement interventions that indirectly affect students' academic achievement through increasing skills in other areas affected by NLD. For example, explicit instruction in metacognitive or behavioral self-monitoring strategies may benefit students who demonstrate NLD-related executive functioning deficits. Additionally, given the high likelihood that individuals with NLD will experience interpersonal difficulties, provision of social skills instruction may be beneficial. Gresham, Sugai, and Horner (2001) note that research on the effectiveness of social skills training has yielded mixed results; however, they report that social skills interventions are more likely to lead to positive outcomes for students when they: are implemented with high levels of frequency and intensity; target the specific skill deficits demonstrated by the student; are based on functional assessments of behavior; differentiate among behavior acquisition, behavior performance, and behavior fluency deficits; are implemented accurately and consistently; and include generalization and maintenance phases. As with any school-based intervention, it is essential that school personnel monitor the implementation of NLD-related interventions to ensure treatment integrity, to record and analyze data to determine intervention efficacy, and to alter interventions if efficacy is not demonstrated.

SUMMARY

This chapter described several models for NLD identification, patterns of cognitive, academic, and socio-emotional assets and liabilities characteristic of the disorder, and considerations for assessment and intervention. As previously noted, since these models are not included in the legal and clinical classification systems most often used by school psychologists, NLD diagnosis often falls outside the scope of practice of the school-based practitioner. However, given increased awareness and clinical use of the diagnosis, it is imperative that school psychologists are aware of NLD symptomatology and of the potential educational implications of the disorder. Additionally, knowledge of comorbid conditions, as well as conditions that may lead to the development of NLD symptoms (e.g., VCFS, brain tumors), may allow school teams to anticipate and prevent or minimize difficulties that have not yet emerged through early intervention. For these reasons, it is important that school-based practitioners are aware of the constellation of symptoms that NLD comprises so that they can comprehensively evaluate the asset and liability areas associated with the disorder and choose interventions appropriate to the diverse needs of students with NLD.

REFERENCES

American Psychiatric Association (2000). *Diagnostic and statistical manual of mental disorders* (4th ed., text revision). Washington, DC: Author.

Antshel, K. M., & Khan, F. M. (2008). Is there an increased familial prevalence of psychopathology in children with nonverbal learning disorders? *Journal of Learning Disabilities, 41*, 208–217.

Buono, L. A., Morris, M. K., Morris, R. D., Krawiecki, N., Norris, F. H., Foster, M. A., & Copeland, D. R. (1998). Evidence for the syndrome of nonverbal learning disabilities in children with brain tumors. *Child Neuropsychology, 4*, 144–157.

Carey, M. E., Barakat, L. P., Foley, B., Gyato, K., & Phillips, P. C. (2001). Neuropsychological functioning and social functioning of survivors or pediatric brain tumors: Evidence of nonverbal learning disability. *Child Neuropsychology, 7*, 265–157.

Cleaver, R. L., & Whitman, R. D. (1998). Right-hemisphere, white matter learning disabilities associated with depression in an adolescent and young adult psychiatric population. *Journal of Nervous and Mental Disease, 186*, 561–565.

Cornoldi, C., Venneri, A., Marconato, F., Molin, A., & Montinari, C. (2003). A rapid screening measure for the identification of visuospatial learning disability in schools. *Journal of Learning Disabilities, 36*, 299–306.

Cutting, L. E., Clements, A. M., Lightman, A. D., Yerby-Hammack, P. D., & Denckla, M. B. (2004). Cognitive profile of Neurofibromatosis Type 1: Rethinking nonverbal learning disabilities. *Learning Disabilities Research and Practice, 19*, 155–165.

Don, A. J., Schellenberg, E. G., & Rourke, B. P. (1999). Music and language skills of children with Williams syndrome. *Child Neuropsychology, 5*, 154–170.

Feifer, S. G., & De Fina, P. A. (2000). *The neuropsychology of reading disorders: Diagnosis and intervention workbook.* Middletown, MD: School Neuropsych Press.

Feifer, S. G., & De Fina, P. A. (2002). *The neuropsychology of written language disorders: Diagnosis and intervention.* Middletown, MD: School Neuropsych Press.

Feifer, S. G., & De Fina, P. A. (2005). *The neuropsychology of mathematics: Diagnosis and intervention*. Middletown, MD: School Neuropsych Press.

Florida Center for Reading Research. (n.d.) Retrieved September 15, 2008, from http://www.fcrr.org.

Forrest, B. J. (2004). The utility of math difficulties, internalized psychopathology, and visual-spatial deficits to identify children with the nonverbal learning disability syndrome: Evidence for a visual-spatial disability. *Child Neuropsychology, 10*, 129–146.

Goldberg, E., & Costa, L. D. (1981). Hemisphere differences in the acquisition and use of descriptive systems. *Brain and Language, 12*, 144–173.

Gresham, F. M., Sugai, G., & Horner, R. H. (2001). Interpreting outcomes of social skills training for students with high-incidence disabilities. *Teaching Exceptional Children, 67*, 331–344.

Griffin, R., Friedman, O., Ween, J., Winner, E., Happé, F., & Brownwell, H. (2006). Theory of mind and the right cerebral hemisphere: Refining the scope of impairment. *Laterality, 11*, 195–225.

Gross-Tsur, V., Shalev, R. S., Manor, O., & Amir, N. (1995). Developmental right-hemisphere syndrome: Clinical spectrum of the nonverbal learning disability. *Journal of Learning Disabilities, 28*, 80–86.

Hale, J. B. (2008). *Response to intervention: Guidelines for parents and practitioners*. Retrieved August 22, 2008, from http://www.wrightslaw.com/idea/art/rti .hale.htm.

Hale, J. B., & Fiorello, C. A. (2004). *School neuropsychology: A practitioner's handbook*. New York: Guilford.

Individuals with Disabilities Education Improvement Act of 2004. (PL No. 108–446, 20 USC 1400).

Johnson, D., & Myklebust, H. (1967). *Learning disabilities: Educational principles and practices*. New York: Grune & Stratton.

Keller, W. D., Tillery, K. L., & McFadden, S. L. (2006). Auditory processing disorder in children diagnosed with nonverbal learning disability. *American Journal of Audiology, 15*, 108–113.

Liddell, G. A., & Rasmussen, C. (2005). Memory profile of children with nonverbal learning disability. *Learning Disabilities Research and Practice, 20*, 137–141.

McDonough-Ryan, P., DelBello, M., Shear, P. K., Ris, M. D., Soutullo, C., & Strakowski, S. M. (2002). Academic and cognitive abilities in children of parents with bipolar disorder: A test of the nonverbal learning disability model. *Journal of Clinical and Experimental Neuropsychology, 24*, 280–285.

Miller, D. C. (2007). *Essentials of school neuropsychological assessment*. Hoboken, New Jersey: John Wiley & Sons.

Mirsky, A. F., Anthony, B. J., Duncan, C. C., Ahearn, M. B., & Kellam, S. G. (1991). Analysis of the elements of attention: A neuropsychological approach. *Neuropsychology Review, 2*, 109–145.

Palombo, J. (2001). *Learning disorders and disorders of the self in children and adolescents*. New York: Norton.

Palombo, J. (2006). *Nonverbal learning disabilities: A clinical perspective.* New York: Norton.

Pennington, B. F. (1991). *Diagnosing learning disorders: A neuropsychological framework.* New York: Guilford.

PDM Task Force. (2006). *Psychodynamic diagnostic manual.* Silver Spring, MD: Alliance of Psychoanalytic Organizations.

Rourke, B. P. (Ed.). (1985). *Neuropsychology of learning disabilities: Essentials of subtype analysis.* New York: Guilford.

Rourke, B. P. (1989). *Nonverbal learning disabilities: The syndrome and the model.* New York: Guilford.

Rourke, B. P. (1995). The NLD syndrome and the white matter model. In B. P. Rourke (Ed.), *Syndrome of nonverbal learning disabilities: Neurodevelopmental manifestations* (pp 1–26). New York: Guilford.

Ryan, T. V., Crews, W. D., Cowen, L., Goering, A. M., & Barth, J. T. (1998). A case of Triple X Syndrome manifesting with the syndrome of nonverbal learning disabilities. *Child Neuropsychology, 4,* 225–232.

Semrud-Clikeman, M., Fine, J. G., & Harder, L. (2005). Providing neuropsychological services to students with learning disabilities. In R. C. D'Amato, E. Fletcher-Janzen, & C. R. Reynolds (Eds.), *Handbook of school neuropsychology* (pp. 403–424). Hoboken, NJ: John Wiley & Sons.

Sundheim, S. T. P. V., & Voeller, K. K. S. (2004). Psychiatric implications of language disorders and learning disabilities: Risks and management. *Journal of Child Neurology, 19,* 814–826.

Swillen, A., Vandeputte, L., Cracco, J., Maes, B., Ghesquière, P., Devriendt, K., & Fryns, J. P. (1999). Neuropsychological, learning, and psychosocial profile of primary school aged children with the velo-cardio-facial syndrome (22q11 deletion): Evidence for a nonverbal learning disability? *Child Neuropsychology, 5,* 230–241.

Tsatsanis, K. D., Fuerst, D. R., & Rourke, B. P. (1997). Psychosocial dimensions of learning disabilities: External validation and relationship with age and academic functioning. *Journal of Learning Disabilities, 30,* 490–502.

Tsatsanis, K. D., & Rourke, B. P. (1995). Conclusions and future directions. In B. P. Rourke (Ed.), *Syndrome of nonverbal learning disabilities: Neurodevelopmental manifestations* (pp. 476–496). New York: Guilford.

Voeller, K. K. S. (1986). Right hemisphere deficit syndrome in children. *American Journal of Psychiatry, 143,* 1004–1009.

What Works Clearinghouse. (n.d.) Retrieved September 15, 2008, from http://www.ies.ed.gov/ncee/wwc

Wodrich, D. L., & Schmitt, A. J. (2006). *Patterns of learning disorders: Working systematically from assessment to intervention.* New York: Guilford.

Woods, S. P., Weinborn, M., Ball, J. D., Tiller-Nevin, S., & Pickett, T. C. (2000). Periventricular leukomalacia (PVL): An identical twin case study illustration of white matter dysfunction and nonverbal learning disability (NLD). *Child Neuropsychology, 6,* 274–285.

World Health Organization. (1993). *International classification of diseases* (10th ed.). Geneva, Switzerland: Author.

Yalof, J. (2006). Case illustration of a boy with nonverbal learning disorder and Asperger's features: Neuropsychological and personality assessment. *Journal of Personality Assessment, 87*, 15–34.

Yalof, J., & Abraham, P. (2006). Personality assessment in schools. In S. R. Smith & L. Handler (Eds.), *The clinical assessment of children & adolescents* (pp. 19–35). Mahwah, NJ: Lawrence Erlbaum Associates.

Yu, J. W., Buka, S. L., McCormick, M. C., Fitzmaurice, G. M., & Indurkhya, A. (2006). Behavioral problems and the effects of early intervention on eight-year-old children with learning disabilities. *Maternal and Child Health Journal, 10*, 329–338.

CLINICAL APPLICATIONS OF SCHOOL NEUROPSYCHOLOGY: PROCESSING DEFICITS

SECTION V

CLINICAL APPLICATIONS
OF SCHOOL
NEUROPSYCHOLOGY:
PROCESSING DEFICITS

CHAPTER 24

Assessing and Intervening in Children with Executive Function Disorders

DENISE E. MARICLE, WENDI JOHNSON, and ERIN AVIRETT

Perhaps the most intriguing, yet least understood, aspect of cognition is executive functioning. There are many who believe that executive functioning is the hallmark of intelligence (Anderson, 2008; Blair, 2006; Duncan, Emslie, Williams, Johnson, & Freer, 1996; Engle, 2002; Friedman et al., 2006; Kane & Engle, 2002). However, there are others who advocate that executive functions are separate and distinct from "g" or general overall intelligence (Ardila, Pineda, & Rosselli, 2000; Baron, 2004; Lidz, 2003). Much of the impetus for this last perspective results from research studies that have found little or no correlation between tasks of executive functioning and IQ scores from standardized measures of intelligence. The study of executive functioning was propelled by the pioneering work of Alexander R. Luria (Luria, 1966; 1973). Luria believed that in order to understand the brain, one must study the interaction of the systems within the brain. Luria was one of the first to propose that the frontal lobes were primarily responsible for behaviors such as planning and regulating one's actions, all of which are strongly associated with executive functioning. Luria's influential work set the foundation for later theoretical definitions, although the nature of the relationship between the frontal lobes and executive functions continues to be debated.

DEFINITION OF EXECUTIVE FUNCTIONS

Attempting to define executive functioning is a difficult task. Currently, there is no universally accepted definition of executive functioning, nor is there a mutually agreed upon list of the cognitive components which comprise

599

executive functions. Lezak, Howieson, and Loring (2004) define executive functions as a set of processes that are essential for engaging in independent, purposeful, self-directed behaviors. Anderson, Levin, and Jacobs (2002) define executive functions as independent but interrelated components of attentional control, goal setting, and cognitive flexibility. Goldberg (2002) views executive functioning as an array of cognitive abilities that makes the human brain a unique, organized, and sophisticated structure. Gioia, Isquith, and Guy (2001) and Baron (2004) identified a list of subdomains implicated in executive functioning, which include set shifting, problem solving, abstract reasoning, planning, organization, goal setting, working memory, inhibition, mental flexibility, initiation, attentional control, and behavioral regulation.

The complex reciprocal nature of executive functioning makes developing a cohesive definition challenging. As early as 1996, Baddeley questioned whether executive functioning was a unified system of multiple functions or a conglomeration of independent processes. Generally speaking, the various cognitive functions that are commonly accepted components of executive function include attentional control, cognitive flexibility, planning and goal setting, inhibition, and self-monitoring (Hughes & Graham, 2002). It is commonly believed that executive functions form the basis for many emotional, social, and cognitive skills. While it is widely accepted that executive functioning can no longer be conceptualized as a single process, the fields of cognitive psychology, developmental psychology, and neuropsychology remain polarized in determining a cohesive definition that all can agree upon.

Given the lack of definitional consensus and the wide range of cognitive abilities subsumed in the term *executive functioning*, competing models and theories have been developed to describe the interrelated processes within the executive system (Busch, McBride, Curtiss, & Vanderploeg, 2005). Executive function models can be categorized based on the way they conceptualize executive functions. Zelazo, Muller, Frye, and Marcovitch (2003) delineate three approaches to conceptualizing executive functioning. The first approach involves models based on abilities that theoretically comprise executive functions, such as conceptualizing executive functioning as a higher order cognitive mechanism involving the component abilities of inhibition, working memory, and planning. An example of this would be Baddeley and Hitch's (1974) model of working memory, which proposes a tripartite model that utilizes the central executive as the "supervisor" of two subordinate systems, the phonological loop and the visual spatial sketchpad.

The second approach involves utilizing factor analytic studies of neuropsychological batteries to determine the functional elements of executive functions (Brookshire, Levin, Song, & Zhang, 2004; Busch et al., 2005; Levin et al., 1991; Mirsky, Anthony, Duncan, Ahearn, & Kellam, 1991; Miyake et al.,

2000; Welsh, Pennington, & Grossier, 1991). This frequently results in 3- or 4-factor solutions that describe separate dimensions of executive functioning. Although this may be misleading in that the labels for each factor are arbitrary, the same assessment may cluster in different ways depending on the categorization of the factors, and the factor structure will at least in part reflect non-executive functioning (van der Sluis, de Jong, & van der Leij, 2007).

A third approach involves conceptualizing the narrow abilities that comprise executive functioning domains and operationalizing tasks based on the multiple narrow abilities that might comprise the domain, or that a specific executive task might require. This approach is most consistent with the CHC (Cattell-Horn-Carroll) theoretical perspective, which currently pervades the field of intellectual assessment. This way of conceptualizing executive functioning avoids aggregating abilities into one unified function and attempts to clarify how the various characteristics of executive functioning operate concurrently. How executive functioning is conceptualized is important because it determines how it is defined as well as how researchers interpret their findings. Currently, there is a wide variety of opinions, hypotheses, and theories regarding executive functioning and subsequently a continuing need for further research to delineate what executive functions are and how they work.

NEUROLOGICAL BASES OF EXECUTIVE FUNCTIONS

An understanding of executive functioning begins with the knowledge of the underlying neural substrates and integrated circuitry involved in higher order cognitive processing (Bauman, 2008). The processes of executive functions are widely associated with the anterior regions of the frontal lobe, known as the prefrontal cortex (PFC). However, exactly how the PFC supports executive functioning remains controversial (Hughes & Graham, 2008; Wood & Grafman, 2003). The PFC constitutes approximately one-third of the adult cortex in humans and does not reach full maturation until young adulthood. The frontal lobes are the last cerebral structures to mature with synaptogenesis, myelination, and pruning of the prefrontal cerebral circuitry and changes in neurochemical activity occurring throughout adolescence (Jacobs & Anderson, 2002). The PFC attends, integrates, formulates, executes, monitors, modifies, and judges (Knight & Stuss, 2002). It has been described as the seat of consciousness, the brain's conductor (Goldberg, 2002), or CEO and management system (Reynolds, 2007). Goldberg (2002) describes the frontal lobes as the part of the brain that "defines your identity, encapsulates your drives, your ambitions, your personality, your essence" (p. 1).

Two hallmark functions attributed to the frontal lobes are cognitive flexibility (set shifting) and inhibition (the ability to inhibit responding or to disengage attention from the immediate environment in order to perform higher level cognitive tasks). Several frontal-subcortical areas originate in the PFC and are evident during the performance of executive functioning tasks. The dorsolateral PFC primarily regulates the more cognitive aspects of executive functions (Miller, 2007; Zillmer, Spiers, & Culbertson, 2008). It is involved in maintaining and shifting set, organizing strategies, performing dual task activities, sustaining attention, and inhibiting responses (Szameitat, Schubert, Muuler, & Cramon, 2002). Defects in control, regulation, and integration of cognitive activities tend to predominate with damage to the dorsolateral PFC. Hale and Fiorello (2004) note that deficits in the dorsolateral PFC lead to the "classic signs of attention deficits" (p. 64). These deficits include inattention, poor problem solving, disorganization, and difficulty monitoring or evaluating one's self. The lateral PFC controls processes such as selective attention and working memory, whereas the lateral orbitofrontal cortex is involved with social aspects such as sensitivity, tact, and attention (Knight & Stuss, 2002).

The orbitofrontal PFC plays a key role in impulse control, in regulation and maintenance of set or ongoing behavior, and in decision making. Damage here can result in disinhibition, impulsivity, aggression, sexual promiscuity, and poor decision making. In recent years, overall differences in the left and right orbitofrontal PFC have been described. The left orbitofrontal PFC is important for the control of self-generated plans and strategies, and the right orbitofrontal PFC monitors externally ordered events (Lezak et al., 2004). A third primary subcortical area involved in executive functioning is the anterior cingulate circuit. This circuitry is involved in the initiation of motor movement as well as in the motivation necessary to complete a task (Miller, 2007).

The anterior cingulate circuit has been implicated in several overlapping functions such as response monitoring, error detection, and conflict resolution in the face of competing responses, inhibition, and selective or divided attention (van Vreen & Carter, 2002; Zillmer et al., 2008). Deficits in the anterior cingulate circuit may involve slow completion time for tasks, lack of persistence, apathy, limited creativity, and difficulty self-monitoring personal performance (Hale & Fiorello, 2004). The anterior cingulate circuit has been hypothesized to operate as an executive attention system (Posner, 1994). This is evident on neuropsychological measures, where the most pronounced deficit associated with damage to the anterior cingulate circuit is the failure of response inhibition (Miller, 2007). The role of the anterior cingulate circuit in inhibition is often stressed, but it appears that it may also play an important role in the initiation of behavior (Cabeza & Nyberg, 2000). The anterior cingulate circuit appears to participate in both the suppression of inappropriate responses and the initiation of appropriate responses.

The proximity and interconnectivity of the orbitofrontal region and the anterior cingulate circuit suggest that they interact to support executive functions (Ullsperger & von Cramon, 2004). The two regions seem to be complementary, with the anterior cingulate circuit monitoring and altering ongoing actions and the orbitofrontal cortex monitoring the external consequences of these actions to guide future actions. Paralleling the anatomical systems are neurochemical systems connecting to the PFC, primarily pathways for dopamine and serotonin. These neuroanatomical and neurochemical systems overlap: For example, the dorsolateral PFC is innervated by ascending dopaminergic neurons contained in the mesocortical dopamine pathway (Casey, Galvan, & Hare, 2005; Robbins, 2005). Thus, the underlying neurophysiology of executive functions is comprised of multiple, interrelated interdependent subsystems. This networked pattern of the frontal lobe to the rest of the brain provides the connectivity necessary to oversee, integrate, and coordinate complex cognitive behaviors (Anderson, P., 2002). However, despite what we know, it is important to note that our knowledge and understanding of how the brain processes and performs executive function tasks is still relatively limited.

DEVELOPMENTAL ASPECTS OF EXECUTIVE FUNCTIONING IN CHILDREN

Historically, it has been postulated that executive functions emerge in late adolescence and play no significant role in normal (or atypical) brain development in infancy and childhood. It has been only recently that researchers have demonstrated that executive functions play a critical role in normal brain development and in some early childhood disorders (Anderson, V., 2002). We now know that higher-order processing skills are developing long before they are observable, functional, and testable (Carlson, 2004; Hughes & Graham, 2008; Lidz, 2003; Welsh et al., 1991). Behaviors such as poor working memory, a lack of self-monitoring, or weak reasoning ability may all be associated with executive functioning deficits, however, when understood in a developmental context, those behaviors would not be deemed atypical at certain ages. It is critical for practitioners to understand the developmental trajectories associated with executive functioning. The emergence of executive functions in childhood does not appear to be linear, nor a gradual developmental progression; rather, it correlates with age-dependent growth spurts of the frontal lobes.

Several studies have demonstrated this interaction between developmental processes and the manifestation of executive functions (Blair, Zelazo, & Greenberg, 2005; Brocki & Bohlin, 2004; Zelazo et al., 2003). The major growth periods in the prefrontal cortex (PFC) occur from birth to age 2, ages 7 to 9, and ages 12 to 19 and may well prove to be associated with myelination, synaptogenesis, and axonal pruning (Byrnes, 2007; Giedd, 2004; Jacobs & Anderson, 2002). Different aspects of executive functioning appear to emerge at different stages of development. For example, organized, strategic, and planned behavior is detected by age 6, whereas organized search, inhibition, and set maintenance seems to mature by age 10. Verbal fluency and complex planning reach adult levels at about age 12. Because of the rapid development of executive functions in early childhood, accurately defining and studying these skills is a challenge. Additionally, Ewing-Cobbs, Prasad, Landry, Kramer, and DeLeon (2004) would argue that because executive functions are rapidly developing they are more vulnerable to disruption during this time period. These difficulties are heightened by the fact that development is not linear and does not occur in stages, but usually takes place in maturational spurts. Therefore, developmental profiles and trajectories vary depending on the executive skill being examined (Archibald & Kerns, 1999; Romine & Reynolds, 2005).

There is no singular core disorder of executive function (Gioia et al., 2001); rather, impairments in executive function tend to show up globally, affecting all aspects of cognition and behavior. Many of the behavioral or cognitive problems associated with impaired executive functions are apparent to the casual observer. Among the symptoms may be limited capacity for self-control or self-direction, emotional lability or flattening of affect, irritability or excitability, impulsivity, difficulty shifting attention or rigidity of thinking, impaired capacity to initiate activity, decreased motivation, impaired ability to inhibit responses, and difficulty with goal-directed behaviors (Lezak et al., 2004). Executive dysfunctions are observed in known neurological disorders resulting from genetic, acquired, or traumatic brain injury; however, problems with the development of executive functions in children are characteristic of several other childhood disorders as well. For example, Attention-Deficit/Hyperactivity Disorder is marked by problems with inhibition and difficulties with attention, which are core attributes of executive functioning (Roth & Saykin, 2004; Shallice et al., 2002). In fact, Barkley (2000) has even suggested that executive dysfunction rather than attention is the core deficit in Attention Deficit Hyperactivity Disorder.

Executive dysfunction has also been associated with children with learning disabilities. Difficulties are often seen with self-regulation, problem solving, cognitive flexibility, and organization (Meltzer & Krishnan, 2007). Children with nonverbal learning disabilities often have weaknesses in fluently shifting attention, adapting to novel situations, self-regulation, and attentional control (Stein & Krishnan, 2007). Executive function deficits are also seen with children on the autism spectrum, most typically those labeled with Asperger's Disorder or High Functioning Autism. These children have problems fluently shifting attention, planning, adapting to novel situations, appropriately responding to social cues, and regulating social interactions (Ozonoff & Schetter, 2007). Currently, there is little consensus and minimal research regarding identifiable patterns of performance on executive function tasks for these various clinical groups. As a result, a desire to better understand developmental disorders and early psychopathology has fueled research into the executive functioning of children (Blair et al., 2005). Because of the importance executive functioning has on daily living, academic success, and social interactions, it is imperative to accurately assess these deficits in children (Bauman, 2008).

ASSESSMENT OF EXECUTIVE FUNCTIONS IN CHILDREN AND ADOLESCENTS

Given the lack of definitional congruence and complexity of executive functions, multiple measurement issues ensue. Obviously, a major hurdle is to determine which executive functions to measure. Because terms for executive functions are used inconsistently and interchangeably, clinicians and researchers do not necessarily agree on which domains are critical to executive functioning and, therefore, should be assessed. Second, the tasks designed to measure executive functions are cognitively complex, often representing multiple underlying cognitive processes. The integrative nature of frontal lobe functioning makes it difficult to parcel out the specific cognitive functions being utilized in each type of task. This interrelatedness of executive functions leaves measurement vulnerable to task impurity (Hughes & Graham, 2002). Romine and Reynolds (2005) go so far as to state, "it is impossible to obtain a pure test of frontal functions because an element of theoretical constraint of frontal lobe functions is that they involve simultaneous management of a variety of cognitive functions" (pp. 198–199). Consequently, tests of executive function tend to have low test-retest reliability (stability) and uncertain validity. Finally, given that the prefrontal cortex does not act in isolation, it is challenging to identify which region of the brain contributes to outcomes on specific executive functioning measures. As a result, a deficit in one area may lead to multiple behaviors or, concurrently, one behavior may be the result of multiple underlying impairments.

In addition to definitional and complexity issues, several early myths involving the assessment of executive functioning persist within the field. One myth of early executive function tests was that deficient performance on such tests directly implicated frontal lobe dysfunction. Subsequent research has shown that successful performance on such tasks requires some combination of more fundamental cognitive skills such as attention, perception, concept formation, working memory, inhibition, planning, or cognitive flexibility. A breakdown in performance can occur at any stage of cognitive processing from lower level basic skills (attention, perception) to higher-level cognitive functions (concept formation, planning) (Delis, Kaplan, & Kramer, 2001). Another myth underlying early assessment of executive functions was that each task tapped a single underlying cognitive function. Again, subsequent research has shown that most executive function tasks require several higher-level cognitive abilities for successful performance.

The majority of the research regarding the assessment of executive functions has occurred with adult populations, and most of the instruments available to assess executive functioning are designed for adults. A few of the instruments currently available to assess executive functioning in children are downward extensions of measures designed for adults, and their psychometric validity and utility with children has never been thoroughly examined. Currently, very few measures of executive functioning are available that were designed specifically for children. An additional factor in assessing executive functioning in children is the intricate interaction of age and development because executive functions are theorized to change with maturation and take different forms at different ages (Archibald & Kerns, 1999). Similar assessment measures that purportedly test the same executive skill area may actually be assessing different cognitive abilities for children at different ages. Depending on the skill being assessed and the type of assessment, the subcomponents of executive functioning may follow different developmental trajectories that mature at different rates (Romine & Reynolds, 2005).

The broad range of skills implicated in executive functioning has led to the use of many different assessment tools. No instrument has been developed to assess for executive functioning in its entirety, but there are assessment tools available that are aimed at measuring specific components of executive function. Several types of instruments claim to include tasks of executive functions. Some of these instruments are cognitive batteries that have components of executive functioning built into a few subtests, such as the *Woodcock Johnson III: Tests of Cognitive Abilities, Normative Update* (WJ III-COG NU: Woodcock, Schrank, Mather, & McGrew, 2007). However, most traditional tests of intelligence and academic functioning fail to capture the executive function skills and abilities that are involved in higher order cognitive tasks. Other instruments were designed as neuropsychological batteries and have specific executive function subtests that contribute to a global or composite executive function score such as the NEPSY/NEPSY II (Korkman, Kirk, & Kemp, 1998, 2007a, 2007b). Finally, a few are stand-alone measures of executive functions or instruments that combine tasks of executive function such as the *Delis-Kaplan Executive Function System* (D-KEFS: Delis et al., 2001).

WOODCOCK JOHNSON III: TESTS OF COGNITIVE ABILITIES, NORMATIVE UPDATE (WJ III COG NU)

The *Woodcock-Johnson III Tests of Cognitive Abilities* (WJ III-COG; Woodcock, McGrew, & Mather, 2001; WJ III Normative Update; Woodcock et al., 2007) is a compilation of tests designed to measure general intellectual ability, broad and narrow cognitive abilities, and aspects of executive functioning in individuals from age 2 to age 95 (Schrank, 2005). The *WJ III COG* measures 7 broad and 25 or more narrow Cattell-Horn-Carroll (CHC) abilities. CHC theory views cognitive abilities as multidimensional and dynamic rather than as static domains of function. Currently, CHC theory does not view executive functioning as a cognitive domain, rather as a cognitive process that is composed of broad (such as *Gf* or *Gs*) and narrow abilities. The cognitive foundation of the *WJ III COG* fits well into a neuropsychological perspective. However, significantly more research needs to be applied to determine if the tasks effectively measure the associated narrow abilities and overarching factors associated with this current structure of human cognitive abilities.

Two clusters are designated as measures of executive functions, the Executive Processes Cluster and the Broad Attention Cluster. The Broad Attention Cluster appears to be a measure of global attention. It assesses four types of attention including attentional capacity, divided attention, selective attention, and sustained attention (Floyd, Shaver, & McGrew, 2003). The Broad Attention Cluster is composed of Numbers Reversed, Auditory Working Memory, Auditory Attention, and Pair Cancellation. Numbers Reversed is a measure of attentional capacity, but also serves as a measure of short-term memory or working memory span. Auditory Working Memory provides a measure of divided attention, but it also contributes as a measure of working memory. To be successful on this task requires the examinee to hold information in short-term memory, divide the information into two groups, and then shift attentional resources to two new groups in order to present a new sequence (Read & Schrank, 2003). Auditory Attention measures selective attention and contributes as a measure of Auditory Processing (*Ga*) since it requires the discrimination of speech sounds in the presence of competing noise. Pair Cancellation contributes to Broad Attention as a measure of sustained attention.

The Executive Processes Cluster was designed to measure core cognitive processes associated with executive functioning, including response inhibition (interference control), cognitive (mental) flexibility, and strategic planning (Floyd et al., 2003). The Executive Processes Cluster is comprised of three subtests: Concept Formation, Planning, and Pair Cancellation. Concept Formation is a controlled learning task that requires rule formation, inductive thinking, categorical reasoning, and logic. Concept formation as a measure of fluid reasoning represents the ability to shift one's mental set, to categorize, and to reason inductively (Ford, Keith, Floyd, Fields, & Schrank, 2003). Planning is a test of complex thinking that utilizes the narrow abilities of visual spatial scanning and sequential reasoning (Read & Schrank, 2003) to trace a stimulus without removing the pencil or retracing any lines. As an executive function measure, the test evaluates the ability to use mental control and the mental processes needed to determine, select, and apply solutions involved in future planning. The planning task was designed to minimize interference from memory and speed, thus providing a "purer" measure of planning. However, the task is vulnerable to the influence of attention and working memory difficulties (Gregg & Coleman, 2003). Pair Cancellation is a complex measure that requires the identification of a specific repeating pattern and involves attention, vigilance, speed, concentration, and interference control.

The majority of research conducted using the *WJ III Tests of Cognitive Abilities* has focused on the broad CHC ability factors and not specifically on the Broad Attention or Executive Processes Clusters. Factor analytic studies (Floyd et al., 2006) using the *WJ III COG* and the *Delis-Kaplan Executive Function System (D-KEFS)* have suggested that both cognitive ability and executive function measures assess a general construct (all correlate moderately to highly with the General Intellectual Ability score) indicating a relationship between the CHC factors and executive functions. The *WJ III Tests of Cognitive Abilities* has also been widely used in studies with clinical populations (e.g. ADHD, Autism Spectrum Disorders, Specific Learning Disabilities), but again such research has focused on the broad ability factors rather than the Broad Attention or Executive Processes Clusters.

Carper (2003) examined the three subtests (Concept Formation, Planning, Pair Cancellation) comprising the WJ III-COG Executive Process Cluster and two subtests (Tower and Design Fluency) from the NEPSY using a sample of typically developing children ($n = 60$). Study results indicated that Design Fluency from the NEPSY correlated with the WJ III-COG Executive Processes Cluster score ($r = .78, p < .01$) but not with the individual subtests comprising the EP cluster, and Tower from the NEPSY showed no significant correlation at all. However, when the sample was broken down by age, Design Fluency only correlated with the EP cluster at the oldest age level (12 years) and showed no correlation at age 10 and 11. Carper than applied a Fisher Z statistic to normalize the sampling distribution and found no age differences.

NEPSY II

The NEPSY (Korkman et al., 1998) and its revision, the NEPSY II (Korkman et al., 2007a; Korkman et al., 2007b), is the first and only neuropsychological battery developed specifically for children and adolescents. The test was designed for use with children ages 3 to 16 and is grounded in the Lurian theoretical model of neuropsychological functioning. The NEPSY II was developed to consist of a series of neuropsychological subtests that could be administered individually or combined as needed to provide insight into cognitive, academic, and neuropsychological functions (Korkman et al., 2007a). The *NEPSY II* purportedly measures six domains of cognitive functioning (Attention/Executive Functions, Language, Sensorimotor Functions, Visuospatial Processing, Memory and Learning, and Social Perception). Korkman and her colleagues (1998) clearly note that these cognitive domains do not develop in isolation, but work in concert together. Additionally, they state that not all cognitive functions comprising a specific domain are assessed and that broad conclusions based on individual subtests that measure only one aspect of a domain should not be drawn. Nevertheless, the domains are considered to be useful specific groupings of cognitive functions.

The tasks of the Attention/Executive Functions domain represent a continuum of skills from simple attention to more complex self-monitoring (Titley & D'Amato, 2008). The subtests that compose the Attention/Executive Functions domain on the *NEPSY II* are Animal Sorting, Auditory Attention and Response Set, Clocks, Statue, Design Fluency, and Inhibition. Examiners familiar with the original *NEPSY* will note that three subtests from the original domain of Attention/Executive Functions have been replaced (e.g. Tower, Visual Attention, and Knock and Tap) by new subtests (Clocks, Animal Sorting, and Inhibition). The *NEPSY II* was designed so that subtests would be selected on the basis of age, referral question, the needs of the child, time constraints, and assessment setting. Of the six subtests that comprise the Attention/Executive Functions domain on the *NEPSY II*, four span the widest age range (7–16), whereas, one is limited to preschoolers (3–6 years) and one to children age 5 to 12.

Animal Sorting (ages 7–16), a card sort task, was designed to measure the ability to form basic concepts, to categorize, and to shift from one concept to another fluently. Animal Sorting does not require the examinee to respond verbally. Auditory Attention and Response Set (ages 5–16) consists of two tasks. The first task, Auditory Attention assesses sustained and selective auditory attention. The second task, Response Set, was designed to assess "the ability to shift and maintain a new and complex set involving both inhibition of previously learned responses and correctly responding to matching or contrasting stimuli" (Korkman, et al., 2007a, p. 43). Clocks (ages 7–16) assesses planning, organization, visual perceptual and visual spatial skills, and the concept of time using analog clocks. In adults with acquired brain injury, performance on clock drawing tasks is frequently impaired.

Additionally, research by Cohen, Riccio, Kibby, and Edmonds (2000) has revealed a development curve, (the ability to draw clocks improved with age) in clock drawing tasks with children. Most 6-year-olds have a basic concept of a clock, and most 10-year-old children can construct a clock face accurately, but number positioning errors and erasures are often still present until age 12. Design Fluency (ages 5–12) assesses the child's ability to generate unique designs by connecting dots, presented in two arrays, structured and random. The Inhibition subtest (ages 5–16) was designed to assess "the ability to inhibit automatic responses in favor of novel responses, and the ability to shift or switch between response types" (Korkman et al., 2007a, p. 71). The Inhibition subtest requires the examinee to look at a series of shapes or arrows, name either the shape or direction or give an alternate response. This subtest has strong roots in the Stroop procedure in which an overlearned response must be inhibited while a conflicting response is given (Korkman et al., 2007b). Statue (ages 3–6) assesses motor persistence and inhibition in preschool children.

Most NEPSY II subtests yield multiple scores (primary scores, process scores, and contrast scores) that reflect overall performance, speed of performance, error rates, or partial scores that measure the subcomponent skills required to complete the task (Korkman et al., 2007a). These scores allow the examiner to understand the cognitive processes underlying task performance. Due to the variety of capacities that constitute the Attention/Executive Functions domain, subtest analysis, process scores, and behavioral observations of test performance are necessary to draw inferences and to formulate appropriate hypotheses. Children who demonstrate impairment in this domain may have underlying deficits in attention, in executive functioning, or in both areas. Further evaluation is likely to be needed in order to determine where the deficits lie.

The Attention/Executive Functions domain is considered to be a valid measure of inhibition, self-monitoring and self-regulation, vigilance, selective and sustained auditory attention, cognitive flexibility, and novel problem solving. The subtests of the NEPSY II that specifically measure the core components of executive functioning examine strategic planning abilities, flexibility, and self-regulatory processes as well as subcomponents of executive functioning such as initiation, fluency, inhibition, and working memory (Kemp, 2007). The NEPSY II does not measure all aspects of attention (e.g., visual attention or scanning) or executive functioning (e.g., reasoning). A major limitation of the Attention/Executive Functions domain of the NEPSY II is the inadequate amount of empirical research on the subcomponents of executive functions and the factors they purport to measure. Additionally, there are some psychometric concerns with several of the subtests comprising the Attention/Executive Functions domain. The authors reported test-retest correlation coefficients for subtest scores in the normative sample. The Design Fluency total score for ages 5 to 12 was .59. Reliabilities that fall below .70 should be approached with caution, and reliability coefficients below .60 are of significant concern. Additionally, the correlations for Animal Sorting within the Attention/Executive Functions domain ranged from .08 to .24 suggesting that it may not measure the same construct as the other subtests of the domain (Korkman et al., 2007a; Titley & D'Amato, 2008). Korkman and her colleagues account for the low correlations by suggesting that the various subtests are measuring different functions within the domain.

Currently, there are no published independent research studies specific to the NEPSY II or examining the subtests included within the Attention/ Executive Functions domain. All of the available research focuses on the original NEPSY with the exception of special group studies conducted by the test's authors to examine the clinical utility of the NEPSY II. The clinical studies reported in the NEPSY II manual include small sample groups of individuals identified on the autism spectrum (Autism, $n = 23$; Asperger's, $n = 19$), with specific learning disorders in reading ($n = 36$) and math ($n - 20$) and with Attention Deficit Hyperactivity Disorder ($n = 55$). Other groups were identified as language impaired, intellectually disabled, deaf or hard of hearing, and emotionally disabled. The group of individuals identified with a learning disability in mathematics displayed lower scores on the Auditory Attention and Response Set subtest, the group of individuals identified with Autism scored significantly lower than the control group on the Animal Sorting subtest, and the ADHD group exhibited significantly lower performance on all subtests that comprise the attention and executive functioning domain, except Animal Sorting. For the ADHD group, Auditory Attention and Response Set had the highest effect size. These results are consistent with research conducted on the original NEPSY (Hooper, Poon, Marcus, & Fine, 2006; Joseph, McGrath, & Tager-Flusberg, 2005; O'Brien et al., 2004; Riddle, Morton, Sampson, Vachha, & Adams, 2005).

DELIS-KAPLAN EXECUTIVE FUNCTION SYSTEM (D-KEFS)

The *Delis-Kaplan Executive Function System* (D-KEFS) (Delis et al., 2001) was the first instrument specifically designed to examine executive functioning. The D-KEFS presents a standardized assortment of existing and modified measures of executive function in children, adolescents, and adults (Delis et al., 2001). The D-KEFS is the only grouping of executive function tests co-normed on a large sample designed to assess mental flexibility, inhibition, problem solving, planning, impulse control, concept formation, abstract thinking, and verbal or spatial creativity (Homack, Lee, & Riccio, 2005).

The D-KEFS was not developed using any single theoretical foundation; rather, it consists of a variety of individual procedures that have been empirically demonstrated to be capable of detecting executive dysfunction. The D-KEFS is a compilation of nine stand-alone tests, each of which is individually aimed at assessing nonverbal and verbal executive functions. Eight of the tests are normed with children, including the Word Context Test, Sorting Test, Twenty Questions Test, Tower Test, Color-Word Interference Test, Verbal Fluency Test, Design Fluency Test, and Trail Making Test. The tests may be administered alone or in combination. Scoring and interpretation of the D-KEFS is based on "a 'cognitive process'" approach, which discourages reliance on a single score and places understanding on how the examinee attempts to solve the task. Each test yields an aggregate score and process scores (e.g., response accuracy, error rates, and response latency). Raw scores are converted to age-corrected scaled scores (mean $= 10$, $sd = 3$) and percentiles. There is no overall composite score as each subtest is scored and interpreted separately.

The D-KEFS was standardized on a stratified sample (matched to the 2000 U.S. Census) of 1,750 individuals of whom 700 were children between the ages of 8 and 15 years. Overall, reliability of the principal scores is generally considered acceptable, but many of the additional process scores demonstrate extremely low reliability. Additionally, there are strong age effects. Children at the youngest ages, 8 to 10 years, generally exhibit the lowest scores and performance on many of the measures is highly dependent on speed of processing until early adolescence (Strauss, Sherman, & Spreen, 2006). Validity evidence is a little scarcer. The authors of the D-KEFS rely on the established validity of previous versions of the tasks to support the validity of the tasks comprising the D-KEFS. For the current combination of tests, validity studies were conducted on only one (Sorting). No other validity studies were conducted on the other eight subtests of the D-KEFS.

The clinical usefulness of the D-KEFS with children is largely unknown. The research literature examining the D-KEFS is scarce, and even more limited when applied to children. A recent study by Wodka et al. (2008) examined the performance of children with ADHD on four subtests of the D-KEFS (Trail Making, Verbal Fluency, Color-Word Interference, and Tower). Wodka and colleagues found that although children with ADHD performed consistently in the average range on all four of the tasks, they exhibited significant differences from the control group on two (Color-Word Interference and Tower) of the four tasks when using summary measures, but no significant differences were observed on the contrast measures. Additionally, there were no significant differences between the ADHD subtype groups, which is consistent with other recent research on the subtypes of ADHD (Pasini, Paloscia, Alessandrelli, Porfrio, & Curatolo, 2007).

Finally, the D-KEFS is a difficult instrument to learn how to administer and interpret. Significant practice and supervision is required to successfully master administration and scoring rules. Additionally, examiners need to have an adequate background in neuropsychological assessment, neuro-development, and cognitive psychology in order to use the D-KEFS appropriately to formulate interpretive hypotheses about an individual child's performance.

BEHAVIOR RATING INVENTORY OF EXECUTIVE FUNCTIONS (BRIEF)

The *Behavior Rating Inventory of Executive Functions* (BRIEF; Gioia, Isquith, Guy, & Kenworthy, 2000) was designed to assess impairment of executive function behaviors in the home and school environments. It is often used in the school setting as the primary measure of executive functioning. The BRIEF defines executive functioning as the ability to self-regulate one's cognitive and social problem solving. The authors designed the instrument to be used with children exhibiting a wide range of neurological, psychiatric, developmental, and medical conditions with the intent of assessing executive dysfunction in an ecologically valid way. The BRIEF is a questionnaire for parents and teachers of school-age children (ages 5–18) comprised of 86 items asking the teacher or parent to determine how often a child performs a behavior. The respondent rates each item's frequency of occurrence on a three-point Likert Scale (Never, Sometimes, Often). The BRIEF utilizes T-scores and yields a global measure of executive functioning (Global Executive Composite) and two indexes, Behavior Regulation and Metacognition. Eight clinical scales are also derived including Inhibit, Shift, Emotional Control, Initiate, Working Memory, Plan/Organize, Organization of materials, and Monitor (the first three subtests make up the Behavior Regulation Index and last five comprise the Metacognition Index). Additionally, there are two validity subscales, which measure inconsistent responses and excessively negative responses of the rater. Higher T-scores indicate more executive dysfunction, with a T-score >65 considered clinically significant.

The normative sample for the parent form consisted of 1,419 parents, primarily mothers, and the sample for the teacher form was comprised of only 720 participants. Only individuals from the state of Maryland were used in the norm sample (broken down by gender, age, ethnicity, and SES), and information in the manual about the representativeness of the norm group to the U.S. population is limited. Thus, a significant limitation to the BRIEF is the adequacy and representativeness of its norm group.

The BRIEF manual reports internal consistency, test-retest, and inter-rater reliability. Internal consistency and test-retest reliabilities were strong, but inter-rater reliabilities for both parent and teacher raters were moderate

(.50 or below). It is important for examiners to know that parents almost always consistently rate both boys and girls as having significantly greater problems on all scales as compared to teacher ratings. In the manual, the authors describe convergent and divergent validity studies comparing the BRIEF and other behavioral measures, such as the *Achenbach System of Empirically Based Assessment* (ASEBA; Achenbach, 2008), the *Behavior Assessment System for Children, 2nd Edition* (BASC II; Reynolds & Kamphaus, 2007), the *Conner's Comprehensive Behavior Rating Scales* and the *Conners, 3rd Edition* (Conners, 2008a; 2008b). The BRIEF correlates moderately to strongly with scales or indices that measure attention on those behavioral measures, but research suggests that the BRIEF does not correlate with direct measures of executive functioning, such as the D-KEFS or the *Wisconsin Card Sorting Test* (Benjamin, 2004; Mangeot, Armstrong, Colvin, Yeates, & Taylor, 2002; Vriezen & Pigot, 2002). Users of the BRIEF need to understand that the BRIEF is an indirect method that does not measure cognitive aspects of executive functioning per se, but rather measures a parent's or teacher's perception of the behavioral manifestations of "executive dysfunction." The BRIEF should never be used as the sole measure of executive functions.

In addition to the BRIEF, there is the *BRIEF-Preschool Version* (Gioia, Espy, & Isquith, 2003) designed for children age 2 to 5–11 and the *BRIEF-Self Report Version* (Gioia, Espy, & Isquith, 2004) designed as a self-report measure for adolescents age 11 to 18. Limited research is available to establish the reliability and validity of measuring the behavioral manifestation of executive dysfunction in preschoolers or through self-report. Pedersen (2005) examined the relationship between parent and teacher ratings on the *BRIEF-Preschool* and performance based measures of executive function in preschool children. Pederson's results indicated that there were no significant differences between parent and teacher ratings on the *BRIEF-Preschool* but that parents' overall ratings were higher than teacher overall ratings, and teachers tended to have higher ratings for males than females. Pederson found no significant correlation between the results of teacher or parent *BRIEF-Preschool* ratings and test performance on cognitive measures of executive functioning. Pederson's results are consistent with the research on older children using the BRIEF.

Gioia, Isquith, Kenworthy, and Barton (2002) used the BRIEF to examine executive function profiles within and between groups of children with Attention-Deficit/Hyperactivity Disorder (ADHD), Traumatic Brain Injury (TBI), Reading Disabilities (RD), and Autism Spectrum Disorders (ASD). Profile differences were evident for the ADHD and ASD groups who exhibited greater problems overall than the RD or TBI groups. The ADHD and ASD groups exhibited elevations across all scales, whereas the RD and TBI groups displayed greater difficulties with working memory, planning, and self-monitoring, but not in inhibiting, shifting, or regulating emotions. However, Gioia and colleagues clearly state that while the BRIEF appears to distinguish between the executive function profiles of these clinical groups, it is not intended to be used to independently diagnose specific disorders; rather, a complete neuropsychological evaluation is recommended.

Anderson, Anderson, Northam, Jacobs, and Mikiewicz (2002) conducted a study using three clinical groups, early treated phenylketonuria, early treated hydrocephalus, and focal frontal lesions, and a healthy control group. They found that the presence of CNS disorder was associated with significantly higher executive dysfunction being reported by parents with the focal lesion group demonstrating the greatest deficits. Anderson and colleagues also reported that deficient performance on the BRIEF was not associated with deficient performance on cognitive measures of executive functioning, suggesting that the measurement domains are tapping into separate dimensions of executive functioning. Mahone and colleagues (2002) examined the validity of the BRIEF with children diagnosed with ADHD and Tourette syndrome, obtaining results similar to Anderson et al. (2005). The ADHD group demonstrated significant behavioral dysfunction as reported by parents on the BRIEF; the BRIEF correlated with other measures of behavioral dysfunction but did not correlate to performance-based measures of executive functions. There was not a significant pattern for the Tourette group, and the mixed group (ADHD and Tourette syndrome) was not significantly different from the ADHD only group. Sesma, Slomine, Ding, and McCarthy (2008) used the BRIEF to examine executive functioning in children during the first year following a traumatic brain injury and found that these children were more likely to exhibit impairments than children who sustained other types of injuries. Additionally, Sesma and her colleagues determined that severity of injury was related to the extent of executive dysfunction, as was premorbid learning and behavioral problems and family functioning and resources. The presence of premorbid learning and behavioral problems and poor family functioning and social disadvantage resulted in significantly higher ratings of executive dysfunction as measured by the BRIEF.

WISCONSIN CARD SORT TEST REVISED AND EXPANDED (WCST)

The *Wisconsin Card Sort Test Revised and Expanded* (WCST; Heaton, Chelune, Talley, Kay, & Curtiss, 1993), originally published in 1981, has been the gold standard of executive function tests and is one of the most widely used tests in adult neuropsychology. The WCST is generally recognized as a measure of concept formation, response inhibition, ability to maintain and shift cognitive set, abstract reasoning and problem solving, and sustained attention. Functional neuroimaging studies with adults have supported the major role of the frontal lobes in performing this task (Berman, Ostrem, & Randolph, 1995; Fallgatter & Strik, 1998; Monchi, Petrides, Petre, Worsley, & Dagher, 2001). Sorting tasks such as the WCST are the most common measure used to assess abstraction and concept formation (Lezak et al., 2004). Most sorting tasks assess the ability to shift concepts as well as the ability to apply newly formed concepts. With children, attention is usually paid to whether the child sorts according to a principle, can formulate the principle verbally, and can follow it consistently. Research suggests that the ability to shift conditions (e.g., shape to color) by rules emerges by about age 4 and increases with age through adolescence (Levin & Hanten, 2005; Levin et al., 1991; Zelazo, Reznick, & Pinon, 1995). Both the D-KEFS and the NEPSY II contain card-sorting tasks similar in nature to the WCST.

The current version of the WCST was designed for use with individuals ages 6 to 89 years old. The test requires the individual to sort cards by a specific characteristic and according to a specified rule. The WCST consists of four stimulus cards and two sets of 64 response cards that depict four forms (circles, crosses, triangles, and stars), four colors (red, yellow, blue, and green), and four numbers (one, two, three and four). Adequate performance requires the individual to determine the correct sorting rule or principle and then to maintain that set across changing stimulus conditions. Raw scores are converted to T-scores, standard scores (mean $= 100$, $sd = 15$), and percentiles.

The WCST was standardized on 899 typically developing individuals between the ages of 6 and 89, of which 453 were children. Limited data is available in the manual regarding the standardization sample; therefore, its representativeness is questionable because demographic information important for interpreting test scores (e.g., race/ethnicity) is not listed. Reliability reported in the manual is limited to inter-rater or inter-scorer, with no evidence provided as to internal consistency or stability. A number of validity studies are reported and overall support the use of the WCST with a variety of neurological and psychological disorders. In particular, studies involving children with TBI, seizures, learning disabilities, and attention deficit hyperactivity disorders indicate that the WCST may be useful in assessing "'executive functions'" in these groups (Clark, n.d.). Normative data for cross-cultural populations (Columbian, Taiwanese, Canadian) of children on the WCST is also available (Paniak, Miller, Murphy, Patterson, & Keizer, 1996; Rosselli & Ardila, 1993; Shu, Tien, Lung, & Chang, 2000).

Research and regression analyses indicate that performance on the WCST steadily increases from age 6–5 through age 19, then stabilizes through age 50 before beginning to decline. Welsh et al. (1991) found that adult level performance was achieved by age 10 on the WSCT. Levin and colleagues (1991) also found large developmental shifts in concept formation and problem solving efficiency between the age groups of 7- to 8-year-olds compared to 9- to 12-year-olds, but also note that further improvements in performance were seen through age 15. Arffa, Lovell, Podell, and Goldberg (1998), using a sample of above average and gifted children (ages 9 to 14 years), found that the performance of these children on the WCST was significantly related to intelligence, with performance clearly improving with increased intellectual functioning and reaching adult levels earlier for the brightest children. These results were similar to those obtained by Slomine et al. (2002) in a sample of children with traumatic brain injuries and by Riccio et al. (1994) in a study with children (9 to 11 years of age) diagnosed with attention deficit hyperactivity disorder, but these results directly contradict those of Welsh et al. (1991) and Levin et al. (1991), which found no relationship between performance and intelligence.

A meta-analytic study conducted by Romine et al. (2004) evaluated 32 journal articles and one dissertation that reported WCST results for children identified with a specific clinical disorder (e.g., ADHD, Learning Disorders, Conduct Disorder, Autism Spectrum Disorders, Mood Disorders, and Psychotic Disorders). The results suggest that individuals with ADHD, Learning Disorders, Conduct Problems, and Autism Spectrum Disorders consistently exhibited poor performance as compared to normal controls on the WCST; however, the ADHD group as a whole performed better than the other clinical groups suggesting that poor performance on the WCST is not sufficient for a diagnosis of ADHD. Romine and colleagues conclude that impaired performance on the WCST may be indicative of a general underlying neurological disorder rather than a specific diagnostic category.

Category Tests

Similar to sorting tasks, category tests are considered measures of concept generation, mental shifting, rule learning and problem solving (Baron, 2004). Category tests assess one's ability to benefit from trial and error experience in response to external feedback, to utilize feedback to accept or reject new hypotheses, and to maintain a successful principle or idea. The inability to do this suggests limited cognitive flexibility, learning inefficiency, and possible memory problems. The original *Category Test* was designed in the 1940s as an integral part of the *Halstead-Reitan Neuropsychological Test Battery* and was used to measure the ability to learn from experience while adaptively integrating new information (Boll, 1993). Assessing concept formation, hypothesis testing, memory, new learning, and abstract reasoning (D'Amato & Hartlage, 2008) is considered a classic measure of executive functioning. The original *Category Test* was designed for use with adults; however, Ralph Reitan later developed downward extensions for the *Halstead-Reitan Neuropsychological Test Battery for Older Children* and the *Reitan-Indiana Neuropsychological Test Battery for Young Children* (Reitan & Wolfson, 1992).

The *Children's Category Test* (CCT; Boll, 1993) was designed to assess nonverbal learning and memory, concept formation, and problem-solving abilities in children ages 5 to 16–11. The CCT follows the theoretical tradition of Halstead and Reitan's original category tests. The standardization sample consisted of 920 children stratified according to the 1988 U.S. Census. Reliability and validity of the CCT is considered to be good, although the test by current standards is now quite dated. An examination of the factor structure of the CCT (Donders, 1999, Nesbit-Greene & Donders, 2002) using the standardization sample and a smaller TBI population resulted in the conclusion that children show variations in both level and pattern of performance across subtests on the CCT. Donders' study strongly suggests that the CCT Level 1 (for 5- to 8-year-olds) and Level 2 (for 9- to 16-year-olds) are measuring different constructs despite their apparent similarities and that age is correlated with performance, with older children performing better than the younger children. In addition, Donders noted that the six subtests comprising each level appear to be measuring different skills or factors that vary in difficulty or complexity, and that a few of the subtests yield little useful information. Nesbit-Greene and Donders conclude that the CCT may measure more than one underlying construct in clinical populations as well, although sensitivity of the CCT with various clinical populations has not been clearly established in the literature. In their TBI sample, Nesbit-Greene and Donders found that intelligence, age, and injury severity were significantly correlated with CCT performance and suggested that the summary total score was insufficient as a marker for diagnostic utility with children.

TRAIL-MAKING TESTS

Trail-making tests derive from the classic test that originated by Partington and the U.S. Army in 1942 for use in the *Army Individual Test Battery* (1944) and was later popularized in the *Halstead-Reitan Neuropsychological Battery* (Halstead, 1952). Trail-making tests have been a popular procedure with both children and adults and have been incorporated into many neuropsychological batteries such as the D-KEFS. Trail-making tests are thought to examine visual attention, visual perception, inhibition, and cognitive processing speed. The task is perceived to be a good measure of global cerebral functioning because of its focus on symbolic recognition (a left hemisphere function) and its visual scanning component (a right hemisphere function) (D'Amato & Hartlage, 2008). The core of the traditional trail-making test is the second task. The first task provides a baseline measure for number sequencing without switching. The second task measures cognitive flexibility (characterized by switching) on a visual-motor sequencing task. A limitation of most trail-making tasks is that poor performance by both adults and children may be the result of a variety of neurocognitive factors such as slow processing speed, poor visual scanning, poor sequencing abilities, or poor fine motor coordination (D'Amato & Hartlage, 2008; Miller, 2007).

The *Comprehensive Trail Making Test* (CTMT; Reynolds, 2002) is a stand-alone measure, which is reported to measure visual scanning, attention, and executive functioning. The CTMT consists of five trials. Trial 1 is similar to the standard first task (baseline) and Trial 5 to the standard second task (requiring switching). Performance on the CTMT is based on the time taken to complete each trial. Raw scores are converted to T-scores and percentiles for each of the five trials, and an overall composite is derived from the five trials. The CTMT appears to have strong psychometric properties and a sufficient normative sample; however, test-retest data are lacking for children, as are research studies on the CTMT's correlation to other tests of executive functioning (Strauss et al., 2006).

The literature is replete with child-based research using trails tasks. However, identifying patterns and trends is difficult because the studies use different tasks, which vary in their format and method of scoring. A recent study by Reitan and Wolfson (2003) examined the performance of children with identified neurological disorders, typically developing children with academic difficulties, and typically developing children on Part B of the Trail Making Test from the *Halstead-Reitan Neuropsychological Battery for Older Children* (Reitan & Wolfson, 1992). They found that 80 percent of the neurologically impaired children, 78 percent of the children with academic difficulties, and 24 percent of the typically developing children evidenced impairment on Trails B. Klemm, Schmidt, Knappe, and Blanz (2006) examined the TMT performance of children at risk for schizophrenia (e.g., had a parent or sibling with schizophrenia) and found a pattern of decreased attentional and cognitive performance compared to a matched control group. Klemm and colleagues suggest that young persons with a genetic risk need more time to achieve the same accuracy as controls during routine work. Armstrong, Allen, Donohue and Mayfield (2007) examined the sensitivity of the *Comprehensive Trail Making Test* (CTMT) to neurocognitive deficits in a sample of adolescents with traumatic brain injury. The TBI group performed significantly below (2 standard deviations) the control group on each CTMT trial, as well as on the overall composite index, indicating that the CTMT is sensitive to neurological disorders.

Tower Tests (Tower of London, Tower of Hanoi)

There are multiple adaptations of tower tasks, including the *Tower of London* (Shallice, 1982), *Tower of London—Drexel University, 2nd Edition* (Culbertson & Zillmer, 2005), and the *Tower of Hanoi* (Simon, 1975). Tower tasks have also been included in some of the standardized batteries of neuropsychological functioning. The D-KEFS includes a tower task among its subtests, and the original version of the NEPSY also contained a tower task, but it has been removed from the second edition of the test (NEPSY II). Tower tests are primarily measures of planning, but also include the narrow abilities of working memory, response inhibition, and visuospatial memory. They are also thought to measure planning and rule application. Imaging has shown that the prefrontal cortex (PFC) plays a major role during tower task performance (Lazeron, Rombouts, & Machielsen, 2000). In most versions, the subject is required to arrange objects from their initial position to a new predetermined configuration in a set number of moves according to specific rules. The various tower tasks differ in terms of the structure of the task, the rules for completing the task, and the way in which performance on the task is evaluated (D'Amato & Hartlage, 2008). Baron (2004) reviewed several studies, which suggest that tower tasks are not interchangeable mostly due to subtle differences in the neurocognitive demands necessary for successful task solution. Several studies (Goel, Pullara, & Grafman, 2001; Humes, Welsh, Retzlaff, & Cookson, 1997) have shown that the *Tower of London* and *Tower of Hanoi* do not correlate, suggesting that they are measuring different cognitive functions. The *Tower of Hanoi* does not appear to measure planning as much as it assesses inhibition of response. There is also some research that suggests tower tasks might not be useful executive function tasks for children (Bishop, Aamodt-Leeper, Creswell, McGurk, & Skuse, 2001) because they might not measure the same functions in children that they do in adults (Baker, Segalowitz, & Ferlisi, 2001).

The *Tower of London—Drexel University, 2nd Edition* (TOL-DX; Culbertson & Zillmer, 2005) was developed to assess higher order problem solving, specifically executive planning abilities, in children and adults (ages 7–80). The process of planning requires the ability to conceptualize, change, anticipate (or look ahead), respond objectively, generate, and select alternatives, all of which requires sustained attention and working memory. Ten problems are administered (at both the child and adult levels) in order of increasing difficulty. Two minutes are allowed for each trial. The *Tower of London—Drexel University, 2nd Edition* was standardized on 990 individuals of whom 446 were children between the ages of 7 and 15. In addition, a small clinical population (ADHD; $n = 129$) was gathered. Reliability and validity studies on this version of the *Tower of London* are limited. Test-retest reliability was conducted only with two small clinical groups, one of which was a child group (ADHD; $n = 31$), and the reliability coefficients were low to moderate. Construct validity studies yielded correlations in the mid .50s showing moderate overlap with other measures of executive functioning and planning.

Culbertson and Zillmer (2005) provide a good deal of information about children's performance on tower tasks, indicating clear developmental differences. Overall, the performance of normal children (ages 7–15) improves with age, and they demonstrate a decrease in rule violations and increased proficiency for solving problems of increasing complexity. Younger children (ages 7–9) show limited planning, frequent rule violations (attributed to difficulty controlling impulses), and a trial-and-error method of problem solving that is dominated by the final goal, whereas older children (ages 10–12) demonstrate more inconsistent planning skill in that they may show sophisticated strategies when solving simpler problems and a reversion to less mature strategies when solving more complex problems. Adult levels are reached at approximately age 13 to 15.

Impaired performance on the *Tower of London* has been reported in the literature for several pediatric disorders including traumatic brain injury, hydrocephalus, focal brain lesions, and phenylketonuria (Fletcher, Brookshire, Landry, & Bohan, 1996; Jacobs & Anderson, 2002; Levin, et al., 1994; Welsh, Pennington, Ozonoff, Rouse, & McCabe, 1990). The primary conclusion of these studies was that while the *Tower of London* was sensitive to brain impairment, its utility in specifically identifying a pattern of deficits specific to a particular form of frontal lobe damage was much less clear. Culbertson and Zillmer (1998) used the TOL-DX to assess age-related changes in executive planning in children with ADHD compared to typically developing children. Both groups demonstrated steady improvement across the age span, exhibiting parallel trajectories, but the ADHD group performed less efficiently.

STROOP COLOR WORD TEST (SCWT)

The Stroop paradigm is one of the oldest and most widely used techniques (MacLeod, 1991), dating back to the work of Raymond Cattell in the nineteenth century (Mitrushina, Boone, Razani, & D'Elia, 2005). The *Stroop Color Word Test* (SCWT; Stroop, 1935) was designed to assess executive functioning in relation to inhibitory responses. The Stroop procedure requires the individual to inhibit a prepotent well-learned verbal response when faced with a novel verbal response (e.g., inhibit an automatized reading response and produce a competing color-naming response). It appears to measure focused and selective attention, the ability to shift cognitive set, and the ability to inhibit automatic responses. Several versions of this classic task are available, but there is no recognized standard version (Homack & Riccio, 2004). Several neuroimaging studies have demonstrated the participation of the superior medial prefrontal cortex, anterior cingulate circuit, and cerebellum during the classic inhibition experimental condition of the Stroop task (Fiez, Petersen, & Cheney, 1992; Gruber, Rogowska, Holcomb, Soraci, & Yurgelun, 2002; Pujol et al., 2001).

The *Stroop Color and Word Test-Revised, Children's Version* (Golden, Freshwater, & Golden, 2003) is an updated norm-referenced standardized version of the initial Stroop test. With most Stroop tasks, the examinee is administered baseline conditions (e.g., naming color patches and reading color words), and then the inhibition condition is administered (naming the ink colors that the color words are printed in). With some tasks, a fourth condition is administered that requires the examinee to switch back and forth between naming the dissonant ink colors and reading the words. Many of the current standardized batteries, such as the D-KEFS and the NEPSY II, incorporate Stroop tasks. Theoretically, the color-word task or inhibition condition is the component that is believed to measure set shifting and inhibition (Homack & Riccio, 2004). Research has shown that Stroop tasks are not necessarily interchangeable and may not tap the same underlying processes (Salthouse & Meinz, 1995; Shilling, Chetwynd, & Rabbit, 2002). As a result, although there is a large literature base, reviewing the literature for consistent results or trends is challenging.

Homack and Riccio (2004) conducted a meta-analysis on the sensitivity and specificity of the *Stroop Color and Word Test* with children. Homack and Riccio noted that while there is a relatively large literature and normative base for Stroop tasks in adults, research with children is limited and no normative base for children exists. In adults, performance on the Stroop task appears to be impacted by intelligence and education level. It is hypothesized that this may be true for children and adolescents as well. Therefore, Homack and Riccio suggest that Stroop performance only be interpreted as reflecting deficits in set shifting and inhibition if the score on the word-reading task is consistent with the child's cognitive ability and there is no evidence of a learning disability. The meta-analysis consisted of 33 articles that reported Stroop results for children and adolescents with various clinical disorders with the largest number involving ADHD and learning disabilities. The evidence suggests that Stroop tasks effectively discriminate children with ADHD and LD from typically developing children (e.g., children with ADHD or LD had impaired performance relative to the control group), but cannot predict within clinical group differences. Homack and Riccio conclude that further research investigating the usefulness of Stroop tasks in the neuropsychological assessment of children is warranted.

THE CONTRIBUTION AND THE ASSESSMENT OF WORKING MEMORY AND ATTENTION
WITHIN THE DOMAIN OF EXECUTIVE FUNCTIONS

Working memory and attention are acknowledged as fundamental aspects of executive functioning (Anderson, Levin & Jacobs, 2002; Baron, 2004; Baddeley, 1996; Hughes & Graham, 2002), and evaluating working memory and attention is seen as a critical component of assessing executive functions. There are numerous instruments available to measure memory skills, specifically working memory skills, in children and adolescents including the *Test of Memory and Learning 2* (TOMAL II; Reynolds & Voress, 2007), the *Wide Range Assessment of Memory and Learning 2* (WRAML 2; Sheslow & Adams, 2003) and the *Children's Memory Scale* (CMS; Cohen, 1997). Additionally, attention can be assessed using subtests comprising the Broad Attention Cluster from the *Woodcock Johnson III: Tests of Cognitive Abilities* and the *Test of Everyday Attention for Children* (TEA-Ch: Manly, Robertson, Anderson, & Nimmo-Smith, 1999). In the interests of space, the reader is referred to Chapter 11 (attention) and Chapter 25 (memory and learning) for a more thorough discussion of these two important topics.

The above review of instruments used to measure executive functions is certainly not encompassing of all the available instruments that could be used to measure the domains of executive functioning. The choice of instrument utilized by any given school psychologist to measure executive functioning within a neuropsychological evaluation is often based on availability, familiarity, client parameters, or the referral question. Overall, there is not yet a full complement of sensitive and reliable measures with good specificity for measuring executive functions in children. Furthermore, a primary issue in the assessment of executive functioning of children and adolescents is that so few school psychologists are trained in the administration, scoring, or interpretation of these instruments. School psychologists who are considering adding one or more of these instruments to their repertoire must understand that neuropsychological assessment is not a collection of tests, but rather a conceptual framework for understanding the integration and manifestation of brain-behavior relationships in child populations (Gioia et al., 2001). School psychologists are well trained in cognitive assessment and child development, but that knowledge and training is simply not sufficient for more specialized neuropsychological assessment of executive functions (or other neuropsychological functions like working memory). School psychologists who attempt to measure executive functions without the proper knowledge or experience risk practicing outside the boundaries of their training and experience, not to mention the potential damage that can be done by inaccurate interpretation of assessment results.

SCHOOL NEUROPSYCHOLOGICAL ASSESSMENT OF EXECUTIVE FUNCTIONS IN CHILDREN AND ADOLESCENTS

The neuropsychological assessment of children in general, and of executive functioning specifically, is complex and requires an understanding of child development, neuropsychological and neuroscientific theory, psychometrics and use of empirical data, as well as knowledge about the impact of social, familial, and cultural variables on brain behavior relationships. A comprehensive assessment of executive functioning should include both formal and informal methods of gathering information.

INFORMAL ASSESSMENT OF EXECUTIVE FUNCTIONS

Valuable information about executive functions can be elicited through a comprehensive interview and completion of a developmental history. The interview and developmental history are important for eliciting information about the presence or absence of executive skills in everyday functioning (Dawson & Guare, 2004). The interview and developmental history should focus on prenatal/birth information, early risk factors, deviations from normal development, related health/medical information (such as exposure to toxins, head injuries, and medications), and descriptions of behavior and cognitive skills. Strauss and colleagues (2006) provide a good example of a background and developmental history questionnaire applicable to neuropsychological assessment in their book *A Compendium of Neuropsychological Tests* (3rd edition).

Behavioral observation and norm-referenced assessment of behavior can also elicit information about executive skills in everyday functioning. Behavioral observation in this context should occur in multiple settings and focus on the child's ability to perform a task independently. The examiner should observe how the child approaches the task and develops the strategies to accomplish the task, initiates the task, sustains attention to the task, problem solves, and self-monitors. In addition to behavioral observations, norm-referenced assessment of behavior, and more specifically attention, can be accomplished using a variety of standardized instruments such as the *Behavior Assessment System for Children-2* (BASC-2; Reynolds & Kamphaus, 2007). The *Behavior Rating Inventory of Executive Functioning* (BRIEF) (Guy, Isquith, et al., 2000) can also be used as long as the examiner understands exactly what is being measured with the test.

NORM-REFERENCED ASSESSMENT OF EXECUTIVE FUNCTIONS

Based on current knowledge of executive functioning in children, to most effectively evaluate executive functions, four specific areas should be thoroughly assessed.

Cognitive (mental) flexibility is the ability to shift one's problem solving strategy during complex or novel tasks. Thinking flexibly and being able to alternate attention is essential to effective problem solving and is a critical element of executive functioning. Set shifting can be easily evaluated using card sorting tasks, Stroop tasks, category tasks, and trail making tasks.

Attention is one of the most difficult domains to separate from executive functioning. To capture the executive functioning aspects of attention, response inhibition, selective attention, and sustained/focused attention should all be evaluated. The Broad Attention Cluster from the *WJ III Tests of Cognitive Abilities* (WJ III COG) provides an excellent measure of these skills. One aspect of attention that warrants particular consideration in the assessment of executive functions is inhibitory control (also referred to as inhibition, interference control, or response inhibition) (Miller, 2007). Inhibition can be cognitive or behavioral and does not appear to be a unitary construct. Inhibitory control can be measured using attention and interference tasks. An example would be the *Conners Continuous Performance Test, 2nd Edition* (Conners, 2004) or the Stroop-like tasks that can be found on the D-KEFS and the NEPSY II. However, recent research has begun to suggest that in children a separate inhibition factor in nonclinical samples cannot be sustained when shared nonexecutive variance is controlled for in the data analysis (Huizinga, Dolan, & van der Molen, 2006; van der Sluis et al., 2007). The reader is referred to Chapter 11 for a more thorough review of attentional constructs.

Planning is the ability to anticipate future events, set goals, and develop appropriate steps to achieve a task. Planning involves sequencing steps or strategies to effectively and efficiently achieve the desired outcome. Planning can be adequately measured using tower tasks and trail making tasks.

Working memory is the process of holding information in mind for the purpose of completing a specific task. Currently, most working memory tasks take one of two forms: span tasks, where information is maintained across a delay, and manipulation tasks in which information is reorganized. Working memory can be assessed with any number of tasks from a variety of instruments. The caveat would be that examiners need to choose measures that evaluate working memory and not other aspects of memory such as short-term immediate memory, associative memory, or long-term retrieval. Working memory should be evaluated in both verbal and visual-spatial formats. The reader is referred to Chapter 25 for a more thorough review of the construct of working memory.

When selecting tasks, it is important to specify the target executive process to be measured, and then to carefully evaluate the assessment tools based on what specific executive component each tool is thought to measure: "Simply relying on a commonly used complex task like the WCST as a general measure of executive functioning will not suffice" (Straus et al., 2006, p. 406). It is important to keep in mind, that regardless of what constructs various tasks purport to measure, there is a paucity of independent research confirming what these tasks actually measure.

When assessing executive functioning, one must carefully observe the child's performance to determine why the child did well or poorly, rather than that he or she simply did or did not arrive at a correct answer (Gioia et al., 2001). Qualitative analysis and process scores are invaluable resources and should not be ignored in favor of scaled scores, T-scores, or standard scores. Because executive functions show differing developmental trajectories, deficits in an executive function should influence performance across two or more specific domains in order to be clinically significant, and the deficit should be both normative and ipsative. Additionally, the examiner needs to consider the particular cognitive skill and behavioral demands of the task, the requirements for success in completing the task, and possible alternative explanations for performance before concluding that there is an executive function deficit (Baron, 2004). A useful, but time-intensive, approach is to select a measure of executive function with relatively minimal executive function demand to establish a baseline of performance, then systematically select and administer measures with increasing executive functioning demands. If present, executive dysfunction will result in decreasing proficiency with tasks as the executive function requirements increase (McCloskey, 2008). It is also critical to remember that a child who exhibits average performance on standardized measures of executive functioning may still be highly dysfunctional in a real world setting as the "absence of EF impairment on neuropsychological testing is not proof of intact EF" (Baron, 2004, p. 134). But, accurate assessment and interpretation can allow for identification of a pattern of strengths and weaknesses in a child's executive skills that can lead to appropriate recommendations for intervention.

EVIDENCE-BASED INTERVENTIONS OF EXECUTIVE FUNCTIONS IN CHILDREN AND ADOLESCENTS

Accurate assessment of executive functions is the key to efficient, effective intervention strategies (Dawson & Guare, 2004), but understanding how executive functions manifest in school and in children of different ages is also important. Children with executive dysfunction may present with academic, social, or behavioral difficulties (or some combination thereof), and they may or may not qualify for special education services using current disability criteria. Executive functions as applied to children and school include the inability to maintain attention, control impulses, resist distraction, maintain effort, engage in mental planning and problem solving, maintain flexibility, manage time, set priorities, organize and execute tasks, and self-monitor. Problems with executive functions may manifest as failing to turn in homework despite having completed it; an inability to initiate and carry out long-term projects; difficulty using mental strategies for memorization and retrieval; trouble initiating tasks, generating ideas independently, and analyzing task requirements; or difficulty regulating impulses or emotion. These are only a few of the difficulties children with executive dysfunction may demonstrate, and it is certainly not an all-inclusive list. These children are often described as lazy, unmotivated, and extremely disorganized. They may have been accurately, or inaccurately, diagnosed with ADHD or ADD because of their difficulties with inhibition, impulsivity, and distraction. Frequently, executive dysfunction does not present itself until the upper elementary or middle school grades, as the demand for executive functions is very limited in the early elementary grades. As children transition from learning specific academic skills like reading and writing to applying those skills to content areas, the demand for executive functions increases rather dramatically (Gioia et al., 2001). The more classroom instruction or activities invoke executive functions, for example, complex task production that requires the individual to figure out what he or she is learning without immediate feedback for correctness, the more executive function difficulties are going to impact learning and performance.

The majority of the published research available on executive function interventions is with adults, and much of that involves single case qualitative studies focusing on recovery from traumatic or acquired brain injury. The research on effective interventions for executive functioning in children is almost nonexistent, and what is available is almost totally focused on recovery from traumatic brain injury or utilizes samples of children with ADHD (Limond & Leeke, 2005; Ylvisaker & DeBonis, 2000). Most of the recommendations available are either based on modified extensions of materials developed for adults, are generic rather than specific to executive functioning, or have no supporting evidence that they actually impact executive functions (Cicerone, 2002). School is a complex environment requiring academic, social, and behavioral skills for success, and executive function interventions with children are challenging because of the complexity of brain function superimposed on a continual developmental process.

Dawson and Guare (2004) in their book *Executive Skills in Children and Adolescents: A Practical Guide to Assessment and Intervention,* provide a behavioral perspective for intervention with executive dysfunction. The ideas and examples provided by Dawson and Guare will not seem particularly new or innovative to most school psychologists; however, the ideas can provide a framework for thinking about how to phrase recommendations and construct interventions. Dawson and Guare clearly note that with executive function deficits, intervention can be focused on the external environment (changing the physical environment, changing the nature of the task, changing the way cues are provided, or changing the way adults interact with the child) or on the person (changing the child's capacity for using executive functions).

Environmentally focused interventions rely on adults to modify the environment by providing support, control, and reinforcement. Environmental management is a critical component in the management of dysexecutive symptoms (Sohlberg & Mateer, 2001). Environmental adjustments might include increasing the structure and routine of the classroom, clarifying classroom expectations (clear communication of expectations, rules, and consequences), teaching and practicing expected behaviors, providing clear directions with positive feedback for performance, structuring tasks into manageable increments, providing explicit instruction for each task component, and teaching the use of strategies and tools such as calendars, graphic organizers, visual schedules, proximity control, or cueing techniques. Environmental adjustments related to school performance that are conducted at home typically center on homework and might include identifying a place and time to complete homework; requiring the parent to structure and monitor the homework; or requiring the parent and teacher to actively coordinate, making sure homework assignments are recorded by the child, sent home with the child for the parent to monitor, completed under parental supervision, and ultimately submitted to the teacher for credit.

Overall, altering the environment typically involves providing greater structure, simplifying tasks or eliminating the need for certain tasks, allowing more time to complete activities, and providing an external oral or written cueing system (Mateer, 1997; Ponsford, 2004). Environmental management structures the environment so as to circumvent or prevent problems arising from executive function difficulties, essentially replacing the role of the frontal lobes. Dawson and Guare note that for children with weak executive skills, the first and often most effective step is to change the environment to adjust to the child's limitations.

Person-focused interventions focus on teaching specific executive skills and motivating the child to use them effectively. In the adult literature this is often referred to as cognitive rehabilitation. This term is commonly used to describe an umbrella of cognitive or cognitive-behavioral interventions, but there is little consensus as to what exactly cognitive rehabilitation entails particularly as applied to executive functioning (Ponsford, 2004). In the field of rehabilitation, person-focused intervention often takes the form of direct retraining of cognitive abilities. In this approach, tasks are designed to provide practice in the underlying cognitive ability such as divided attention or inhibition. Mahone and Slomine (2007) provide an example of this approach in their discussion of interventions strategies for children as they relate to the various skills of executive functioning (e.g., initiation, planning, working memory). In school settings, instructional strategies will vary with the executive skill to be learned, but in general cognitive behavioral strategies tend to be the most effective, and training task-specific routines incorporates many features of behavioral programming. Important features in direct retraining include writing a task analysis that breaks the task into single logically sequential steps, developing explicit instructions for each step in the sequence, providing sufficient practice on each step, and ensuring that reinforcement and motivation to succeed are embedded into the training (Sohlberg & Mateer, 2001). Before using a reinforcement or incentive program to motivate the child to perform the skill, it is imperative that the child actually be able to execute the skill. Most children fail to use executive skills because they do not have them, not because they do not want to apply them. Teaching skills is not sufficient; skills must be coached, rehearsed, and practiced preferably in the environment in which they need to be performed (Mahone & Slomine, 2007). Person-focused interventions for executive functions must be viewed developmentally. Because executive skills develop over time with the progression from external (someone else monitors) to internal (internalized and self-monitored), parents and teachers must first teach the skill, provide the external support and monitoring of the skill, and provide time for the skill to be incorporated into the child's repertoire.

A promising person-focused intervention applicable to executive functions is self-instructional training. Children are taught to regulate their behavior via self-talk. The foundation of this approach stems from the work of Vygotsky and Luria, both of whom suggested that volitional behavior is mediated by inner speech rather than mental acts (Sohlberg & Mateer, 2001). Verbal self-instruction and self-regulation techniques have been effective in the remediation of impulsivity, planning, and problem-solving deficits in children (Alderman, Fry, & Youngson, 1995).

Ultimately, the goal of intervention is to improve functioning on daily activities in the school and home environments. Unfortunately, little information is available regarding the generalizability of gains made on experimental tasks to real-world tasks or on the maintenance of treatment effects over time. Further research needs to be conducted on effective interventions for executive functions, the use of interventions with different age ranges, and long-term followup of treatment efficacy.

An alternative to the individualized approach to intervention is provided in Lynn Meltzer's (2007) book, *Executive Function in Education: From Theory to Practice*. Six chapters in the third section of the book discuss the need to apply executive functioning training as a component of regular education classroom practices and curriculum for all children. The authors of these chapters in Meltzer's book basically posit that interventions that focus on rehabilitating or remediating students with deficits are not robust enough and that it is the educational system that needs to change to accommodate all students. These authors acknowledge significant barriers to this approach, including teachers who are not trained to teach executive function skills and strategies; limited opportunity within the educational environment to frequently practice such skills with plentiful individualized feedback; and the inability to provide ongoing support and adaptation within the curriculum and regular classroom for children with executive functioning deficits to make progress. Yet, they advocate for further research into the effectiveness of this approach and the development of specific curriculum or instructional methods for addressing executive functions in the regular education environment.

Finally, there are promising pharmacological interventions. The stimulant medications used to treat attention-deficit disorders have been consistently associated with improvements in executive functions (working memory, inhibition, and motor planning) for children with traumatic brain injuries, epilepsy, leukemia and ADHD (Weber & Lutschg, 2002). Other medications, amantadine hydrochloride (Beers, Skold, Dixon, & Adelson, 2005) and guanfacine (Cummings, Singer, Krieger, Miller, & Mahone, 2002) also show promising results.

SUMMARY

In summary, the study of executive functions is an emerging field that is still grappling to develop a unitary definition and to describe the relationship among executive functions, cognition, and behavior. This is compounded by a disconnect between theory, assessment, and intervention, as well as by limited research on the developmental nature of executive functions in children, how best to assess these functions, and effective ways to intervene when executive dysfunction is identified. Regardless, school psychologists are increasingly using neuropsychological measures to enhance their standard assessment practices and to measure cognitive functions such as executive functioning. Thus, it is important for these school psychologists to have the appropriate training in the administration, scoring, and interpretation of neuropsychological tests and to restrict their interpretive inferences to a level consistent with their background and training. The school psychologist practicing school neuropsychology should be familiar with basic neuropsychological principles and be well versed in pediatric psychopathology and neurology when using neuropsychological tests to diagnose neurological, developmental, or neuropsychiatric disorders.

REFERENCES

Achenbach, T. M. (2008). *Achenbach systems of empirically based assessment (ASEBA).* Burlington, VT: ASEBA.

Alderman, N., Fry, R. K., & Youngson, H. A. (1995). Improvement of self-monitoring skills, reduction of behavior disturbance and the dysexecutive syndrome: Comparison of response-cost and a new programme of self-monitoring training. *Neuropsychological Rehabilitation, 5,* 193–221.

Anderson, M. (2008). The concept and development of general intellectual ability. In J. Reed & J. Warner-Rogers (Eds.), *Child neuropsychology: Concepts, theory, and practice.* New York: Wiley-Blackwell.

Anderson, P. (2002). Assessment and development of executive function during childhood. *Child Neuropsychology, 8,* 71–82.

Anderson, V. (2002). Executive functions in children: Introduction. *Child Neuropsychology, 8,* 69–70.

Anderson, V. A., Anderson, P., Northam, E., Jacobs, R., & Mikiewicz, O. (2002). Relationships between cognitive and behavioral measures of executive functions in children with brain disease. *Child Neuropsychology, 8,* 231–240.

Anderson, V., Levin, H. S., & Jacobs, R. (2002). Executive functioning after frontal lobe injury: A developmental perspective. In D. T. Stuss & R. T. Knight (Eds.), *Principles of frontal lobe function* (pp. 504–527). New York: Oxford University Press.

Archibald, S. J., & Kerns, K. A. (1999). Identification and description of new tests of executive functioning in children. *Child Neuropsychology, 5,* 115–129.

Ardila, A., Pineda, D., & Rosselli, M. (2000). Correlation between intelligence test scores and executive function measures. *Archives of Clinical Neuropsychology, 15,* 31–36.

Arffa, S., Lovell, M., Podell, K., & Goldberg, E. (1998). Wisconsin Card Sorting Test performance in above average and superior school children: Relationship to intelligence and age. *Archives of Clinical Neuropsychology, 13,* 713–720.

Armstrong, C. M., Allen, D. N., Donohue, B., & Mayfield, J. (2007). Sensitivity of the Comprehensive Trail Making Test to traumatic brain injury in adolescents. *Archives of Clinical Neuropsychology, 23,* 351–358.

Army Individual Test Battery, (1944). Manual of directions and scoring, War Department, Adjutant General's Office, Washington, DC.

Baddeley, A. (1996). Exploring the central executive. *Quarterly Journal of Experimental Psychology: Section A, 49,* 5–28.

Baddeley, A., & Hitch, G. (1974). Working memory. In G. H. Bower (Ed.), *The psychology of learning and motivation* (Vol. 8, pp. 47–89). New York: Academic Press.

Baker, K., Segalowitz, S. J., & Ferlisi, M. C. (2001). The effect of differing scoring methods for Tower of London task on developmental patterns of performance. *The Clinical Neuropsychologist, 15*, 309–313.

Barkley, R. A. (2000). The executive functions and ADHD. *Journal of the American Academy of Child and Adolescent Psychiatry, 39*, 1064–1068.

Baron, I. S. (2004). *Neuropsychological evaluation of the child.* New York: Oxford University Press.

Bauman, W. (2008). *Executive functioning in children and adolescents with traumatic brain injuries: Utilization of the Comprehensive Trail Making Test.* Unpublished doctoral dissertation. Texas Woman's University.

Beers, S. R., Skold, A., Dixon, C. E., & Adelson, D. (2005). Neurobehavioral effects of amantadine after pediatric traumatic brain injury: A preliminary report. *Journal of Head Trauma Rehabilitation, 20*, 450–463.

Benjamin, M. L. (2004). *Pilot data on the Behavioral Rating Inventory of Executive Function (BRIEF) and performance measures of executive function in pediatric traumatic brain injury.* Unpublished master's thesis. University of Florida.

Berman, K. F., Ostrem, J. L., & Randolph, C. (1995). Physiological activation of a cortical network during performance of the Wisconsin Card Sort Test: A positron emission tomography study. *Neuropsychologia, 33*, 1027–1046.

Bishop, D. V. M., Aamodt-Leeper, G., Creswell, C., McGurk, R., & Skuse, D. H., (2001). Individual differences in cognitive planning on the Tower of Hanoi task: Neuropsychological maturity or measurement error? *Journal of Child Psychology and Psychiatry, 42*, 551–556.

Blair, C. (2006). Toward a revised theory of general intelligence: Further examination of fluid cognitive abilities as unique aspects of human cognition. *Behavioral and Brain Sciences, 29*, 145–153.

Blair, C., Zelazo, P. D., & Greenberg, M. T. (2005). The measurement of executive function in childhood. *Developmental Neuropsychology, 28*, 561–571.

Boll, T. (1993). *Children's category test.* San Antonio, TX: The Psychological Corporation.

Brocki, K. C., & Bohlin, G. (2004). Executive functions in children aged 6–13: A dimensional and developmental study. *Developmental Neuropsychology 26*, 571–593.

Brookshire, B., Levin, H. S., Song, J. X., Zhang, L. (2004). Components of executive function in typically developing and head injured children. *Developmental Neuropsychology, 25*, 61–83.

Busch, R. M., McBride, A., Curtiss, G., & Vanderploeg, R. (2005). The components of executive functioning in traumatic brain injury. *Journal of Clinical and Experimental Neuropsychology, 27*, 1022–1032.

Byrnes, J. P. (2007). Some ways in which neuroscientific research can be relevant to education. In D. Coch, K. W. Fischer, & G. Dawson. *Human behavior, learning and the developing brain.* New York: Guilford Press.

Cabeza, R., & Nyberg, L. (2000). Imaging cognition II: An empirical review of 275 PET and fMRI studies. *Journal of Cognitive Neuroscience, 12*, 1–47.

Carlson, N. R. (2004). *Physiology of behavior* (8th ed.). New York: Pearson.

Carper, M. S., (2003). *A concurrent validity study comparing executive functioning of the Woodcock Johnson III Tests of Cognitive Ability and the NEPSY.* Unpublished doctoral dissertation. Texas Woman's University.

Casey, B. J., Galvan, A., & Hare, T. A. (2005). Changes in cerebral functional organization during cognitive development. *Current Opinion in Neurobiology, 15,* 239–244.

Cicerone, K. D. (2002). The enigma of executive functioning: Theoretical contributions to therapeutic interventions. In P. J. Eslinger (Ed.), *Neuropsychological interventions* (pp. 246–265). New York: Guilford.

Clark, E. (n.d.). Review of the Wisconsin Card Sorting Test, Revised and Expanded. [Electronic version] *14th Mental measurements yearbook.* Retrieved August 13, 2008, from http://www.ovidweb.cgi.

Cohen, M. J. (1997). *Children's memory scale.* San Antonio, TX: The Psychological Corporation.

Cohen, M. J., Riccio, C. A., Kibby, M. Y., & Edmonds, J. E. (2000). Developmental progression of clock face drawing in children. *Child Neuropsychology, 6,* 64–76.

Conners, K. (2004). *Continuous performance test* (2nd ed.). Toronto: Multi-Health Systems.

Conners, K. (2008a) *Conners 3rd edition* North Tonawanda, NY: Multi-Health Systems.

Conners, K. (2008b) *Conners comprehensive behavior rating scales.* North Tonawanda, NY: Multi-Health Systems.

Culbertson, W. C., & Zillmer, E. A. (1998). The construct validity of the Tower of London-Drexel University as a measure of executive functioning of ADHD children. *Assessment, 5,* 215–226.

Culbertson, W. C., & Zillmer, E. A. (2005). *Tower of London—Drexel University* (2nd ed.). Chicago, IL: Multi-Health Systems.

Cummings, D. D., Singer, H. S., Krieger, M., Miller, T., & Mahone, R. M. (2002). Neuropsychiatric effects of guanfacine in children with mild Tourette syndrome: A pilot study. *Clinical Neuropharmacology, 25,* 325–332.

D'Amato, R. C., & Hartlage, L. C. (2008). *Essentials of neuropsychological assessment* (2nd ed.). New York: Springer.

Dawson, P., & Guare, R. (2004). *Executive skills in children and adolescents: A practical guide to assessment and intervention.* New York: Guilford.

Delis, D. C., Kaplan, E., & Kramer, J. (2001). *Delis Kaplan executive function system.* San Antonio, TX: The Psychological Corporation.

Donders, J. (1999). Latent structure of the Children's Category Test at two age levels in the standardization sample. *Journal of Clinical and Experimental Neuropsychology, 21,* 279–282.

Duncan, J., Emslie, H., Williams, P., Johnson, R., & Freer, C. (1996). Intelligence and the frontal lobe: The organization of goal directed behavior. *Cognitive Psychology, 30,* 257–303.

Engle, R. W. (2002). Working memory capacity as executive attention. *Current Directions in Psychological Science, 11,* 19–23.

Ewing-Cobbs, L., Prasad, M. R., Landry, S. H., Kramer, L., & DeLeon, R. (2004). Executive functions following traumatic brain injury in young children: A preliminary analysis. *Developmental Neuropsychology, 26,* 487–512.

Fallgatter, A. J., & Strik, W. K. (1998). Frontal brain activation during the Wisconsin Card Sorting Test assessed with two-channel near-infrared spectroscopy. *European Archives of Psychiatry and Clinical Neuroscience, 248,* 245–249.

Fiez, J. A., Petersen, S. E., & Cheney, M. K. (1992). Impaired non-motor learning and error detection associated with cerebellar damage. *Brain, 115,* 155–178.

Fletcher, J. M., Brookshire, B. L., Landry, S. H., & Bohan, T. P. (1996). Attentional skills and executive functions in children with early hydrocephalus. *Developmental Neuropsychology, 12,* 53–76.

Floyd, R. G., McCormack, A. C., Ingram, E. L., Davis, A. E., Bergeron, R., & Hamilton, G. (2006). Relations between the Woodcock Johnson III clinical clusters and measures of executive functions from the Delis-Kaplan Executive Function System. *Journal of Psychoeducational Assessment, 24,* 303–317.

Floyd, R. G., Shaver, R. B., & McGrew, K. S. (2003). Interpretation of the Woodcock Johnson III Tests of Cognitive Abilities: Acting on evidence. In F. A. Schrank & D. P. Flanagan (Eds.), *WJ III clinical uise and interpretation: Scientist-practitioner perspectives* (pp. 29–46). New York: Academic Press.

Ford, L., Keith, T. Z., Floyd, R. G., Fields, C., & Schrank, F. A. (2003). Using the WJ III: Tests of Cognitive Abilities with Attention Deficit Hyperactivity Disorder. In F. A. Schrank & D. P. Flanagan (Eds.), *WJ III Clinical Use and Interpretation: Scientist-Practitioner Perspectives* (pp. 319–344). New York: Academic Press.

Friedman, N. P., Miyake, A., Corley, R. P., Young, S. E., DeFries, J. C., & Hewitt, J. K. (2006). Not all executive functions are related to intelligence. *Psychological Science, 17,* 172–179.

Giedd, J. N. (2004). Structural magnetic resonance imaging of the adolescent brain. *Annals of New York Academy of Science, 1021,* 77–85.

Gioia, G. A., Espy, K., & Isquith, P. K. (2003). *Behavior rating inventory of executive function—Preschool version.* Odessa, FL: Psychological Assessment Resources.

Gioia, G. A., Espy, K., & Isquith, P. K. (2004). *Behavior rating inventory of executive function—Self report.* Odessa, FL: Psychological Assessment Resources.

Gioia, G. A., Isquith, P. K., & Guy, S. C. (2001). Assessment of executive functions in children with neurological impairment. In R. J. Simeonsson & S. L. Rosenthal (Eds.), *Psychological and developmental assessment: Children with disabilities and chronic conditions.* New York: Guilford.

Gioia, G. A., Isquith, P. K., Guy, S. C., & Kenworthy, L. (2000). *Behavior Rating Inventory of Executive Function.* Odessa, FL: Psychological Assessment Resources.

Gioia, G. A., Isquith, P. K., Kenworthy, L., & Barton, R. M. (2002). Profiles of everyday executive function in acquired and developmental disorders. *Child Neuropsychology, 8,* 121–137.

Goel, V., Pullara, S. D., & Grafman, J. (2001). A computational model of frontal lobe dysfunction: Working memory and the Tower of Hanoi task. *Cognitive Science, 25,* 287–313.

Goldberg, E. (2002). *The executive brain: Frontal lobes and the civilized mind.* New York: Oxford University Press.

Golden, C., Freshwater, S. M., & Golden, Z, (2003). *Stroop color and word test—Revised, children's version.* Wooddale, IL: Stoelting.

Gregg, N., & Coleman, C. (2003). Use of the Woodcock Johnson III in the diagnosis of learning disabilities. In F. A. Schrank & D. P. Flanagan (Eds.), *WJ III clinical use and interpretation: Scientist-practitioner perspectives* (pp. 125–174). New York: Academic Press.

Gruber, S. A., Rogowska, J., Holcomb, P., Soraci, S., & Yurgelun, D. (2002). Stroop performance in normal control subjects: An fMRI study. *Neuroimage, 16*, 349–360.

Hale, J. B., & Fiorello, C. A. (2004). *School neuropsychology: A practitioner's handbook.* New York: Guilford.

Halstead, W. (1952). The forntal lobes and the highest integrating capacities of man. *Halstead papers.* M175, p. 26. Akron, OH: Archives of the History of American Psychology.

Heaton, R. K., Chelune, G. J., Talley, J. L., Kay, G., & Curtiss, G. (1993). *Wisconsin card sorting test.* Odessa, FL: Psychological Assessment Resources.

Homack, S., Lee, D., & Riccio, C. A. (2005). Test review: Delis Kaplan executive function system. *Journal of Clinical and Experimental Neuropsychology, 27*, 599–609.

Homack, S., & Riccio, C. A. (2004). A meta-analysis of the sensitivity and specificity of the Stroop color and word test with children. *Archives of Clinical Neuropsychology, 19*, 725–743.

Hooper, S. R., Poon, K. K., Marcus, L., & Fine, C. (2006). Neuropsychological characteristics of school-age children with high functioning autism: Performance on the NEPSY. *Child Neuropsychology, 12*, 299–305.

Hughes, C., & Graham, A. (2002). Measuring executive functions in childhood: Problems and solutions. *Child and Adolescent Mental Health. 7*, 131–142.

Hughes, C., & Graham, A. (2008). Executive functions and development. In J. Reed & J. Warner-Rogers (Eds.), *Child Neuropsychology: Concepts, Theory, and Practice.* New York: Wiley-Blackwell.

Humes, G. E., Welsh, M. C., Retzlaff, P., & Cookson, N. (1997). Towers of Hanoi and London: Reliability of two executive function tasks. *Assessment, 4*, 249–257.

Huizinga, M., Dolan, C. V., & van der Molen, M. W. (2006). Age related change in executive function: Developmental trends and a latent variables analysis. *Neuropsychologia, 44*, 2017–2036.

Jacobs, R., & Anderson, V. (2002). Planning and problem solving skills following focal frontal brain lesions in childhood: Analysis using the Tower of London. *Child Neuropsychology, 8*, 93–106.

Joseph, R. M., McGrath, L. M., & Tager-Flusberg, H. (2005). Executive dysfunction and its relation to language ability in verbal school-age children with autism. *Developmental Neuropsychology, 27*, 361–378.

Kane, M. J., & Engle, R. W. (2002). The role of prefrontal cortex in working memory capacity, executive attention, and general fluid intelligence: An individual differences perspective. *Psychonomic Bulletin and Review, 9*, 637–671.

Kemp, S. (2007, July). *Introduction to the clinical development and applications of the NEPSY II*. Paper presented at the National School Neuropsychology Conference, Grapevine, TX.

Klemm, S., Schmidt, B., Knappe, S., & Blanz, B. (2006). Impaired working speed and executive functions as frontal lobe dysfunctions in young first-degree relatives of schizophrenic patients. *European Child and Adolescent Psychiatry, 15*, 400–408.

Knight, R. T., & Stuss, D. T. (2002). *Principles of frontal lobe function*. New York: Oxford University Press.

Korkman, M., Kirk, U., & Kemp, S. L. (1998). *NEPSY: A developmental neuropsychological assessment*. San Antonio, TX: The Psychological Corporation.

Korkman, M., Kirk, U., & Kemp, S. L. (2007a). *NEPSY II: A developmental neuropsychological assessment: Administration Manual*. San Antonio, TX: The Psychological Corporation.

Korkman, M., Kirk, U., & Kemp, S. L. (2007b). *NEPSY II: A developmental neuropsychological assessment: Clinical and Interpretive Manual*. San Antonio, TX: The Psychological Corporation.

Lazeron, R. H., Rombouts, S. A., & Machielsen, W. C. (2000). Visualizing brain activation during planning: The Tower of London Test adapted for functional MR imaging. *American Journal of Neuroradiology, 21*, 1407–1414.

Levin, H. S., Culhane, K. A., Hartmann, J., Evankovich, K., Mattson, A. J., Harward, H., Ringholz, G., Ewing-Cobbs, L., & Fletcher, J. M. (1991). Developmental changes in performance on tests of purported frontal lobe functioning. *Developmental Neuropsychology, 7*, 377–395.

Levin, H. S., & Hanten, G. (2005). Executive functions after traumatic brain injury in children. *Pediatric Neurology, 33*, 79–93.

Levin, H. S., Mendelsohn, D., Lily, M., Fletcher, J., Culhane, K., Chapman, S., Howard, H., Kusnerik, L., Bruce, D., & Eisenberg, H. (1994). Tower of London performance in relation to magnetic resonance imaging following closed head injury in children. *Neuropsychology, 8*, 171–179.

Lezak, M. D., Howieson, D. B., & Loring, D. W. (2004) *Neuropsychological assessment* (4th edition). New York: Oxford University Press.

Lidz, C. (2003). *Early childhood assessment*. New York: John Wiley & Sons.

Limond, J., & Leeke, R. (2005). Practitioner review: Cognitive rehabilitation for children with acquired brain injury. *Journal of Child Psychology and Psychiatry, 46*, 339–352.

Luria, A. R. (1966). *Higher cortical functions in man* (2nd ed.). New York: Basic Books.

Luria, A. R. (1973). *The working brain: An introduction to neuropsychology*. New York: Basic Books.

MacLeod, C. M. (1991). Half a century of research on the Stroop effect: An integrative review. *Psychological Bulletin, 109*, 163–203.

Mahone, E. M., Cirino, P. T., Cutting, L. E., Cerrone, P. M., Hagelthorn, K. M., Hiemenz, J. R., Singer, H. S., & Denckla, M. B. (2002). Validity of the Behavior Rating Inventory of Executive Function in children with ADHD and/or Tourette Syndrome. *Archives of Clinical Neuropsychology, 17*, 643–662.

Mahone, E. M., & Slomine, B. S. (2007). Managing dysexecutive disorders. In S. J. Hunter & J. Donders (Eds.), *Pediatric neuropsychological intervention: A critical review of science & practice*. London: Cambridge University Press.

Mangeot, S. D., Armstrong, K., Colvin, A. N., Yeates, K. O., & Taylor, H. G. (2002). Long term executive deficits in children with traumatic brain injuries: Assessing using the Behavior Rating Inventory of Executive Function (BRIEF). *Child Neuropsychology, 8*, 271–284.

Manly, T., Robertson, I. H., Anderson, V., & Nimmo-Smith, I. (1999). *TEA-Ch: The test of everyday attention for children*. San Antonio, Texas: The Psychological Corporation.

Mateer, C. A. (1997). Rehabilitation of individuals with frontal lobe impairment. In J. Leon-Carrion (Ed.), *Neuropsychological rehabilitation: Fundamentals, innovations, and directions*. Delray, FL: St. Lucie Press.

McCloskey, G. (2008). *Executive functions: Definitions, assessment and education/intervention*. Retrieved October 1, 2008, from http://www.ospaonline.org/pdf/presentations/mccloskey_EF.ppt.

Meltzer, L. (2007). *Executive function in education: From theory to practice*. New York: Guilford.

Meltzer, L., & Krishnan, K. (2007). Executive function difficulties and learning disabilities: Understandings and misunderstandings. In L. Meltzer (Ed.), *Executive function in education: From theory to practice* (pp. 77–105). New York: Guilford.

Miller, D. C. (2007). *Essentials of school neuropsychology assessment*. Hoboken, NJ: John Wiley & Sons.

Mirsky, A. F., Anthony, B. J., Duncan, C. C., Ahearn, M. B., & Kellam, S. J. (1991). Analysis of the elements of attention: A neuropsychological approach. *Neuropsychology Review, 2*, 109–145.

Mitrushina, M. M., Boone, K. B., Razani, J., & D'Elia, L. F. (2005). *Handbook of normative data for neuropsychological assessment* (2nd ed.). New York: Oxford University Press.

Miyake, A., Friedman, N. P., Emerson, M. J., Witzki, A. H., Howerter, A., & Wager, T. D. (2000). The unity and diversity of executive functions and their contributions to complex 'frontal lobe' tasks: A latent variable analysis. *Cognitive Psychology, 41*, 49–100.

Monchi, O., Petrides, M., Petre, V., Worsley, K., & Dagher, A. (2001). Wisconsin card sorting revisited: Distinct neural circuits participating in different stages of the task identified by event related functional magnetic resonance imaging. *Journal of Neuroscience, 21*, 7733–7741.

Nesbit-Greene, K., & Donders, J. (2002). Latent structure of the Children's Category Test after pediatric traumatic head injury. *Journal of Clinical and Experimental Neuropsychology, 24*, 194–199.

O'Brien, L. M., Mervis, C. B., Halbrook, C. R., Bruner, J. L., Smith, N., McNally, N., et al. (2004). Neurodevelopmental profiles for a sample of children diagnosed with ADHD. *Journal of Sleep Research, 13*, 165–172.

Ozonoff, S., & Schetter, P. (2007). Executive dysfunction in autism spectrum disorders: From research to practice. In L. Meltzer (Ed.), *Executive function in education: From theory to practice* (pp. 133–160). New York: Guilford.

Paniak, C. E., Miller, H. B., Murphy, D., Patterson, L., & Keizer, J. (1996). Canadian developmental norms for 9- to 14-year-olds on the Wisconsin card sorting test. *Canadian Journal of Rehabilitation, 9*, 233–237.

Pasini, A., Paloscia, C., Alessandrelli, R., Porfrio, M. C., & Curatolo, P. (2007). Attention and executive functions profile in drug naïve ADHD subtypes. *Brain and Development, 29*, 400–408.

Pederson, L. L. (2005). *The relationship between behavioral and performance-based measures of executive function in preschool children*. Unpublished dissertation. Texas Woman's University.

Ponsford, J. (2004). *Cognitive and behavioral rehabilitation: From neurobiology to clinical practice*. New York: Guilford.

Posner, M. I. (1994). Attention: The mechanisms of consciousness. *Proceedings of the National Academy of Science, 91*, 7398–7403.

Pujol, J., Vendrell, P., Deus, J., Junque, C., Bello, J., Marti-Vilat, J. L., & Capdevila, A. (2001). The effect of medial frontal and posterior parietal demyelinating lesions on Stroop interference. *Neuroimage, 13*, 68–75.

Read, B. G., & Schrank, F. A. (2003). Qualitative analysis of Woodcock Johnson III test performance. In F. A. Schrank & D. P. Flanagan (Eds.), *WJ III clinical use and interpretation: Scientist-practitioner perspectives* (pp. 47–91). New York: Academic Press.

Reitan, R. M., & Wolfson, D. (1992). *Neuropsychological evaluation of older children*. Tucson, AZ: Neuropsychology Press.

Reitan, R. M., & Wolfson, D. (2003). The Trail Making Test as an initial screening procedure for neuropsychological impairment in older children. *Archives of Clinical Neuropsychology, 19*, 281–288.

Reynolds, C. R. (2002). *Comprehensive trail making test*. Austin, TX: Pro-Ed.

Reynolds, C. R. (2007, July). *Frontal lobe development: What is it and when does it end?* Paper presented at the National School Neuropsychology Conference, Grapevine, TX.

Reynolds, C. R., & Kamphaus, R. W. (2007). *Behavior assessment system for children* (2nd ed.). New York: Pearson Assessments.

Reynolds, C. R., & Voress, J. K. (2007). *Test of memory and learning* (2nd ed.). Austin, TX: Pro-Ed.

Riccio, C. A., Hall, J., Morgan, A., Hynd, G. W., Gonzalez, J. J., & Marshall, R. M. (1994). Executive function and the Wisconsin Card Sorting Test: Relationship with behavioral ratings and cognitive ability. *Developmental Neuropsychology, 10*, 215–229.

Riddle, R., Morton, A., Sampson, J. D., Vachha, B., & Adams, R. (2005). Performance on the NEPSY among children with spina bifida. *Archives of Clinical Neuropsychology, 20*, 243–248.

Robbins, T. (2005). Chemistry of the mind: Neurochemical modulation of prefrontal cortical function. *Journal of Comparative Neurology, 493*, 140–146.

Romine, C. B., Lee, D., Wolfe, M. E., Homack, S., George, C., & Riccio, C. A. (2004). Wisconsin Card Sorting Test with children: A meta-analytic study of sensitivity and specificity. *Archives of Clinical Neuropsychology, 19*, 1027–1041.

Romine, C. B., & Reynolds, C. R. (2005). A model of the development of frontal lobe functioning: Findings from a meta-analysis. *Applied Neuropsychology, 12,* 190–201.

Rosselli, M., & Ardila, A. (1993). Developmental norms for the Wisconsin Card Sorting Test in 5- to12-year-old children. *The Clinical Neuropsychologist, 7,* 145–154.

Roth, R. M., & Saykin, A. J. (2004). Executive dysfunction in attention-deficit hyperactivity disorder: Cognitive and neuroimaging findings. *Psychiatric Clinics of North America, 27,* 83–96.

Salthouse, T. A., & Meinz, E. J. (1995). Aging, inhibition, working memory and speed. *Journal of Gerontology, 50,* 297–306.

Schrank, F. A. (2005). Woodcock Johnson III Tests of Cognitive Abilities. In D. P. Flanagan & P. L. Harrison (Eds.), *Contemporary intellectual assessment: Theories, tests, and issues.* New York: Guilford.

Sesma, H. W., Slomine, B. S., Ding, R., & McCarthy, M. L. (2008). Executive functioning in the first year after pediatric traumatic brain injury. *Pediatrics,* 121, 1686–1695.

Shallice, T. (1982). Specific impairments of planning. *Philosophical Transactions of the Royal Society of London, 298,* 199–209.

Shallice, T., Marzocchi, G. M., Coser, S., Del Savio, M., Meuter, R. F., & Rumaiti, R. I. (2002). Executive function profile of children with attention deficit hyperactivity disorder. *Developmental Neuropsychology, 21,* 43–71.

Sheslow, D., & Adams, W. (2003). *Wide range assessment of memory and learning* (2nd ed.). Wilmington, DE: Wide Range.

Shilling, V. M., Chetwynd, A., & Rabbit, P. M. A. (2002). Individual inconsistency across measures of inhibition: An investigation of the construct validity of inhibition in older adults. *Neuropsychologia, 40,* 605–619.

Shu, B., Tien, A. Y., Lung, F. W., & Chang, Y. Y. (2000). Norms for the Wisconsin Card Sorting Test in 6- to 11- year -old children in Taiwan. *The Clinical Neuropsychologist,* 14, 275–286.

Simon, H. A. (1975). The functional equivalence of problem solving skills. *Cognitive Psychology, 7,* 268–288.

Slomine, B. S., Gerring, J. P., Gradose, M. A., Vasa, R., Brady, K. D., Christensen, J. R., & Denckla, M. B. (2002). Performance on measures of 'executive function' following pediatric traumatic brain injury. *Brain Injury, 16,* 759–772.

Sohlberg, M. M., & Mateer, C. A. (2001). *Cognitive rehabilitation: An integrative neuropsychological approach.* New York: Guilford Press.

Stein, J., & Krishnan, K. (2007). Nonverbal learning disabilities and executive functions: The challenges of effective assessment and teaching. In L. Meltzer (Ed.), *Executive function in education: From theory to practice* (pp. 106–132). New York: Guilford.

Strauss, E., Sherman, E. M. S., Spreen, O. (2006). *A compendium of neuropsychological tests: Administration, norms, and commentary* (3rd ed.). New York: Oxford University Press.

Stroop, J. R. (1935). Studies of interference in serial verbal reaction. *Journal of Experimental Psychology, 18,* 643–662.

Szameitat, A. J., Schubert, T., Muuler, K., & Cramon, D. Y. (2002). Localization of executive functions in dual-task performance with fMRI. *Journal of Cognitive Neuroscience, 14,* 1148–1199.

Titley, J., & D'Amato, R. C. (2008). Understanding and using the NEPSY II with young children, children and adolescents. In R. C. D'Amato and L. C. Hartlage (Eds.), *Essentials of neuropsychological assessment* (2nd ed.). New York: Springer.

Ullsperger, M., & von Cramon, D. Y. (2004). Decision making, performance, and outcome monitoring in frontal cortical areas. *Nature Neuroscience, 7,* 1173–1174.

van der Sluis, S., de Jong, P. F., & van der Leij, A. (2007). Executive functioning in children and its relations with reasoning, reading, and arithmetic. *Intelligence, 35,* 427–449.

van Vreen, V., & Carter, C. S. (2002). The timing of action-monitoring processes in the anterior cingulated cortex. *Journal of Cognitive Science, 14,* 593–602.

Vriezen, E. R., & Pigott, S. E. (2002). The relationship between parental report on the BRIEF and performance based measures of executive function in children with moderate to severe brain injury. *Child Neuropsychology, 8,* 296–303.

Weber, P., & Lutschg, J. (2002). Methylphenidate treatment. *Pediatric Neurology, 26,* 261–266.

Welsh, M. C., Pennington, B. F., & Grossier, D. B., (1991). A normative developmental study of executive function: A window on prefrontal function in children. *Developmental Neuropsychology, 7,* 131–149.

Welsh, M. C., Pennington, B. F., Ozonoff, S., Rouse, B., & McCabe, E. R. B. (1990). Neuropsychology of early treated phenylketonuria: Specific executive function deficits. *Child Development, 61,* 1697–1713.

Wodka, E. L., Loftis, C., Mostofsky, S. H., Prahme, C., Gridley-Larson, J. C., Denckla, M. B., & Mahone, E. M. (2008). Predictions of ADHD in boys and girls using the D-KEFS. *Archives of Clinical Neuropsychology, 23,* 283–293.

Wood, J. N., & Grafman, J. (2003). Human prefrontal cortex: Processing and representational perspectives. *Nature Reviews Neuroscience, 4,* 139–147.

Woodcock, R. W., McGrew, K. S., & Mather, N. (2001). *Woodcock-Johnson III: Tests of Cognitive Abilities.* Rolling Meadows, IL: Riverside Publishing.

Woodcock, R. W., Schrank, F. A., Mather, N., & McGrew, K. S. (2007). *Woodcock-Johnson III normative update.* Rolling Meadows, IL: Riverside Publishing.

Ylvisaker, M., & DeBonis, D. (2000). Executive function impairment in adolescence: TBI and ADHD. *Topics in Language Disorders, 20,* 29–57.

Zelazo, P. D., Muller, U., Frye, D., & Marcovitch, S. (2003). The development of executive function in early childhood. *Monographs of the Society for Research in Child Development, 68* (Serial No. 274).

Zelazo, P. D., Reznick, J. S., & Pinon, D. E. (1995). Response control and the execution of verbal rules. *Developmental Psychology, 31,* 508–517.

Zillmer, E. A., Spiers, M. V., & Culbertson, W. C. (2008). *Principles of neuropsychology* (2nd ed.). Belmont, CA: Thomson.

CHAPTER 25

Assessing and Intervening with Children with Memory and Learning Disorders

JEFFREY A. MILLER and JESSICA L. BLASIK

T HIS CHAPTER BEGINS by describing overarching theories of working memory and long-term memory. Particular attention is paid to the connection between working and long-term memory in terms of learning and retrieval. Next, the neurobiology of the memory system is described including coverage of the neurocellular correlates of learning. Then, brief coverage of memory deficits associated with childhood developmental disorders is provided. It is argued that learning disabilities are associated with a variety of memory problems, which should be a focus of assessment and intervention. Finally, reviews of major memory and learning test batteries and empirically based interventions are provided.

MEMORY AND LEARNING

Memory and learning are very similar and can become easily confused. Memory and learning can be distinguished in the following way. Memory is the ability to recall past events and information. Learning is a process of linking memories with new experience; therefore, memory is essential to learning and memory is dependent upon learning. Simply put, the more information one has stored and can access in memory, the easier it is to link new information to and among memory, thus facilitating learning. There are three stages of memory and learning: encoding, storage, and retrieval. Encoding involves the processing of afferent information that will be stored in memory. Storage entails the consolidation of new information with information in memory. Finally, retrieval is the act of consciously accessing memories or automatically executing learned behaviors. The processes of memory and learning can break down at any of these stages.

OVERVIEW OF MEMORY SYSTEMS

The human memory system can be fractionated into several major divisions based on the temporal nature (temporary or longer term) of information storage. In the following the memory systems will be described according to two perspectives. The first perspective is from cognitive neuroscience and includes sensory memory, short-term memory, working memory, and long-term memory. It is important for the school neuropsychologist to understand the cognitive neuroscience perspective on memory organization as it will allow access to the broad empirical literature generated by the field of neuroscience. These memory systems are outlined in Table 25.1. The second perspective is from the school neuropsychology perspective, which draws its constructs from extant tests that are used to assess memory and learning. As will be seen, a one-to-one relationship does not always exist between the definitions used in cognitive neuroscience and the labels assigned to different memory and learning tests. It becomes the responsibility of school neuropsychologists to conduct demands and task analyses (cf. Hale &

Table 25.1
Memory and Learning Terms from Cognitive Neuroscience

Sensory Memory—Echoic

Sensory Memory—Iconic

Working Memory—Phonological Loop
- Phonological Store (Phonological STM)
- Articulatory Control Process (Verbal WM)

Working Memory—Visuospatial Sketchpad
- Visual Cache (Visuospatial STM)
- Inner Scribe (Visual WM)

Working Memory—Episodic Buffer

Working Memory—Central Executive (Executive WM)

Long-Term Memory—Explicit (Long-Term Retrieval)
- Semantic
- Episodic
- Lexical

Long-Term—Implicit

(Learning)

Note: Labels in parentheses are suggested by Dehn (2008). STM = short term memory, WM = working memory.

Fiorello, 2004) of memory and learning tests to determine whether the test evidences substantive validity (Messick, 1995) for the theoretical and empirical foundation for memory and learning constructs.

ORGANIZATION OF MEMORY FROM THE COGNITIVE NEUROSCIENCE PERSPECTIVE

SENSORY MEMORY

Sensory memory is associated with perception and is the ability to briefly retain a visual, auditory, or tactile perception after the original stimulus is removed (Baddeley, 2004). The sensory impression is ephemeral, lasting less than two seconds. The most frequently studied forms of sensory memory are visual, known as iconic, and auditory, known as echoic memory. Studies have shown that echoic memory persists longer than iconic memory (Baddeley, 2004). Less well studied is tactile memory, also known as haptic memory, which can hold up to five tactile stimuli at a time (Gallace, Tan, Haggard, & Spence, 2008). Like most of the memory system, sensory memory requires the allocation of attention and is dependent on executive functioning of the prefrontal lobe (Kaiser, Walker, Leiberg, & Lutzenberger, 2005). Further, there is an alignment of echoic and iconic memory with the visual and auditory components of the working memory system described next.

SHORT-TERM AND WORKING MEMORY

Short-term memory is a term historically used to describe all temporary memory that occurs subsequent to sensory memory (Atkinson & Shiffrin, 1968). However, the development of more articulated theories of working memory have shown that short-term memory is just one aspect of the more general working memory system. Therefore, short-term memory will be described in the context of working memory.

There are several theories of working memory (see Dehn, 2008; Leffard et al., 2006 for reviews). One primary point of departure between these different theories is the capacity of working memory. Studies of working memory capacity show that, depending on the research paradigm, capacity can range from 4 to 7 +/− 2 units of information (Cowan et al., 2005; Miller, 1956). Miller proposed that people are able to retain about seven chunks of information, while Cowan (2001) has more recently suggested about four units is the capacity of working memory. Despite these debates, it is clear that working memory has limited capacity.

The most frequently cited and thoroughly researched model of working memory is Baddeley and Hitch's (1974) multicomponent model. This model provides an organizing framework for assessment and intervention. The model originally had three components, but was updated by Baddeley (2000; 2001) to include a fourth component responsible for transfer of information between working memory and long-term memory. The four components of the model are (a) the central executive, (b) the phonological loop, (c) the visuospatial sketchpad, and (d) the episodic buffer.

The central executive is responsible for controlling attention to the other components of the model. Specifically, Baddeley (2003) has argued that the central executive is responsible for focusing, dividing, and shifting attentional resources. Other researchers have argued that the central executive can be fractionated into the following components: inhibition, updating, and shifting (Miyake, Friedman, Emerson, Witzki, & Howerter, 2000). Inhibition is responsible for suppressing attention to irrelevant stimuli and prepotent responses. Updating refreshes information in the other working memory systems. Finally, shifting is the ability to shift attention between different tasks or stimuli.

Utilizing articulatory suppression research paradigms, Baddeley (2003) was able provide compelling support for the phonological component of working memory. The phonological loop has limited capacity, is under the control of the central executive, and has been described as a slave system. However, research by Engle, Tuholski, Laughlin, and Conway (1999) suggests the phonological loop is actually actively involved in maintaining rules for problem solving and learning. This suggests the phonological loop is more active than once thought. Burgess and Hitch (1999) indicated that the phonological loop can be fractionated into two components: the *phonological store* for storing information and the *articulatory control process* for rehearsal and recoding. It is this latter aspect of the phonological loop that correlates with Engle's findings described above.

Less well studied, but receiving increased attention, is the visuospatial sketchpad. This system has limited capacity, is also under the control of the central executive, and is responsible for visual and spatial information. Logie (1995) fractionated the visuospatial sketchpad into two subcomponents. The *visual cache* is the storage component for visual information, and the *inner scribe* is the more active component responsible for rehearsal of perceived movement and spatial information. Thus, it can be seen that both the phonological loop and the visuospatial sketchpad have both short-term storage and active rehearsal functions.

The final component is the episodic buffer. Information travels bi-directionally between the other components of working memory and long-term memory (Baddeley, 2001). Information stored in long-term memory is brought into consciousness and assimilated with new information from the external environment (Baddeley, 2003). The episodic buffer is hypothesized to update stored long-term memory directly, thus allowing for new knowledge to be rapidly assimilated or accommodated into existing information networks.

Short-term memory is often confused with working memory; this confusion is exacerbated by the sometimes interchangeable use of the terms. However, short-term memory is best used to describe temporary memories that are simply repeated without transformation. Working memory, on the other hand, involves active transformation via the recruitment of additional attentional resources. That is, short-term memory is a lower order process of the working memory system of both the phonological loop and the visuo-spatial sketchpad, specifically the phonological store and the visual cache respectively (Leffard et al., 2006). As an example, Reynolds (1997) examined digit span tasks using factor analysis and found that 25 to 30 percent of normal children have one standard deviation difference between digit span forward and digit span backward. This example provides a good paradigm because digit span forward requires simple recall while digit span backward requires additional attentional resources invoked by the central executive.

LONG-TERM MEMORY

In this section the theoretical organization of long-term memory is provided. In the next section the neurobiology that accounts for memory is described. At the most global level, long-term memory can be fractionated into two types based on the effortfulness of recall: explicit (or declarative) and implicit (or nondeclarative). The explicit memory system requires intentional, conscious effort through the activation of working memory and the episodic buffer (Postle, 2007). On the other hand, implicit memory is unintentional, automatic, and does not require conscious activation.

Explicit memories are derived from experiences with the external world and come in several forms: semantic, episodic, and lexical. *Semantic memory* is a collection of all of one's knowledge about facts and objects; it is large, complex, and structured. Information can be both representational and consistent with the external world or propositional and symbolic (Tulving & Markowitch, 1998). *Episodic memory* includes the storage and retrieval of personal events in a temporal context. It is the what, when, and where of events that can be recalled. As Tulving stated, episodic memory is a "memory system that allows people to consciously re-experience past experiences" (2002, p. 6). Episodic memory is last to develop in children and the first to be compromised in older adulthood (Clayton & Griffiths, 2002; Tulving, 2002). Finally, *lexical memory* is specific to decoding spoken and written language (Martin, 2003). It is particularly important for the school neuropsychologist to understand the lexical memory system because its fluent operation allows for listening comprehension, oral expression, reading, mathematics, and writing. Specifically, there is a phonological lexicon that stores known phonemes used to interpret and comprehend heard phonemes and used to generate fluent spoken language. The orthographic lexicon stores known graphemes that are associated with read graphemes for word reading and are used to generate written language (Andrewes, 2001; Martin, 2003; Tulving, 1995). There are orthography-phonology and phonology-orthography converter processes (Martin, 2003) that allow such behaviors as reading aloud or taking notes during a lecture.

Implicit memory, also known as nondeclarative memory, can be considered procedural memory as it stores automatic schemas that facilitate other cognitive tasks, skills, and behaviors (Marsolek, Squire, Kosslyn, & Lulenski, 1994). Implicit memory is about automaticity. Learning a new skill such as driving a car requires a large amount of attentional resources and conscious recall of explicit memory. In the process of learning the task, such as driving a car, schemas are formed that handle many aspects of driving, thus freeing up attentional resources for other tasks, such as listening to the radio or talking to a passenger. This transfer of information from explicit to implicit is necessary to scaffold more complex and higher-order reasoning. For example, until reading becomes fluent and automatic, high-level comprehension is very difficult, if not impossible.

ORGANIZATION OF MEMORY FROM THE SCHOOL NEUROPSYCHOLOGY PERSPECTIVE

Miller (2007) proposed a model of memory for school neuropsychology that is easily transferable to the measures that are available for assessing memory and learning. His model includes three components: immediate, delayed memory (long-term memory), and working memory. Table 25.2 provides an overview of these memory systems. As indicated above, the school neuropsychological memory model provides a useful heuristic for organizing results from memory assessment battery tests.

Immediate memory is akin to the short-term memory system in which information is maintained in conscious awareness for a brief period of time, but is not transformed in any way. Immediate memory is fractionated into three components: verbal, visual, and verbal-visual. Verbal-visual immediate memory is a form of associative memory between the visual and the verbal systems.

Delayed memory can be broken down into four components: verbal, visual, delayed verbal-visual, and semantic. According to Miller's (2007) approach, verbal and visual delayed memories are for newly learned information in the context of neuropsychological testing, such as in a list-learning task. Each of

Table 25.2
School Neuropsychology Organization of Memory

Verbal

- Verbal Immediate Memory
- Verbal Working Memory
- Verbal Delay Memory
- Semantic

Visual

- Visual Immediate Memory
- Visual Working Memory
- Visual-Verbal Associative Delay Memory
- Visual Delay Memory

Associative

- Visual-Verbal Associative Memory
- Visual-Verbal Associative Delay Memory

these can be broken down into measures of learning, delayed free-recall, and delayed recognition. Neuropsychological tests of delayed memory typically include test phases for learning such as selective reminding, an interference trial or time delay, and then free or cued recall, which align with the three forms of verbal and visual delayed memory. Semantic memory, sometimes referred to as comprehension-knowledge, is similar to the semantic memory described in the cognitive neuroscience section above and comprises memories of knowledge and facts. The final classification is delayed associative memory, which is recall of prior verbal-visual associative learning.

Working memory is divided into verbal working memory and nonverbal, or visual, working memory tasks. These processes are similar to the articulatory control process of the phonological loop and the inner scribe of the visuospatial sketchpad, Baddeley's (2001) working memory model.

NEUROBIOLOGY OF MEMORY AND LEARNING

Early brain development, including the prenatal period, is critical to a person's later ability to encode, store, and recall information. The brain undergoes significant transformation as it develops and becomes the functioning organ used for tasks of varying difficulties. At the core of brain functioning, lay neurons which are differentiated by certain roles. These neurons take on specific tasks of transmitting afferent (incoming) and efferent (outgoing) information. During early development the brain undergoes synaptogenesis, where the connections are made between neurons to form synapses. The proliferation of synapses through the growth of dendrites is referred to as aborization and increases the complexity of the connections of neurons in the brain during normal development. The new networks must be stimulated through exposure to primary caregivers to begin to strengthen networks responsible for neuropsychological functioning. Memory and learning derive from and further build these networks through receiving, consolidating, and accessing information.

NEUROBIOLOGY OF WORKING MEMORY

Brain activity associated with working memory tasks, in general, has been localized in the frontal lobes. Studies on brain activation indicated information held in the phonological loop activates the left ventrolateral prefrontal cortex, and visuospatial sketchpad activation takes place in the corresponding (homologous) right ventrolateral prefrontal cortex (Osaka & Osaka, 2007; Postle, 2007). Osaka and Osaka (2007) summarize what is known about brain structures and central executive functioning in working memory. Via neuro-imaging studied, the prefrontal cortex has been shown to be involved in the central executive role in working memory tasks, specifically the dorsolateral prefrontal cortex and anterior cingulate cortex. Further, there is a relationship between complexity and activation. That is, as tasks require increased attentional control, associated increases in activation of the dorsolateral prefrontal cortex have been observed. It has also been found that individuals with larger memory spans have a more effective anterior cingulate cortex and a stronger network with the dorsolateral prefrontal cortex, which is presumed to account for individual differences in executive function for span related tasks. The higher connectivity between the dorsolateral prefrontal cortex and anterior cingulate cortex are also associated with better attention control and inhibition.

NEUROBIOLOGY OF LONG-TERM MEMORY

New explicit long-term memories are formed through the processes of long-term potentiation (LTP) and consolidation shown to be localized bilaterally in the medial temporal lobes—specifically the hippocampus. Long-term potentiation is a process of learning evidenced by synaptic change that can last for weeks or even months (Bruel-Jungerman, Davis, & Laroche, 2007). Consolidation is a process by which information begins to be stored more permanently and incorporated into the existing network of memories (Andrewes, 2001; McGaugh, 2000).

Over the past thirty years, research on neuronal changes has expanded, and great advances in how the brain is understood have been a result. For example, there is evidence to support that patterns of activity between neurons cause changes to the synapses, thus allowing learning to take place (Leff et al., 2004). The brain shows its ability to learn through changes within its neuronal interconnections due to synaptic plasticity. There are different ways that brains show plasticity, suggesting memory and learning consolidation occur in multiple ways: synaptic weakening, synaptic strengthening, synaptogenesis/remodeling, and neurogenesis (the growth of new neurons) (Bruel-Jungerman et al., 2007). In addition to the hippocampus, plasticity has been found in other regions of the brain as well, such as the motor cortex for procedural learning and the amygdala (Bruel-Jungerman et al., 2007; Giap, Jong, Ricker, Cullen, & Zafonte, 2000).

Synaptic strengthening takes place in the neural circuits of the hippocampus, supporting and strengthening memories, and is the most widely held view of plasticity in the brain (Bruel-Jungerman et al., 2007). This process of LTP is believed to be vital to the transfer of information from immediate memory and long-term memory. Long-term potentiation is found most commonly in the hippocampus, as this is the site for integration of both input (afferent) and output (efferent) forms of information and the area where new learning takes place (Giap et al., 2000). In contrast to LTP, a more recently discovered involvement in memory is long-term depression (LTD), which is the weakening of synaptic strength, and it is activity dependent. That is, if you don't use it you lose it (Bruel-Jungerman et al., 2007; Giap et al., 2000). Studies have made a connection between synaptic changes that occur while biochemical and molecular mechanisms that underlie LTP are activated. Studies of the simultaneous events of chemical reactions and changes support the hypothesis that these brain chemicals are involved in LTP and LTD, and thus in memory and learning (Bruel-Jungerman et al., 2007). The connections between two neurons, the presynaptic and postsynaptic events, are strengthened or weakened through these chemical changes (Leff et al., 2004).

The neurotransmitter dopamine is believed to play a role in the protein synthesis phase of LTP as well as serve as a natural reward to learning (Hyman, Malenka, & Nestler, 2006; O'Carroll, Martin, Sandin, Frenguelli, & Morris, 2006; Wise, 2004). More specifically, dopamine is believed to be related to exposure to novel situations and stimuli, becoming involved in the protein synthesis of LTP and its association with long-term memory formation. Dopamine may have some affect on the strength of hippocampal-dependent memory and play a key role in accessing memories (O'Carroll et al., 2006). Other brain structures involved with dopamine are the prefrontal cortex for goal setting, as well as the ventral striatum, where dopamine plays a role in reward-related behaviors and learning. In this case, dopamine serves as a motivation source, but in a broad range of brain structures it serves as a catalyst for storage of memories (Hyman et al., 2006).

The amygdala is known to be critically involved in the process of memory consolidation. Recent research has shown the role the amygdala plays in transferring an immediate memory to long-term memory is its involvement in modulating the consolidation of many forms of memory through the basolateral nucleus (BLA) region (McGaugh, 2002). Additionally, the amygdala has been shown to be associated with enhancing memory consolidation during periods of emotional arousal. Numerous studies indicate that adrenal stress hormones related to emotional arousal mediate memory consolidation. Miller (2007) discusses *flashbulb memories* of highly emotional experiences as being stored via the cooperation between the amygdala and hippocampus (Feifer & Della Toffalo, 2007).

As discussed above, when beginning to learn a motor skill, conscious cognitive involvement is necessary until the skill becomes overlearned at which time conscious involvement is no longer necessary (Doyon, Penhune, & Ungerleider, 2003). Studies have found that brain structures such as the striatum, cerebellum, and motor cortical regions of the frontal lobe are associated with the learning of these motor skills (Doyon et al., 2003; Nyberg, Eriksson, Larsson, & Marklund, 2006). PET scans and fMRIs have verified that there are two different loops at work when learning and developing motor skills: the cortico-basal ganglia-thalamo-cortical loop (cortical-striatal) and the cortico-cerebello-thalamo-cortical loop (cortical cellebellar) (Doyon et al., 2003). When learning a new skill, the cerebellum is highly active and gradually has less workload as the skill becomes well learned. Once the skill is learned, the striatum becomes increasingly more involved, suggesting a switch in loop activation from learning new skills to well learned skills (Nyberg et al., 2006).

EXAMPLES OF THE ASSESSMENT OF MEMORY AND LEARNING

Best practices for assessing memory and learning include conducting broadband assessments of verbal and nonverbal memory followed by narrowband measures of specific memory functions to examine hypotheses of strengths and weaknesses found in broadband measures (Hale & Fiorello, 2004). Modern school neuropsychologists are fortunate to have available to them a variety of broadband memory and learning test batteries designed for children. These test batteries are relatively well-normed and allow for more certitude in test-by-test comparisons than was previously available. This is not to say that cognitive demands analysis is not necessary (Hale & Fiorello, 2004) because many of the tests' names may be deceiving as to the construct assessed or measure irrelevant variance. Historically, the typical neuropsychological assessment battery was conducted by starting with an intelligence test such as a Wechsler scale followed by a variety of tests of individual memory and learning abilities that had less than stellar norms. Now, there are research-based tests and test batteries available that have national norms.

The proliferation of co-normed test batteries has served to continue the debate between the fixed versus flexible battery approach to neuropsychological assessment (e.g., Russell, 2007). Traditionally, fixed-batteries of tests were preferred such as the *Halstead-Reitan Neuropsychological Test Battery* (Reitan & Wolfson, 1993). Arguments against the fixed battery approach included the claim that such a battery assumed that all relevant neuropsychological processes were assessed by the test battery. Then there was a proliferation of support for the flexible battery approach because it was viewed as more economical and allowed for a more comprehensive assessment of neuropsychological processes. The field of school psychology has become friendlier to the concept of the flexible battery approach with the rise of the *cross-battery approach* described by Flanagan and McGrew (1997). Hale and Fiorello (2004), in their seminal book on school neuropsychology, advocate for a flexible battery approach, suggesting a combination of fixed/flexible in which the evaluator has a core, fixed battery that is sufficiently broad to pick up a wide range of neuropsychological strengths and deficits. Then, the school neuropsychologist makes hypotheses about the nature of the neuropsychological deficit. The hypothesis is followed up with more specific tests that will increase the reliability of the assessment and allow for the partitioning of irrelevant variance through triangulation and task demand analysis. The advantage of a combined approach is that the evaluator can pick up possibly subtle neuropsychological deficits as well as provide a consistent set of measures the evaluator has observed over large numbers of individuals. The fixed battery aspect of the assessment also allows the evaluator to subsequently publish nomothetic studies based on client databases.

MAJOR COGNITIVE ASSESSMENT INSTRUMENTS

The inclusion of major cognitive batteries in the comprehensive assessment of children is common and well advised. These batteries include the *Wechsler Intelligence Scale for Children IV* (WISC-IV; Wechsler, 2003), the *Stanford-Binet, 5th Edition* (SB5; Roid, 2003), and the *Woodcock-Johnson III Tests of Cognitive Abilities* (WJIII-COG; McGrew & Woodcock, 2001). Inclusion of one of these major instruments allows for the assessment of a broad range of cognitive abilities. All of these batteries utilize some variation on the Cattell-Horn-Carroll (Carroll, 1993) model of cognitive functioning and therefore assess a broad range of skills. Leffard and colleagues (2006) examined the assessment of working memory by these major instruments. Table 25.3 provides a summary of their analysis.

The WISC-IV has been extended to assess neuropsychological functioning at a more comprehensive level. The *WISC-IV Integrated* (WISC-IV-I; Wechsler et al., 2004) provides a wider range of memory assessment than the WISC-IV, as can be seen in Table 25.3. The WISC-IV-I adds several *process* subtests that are designed to test hypotheses about underlying cognitive processes. The WISC-IV-I includes sixteen additional subtests in the domains of verbal, perceptual, working memory, and processing

Table 25.3

Comparison of Reported Tapped Processes with Working Memory Components Measured

Subtest	Reported to Measure	WM Component Measured
WISC-IV		
Digit Span Forward	Rote learning and memory, attention, encoding, auditory processing[a]	Phonological loop, rehearsal
Digit Span Backward	Working memory, transformation of information, mental manipulation, visuospatial imaging[a]	Phonological loop, transformation
Letter-Number Sequencing	Sequencing, mental manipulation, attention, short-term auditory memory, visuospatial imaging, processing speed[a]	Phonological loop, transformation
Arithmetic	Mental manipulation, concentration, attention, STM and LTM, numerical reasoning ability, mental alertness[a]	Phonological loop, transformation, math skills
WISC-IV Integrated		
Visual Digit Span	Visuospatial STM, registration, sequencing, WM capacity, attention, concentration[b]	Phonological loop, rehearsal
Spatial Span Forward	Rote learning and memory abilities, attention, encoding, spatial processing[b]	Visuospatial sketchpad, rehearsal
Spatial Span Backward	Rote learning and memory abilities, attention, encoding, spatial processing[b]	Visuospatial sketchpad, transformation
Letter Span	Auditory STM, registration, sequencing, attention, concentration[b]	Phonological loop, rehearsal
Letter-Number Sequencing Process Approach	Sequencing, mental manipulation, attention, auditory STM, visuospatial imaging, processing speeds[b]	Phonological loop, transformation
Arithmetic Process Approach	Mental manipulation skills, concentration, numerical reasoning ability, and mental alertness[b]	None
Written Arithmetic	Numerical reasoning with limited demands on attention, mental efficiency[b]	None
WJIII-COG		
Numbers Reversed	STM, WM, attentional capacity[c]	Phonological loop, transformation
Memory for Words	Auditory STM[c]	Phonological loop, rehearsal

Table 25.3
Continued

Subtest	Reported to Measure	WM Component Measured
Auditory WM	Auditory STM, WM, divided attention[c]	Phonological loop, transformation
Picture Recognition	Visual memory[c]	Visuospatial sketchpad, rehearsal
SBb		
Last Word	Verbal STM[d]	Phonological loop, transformation
Delayed Response	STM, attention, rudimentary WM[d]	Visuospatial sketchpad, rehearsal
Block Tapping	STM, transformation[d]	Visuospatial sketchpad, rehearsal, transformation (advanced levels only)
Memory for Sentences	STM[d]	Phonological loop, rehearsal

[a](Wechsler, 2003)
[b](Wechsler et al., 2004)
[c](Mather & Woodcock, 2001)
[d](Roid, 2003)

© Leffard, S. A., Miller, J. A., Bernstein, J. H., DeMann, J. J., Mangis, H. A., & McCoy, E.L.B. (2006). Substantive validity of working memory measures in major cognitive functioning test batteries for children. *Applied Neuropsychology, 13*, 230–241.

speed. With the additional subtests, the WISC-IV-I measures the following components of memory:

- Verbal Immediate Memory
  - Digit Span-Forward
  - Letter Span-Forward
- Visual Immediate Memory
  - Visual Digit Span-Forward
  - Spatial Span-Forward
- Working Memory
  - Arithmetic Process Approach
  - Digit Span-Backward
  - Letter-Number Sequencing Process Approach
  - Spatial Span-Backward
- Semantic Memory
  - Comprehension Multiple Choice
  - Information Multiple Choice

- ○ Vocabulary Multiple Choice
- ○ Picture Vocabulary Multiple Choice

Memory and Learning Test Batteries

As discussed above, several well-normed test batteries of memory and learning are available and some are now in their second editions. Each of these test batteries could be useful in the neuropsychological assessment of children. A brief summary of each test battery follows.

Test of Memory and Learning (2nd Edition)   The *Test of Memory and Learning, 2nd Edition* (TOMAL-2; Reynolds & Voress, 2007) provides tests of verbal and nonverbal short-term, working, and long-term memory. The TOMAL-2 is normed on individuals 5 to 59 years of age and includes 14 subtests. The composite scores are Verbal Memory Composite Index and Nonverbal Memory Composite Index, Composite Memory Index, and Verbal Delayed Recall Index. The Verbal Delayed Recall Index is measured by a delay component of the Memory for Stories and Word Selective Reminding subsets. Additional composites that can be derived from combinations of subtests are: Attention/ Concentration, Sequential Recall, Free Recall, Associative Recall, and Learning Supplementary Composite Indexes. Core subtests are organized as follows:

- Verbal Memory Composite
  - ○ Memory for Stories
  - ○ Word Selective Reminding
  - ○ Object Recall
  - ○ Paired Recall
- Nonverbal Memory Composite
  - ○ Facial Memory
  - ○ Abstract Visual Memory
  - ○ Visual Sequential Memory
  - ○ Memory for Location

The test battery evidences very good reliability for composites and subtests (Schmitt & Decker, in press). The TOMAL-2 has the most current norms and provides the widest range of memory measures of the current memory batteries available for children. A notable feature is that digits forward and digits backward are provided with separate norms consistent with Baddeley's (2004) differentiation between short-term and working memory.

Wide Range Assessment of Memory and Learning, 2nd Edition   The *Wide Range Assessment of Memory and Learning, 2nd Edition* (WRAML-2; Sheslow &

Adams, 2003) is greatly expanded from the first edition and now has extended age-range norms for individuals from 5 to 90 years of age. The core battery includes two subtests for each of three composite scores (Verbal Memory, Visual Memory, and Attention/Concentration) that also yield a General Memory Index. The six core subtests are organized as follows.

- Verbal Memory Composite
  - Story Memory
  - Verbal Learning
- Visual Memory
  - Design Memory
  - Picture Memory
- Attention/Concentration
  - Finger Windows
  - Number Letter

Delayed memory is assessed from the core battery via Story Memory Delay Recall and Verbal Learning Delay Recall. An optional subtest, Sound Symbol, also has an associated delayed memory subtest Sound Symbol Delay Recall. There is also a Working Memory Index comprised of Verbal Working Memory and Symbolic Working Memory subtests. It is recommended that, when administering the WRAML-2, the subtests of the Working Memory Index and delayed recall subtests be administered routinely for comprehensive assessment of memory. The test stimuli are engaging for children, but can be taxing for the evaluator who must keep track of numerous stimulus materials (Dunn, 2005). The WRAML-2 evidences good reliability for the core subtests and index scores. The range of constructs measured in WRAML-2 is not as wide as in the TOMAL-2, but the WRAML-2 is a well-normed, psychometrically sound assessment battery suitable for school neuropsychology practice.

Children's Memory Scale The *Children's Memory Scale* (CMS; Cohen, 1997) provides standardized assessment of memory function for children between the ages of 5 and 16 years old. The CMS is a downward extension of the Wechsler Memory Scale series for adults and has therefore been criticized as not attending to the memory and learning difficulties specific to children (Baron, 2004). This test has been around for quite a while and was co-normed with the *Wechsler Intelligence Scale for Children-III* (Wechsler, 1991). The CMS includes 14 core subtests resulting in the following composite scores: Visual Immediate, Visual Delayed, Verbal Immediate, Verbal Delayed, General Memory, Attention/Concentration, Learning, and Delayed Recognition. The CMS evidences slightly lower reliabilities than other test batteries, and reviewers have raised concerns about the floor and ceiling effects of some subtests (Vaupel, 2001). The CMS has been touted as being user friendly and engaging to children (Napolitano, 2001); however, the test is a bit dated and due for renorming.

NEPSY-II   The NEPSY-II (Korkman, Kirk, & Kemp, 2007) is a battery of neuropsychological tests normed for children (ages 3 years to 16 years, 11 months) that provides a comprehensive picture of a child's neuropsychological functioning. Unfortunately, the test is often administered by individuals with little training in school neuropsychology who then claim that a school neuropsychological assessment has been conducted. The NEPSY-II requires specialized training in neuropsychological assessment to accurately interpret the results of the battery. It is notable for this chapter that the NEPSY-II includes a Memory and Learning Domain comprised of:

- Verbal Memory Subtests
  - Narrative Memory
  - Sentence Repetition
  - Word List Interference
  - Repetition of Nonsense Words
- Visual Memory Subtests
  - Memory for Faces
  - Memory for Design
- Learning Subtests
  - Memory for Names
  - List Learning
- Long-Term Memory Subtests
  - Speeded Naming
  - Verbal Fluency

The NEPSY-II provides a surprisingly comprehensive assessment of memory and learning for being just one domain in the assessment battery. In addition to Memory and Learning, the other domains measured by the NEPSY-II are Social Perception, Executive Functioning, Language, Sensorimotor Functioning, and Visuospatial Processing.

NARROWBAND TESTS OF MEMORY AND LEARNING

There are a variety of measures that assess specific aspects of verbal and nonverbal memory and learning. Although most of the domains that need to be assessed can be selected from extant test batteries, the following provide additional instruments for hypothesis testing as well as potential use in a flexible battery wherein targeted memory assessment is indicated (see Baron, 2004 for a review).

Verbal Memory and Learning Tests For the assessment of learning, including a test of verbal selective reminding such as the *California Verbal Learning Test-Children's Version* (CVLT-C; Delis, Kramer, Kaplan, Ober, & Fridlund, 1989) or the *Children's Auditory Verbal Learning Test-2* (Talley, 1988) is useful. These are list-learning tests that include feedback from the examiner over repeated trials as well as memory for the list of words after interference lists have been introduced. Sentence memory (sentence repetition), story memory, and paired associate learning are also important areas of verbal memory to be assessed, and tests of these constructs are available in the batteries described above.

Nonverbal Memory and Learning The *Benton Visual Retention Test* (BVRT; Benton, 1992) provides a versatile test of visual memory. The test provides assessment of visual perception, visual memory, and visual-motor integration. Unlike the Beery-Buktenica *Developmental Test of Visual-Motor Integration* (VMI; Beery, Buktenica, & Beery, 2004), the BVRT allows for assessment of visual perception after a delay of exposure to the stimuli. It also allows for error analysis including omissions, distortions, perseverations, rotations, misplacements, and size errors. Other specific components of nonverbal memory that should be assessed include memory for faces and nonverbal selective reminding tests that measure learning for nonverbal stimuli over trails. Subtests of the above-described batteries are available for these areas of memory assessment.

Automated Working Memory Assessment The *Automated Working Memory Assessment* (AWMA) developed by Alloway (2007) provides computer administration of a comprehensive assessment of working memory assessment. The AWMA includes a screener form, a short form, and the complete long form that includes 12 subtests. As Dehn (2008) points out, the AWMA is unique in that it attempts to clearly differentiate measures of short-term memory and working memory by including additional processing tasks for the working memory measures. The subtests included are the following:

- Phonological STM Subtests
  - Digit Recall
  - Word Recall
  - Nonword Recall
- Verbal WM Subtests
  - Listening Recall

- ○ Counting Recall
- ○ Backward Digit
- Visuospatial STM Subtests
  - ○ Dot Matrix
  - ○ Mazes Memory
  - ○ Block Recall
- Visuospatial WM
  - ○ Odd-One-Out (recall the location of the shape that did not match the others in a grid)
  - ○ Mr. X (a test using cartoon characters to recall the location of a ball)
  - ○ Spatial Span

The subtests evidence moderate to good reliability (Dehn, 2008). One issue that may require further study is that the voice in the English version of the test is British and may introduce additional error variance to youth in the United States taking the test. The AWMA does provide school neuropsychologists with a progressive, computer-based measure of short-term and working memory.

MEMORY AND LEARNING RATING SCALES

There are now a few parent, teacher, and self-rating scales that include assessments of memory functioning. The argument for the use of rating scales of cognitive processes such as memory and executive function is that they provided a more ecologically valid assessment of the constructs compared to individually administered tests which capture a snapshot of a child's neuropsychological functioning. Rating scales can provide useful, structured information about parents, teachers, or self-perceptions of memory function as these assessments can be examined in relation to individually administered measures of memory to help raters identify discrepancies or consistencies in regard to whether there is a real memory or learning problem. Further, rating scale assessment of memory can provide a low-cost screening of potential problems with memory and learning because the measure can be administered without significant involvement of school neuropsychologists. The following identifies some current rating scale measures of memory and learning.

The *Working Memory Rating Scale* (WMRS; Alloway, Gathercole, & Kirkwood, 2008) is a 22-item rating scale that uses a four-point Likert scale. The authors state the advantages of the test are that it only takes 5 minutes to administer and that it was co-normed with the *Automated Working Memory Assessment* (Alloway, 2007). The WMRS was shown to have good reliability and correlation with the WISC-IV Working Memory Index (Alloway, Gathercole, Kirkwood, & Elliott, in press).

The *Behavior Rating Inventory for Executive Function* (BRIEF; Gioia, Isquith, Guy, & Kenworthy, 2000) is a rating scale that measures several components of executive function. There are several versions of the BRIEF, including a preschool version and a self-report adolescent version. Working memory is considered a component of executive function on the BRIEF and is measured by the Working Memory subscale. The scale also measures other important executive function abilities that are associated with the central executive such as the ability to shift attention, inhibit, and self-monitor. The BRIEF has evidenced good reliability and validity; however, the authors caution that the BRIEF is not diagnostic and should be used in the context of a comprehensive evaluation (Gioia, Isquith, Rezlaff, & Espy, 2002).

EVIDENCE-BASED INTERVENTIONS FOR THE TREATMENT OF CHILDREN WITH MEMORY AND LEARNING DYSFUNCTIONS

The depth of the evidence base for memory and learning interventions in children is dependent on the type of deficit. Certainly there is a large literature base on the treatment of learning disabilities. However, despite the advancement in theory and assessment of memory and learning described above, the treatment of learning or memory, in general, is not well established or associated with the strong theoretical base previously described. In the following, the general approaches to best practices for intervening on memory and learning deficits are described and followed by specific evidence-based treatment protocols.

ROURKE'S DEVELOPMENTAL REHABILITATION MODEL

The treatment of memory and learning problems, as is the case with many acquired neuropsychological deficits, starts with a determination of the expected level of recovery to the acquired loss of functioning. For developmental memory functioning deficits, consideration is given to current levels of function and projected improvement. Rourke, Bakker, Fisk and Strang (1983) developed the *Developmental Rehabilitation Model* (DRM; Rourke, 1994; Work & Choi, 2005) that does just this; it takes into consideration the presentation of the problem, examines the probability of recovery, and charts a course for treatment in both the child's academic and societal contexts. Rourke and colleagues' model provides a pragmatic, yet comprehensive, approach to conceptualizing treatment approaches to children with learning and memory problems. The DRM starts off with a biopsychosocial examination of the status of the child's learning problems. These data are derived from a comprehensive evaluation including observation, interview, neuropsychological evaluation data, and neurological data if available. Next, two levels of analysis are conducted. First, the school neuropsychologist asks what the demands of the immediate environment are in terms of academic and social functioning. Second, the long-term demands of early adulthood in the realms of work and social interaction are examined. It can be seen that there is an alignment of academic functioning with work in adulthood, as well as an alignment of social functioning in childhood with social interaction and leisure activities in adulthood. This aspect of the DRM is important as it causes the school neuropsychologist to evaluate the real developmental eventualities that will guide immediate intervention strategies. From these projections, an optimal short- and long-term intervention plan is considered. This plan is moderated by the realistic availability of resources across family, school, and service provider domains. In most cases the "realistic" treatment plan would be less than the optimal plan. This is particularly the case in schools where federal mandates do not require optimal services, but rather, only require minimal services to allow the child to benefit from a public education, or in situations in which the family cannot provide optimal support for a variety of reasons. Thus, the model allows for the consideration of broad influences on the child such as the political climate toward insurance reimbursements or the social stress within a family.

After conducting the DRM, the school neuropsychologist has four basic approaches to treatment: improvement, restoration, accommodation, and compensation. *Improvement* of functioning has to do primarily with developmental memory dysfunction that can be either significantly impaired or moderately impaired. Research shows that even those with so-called normal memory can improve their memory functioning with intervention (Lee, Lu, & Ko, 2007; Oberauer, 2006). In more severe developmentally delayed cases, there is additional room to improve, and intervention has been shown effective (Comblain, 1994; Conners, Rosenquist, Arnett, Moore, & Hume, 2008). *Restoration* has to do with loss of memory and learning functioning after injury or insult. Maximal recovery typically occurs within one year of a traumatic brain injury (Arffa, 2006). The goal of restoration intervention is to return the individual to premorbid levels of functioning and to decrease the time to return to normal functioning. Cognitive rehabilitation should be provided weekly for children who have suffered injury or insult that has resulted in a significant loss of functioning until they reach premorbid levels of functioning or until it is clear further gains will not achieved. *Accommodation* has to do with organizing the child's environment for maximal success, which is quite doable in school settings in association with individualized education programs (IEP) for children with memory loss associated with traumatic brain injury, an eligibility category for IDEIA (2004). Finally, *compensation* includes the introduction of memory and learning aids such as notebooks, personal digital assistants, digital recorders, etc. that the individual can utilize across contexts to improve memory and learning.

INTERVENTIONS SPECIFIC TO MEMORY

Glisky and Glisky (2002) provide a clear summary of many evidence-based memory and learning interventions currently used in practice. They organize memory and learning intervention into four categories: (a) practice and rehearsal, (b) mnemonic strategies, (c) environmental supports and external aids, and (d) domain-specific learning. The first category, practice and rehearsal, is indicated for all levels of memory problems including new learning. The approach to distributed practice through repetition is consistent with the transfer of explicit memory to implicit memory and consistent with consolidation theory (McGaugh, 2000) described above; that is, the more the memory is practiced the more likely it is to be retained over time (Ellmore, Stouffer, & Nadel, 2008). Intervention plans that include practice and rehearsal should include breaks between learning and rehearsal that increase over time. For example, learning is facilitated by a review of material 5 minute after exposure, then a few hours after exposure, and later several days or weeks after exposure. This is consistent with the notion of a *spiral curriculum* in which ideas are revisited repeatedly (Dever & Hobbs, 2000). Mather and Jaffe (2002) point out that it is useful to provide practice and rehearsal across multiple modalities such as visual and verbal practice.

Mnemonic strategies are indicated for individuals with less severe memory deficits, according to Glisky and Glisky (2002). Direct instruction on the use of mnemonic strategies is a frequent component of memory rehabilitation. Mnemonic strategies are also common teaching tools as many of us remember the colors of the rainbow by the mnemonic Roy G. Biv. However, for children with memory problems, the use of mnemonic strategies requires intention in a variety of ways. First, the child must understand processes of associating material with visual images or making associations with the first letter of each word in a list. Mather and Jaffe (2002) recommend the PAR technique in which the child is taught to "Picture it, Associate it, and Review it" (p. 274). Once one is able to generate mnemonic strategies, one must be able to intentionally identify opportunities to use these strategies. This can occur through cuing when opportunities to use mnemonics present themselves, then gradually fading the cues. Glisky and Glisky (2002) include strategies such as organized study methods like STORE, the story approach, in which stories are analyzed for the following components: *Setting, Trouble* (i.e., what is the trouble or problem in the story), *Order* of events, *Resolution*, and *End*

(Mather & Jaffe, 2002). Somewhat associated with mnemonics is the use of graphic organizers (Alvermann, 1986; Robinson & Kiewra, 1995), which allow the child to reorganize information to be learned in a visual structure that facilitates multimodal pathways to encoding and recall.

Computer technology has provided an array of external memory aides. The use of portable digital assistants (PDAs; Churchill, 2008) can be taught to children to improve memory for events such as homework due dates and social events. Further, notes and to-do lists can be created in the PDA that are readily searchable. Computer technology, however, is not always necessary. Teaching children with memory problems to use calendars, to-do lists, notebooks and alarm clocks are all effective strategies that can provide valuable skills for adulthood.

The final category of intervention described by Glisky and Glisky (2002) is domain-specific learning. Based on the notion that procedural memory is preserved even after significant head injury, this approach is indicated for those with more severe injuries and for new procedural learning. One form of domain-specific learning has to do with learning vocational skills such as computer skills through the use of fading cues and repetition. Another approach is *errorless learning*, which contrasts trial and error learning. Clare and Jones (2008) provide a review of procedures and outcomes for the errorless learning approach. Finally, Glisky and Glisky suggest that combining vanishing cuing with errorless learning may provide an optimal learning approach for procedural learning for individuals with more severe memory impairments.

WORKING MEMORY OVERLOAD AND INTERVENTION IN THE CLASSROOMS

Gathercole and Alloway (2004) identified *working memory overload* as a cause of the difficulty to learn for many children with working memory problems. The objective of their recommended intervention on working memory overload is to reduce the working memory demands in the instructional environment. Gathercole and Alloway recommend the following sequence for reducing working memory overload. Teachers in the classroom should be able to identify instances of memory overload, monitor for their occurrence, and evaluate the severity of the overload. Once the teacher has identified the memory overload as significant enough to interfere with learning, the teacher should reduce the working memory load of the task and be prepared to repeat and/or encourage (cue) the use of memory aids. Through these interventions the teacher then works to develop the child's independent use of the strategies. Dehn (2008) reviews several techniques that can be effective at reducing working memory overload. These strategies include using simplified language, breaking tasks down into smaller parts, repetition, providing extra time for rehabilitation, providing information in an organized manner, and scaffolding.

ATTENTION AND EXECUTIVE FUNCTION INTERVENTION

Baddeley's (2000) working memory model points to the importance of attention and attentional control through the central executive to normal memory functioning. Thus, it cannot be ignored that memory problems may also be associated with attention and attention control problems. There are now numerous attention training programs available that are beyond the scope of this chapter, but they should be considered if assessment suggests problems in these areas are associated with memory difficulties. It is encouraging to note that interventions from attention and control of attention are being shown effective in children as young as preschool age (Diamond, Barnett, Thomas, & Munro, 2007).

CASE EXAMPLE: FROM ASSESSMENT TO INTERVENTION

Upon receiving the referral for assessment and intervention, one should consider if memory and learning problems could be associated with referral concern. As can be seen in Table 25.3, many of the common problems that may be referred to a school neuropsychologist include symptoms of memory deficits. Whether the evaluator uses a fixed or flexible approach, the assessment battery should be reviewed to ensure that memory related functions relevant to the referral concern are assessed. Should a specific memory or learning problem emerge, then targeted interventions to remediating or compensating for the area of deficit should be implemented.

Intervention on core cognitive processes such as memory has valued-added benefits beyond remediating a problem. Certainly the child benefits by being able to read better or write better, but memory improvement through strategy development and the habits that develop from learning these strategies can serve the child in a variety of contexts. Interventions for memory include direct instruction on and practice becoming fluent at using memory-enhancing strategies. Therefore, the child can apply the strategies to future learning experiences. For example, if a child has difficulty with immediate memory associated with basic reading and subsequently responds to intervention, the child will have gained a skill that will be useful when taking written notes in a classroom or remembering the names of new friends.

As an example, consider the case of a child referred for reading comprehension difficulties. Referring to Table 25.3, the school neuropsychologist should anticipate that there may be problems with verbal working memory, delayed verbal memory, and/or semantic memory. The overview of the strategy for the assessment and intervention for reading comprehension with respect to working memory is provided in Table 25.4. Using the WJIII-COG as the core cognitive battery, the evaluator would determine which subtests are necessary to assess these areas. Numbers Reversed and Auditory Working Memory would be identified as measures of verbal working memory. Retrieval Fluency and Visual-Auditory Learning Delayed would be identified as measures of delayed verbal memory. Finally, Verbal Comprehension and General Information could serve as measure of semantic memory. As indicated above, assessing attention is important when there is a concern about

Table 25.4
Memory Assessment to Intervention in Reading Comprehension

Memory Function	Assessment Instrument	Intervention Approaches
Verbal Working Memory	**WJ III COG** • Numbers Reversed • Auditory Working Memory **TOMAL-2** • Digits Backward • Letters Backward	• Direct instruction for memory strategy development • Teacher management of verbal working memory overload • Encourage independence of strategy use
Delayed Verbal Memory	**WJ III COG** • Retrieval Fluency • Visual-Auditory Learning Delayed **TOMAL-2** • Word Selective Reminding-Delayed Recall • Memory for Stories-Delayed Recall	• Direct instruction on strategies to identify salient stimuli in written or oral information • Use graphic organizers to organize the information being learned • Provide multiple exposures to the information
Semantic Memory	**WJ III COG** • Verbal Comprehension • General Information **TOMAL-2** • Word Selective Reminding • Paired Recall	• Direct instruction on how to practice newly learned information via distributive practice • Refer to and expand graphic organizers as an external representation of memory networks

memory. The WJIII-COG does not measure attention directly, so it would be necessary to add a measure of attention such as a continuous performance test (Riccio, Reynolds, Lowe & Moore, 2002). The WJIII-COG can be supplemented by subtests from the TOMAL-2. The Verbal Memory Index, Verbal Delayed Recall Index, and Learning Index composites will be particularly relevant to this case. Specific subtests to be examined for verbal working memory are Digits Backward and Letters Backward, for verbal delayed memory Word Selective Reminding-Delayed Recall and Memory for Stories-Delayed Recall. Although not a direct measure of semantic memory, it would be useful to examine the verbal learning subtests of the Learning Index for markers of how the child is learning information during structured performance subtests that comprise the index: Word Selective Reminding and Paired Recall.

For illustrative purposes, assume there are memory and learning deficits in each of the three areas described above, including evidence of inattention. Intervention for verbal working memory should include direct instruction and practice in developing attention to incoming stimuli, ignoring irrelevant stimuli, specific mnemonic strategies, and practice and rehearsal of new concepts. Further, the school neuropsychologist should provide consultation to the teacher on how to reduce working memory overload as described above and how to encourage the child to independently apply memory support strategies. For delayed verbal memory, the child should learn to notice cues that indicate the necessity to focus attention. At first these cues would need to be introduced by the teacher and parent. For example, make sure there is eye contact with the child and verbal orientation to what is about to be said. Next, the child may get direct advice on how to focus on the important information by noticing words in lectures or readings that indicate important information will follow. Teach the child to listen for words such as "most important," "there are x number of things to know," or "in summary." Teach methods of graphical representations of information as described above and ensure multiple exposures to the information. Problems with verbal delayed memory are certainly indicators of difficulty encoding information into semantic memory. To facilitate retrieval, interventions should focus on helping the child refresh and update information as well as to support associations with known information already in memory. Directing instruction on how to practice very recently learned material, such as review after 5 minutes, then again after a half hour, will greatly improve verbal delayed memory and ultimately facilitate long-term potentiation via the hippocampus. Electronic graphic organizers available now can be easily added to and can provide an external representation of memory networks. Teaching children to use and routinely update such graphic organizers can facilitate deep semantic memory for specific topical areas. In this way, the child is encouraged in a visual way to attach new information with known information.

SUMMARY

Memory and learning have been shown to have rich theoretical bases that should be consulted for assessment and intervention planning. Baddeley's (2001; 2003; 2004) working memory model has particularly strong support. Efforts to translate extant measures of memory and learning have resulted in the school neuropsychological model of memory. The processes of storing and consolidating memories are being informed by the proliferation of neuroscience and neuroimaging studies. It is notable that the whole process of learning and remembering involves cortical and subcortical structures that work collectively to move learning from explicit to implicit. It was noted that working and long-term memory are associated with all learning disabilities and other common childhood disorders. As such, memory and learning assessment should be included in any comprehensive evaluation of a child suspected of having a learning disability. It is promising that the field of school neuropsychology has evolved to have well-normed test batteries for assessing memory and learning. Finally, it was noted that the field of intervention for memory problems does not have an extensive evidence base, but there are various cognitive rehabilitation techniques currently available that show promise.

REFERENCES

Alloway, T. P. (2007). *Automated working memory assessment*. London: Pearson Assessment.

Alloway, T. P., Gathercole, S. E., & Kirkwood, H. (2008). *The working memory rating scale*. London: Pearson Assessment.

Alloway, T. P., Gathercole, S. E., Kirkwood, H., & Elliott, J. (in press). The Working Memory Rating Scale: A classroom-based behavioral assessment of working memory. *Learning and Individual Differences*.

Alvermann, D. (1986). Graphic organizers: Cueing devices for comprehending and remembering main ideas. In J. Baumann (Ed.), *Teaching main idea comprehension*. Newark, DE: International Reading Association.

Andrewes, D. (2001). *Neuropsychology: From theory to practice*. New York: Psychology Press.

Arffa, S. (2006). Traumatic brain injury. In C. E. Coffey, R. A. Brumback, D. R. Rosenberg, & K. Voeller (Eds.), *Textbook of essential pediatric neuropsychiatry* (pp. 507–548). Philadelphia: Lippincott Williams & Wilkins.

Atkinson, R. C., & Shiffrin, R. M. (1968). Human memory: A proposed system and its control processes. In *The psychology of learning and motivation: II*. Oxford, UK: Academic Press.

Baddeley, A. (2000). The episodic buffer: A new component of working memory? *Trends in Cognitive Sciences, 4*, 417–423.

Baddeley, A. (2001). Is working memory still working? *American Psychologist, 56*, 851–864.

Baddeley, A. (2003). Working memory: Looking back and looking forward. *Nature Reviews Neuroscience, 4*, 829–839.

Baddeley, A. (2004). *Your memory: A user's guide.* Buffalo, NY: Firefly Books.

Baddeley, A., & Hitch, G. J. (1974). Working memory. In G. H. Bower (Ed.), *The psychology of learning and motivation: Advances in research and theory* (Vol. 8, pp. 47–89). New York: Academic Press.

Baron, I. S. (2004). *Neuropsychological evaluation of the child.* New York: Oxford University Press.

Beery, K. E., Buktenica, N. A., & Beery, N. A. (2004). *Beery-Buktenica developmental test of visual-motor integration* (5th ed.). Bloomington, MN: Pearson.

Benton, A. L. (1992). *Benton visual retention test* (5th ed.). San Antonio, TX: The Psychological Corporation.

Bruel-Jungerman, E., Davis, S., & Laroche, S. (2007). Brain plasticity mechanisms and memory: A party of four. *Neuroscientist, 13*, 492–505.

Burgess, N., & Hitch, G. J. (1999). Memory for serial order: A network model of the phonological loop and its timing. *Psychological Review, 106*, 551–581.

Carroll, J. B. (1993). *Human cognitive abilities: A survey of factor analytic studies.* New York: Cambridge University Press.

Churchill, D. (2008). Learning objects for educational applications via PDA technology. *Journal of Interactive Learning Research, 19*, 5–20.

Clare, L., & Jones, R. S. P. (2008). Errorless learning in the rehabilitation of memory impairment: A critical review. *Neuropsychology Review, 18*, 1–23.

Clayton, N. S., & Griffiths, D. P. (2002). Testing episodic-like memory in animals. In L. R. Squire & D. L. Schacter (Eds.), *Neuropsychology of memory* (pp. 492–507). New York: Guilford.

Cohen, M. J. (1997). *Children's memory scale.* San Antonio, TX: The Psychological Corporation.

Comblain, A. (1994). Working memory in Down's syndrome: Training the rehearsal strategy. *Down Syndrome: Research & Practice, 2*, 123–126.

Conners, F. A., Rosenquist, C. J., Arnett, L., Moore, M. S., & Hume, L. E. (2008). Improving memory span in children with Down syndrome. *Journal of Intellectual Disability Research, 52*, 244–255.

Cowan, N. (2001). The magical number 4 in short-term memory: A reconsideration of mental storage capacity. *Behavioral Brain Science, 24*, 87–185.

Cowan, N., Elliott, E. M., Scott-Saults, J., Morey, C. C., Mattox, S., Hismjatullina, A., et al. (2005). On the capacity of attention: Its estimation and its role in working memory and cognitive aptitudes. *Cognitive Psychology, 51*, 42–100.

Dehn, M. J. (2008). *Working memory in academic learning: Assessment and intervention.* Hoboken, NJ: John Wiley & Sons.

Delis, D. C., Kramer, J. H., Kaplan, E., Ober, B. A., & Fridlund, A. J. (1989). *California verbal learning test, children's version.* San Antonio, TX: The Psychological Corporation.

Dever, M. T., & Hobbs, D. E. (2000). Curriculum connections. The learning spiral-toward authentic instruction. *Kappa Delta Pi Record, 36,* 131–133.

Diamond, A., Barnett, W. S., Thomas, J., & Munro, S. (2007). Preschool program improves cognitive control. *Science, 318,* 1387–1388.

Doyon, J., Penhune, V., & Ungerleider, L. G. (2003). Distinct contribution of the cortico-striatal and cortico-cerebellar systems to motor skill learning. *Neuropsychologia, 41,* 252–262.

Dunn, T. M. (2005). Review of the Wide Range Assessment of Memory and Learning, 2nd Edition. In B. S. Plake & J. C. Impara (Eds.), *The sixteenth mental measurements yearbook* [Electronic version]. Retrieved October 27, 2008, from http://www .ebscohost.com.

Ellmore, T. M., Stouffer, K., & Nadel, L. (2008). Divergence of explicit and implicit processing speed during associative memory retrieval. *Brain Research, 1229,* 155–166.

Engle, R. W., Tuholski, S. W., Laughlin, J. E., & Conway, A. R. A. (1999). Working memory, short-term memory, and general fluid intelligence: A latent-variable approach. *Journal of Experimental Psychology: General, 128,* 309–331.

Feifer, S. G., & Della Toffalo, D. A. (2007). *Integrating RTI with cognitive neuropsychology: A scientific approach to reading.* Middletown, MD: School Neuropsych Press.

Flanagan, D. P., & McGrew, K. S. (1997). A cross-battery approach to assessing and interpreting cognitive abilities: Narrowing the gap between practice and cognitive science. In D. P. Flanagan, J. L. Genshaft, & P. L. Harrison (Eds.), *Contemporary intellectual assessment: Theories, tests, and issues* (pp. 314–325). New York: Guilford.

Gallace, A., Tan, H. Z., Haggard, P., & Spence, C. (2008). Short term memory for tactile stimuli. *Brain Research, 1190,* 132–142.

Gathercole, S. E., & Alloway, T. P. (2004). *Understanding working memory: A classroom guide.* London: Medical Research Council.

Giap, B. T., Jong, C. N., Ricker, J. H., Cullen, N. K., & Zafonte, R. (2000). The hippocampus: Anatomy, pathophysiology, and regenerative capacity. *Journal of Head Trauma Rehabilitation, 15,* 875–894.

Gioia, G. A., Isquith, P. K., Guy, S. C., & Kenworthy, L. (2000). *Behavior Rating Inventory of Executive Function (BRIEF) manual.* Lutz, Fl: Psychological Assessment Resources.

Gioia, G. A., Isquith, P. K., Retzlaff, P. D., & Espy, K. A. (2002). Confirmatory factor analysis of the Behavior Rating Inventory of Executive Function (BRIEF) in a clinical sample. *Child Neuropsychology, 8,* 249–257.

Glisky, E. L., & Glisky, M. L. (2002). Learning and memory impairments. In P. J. Eslinger (Ed.), *Neuropsychological interventions: Clinical research and practice.* New York: Guilford.

Hale, J. B., & Fiorello, C. A. (2004). *School neuropsychology: A practitioner's handbook.* New York: Guilford.

Hyman, S. E., Malenka, R. C., & Nestler, E. J. (2006). Neural mechanisms of addiction: The role of reward-related learning and memory. *Annual Review of Neuroscience, 29,* 565–598.

Individuals with Disabilities Education Improvement Act (IDEIA), P.L. 108–446, 20 U.S.C. 1400–87 December, 2004.

Kaiser, J., Walker, F., Leiberg, S., & Lutzenberger, W. (2005). Cortical oscillatory activity during spatial echoic memory. *European Journal of Neuroscience, 21*, 587–590.

Korkman, M., Kirk, U., & Kemp, S. (2007). *NEPSY-II: A developmental neuropsychological assessment*. San Antonio, TX: The Psychological Corporation.

Lee, Y., Lu, M., & Ko, H. (2007). Effects of skill training on working memory capacity. *Learning and Instruction. 17,* 336–344

Leff, P., Retana, I., Arias-Caballero, A., Zavala, E., Loria, F., Pavón, L., et al. (2004). Understanding the neurobiological mechanisms of learning and memory: Cellular, molecular, and gene regulation implicated in synaptic plasticity and long-term potentiation. Part IV A. *Salud Mental, 27*, 39–52.

Leffard, S. A., Miller, J. A., Bernstein, J. H., DeMann, J. J., Mangis, H. A., & McCoy, E. L. B. (2006). Substantive validity of working memory measures in major cognitive functioning test batteries for children. *Applied Neuropsychology, 13*, 230–241.

Logie, R. H. (1995). *Visuo-spatial working memory*. Hove, UK: Erlbaum.

Marsolek, C. J., Squire, L. R., Kosslyn, S. M., & Lulenski, M. E. (1994). Form-specific explicit and implicit memory in the right cerebral hemisphere. *Neuropsychology, 8*, 588–597.

Martin, R. C. (2003). Language processing: Functional organization and neuroanatomical basis. *Annual Review of Psychology, 54*, 55–89.

Mather, N., & Jaffe, L. E. (2002). *Woodcock-Johnson III: Reports, recommendations, and strategies*. New York: John Wiley & Sons.

Mather, N., & Woodcock, R. W. (2001). *Examiner's manual. Woodcock-Johnson III tests of cognitive abilities*. Itasca, IL: Riverside.

McGaugh, J. L. (2000). Memory-A century of consolidation. *Science, 287*, 248–251.

McGaugh, J. L. (2002). The amygdala regulates memory consolidation. In L. R. Squire & D. L. Schacter (Eds.), *Neuropsychology of memory* (pp. 437–449). New York: Guilford.

McGrew, K. S., & Woodcock, R. W. (2001). *Technical manual. Woodcock-Johnson III*. Itasca, NY: Riverside Publishing.

Messick, S. (1995). Validity of psychological assessment: Validation of inferences from persons' responses and performances as scientific inquiry into score meaning. *American Psychologist, 50*, 741–749.

Miller, D. C. (2007). *Essentials of school neuropsychological assessment*. Hoboken, NJ: John Wiley & Sons.

Miller, G. A. (1956). The magical number seven, plus or minus two: Some limits on our capacity for processing information. *Psychological Review, 63*, 81–97.

Miyake, A., Friedman, N. P., Emerson, M. J., Witzki, A. H., & Howerter, A. (2000). The unity and diversity of executive functions and their contributions to complex "frontal lobe" tasks: A latent variable analysis. *Cognitive Psychology, 41*, 49–100.

Napolitano, S. A. (2001). Review of the Children's Memory Scale. In B. S. Plake & J. C. Impara (Eds.), *The fourteenth mental measurements yearbook* [Electronic version]. Retrieved October 27, 2008, from http://www.ebscohost.com.

Nyberg, L., Eriksson, J., Larsson, A., & Marklund, P. (2006). Learning by doing versus learning by thinking: An fMRI study of motor and mental training. *Neuropsychologia, 44*, 711–717.

Oberauer, K. (2006). Is the focus of attention in working memory expanded through practice? *Journal of Experimental Psychology: Learning, Memory, and Cognition, 32*, 197–214.

O'Carroll, C. M., Martin, S. J., Sandin, J., Frenguelli, B., & Morris, R. G. M. (2006). Dopaminergic modulation of the persistence of one-trial hippocampus-dependent memory. *Learning & Memory, 13*, 760–769.

Osaka, M., & Osaka, N. (2007). Neural bases of focusing attention in working memory: An fMRI study based on individual differences. In N. Osaka, R. H. Logie, & M. D'Esposito (Eds.), *The cognitive neuroscience of working memory* (pp. 99–117). New York: Oxford University Press.

Postle, B. R. (2007). Activated long-term memory? The bases of representation in working memory. In N. Osaka, R. H. Logie, & M. D'Esposito (Eds.), *The cognitive neuroscience of working memory* (pp. 333–349). New York: Oxford University Press.

Reitan, R. M., & Wolfson, D. (1993). *The Halstead-Reitan neuropsychological test battery: Theory and clinical interpretation* (2nd ed.). Tucson: Neuropsychology Press.

Reynolds, C. R. (1997). Forward and backward memory span should not be combined for clinical analysis. *Archives of Clinical Neuropsychology, 12*, 29–40.

Reynolds, C. R., & Voress, J. K. (2007). *Test of memory and learning* (2nd ed.). Austin, TX: Pro-Ed.

Riccio, C. A., Reynolds, C. R., Lowe, P., & Moore, J. J. (2002). The continuous performance test: A window on the neural substrates for attention? *Archives of Clinical Neuropsychology, 17*, 235–272.

Robinson, D. H. & Kiewra, K. A. (1995). Visual argument: Graphic organizers are superior to outlines in improving learning from text. *Journal of Educational Psychology, 87*, 455–467.

Roid, G. H. (2003). *Examiner's manual. Stanford-Binet intelligence scales* (5th ed.). Itasca: Riverside Publishing.

Rourke, B. P. (1994). Neuropsychological assessment of children with learning disabilities: Measurement issues. In C. R. Lyon (Ed.), *Frames of reference for the assessment of learning disabilities: New views on measurement issues* (pp. 475–514). Baltimore: Paul H. Brookes.

Rourke, B. P., Bakker, D. J., Fisk, J. L., & Strang, J. D. (1983). *Child neuropsychology: An introduction to theory, practice, and clinical practice.* New York: Guilford.

Russell, E. W. (2007). Commentary on "A motion to exclude and the 'fixed' versus 'flexible' battery in forensic neuropsychology." *Archives of Clinical Neuropsychology, 22*, 787–790.

Schmitt, A. J., & Decker, S. L. (in press). Review of the test of memory and learning (2nd ed.) (TOMAL-2). *Journal of Psychoeducational Assessment.*

Sheslow, D., & Adams, W. (2003). *Wide range assessment of memory and learning* (2nd ed.). Wilmington, DE: Wide Range.

Talley, J. L. (1988). *Children's auditory verbal learning test-2.* Odessa, FL: Psychological Assessment Resources, Inc.

Tulving, E. (1995). Organization of memory: Quo vadis? In M. S. Gazzaniga (Ed.), *The cognitive neurosciences* (pp. 839–847). Cambridge, MA: MIT Press.

Tulving, E. (2002). Episodic memory: From mind to brain. *Annual Review of Psychology, 53*, 1–25.

Tulving, E., & Markowitsch, H. J. (1998). Episodic and declarative memory: Role of the hippocampus. *Hippocampus, 8*, 198–204.

Vaupel, C. A. (2001). Review of the children's memory scale. *Journal of Psychoeducational Assessment, 19*, 392–400.

Wechsler, D. (1991). *Wechsler intelligence scale for children* (3rd ed.). San Antonio, TX: The Psychological Corporation.

Wechsler, D. (2003). *Wechsler intelligence scale for children* (4th ed.), *Technical and interpretive manual*. San Antonio, TX: Harcourt Assessment.

Wechsler, D., Kaplan, E., Fein, D., Kramer, J., Morris, R., Delis, D., & Maerlender, A. (2004). *Wechsler intelligence scale for children, 4th edition integrated—Technical and interpretive manual*. San Antonio, TX: Harcourt Assessment.

Wise, R. A. (2004). Dopamine, learning and motivation. *Nature Reviews Neuroscience, 5*, 483–494.

Work, P. H. L., & Choi, H. (2005). Developing classroom and group interventions based on a neuropsychological paradigm. In R. C. D'Amato, E. Fletcher-Janzen & C. R. Reynolds (Eds.), *Handbook of school neuropsychology* (Vol. 663-683). Hoboken, NJ: John Wiley & Sons.

CHAPTER 26

Assessing and Intervening with Children with Sensory-Motor Impairment

SCOTT L. DECKER and ANDREW DAVIS

T HE PURPOSE OF this chapter is to review techniques and methodology in sensory-motor assessment and the determination of sensory-motor impairment. Additionally, models of rehabilitation of sensory-motor functions will be discussed. Sensory and motor tests have been part of neurological exams for over a century (Finger, 1994) and have become an area of increasing interest in other fields. Measures of sensory and motor function are currently used by numerous professions including neurologists, neuropsychologists, psychiatrists, and school psychologists. Traditionally, such measures were administered for the purpose of localizing brain injury and investigating lateralization. Sensory-motor measures are also reliable indicators of the overall integrity of the central nervous system and are sensitive to cortical and subcortical injury or impairment.

Typically, the term *sensory-motor* in neuropsychology involves an assessment of basic input and output functions that are more complex than basic reflexes, but less complex than effortful cognition involving reasoning or executive functions. Although presented as theoretically isolated, sensory-motor functions are closely integrated with other "higher" level cognitive abilities. In fact, fidelity of sensory function was historically viewed as the essential quality of intelligence (Galton, 1883). Although subsequent research has suggested this is not the case, contemporary research has indicated measures of basic sensory-motor skills are correlated with measures of intellectual functioning (Acton & Schroeder, 2001; Baltes & Lindenberger, 1997; Carroll, 1993; Deary, 1994; Roberts, Pallier, & Goff, 1999; Roberts, Stankov, & Pallier, 1997; Stankov, Seizova-Cajic, & Roberts, 2001) as well as academic success (Decker, 2004; Fletcher, Taylor, Morris, & Satz, 1982; Satz,

Taylor, Friel, & Fletcher, 1978). Sensory-motor mechanisms may be viewed as a prerequisite, but not sufficient, condition for the development of more complex levels of cognitive function that are cross modal (not dependent on a particular sensory modality). This makes sense in that all measures of higher cognitive functions involve or require sensory information but also require more integrated cortical involvement that contributes and adds to sensory information.

Part of the value of including sensory and motor tests in school neuropsychological assessment is the specific neurological correlates of sensory and motor functioning to common neurodevelopmental disorders. Deficits in sensory and motor functioning more reliably predict the nature and localization of neurological impairment than measures of complex cognitive ability. This is primarily a result of genetic influences in how the brain and nervous system are "wired." Sensory receptors communicate information to specific primary sensory reception areas in the brain. The eyes are connected via the optic nerve to the occipital lobe, the ear to the superior temporal area, and tactile senses to the post-central gyrus (Berninger & Richards, 2002; Carlson, 2004; Kolb & Whishaw, 2003). The eyes, ears, and skin are contralaterally connected to brain regions. Damage to a primary sensory area in the brain will invariably create functional deficits on the opposite side of the body. The reliable localization of brain injury from functional sensory or motor deficits accounts for part of the basis and success of early neuropsychological batteries (Dean & Woodcock, 2003; Halstead, 1947).

One problem that emerged from using traditional sensory-motor measures borrowed from neurology is that interpretive patterns of deficits reliable with adults were assumed to generalize to children. This has not been supported by research, which suggests that developmental differences in sensory-motor functioning must be taken into account (Dean & Woodcock, 2003; Dean, Woodcock, Decker, & Schrank, 2003; Reitan & Wolfson, 2003). As such, age-based normative information is essential for sensory-motor assessment with children to control for developmental differences, despite the simplicity of the tasks.

SENSORY AND MOTOR FUNCTIONS

One limitation to both research and treatment of sensory-motor deficits is the lack of consensus in the component processes of sensory and motor functions. For heuristic value, tentative definitions and descriptions will be provided here. Primary sensory functions typically refer to biological mechanisms that encode stimulus energy (sight, sound, smell, and touch) from the external environment for the purpose of guiding a volitional or involuntary motor response. The process in which external stimulus energy is transformed into a neural code through sensory receptors is known as *sensory transduction*. For example, the eye consists of multiple mechanisms that transduce electromagnetic energy with wavelengths approximately 380 nanometers (blue light) to about 750 nanometers (red light). Similarly, the human ear captures vibrational differences in air waves between 20 Hz to about 20 kHz (Carlson, 2004). These mechanisms are often referred to as "lower" level processing in that conscious or deliberative thinking is often not a component of sensory functioning and effortful processing or directed attention is not necessary for the functioning of sensory mechanisms. However, attention and sensory-perception are intimately connected. Although clear demarcations do not exist, primary sensory functions may also involve post-transduction to cortical perception of stimulus information. Additionally, such mechanisms generally involve the peripheral nervous system (i.e., cranial nerves) and function to provide information to the central nervous system and cortical regions for the purpose of guiding motor acts. Primary sensory functions may also include functions that represent internal bodily processes such as balance (vestibular) and position in space (proprioception), although such information does not involve the transduction of external stimulus energy.

Motor functions broadly refer to a host of mechanisms that influence behavioral actions, or output processes, that range from reflexive to controlled or deliberative responses. Motor acts involve a hierarchy of processing along the neural axis that may involve the spinal cord, at the lowest level, to the cerebral cortex, at the highest level. For example, touching a hot stove may reflexively cause a withdraw motor response that is triggered by lower spinal and/or brain stem areas, whereas a consciously deliberated motor response may involve higher level (on the neuroaxis) cortical involvement (e.g., upper motor neurons). Both involve motor responses but involve different levels of cortical integration. Generally, the level of processing is dependent on the stimulus and the complexity of the response.

SENSORY-MOTOR AND PERCEPTUAL-MOTOR INTEGRATION

Visual construction measures evaluate motor responses to different tasks that require the integration and ordering of various isolated pieces or aspects of visual information (Lezak, 1995). Visual-motor construction measures range from graphic copying of two-dimensional geometric figures to block building. Figure copying has perhaps the longest history of use in visual-motor assessment. Despite its simplicity, figure copying requires numerous cognitive processes. First, the task requires an orientation to a particular stimulus within the visual field (Posner, 1980). Next, the external stimuli must be accurately perceived. Primary visual sensory mechanisms are crucial in this step as well as the fidelity in which a visual image is constructed that represents the external stimuli, initially in the striate area of the occipital lobes.

Research in neuroscience has suggested the visual stream is divided into a dorsal stream for perceptual-motor tasks and a ventral stream for object recognition tasks (Ungerleider & Mishkin, 1982). These two streams have been interpreted as the "where" and "what" streams (Kolb & Whishaw, 2003). Clinical observations of brain-injured subjects have supported this distinction (Goodale & Milner, 1992). Additionally, significant connections between the dorsal stream in the parietal lobes with the frontal lobes of the brain has led researchers to conclude that the fronto-parietal network functions as a visual-motor controller (Wise, Boussaoud, Johnson, & Caminiti, 1997). Other research has suggested the posterior parietal lobes serve to code information related to spatial locations of external objects and the integration of bodily position and movements (e.g., eye, head, body, arm) that are then integrated to motor action maps. Essentially, the parietal lobe is necessary for sensory-motor transformations from sensory coordinates to motor coordinates (Andersen, Snyder, Bradley, & Xing, 1997).

This model is consistent with clinical neuropsychological studies as well. For example, numerous studies have suggested deficits in copying geometric designs from the Bender-Gestalt test is most affected by brain damage in the posterior right parietal lobe of the brain (Lacks, 1999). Similarly, damage to the right parietal lobe is more likely to result in deficits in the analysis of spatial relations (Wilson, 2004). Clinical research has also suggested damage to the right parietal area is more likely to result in problems with analyzing global or structural features of drawings; whereas damaged left parietal regions may result in spared structural components of drawings that lack detail. Additionally, right parietal lobe damage may likely result in anosognosia (deficits in self-awareness) and neglect (inability to attend to stimuli in a visual field, typically left). Taken together, there is an emerging conceptualization of parietal lobe involvement with sensory-motor tasks of a "mental space" for the flexible integration of information from various sensory modalities with spatial coordinates of external space relative to somatic or bodily position and object orientation. The integration of this information is connected, or mapped, to motor action and action planning forming a hierarchy of sensory-motor functioning.

SENSORY-MOTOR IMPAIRMENTS IN CHILDHOOD DISORDERS AND LEARNING DISABILITIES

Sensory or motor deficits may have clinical significance for many childhood disorders. Table 26.1 provides terminology used to describe various neuropsychological deficits and the corresponding neurological areas typically

Table 26.1
Examples of Neuropsychological Terminology in Sensory-Motor Deficits
and Associated Neurological Area

	Disorder of Visual Pathway	Description	Neurological Correlate
Primary Visual Sensory	Monocular Blindness	Loss of vision in complete left or right visual field.	Eye, optic nerve, optic tract
	Bitemporal Hemianopia	Loss of vision in complete right and left outer visual fields.	Optic chiasm
	Nasal Hemianopia	Loss of vision in either left or right inner right visual field.	Lateral optic nerve
	Homonymous Hemianopia	Loss of vision in same visual field of each eye (e.g., left temporal and right nasal or right temporal and left nasal).	Optic tract
	Quadrantanopia	Loss of vision.	Optic tract
Primary Sensory Auditory	Deafness	Total loss of hearing.	Auditory nerve, Cochlear
	Bilateral Deafness	Loss of hearing in one ear.	Auditory nerve, Cochlear
Primary Sensory Tactile	Numbness	Loss of feeling in area of body; typically unilateral.	Contralateral somatosensory strip
	Proprioception	Sense of spatial orientation based on body position.	Vestibular, somatosensory strip, parietal lobe
Cortical Sensory	Asterognosia	Inability to recognize object by touch.	Cortical Anterior Parietal-Temporal
	Agnosia	Inability to recognize or name visual stimuli or part of body (Visual, Auditory, Finger).	Cortical Occipital-Temporal (Ventral Stream)
	Simultanagnosia	Inability to represent multiple visual objects in awareness.	Occipital – Posterior Parietal Lobe
	Sensory Integration	Combining information from difference senses into whole perception.	Multiple cortical areas
Primary Motor	Paralysis, Hemiplegia	Complete loss of movement.	Peripheral Nervous System, Spinal cord, Cortical frontal
	Hemiparesis	Loss of movement on one side of the body.	Corticospinal tract, Lateral frontal

(continued)

Table 26.1
Continued

	Disorder of Visual Pathway	Description	Neurological Correlate
Cortical Motor	Agraphia	Inability to write.	Multiple cortical areas (Left posterior temporal)
	Dyspraxia	Coordination of intention and action.	Multiple cortical areas
	Optic Ataxia	Deficit in visual guidance in reaching for objects.	Parietal-frontal
	Ocular apraxia	Deficit in visual scanning particularly horizontal eye movement.	Cerebellum, Optic-motor coordination

involved. The focus of this review will include disorders primarily from the DSM-IV (American Psychiatric Association, 2000) and federal guidelines for identifying children in schools (IDEA, 2004).

Primary areas are indicated by measures that predominantly involve sensory detection. Secondary measures involve the integration of sensory information with higher cortical functions, such as memory or language. Similarly, primary motor function is involved with simple isolated motor movements. Secondary motor movements are involved with functional integration of higher cortical functions involving complex sequential or coordinated movements, such as writing or playing a musical instrument.

Numerous childhood disorders are known to have sensory-motor impairments as primary symptoms of the disorder. Often in clinical practice, the difficulty is determining the specific processing breakdown contributing to impairment. Nonetheless, specific sensory impairment has long been part of various developmental disorders. For example, tactile sensory impairment in the fingers (finger agnosia) has historically been found to be an essential part of a cluster of symptoms including acalculia (math calculation disability) known as Gerstmann syndrome (Gerstmann, 1940), although the qualification of Gerstmann as a true "syndrome" has been questioned (Miller & Hynd, 2004). Visual-motor deficits have been reliably found in children with other neurological disorders, such as fetal alcohol syndrome (Uecker & Nadel, 1996), periventricular leukomalacia (PVL), seizure disorders, and cerebral palsy (CP). It is important to consider the synergistic and/or exacerbating effect that motor deficits can have on other areas of development, including social skills and language and cognitive development. Thus, it is important for school neuropsychologists to recognize they must consider sensory-motor deficits in their assessment of a child with known or suspected neurological impairment and not relegate this domain to other professionals.

Developmental Coordination Disorder (DCD) is a childhood motor disorder involving substantially below average motor coordination that significantly interferes in daily activities. Children with DCD typically fail to meet normal motor milestones, such as walking or running. Visual-spatial processing deficits are a hallmark symptom in children with developmental coordination disorder (Wilson & McKenzie, 1998). Nonverbal Learning Disabilities (NVLD) is another condition in which visual-spatial deficits are a hallmark feature and includes perceptual disturbances as a primary characteristic of the syndrome (Rourke, 1989). A common component of NVLD is visual-perceptual deficits with relatively intact or superior auditory memory skills. Additionally, children with NVLD have delayed motor skill development.

Many other childhood disorders have sensory-motor impairment as secondary symptoms, some of which may be misattributed to other symptomology. This includes conditions such as learning disabilities and Attention Deficit Hyperactivity Disorder (ADHD). As such, competency in assessing sensory-motor functions is essential in diagnosing these disorders and ensuring that the appropriate interventions are being used. A few studies have documented sensory impairment in children diagnosed with ADHD. Motor impulsivity is a hallmark feature of ADHD. However, motor impulsivity in ADHD has primarily been attributed to cortical factors involved with the control and regulation of motor output by executive function control, rather than a more basic deficit of motor control that may involve lower level or peripheral nervous system involvement. As such, research indicating deficits in basic sensory and motor measures in children with ADHD may involve the confounding effects of attention and other higher-level response mediators. It is difficult to determine whether such children have primary sensory-motor deficits or whether such deficits are secondary to attention and/or executive processes registering sensory information.

The primary symptoms of children with autism involve language and social deficits. However, many children with autism have sensory-integration issues as well as gross and fine motor problems (Smith, 2004). Children with autism are frequently overwhelmed by sensory stimuli, particularly if the stimulus is new or novel. Additionally, motor-mannerisms have been included as a diagnostic indicator of the disorder. There is some evidence that sensory-motor problems early in life may be good predictors of autism, and several studies have attempted to understand the precise nature of the motor problems in children with autism. There is some evidence for motor preparation deficits in children with autism (Hughes, 1996). Additionally, some studies have found apraxic and proprioception deficits in children with autism (Weimer, Schatz, Lincoln, Ballantyne, & Trauner, 2001). Although motor problems have been reliably associated with autism, some of the impairment in both sensory and motor problems may be accounted for by global intellectual impairment, which may also account for social-cognitive deficits. However, some of the core deficits in higher-level social cognition may in turn have origins in the disruption of basic sensory-motor processes in early development, which cause impairment in social-cognitive processes like facial recognition (Smith, 2004)

Deficits in sensory-motor functioning may significantly impact academic learning. However, Specific Learning Disabilities (SLD), according to federal guidelines (IDEA, 2004) excludes sensory-motor impairments by definition. As such, prior to diagnosing a learning disability, sensory and motor problems must be ruled out as the primary factor in the etiology of SLD. These guidelines are provided to essentially isolate the cause of a learning disability to the higher-order cognitive processing component of the central nervous system, typically in the information-processing area of the cerebral cortex. As such, a child who is blind and cannot read would not be considered to have a learning disability, but rather a sensory impairment. It is also important to consider that sensory-motor deficits may exacerbate a subclinical level of SLD, and thus may not be the sole factor in the child's failure to learn, but should be considered a contributor. Failure to assess or account for sensory-motor deficits in children with SLD could lead to the subclinical SLD receiving an inappropriate level of intervention.

Determining where sensory processes stop and higher-level information processing mechanisms start is difficult, particularly when one considers the integral involvement of the sensory system in higher-order processing. For example, the optic nerve initially brings visual information from the eye to the lateral geniculate nucleus in the mid-brain prior to the occipital lobe and the reading systems of the cortex. The lateral geniculate nucleus divides the visual stream into multiple layers, broadly grouped as the magnocellular and parvocelluar pathways. One theory of dyslexia, although controversial, has suggested dyslexia is caused, or at least influenced, by developmental anomalies in the magnocellular pathway, which is involved with contrast sensitivity of rapidly detecting a target (e.g., letters or words) with a background (Stein & Walsh, 1997). Thus, would this be considered a sensory deficit and excluded from the current definition of an IDEA reading disorder? This raises an important issue about the role of sensory-motor impairment in diagnosing a learning disability and the complexities involved in disentangling sensory deficits from non-sensory deficits. Additionally, sensory and motor difficulties could conceivably exacerbate a subclinical learning problem to a diagnostic level. Regardless of conceptualizing sensory-motor measures as a "rule-out" or as an attribute of a condition, this demonstrates the importance of including sensory-motor measures in a neuropsychological evaluation as well as understanding how sensory, cognitive, and motor processes are integrated.

SCHOOL NEUROPSYCHOLOGICAL ASSESSMENT OF SENSORY-MOTOR FUNCTIONS

There is a considerable range in the sensory and motor functions that are assessed by different batteries and by different measures. Typically, measures of sensory and motor functioning are given selectively when the results of a more comprehensive battery of cognitive tests suggest the possibility of sensory-motor deficits. As such, it is critical to understand the measurement characteristics of different tests (Miller, 2007; Wodrich & Schmitt, 2006). Additionally, it is important to understand what the test is measuring beyond the name of the tests. There are many tests of "sensory-motor" functioning, which may drastically differ in the functions being measured along the neuroaxis (sensory reception to complex perceptual processing). Below is a review of a few sensory-motor measures with emphasis on the functional and conceptual aspects of the constructs and

DEAN-WOODCOCK SENSORY-MOTOR BATTERY

The *Dean-Woodcock Sensory Motor Battery* (DWSMB; Dean & Woodcock, 2003) consists of eight measures of sensory functioning, nine measures of motor functioning, and one measure of lateral preference. The DWSMB was designed in part to overcome some of the psychometric limitations of "traditional" neuropsychological batteries, including multiple sets of normative data and a focus on upper extremity motor functioning. Many of the measures used in the DWSMB are similar to historically used measures in other neuropsychological batteries, such as the Halstead-Reitan (Reitan & Wolfson, 1993). The DWSMB has a normative sample of over 1,000 individuals that range in age from 4 years to 90 years plus. The DWSMB was co-normed with the *Woodcock-Johnson, 3rd Edition*. One valuable aspect of the DWSMB is the use of Rasch modeling in scale development. The Rasch model produces interval level metrics with a "ruler-like" measurement quality. Such metrics are ideal to use in monitoring functional gain as a result of treatment.

The Near Point Visual Acuity exam measures primary visual acuity. It uses a version of Snellen notations to determine if visual processes are intact and to determine the functional proficiency of vision at a certain distance, comparable to the distance involved in completing most psychological tests. Deficits on this test indicating primary visual deficits may impact the results of other measures involving primary visual ability in cognitive ability and/or academic achievement tests. Recent research has suggested that even corrected visual acuity may account for a substantial portion of the variance in visual attention tasks and thus may need to be formally assessed, as opposed to simply checking if the examinee is wearing prescribed lenses (Davis, Hertza, Williams, Gupta, & Ohly, in press).

The Visual Confrontation test is another measure of primary visual ability, although slightly further along the visual-processing stream. Specifically, Visual Confrontation is a measure of the visual fields. The visual field is divided into different quadrants, typically left and right and above eye level, at eye level, and below eye level. Additionally, the inner side of each visual field is referred to as nasal (toward the nose) and the outer side is referred to as temporal. Each quadrant has a unique neurological localization such that the upper right visual field corresponds to the lower left occipital lobe. Similarly, the lower left visual field corresponds to higher areas in the right occipital lobe and greater loss of vision in the visual fields corresponds to greater cortical damage (Kolb & Whishaw, 2003). Table 26.1 provides a list of terms to describe various deficits in the visual field. Taken together, these measures comprehensively measure the range of deficits found in primary visual deficits.

Naming Pictures of Objects measures the ability to volitionally access the correct word and is a skill that can be lost due to a variety of neuro-psychological conditions that can affect children and adults, such as traumatic brain injury (Lezak, 1995). The test consists of 21 pictures of everyday objects and is used to screen for dysnomia (difficulty naming objects), for visual agnosia (failure to visually recognize objects), or for a motor coordination problems with the speech muscles. Auditory Acuity screens for simple hearing difficulties. Although most subjects are aware of a hearing loss, some subjects who may have recently incurred a brain trauma may be unaware of the deficit, especially when the hearing loss is slight or when aphasic deficits are contributing to speech problems (Lezak, 1995). Auditory Acuity aids in determining laterality impairment when there is a difference in performance between the left and right auditory channels (Dean & Woodcock, 2003). Additionally, auditory acuity is rarely formally assessed, which may be an oversight as mild hearing loss has an obvious impact on receptive language and may go undetected until a formal hearing screen is conducted.

The tactile examination subtests are classic tests of perceptual discrimination, versions of which can be found on the *Halstead-Reitan Neuropsychological Test Battery* (Reitan & Wolfson, 1993). The first aspect of Tactile Examination-Palm Writing requires the subject to identify if an X or an O is written on his or her palm, while the second task requires the subject to identify numbers. Differences in errors between hands provide evidence for contralateral cerebral impairment. Deficits on this task can also indicate a tactile discrimination problem, which can present as clumsiness and difficulty with dexterity, which may affect fine motor movements and interaction with manipulatives (Dean & Woodcock, 2003). Object Identification tests the ability to identify common objects by tactile stimulation without vision. Inability to perform this task is described as astereognosis (loss of an ability to recognize objects by touch) (Luria, 1966; Reitan & Wolfson, 1993). Generally, normal individuals are able to easily complete this task, and even one error or indication of hesitation may indicate cerebral dysfunction (Dean & Woodcock, 2003). Finger Identification requires subjects to identify fingers by touch while blindfolded and assesses finger agnosia (inability to recognize tactile stimulation in one's own fingers). Errors on this task are associated with contralateral parietal lobe lesions (Reitan & Wolfson, 1993). Simultaneous Localization uses double sensory stimulation of the child's hands and cheeks in a combination of right only, left only, and right and left together. Double and unilateral stimulation provides a validated method to detect sensory cortical deficits (Dean & Woodcock, 2003; Kahn, Goldfarb, Pollack, & Peck, 1960).

The DWSMB also has a variety of motor measures, including standardized and norm-referenced assessments of lower extremity functioning, which separates it from most other neuropsychological sensory-motor measures. Gait and Station is comprised of three separate tasks that broadly assess gait problems, which is the loss of or difficulty with an ability to coordinate lower extremity motor movement, which can result in difficulty in a broad array of abilities (Dean & Woodcock, 2003; Sattler & D'Amato, 2002), and which may be sensitive to subcortical lesions (Dean & Woodcock, 2003). The Romberg is a classic neurological test to measure postural instability when standing with the eyes closed. The positions become increasingly difficult for the child, and hence more subcortically dependent (Dean & Woodcock, 2003). Construction is a simple drawing test requiring subjects to copy a cross and a clock and is designed to detect construction dyspraxia (difficulty in motor tasks involving the construction of figures), visual motor integration, and visuospatial awareness and memory.

Like other drawing tests, including the *Bender Visual-Motor Gestalt Test, 2nd Edition* (Brannigan & Decker, 2003) and the *Reitan-Indiana Aphasia Screening Test* (Reitan & Wolfson, 1992), drawing measures are central in that they are sensitive to brain impairment (Lezak, 1995; Sattler & D'Amato, 2002) and degenerative diseases such as Alzheimer's disease (Dean & Woodcock, 2003). Coordination assesses an individual's upper extremity motor functioning by requiring the subject to first touch the tip of the nose with the index finger, and then touch the examiner's finger as the examiner moves his or her finger across the subject's field of vision. A second part of the exam requires the subject to rapidly alternate between the front and back of the hand on the thigh. Both tasks assess coordinated motor movement at the cerebral and cerebellar levels (Dean & Woodcock, 2003). Mime Movements assesses an individual's ability to follow simple directions and execute skilled motor movements and thus provides an indicator of ideomotor dyspraxia (an inability to perform simple motor tasks when requested to do so) (Dean & Woodcock, 2003).

Left-Right Movements assesses left-right confusion by asking the subject to perform a number of very simple tasks with both hands. As with any task, it is important for the school neuropsychologist to consider alternate explanations of why these seemingly simple motor tasks may be impaired. For example, it is important to rule out receptive language and attention prior to assigning deficit to the motor system. Finger Tapping assesses fine motor speed and dexterity and provides an indicator of the overall functioning of the motor strip and precentral gyrus (Dean & Woodcock, 2003). Expressive Speech assesses for the presence of dysarthria by asking subjects to repeat a series of simple words and phrases. This subtest can be negatively impacted by language abilities such as those seen following a left-hemisphere stroke. Finally, Grip Strength requires a hand dynometer to measure the strength of each hand. Impaired performance with either hand is associated with contralateral motor strip, overall integrity of the cerebral hemispheres, and peripheral nerve and muscle functioning (Dean & Woodcock, 2003).

OTHER SENSORY-MOTOR BATTERIES

Although not a full battery or as comprehensive as the DWSMB, the NEPSY-II (Korkman, Kirk, & Kemp, 2007) includes a Sensorimotor Core with three measures of sensory-motor functioning. The Fingertip Tapping subtest, similar to versions on the *Halstead-Reitan Neuropsychological Battery* (Reitan & Wolfson, 1993) and the DWSMB (Dean & Woodcock, 2003), requires the child to rapidly tap the tip of the index finger against other fingers. Scores are tallied based on the completion time to complete the requisite number of fingertip taps for each task. Imitating Hand Positions subtest is administered to children of all ages on the NEPSY-II. The examiner models a variety of hand positions, which the children must imitate, first with the preferred hand, and then with the nonpreferred hand. Korkman et al. (1998) indicate that difficulty with this task may be linked to kinesthetic praxis, processing of tactile information, and fine motor skills. Visuomotor Precision subtest requires the use of a pencil to quickly draw a line inside a track that resembles a racing track or train tracks, which measures graphomotor skills, fine motor ability, and visual-spatial integration. Korkman et al. (2007) also noted that poor performance could indicate impulsivity, poor visuomotor coordination, and poor planning.

There are several other batteries of sensory-motor assessment that are less often used in school neuropsychological assessment evaluations. The *Wide Range Assessment of Visual Motor Abilities* (Adams & Sheslow, 1995) consists of Drawing, Matching, and Pegboard tests that are appropriate for ages 3 to 17. The *Bayley Scales of Infant Development, 3rd Edition* (Bayley, 2005) includes not only measures of motor development but also cognitive, language, and social-emotional development. The test is used for early development assessment in children from 1 to approximately 4 years of age. Similarly, the *Peabody Developmental Motor Scales, 2nd Edition* (Folio & Fewell, 2000) is used in young children from birth to 5 years of age and measures a variety of motor skills and developmental motor milestones.

SINGLE MEASURES OF SENSORY-MOTOR FUNCTIONS

A variety of other measures may be considered measures of sensory-motor functioning. These measures are described as visual-motor, perceptual-motor, visual-motor integration, perceptual-motor integration, and other similar terminologies. Only a few of the most frequently used measures will be reviewed here (see Miller 2007 for a more complete listing).

The *Beery-Buktenica Visual Motor Integration* test (VMI; Beery, Buktenica, & Beery, 2004) consists of 30 geometric designs that are copied with a pencil on a response booklet. Each design is copied within a provided area on the response booklet. The test purportedly measures the coordination between visual perception and motor output. Normative information is available for individuals from 2 to 18 years of age. The VMI consists of both a short and long form and has two supplemental tests to measure more specific aspects of visual-perception and motor precision.

The *Bender Visual Motor Gestalt Test*, popularly referred to as the Bender-Gestalt measure (Bender, 1938), has been one of the most frequently used measures in psychology. The *Bender-Gestalt, 2nd Edition* (BGII; Brannigan & Decker, 2003) improves on many psychometric shortcomings of the original edition. Additionally, the construct is more focused on visual perceptual-motor ability, rather than on personality assessment. Items were added to extend the measurement scale, and normative information was collected on ages 4 to 80 years of age. Standard scores are provided for both a Copy procedure in which geometric designs are drawn on a blank piece of paper as well as a Recall procedure in which the designs are recalled from memory. Because drawings are made on a blank piece of paper, examinees must impose an organization onto the paper, which provides a valuable qualitative observation of performance. Demonstrations of how to use Rasch scoring metrics, similar to W-scores found on the DWSMB, for measuring intervention changes is also available (Decker, 2008b).

EVIDENCE-BASED INTERVENTIONS FOR THE TREATMENT OF CHILDREN WITH SENSORY-MOTOR IMPAIRMENTS

Treatment options for sensory-motor impairment depend on the nature and extent of the deficit. Complete loss of sensory functioning from damage or dysfunction to primary sensory systems (e.g., eye, optic nerve, ear) typically requires a high level of accommodation. Most children with these conditions are covered under the 504 Americans Disability Act. Standard accommodations for children who are hard of hearing may require hearing aids and/or an amplification system for the teacher. Children with hearing loss may require extended time to complete academic assignments and may require interpreters. If vision is intact, children may benefit from increased visual supplements to instruction. Some children with congenital hearing loss also experience problems with articulation and expressive speech, suggesting assistive technology may be beneficial. Similarly, children with vision loss or low vision may require accommodations in academic assignment as well as text in Braille. If auditory acuity is intact, an increased use of verbal supplements will be of obvious value.

Children with disorders involving gross motor deficits, such as cerebral palsy, may require accommodations for movement including wheelchair and handicapped accessory facilities. Gross motor deficits can also limit participation in social aspects of school. For example, children may not be able to participate to the full extent in physical education or recess activities. Developing interventions to ensure social participation can be crucial, such as having a child with severe gross motor problems act as a coach, referee, or scorekeeper to increase involvement. Children with fine-motor difficulties may require accommodations in writing. Often, accommodations that allow the child to type using an electronic keyboard, or substitute voice response instead of requiring handwritten responses on assignments, improves the child's academic participation. If the child's impairment is severe enough to drastically interfere with taking statewide achievement tests, alternative assessments may be an option. These accommodations should be specified in the child's Individualized Educational Plan.

Treatment options for sensory-motor impairment that involves more cortical involvement may more likely benefit from remediation, although accommodations may also be needed. Treatments for sensory and motor deficits range from rehabilitative to compensatory. In schools, children with primary sensory or motor deficit usually received physical or occupational therapy, typically fine motor or gross motor. Such treatment focuses on basic functions such as using scissors, pencils, or other functions needed in school.

Children with more subtle sensory-motor deficits may also benefit from accommodations. This is particularly important for school psychologists to consider, as these subtle, or hidden, deficits may not have required attention from an occupational or physical therapist. The presence of mild sensory and motor skill impairment may exacerbate learning and attention problems and, without detection, may lead to interventions that are not targeting the correct construct. For example, a child with mild agraphesthesia or astereognosis may be slow in or have difficulty with turning pages, which could present as a deficit in reading fluency. The impact on academics of mild fine motor deficits may be overlooked if not quantitatively assessed. For example, slow or unsteady handwriting as a result of a motor coordination, sequencing, or planning deficit could result in slow or inaccurate note taking or copying from the board. Providing notes prior to lectures, having a "scribe" and providing the student copies of what is on the board are all reasonable accommodations for these children. Without knowledge of the sensory deficit, interventions could unnecessarily address reading speed. This magnifies the importance of assessing sensory-motor deficits in children with suspected cognitive and/or academic problems.

Most interventions are conceived to be restorative of deficient or impaired sensory-motor functioning. However, tactile stimulation has been found to have protective effect. Tactile development occurs earlier than other sensory modalities. Hypoxic-ischemic encephalopathy occurs when the brain is deprived of oxygen, which often occurs due to perinatal complications and frequently results in specific damage to the hippocampus due to glutamate excitotoxicity. Recent studies have found that tactile stimulation has a neuroprotective effect on the brain and reduces the harmful effects of early brain injury in animals (Rodrigues et al., 2004). Such research is supported by other observations of adverse behavioral consequences in primates isolated from social contact (Harlow, Dodsworth, & Harlow, 1965) and in human children with reactive attachment disorder (American Psychiatric Association, 2000).

More formalized investigations of empirically based interventions for motor problems have lacked a consensus in treatment recommendations. In a review of treatments for motor problems, Polatajko, Rodger, Dhillon, & Hirji (2004) reviewed six categories of treatment approaches: (1) neuro-developmental, (2) sensory integrative therapy, (3) conductive education, (4) cognitive approaches, (5) compensatory approaches, and (6) exercise therapy. Research, categorized by quality, was reviewed for a variety of motor disorders including Developmental Coordination Disorder, Cerebral Palsy, Muscular Dystrophy, and Spina Bifida. Although a few treatments seemed promising for some disorders, overall it was concluded, "there is no proven best practice approach for any specific disorder" (p. 482). These authors also note the heterogeneous nature of many of these disorders complicates the study of treatment outcomes, and clinicians must rely on clinical judgment to determine the best approach. The Committee on Children with Disabilities (CCD, 1996) similarly concluded from meta-analyses of research that "Clear documentation of efficacy has continued to be elusive" and "This problem may in part reflect difficult issues of methodology associated with the study of therapeutic efficacy in children because of their changing maturation and the need to identify and measure appropriate outcome criteria" (p. 308). The difficulty with methodological issues has been reiterated in a more recent statement as well as a caution in prescribing therapies with no known therapeutic value (Michaud, 2004).

Although the methodological issues are numerous, having well-designed measures of sensory-motor functioning that are sensitive to behavioral changes in performance are essential. Decker (2008a; 2008b) has argued for the use of Item Response Theory (IRT) metrics in scale development to serve this purpose. Item Response Theory models provide equal interval metrics that are not sample dependent and are modeled with a logistics curve. The model assumes a person's raw score is an interaction of the person's ability interacting with the difficulty of an item (ability-item). One familiar application of this scale is the W-score on the WJIII, also featured on the DWSMB. Decker (2008a) provided a demonstration of the use of W-scores to monitor treatment outcomes. In this example, the W-score for Letter-Word Identification on the WJIII Tests of Achievement was tested pre and post an academic reading intervention to increase word identification for a particular child. The W-score from the normative sample corresponding to the person's age in months at the first and second time periods was used as a reference for comparing the rate of change between the child's pre and post measures. Parallel lines would indicate equal slopes and no change in academic functioning. Projected overlapping lines would indicate the intervention was successful. This method is recommended as an additional check on intervention determination when curriculum based measures are used. Although W-scores for academic achievement were used in this study, the same methodology may be applied to the W-scores on the DWSMB.

Decker (2008b) used Item Response Theory to analyze the growth and decline in visual-motor ability on the Bender-Gestalt II. The theta values derived in this study are equivalent to W-scores. Using the theta values, an example was provided in using a test-retest procedure to determine significant performance change on the BG II that controls for developmental change. This method of determining change in performance as a result of intervention may be generalized to any measure so long as theta values, or equivalent (i.e., W-scores), and standard errors are available. Although often underutilized, the IRT scales provided on many sensory-motor measures are ideal for empirically determining treatment efficacy.

SUMMARY

Sensory-motor assessment involves a wide range of measures that assess a variety of processes. Sensory functioning begins with transduction and blends into perception. Motor functioning also has a range from simple motor responses to complex motor responses. Sensory-motor assessment is illustrative in that there is a high correspondence between sensory-motor functioning and the neurological substrate that supports it. Damage to particular neurological areas of the brain or spinal cords reliably produce predictable deficits in sensory and motor functioning. This not only makes sensory-motor assessment an important competency for school neuropsychologists but also provides a low-inference model of neuropsychology important for training school neuropsychologists. Effectiveness of sensory-motor interventions has been slowed by the lack of component processes specification of sensory-motor measures, such as primary from secondary components. Additionally, measurement of intervention change has also been an impediment to determining intervention effectiveness. Some of these limitations are beginning to be overcome in contemporary sensory motor measures.

REFERENCES

Acton, G. S., & Schroeder, D. H. (2001). Sensory discrimination as related to general intelligence. *Intelligence, 29*, 263–271.

Adams, W., & Sheslow, D. (1995). *Wide range assessment of visual motor abilities.* Odessa, FL: Psychological Assessment Resources.

American Psychiatric Association. (2000). *Diagnostic and statistical manual of mental disorders* (4th ed., Text Revision). Washington, DC: Author.

Andersen, R. A., Snyder, L. H., Bradley, D. C., & Xing, J. (1997). Multimodal representation of space in the posterior parietal cortex and its use in planning movements. *Annual Review of Neuroscience, 20*, 303–330.

Baltes, P. B., & Lindenberger, U. (1997). Emergence of a powerful connection between sensory and cognitive functions across the adult lifespan: A new window to the study of cognitive aging? *Psychology and Aging, 12*, 12–21.

Bayley, N. (2005). *Bayley scales of infant development* (3rd ed.). San Antonio, TX: Harcourt Assessment.

Beery, K. E., Buktenica, N. A., & Beery, N. A. (2004). *The Beery-Buktenica developmental test of visual-motor integration* (5th ed.). Minneapolis, MN: NCS Pearson.

Bender, L. (1938). *A visual motor gestalt test and its clinical use.* New York: American Orthopsychiatric Association.

Berninger, V. W., & Richards, T. L. (2002). *Brain literacy for educators and psychologists.* San Diego: Academic Press.

Brannigan, G. G., & Decker, S. L. (2003). *Bender-Gestalt II examiner's manual.* Itasca, IL: Riverside Publishing.

Carlson, N. R. (2004). *Physiology of behavior.* Boston: Pearson.

Carroll, J. B. (1993). *Human cognitive abilities: A survey of factor-analytic studies.* Cambridge, UK: Cambridge University Press.

Committee on Children with Disabilities. (1996). The role of the pediatrician in prescribing therapy services for children with motor disabilities. *Pediatrics, 98*(2), 308–310.

Davis, A. S., Hertza, J., Williams, R. N., Gupta, A. S., & Ohly, J. (in press). The influence of corrected visual acuity on visual attention and incidental learning in patients with multiple sclerosis. *Applied Neuropsychology.*

Dean, R. S., & Woodcock, R. W. (2003). *Examiner's manual. Dean-Woodcock neuropsychological battery.* Itasca, IL: Riverside Publishing.

Dean, R. S., Woodcock, R. W., Decker, S. L., & Schrank, F. A. (2003). A cognitive neuropsychological assessment system. In F. L. Schrank & D. P. Flanagan (Eds.), *WJ III clinical use and interpretation.* San Diego: Elsevier Science.

Deary, I. J. (1994). Sensory discrimination and intelligence: Postmortem or resurrection? *American Journal of Psychology, 107,* 95–115.

Decker, S. L. (2004). Incremental validity of tactile measures in predicting letter-word identification skills. *Archives of Clinical Neuropsychology, 19,* 907–908.

Decker, S. L. (2008a). Intervention psychometrics. *Assessment for Effective Intervention, 34,* 52–61.

Decker, S. L. (2008b). Measuring growth and decline in visual-motor processes with the Bender-Gestalt (2nd ed.). *Journal of Psychoeducational Assessment, 26,* 3–15.

Finger, S. (1994). *Origins of neuroscience: A history of explorations into brain functions.* New York: Oxford University Press.

Fletcher, J. M., Taylor, H. G., Morris, R., & Satz, P. (1982). Finger recognition skills and reading achievement: A developmental neuropsychological perspective. *Developmental Psychology, 18,* 124–132.

Folio, M. R., & Fewell, R. R. (2000). *Peabody developmental motor scales* (2nd ed.). San Antonio: Harcourt Assessment.

Galton, F. (1883). *Inquiries into human faculty.* London: Dent.

Gerstmann, J. (1940). Syndrome of finger agnosia, disorientation for right and left, agraphia and acalculia. *Archives of Neurology and Psychiatry, 44,* 398–408.

Goodale, M. A., & Milner, D. A. (1992). Separate visual pathways for perception and action. *Trends in Neuroscience, 15,* 20–25.

Halstead, W. C. (1947). *Brain and intelligence: A quantitative study of the frontal lobes.* Chicago: University of Chicago Press.

Harlow, H., Dodsworth, R. O., & Harlow, M. K. (1965). Total social isolation in monkeys. *Proceedings of the National Academy of Sciences of the United States of America, 54,* 90–97.

Hughes, C. (1996). Planning problems in autism at the level of motor control. *Journal of Autism and Developmental Disorders, 26,* 90–107.

Individuals with Disabilities Education Improvement Act of 2004 (IDEA), Pub. L. No. 108–446, 118 Stat 2647 (2004).

Kahn, R. L., Goldfarb, A. I., Pollack, M., & Peck, A. (1960). Brief objective measures for the determination of mental status in the aged. *American Journal of Psychiatry, 117,* 326–328.

Kolb, B., & Whishaw, I. Q. (2003). *Fundamentals of human neuropsychology* (5th ed.). New York: Worth Publishers.

Korkman, M., Kirk, U., & Kemp, S. (2007). *NEPSY-II: A developmental neuropsychological assessment.* San Antonio, TX: The Psychological Corporation.

Lacks, P. (1999). *Bender-Gestalt screening for brain dysfunction* (2nd ed.). New York: John Wiley & Sons.

Lezak, M. D. (1995). *Neuropsychological assessment* (3rd ed.). New York: Oxford University Press.

Luria, A. R. (1966). *Higher cortical functions in man.* New York: Basic Books.

Michaud, L. J. & Committee on Children with Disabilities. (2004). Prescribing therapy services for children with motor disabilities. *Pediatrics, 113*(6), 1836–1838.

Miller, C. J., & Hynd, G. W. (2004). What ever happened to developmental Gerstmann's Syndrome? Link to other pediatric, genetic, and neurodevelopmental syndromes. *Journal of Child Neurology, 19,* 282–289.

Miller, D. C. (2007). *Essentials of school neuropsychological assessment.* New York: John Wiley & Sons.

Polatajko, H. J., Rodger, S., Dhillon, A., & Hirji, F. (2004). Approaches to the management of children with motor problems. In D. Dewey & D. E. Tupper (Eds.), *Developmental motor disorders: A neuropsychological perspective* (pp. 461–486). New York: Guilford.

Posner, M. I. (1980). Orienting of attention. *Quarterly Journal of Experimental Psychology: Human Experimental Psychology, 32,* 3–25.

Reitan, R. M., & Wolfson, D. (1992). *Neuropsychological evaluation of older children.* South Tucson, AZ: Neuropsychology Press.

Reitan, R. M., & Wolfson, D. (1993). *The Halstead-Reitan neuropsychological test battery: Theory and clinical interpretation.* Tucson, AZ: Neuropsychology Press

Reitan, R. M., & Wolfson, D. (2003). The significance of sensory-motor functions as indicators of brain dysfunction in children. *Archives of Clinical Neuropsychology, 18,* 11–18.

Roberts, R. D., Pallier, G., & Goff, G. N. (1999). Sensory processes within the structure of human cognitive abilities. In *Learning and individual differences.* Washington DC: American Psychological Association.

Roberts, R. D., Stankov, L., & Pallier, G. (1997). Charting the cognitive sphere: Tactile-kinesthetic performance within the structure of intelligence. *Intelligence, 25,* 111–148.

Rodrigues, A. L., Arteni, N. S., Abel, C., Zylbersztejn, D., Chazan, R., Viola, G., et al. (2004). Tactile stimulation and maternal separation prevent hippocampal damage in rats submitted to neonatal hypoxia-ischemia. *Brain Research, 1002,* 94–99.

Rourke, B. P. (1989). Introduction. In *The NLD syndrome and the white matter model.* New York: Guilford.

Sattler, J. M., & D'Amato, R. C. (2002). Brain injuries: Formal batteries and informal measures. In J. M. Sattler (Ed.), *Assessment of children: Behavioral and clinical Applications* (4th ed., pp. 440–469). San Diego, CA: J. M. Sattler Publisher.

Satz, P., Taylor, H. G., Friel, J., & Fletcher, J. M. (1978). Some developmental and predictive precursors of reading disabilities: A six-year follow-up. In

A. L. Benton & D. Pearl (Eds.), *Dyslexia* (pp. 313–347). New York: Oxford University Press.

Smith, I. M. (2004). Motor problems in children with Autistic Spectrum Disorder. In D. Dewey & D. E. Tupper (Eds.), *Developmental motor disorders: A neuropsychological perspective*. New York: Guilford.

Stankov, L., Seizova-Cajic, T., & Roberts, R. D. (2001). Tactile and kinesthetic perceptual processes within the taxonomy of human cognitive abilities. *Intelligence, 29*, 1–29.

Stein, J., & Walsh, V. (1997). To see but not to read; the magnocellular theory of dyslexia. *Trends in Neuroscience, 20*, 147–152.

Uecker, A., & Nadel, L. (1996). Spatial locations gone awry: Object and spatial memory deficits in children with fetal alcohol syndrome. *Neuropsychologia, 34*, 209–223.

Ungerleider, L. G., & Mishkin, M. (Eds.). (1982). *Two cortical visual systems*. Cambridge, MA: The MIT Press.

Weimer, A. K., Schatz, A. M., Lincoln, A., Ballantyne, A. O., & Trauner, D. A. (2001). "Motor" impairment in Asperger syndrome: Evidence for a deficit in proprioception. *Developmental and Behavioral Pediatrics, 22*, 92–101.

Wilson, P. (2004). Visuospatial, kinesthetic, visuomotor integration, and visuoconstructional disorders. In D. Dewey & D. E. Tupper (Eds.), *Developmental motor disorders: A neuropsychological perspective* (pp. 291–312). New York: Guilford.

Wilson, P. H., & McKenzie, B. E. (1998). Information processing deficits associated with developmental coordination disorder: A meta-analysis of research findings. *Journal of Child Psychology and Psychiatry, 39*, 829–840.

Wise, S. P., Boussaoud, D., Johnson, P. B., & Caminiti, R. (1997). Premotor and parietal cortex: Corticocortical connectivity and combinatorial computations. *Annual Review of Neuroscience, 20*, 25–42.

Wodrich, D. L., & Schmitt, A. J. (2006). *Patterns of learning disabilities*. New York: Guilford.

CHAPTER 27

Assessing and Intervening with Chronically Ill Children

BETH COLALUCA and JONELLE ENSIGN

T HE FOCUS OF the present chapter is to review common chronic childhood illnesses that either directly or indirectly impact cognitive functioning. Children with a history of central nervous system (CNS) infection or compromise, chronic medical illnesses, acquired or congenital brain damage, and neurodevelopmental risk factors are included. The purpose of this chapter is to provide a "snapshot" overview of neurocognitive sequelae associated with chronic medical conditions; the reader is encouraged to refer to additional references for more in-depth information.

CENTRAL NERVOUS SYSTEM (CNS) INFECTION OR COMPROMISE

ASTHMA

Asthma is a chronic respiratory disease characterized by coughing, wheezing, and shortness of breath resulting from airway obstruction and irritability, tissue inflammation, congestion, and muscle constriction. Asthmatic attacks can be caused by viral infections, allergies, airborne irritants, strenuous exercise, weather and temperature fluctuations, as well as emotional reactions (Bray, Kehle, Theodore, & Peck, 2006). Not surprisingly, it has been found that children with asthma have increased absences from school (as cited in Bray et al., 2006).

Neurocognitive deficits are not often found in children with mild to moderate asthma (Annett, Aylward, Lapidus, Bender, & DuHamel, 2000). Nevertheless, some differences between children with and without asthma have been observed. Specifically, children with asthma have been found to have difficulties with modulation and control of impulsive behaviors (Annett et al., 2000), and parents report more learning problems (Blackman & Gurka, 2007; Stores, Ellis, Wiggs, Crawford, & Thomson, 1998). In children diagnosed with nocturnal asthma, marginal disturbances of attention and memory have been found (Stores et al., 1998). Some aspects of cognitive function, mood, and behavior seem to improve following treatment of nocturnal asthma (Stores et al., 1998).

Youth with asthma often meet DSM-IV criteria for anxiety and depressive disorders (Blackman & Gurka, 2007; Katon et al., 2007; Stores et al., 1998). These children also tend to experience psychosomatic symptoms (Stores et al., 1998); disturbances in their social relationships, self-esteem, sense of hopefulness, self-worth, and sense of well-being (as cited in Bray et al., 2006). Also reported by parents are behavior and conduct problems including symptoms of Attention Deficit Hyperactivity Disorder (ADHD) (Blackman & Gurka, 2007; Stores et al., 1998). Besides asthma itself, other risk factors for mood disorders in these youth include female gender, living in a single-parent household, higher externalizing behavior scores, more recent asthma diagnosis, and greater functional impairment. Interestingly, severity of asthma was not found to be a significant contributor to mood disturbance (Katon et al., 2007). Due to the important mind-body connection evident in a medical condition like asthma, psychologically based treatments such as family therapy, biofeedback, yoga, hypnosis, stress management, relaxation techniques, guided imagery, and written-emotional expression have proven successful (as cited in Bray et al., 2006).

HIV/AIDS

Acquired immunodeficiency syndrome (AIDS) is caused by the human immunodeficiency virus (HIV), which can be contracted through infected blood products, sexual contact, and from mother to child (vertical transmission). The present chapter will refer only to children affected via vertical transmission as this is the most common means of transmission for children, and neuropsychological sequelae are more prominent (Pulsifer & Aylward, 2000; Schneider & Walsh, 2008). Developmental delay and neurologic compromise have been well documented in the literature for HIV-infected children (as cited in Jeremy et al., 2005) and are often observed early in the course of the disease (Pulsifer & Aylward, 2000). Cortical atrophy, white matter hyperintensities, and basal ganglia calcifications are common and are consistent with the neuropsychological deficits observed, including delayed cognitive development and motor impairment (Pulsifer & Aylward, 2000; Steele, Nelson, & Cole, 2007). Early studies showed that children with AIDS exhibit greater neuropsychological impairment than those who were

HIV-infected without AIDS (as cited in Pulsifer & Aylward, 2000). However, HIV-infected children also tend to have poorer overall neuropsychological functioning, particularly in children with higher viral loads (Jeremy et al., 2005; Pulsifer & Aylward, 2000). Several studies have documented declines in neurocognitive scores and loss of developmental milestones for HIV-infected children despite the introduction of antiretroviral therapy, which is known to suppress HIV (Shanbhag et al., 2005). Pearson et al. (2000) found that children with more global cognitive impairment, cortical atrophy, and motor dysfunction were at greater risk for disease progression. Neuropsychological test performance at week 48 of antiretroviral therapy provided stronger predictive power of disease progression than physiological measures.

Some studies have found lower IQ in HIV-infected children even after antiretroviral therapy (Jeremy et al., 2005), whereas others have not (as cited in Pearson et al., 2000). Lack of normal fine and gross motor development is often observed in HIV-infected children (as cited in Pearson et al., 2000), yet there is some evidence that impairments observed in infancy may improve with age (Pulsifer & Aylward, 2000). Deficits in attention and executive functioning have been seen even in the absence of physical symptoms of the disease (as cited in Schneider & Walsh, 2008). Other common neuropsychological deficits include problems with visual integration and perceptual-motor functioning (as cited in Pulsifer & Aylward, 2000), visual scanning, verbal and nonverbal memory, expressive and receptive language, and psychomotor speed (as cited in Pearson et al., 2000). Research indicates academic deficits in the areas of mathematics (as cited in Pearson et al., 2000) and writing (Fundarò et al., 1998). These children experience more environmental stress due to the increased likelihood of parental death, frequent hospitalization, as well as the stigma associated with their diagnosis. However, Steele et al. (2007) found that when the illness is disclosed, HIV-infected children tend to adjust better. Furthermore, their research found that an enriching home environment can moderate the association between HIV infection and cognitive functioning. Finally, they failed to find differences in rates of emotional and behavioral problems between HIV-positive and healthy samples.

ACUTE LYMPHOCYTIC LEUKEMIA

Acute lymphocytic leukemia (ALL), a fast-growing cancer of the lymphocytes, is the most common pediatric malignancy with a high risk for neurocognitive sequelae as the treatment directly involves the central nervous system (CNS). A recent meta-analysis found deficits in psychomotor skills, attention, visual-spatial processing, verbal and visual memory, and executive functioning following administration of both cranial radiation therapy (CRT) and chemotherapy (CTX) (Campbell et al., 2007). Research has demonstrated that there may be a delayed onset of decline in IQ, up to seven years after the start of CRT (Mulhern, Fairclough, & Ochs, 1991), which may be mediated by working memory and processing speed deficits (Schatz, Kramer, Ablin, & Matthay, 2000). Attention problems are common with more intensive therapy related to more severe attention deficits (as cited in Butler & Haser, 2006). Extensive research has shown that pediatric ALL survivors often exhibit a specific learning disability in the area of mathematics following CRT and/or CTX (Brown et al., 1992; Copeland et al., 1988; Raymond-Speden, Tripp, Lawrence, & Holdaway, 2000), whereas spelling appears relatively preserved (Mulhern et al., 1991). Younger age at time of treatment, particularly with administration of CRT, female gender (Mulhern et al., 1991), neurologic severity (e.g., preexisting neurologic impairment and/or perioperative or postoperative neurologic events) and time since treatment have all been associated with poorer neurocognitive outcome (as cited in Moore, 2005).

Fortunately, protocols for standard risk ALL patients no longer include CRT as a part of treatment due to the significant neurocognitive sequelae without noted additional therapeutic benefit. Nonetheless, a recent meta-analysis evaluating the effects of CTX alone revealed deficits in fine motor functioning, attention, visual-spatial processing, verbal memory, speed of information processing, overall intellectual ability, reading and math achievement, and possibly executive functioning (Peterson et al., 2008). One positive finding from this meta-analysis was that verbal skills are often spared with CTX only, although there is some evidence of verbal fluency deficits (as cited in Butler & Haser, 2006). Additional research suggests problems with visual-motor integration (as cited in Butler & Haser, 2006), hand-eye coordination (Brown et al., 1992), and a potential decline with perceptual motor skills over time following CTX (as cited in Moore, 2005). Other research has shown that the transient effects of vincristine (CTX drug often included in protocols for ALL) on fine motor functioning may disappear after discontinuation of treatment (Copeland et al., 1988).

Efforts aimed toward remediating the late cognitive effects of treatment for ALL have been made. Stimulant medications used to treat ADHD have been used to treat attention problems in leukemia survivors with some success (as cited in Moore, 2005). Butler et al. (2008) recently completed a multicenter study evaluating the efficacy of a cognitive remediation program upon attention deficits in 161 survivors of childhood cancer, including ALL. Their results were equivocal, indicating only mildly improved cognitive functioning. Parent report of attention, reported use of metacognitive strategies, and math achievement were improved in the research group.

An estimated 25 to 30 percent of families who have a child diagnosed with cancer experience significant coping difficulties (as cited in Patenaude &

Kupst, 2005). Problems with peer relationships, self-esteem, and/or identity are common, and young adult survivors of childhood cancer are at risk for development of posttraumatic stress symptoms (as cited in Patenaude & Kupst, 2005). Patients who experience insults to the central nervous system are at higher risk for adverse psychosocial outcomes (as cited in Patenaude & Kupst, 2005). Fortunately, however, all pediatric cancer patients generally experience positive adjustment and fewer emotional and behavioral problems. There is some evidence that rates of depression are similar to the general population (as cited in Patenaude & Kupst, 2005).

END STAGE RENAL DISEASE

As its name implies, end stage renal disease (ESRD) is defined as chronic, irreversible kidney failure. Neurologic sequelae associated with renal failure include cerebral atrophy, microcephaly (small head size), and central nervous system infarcts (tissue death due to lack of oxygen). Uremic encephalopathy has been identified as resulting in problems with memory, attention, and perceptual-motor difficulties (Baum, Freier, & Chinnock, 2003). There is increased risk of neurocognitive delay with ESRD, particularly in toddlers (as cited in Gerson et al., 2006). Children with congenital renal disease tend to exhibit worse neuropsychological outcome as opposed to children whose disease is from other causes (Fennell, 2000). Additionally, the longer the child has struggled with the disease, as well as disease severity, appear related to greater risk of neurocognitive impairment. Finally, children undergoing hemodialysis versus other forms of dialysis perform less well on neuropsychological measures (Fennell, 2000).

Children in ESRD often exhibit copying skills deficits (as cited in Fennell, 2000), lower IQ, and impaired concentration (Groothoff et al., 2002), problems with sustained attention and initiation of behavior (as cited in Gerson et al., 2006), as well as problems with verbal learning, short-term memory (as cited in Fennell, 2000), and general memory (as cited in Gerson et al., 2006). There is mixed evidence regarding whether children in ESRD exhibit visual-spatial and/or language deficits (as cited in Gerson et al., 2006). Longer duration of chronic kidney disease, younger age, and mother/caregiver's lower educational level is associated with poorer academic achievement (Brouhard et al., 2000).

Several studies have suggested that neurocognitive impairment in ESRD can be reversed, at least to some degree, following kidney transplant (as cited in Brouhard et al., 2000). Specifically, there is evidence of improved sustained attention and mental processing speed (Mendley & Zelko, 1999), memory and learning (as cited in Fennell, 2000; as cited in Gerson et al., 2006), verbal IQ (as cited in Groothoff et al., 2002), or even full-scale IQ (as cited in Baum et al., 2003) post-transplant. Furthermore, educational functioning may improve with successful renal transplant (as cited in Brouhard et al., 2000). However, some studies have found persistent deficits in visuospatial construction, and still others have found persistent delays in intellectual functioning (Groothoff et al., 2002).

Patients undergoing hemodialysis often report feeling physically different from their peers and have lower self-esteem, higher anxiety, and sad mood (as cited in Fennell, 2000). Post-transplant patients continue to be at risk for psychiatric problems and lower adaptive behavior functioning (as cited in Fine et al., 2004), yet there is no evidence of increased prevalence of psychological disorders (as cited in Gerson et al., 2006). Renal transplant is associated with better psychosocial outcomes than for children treated with dialysis only (as cited in Fine et al., 2004).

CHRONIC MEDICAL ILLNESSES

CEREBROVASCULAR ACCIDENT (CVA)

The literature clearly documents that children who experience CVA from a variety of etiologies often experience significant, sometimes permanent neuropsychological impairment including deficits in intellectual functioning (Lansing et al., 2004), language (Ballantyne, Spilkin, & Trauner, 2007), attention (Max et al., 2004), verbal learning and memory (Lansing et al., 2004), visual-spatial processing (Schatz, Craft, Koby, & DeBaun, 2004), and processing speed (Hartel, Schilling, Sperner, & Thyen, 2004). Hemiparesis (weakness on one side of the body) is the most common finding following unilateral CVA (Hogan, Kirkham, & Isaacs, 2000). Earlier age of CVA correlates with poorer attention independent of lesion size (Max et al., 2004) and anterior infarcts are related to impaired attention (Craft, Schatz, Glauser, Lee, & DeBaun, 1993). There is some evidence suggesting a lack of lateralized findings with children that is typically seen in adults (Hogan et al., 2000). Thus, children with CVA often exhibit diffuse deficits. Some research indicates that the likelihood of lateralized findings increases when the CVA occurs after 5 years of age (Hogan et al., 2000).

A review of the literature found that mean IQ often remains in the average range following either left hemisphere (LH) or right hemisphere (RH) CVA albeit scores are often significantly lower than the population mean (Hogan et al., 2000). A mild PIQ > VIQ split has been seen in children with LH CVA, whereas a more marked pattern of VIQ > PIQ split has been observed in children with RH CVA (Cohen, Branch, McKie, & Adams, 1994). Some research has found that children with either RH or LH CVA experience more problems with visual-spatial as opposed to verbal/language functioning

(Schatz et al., 2004), although there is also evidence of long-term deficits in language production following RH or LH CVA (Ballantyne et al., 2007; Hartel et al., 2004). Visual-spatial memory deficits are often associated with RH CVA in children (Cohen et al., 1994). Verbal learning and memory deficits have been observed in children with either RH or LH CVA with earlier lesions resulting in greater recall and recognition deficits (Lansing et al., 2004). Long-term verbal memory and functional memory deficits have also been observed following childhood CVA (as cited in Hartel et al., 2004). Children with a history of LH CVA often demonstrate academic problems in the areas of reading and writing, whereas math difficulties are often seen in children with a history of RH CVA (Cohen et al., 1994).

Some studies have found problems with emotional expression and social skills in children with history of neonatal CVA, whereas others have failed to find significant emotional/behavioral problems post-CVA (as cited in Hartel et al., 2004). Patients with early onset unilateral CVA (in either hemisphere) exhibit more problems with social competence, emotional behavior, as well as cognitive and academic functioning (Trauner, Panyard-Davis, & Ballantyne, 1996). Posterior lesions appear to be more likely to result in social deficits (Trauner et al., 1996).

SICKLE CELL DISEASE (SCD)

Sickle cell disease is comprised of a group of autosomal recessive disorders in which inherited abnormal hemoglobin causes distorted "sickled" red blood cells resulting in anemia. SCD is one of the most common genetic disorders and primarily affects individuals of African American descent (Wang, 2007). The most severe form is hemoglobin (Hb) SS disease. Central nervous system complications of SCD include CVA, "silent" stroke, seizures, as well as chronic hypoxia and vaso-occlusion (Wang, 2007). Although neuropsychological deficits are common in this population, the precise etiology is unknown. There is evidence of developmental declines in the areas of motor functioning and language in very young children with SCD (Schatz & Roberts, 2007), and a decline in IQ over time has been observed in older children (Steen et al., 2005).

Grueneich et al. (2004) found that a greater degree of abnormality on brain imaging, even in the absence of known neurologic impairment, is related to more neurocognitive variability. Lower full-scale, verbal, and performance IQs have been observed in children with SCD with silent or clinical infarct, or even in the absence of abnormalities on brain MRI compared with published norms (as cited in Berkelhammer et al., 2007). Mildly deficient to borderline IQ is often seen in children with SCD who have suffered a CVA (Gruenich et al., 2004). There appears to be a correlation between IQ and level of neurological involvement in children with SCD (Berkelhammer et al., 2007). Likewise, impaired attention appears to be related to the presence and severity of cerebral damage with deficits in sustained attention, auditory attention, and working memory representing common findings (Berkelhammer et al., 2007; Lansing et al., 2004). However, attention problems have also been observed in children with SCD in the absence of CVA (as cited in Gruenich et al., 2004). Children with SCD and history of LH CVA exhibit problems with linguistic functioning (Cohen et al., 1994), yet impaired verbal/language skills have also been observed in children with SCD compared with sibling controls regardless of neuroimaging results (Berkelhammer et al., 2007). Children with SCD and diffuse stroke (either overt or silent) tend to exhibit spatial difficulties as opposed to those who suffer anterior lesions (Craft et al., 1993). In the absence of CVA, children with SCD may not demonstrate slower processing speed (Schatz et al., 2004).

Memory deficits are commonly observed in children with SCD and clinical infarct with retrieval deficits often associated with frontal infarct (as cited in Berkelhammer et al., 2007). Short-term memory problems may exist even in the absence of CVA (as cited in Gruenich et al., 2004). Auditory-verbal memory and visual-spatial memory impairment has been seen in children with SCD and LH CVA (Cohen et al., 1994). Executive functioning deficits (primarily working memory) have been documented in children with higher risk SCD (Schatz & Roberts, 2007). Christ, Moinuddin, McKinstry, DeBaun, & White (2007) found that children with SCD and frontal lobe infarct performed less well on a measure of inhibitory control. Visual-motor constructional deficits are common in children with SCD who have a history of either LH or RH CVA (Cohen et al., 1994). Some research indicates that visual-motor coordination deficits may be seen even in the absence of CVA (as cited in Gruenich et al., 2004), whereas other research has demonstrated relatively spared visual-motor integration skills in SCD patients with no neurologic disease compared with sibling controls (Schatz et al., 2004; Swift et al., 1989). Swift et al. (1989) found attention/distractibility, verbal functioning, and memory scores were lower in children diagnosed with SCD versus sibling controls. Children with SCD often demonstrate deficient school readiness (as cited in Wang, 2007). Reading and math deficits are common in children with SCD who also have a history of CVA, and there is some evidence of declines in math scores over time (Wang et al., 2001). There is some research suggesting that children with SCD and no history of CVA appear to be as well adjusted emotionally and socially as their peers (Noll, Reiter-Purtill, Vannatta, Gerhardt, & Short, 2007).

Reducing the likelihood of CVA in children with SCD has become possible through careful monitoring (transcranial Doppler ultrasonography), and chronic transfusion reduces the risk of secondary CVA (Wang, 2007). Bone marrow transplantation nearly eliminates the risk of secondary CVA, yet it is unclear whether this treatment halts neurocognitive deterioration (Wang, 2007). Hydroxyurea is often used for treatment of SCD, yet it is also uncertain whether patients experience subsequent cognitive benefits (Berkelhammer et al., 2007).

Cystic Fibrosis

Cystic fibrosis (CF) is the most common life-shortening autosomal recessive genetic illness caused by a single gene that affects multiple organ systems. CF is caused by an imbalance of salt in the body, which results in build-up of thick, abundant mucus that clogs organs and traps infection. Although CF does not directly affect the brain and central nervous system, malnutrition (particularly early in life), increased airway resistance, and potentially decreased cerebral oxygenation can result in neurobehavioral sequelae (Stewart et al., 1995). Koscik et al. (2005) found that vitamin E deficiency in patients with CF was associated with lower cognitive functioning in later childhood and thus recommend newborn screening for early identification and treatment. Very few studies have been conducted with regard to cognitive and psychosocial outcomes associated with cystic fibrosis. Stewart et al. (1995) found that scores on measures of sensorimotor functioning, language, abstraction, and academic achievement were similar to that of controls. Furthermore, they found that children over 5 years of age demonstrated average IQ. There was, however, evidence of delays in IQ prior to age 5 years that may remit over time. Stewart et al. suggested that verbal IQ and possibly tactile perception correlate with disease severity. Thompson, Gustafson, Gil, Godfrey, & Murphy (1998) found higher rates of oppositional and conduct disorders in children diagnosed with cystic fibrosis when compared with a group of children diagnosed with sickle cell disease.

Juvenile Diabetes

Insulin-dependent diabetes mellitus (IDDM), a disorder of glucose metabolism, is one of the most common childhood chronic diseases. Glucose is essential for normal brain metabolism, particularly in children whose brains are still developing. Treatment requires daily insulin injections and diet regulation, yet even the best followed regimen is not equivalent to normal physiological functioning leaving patients vulnerable to having glucose levels outside normal ranges. Hypoglycemia occurs as a result of too much insulin from treatment for IDDM and is more common in patients with good disease control (Rovet, 2000). Hyperglycemia occurs when there is too much glucose as a result of not enough insulin. Both hypoglycemia and hyperglycemia often occur throughout the course of the disease. Unfortunately, both may result in neuropsychological deficits (Desrocher & Rovet, 2004).

Children under 5 years of age are thought to be more susceptible to hypoglycemic episodes and the associated damage to the brain, including disruption of cerebral blood flow and neurotransmission as well as possible seizures (Desrocher & Rovet, 2004; Rovet, 2000). Neuroanatomical changes, including ventricular enlargement, white matter lesions in the hippocampus, and generalized cortical atrophy, have been associated with recurrent hypoglycemic episodes (Fontaine & Snyder, 2008). It is therefore no surprise that these children, in addition to those with long-standing IDDM, often experience a higher prevalence of cognitive and psychoeducational problems (Desrocher & Rovet, 2004; Fontaine & Snyder, 2008). Some research suggests a relationship between hypoglycemia and motor speed as well as selective and focused attention (Desrocher & Rovet, 2004), whereas other research has failed to find deficits in these areas (Hershey, Lillie, Sadler, & White, 2003). Hypoglycemia may also result in poor complex visual organization (Fontaine & Snyder, 2008), visual abstract reasoning (Rovet, 2000), decision making and planning (Desrocher & Rovet, 2004), verbal fluency (as cited in Hershey et al., 2003), as well as visual and short-term memory deficits (Desrocher & Rovet, 2004; as cited in Hershey et al., 2003). The evidence regarding a relationship between hypoglycemia and verbal memory deficits is mixed (Desrocher & Rovet, 2004; as cited in Anderson, Northam, Hendy, & Wrennall, 2001). Research suggests that repeated episodes of hypoglycemia may not result in cognitive decline, at least in adults (as cited in Hershey et al., 2003). Hyperglycemia has been associated with deficits of motor speed (Fontaine & Snyder, 2008), shifting attention (Rovet, 2000), as well as problems with selective reminding, executive functioning, visual-spatial processing, and verbal abilities (Desrocher & Rovet, 2004).

Some research has shown that children with IDDM diagnosed before 5 years of age score 10 to 20 points below average on IQ measures, apparently due primarily to motor slowing on performance tasks (as cited in Desrocher & Rovet, 2004). Children with IDDM are at risk for deficits with general fund of knowledge, word knowledge, as well as a decline with vocabulary scores over time (as cited in Anderson et al., 2001). However, there is also evidence of intact receptive and expressive language even in children with early onset disease (as cited in Desrocher & Rovet, 2004). These children also demonstrate impaired abstract reasoning and problem solving as well as problems with verbal fluency, working memory, speed of processing, mental flexibility, planning, and organizational skills (as cited in Anderson et al., 2001). Attention problems have been linked to early age of onset of IDDM and hypoglycemia (Rovet, 2000), and males have been found to exhibit more attention problems than females (as cited in Anderson et al., 2001). Memory problems appear to become more pronounced with longer disease duration (Desrocher & Rovet, 2004). Sensory-motor and visual-spatial weaknesses have been associated with disease onset early in life and longer disease duration (Desrocher & Rovet, 2004). Children with IDDM often experience difficulties with new learning (as cited in Anderson et al., 2001). School problems have been associated with hypoglycemic convulsions, greater than five years of disease duration, and frequent school absenteeism (as cited in Rovet, 2000). Poorer reading and math abilities have been found in children with early onset IDDM (as cited in Rovet, 2000). Although there is evidence of some neuropsychological deficits in children with IDDM, many studies have found that patients score within the average range on most measures, albeit their scores are often lower than controls (as cited in Anderson et al., 2001).

Children with IDDM are at risk for behavioral and psychosocial problems, yet it appears that the greatest risk groups are males diagnosed after age 5 and adolescent females (Rovet, 2000). Contrary to what might be expected, there is evidence of poorer psychological adjustment in children with better glycemic control (as cited in Anderson et al., 2001).

Spina Bifida and Hydrocephalus

Spina bifida (SB) occurs when the neural tube fails to fuse early in the course of gestation (3–6 weeks). It represents the second most common birth defect, the cause of which is unknown (Anderson et al., 2001), although a deficiency in folic acid has been implicated (Cascio & Ries, 2008). There are three types of SB: occulta, meningocele, and myelomeningocele (MM). MM represents the most common (approximately 70 percent of all cases) and severe form. It occurs when there is incomplete formation of the meninges and the spinal cord protrudes through the midline defect (Anderson et al., 2001). It has been estimated that 80 to 95 percent of those with MM have hydrocephalus (HYD). HYD occurs when the volume of cerebrospinal fluid (CSF) increases within the ventricles of the brain, and they become enlarged, resulting in increased intracranial pressure (Erickson, Baron, & Fantie, 2001). The present chapter will focus on children with SB/MM and hydrocephalus (SBH), as the associated neuropsychological sequelae are greatest in this group.

There are a variety of neuropsychological deficits associated with SBH that appear to be influenced, at least in part, by the level of the spinal cord lesion (the higher the lesion, the more impairment), as well as the number of shunt revisions (Baron, Fennell, & Voeller, 1995; as cited in Huber-Okrainec, Dennis, Brettschneider, & Spiegler, 2002). Children with SB who have higher spinal cord lesions have limited mobility, which restricts their opportunities for visuo-motor and visual-spatial learning. Eye-movement disorders often co-occur with spina bifida, which has also been associated with visual-perception problems (as cited in Dennis, Fletcher, Rogers, Hetherington, & Francis, 2002). HYD in children with SBH is often associated with the Arnold Chiari II malformation, or downward displacement of the cerebellar tonsils into the cervical spinal canal. It is noted that many of the perceptual-motor and motor speech deficits observed in children with SBH are associated with cerebellar dysfunction (Huber-Okrainec et al., 2002). A recent study also suggested that unusual development of the cerebellum is related to poor verb generation accuracy (Dennis et al., 2008).

Children with SBH often exhibit fine and gross motor impairment (Baron et al., 1995) and difficulties with temporally organized movements (as cited in Huber-Okrainec et al., 2002). Problems with visual-motor integration, disembedding figures, and matching patterns are also common, whereas facial recognition appears to be relatively spared (as cited in Dennis et al., 2002). These children also tend to demonstrate slower visual tracking and hand-eye coordination speed, as well as slower speed on tasks that do not require visual or motor output (Anderson et al., 2001). The typically observed VIQ > PIQ pattern has been well documented for children with SBH and does not appear to be explained completely by the motor demands of performance tasks (as cited in Anderson et al., 2001; as cited in Erickson et al., 2001). Some research has found that children with SBH exhibit lower IQ than children with HYD associated with a different etiology (as cited in Anderson et al., 2001). Nonetheless, some studies have found that children with SBH often exhibit average intellectual functioning even in the presence of motor impairment (as cited in Cascio & Ries, 2008).

The incidence of ADHD is greater for children with SBH compared to the general population and appears unrelated to IQ (as cited in Cascio & Ries, 2008). There is also some evidence of executive functioning deficits, apparently unrelated to IQ, including problems with visual planning and sequencing, problem solving, abstraction, and cognitive flexibility (Snow, 1999). It has been suggested that the attention and organizational problems that children with SBH exhibit may contribute to learning problems (Erickson et al., 2001). Children with SBH have difficulties with verbal short-term and long-term retrieval on word list tasks, sentence repetition, and literal text recall of stories, yet semantic recall of stories is relatively intact (as cited in Erickson et al., 2001). Nonverbal recall and recognition may also be impaired (as cited in Erickson et al., 2001). These children tend to acquire new information slower than their peers in verbal, tactile, motor, and visuospatial modalities (as cited in Erickson et al., 2001). Memory and learning deficits have been observed in children with SBH that demonstrate average to above average IQ (as cited in Cascio & Ries, 2008).

More recent research has investigated the pattern of language skills in children with SBH. Although vocabulary, syntax, and language tasks relying upon repetition and rote memory are often intact, these children typically have difficulties explaining the meaning of words and comprehending complex grammar (as cited in Anderson et al., 2001). Children with SBH tend to demonstrate extreme verbosity and repetitive speech that may be well articulated, yet superficial in content (Baron et al., 1995; as cited in Erickson et al., 2001). They tend to struggle with structured productive language tasks, whereas language difficulties are likely less detectable in conversational speech (Erickson et al., 2001). Finally, there is evidence of motor-based speech deficits affecting fluency and rate of speech (Huber-Okrainec et al., 2002).

The profile of cognitive and achievement deficits in patients with SBH has been likened to Dr. Byron Rourke's nonverbal learning disability syndrome in which deficits are observed in visual-spatial processing, nonverbal reasoning, visual motor and fine motor functioning, math and social skills (as cited in Cascio & Ries, 2008). Indeed, these children demonstrate problems in all of these areas, yet they also commonly exhibit the aforementioned higher level language difficulties and problems with executive functioning rendering them a rather unique group. Common academic problems include reading comprehension and writing fluency, whereas word decoding, reading fluency, and spelling often remain intact (Barnes, Dennis, & Hetherington, 2004). Some children with SBH exhibit inappropriate social and emotional behavior typically associated with difficulties comprehending nonverbal cues, and these difficulties have been found to correlate with IQ (Erickson et al., 2001).

SLEEP-DISORDERED BREATHING

Breathing during sleep falls on a spectrum ranging from unobstructed respiration to severe obstructive sleep apnea (OSA) verified by polysomnography (PSG). The term sleep-disordered breathing (SDB) has been used in the research to describe the various forms of pathological nocturnal respiratory functioning, including OSA, or obstructive sleep apnea syndrome (OSAS) (Beebe, 2006). PSG is the standard measure for sleep disturbance and provides indices of sleep-wake states, respiratory and cardiac activity, oxygen saturation, carbon dioxide tension, and body movement (Halbower & Mahone, 2006). Although there is disagreement regarding the criteria that should be used as the standard to define sleep-disordered breathing and its level of severity (Halbower & Mahone, 2006), general definitions are available.

OSA or OSAS is characterized by a lack of airflow as a result of upper airway obstructions and frequently includes snoring as a symptom (Halbower & Mahone, 2006). An apnea/hypopnea index (AHI) is defined as the number of episodes per hour in which airflow ceases or is reduced. An AHI greater than even one per hour is outside of the normal range for children. However, the AHI threshold at which morbidity occurs is not known (Halbower & Mahone, 2006). Some research has suggested that several domains of neuro-cognitive functioning are often spared in children with OSA or OSAS including sustained attention, verbal memory, and processing speed (Beebe et al., 2004); copying line drawings, vocabulary, and expressive language (as cited in Beebe, 2006); immediate recall (Kaemingk, Pasvogel, et al., 2003); long-term memory (Uema et al., 2007); working memory (Archbold, Giordani, Ruzicka, & Chervin, 2004); as well as general intelligence (Archbold et al., 2004; Beebe et al., 2004; Kaemingk, Pasvogel, et al., 2003). Likewise, academic achievement appears generally unaffected (Archbold et al., 2004; Kaemingk, Pasvogel, et al., 2003), and there is no evidence of clinically significant symptoms of anxiety and depression (Beebe et al., 2004).

Researchers suspect that when neuropsychological dysfunction does occur, it can be attributed to percentage of REM sleep, percentage of Stage 1 sleep, movement-related arousals, or hypoxia (Archbold et al., 2004; Beebe et al., 2004; O'Brien et al., 2004). In children with SDB, including OSA/OSAS, deficits in attention, memory and learning, executive functioning, intellectual ability, and social-emotional functioning have been reported. More specifically, problems with impulse control and behavioral inhibition (Beebe et al., 2004) and sustained attention and vigilance (Archbold et al., 2004) have been observed. Further, symptoms of ADHD, especially those related to hyper-activity-impulsivity, have been related to sleep efficiency (Suratt et al., 2006). Within the memory and learning domain, impaired acquisition or recall across trials has been found (Kaemingk, Pasvogel, et al., 2003). Parents have reported problems with self-initiation, working memory, planning, organization, and self-monitoring. Teachers have reported impaired behavior regulation, mental flexibility, emotional control, and metacognitive skills in children with OSA (Beebe et al., 2004).

In children with more general SDB, impaired mental flexibility has been reported (Archbold et al., 2004), and lower scores on the executive functions domain of the *NEPSY* have been observed (O'Brien et al., 2004). Difficulties with tasks involving higher cognitive function have also been found in these children using tests of general intellectual ability (O'Brien et al.), particularly in the areas of analytical thinking, auditory-visual integration, and auditory-motor memory (Friedman et al., 2003). Emotionally, parents have reported conduct problems including hyperactivity, rebelliousness, and aggression (as cited in Beebe, 2006).

Multiple studies have found that children who are primarily snorers actually perform less well on neuropsychological measures than children diagnosed with a specific sleep disorder like OSA (Beebe, 2006; Emancipator et al., 2006; Giordani et al., 2008; Suratt et al., 2006; Uema et al., 2007). For instance, problems with short-term attention, sustained attention (Giordani et al., 2008), attentional capacity (Blunden, Lushington, Kennedy, Martin, & Dawson, 2000), and visual attention (Hill et al., 2006) have been observed. Deficits in memory and learning including recall following multiple repetitions (Uema et al., 2007), visual delayed recall of visual-spatial information, working memory (Giordani et al., 2008), and verbal memory (Suratt et al., 2006) have been associated with snoring in children. Visual-spatial problem solving difficulties (Giordani et al., 2008), slow processing speed (Hill et al., 2006), weaker vocabulary (Emancipator et al., 2006; Suratt et al., 2006), poor abstract reasoning (Suratt et al., 2006), and problems with academic functioning, including poorer math, spelling, reading, and listening comprehension scores (Giordani et al., 2008) have also been observed. As a result, it may be useful to obtain a history of snoring and nocturnal functioning for those children at risk for cognitive and achievement deficits and to refer to a pediatric sleep specialist if concerns regarding sleep arise (Beebe et al., 2004; Emancipator et al., 2006).

Adenotonsillectomy (AT), or surgical removal of the tonsils and adenoids, is a common treatment for OSA. Fortunately, some of the neuropsychological impairments associated with mild childhood OSA appear to be largely reversible with treatment. For example, Friedman and colleagues (2003) found that perceptual closure, visual and auditory short-term memory skills, and executive functioning skills such as inference, organization, problem solving, and analytical thinking, improved following treatment for OSAS. Further, hyperactivity and attention deficit seen prior to AT surgery related to sleepiness were no longer apparent one year later (Chervin et al., 2006).

ENDOCRINOLOGICAL DISORDERS

Adrenal Gland Disorders   Primary hypoadrenalism (also known as adrenal insufficiency or AI) is uncommon, and secondary causes are largely unknown. The incidence of AI secondary to congenital adrenal hyperplasia (CAH) is approximately 1 per 16,000 births (Rozenblatt, 2008). CAH occurs when a fetus is exposed to an abnormally high level of androgens leading to an increased level of adrenocorticotrophic hormone (ACTH) and corticotropin-releasing hormone. Research suggests that early exposure to high levels of testosterone can suppress the development of the left cerebral hemisphere (Kelso, Nicholls, Warne, & Zacharin, 2000). Indeed, studies have found a higher prevalence of left-hand dominance, language disorders, and language-based learning disorders in children diagnosed with CAH (Kelso et al., 2000). Furthermore, children treated prenatally with dexamethasone tend to demonstrate slower verbal processing speed (as cited in Rozenblatt, 2008). Children with CAH often exhibit enhanced spatial ability and higher nonverbal versus verbal IQ, as well as above average overall IQ (as cited in Kelso et al., 2000). White matter abnormalities and temporal lobe atrophy without associated neuropsychological sequelae have been observed in children with CAH (as cited in Rozenblatt, 2008).

Cushing's disease is caused by an adenoma of the pituitary gland, which produces ACTH, stimulating the adrenal glands (Rozenblatt, 2008). With adults, cognitive functioning often improves following successful treatment. However, there is some evidence that this is not the case for children. In fact, one study found a decline in IQ as well as academic achievement following successful treatment that could not be explained by psychopathology (Merke et al., 2005). In this study, children with Cushing's disease exhibited average to above average IQ before treatment. Other research has found that children with Cushing's disease demonstrate deficits in working memory, attention, and self-regulation, as well as verbal learning difficulties associated with hippocampal volume loss (Rozenblatt, 2008). With regard to emotional functioning, there is evidence of depression, anxiety, and obsessive-compulsive symptoms in children with Cushing's disease (Rozenblatt, 2008).

Thyroid Disorders   Early deficiency of the thyroid hormone can have a large impact upon brain development (Anderson et al., 2001). Hypothyroidism is the most common disorder of the thyroid gland, affecting more females than males. Hypothyroidism results from primary dysfunction of the thyroid gland, problems involving the pituitary gland or hypothalamus, or resistance to the thyroid hormone (Anderson et al., 2001; as cited in Rozenblatt, 2008). Hashimoto's thyroiditis is the most common cause of hypothyroidism in children over 6 years of age (Rozenblatt, 2008).

Children with congenital hypothyroidism (CH) demonstrate average intelligence, yet their scores are often lower than controls. Earlier intervention is associated with higher level of intellectual functioning (Anderson et al., 2001; Oerbeck, Sundet, Kase, & Heyerdahl, 2003). The type and severity of neuropsychological deficits may also be related to the age of disease onset, disease severity, and treatment related issues including compliance (as cited in Anderson et al., 2001; as cited in Oerbeck et al., 2003). Subtle, persistent deficits associated with CH have been observed in the areas of visual-spatial functioning, language, and memory (Rovet & Ehlrich, 2000), although some research has shown that visual-spatial deficits are uncommon (as cited in Anderson et al., 2001). Furthermore, one study failed to find differences in memory between children with CH and controls (Rovet & Ehrlich, 2004). Verbal functions appear favorable in patients treated with L-thyroxine (Oerbeck et al., 2003; Rovet & Ehrlich, 2004). The research regarding attention problems is mixed with some research associating CH with attention deficits that persist over time (Rovet & Ehrlich, 2004) and other research indicating that attention is less often a problem in these children (as cited in Anderson et al., 2001). Executive functioning deficits, including problems with inhibition and cognitive flexibility, have been reported in children with CH (Rozenblatt, 2008). Motor outcome has been linked to disease severity (Oerbeck et al., 2003). Academic problems have been observed in the areas of reading and math (Oerbeck et al., 2003), whereas writing and spelling appear relatively spared (Rovet & Ehrlich, 2004). CH has been associated with a difficult temperament in infancy and more behavior problems in middle childhood (as cited in Anderson et al., 2001). Some research has found that parents rate their children with CH as having more behavior problems than controls, and teachers endorse more internalizing problems, less academic effort and performance, as well as mild attention problems (Rovet & Ehrlich, 2004). However, a meta-analysis failed to find increased rates of behavioral problems in children with CH (as cited in Anderson et al., 2001).

Hyperthyroidism in childhood is most often a result of Grave's disease and may also result in neuropsychological dysfunction, although research in children is limited. Studies with adults have found problems with executive functioning, and there is some evidence that children may experience problems with attention/concentration, inhibition, planning, and organization (as cited in Rozenblatt, 2008).

Parathyroid Disorders   Hypoparathyroidism is associated with certain genetic disorders, whereas hyperparathyroidism is rare in children (Rozenblatt, 2008). Little research has been conducted with children diagnosed with these conditions. In adults, hypoparathyroidism has been associated with problems in executive functioning including processing speed, word fluency, and attention (as cited in Rozenblatt, 2008). Unspecified cognitive impairment and psychiatric symptoms, including depression, anxiety, and even psychosis, have been reported in patients with hypoparathyroidism (as cited in Rozenblatt, 2008).

ORGAN TRANSPLANTS

When an organ is compromised, it may lead to either direct or indirect cognitive dysfunction (Wetherington & Duquette, 2008). Some authors have suggested that improvements in cognitive functioning are observed in children following any type of organ transplant (as cited in Wetherington & Duquette, 2008).

Heart Transplants   Children and adolescents typically function in the normal range on measures of cognitive ability following heart transplant unless they experience a complicated transplant course (Brosig, Hintermeyer, Zlotocha, Behrens, & Mao, 2006). However, their scores are still often lower than healthy children (Wray, Long, Radley-Smith, & Yacoub, 2001) or children who have undergone a different type of cardiac surgery (as cited in Fine et al., 2004). Likewise, academic functioning for post-heart transplant patients tends to be within normal limits, yet scores are often lower when compared with healthy children, and academic problems may increase over time (Wray et al., 2001). A risk factor for transplant-related complications includes donor organ size mismatch, which can result in hypertension and seizures (Baum et al., 2003). It appears that the age of the child at the time of transplant may also impact cognitive outcome. Most notably, children receiving heart transplants in the first year of life tend to exhibit developmental delays (as cited in Baum et al., 2003). Specifically, motor delays have been reported in children 2 to 38 months of age who underwent heart transplant during infancy. Fortunately, there is evidence that these delays tend to improve by 36 to 38 months (Freier et al., 2004). Freier et al. (2004) found delays in the areas of language, nonverbal processing, as well as abstract reasoning and goal directed behavior in older infants who had undergone heart transplant.

Heart transplant recipients and their parents appear to experience improved quality of life after transplant (Brosig et al., 2006), yet a small percentage of children experience significant psychological distress during the first year after transplant (Todaro, Fennell, Sears, Rodrigue, & Roche, 2000). There is also evidence of continued psychological difficulties even three years post heart or heart-lung transplant (Wray & Radley-Smith, 2006). The incidence of behavior problems in post heart or heart-lung transplant recipients was higher than for a group of healthy controls in one study (Wray & Radley-Smith, 2006).

Lung Transplants   Children who are younger, more physically developed, and have a shorter duration of their illness prior to lung transplant are likely to experience less cognitive impairment (Kaller et al., 2005). Wray and Radley-Smith (2006) found that children who underwent heart or heart-lung transplant under 3½ years of age demonstrated declines on several developmental measures over time, even though scores fell within the average range compared with the normative sample. Research is limited in pediatric lung transplant recipients, possibly due to the high mortality rate (Wetherington & Duquette, 2008).

Liver Transplants   Developmental delay is common in children who have undergone liver transplant and seems to be correlated with age at onset of disease as well as duration of illness (Kaller et al., 2005). However, specific causes of the delay are unknown (Fine et al., 2004). Krull, Fuchs, Yurk, Boone, and Alonso (2003) found that prolonged hospitalization was associated with lower scores on certain cognitive tests in liver transplant recipients. There is some evidence that intellectual functioning tends to fall in the lower end of the average range (Kaller et al., 2005) with relatively preserved expressive vocabulary (Adebäck, Nemeth, & Fischler, 2003). One study found children who are post-liver transplant have lower verbal intelligence than patients diagnosed with cystic fibrosis, whereas another study found lower performance IQ when compared with cystic fibrosis patients (Adebäck et al., 2003). Kaller et al. found scores on measures of sequential processing to be below the norm in liver recipients. There is mixed evidence regarding the presence of motor (as cited in Wetherington & Duquette, 2008; as cited in Fine et al., 2004) and visuospatial deficits (Krull et al., 2003; as cited in Baum et al., 2003; as cited in Fine et al., 2004). Pediatric liver recipients have been found to score lower on measures of receptive language (Krull et al., 2003), flexibility in thinking, logical analysis, abstract thinking, and memory compared with patients diagnosed with cystic fibrosis (as cited in Adebäck et al., 2003). There is some evidence of learning disabilities in post-liver transplant patients (as cited in Fine et al., 2004), yet other studies have found that these patients perform better academically than would be expected based upon their measured intelligence (as cited in Baum et al., 2003). Krull et al. (2003) failed to find significant differences on measures of academic achievement between liver transplant patients and children diagnosed with cystic fibrosis. Fortunately, some research has found that mental development tends to improve over time after transplantation (as cited in Fine et al., 2004).

Fine et al. (2004) found that approximately 50 percent of post-liver transplant patients exhibited significant behavioral and/or emotional problems, and rates of depression were higher than for other chronic illnesses (Fine et al., 2004). Adebäck et al. (2003) found that low IQ correlated with low scores on a self-concept scale and indicators of emotional difficulties.

CHILDREN WITH A HISTORY OF ACQUIRED OR CONGENITAL BRAIN DAMAGE

ANOXIA/HYPOXIA/ASPHYXIA

Oxygen deprivation in children creates a vulnerability to pathological brain changes and negative neurodevelopmental outcomes given the prevailing idea that brain damage occurs once the degree of asphyxia reaches a particular threshold (as cited in Raz et al., 1998). In general, a hypoxic-ischemic insult (i.e., inadequate oxygen) is considered necessary in order to diagnose birth asphyxia. Blood pH level is used as the standard, with a pH value between 7.0 and 7.1 being the threshold for severe and profound birth asphyxia (Hopkins-Golightly, Raz, & Sander, 2003). It has been difficult to determine "dose-response" relationships between the extent of hypoxic-ischemic insult and neurocognitive deficits (Raz et al., 1998), yet there is evidence that even relatively minor birth hypoxia may result in significant effects on cognitive development (Hopkins-Golightly et al., 2003). More specifically, impaired abilities cited in the research include selective and sustained attention, including signal discrimination (Espy, Senn, Charak, Tyler, & Wiebe, 2007; O'Dougherty, Wright, Loewenson, & Torres, 1985); receptive vocabulary in preschoolers, and emergent math skills (Espy et al., 2007); overall cognitive functioning and school achievement (O'Dougherty et al., 1985); and social-emotional skills including assertiveness, independence, and self-confidence (O'Dougherty et al., 1985). Although balance and gait often remain intact, significant differences have been found in these children's ability to complete complex, visually guided motor movements of the upper extremities (Raz et al., 1998).

ENCEPHALITIS AND MENINGITIS

Acute encephalitis is an inflammation of the brain, the etiology of which is seldom established. Symptoms at the acute stage include fever, altered consciousness, seizures, disorientation, and memory defects. Forms of encephalitis are classified according to type of onset as acute, sub-acute, or chronic, and according to dispersal as sporadic (i.e., individual cases scattered around the world) or epidemic (i.e., many cases in a distinct geographical area). Sporadic infections due to herpes simplex 1 virus are most common (Hokkanen & Launes, 2007). In 1958, Rasmussen described an intractable focal epilepsy that presented in children as focal motor seizures and associated progressive hemiparesis, cognitive impairment, and dysphasia. Now called Rasmussen's encephalitis, this rare illness usually presents between 14 months and 14 years of age, and radiological evidence reveals that cerebral atrophy is progressive and usually unilateral. Seizures are the most common initial symptom, and cognitive and behavioral deterioration are typically observed after the onset of hemiparesis. Neurological deterioration can progress over a period from months to ten years, with the median being three years (Hart, 2004).

Although the literature regarding neuropsychological sequelae following encephalitis in children is lacking, Hokkanen and Launes (2007) reported findings with adults. Specifically, they reported that perceptual, intellectual, and linguistic abilities as well as short-term memory often remain intact. However, consolidation deficits often occur that may prevent new learning. Furthermore, when the virus involves the temporal lobes, anterograde memory loss occurs. These authors note that this has been the most consistent finding in herpes simplex virus encephalitis (HSVE). However, remote memory deficits (retrograde amnesia) are also common and explicit memory seems especially vulnerable. Language defects in adults with encephalitis are usually characterized by anomia. Although most cognitive deficits diminish over time or remain the same, in some individuals, a more global cognitive deterioration may occur. Psychiatric and behavioral symptoms have been found to precede, accompany, and follow the illness in adults. In some cases, these symptoms may be explained as an emotional reaction to having a potentially fatal illness; however, the damage to the limbic system and amygdalo-frontal pathways that occurs as a result of encephalitis can also result in symptoms such as emotional or mood disorders, delusions, hallucinations, and anxiety and dissociative disorders.

Meningitis is an infectious disease of the membranes surrounding the brain, with diagnosis made when the presence of bacteria or bacterial antigens are located in the cerebrospinal fluid (CSF) (Koomen et al., 2004). Fortunately, the introduction of effective immunizations in the 1980s has greatly reduced the incidence of meningitis (Taylor, Schatschneider, & Minich, 2000). Two theories have been described in the literature in an attempt to explain the neurocognitive deficits observed with meningitis. The delay theory, described by Grimwood, Anderson, Tan, and Nolan (2000), suggests that bacterial meningitis causes developmental delay. The impairment theory, described by Taylor and colleagues (2000), suggests that cognition is irreparably impaired during the course of meningitis. There is some discrepancy in the literature regarding the effect of acute neurological complications at the time of illness; however, most researchers have found that those children who do experience neurological complications during the acute phase of the disease are at the greatest risk for negative long-term sequelae (Grimwood et al., 2000; Grimwood et al., 1995). Other factors found to be predictive of outcome include socioeconomic status (SES), access to rehabilitation, and age at illness (Anderson, Anderson, Grimwood, & Nolan, 2004). Interestingly, it is children suffering from illness prior to 12 months of age who have been found to experience greater difficulties, which is in contrast to neural plasticity theories (Anderson et al., 2004).

The literature indicates that there may be mild impairment in all neuropsychological domains rather than selective impairments in children with meningitis (Koomen et al., 2004). More specifically, Koomen and colleagues reported impaired manual steadiness, divided and sustained attention, copying of geometric figures, immediate memory capacity and spatial memory, and intellectual ability. Other researchers have reported deficits in cumulative learning and verbal sequential memory. Additionally, parent and teacher reports indicate lower adaptive functioning as well as poorer reading and spelling skills (Taylor et al., 2000). Even many years post meningitis, difficulties with executive functions such as efficiency, conceptualization, abstraction, organization, verbal fluency, mental flexibility, and problem solving; lower range IQs, and parent and teacher rated behavior problems have been reported (Anderson et al., 2004; Grimwood et al., 1995; Grimwood et al., 2000). Although only 8.5 percent of one sample of school-age survivors had major neurological, intellectual, or audiological sequelae five to ten years after meningitis, a much larger 27 percent had functionally important disabilities, including mild to moderate hearing loss and neurologic or central audiologic perceptual dysfunction (Grimwood et al., 1995). Nevertheless, some gains over time are seen, particularly in the areas of central auditory function, immediate memory capacity, processing speed (Grimwood et al., 2000), and goal-setting skills (Anderson et al., 2004).

Given the auditory problems, language deficits, and problems comprehending language-based material commonly following meningitis, these children often experience difficulty hearing and/or comprehending instructions in a regular classroom. Therefore, researchers suggest accommodations including ensuring quieter classrooms, sitting close to the teacher, small group teaching, repetition of information, and rephrasing verbal material in an effort to positively impact academic achievement, behavior, and self-esteem (Grimwood et al., 2000).

CHILDREN WITH NEURODEVELOPMENTAL RISK FACTORS

Fetal Alcohol Spectrum Disorders

Fetal Alcohol Syndrome (FAS) has traditionally been diagnosed when various growth and facial abnormalities, including significant growth retardation, short palpebral fissures (i.e., openings for the eyes), thin upper lip, elongated and flattened mid-face, and central nervous system (CNS) involvement, are present. Individuals who only partially met these diagnostic criteria were previously been diagnosed with Fetal Alcohol Effects (FAE) (Kaemingk, Mulvaney, & Halverson, 2003). However, more recently, the term Fetal Alcohol Spectrum Disorder (FASD) has been used to refer to the full spectrum of morphological and cognitive-behavioral outcomes associated with the various presentations of the disorder. The terms alcohol-related neurodevelopmental disorder (ARND) and alcohol-related birth defects (ARBD) have been used to replace FAE (Cone-Wesson, 2005; Kodituwakku, 2007). These terms have been proposed because it has been found that relatively few children exposed to alcohol prenatally develop the growth and facial abnormalities previously required for the FAS diagnosis. Further, it has been found that neuropsychological deficits occur similarly in children with and without growth and facial abnormalities (Kodituwakku, 2007; Rasmussen, Horne, & Witol, 2006) and that, while physical dysmorphic features seem to attenuate over time, neurobehavioral deficits do not (Streissguth, Barr, Bookstein, Sampson, & Olson, 1999).

Four primary areas of the brain are typically involved with FASD, including the cerebellum, basal ganglia, corpus callosum, and hippocampus. Furthermore, studies have demonstrated that neuronal development is significantly impaired due to abnormal cell death and problems with differentiation (Wacha & Obrzut, 2007). Neurocognitive sequelae range from no measureable effects to generalized retardation and severe neuropsychiatric and/or behavioral disorders (as cited in Korkman, Kettunen, & Autti-Rämö, 2003). The severity of effects is related to the quantity of maternal alcohol intake, with binge-type drinking being the most dangerous (Streissguth et al., 1999). Timing of intake of alcohol is another crucial factor, with the most dangerous periods being the first trimester and the last two months of pregnancy (Wacha & Obrzut, 2007). It has been suggested that the cognitive deficits related to FASD are the primary disabilities, while the negative behavioral outcomes represent secondary disabilities (Kodituwakku, 2007). The essence of the cognitive-behavioral phenotype associated with FASD has been defined as a generalized deficit in processing complex information with unimpaired performance on simpler tasks (Kodituwakku, 2007).

Fetal alcohol exposure is one of the leading causes of mental retardation (Cone-Wesson, 2005). IQs typically fall in the mildly impaired to the borderline range (60–85) (Cone-Wesson, 2005; Streissguth et al., 1999) with greater deficits in the verbal compared to performance domains (Korkman, Autti-Rämö, Koivulehto, & Granström, 1998; Rasmussen et al., 2006). Nonetheless, additional research supports the presence of impaired visual-spatial and motor functioning. Whereas motor precision and kinesthetic and tactile differentiation are typically spared, the ability to learn motor series and sequential motor movements are often impaired (Korkman et al., 1998). In addition, Streissguth and colleagues (1999) found that fine motor speed and coordination were impaired. Visual-motor integration (Coles et al., 1997); spatial localization, or forming internal representations of spatial relations (Uecker & Nadel, 1996); and visuo-motor production, or design copying (Korkman et al., 1998; Uecker & Nadel, 1996) represent areas of weakness in these children.

Focused and sustained attention to visual and stimuli has been found to be significantly impacted in children with FASD, as evidenced by lower accuracy and slower reaction times (Mattson, Calarco, & Lang, 2006; Streissguth et al., 1999). Decreased vigilance has also been observed (Streissguth et al., 1999). Slower processing of numbers (Burden, Jacobson, & Jacobson, 2005) and verbal information (Rasmussen et al., 2006) has been reported in the literature. Impairments of immediate visual and verbal learning (Kaemingk, Mulvaney, et al., 2003; Streissguth et al., 1999) and immediate and delayed spatial memory (Streissguth et al., 1999; Uecker & Nadel, 1996) have also been observed, although relative retention of information learned, or forgetting rate, is often spared (Kaemingk, Mulvaney, et al., 2003). Academic deficits have been observed in the foundation areas of math (Burden et al., 2005; Goldschmidt, Richardson, Cornelius, & Day, 2004; Streissguth et al., 1999), reading, and spelling (Goldschmidt et al., 2004).

Deficits within the executive functioning domain include problems with response inhibition and monitoring accuracy of recall (Noland et al., 2003) and flexibility in problem solving (Coles et al., 1997; Streissguth et al., 1999). Functional executive functioning deficits as reported by parents include problems with planning, organizing, and working memory (Rasmussen et al., 2006). These functional impairments have been found to be predictive of social behaviors observed by both parents and teachers, suggesting that children's executive functioning deficits are pervasive enough to impact social behaviors across multiple settings (Schonfeld, Paley, Frankel, & O'Connor, 2006). In the classroom, executive functioning deficits may manifest as an inability to follow instructions, retain information, generalize information, organize events into a logical sequence, organize personal belongings, and/or organize a learning task into a sequence for completion. Socially, these children tend to be impulsive (i.e., act before considering consequences), intrude into others' personal space, and have difficulty inhibiting responses. As a result, their ability to make and maintain friendships is negatively affected (Kalberg & Buckley, 2007). Interventions are better designed when the executive function deficits experienced by these children are clearly understood (Schonfeld et al., 2006).

It is evident that, although a continuum of language outcomes exists, no specific pattern of deficits has emerged in children with FASD. Specifically, deficits have been found within the syntactic and semantic domains (Cone-Wesson, 2005) and in naming ability (Korkman et al., 1998). Deficits in receptive language are primarily related to poor phonological analysis and production rather than in comprehension of instructions (Korkman et al., 1998). Social communication, including the referential and pragmatic aspects of narrative production in older children, represents another area of weakness in children with FASD (Coggins, Timler, & Olswant, 2007). Researchers suggest that, because social communication is a key deficit in children with FASD, a comprehensive evaluation of social communication should be completed even when performance on standardized language measures is within the normal range. Specifically, these assessments should include more integrative tasks such as narratives and observations of peer interactions in order to more closely assess the demands of everyday social interactions (Coggins et al., 2007).

In general, interventions should target multisystem and multilevel processes. The mnemonic "ENEMIES" (Executive functioning, Neuromotor, Emotional, Medical, Interpersonal, Environment, and Speech/Language) has been proposed as a framework for ensuring that important areas are addressed when planning interventions (Premji, Benzies, Serrett, & Hayden, 2006). Researchers suggest that structure will help these children know what is expected of them. Specifically, visual (e.g., visual organization such as containers to separate materials, visual instructions such as providing a finished example of an assigned task, and visual schedules), environmental (e.g., keeping space clear of visual and auditory distractions and clearly defining work centers), and task (e.g., delineating steps of a task by color-coding materials) structure interventions should be included (Kalberg & Buckley, 2007). A successful math intervention program included case management, parent training, teacher consultation, and individual instruction with the child. Math tutoring included several key components in an effort to compensate for common neurodevelopmental difficulties in children with FASD. For instance, to compensate for slower speed of processing, a slower pace of instruction using interactive experiences was used. Deficits in visual/spatial processing and working memory were targeted by using tangible objects and tools (e.g., number lines), while poor interhemispheric transfer of information was targeted by using repetitive experiences in which students labeled (left-hemisphere function) their visual-spatial perceptions (right-hemisphere function). To improve integration, feedback regarding patterns of errors and mediation of the experience were provided. Finally, to compensate for poor graphomotor skills, writing materials were adapted to facilitate understanding of starting points, and column alignment and the program "Handwriting Without Tears" was used (Kable, Coles, & Taddeo, 2007).

Low Birth Weight or Prematurity

Tens of thousands of children are born each year in the United States with birthweights considered low (LBW, <2500 g). Birthweight can also be classified as very low (VLBW, <1500 g) or extremely low (ELBW, <1000 g or < 750 g). Short gestational period is an alternate means of defining preterm infants, with preterm usually defined as a gestation of less than 37 weeks. However, gestation is measured less reliably, so birthweight is most often used as the marker (Taylor, Minich, Bangert, Filipek, & Hack, 2004).

Medical and neurodevelopmental problems are often observed in these children, although individual outcomes are highly variable with detectable brain damage being either absent, relatively localized, or diffuse. Common sequelae of VLBW include deficits in motor and visual-perceptual skills, memory, attention, and executive function. More specifically, although gross motor coordination and motor steadiness seem unaffected (Pietz et al., 2004), visuomotor performance (Esbjørn, Hansen, Greisen, & Mortensen, 2006; Peterson, Taylor, Minich, Klein, & Hack, 2006), visual-spatial processing (Vicari, Caravale, Carlesimo, Casadei, & Allemand, 2004) and small, precise arm-hand movements including finger dexterity and wrist-finger speed (Pietz et al., 2004) are often impaired.

Regarding language outcomes, Jansson-Verkasalo and colleagues (2004) found development of morphology within the normal range but observed deficits in language comprehension, vocabulary acquisition, and auditory discrimination in young children. In studying memory of spatial configurations, Vicari and colleagues (2004) observed that, while children were able to effectively store these configurations, they were not able to effectively rehearse spatial representations in order to prevent memory decay. Researchers have also reported deficits in general cognition (Anderson et al., 2003; Esbjørn et al., 2006; Peterson et al., 2006; Schneider, Wolke, Schlagmüller, & Meyer, 2004) and adaptive behavior (Peterson et al., 2006). Academically, these children often exhibit deficits in math, reading, and spelling (Anderson et al., 2003; Peterson et al., 2006; Schneider et al., 2004) as well as with their academic self-concept (Schneider et al., 2004). Regarding social-emotional functioning, parents have reported hyperactivity, somatic complaints, atypical behaviors, and poor social and leadership skills. Teachers have reported symptoms of depression, atypical behaviors, poor adaptability, and poor social and leadership skills (Anderson et al., 2003). Further, another study reported that VLBW adolescents exhibited more psychiatric symptoms than controls, yet an increased prevalence of depression was not found (Indredavik, Vik, Heyerdahl, Kulseng, & Brubakk, 2005).

Social-environmental factors may moderate neurocognitive outcomes in low birthweight children (Ment et al., 2003; Taylor, Minich, Bangert, et al., 2004). In addition, although the risks for cognitive sequelae extend across the range of birthweights less than 1500 g, deficits have been found to be most pronounced in children with the lowest birthweights. However, weight for gestational age has failed to account for poorer outcomes independent of other complications, limiting the predictive value of prematurity. For example, children needing oxygen for longer periods of time had poorer outcomes even when birthweight and weight for gestational age were taken into account (Taylor, Minich, Bangert, et al., 2004).

Impairments observed in VLBW children have persisted throughout the school-age years, even into the high school years (Taylor, Minich, Bangert, et al., 2004; Taylor, Minich, Klein, & Hack, 2004). For instance, Taylor and colleagues reported deficits in executive functioning skills such as attention shifting (Taylor, Minich, Bangert, et al., 2004; Taylor, Minich, Klein, et al., 2004); organizing one's approach to self-directed, multi-step tasks and spatial planning (Taylor, Minich, Bangert, et al., 2004); and perceptual-motor planning (Taylor, Minich, Klein et al., 2004) in adolescence. Deficits were also observed in general cognition; memory and learning outcomes including spatial recognition, working memory, visual memory, and use of semantic clustering in verbal recall (Taylor, Minich, Bangert, et al., 2004); and process-ing speed (Taylor, Minich, Klein, et al., 2004). It should be kept in mind, however, that some findings suggest that, while the level of cognitive performance may be impaired, the rate of skill acquisition may be unaffected (Taylor, Minich, Klein, et al., 2004). Therefore, repeated assessments into adolescence are justified, and long-term special education planning is impor-tant (Taylor, Minich, Klein, et al., 2004).

Although ADHD is diagnosed with a higher incidence in children born prematurely (Davis, Burns, Snyder, & Robinson, 2007; Potgieter, Vervisch, & Lagae, 2003), results of studies have shown that the pattern of attention problems in VLBW children are different from those in other children with attention problems (Davis et al., 2004; Snyder, Davis, Burns, & Robinson, 2007). In fact, researchers have suggested a unique prematurity pattern of attention disorders (PPAD) that may be best understood using a framework that considers attention problems within the larger context of self-regulation and may not be best measured using current rating checklists (Davis et al., 2004). Delays in orienting and engaging attention may result in VLBW children missing important information such that subsequent information does not make sense (Snyder et al., 2007). Therefore, educational recommen-dations in the research have included direct teaching of organizational strategies, providing extra time and direction in preparation for and taking tests, encouraging use of verbal mediation, and using repetitive or process-oriented instructional approaches (Schneider et al., 2004; Taylor, Minich, Bangert, et al., 2004).

EXPOSURE TO LEAD AND OTHER ENVIRONMENTAL TOXINS

The toxins most known to cause harm to the nervous system include lead, polychlorinated biphenyls (PCBs, or industrial pollutants), mercury, ethanol, polybrominated diphenyl ethers (PBDEs, or compounds used as a flame retardant), and nicotine from tobacco smoke (Burstyn & Fenton, 2006).

Although lead exposure has been one of the most researched areas, a distinct neurobehavioral phenotype has not emerged (Williams & Ross, 2007). Additionally, the effects of lead exposure are relatively subtle, and there is not an apparent threshold (Chiodo, Jacobson, & Jacobson, 2004). Although the Centers for Disease Control (CDC) has lowered the allowable amount of lead in a child's blood from 25 to 10 µg/dl (as cited in Burstyn & Fenton, 2006), negative associations with attention and withdrawal behaviors, reaction time, and auditory attention have been found at levels as low as 3 µg/dl (Chiodo et al., 2004). In addition, symptoms of ADHD-Combined Type, especially the symptoms related to hyperactivity-impulsivity, have been associated with low-level blood exposure (Nigg et al., 2008). At levels of blood exposure less than 6 μg/dl, children have been found to demonstrate difficulties with visual-motor integration (Chiodo et al., 2004), yet they appear to retain the ability to transfer use of an efficient attention allocation strategy from one task to another (Davis, Chang, Burns, Robinson, & Dossett, 2004). This ability was not retained, however, in children exposed at a higher level (10–29 μg/dl) (Davis et al., 2004). Another study revealed that children with lead exposure suffered from difficulties with spatial span due to insufficient allocation of attention to the initial presentation; attentional flexibility; planning and problem solving due to reliance upon a trial and error strategy; and rule-based responding. The authors suggested several explanations for the lower performance on tasks requiring rule-based responding, including that children may have favored speed over accuracy, also held a weaker representation of the explicit rule in working memory, or responded impulsively (Canfield, Gendle, & Cory-Slechta, 2004). Other studies have found deficits in working memory (Chiodo et al., 2004), rule learning and reversal (Froehlich et al., 2007), and deficits in overall intellectual ability (Burstyn & Fenton, 2006; Chiodo et al., 2004; Williams & Ross, 2007). Lead-exposed children have more difficulties handling stress and are prone to depression. They also tend to exhibit increased frustration, volatility, and failure resulting in a greater predisposition to violence, addiction, and criminal behavior (as cited in Burstyn & Fenton, 2006). It is noteworthy, however, that effects of lead exposure are attenuated when social-environmental variables are taken into consideration. As a result, the independent effect of lead is difficult to isolate (Chiodo et al., 2004).

Assessing the effects of PCBs is difficult because PCBs are compounds and there are differences associated with the source of exposure (e.g., placental, breast milk) (Cook-Cottone, 2004). Although these industrial pollutants have been banned in most industrial countries, PCBs have remained in the environment and have accumulated in the food chain (Cook-Cottone, 2004; Williams & Ross, 2007). Despite a lack of set guidelines for classifying the toxicity of exposure levels, the CDC has released national averages of levels found in adolescents ages 12 to 19, and they recommend comparing an individual's levels with these averages to estimate level of exposure (as cited in Cook-Cottone, 2004). Subtle effects on sustained attention, impulsivity, attentional flexibility, and working memory have been found (as cited in Williams & Ross, 2007). In addition, Cook-Cottone reported deficits in verbal ability, memory, and information processing along with inconsistent evidence of problems with psychomotor development, decreased sustained activity, and increased withdrawn and depressed behavior. Overall intellectual ability has also been found to be affected (as cited in Cook-Cottone, 2004; Stewart, Reihman, Lonky, Darvill, & Pagano, 2003).

Organophosphate (OP) pesticides are a group of insecticides commonly used for agricultural and household purposes. Major symptoms of OP pesticide poisoning appear within twelve hours of exposure and include dizziness, anxiety, restlessness, muscle twitching, weakness, tremor, unco-ordination, hypersecretion (i.e., excessive production of a bodily secretion), miosis (i.e., pupil contraction), and pulmonary edema (i.e., abnormal buildup of fluid in the lungs). Repeated exposure can further result in anorexia (loss of appetite), weakness, and malaise. Although there currently is a limited amount of research available on the risks of OP pesticide exposure, there is some evidence that a threshold exists in detecting cognitive dysfunction (Lizardi, O'Rourke, & Morris, 2007). Lizardi and colleagues reported deficits in sensory-motor skills such as physical endurance, ball catching, and fine eye-hand motor coordination; long-term memory; executive functions including speed of attention, sequencing, mental flexibility, visual search, concept formation, and conceptual flexibility; and in the number of body parts drawn when drawing a picture of a person (1.6 compared to 4.4 in controls).

Mercury or methylmercury (MeHg) is a neurotoxin affecting the brain, spinal cord, kidneys, and liver (Burstyn & Fenton, 2006). In high doses, MeHg has been associated with intellectual impairment, cerebral palsy, and micro-cephaly (Davidson et al., 2006). Fish contain small amounts of MeHg, and current data suggest that negative neurocognitive outcomes could result from exposure at a rate as low as 10 ppm as measured in maternal hair (Davidson et al., 2006). The Seychelles Child Development Study (SCDS) is a longitudinal study of children whose mothers reported eating an average of twelve fish meals per week throughout pregnancy. Cross-sectional research conducted at six different ages through age 11 has revealed few significant negative associations as a result of MeHg exposure in this popu-lation (Thompson et al., 2007). For instance, Davidson and colleagues found that, over the first ten years of life, there was no effect on memory skills, global cognition, scholastic readiness, or social-behavioral development.

DRUG EXPOSURE

A review of the literature regarding drug exposure in utero revealed a variety of neuropsychological deficits associated with different substances. The present chapter includes research regarding prenatal exposure to metham-phetamines, cocaine, tobacco, and marijuana. While there is little research regarding the effects of prenatal methamphetamine exposure, deficits have been reported in the areas of selective and visual attention, verbal and spatial memory, and visual-motor integration (Chang et al., 2004).

Despite cocaine decreasing blood flow to the fetus via vasoconstriction of the placenta, cocaine by itself has not been shown to have a negative effect on physical growth or cognitive development (as cited in Cone-Wesson, 2005). Rather, it is cocaine exposure combined with social-environmental factors such as quality of the caregiving environment (Singer et al., 2004), poverty and birthweight (Savage, Brodsky, Malmud, Giannetta, & Hurt, 2005) that create the deleterious effects. There is mixed evidence regarding the impact of prenatal cocaine exposure (PCE) upon neuropsychological functioning. It has been reported that receptive language (Kilbride, Castor, & Fuger, 2006; Morrow et al., 2004), articulation in spontaneous language (Delaney-Black et al., 2000), knowledge of linguistic concepts, word structure, and ability to recall sentences (Lewis et al., 2004) remain unaffected following exposure to cocaine in utero. On the other hand, some research has found that PCE children at age 4 continue to lag behind non-exposed peers in their language skills. For instance, exposed children performed more poorly on tests of basic concepts, including knowledge of attributes, dimension/size, direction, location, position, number, quantity, and equality (Lewis et al., 2004). Another study found increasingly poor expressive language, but not receptive language with increased level of PCE (Morrow et al., 2004). More generally, PCE has been associated with deficits in aptitude of language performance but not in the trajectory of language development during the preschool years (Lewis et al., 2007).

Some studies have found relatively spared executive functions, including category fluency and motor planning (Noland et al., 2003) and motor inhibition (Warner et al., 2006) following PCE. Deficits in selective attention have been reported (Noland et al., 2005). One study found problems with sustained attention under conditions of higher arousal that required greater control over impulsivity, although teachers did not identify the cocaine-exposed children to have more problems with inhibitory control in the classroom than a control group (Savage et al., 2005). An association between PCE and increased difficulty inhibiting salient responses has also been hypothesized (Bendersky, Gambini, Lastella, Bennett, & Lewis, 2003) although in one study, indicators of impulsivity or response inhibition were not observed (Accornero et al., 2007). Deficits have been observed on tasks involving fine motor skills and visual-motor integration (Arendt et al., 2004), and PCE children have shown slower response times (Accornero et al., 2007; Warner et al., 2006). While overall cognitive development has been found to be spared (Kilbride et al., 2006; Pulsifer, Radonovich, Belcher, & Butz, 2004; Singer et al., 2004), children were less likely to have an IQ above the normative mean (Singer et al., 2004). There is some evidence of gender effects as boys have been found to exhibit abstract/visual reasoning deficits (Bennett, Bendersky, & Lewis, 2008). PCE children have exhibited lower scores on short-term memory tasks (Bendersky et al., 2003). Significant difficulties in several aspects of visuospatial memory have been found in PCE children. Specifically, these children's visuomotor speed was slowed, and they had more difficulty efficiently accessing and using an internal spatial map. Thus, results suggest a mild impairment in information processing speed and/or procedural learning but not in accuracy (Schroder, Snyder, Sielski, & Mayes, 2004). Finally, there is evidence that these children do not exhibit deficits in general school readiness (Pulsifer et al., 2004) and there is no significant difference in the frequency at which parents report emotional and behavioral problems (Kilbride et al., 2006).

A dose-response relationship has been found between maternal tobacco use and childhood hyperactivity independent of sociodemographic factors (Kotimaa et al., 2003). However, another study found sociodemographic factors to be important predictors in behavioral outcome. Specifically, prenatal smoking exposure was highly confounded with factors such as maternal education and maternal history of substance use disorder in the prediction of behavior disorders (Nigg & Breslau, 2007). Results have been mixed regarding the effect of tobacco exposure upon general cognition and academic achievement (as cited in Howell, Coles, & Kable, 2008). Smoking during or after pregnancy has been associated with slightly poorer academic achievement in some studies. IQs of children of heavy smokers have been found to be significantly lower than for children of non-smokers (as cited in Williams & Ross, 2007). Consistent findings regarding underlying auditory processing deficits have been found, with these deficits manifesting in delays in early language development and later reading and academic skills (as cited in Howell et al., 2008). Results of studies have also found subtle deficits in the ability to control and regulate behavior in order to meet environmental demands, as well as lower attention span, greater motor activity, and poorer auditory and visual vigilance (as cited in Howell et al., 2008). A review by Williams and Ross cited research associating nicotine exposure with the ability to encode and retain information in memory, and paternal smoking history was found to be just as strongly related to increased ADHD and aggression as maternal smoking during pregnancy. Finally, Noland and colleagues (2005) found that children with prenatal cigarette exposure had higher rates of commission errors on tests of selective attention.

Heavy use of marijuana, defined as the use of at least one marijuana cigarette each day, has been associated with neuropsychological deficits in prenatally exposed children (Goldschmidt, Richardson, Willford, & Day, 2008). Lower IQ scores have been observed even after controlling for significant covariates in children with prenatal marijuana exposure. Exposure during the first trimester has been related to verbal reasoning deficits, and exposure during the second trimester has been found to be the best predictor of lower IQ scores (Goldschmidt et al., 2008). With regard to academic functioning, exposure to marijuana during the first trimester has been associated with lower reading and spelling scores as well as poorer teacher evaluation, while exposure during the second trimester has been associated with deficits in reading comprehension and general underachievement (Goldschmidt et al., 2004). Other studies have suggested failure to maintain vigilance (Noland et al., 2005) as well as other symptoms of ADHD (as cited in Howell et al., 2008; Williams & Ross, 2007), but no relationship to performance on executive functioning tasks including category fluency, motor planning, and response inhibition has been established (Noland et al., 2003). There appears to be an increased risk of depression and conduct disorder in children prenatally exposed to marijuana (as cited in Williams & Ross, 2007).

Various interventions described by McLaughlin, Williams, and Howard (1998) have proven highly effective in managing the behavior problems that may be observed in children who have been prenatally exposed to drugs. For instance, these researchers reported that three contingency management methods, including token reinforcement, contracting, and daily report cards, produced positive outcomes. In addition, they report that self-monitoring has been used across age and grade levels to modify social and academic behaviors. Self-instruction training was also described as being well suited for secondary students for whom independence is often expected. For instance, the self-managed drill and practice intervention called the Cover, Copy, and Compare method has been demonstrated to be effective across curricula objectives, students, and environments. Peer tutoring strategies have also produced positive outcomes. Classwide Peer Tutoring involves the use of peers to supervise responding and practice, the use of a game format to increase motivation and interest and the use of weekly evaluations for the purpose of progress monitoring. Direct instruction of students should include frequent teacher-student interactions that are guided by carefully sequenced lessons. Efficiency is increased by providing small group instruction whenever possible, maintaining a fast pace, devising strategies for generalization, providing immediate and positive correction, and carefully sequencing instruction. These strategies have been proven effective with preschool, elementary, and secondary regular and special education students.

SUMMARY

The present chapter details several medical conditions that impact neurocognitive functioning either directly or indirectly. Although some of the diseases discussed are rather rare and school neuropsychologists may not see children with these conditions often, awareness of the associated neuropsychological deficits is imperative to provide appropriate services for these children in school. The information provided in this chapter provides a guideline to frequently observed deficits, yet much research remains to further clarify neuropsychological sequelae associated with medical conditions. Furthermore, individual differences must always be taken into account when assessing children.

REFERENCES

Accornero, V. H., Amado, A. J., Morrow, C. E., Xue, L., Anthony, J. C., & Bandstra, E. S. (2007). Impact of prenatal cocaine exposure on attention and response inhibition as assessed by continuous performance tests. *Journal of Developmental and Behavioral Pediatrics, 28,* 195–205.

Adebäck, P., Nemeth, A., & Fischler, B. (2003). Cognitive and emotional outcome after pediatric liver transplantation. *Pediatric Transplantation, 7*(5), 385–389.

Anderson, P., Doyle, L. W., Callanan, C., Carse, E., Casalaz, D., Charlton, M. P., et al. (2003). Neurobehavioral outcomes of school-age children born extremely low birth weight or very preterm in the 1990s. *Journal of the American Medical Association, 289,* 3264–3272.

Anderson, V., Anderson, P., Grimwood, K., & Nolan, T. (2004). Cognitive and executive function 12 years after childhood bacterial meningitis: Effect of acute neurologic complications and age of onset. *Journal of Pediatric Psychology, 29,* 67–81.

Anderson, V., Northam, E., Hendy, J., & Wrennall, J. (2001). *Developmental psychology: A clinical approach.* Philadelphia: Psychology Press.

Annett, R. D., Aylward, E. H., Lapidus, J., Bender, B. G., & DuHamel, T. (2000). Neurocognitive functioning in children with mild and moderate asthma in the Childhood Asthma Management Program. *Journal of Allergy and Clinical Immunology, 105,* 717–724.

Archbold, K. H., Giordani, B., Ruzicka, D. L., & Chervin, R. D. (2004). Cognitive executive dysfunction in children with mild sleep-disordered breathing. *Biological Research for Nursing, 5,* 168–176.

Arendt, R. E., Short, E. J., Singer, L. T., Minnes, S., Hewitt, J., Flynn, S., et al. (2004). Children prenatally exposed to cocaine: Developmental outcomes and environmental risks at 7 years of age. *Developmental and Behavioral Pediatrics, 25,* 83–90.

Ballantyne, A. O., Spilkin, A. M., & Trauner, D. A. (2007). Language outcome after perinatal stroke: Does side matter? *Child Neuropsychology, 13,* 494–509.

Barnes, M., Dennis, M., & Hetherington, R. (2004). Reading and writing skills in young adults with spina bifida and hydrocephalus. *Journal of the International Neuropsychological Society, 10,* 655–663.

Baron, I. S., Fennell, E. B., & Voeller, K. K. S. (1995). Hydrocephalus and myelomeningocele. In I. S. Baron, E. B. Fennell, & K. K. S. Voeller (Eds.), *Pediatric neuropsychology in the medical setting* (pp. 221–240). New York: Oxford University Press.

Baum, M., Freier, M. C., & Chinnock, R. E. (2003). Neurodevelopmental outcome of solid organ transplantation in children. *Pediatric Clinics of North America, 50*(6), 1493.

Beebe, D. W. (2006). Neurobehavioral morbidity associated with disordered breathing during sleep in children: A comprehensive review. *Sleep, 29*, 1115–1134.

Beebe, D. W., Wells, C. T., Jeffries, J., Chini, B., Kalra, M., & Amin, R. (2004). Neuropsychological effects of pediatric obstructive sleep apnea. *Journal of the International Neuropsychological Society, 10*, 962–975.

Bendersky, M., Gambini, G., Lastella, A., Bennett, D. S., & Lewis, M. (2003). Inhibitory motor control at 5 years as a function of prenatal cocaine exposure. *Journal of Developmental and Behavioral Pediatrics, 24*, 345–351.

Bennett, D. S., Bendersky, M., & Lewis, M. (2008). Children's cognitive ability from 4 to 9 years old as a function of prenatal cocaine exposure, environmental risk, and maternal verbal intelligence. *Developmental Psychology, 44*, 919–928.

Berkelhammer, L. D., Williamson, A. L., Sanford, S. D., Dirksen, C. L., Sharp, W. G., Margulies, A. S., & Prengler, R. A. (2007). Neurocognitive sequelae of pediatric sickle cell disease: a review of the literature. *Child Neuropsychology, 13*, 120–131.

Blackman, J. A., & Gurka, M. J. (2007). Developmental and behavioral comorbidities of asthma in children. *Journal of Developmental and Behavioral Pediatrics, 28*, 92–99.

Blunden, S., Lushington, K., Kennedy, D., Martin, J., & Dawson, D. (2000). Behavior and neurocognitive performance in children aged 5–10 years who snore compared to controls. *Journal of Clinical and Experimental Neuropsychology, 22*, 554–568.

Bray, M. A., Kehle, T. J., Theodore, L. A., & Peck, H. L. (2006). Respiratory impairments. In L. Phelps (Ed.), *Chronic health-related disorders in children: Collaborative medical and psychoeducational interventions* (pp. 237–251). Washington, DC: American Psychological Association.

Brosig, C., Hintermeyer, M., Zlotocha, J., Behrens, D., & Mao, J. (2006). An exploratory study of the cognitive, academic, and behavioral functioning of pediatric cardiothoracic transplant recipients. *Progress in Transplantation (Aliso Viejo, Calif.), 16*(1), 38–45.

Brouhard, B. H., Donaldson, L. A., Lawry, K. W., McGowan, K. R., Drotar, D., Davis, I., et al. (2000). Cognitive functioning in children on dialysis and post-transplantation. *Pediatric Transplantation, 4*(4), 261–267.

Brown, R. T., Madan-Swain, A., Pais, R., Lambert, R. G., Sexson, S., & Ragab, A. (1992). Chemotherapy for acute lymphocytic leukemia: Cognitive and academic sequelae. *Journal of Pediatrics, 121*, 885–890.

Burden, M. J., Jacobson, S. W., & Jacobson, J. L. (2005). Relation of prenatal alcohol exposure to cognitive processing speed and efficiency in childhood. *Alcoholism: Clinical and Experimental Research, 29*, 1473–1483.

Burstyn, V., & Fenton, D. (2006). Toxic world, troubled minds. In S. Olfman (Ed.), *No child left different* (pp. 49–71). Westport, CT: Praeger Publishers/Greenwood Publishing Group.

Butler, R. W., Fairclough, D. L., Katz, E. R., Noll, R. B., Copeland, D. R., Mulhern, R. K., et al. (2008). A multicenter, randomized clinical trial of a cognitive remediation program for childhood survivors of a pediatric malignancy. *Journal of Consulting and Clinical Psychology, 76*(3), 367–378.

Butler, R. W., & Haser, J. K. (2006). Neurocognitive effects of treatment for childhood cancer. *Mental Retardation and Developmental Disabilities, 12*, 184–191.

Campbell, L. K., Scaduto, M., Sharp, W., Dufton, L., Van Slyke, D., Whitlock, J. A., et al. (2007). A meta-analysis of the neurocognitive sequelae of treatment for childhood acute lymphocytic leukemia. *Pediatric Blood Cancer, 49*, 65–73.

Canfield, R. L., Gendle, M. H., & Cory-Slechta, D. A. (2004). Impaired neuropsychological functioning in lead-exposed children. *Developmental Neuropsychology, 26*, 513–540.

Cascio, D. P., & Ries, J. K. (2008). Spina bifida. In C. L. Castillo (Ed.), *Children with complex medical issues in schools* (pp. 435–455). New York: Springer.

Chang, L., Smith, L. M., LoPresti, C., Yonekura, M. L., Kuo, J., Walot, I., et al. (2004). Small subcortical volumes and cognitive deficits in children with prenatal methamphetamine exposure. *Psychiatry Research, 132*, 95–106.

Chervin, R. D., Ruzicka, D. L., Giordani, B. J., Weatherly, R. A., Dillon, J. E., Hodges, E. K., et al. (2006). Sleep-disordered breathing, behavior, and cognition in children before and after adenotonsillectomy. *Pediatrics, 117*, 769–778.

Chiodo, L. M., Jacobson, S. W., & Jacobson, J. L. (2004). Neurodevelopmental effects of postnatal lead exposure at very low levels. *Neurotoxicology and Teratology, 26*, 359–371.

Christ, S. E., Moinuddin, A., McKinstry, R. C., DeBaun, M., & White, D. A. (2007). Inhibitory control in children with frontal infarcts related to sickle cell disease. *Child Neuropsychology, 13*, 132–141.

Coggins, T. E., Timler, G. R., & Olswant, L. B. (2007). A state of double jeopardy: Impact of prenatal alcohol exposure and adverse environments on the social communicative abilities of school-age children with fetal alcohol spectrum disorder. *Language, Speech, and Hearing Services in Schools, 38*, 117–127.

Cohen, M. J., Branch, W. B., McKie, V. C., & Adams, R. J. (1994). Neuropsychological impairment in children with sickle cell anemia and cerebrovascular accidents. *Clinical Pediatrics, 33*, 517–524.

Coles, C. D., Platzman, K. A., Raskind-Hood, C. L., Brown, R. T., Falek, A., & Smith, I. E. (1997). A comparison of children affected by prenatal alcohol exposure and attention deficit, hyperactivity disorder. *Alcoholism: Clinical and Experimental Research, 21*, 150–161.

Cone-Wesson, B. (2005). Prenatal alcohol and cocaine exposure: Influences on cognition, speech, language, and hearing. *Journal of Communication Disorders, 38*, 279–302.

Cook-Cottone, C. (2004). Exposure to polychlorinated biphenyls (PCBs): Implications for school psychologists. *Psychology in the Schools, 41*, 709–714.

Copeland, D. R., Dowell, R. E., Fletcher, J. M., Bordeaux, J. D., Sullivan, M. P., Jaffe, N., et al. (1988). Neuropsychological effects of childhood cancer treatment. *Journal of Child Neurology, 3*, 53–62.

Craft, S., Schatz, J., Glauser, T. A., Lee, B., & DeBaun, M. R. (1993). Neuropsychologic effects of stroke in children with sickle cell anemia. *Journal of Pediatrics, 123*, 712–717.

Davidson, P. W., Myers, G. J., Cox, C., Wilding, G. E., Shamlaye, C. F., Huang, L. S., et al. (2006). Methylmercury and neurodevelopment: Longitudinal analysis of the Seychelles child development cohort. *Neurotoxicology and Teratology, 28*, 529–535.

Davis, D. W., Burns, B., Snyder, E., & Robinson, J. (2007). Attention problems in very low birth weight preschoolers: Are new screening measures needed for this population? *Journal of Child and Adolescent Psychiatric Nursing, 20*, 74–85.

Davis, D. W., Chang, F., Burns, B., Robinson, J., & Dossett, D. (2004). Lead exposure and attention regulation in children living in poverty. *Developmental Medicine and Child Neurology, 46*, 825–831.

Delaney-Black, V., Covington, C., Templin, T., Kershaw, T., Nordstrom-Klee, B., Ager, J., et al. (2000). Expressive language development of children exposed to cocaine prenatally: Literature review and report of a prospective cohort study. *Journal of Communication Disorders, 33*, 463–481.

Dennis, M., Fletcher, J. M., Rogers, T., Hetherington, R., & Francis, D. J. (2002). Object-based and action-based visual perception in children with spina bifida and hydrocephalus. *Journal of the International Neuropsychological Society, 8*, 95–106.

Dennis, M., Jewell, D., Hetherington, R., Burton, C., Brandt, M. E., Blaser, S. E., et al. (2008). Verb generation in children with spina bifida. *Journal of the International Neuropsychological Society, 14*, 181–191.

Desrocher, M., & Rovet, J. (2004). Neurocognitive correlates of type 1 diabetes mellitus in childhood. *Child Neuropsychology, 10*, 36–52.

Emancipator, J. L., Storfer-Isser, A., Taylor, H. G., Rosen, C. L., Kirchner, H. L., Johnson, N. L., et al. (2006). Variation of cognition and achievement with sleep-disordered breathing in full-term and preterm children. *Archives of Pediatric and Adolescent Medicine, 160*, 203–210.

Erickson, K., Baron, I. S., & Fantie, B. D. (2001). Neuropsychological functioning in early hydrocephalus: Review from a developmental perspective. *Child Neuropsychology, 7*, 199–229.

Esbjørn, B. H., Hansen, B. M., Greisen, G., & Mortensen, E. L. (2006). Intellectual development in a Danish cohort of prematurely born preschool children: Specific or general difficulties? *Developmental and Behavioral Pediatrics, 27*, 477–484.

Espy, K. A., Senn, T. E., Charak, D. A., Tyler, J., & Wiebe, S. A. (2007). Perinatal pH and neuropsychological outcomes at age 3 years in children born preterm: An exploratory study. *Developmental Neuropsychology, 32*, 669–682.

Fennell, E. B. (2000). End-stage renal disease. In K. O. Yeates, M. D. Ris, & H. G. Taylor (Eds.), *Pediatric neuropsychology: Research, theory, and practice* (pp. 25–46). New York: Guilford.

Fine, R. N., Alonso, E. M., Fischel, J. E., Bucuvalas, J. C., Enos, R. A., & Gore-Langton, R. E. (2004). Pediatric transplantation of the kidney, liver and heart: summary report. *Pediatric Transplantation, 8*(1), 75–86.

Fontaine, E. N., & Snyder, G. (2008). Diabetes. In C. L. Castillo (Ed.). *Children with complex medical issues in schools* (pp. 105–134). New York: Springer.

Freier, M. C., Babikian, T., Pivonka, J., Burley Aaen, T., Gardner, J. M., Baum, M., et al. (2004). A longitudinal perspective on neurodevelopmental outcome after infant cardiac transplantation. *The Journal of Heart and Lung Transplantation, 23*(7), 857–864.

Friedman, B., Hendeles-Amitai, A., Kozminsky, E., Leiberman, A., Friger, M., Tarasiuk, A., et al. (2003). Adenotonsillectomy improves neurocognitive function in children with obstructive sleep apnea syndrome. *Sleep, 26*, 999–1005.

Froehlich, T. E., Lanphear, B. P., Dietrich, K. N., Cory-Slechta, D. A., Wang, N., & Kahn, R. S. (2007). Interactive effects of a DRD4 polymorphism, lead, and sex on executive functions in children. *Biological Psychiatry, 62,* 243–249.

Fundarò, C., Miccinesi, N., Baldieri, N. F., Genovese, O., Rendeli, C., & Segni, G. (1998). Cognitive impairment in school-age children with asymptomatic HIV infection. *AIDS Patient Care and STDs, 12*(2), 135–140.

Gerson, A. C., Butler, R., Moxey-Mims, M., Wentz, A., Shinnar, S., Lande, M. B., et al. (2006). Neurocognitive outcomes in children with chronic kidney disease: Current findings and contemporary endeavors. *Mental Retardation and Developmental Disabilities Research Reviews, 12*(3), 208–215.

Giordani, B., Hodges, E. K., Guire, K. E., Ruzicka, D. L., Dillon, J. E., Weatherly, R. A., et al. (2008). Neuropsychological and behavioral functioning in children with and without obstructive sleep apnea referred for tonsillectomy. *Journal of the International Neuropsychological Society, 14,* 571–581.

Goldschmidt, L., Richardson, G. A., Cornelius, M. D., & Day, N. L. (2004). Prenatal marijuana and alcohol exposure and academic achievement at age 10. *Neurotoxicology and Teratology, 26,* 521–532.

Goldschmidt, L., Richardson, G. A., Willford, J., & Day, N. L., (2008). Prenatal marijuana exposure and intelligence test performance at age 6. *Journal of the American Academy of Child and Adolescent Psychiatry, 47,* 254–263.

Grimwood, K., Anderson, V. A., Bond, L., Catroppa, C., Hore, R. L., Keir, E. H., et al. (1995). Adverse outcomes of bacterial meningitis in school-age survivors. *Pediatrics, 95,* 646–656.

Grimwood, K., Anderson, V., Tan, L., & Nolan, T. (2000). Twelve year outcomes following bacterial meningitis: Further evidence for persisting effects. *Archives of Disease in Childhood, 83,* 111–116.

Groothoff, J. W., Grootenhuis, M., Dommerholt, A., Gruppen, M. P., Offringa, M., & Heymans, H. S. A. (2002). Impaired cognition and schooling in adults with end stage renal disease since childhood. *Archives of Disease in Childhood, 87*(5), 380–385.

Grueneich, R., Ris, M. D., Ball, W., Kalinyak, K. A., Noll, R., Vannatta, K., et al. (2004). Relationship of structural magnetic resonance imaging, magnetic resonance perfusion, and other disease factors to neuropsychological outcome in sickle cell disease. *Journal of Pediatric Psychology, 29,* 83–92.

Halbower, A. C., & Mahone, E. M. (2006). Neuropsychological morbidity linked to childhood sleep-disordered breathing. *Sleep Medicine Reviews, 10,* 97–107.

Hart, Y. (2004). Rasmussen's encephalitis. *Epileptic Disorders, 6,* 133–144.

Hartel, C., Schilling, S., Sperner, J., & Thyen, U. (2004). The clinical outcomes of neonatal and childhood stroke: review of the literature and implications for future research. *European Journal of Neurology, 11,* 431–438.

Hershey, T., Lillie, R., Sadler, M., & White, N. H. (2003). Severe hypoglycemia and long-term spatial memory in children with type 1 diabetes mellitus: A retrospective study. *Journal of the International Neuropsychological Society, 9*(5), 740–750.

Hill, C. M., Hogan, A. M., Onugha, N., Harrison, D., Cooper, S., McGrigor, V. J., et al. (2006). Increased cerebral blood flow velocity in children with mild sleep-disordered breathing: A possible association with abnormal neuropsychological function. *Pediatrics, 118*, 1100–1108.

Hogan, A. M., Kirkham, F. J., & Isaacs, E. B. (2000). Intelligence after stroke in childhood: Review of the literature and suggestions for future research. *Journal of Child Neurology, 15*, 325–332.

Hokkanen, L., & Launes, J. (2007). Neuropsychological sequelae of acute-onset sporadic viral encephalitis. *Neuropsychological Rehabilitation, 17*, 450–477.

Hopkins-Golightly, T., Raz, S., & Sander, C. J. (2003). Influence of slight to moderate risk for birth hypoxia on acquisition of cognitive and language function in the preterm infant: A cross-sectional comparison with preterm-birth controls. *Neuropsychology, 17*, 3–13.

Howell, K. K., Coles, C. D., & Kable, J. (2008). The medical and developmental consequences of prenatal drug exposure. In J. Brick (Ed.), *Handbook of the medical consequences of alcohol and drug abuse* (pp. 281–302). New York: Haworth Press.

Huber-Okrainec, J., Dennis, M., Brettschneider, J., & Spiegler, B. J. (2002). Neuromotor speech deficits in children and adults with spina bifida and hydrocephalus. *Brain and Language, 80*, 592–602.

Indredavik, M. S., Vik, T., Heyerdahl, S., Kulseng, S., & Brubakk, A. (2005). Psychiatric symptoms in low birth weight adolescents, assessed by screening questionnaires. *European Child & Adolescent Psychiatry, 14*, 226–236.

Jansson-Verkasalo, E., Valkama, M., Vainionpää, L., Pääkkö, E., Ilkko, E., & Lehtihalmes, M. (2004). Language development in very low birth weight preterm children: A follow-up study. *Folia Phoniatrica et Logopaedica, 56*, 108–119.

Jeremy, R. J., Kim, S., Nozyce, M., Nachman, S., McIntosh, K., Pelton, S. I., et al. (2005). Neuropsychological functioning and viral load in stable antiretroviral therapy-experienced HIV-infected children. *Pediatrics, 115*(2), 380–387.

Kable, J. A., Coles, C. D., & Taddeo, E. (2007). Socio-cognitive habilitation using the math interactive learning experience program for alcohol-affected children. *Alcoholism: Clinical and Experimental Research, 31*, 1425–1434.

Kaemingk, K. L., Mulvaney, S., & Halverson, P. T. (2003). Learning following prenatal alcohol exposure: Performance on verbal and visual multitrial tasks. *Archives of Clinical Neuropsychology, 18*, 33–47.

Kaemingk, K. L., Pasvogel, A. E., Goodwin, J. L., Mulvaney, S. A., Martinez, F., Enright, P. L., et al. (2003). Learning in children and sleep disordered breathing: Findings of the Tucson Children's Assessment of Sleep Apnea (TuCASA) prospective cohort study. *Journal of the International Neuropsychological Society, 9*, 1016–1026.

Kalberg, W. O., & Buckley, D. (2007). FASD: What types of intervention and rehabilitation are useful? *Neuroscience and Biobehavioral Reviews, 31*, 278–285.

Kaller, T., Schulz, K., Sander, K., Boeck, A., Rogiers, X., & Burdelski, M. (2005). Cognitive abilities in children after liver transplantation. *Transplantation, 79*(9), 1252–1256.

Katon, W., Lozano, P., Russo, J., McCauley, E., Richardson, L., & Bush, T. (2007). The prevalence of DSM-IV anxiety and depressive disorders in youth with asthma compared with controls. *Journal of Adolescent Health, 41*, 455–463.

Kelso, W. M., Nicholls, M. E., Warne, G. L., & Zacharin, M. (2000). Cerebral lateralization and cognitive functioning in patients with congenital adrenal hyperplasia. *Neuropsychology, 14,* 370–378.

Kilbride, H. W., Castor, C. A., & Fuger, K. L. (2006). School-age outcome of children with prenatal cocaine exposure following early case management. *Developmental and Behavioral Pediatrics, 27,* 181–187.

Kodituwakku, P. W. (2007). Defining the behavioral phenotype in children with fetal alcohol spectrum disorders: A review. *Neuroscience and Biobehavioral Reviews, 31,* 192–201.

Koomen, I., van Furth, A. M., Kraak, M. A. C., Grobbee, D. E., Roord, J. J., & Jennekens-Schinkel, A. (2004). Neuropsychology of academic and behavioural limitations in school-age survivors of bacterial meningitis. *Developmental Medicine and Child Neurology, 46,* 724–732.

Korkman, M., Autti-Rämö, I., Koivulehto, H., & Granström, M. (1998). Neuropsychological effects at early school age of fetal alcohol exposure of varying duration. *Child Neuropsychology, 4,* 111–140.

Korkman, M., Kettunen, S., & Autti-Rämö, I. (2003). Neurocognitive impairment in early adolescence following prenatal alcohol exposure of varying duration. *Child Neuropsychology, 9,* 117–128.

Koscik, R. L., Lai, H. J., Laxova, A., Zaremba, K. M., Kosorok, M. R., Douglas, J. A., et al. (2005). Preventing early, prolonged vitamin E deficiency: An opportunity for better cognitive outcomes via early diagnosis through neonatal screening. *The Journal of Pediatrics, 147,* S51–6.

Kotimaa, A. J., Moilanen, I., Taanila, A., Ebeling, H., Smalley, S. L., McGough, J. J., et al. (2003). Maternal smoking and hyperactivity in 8-year-old children. *Journal of the American Academy of Child and Adolescent Psychiatry, 42,* 826–833.

Krull, K., Fuchs, C., Yurk, H., Boone, P., & Alonso, E. (2003). Neurocognitive outcome in pediatric liver transplant recipients. *Pediatric transplantation, 7,* 111–118.

Lansing, A. E., Max, J. E., Delis, D. C., Fox, P. T., Lancaster, J., Manes, F. F., et al. (2004). Verbal learning and memory after childhood stroke. *Journal of the International Neuropsychological Society, 10,* 742–752.

Lewis, B. A., Kirchner, H. L., Short, E. J., Minnes, S., Weishampel, P., Satayathum, S., et al. (2007). Prenatal cocaine and tobacco effects on children's language trajectories. *Pediatrics, 120,* 78–85.

Lewis, B. A., Singer, L. T., Short, E. J., Minnes, S., Arendt, R., Weishampel, P., et al. (2004). Four-year language outcomes of children exposed to cocaine in utero. *Neurotoxicology and Teratology, 26,* 617–627.

Lizardi, P. S., O'Rourke, M. K., & Morris, R. J. (2007). The effects of organophosphate pesticide exposure on Hispanic children's cognitive and behavioral functioning. *Journal of Pediatric Psychology, 33,* 1–11.

Mattson, S. N., Calarco, K. E., & Lang, A. R. (2006). Focused and shifting attention in children with heavy prenatal alcohol exposure. *Neuropsychology, 20,* 361–369.

Max, J. E., Robin, D. A., Taylor, H. G., Yeates, K. O., Fox, P. T., Lancaster, J. L., et al. (2004). Attention function after childhood stroke. *Journal of the International Neuropsychological Society, 10,* 976–986.

McLaughlin, T. F., Williams, B. F., & Howard, V. F. (1998). Suggested behavioral interventions in the classroom to assist students prenatally exposed to drugs. *Behavioral Interventions, 13*, 91–109.

Mendley, S. R., & Zelko, F. A. (1999). Improvement in specific aspects of neuro-cognitive performance in children after renal transplantation. *Kidney International, 56*, 318–323.

Ment, L. R., Vohr, B., Allan, W., Katz, K. H., Schneider, K. C., Westerveld, M., et al. (2003). Change in cognitive function over time in very low-birth-weight infants. *Journal of the American Medical Association, 289*, 705–711.

Merke, D. P., Giedd, J. N., Keil, M. F., Mehlinger, S. L., Wiggs, E. A., Holzer, S., et al. (2005). Children experience cognitive decline despite reversal of brain atrophy one year after resolution of Cushing syndrome. *The Journal of Clinical Endocrinology and Metabolism, 90*, 2531–2536.

Moore, B. D. (2005). Neurocognitive outcomes in survivors of childhood cancer. *Journal of Pediatric Psychology, 30*, (1), 51–63.

Morrow, C. E., Vogel, A. L., Anthony, J. C., Ofir, A. Y., Dausa, A. T., & Bandstra, E. S. (2004). Expressive and receptive language functioning in preschool children with prenatal cocaine exposure. *Journal of Pediatric Psychology, 29*, 543–554.

Mulhern, R. K., Fairclough, D., & Ochs, J. (1991). A prospective comparison of neuropsychologic performance of children surviving leukemia who received 18-Gy, or 24-Gy, or no cranial irradiation. *Journal of Clinical Oncology, 9*, 1348–1356.

Nigg, J. T., & Breslau, N. (2007). Prenatal smoking exposure, low birth weight, and disruptive behavior disorders. *Journal of the American Academy of Child and Adolescent Psychiatry, 46*, 362–369.

Nigg, J. T., Knottnerus, G. M., Martel, M. M., Nikolas, M., Cavanagh, K., Karmaus, W., et al. (2008). Low blood lead levels associated with clinically diagnosed attention-deficit/hyperactivity disorder and mediated by weak cognitive control. *Biological Psychiatry, 63*, 325–331.

Noland, J. S., Singer, L. T., Arendt, R. E., Minnes, S., Short, E. J., & Bearer, C. F. (2003). Executive functioning in preschool-age children prenatally exposed to alcohol, cocaine, and marijuana. *Alcoholism: Clinical and Experimental Research, 27*, 647–656.

Noland, J. S., Singer, L. T., Short, E. J., Minnes, S., Arendt, R. E., Kirchner, H. L., et al. (2005). Prenatal drug exposure and selective attention in preschoolers. *Neurotoxicology and Teratology, 27*, 429–438.

Noll, R. B., Reiter-Purtill, J., Vannatta, K., Gerhardt, C. A., & Short, A. (2007). Peer relationships and emotional well-being of children with sickle cell disease: A controlled replication. *Child Neuropsychology, 13*, 173–187.

O'Brien, L. M., Mervis, C. B., Holbrook, C. R., Bruner, J. L., Smith, N. H., McNally, N., et al. (2004). Neurobehavioral correlates of sleep-disordered breathing in children. *Journal of Sleep Research, 13*, 165–172.

O'Dougherty, M., Wright, F. S., Loewenson, R. B., & Torres, F. (1985). Cerebral dysfunction after chronic hypoxia in children. *Neurology, 35*, 42–46.

Oerbeck, B., Sundet, K., Kase, B. F., & Heyerdahl, S. (2003). Congenital hypothyroidism: influence of disease severity and L-thyroxine treatment on intellectual, motor, and school-associated outcomes in young adults. *Pediatrics, 112*(4), 923–930.

Patenaude, A. F., & Kupst, M. J. (2005). Psychosocial functioning in pediatric cancer. *Journal of Pediatric Psychology, 30,* 9–27.

Pearson, D. A., McGrath, N. M., Nozyce, M., Nichols, S. L., Raskino, C., Brouwers, P., et al. (2000). Predicting HIV disease progression in children using measures of neuropsychological and neurological functioning. *Pediatrics, 10*(6). Available at: http://www.pediatrics.org/cgi/content/full/106/6/e76.

Peterson, C. C., Johnson, C. E., Ramirez, L. Y., Huestis, S., Pai, A. L. H., Demaree, H. A., et al. (2008). A meta-analysis of the neuropsychological sequelae of chemotherapy-only treatment for pediatric acute lymphoblastic leukemia. *Pediatric Blood Cancer, 51,* 99–104.

Peterson, J., Taylor, H. G., Minich, N., Klein, N., & Hack, M. (2006). Subnormal head circumference in very low birth weight children: Neonatal correlates and school-age consequences. *Early Human Development, 82,* 325–334.

Pietz, J., Peter, J., Graf, R., Rauterberg-Ruland, I., Rupp, A., Sontheimer, D., et al (2004). Physical growth and neurodevelopmental outcome of nonhandicapped low-risk children born preterm. *Early Human Development, 79,* 131–143.

Potgieter, S., Vervisch, J., & Lagae, L. (2003). Event related potentials during attention tasks in VLBW children with and without attention deficit disorder. *Clinical Neurophysiology, 114,* 1841–1849.

Premji, S., Benzies, K., Serrett, K., & Hayden, K. A. (2006). Research-based interventions for children and youth with a fetal alcohol spectrum disorder: Revealing the gap. *Child: Care, Health, and Development, 33,* 389–397.

Pulsifer, M. B., & Aylward, E. H. (2000). Human immunodeficiency virus. In K. O. Yeates, M. D. Ris, & H. G. Taylor (Eds.), *Pediatric neuropsychology research, theory, and practice* (pp. 381–402). New York: Guilford.

Pulsifer, M. B., Radonovich, K., Belcher, H. M., & Butz, A. M. (2004). Intelligence and school readiness in preschool children with prenatal drug exposure. *Child Neuropsychology, 10,* 89–101.

Rasmussen, C., Horne, K., & Witol, A. (2006). Neurobehavioral functioning in children with fetal alcohol spectrum disorder. *Child Neuropsychology, 12,* 453–468.

Raymond-Speden, E., Tripp, G., Lawrence, B., & Holdaway, D. (2000). Intellectual, neuropsychological, and academic functioning in long-term survivors of leukemia. *Journal of Pediatric Psychology, 25,* 59–68.

Raz, S., Glogowski-Kawamoto, B., Yu, A. W., Kronenberg, M. E., Hopkins, T. L., Lauterbach, M. D., et al. (1998). The effects of perinatal hypoxic risk on developmental outcome in early and middle childhood: A twin study. *Neuropsychology, 12,* 459–467.

Rovet, J. F. (2000). Diabetes. In K. O. Yeates, M. D. Ris, & H. G. Taylor (Eds.), *Pediatric neuropsychology research, theory, and practice* (pp. 336–365). New York: Guilford.

Rovet, J. F., & Ehrlich, R. (2000). Psychoeducational outcome in children with early-treated congenital hypothyroidism. *Pediatrics, 105*(3), 515–522.

Rozenblatt, S. (2008). Endocrinological disorders. In C. L. Castillo (Ed.), *Children with complex medical issues in schools* (pp. 185–212). New York: Springer.

Savage, J., Brodsky, N. L., Malmud, E., Giannetta, J. M., & Hurt, H. (2005). Attentional functioning and impulse control in cocaine-exposed and control children at age 10 years. *Developmental and Behavioral Pediatrics, 26,* 42–47.

Schatz, J., Craft, S., Koby, M., & DeBaun, M. R. (2004). Asymmetries in visual-spatial processing following childhood stroke. *Journal of the International Neuropsychological Society, 10,* 340–352.

Schatz, J., Kramer, J. H., Ablin, A., & Matthay, K. K. (2000). Processing speed, working memory, and IQ: A developmental model of cognitive deficits following cranial radiation therapy. *Neuropsychology, 14,* 189–200.

Schatz, J., & Roberts, C. W. (2007). Neurobehavioral impact of sickle cell disease in early childhood. *Journal of the International Neuropsychological Society, 13,* 933–943.

Schneider, J. C., & Walsh, K. S. (2008). HIV/AIDS. In C. L. Castillo (Ed.), *Children with complex medical issues in schools* (pp. 253–277). New York: Springer.

Schneider, W., Wolke, D., Schlagmüller, M., & Meyer, R. (2004). Pathways to school achievement in very preterm and full term children. *European Journal of Psychology of Education, 19,* 385–406.

Schonfeld, A. M., Paley, B., Frankel, F., & O'Connor, M. J. (2006). Executive functioning predicts social skills following prenatal alcohol exposure. *Child Neuropsychology, 12,* 439–452.

Schroder, M. D., Snyder, P. J., Sielski, I., & Mayes, L. (2004). Impaired performance of children exposed in utero to cocaine on a novel test of visuospatial working memory. *Brain and Cognition, 55,* 409–412.

Shanbhag, M. C., Rutstein, R. M., Zaoutis, T., Zhao, H., Chao, D., & Radcliffe, J. (2005). Neurocognitive functioning in pediatric human immunodeficiency virus infection: Effects of combined therapy. *Archives of Pediatrics & Adolescent Medicine, 159,* 651–656.

Singer, L. T., Minnes, S., Short, E., Arendt, R., Farkas, K., Lewis, B., Klein, N., Russ, S., Min, M., Meeyoung, O., & Kirchner, H. L. (2004). Cognitive outcomes of preschool children with prenatal cocaine exposure. *Journal of American Medical Association, 29,* 2448–2456.

Snow, J. H. (1999). Executive processes for children with spina bifida. *Children's Health Care, 28,* 241–253.

Snyder, E. H., Davis, D. W., Burns, B. M., & Robinson, J. B. (2007). Examining attention networks in preschool children born with very low birth weights. *Journal of Early Childhood and Infant Psychology, 3,* 185–203.

Steele, R. G., Nelson, T. D., & Cole, B. P. (2007). Psychosocial functioning of children with AIDS and HIV infection: Review of the literature from a socioecological framework. *Journal of Developmental and Behavioral Pediatrics, 28,* 58–69.

Steen, R. G., Fineberg-Buchner, C., Hankins, G., Weiss, L., Prifitera, A., & Mulhern, R. K. (2005). Cognitive deficits in children with sickle cell disease. *Journal of Child Neurology, 20,* 102–107.

Stewart, P. W., Reihman, J., Lonky, E. I., Darvill, T. J., & Pagano, J. (2003). Cognitive development in preschool children prenatally exposed to PCBs and MeHg. *Neurotoxicology and Teratology, 25,* 11–22.

Stewart, S., Campbell, R. A., Kennard, B., Nici, J., Silver, C. H., Waller, D. A., et al. (1995). Neuropsychological correlates of cystic fibrosis in patients 5 to 8 years old. *Children's Health Care, 24,* 159–173.

Stores, G., Ellis, A. J., Wiggs, L., Crawford, C., & Thomson, A. (1998). Sleep and psychological disturbance in nocturnal asthma. *Archives of Disease in Childhood, 78,* 413–419.

Streissguth, A. P., Barr, H. M., Bookstein, F. L., Sampson, P. D., & Olson, H. C. (1999). The long-term neurocognitive consequences of prenatal alcohol exposure: A 14-year study. *Psychological Science, 10,* 186–190.

Suratt, P. M., Peruggia, M., D'Andrea, L., Diamond, R., Barth, J. T., Nikova, M., et al. (2006). Cognitive function and behavior of children with adenotonsillar hypertrophy suspected of having obstructive sleep-disordered breathing. *Pediatrics, 118,* 771–781.

Swift, A. V., Cohen, M. J., Hynd, G. W., Wisenbaker, J. M., McKie, K. M., Makari, G., et al. (1989). Neuropsychologic impairment in children with sickle cell anemia. *Pediatrics, 84*1077–1085.

Taylor, H. G., Minich, N., Bangert, B., Filipek, P. A., & Hack, M. (2004). Long-term neuropsychological outcomes of very low birth weight: Associations with early risks for periventricular brain insults. *Journal of the International Neuropsychological Society, 10,* 987–1004.

Taylor, H. G., Minich, N. M., Klein, N., & Hack, M. (2004). Longitudinal outcomes of very low birth weight: Neuropsychological findings. *Journal of the International Neuropsychological Society, 10,* 149–163.

Taylor, H. G., Schatschneider, C., & Minich, N. M. (2000). Longitudinal outcomes of Haemophilus influenzae meningitis in school-age children. *Neuropsychology, 14,* 509–518.

Thompson, R. J., Gustafson, K. E., Gil, K. M., Godfrey, J., & Murphy, L. M. (1998). Illness specific patterns of psychological adjustment and cognitive adaptational processes in children with cystic fibrosis and sickle cell disease. *Journal of Clinical Psychology, 54,* 121–128.

Thompson, W. W., Price, C., Goodson, B., Shay, D. K., Benson, P., Hinrichsen, V. L., et al. (2007). Early thimerosal exposure and neuropsychological outcomes at 7 to 10 years. *New England Journal of Medicine, 357,* 1281–1292.

Todaro, J. F., Fennell, E. B., Sears, S. F., Rodrigue, J. R., & Roche, A. K. (2000). Review: Cognitive and psychological outcomes in pediatric heart transplantation. *Journal of Pediatric Psychology, 25,* 567–576.

Trauner, D. A., Panyard-Davis, J. L., & Ballantyne, A. O. (1996). Behavioral differences in school age children after perinatal stroke. *Assessment, 3,* 265–276.

Uecker, A., & Nadel, L. (1996). Spatial locations gone awry: Object and spatial memory deficits in children with fetal alcohol syndrome. *Neuropsychologia, 34,* 209–223.

Uema, S. F. H., Pignatari, S. S. N., Fujita, R. R., Moreira, G. A., Pradella-Hallinan, M., & Weckx, L. (2007). Assessment of cognitive learning function in children with obstructive sleep breathing disorders. *Brazilian Journal of Otorhinolaryngology, 73,* 315–320.

Vicari, S., Caravale, B., Carlesimo, G. A., Casadei, A. M., & Allemand, F. (2004). Spatial working memory deficits in children at ages 3–4 who were low birth weight, preterm infants. *Neuropsychology, 18*, 673–678.

Wacha, V. H., & Obrzut, J. E. (2007). Effects of fetal alcohol syndrome on neuropsychological function. *Journal of Developmental and Physical Disabilities, 19*, 217–226.

Wang, W. (2007). Central nervous system complications of sickle cell disease in children: an overview. *Child Neuropsychology, 13*, 103–119.

Wang, W., Enos, L., Gallagher, D., Thompson, R., Guarini, L., Vichinsky, E., et al. (2001). Neuropsychologic performance in school-aged children with sickle cell disease: A report from the Cooperative Study of Sickle Cell Disease. *Journal of Pediatrics, 139*, 391–397.

Warner, T. D., Behnke, M., Eyler, F. D., Padgett, K., Leonard, C., Hou, W., et al. (2006). Diffusion tensor imaging of frontal white matter and executive functioning in cocaine-exposed children. *Pediatrics, 118*, 2014–2024.

Wetherington, C. E., & Duquette, P. J. (2008). Solid organ transplant. In C. L. Castillo (Ed.), *Children with complex medical issues in schools* (pp. 407–433). New York: Springer.

Williams, J. H. G., & Ross, L. (2007). Consequences of prenatal toxin exposure for mental health in children and adolescents: A systematic review. *European Journal of Child and Adolescent Psychiatry, 16*, 243–253.

Wray, J., Long, T., Radley-Smith, R., & Yacoub, M. (2001). Returning to school after heart or heart-lung transplantation: How well do children adjust? *Transplantation, 72*, 100–106.

Wray, J., & Radley-Smith, R. (2006). Longitudinal assessment of psychological functioning in children after heart or heart-lung transplantation. *The Journal of Heart and Lung Transplantation, 25*, 345–352.

CHAPTER 28

Assessing and Intervening with Children with Brain Tumors

ELIZABETH L. BEGYN and CHRISTINE L. CASTILLO

P EDIATRIC CANCER, INCLUDING brain tumors and leukemia, is the second leading cause of death in children under the age of 15 in the United States, with 9,100 new cases diagnosed each year. With medical advances in treatment, the current five-year survival rate for brain tumor survivors has increased from 50 percent to 75 percent in the last 25 years (Bleyer, 1999). Leukemia and central nervous system (CNS) tumors account for over half of new cancer cases each year (Altman & Sarg, 2000). Improvements in survival can be attributed to the introduction of new and improved therapies, namely chemotherapy, bone marrow transplants (BMT), and radiation therapy; centralization of care; and improved supportive care, including the introduction of antiemetic drugs and central venous catheters (Eiser, 2004).

The American Brain Tumor Association (ABTA) defines brain tumors as "abnormal growths in the brain resulting from cells reproducing in an uncontrolled manner" (2005). Each year, 2,200 brain tumors are diagnosed in children and adolescents in the United States (Bleyer, 1999). Brain tumors represent the second most common form of pediatric cancer (affecting 3.45 per 100,000 children younger than age 15), secondary to leukemia, and are the leading cause of death from childhood cancer (Tomita, 2000). However, survival rates vary given the type of tumor (Butler & Haser, 2006). Depending on the type and location of the brain tumor, late medical effects may include poor manual dexterity, seizures, hand-eye coordination deficits, hemiplegia (i.e., paralysis on one side of the body), primary thyroid dysfunction, infertility, chronic pain, or vision or hearing loss (Anderson et al., 2001; Barr et al., 1999).

MAJOR TYPES OF BRAIN TUMORS

Glial cell tumors, also known as astrocytomas and gliomas, account for 52 percent of all CNS malignancies in children and are the most common type of pediatric brain tumor (Fuemmeler, Elkin, & Mullins, 2002). Astrocytes are star-shaped cells arising from connective tissue. When they form tumors, they are known as astrocytomas, mostly in the cerebrum, and described by their degree of malignancy (i.e., low-grade, mid-grade, and high-grade). Juvenile benign pilocytic astrocytomas, a common low-grade astrocytoma, are most commonly found in the cerebellum, with peak incidence between 5 and 14 years of age (Armstrong & Mulhern, 1999; Buschmann, Gers, & Hildebrandt, 2003; Lo et al., 2008). Up to 70 percent of cases are completely resected, although radiation and chemotherapy may also be necessary. The five-year survival rate for low-grade astrocytomas is promising and has been reported to be up to 95 percent. High-grade gliomas, such as anaplastic astrocytomas or glioblastomas, are aggressive tumors that are more likely to spread to neighboring healthy tissue (ABTA, 2005). The median age of diagnosis for children with high-grade gliomas is between 9 and 10 years, and they occur primarily in the cerebral hemispheres (Children's Hospital Boston, n.d.). Treatment usually involves neurosurgery in combination with radiation therapy and chemotherapy. The five-year survival rate for high-grade gliomas is less than 30 percent, with some documenting survival to be as low as 10 percent (Tamber & Rutka, 2003). For a review of these and other common pediatric tumors, please see Table 28.1.

Brain stem gliomas account for 10 to 20 percent of pediatric brain tumors (Fuemmeler et al., 2002). Approximately three-fourths of cases are diagnosed before the age of 20 (Landolfi & Venkataramana, 2006), with a mean age of onset around 6 years. These tumors are typically highly aggressive and can be characterized by their distinct anatomical locations within the diffuse intrinsic pontine, tectal, and cervicomedullary regions (Landolfi & Venkataramana, 2006). Surgical resection is possible for isolated tumors that arise out of the brain stem, medulla, and upper portion of the spinal cord. However, they are not typically treated via neurosurgery due to their remote location and the complex functions they support (Medical Center of Central Georgia, 2002). Rather, treatment typically involves radiation therapy and/or chemotherapy. The survival rate for the majority of children diagnosed with a typical brain stem glioma is less than one year (St. Jude Children's Research Hospital, 2008) and has been documented to be less than 5 percent.

Primary neuroectodermal tumors (PNETs) are also a common type of pediatric brain tumor. Medulloblastomas are the most common form of PNET and account for 10 to 20 percent of all pediatric brain tumors (Fuemmeler et al., 2002; Ulrich & Pomeroy, 2003). Medulloblastomas are localized to the

Table 28.1
Major Types of Pediatric Brain Tumors

Type of Tumor	Typical Location	Age of Onset/ Diagnosis	Treatment	5-year Survival Rate
Gliomas				
Low-grade	Mostly in the cerebellum	Peak incidence between 5 and 14 years	NS, possibly RT or CT	65–95%
High-grade	Mostly in the cerebral hemispheres	Median age is between 9 and 10 years	NS, RT, and CT	<30%
Brain stem glioma	Brainstem	Peak incidence between 5 and 10 years	RT and/or CT	<5%
PNETs— Medulloblastoma	Cerebellum	80% identified before age 14, with mean age at 6 years	NS, RT, and/or CT	65–80%
Ependymoma	Cerebellum (<4 years), cerebral hemispheres (>4 years)	60% identified before 5 years	NS and RT and/or CT	>70%

Note: CT = Chemotherapy; NS = Neurosurgery; PNET = Primary Neuroectodermal Tumor; RT = Radiation therapy.

cerebellum and affect males four times more frequently than females. While 80 percent of cases are identified in children before the age of 14, the mean age at diagnosis is 6 years (Armstrong & Mulhern, 1999). Treatment typically involves neurosurgery, followed by chemotherapy and radiation therapy. The five-year survival rate is approximately 65 percent (Butler & Haser, 2006), although others have documented up to 80 percent survival rate.

Finally, *ependymal tumors* account for 5 to 10 percent of all pediatric brain tumors (Ater, Weinberg, Maor, Moore, & Copeland, 2005). Approximately 60 percent of cases are diagnosed in children before the age of 5 years (Varni, Blount, & Quiggins, 1998). While the majority of ependymomas arise in the posterior fossa region (i.e., cerebellum) in children younger than 4 years at diagnosis, these tumors are often located in the cerebral hemispheres in older children (Sala et al., 1998). Treatment usually involves surgical resection followed by radiation therapy and/or chemotherapy. Additionally, a shunt is often required to reduce intracranial pressure in the patient (ABTA, 2005). The current five-year survival rate for children with ependymal tumors with no residual tumor found on postoperative brain images is over 70 percent (Beers & Berkow, 1999).

VARIABLES CONTRIBUTING TO NEUROCOGNITIVE FUNCTIONING

Type of Treatment

Most treatment regimens are multimodal and include a combination of surgery, chemotherapy, and radiation therapy. Given the complex interaction and exacerbation of treatment effects when multiple methods are used, it is often difficult to distinguish specific treatment effects (Moore, 2005). Nevertheless, the following sections attempt to detail the common effects of each treatment modality in isolation, as well as the combined effect of multiple treatment methods.

Neurosurgery

Neurosurgery is typically the primary treatment for pediatric brain tumors, which unfortunately places brain structures at additional risk for further damage because healthy tissue may also be removed in order to resect as much of the tumor as possible (Armstrong, Blumberg, & Toledano, 1999). Postoperative complications can include infection, hydrocephalus, vision loss, speech and language impairments, severe coordination problems, seizures, and ataxia (Mulhern, 1994; Schwartz, Hobbie, & Constine, 2005).

Children treated by neurosurgery alone demonstrate less severe declines in their intelligence scores over time than children treated with additional therapies (e.g., radiation therapy; Mulhern, Merchant, Gajjar, Reddick, & Kun, 2004), but may still experience a decline in certain functions based on the area of the brain involved. For example, children who underwent surgical resection for a posterior fossa tumor were more likely to exhibit short-term memory impairments, attention (i.e., sustained attention) deficits, executive functioning (e.g., organization and planning) deficits, slower processing speed, semantic memory deficits, and visual-constructive difficulties (Steinlin et al., 2003). Furthermore, children treated via neurosurgery are placed at increased risk for mild to moderate deficits in the areas of nonverbal reasoning, motor output, verbal memory, and visuospatial processing and memory (Carpentieri et al., 2003). For the most part, more complete resections improve the efficacy of additional therapies (i.e., chemotherapy and radiotherapy) and are associated with better cognitive outcomes (Ater et al., 2005; Strother et al., 2002).

Chemotherapy

Chemotherapy drugs are highly toxic medications that prevent and interfere with the growth and reproduction of cancer cells. Common chemotherapy agents used in children include vincristine, carboplatin, methotrexate, and cyclophosphamide (Ulrich & Pomeroy, 2003). Chemotherapy agents are used in the pediatric cancer population for several reasons. After radiation therapy and/or surgery, chemotherapy is used to reduce the risk of metastatic recurrence; this is known as adjuvant chemotherapy (Venes & Thomas, 2001). In multi-drug regimens, which is quite common, more than one chemotherapy agent is used to overcome drug resistance and increase chances for complete cancer remission; this is known as combination chemotherapy. A common method of chemotherapy involves intrathecal chemotherapy (ITC), which is a technique used to administer chemotherapeutic agents directly into the cerebral spinal fluid (CSF) space, allowing tumor cells to be exposed to higher concentrations of the drugs (Tomita, 2000).

Although most studies have found that chemotherapy is less harmful than cranial irradiation, approximately 20 to 30 percent of children treated with chemotherapy demonstrate neurocognitive impairments (Mulhern & Butler, 2004). Children treated via intrathecal chemotherapy are at risk for developing nonverbal learning difficulties, potentially requiring special education services (Armstrong et al., 1999). After reviewing available literature in the pediatric leukemia population, Moleski (2000) concluded that CNS chemotherapy is harmful and should not be considered safer than cranial irradiation, cautioning that the late effects are still largely unknown.

RADIATION THERAPY

Radiation therapy is often used in children with brain tumors, either locally to the tumor site or to the entire brain and spinal cord (Anderson et al., 2001), with typical doses ranging between 30 gray (Gy) to 60 Gy. Different types of radiation therapy include conventional radiotherapy, focal radiotherapy, craniospinal radiotherapy, stereotactic radiotherapy, and brachytherapy. Although the goal of irradiation is to damage the reproductive ability of tumor cells and is seen as an effective treatment modality, use of such therapy in the brain has been documented to cause demyelination and white matter disease (Burger & Boyko, 1991).

Neurocognitive decline associated with cranial irradiation has been identified in the areas of visual memory, verbal fluency, executive functioning, and visuomotor integration (Spiegler, Bouffet, Greenberg, Rukta, & Mabbott, 2004). Mulhern and colleagues (2001) reported that the late effects of radiation therapy are largely responsible for the gradual decline in neurocognitive abilities often found in pediatric brain tumor survivors. Furthermore, children treated with cranial irradiation are at increased risk for adjustment difficulties (Armstrong & Mulhern, 1999). Children treated before age 4 with whole brain radiation are at the greatest risk for cognitive decline (Mulhern, Hancock, Fairclough, & Kun, 1992).

COMBINATION TREATMENT

Survivors treated with a combination of treatments (e.g., cranial irradiation, intrathecal chemotherapy, and/or neurosurgery) are at increased risk for neurocognitive impairments. Treatment involving cranial irradiation in combination with intrathecal methotrexate has devastating effects on cognitive abilities (Butler, Hill, Steinherz, Meyers, & Finley, 1994). Childhood survivors of medulloblastomas previously treated with chemotherapy in addition to craniospinal irradiation are at increased risk for declines in health status, quality of life, physical activity, and behavioral and emotional functioning, requiring more therapeutic support than children treated with craniospinal irradiation alone (Bull, Spoudeas, Yadegarfar, & Kennedy, 2007). Furthermore, children treated with a combination of chemotherapy and cranial irradiation exhibit more significant attention and information processing speed deficits than children treated with chemotherapy alone (Anderson, Godber, Smibert, Weiskop, & Ekert, 2004).

LOCATION OF THE BRAIN TUMOR

Although Mulhern and colleagues (1992) found that tumor location has minimal effect on neurocognitive abilities in survivors, the areas of neurocognitive deficits may indeed vary depending on the location of the tumor. For example, children with tumors in the cerebral hemispheres are at increased risk for verbal or nonverbal deficits, while children with midline tumors are more susceptible to attention, memory, and motor deficits (Moore, 2005). While children surviving brain stem tumors may exhibit average neurocognitive abilities, they may present with gross motor impairments.

AGGRESSIVENESS OF TREATMENT

Survivors of brain tumors are at increased risk for more severe cognitive deficits based on the aggressiveness of their treatment (Armstrong et al., 1999; Butler & Copeland, 1993; Fuemmeler et al., 2002; Winqvist, Vainionpaa, Kokkonen, & Lanning, 2001). Kieffer-Renaux and colleagues (2000) reported that survivors of medulloblastomas treated with 25 Gy of radiation demonstrate higher overall intelligence compared to children treated with 35 Gy, concluding that there is a negative correlation between strength of the radiation dose and intelligence. Furthermore, children treated with radiation doses of 36 Gy or higher exhibited more rapid cognitive decline than lower doses in children treated for medulloblastomas (Palmer et al., 2001). In addition, more intensive chemotherapy regimens have been associated with more adjustment problems (Vainionpaa, 1993; Zebrack & Zeltzer, 2003).

The age of diagnosis is another important contributor to neurocognitive functioning in pediatric brain tumor survivors. Vainionpaa (1993) suggested that younger children with less mature central nervous systems are more susceptible to cytotoxic therapy, causing greater mobility struggles than older children being treated for cancer. Palmer and colleagues (2001) reported that children with medulloblastomas treated before the age of 8 years demonstrated greater declines in the area of nonverbal abstract reasoning, general fund of information, and overall cognitive ability compared to children treated after 8 years of age. Additional studies have found that children treated before the age of 5 years exhibited more cognitive decline, memory deficits, and motor problems than children treated after the age of 5 (Armstrong et al., 1999; Winqvist et al., 2001). Overall, substituting or delaying the use of treatment, especially cranial irradiation, may reduce the negative effects on neurocognitive development (Ater et al., 1997).

TIME SINCE TREATMENT

The time that has lapsed since termination of treatment is another factor affecting the neurocognitive outcome of pediatric cancer survivors. Neurocognitive deficits tend to be progressive and emerge gradually following treatment (Moore, 2005; Mulhern, 1994). Survivors may evidence a plateau in their skills, a slower achievement of skills relative to their peers, or potentially a decline in skill set. Overall, deficits are likely related to difficulty learning and acquiring new information after treatment, as opposed to loss of previously learned information (Mulhern, Merchant, et al., 2004).

REVIEW OF NEUROCOGNITIVE ABILITIES IN PEDIATRIC BRAIN TUMOR SURVIVORS

VISUAL-MOTOR INTEGRATION AND SENSORY-MOTOR ABILITIES

Visual-motor integration deficits and slower motor output have been noted in children with brain tumors (Carpentieri et al., 2003; Coniglio & Blackman, 1995; Winqvist et al., 2001). Kieffer-Renaux and colleagues (2000) found that survivors of medulloblastomas demonstrate deficits in visuo-constructive skills and manual dexterity, regardless of the strength of radiation dose. Fine motor skills and perceptual-motor skills have also been found to be negatively affected by inthrathecal chemotherapy during the acute phase of treatment (Moleski, 2000). Given this set of difficulties, children may evidence functional fine motor difficulties that impact their ability to take care of daily hygiene needs (e.g., dressing, toileting, bathing). They may also struggle with academic tasks, especially those that require writing or manipulation of materials.

ATTENTION AND CONCENTRATION

The most profound neurocognitive deficits that have been documented in pediatric cancer survivors involve attention and concentration abilities, which are related to a decrease in the volume of white matter (Mulhern & Butler, 2004; Reddick et al., 2003). Specifically, exposure to cranial irradiation places survivors at increased risk for impairments in filtering, focusing, and sustained attention (Lockwood, Bell, & Colegrove, 1999; Mulhern et al., 2001). Additionally, survivors have demonstrated increased susceptibility to distraction, and evidence greater difficulty focusing during conditions requiring attentional processing (Rodgers, Horrocks, Britton, & Kernahan, 1999). Attentional deficits may then increase the risk for observed cognitive and academic decline (Reddick et al., 2003). Although the etiology of these attention difficulties is quite different than for children without significant medical histories but with a diagnosis of Attention Deficit Hyperactivity Disorder—Predominantly Inattentive Type (ADHD-I), environmental modifications and interventions can be just as helpful.

VISUAL-SPATIAL PROCESSES

Johnson and colleagues (1994) found that childhood survivors of medulloblastomas exhibit significant perceptual organization deficits. While some studies have documented visual-spatial impairments in survivors of other posterior fossa tumors (Schmahmann, 2004; Steinlin et al., 2003), other studies have documented intact skills (Ater et al., 1996). For those children who do indeed experience difficulty, processing of visual information can be quite challenging. It may impact their ability to complete mathematics problems (e.g., errors in computation due to misalignment of the columns in numerical operations, poor spatial reasoning in geometry), or complete other visually demanding tasks (e.g., copying information from the chalkboard).

LANGUAGE PROCESSES

Language functioning in pediatric brain tumor survivors depends largely on the area and type of tumor they experience. For example, expressive language impairments have been documented in children treated for posterior fossa tumors via neurosurgery (Schmahmann, 2004). Ribi and colleagues (2005) reported that approximately half of a sample of childhood survivors of medulloblastomas exhibited language deficits.

LEARNING AND MEMORY

Memory impairments have been reported in 50 to 75 percent of children with brain tumors (Armstrong et al., 1999). Working memory abilities are reportedly quite vulnerable to cranial irradiation, with processing speed deficits thought to be at least partially responsible for working memory impairments observed in survivors (Butler & Mulhern, 2005). Reddick and colleagues (2003) found that survivors exhibit verbal memory deficits. More specifically, Reeves and colleagues (2006) hypothesized that survivors exhibit an immediate, mild, and stable insult on verbal memory that does not change with time.

EXECUTIVE FUNCTIONS

Executive functioning skills "allow an individual to perceive stimuli from his or her environment, respond adaptively, flexibly change direction, anticipate future goals, consider consequences, and respond in an integrated or common-sense way" (Baron, 2004, p. 135). Lezak (1995) defines the four main components of executive functioning as volition, planning, purposive action, and effective performance. Some common subdomains of executive functioning include attention and concentration, planning and organization, working memory, set-shifting, concept formation, problem-solving, and self-regulation and inhibition, among others. Given that many of these skills are not expected to fully develop until later adolescence or even early adulthood, it is sometimes difficult to determine if a child who has been treated for a brain tumor will exhibit such difficulties. Due to the delayed effects on neurocognitive skills that result from demyelination and general white matter dysfunction from chemo therapy and radiation (Burger & Boyko, 1991; Mulhern et al., 2001), it is not often until early to middle adolescence that significant difficulties with some of these functions are noticed. Specifically, neurocognitive decline is not unexpected in the areas of verbal fluency and executive functioning (Spiegler et al., 2004). Specifically for children who have undergone neurosurgical resection of posterior fossa tumors, difficulties with organization, planning, and other executive functions have been revealed (Steinlin et al., 2003).

PROCESSING SPEED

Slower general processing speed and reduced information processing efficiency has consistently been documented as significant areas of weakness for survivors of pediatric brain tumors treated with cranial radiation, mostly due to the global white matter pathology following treatment (Schatz, Kramer, Ablin, & Matthay, 2000). Palmer and colleagues (2001) postulated that underlying memory impairments and speed of processing deficits may be responsible for documented cognitive decline in survivors of medulloblastomas.

Cognitive Functioning

Pediatric cancer survivors exhibit more cognitive deficits compared to healthy peers (Winqvist et al., 2001). Nonverbal cognitive abilities are more susceptible to cancer treatment compared to verbal reasoning abilities, averaging a mean difference of 7.3 standard score points between these cognitive domains (Poggi et al., 2005). Spiegler and colleagues (2004) found a gradual decline in cognitive abilities in survivors of posterior fossa brain tumors over a four-year time period, especially in younger patients.

Radiation therapy has been found to be the most important treatment factor affecting a child's cognitive functioning, with craniospinal irradiation having both an immediate impact along with a continuing pattern of decline over time (Palmer et al., 2001). Furthermore, radiation therapy in combination with intrathecal methotrexate, history of hydrocephalus requiring shunt placement, or younger age at diagnosis have been documented to be significant risk factors for cognitive dysfunction in survivors (Butler et al., 1994; Johnson et al., 1994; Mabbott, Penkman, Witol, Strother, & Bouffet, 2008; Reimers et al., 2003).

Academic Functioning

As a result of cancer and/or its treatment, pediatric brain tumor survivors are at heightened risk for future learning impairments (Armstrong & Mulhern, 1999). Survivors are at risk for academic difficulties due to loss of opportunity to learn related to hospitalization, multiple clinic visits, and treatment side effects (Armstrong et al., 1999). Many brain tumor survivors previously treated with high doses of cranial irradiation require ongoing special education services. For example, Brown and colleagues (1998) found that more than one-third of survivors received part-time special education services following treatment, while 7 percent required full-time services; the majority of those who received services did so based on their medical diagnosis. Hays and colleagues (1997) found that adult survivors of pediatric cancer completed fewer years of school and experienced higher rates of unemployment, lower occupational status, and lower annual incomes compared to matched controls.

Psychosocial Functioning

The research is mixed as to the effect of childhood cancer on survivors' emotional and behavioral functioning. More specifically, internalizing behaviors (e.g., depression, anxiety, poor self-image, social withdrawal, somatic complaints), as well as externalizing behaviors (e.g., aggression and substance abuse), have been inconsistently reported in pediatric brain tumor survivors.

Interestingly, most studies have found minimal evidence that survivors of childhood cancer experience significant symptoms of maladjustment

(Patenaude & Kupst, 2005). Research has indicated that pediatric cancer survivors do not exhibit significantly different levels of depression, anxiety, or self-esteem compared to population norms or matched controls (Eiser, Hill, & Vance, 2000). In fact, survivors tend to endorse a positive quality of life and rate themselves as being able to effectively cope with their illness, with a high level of satisfaction in their social relationships (Zebrack & Chesler, 2002). Survivors also report a high level of satisfaction in social relationships, exhibit minimal social skills deficits, and are less likely to engage in illicit drug use and experimentation (Newby, Brown, Pawletko, Gold, & Whitt, 2000; Verrill, Schafer, Vannatta, & Noll, 2000; Zebrack & Chesler, 2002). In fact, many survivors described their experience with cancer as positive, leading to positively perceived changes, reordering of life priorities, and greater appreciation of life and relationships (Eiser et al., 2000; Zebrack & Chesler, 2002). Furthermore, when adjustment problems occur, they are likely transient, mild, and related to an aspect of the cancer or its treatment (Butler, Rizzi, & Bandilla, 2000; Van Dongen-Melman & Saunders-Woudstra, 1986).

However, research has consistently documented that a small subset of approximately 25 to 30 percent of survivors and their families exhibit significant symptoms of maladjustment, likely in areas of academic achievement, social relationships, employment, self-identity, and self-esteem (Patenaude & Kupst, 2005). Variables that have been found to contribute to survivors' psychosocial functioning include the type of disease, the form of treatment, personal characteristics, and family or other environmental factors. Better psychosocial functioning has been associated with shorter treatment duration (Koocher & O'Malley, 1981) and less functional impairment (Elkin, Phipps, Mulhern, & Fairclough, 1997). Personal factors found to be related to positive psychological functioning include older age at diagnosis; better level of functioning before diagnosis; lower level of personal distress; better cognitive functioning; positive expectations of the future; use of a repressive adaptive coping style (low distress, high restraint); and acknowledgment that a certain level of denial and avoidance can be adaptive (Boman & Bodegard, 2000; Elkin et al., 1997; Erikson & Steiner, 2001; Koocher & O'Malley, 1981; Kupst et al., 1995; Last & Grootenhuis, 1998; Mulhern, Wasserman, Friedman, & Fairclough, 1989).

COMORBIDITY

In a sample of 18 children treated for medulloblastomas between 1980 and 2000, 39 percent presented with cognitive deficits; 79 percent with attention and processing speed deficits; 64 percent with executive functioning impairments; 64 percent with significant school difficulties; 88 percent with learning and memory impairments; 56 percent with language deficits; and 50 percent with visual perception deficits (Ribi et al., 2005). Even in this small sample, it is quite apparent that children who are treated for brain tumors do not eacape at least some deleterious impact to their neurocognitive, emotional, or behavioral functioning.

While pediatric brain tumor survivors are at increased risk for neuro-cognitive impairment, it is important to note that their weaknesses may not be appropriately categorized with standard diagnostic tools. That is, many survivors may present with symptoms that resemble other childhood dis-orders, such as Attention Deficit Hyperactivity Disorder (ADHD), though the underlying etiology of their symptoms is inherently different. For exam-ple, a child who has been treated with neurosurgery, chemotherapy, and radiation is very likely to exhibit problems with sustained attention and behavioral inhibition. This child's performance on a continuous performance test may be quite impaired. However, their symptoms of inattention and impulsivity cannot be isolated from their medical history and described in a diagnosis such as ADHD. As a result, although it may be helpful to identify the extent of impairment as it relates to learning, attention, behavioral inhibition, or other similar concerns, provision of clinical diagnoses may not be appropriate. School professionals who are not aware of the child's medical history may not understand the child's limitations if only a clinical label like ADHD is used for ease of communication and service provision. Moreover, individuals providing evaluation or intervention for children with brain tumors need to cognizant of the common neurocognitive impairments (described above), despite the fact that they may meet criteria for a clinical diagnosis.

COMPONENTS OF A SCHOOL NEUROPSYCHOLOGICAL EVALUATION

Before the inception of Response-to-Intervention (RTI), standard psycho-educational batteries used in the public school system were used to identify significant discrepancies between a child's performance on measures of cognitive functioning (e.g., *Wechsler Intelligence Scale for Children, 4th Edition*; WISC-IV) and academic achievement (e.g., *Woodcock-Johnson Tests of Achieve-ment, 3rd Edition*; WJ-III). Although these measures are still used at the present time, these evaluation tools often do not adequately capture the range of strengths and weaknesses that are necessary to identify in children with diseases and disorders that affect the CNS (Fletcher-Janzen, 2005). In the pediatric brain tumor population, a standard neuropsychological evaluation is complicated by several factors. That is, neurocognitive deficits may not become evident until several years after completion of treatment. In addition, survivors of brain tumors may present with significant scatter among sub-tests; therefore, composite scores may not be a valid indicator of true functioning. Global assessments of intelligence and standardized achievement may provide useful information in terms of comparing survivors to their peers, but are limited in their function in determining adequate intervention plans.

Armstrong and colleagues (1999) proposed a developmental model to diagnose learning strengths and weaknesses within this population. Particular clinical attention should be devoted to assessing survivors' attention and concentration, processing speed, visual-motor integration, and fine motor speed and accuracy. Clinicians are urged to be cognizant of the neurocognitive instability in the brain tumor population. Retesting may be warranted at twelve- to eighteen-month intervals with ongoing content-specific assessments. Comparison of baseline and follow-up testing may demonstrate a gradual decline in the child's abilities.

The ultimate goal of neuropsychological assessment is to provide ecologically valid interventions that can be implemented in the home and school environments (Fletcher-Janzen, 2005) and should be a priority of clinicians. Collaboration between school- and hospital-based personnel involved with the child's treatment and recovery is paramount (Armstrong et al., 1999; Fletcher-Janzen, 2005). The neuropsychological assessment of pediatric cancer survivors is complex, given the unique nature of the child's medical history and the diversity of treatment within the population. Consideration of the type of treatment (e.g., neurosurgery with intrathecal methotrexate, oral vincristine, and craniospinal irradiation) must be taken into account. An ethical and competent pediatric neuropsychologist should have expertise and experience in pediatric neuro-oncology to best serve this population. School psychologists are strongly encouraged to consult with other school-based disciplines (e.g., speech-language pathologists, occupational therapists) and outpatient providers such as neurosurgeons, neuro-oncologists, and pediatric neuropsychologists.

INTERVENTIONS FOR CHILDREN WITH BRAIN TUMORS

Due to the aforementioned variability in outcome for children with brain tumors, it is impossible to describe a single intervention technique that is appropriate for all members of this group of children. Rather, intervention, and certainly accommodation, should be based on a well-defined individual evaluation that elucidates a child's strengths and weaknesses. The resulting neuropsychological profile will then lead clinicians and educators to the appropriate targets for intervention.

Before entering into a review of helpful intervention techniques and accommodations, it is perhaps more important to describe the difference between the medical and educational models of intervention, especially for caregivers and medical personnel who may be unfamiliar with these differences. When these differences are not well explained, frustration and miscommunication can certainly occur. To help clarify the difference between these models of intervention, the reader is asked to consider Susan, an 11-year-old student with mild anxiety. Under a medical model, concerns such as anxiety or excessive worry may be addressed in numerous ways, and may included implementation of psychotherapy and provision of psychotropic medication, in addition to environmental modifications. Susan's parents will likely seek assistance from their pediatrician and request additional resources. Under the educational model of treatment, only the issues that impact educational progress are typically addressed. Well-trained teachers and other school personnel may "intervene" by providing Susan frequent reassurance and praise and implementing other methods that are useful for most any child despite his or her level of anxiety. However, intervention, especially in the way of providing special education accommodations and services, would only be warranted for Susan if her anxiety is long-standing and great enough in intensity that it significantly interferes with her ability to perform on tests and interact with peers and teachers. If Susan is able to maintain her composure, despite continuing to experience elevated levels of worry, the educational model would fail to identify a significant need that requires intervention in the school setting.

Attention problems, slow processing speed, and difficulties with executive functioning skills are exceedingly common for children with brain tumors; however, there are not many evidenced-based interventions available as of yet for some of these issues specifically as they relate directly to the late effects of treatment (i.e., chemotherapy, radiation) for childhood brain tumor. There has been investigation of traditional cognitive rehabilitation models, but their use in populations other than those with traumatic brain injuries, stroke, dementia, or schizophrenia is still somewhat limited at the present time. Adaptation to weakness, coping with a decreased level of functioning, and secondary mood and anxiety difficulties are also common problems for these children following treatment, and therefore intervention methods will also be provided to address these issues. It is not possible to provide an exhaustive list of appropriate interventions for all areas of weakness; therefore, the reader is referred to additional literature for a more comprehensive look at appropriate methods of intervention for this population of children (see Schnoebelen, Perez, & Stavinoha, 2008).

The History of Cognitive Rehabilitation in Traumatic Brain Injury and Stroke

Cognitive rehabilitation, or remediation as it is sometimes called, is based upon the idea that the brain is able to change and improve given certain interventions; this idea was originally proposed by Alexander Luria in 1948. Review of the literature indicates early attempts at cognitive rehabilitation, starting most notably with Sohlberg and Mateer (1986, 1989) who were some of the earlier pioneers in developing a structured method of rehabilitation for individuals with brain injuries.

In 1997, Laatsch and colleagues (Laatsch, Jobe, Sychra, Lin, & Blend) investigated the benefits of a program called Cognitive Rehabilitation Therapy (CRT) in three adult patients with brain injury; the program was provided to the patients for a duration up to six months. The authors discovered increased regional cerebral blood flow (rCBF), as measured by single photo emission computed tomography (SPECT), in the areas of the brain that were affected by the brain injury. In addition, the authors further discovered improvements on specific measures of neuropsychological functioning, including increase in cognitive, memory, and problem-solving skills.

Cicerone and colleagues (2000) published a review article detailing the evidence-based recommendations for specific cognitive rehabilitation interventions with stroke and traumatic brain injury (TBI) survivors. At that time, 20 out of 29 Class I studies (i.e., well designed, prospective, randomized control trials) proved that cognitive rehabilitation was an effective intervention for TBI and stroke patients. Some of the functional areas improved in the various research trials include attention, communication, memory, and problem-solving. Based on the broad review of the literature at that time, practice standards were indicated for four skill domains, including visuospatial ability, cognitive-linguistic skills, functional communication, and memory. Additional practice guidelines were also formulated for numerous areas, including attention, reading comprehension, language formation, and problem-solving.

In 2005, an updated review by Cicerone and colleagues was published, indicating that cognitive rehabilitation continued to be "of significant benefit when compared with alternative treatments" (p. 1689) for individuals with a history of TBI and stroke. There was some change in the delineation of practice standards and guidelines. Specifically, standards of practice were indicated for visuospatial ability, cognitive-linguistic skills, functional communication (pragmatic language, gestural training), memory, and attention. Guidelines of practice included remediation of visual scanning, reading comprehension, language formulation, problem- solving, and unilateral left neglect.

Cognitive Rehabilitation Techniques

Research has indicated that rehabilitation should "facilitate and guide natural recovery, reinforcing positive compensation, and suppressing maladaptive behaviors" (Salazar et al., 2000, p. 3080). There are two basic methods for rehabilitation of skills: restoration and compensation. Ideally, clinicians and caregivers would have all of a child's skills restored to premorbid levels of functioning. Unfortunately, that does not occur very often, so intervention techniques offered in this section are geared more toward compensation and supplementation of weaknesses rather than toward full restoration.

Some of the methods for cognitive rehabilitation include psychotherapy, medication, computer-assisted training, behavior management, and instruction in cognitive strategies. Improvement in cognitive and language skills has also been shown following cognitive rehabilitation with computer- and telephone-assisted methods (Lo Priore, Castelnuovo, Liccone, & Liccone, 2003; Schoenberg et al., 2008; Tam et al., 2003), although these are relatively rare.

In general, rehabilitation methods are thought to be best employed in a multidisciplinary manner so that all involved individuals are actively engaged in the intervention. In the medical setting, members of the multidisciplinary team include physiatrists (rehabilitation physicians), rehabilitation therapists (physical, occupational, speech/language), social workers, neuropsychologists, psychiatrists, and many others. For children, many of these same individuals are important for the implementation of a rehabilitation program. At schools, individuals important and necessary for providing intervention include parents, teachers, therapists, and even peers. Notably, Braga, Da Paz Júnior, and Ylvisaker (2005) discovered that children with TBI participating in a cognitive rehabilitation program demonstrated greater physical and cognitive improvements when it was implemented in the context of their everyday life, rather than in a clinical environment. This finding is especially exciting in that school resources can be better utilized if information, expertise, and clinical skills are more widely disseminated for use beyond the school setting.

The following sections include a brief review of how certain techniques may be utilized specifically for children with brain tumors, including broad cognitive rehabilitation techniques designed to target general cognitive weaknesses, including executive functioning and attention; and specific techniques intended to address difficulties with attention, emotional coping, and school re-entry. Readers are referred to other chapters in this volume for a more comprehensive review of general techniques applicable to children with speech and language disorders, mood and behavior disorders, problems with memory and learning, attention problems, and executive dysfunction, which often occur for children with brain tumors.

BROAD COGNITIVE REHABILITATION IN CHILDHOOD CANCER

Taking from previous research on cognitive rehabilitation in other populations, Robert Butler (1998) first described his use of a modified Attention

Process Training (APT; Sohlberg & Mateer, 1986) with childhood cancer survivors, aptly named Cognitive Remediation Program (CRP). CRP combines the massed practice approach from APT with additional focus on attention and learning strategies in weekly two-hour sessions over the course of six months. It draws upon theories of general brain injury rehabilitation, special education and educational psychology, and clinical psychology (Spencer, 2006). The CRP model of cognitive rehabilitation includes strategies for task preparation, on-task behavior, and post-task behavior. Spencer reviewed the CRP model and detailed some of the tasks involved in the program. The first aspect required participants to focus on a learning task for 15 minutes in an effort to increase stamina for the course of the two-hour sessions. The second aspect is designed to instruct participants in metacognitive strategies based on their individual learning styles. These include planning and preparing for a task, maintaining performance, and checking performance after completion of a task. The third aspect involves teaching the participants to use cognitive behavioral strategies such as stress inoculation, reframing negatives into positives, and utilizing psychotherapeutic support, among others.

Results of a 1998 study (Butler) indicated that participants made significant improvements in arithmetic ability and attention. Additional research of the efficacy of the CRP on childhood cancer survivor's attention and arithmetic abilities was published in 2002 by Butler and Copeland. Based on the investigation using a comparison group that had not yet received any form of cognitive intervention, the patients who participated in CRP demonstrated a significant improvement in attention and concentration. Contrary to the previous research by Butler (1998), no improvements were noted in mathematics tasks for either group.

Several review articles (Butler & Mulhern, 2005; Mulhern & Butler, 2004; Mulhern, Merchant, et al., 2004) have been published since the initial studies on CRP that advocate for its use in combination with the application of pharmacological interventions (e.g., stimulant medication to improve attention) and environmental modifications.

In 2008, Butler and colleagues published the results of their randomized multicenter clinical trial that investigated the CRP in children with a history of cancer who were at least one year off treatment and had identified difficulties with attention. The CRP involved a two-hour weekly session occurring over the course of four to five months, for up to 20 sessions. The program included massed practice, strategy acquisition, and cognitive-behavioral interventions. At follow-up assessment, children demonstrated increased attention based on parent report and improved academic achievement. Contrary to expectations, there were no statistically significant improvements in neurocognitive function.

There are numerous other methods designed specifically for the rehabilitation of executive dysfunction, which most often have been utilized with the brain injury population. Some of these interventions include NeuroPage (Evans, Emslie, & Wilson, 1998; Hersch & Treadgold, 1994), Goal Management Training (Levine et al., 2000; Robertson, 1996), Periodic Auditory Alerts (Manly, Hawkins, Evans, Woldt, & Robertson, 2002), The Executive Plus Model (Gordon, Cantor, Ashman, & Brown, 2006), and Cogmed Working Memory Training (Klingberg et al., 2005; Westerberg & Klingberg, 2007). To date, there does not appear to be any studies utilizing these methods with the pediatric brain tumor population, and so readers are referred to the respective sources in order to review these methods.

Attention and Concentration

As previously noted, a large percent of children with a history of brain tumor and related treatment develop attention problems (Ribi et al., 2005). As a result, this is an appropriate area of initial intervention, especially since attention problems impact nearly every other area of functioning, including memory, academic performance, and even language. Although the term *attention* has numerous meanings, in this section *attention* will be conceptualized as an individual's ability to direct his or her focus for a certain period of time on specific stimuli. The definition of attention in the literature has also included processing speed; attentional control; and sustained, selective, and divided attention (Sohlberg & Mateer, 1989). Previous studies have examined the efficacy of pharmacological treatment, behavioral therapy, psychosocial interventions, biofeedback (i.e., neurofeedback), and other interventions for children with attention problems, usually in the context of a diagnosis of ADHD. Although it is assumed that some of the interventions typically used for children with ADHD may also result in benefits for children with brain tumors who develop attention problems, this cannot be guaranteed. Children who have undergone treatment for brain tumor have had their brain changed in a manner unlike children with only ADHD alone.

There have been numerous studies investigating the effects of methylphenidate (MPH) on survivors of childhood cancer. Thompson and colleagues (2001) completed a randomized, double-blind, placebo-controlled trial of MPH in children with a history of brain tumor or acute lymphoblastic leukemia (ALL) who were off-treatment (chemotherapy and/or radiation), free of cancer for at least 24 months, and performed below the 16th percentile in one or more academic areas. It was found that the children prescribed MPH demonstrated a statistically significant improvement in general attention as measured by a continuous performance test (CPT). Although there were trends for improvement on tasks of verbal memory, there were no statistically significant improvements compared to the control group.

A similar study was completed by Mulhern, Khan, and colleagues in 2004, measuring outcome by parent and teacher ratings of participants receiving a low dose (LD) or moderate dose (MD) of MPH. Compared to the placebo group, the children in the methylphenidate group demonstrated statistically significant improvements in inattention and cognitive problems according to their caregivers' responses to the *Conners' Rating Scales* (CRS); teachers also reportedly a statistically significant improvement in the level of hyperactivity. Notably, there were no differences between the LD and MD participants on the CRS findings. Teachers further noted improvements in social and academic competence on the *Social Skills Rating System* (SSRS), without differences between the LD and MD groups. For problem behaviors as rated by the SSRS, teachers also reported significant improvements, but only for the MD group.

More recently, another MPH trial was completed with childhood cancer survivors (Conklin et al., 2007). At the outset, participants were required to have omissions errors at or above the 75th percentile on a CPT; parent ratings on the ADHD Index, Hyperactivity, or Cognitive Problems/Inattention on the *Conners' Rating Scales—Revised* (CRS-R) at or above the 75th percentile; and scores in one or more areas of academic achievement at or below the 25th percentile. Following administration of MPH or a placebo, the participants completed a brief CPT, in addition to measures of verbal learning and memory; visual-auditory learning; selective attention, impulsivity, and cognitive flexibility; and academic achievement. Compared to the placebo group, the participants receiving MPH demonstrated significant gains on the measure of selective attention, impulsivity, and cognitive flexibility. The researchers also discovered that male children who were older at age of treatment and had a higher intelligence responded better to the medication intervention.

As so aptly noted by Weber and Lütschg (2002), due to the very high degree of impact on attention for childhood cancer survivors, "we have to aim to increase the quality of life by reducing the negative therapeutic sequelae" (p. 262). Overall, the use of stimulant medication, specifically MPH, may be a useful way to help improve a child's attention. As a child's attention improves, perhaps so may his or her reaction time, associative learning, and perceptual skills (Brown, Dreelin, & Dingle, 1997).

EMOTIONAL COPING

Children with a history of brain tumor and related treatments are at greater risk for developing depression and anxiety compared to their healthy peers (Cohen, 1999). They often experience a decline or loss of functioning (e.g., motor, cognitive, language). As a result, they may have to participate in hours of physical rehabilitation or other interventions that are painful and frustrating. They may also have to continue to endure frequent medical appointments and laboratory tests (e.g., brain scans, blood work), which sets them apart from their peers. Adapting to a decreased level of functioning and its impact on daily routines can lead to secondary mood dysregulation and anxiety.

As has been indicated for primary mood and anxiety disorders, cognitive behavioral therapy (CBT) paradigms and techniques can also be very effective for children who experience secondary internalizing problems. Some of the intervention methods include relaxation strategies, stress inoculation, and reframing, and are used in combination with other cognitive remediation techniques in Butler's (1998) CRP. Summarizing the National Institute for Health and Clinical Excellence's clinical reviews and guidelines for the use of CBT in children and adolescents, Muñoz-Solomando, Kendall, and Whittington (2008) found that CBT is best employed in children with anxiety, depression, obsessive-compulsive disorder, and post-traumatic stress disorder. More specifically, recent research has demonstrated that children with anxiety can be effectively treated through individual or group CBT (Liber et al., 2008), which provides flexibility to school psychologists and neuropsychologists who may have limited time to provide individual intervention to students.

It is extremely important to monitor children with a history of brain tumor for symptoms of depression and anxiety. Chronic irritability, social withdrawal, excessive worry regarding performance, and feelings of ineptitude should raise concern from teachers and other school personnel. For these children, identification and appropriate treatment is important. Identification of strengths, appropriate coping skills, and sources of support (e.g., parents, clergy) should be a part of the intervention. Worksheets and ideas for intervention can be found in the "Coping with Chronic Health Conditions" chapter of *Helping Schoolchildren with Chronic Health Conditions* (Clay, Maloney, & Gross, 2004).

School Reentry

Many children who have endured long absences from school due to their medical treatment are at risk for having difficulties with school reentry. Some of the reasons for failing to return to school for an extended period of time may include cognitive and physical fatigue, anxiety about changes in appearance (e.g., alopecia due to chemotherapy, visible surgical scars), fears of feeling left behind by peers, and other emotional factors. Prevatt, Heffer, and Lowe (2000) provided a review of school reintegration programs that targeted one or more of five target groups: the child, the family, teachers and other school personnel, the child's peers, and medical personnel. The programs included school personnel workshops, peer education, and more comprehensive programs aimed at multiple recipient groups. Prevatt and colleagues (2000) found that the programs geared toward even one recipient group (i.e., school personnel workshops, peer education) were cost effective and resulted in an increase in knowledge about the medical condition and increased comfort in interacting with the affected child. Due to the primary use of case studies in reviewing the comprehensive programs, the authors were unable to comment on the overall effectiveness.

As should occur regardless of the child's medical condition, Armstrong and colleagues (1999) recommended frequent consultation between school- and hospital-based personnel to facilitate a child's smooth transition back into school, track his or her progress, and monitor for necessary interventions. In order to facilitate this process, many hospitals offer programs that send personnel, such as education specialists or child life specialists, to the school prior to a child's return to explain the illness to their classmates and teachers. Such interventions have been found to increase self-esteem and decrease depression in survivors (Katz, Rubenstein, Hubert, & Blew, 1988). However, this should be cleared with the child and his or her parents, as some may not feel comfortable disclosing information. For ideas on how school personnel can seek consent to release this type of information, and for a list of important questions to answer, readers are directed to the school reintegration chapter in *Helping Schoolchildren with Chronic Health Conditions* (Clay, 2004).

Additionally, Eiser (2004) recommended that a manual for teachers should be available in order to provide methods to reduce anxiety about school and encourage teachers to support the child by facilitating peer interactions. Due to the long-term follow-up that many pediatric brain tumor survivors receive from medical and neuropsychological services at the local medical center, these professionals should be consulted on a regular basis and incorporated into the school treatment team.

SUMMARY

It is apparent that children who have been treated for brain tumors are at risk for a plethora of physical, cognitive, academic, and social challenges. However, with supportive and understanding school personnel, their reintegration back into the school setting after prolonged treatment can be a positive experience for all involved individuals. It is of primary importance that all school professionals who may have contact with survivors of brain tumors arm themselves with knowledge and patience so that each student's educational experience is not wrought with frustration and isolation, but with feelings of acceptance, competence, and support.

REFERENCES

Altman, R., & Sarg, M. (Eds.). (2000). *The cancer dictionary* (Rev. ed.). New York: Checkmark Books.

American Brain Tumor Association (ABTA). (2005). *A primer of brain tumors: A patient's reference manual.* Retrieved August 15, 2008, at http://www.neurosurgery.mgh. harvard.edu/abta/primer.htm.

Anderson, D. M., Rennie, K. M., Ziegler, R. S., Neglia, J. P., Robinson, L. R., & Gurney, J. G. (2001). Medical and neurocognitive late effects among survivors of childhood central nervous system tumors. *Cancer, 92,* 2709–2719.

Anderson, V. A., Godber, T., Smibert, E., Weiskop, S., & Ekert, H. (2004). Impairments in attention following treatment with cranial irradiation and chemotherapy in children. *Journal of Clinical and Experimental Neuropsychology, 26,* 684–697.

Armstrong, F. D., Blumberg, M. J., & Toledano, S. R. (1999). Neurobehavioral issues in childhood cancer. *School Psychology Review, 28,* 194–203.

Armstrong, F. D., & Mulhern, R. K. (1999). Acute lymphoblastic leukemia and brain tumors. In R. T. Brown (Ed.), *Cognitive aspects of chronic illnesses in children* (pp. 47–78). New York: Guilford.

Ater, J. L., Moore, B. D., Francis, D. J., Castillo, R., Slopis, J., & Copeland, D. R. (1996). Correlation of medical and neurosurgical events with neuropsychological status in children at diagnosis of astrocytoma: Utilization of neurological severity score. *Journal of Clinical Neurology, 11,* 462–469.

Ater, J. L., van Eys, J., Woo, S. Y., Moore, B., Copeland, D. R., & Bruner, J. (1997). MOPP chemotherapy without irradiation as primary postsurgical therapy for brain tumors in infants and young children. *Journal of Neurooncology, 32,* 243–252.

Ater, J. L., Weinberg, J. S., Maor, M. H., Moore, B. D., & Copeland, D. R. (2005). Brain tumors: Diagnosis, surgery and radiotherapy, and supportive care. In K. W. Chan & R. B. Raney, Jr. (Eds.), *Pediatric oncology* (pp. 30–49). New York: Springer.

Baron, I. S. (2004). *Neuropsychological evaluation of the child.* New York: Oxford University Press.

Barr, R. D., Simpson, T., Whitton, A., Rush, B., Furlong, W., & Feeny, D. H. (1999). Health-related quality of life in survivors of tumours of the central nervous system in childhood—a preference-based approach to measurement in a cross-sectional study. *European Journal of Cancer, 35,* 248–255.

Beers, M. H., & Berkow, R. (1999). *The Merck manual of diagnosis and therapy* (17th ed.). Whitehouse Station, NJ: Merck Research Laboratories.

Bleyer, W. A. (1999). Epidemiology of childhood brain tumors. *Child's Nervous System, 15,* 758–763.

Boman, K., & Bodegard, G. (2000). Long-term coping in childhood cancer survivors: Influence of illness, treatment and demographic background factors. *Acta Paediatrica, 89,* 105–111.

Braga, L. W., Da Paz Júnior, A. C., & Ylvisaker, M. (2005). Direct clinician-delivered versus indirect family-supported rehabilitation of children with traumatic brain injury: A randomized controlled trial. *Brain Injury, 19*, 819–831.

Brown, R. T., Dreelin, B., & Dingle, A. (1997). Neuropsychological effects of stimulant medication on children's learning and behavior. In C. R. Reynolds & E. Fletcher-Janzen (Eds.), *Handbook of clinical child psychology* (2nd ed., 539–572.). New York: Plenum Press.

Brown, R. T., Madan-Swain, A., Walco, G. A., Cherrick, I., Ievers, C. E., Conte, P. M., et al. (1998). Cognitive and academic late effects among children previously treated for acute lymphocytic leukemia receiving chemotherapy as CNS prophylaxis. *Journal of Pediatric Psychology, 23*, 333–340.

Bull, K. S., Spoudeas, H. A., Yadegarfar, G., & Kennedy, C. R. (2007). Reduction in health status 7 years after addition of chemotherapy to craniospinal irradiation for medulloblastoma: A follow-up study in PNET 3 trial survivors-on behalf of the CCLG (formerly UKCCSG). *Journal of Clinical Oncology, 25*, 4239–4245.

Burger, P. C., & Boyko, O. B. (1991). The pathology of CNS radiation injury. In P. H. Gutin, S. A. Leibel, & G. E. Sheline (Eds.), *Radiation injury to the nervous system* (pp. 3–15). New York: Raven.

Buschmann, U., Gers, B., & Hildebrandt, G. (2003). Pilocytic astrocytomas with leptomeningeal dissemination: Biological behavior, clinical course, and therapeutical options. *Child's Nervous System, 19*, 298–304.

Butler, R. W. (1998). Attentional processes and their remediation in childhood cancer. *Medical and Pediatric Oncology, Suppl 1*, 75–78.

Butler, R. W., & Copeland, D. R. (1993). Neuropsychological effects of central nervous system prophylactic treatment in childhood leukemia: Methodological considerations. *Journal of Pediatric Psychology, 18*, 319–338.

Butler, R. W., & Copeland, D. R. (2002). Attentional processes and their remediation in children treated for cancer: A literature review and the development of a therapeutic approach. *Journal of the International Neuropsychological Society, 8*, 115–124.

Butler, R. W., Copeland, D. R., Fairclough, D. L., Mulhern, R. K., Katz, E. R., Kazak, A. E., et al. (2008). A multicenter, randomized clinical trial of a cognitive remediation program for childhood survivors of a pediatric malignancy. *Journal of Consulting and Clinical Psychology, 76*, 367–378.

Butler, R. W., & Haser, J. K. (2006). Neurocognitive effects of treatment for childhood cancer. *Mental Retardation and Developmental Disabilities, 12*, 184–191.

Butler, R. W., Hill, J. M., Steinherz, P. G., Meyers, P. A., & Finley, J. L. (1994). Neuropsychologic effects of cranial irradiation, intrathecal methotrexate, and systemic methotrexate in childhood cancer. *Journal of Clinical Oncology, 12*, 2621–2629.

Butler, R. W., & Mulhern, R. K. (2005). Neurocognitive interventions for children and adolescents surviving cancer. *Journal of Pediatric Psychology, 30*, 65–78.

Butler, R. W., Rizzi, L., & Bandilla, E. (2000). The effects of childhood cancer and its treatment on two objective measures of psychological functioning. *Children's Health Care, 28*, 311–327.

Carpentieri, S. C., Waber, D. P., Pomeroy, S. L., Scott, R. M., Goumnerova, L. C., Kieran, M. W., et al. (2003). Neuropsychological functioning after surgery in children treated for brain tumor. *Neurosurgery, 52,* 1348–1357.

Children's Hospital Boston. (n.d.). *Anaplastic astrocytoma.* Retrieved October 1, 2008, from http://www.childrenshospital.org/az/Site565/mainpageS565P0.html.

Cicerone, K. D., Dahlberg, C., Kalmar, K., Langenbahn, D. M., Malec, J. F., Berquist, T. F., et al. (2000). Evidence-based cognitive rehabilitation: Recommendations for clinical practice. *Archives of Physical Medicine and Rehabilitation, 81,* 1596–1615.

Cicerone, K. D., Dahlberg, C., Malec, J. F., Langenbahn, D. M., Felicetti, T., Kneipp, S., et al. (2005). Evidence-based cognitive rehabilitation: Updated review of the literature from 1998 through 2002. *Archives of Physical Medicine and Rehabilitation, 86,* 1681–1692.

Clay, D. L. (2004). Integration/reintegration into the school setting. In D. L. Clay (Ed.), *Helping schoolchildren with chronic health conditions* (p. 61–79). New York: Guilford.

Clay, D. L., Maloney, R., & Gross, J. (2004). Coping with chronic health conditions. In D. L. Clay (Ed.), *Helping schoolchildren with chronic health conditions* (p. 81–141). New York: Guilford.

Cohen, M. S. (1999). Families coping with childhood chronic illness: A research review. *Families, Systems, and Health, 17,* 149–164.

Coniglio, S. J., & Blackman, J. A. (1995). Developmental outcomes of childhood leukemia. *Topics in Early Childhood Special Education, 15,* 2–9.

Conklin, H. M., Khan, R. B., Reddick, W. E., Helton, S., Brown, R., Howard, S. C., et al. (2007). Acute neurocognitive response to methylphenidate among survivors of childhood cancer: A randomized, double-blind, cross-over trial. *Journal of Pediatric Psychology, 32,* 1127–1139.

Eiser, C. (2004). Measuring outcomes: Children adjusting to cancer. In *Children with cancer: The quality of life* (pp. 66–79). Mahwah, NJ: Lawrence Erlbaum.

Eiser, C., Hill, J. J., & Vance, Y. H. (2000). Examining the psychological consequences of surviving childhood cancer: Systematic review as a research method in pediatric psychology. *Journal of Pediatric Psychology, 25,* 582–588.

Elkin, T. D., Phipps, S., Mulhern, R. K., & Fairclough, D. (1997). Psychological functioning of adolescent and young adult survivors of pediatric malignancy. *Medical and Pediatric Oncology, 29,* 582–588.

Erikson, S. J., & Steiner, H. (2001). Trauma and personality correlates in long term pediatric cancer survivors. *Child Psychiatry and Human Development, 33,* 195–213.

Evans, J. J., Emslie, H., & Wilson, B. A. (1998). External cueing systems in the rehabilitation of executive impairments of action. *Journal of the International Neuropsychological Society, 4,* 399–408.

Fletcher-Janzen, E. (2005). The school neuropsychology examination. In R. C. D'Amato, E. Fletcher-Janzen, & C. R. Reynolds (Eds.), *Handbook of school neuropsychology* (pp. 172–212). Hoboken, NJ: John Wiley & Sons.

Fuemmeler, B. F., Elkin, T. D., & Mullins, L. L. (2002). Survivors of childhood brain tumors: Behavioral, emotional, and social adjustment. *Clinical Psychology Review, 22,* 547–585.

Gordon, W. A., Cantor, J., Ashman, T., & Brown, M. (2006). Treatment of post-TBI executive dysfunction: Application of theory to clinical practice. *Journal of Head Trauma Rehabilitation, 21*, 156–167.

Hays, D. M., Dolgin, M., Steele, L. L., Patenaude, A. F., Hewitt, K. D., Ruymann, F., et al. (1997). Educational achievement, employment, and work-place experience of adult survivors of childhood cancer. *International Journal of Pediatric Hematology/ Oncology, 4*, 327–337.

Hersch, N., & Treadgold, L. (1994). NeuroPage: The rehabilitation of memory dysfunction by prosthetic memory and cueing. *NeuroRehabilitation, 4*, 187–197.

Johnson, D. L., McCabe, M. A., Nicholson, H. S., Joseph, A. L., Getson, P. R., Byrne, J., et al. (1994). Quality of long-term survival in young children with medulloblastoma. *Journal of Neurosurgery, 20*, 1004–1010.

Katz, E. R, Rubenstein, C. L., Hubert, N. C., & Blew, A. (1988). School and social reintegration of children with cancer. *Journal of Psychosocial Oncology, 6*, 123–140.

Kieffer-Renaux, V., Bulteau, C., Grill, J., Kalifa, C., Viguier, D., & Jambaque, I. (2000). Patterns of neuropsychological deficits in children with medulloblastoma according to craniospinal irradiation doses. *Developmental Medicine & Child Neurology, 42*, 741–745.

Klingberg, T., Fernell, E., Olesen, P. J., Johnson, M., Gustafsson, P., Dahlström, K., et al. (2005). Computerized training of working memory in children with ADHD: A randomized, controlled trial. *Journal of the American Academy of Child and Adolescent Psychiatry, 44*, 177–186.

Koocher, G. P., & O'Malley, J. E. (Eds.). (1981). *The Damocles syndrome: Psychosocial consequences of surviving childhood cancer*. New York: McGraw-Hill.

Kupst, M. J., Natta, M. B., Richardson, C. C., Schulman, J. L., Lavigne, J. V., & Das, L. (1995). Family coping with pediatric leukemia: Ten years after treatment. *Journal of Pediatric Psychology, 20*, 601–617.

Laatsch, L., Jobe, T., Sychra, J., Lin, Q., & Blend, M. (1997). Impact of cognitive rehabilitation therapy on neuropsychological impairments as measured by brain perfusion SPECT: A longitudinal study. *Brain Injury, 11*, 851–863.

Landolfi, J. L., & Venkataramana, A. (2006). Brainstem gliomas. Retrieved September 5, 2008, at http://www.emedicine.com/neuro/TOPIC40.HTM.

Last, B. F., & Grootenhuis, M. A. (1998). Emotions, coping and the need for support in families of children with cancer: A model for psychosocial care. *Patient Education and Counseling, 22*, 169–179.

Levine, B., Robertson, I. H., Clare, L., Carter, G., Hong, J., Wilson, B. A., et al. (2000). Rehabilitation of executive functioning: An experimental-clinical validation of Goal Management Training. *Journal of the International Neuropsychological Society, 6*, 299–312.

Lezak, M. D. (1995). *Neuropsychological assessment* (3rd ed.). New York: Oxford University Press.

Liber, J. M., Van Widenfelt, B. M., Utens, E. M. W. J., Ferdinand, R. F., Van der Leeden, A. J. M., Van Gastel, W., et al. (2008). No differences between group versus individual treatment of childhood anxiety disorders in a randomized clinical trial. *Journal of Child Psychology and Psychiatry, 49*, 886–893.

Lo, S., Kish, K. K., Chang, E. L., Levin, K. J., Keole, S. R., & Sloan, A. E. (2008). *Juvenile pilocytic astrocytoma*. Retrieved October 1, 2008, from http://www.emedicine .com/Radio/topic367.htm.

Lockwood, K. A., Bell, T. S., & Colegrove, R. W. (1999). Long-term effects of cranial radiation therapy on attention functioning in survivors of childhood leukemia. *Journal of Pediatric Psychology, 24,* 55–66.

Lo Priore, C., Castelnuovo, G., Liccone, D., & Liccone, D. (2003). Experience with the V-STORE: Considerations on presence in virtual environments for effective neuropsychological rehabilitation of executive functions. *Cyberpyschology & Behavior, 6,* 281–287.

Mabbott, D. J., Penkman, L., Witol, A., Strother, D., & Bouffet, E. (2008). Core neurocognitive functions in children treated for posterior fossa tumors. *Neuropsychology, 22,* 159–168.

Manly, T., Hawkins, K., Evans, J., Woldt, K., & Robertson, I. H. (2002). Rehabilitation of executive function: Facilitation of effective goal management on complex tasks using periodic auditory alerts. *Neuropsychologia, 40,* 271–281.

Medical Center of Central Georgia. (2002). *Neurological disorders: Brain tumors*. Retrieved September 15, 2008, from http://www.mccg.org/childrenshealth/ content.asp?pageid =P02627.

Moleski, M. (2000). Neuropsychological, neuroanatomical, and neurophysiological consequences of CNS chemotherapy for acute lymphoblastic leukemia. *Archives of Clinical Neuropsychology, 15,* 603–630.

Moore, B. D. (2005). Neurocognitive outcomes in survivors of childhood cancer. *Journal of Pediatric Psychology, 30,* 51–63.

Mulhern, R. K. (1994). Neuropsychological late effects. In D. J. Bearison & R. K. Mulhern (Eds.), *Pediatric psychooncology: Psychological perspectives on children with cancer* (pp. 99–121). New York: Oxford Press.

Mulhern, R. K., & Butler, R. W. (2004). Neurocognitive sequelae of childhood cancers and their treatment. *Pediatric Rehabilitation, 7,* 1–14.

Mulhern, R. K., Hancock, J., Fairclough, D., & Kun, L. (1992). Neuropsychological status of children treated for brain tumors: A critical review and integration. *Medical and Pediatric Oncology, 20,* 181–192.

Mulhern, R. K., Khan, R. B., Kaplan, S., Helton, S., Christensen, R., Bonner, M., et al. (2004). Short-term efficacy of methylphenidate: A randomized, double-blind, placebo-controlled trial among survivors of childhood cancer. *Journal of Clinical Oncology, 22,* 4795–4803.

Mulhern, R. K., Merchant, T. E., Gajjar, A., Reddick, W. E., & Kun, L. E. (2004). Late neurocognitive sequelae in survivors of brain tumours in childhood. *The Lancet, 5,* 399–408.

Mulhern, R. K., Palmer, S. L., Reddick, W. E., Glass, J. O., Kun, L. E., Taylor, J., et al. (2001). Risks of young age for selected neurocognitive deficits in medulloblastoma are associated with white matter loss. *Journal of Clinical Oncology, 2,* 472–479.

Mulhern, R. K., Wasserman, A. L., Friedman, A. G., & Fairclough, D. (1989). Social competence and behavioral adjustment of children who are long-term survivors of cancer. *Pediatrics, 83,* 18–25.

Muñoz-Solomando, A., Kendall, T., & Whittington, C. J. (2008). Cognitive behavioural therapy for children and adolescents. *Current Opinion in Psychiatry, 21,* 332–337.

Newby, W., Brown, R., Pawletko, T., Gold, S., & Whitt, K. (2000). Social skills and psychological adjustment of child and adolescent cancer survivors. *Psycho-Oncology, 9,* 113–126.

Palmer, S. L., Goloubeva, O., Reddick, W. E., Glass, J. O., Gajjar, A., Kun, L., et al. (2001). Patterns of intellectual development among survivors of pediatric medulloblastoma: A longitudinal analysis. *Journal of Clinical Oncology, 19,* 2302–2308.

Patenaude, A. F., & Kupst, M. (2005). Psychosocial functioning in pediatric cancer. *Journal of Pediatric Psychology, 30,* 9–27.

Poggi, G., Liscio, M., Galbiati, S., Adduci, A., Massimino, M., Gandola, L., et al. (2005). Brain tumors in children and adolescents: Cognitive and psychological disorders at different ages. *Psycho-Oncology, 14,* 386–395.

Prevatt, F. F., Heffer, R. W., & Lowe, P. A. (2000). A review of school reintegration programs for children with cancer. *Journal of School Psychology, 38,* 447–467.

Reddick, W. E., White, H. A., Glass, J. O., Wheeler, G. C., Thompson, S. J., Gajjar, A., et al. (2003). Developmental model relating white matter volume to neurocognitive deficits in pediatric brain tumor survivors. *Cancer, 97,* 2512–2519.

Reeves, C. B., Palmer, S. L., Reddick, W. E., Merchant, T. E., Buchanan, G. M., Gajjar, A., et al. (2006). Attention and memory functioning among pediatric patients with medulloblastoma. *Journal of Pediatric Psychology, 31,* 272–280.

Reimers, T. S., Ehrenfels, S., Mortensen, E. L., Schmiegelow, M., Sonderkaer, S., Carstensen, H., et al. (2003). Cognitive deficits in long-term survivors of childhood brain tumors: Identification of predictive factors. *Medical and Pediatric Oncology, 40,* 26–34.

Ribi, K., Relly, C., Landolt, M. A., Alber, F. D., Boltshauser, E., & Grotzer, M. A. (2005). Outcome of medulloblastoma in children: Long-term complications and quality of life. *Neuropediatrics, 36,* 357–365.

Robertson, I. H. (1996). *Goal management training: A clinical manual.* Cambridge, UK: PsyConsult.

Rodgers, J., Horrocks, J., Britton, P., & Kernahan, J. (1999). Attentional ability among survivors of leukaemia. *Archives of Disease in Childhood, 80,* 318–323.

Sala, F., Talacchi, A., Mazza, C., Prisco, R., Ghimenton, C., & Bricolo, A. (1998). Prognostic factors in childhood intracranial ependymomas: The role of age and tumor location. *Pediatric Neurosurgery, 28,* 135–142.

Salazar, A. M., Warden, D. L., Schwab, K., Spector, J., Braverman, S., Walter, J., et al. (2000). Cognitive rehabilitation for traumatic brain injury: A randomized trial. *Journal of the American Medical Association, 283,* 3075–3081.

Schatz, J., Kramer, J. H., Ablin, A., & Matthay, K. K. (2000). Processing speed, working memory, and IQ: A developmental model of cognitive deficits following cranial radiation therapy. *Neuropsychology, 14,* 189–200.

Schmahmann, J. D. (2004). Disorders of the cerebellum: Ataxia, dysmetria of thought, and the cerebellar cognitive affective syndrome. *Journal of Neuropsychiatry and Clinical Neurosciences, 16,* 367–378.

Schnoebelen, S., Perez, R., & Stavinoha, P. L. (2008). Brain tumors. In C. L. Castillo (Ed.), *Children with complex medical issues in schools: Neuropsychological descriptions and interventions* (p. 39–64). New York: Springer.

Schoenberg, M. R., Ruwe, W. D., Dawson, K., McDonald, N. B., Houston, B., & Forducey, P. G. (2008). Comparison of functional outcomes and treatment cost between a computer-based cognitive rehabilitation teletherapy program and a face-to-face rehabilitation program. *Professional Psychology: Research and Practice, 29,* 169–175.

Schwartz, C. L., Hobbie, W. L., & Constine, L. S. (2005). Algorithms of late effects of disease. In C. L. Schwartz, W. L. Hobbie, L. S. Constine, & U. S. Raccione (Eds.), *Survivors of childhood cancer: A multidisciplinary approach* (2nd ed., pp. 5–16). Heidelberg, Germany: Springer.

Sohlberg, M. M., & Mateer, C. A. (1986). *Attention Process Training (APT).* Puyallup, WA: Washington Association for Neuropsychological Research and Development.

Sohlberg, M. M., & Mateer, C. A. (1989). *Introduction to cognitive rehabilitation.* New York: Guilford.

Spencer, J. (2006). The role of cognitive remediation in childhood cancer survivors experiencing neurocognitive late effects. *Journal of Pediatric Oncology Nursing, 23,* 321–325.

Spiegler, B. J, Bouffet, E., Greenberg, M. L., Rukta, J. T., & Mabbott, D. J. (2004). Change on neurocognitive functioning after treatment with cranial radiation in childhood. *Journal of Clinical Oncology, 22,* 706–713.

Steinlin, M., Imfeld, S., Zulauf, P., Boltshauser, E., Lövblad, K. O., Ridolfi Lüthy, A., et al. (2003). Neuropsychological long-term sequelae after posterior fossa tumour resection during childhood. *Brain, 126,* 1998–2008.

St. Jude Children's Research Hospital. (2008). *Brain tumor: Brain stem glioma.* Retrieved October 1, 2008, from http://www.stjude.org/stjude/v/index.jsp?vgnextoid= b86c061585f 70110VgnVCM1000001e0215acRCRD&vgnextchannel=b4dcbfe82e11 8010VgnVCM1000000e2015acRCRD.

Strother, D. R., Pollack, I. F., Fisher, P. G., Hunter, J. V., Woo, S. Y., Pomeroy, S. L., et al. (2002). Tumors of the central nervous system. In P. A. Pizzo & D. G. Poplack (Eds.), *Principles and practice of pediatric oncology* (pp. 751–824). Philadelphia: Lippincott Williams & Wilkins.

Tam, S.-F., Man, W. K., Hui-Chan, C. W. Y., Lau, A., Yip, B., & Cheung, W. (2003). Evaluating the efficacy of tele-cognitive rehabilitation for functional performance in three case studies. *Occupational Therapy International, 10,* 20–38.

Tamber, M. S., & Rutka, J. T. (2003). Pediatric supratentorial high-grade gliomas. *Neurosurgical Focus, 14.* Retrieved September 30, 2008, from http://www .medscape.com/viewarticle/449870.

Thompson, S. J., Leigh, L., Christensen, R., Xiaoping, X., Kun, L. E., Heideman, R. L., et al. (2001). Immediate neurocognitive effects of methylphenidate on learning-impaired survivors of childhood cancer. *Journal of Clinical Oncology, 19,* 1802–1808.

Tomita, T. (2000, Fall). Pediatric brain tumors: Overall review. *The Child's Doctor, Journal of Children's Memorial Hospital Chicago.* Retrieved August 25, 2008, from http://www.childsdoc.org/fall2000/braintumors.asp.

Ulrich, N., & Pomeroy, S. (2003). Pediatric brain tumors. *Neurologic Clinics of North America, 21,* 897–913.

Vainionpaa, L. (1993). Clinical neurological findings of children with acute lympho-blastic leukemia at diagnosis and during treatment. *European Journal of Pediatrics, 152,* 115–119.

Van Dongen-Melman, J. E. W. M., & Saunders-Woudstra, J. A. R. (1986). Psychologi-cal aspects of childhood cancer. *Journal of Child Psychology and Psychiatry, 27,* 148–180.

Varni, J. W., Blount, R. L., & Quiggins, D. J. (1998). Oncologic disorders. In R. T. Ammerman & J. V. Campo (Eds.), *Handbook of pediatric psychology and psychiatry: Vol. II* (pp. 313–347). Boston: Allyn & Bacon.

Venes, D. & Thomas, C. L. (Eds.). (2001). *Taber's cyclopedic medical dictionary* (19th ed.). Philadelphia: F. A. Davis Company.

Verrill, J. R., Schafer, J., Vannatta, K., & Noll, R. B. (2000). Aggression, antisocial behavior, and substance abuse in survivors of pediatric cancer: Possible protective effects of cancer and its treatment. *Journal of Pediatric Psychology, 25,* 593–502.

Weber, P., & Lütschg, J. (2002). Methyphenidate treatment. *Pediatric Neurology, 26,* 261–266.

Westerberg, H., & Klingberg, T. (2007). Changes in cortical activity after training of working memory: A single-subject analysis. *Physiology & Behavior, 92,* 186–192.

Winqvist, S., Vainionpaa, L., Kokkonen, J., & Lanning, M. (2001). Cognitive functions of young adults who survived childhood cancer. *Applied Neuropsychology, 8,* 224–233.

Zebrack, B. J., & Chesler, M. A. (2002). Quality of life in childhood cancer survivors. *Psycho Oncology, 11,* 132–141.

Zebrack, B. J., & Zeltzer, L. K. (2003). Quality of life issues and cancer survivorship. *Current Problems in Cancer, 27,* 198–211.

CHAPTER 29

Assessing and Intervening with Children with Seizure Disorders

AUDREA R. YOUNGMAN, CYNTHIA A. RICCIO, and NICHOLE WICKER

THE PURPOSE OF this chapter is to discuss seizures disorders, what is known about seizure disorders, their potential impact on cognitive and behavioral functioning, neuropsychological assessment of a child with a seizure disorder, and the complement of possible treatment approaches. Seizure disorders comprise one of the most common and complex classes of neurological disorders that affect people of all ages; at least 3 percent of the U.S. population will have some form of a seizure disorder at some point in their lives (Elger & Schmidt, 2008). It has been estimated that in the United States, approximately 5 percent of children will experience a seizure before the age of 20 (Hauser, Annegers, & Rocca, 1996); of these, about 25 percent will meet formal criteria for some form of epilepsy (Elger & Schmidt, 2008). The incidence of epilepsy is highest in the first year of life and increases after the age of 60 (Elger & Schmidt, 2008).

A seizure may be initiated by internal or external central nervous system (CNS) processes. Fever, electroconvulsive therapy (ECT), and drug withdrawal, for example, are considered external to the CNS, but may precipitate a seizure. Seizures are changes in consciousness that occur during periods of expected wakefulness. During a seizure, neurons fire excessively in a synchronized pattern that may be up to six times faster than the normal rate (Zillmer, Spiers, & Culbertson, 2008). The seizure is called an *ictal* event; the time period preceding the seizure is referred to as *pre-ictal*; the time period following a seizure is referred to as *post-ictal*. When discussing seizure disorders, most often one is concerned with epilepsy rather than a single seizure. In contrast to a seizure, epilepsy is defined by paroxysmal and noticeable changes in neuron firing that may or may not be accompanied by affects on consciousness or perceptual motor functions (Neppe & Tucker, 1994). By definition, with epilepsy, the changes must be initiated by internal CNS processes; however, these processes may have been initially triggered by an external occurrence (e.g., head injury). A second underlying feature of epilepsy is a tendency to experience at least two unprovoked seizures (Elger & Schmidt, 2008; Fisher et al., 2005).

CLASSIFICATION OF SEIZURE DISORDERS IN CHILDREN

Epilepsy encompasses several types of seizure disorders (see Table 29.1) because each disorder is categorized by different and complex signs and symptoms (MacAllister & Schaffer, 2007). There is a hierarchical classification system that consists of three tiers (Fisher et al., 2005; MacAllister & Schaffer, 2007). Although the classification system is multifaceted and subject to debate by researchers, it is beneficial for diagnosis and treatment because it can encompass the wide array of epileptic disorders, while differentiating by lesion detection (Elger & Schmidt, 2008). The first tier is related to the seizure type: generalized, localization-related, or undetermined. The second tier classifies seizures based on the detection of any brain lesions and states whether seizures are idiopathic, symptomatic, or cryptogenic. It is important to note that in a majority of cases, there is no specific neurological problem identified; the cause of the epilepsy is idiopathic. The final tier classifies the specific syndrome.

At the first tier, seizures are classified according to the type of abnormal neuronal activity observed. In partial seizures, the first observed EEG changes are limited to one area of the cerebral hemisphere. Complex partial seizures may begin as a partial seizure, but there is an alteration of consciousness such that there may be changes in mood, cognition, memory, or behavior. Temporal lobe epilepsy (TLE) is ascribed to the category of complex partial seizures and may be associated with fear and rage, dissociative symptoms (periods of confusion, impaired memory, distorted sense of time), and other behavioral problems. Automatisms (lip smacking or other repetitive motor movements) may be associated with complex partial seizures. In addition, either prodromal symptoms or auras may be associated with complex partial seizures; these include a sense of déjà-vu or olfactory hallucinations. With complex partial seizures, once the seizure is over, the person will generally be disoriented and will not recall the events that occurred (Zillmer et al., 2008). In contrast, primary generalized seizures are those where the first clinical signs occur in both hemispheres; thus, any motor symptoms are bilateral. Absence seizures are one type of generalized seizure. Absence seizures involve brief periods of loss of consciousness without accompanying motor activity, although eyelid flickering (rate of 3/second) is common. Absence seizures may appear as momentary lapses of attention; automatisms of lip smacking or head drooping may or

Table 29.1

Classification of Seizure Disorders

	Syndromes Included	Etiology/Mechanism	Characteristics
Idiopathic Generalized Epilepsies (IGE)	• Juvenile myoclonic epilepsy • Myoclonic epilepsy in infancy • Childhood absence epilepsy • Juvenile absence epilepsy • Generalized epilepsy with generalized tonic-clonic seizures	• Undetermined, but believed to have a genetic component with linkages to chromosomes 5, 2, 3, and 6 (Beghi, Beghi, Cornaggia, & Gobbi, 2006; Hommet, Sauerwein, De Toffol, & Lassonde, 2005). • Ion channel defect accounts for a small number of cases (Elger & Schmidt, 2008). • Theorized that the cause is multifactorial with an interaction of environmental effects and genetic variations (Duncan, Sander, Sisodiya, & Walker, 2006; Elger & Schmidt, 2008).	• Seizures have bilateral, synchronous, and symmetrical spikes and waves or polyspike-waves (Elger & Schmidt, 2008). • Seizures occur throughout the cortex due to a generalized lowering of the seizure threshold (Elger & Schmidt, 2008).
Focal Epilepsies	• Benign rolandic epilepsy • Occipital epilepsy • Temporal lobe epilepsy • Frontal lobe epilepsy	• Benign rolandic epilepsy has been linked to chromosome 15q14, but there is evidence to suggest its etiology is multifactorial (MacAllister & Schaffer, 2007).	• EEG findings suggest individuals with benign rolandic epilepsy have high voltage centrotemporal spikes followed by slow waves (MacAllister & Schaffer, 2007). • Frontal lobe epilepsy is typically associated with little or no interictal or ictal EEG abnormalities (MacAllister & Schaffer, 2007).

(continued)

Table 29.1
Continued

	Syndromes Included	Etiology/Mechanism	Characteristics
Epileptic Encephalo-pathies	• Dravet's syndrome • West syndrome • Lennox-Gastaut Syndrome • Myoclonic astastic epilepsy • Landau-Kleffner syndrome	• There is evidence to suggest Dravet's is associated with mutations on the SCNA1 gene (Oguni et al., 2005; Ohtsuka, Maniwa, Ogino, Yamatogi, & Ohtahara, 1991). • Factors associated with the etiology of West Syndrome include neurological insult, cortical malformations, neurocutaneous syndrome, chromosomal disorder, or inborn error of metabolism (Wirrell, Farrell, & Whiting, 2005). • Lennox-Gastaut syndrome usually results from focal, multifocal, or diffuse brain damage (Nabbout & Dulac, 2003). • The etiology of myoclonic astatic epilepsy is likely associated with genetic factors (MacAllister & Schaffer, 2007).	• Epileptic encephalopathies characterized by deterioration of sensory, motor, or cognitive functions in relation to epileptic or seizure activity (Nabbout & Dulac, 2003). • Lennox-Gastaut syndrome is characterized by slow generalized spike-and-wave discharges on EEG (MacAllister & Schaffer, 2007). • Landau-Kleffner Syndrome is characterized by continuous spike-and-waves during slow-wave sleep (Kramer et al., 1998).

may not be present (Zillmer et al., 2008). The seizure can be as brief as 1 second, but usually lasts 5 to 10 seconds. There is no aura or warning; the individual usually is not aware anything has occurred. The second type of generalized seizure is tonic-clonic. Tonic-clonic seizures may present with or without warning or aura. If there is an aura, it may be abdominal discomfort, irritability, or dizziness. With tonic-clonic seizures, there is loss of consciousness, rigidity with extension of extremities, and arching the back (tonic phase) followed by rhythmic contractions (clonic phase) (Zillmer et al., 2008).

NEUROCOGNITIVE DEFICITS ASSOCIATED WITH SEIZURE DISORDERS

The appearance of epilepsy throughout childhood has varied characteristics, treatment interventions, and outcomes. It is generally presumed that the type and severity of epilepsy is related to outcome; however, research findings are equivocal. For example, while some studies have suggested that children with generalized seizures are more at risk than those with partial seizures for cognitive or educational difficulties (Mandelbaum & Burack, 1997; Seidenberg, Beck, & Geisser, 1986), others have found no significant association between seizure type and academic outcome (Mitchell, Chavez, Lee, & Guzman, 1991; Sturnniolo & Galletti, 1994; Williams et al., 2001a). Age of onset has been found to be associated with poorer cognitive function in some studies (Bulteau et al., 2000; Mitchell et al., 1991; O'Leary et al., 1983; Schoenfeld et al., 1999); yet, other studies have not found a similar pattern (Sturnniolo & Galletti, 1994). As can be seen from Table 29.2, various functional domains may be spared or impaired in children with seizure disorders, depending on seizure type, duration, age of onset, medication, and other variables. Using structural equation modeling, a three-factor model of neuropsychological function, comprised of verbal/memory/executive, rapid naming/working memory, and psychomotor skills, was identified to predict academic difficulties in children with epilepsy (Fastenau et al., 2004). Home environment (e.g., level of organization and support) was found to be a moderating variable.

Cognition

The more significant effects on cognition are the result of four factors that include early age onset of the seizure disorder, extent to which the individual has seizure control, duration of the seizure disorder, and whether the person demonstrates multiple seizure types or a single type (Besag, 1995, 2004; Dodrill, 1993; Kopp et al., in press). Complex partial seizures occurring in the temporal lobe region of the brain produce more obvious behavior and cognitive changes than most of the other seizure types (Bortz, Prigatano, Blum, & Fisher, 1995). Studies of intellectual and neuropsychological functioning in children with

Table 29.2
Neurocognitive Domains and Seizure Disorders

Domain	Expected Functional Status
Sensory-Motor Functions	• Children with temporal lobe epilepsy may experience auras of somatosensory symptoms prior to seizures (MacAllister & Schaffer, 2007). • Epilepsy associated with significant slowing of psychomotor speed (Boelen et al., 2005). • Children with frontal lobe epilepsy demonstrate motor difficulties (Hernandez et al., 2002). • IGE associated with deficits in sequential fine motor responses (Henkin, Sadeh, & Gadoth, 2007). • Difficulty in gross as well as in fine motor functions is associated with seizure disorders, particularly in the areas of running speed, balance, response speed and bilateral coordination, but also in upper-limb speed, dexterity and coordination (Beckung & Uvebrant, 1997).
Attentional Processes	• Juvenile myoclonic epilepsy is associated with impaired attention (Pascalicchio et al., 2007). • Benign childhood epilepsy with centrotemporal spikes associated with impaired attentional functions (Deltour, Quaglino, Barathon, De Broca, & Berquin, 2007). • Idiopathic generalized epilepsy is associated with attentional deficits (Henkin et al., 2007). • There are some indications that auditory attention deficits are associated with decreased academic performance (Williams et al., 2001a).
Visual-Spatial Processes	• Visual spatial functioning may be one area that is spared, particularly if graphomotor and speed components are eliminated (Bender, Marks, Brown, Zach, & Zaroff, 2007). • Juvenile myoclonic epilepsy is associated with difficulty on visuospatial tests that assess right hemisphere function (Sonmez, Atakli, Sari, Atay, & Arpaci, 2004). • Children with absence seizures typically demonstrate difficulties with visuospatial skills (Pavone et al., 2001).
Language Processes	• Language disturbances are often associated with temporal lobe epilepsy (Bigel & Smith, 2001; Lendt, Helmstaedter, & Elger, 1999). • Benign rolandic epilepsy has been associated deficient performance on tests of vocabulary, verbal fluency, and verbal memory (Croona, Kihlgren, Lundberg, Eeg-Olofsson, & Eeg-Olofsson, 1999; Gündüz, Demirbilek, & Korkmaz, 1999). • Children with left temporal lobe epilepsy are likely to display difficulties with verbal fluency; verbal learning, verbal memory, and delayed recall of verbal learning (Guimaràes et al., 2007; Jambaqué et al., 2007). • Children with absence seizures generally do not demonstrate any deficits in verbal memory or language skills (Pavone et al., 2001).

Table 29.2
Continued

Domain	Expected Functional Status
Memory and Learning Processes	• Verbal and nonverbal memory (e.g., immediate and working memory) appear to be impaired in children with idiopathic generalized epilepsies (Henkin et al., 2007; Prassouli, Katsarou, Attilakos, & Antoniadou, 2007). • Focal epilepsy is associated with difficulty with auditory memory processing (Jocic-Jakubi & Jovic, 2006; Krause, Boman, Sillanmäki, Varho, & Holopainen, 2008). • Deficits are evidenced in long term delayed recall, but not in new learning or short term memory tasks evidenced (Williams et al., 2001b). • Temporal lobe epilepsy is associated with deficits in verbal and visual memory, delayed recall, and recognition (Guimaràes et al., 2007).
Executive Functions	• Children with epilepsy (localized or IGE) demonstrated impaired performance on executive function tasks (Parrish et al., 2007). • Juvenile myoclonic epilepsy is associated with difficulty in resisting interference and changing categories, as well as maintaining perseverance, fluency, and mental retrieval (Sonmez et al , 2004). • Executive dysfunction appears to have an adverse influence on quality of life (QOL) in children with epilepsy (Sherman, Slick, Connolly, & Eyrl, 2007). • Results of several studies revealed that frontal lobe metabolic values were strong predictors of executive functioning in patients with epilepsy, but not in healthy controls (McDonald et al., 2006). • Resting hypometabolism can be a useful predictor of executive dysfunction in patients with epilepsy (McDonald et al., 2006). • Juvenile myoclonic epilepsy is associated with impaired control of inhibition, decreased cognitive speed, and decreased mental flexibility in comparison to the matched control group (Pascalicchio et al., 2007).
Speed and Efficiency of Cognitive Processing	• Juvenile myoclonic epilepsy has been associated with impaired processing speed (Pascalicchio et al., 2007). • Children with epilepsy are more likely to have decreased processing speed than children with epilepsy who do not have any brain structure abnormalities (Byars et al., 2007).
General Cognitive Ability	• Children with epilepsy typically experience specific cognitive disabilities rather than a global deficit in general cognitive ability (Palade & Benga, 2007). • Children with epilepsy appear to be functioning in the average range (Bourgeois, 1998; Bourgeois, Prensky,

(continued)

Table 29.2

Continued

Domain	Expected Functional Status
	Palkes, Talent, & Busch, 1983); however, the distribution of intelligence (IQ) scores of children with epilepsy appears to be skewed towards lower values (Chaix et al., 2006).
	• Children with occipital lobe epilepsy and temporal lobe epilepsy typically perform lower on measures of intellectual functioning, while children with juvenile myoclonic epilepsy do not generally display any deficits in global cognitive functioning (Pascalicchio et al., 2007; Sonmez et al., 2004).
	• Children with epileptic encephalopathies including Dravet's syndrome, West syndrome, Lennox-Gastaut syndrome, Myoclonic astastic epilepsy, and Landau-Kleffner syndrome often experience a regression or developmental delay in cognitive development (MacAllister & Schaffer, 2007).
	• For individuals with complex partial seizures, age of onset and recurrence of seizures are strongest predictors of cognitive functioning (Schoenfeld et al., 1999).
	• Decreased cognitive ability is associated with co-morbidity of other disorders (e.g., tuberous sclerous) (Kopp, Muzykewicz, Staley, Thiele, & Pulsifer, in press).
Academic Achievement	• Children with epilepsy are at a greater risk than other children to demonstrate academic difficulties (Austin, Huberty, Huster, & Dunn, 1998; Bourgeois, 1998; Fowler, Johnson, & Atkinson, 1985; Westbrook, Silver, Coupey, & Shinnar, 1991); but research is equivocal with regard to type of seizure disorder and association with academic difficulties (Germanó et al., 2005; Gülgönen, Demirbilek, Korkmaz, Dervent, & Townes, 2000; Katzenstein, Fastenau, Dunn, & Austin, 2007).
	• Approximately one-half of children with epilepsy meet criteria for LD with the majority of difficulties occurring in writing, followed by math, and then reading (Fastenau, Shen, Dunn, & Austin, 2008).
Social Emotional Functioning	• Individuals with epilepsy have high prevalence of psychosocial problems, are less likely to marry, and evidence higher rates of social isolation (Camfield & Camfield, 2003; Kokkonen, Kokkenen, Saukkonen, & Pennanen, 1997; Parker & Asher, 1987).
	• Specific problems include immaturity, emotional lability, and disinhibition (Janz, 1985), as well as difficulties with social integration and social adjustment (Hommet et al., 2005).
	• With complex partial epilepsy, frequency of seizures in the past year is a strong predictor of behavioral difficulties (Schoenfeld et al., 1999).

Table 29.2
Continued

Domain	Expected Functional Status
	• Temporal lobe epilepsy is often associated with depression even when cognitive abilities are not impaired (Tracy et al., 2007).
	• Comorbidity with ADHD can affect quality of life significantly (Sherman et al., 2007).
	• Children with more visible forms of epilepsy report greater perceived loneliness, but fewer problems with illness adjustment (Curtin & Siegel, 2003).

epilepsy, regardless of seizure type, indicate that onset of seizures early in life and a long duration of seizure disorder place children at higher risk for cognitive dysfunction (Bortz et al., 1995). Both groups of children, with either partial or generalized seizures and an early seizure onset, demonstrated poorer performance on neuropsychological measures than children whose seizures started at a later age (O'Leary et al., 1983).

Alternatively, many children with epilepsy do not differ from other children with regard to general cognitive functioning. For example, children with Juvenile Myoclonic Epilepsy do not typically exhibit general cognitive performance that is significantly different from their peers (Pascalicchio et al., 2007; Sonmez et al., 2004). No difference in cognitive function was found that could be explained by medication dosage, duration of pharmacotherapy, or serum drug concentration (Sonmez et al., 2004). In contrast, comorbid conditions, such as Tuberous Sclerosis, affect the extent to which functional domains are compromised; nearly one-half of children with Tuberous Sclerosis Complex are likely to demonstrate mental retardation (Kopp et al., in press).

Academic Underachievement

Children with epilepsy are at a greater risk than other children to demonstrate academic difficulties including learning and behavior problems (Austin et al., 1998; Bourgeois, 1998; Fowler et al., 1985; Westbrook et al., 1991). Under- or low achievement is frequent among children with epilepsy, but no discernible connection between severity or duration of seizure disorder and achievement has been identified (Mitchell et al., 1991). Similarly, using an IQ-achievement discrepancy for specific learning disability (SLD), approximately one-half of children with epilepsy met criteria for SLD with the majority of difficulties in writing, followed by math, and then reading (Fastenau et al., 2008; Fastenau et al., 2004). The relationship between epilepsy and SLD is not clear. It is possible that both may be the result of brain damage/dysfunction, that epilepsy may cause brain damage/dysfunction and subsequently lead to SLD, or epilepsy may cause SLD directly without any evident brain damage. Alternatively, there are some indications that teachers underestimate the academic abilities of children they know to have epilepsy, potentially setting lower expectations and exacerbating their academic difficulties (Katzenstein et al., 2007). There is also a potential issue of chronic absences caused by the seizure disorder that in turn leads to underachievement.

Learning and Memory

Depending on the seizure classification, some children may demonstrate impaired verbal and visual immediate and working memory, attention, and slower processing speed (Pascalicchio et al., 2007; Sonmez et al., 2004). There are some indications that deficits in auditory attention and memory are associated with decreased academic performance in children with epilepsy (Williams et al., 2001a). Younger age, family history of seizure activity, and experience with absence seizures are associated with greater levels of difficulty with verbal memory, general cognitive functioning, and short-term memory (Sonmez et al., 2004). Adults and children with focal seizures of the left temporal lobe generally have greater verbal than nonverbal deficits, whereas seizures emanating from the right temporal lobe have greater nonverbal than verbal deficits. Notably, long-term memory appears to be more significantly affected than short-term memory (Bortz et al., 1995; Williams et al., 2001b). Comparing the differences in qualitative aspects of verbal memory between the left and right temporal foci and no seizure disorder, individuals with left temporal lobe seizures have more intrusion errors on delayed and free recall tasks and have evidence of response bias. Those with right temporal lobe seizures did not demonstrate any response bias (Bortz et al., 1995). This is most evident with consolidation of new materials, as well as with difficulty in initial learning of verbal materials in conjunction with left temporal seizures.

Executive Function

The executive functions of the brain involve processes such as logical analysis, conceptualization, reasoning, planning, sequential thinking, and self-monitoring (Zillmer et al., 2008). These functions are negatively impacted when a person is distractible, has a poor memory, has language deficits, or has difficulty with perceptual motor skills. These impairments are commonly seen in individuals with epilepsy. Difficulty may be evidenced in resisting interference and shifting cognitive sets, as well as maintaining perseverance, fluency, and mental retrieval (Guimarães et al., 2007; Pascalicchio et al., 2007;

Sonmez et al., 2004). Across measures of executive function, children with recent onset and well-controlled epilepsy exhibited significantly more difficulty than controls despite average mean cognitive ability (Parrish et al., 2007). Deficits in executive functioning directly relate to cognitive performance; further, executive function deficits influence the quality of life for children with epilepsy (Sherman et al., 2007).

Associated Problems

Children with epilepsy are at a greater risk of experiencing some form of psychological disorder. Psychiatric problems are estimated to co-occur in 37 to 77 percent of children with epilepsy (Plioplys, Dunn, & Caplan, 2007). For individuals over age 15, controlling for a number of confounding factors, psychological comorbidity was evident in 35 percent of participants with juvenile myoclonic epilepsy (Trinka et al., 2006). Within the sample in the Trinka et al. study, 19 percent displayed Axis I disorders, and 23 percent exhibited Axis II disorders. The incidence of psychological impairment in these individuals was slightly higher than a representative community-based sample; however, it is difficult to tease out psychosocial and environmental effects associated with the epilepsy (Trinka et al., 2006).

It is believed that psychological comorbidity is the result of multiple factors including social prejudice, the side effects of antiepileptic drugs (AEDs), and adjustments similar to other chronic illnesses (Fowler et al., 1985). Linguistic and cognitive abilities are believed to moderate the manifestation of psychopathology, such that there is less consistent psychopathology in children of average ability with epilepsy. Alternatively, when there is also developmental and cognitive delay, there is a higher likelihood of autistic-like behaviors and behaviors associated with Attention Deficit Hyperactivity Disorder or ADHD (Plioplys et al., 2007; Sherman et al., 2007). The prevalence of autism in children with epilepsy ranges from 5 to 38 percent (Danielsson, Gillberg, Billstedt, Gillberg, & Olsson, 2005; Rossi, Parmeggiani, Bach, Santucci, & Visconti, 1995; Tuchman & Rapin, 2002), and the likelihood increases if a child has severe mental retardation or cerebral palsy (Tuchman & Rapin, 2002). Similarly, parent reports suggest that children with epilepsy, in conjunction with Tuberous Sclerosis Complex, exhibit clinically significant behavior problems with high rates of autistic-like behaviors, withdrawal, hyperactivity, and attention problems (Kopp et al., in press). Because of their difficulties with inattention and restlessness, children with epilepsy are likely to be diagnosed with ADHD (Hirshberg, Chui, & Frazier, 2005).

In the cases of internalizing disorders, attention problems, and thought problems, it is believed that the problems may be directly related to the epilepsy. Of the psychiatric disorders, depression is typically the most common, followed by anxiety disorders and personality disorders. The duration of the disease, age at onset, and receiving polypsychopharmacological treatment are related to higher levels of interpersonal problems, ineffectiveness, negative self-esteem, or all-around greater depression level (Cushner-Weinstein et al., 2008). Externalizing or behavior problems may also be present in children with epilepsy. Children with low cognitive or adaptive abilities, the presence of a mixed seizure disorder, or greater seizure frequency are more likely to present behavioral concerns. Epilepsy is associated with social and cultural implications. Although epilepsy is widely recognized in U.S. society, it is often misunderstood and has been associated with negative beliefs and attitudes (Hargis, 2008). Children with epilepsy may experience difficulties in initiating social behaviors or responding to the actions of others (Tse, Hamiwka, Sherman, & Wirrell, 2007). They may demonstrate trends towards poorer peer relations and poorer interactions in the school environment (Yu, Lee, Wirrell, Sherman, & Hamiwka, 2008). It is not clear whether social stigma, neuropsychological functioning, or the interaction of these two factors accounts for the difficulty some children with epilepsy may face in the social arena. Similar discrepancies are found in health behaviors between children with epilepsy and their same-age peers. These children tend to exhibit less healthy eating and exercise habits, and often feel less positive about their health than their peers (Ben-Menachem, 2007; Yu et al., 2008)

SCHOOL NEUROPSYCHOLOGICAL ASSESSMENT OF CHILDREN WITH SEIZURE DISORDERS

As can be seen from previous discussion and Table 29.2, it is important to ensure that all domains of functioning are assessed for a child with a seizure disorder. Neuropsychological assessment can assist in the formulation of hypotheses regarding potential instructional methods/materials, as well as treatment supports, for a particular child (Reynolds, Kamphaus, Rosenthal, & Hiemenz, 1997). Data generated from the assessment process should be used to develop recommendations regarding whether the individual would profit from compensatory strategies, remedial instruction, or a combination (Gaddes & Edgell, 1994). By identifying both strengths and weaknesses, intact functional systems can be maximized in the rehabilitation and remediation efforts (Riccio & Reynolds, 1998). The intact systems that have been identified can be used to develop compensatory behaviors as part of the rehabilitation program. Further, identification of intact systems suggests a more positive outcome and increases the likelihood of motivated support systems for the child with a seizure disorder (Riccio & Reynolds, 1998). A suggested battery of measures that might be appropriate is provided in Table 29.3. In choosing

Table 29.3
Possible Components to Pediatric Neuropsychological Assessment for Epilepsy

Domain	Possible Measure(s) or Battery (if part of battery)
Sensory-Motor Functions	**Sensory Functions:** • Finger Discrimination (NEPSY-II) **Motor Functions:** • Finger Tapping, Imitating Hand Positions, Visuomotor Precision, Manual Motor Sequences, Design Copy, Oromotor Sequences (NEPSY-II)
Attentional Processes	• Trails (HRNB), Comprehensive Trail Making Test, or Color Trails Test • Continuous Performance Tests (Gordon, Conners', IVA, TOVA) • Auditory Attention and Response Set, Visual Attention, Statue (NEPSY-II) • Cancellation Tests (e.g., Wechsler scales)
Visual-Spatial Processes	• Arrows, Block Construction, Route Finding, Design Copy from NEPSY-II • Block Design, Matrix Reasoning of Wechsler Scales
Language Processes	• Auditory Attention and Response Set, Phonological Processing, Comprehension of Instructions, Oromotor Sequences, and Verbal Fluency tests from NEPSY-II • Vocabulary, Similarities, Comprehension of Wechsler Scales • Peabody Picture Vocabulary Test – 4 • Expressive Vocabulary Test
Memory and Learning	• Digit Span Forward (e.g., Wechsler Scales) • List Learning, Story Recall, Memory for Faces, Memory for Names, Sentence Repetition (NEPSY-II or comparable subtests from memory battery) • Digit Span Backward (e.g., Wechsler scales) • Letter Number Sequencing (e.g., Wechsler scales)
Executive Functions	• Card Sorting Task (Wisconsin, DKEFS) • Tower Tasks (Tower of Hanoi, Tower of London, DKEFS)
Speed and Efficiency of Cognitive Processing	• Rapid Naming (NEPSY-II) • Symbol Search, Digit Symbol/Coding, Cancellation (e.g., Wechsler Scales)
General Cognitive Abilities	• Major Intelligence Measure
Academic Achievement	• Norm-Referenced Measures (e.g., WJ-III, WIAT-2, KTEA-2) • Curriculum Based Measurement (e.g., DIBELS, AIMSweb) • Permanent Product Review, Portfolio Assessment
Social-Emotional Functioning	• Behavior Assessment Scale for Children-II

measures across domains, it is important to ensure that both anterior and posterior functioning, as well as left and right hemisphere functioning are covered (Riccio & Reynolds, 1998). At the same time, to decrease measurement variance and facilitate comparison, it is important to limit the number of normative samples.

INTERVENTION APPROACHES FOR CHILDREN
WITH SEIZURE DISORDERS

The choice of interventions depends on the targeted behavior, the desired outcome, and the needs of the individual child. The occurrence of seizures often is addressed through medical interventions—pharmacologically or surgically or both; educational and psychosocial effects may require more behavioral or ecological interventions, accommodations, or compensatory skills. It should be noted that the evidence base specific to outcomes with medical intervention generally focuses on the frequency of seizures following the intervention, with less information on functional or educational outcomes.

MEDICAL INTERVENTION

Pharmacology   From a medical perspective and with the goal of seizure control, medication is usually the initial approach. The type of drug recommended depends on the type of seizure. An analysis of 27 published, randomized trials of antiepilepsy drugs (AEDs) in children demonstrated equal efficacy with carbamazepine (Tegretol), oxcarbazepine, phenytoin (Dilantin), valproic acid (Depakote), clobazam, and phenobarbital (Camfield & Camfield, 2003). While controlling the frequency of seizures, the medications may also affect current overall functioning and impact development over time (Ortinski & Meador, 2004). Effects of AEDs on neurocognitive functioning in children have not been studied extensively despite findings in the adult literature that suggest their possible effects on learning and memory; some of the older AEDs are believed to have compromised cognitive functioning, particularly processing speed and attention (Loring & Meador, 2004; Prevey et al., 1996). Newer AEDs may not have the same negative effects as the older ones, but current research is insufficient (Bourgeois, 1998). It should be noted that AED polypsychopharmacological treatment is associated with social problems, aggression, and inattention (Freilinger et al., 2006).

Surgery   In cases where seizures cannot be controlled by drugs, surgery as a treatment method has been used. If the area where the seizures occur can be identified, it is removed. Epilepsy surgery has been demonstrated to be a safe and effective treatment for refractory epilepsy and, compared to pharmacotherapy, is associated with decreased frequency of seizures (Hakimi, Spanaki, Schuh, Smith, & Schultz, 2008). In general, there is a significant delay from the onset of epilepsy to the use of surgery as a method of treatment. Once the first AED fails, the chances of control with a second drug trial is about 14 percent. This decreases with each subsequent trial; however, more than one-third of the neurologists indicated that failure on four monotherapy AED trials is needed for consideration for epilepsy surgery (Kwan & Brodie, 2000). Additionally, as many as 77 percent of the neurologists in Kwan and Brodie (2000) study used a criterion of failure of at least two drug combination therapy trials. Alternatively, Hakimi et al. (2008) found that seizure frequency was the key determinant in whether to refer a person for surgery; the majority of neurologists surveyed indicated that the frequency of seizures must be every three months before considering surgery as an option. Best practices suggest that for any surgical intervention to be considered appropriate, it must be offered before the duration and frequency of the seizures cause irreversible psychosocial consequences (Shevell et al., 2003); however, it is difficult to know when surgery is most beneficial or if irreversible consequences will occur with this course of treatment.

Another form of nonpharmacological treatment for medically intractable epilepsy is vagus nerve stimulation. The vagus nerve stimulator (VNS) is made up of a signal generator that is programmed and implanted under the skin in the child's left upper chest. A battery powers the VNS, while the system delivering intermittent electrical stimulation to the left vagus nerve in the neck through a connecting lead. VNS has demonstrated efficacy against partial onset and generalized seizures, although few patients have become seizure free. It is generally well tolerated, and implantation is not technically demanding (Kwan & Brodie, 2005).

Dietary Modifications   Dietary treatment called the "ketogenic diet" (initially developed in the 1920s) mimics the effects of biochemical changes that occur during fasting (acidosis, dehydration, and ketosis). The ketogenic diet is a low carbohydrate diet, based on an intake of fats and proteins with minimal carbohydrate consumption (Bergqvist, Schall, Gallagher, Cnaan, & Stallings, 2005). This treatment is generally used when seizures are difficult to control, when the patient is unresponsive to medications, or when the drugs are not tolerated well. Studies have demonstrated a 90 percent reduction rate of seizures on 37 percent of patients (Freeman et al., 1998). Additionally, 30 percent receive reductions ranging from 50 to 90 percent (Thiele, 2003). This type of diet has demonstrated effectiveness in children and has positive results in adults as well (Vining, 1999; Vining et al., 2002). One major problem in the use of the ketogenic diet is the need for adherence to the restrictive dietary regime (Benbadis, Tatum, & William, 2001). It is important for the whole family to become involved, and close collaboration between the child, family, pediatrician, and dietician are essential to successful implementation. While the ketogenic diet does not have the tranquilizing and cognitive effects of antiepileptic drugs, there are some potential concerns regarding its effects on growth in children (Benbadis et al., 2001).

BEHAVIORAL APPROACHES

Behavioral approaches have been used to address some components of seizure disorders with some success across studies (Efron, 1957; Pritchard, Holmstrom, & Giacinto, 1985); however, no agreement in the efficacy or effectiveness of behavioral approaches has been reached due to the lack of available studies and the limited control in the experimental designs. Specific techniques vary, and the type, duration, and severity of the seizure disorder may also vary. For those individuals who experience an aura or identifiable trigger to the seizure, one component may include habituation training (Noeker & Haverkamp, 2001). This training may help an individual become aware of his or her auras in order to stop the escalation of neuronal activity before the seizure occurs (Wagner & Smith, 2005). Sensory auras such as smell, touch, and taste, appear to be most successful when using this type of intervention. Habituation training includes strongly stimulating the part most threatened by the seizure. For example, tactile auras have been remediated by using tickling and squeezing methods (Wagner & Smith, 2005).

In addition to these techniques, stress reduction measures and biofeedback have been used (Bortz et al., 1995; Wagner & Smith, 2005). Progressive relaxation strategies have demonstrated some effectiveness (Wagner & Smith, 2005). This technique involves the tightening and relaxing of certain muscle groups and the application of this strategy when confronted by stressful situations and feelings that are associated with high risk for seizure activity. In addition to stress, sudden changes in arousal may be associated with the instances of seizure occurrence. As a result, a technique called "countermeasures" has been used to fight the initial stages of the seizures (Hirshberg et al., 2005). The goal of this behavioral approach is to change the arousal level. For example, if seizures are triggered by feelings of drowsiness, the goal of the countermeasure approach is to teach the individual to attain a state of hyperarousal to prevent the progression of the seizure.

Biofeedback is another method that has been utilized to gain seizure reduction for those who do not respond to medications. The individual is trained to understand his or her brain and mind states using operant conditioning principles to direct brain activity (Sterman & Egner, 2006). With children, it is typically done by presenting the child with a reward for desired movement of brain signals in the desired direction and by presenting his or her brain activity in a creative way. A recent meta-analysis indicated that 82 percent of patients demonstrated more than 30 percent reduction of seizures, with an average of more than a 50 percent reduction (Sterman, 2000). In general, biofeedback for the treatment of epilepsy has demonstrated positive results; however, no consensus has been reached as to which variation of this feedback works best due to the limited studies available. Additionally, the studies that do exist come from varying populations with a lack of control in the designs (Hirshberg et al., 2005). The participants in these studies were nonresponsive to medical treatment; for many, the only other alternative was surgery.

PSYCHOSOCIAL INTERVENTIONS

Research suggests that oftentimes the mental health needs of children with seizure disorders are not identified or addressed. Survey and educational sessions with various groups of professionals indicated that pediatricians often do not consider mental health issues, while mental health professionals may not be comfortable or feel competent to work with children with epilepsy (Smith et al., 2007). With concerns for depression and its effect on child quality of life as well as parental stress (Cushner-Weinstein et al., 2008), screening for possible depression may be appropriate. In general, consideration of parental comfort level with their child's diagnosis and acceptance of the treatments may also need to be addressed through educational supports. Enhancing a more positive attitude toward having epilepsy might help improve problems with poor self-concept or behavior problems, but might not influence social competence (Tse et al., 2007).

EDUCATIONAL MODIFICATIONS AND ACCOMMODATIONS

With potential side effects of medications and seizure disorder both impacting speed of processing as well as fatigue, it is important to consider modification of time allowances or reduction of workload for students with seizure disorders. Because of the heterogeneous nature of children with seizure disorders, and the potential functional domains affected, it is important to identify (a) strengths and weaknesses of the student, (b) any psychosocial factors that may exacerbate difficulties, and (c) medication effectiveness and potential side effects.

Research suggests that awareness about epilepsy is low, and individuals with epilepsy are more affected by the social and psychological aspects of epilepsy than the seizures themselves (Martinuik, Speechley, Seeco, Campbell, & Donner, 2007). In-service or educational information for staff, teachers, and students who work and interact with a child with a seizure disorder, as well as with the child and family members, may increase their level of comfort and ease, ultimately improving the outcome for the child. Researchers investigated the effects of an epilepsy education program on the awareness of fifth-grade students. Results of the study indicated that children who participated in the educational intervention demonstrated an increase in knowledge and positive attitude about epilepsy as compared to control counterparts a month after completion of the program (Martinuik et al., 2007). For many individuals, changes may be needed in level of intervention or type of intervention as physiological changes occur; for this reason, frequent monitoring of progress and data-based decision making, whenever an intervention (medical, psychological or education) is instituted, always constitutes best practice.

THE ROLE OF A SCHOOL NEUROPSYCHOLOGIST IN WORKING WITH CHILDREN SUSPECTED OR HAVING SEIZURE DISORDERS

As previously demonstrated, children with epilepsy may present a variety of symptoms based on the type of disorder, the intensity of the disorder, neuropsychological impairments, and social or familial support. In order to accurately identify seizure disorders and provide the necessary interventions or accommodations, school neuropsychologists need to be aware of the variety of impacts seizure disorders may have, as well as the overlap in symptom presentation with other disorders. In particular, children with absence seizures are often differentially diagnosed with Attention Deficit Hyperactivity Disorder, Predominately Inattentive Type. The misclassification often occurs because both sets of children typically demonstrate sustained staring episodes; however, children with ADHD display greater levels of inattention and difficulty completing assigned work (Williams et al., 2002). The inaccurate diagnosis of seizure disorders can lead to delayed access of appropriate treatment and can place the child at risk for continued or enhanced seizure activity (Williams et al., 2002). Given the dangers of misclassification, it is important for school neuropsychologists to help provide information to parents and educators on the symptoms associated with seizure disorders. Increasing school-based awareness of seizures and the role individuals can take during a major seizure episode can help lessen social stigma or any negative social consequences.

Working with children with seizure disorders also requires that school neuropsychologists know, understand, and feel comfortable utilizing proper first aid care for all types of seizures ranging from absence seizures to epileptic encephalopathies. It is also important to become familiar with the type(s) of anti-seizure medication a child may be taking. The side effects or interactive effects with other medications a child may experience may easily impact educational and behavioral functioning to a similar degree as the actual seizures. If a child is suspected of having a seizure disorder, it is recommended that the child be referred to a pediatric neurologist for a 24-hour ambulatory EEG study. This procedure allows for a sustained period of time to measure and account for any seizure activity that may be occurring.

SUMMARY

Seizure disorders encompass several different syndromes. Each of these has a different impact on brain functioning, cognitive performance, as well as personality and behavior characteristics. Issues about medication compliance, society stigma, and executive function impairments are concerns as well. Children with seizure disorders are often subject to comorbid cognitive difficulties, psychopathology, or unmet mental and social health needs. Impairments exhibited by children may vary based on variables associated with the seizures. Further, it is theorized that the relationship between seizures and other comorbid conditions is multifactorial and involves the complex relationship of social, familial, personal, and biological factors (Fastenau, Dunn, & Austin, 2003; Fastenau et al., 2008). This relationship accounts for the fact that some children with epilepsy may not exhibit the same deficits as others and underscores the need for assessment and treatment to be tailored to the individual child (Besag, 2006).

REFERENCES

Austin, J. K., Huberty, T. J., Huster, G. A., & Dunn, D. W. (1998). Academic achievement in children with epilepsy or asthma. *Developmental Medicine & Child Neurology, 40*, 248–255.

Beckung, E., & Uvebrant, P. (1997). Hidden dysfunction in childhood epilepsy. *Developmental Medicine & Child Neurology, 39*, 72–79.

Beghi, M., Beghi, E., Cornaggia, C. M., & Gobbi, G. (2006). Idiopathic generalized epilepsies of adolescence. *Epilepsia, 47*, 107 110.

Benbadis, S. R., Tatum, I. V., & William, O. (2001). Advances in the treatment of epilepsy. *American Family Physician, 64*, 91–99.

Bender, H. A., Marks, B. C., Brown, E. R., Zach, L., & Zaroff, C. M. (2007). Neuropsychologic performance of children with epilepsy on the NEPSY. *Pediatric Neurology, 36*, 312–317.

Ben-Menachem, E. (2007). Weight issues for people with epilepsy—a review. *Epilepsia, 48*, 42–45.

Bergqvist, A. G., Schall, J. J., Gallagher, P. R., Cnaan, A., & Stallings, V. A. (2005). Fasting versus gradual initiation of the ketogenic diet: A prospective, randomized clinical trial of efficacy. *Epilepsia, 46*, 1810–1819.

Besag, F. M. C. (1995). Myoclonus and infantile spasms. In M. M. Robertson & V. Eapen (Eds.), *Movement and allied disorders in childhood* (pp. 149–175). Oxford, UK: Wiley.

Besag, F. M. C. (2004). Behavioral aspects of pediatric epilepsy syndromes. *Epilepsy and Behavior, 5*(Suppl.), S3–S13.

Besag, F. M. C. (2006). Cognitive and behavioral outcomes of epileptic syndromes: Implications for education and clinical practice. *Epilepsia, 47*(Suppl. 2) 119–125.

Bigel, G. M., & Smith, M. L. (2001). The impact of different neuropathologies on pre- and postsurgical neuropsychological functioning in children with temporal lobe epilepsy. *Brain and Cognition, 46,* 46–49.

Boelen, S., Nieuwenhuis, S., Steenbeek, L., Veldwijk, H., van de Ven-Verest, M., Tan, I. Y., et al. (2005). Effect of epilepsy on psychomotor function in children with uncomplicated epilepsy. *Developmental Medicine & Child Neurology, 47,* 546–550.

Bortz, J. J., Prigatano, G. P., Blum, D., & Fisher, R. S. (1995). Differential response characteristics in the nonepileptic and epileptic seizure patients on a test of verbal learning and memory. *Neurology, 45,* 2029–2034.

Bourgeois, B. F. (1998). Antiepileptic drugs, learning, and behavior in childhood epilepsy. *Epilepsia, 39,* 913–921.

Bourgeois, B. F., Prensky, A. L., Palkes, H. S., Talent, B. K., & Busch, G. B. (1983). Intelligence in epilepsy: A prospective study in children. *Annals of Neurology, 14,* 438–444.

Bulteau, C., Jambaque, I., Viguier, D., Kieffer, V., Dellatolas, G., & Dulac, O. (2000). Epileptic syndromes, cognitive assessment and school placement: A study of 251 children. *Developmental Medicine & Child Neurology, 42,* 319–327.

Byars, A. W., deGrauw, T. J., Johnson, C. S., Fastenau, P. S., Perkins, S. M., Egelhoff, J. C., et al. (2007). The association of MRI finding and neuropsychological functioning after the first recognized seizure. *Epilepsia, 48,* 1067–1074.

Camfield, P., & Camfield, C. (2003). Childhood epilepsy: What is the evidence for what we think and what we do? *Journal of Child Neurology, 18,* 272–278.

Chaix, Y., Laguitton, V., Lauwers-Cances, V., Daquin, G., Cances, C., Demonet, J., et al. (2006). Reading abilities and cognitive functions of children with epilepsy: Influence of epileptic syndrome. *Brain & Development, 28,* 122–130.

Croona, C., Kihlgren, M., Lundberg, S., Eeg-Olofsson, O., & Eeg-Olofsson, K. E. (1999). Neuropsychological findings in children with benign childhood epilepsy with centrotemoral spikes. *Developmental Medicine & Child Neurology, 41,* 813–818.

Curtin, L. S., & Siegel, A. W. (2003). Social functioning in adolescents with epilepsy. *Children's Health Care, 32,* 103–114.

Cushner-Weinstein, S., Dassoulas, K., Salpekar, J., Henderson, S. E., Pearl, P. L., Gaillard, W. D., et al. (2008). Parenting stress and childhood epilepsy: The impact of depression, learning, and seizure-related factors. *Epilepsy & Behavior, 13,*109–114.

Danielsson, S., Gillberg, I. C., Billstedt, E., Gillberg, C., & Olsson, I. (2005). Epilepsy in young adults with autism: A prospective population-based follow-up study of 120 individuals diagnosed in childhood. *Epilepsia, 46,* 918–923.

Deltour, L., Quaglino, V., Barathon, M., De Broca, A., & Berquin, P. (2007). Clinical evaluation of attentional processes in children with benign childhood epilepsy with centrotemporal spikes (BCECTS). *Epileptic Disorders, 9,* 424–431.

Dodrill, C. B. (1993). Neuropsychology. In J. Laidlaw, A. Richens, & D. Chadwick (Eds.), *A textbook of epilepsy* (pp. 459–473). New York: Churchill Livingstone.

Duncan, J. S., Sander, J. W., Sisodiya, S. M., & Walker, M. C. (2006). Adult epilepsy. *Lancet, 367,* 1087–1187.

Efron, R. (1957). The conditioned inhibition of uncinate fits. *Brain, 80,* 251–262.

Elger, C. E., & Schmidt, D. (2008). Modern management of epilepsy: A practical approach. *Epilepsy and Behavior, 12,* 501–539.

Fastenau, P. S., Dunn, D. W., & Austin, J. K. (2003). Pediatric epilepsy. In M. R. P. J. Eslinger (Ed.), *Principles and practice of behavioral neurology and neuropsychology* (pp. 965–982). New York: Saunders/Churchill Livingstone/Mosby.

Fastenau, P. S., Shen, J., Dunn, D. W., & Austin, J. K. (2008). Academic underachievement among children with epilepsy: Proportion exceeding psychometric criteria for learning disability and associated risk factors. *Journal of Learning Disabilities, 41,* 195–207.

Fastenau, P. S., Shen, J., Dunn, D. W., Perkins, S. M., Hermann, B. P., & Austin, J. K. (2004). Neuropsychological predictors of academic underachievement in pediatric epilepsy: Moderating roles of demographic, seizure, and psychosocial variables. *Epilepsia, 45,* 1261–1272.

Fisher, R. S., van Emde, B. W., Blume, W., Elger, C. E., Genton, P., Lee, P., et al. (2005). Epileptic seizures and epilepsy: Definitions proposed by the International League Against Epilepsy (ILAE) and the International Bureau for Epilepsy (IBE). *Epilepsia, 46,* 470–472.

Fowler, M. G., Johnson, M. P., & Atkinson, S. S. (1985). School achievement and absence in children with chronic health conditions. *Journal of Pediatrics, 106,* 683–687.

Freeman, J. M., Vining, E. P., Pillas, D. J., Pysik, P. L., Casey, J. C., & Kelly, M. T. (1998). The efficacy of the ketogenic diet—1998: A prospective evaluation in 150 children. *Pediatrics, 102,* 1358–1363.

Freilinger, M., Reisel, B., Reiter, E., Zelenko, M., Hauser, E., & Seidl, R. (2006). Behavioral and emotional problems in children with epilepsy. *Journal of Child Neurology, 21,* 939–945.

Gaddes, W. H., & Edgell, D. (1994). *Learning disabilities and brain function: A neurodevelopmental approach.* New York: Springer-Verlag.

Germanó, E., Gagliano, A., Magazù, A., Sferro, C., Calarese, T., Mannarino, E., et al. (2005). Benign childhood epilepsy with occipital paroxysms: Neuropsychological findings. *Epilepsy Research, 64,* 137–150.

Guimaràes, C. A., Li, L. M., Rzezak, P., Fuentes, D., Franzon, R. C., Montenegro, M. A., et al. (2007). Temporal lobe epilepsy in childhood: Comprehensive neuropsychological assessment. *Journal of Child Neurology, 22,* 836–840.

Gülgönen, S., Demirbilek, V., Korkmaz, B., Dervent, A., & Townes, B. D. (2000). Tonic seizures in subacute sclerosing panencephalitis: A video-illustration of two cases. *Epilepsia, 41,* 405–411.

Gündüz, E., Demirbilek, V., & Korkmaz, B. (1999). Benign rolandic epilepsy: Neuropsychological findings. *Seizure, 4,* 246–249.

Hakimi, A. S., Spanaki, M. V., Schuh, L. A., Smith, B. J., & Schultz, L. (2008). A survey of neurologists' views on epilepsy surgery and medically refractory epilepsy. *Epilepsy & Behavior, 13,* 96–101.

Hargis, E. R. (2008). *Targeting epilepsy: One of the nation's most common disabling neurological conditions at a glance.* Retrieved June 27, 2008, from http://www.cdc.gov.

Hauser, W. A., Annegers, J. F., & Rocca, W. A. (1996). Descriptive epidemiology of epilepsy: Contributions of population-based studies from Rochester, Minnesota. *Mayo Clinic Proceedings. Mayo Clinic, 71,* 576–586.

Henkin, Y., Sadeh, M., & Gadoth, N. (2007). Learning difficulties in children with epilepsy with idiopathic generalized epilepsy and well-controlled seizures. *Developmental Medicine & Child Neurology, 49*, 874–875.

Hernandez, M. T., Sauerwein, H. C., Jambaqué, I., De Guise, E., Lussier, F., Lortie, A., et al. (2002). Deficits in executive functions and motor coordination in children with frontal lobe epilepsy. *Neuropsychologia, 4*, 384–400.

Hirshberg, L. M., Chui, S., & Frazier, J. A. (2005). Emerging brain-based interventions for children and adolescents: Overview and clinical perspective. *Child and Adolescent Pediatric Clinics of North America, 14*, 1–19.

Hommet, C., Sauerwein, H. C., De Toffol, B., & Lassonde, M. (2005). Idiopathic epileptic syndromes and cognition. *Neuroscience and Biobehavioral Reviews, 30*, 85–96.

Jambaqué, I., Dellatolas, G., Fohlen, M., Bulteau, C., Watier, L., Dorfmuller, G., et al. (2007). Memory functions following surgery for temporal lobe epilepsy in children. *Neuropsychologia, 45*, 2850–2862.

Janz, D. (1985). Epilepsy with impulsive petit mal (juvenile myoclonic epilepsy). *Acta Neurologica Scandinavica, 72*, 449–459.

Jocic-Jakubi, B., & Jovic, N. J. (2006). Verbal memory impairment in children with focal epilepsy. *Epilepsy & Behavior, 9*, 432–439.

Katzenstein, J. M., Fastenau, P. S., Dunn, D. W., & Austin, J. K. (2007). Teachers' ratings of the academic performance of children with epilepsy. *Epilepsy & Behavior, 10*, 426–431.

Kokkonen, J., Kokkenen, E. R., Saukkonen, A. L., & Pennanen, P. (1997). Psychosocial outcome of young adults with epilepsy in childhood. *Journal of Neurology, Neurosurgery, and Psychiatry, 62*, 265–268.

Kopp, C. M. C., Muzykewicz, D. A., Staley, B. A., Thiele, E. A., & Pulsifer, M. B. (in press). Brain oscillatory EEG event-related desynchronization (ERD) and event-related synchronization (ERS) responses during an auditory memory task are altered in children with epilepsy. *Epilepsy & Behavior.*

Kramer, U., Nevo, Y., Neufeld, M. Y., Fatal, A., Leitner, Y., & Harel, S. (1998). Epidemiology of epilepsy in childhood: A cohort of 440 consecutive patients. *Pediatric Neurology, 18*, 46–50.

Krause, C. M., Boman, P., Sillanmäki, L., Varho, T., & Holopainen, I. E. (2008). Brain oscillatory EEG event-related desynchronization (ERD) and event-related synchronization (ERS) responses during an auditory memory task are altered in children with epilepsy. *Seizure, 17*, 1–10.

Kwan, P., & Brodie, M. J. (2000). Early identification of refractory epilepsy. *New England Journal of Medicine, 3*, 314–319.

Kwan, P., & Brodie, M. J. (2005). Provision of care. In W. H. Organization (Ed.), *Atlas Epilepsy Care in the World* (pp. 34–35). Geneva, Switzerland: World Health Organization.

Lendt, M., Helmstaedter, C., & Elger, C. E. (1999). Pre- and postoperative neuropsychological profiles in children and adolescents with temporal lobe epilepsy. *Epilepsia, 40*, 1543–1550.

Loring, D. W., & Meador, K. J. (2004). Cognitive side effects of antiepileptic drugs in children. *Neurology, 62*, 872–877.

MacAllister, W., & Schaffer, S. G. (2007). Neuropsychological deficits in childhood epilepsy syndromes. *Neuropsychological Review, 17,* 427–444.

Mandelbaum, D. E., & Burack, G. D. (1997). The effect of seizure type and medication on cognitive and behavioral functioning in children with idiopathic epilepsy. *Developmental Medicine & Child Neurology, 39,* 731–735.

Martinuik, A. L. C., Speechley, K. N., Seeco, M., Campbell, M. K., & Donner, A. (2007). Evaluation of an epilepsy education program for grade 5 students: A cluster randomized trial. *Epilepsy & Behavior, 9,* 58–67.

McDonald, C. R., Swartz, B. E., Halgren, E., Patell, A., Daimes, R., & Mandelkern, M. (2006). The relationship of regional frontal hypometabolism to executive function: A resting fluorodeoxyglucose PET study of patients with epilepsy and healthy controls. *Epilepsy & Behavior, 9,* 58–67.

Mitchell, W. G., Chavez, J. M., Lee, H., & Guzman, B. L. (1991). Academic underachievement in children with epilepsy. *Journal of Child Neurology, 6,* 65–72.

Nabbout, R., & Dulac, O. (2003). Epileptic encephalopathies: A brief overview. *Journal of Clinical Neurophysiology, 20,* 393–397.

Neppe, V. M., & Tucker, G. J. (1994). Neuropsychiatric aspects of epilepsy and atypical spells In S. C. Yudofsky & R. E. Hales (Eds.), *Synopsis of neuropsychiatry* (pp. 307–328). Washington, DC: American Psychiatric Association.

Noeker, M., & Haverkamp, F. (2001). Successful cognitive-behavioral habituation training toward photophobia in photogenic partial seizures. *Epilepsia, 42,* 689–691.

Oguni, H., Hayashi, K., Osawa, M., Awaya, Y., Fukuyama, Y., Fukuma, G., et al. (2005). Severe myoclonic epilepsy in infancy: Clinical analysis and relation to SCN1A mutations in a Japanese cohort. *Advances in Neurology, 95,* 103–117.

Ohtsuka, Y., Maniwa, S., Ogino, T., Yamatogi, Y., & Ohtahara, S. (1991). Severe myoclonic epilepsy in infancy: A long-term follow-up study. *The Japanese Journal of Psychiatry and Neurology, 45,* 416–418.

O'Leary, D. S., Lovell, M. R., Sackellares, J. C., Berent, S., Giordani, B., Seidenberg, M., et al. (1983). Effects of age of onset of partial and generalized seizures on neuropsychological performance in children. *Journal of Nervous and Mental Disease, 171,* 623–629.

Ortinski, P., & Meador, K. J. (2004). Cognitive side effects of antiepileptic drugs. *Epilepsy and Behavior, 5,* 560–565.

Palade, S., & Benga, I. (2007). Neuropsychological impairments on the CANTAB test battery: Case reports of children with frontal and temporal lobe epilepsy. *Cognition, Brain, & Behavior, 11,* 539–552.

Parker, J. G., & Asher, S. R. (1987). Peer relations and later personal adjustment: Are low-accepted children at risk? *Psychological Bulletin, 102,* 357–389.

Parrish, J., Geary, E., Jones, J., Seth, R., Hermann, B., & Seidenberg, M. (2007). Executive functioning in childhood epilepsy: Parent-report and cognitive assessment. *Developmental Medicine & Child Neurology, 49,* 412–416.

Pascalicchio, T. F., de Araujo Filho, G. M., da Silva Noffs, M. H., Lin, K., Cabocio, L. O. S. F., Vidal-Dourado, M., et al. (2007). Neuropsychological profile of patients with juvenile myoclonic epilepsy: A controlled study of 50 patients. *Epilepsy and Behavior, 10,* 263–267.

Pavone, P., Bianchini, R., Trifiletti, R. R., Incorpora, G., Pavone, A., & Parano, E. (2001). Neuropsychological assessment in children with absence epilepsy. *Neurology, 56*, 1047–1051.

Plioplys, S., Dunn, D. W., & Caplan, R. (2007). Ten-year research update review: Psychiatric problems in children with epilepsy. *Journal of the American Academy of Child & Adolescent Psychiatry, 46*, 1389–1402.

Prassouli, A., Katsarou, E., Attilakos, A., & Antoniadou, I. (2007). Learning difficulties in children with epilepsy with idiopathic generalized epilepsy and well-controlled seizures. *Developmental Medicine & Child Neurology, 49*, 874.

Prevey, M. L., Delaney, R. C., Cramer, J. A., Cattanach, L., Collins, J. F., & Mattson, R. H. (1996). Effect of valproate on cognitive function: Comparison with carbamazepine. *Archives of Neurology, 53*, 1008–1016.

Pritchard, P. B., Holmstrom, V. L., & Giacinto, J. (1985). Self-abatement of complex partial seizures. *Annals of Neurology, 18*, 265–267.

Reynolds, C. R., Kamphaus, R. W., Rosenthal, B. L., & Hiemenz, J. R. (1997). Application of the Kaufman assessment battery for children (K-ABC) in neuropsychological assessment. In C. R. Reynolds & E. Fletcher-Janzen (Eds.), *Handbook of clinical child neuropsychology* (2nd ed., pp. 252–269). New York: Plenum.

Riccio, C. A., & Reynolds, C. R. (1998). Neuropsychological assessment of children. In A. S. Bellack & M. Hersen (Eds.), *Comprehensive clinical psychology* (Vol. 4, pp. 267–301). New York: Pergamon.

Rossi, P. G., Parmeggiani, A., Bach, V., Santucci, M., & Visconti, P. (1995). EEG features and epilepsy in patients with autism *Brain & Development, 17*, 169–174.

Schoenfeld, J., Seidenberg, M., Woodard, A., Hecox, K., Inglese, C., Mack, K., et al. (1999). Neuropsychological and behavioral status of children with complex partial seizures. *Developmental Medicine & Child Neurology, 41*, 724–731.

Seidenberg, M., Beck, N., & Geisser, M. (1986). Academic achievement of children with epilepsy. *Epilepsia, 27*, 753–759.

Sherman, E. M. S., Slick, D. J., Connolly, M. B., & Eyrl, K. L. (2007). ADHD, neurological correlates and health-related quality of life in severe pediatric epilepsy. *Epilepsia, 48*, 1083–1091.

Shevell, M., Ashwal, S., Donley, D., Flint, J., Gingold, M., Hirtz, D., et al. (2003). Practice parameter: Evaluation of the child with global developmental delay report of the quality standards subcommittee of the American Academy of Neurology and the Practice Committee of the Child Neurology Society. *Neurology, 60*, 367–380.

Smith, K., Siddarth, P., Zima, B., Sankar, R., Mitchell, W., Gowrinathan, R., et al. (2007). Unmet mental health needs in pediatric epilepsy: Insights from providers. *Epilepsy & Behavior, 11*, 401–408.

Sonmez, F., Atakli, D., Sari, H., Atay, T., & Arpaci, B. (2004). Cognitive function in juvenile myoclonic epilepsy. *Epilepsy and Behavior, 5*, 329–336.

Sterman, M. B. (2000). Basic concepts and clinical findings in the treatment of seizure disorders with EEG operant conditioning. *Clinical Electroencephalography, 31*, 45–55.

Sterman, M. B., & Egner, T. (2006). Foundation and practice of neurofeedback for the treatment of epilepsy. *Applied Psychophysiology and Biofeedback, 31*, 21–35.

Sturnniolo, M. G., & Galletti, F. (1994). Idiopathic epilepsy and school achievement. *Archives of Disease in Childhood, 70,* 424–428.

Thiele, E. A. (2003). Assessing the efficacy of antiepileptic treatments: The ketogenic diet. *Epilepsia, 44*(7), 36–29.

Tracy, J. I., Lippincott, C., Mahmood, T., Waldron, B., Kanauss, K., Glosser, D., et al. (2007). Are depression and cognitive performance related in temporal lobe epilepsy? *Epilepsia, 48,* 2327–2335.

Trinka, E., Kienpointner, G., Unterberger, I., Luef, G., Bauer, G., Doering, L. B., et al. (2006). Psychiatric comorbidity in juvenile myoclonic epilepsy. *Epilepsia, 47,* 2086–2091.

Tse, E., Hamiwka, L., Sherman, E. M. S., & Wirrell, F. (2007). Social skills problems in children with epilepsy: Prevalence, nature, and predictors. *Epilepsy & Behavior, 11,* 499–505.

Tuchman, R., & Rapin, I. (2002). Epilepsy in autism. *Lancet Neurology, 1,* 352–358.

Vining, E. P. (1999). Clinical efficacy of the ketogenic diet. *Epilepsy Research, 37,* 181–190.

Vining, E. P., Pyzik, P., McGrogan, J., Hladky, H., Anand, A., Kriegler, S., et al. (2002). Growth of children on the ketogenic diet. *Developmental Medicine and Child Neurology, 44,* 796–802.

Wagner, J. L., & Smith, G. (2005). Psychosocial intervention in pediatric epilepsy: A critique of the literature. *Epilepsy and Behavior, 8,* 39–49.

Westbrook, L. E., Silver, E. J., Coupey, S. M., & Shinnar, S. (1991). Social characteristics of adolescents with idiopathic epilepsy: A comparison to chronically ill and non-chronically ill peers. *Journal of Epilepsy, 4,* 87–94.

Williams, J., Lange, B., Phillips, T., Sharp, G. B., De los Reyes, E., Bates, S., et al. (2002). The course of inattentive and hyperactive-impulsive symptoms in children with new onset seizures. *Epilepsy & Behavior, 3,* 517–521.

Williams, J., Phillips, T., Griebel, M. L., Sharp, G. B., Lange, B., Edgar, T., et al. (2001a). Factors associated with academic achievement in children with controlled epilepsy. *Epilepsy & Behavior, 2,* 217–223.

Williams, J., Phillips, T., Griebel, M. L., Sharp, G. B., Lange, B., Edgar, T., et al. (2001b). Patterns of memory performance in children with controlled epilepsy on the CVLT-C. *Child Neuropsychology, 7,* 15–20.

Wirrell, E., Farrell, K., & Whiting, S. (2005). The epileptic encephalopathies of infancy and childhood. *The Canadian Journal of Neurological Sciences [Le Journal Canadien Des Sciences Neurologiques], 32,* 409–418.

Yu, C. G., Lee, A., Wirrell, E., Sherman, E. M. S., & Hamiwka, L. (2008). Health behavior in teens with epilepsy: How do they compare with controls? *Epilepsy & Behavior, 13,* 90–95.

Zillmer, E. A., Spiers, M. V., & Culbertson, W. C. (2008). *Principles of neuropsychology.* Belmont, CA: Thompson Wadsworth.

CHAPTER 30

Assessing and Intervening with Children with Traumatic Brain Injury

JENNIFER R. MORRISON

T HE PURPOSE OF this chapter is to discuss the implications of traumatic brain injury on a school-based population. This will be accomplished by describing the epidemiological data, injury types and categories of severity, common neurocognitive sequelae that could be anticipated, the possible impact of traumatic brain injury on education and learning, pertinent literature regarding recovery and progression of symptoms, and considerations for assessment and intervention.

INTRODUCTION AND OVERVIEW

In a report to congress, the Centers for Disease Control's (CDC) Center for Injury Prevention and Control estimated that 5.3 million citizens in the United States, roughly 2 percent of the population, are living with one or more disabilities resulting from a traumatic brain injury (TBI; CDC, 2002). Head injury is the leading cause of death in persons under the age of 35 (Fletcher, Ewing-Cobbs, Francis, & Levin, 1995). The portions of the population that are at highest risk for sustaining a TBI are adolescents and young adults between 15 and 24 years of age (CDC). Of those who are treated at a hospital for their injuries, about 50 percent will have major neurological sequelae (Di Scala, Osberg, Gans, Chin, & Grant, 1991). TBIs are classified into two categories: open and closed head injuries (Youse, Le, Cannizzaro, & Coetho, 2002). Open head injuries are characterized by penetration of the skull and disruption to the meninges that surround and protect the brain. This is most often associated with a gunshot wound. As this type of injury is less common, occurring in a fraction of the pediatric population, and presents with more focal and predictable sequelae, most of the discussion in the current chapter will pertain to the other form of head injury. Closed head injuries involve trauma to the head from an external force that does not penetrate the skull or compromise the meninges (Youse et al., 2002). This includes insult to the brain associated with incidences such as car accidents, falls, impacts to the head, and being struck by or thrown from something. Each of these injuries is distinct; with no one head injury presenting the same, even if the mechanism of injury is the same. Thus, there needs to be some generally recognized way of categorizing injury levels in order to more quickly assess the degree of potential disability and need.

TBI severity is generally classified into mild, moderate, and severe categories. Several different measures have been used to describe the levels of TBI severity. The most common is the Glasgow Coma Scale (GCS; Teasdale & Jennett, 1974), which is a 15-point scale that measures aspects of brain injury by assessing brain activity at certain levels. This scale includes consideration for level of eye opening, motor movement, and verbal responses. The patient's quality of response in each of these categories is coded and combined to arrive at a composite GCS score. Another common measure of TBI severity is the level of post-traumatic amnesia (PTA), a form of injury-related anterograde amnesia that is characterized by the inability to store new memories or acquire new learning (Youse et al., 2002). Often, these and other measures, such as neuroimaging results and duration of coma, are used in combination to estimate severity levels. This information is used to establish the overall prevalence of TBI. It has been estimated that as many as 75 percent of TBIs are mild in nature, those falling from 13 to 15 on the GCS (Youse et al., 2002, p. 5). The Centers for Disease Control estimates that the remaining cases are split relatively evenly between those with moderate and severe injuries (2002). Youse and associates defined moderate TBI as involving a GCS of 9 to 12 and coma of less than 6 hours. Severe TBI was defined as an injury that was characterized by a GCS of 3 to 8 and more than 6 hours in a coma (Youse et al., 2002). These designations are somewhat arbitrary with mixed efficacy in the literature; however, these sources of information can provide a rough point of reference for establishing the possible severity of sequelae that could be expected (e.g. Levin & Eisenberg, 1979; Winogron, Knights, & Bawden, 1984).

In regard to the specific mechanisms of neural injury that may occur, the forces inflicted on the head in TBI produce a complex mixture of consequences, including diffuse and focal lesions within the brain. Damage resulting from an injury can be immediate (primary) or secondary in nature. Although primary insults are often readily apparent, secondary injury resulting from disordered autoregulation and other pathophysiological changes within the brain occur in the days and even weeks after injury (Leddy, Kozlowski, Fung, Pendergast, &

Willer, 2007). Urgent neurosurgical intervention for intracerebral (between the two hemispheres of the brain), subdural (between the dura and the brain), or epidural (between the skull and the outer covering of the brain) hemorrhages can mitigate the extent of secondary injury. Hypoxic or ischemic injuries resulting from lack of adequate blood flow to the brain or poor oxygenation of the blood also significantly affect recovery and can be either primary or secondary in nature.

Because of the shape of the inner surface of the skull, focal injuries are most commonly seen in the frontal and temporal lobes, but can occur anywhere (Leddy et al., 2007). Cerebral contusions are readily identifiable on computed tomography (CT) scans, but may not be evident immediately, only becoming visible after two to three days. Deep intracerebral hemorrhages can result from arterial damage from either focal or diffuse damage. Diffuse injury (referred to as diffuse axonal injury or DAI) is only visible on CT scan in the worst 5 to 10 percent of cases, and most commonly seen as multiple punctate subcortical lesions in and around the corpus callosum and deep white matter and/or as intraventricular hemorrhages (Scheid, Walther, Guthke, Preul, & von Cramon, 2006). The most consistent effect of diffuse brain damage, even when mild, is the presence of altered consciousness. The depth and duration of coma provide the best guide to the severity of the diffuse damage. The majority of children with DAI will not have any CT evidence to support the diagnosis. Other clinical markers suggesting the possible presence of DAI include high speed of injury and prolonged retrograde and anterograde amnesia (Scheid et al., 2006).

Prior to the advent of modern emergency care techniques and the availability of regional trauma facilities, children and adolescents with acquired brain injuries were subject to increased mortality rates associated with both primary and secondary complications (Mateer, Kerns, & Eso, 1996). Current technologies have allowed many of these youth to survive, and eventually return to normal daily activities. Despite this increase in the survival rate and subsequent needs in the TBI population, the educational assistance demanded by these children and adolescents has only recently been the topic of special education legislation. Regardless of the less severe cognitive sequelae usually associated with mild TBI, which constitute a large percentage of youth with acquired head injuries, these children, with documentation of their injuries paired with educational needs, will qualify for special education services. Within days to weeks of the head injury approximately 40 percent of children with a history of TBI develop a host of troubling symptoms collectively called post-concussion syndrome (PCS; McCrea, 2008). A child need not have suffered a concussion or loss of consciousness to develop the syndrome, and many children and adolescents with mild TBI suffer from PCS. Symptoms include headache, dizziness, vertigo (a sensation of spinning around or of objects spinning around the child), memory problems, trouble concentrating, sleeping problems, restlessness, irritability, apathy, depression, and anxiety. These symptoms may last for a few weeks after the head injury. Many children with mild to moderate head injuries who experience cognitive deficits become easily confused or distracted and have problems with concentration and attention. They also have problems with higher-level executive functions, such as planning, organizing, abstract reasoning, problem solving, and making judgments, which may make it difficult to resume pre-injury school-related activities. Recovery from cognitive deficits is greatest within the first six months after the injury and more gradual after that (McCrea, 2008). Thus, the provision of special education services is indicated, if not required, for such individuals to make educational progress.

The remaining cases of TBI, classified as moderate or severe, will be more likely to meet full criteria for special education services as indicated by academic need. Research has suggested that the post-injury period for children with TBI is characterized by severely decreased cognitive functioning in many areas. This "acute stage" of recovery involves drastic improvements from the time of injury, lasting as long as three to six months post-injury (Catroppa & Anderson, 2002). Some have estimated that the acute stage lasts as long as twelve months past the time of injury. Despite disagreement as to the length of time over which recovery of function occurs, a general consensus exists in the literature regarding the persistent problems evident in TBI patients well past the acute stage of recovery (e.g., Lord-Maes & Obrzut, 1996). This level of deficit, which is often apparent at first with the more severely injured children, is often dynamic and emergent as the child progresses developmentally.

It has been asserted that rapid improvements made in physical recovery during the acute stage following an acquired TBI in children mask possible underlying cognitive deficits that remain (Johnson, 1992). Johnson's research suggested that cognitive deficiencies not readily apparent during the acute stages of development arose well past recovery from physical injuries. He further asserted that "return to school" was not an acceptable indicator that the child had fully recovered from his or her injuries. Hawley, Ward, Magnay, and Long (2002) found that in addition to difficulty associated with recovery of cognitive function, parental reports indicated that a majority (72.6 percent) of the students missed school as a result of their injuries. Sixty-nine percent of the children in the mild TBI group missed school, with a mean of 16.1 days being missed. Those in the moderate TBI group were absent an average of 30.6 days, totaling 82.5 percent of the sample. Of those in the severe TBI group, 91.8 percent reportedly missed school, with an average of 140.6 days missed across the group (Hawley et al., 2002). This suggests that those who have acquired a TBI not only have to cope with recovery of cognitive function but must also compensate for up to a full school semester of lost learning. This implies that the child with a TBI will be at a great disadvantage upon reentry into the school system.

The 21st Annual Report of the Office of Special Education Programs (U.S. Department of Education, 2003) indicated that 11,895 students had been classified under the TBI handicapping code that year. This number is in stark contrast to the estimated 1.5 million people, a portion of which will be children and adolescents, who acquire a TBI annually (Youse et al., 2002). This dichotomy between the total number of brain injuries and the number of children receiving special education services as a result of such injuries indicates that these children and adolescents either do not meet the full IDEA criteria needed to receive services, have not informed their school district of their injury, and/or are physically unable to return to public school after their injuries. Ewing-Cobbs, Fletcher, Levin, Iovino, and Miner (1998) noted that 73 percent of their severely injured sample had been receiving special education services, and 39 percent of the children had failed a grade following their head injury. These percentages were present despite lower but overall average performance on measures of achievement, an indication of previously acquired school-based learning.

Research on TBI has shown a variety of neurocognitive deficits in youth with mild, moderate, and severe TBIs. In a study of 525 British children with mild, moderate, and severe TBIs, parents indicated that many changes were evident. Cognitive differences included personality changes, poor concentration, memory problems, and mobility problems (Hawley et al., 2002). Chadwick, Rutter, and Schaffer (1981) found that children with TBI were deficient in tasks involving reaction time, manual dexterity, and measures of nonverbal intelligence. Hawley and colleagues cited deficits in intellectual, academic, and personality domains. Results such as these suggest that the use of a unitary measure of cognitive ability, as has been the trend previously, is not sufficient to elucidate the many cognitive and psychosocial sequelae associated with TBI. Further, comparisons focusing on global areas of dysfunction in children with TBI provide little information in regard to linking appropriate interventions for remediation with noted areas of deficiency. A proactive stance in which assessment was used to ascertain a child's level of functioning across all major areas of ability would be most beneficial when designing academic interventions (see Table 30.1 for possible neurocognitive sequelae). In order to establish goals, modifications, and accommodations that can effectively address the needs of these children, professionals should seek to educate themselves on the common physical, cognitive, and social-emotional side effects that could be associated with this diagnosis.

Table 30.1
Possible Consequences of Traumatic Brain Injury

Neurological impairment (motor, sensory and autonomic)

- Motor function impairment—coordination, balance, walking, hand function, speech
- Sensory loss—taste, touch, hearing, vision, smell
- Sleep disturbance—insomnia, fatigue
- Medical complications—spasticity, post-traumatic epilepsy, hydrocephalus, heterotopic ossification

Cognitive impairment

- Memory impairment, difficulty with new learning, attention and concentration; reduced speed and flexibility of thought processing; impaired problem-solving skills
- Problems in planning, organizing, and making decisions
- Language problems—dysphasia, problems finding words, and impaired reading and writing skills
- Impaired judgment and safety awareness

Personality and behavioral changes

- Impaired social and coping skills, reduced self-esteem
- Altered emotional control; poor frustration tolerance and anger management; denial, and self-centeredness
- Reduced insight, disinhibition, impulsivity
- Psychiatric disorders—anxiety, depression, post-traumatic stress disorder, psychosis
- Apathy, amotivational states

Common lifestyle consequences

- Inadequate academic achievement
- Lack of transportation alternatives
- Inadequate recreational opportunities
- Difficulties in maintaining interpersonal relationships, breakdown of established romantic relationships
- Loss of preinjury roles; loss of independence

Adapted from information provided by the Brain Injury Association of America, 2006.

SPECIAL CONSIDERATIONS FOR PEDIATRIC TBI

There are significant age-related variables that need to be considered when pediatric TBI is discussed, since much of the adult TBI literature does not accurately reflect what is seen in children and adolescents upon downward extension alone. For instance, contemporary research has suggested that there is a higher incidence of diffuse brain swelling in children following a TBI, which has commonly been associated with devastating secondary injuries as the brain presses against the bony ridges lining the skull. Neurobiological studies have indicated that children are more likely than adults to experience exacerbated edema of brain tissue due to differences in neurotransmitter distribution and a more sensitive inflammatory response (Kochanek, 2006). Because the skull is comparatively compliant due to the presence of membranous sutures in infants and young children, there is an increased range of cranial distortions that are possible as the ever-swelling brain pushes outward, and the cranium is forced to change its shape to accommodate. In addition, there is a natural process referred to "pruning," which describes the developmental tendency of the pediatric brain to selectively kill neurons that were generated in excess in early brain formation. Because the pediatric brain is disposed to initiating a process of cell death as part of the natural selection of cells for retention while "weeding out" cells that are less efficient and useful, it is possible that a child's brain will respond with this type of response after a head injury at a higher rate than would be seen in an adult. Consequently, more neurons would be lost in a child versus an adult (Kochanek, 2006). As a result of the initial impact of the TBI itself and any further secondary damage, there are many possible neurocognitive domains that could be negatively affected by a TBI.

NEUROCOGNITIVE DEFICITS ASSOCIATED WITH TBI

Sensory Processing and Motor Control Deficits Associated with TBI

Acute presentation of a child after experiencing a TBI will be varied depending on the type of injury, severity, location of cerebral insult, and extent of localized versus diffuse injuries. Thus, an overall generalization regarding functional implications to any one cognitive or behavioral domain is impossible. However, there are some overarching themes that can be discussed in this regard. Sensory processing is thought to exist within three functional units: specifically, one zone for primary sensory input, one for secondary sensory response programming and output, and one for tertiary arousal. The primary zones are the smallest and most specific, consisting of brain regions where visual, auditory, and tactile sensations are registered as they come in. The secondary zones allow for the individual sensory bits of information to gather together to culminate in a perception including input from multiple sensory modalities. Finally, the tertiary zones overlap between the parietal (somatosensory), temporal (auditory), and occipital (visual) lobes and are responsible for the integration of sensory perception into something meaningful. Total sensory loss, such as blindness or deafness, is rare in closed head injuries, as the anatomical location of these primary functioning zones does not lend itself to direct impact. The tertiary zones, in contrast, are more vulnerable because they are larger and more diffuse. Additionally, small areas of damage across the primary and secondary regions aggregate into larger more pronounced deficits at the tertiary level (Glozman, 2007).

At the most basic level, it is possible for the child, based on the location of the cerebral damage, to exhibit a range of motor deficits from complete inability to move one side of the body (e.g., hemiplegia, possibly through damage to the posterior limb of the internal capsule), to weakening of the muscles on one side of the body (e.g., hemiparesis, caused by damage to the corticospinal tract), to poor coordination associated with a range of lesion sites including the somatosensory regions, basal ganglia, and/or cerebellum. This may translate into functional impairments including gait disturbances (unsteady or uncoordinated), difficulty with oromotor control affecting eating and talking, and impairments in fine motor coordination needed for writing, drawing, and daily self-help skills such as grooming, dressing, and feeding. However, sensory processing deficits may also manifest as sensitivity or alterations in the processing of visual inputs, sounds, taste, and smell. Children with TBI may present in a way that is consistent with what is seen in a Sensory Processing Disorder. If so, assessment and intervention typically used for youth with sensory processing differences would be equally effective with those suffering from a head injury (Schoenbrodt, 2001).

Attention and Executive Functioning Deficits Associated with TBI

Although younger children's developmental readiness opens the door for possible plasticity, this variable allows for less predictability in the manifestation and developmental progression of deficit expression. This is most apparent with the attention and executive functioning systems, which are attributed in large part to the frontal lobes. The frontal lobes are the last of the cerebral lobes to develop, with neuronal proliferation and synaptogenesis (formation of new brain cells) peaking between 1 and 2 years of age (Milner & Petrides, 1984 as cited in Catroppa & Anderson, 2006). However, a variety of research studies have suggested developmental age ranges during which particular skill sets emerge and are honed extending into the early to middle twenties (see Catroppa & Anderson for a full review). Additionally, the shape and structure of the skull and its relation to the anterior portions of the frontal lobe and bilateral temporal lobes leave the circuitry involved in attention and executive functioning at risk, particularly when injuries involve acceleration/deceleration insults, such as those seen in a motor vehicle accident (Mateer et al., 1996). When you take this factor into consideration with the developmental trajectory seen in normal neurocognitive development, deficits in attention and executive functioning may not become clear until late childhood and adolescence, when children are required to act upon their environments and express a more independent behavioral and functional range of skills. These areas of functioning include planning, problem solving, processing speed, abstract thought, multitasking, cognitive flexibility, and metacognition. Any or all of these areas may be impacted following a TBI (Schoenbrodt, 2001). A specific example of a focal injury that may be linked to observed functional deficits includes injuries involving the prefrontal cortex. In this case, research has clearly delineated that this structural area is typically responsible for skills such as temporal organization, integration, formulation, and execution of novel behavioral sequences requiring the person to respond to both environmental feedback and internal motivational states (Sohlberg & Mateer, 2001).

When focal frontal lobes lesions exist as a result of impact to the head, the possibility of subsequent attention and executive functioning problems increases. However, diffuse axonal shearing and damage to cortical tracts that extend from the front to the back of the brain can also cause functional deficits. For example, the dorsolateral prefrontal cortex, which is thought to be the highest cortical area responsible, at least in part, for motor planning, organization, and regulation, integration of sensory and mnemonic information, regulation of intellectual function and action, and working memory, is connected to the orbitofrontal cortex and to a variety of brain areas, including the thalamus, parts of the basal ganglia (the dorsal caudate nucleus), the hippocampus, and primary and secondary association areas of neocortex, including posterior temporal, parietal, and occipital areas. Damage to any of these areas may disrupt the executive functions attributed to a portion of the brain along the connection, as it appears that the executive system in children differs from that of adults and includes a wider neural substrate that extends well beyond the frontal lobes. This diverse set of skills is essential in developing new knowledge and capabilities and the establishment of advanced functioning in the domains of independent life skills needed in adolescence and adulthood (Power, Catroppa, Coleman, Ditchfield, & Anderson, 2007). It should be clear why executive functioning deficits have been deemed the most devastating and pervasive effect seen after a TBI.

VISUAL PERCEPTION AND VISUAL-MOTOR INTEGRATION DEFICITS ASSOCIATED WITH TBI

Vision problems are a possible sequelae associated with traumatic brain injury. These visual problems range from dry eyes to visual field loss to double vision. Each case is different, and the difficulty each patient has depends on the severity and location of the injury. A common visual effect of brain injury is the loss of one's visual field or ability to see to the side. There are many types of visual field losses that can occur, but the most common form is called a homonymous hemianopsia, or loss of half of the field of vision in each eye. If the posterior portion of the brain (occipital lobe) is damaged on one side, a loss of visual field occurs to the opposite side in both eyes. Students experiencing this type of problem frequently bump into objects and easily trip or fall over objects in the lost visual field. Going into crowded areas, such as schools, may become quite difficult because people and objects suddenly appear in front of them from the blind side. Additionally, the loss of visual field may also cause children to miss words and have difficulty reading. When certain portions of the brain are damaged (typically in the right hemisphere), the child may fail to appreciate space to one side, which is usually to the left (the contralateral side). Unlike visual field loss, this problem, called visual neglect, is not a physical loss of sensation, but rather a loss of attention to the visual area. For instance, a child with neglect may no longer brush one side of his hair. Patients with visual neglect have more difficulties than those with only visual field loss. Unfortunately, both neglect and field loss may be observed together in some cases (Clark, 1996; Hellerstein & Kadet, 1999; Schoenbrodt, 2001).

Other visual-spatial disorders may occur as well. Children may experience difficulty navigating themselves, even in familiar areas. They may also misjudge the straight-ahead position and can confuse right and left. In addition to perceptual and attention problems in the visual-spatial domain, physical limitations may arise subsequent to a TBI. Smooth and accurate eye movements are essential in reading, tracking objects, and compensating for body movements. Following injury to the brain, movements may become jerkier. Nystagmus, a jerky motion of the eyes, may also occur. When acquired later in life, nystagmus results in a vertigo-like sensation or a feeling that the world is moving. The sensation of dizziness or tilting may also occur following damage to the brain stem. Children and adolescents with a history of head injury commonly experience blurred or double vision. Each eye has six external muscles that move the eyes together as a team. If control is impaired to one or more muscles, the eyes cannot maintain alignment in all positions required to direct their gaze or line of sight. This may occur due to damage to the control centers for several cranial nerves. Double vision may be constant or intermittent. The patient may experience normal single vision in the straight-ahead position, but suddenly have double vision when looking to one side. As we bring reading material close to our eyes, both eyes must turn in together as a team, which is called ocular convergence. This ability is frequently impaired in brain injury, resulting in eye fatigue or discomfort while reading. After TBI, younger patients may experience more problems focusing on near objects and material. This may present simply as difficulty in reading. This is usually due to damage to the oculomotor nerve, which is responsible for controlling the eye's ability to focus by changing the shape of the lens. Another impairment that may impact reading when a child with a TBI returns to school involves eye movements called saccades. These small movements are used to jump from word to word as we read. Impairments in saccades may result in difficulty reading smoothly along a line of print (Clark, 1996; Hellerstein & Kadet, 1999; Schoenbrodt, 2001).

LANGUAGE DEFICITS ASSOCIATED WITH TBI

Language and communication problems are common disabilities in children with TBI. Some may experience aphasia, defined as difficulty understanding and producing spoken and written language; others may have difficulty with the more subtle aspects of communication, such as body language and emotional, nonverbal signals. In Broca's aphasia or motor aphasia, Children with TBI have trouble recalling words and speaking in complete sentences. They may speak in broken phrases and pause frequently. Most children are aware of these deficits and may become extremely frustrated. Children with Wernicke's aphasia or fluent aphasia, display little meaning in their speech, even though they speak in complete sentences and use correct grammar. Instead, they speak in flowing gibberish, drawing out their sentences with nonessential and, sometimes, invented words. Many children with fluent aphasia are unaware that they make little sense and become angry with others for not understanding them. Children with global aphasia have extensive damage to the portions of the brain responsible for language and often suffer severe communication disabilities. Youth with TBI may have problems with expressive language if the part of the brain that controls speech muscles is damaged. In this disorder, called dysarthria, children can think of the appropriate language but cannot easily speak the words because they are unable to use the muscles needed to form the words and produce the sounds. Speech is often slow, slurred, and garbled. Some children may have problems with intonation or inflection, called prosodic dysfunction. An important aspect of speech, inflection conveys emotional meaning and is necessary for certain aspects of language, such as irony. These language deficits can lead to miscommunication, confusion, and frustration for the child as well as those interacting with him or her (Demir, Altinok, Aydin, & Köseoglu, 2006; Schoenbrodt, 2001).

MEMORY DEFICITS ASSOCIATED WITH TBI

Overall, the mechanisms of memory are not completely understood. Specific brain areas, such as the hippocampus, amygdala, striatum, and the mammillary bodies, are thought to be involved in memory functioning with each implicated in a specific role (Blumenfeld, 2002). For example, the hippocampus is believed to be involved in declarative learning, while the amygdala is thought to be involved in attaching an emotional linkage to memory traces. Research on specific case studies citing anatomical areas damaged in trauma patients, paired with findings from animal models, has allowed the ability to describe the neuroanatomical correlates associated with memory deficits as a primary source of information (Blumenfeld, 2002) However, rather than implicating a specific area (such as in a focal injury), it could be that damage to adjacent areas, or to a pathway traveling through the area, is actually responsible for the observed deficit (such as in shearing and axonal injuries). Further, it is not sufficient to describe memory and its counterpart, learning, as solely dependent on specific brain regions. Learning and memory are attributed not only to structural functioning but also to changes in neuronal synapses, thought to be mediated by long-term potentiation and long-term metabolic depression at the microscopic level. Certainly this process cannot be localized to a specific focal point (Blumenfeld, 2002). Thus, although memory deficits are one of the most common neurocognitive sequelae, following a closed head injury, deficits may arise from focal injuries, diffuse injuries, secondary damage associated with cerebral swelling, subsequent pathophysiological cascades, or any combination of these factors (Squire, Stark, & Clark, 2004).

Research regarding memory functioning in children following a TBI indicates that there is a relative sparing of some, usually simpler, memory functions. Specific areas of memory difficulty are suggested in the literature including recall of large amounts of verbal information such as sentences, paragraphs, and stories of varying lengths (Anderson et al., 1997; Catroppa & Anderson, 2002; Chadwick et al., 1981; Farmer et al., 1999; Hanten, Levin, & Song, 1999; Max et al., 1999). This suggests that children and adolescents who have sustained TBIs are able to successfully complete simple verbal memory tasks, such as memory for smaller pieces of verbal information— digits, letters, words, and sometimes sentences— but demonstrate increased difficulty as the complexity of the stimuli and task requirements become more demanding. Difficulty remembering large amounts of verbal information also extends to recall after a delay. This effect is present across the spectrum of injury severity (Donders, 1993). In regard to memory for lists of verbal information, participants with less severe injuries seem to retain function in comparison with more acutely injured children.

Research exploring the effects of TBI on visual memory in children suggests differing results. In regard to immediate visual memory, basic sequential recall of information seems to remain intact despite TBI, regardless of severity. When assessed in regard to spatial placement of visual stimuli and sequential block tapping, Anderson et al. (1997) found that children with severe head injuries were initially impaired in comparison to less injured and control groups, but that these differences had resolved themselves by twelve months after their injuries. Another set of visual memory assessments indicates significantly lower performance by a severe TBI sample. Despite clinical significance, all groups in this study exhibited performance in the average range (Farmer et al., 1999). Some methodological differences in this set of literature indicates varying results, often showing decreased performance in the more severely injured participants (Anderson et al., 1997; Catroppa & Anderson, 2002; Donders, 1993; Farmer et al., 1999; Max et al., 1999).

SOCIAL-EMOTIONAL AND BEHAVIORAL DEFICITS ASSOCIATED WITH TBI

Some children with a history of TBI have emotional or behavioral problems that fit criteria for a psychiatric disorder. Family members of TBI children often find that personality changes and behavioral problems are among the most unexpected and problematic disabilities to handle. Psychiatric problems that may surface include depression, apathy, anxiety, irritability, anger, paranoia, confusion, frustration, agitation, insomnia and other sleep problems, and mood swings (Yeates & Taylor, 2006). Problem behaviors may include aggression and violence, impulsivity, disinhibition, acting out, noncompliance, social inappropriateness, emotional outbursts, immature and overly dependent behavior, impaired self-control, decreased self-awareness, inability to take responsibility or accept criticism, egocentrism, inappropriate sexual activity or behavior, and alcohol or drug abuse/addiction. Sometimes, children and adolescents with TBI suffer from developmental stagnation, meaning that they fail to mature emotionally, socially, or psychologically after the trauma. This is a serious problem, as attitudes and behaviors that are appropriate for a child or teenager become inappropriate as they near adulthood (Savage & Wolcott, 1994; Schoenbrodt, 2001). Thus, the presentation of youth who have sustained a TBI may be similar to that of a child or adolescent suffering from a mental health diagnosis alone. Also, those with traumatic injuries to the brain may exhibit emotional and psychological problems that are even more pronounced than would be expected from adjustment to changes in functional skills alone, such as those evident in an Adjustment Disorder. As can be seen, there are a variety of factors that should be explored when working with children who have a history of head injuries, even those that were mild in nature.

These behavioral, personality, and psychological changes may be due to a variety of neurological factors. For instance, frontotemporal-limbic circuitry appears to be particularly implicated in a range of emotional disturbances. Additionally, ventro-medial frontal areas are thought to play an important role in motivation and anticipation, and right hemisphere and subcortical lesions have been associated with disorders of motivation (Blumenfeld, 2002; Milner, 1995). Impairments in affect recognition often result in difficulties responding appropriately in interpersonal situations. Sensory changes such as intolerance of light or noise, in addition to the secondary psychological impact of other physical and cognitive impairments, are also relevant. Literature in this area suggests that there is a range of possible focal or diffuse lesions that could contribute to the psychological presentation of a child after a head injury. However, physiological changes alone cannot account for the increased prevalence of emotional disturbances in the TBI population.

Gainotti (1999) draws on psychodynamic theories of denial in issues of emotional adjustment following brain injury. His review suggested that other researchers have highlighted the importance of pre- and post-morbid coping style, personality, clients' own causal explanations for their difficulties, and pre-injury psychopathology as factors influencing emotional outcome. Work focusing on the TBI survivor's adjustment to his or her injury in terms of subjective experience of the self has demonstrated how survivors may experience distressing threats to their sense of identity. Additionally, when an individual suffers from a TBI there is a possibility that the child or adolescent is functionally unable to recognize his or her own level of impairment in a variety of domains due to frontal lobe deficits affecting self-monitoring and metacognition in isolation or in combination with psychological difficulty adjusting to cognitive and physical alterations. Further, environmental changes can exacerbate physiological changes. These may include reduction in the size of social system, nature of relationships (e.g., changes in intimacy and romantic relationships), changes in roles, and increased financial burden, which are highlighted as imposing a significant burden on both the individual and the family. Gainotti (1999) noted that family members cope with the physical consequences better than the emotional or behavioral difficulties. This is exacerbated by the common, but erroneous, belief that the trajectory of cognitive improvement will mirror that of physical recovery.

RECOVERY FROM TBI AND LONG-TERM IMPLICATIONS

When practitioners are charged with the goal of determining which children with a history of TBI are at risk for developing long-term problems, research suggests that there are several factors that may be prognostic. Specifically, variables that appear to be important in outcome include younger age at injury, severity of the injury, psychosocial factors, and pre-morbid functioning (e.g., Power et al., 2007). Much research has alluded to the plasticity effect seen following a head injury, with the implication that because children have immature brains, which are more apt to regenerate and reorganize themselves when compared with adults, that they are more capable of functional recovery. There is certainly a potential for increased plasticity in children versus older adults and the elderly; however, age-related variables exist within the pediatric TBI population as well. Levin et al. (1992) suggested that children 4 years and younger had the poorest outcome following severe TBI when compared with other children due to the more likely presence of subdural hematomas (bleeding between the brain and the skull that presses on surrounding brain tissue and causes cell death) or secondary hypotension (low blood pressure). Overall findings from this study indicated that children in the 5- to 10-year range fared better in comparison with younger children, adolescents, and adults (Levin et al., 1992). Given this information, the professional working with children must be mindful of the developmental context within which the maturing brain must be conceptualized. It is common for children to present with a phenomenon that is likened to "growing into a disability." For instance, Barlow, Thompson, Johnson, and Minns (2005) reported that extended followup of preschool-aged children after a severe TBI revealed learning difficulties, attention problems, and memory deficits that were not readily apparent when they were at home. It is possible that once the child is required to perform more demanding, complex cognitive tasks in a school-based setting, deficits are more easily observed, as there is an available peer comparison and more opportunities to demonstrate skills or evidence impairments. Additionally, it is possible for a young child to plateau in his or her cognitive recovery, only to begin having functional problems in a neurocognitive domain that was not used as frequently at a younger age. For instance, problems with inhibition, impulsivity, emotional regulation, and executive functioning have all been noted to "appear" in children who sustained TBIs as they develop into adolescents. This is not a new set of deficits; rather, it is the manifestation of frontal lobe dysfunction that may have been relatively subtle prior to the additional development of the frontal portion of the brain. As the child was required by the environment to use these skills with more frequency and facility, deficits became more observable.

Abnormalities in neuronal pathways and lesions subsequent to a TBI can cause secondary problems. One of the more common is a related seizure disorder, which may be observed immediately (within 24 hours of the injury), early on (within the first week), or late (more than one week after an injury). Of all patients who are hospitalized in association with a sustained TBI, 5 to 7 percent will experience post-traumatic seizures (Teasell et al., 2007). As the severity increases, seizure activity is more common. Upwards of 11 percent of individuals diagnosed with a severe closed head injury and 35 to 50 percent of those with open head injuries were reported to have associated seizure activity (Teasell et al., 2007). Post-traumatic seizure risk is compounded for those with moderate to severe injuries, cortical contusion, depressed skull fracture, epidural or intracerebral hematoma, wounds with penetration into the dura, presence of seizures within the first week, prolonged coma, and an extended period of post-traumatic amnesia. Although the risk of developing epilepsy associated with a TBI is at its highest in the first few months after an injury, the risk remains up to five years post-injury (Teasell et al., 2007). Research has suggested that seizure activity that occurs shortly after a TBI may cause additional brain damage, because associated intracranial pressure, excessive neurotransmitter release, and abnormal brain metabolism can lead to excessive cell death. Thus, it is common for physicians to prescribe anticonvulsants as a preventive when TBI had occurred in addition to its traditional usage for already existing seizures. This use of anti-seizure medication as a prophylactic has been demonstrated to decrease the presence of early onset seizure activity but has been deemed relatively ineffective in treating seizures that begin a week or more post-injury (Young et al., 2004 in Teasell, et al., 2007). This should be taken into consideration, since there are many notable cognitive deficits that are attributed to anticonvulsants (e.g., slow motor and psychomotor speed, decreased attention, memory impairments, somnolence), and when added to the already existing neurocognitive deficits seen in children with TBI, functional implications are significantly increased.

SCHOOL NEUROPSYCHOLOGICAL ASSESSMENT OF CHILDREN WITH TBI

When a professional is faced with the task of assessing a student with TBI there are a variety of factors that will influence decision making. Sohlberg and Mateer (2001) provided an excellent discussion of assessment considerations when working with children and adolescents with a history of brain injury. For the purpose of this chapter, several broad concepts will be discussed. First, when assessing those with TBI one should consider the testing materials to be chosen. For instance, the most accepted method for choosing assessment measures is the flexible-battery approach (Sohlberg & Mateer, 2001). However, this can sometimes lead to extension of the number of hours needed for testing, given the physical and cognitive limitations of a child with TBI. Possible deficits include decreased visual field functioning, hemiparesis, poor visual acuity, hearing problems, anxiety, boredom, preoccupation, hunger, fatigue, and pain. One can see that testing should be limited to the shortest amount of time possible to discern neurocognitive profiles. Additionally, the nature of cognitive deficits that are typically present, such as those concerning slowed processing speed, decreased attention and concentration, poor memory, and difficulty with executive functioning and emotional regulation, necessitates that the professional be succinct, efficient, and adept at fluid administration of chosen measures. This will limit the exacerbation of already present cognitive deficits by controlling the pace of the testing session, the order of items and tasks presented, and the complexity of the measures presented. Thus, a flexible approach, although ideal, may not be the most effective way of gleaning information. Instead, Sohlberg and Mateer

(2001) suggested a mixed-model approach. This includes using several standard global measures of skill, such as intellectual, academic, and memory batteries, and then including individualized choices in the language, visual-perceptual, attention and executive functioning, and social-emotional/behavioral realms. All of these areas should be addressed as part of a thorough neuropsychological assessment, but the trained professional should be able to determine, based on observations during testing and needs of the family and child, to limit or expand each as needed.

The procedure for testing children with head injuries is typically different in trajectory than those who have diagnoses such as learning disabilities or significant attention problems. Children and adolescents with sustained trauma to the head often return to school during the so-called "acute phase," a period of tremendous recovery of function. As such, assessments completed upon return to school that are used to establish neurocognitive skills and develop initial IEP goals are only accurate for a short period of time. Thus, in opposition to the standard three-year re-evaluation plan that is often seen in children receiving services through the special education program, these children should be assessed based on the length of time since their injury and developmentally important transitions in their educational progression. For instance, a child with a moderate to severe head injury would be best served through an assessment when returning to school and then again twelve months later. Further, after the initial period of recovery, it is important to provide comprehensive assessments when the demands of an educational placement change. This includes the transition between elementary and middle school, middle and high school, and before graduation. Serial testing allows for consistent monitoring of changes in skills over time. Also, in light of the potential for a child's developing disabilities that may not be present initially after an injury, the baseline assessment of skills is not sufficient for development of IEP goals on an ongoing basis or account for the potential range of functional deficits over time. This suggests that a possible route for providing assessment for these children is to combine consistent serial testing using norm referenced materials at developmental intervals paired with curriculum-based measures. School-based professionals would then be able to establish individualized goals that were informed enough to anticipate ongoing behavioral and educational needs, which are particularly dynamic in the pediatric TBI population (Sohlberg & Mateer, 2001; Ylvisaker & Feeney, 1998).

TBI REHABILITATION AND INTERVENTION

The effects of TBI can be far-reaching and profound. While TBI can cause long-term physical disability, it is the complex neurobehavioral sequelae that produce the greatest disruption to quality of life. Cognitive and behavioral changes, difficulties maintaining personal relationships, and coping with school are reported by survivors as more disabling than any residual physical deficits. TBI displays an extremely varied spectrum of possible lesions and resulting potential disabilities. Moreover, each person has a different set of pre-morbid abilities and psychosocial situations. Because of this, the goals of rehabilitation need to be holistic, long term, and individualized to each survivor and his or her family. In-patient management is often required for those with more severe and acute physical, cognitive, and/or behavioral deficits. The focus is on issues such as PTA monitoring, retraining in activities of daily living, pain management, cognitive and behavioral therapies, pharmacological management, assistive technology (e.g., prescription wheelchairs and gait aids), environmental manipulation (e.g., installation of lifts, ramps, rails, and bathroom alterations), as well as family education and counseling (Sohlberg & Mateer, 2001). Most children also require physical and/or occupational rehabilitation for associated trauma (e.g., fractures).

Determining the combination of cognitive, behavioral, and physical deficits is an important first step in setting goals for rehabilitation on an out-patient or school basis. Prioritizing goals should be undertaken with the assistance of both the person and the family. Children for whom there is no support, or for whom such support is inadequate or inappropriate, fare worse despite the degree or type of rehabilitation (Max et al., 1999). A combination of deficits leads to a greater degree of social disability than would be expected from isolated single impairment. Community living skills, domestic and household duties, communication (reading, writing, using the telephone), money management, time management, driving and public transport, and social skills may require retraining. Returning to school is an important factor that contributes to satisfaction and quality of life. On first returning to the community, people with TBI may have reduced awareness of their cognitive deficits and can fail or do badly if pressured to return to study or household responsibilities too soon. Vocational and leisure options may include retraining, rehabilitation, or supported employment services. Behavioral changes may alienate family and friends, with families sometimes perceiving the person as a "difficult stranger." Aggression, substance misuse, and lack of empathy particularly strain relationships for others who may see the child as unmotivated and lazy (Max et al., 1999). Ignorance and misperceptions of families, classmates, and healthcare professionals about the effects of TBI may make matters worse. Behavioral management may be necessary to increase independence and reduce maladaptive social behaviors such as agitation, irritability, combative outbursts, lethargy, and abnormal or foul language.

Although there remains a great need for experimentally derived, prospective studies with randomly assigned experimental-control groups, the most recent federal legislation changes and their emphasis on establishing empirically based interventions make it necessary that professionals designing intervention plans for children with a history of head injury remain vigilant in attempting to ascertain those techniques and systems that are borne out in the literature. Of the findings that were gleaned from a recent meta-analysis, research (Laatsch et al., 2007) has suggested that children with severe TBI respond to structured cognitive rehabilitation. Specifically, findings indicated that the children who received intervention from trained practitioners as well as family members using home retraining programs achieved clinically significant gains. Because research has suggested that psychoeducation is helpful when provided in an emergency room, it is further indicated that rehabilitation and intervention with children and adolescents with TBI should include a family education module to explain the effects of TBI and common sequelae (see Laatsch et al., 2007, for a review of pertinent studies).

Significant improvements on neuropsychological, academic, and adaptive/ behavioral functioning post brain injury were also seen following utilization of a program focusing on transition back to school. The goal was to assist children with brain injuries to adjusting to and compensate for their learning deficits by using techniques to increase problem-solving and metacognitive strategies paired with individualized tutoring. At the followup assessment, participants across both the control and clinical groups had improved on most neuropsychological measures relative to their respective baseline scores; but significant differences were seen on measures of simultaneous processing and expressive vocabulary across all participants. Adaptive behavior and functional communication measures also improved in both groups with greater improvements in the intervention group than in the comparison group (Laatsch et al., 2007). Another study suggested that statistically significant improvement within the experimental group was demonstrated on sustained and short-term attention tests and on a delayed word memory test, compared to no changes in the control group when they were provided with consistent, structured, skill-based memory retraining (see Laatsch et al., 2007, for a review of pertinent research).

With regard to specific neurocognitive domains and the remediation of functional impairments, memory deficits are perhaps one of the most problematic. In addition to the large percentage of those with a history of TBI exhibiting memory deficits, these impairments appear to be persistent. Research (Raymond, Malia, Bewick, & Bennett, 1996) has suggested that upwards of 75 percent of some samples of people with severe TBI noted deficits in the domain of memory functioning at ten to fifteen years post-injury. Memory functioning is a complex area of skill that is impacted by factors such as cognitive fatigue, processing speed, and/or attention and concentration. For individuals who experience impairments because of these associated variables, their problems with encoding, storage, and retrieval of information are alleviated as the other domains are increased. However, those who struggle with memory deficits due to primary consolidation problems (usually associated with damage to the medical temporal lobe or diencephalon), where the process of transferring information from short-term to long-term memory is impacted, exhibit no significant rebound of skills as other neurocognitive domains evidence improvement. These individuals may be left with permanent memory problems and may have to resort to external compensatory strategies and aids to improve functional skills (Raymond et al., 1996).

Rehabilitation and intervention techniques are also commonly targeted at addressing attention and executive functioning deficits. Brain-injured patients often show very specific attention deficits in neuropsychological assessment; however, everyday situations are mostly characterized by a mixture of different attention requirements. This makes it nearly impossible to look for specific deficits in activities of daily living, because there is significant overlap between these more singular skills when executing real-world activities. This, however, does not imply that it is not necessary to disentangle these everyday attention requirements to look for specific impairments in the individual patient and to address them with targeted therapeutic methods. Only after having looked at these more theoretically based questions should one start to study the effects of these training programs on everyday life attention performance (Sturm, Willmes, Orgass, & Hartje, 1997). The observations of one specific study supports the hypothesis that impairments on a given level can only be approached by training on the same or a subordinate level. This means that training effects occur simply after having carried out the tasks by repeatedly stimulating the impaired attention function (Sturm et al., 1997). After training for sustained attention, it was found that there was significant improvement not only for a sustained attention task but also for spatial neglect symptoms in right brain-damaged patients (Robertson et al., 1995 as cited in Sturm et al., 1997). This was attributed to a spreading of activation from anterior to posterior attention systems within the same hemisphere. During training, only strategies to improve the sustained attention deficits were presented, but the neglect problem per se was not addressed at all by the intervention.

SUMMARY

Working with children who have suffered from a head injury is a complex endeavor. When the range of possible presentations is considered, the application of the federal handicapping code for traumatic brain injury does relatively little to describe the child's capabilities and associated needs. With information regarding the clinical presentation of the injury including severity, provision of acute medical care techniques, neuroimaging confirming the presence of focal lesions, indications of diffuse brain trauma, and information regarding pre-morbid functioning and current psychosocial stressors and/or family supports, a more detailed picture of a child's neuro-cognitive and social-emotional profile can be estimated. However, more intensive observation and assessment is needed to fully conceptualize the functional strengths and weaknesses that each of these youth will exhibit. At the most basic level, clinical evaluation of these children will often be completed by several professionals, each with his or her own interpretive lens. For instance, the physical therapist will best be able to describe the child's gait and station, physical strength, range of motion, gross motor control and coordination, and balance. The occupational therapist is most adept at exploring a child's visual perceptual skills, fine motor speed and dexterity, proprioceptive abilities, adaptive functioning in daily living skills, and visual acuity, responsiveness, and tracking. The speech and language pathologist is the foremost expert on the post-traumatic linguistic problems that may arise, including aphasias, dysphagia, decreased listening comprehension, and poor organization in expression. The psychologist is the clinical expert needed to fully elucidate the child's ability to cope with extensive changes in independence, family and social status, interpersonal functioning, and psychological stressors.

As can be seen, many professionals are potentially involved when working with these children and adolescents. Unfortunately, very few have the breadth of training to conceptualize the child as a dynamic individual experiencing a variety of disability areas that are often layered. As such, the ability of the school-based practitioner with professional experience working with the TBI population is able to assist parents, staff members, and the students themselves through the recovery, adjustment, and ultimately, the compensatory stages following the injury. The recognition that functional deficits exist is not sufficient; one must understand that the individual is not a conglomeration of different diagnoses. Although students may present with a mixed expressive and receptive language disorder, sensory processing disorder, orthopedic impairments, and a plethora of neurocognitive and behavioral changes, it is the neuropsychologist who is best equipped to discuss the synergy between these factors. In summary, school psychologists and licensed psychologists working with children and adolescents suffering from traumatic brain injuries have a unique and valuable perspective that allows them to guide an individual, the family, and the teachers and school faculty who interact with the child through an exceedingly difficult transition. Through competent use of consultation, behavioral observation, psychoeducation, assessment, and direct intervention through rehabilitation and/or counseling, it is possible to provide knowledgeable support to such families.

REFERENCES

Anderson, V., Morse, S., Klug, G., Catroppa, C., Haritou, F., Rosenfeld, J., et al. (1997). Predicting recovery from head injury in young children: A prospective analysis. *Journal of the International Neuropsychological Society, 3*, 568–580.

Barlow, K., Thompson, E., Johnson, D., & Minns, R. (2005). Late neurological and cognitive sequelae of inflicted traumatic brain injury in infancy. *Pediatrics, 116*, 174–185.

Blumenfeld, H. (2002). *Neuroanatomy through clinical cases.* Sunderland, MA: Sinauer Associates.

Catroppa, C., & Anderson, V. (2002). Recovery in memory function in the first year following TBI in children. *Brain Injury, 16*, 369–384.

Centers for Disease Control's Center for Injury Prevention and Control. (2002). *Traumatic brain injury in the United States: A report to congress.* Retrieved from http://www.cdc.gov on 03/01/2002.

Chadwick, O., Rutter, M., & Schaffer, D. (1981). A prospective study of children with head injuries: IV, Specific cognitive deficits. *Journal of Clinical Neuropsychology, 3*, 101–120.

Clark, E. (1996). Children and adolescents with traumatic brain injury: Reintegration challenges in educational settings. *Journal of Learning Disabilities, 29*, 549–561.

Demir, S., Altinok, N., Aydin, G., & Köseoglu, F. (2006). Functional and cognitive progress in aphasic patients with traumatic brain injury during the post-acute phase. *Brain Injury, 20*, 1383–1390.

Di Scala, C., Osberg, J. S., Gans, B. M., Chin, L. J., & Grant, C. C. (1991). Children with traumatic head injury: Morbidity and post-acute treatment. *The Archives of Physical Medicine and Rehabilitation, 72*, 662–666.

Donders, J. (1993). Memory functioning after traumatic brain injury in children. *Brain Injury, 7*, 431–437.

Ewing-Cobbs, L., Fletcher, J., Levin, H., Iovino, I., & Miner, M. (1998). Academic achievement and academic placement following traumatic brain injury in children and adolescents: A two-year longitudinal study. *Journal of Clinical and Experimental Neuropsychology, 20*, 769–781.

Farmer, J. E., Haut, J. S., Williams, J., Kapila, C., Johnstone, B., & Kirk, K. S. (1999). Comprehensive assessment of memory functioning following traumatic brain injury in children. *Developmental Neuropsychology, 15*, 269–289.

Fletcher, J., Ewing-Cobbs, L., Francis, D., & Levin, H. (1995). Variability in outcome after traumatic brain injury in children: A developmental perspective. In S. Broman & M. Michels (Eds.), *Traumatic head injury in children.* New York: Oxford University Press.

Gainotti, G. (1999). Neuropsychology of emotions. In G. Denes & L. Pizzamiglio (Eds.), *Handbook of clinical and experimental psychology.* Hove, UK: Erlbaum.

Glozman, J. (2007). A. R. Luria and the history of Russian neuropsychology. *Journal of the History of the Neurosciences 16*, 168–180.

Hanten, G., Levin, H., & Song, J. (1999). Working memory and metacognition in sentence comprehension by severely head-injured children: A preliminary study. *Developmental Neuropsychology, 16,* 393–414.

Hawley, C., Ward, A., Magnay, A., & Long, J. (2002). Children's brain injury: A postal follow-up of 525 children from one health region in the UK. *Brain Injury, 16,* 969–985.

Hellerstein, L., & Kadet, T. (1999). Visual profile of patients presenting with brain trauma. *Journal of Optometric Vision Development, 30*(2), 51–54.

Johnson, D. A. (1992). Head injured children and education: A need for greater delineation and understanding. *British Journal of Educational Psychology, 62,* 404–412.

Kochanek, P. (2006). Pediatric traumatic brain injury: Quo vadis? *Developmental Neuroscience, 28,* 244–255.

Laatsch, L., Harrington, D., Hotz, G., Marcantuono, J., Mozzoni, M., Walsh, V., et al. (2007). An evidence-based review of cognitive and behavioral rehabilitation treatment studies in children with acquired brain injury. *Journal of Head Trauma Rehabilitation, 22,* 248–256.

Leddy, J., Kozlowski, K., Fung, M., Pendergast, D., & Willer, B. (2007). Special issue: Sports and concussion. *NeuroRehabilitation, 22,* 199–205.

Levin, H. S., & Eisenberg, H. M. (1979). Neuropsychological impairments after closed head injury in children and adolescents. *Journal of Pediatric Psychology, 4,* 389–402.

Levin, H., Williams, D., Eisenberg, H., & High, W. (1992). Serial MRI and neuro-behavioural findings after mild to moderate closed head injury. *Journal of Neurology, Neurosurgery and Psychiatry, 55,* 255–262.

Lord-Maes, J., & Obrzut, J. E. (1996). Neuropsychological consequences of traumatic brain injury in children and adolescents. *Journal of Learning Disabilities, 29,* 609–617.

Mateer, C. A., Kerns, K. A., & Eso, K. L. (1996). Management of attention and memory disorders following traumatic brain injury. *Journal of Learning Disabilities, 29,* 618–632.

Max, J. E., Roberts, M. A., Koele, S. L., Lindgren, S. D., Robin, D. A., Arndt, S., et al. (1999). Cognitive outcome in children and adolescents following severe traumatic brain injury: Influence of psychosocial, psychiatric, and injury-related variables. *Journal of the International Neuropsychological Society, 5,* 58–68.

McCrea, M. A. (2008). *Mild traumatic brain injury and postconcussion syndrome: The new evidence base for diagnosis and treatment.* Oxford, UK: Oxford University Press.

Milner, B. (1995). Epilepsy and the functional anatomy of the frontal lobe. In H. Jasper, S. Riggio, & P. S. Goldman-Rakic (Eds.), *Aspects of Human Frontal Lobe Function.* New York: Raven Press.

Power, T., Catroppa, C., Coleman, L., Ditchfield, M., & Anderson, V. (2007). Do lesion site and severity predict deficits in attentional control after preschool traumatic brain injury (TBI)? *Brain Injury, 21,* 279–292.

Raymond, M., Malia, K., Bewick, K., & Bennett, T. (1996). A comprehensive approach to memory rehabilitation following brain injury. *Journal of Cognitive Rehabilitation, 14,* 18–23.

Savage, R., & Wolcott, G. (1994). *Emotional dimensions of acquired brain injury*. Austin, TX: Pro-Ed.

Scheid, R., Walther, K., Guthke, T., Preul, C., & von Cramon, Y. (2006). Cognitive sequelae of diffuse axonal injury. *Archives of Neurology, 63*, 418–424.

Schoenbrodt, L. (2001). *Children with traumatic brain injury: A parents' guide*. Bethesda, MD: Woodbine House.

Sohlberg, M., & Mateer, C. A. (2001). *Cognitive rehabilitation: An integrative neuropsychological approach*. New York: Guilford.

Squire, L., Stark, C., & Clark, R. (2004). The medial temporal lobe. *Annual Review of Neuroscience, 27*, 279–306.

Sturm, W., Willmes, K., Orgass, B., & Hartje, W. (1997). Do specific attention deficits need specific training? *Neuropsychological Rehabilitation, 7*, 81–103.

Teasdale, G., & Jennett, B. (1974). Assessment of coma and impaired consciousness: A practical scale. *Lancet, 2*, 81–84.

Teasell, R., Bayona, N., Marshall, S., Cullen, N., Bayley, M., Chundamala, J., Villamere, J., Mackie, D., Rees, L., Hartridge, C., Lippert, C., Hilditch, M., Welch-West, P., Weiser, M., Ferri, C., McCabe, P., McCormick, A., Aubut, J., Comper, P., Salter, K., Van Reekum, R., Collins, D., Foley, N., Nowak, J., Jutai, J., Speechley, M., Hellings, C., & Tu, L. (2007). A systematic review of rehabilitation of moderate to severe acquired brain injuries. *Brain Injury, 21*, 107–112.

U.S. Department of Education (2003). *25th Annual Report to Congress on the Implementation of the Individuals with Disabilities Education Act*. Retrieved from http://www.ed.gov/about/reports/annual/osep/2003/25th-vol-1.doc.

Winogron, H. W., Knights, R. M., & Bawden, H. N. (1984). Neuropsychological deficits following head injury in children. *Journal of Clinical Neuropsychology, 6*, 269–286.

Yeates, K., & Taylor, H. (2006). Behavior problems in school and their educational correlates among children with traumatic brain injury. *Exceptionality, 14*, 141–154.

Ylvisaker, M., & Feeney, T. (1998). School reentry after traumatic brain injury. In M. Ylvisaker (Ed.), *Traumatic brain injury rehabilitation: Children and adolescents* (2nd ed., pp. 369–387). Woburn, MA: Butterworth-Heinemann.

Youse, K. M., Le, K. N., Cannizzaro, M. S., & Coetho, C. A. (2002). *Traumatic brain injury*. The ASHA Leader. Retrieved 3/1/2005 from http://www.asha.org/about/publications/leader-online/archives/2002/q2/020625a4.htm.

APPENDIX

Resources for School Neuropsychology

Table A.1

Major School Neuropsychology Publications (most recent to oldest)

Miller, D. C. (Ed.). (2009). Best practices in school neuropsychology: Guidelines for effective practice, assessment, and evidence-based intervention. Hoboken, NJ: John Wiley & Sons.

Feifer, S. G., & Rattan, G. (2009). Emotional disorders: A neuropsychological, psychopharmacological, and educational perspective. Middletown, MD: School Neuropsych Press.

Reynolds, C. R., & Fletcher-Janzen, E. (Eds.). (2008). Handbook of clinical child neuropsychology (3rd ed.). New York: Plenum Press.

Castillo, C. L. (Ed.). (2008). Children with complex medical issues in schools: Neuropsychological descriptions and interventions. New York: Springer.

Fletcher-Janzen, E., & Reynolds, C. R. (Eds.). (2008). Neuropsychological perspectives on learning disabilities in the era of RTI: Recommendations for diagnosis and intervention. Hoboken, NJ: John Wiley & Sons.

Dehn, M. J. (2008). Working memory and academic learning: Assessment and intervention. Hoboken, NJ: John Wiley & Sons.

Miller, D. C. (2007). Essentials of school neuropsychological assessment. Hoboken, NJ: John Wiley & Sons.

Feifer, S. G., & Della Toffalo, D. (2007). Integrating RTI with cognitive neuropsychology: A scientific approach to reading. Middletown, MD: School Neuropsych Press.

D'Amato, R. C., Fletcher-Janzen, E., & Reynolds, C. R. (Eds.). (2005). Handbook of school neuropsychology. New York: John Wiley & Sons.

Feifer, S. G., & De Fina, P. A. (2005). The neuropsychology of mathematics: Diagnosis and intervention. Middletown, MD: School Neuropsych Press.

Hale, J. B., & Fiorello, C. A. (2004). School neuropsychology: A practitioner's handbook. New York: Guilford.

Jiron, C. (2004). Brainstorming: Using neuropsychology in the schools. Los Angeles: Western Psychological Services.

(*continued*)

817

Table A.1

Continued

Baron, I. S. (2004). Neuropsychological evaluation of the child. New York: Oxford University Press.

Shaywitz, S. (2003). Overcoming dyslexia: A new and complete science-based program for reading problems at any level. New York: Alfred A. Knopf.

Eslinger, P. J. (Ed.). (2002). Neuropsychological interventions. New York: Guilford.

Berninger, V. W., & Richards, T. L. (2002). Brain literacy for educators and psychologists. New York: Academic Press.

Feifer, S. G., & De Fina, P. A. (2002). The neuropsychology of written language disorders: Diagnosis and intervention. Middletown, MD: School Neuropsych Press.

Semrud-Clikeman, M. (2001). Traumatic brain injury in children and adolescents. New York: Guilford.

Feifer, S. G., & De Fina, P. A. (2000). The neuropsychology of reading disorders: Diagnosis and intervention. Middletown, MD: School Neuropsych Press.

Goldstein, S., & Reynolds, C. R. (Eds.). (1999). Neurodevelopmental and genetic disorders in children. New York: Guilford.

Siantz-Tyler, J., & Mira, M. P. (1999). Traumatic brain injury in children and adolescents: A sourcebook for teachers and other school personnel. Austin, TX: Pro-Ed.

Table A.2

Journals Relevant to School Neuropsychology

Journal	Number of Articles (1991–2008) Related to School Neuropsychology
Neuropsychology	2255
Child Neuropsychology[1]	682
Journal of Clinical and Experimental Neuropsychology	177
Archives of Clinical Neuropsychology	116
Applied Neuropsychology	75
Journal of Learning Disabilities	37
The Clinical Neuropsychologist	29
Neuropsychology Review	29
Journal of the International Neuropsychological Society	22
Journal of Cognitive Neuroscience	16
Psychology in the Schools	11
School Psychology Review	11
Developmental Psychology	6

Table A.2

Continued

Journal	Number of Articles (1991–2008) Related to School Neuropsychology
Mind, Brain, and Education[2]	6
Psychological Assessment	5
School Psychology Quarterly	4
Journal of Psychoeducational Assessment	3

[1] The Child Neuropsychology journal was introduced in 1995.

[2] Mind, Brain, and Education journal was introduced in 2007.

Note: These figures were derived by entering the words "neuropsychology" and "child" in the online search engines, PsycInfo, MEDLINE, and Psychology and Behavioral Sciences Collection online databases for the 1991 to 2008 period.

AUTHOR INDEX

SUBJECT INDEX